the knowledgebook

idea

the knowledgebook

Everything you need to know to get by in the 21st century

Washington, D.C.

The Universe: *The Orion Nebula, birthplace of many stars, p. 12*

The Earth: *71 percent of the Earth's surface is covered by water, p. 46*

Biology: *Beauty and functionality often go together in nature, p. 63*

Chemistry: *Carbon nanotubes may play a huge role in the future, p. 105*

THE BLUE PLANET

The Earth: *Our planet reached its present form ca 30 million years ago, p. 26*

DISCOVERIES AND INVENTIONS

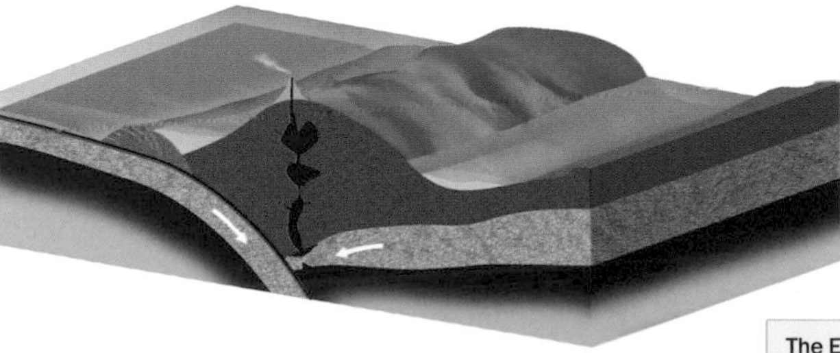

The Earth: *The formation of mountains through subduction, p. 36*

Physics and Technology: *Components of a CPU, p. 140*

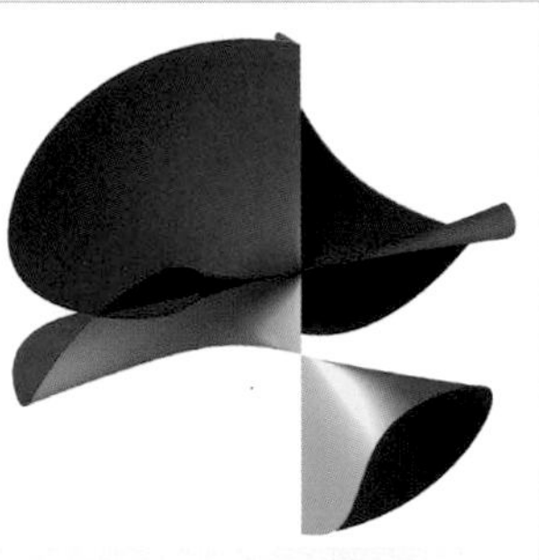

Mathematics: *A graphic produced by a mathematical formula, p. 163*

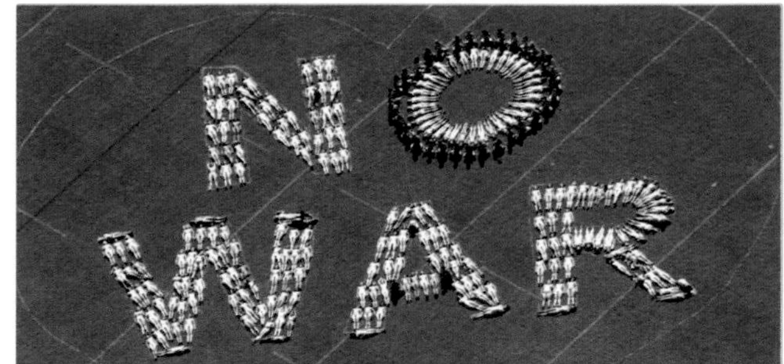

Politics, Law, and Economy: *Peace activists repeatedly draw attention to their cause through spectacular actions, p. 185*

SOCIAL LIFE

Biology: *Hummingbirds flap their wings 80 times per second, p. 73*

Politics, Law, and Economy: *Justitia, a symbol of justice, p. 190*

Religion: *The Jewish holiday of Hanukkah celebrates the miraculous replenishment of the lanterns of the temple in 164 B.C., p. 233*

Psychology: *Facial expressions speak a universal language, p. 274*

Visual Arts: *Vermeer's "Girl With a Pearl Earring," p. 301*

MIND AND SOUL

Religion: *Hindu god Shiva performing a sacred dance, p. 223*

THE ARTS

Philosophy: *Erasmus of Rotterdam was a significant Humanist, p. 253*

Architecture: *With the Bilbao branch of the Guggenheim Museum, Frank Gehry created an internationally acclaimed icon of modern architecture, p. 333*

Literature: *Nobel Prize-winning author Orhan Pamuk, p. 359*

Music: *Sun King Louis XIV performs in a ballet by J. P. Lully, p. 366*

Film: *"Star Wars" made R2-D2 and C-3PO pop culture icons, p. 392*

Monographic Boxes

Analytic Boxes

THE UNIVERSE

The universe consists of innumerable stars, planets, galaxies, and, above all, an unimaginable amount of space. Humankind has taken a deep look into this space; we examine its radiation and celestial bodies; we survey the design of our solar system, understand the energy production of the stars and from this have even derived models of how the universe began and developed. At the same time we recognize that human beings could not possibly live isolated away from these cosmic events. The universe offers the best conditions for the development of life and also for its annihilation. The more we know of our cosmic environment, the better we can understand our position within it. This is the drive behind humankind's next great adventure—breaking out further into space.

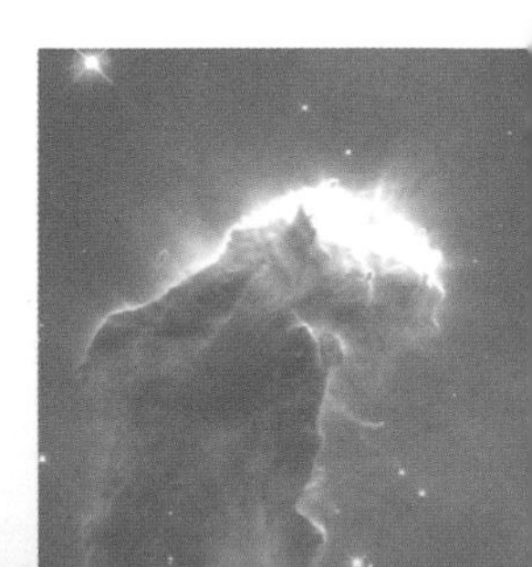

KEY FACTS

ACCORDING TO OBSERVATIONS *of the oldest stars and the standard big bang model, the universe is approximately 14 billion years old.*

EVERYTHING, INCLUDING SPACE AND TIME, *originated in a cosmic instantaneous expansion.*

MATTER *is distributed uniformly throughout the universe.*

THE HEAT *remaining from the big bang is measurable throughout space.*

Searching for a model of the universe | Structures of infinity

THE THEATER OF OUR EXISTENCE

What does the entire universe look like? How was it created and how did it develop? Cosmology attempts to address these questions. The only source of information available is the radiation (light or energy) that reaches the Earth from across outer space that is emitted by objects in the universe. Based on this information, humans use their intellect and reason to develop physical models of the world. Of course, these models can change with new discoveries; what is considered true today may be viewed as wrong tomorrow.

According to the big bang theory, the entire universe started out smaller than the size of a pea.

SEARCHING FOR A MODEL OF THE UNIVERSE

A standard model of the universe's origin is the big bang theory. The universe was initially extremely dense, but has since expanded to be infinitely large, containing less than one atom per cubic meter.

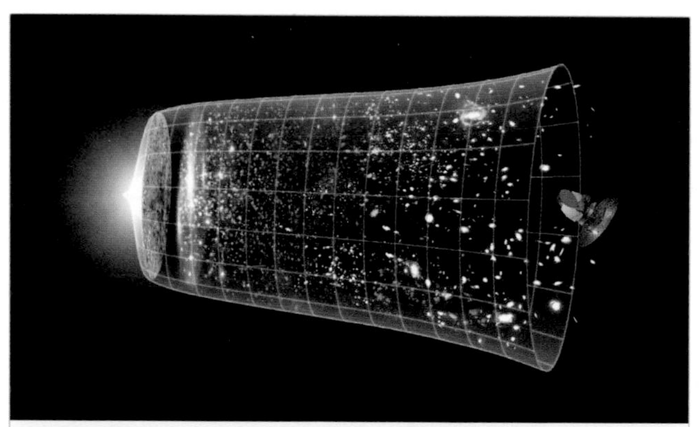

Since the big bang, space has been constantly expanding. As the hot mixture of matter and radiation cooled down, stars and galaxies emerged. Today, space probes investigate the remaining radiation.

Scientific models of the universe describe its origin and development. In particular, they must be able to explain its current characteristics. These include the types of matter and their arrangement. One characteristic is particularly striking: Galaxies (p. 11) appear to be moving away from one another. As there is no apparent starting point for this movement, the expanding universe has no center.

The Big Bang Theory

Data from scientific measurements do not always lend themselves to a single interpretation. Nevertheless, most cosmologists today have confidence in the theory of the big bang. According to this, the universe had a beginning, although no one knows exactly what happened in that very first moment. The development of the universe began about 14 billion years ago with an expansion known as the big bang. This instantaneous expansion was unique because there was no surrounding space into which the resulting debris could disperse. Space itself began to expand exponentially and ruptured in the process. The big bang occurred everywhere, not just in a single place.

In its initial phase, the universe expanded in size within the time frame of a fraction of a second. After this so-called inflationary phase, the expansion continued, but much more slowly.

Matter and Radiation

Primordial matter emerged out of the smallest elementary particles and was inconceivably hot at first. As the universe expanded, however, the matter cooled down. Particles no longer collided against each other and began to merge into larger pieces. After a few seconds, the universe was full of the components that later developed into atoms: protons, neutrons, and electrons. The primordial matter was hot and dense. The early universe was dominated by radiation (p. 11) because the density of photons was greater than that of matter. They corresponded to light at very short wavelengths and thus had high energy: (Energy = constant x 1/wavelength).

According to the theory of the big bang, space, time, and matter expanded into existence.

Redshift

THE HUBBLE LAW states that galaxies that are farther away have larger velocities than galaxies that are closer, i.e., distant galaxies move away from us at higher speeds than galaxies that are closer. The "redshift" is the effect of light moving away from us, which appears to have a longer wavelength, i.e., blue light "stretches" to become red light. Gas and dust clouds within a galaxy will absorb light emitted by the stars. The redshift depends on the galaxy's velocity.

The redshift of light grows with distance. This shows a comparison of the light spectrum of a nearby star (bottom) and a distant galaxy (top).

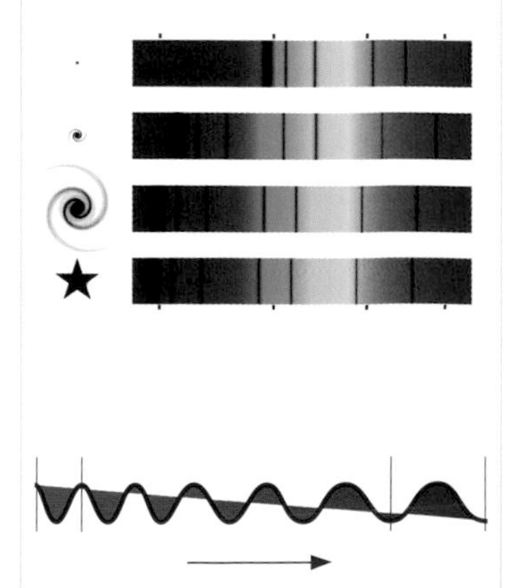

The longer a light wave is in transit in the expanding space, the more it is stretched. This causes it to appear redder.

STRUCTURES OF INFINITY

Already in the early stages of the universe, the first chemical elements were forming. Subsequently, stars, galaxies, and surprisingly large cosmic structures began to take form.

A few minutes after the big bang, protons and neutrons merged into light atomic nuclei. About 380,000 years later, these atomic nuclei began to capture electrons and form atoms. The first chemical elements emerged: hydrogen, helium, and lithium. Radiation and matter now had less influence upon each other, and the radiation could freely expand; the universe became transparent. With the increasing expansion of space, radiation waves stretched and their energy diminished. In these dark ages, gas was the predominant form of matter as there were still no light-emitting stars (p. 12).

Formation of Structures

Regions with a slight over-density of matter in the early universe are where structures (stars, galaxies, galaxy clusters, and superclusters) formed. Matter clumped together under its own gravity. As the resulting clumps grew, they attracted additional material (also through gravity). Current simulations and data favor the "cold matter scenario" in which structures form from the bottom up: stars to galaxies to clusters to superclusters.

The details of these processes, however, have not been conclusively explained. Scientists assume that matter from the big bang was uniformly distributed and that the clumping of "dark matter," among other things, was assisted by compression. The nature of dark matter is not understood, as it is invisible and is only observable through its gravitational force, which influences regular forms of matter.

Galaxies

Galaxies are huge rotating collections of stars, gas, and dust. There is a considerable amount of empty space between these components. Their form is generally elliptical or spiral. Our sun is located in the spiral arm of a galaxy of approximately 100 billion stars—the Milky Way. Light requires 100,000 years to cross the Milky Way Galaxy. The next largest galaxy is the Andromeda Galaxy. Its light travels more than 2 million years by the time it reaches Earth. Many galaxies existing together form a galaxy cluster.

above: *Spiral galaxy NGC 3370*

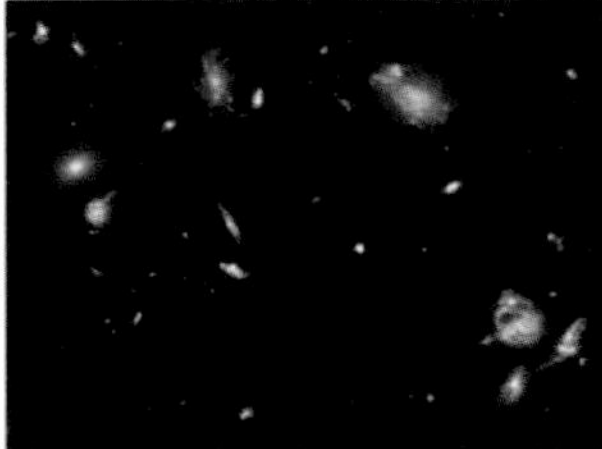

This shot from the Hubble Space Telescope shows the most distant visible galaxies.

21ST CENTURY

ORDINARY, KNOWN MATTER *constitutes only 4% of the universe, according to the big bang theory.*

OF THE REMAINDER, *23% is attractive dark matter and 73% is repellent dark energy.*

SOME THEORISTS *are tweaking the big bang model of the universe.*

Distances in the Universe

Inside the vacuum of space, light travels at a speed of nearly 190,000 miles/sec (300,000 km/sec). It covers about 5,900 billion miles (9,500 billion km) in one year, which is known as a light year. The light year (ly) is a unit of measurement for the inconceivable distances of the universe. The star closest to the sun is 4.3 ly away from Earth.

Superclusters and Galaxy Clouds

Galaxies are not evenly distributed in outer space. The force of gravity causes them to form clusters of galaxies. Galaxy clusters unite to form even larger groups known as superclusters. These can stretch more than 100 million ly and comprise thousands of galaxies.

These superclusters are bound together by gravity and lie along filaments (much like the film on soap bubbles). The largest known structure of this kind is the Great Wall, discovered in 1989. More than 2,000 galaxies are distributed across its 500-million-ly-long, at least 200-million-ly-wide, and 15-million-ly-deep area.

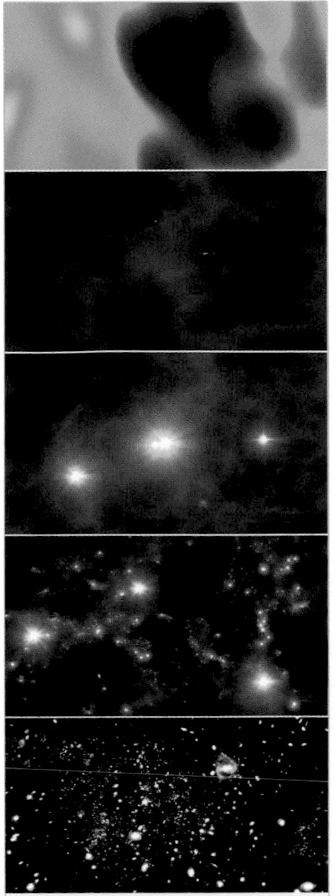

The smallest differences in temperature (above) lead to matter consolidating into stars and galaxies.

Cosmic Background Radiation

THE ENTIRE UNIVERSE is full of cosmic background radiation (CMB). It is generally considered to be residual radiation from the big bang expansion. As a result of the expanding of the universe, the wavelength of this radiation stretched and its energy dissipated. In the early stages, its energy corresponded to the heat of the universe, but today it just 2.7 K (degrees Kelvin), or 2.7 degrees above absolute zero (−459.67°F or −273.15°C). Otherwise, the radiation has remained unchanged. Since radiation and matter were at first closely related, cosmic background radiation must reflect the distribution of matter shortly after the big bang.

A temperature map of the sky, provided with measurement data from the research probe WMAP (Wilkinson Microwave Anisotropy Probe). Variations in temperature between warmer (red) and cooler (blue) regions amounted to only thousandths of degrees.

THE UNIVERSE

KEY FACTS

STARS *are massive, glowing balls of hot gas.*

RADIATION *from the release of energy during the fusion of hydrogen atomic nuclei into helium nuclei causes stars to shine.*

CHEMICAL ELEMENTS *are produced in the stars.*

LIFE AND EXISTENCE *as we know them are both made possible and supported by the sun.*

The birth of stars | Death and legacy of stars | The sun—our energy provider | The view of the starry sky

STARS—IT BECOMES LIGHT

As the central star of our solar system, the sun provides a gigantic power source to humankind. Its energy influences various processes on Earth such as the weather and photosynthesis (p. 66). At the same time, the sun can also have a destructive effect. It is only one of the billions of stars that supply the universe with light, structure, and chemical components. They are all integrated within the cosmic cycle of future star generations. All of the stars that are viewable to the naked eye are a part of the Milky Way Galaxy.

The material of planets, like that of a human body, is in large part produced by stars.

THE BIRTH OF STARS

Stars are formed in massive nebulas of gas and dust, which condense into gas balls through their own gravitational force. They differ in mass, color, and brightness, but share the same energy source: nuclear fusion.

The cosmic breeding grounds of stars lie in expanded clouds consisting predominantly of hydrogen gas, for example, in the Orion Nebula. Despite its high density, it has a reddish appearance with a patchwork of opaque regions where dust absorbs the light from stars, preventing it from being transmitted.

Stars are formed from the gas and dust of the Eagle Nebula. Its radiation makes the gas glow.

If a nebula possesses enough mass, it gradually collapses under its own weight. The gas separates into individual clouds, which compress themselves into rotating gas balls. As the gas is compressed more and more, the inner pressure increases. As soon as the pressure within the gas ball is high enough, it can oppose the force of gravity and effectively halt further collapse. In a very large and gaseous nebula, the gas does not dissolve, but rather the large ball breaks up into smaller balls. These will eventually become individual stars or star systems.

Ignition of Nuclear Fusion

The temperature of the gas increases drastically. The hydrogen atoms pelt against each other in the embryo of the star and knock away their electrons. If the temperature of this plasma exceeds around 18 million°F (10 million°C), nuclear fusion ignites and the hydrogen atomic nuclei fuse into helium atomic nuclei. An enormous amount of energy is set free in the process; the star begins to radiate.

The Orion Nebula can be observed in the constellation of the same name. Its densest regions are the birthplaces of quite a few stars.

Cosmic Lifespans

According to human perceptions, a star radiates for an inconceivably long time. Our sun (p. 14) has a life expectancy of around 10 billion years. The higher the mass of the star, the quicker the depletion of its energy supply.

Giants and Dwarves

STARS vary from one another in terms of their mass, dimension, and temperature. Red dwarves, stars with just 8 to 60 percent of the sun's mass (a solar mass), emit their energy sparingly, and therefore will have long life spans because their conversion of hydrogen nuclei to helium requires less power. Higher-mass stars can be as much as 100 times the mass of the sun and shine 10,000 times brighter, thus exhausting their energy faster. Red giants (p. 13) are stars at the end of their life and can expand up to 100 times their original diameter.

A COMPARISON OF STAR SIZES

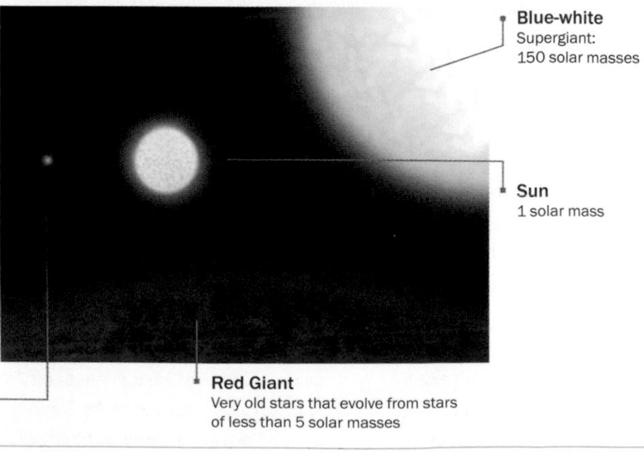

DEATH AND LEGACY OF STARS

The last phase of the life cycle of a star can be turbulent. Stars with high masses balloon or even explode. Often bizarre celestial bodies are all that remain of dissipated stars.

When the hydrogen supply in the center of the star is exhausted, the lessened output of energy results in a decrease of its inner pressure. The core of the star contracts under its own gravitational force, thus compressing itself and reheating. If the core is hot enough, the helium can fuse into carbon as well as oxygen, and can therefore continue to produce energy for a while.

The Star Inflates

To transform into a red giant, the star bursts with energy one more time, and the diameter of its outer gas layers expands a hundredfold. Its surface cools and appears reddish in the process. It gets so extremely hot in the center of a high-mass giant star that heavy chemical elements, such as iron, can form through nuclear fusion.

"Red giants" are not particularly balanced. These variable stars pulsate periodically or irregularly, and often expel their outer layer in the form of a planetary nebula. When this happens, a star with a mass comparable to that of the sun thus reaches the end of its existence. The bright, compact core of the star remains, which is roughly the size of Earth. The resulting "white dwarf" continues to cool down gradually.

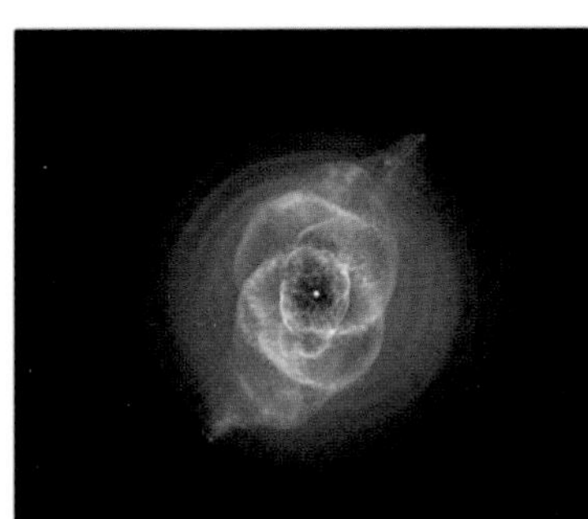

The Helix Nebula is an especially complex planetary nebula. Some astronomers believe that there are two stars located at its center.

Neutron Star and Pulsar

A star with more than about eight solar masses awaits a different fate. Following the depletion of fuel, the outer layers of the star are blown away in one last massive release of energy during the collapse of its center. The star explodes as a "supernova," while the core of the star simultaneously continues to collapse. Its inner pressure increases dramatically and the atomic components are pressed against one another. Electrons and protons are converted to neutrons, and empty spaces disappear. This neutron star has a mass comparable to that of the sun; however, its diameter is around 6 to 12 miles (10 to 20 km). A teaspoon of neutron material has about the mass of one billion small cars. Neutron stars rotate quickly and can send a periodic radio signal. The Crab Nebula is the best known example of a supernova remnant. Inside, a pulsar rotates 30 times per second.

Final Destination "Black Hole"

The neutron star is stable only if it has less than around three solar masses. Otherwise, it cannot resist its own gravitational force and continues to break down, this time completely. It is in this way that a black hole is created, in which neither light nor matter can escape due to its incredible force of gravitational pull. Space is so compressed within a black hole that the normal laws of physics no longer apply.

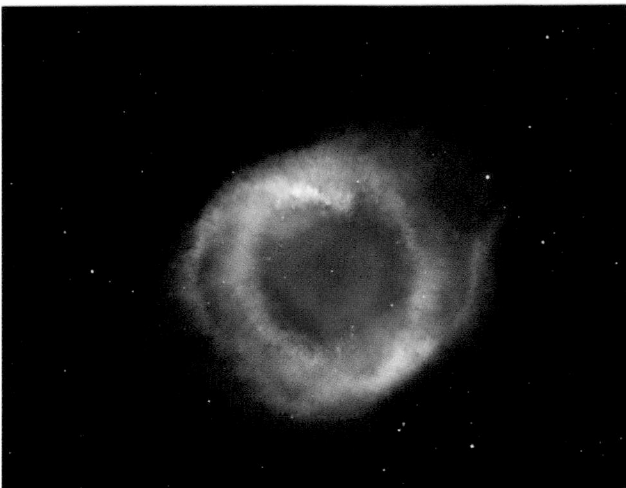

The Cat's Eye Nebula is the expelled gas cover of a previously sunlike star. The white dwarf at its center radiates intensively.

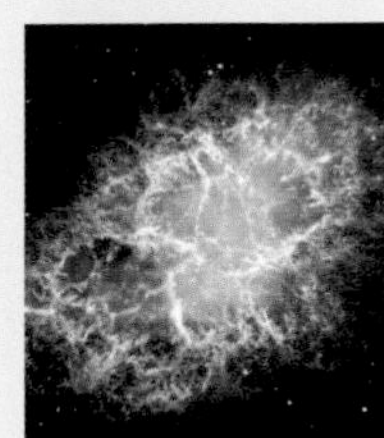

SUPERNOVA EXPLOSIONS occur at the final life stage of high mass stars.

THE LUMINOSITY increases by a billion times in the process. An exploded star will be as bright as its entire galaxy for a short period of time.

The Crab Nebula is the remnant of a supernova explosion that was observed by East Asian astronomers in 1054.

Supernova

ON AVERAGE, a supernova explodes once every 50 years in a normal galaxy.

THE RADIATION from a supernova explosion at a distance of just a few dozen light-years can be very destructive. The atmosphere of a planet—and possibly life on the planet—can be damaged.

HEAVY CHEMICAL ELEMENTS—for example, phosphorus, iron, and uranium—are produced in large quantities in a supernova. Many of these elements are important for life on Earth. The material of a supernova can once again become part of a gas or dust nebula, while the next generation of stars and planets can also be formed. All matter on Earth is made up of such material.

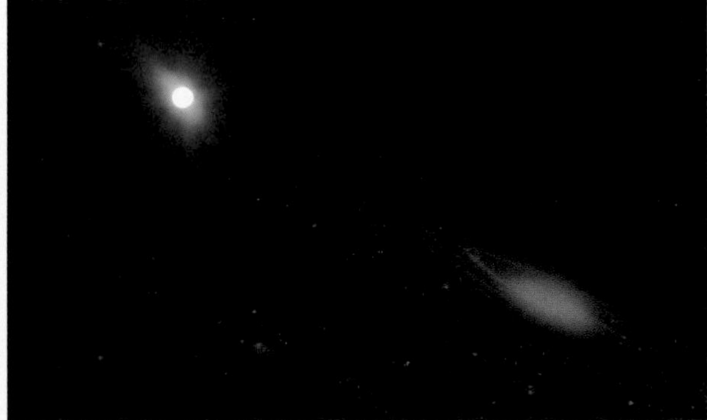

For a few days, a supernova radiates brighter than its home galaxy.

THE SUN—OUR ENERGY PROVIDER

The sun not only stands at the center of our solar system but is also the center of life. As a gigantic power plant, the sun provides the Earth with light and warmth.

Like all stars, the sun is a sphere of hot gases. Its diameter is 109 times larger than that of the Earth. While consisting primarily of hydrogen, the sun also contains a very small amount of helium and various other heavy elements.

Aurora borealis: Polar lights appear when solar wind particles collide with atoms and molecules in the Earth's atmosphere.

Inside the Sun

At the sun's core region, gas is strongly pressed together under its own weight and is heated to a temperature of around 27 million°F (15 million°C). Hydrogen atoms collide against one another and break up into hydrogen nuclei and electrons. The hydrogen nuclei merge to become helium nuclei, releasing large amounts of energy.

The energy released through nuclear fusion is in the form of "neutrinos" (a massless, non-interacting particle) that carries energy directly out of the sun. Some of the radiation energy goes into heating a region of the sun's interior because the energy heats up bubbles of gas. These rise and release energy into the photosphere—the outer, visible region of the sun's surface. Then, they cool and sink. In the photosphere, the photons are absorbed and re-radiated.

The Exterior Solar Layers

Two layers are almost transparent around the dazzling photosphere and can only be seen during a solar eclipse (p. 20). The chromosphere is then recognizable as a pale red shimmer, while the whitish corona surrounds it in a frayed wreath shape. The temperature in the corona increases to over 1.8 million°F (1 million°C). The photosphere gives sunlight, as the chromosphere and the corona emit radio and x-ray radiation.

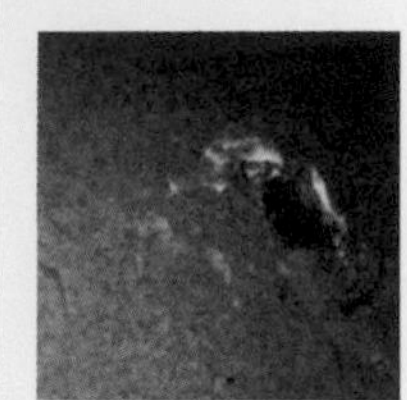

RADIATION CONDITIONS *in space and in the Earth's atmosphere are termed space weather.*

RADIATION ERUPTIONS *on the sun's surface cause temporary changes in space weather.*

The frequency of sunspots and radiation outbursts fluctuates clearly in a rhythm of 11 years.

Space Weather

GEOMAGNETIC STORMS develop when the sun explosively hurls more radiation and small particles than usual into space. After one to four days, the electrically charged particles reach the Earth and form electric currents in its magnetic field (p. 27).

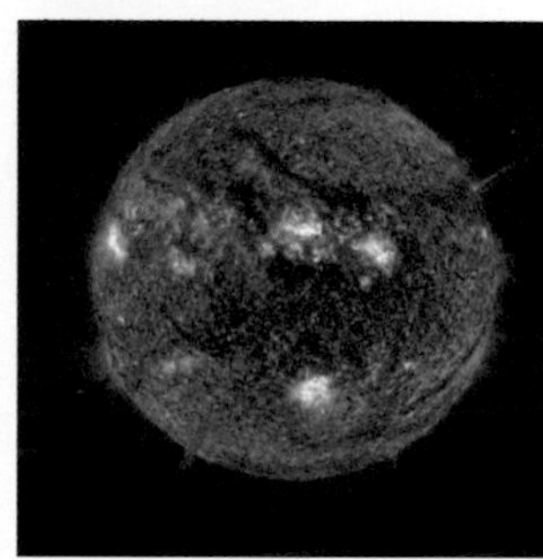

THROUGH INTENSIFIED ULTRAVIOLET AND X-RAYS, the Earth's upper atmosphere expands. While the Earth's satellites are slowed, the outbreaks of radiation can damage satellites and spaceships while also endangering the health of astronauts. A long-term alteration in space weather could result in climatic change on Earth.

Flares and solar winds influence space weather.

The Restless Sun

A tremendous amount of activity takes place on the sun's surface that is detectable through sunspots. Appearing to be darker than the environment around them, these areas result from cooling. They occur in the extraordinarily strong magnetic fields of the sun, which cause the lower-level energy in the cooler areas to be pushed outward. Close to the sunspots are solar chromospheric eruptions known as flares. These result from spectacular outbreaks of ultraviolet and x-ray radiation. A single flare can release almost as much energy as the whole sun in only a second. These flares also create explosive emissions of solar material that can reach the Earth. The solar corona hurls small particles into space; collectively these particles are known as the solar wind. Consisting of electrons, hydrogen, and helium nuclei, it reaches the Earth at speeds of almost 250 miles/sec (400 km/sec). The solar wind can create a storm that disturbs radio communication and electricity networks.

The Sun as an Energy Source

Although the Earth catches only a small fraction of the sun's radiation energy, there is still a considerable volume of energy emitted. Just one minute of solar energy on 10 ft^2 (1 m^2) of the Earth's surface is enough to easily warm up 1 qt (1 l) of water by more than 50°F (10°C).

During a solar eclipse, the moon passes before the sun and casts its shadow on the Earth.

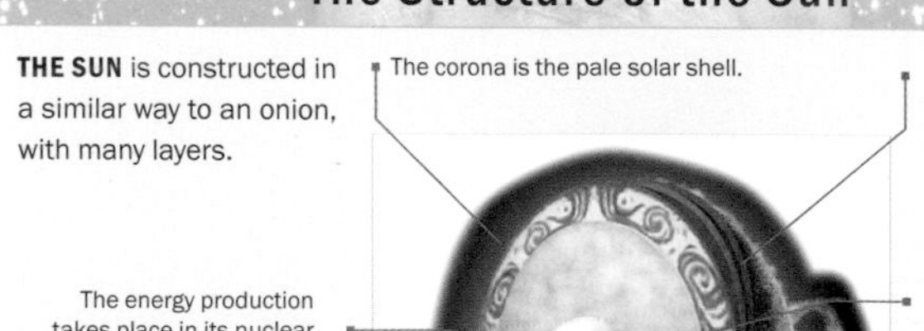

The Structure of the Sun

THE SUN is constructed in a similar way to an onion, with many layers.

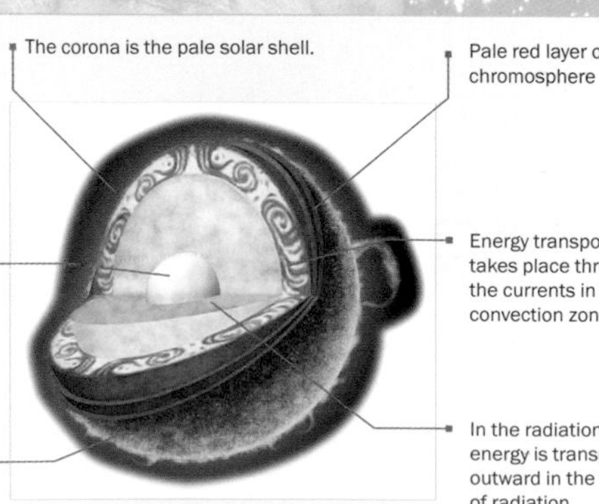

The corona is the pale solar shell.
Pale red layer of the chromosphere
The energy production takes place in its nuclear center at about 27 million°F (15 million°C).
Energy transport takes place through the currents in the convection zone.
The photosphere consumes most of the sunlight; it is about 9900°F (5500°C).
In the radiation zone, energy is transported outward in the form of radiation.

THE VIEW OF THE STARRY SKY

Light from cities often prevents an unclouded view of the star-filled sky. Only away from this "light pollution" can the sky reveal its magnificence.

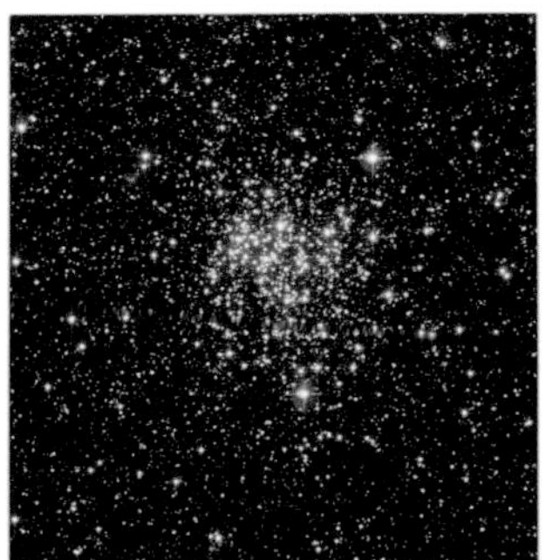

The open star cluster NGC 265 is held together only weakly through the gravitational force of its stars.

The sky is full of stars even during the daytime, but only one of them is visible: The sun, which shines brighter than the rest of them.

Because the Earth rotates around its axis, the sun appears to run along a course in the sky. As soon as the sun sets, our eyes can discern the faint light of the other stars. Like the sun, they also drift slowly in circles, orbiting around one common point. Extending the Earth's axis upward into space, it points to this fulcrum. For an observer standing in the Northern Hemisphere, this is the sky's North Pole—it is in almost the same position as the northern star.

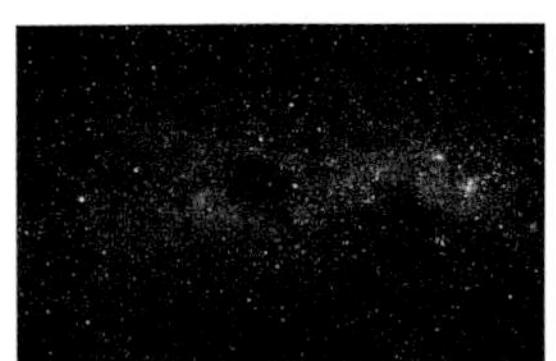

Alpha Centauri—Our Neighboring System

The stars close to the sun shine in the south sky in the constellation Centaurus. Its brightest star is Alpha Centauri, which is possible to see as a double star through a telescope. Its two stars orbit each other about every 80 years in a distance similar to that from which Uranus (p. 21) orbits the sun. The Alpha Centauri is about 4.4 ly away from the Earth and is accompanied by the faint Proximal Centauri, which is about 4.3 ly away and a little closer to the sun.

above: *Region around Alpha Centauri in the southern sky*

The Sparkling of Stars

When viewed from the Earth, some stars appear brighter than others. Differences in brightness are due to the fact that stars are at varying distances from the Earth and glow with different levels of intensity. The Earth's atmosphere is made up of different layers. Some layers are thicker, some are hotter. "Pockets" or cells of air move together at different speeds, acting like moving lenses. This causes the light to deviate from a straight path, making it appear as though a star or planet (p. 16) is twinkling or shimmering. Planets are much closer to the Earth than stars and appear as tiny disks, not as points; therefore, their image is not so easily distorted by restless atmospheric winds.

Constellations

Long before modern astronomy and space flight, people tried to find order in the myriad of stars. They connected individual stars through imaginary lines, drawing figures in the sky based on myths and legends. Each culture developed its own constellations.

Today's constellations do not have any meaning in the science of astronomy, but they can be helpful when searching for certain stars or planets. Sirius, the brightest star after the sun, can be found by extending three bright stars that form Orion's belt to the left and down.

The Milky Way

In a clear night sky, the pale, milky light band of the Milky Way shines across the sky in soft contours, showing the symmetry of Earth's galaxy (p. 11). Innumerable stars widely separated from each other, along with clouds of gas and dust, rotate in the spiral arms around the center of the Milky Way galaxy. From Earth, the entirety of their light is observable. The light band is brightest in the area around the constellation Sagittarius, which is also the center of the galaxy.

The Milky Way observed through a telescope

Clusters of Stars

Like many other stars in the Milky Way, Sirius is a double star. It rotates with an accompanying star that has a faint light. Sirius and its companion are bound together by gravity and orbit around a common point. Star clusters are common. A group of a few to several hundred stars, weakly bound by gravity, form open star clusters. They do not have a "core." Globular clusters, on the other hand, are tight groups of several thousand to hundreds of thousands of stars, whose appearance is spherical. Globular clusters are distributed evenly in a sphere around the "bulge" or center of galaxies (p. 11).

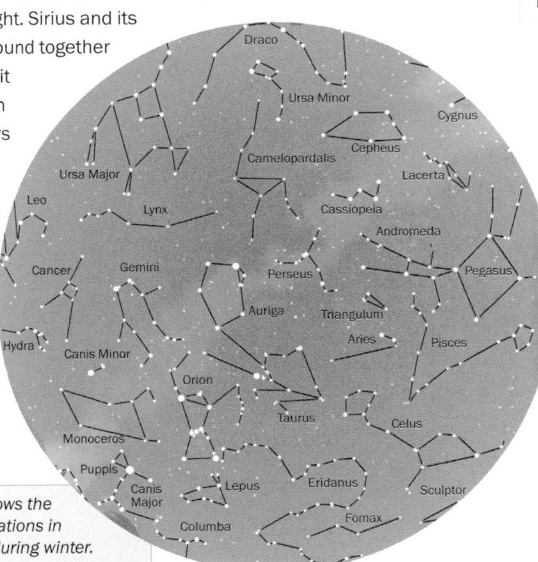

This star chart shows the stars and constellations in the northern sky during winter.

All of the stars that are visible in the night sky belong to our galaxy. Others at farther distances are not detectable as individual stars, but together they form the pale glowing band of the Milky Way, which is about 90,000 ly in diameter and about 275,000 ly in circumference.

Jupiter is sometimes spotted in the night sky near Venus and Mars.

KEY FACTS

THE SOLAR SYSTEM *originated about 4.6 billion years ago from a gigantic cloud of gas and dust.*

PLANETS, *dwarf planets, and countless smaller celestial bodies orbit the sun.*

EXOPLANETS, *or extrasolar planets, are planets that orbit stars outside of our solar system.*

AN ASTEROID BELT *divides the inner and outer planets.*

The solar system—oasis in the universe | Distant planetary systems

PLANETARY SYSTEMS—COSMIC CAROUSELS

The Earth and many other celestial bodies orbit around the sun like a cosmic carousel. Since planets have also been discovered around other stars, it is clear that our solar system is not a unique case in the universe. The question of whether the other solar systems accommodate life still remains unsolved.

Although planetary systems always develop in a similar manner, they are distinctly diverse.

THE SOLAR SYSTEM—OASIS IN THE UNIVERSE

The solar system is an oasis in the universe because it offers human beings a life-sustaining home in the middle of the inhospitable expanse of space.

The sun (p. 14) and all the celestial bodies belong to the solar system. These include the planets and their moons, dwarf planets, asteroids (p. 22), and other even smaller celestial bodies. The gravitational force of the sun keeps the planets in elliptical orbits around the sun.

Orbits of celestial bodies around the sun

Planets and Asteroids

Apart from the sun, the planets are the largest celestial bodies in the solar system. Their orbital paths are found more or less on the same plane. Viewed from above, the components of the solar system can be distinguished. The inner planets (p. 18) include Mercury, Venus, Earth, and Mars (p. 19), which are relatively small and rocky. The much larger outer planets (p. 21) are Jupiter, Saturn, Uranus, and Neptune. Extended shells made of hydrogen, helium, and methane surround their cores, which consist of rock and ice. Separating these two planet groups is an asteroid belt (p. 22). These irregularly formed pieces of rock include some that are more than 62 miles (100 km) in diameter. The dwarf planet Ceres is also present in the asteroid belt.

Beyond Neptune's Orbit

The dwarf planets Pluto and Eris orbit the sun from a distance beyond Neptune's orbital path. In this distant area, innumerable small celestial bodies also complete revolutions.

The Milky Way Galaxy's Sun

The solar system belongs to the Milky Way Galaxy (p. 11) along with billions of other stars. It is found in one of the spiral arms and circles around the galactic center at a distance of about 25,000 ly. Despite its speed of about 137 miles/sec (220 km/sec), it takes around 250 million years to complete one orbit.

What Is a Planet?

Since its discovery in 1930, Pluto was classified as a planet. Later, many similar bodies were found in its vicinity. In 2006, the word "planet" was redefined based on three determinants: First, it orbits a star and is itself neither a star nor a moon; second, it is roughly spherical in shape; third, in the development phase of the solar system it cleared its orbital environment of other cosmic material. As Pluto does not fulfill the third condition, it is classified as a dwarf planet like Eris and Ceres.

above: *Dwarf planet Pluto and its moon Charon*

The Life Zone

The Earth orbits the warmth-providing sun at just the "right" distance: The sun's heat is not too hot and not too cold. This allows the Earth to have continuously flowing water—not just ice or vapors—which is necessary for the existence of life. The "life zone" is an area within the distance from a star at which water can flow. For a faint star, this zone is relatively close, while it is farther away for a more brightly shining star. The temperature on a planet's surface also depends on its atmosphere.

above: *Life depends on the distance between the sun and Earth.*

Planets in Comparison

AS THE LARGEST PLANET in the solar system, Jupiter is 11 times larger and 318 times heavier than Earth. Earth is slightly larger than Venus, 2.5 times larger than Mercury, and about the same size as Mars. Dwarf planet Pluto is a little smaller than Earth's moon. The distances between the planets are not shown according to scale: The distance between Earth and the sun is about 93 million miles (150 million km). Jupiter is five times farther away.

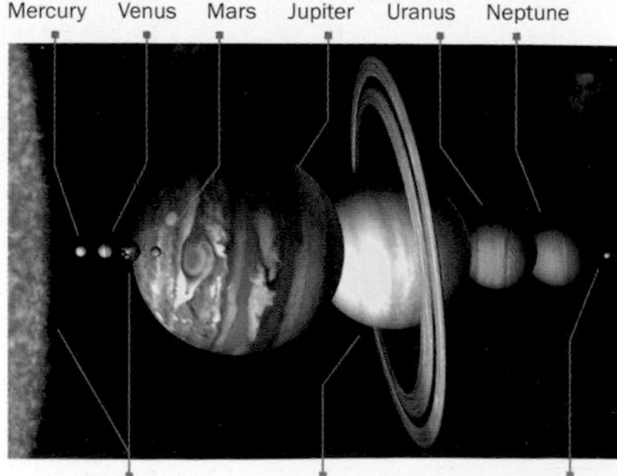

see also: Water, *Earth Chapter, pp. 44–47*

DISTANT PLANETARY SYSTEMS

Gigantic gas and dust disks from which planetary systems originate have been observed in the universe. It is difficult to discover planets around distant stars, but the hunt is on.

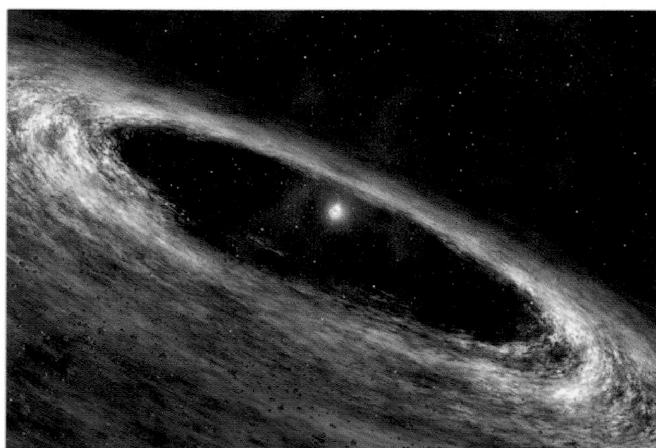

Young stars are often orbited by protoplanetary disks made of gas and dust, from which planets can form.

The solar system is not a unique case. Planets surround stars in many areas of our galaxy while in other places, entirely new planetary systems are forming. Although there are many details that are not completely understood, our solar system could have originated from a gigantic cloud of gas and dust that was compressed under its own gravitational force. As a star formed in its center (p. 12), the cloud would have turned faster and faster, resembling a skater when she pulls in her arms during a pirouette. The exterior area of the dust cloud would have flattened itself due to the centrifugal force. The protoplanetary disk formed as multiple inelastic collisions of particles created masses of self-gravitating material, which then formed into planets, asteroids, etc.

INSIDER KNOWLEDGE

ABOUT 99.9% *of our solar system's mass is found in the sun.*

THE FIRST TWO EXOPLANETS *were seen in 1992 close to a pulsar, a burnt-out star (p. 13).*

PHOTOGRAPHIC EVIDENCE *of exoplanets has so far been gathered only in exceptional cases of particularly dark stars.*

Difficult to Find

Using some of the world's best telescopes, it is now possible to photograph "exoplanets," planets near stars that are similar to the sun or other bright stars. Even the stars closest to the sun are several light-years away (p. 11).

At such a distance, stars and planets appear too close to one another to distinguish them from one another. When a car is far away with its headlights on, it is difficult to make out each headlight. It is even more difficult to distinguish two celestial bodies when one shines a billion times brighter than the other.

Search Methods

Aside from astrometry, exoplanets can be found in many different ways. In transit photometry, the planet passes in front of the central star, causing its own light to dim. With the Doppler spectroscopy or radial velocity method, the planet's motion around the star causes shifts in its spectral lines. Another way is by monitoring the varying pulses of a pulsar that are caused by the arrival of an orbiting planet.

Scientists are currently searching for ways to pierce the glaring light of stars in order to directly observe extrasolar planets. Gravitational fields of galaxies can also distort the path of light from distant objects. With the help of increasingly high-tech telescopes, large extrasolar planets could be discovered, such as those that orbit smaller massed stars.

In the next century, it should also be possible, with the help of improved space telescopes and star-gazing techniques, to systematically find extrasolar planets that are similar in size to Earth. As long as they have atmospheres, these planets can be searched for signs of existing life. Such signs would include, for example, oxygen, which is generated by plants and appears in Earth's atmosphere.

51 Pegasi

51 Pegasi is the first sunlike star that was discovered to have an orbiting planet. The star in the constellation Pegasus is about 50 ly in distance from the Earth. Its planet has approximately half the mass of Jupiter, or 160 times Earth's. Its distance from the star is equal to 20 times the distance between the Earth and the sun. Therefore, the planet may be as hot as 1832°F (1000°C). It takes only 4.2 days to complete an orbit around its star. This exoplanet was discovered in 1995. Since then, more than 300 others have been identified.

above: *51 Pegasi is comparable to the sun in mass and size.*

Planetary Systems in Comparison

NO PLANETARY SYSTEMS discovered so far are the same as our solar system. A bulky exoplanet often orbits closely around its star. There are likely to be more planets in these systems, but they cannot be identified using current methods. Small planets may be seen through gravitational microlensing, or during the rare event of the planet and its central star passing in front of another star. This acts as a lens through which the background star's light is amplified.

ARRANGEMENT OF OUR INNER SOLAR SYSTEM:

Name of the star around which the exoplanet orbits

Exoplanet with 6.6 times the mass of Jupiter

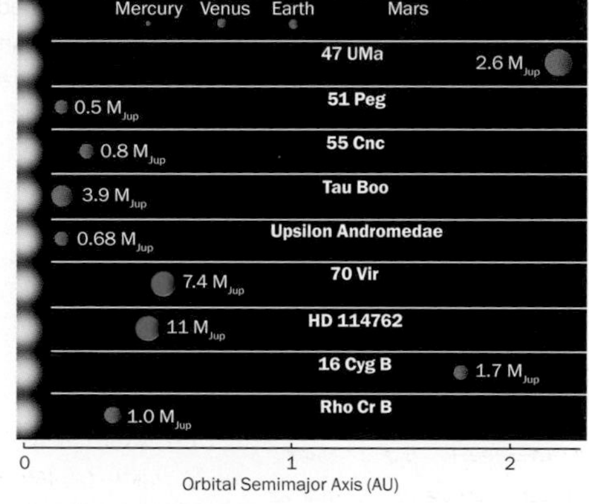

Distance from the star around which the exoplanet orbits

THE UNIVERSE

➔ **see also: Photosynthesis,** *Biology Chapter, p. 66*

KEY FACTS

THE INNER PLANETS *are rocky celestial bodies all with distinctly different atmospheres.*

THE OUTER PLANETS *are gas giants with multiple moons.*

ASTEROIDS AND COMETS *are remnants from when the solar system was created; they orbit between the planets.*

SPACE TRAVEL, *even today, serves as a way to secure political supremacy.*

Inner planets | Mars | The moon | Outer planets | Asteroids and comets | Humankind conquers the solar system

CELESTIAL BODIES OF OUR SOLAR SYSTEM

Planets, their moons, and innumerable small celestial bodies revolve in an orbit around the sun. While vastly different environmental conditions prevail, they are mostly hostile to life. People explore these celestial bodies using space probes—taking the first steps toward following them into space. Though man can see millions of light-years into space, the Milky Way can still surprise.

The surface of Mars most closely resembles that of Earth, but it does not have liquid water and its atmosphere is thinner.

THE UNIVERSE

THE INNER PLANETS

The surfaces of Mercury, Venus, Earth, and Mars are clearly distinguishable, primarily due to their differences in size and distance from the sun. Only Earth is habitable.

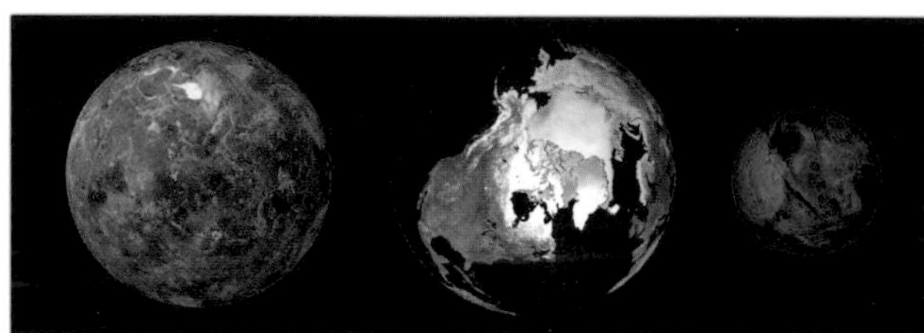

From the left: Venus, Earth, and Mars in comparison.

The inner planets have rocky surfaces and extremely differentiated atmospheres. Only Earth offers a livable environment with breathable air and lasting liquid water. Mercury and Venus are extremely hot—Mercury due to its proximity to the sun and Venus due to its greenhouse atmosphere. Mars is nearly habitable, even though its carbon dioxide atmosphere is very thin. Contrary to Mercury and Venus, both the Earth and Mars are orbited by moons.

The Greenhouse Climate of Venus

THE CLOUD BLANKET around Venus consists of droplets of corrosive sulfuric acid. It is around 12 miles (20 km) thick; therefore, only a small amount of sunlight heats the surface of the planet. But the atmosphere traps the heat radiation from the soil and heats the surface up to more than 860°F (460°C). The hostile gas envelope consists almost completely of carbon dioxide; some nitrogen; and traces of sulfur dioxide, water, and other substances. Its pressure corresponds to the hydrostatic pressure at around 3,000 ft (900 m) sea depth. Only a moderate breeze blows on the surface of Venus. Even though Venus itself rotates very slowly, the upper cloud layers complete a cycle around the planet in only four days.

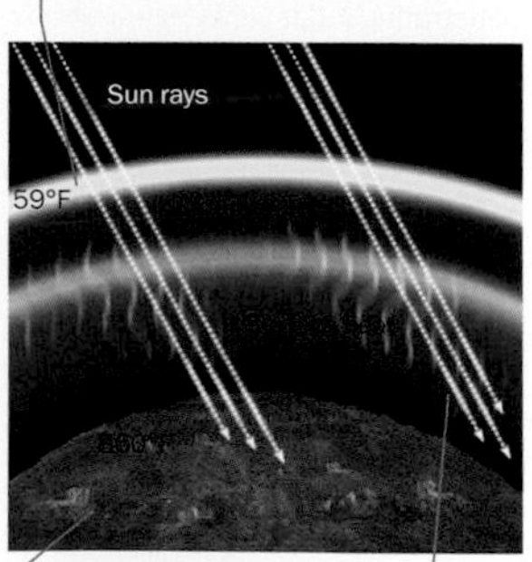
Cloud cover reflects most of the solar radiation.
Sun rays
59°F
Heat radiation on the surface is trapped by the atmosphere.
A small amount of solar radiation heats the surface of Venus.

Mercury

As the closest planet to the sun, Mercury requires only about 88 Earth-days to make one orbit. The Earth is almost three times farther from the sun. At first glance, Mercury is hardly distinguishable from our moon, yet it is somewhat larger.

Mercury's low gravity makes it unable to sustain a proper atmosphere. Therefore it possesses only a hint of a gas "envelope" that probably consists of fragments that were ejected by the sun (p. 14) and of dispersed articles from the planet's soil. Since the atmosphere cannot store heat, the temperature on Mercury's surface is extremely volatile. It fluctuates between around 806°F (430°C) during the day and −275°F (−170°C) at night.

The dense cloud blanket of Venus exhibits obvious flow patterns.

Venus

Venus, the second closest planet to the sun, is almost as large as Earth, causing it to be known as Earth's "sister planet." It is also known to us as the bright morning or evening star. Sometimes it can even be seen during the day, since it reflects around 75 percent of the radiation it receives from the sun because of its dirty yellow cloud blanket. The Earth is only half as reflective. Owing to its atmosphere, the surface temperature on Venus stays nearly level at over 860°F (460°C). Its surface cannot be seen through the clouds but can be mapped by space probes through radar. About 70 percent of Venus's terrain consists of wide, rocky plains. Jutting out from these are highlands the size of continents. Some regions of Venus have mighty mountain ranges. The terrain is further characterized by several depressions, valleys, elongated craters, and shield volcanoes.

With the space probe Mariner 10, 45% of Mercury's surface has been mapped photographically.

MARS—ALMOST HABITABLE

Although only half as large as Earth, Mars has the most similar surface to our planet in the whole solar system. It is still unclear whether or not there is, or ever was, life on Mars.

Valles Marineris, the gigantic system of canyons on Mars

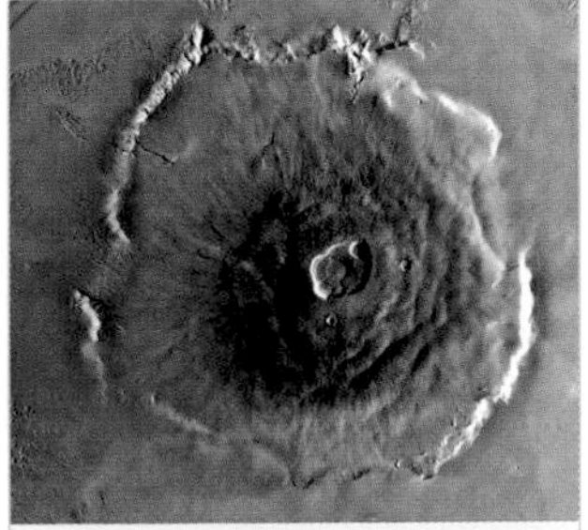

The volcano Olympus Mons is the solar system's highest mountain.

Mars is about one and a half times farther away from the sun than the Earth and requires 687 Earth days to complete one orbital revolution. A day on Mars lasts only a little longer than one day on Earth.

INSIDER KNOWLEDGE

MERCURY *is smaller than Jupiter's moon Ganymede and Saturn's moon Titan, even though it is a planet.*

CARBON DIOXIDE, *like water vapor, is a greenhouse gas also found on Earth, where it is mainly found in the oceans or rocks.*

DUST STORMS *engulf large parts of Mars every few years.*

Layers of frozen water are visible in the summer on the northern polar cap of Mars. The carbon dioxide ice has vaporized and will freeze once again in winter.

Atmosphere

The atmosphere on Mars consists of around 95 percent carbon dioxide, some nitrogen, argon, and traces of oxygen and water. The pressure on the planet's surface is typically a little bit more than 6 millibars, which is about the pressure one feels on Earth at a height of about 21 miles (34 km). It is not possible for a person to survive on Mars without an oxygen supply and a pressure suit.

The thin atmosphere does not provide a buffer against heat. In summer, the temperature near its equator can fluctuate between 68°F (20°C) during the day and –112°F (–80°C) at night. Large windstorms can rage for months.

Surface

Mars stands out in the night sky because of its reddish-brown color, which is due to its weathered rocks. Unlike Earth, Mars's surface does not have any active horizontal movement, or tectonic plates. The rocky dust contains a large amount of ferrous oxide, which is also known to us as rust. Wind and somewhat violent storms scatter the dust over the entire planet.

The northern and southern hemispheres of Mars are entirely different. The north is dominated by plains with scattered craters. Slightly north of the equator, the volcano Olympus Mons looms at a height of 15.6 miles (26 km). At nearly three times the height of Mount Everest, it is the highest mountain in the solar system. It has a diameter of 360 miles (600 km). The highland of the southern hemisphere is dotted with impact craters. A few especially large impact basins can also be found there with diameters of up to 1,200 miles (2,000 km). Just south of the equator, there is a system of massive canyons, the Valles Marineris, which is more than 2,400 miles (4,000 km) in length and 420 miles (700 km) in width. If one were to place the Grand Canyon there, it would hardly be noticeable.

Flood Catastrophes

The terrain of Mars reflects signs of devastating floods that occurred in the Valles Marineris during an earlier age. Bodies of water must have traveled along a north-sloped gradient, causing abrupt channels in the ground and transforming greater obstructions into streamlined islands. The floods were perhaps caused by ice locked under the surface that was melted by volcanic heat. This early surface water, however, can no longer be seen today, as Mars's atmosphere is so thin that the unfiltered energy from the sun would cause it to evaporate instantaneously. While liquid water remains elusive, frozen water at the poles appears extensive.

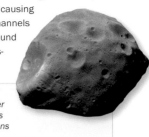

Phobos, the larger of Mars's two moons

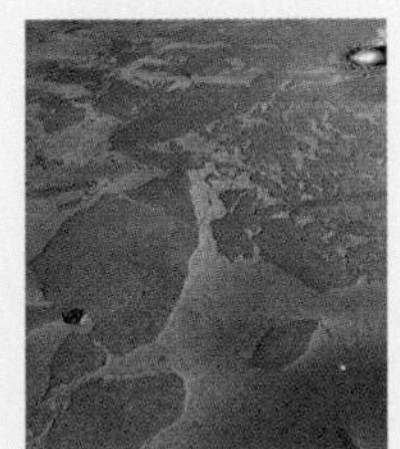

WATER *exists today in the soil of Mars in the form of ice; earlier it seems that there was even liquid water.*

AS YET, THE EXISTENCE OF *life on Mars has not been proved. It is presumed that the earliest form of life would have been microorganisms.*

This view of the surface structure of Mars is made up of dust-covered ice sheets.

Water and Life on Mars

DATA FROM MARS SPACE PROBES and the Phoenix Lander have shown that there are carbonate minerals in some regions of Mars. This indicates that there may have been a denser atmosphere and liquid water in the past. Deep-penetrating radar waves show abundant ice deposits at the poles.

METEORITE ALH84001 consists of Mars rock (p. 22). Microscopically small crystal chains were discovered inside of it, which resemble parts of bacteria found on Earth. It is debatable whether or not they originate from bacteria on Mars. They could even have been formed minerally. Similar traces were found in other Mars meteorites.

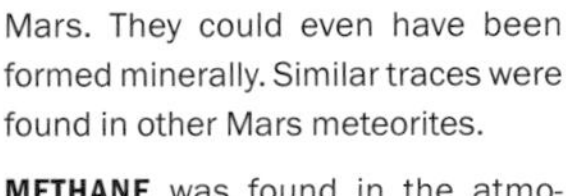

METHANE was found in the atmosphere of Mars. Whether it was formed by geological processes or by microorganisms is unclear.

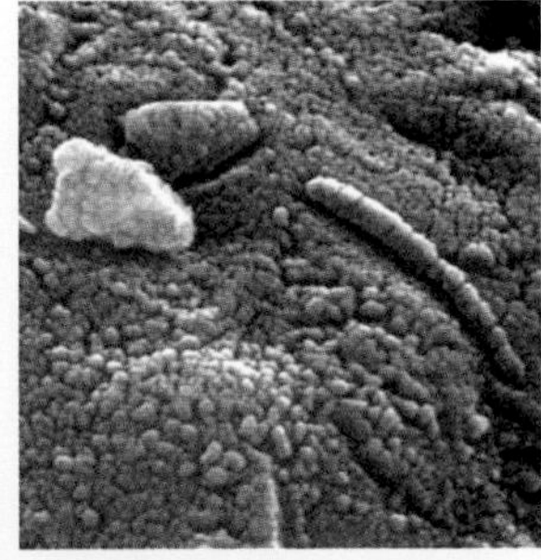

The Mars meteorite ALH84001 seen through an electronic microscope

THE MOON—EARTH'S COMPANION

The moon revolves around the Earth at a distance of around 230,000 miles (384,000 km). No other celestial body is as continuously close to our planet or as well researched as the moon.

The moon's surface resembles a rocky desert. It is characterized by impact craters, basins, and depressions, which are full of solidified lava.

When compared with the other planets in the solar system, the Earth has by far the largest moon in proportion to its own size. Its diameter of around 2,088 miles (3,480 km) corresponds to more than 25 percent of the Earth's diameter. Consequently, the Earth and moon are sometimes called dual planets. The mass of the moon is, however, not large enough to hold a gas envelope worth mentioning. As a result, its temperature fluctuates between 266°F (130°C) on the lighted side and –256°F (–160°C) on the darkened side.

The side of the moon facing away from the Earth: more craters, fewer plains.

Craters and Seas

The crater-scarred moon shows how the Earth looked around 4 billion years ago. At that time, the newly formed planets were exposed to a hailstorm of asteroids (p. 22). The Earth's craters were worn off or covered through the course of time by wind, water, and cataclysms of the crust. These forces are absent on the moon. Its appearance has hardly changed since the creation of its dark lowlands, which can be recognized with the naked eye.

Earlier they were regarded as seas, and thus named accordingly. The "Sea of Tranquility" lies at the center of the moon's western hemisphere. The first men on the moon left their footprints in the gray dust of this sea in 1969 (p. 23). It is now known that the moon's seas are solidified lava rivers in impact craters.

Moon crater Eratosthenes has a diameter of ca 35 miles (58 km).

Moonlight and Earthlight

For most of the month, the moon lights up the night sky by reflecting sunlight. Most of the time we see only part of the sunlit hemisphere of the moon, for example, as a crescent. It appears as a full moon only when the moon's revolution sets the Earth between the moon and the sun.

Yet even the darkened part of the moon facing Earth, opposite to the sun, is never completely dark. It is lit by "earthlight," the sunlight that is reflected primarily by clouds around the Earth. This phenomenon is interesting for climate researchers since it enables the measurement of the Earth's reflection, which is partly influencing the warming of its atmosphere and climate change.

How Did the Earth Acquire Its Moon?

The moon is unique. Mercury and Venus do not have any moons, while the tiny moons around Mars are probably trapped asteroids. The proposed explanation is that about 4.5 billion years ago, a planet the size of Mars collided with the young Earth. The iron cores of the planets melted, while their rocky material evaporated or was thrown into space. This material massed together in the Earth's orbit to create the moon. One fact that substantiates this theory is that the moon contains little iron.

above: *According to computer simulation, the Earth acquired its moon thanks to a cosmic collision.*

Orbiting Time and Rotation

Anyone who observes the moon over days and weeks might notice that it always presents the same side. This means it takes the same amount of time to complete one rotation around its own axis as it does to complete one revolution around the Earth: about 27 days. After half a revolution, it faces the opposite direction as at the start of the revolution. After another half revolution, it again faces the original direction.

Occurrence of Lunar and Solar Eclipse

THE MOON IS ECLIPSED when it passes through the Earth's shadow. The sun is eclipsed when the moon's shadow falls on the Earth. For this to happen, the moon must position itself between the Earth and the sun. Since the shadow of the moon is smaller than Earth, we can perceive the solar eclipse only in certain regions (p. 14). In the surrounding areas, a part of the sun appears darkened.

FOR AN ECLIPSE to occur, the Earth, moon, and sun must align in a nearly straight line. Yet, because the moon's orbit is slanted compared to the Earth's orbit, eclipses do not occur with each revolution of the moon around Earth.

Solar eclipse: The shadow of the moon falls on the Earth (2 and 3).

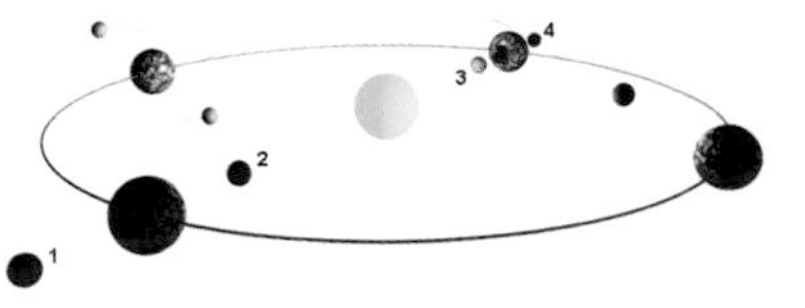

Lunar eclipse: The moon passes through the Earth's shadow (1 and 4).

At all other positions, the shadows of the moon and the Earth fall on empty space.

➲ see also: Global Warming, *Earth Chapter*, p. 51

THE OUTER PLANETS

The four gigantic outer planets are clearly distinguishable from the four inner rocky planets. They possess relatively small rocky cores, massive atmospheres, and many moons.

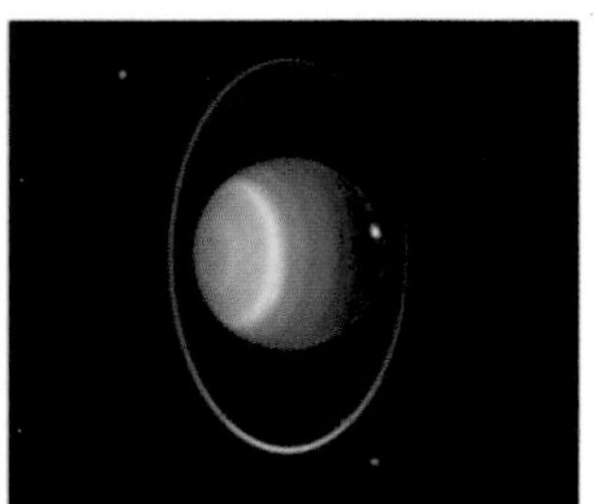

Uranus shows its atmosphere, moons, and fine rings under an infrared light.

Jupiter is the largest planet in the solar system, with 11 times Earth's diameter and 318 times its mass. Saturn is hardly less impressive, with nine times Earth's diameter, while the diameters of Uranus and Neptune are around four times greater than Earth's. All of the outer planets revolve around the sun outside the asteroid belt (pp. 16, 22). As the innermost of the outer planets, Jupiter is about five times farther from the sun than Earth; the others are about 10, 20, and 30 times as distant.

Massive Atmospheres

The brownish-red and yellow cloud bands of Jupiter are conspicuous, along with the Great Red Spot, a high-pressure storm that revolves around the planet. Based on its dimensions, it could easily engulf the Earth. Furthermore, the storm has a very long life, as astronomers have observed it as far back as the 17th century.

All cloud bands are composed largely of the gases that also make up the sun: hydrogen and helium. Their colorful variety results from differing proportions of chemical substances.

Solar wind particles generate circular polar lights at the south pole of Saturn.

Planetary Ring Systems

All outer planets are orbited by ring systems. That of Saturn is the largest and most spectacular. The numerous rings consist of dust, ice crystals, and ice and rock fragments. Presumably, Saturn's rings are remnants of ruptured comets, asteroids, and moons. They are structured with spokes, waves, and interweaving patterns. Some could have resulted from gravitational forces of Saturn's moons or hurtling asteroids. Many have remained unexplained.

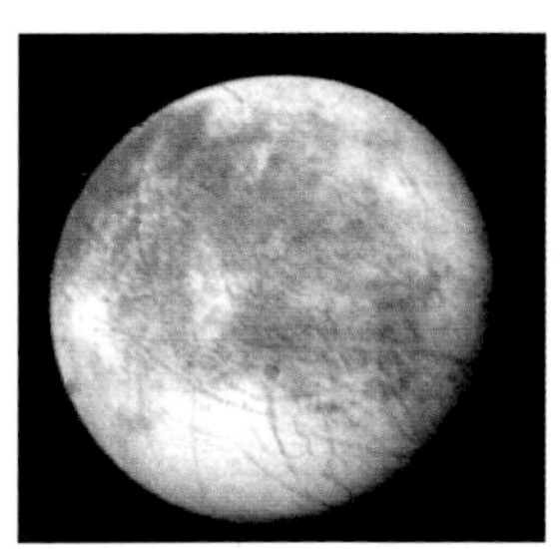

Europa's Ocean

The surface of Jupiter's moon Europa is a thick ice crust. Underneath it is believed that there are deep oceans, because the moon during its slightly elliptical orbit is heated through the compression and repression caused by the periodically changing force of Jupiter. Europa could, therefore, offer a habitat for microorganisms. Yet there are also signs of hydrogen peroxide and sulfuric acid, which largely decompose organic matter. However, there are bacteria on Earth that are able to live under extremely aggressive conditions.

above: *Europa's surface resembles ice fields on Earth.*

Composition of the Gas Giants

THE ATMOSPHERES OF THE OUTER PLANETS consist primarily of hydrogen and helium, as well as smaller amounts of methane, ammonia, sulfur, water, and other substances. Deeper within the planets, gas is liquefied due to enormous pressure caused from the layers lying above.

UNDER THEIR LIQUID LAYERS, Uranus and Neptune have ice-like coats. Deep inside Jupiter and Saturn, the pressure is a million times greater than at the surface. The hydrogen there resembles an electrically conducting metal. All outer planets are presumed to have rocky cores.

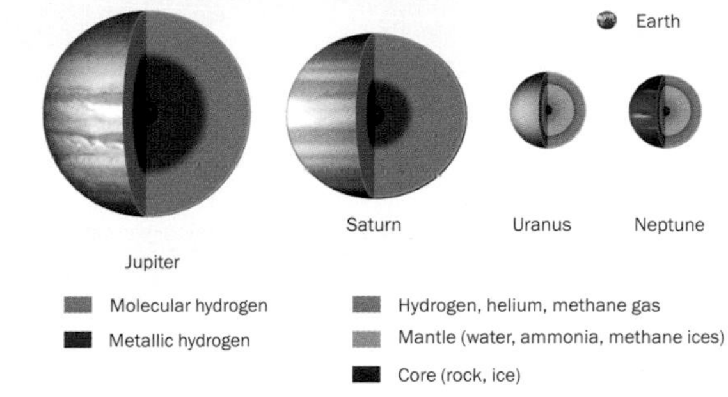

The outer layers of Jupiter and Saturn consist of sulfur compounds and ammonia crystals, among other things.

The bluish coloring of Uranus and Neptune is caused by methane in their atmospheres.

Numerous Moons

Like small planetary systems, numerous and variously shaped moons orbit the outer planets. More than 150 have been discovered so far. The greatest moons of Jupiter are Io, Europa, Ganymede, and Calisto. While the surface of Europa consists of ice, the sulfur-covered Io is the most volcanically active celestial body in the solar system. With a diameter of around 3,268 miles (5,260 km), Ganymede is the largest moon in the solar system. Calisto is heavily scarred by impact craters.

Among Saturn's moons, Titan is especially conspicuous. It is the second largest moon in the solar system and possesses a dense atmosphere of nitrogen. It resembles the original atmosphere on Earth, but is much colder. The surface area of Uranus's moon Miranda is covered with canyons. Neptune's moon Triton has a thin atmosphere and a temperature of 38 kelvin (–390°F or –235°C).

This infrared photograph allows a glimpse through the dense atmosphere of Saturn's moon Titan.

INSIDER KNOWLEDGE

THE DISTANCE *between the moon and the Earth increases by almost 1.6 inches (4 cm) annually.*

JUPITER'S RINGS *are extremely fine: no ice fragments, no ice crystals, no rock fragments, no dust particles.*

THE VOLCANOES *of some moons spew ice instead of lava.*

ASTEROIDS AND COMETS: WANDERING SPACE DEBRIS

Asteroids and comets have roamed around the planets since the start of the solar system. Now and then, they draw attention to themselves through glorious bursts of light.

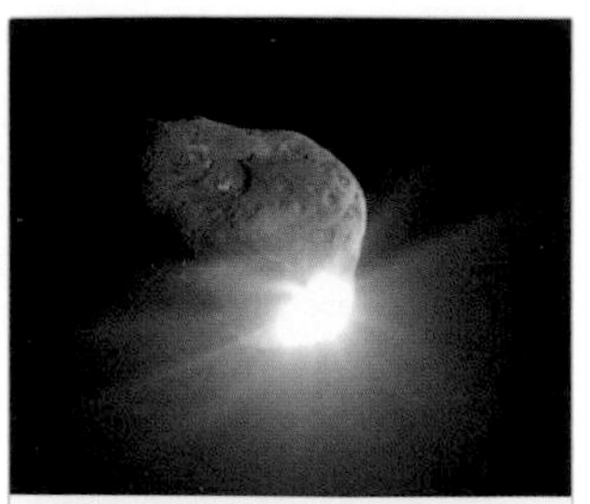

Comet Tempel 1 was examined in 2005 by means of the controlled impact of a space probe.

Asteroids and comets are remnants that originate from the time of the solar system's creation (p. 16). They consist of material that could not agglomerate into planets. Asteroids are irregularly shaped rocks; some are several hundred miles (kilometers) long, but many are shorter than one mile (kilometer).

Comets are large clumps of dust and rock, which are held together by ice. They can be a few miles (kilometers) long. Asteroids and comets cannot always be distinguished, as some celestial bodies have properties of both.

Asteroids are spectrally classified: They are either carbonaceous (75 percent of known asteroids), silicaceous (17 percent), or metallic (8 percent).

This meteorite crater in the desert of Arizona is 3,891 ft (1,186 m) long and about 50,000 years old.

A Comet Awakens

If a comet penetrates into the inner solar system, the sun heats it up, which typically results in a part of its matter evaporating and forming an elongated atmosphere, a so-called coma. The comet reflects sunlight, and the sun-rays incite its gases to radiate themselves.

A few comets develop a characteristic comet tail in the vicinity of the sun. The radiation pressure on the particles and light from the sun drive gas pieces and fine dust out of the coma. Therefore with every orbit around the sun, a comet loses matter until it ultimately disintegrates completely.

The asteroid Gaspra was measured in 1991 by the space probe Galileo.

Home of Comets and Asteroids

Most comets revolve around the sun on elongated elliptical orbits. A few originate from the area of space directly behind the outer planets (p. 21). In that region, there are a large number of widely scattered celestial bodies made of ice or rock. Other comets appear to originate from the edge of the solar system. There, the gravitational pull of the sun disappears and the "no man's land" between the stars begins. Even light takes one to two years to reach that area. These comets possibly form the Oort cloud around the solar system.

Most asteroids revolve around the sun between the orbits of Mars and Jupiter in the asteroid belt (p. 48).

On Collision Course

When asteroids and comets come too close to a planet, they can be hurled into another orbit, trapped by the gravitational force as moons, or can collide. During the early history of the solar system, the latter possibility occurred quite frequently. There are indications that collisions occurred even on Earth. The extinction of dinosaurs 65.5 million years ago could have been caused by an asteroid impact.

Meteors

Meteors are the streaks that occasionally illuminate the night sky. They originate from small pieces of matter that penetrate the atmosphere at high speeds. The air friction causes them to evaporate, while the energy released from the separated particles incites a glow. Sometimes they do not die down completely, and residues appear on the Earth's surface as meteorites. Most of the meteorites are fragments from asteroids.

above: *If the Earth crosses the path of a disintegrating comet, one can observe a meteor shower.*

Asteroids that intersect the Earth's orbit are being observed today. Methods are being developed for possibly deflecting such asteroids from their path, even if there is no direct threat perceived.

Halley's Comet

THIS COMET has been observed for centuries. Astronomer Edmond Halley calculated its elongated elliptical orbit and its periodical return. The comet reaches behind the orbit of Neptune and requires on an average 76 years to complete a revolution around the sun. Deviations occur through gravitational forces of the planets. During its last transit in the vicinity of Earth in 1986, it was analyzed by several space probes. The core of the comet is about 9 miles (15 km) large and surprisingly dark like coal.

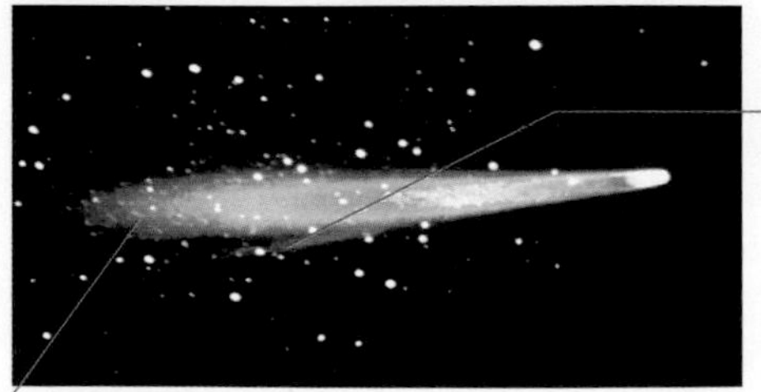

Gas or plasma tail: The light gas is torn away by the sun's radiation. The tail can stretch over 62 million miles (100 million km).

Dust tail: The dust is slowly pushed away by the sun's radiation and traces the comet's curved path.

see also: Meteorite Impact, *Earth Chapter, p. 33*

HUMANKIND CONQUERS THE SOLAR SYSTEM

What was once considered impossible has become reality. Rockets bring people into space, probes research the universe, and man-made satellites leave their mark on our daily lives.

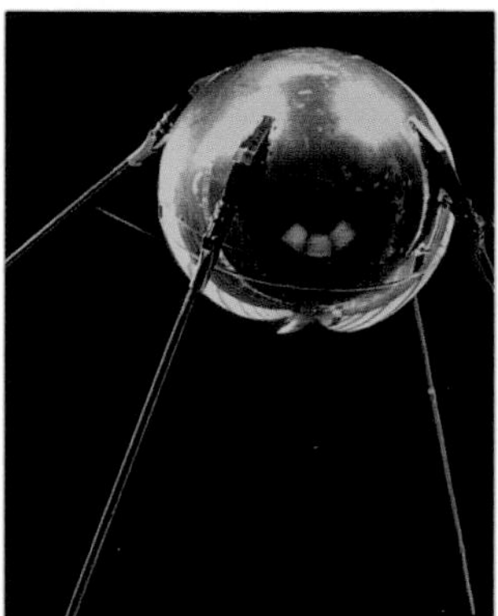

The Soviet Sputnik 1 was the first man-made satellite to orbit around Earth. With it began the era of space travel in 1957.

The Apollo project of the U.S. set man on a foreign celestial body in 1969 and brought him safely back to Earth.

At the start of the 20th century, pioneers worldwide began to substantiate visions of space travel through facts. As scientists examined its feasibility in theory, they looked for solutions to the propulsion and steering problems of rockets.

Military Developments

The military evolution of the rocket brought the German V2 to the forefront in the Second World War. It

Space probes and robots are supposed to explore Mars.

was the first rocket to penetrate the frontiers of space at a height of more than 50 miles (80 km).

In the Cold War, the possibilities of rocket technology were further exploited. Spy satellites were launched into orbit around the Earth, threatening the scenario of atomic destruction. The nuclear threat has been mitigated today; nonetheless, space technology remains a significant means for securing political and military power for the former superpowers.

Science and Technology

The modern world cannot survive without space travel. Satellites transmit news, telephone conversations, stock information, and computer data worldwide. They facilitate the navigation of cars and of cruise missiles. Satellites transmit data for weather forecasts, warn of environmental catastrophes, measure the ozone layer, and survey crops.

Other satellites peer into space. There, they not only perceive visible light, but also infra-red, ultra-violet, and x-rays. They deliver valuable information through which we can better understand the universe, and our place therein. Furthermore, celestial bodies and solar systems are explored on-site by means of planetary probes and robots.

Manned Space Travel

The magic moment of space travel struck shortly after man personally ventured into space at the edges of Earth. In a forceful act of discovery between 1969 and 1972, the Apollo project by the U.S. set man on the moon and brought him back safely to Earth.

Today, astronauts from many nations work collectively at the International Space Station. In conditions of zero gravity, they are researching, among other things, medicine, industrial materials, space travel technology, and astrophysics. Internationally, work is under way on technologies that will enable the installation of outposts on the moon and Mars in the next 15 to 30 years.

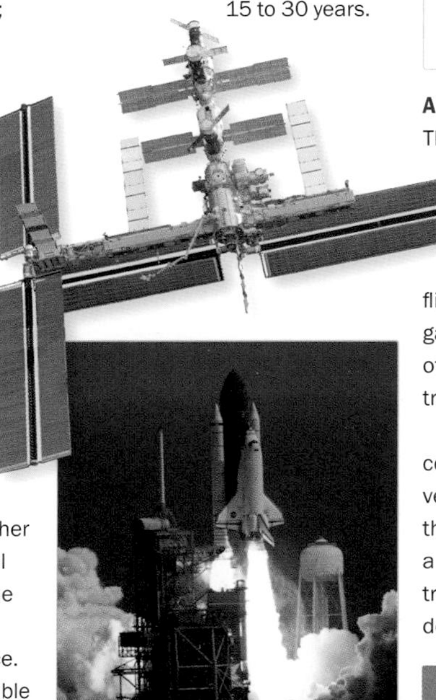

The space shuttle brings material and astronauts to the International Space Station (ISS).
above: *ISS with solar cell surfaces and a robotic arm.*

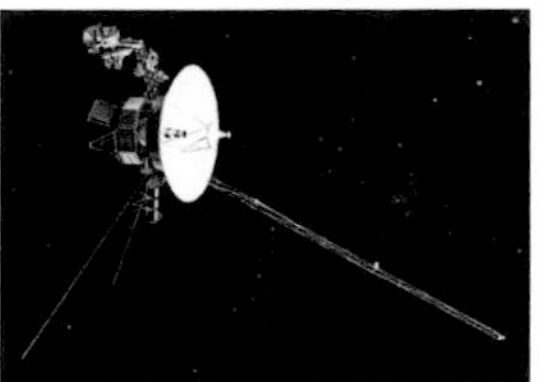

At the Edge of the Solar System

The U.S. space probe Voyager 1 embarked on a long journey in 1977. It transmitted valuable data on the outer planets and is now at the far edge of the solar system. The probe is at a distance of around 9.3 billion miles (15 billion km) from the sun, two and a half times farther than the dwarf planet Pluto. Voyager 1 is, therefore, the farthest man-made object in space. It travels at a speed of 10.5 miles/sec (17 km/sec) and still transmits measured data. According to information from NASA, its energy supply is ensured theoretically until 2020.

above: *Space Probe Voyager 1*

Alternative Space Travel

The rocket aircraft SpaceShipOne reached an altitude of over 62 miles (100 km) in 2004. It was the first privately developed and financed space flight to the borders of space—and gave a signal for the establishment of the first non-governmental space travel enterprises.

They wish to exploit space commercially after further developmental work, for instance, through world space travel, as a provider for state-owned space travel as well as for industrial development research.

21ST CENTURY

SATELLITES *offer optimum possibilities for researching our planet in its entirety.*

SPACE RESEARCH *shows how closely the Earth is integrated in the cosmic experience.*

COLONIZATION OF SPACE *could protect humanity from global catastrophes.*

➔ **see also: Rockets,** *Physics and Technology Chapter, p. 123*

Monographic Boxes

Analytic Boxes

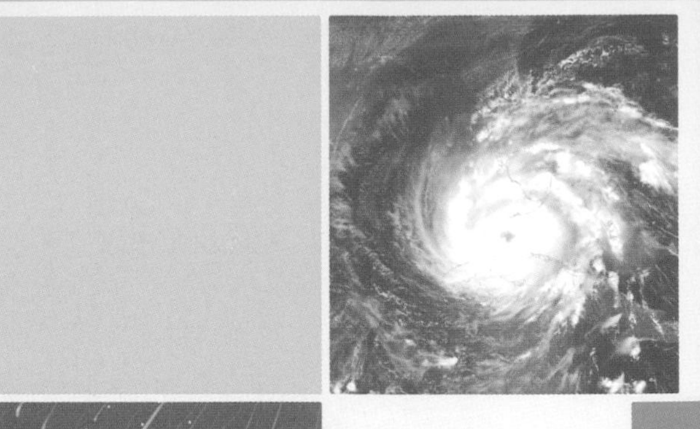

THE EARTH

With his novels "20,000 Leagues under the Sea" and "Journey to the Center of the Earth," Jules Verne became one of the most prominent visionaries of geology. His stories inspired have often inspired the very research that have allowed his wild imaginings to become a reality. The technological and scientific advancements we have made have not only opened up unexplored worlds for us, like the depths of the sea or the distant past of the dinosaurs, but have also given us important insights into the very workings of the Earth. Global warming, rising sea levels, and tsunamis are the concerns of the 21st century. It is going to be one of the principal duties of scientific research to investigate the Earth's system in a more effective way to find solutions for the threat of climatic catastrophe.

KEY FACTS

THE SUN *first shone around 4.6 billion years ago.*

THE AGE OF EARTH *is estimated to be 4.55 billion years.*

THE MOON *resulted from a meteor strike on the Earth around 4.53 billion years ago.*

THE FIRST ATMOSPHERE *developed around 4 billion years ago.*

CONTINENTS FIRST *emerged around 4 billion years ago.*

Birth of the Earth | Earth's system

EARTH'S ORIGIN

After the big bang 14 billion years ago, around 9 billion years passed before our solar system developed. The birth of the sun around 4.6 billion years ago led to the creation of the solar system, our Earth, and the other planets. The story of Earth's development provides answers to questions about its current form and many geological phenomena. It explains, for example, the inner structure of the Earth, formation of the atmosphere and magnetic field surrounding the Earth, and origin of oceans and continents.

The structure of the Earth developed in the first eon of Earth's history between 4.57 and 3.8 billion years ago.

BIRTH OF THE EARTH

Earth reached its present form within approximately 50 million years, merely the blink of an eye relative to its age of 4.55 billion years. The geological conditions today mirror those of the past.

After its birth (p. 10), a vast number of celestial bodies moved in a path around the young sun. These planetary predecessors, known as planetesimals, varied in size from a few millimeters to several hundred miles. They collided with each other and either smashed into smaller fragments or, through the sun's heat, clumped into larger objects. Over the course of millions of years, some of these steadily growing balls of matter attained a certain level of mass, hence gravity, and began to revolve in stable trajectories around the sun. One of these satellites, or protoplanets, was the Earth.

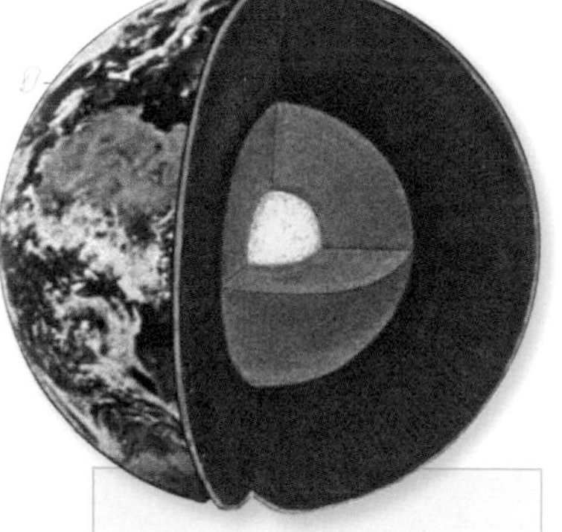

The layered structure of the Earth from the inside out: core, mantle, and crust.

The Young Earth

The young Earth differed fundamentally from the planet we know today. Because of extremely high temperatures, all volatile elements evaporated. The "proto-Earth" was a gas-free, shapeless, solid clump of rock that moved unevenly around the sun. The Earth's rotation only stabilized about 4.5 billion years ago with the creation of the moon.

Around the same time, the inner structure of Earth was on the verge of restructuring itself. Solar energy, continual collisions with other celestial bodies, and radioactive decay in the Earth's interior produced so much heat that the young Earth began to melt. Heavy elements such as iron sank in the molten stone and concentrated within the Earth's core, while lighter elements collected on the surface. Eventually, the layered structure of the Earth was formed.

Layered Structure of the Earth

Present-day Earth is constructed like an onion. Its core has a diameter of about 4,000 miles (7,100 km). It consists primarily of iron, as well as a few parts nickel, and has a temperature upwards of 7000°F (3900°C). Only its innermost area, about 746 miles (1,200 km) in diameter, is solid; the rest is liquid. The Earth's core is enclosed by a powerful 1,771 mile (2,850 km) mantle. The mantle's pressure and temperature are so high that the rocks, despite their solid state, react like modeling clay and do not break in spite of the immense pressure.

The Earth's surface forms a solid external crust. It is relatively thin, composing less than 1 percent of the Earth's total volume and contains a high concentration of aluminum and silicon (p. 24). There are two types of crust material: The oceanic crust, up to 6 miles (10 km) thick, and the continental crust, up to 25 miles (40 km) thick. The movements occurring on the crust are caused by tectonic plates, which are broken portions of the lithosphere (the crust and upper part of the mantle).

A steady 40,000 year rain formed the original oceans.

The Age of Rocks

RADIOMETRIC DATING IS A METHOD OF calculating the age of rocks. It was a great leap forward, since the age of rocks could previously only be estimated. The method is based on the fact that radioactive elements decay at a consistent rate. Each radioactive element requires a certain amount of time for its original mass to decay by half. This amount of time is known as the element's half-life. Using a mass spectrometer, the quantity of original elements and their decay products can be measured in a rock. Its age is calculated based on the proportion and half-life of the radioactive elements.

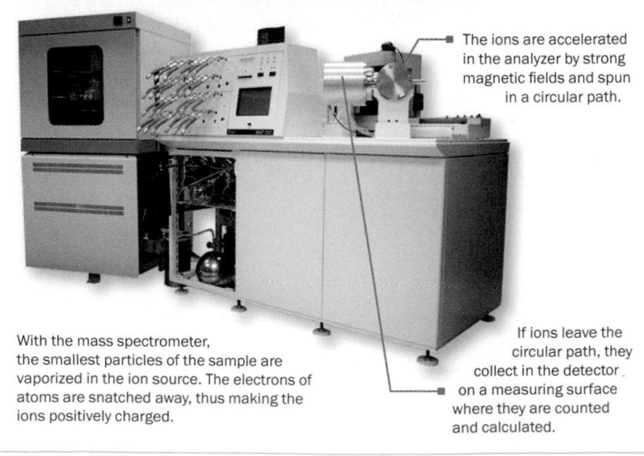

The ions are accelerated in the analyzer by strong magnetic fields and spun in a circular path.

With the mass spectrometer, the smallest particles of the sample are vaporized in the ion source. The electrons of atoms are snatched away, thus making the ions positively charged.

If ions leave the circular path, they collect in the detector on a measuring surface where they are counted and calculated.

see also: **Sun and Moon**, *Universe Chapter, pp. 14, 20*

EARTH'S SYSTEM

After the formation of Earth 4.55 billion years ago, about 500 million years passed before the first atmosphere, ocean, and continents came into being.

When Earth reached its current size, gravity enabled it to retain gases in its atmosphere which had previously evaporated into the universe. For millions of years, the planet was surrounded by a dense, hot cloud of hydrogen, carbon dioxide, nitrogen, ammonia, methane, and hydrogen sulfide.

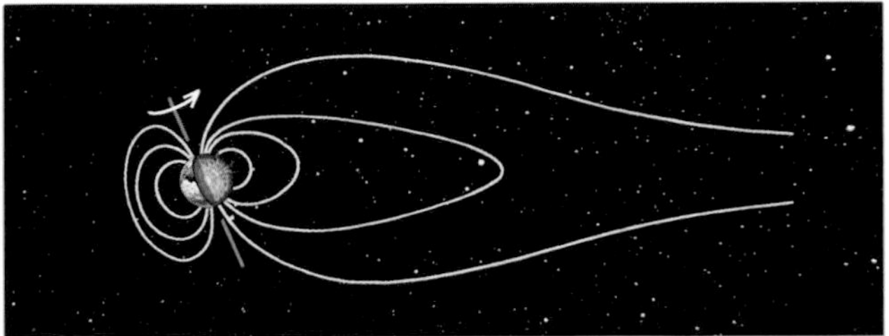

The Earth's magnetic field deflects the high-energy particles of the solar wind and becomes deformed as a result. It forms a magnetic tail.

The Great Rain

The solar system still contained much matter that was not bound to the planets; however, as the number of collisions with this matter declined and the Earth slowly cooled down, hydrogen began to condense. A torrential rain set in which lasted 40,000 years. Water collected in depressions and rose incessantly until it formed the first globe-spanning ocean.

New Land

Wind and rain eroded the landmasses that projected out of the ocean. Loose, crushed rocks collected in hollows, were carried by rivers to the sea, and were deposited at the bottom as sediment. This formation of rocks continued for millions of years.

Because of their increasing weight, sediments pressed the oceanic crust into the upper mantle where it melted. The molten stone rose up and reacted chemically with the sediment. This reaction led to the development of granite. Because of the lower density of this stone, granite eventually raised itself out of the sea and formed the first non-volcanic continents.

INSIDER KNOWLEDGE

OLDEST ROCK: *4.03-billion-year-old gneiss at Great Slave Lake*

EARTH'S WEIGHT: *about 13.2 x 10^{24} lbs (6 x 10^{24} kg)*

EARTH'S SURFACE AREA: *about 196.9 x 10^6 miles^2 (510.1 x 10^6 km^2)*

EARTH'S DIAMETER: *7,928 miles (12,756 km) at Equator, 7,902 miles (12,714 km) at Poles*

EARTH'S CIRCUMFERENCE: *24,901 miles (40,075 km) at Equator, 24,859 miles (40,008 km) at Poles*

Cracks formed at the edge of the oceanic crust. Consequently, powerful bodies of granite as large as islands broke loose and began to drift towards the outer mantle. Some of the stone bodies collided and united to form larger landmasses; others were eroded over time due to wind and rain, and disappeared.

Earth's Magnetic Field

The Earth's magnetic field developed about 4 billion years ago, probably simultaneously with the formation of Earth's layered structure. As with a direct current generator, there is an interaction between the Earth's rotation and the flow of liquid iron in the outer core. The resulting electrical current formed a magnetic field that served as effective protection against cosmic radiation and was an important precondition for the development of life on Earth.

EARTH'S DISK: *The conception of Earth as a disk had already been rejected in antiquity. Its spherical shape was generally well-known and accepted in the Middle Ages.*

GEOCENTRIC WORLDVIEW: *The Earth was considered the center of the universe—the Church maintained that view into the 17th century.*

The Greek philosopher Aristotle is considered the father of natural sciences.

Aristotle and Company

ARISTOTLE, in the fourth century B.C., held a belief that all celestial bodies circle around a stationary Earth which reigned for nearly 2,000 years. One of its most important proponents in the second century was Ptolemy; therefore, one also hears of a Ptolemaic worldview. In 1509, Nicolaus Copernicus discovered that celestial bodies orbit the sun. Galileo Galilei succeeded in physically proving the theory of heliocentrism, also known as the Copernican worldview. Consequently, he was treated with great hostility by the Church.

THE GREEKS also employed their own theory about the creation of the Earth. They formulated a theory of four elements, according to which all matter originated from four classical elements: fire, water, air, and earth. They certainly made no attempt to find proof for their theories, and this distinguishes them from today's natural scientists.

This illustration depicts symbolically the break from the medieval worldview.

THE EARTH

KEY FACTS

THERE ARE OVER 4,000 *minerals.*

ABOUT 30 MINERALS *form into rocks, which are more common than all the other minerals.*

THE LARGEST CRYSTAL *is a beryl from Madagascar: length 59.1 ft (18 m), diameter 11.5 ft (3.5 m), volume 5,050 ft³ (143 m³), weight 380 tons.*

A MONOLITH *is a geological feature composed of one stone or rock.*

Glittering variety—minerals | The world of rocks

BUILDING MATERIALS OF EARTH—MINERALS AND ROCKS

Since the Stone Age, humans have mined rocks and minerals to use them as raw materials. Because they are specially valued for their form, color and luster, gems or precious stones are frequently used for jewelry. The studies of the origin, characteristics and composition of rocks and minerals are known as petrology and mineralogy, respectively.

Every rock on Earth contains minerals.

GLITTERING VARIETY—MINERALS

Minerals are the solid building materials of the Earth, which include metals and salts. They can develop through vastly different geological processes.

Minerals consist of solid matter that, as a rule, takes on a crystalline structure. They can be either pure elements (e.g., gold, silver, or sulfur) or chemical compounds. Minerals can also be classified by the way they are formed; the different types include igneous, sedimentary, metamorphic, and weathered minerals. Some minerals, such as garnet, can take shape in multiple ways.

Igneous Minerals

Igneous minerals such as feldspar, quartz, and mica form when magma rising out of the Earth's mantle cools at a temperature of 2732°F (1500°C). As a result of this cooling, crystallization occurs until the chemical composition of the molten rock has changed to such an extent that it is not possible for any new minerals to emerge.

Sedimentary Minerals

Many minerals form through sedimentation (p. 29). For example, if seawater were to evaporate then minerals such as calcite, dolomite, anhydrite, gypsum, halite (rock salt), and potassium chloride would be left behind. In addition, compression of loose particles by increased temperature and pressure, as well as chemical reactions, leads to the formation of sedimentary minerals like clay. These rocks cover nearly 75 percent of the Earth's surface.

Metamorphic Minerals

Under conditions of high temperatures or intense pressure, the original crystal lattice of minerals becomes unstable. Meanwhile, their components take the form of other structures that can withstand the changed conditions. These resulting minerals are metamorphic: graphite, talc, and garnet.

Weathered Minerals

Over time, weathering can form minerals like malachite, which results from the oxidation of copper ores (p. 43). Some clay minerals, such as kaolinite, result from chemical decomposition occurring above ground.

Garnet develops from the cooling of magma or through metamorphism.

ONLY RARELY *do minerals consist of a uniform crystal lattice; poly-crystal minerals are made up of many small crystals.*

CONTRARY *to the naturally occurring process of crystallization, crystal breeding produces artificial crystals.*

Cubic crystal lattice of rock salt crystals (sodium chloride)

What Is a Crystal?

CRYSTALS ARE solid bodies whose ions, atoms, or molecules are strictly arranged in a three-dimensional lattice. The structure of the crystal lattice depends on its chemical composition as well as the conditions under which it formed. The lattice presents different types of symmetry, which are used to differentiate crystals within 32 classes and then into seven different systems. Only a few minerals, such as glass or opal, do not contain crystal formations; they are called amorphous or shapeless.

WITHIN THE SEMICONDUCTOR INDUSTRY, in which the most important basic material is silicon, crystals are being "bred" even today. Not only are synthetic crystals purer than natural crystals, but they are also much more convenient to produce, as no digging is involved.

Triclinic | Monoclinic | Orthorhombic | Trigonal

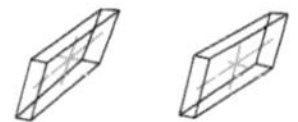
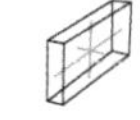
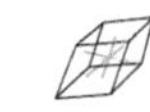

Hexagon | Tetragon | Cubic

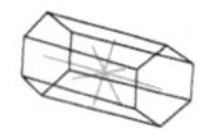

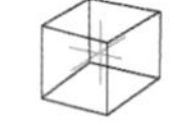

The seven crystal systems

Mineral	Hardness
Talc	1
Gypsum	2
Calcite	3
Fluorite	4
Apatite	5
Orthoclase	6
Quartz	7
Topaz	8
Corundum	9
Diamond	10

Mineral Hardness

The hardness of a mineral is indicated by its resistance to mechanical stress. In mineralogy and geology, the scratch hardness test is especially used during analysis. The Mohs Hardness Scale, named after the German mineralogist Friedrich Mohs, is based on the idea that each mineral is able to scratch those that are below it on the scale. The lowest hardness grade is talc while the highest is diamond, which can only be scratched by itself.

above: *Mohs Hardness Scale*

see also: Semiconductors, *Chemistry Chapter, p. 102* | *Physics and Technology Chapter, p. 140*

THE WORLD OF ROCKS

According to geologists, all rocks are naturally occurring aggregates of minerals, rock fragments, or remnants of organisms.

Mount Augustus in Australia is the largest monolith at 5 miles (8 km) long, over 2,297 ft (700 m) tall, and covering 18.5 miles² (48 km²).

There are three primary types of rock formation through which rocks are differentiated.

Igneous Rocks

Igneous rocks form when liquid magma cools, leading minerals to crystallize and attach themselves to larger, firmer objects. They are differentiated by whether they were formed within the Earth (intrusive or plutonic rocks) or on the surface (extrusive or volcanic rocks).

When magma solidifies within the Earth's crust, these enormous masses are known as plutons. Plutons include batholiths, dikes, sills, laccoliths, and lopoliths. These deeply embedded rocks (i.e., granite and diorite) have especially large crystals that are caused by the slow cooling process.

Igneous rock: Cross-section of a round lava bomb, Black Butte Crater, Oregon.

If magma reaches the Earth's surface through a volcanic eruption, after which it is called lava, then only small crystals are formed. Typical extrusive igneous rocks are basalt and rhyolite. Some vulcanites also have separate large crystals. These external crystals, such as diamonds (p. 43), are dragged along and eventually brought to the surface. During the quick cooling of lava, no mineral crystallization takes place. Instead, volcanic glass such as obsidian is formed.

Sedimentary Rocks

Loose sediments can result from deposits of weathered rock fragments, remnants of plants and animals or chemical precipitations. Through the stresses of pressure and temperature, they are dehydrated and compressed into sedimentary rocks.

Sedimentary rocks are classified into several main groups: clastic sediments (fragmental rocks), chemical sediments, biogenous sediments, and a special form of residue sediments (residual rocks).

Clastic sediments form from other mechanically destroyed rocks. They are differentiated according to the size of their components or grains: clay, silt, sand, or gravel. Chemical sediments such as salt rocks, sinter, and stalactites are the result of vaporization from watery solutions. Biogenous sedimentary rocks, which develop from organic remains, include coal as well as sediments of reef debris found on beaches. Residual rocks form as a result of the chemical breakdown of rocks on the Earth's surface and sedimentation of the decomposed remains.

Metamorphic Rocks

Metamorphism means transformation; hence metamorphic rocks form from the transformation of a pre-existing rock (referred to as a protolith) within the Earth's crust. Necessary prerequisites for this mutation are high temperature and intense pressure. Under these conditions, the parent rocks melt and their structure is changed. Marble, for instance, is created from the transformation of sedimentary rock. The metamorphism of igneous rocks results in orthorocks such as mica. One distinct characteristic of many metamorphic rocks is their "foliation," or layered structure. The rock is divided into thin plates along these splintering surfaces, or "cleavage."

Metamorphic rock: Marble formed from the transformation of limestone.

INSIDER KNOWLEDGE

EARTH'S MINERAL COMPOSITION

Plagioclase—Silicate—39%
Alkali feldspar—Silicate—12%
Quartz—Silicate—12%
Pyroxene—Silicate—11%
Amphibole—Silicate—5%
Mica—Silicate—5%
Olivine—Silicate—3%
Clay—Chlorite—Silicate—4.6%
Calcite and Aragonite 1.5%
Magnetite, Titanmagnetite 1.5%
Dolomite 0.5%
Other minerals 4.9%

Layered sedimentary rocks in Paria Canyon, Utah

Sedimentation

THE DEPOSITION OF SOLID MATERIALS that are heavier than the surrounding medium is called sedimentation. With chemical sediments and certain biogenic sediments, such as reef limestone, the sedimentation, and perhaps secretions of material, takes place locally, although normally transport takes place at an earlier time. Sediment grains become more rounded the longer they have traveled. Sedimentation is distinguished based on the medium of transport: Either through the air or through the water. The first sedimentation led to the formation of dunes, among other things.

ONE TYPICAL CHARACTERISTIC of sedimentary rocks is stratification. This occurs due to differences in mineralogical composition, grain size, or coloring of the deposited material.

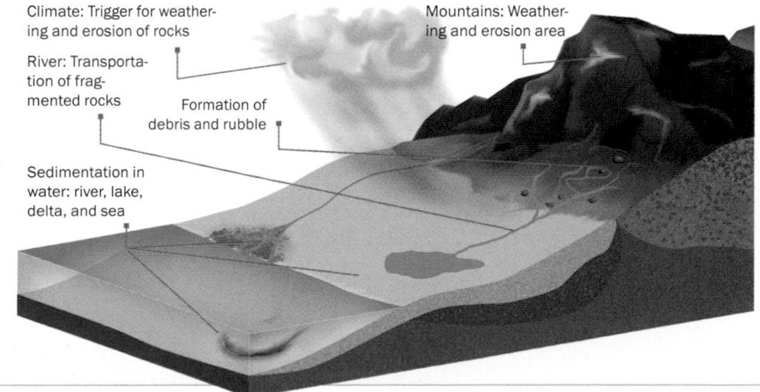

KEY FACTS

DEEP-SEA HYDROTHERMAL VENTS, *known as black smokers, are the possible origin of life.*

CYANOBACTERIA *began to produce oxygen 3.5 billion years ago.*

EUKARYOTES, *living creatures with cell nuclei and cell membranes, have existed for 1.5 billion years.*

HOMO SAPIENS, *the latest stage of human development, first appeared on the planet 160,000 years ago.*

Time before life | New life | The ancient Earth | Earth's middle age to today

HISTORY OF THE EARTH—STATIONS OF LIFE

Not only cosmic processes were responsible for the Earth's formation. Animals, plants, and micro-organisms had a substantial influence on planetary structures in the course of Earth's history. Without them, there would be no oxygen atmosphere, no coral islands, and no fertile ground or raw materials such as petroleum or coal (p. 42).

Humans destroy species around 1,000 to 10,000 times faster than evolution.

TIME BEFORE LIFE

Durings its beginning phase, the Earth was a hostile world for life. Later, however, water, one of the most important prerequisites for the birth of life, became available.

Four billion years ago, the Earth cooled enough to allow water to exist in liquid form. It vaporized, accumulated in clouds, and then rained down again.

Water in the Air

This cycle led to the formation of Earth's first stable hydrosphere (p. 52). Just like today, the carbon dioxide that was bound in water as carbonic acid was released into the atmosphere through evaporation. In the course of time, the proportions of water vapor, carbon dioxide, and methane leveled off at a fixed ratio. However, they were at a much higher level than today, which caused an extreme greenhouse effect (p. 51). The further cooling of the Earth and the slowing of volcanic activity (p. 38) allowed the temperature at the surface to drop below 212°F (100°C). Despite this, the young Earth remained hostile to life. It was the equivalent of a 140°F (60°C) hot sauna with an oxygen-free atmosphere containing large amounts of carbon dioxide, nitrogen, methane, and ammonia. Thunderstorms raged frequently, and a pelting rain of carbonic acid, sulfuric acid, and phosphoric acid was prevalent.

Some volcanic eruptions in the Earth's history have played a role in the world's climate.

The Soda-Ocean

Together with the water cycle, the "rock cycle" set in. Wind and rain worked on the Earth's surface and transported eroded rock (p. 29) fragments and materials through the rivers and into the oceans. It was with this process that materials accumulated into the seas. The first ocean was primarily alkaline because high amounts of sodium carbonate (soda) were dissolved into its water. Through the chemical reactions between seawater and the Earth's crust as well as the steady input of materials, the "soda-ocean" was transformed in 3.46 billion years. Today's "halite ocean" consists of dissolved common salt.

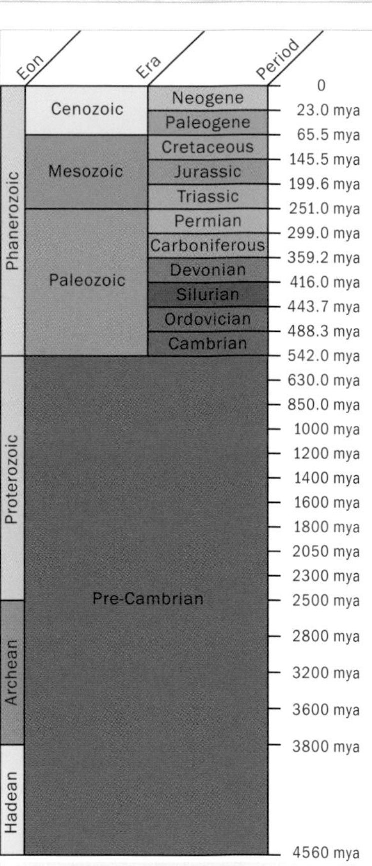

Chronology of the Earth's ages (mya = millions of years ago) in international standard colors

Primordial Soup Theory

PRIMITIVE STATE: In 1953, American biologist and chemist Stanley Lloyd Miller conducted an experiment that astonished experts. In a system of glass tubes, he had imitated the first atmosphere, ocean, and thunderstorm. Within a few days, complex organic compounds such as amino acids and sugar formed in the water. The mystery of the original foundation of life appeared to be solved. The term "primordial soup" was coined.

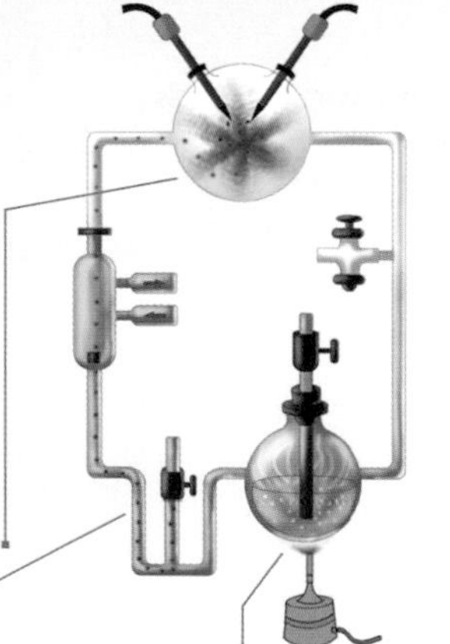

The gas-mixture was exposed to an electric current.

In the U-shaped collecting pipes, an organic mixture forming a brown oily mass was collected.

Miller brought water to a boil then added ammonium, methane, and hydrogen to the water vapor.

INSIDER KNOWLEDGE

FROM WATER DROPLETS *enclosed within salt crystals, scientists have isolated and brought back to life bacteria that were 250 million years old.*

see also: **Primordial Experiment,** *Biology Chapter, p. 58*

NEW LIFE

No one can say with certainty whether life came from outer space, developed in ice, or had its beginnings in the primordial oceans. The origin of life remains a mystery.

After the primordial soup theory (p. 30), the most popular theory of the origin of life is the biofilm theory. It assumes that the first components, and life itself, originated around hot sources in the sea.

Black Smokers—Breeding Grounds of Life

"Black smokers" of the deep sea are especially significant. Their hot water is dark due to its high mineral content. Pyrite is a mineral that forms through contact with cold seawater. It has the special ability to form molecules on its crystal surface that accumulate as biofilms into thin skins. It is this characteristic that has pushed this mineral into the focus of research. According to scientific opinion, it was only a matter of time until the components connected into organic molecules and ultimately to a primitive form of life.

Many cells developed only around 600 million years ago.

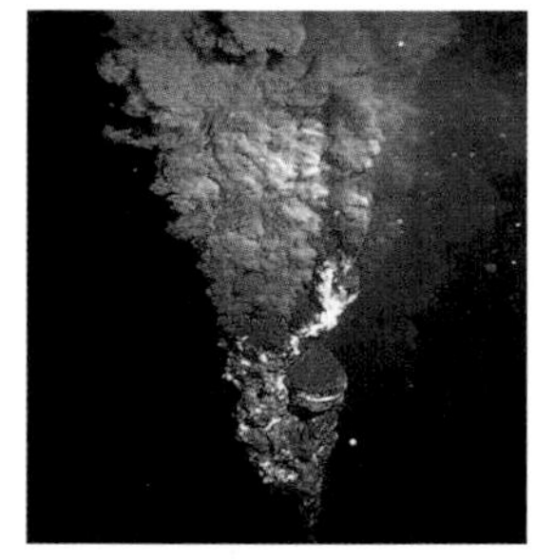

Black Smokers—Hot Springs of the Deep Sea

Water as hot as 752°F (400°C) bubbles up out of the 6.6–13.1 ft (2–4 m) high chimneys of black smokers, reacting with metal sulfides and oxides as gases. During contact with the cold seawater, minerals which had been stored at the chimney and in the environment break down. Around the chimney, a whole host of live communities have been formed; these consist of bacteria, worms, crabs, and other organisms. Many scientists believe that the beginning of life took place here.

above: *Black smoker*

The "snowball Earth" challenged the evolution of life.

Cyanobacteria—Oxygen Workshops

With their age of 3.46 billion years, cyanobacteria have proved to be the first living creatures on Earth. For 1.5 billion years, they were the only organisms in the biosphere. Unicellular organisms played a special role in Earth's history because they were capable of photosynthesis. In the beginning, oxygen was connected with iron that had been diluted in seawater to form different iron oxides that accumulated in the seabed (bedrock). Only after all the iron was oxidized around 2 billion years ago was the oxygen formed during photosynthesis released into the atmosphere. With this, the development of an oxygen atmosphere began around 350 million years ago. The oxygen content leveled off at today's 21 percent. With carbon, the forests expanded and more and more oxygen was produced. The oxygen content reached its highest level in Earth history at 35 percent, 300 million years ago. Since the Triassic period, the value sank back to today's level.

Repeating Ice Ages

Time and again, the Earth was afflicted by ice ages. Such cold phases occurred regularly due to planetary movements which changed the distance and the position of the Earth relative to the sun. However, natural catastrophes such as meteorite collisions and volcanic eruptions can also trigger an ice age.

One of the longest ice ages occurred 750 million years ago; it lasted 120 million years. Traces such as glacier scars on rocks were found in the proximity of the Equator and prove that the Earth's sphere was fully covered with ice. Organisms probably survived this hostile period in the hot springs of the deep sea. Still, very little is known about the ecosystem of the black smokers. Yet, a complete nutrition cycle exists in them in which all creatures live directly or indirectly from bacteria and can exist independent of their inhospitable environment.

Cyanobacteria can flourish under extreme conditions such as Arctic ice, hot sulfuric springs, or warm salt and soda seas.

INSIDER KNOWLEDGE

EARLIEST EVIDENCE OF LIFE: *In Western Australia, 11 different kinds of bacteria have been found in 3.46-billion-year-old rocks.*

STROMATOLITES, *structures on which the limestone accumulations of cyanobacteria are arranged, are the oldest living images of the Earth. They have existed since the Pre-Cambrian era.*

Warm and Cold Phases

RESEARCHING THE ICE AGES helps to understand the climatic changes experienced today. It is important to differentiate between periodically occurring natural changes and the changes in climate caused by humans. The theory that humankind has had an impact on the weather since at least the period of industrialization is rapidly gaining support.

The world climate during the Pre-Cambrian can only be roughly construed since its rocks can be analyzed only rarely and with difficulty.

Pre-Cambrian
Precipitation
wetter
drier
Temperature
wetter
drier
W = Iceless climate
E = Ice ages
W W W W W W
E E E E E
4 3 2 1
Time in billions of years before today

The average temperatures and precipitation were found to be much higher throughout the whole Pre-Cambrian era than in any other geologic period.

Only starting from the Paleozoic era is there enough reliable data from rocks available to provide measurements that help to better understand world climate.

➲ see also: Photosynthesis, *Biology Chapter*, p. 66

THE ANCIENT EARTH

During ancient Earth history, known as the Paleozoic age, the forerunners of all of today's animal groups developed. The individual landmasses were combined to form one "super" continent. At the end of this period of over 290 million years, a mass extinction took place.

The warm swamp forest of the Carboniferous shows evidence of a rich plant and animal world. Insects and amphibians were widely dispersed.

With the emergence of eukaryotes (living creatures with a real cell nucleus and cell membrane), the basis for the evolution of higher organisms appeared about 1.5 billion years ago. The fossilized imprints of worms, leaves, and pillow-shaped organisms within the 640-million-year-old sandstone is evidence that the first multiple-celled creatures developed during the span of the Pre-Cambrian period.

The Paleozoic

The first limestone-shelled organisms appeared 543 million years ago. This small, shelly fauna indicates the beginning of the Paleozoic age, which is classified into six periods: Cambrian, Ordovician, Silurian, Devonian, Carboniferous, and Permian (p. 30).

At this time, today's southern continents were joined to form one landmass. This large continent in the Southern Hemisphere was called Gondwana. The northern continents of today were located in the equatorial zone and were separated from one another by the Lapetus Ocean. In the Silurian, the northern continents merged to form the continent Lauruasia. Both continents moved around during the Devonian until, by the end of the Paleozoic, they had formed the huge continent of Pangaea that was surrounded by the vast Panthalassa Ocean.

The Cambrian Explosion

After the first multiple-celled organisms appeared, the development of life in water made quick progress in a geologically short time period of 50 million years. Many of the animal groups that are known today developed during the Cambrian including gliding animals, mollusks, and fish—the first invertebrates. Fossils are available from the creatures that possessed shells or skeletons, which play an important role in ageing rock layers.

Fossils of the Mesosaurus are found both in South America and in Africa. This provides evidence that the continents were joined together in the Triassic period.

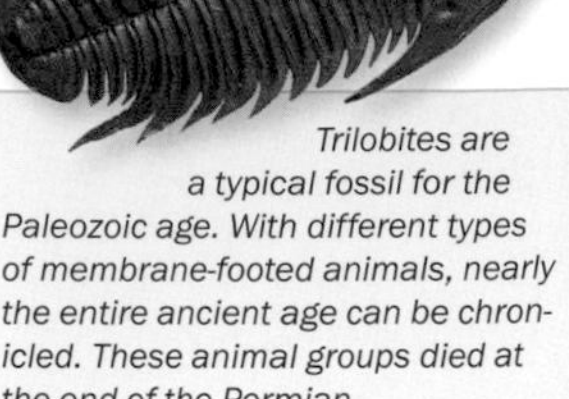

Trilobites are a typical fossil for the Paleozoic age. With different types of membrane-footed animals, nearly the entire ancient age can be chronicled. These animal groups died at the end of the Permian.

During the Devonian, they were followed by amphibians, which developed from fish.

The abundance of plants reached a high point during the Carboniferous period. The gigantic swamp forests with ferns, club moss growths, and horsetail plants are the source material for today's supply of coal (p. 42).

Plants and Animals Conquer the Land

In the Ordovician, the first moss-like plants developed from green algae. From these, the first vascular plants developed in the earlier part of the Silurian period. Their vascular structure was favorable to the quick propagation of plants.

The development of a plant world was a prerequisite for the animals' first arrival on land. Already during the Silurian period, gliding animals conquered the Earth.

The Permian and Pangaea

The climate of the Permian was hot and dry. During an extreme drought on the supercontinent Pangaea, the interior seas dried up and left huge deposits of rock salt (p. 43).

The ancient Earth period ended after 251 million years with a natural catastrophe: Volcanic eruptions consumed Pangaea for several hundred thousand years, which changed the climate. As a result, 95 percent of all sea species and 75 percent of all land species died.

The Golden Nail

MASS EXTINCTIONS, NEW SPECIES, and volcanic eruptions are all events that have the potential to leave behind traces in the formation of rock. Geologists can study the type of rock, its chemical composition, and any fossil remains in the old layers to piece together the story of Earth's history. In early geology, a rock layer that marked a global transition, and thus divided two major geological time periods, was marked with a distinctive golden nail. This method is no longer used, but golden nails are still sometimes awarded as a symbolic gesture for notable work.

The iridium-rich layer called the Cretaceous-Tertiary (or K-T) boundary shows evidence of a meteorite collision.

Above the K-T boundary, there are no longer fossils of ammonites and dinosaurs.

Typical fossils of the Cretaceous period, like ammonites and dinosaurs, are located in the lower rock layers.

INSIDER KNOWLEDGE

EXTRATERRESTRIAL: *The first rock from Mars (p. 19) was discovered in 1911; its origin was proved without doubt through geochemistry.*

THE 900,000-YEAR-OLD ICE *found in the Antarctic region up to approximately 10,499 ft (3,200 m) deep provides information about the climate and atmosphere of that time.*

see also: Evolution of Animals, *Biology Chapter*, p. 68

EARTH'S MIDDLE AGE TO TODAY

The middle period of Earth's history was the time of the reptiles. Only with the mass extinction at the end of the Cretaceous period did mammals have their chance to conquer the Earth.

During the Jurassic and Cretaceous periods, large predatory reptiles such as the plesiosaur and icthyosaur ruled the sea.

The Mesozoic

At the end of the Paleozoic, reptiles developed from amphibians. During the Mesozoic, they came to rule the animal world, namely the dinosaurs. Mammals also developed from an earlier line of reptiles; however, they initially led a comparatively silent life. With the appearance of flowering plants, an era of insects began. The oceanic world was similar to that of today, except that there were enormous reptiles and ammonites, which were similar to squid, living in the sea.

The Mesozoic covers a time period of 185 million years and is sub-classified as the Triassic, Jurassic, and Cretaceous periods. The Triassic was one of the warmest phases of the Earth's history. Deserts dominated the Earth while the polar regions remained unformed. The large continent Pangaea was still in existence as animals and plants could disperse without interruption. In the middle of the Jurassic period, the first crack took place as Pangaea began to separate itself between the northern continent Laurasia and the southern continent Gondwana, thus forming the Atlantic Ocean and the Tethys Ocean. The climate remained hot and dry, although the polar ice caps developed at this time.

Most geographic changes took place in the Cretaceous period. With their complete separation, Laurasia and Gondwana developed their own ecosystems. The wet, mild climate became warmer as the melted polar ice caps made the seas reach their highest level. At the end of the Cretaceous period, the Earth appeared almost as it does today.

Gigantic Insects

About 300 million years ago, insects with gigantic bodies emerged. Lengthy millipedes, giant spiders, and dragonflies with a wingspan of 27.6 inches (70 cm) crawled and flew through the swamp forests. The enormous size gives indirect evidence that the oxygen content of the air in the Carboniferous must have been substantially higher than it is today (p. 31). Insects are trachea breathers, meaning air streams through pipes or tracheas directly to the organs. Past a certain body size, oxygen cannot be efficiently distributed, thus it is assumed that the oxygen content was close to 35%, compared with today's 21%.

above: *Today's largest millipedes can grow up to 11.8 inches (30 cm) in length.*

Up to 40 tons of meteorite material pelts down on the Earth each day. The vast majority, however, is burnt up in the atmosphere.

EXTINCTION IN ONE ROCK SUCCESSION *and the sudden appearance of innumerable fossil organism groups in the same rock layer is an indication of a natural catastrophe.*

THE LAZARUS EFFECT *is the rediscovery of animal and plant species that were thought to be extinct.*

The meteorite collision at the end of the Cretaceous period was one of the reasons for the extinction of dinosaurs.

Mass Extinction in Earth's History

FIVE LARGE MASS EXTINCTIONS and about 20 other smaller periods of widespread death have taken place in the last 440 million years as large portion sof life were extinguished. At the end of the Ordovician, a climatic cooling destroyed 60 to 80% of the creatures living in the sea. Something similar occurred in the upper Devonian period.

CONTINUOUS VOLCANIC ACTIVITY and the climatic changes connected with it triggered the most thorough mass extinction of the Earth's history during the Permian period, called the Permian-Triassic extinction event. Changes extinguished the lives of 95% of marine and 70% of terrestial creatures. At the end of the Crctaceous period the last mass extinction took place, when the climate changes from a meteorite impact destroyed 75% of sea creatures and 20% of creatures living on land.

Ammonites are the most significant fossil group in determining the age of marine rock layers. They first appeared during the Devonian period and became extinct at the end of the Cretaceous period.

An Enormous Meteor—End of the Cretaceous Period

About 65.5 million years ago, the Earth was struck by a meteorite several miles (kilometers) across. The resulting crater can still be seen today in the Gulf of Mexico. There is yet more proof for this incident: The dust cloud from the collision settled across the Earth as a thin pitch in which a high concentration of iridium can be measured. While this metal is found very seldom on Earth, stone meteorites contain a high concentration of it. Evidence of the impact is also clearly present in studying the rock layer between the Cretaceous and Cenozoic period and noting the limited presence of organic life.

The Cenozoic Period

With the Cenozoic period, the rise of mammals began as they, contrary to the dinosaurs, outlived the mass extinction that followed the meteorite collision and subsequent climate change. The first herbivores soon became prey for carnivorous animals. Apes first appeared in Africa 22 million years ago while the modern humans of today emerged between 200,000 to 150,000 years ago. Today's climatic conditions were established during the ice age (p. 31), which was about 2.8 million years ago.

21ST CENTURY

ARMAGEDDON: *Orbiting dangerously close to the Earth are around 4,300 asteroids, of which about 600 regularly cross the orbit of the Earth. According to statistics, a collision of seismic proportions is to be expected every 100 million years.*

HOMO SAPIENS: *The spread and dominance of modern human beings may lead to the sixth mass extinction in the history of Earth.*

➲ see also: Meteorites and Asteroids, *Universe Chapter*, p. 22

KEY FACTS

MOUNTAINS *are formed mostly via subduction of oceanic plates and collision of continental plates.*

THE OCEAN FLOOR *is constantly transformed due to the subduction of oceanic plates and at no point is it older than 190 million years.*

VOLCANOES AND EARTHQUAKES *almost always occur on the boundaries of the Earth's plates. These boundaries are especially active zones.*

THE EARTH IN MOTION

Devastating earthquakes in Afghanistan, volcanoes billowing ash in Java, huge mid-oceanic ridges, oceanic trenches in the ocean floor, and mighty ice-covered mountain chains in South America—all of these natural phenomena are closely linked to one another. Their common origin lies in the shifting of the continents or the formation of oceans. Both are in turn driven by the internal forces of the Earth, which constantly alter the face of the planet. To understand the Earth today, it is imperative to understand these driving mechanisms.

In approximately 250 million years, all landmasses on Earth will recombine to form one massive continent.

PLATE TECTONICS—TRANSFORMATION OF EARTH'S MASSES

How is it that the Atlantic Ocean spread across to Africa and then subsequently split about 30 million years ago? This can be explained with the model of plate tectonics.

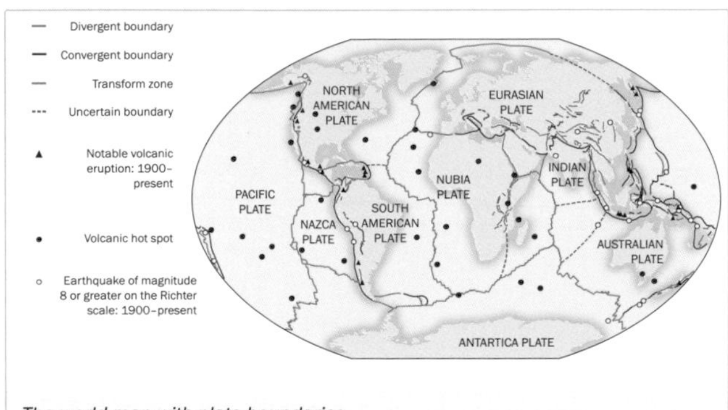

The world map with plate boundaries.

The Earth's crust, together with the uppermost mantle, compose the lithosphere, which is about 62 miles (100 km) thick. Depending on the crust type (p. 26), it is possible to differentiate between the oceanic and continental lithosphere. The solid, outer shell of the Earth forms a mosaic of seven large and approximately ten smaller plates.

The soft, partly molten asthenosphere lies under the plates, which in turn is a part of the Earth's mantle. The lithospheric plates glide slowly over this layer. The cause of this sliding movement lies deep within the interior of the Earth.

The Driving Mechanism of Plate Tectonics

The underlying layers of the Earth's mantle are heated by radioactive decay. The heated mantle material rises up and cools down in the process. Due to the constant supply of such material, however, it cannot sink directly back to the bottom, instead it is pushed up and sinks back in a periodic motion. This cycle is called mantle convection.

The mantle material in turn pushes up the Earth's crust until it ultimately breaks open. Along the line of fracture, the magma solidifies beneath the Earth's surface; in the case of intense volcanic activity, this lava spills out. Both lead to the formation of new ocean crusts.

These cracks continually break open and form further crusts. In this way, two separate oceanic lithospheric plates are formed, which gradually grow and drift apart. Active faults and volcanoes form the Mid-Atlantic Ridge on the ocean floor. If the crust within a continent breaks open, new oceans can form. The East African Trench is the beginning stage of an ocean, which could divide Africa in about 10 million years.

At the San Andreas Fault in California, the Pacific plate is being pushed and moves north of the North American plate.

Production of Crust in the Mid-Oceanic Ridge

THE REPEATED SPLITTING OPEN of the crust in a mid-oceanic ridge leads to the breaking up of pieces of crust. As a result, a central trench is created over time, which can measure up to 31 miles (50 km) in width and over 2 miles (3 km) in height, but is never a continuous stretch. Portions of the ridge are pushed alongside each other's lines of fracture and trenches are thus formed. Often hot springs can be found in these fractures, the black smokers (p. 31).

Because the ocean floor is spreading, the sediment layer nearest to the ridge is younger and thinner than farther away.

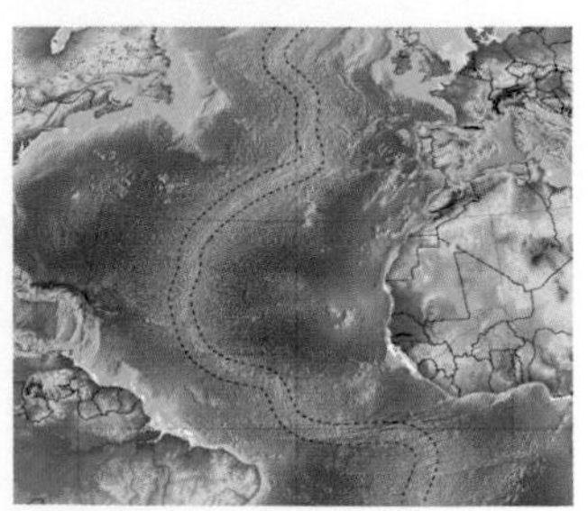

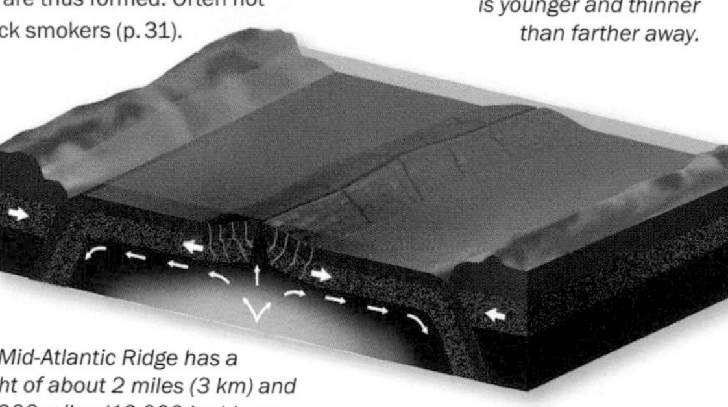

The Mid-Atlantic Ridge has a height of about 2 miles (3 km) and is 9,900 miles (16,000 km) long.

SUBDUCTION—THE DESCENDING OF THE OCEAN CRUST

The continuous formation of new ocean crusts means that at other places, older ones need to be destroyed. This occurs where plates move against each other.

Mauna Kea is the youngest volcano of Hawaii, and at a height of 13,796 ft (4,205 m), the highest mountain in the Pacific.

Where lithospheric plates meet, one descends below the other. This process is called subduction. The time it takes for this to happen depends on the intensity and movement of the plates. The East Pacific Ridge, for example, spreads at a rate of 5 inches (12 cm) per year, while in the Mid-Atlantic Ridge it is only 2 inches (5 cm) per year. Areas where the plates drift away from each other are called divergent plate boundaries; a collision of two plates is called a convergent plate boundary.

Island Arcs—Volcanoes Under Water

The longer an oceanic plate takes to drift, the cooler, and consequently heavier, it becomes. If two plates collide, subduction of the plate with the higher weight takes place. On one hand, the individual weight of the plate pulls it down; on the other, it is pushed back by the accumulation of new crusts.

The crust's rocks and the sediments that have been deposited on it melt in the upper mantle. Magma is formed that rises to the surface and flows from volcanoes as lava. When the volcanoes lie above the mean sea level, a chain of islands with corresponding height can be identified which will bend in the direction of the descending plate; this form is related to the bending of the Earth's surface.

Oceanic Trenches—Volatile Regions

An oceanic trench is part of every island arc, and indicates the point of contact for both of the plates. If the angle of descent of the subducting plate is less, the distance to the melting zone is farther apart. Oceanic trenches and island arcs are then located far away from each other and the channel is flat. The greater the angle of descent, the faster the subduction of the plate into the Earth's interior will be. The oceanic trench is then located in close proximity to the island arc.The deepest point of the ocean with a depth of up to 36,200 ft (11,034 m) can be found in the Mariana Trench in the Pacific Ocean, where the Pacific plate has been subducted below the Philippine plate.

On a Collision Course

Ocean crusts are mainly composed of rocks like basalt and gabbro, and are therefore heavier than the continental crusts, which are primarily composed of granite and gneiss. If they come into contact due to plate tectonic movements, the oceanic plate will always subside below the continental plate. There are frequent earthquakes and volcanic eruptions in the subduction zones.

Subduction does not take place during the collision of two continental plates. Instead the plates push against each other, which leads to the formation of mountains (p. 36).

Shifting With Consequences

At certain places, neither subduction nor collision takes place; instead both plates slide against each other. However, it is not a smooth flow even in these "shearing zones." The plates come into contact, interlock, and can cause earthquakes once they free themselves from each other. The most well-known shear zone is the San Andreas Fault. However, even the lines of fracture in the mid-oceanic ridges, which form individual blocks via different spreading rates, display high earthquake activity.

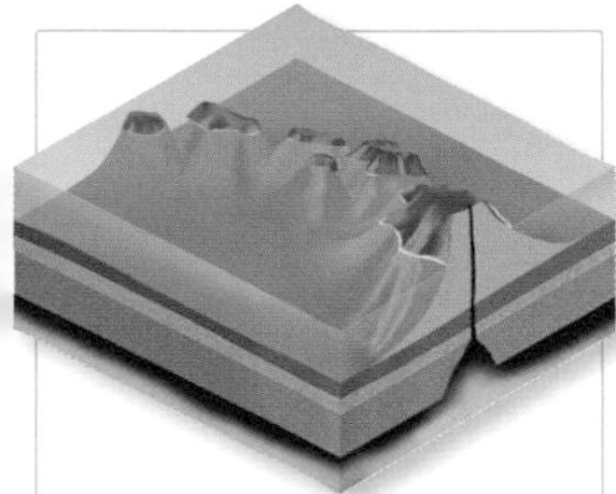

Hot Spots

The "hot spots" are located in the center of the Pacific. Here, flows of magma constantly rise from within a depth of almost 10,000 ft (3,000 m) and lava is ejected from the Earth. While the Pacific plate skims over the hot spots, volcanic islands were and continue to be formed: the Hawaiian islands. The oldest is located in the northwest, the youngest in the southwest. As the position of the hot spot has changed over time, the chain of islands follows a slight bend in formation. The first volcano that was formed here has already completely sunk into the ocean due to its own weight.

above: *Cross-section of the Pacific plate under the Hawaiian islands*

THE LAND BRIDGE THEORY: *Earlier theories assumed stationary continents, and supposed that they were originally linked by land bridges that sunk into the sea at at a later stage.*

IN 1915, ALFRED WEGENER *published his work "The Origin of Continents and Oceans."*

HIS THEORY *of continental drift was acknowledged only after his death.*

Alfred Wegener

The Continental Drift Theory

ALL ALONG THE ATLANTIC COASTS, Africa and South America fit like pieces of a jigsaw puzzle. The same sediments and reptiles from the Paleolithic and Mesozoic ages can be found on both continents. Closely related plants of the same family grew 200 million years ago in India, Australia, and the Antarctic. Based on these observations, the German meteorologist and geoscientist Alfred Wegener concluded toward the beginning of the 20th century that in the past there was one big landmass composed of all the continents. After the breaking up of this super continent, the individual pieces of landmasses drifted to their current positions.

THE CAUSE for their drifting apart could not be clarified by Wegener, for which he also faced criticism. Around 50 years later, his theory and its validity was confirmed with the model of plate tectonics.

The Lystrosaurus lived during the early Triassic period in what is today Africa, India, and in the Antarctic—biological proof of continental drift.

THE EARTH

MOUNTAINS AND THEIR FORMATION

One-fourth of the Earth's surface is covered with mountains. Rugged and majestic, these mighty peaks tower over 3,280 ft (1,000 m) above sea level.

The Himalaya as well as the peaks of the Andes attribute their origins to plate tectonics (p. 34). The collision of two continents that led to the rise of the Himalaya continues to date. The "rooftop of the world" thus continues to grow at a rate that is less than half a millimeter per year. The Andes were formed due to the descending Nazca plate under the South American continent through a process of mountain formation called orogeny. Mountains themselves are referred to as orogens.

Range of mountain folds

Horst

Nappe system

Fault-block mountain

Different geological processes can lead to the formation of mountains and mountain ranges.

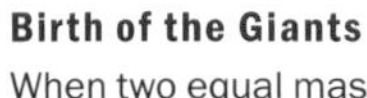

Birth of the Giants

When two equal masses of continental plates collide, the Earth's crusts of both plates come in contact with each other and the sedimentary layers are folded upward. Depending on the intensity of the pressure exerted, large sedimentary masses, or "covers," are thus subjected to a thrust action from their base. These are transported across vast distances and deposited over one another. The Alps are a combination of both fold and thrust mountain formation.

Even the process of lithospheric plates drifting apart (continental drift) results not only in mountains on the ocean floor, but also forms mountains on continents. For example, huge faults have developed along the East African rift zone which were formed via plate tectonic movements 2 to 3 million years ago. Here, magma rose from the inner core of the Earth. Magma and volcanoes that have solidified within the Earth's crust resulted in the upheaval of huge mountains in Africa such as Mount Kilimanjaro at a height of 19,340 ft (5,895 m).

The Alps were formed 30–35 million years ago through the collision of plates. The folded mountain body continues to rise to this day.

Highlands and Mountains

The smaller relatives of the high mountains are the highlands, which are between 4,900 ft and 6,500 ft (1,500 m to 2,000 m). The mountains of today will be reduced to highlands or low mountain ranges due to weathering and erosion within a span of millions of years.

Low mountain ranges or highlands are usually "block mountains." Fractures are created by the Earth's crust being stretched and extended as individual rock segments, or "blocks," are formed. As these rock masses slip through fault lines, they form rifts and horsts, or high ridges. These blocks remain intact and subsequently protrude as mountains. The blocks can also tilt and form the "scarp" or "tilt-block mountains."

When such blocks contain folded rock layers, it denotes the existence of an ablated fold mountain in which fractures have developed. In this case, they are referred to as fault-block fold mountains.

INSIDER KNOWLEDGE

THE ANDES, *spanning 4,660 miles (7,500 km) of South America, is Earth's longest mountain range. The underwater Mid-Atlantic Ridge is 9,942 miles (16,000 km) long.*

THE VOLCANO MAUNA KEA *in Hawaii, of which about 3.7 miles (6 km) lies underwater, is over 0.6 mile (1 km) taller than Mount Everest.*

MOUNTANEOUS GLACIERS *can flow at a daily velocity of over 328 ft (100 m), but rarely move more than a few yards or meters in a year.*

Formation of Mountains Through Subduction

THE ANDES are an example of mountain ranges that have been formed through subduction. During subduction (p. 35), a portion of the oceanic crust is scraped and raised to form a "wedge" on the continental plate. Simultaneously, the continental crust is chipped. Hence, the continental crust is shortened and the zone comprising volcanic belts and magma, the so-called intrusions beneath the surface, now emplaces the internal "bed." In this manner, several such parallel belts are formed—hence the term "chain mountains." There is a basin at the foot of the mountains, which is mainly composed of material from erosion and denudation.

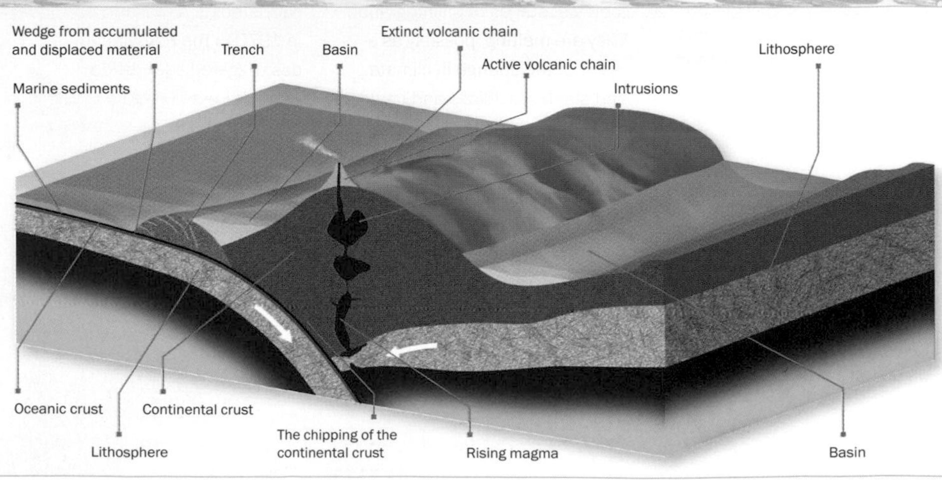

PEOPLE AND MOUNTAINS

One-tenth of the world's population lives on mountains. They are an important means of subsistence not just for these inhabitants, but also for the rest of humankind.

Together with the melting snow on the Alps, the water derived from the snow of Alpine glaciers provides drinking water (p. 45) to more than half the world's population.

Avalanche Protection

The best protection against avalanches is thick forests and vegetation as these are not conducive to the accumulation of large snow masses. If afforestation is not possible, then one needs to employ artificial protective barriers like a fence that reduces the wind intensity, restricting the formation of snowbanks. Barriers made both of steel or concrete divide the incline into smaller partitions, so snow cover does not slip down the slope as one mass. Another measure to protect against avalanches is controlled snow blasts. One can prevent the uncontrolled descent of avalanches by triggering smaller avalanches in a controlled manner with the help of explosives or blasting agents.

above: *A dust avalanche*

21ST CENTURY

TO MONITOR *the probability and danger of landslides on mountain sides, a pre-warning system with soil probes is being developed.*

GLOBAL WARMING *could melt more than half of the world's mountainous glaciers within the next 50 years. Catastrophic droughts and floods could be some of the consequences.*

Eternal Ice

Glaciers are formed in places where there is abundant snowfall in quantities that exceed the capacity to defrost. The snow crystals thicken, solidify, and form solid glacial ice.

This accumulation area, the source of a glacier, is usually situated at a height of over 9,800 ft (3,000 m). The end, the glacier tongue, can be situated as low as 4,900 ft (1,500 m). On their way down the valley, glaciers scrape off rocks on the edges and under the surface of the adjoining landmass of the glacier tongue, and thereby transform the original V-shaped valleys into broad U-shaped valleys. Disintegration of a glacier tongue often results in the formation of a lake between the tongue and the end or terminal moraine. This explains the formation of lakes like Lake Constance and the Donner Lake in California.

Most of the world's glaciers are currently in their last stages of disintegration. They are melting, possibly as a result of the change in climate, and steep precipices and boulder masses are being freed as a result of this. Increased landslides are a possible consequence of this phenomenon.

Protective measures adopted to counter falling boulders include steel nets, the latest model being able to collect up to 15 tons of rocks and boulders.

Landslides

Humankind is partially responsible for the fact that mountains have become danger zones. Clearing and road construction have destroyed the basic framework and vegetative binding of roots in many areas of the mountainsides. These slopes are then more susceptible to landslides or are at times also drastically eroded. A massive earthquake in 1970 in the Peruvian Andes triggered a landslide which buried 70,000 people under rocks, ice, and silt.

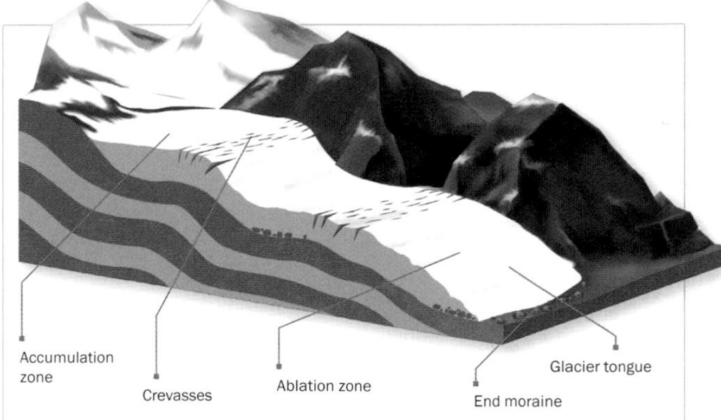

A longitudinal section of a valley glacier (or alpine glacier) in high mountains. Such glaciers can attain a length of over 43 miles (70 km). They constitute only one portion of about 1% of the total ice surface worldwide.

The growth of tourism disturbs the delicate equilibrium of the mountian eco-system.

Snow Avalanches

Most avalanches occur with a slope inclination between 30° and 50°. If the incline is greater, then large snow masses cannot be sustained on the slope; if it is less, then the snow cannot flow.

Avalanches are caused by instability of the snow cover when an underlying snow layer is loosened and released. With rising temperatures, the crystals lose their binding properties.

There is also a danger when wind blows alongside mountain ridges with hanging snow masses, or cornices. Dust avalanches are especially destructive. Snow races down at speeds over 180 mph (300 km/h). Accompanying wind storms and air pressure variations are comparable to a hurricane. Inhaling this combination of air and snow could lead to asphyxiation.

Mount Everest between Nepal and Tibet with a height of 29,028 ft (8,848 m) is the highest geographical elevation above sea level.

ANATOMY OF VOLCANOES

Volcanoes have existed ever since the Earth's inception 4.5 billion years ago. While volcanic eruptions can destroy the animal and plant world, lava also enriches the soil with minerals.

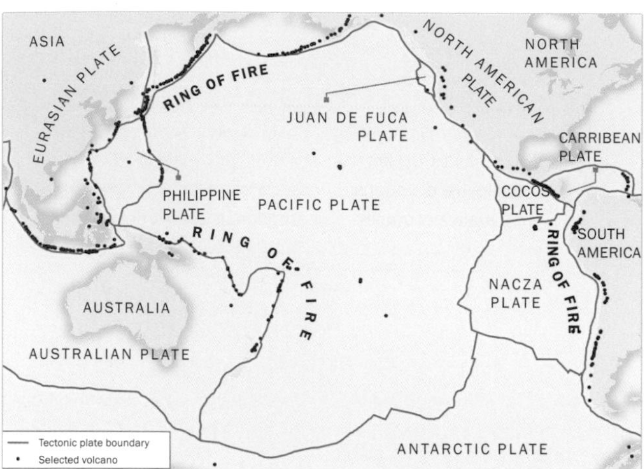

A "ring of fire," which is composed of numerous volcanoes, surrounds the Pacific Ocean. Earthquakes are also especially prevalent along this belt.

Joints of the Earth

Most volcanoes are located alongside the active borders of continental plates (p. 40). Undersea volcanoes are situated in regions where new crust formations take place, such as the Mid-Oceanic Ridge. These are volcanoes that form islands. Land volcanoes are usually found in zones where one plate has been pushed beneath another as the Earth's crust merges. Such subduction zones are distributed around the Pacific Ocean. Volcanoes situated in coastal regions are distributed like a string of pearls on a necklace and constitute the "ring of fire," which accounts for over 80 percent of today's volcanoes. "Hot zones," where the internal merging of the Earth's crust creates magma, result in volcanoes that are independent of continental plates and borders. One example of this group is the volcanoes of Hawaii.

Inside a Volcano

Volcanoes are fed by magma chambers, which are pockets of molten rock that lie about a half of a mile beneath the Earth's crust. If the existing pressure in the chamber exceeds a certain level, then the magma rises through fissures and cracks to form a volcanic vent. The rising magma can either remain below the surface or it can reach the surface and break out as lava. The rising of molten rock to the surface is known as volcanism; if magma solidifies while still within the Earth, it is called subvolcanism.

The Lifeblood of Magma

The composition of the molten rock determines the type of volcanic eruption. If the silica (SiO_2) content exceeds 66 percent, then it is referred to as acid magma; when silica content is 52 percent, then it is referred to as basic magma. Magma releases gases as it rises, decreasing the pressure—like carbon dioxide when a soda bottle is opened. The higher the rise of the magma, the more "degasification" takes place. The enormous pressure exerted by this volume of gases forces itself up the volcano vent and blasts open onto the surface. Acid magma is viscous so gases cannot escape easily. Thus, eruptions of acidic volcanoes are explosive. Gases are released more readily in basic magma, on the other hand, as it is less viscous.

Satellite images from an eruption of Mount Etna: White smoke and black ash clouds are emitted from the crater.

An eruption spreads molten rock and lava around the crater of this volcano in Réunion, which then forms a cinder cone.

INSIDER KNOWLEDGE

THE LARGEST VOLCANO ON EARTH *is Ojos de Salado in the Andes with a height of 22,614.8 ft (6,893 m).*

THE SOLAR SYSTEM'S LARGEST VOLCANO *is the Olympus Mons on Mars, which is 14.9 miles (24 km) high.*

IN 1815, THE TAMBORA *in Indonesia ejected 62 mile³ (100 km³) material—the size of a cube with an edge length of 2.8 miles (4.7 km).*

Types of Volcanoes

THERE ARE DIFFERENT TYPES of volcanoes. In linear volcanoes, volcano cones, or cinder cones, lava is ejected through linear shafts. In central volcanoes, lava flows from a central tube-like vent. Shield volcanoes have viscous lava; stratovolcanoes, or composite cones, have less viscous lava.

CROSS SECTION OF A STRATOVOLCANO: If the pressure in the magma chamber is too high, then the lava tries to reach the surface via columns and fissures.

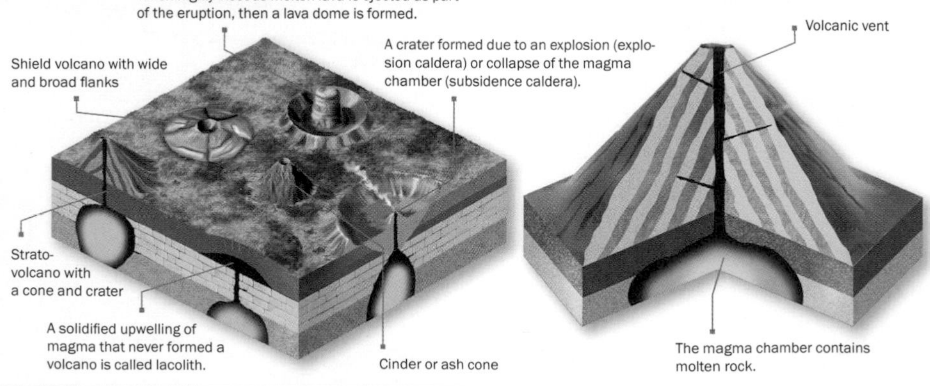

VOLCANIC ERUPTIONS

Some people live with the threat of death in the event of possible volcanic eruptions. It is only in the last few years that scientists have been able to exactly predict their occurrence.

Many volcanic areas are very fertile, as lava and ash are rich in minerals and can improve the quality of the soil in the long run. Hence, as a rule, these areas are densely populated. In order to be able to predict the danger of a possible eruption, volcanologists constantly monitor volcanoes that tend to periodically resume activity.

Warning Signals

As all eruptions are preceded by earthquakes, volcanoes and their activities can be monitored with seismic instruments. Another indication of an impending eruption is an intensified release of gases. Sulfur dioxide concentration in the gases, which flows out of fissures and cracks, increases considerably.

Laser-equipped measuring devices, which measure the volcano with high precision, record surface deformations and provide information regarding the dilation (expansion) of the magma chamber, which is a result of increased pressure within the chamber.

Volcanic craters are often filled with rain and groundwater. Such crater lakes are formed in areas like this one in Costa Rica.

Lava

Depending on conditions while being ejected from the surface and during cooling, lava manifests itself in various forms. Thin, smooth flowing magma forms the "pahoehoe-lava," with a smooth, billowy, undulating surface. Viscous "aa-lava" solidifies to form sharp, edgy blocks. If acidic lava froths during degasification, pumice is formed. If it cools abruptly, non-crystalline or glassy vitreous rocks such as obsidian are formed. When lava enters the ocean or is released underwater, pillow lava is formed with rock masses ranging up to 3 ft (0.9 m) in diameter.

above: *A stream of lava flows through the landscape.*

The Eruption

Volcanoes eject gas-like liquid and solid emissions. In the case of an effusive eruption, less viscous, basic lava flows out that is capable of flooding large areas before solidifying. These eruptions can last for centuries and, as history has shown, can have devastating effects on the climate. This is because large quantities of greenhouse gases, steam, and carbon dioxide are released in the process. Viscous lava explodes during the process of degasification and this explosion is accompanied by rocks. These explosive eruptions result in the surrounding areas being bombarded with material and buried under several feet of ash within a short span of time.

This emission is called pyroclastic. Fine pyroclastic material can collect to form a pyroclastic cloud with a temperature of about 1800°F (1000°C) and can flow at a speed of 620 mph (1,000 km/h).

Explosive eruptions are usually accompanied by heavy rainfall, as the released steam condenses with the ash in the air. If water combines with the ash, destructive mud or debris called a lahar flows down the slopes of the volcano.

New Beginnings

Often thousands of square miles of land are destroyed after a volcanic eruption. It seems unthinkable that nature would ever be able to recuperate. However, after the eruption of Mount St. Helens in Washington, U.S. in 1980, it was only a matter of months before the first vegetative growth reappeared on the surrounding, nutrient-rich ash fields. Animals returned to the area soon after. However, it could take close to 200 years before the local ecosystem returns to its pre-eruption state.

21ST CENTURY

A SUPERVOLCANO *lies beneath Yellowstone National Park in the U.S. There is a 37-mile-(60-km)-long, 25-mile-(40-km)-wide and 6-mile-(10-km)-deep magma chamber approximately 5 miles (8 km) under the surface, which contains about 5,800 miles³ (24,000 km³) of magma. An eruption could lead to earthquakes, flood waves, and a global climatic catastrophe.*

THE ROMAN AUTHOR *Gaius Plinius Secundas (Pliny the Elder), driven by his scientific curiosity, wanted to observe the eruption of Mount Vesuvius. He died of asphyxiation due to the sulfur vapors.*

KATIA AND MAURICE KRAFFT *are two of the world's most famous volcanologists. The couple was killed in the eruption of the Japanese volcano Unzen in 1991.*

The inhabitants of Pompeii were caught unawares by the eruption of Mount Vesuvius in 79 A.D.

Volcanic Eruptions in History

THE ERUPTION OF MOUNT VESUVIUS is one of the most famous volcanic eruptions in history. In 79 A.D., a fatal pyroclastic cloud caused the burial of the Roman city of Pompeii under an 82-ft-(25-m)-thick ash cover. The eruption of Mount Tambora in Indonesia in 1815 caused the death of about 10,000 people. The wind currents spread the volcanic dust particles all over the Earth, leading to crop failures and starvation in Europe, and causing as many as 90,000 additional deaths. The fact that the eruption of Mount Pinatubo in the Philippines in 1991 did not kill more than 500 people is attributable to the early prediction of volcanologists.

The eruption of Mount Pinatubo had global consequences. The gases and pyroclastic material released caused a temperature drop of one degree Fahrenheit.

EARTHQUAKES—CAUSES AND CONSEQUENCES

Earthquakes are the result of dynamic processes with our planet's core. The results on the surface are felt in the form of the most destructive natural catastrophes that are possible.

About 90 percent of all earthquakes occur in places on continental plates where lithospheric plates are being re-formed, subducted, or are sliding past one another (p. 34).

The ground undergoes tremendous tension in these zones, as the plates collide and restrict any lateral movement. If tension increases, the rocks break and the crust experiences tremors. The pressurizing forces can also create cracks within the plates as rocks are pushed alongside. Even these sudden jerks on the surface are considered earth quakes. Tremors or earthquakes mostly occur at a depth that is less than 37 miles (60 km); occurrences at core depths between 190 and 430 miles (300 and 700 km) are rare. The point of origin of an earthquake is called the hypocenter. The epicenter lies above the hypocenter on the Earth's surface. As a rule, high-intensity tremors are recorded in this region.

INSIDER KNOWLEDGE

THE RING OF FIRE *is a geologically active zone around the Pacific, where most earthquakes occur.*

OVER 800,000 TIMES *in a year tremors occur; however, nearly 95% of these earthquakes are imperceptible to people.*

SEAQUAKES *are earthquakes that take place under the sea.*

above and below: *More destructive than the earthquake itself in San Francisco in 1906 was the subsequent conflagration.*

Seismic Waves

When rocks break, the energy is released in the form of waves. These seismic waves are the actual cause of an earthquake. There are many types of seismic waves. The two main types are "body waves" and "surface waves." Body waves are formed in the hypocenter and spread out in a circular motion through the Earth's internal core. These help create surface waves that travel along the Earth's surface.

Causes

The cause of non-tectonic earthquakes is usually volcanic eruptions. Molten rock seething in the magma chamber (p. 38) or the ascent of magma causes tremors on Earth. Hundreds of smaller earthquakes usually occur prior to an eruption (p. 39).

Also, humans have directly caused a few earthquakes: Collapsed mines and tunnels, as well as sub-surface atom bomb tests, cause tremors that are strong enough to trigger an earthquake.

Consequences of an Earthquake

On the morning of January 23, 1556, the Chinese province of Shaanxi experienced tremors with a recorded magnitude of 8.0 (p. 41). The death toll was 830,000 people—most of whom were killed in their sleep as their houses collapsed. Since then, no earthquake has cost so many lives.

The first seismographs were developed at the end of the 19th century. They are used to detect and record earthquake waves and seismic activity.

The consequences and by-product phenomena of an earthquake can be as destructive as the tremors themselves. Following earthquakes in San Francisco in 1906 and Kobe, Japan, in 1995, extensive fires broke out that continued to rage for days. After a violent earthquake in 1755, Lisbon, the capital of Portugal, faced the onslaught of a tsunami and the city was submerged.

In remote inaccessible regions, it is more difficult to provide timely assistance. Starvation and epidemics often result. Survivors are often left without shelter and many consequently die due to the elements. This was the case after a devastating earthquake in Kashmir in 2005, when winter set in soon afterwards. In 1975, Chinese seismologists were able to accurately predict the occurrence of an earthquake. A large number of inhabitants in the area were evacuated on time. However, one year later, 100,000 people died from an earthquake in another northern Chinese city. This time the scientists had not noticed any indications of an impending earthquake.

Epicenter and the Distribution of Waves

THE FASTEST SEISMIC WAVES are "P" or primary waves, which travel through rocks, liquids, and gases with a speed of 4–9 miles/sec (6–14 km/sec). The "S" or secondary waves are only half as fast and can only pass through solid material. The distance of the recording station from the epicenter can thus be determined by the time interval between the occurrence of P and S waves. With these measurements from three separate seismological stations, the location of the epicenter can be determined from the intersection of the data points.

LOVE AND RAYLEIGH WAVES travel on the Earth's surface and have been named after two scientists. These surface waves are indeed slower than S waves, but they can also cause large-scale damage. Most vibrations or tremors that are felt from earthquakes are Rayleigh waves.

P waves: Longitudinal or compressional waves in the direction of propagation
S waves: Transverse shear movement in the direction of propagation
Love waves: Shear movements parallel to the Earth's surface
Rayleigh waves: Vertical elliptical movement

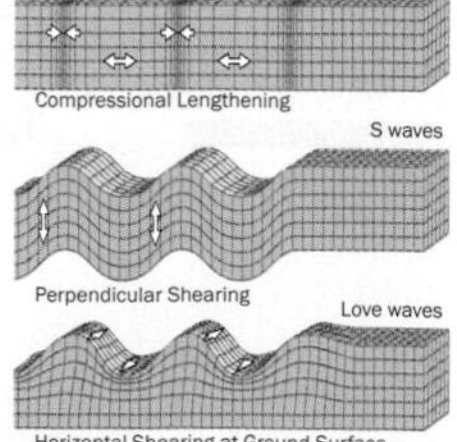

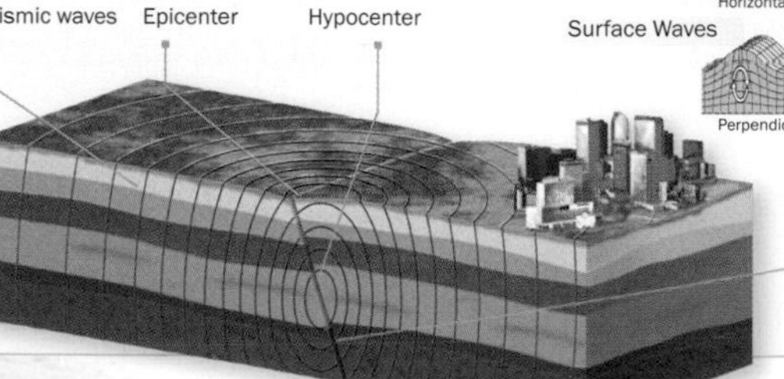

MEASUREMENT AND PREDICTION OF EARTHQUAKES

As we are only partially capable of protecting against the devastating effects of earthquakes, research continues on how they can be predicted beforehand.

Early seismographs, used to measure vibrations of an earthquake, were composed of a weighted, hanging pendulum attached to a pen to etch or draw vibrations onto glass or a paper roll. The stronger the earthquake, the greater the amplitude. Modern seismographs employ more sophisticated recording instruments with electronic sensors and amplifiers. Groups of seismographs can accurately locate an earthquake's epicenter.

Japan's Hanshin highway was considered to be earthquake-proof prior to the earthquake of 1995.

Three Scales of Measurement

At the beginning of the 20th century, the volcanologist Giuseppe Mercalli categorized earthquakes based on perceivable and visible damages. The "Mercalli intensity scale" consists of 12 levels. The first level cannot be felt by humans and is registered only by seismographs. Level 12 is described as severe changes on the Earth's surface and the destruction of almost all buildings. The Richter scale, developed by Charles Francis Richter in 1935, represents the intensity of an earthquake as "magnitude" (M). This value is determined by the distance between the hypocenter and seismological recording station, and the amplitudes recorded on seismographs. Each number on the Richter scale represents an earthquake that is ten times as powerful as the number below it. Today, scientists use the more precise moment-magnitude scale to measure the energy released by an earthquake. The magnitude is measured by multiplying the surface area of the fault's rupture by the distance that earth is displaced along the fault.

Prospective Early Warning System?

Many phenomena can precede an earthquake. Rock deformations lead to changes in the active plate boundaries of the Earth's magnetic field. If water seeps from rock pores, the groundwater level can change. Earth columns that open up also influence the electrical conductivity of the soil. Rock fissures release radioactive gases on the Earth's surface. Eventually, smaller tremors result in a large, concluding quake. All these events can be measured in seismological stations. Frequently, unusual animal behavior is also noticeable. However, the problem is that the Earth can also experience earthquakes and tremors without any of these indications.

21ST CENTURY

"THE BIG ONE": *The high possibility of the occurrence of a very destructive earthquake in the next 50 years in San Francisco or Los Angeles.*

WITH THE HELP OF A CELL SIGNAL *in a tsunami early-warning system that has been developed by German scientists, it is possible to inform people about an impending tsunami in their region.*

Recently, the activity of positively charged oxygen (O_2) ions has been used to predict seismic activity. They originate in the interior of the Earth, when O_2 molecules are destroyed and rise to the Earth's surface. In doing so, they combine with oxygen in rocks. This results in the release of infrared heat. A satellite-supported early warning system could possibly detect these infrared rays and raise an alarm.

Earthquake-Proof

Modern skyscrapers like Taipei 101 in Taiwan are supposed to be able to survive earthquakes up to an intensity of 8.0 on the Richter scale. The buildings are supported by large steel-concrete columns, which are interconnected in an intertwined layout—a movable "corset" that swings along with the tremors. Other tall buildings are built on roller bearings that can neutralize the effects of the Earth's tremors. A specialty of Taipei 101 is the built-in vibration compensator (above): a steel ball that weighs over 600 tons and hangs from a steel rope on the uppermost floor. To a certain extent, the ball at the top of the building is able to reduce the effects of earthquake vibrations.

right: *Earthquake-proof Taipei 101 at 1,670 ft (509 m) is the tallest building in the world.*

THE TSUNAMI EARLY-WARNING SYSTEM *in the Indian Ocean comprises seismographs, GPS-buoys that are capable of measuring the wave heights of the ocean, and seawater level gauges and stations along the coast.*

THE HIGHEST RECORD *of a tsunami-tidal wave on a flat coast is 279 ft (85 m).*

Computerized tsunami early-warning station for the Pacific Ocean in Malaysia.

Tsunami—"Big Wave in the Port"

MOST TSUNAMIS are triggered by seaquakes. These cause a vertical shift of the ocean floor, which sets the overlying water column in motion. Waves are formed on the open sea which are circular in shape. Contrary to a storm wave, where only the uppermost layer of water is raised, in the case of a tsunami, all the layers of water are raised. When approaching the coastal areas, the waves become higher due to a decrease in water depth, but also decrease in speed. Not only do the rising waves cause wide-scale damage, even the wave troughs are capable of causing havoc, whose suction pulls in anything that comes in contact with it—often a mile into the sea.

In 2004, a tsunami ravaged many coasts of Southeast Asia. The trigger was a seaquake measuring 9.3 M in the Indian Ocean.

THE EARTH

KEY FACTS

RESERVES *refer to the amount of a raw material extractable with today's technology.*

RESOURCES *refer to the amount of raw material which is available, but not currently promotable economically or geologically.*

THE WORLDWIDE ENERGY REQUIREMENT *is satisfied approximately 35% by crude oil, 23% by natural gas, 25% by bituminous coal, and 6% by nuclear energy.*

Fossils—raw materials | Natural minerals | Water—a precious substance | The Earth's most valuable resource

RAW MATERIALS OF THE EARTH

Unprocessed or raw materials are the very basis of human life on this planet. They are found on the Earth's surface, within the Earth's crust, and in the sea. While many resources of nature such as wood and grain can be grown, raw materials are limited. Because of our dependence and rapid use of them, the ultimate drying up of the Earth's oil resources is foreseeable. Additionally, there will eventually be a shortage (p. 45) of essential foodstuffs and clean drinking water for the world's population.

Due to their economic significance, raw materials are often an object of political conflicts.

FOSSILS—RAW MATERIALS

Crude oil, natural gas, and coal are fossilized elements. They are used especially as fuel and for the production of plastics.

Fossil materials have formed from the pressurizing and burial of organic matter though the course of millions of years to become the world's most important source of energy. However, they are being consumed at an alarming rate, which has initiated a search for new raw materials. Methane hydrate, which is found on the ocean floor and in Arctic permafrost regions, is just one of these possible energy alternatives (p. 43).

Crude Oil and Natural Gas

Almost 100 percent of today's required "black gold" is conventional crude oil. It is easily and cheaply accessible with the help of drill towers and offshore-platforms. Oil can also be extracted from oil shale or oil sands, but requires a greater financial expenditure and causes a considerable amount of environmental pollution, which is why the large oil sand deposits in Canada and Venezuela have had little strategic significance so far.

A quarter of world energy consumption has been covered by natural gas, which is found alongside crude oil. About two-thirds of all fossil fuels are found in the stretch from the Middle East over the Caspian area up to Siberia.

Coal

The primeval swamp forests that covered large surfaces of the Earth 300 million years ago have formed the source material for coal. Dead plants were covered by sand and mud; bacteria and chemical processes had caused petrification. Over millions of years, the growing sediment layers caused pressure and warmth to ascend upward, forcing cell water and gases out. During carbonization, there was an increase in the content of carbon. Bituminous coal was formed out of brown coal (lignite). Today, the deposits of lignite are about 15 million years old.

Drilling rig off the coast of Nanhai in the South Chinese Sea.

Poisoned Environment

Tar lumps from damaged tanks pollute the European coasts. African land is contaminated with the poisonous residues caused by lead extraction. The air in Siberia contains enormous amounts of sulfur dioxide as a result of heavy metal extraction. The exploitation of fossil and mineral raw material leads to an increased destruction of the environment. Yet humans are not only the ones who cause this, but are also the ones affected. Enacting measures such as the Agenda-21, an international environmental program for the 21st century, have become increasingly important.

above: *Crude oil pollution in a poisoned environment.*

Origin of Crude Oil and Natural Gas

CRUDE OIL AND NATURAL GAS have developed from small living organisms, which sank to the ocean bed. Layers of sediment enclosed the remains while bacteria transformed the dead organisms into simpler carbon compounds. Through the pressure and high temperatures created by the sediments, liquid (crude oil) and a gas form of hydrocarbon (natural gas) were created. The high pressure pressed the hydrocarbons from the surrounding rock and, due to their low density, they rose to the surface. Below a non-transparent covering layer, the crude oil and natural gases have accumulated in the pores of reservoir rocks.

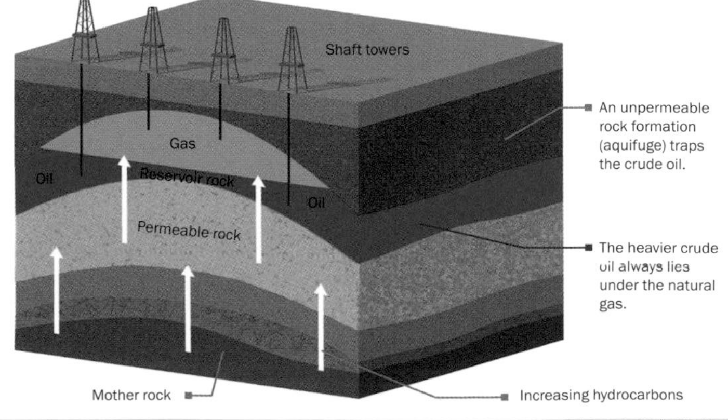

see also: **Fossil Fuel,** *Physics and Technology Chapter, p. 132* | **Production of Coal,** *Biology Chapter, p. 62*

NATURAL MINERALS

Natural minerals are essential for today's world: Metals are necessary in computers, sand is required for the production of glass and cement, and salt is an essential food.

Whether hidden in the mountains or deep underwater, the gems of the Earth are sought after, uncovered, and exploited.

Metals

Most of the metals are found in nature as minerals or mineral conglomerates (p. 28). The rock that has a high enough mineral content that it is worthwhile to extract is described as ore. It is usually found where the Earth's crust experiences tectonic movements or where new crust is developed and magma comes out from the interior—a process in which metals crystallize (p. 28). Therefore, for instance, the Andes Mountains are full of copper, lead, tin, and zinc ore. But also the mid-oceanic ridges and undersea mountains contain metals such as nickel and platinum.

Around 4000 B.C. the mountain inhabitants dug the first copper mine in Timna, Israel.

A vast ore deposit is also displayed in the huge fields of manganese nodules, which can also be found on the seabed. The nodules, which contain copper, nickel, and cobalt apart from manganese, grow probably through the storage of elements flowing into the spreading seafloor.

One metal that is frequently detached through wind and water from its parent rock is gold. It is then stored in river or sand sediments. In 1972, the Holtermann specimen was discovered in Australia. It is the largest gold mass in the world at a weight of over 472 lbs (214 kg).

Salts

Our table salt is usually obtained from seawater or taken from dried saltwater rivers. The salt flats of Salar de Uyuni in the Bolivian Andes are the largest of their kind at around 4,600 miles^2 (12,000 km^2). However, most of this "white gold" comes from subterranean deposits. Fresh water that is forced through pipes under the ground releases these salty layers. When it is pumped to the surface, the resulting brine solution is steamed. Thus cooking salt is produced as a subsequent sediment. The provision industry uses the potassium phosphates and sodium phosphates as preservatives. Additionally, phosphate and potassium salts are used as fertilizer products in agriculture.

The large salt deposits are also a good example of how mineral deposits can provide information about the history of the Earth. They indicate an intense humidification of seawater and show that continental shallow sea has always been separated from the open ocean. Due to the intense radiation of the sun, the seawater has evaporated in isolated areas, leaving salt deposits. Table salt, potassium salt, and gem salts are all also harvested from mines deep in the ground.

above: *The first diamond was found in fourth-century B.C. India.*

left: *For over 3,000 years salt has been extracted from the Earth.*

Diamonds

Diamonds are formed deep in the upper mantle at temperatures of about 2700°F (1500°C) and at a pressure of over 40,000 bar. The coveted mineral is found in the rocks of extinct dikes, or kimberlites, which could be over 3 billion years old. They are extracted through open-cast mining in deep sections of tunnels, and in lugs. However, diamond placers are more productive and produce diamonds with gemstones of much higher quality.

About 80 percent of diamonds in the world are used in industry. They are used in drill heads, as abradants, and in semiconductor technology. The remaining 20 percent are gemstones and high-value collectibles. The largest diamond deposits are found in Africa.

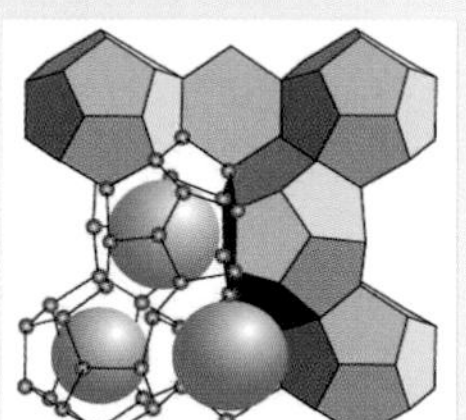

FROZEN GAS RESERVES *are estimated to exceed the current energy capacity of oil, natural gas, and coal combined by approximately two times.*

A COMMERCIAL APPLICATION *has, however, not yet been devised.*

Water molecules form cave-like rooms, in which methane molecules are stored.

Methane Hydrate—Future Raw Material?

"COMBUSTIBLE ICE" is found in the ocean between 1,000–13,000 ft (300–4,000 m) where water, under pressure, freezes from 32°F (0°C). Within the crystal of the ice, methane can be stored that has been produced by the bacterial decomposition of dead organisms.

PROMOTION in the sea comes with a lot of dangers, because methane hydrate occurs there mostly as a stabilizer in the sediments of continental slopes. A breakup could disintegrate the great undersea landslides which, among other things, trigger tsunamis. Simultaneously, it would lead to an uncontrolled release of large quantities of methane which, as a greenhouse gas, would lead to a warming of the atmosphere, and ultimately an increasing of the sea temperature as a result. An alternative is the deposit of methane hydrate in continuously frozen ground, for example, in Alaska. At a depth of about 1,600 ft (500 m), far larger amounts of methane have been extracted for several years.

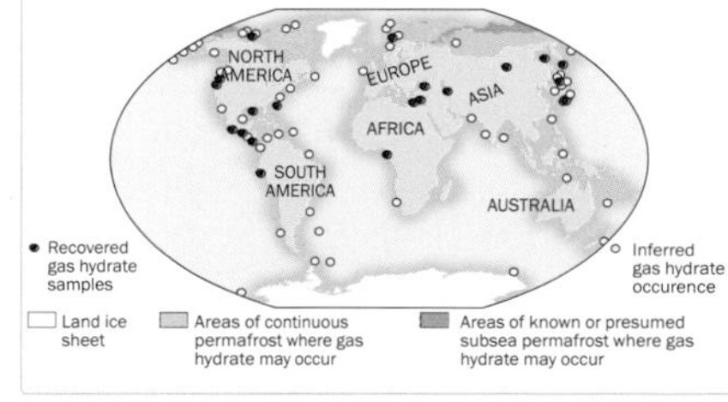

Methane hydrate deposits in continuous frozen areas and in the ocean.

INSIDER KNOWLEDGE

RAW MATERIAL EXPORTS

Aluminum	*Russia*
Lead	*China*
Diamonds	*Botswana*
Iron	*Brazil*
Natural Gas	*Russia*
Crude Oil	*Saudi Arabia*
Gold	*South Africa*
Copper	*Chile*
Nickel	*Russia*
Bituminous Coal	*Australia*
Uranium	*Canada*

➔ see also: Fertilization and Nutrition, *Chemistry Chapter, p. 100*

WATER—A PRECIOUS SUBSTANCE

When viewed from space, the planet Earth shines a deep blue. Across the stretches of the universe, no other blue planet has yet been discovered.

The limestone of the "stone forest" of Shilin in southwestern China, up to 100 ft (30 m) high, was formed over millennia.

Most of the Earth's surface, 71 percent, is covered with an estimated 330 million cubic miles (1.38 billion km^3) of water. Of this, only about three percent is fresh water, two-thirds of which exists in the form of mountain glaciers and polar ice. Salt water makes up the remaining 97 percent.

Pure water has no taste, odor, or color. Since it absorbs infrared and visible red light, it appears blue.

Mysterious Elixir of Life

Water is the only molecular substance that can be found in nature in its solid, liquid, and gaseous states.

With its 2:1 ratio of hydrogen and oxygen, the water molecule H_2O is one of the smallest and lightest substances on Earth. In each molecule, two hydrogen atoms bind to an oxygen atom with an angle of 104.45° between them. Thanks to this unique geometry, water is positively charged on one side and negatively on the other. This bipolarity helps explain water's ability to take different forms and combine with many other substances.

Many of water's physical and chemical properties are not yet fully understood. For example, scientists cannot accurately predict its dynamic behavior in a flowing river.

One characteristic of water presents a very special anomaly: It reaches its greatest density and smallest volume at a temperature of 39°F (4°C). At higher or lower temperatures, it expands and becomes lighter. This explains why ice floats and bodies of water freeze from top to bottom. The water temperature increases with depth, hence the deepest areas do not freeze completely. This makes it possible for aquatic animals like fish to survive through the winter.

Life depends on water; in fact, it is even believed to have originated underwater 3.5 billion years ago (p. 31). The metabolic processes that take place within the cells of living things can only happen in a water-based solution.

Shaping the Earth's Surface

Along with wind, water is one of the forces responsible for the weathering of rock.

The geological workings of water begin when rain falls to the ground. The water first collects in small rivulets while soil and rock particles are carried and soluble substances are washed out of the ground. This process, known as erosion, leaves a path of cracks and furrows on the surface of the land.

Following the contour of the land, the water collects in streams, which in turn merge to form rivers. The erosive power of water increases along with the volume and speed of the current. On their way to the sea, rivers transport huge amounts of soil and minerals, thus constantly altering the Earth's surface.

Over the course of millennia, the erosive forces of wind and water serve to flatten out the Earth's landscape. Scientists estimate that rugged mountain ranges are worn down approximately 16 ft (5 m) over every 10,000 years. Plateaus and plains experience lower rates of erosion of about 3 ft (1 m) and only 1 inch (3 cm), respectively, in the same amount of time. This is because the products of weathering are carried away more slowly over the gentler slope of the land.

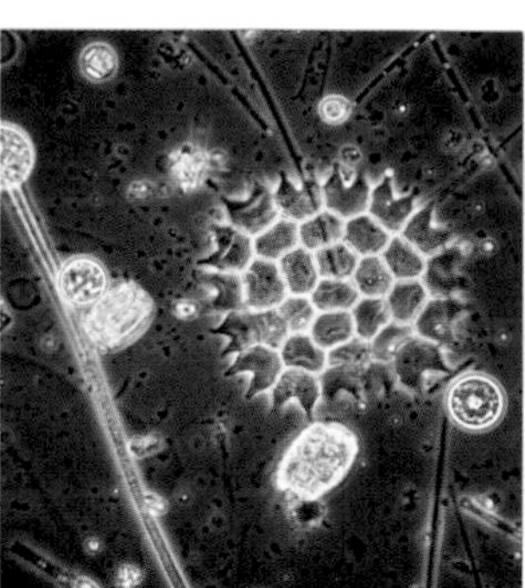

A single drop of lake water contains countless microorganisms.

The Water Cycle

THE SUN DRIVES the water cycle. Its rays warm the air, causing water to evaporate from landmasses and the oceans. The water vapor rises into the atmosphere, where it condenses again and falls to Earth as rain or snow. Most precipitation falls directly back into the sea. On land, it collects into streams, rivers, and groundwater. From these, some will flow once again into the oceans and seas.

Six times as much water evaporates from oceans (102,000 miles^3 or 424,700 km^3) as land (17,000 miles^3 or 71,400 km^3) each year.

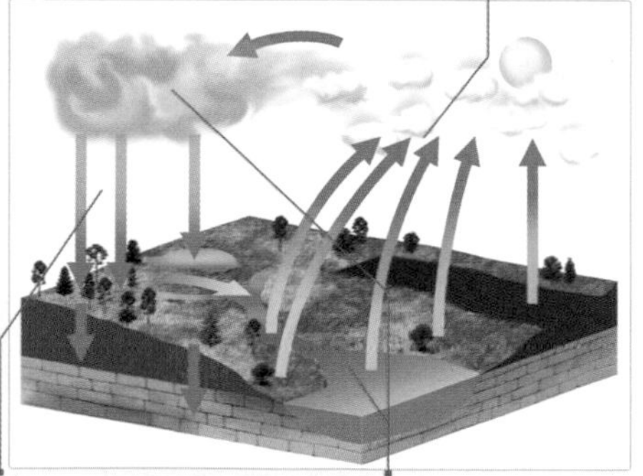

Most precipitation each year (92,000 miles^3 or 385,000 km^3) falls directly into the oceans and seas. Only a fifth falls onto land (26,600 miles^3 or 111,000 km^3).

Annually, 9,500 miles^3 (39,700 km^3) of water is carried in the air from the oceans to land in the form of humidity. The same amount returns to the sea through rivers and groundwater channels.

INSIDER KNOWLEDGE

FOSSIL WATER: *There are deposits of water deep within the Earth that have never been exposed since the planet's formation.*

ICY DIVERSITY: *Ice can form 13 different types of crystals.*

RAINFOREST: *A tree in the rainforest can release 200 gal (760 l) of water into the atmosphere daily.*

see also: The Origin of Life, *Biology Chapter, pp. 58–61*

THE EARTH'S MOST VALUABLE RESOURCE

As most developing countries cannot afford to implement environmentally friendly water usage policies, the responsibility for the planet's water resources lies with the industrialized nations.

The Use of Water

Since humans began to plant crops and raise animals, water has been needed not only for drinking, but as a resource. The first human settlements arose in the vicinity of rivers, lakes, and natural springs.

Even today, coastal regions and areas near rivers or lakes are heavily populated as well as centers for industry. The enormous demand for water in both industry and agriculture, along with its use in energy production, is gradually depleting natural water reserves.

> **INSIDER KNOWLEDGE**
>
> **OASES:** *The groundwater deposits under the Sahara are up to 1 million years old. Exploited for irrigation projects, these water resources are not replenished due to the low levels of precipitation.*
>
> **MEXICO CITY:** *As the groundwater beneath the city is pumped out, Mexico's capital sinks about 8 inches (20 cm) each year.*

Clean Water

The intensive use of water by people has also led to high levels of pollution and contamination. As a result, water must be treated in complex and costly processes before it is safe to drink. Desalination plants that remove salt from seawater are not a useful alternative, since the process is less efficient and the costs are even greater.

Water Shortages

Only 0.03 percent of the Earth's entire water supply is readily available for use as drinking water. However, even that amount would be sufficient if global water resources were more evenly distributed and populations around the world enjoyed better access to water treatment facilities.

Water shortages occur primarily in areas where low precipitation levels are combined with economic weaknesses or high population concentrations, as seen in parts of Africa and China. Some one billion people around the world lack access to clean drinking water. Each year, approximately five million people die from water shortages or diseases caused by contaminated water. The need for clean drinking water may soon become a worldwide problem. According to UN forecasts, nearly nine billion people will have to share the Earth's freshwater resources by 2050.

Water Pollution

Environmental regulations and restrictions aimed at keeping water clean exist in only a few industrialized nations. Wastewater is processed in treatment plants before it is released back into rivers.

Agricultural practices also cause problems around the world. Farming accounts for some 70 percent of global water use. When fields are irrigated, fertilizers and pesticides are washed into the groundwater or nearby rivers. Meanwhile, the world's oceans are often used as dumping grounds for excess chemicals and other waste.

The 2002 wreck of the oil tanker Prestige off the coast of northern Spain caused Europe's worst oil spill.

The disposal of used oil and industrial or radioactive waste directly into the sea is a common practice. About one million tons of oil are discharged into the world's oceans and seas each year. Many rivers, lakes, and seas have already suffered ecological destruction or long-term damage due to these short-sighted disposal strategies.

CONSTRUCTION: *From 1993 to 2006, up to 18,000 workers were employed at the site.*

COST: *At 50 billion dollars, the expenditures for the dam are twice as high as originally projected.*

POWER OUTPUT: *The dam's 26 turbines are expected to generate 18,200 megawatts of electricity; the equivalent of nine nuclear power plants.*

China's Three Gorges Dam was placed in service in May 2006.

The World's Largest Dam

CONCRETE COLOSSUS: Behind a wall 600 ft (185 m) high and 7,570 ft (2,310 m) long, the Yangtze River has been contained to produce a lake 410 miles (660 km) wide. The Three Gorges Dam is a controversial construction project since it represents a massive human intervention in natural processes.

PROS AND CONS: Supporters argue that the benefits of the project are flood control and energy production. Yet in order to build the dam, 23,800 hectares of land, 13 towns, and 657 factories were flooded, which displaced 2 million people. The long-term ecological consequences are impossible to predict.

The energy produced by the Three Gorges Dam is not intended to supply private households, but rather to power industrial facilities in eastern China.

Arctic and Antarctic

Over two-thirds of the world's freshwater reserves are locked up in the form of Arctic and Antarctic ice. Because these regions are so isolated, the water is not considered accessible for human use. In addition to this, Antarctica is believed to harbor valuable resources such as oil, natural gas, coal, uranium, iron, and precious metals. Seven countries have already claimed large portions of Antarctica. The Antarctic Treaty of December 1, 1959, prohibits mining on the continent until 2041.

above: *If global warming does not cease, the Arctic will be ice-free by the end of this century.*

KEY FACTS

MARINE SPECIES: *Of the nearly 2 million identified species of living organisms on Earth, around 13% of them live in the sea. Many more are presumed to exist in unexplored areas.*

CORAL REEFS *are the world's second most species-rich habitats, after tropical rain forests.*

OVER 1 BILLION PEOPLE *obtain the majority of their food from the sea.*

The sea | Ocean currents and tides | Islands and coral reefs | Humans and the sea

OCEANS AND SEAS

Populated by a multitude of swimming, drifting, and bottom-dwelling organisms, oceans and seas cover more than two-thirds of the Earth's surface. For humans, the oceans serve as a key food source. They also play a central role in climate regulation, since they store and release enormous amounts of heat. Many areas of the world's oceans have not yet been explored. It seems easier to launch a rocket into space than it would be to investigate the seemingly limitless depths of the ocean in a submarine.

Melting of the polar ice would raise sea levels around the world by nearly 213 ft (65 m).

THE SEA

The great portion of the salt water on our planet is contained within Earth's vast oceans. Smaller seas lie between oceans and the continents.

Nearly all of the Earth's 311 million cubic miles (1.3 billion km^3) of salt water is divided among five gigantic basins: the Atlantic, Pacific, Indian, Southern, and Arctic Oceans. Smaller seas are separated from the main bodies of water by island chains, straits, or peninsulas. For example, the North, Mediterranean, and Caribbean Seas are adjacent to the Atlantic Ocean. Many of these smaller bodies of water are "shelf" seas, which are quite shallow in comparison with oceans. In these, the seafloor lies no more than 656 ft (200 m) below the surface. Individual oceans and seas differ in their salt content, surface temperature, depth, and currents, as well as the plant and animal life within.

Sand and rock eroded by waves adds dissolved salts to sea water.

Ocean Habitats

THE SEA is divided into coastal (littoral) and open sea (pelagic) zones, as well as various regions classified by depth. Specific fish and marine organisms live in each habitat. There are also some living things that move between the zones.

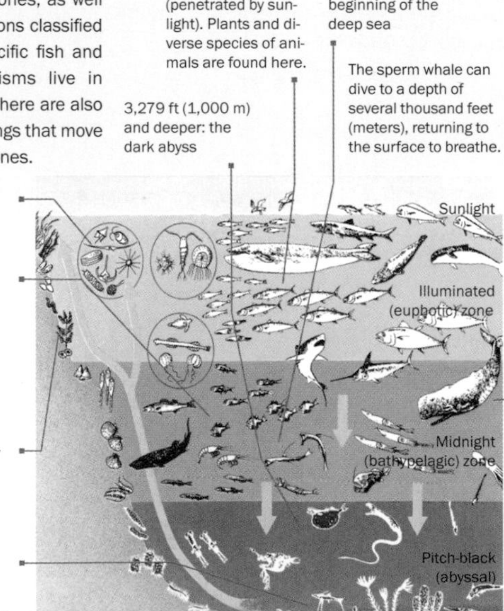

0–656 ft (0–200 m): epipelagic or euphotic zone (penetrated by sunlight). Plants and diverse species of animals are found here.
656+ ft (200+ m): the mesopelagic or "twilight" zone; the beginning of the deep sea
The sperm whale can dive to a depth of several thousand feet (meters), returning to the surface to breathe.
3,279 ft (1,000 m) and deeper: the dark abyss
Littoral zone: sea area above the continental shelf
Pelagic zone: open sea beyond the shelf
Shelf: underwater extension of a continent
The benthos: organisms and habitats on and within the seafloor
Sunlight
Illuminated (euphotic) zone
Midnight (bathypelagic) zone
Pitch-black (abyssal)

Salty Seas

Day after day, large amounts of a variety of substances are carried into the sea by rivers, coastal waves, melt water, precipitation, and winds. These substances may dissolve in the water or accumulate as sediment on the seafloor. Almost all of the chemical elements on Earth can be found in seawater. However, the greatest proportion of the dissolved mixture consists of salts.

The average salt content, or salinity, of the world's oceans and seas is 3.5 percent. This means that an average of 1.2 oz (35 g) of salt are dissolved in each quart (liter) of seawater. Over half of this amount is table salt, or sodium chloride. Near the mouths of rivers, where fresh and salt water come together, salinity levels are comparable to those observed in the open ocean.

When seawater evaporates (p. 44), the salts dissolved in the water are left behind. The hotter and drier the climate, the more evaporation occurs and the saltier the water becomes. Particularly high salt concentrations can be found in smaller seas under these conditions. Because of their limited connections to the ocean, less mixing of the water occurs. Therefore, the Persian Gulf has a salt content of 4 percent, while the average value in the Indian Ocean is only 3.48 percent. At the Poles seasonal variations in the sea ice affect salinity. Salt is not incorporated into ice crystals. Thus, ice formation leaves the surrounding water with a higher salt content, while melting ice dilutes the water and creates areas of low salinity.

Most marine species are found in the sea's sunny upper reaches.

21ST CENTURY

GULF STREAM: *Its weakening would lead to chilly temperatures in northern, western, and central Europe.*

THE SEA AS PHARMACY: *Marine organisms offer great potential for medicinal applications. For example, the poison of the cone snail can serve as a painkiller while the substances produced by sponges and algae are used to prepare medications.*

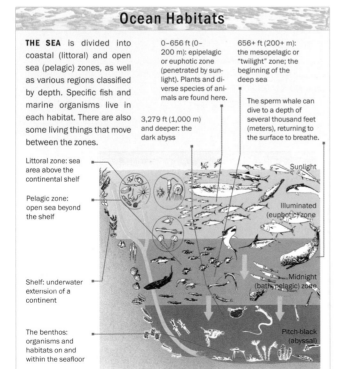

see also: Fish, *Biology Chapter*, p. 70

OCEAN CURRENTS AND TIDES

In the oceans, winds and varying salt concentrations drive huge masses of water over long distances. The moon also affects the oceans from afar and lifts waves onto the shore.

Like gigantic conveyor belts, numerous surface and deep-water currents circulate through the world's oceans. The result is a complete turnover of the Earth's ocean waters over a period of a few hundred to 2,000 years.

Influence of the Winds

Surface currents in the oceans are driven by the prevailing winds. The circulating trade winds (p. 53) create current systems that transport warm water away from the Equator and cold water toward it.

Cold ocean currents near the shore lead to the development of coastal deserts. Since the air masses near the water are cooler than the air above it, the moist air does not rise, and clouds and rain do not form.

The wetness of the sand shows the tidal amplitude of a port.

Without warm ocean currents, many regions of the Earth would experience significantly lower average temperatures because the currents also warm the nearby land. One component of this gigantic water transportation system is the salt-rich Gulf Stream, which forms in the Caribbean and flows across the North Atlantic toward Europe.

Deep-Water Currents

Between Greenland and Norway, the Gulf Stream waters begin a journey into the depths. Along the way, the water is sharply cooled by frigid winds from the North Pole, and its salt content increases due to the formation of sea ice. Both factors raise the water's density as well as its weight. The heavier water sinks through layers of lighter water in the polar zone until it reaches the seafloor. There, it flows at great depths toward the southern end of the Atlantic. Upon arrival, the current is channeled through the Indian Ocean to the Southern Pacific, where it gradually warms. After its long journey through the depths, the water rises to the surface again. Off the coast of South America, it is picked up by a circulating current and transported back into the Caribbean Sea, where it once again becomes the Gulf Stream.

The Gulf Stream—Warmth for Europe

THE GULF STREAM splits into smaller circulating currents, or "eddies," on its way across the Atlantic. These mix with the colder surrounding water, producing lukewarm water that bathes the coasts of western and northern Europe. Because of this, the region enjoys an unusually mild climate compared with countries at similar latitudes such as Canada. Thus, species of palm trees can grow in Ireland, and fjords of the Norwegian coast are ice-free all year.

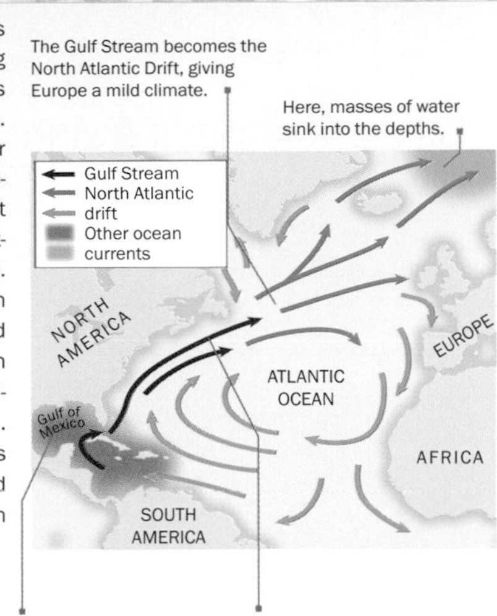
The Gulf Stream becomes the North Atlantic Drift, giving Europe a mild climate.
Here, masses of water sink into the depths.
Gulf Stream
North Atlantic drift
Other ocean currents
NORTH AMERICA
Gulf of Mexico
ATLANTIC OCEAN
EUROPE
AFRICA
SOUTH AMERICA
In the Gulf of Mexico, the Gulf Stream soaks up large amounts of heat. Its salt content also increases through evaporation.
Off the coast of North America, the Gulf Stream flows into the open Atlantic, where it becomes unstable and forms eddies, which are circulating streams of warm water.

The Power of the Moon

The moon's gravity and the Earth's centrifugal force cause a "bulge" of ocean water to form on the side of the planet facing the moon. The same thing happens on the opposite side due to the Earth's centrifugal force. Between the two bulges of water lie lower "troughs."

Because of the Earth's rotation, this phenomenon causes sea levels to rise and fall twice each day. The period when the water is rising is called flood tide, and the time when it is receding is called ebb tide.

The difference between the high and low tide levels varies around the world. The narrow bays of Canada's east coast act as funnels due to their shape, so especially large tidal differences, or amplitudes, are observed there: 49.2 ft (15 m) in the Bay of Fundy. In contrast, tidal amplitudes on the North Sea coast are 11.5 ft (3.5 m).

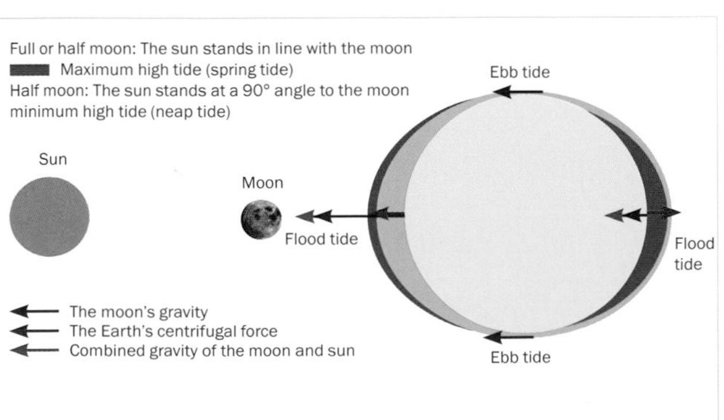
Full or half moon: The sun stands in line with the moon
Maximum high tide (spring tide)
Half moon: The sun stands at a 90° angle to the moon
minimum high tide (neap tide)
Sun
Moon
Flood tide
Ebb tide
Flood tide
Ebb tide
The moon's gravity
The Earth's centrifugal force
Combined gravity of the moon and sun

The tides

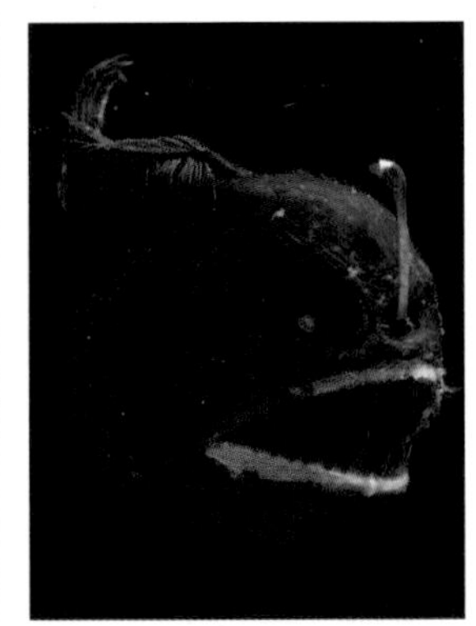

The Deep Sea

Absolute darkness, icy temperatures of 30.2 to 39.2°F (-1 to 4°C) and pressures that can exceed 1000 bar; the conditions in the planet's largest habitat are extreme. It is not surprising that only about 20% of all marine organisms are found below 3,279 ft (1,000 m). Here, life burns on a low flame; animals reduce their metabolic rates in order to survive. "Black smokers" (p. 31), hot springs populated by bacteria, shellfish, worms, crabs, and bizarre-looking fish, can be viewed as "oases" of the ocean depths.

above: *A resident of the abyss: the deep-sea anglerfish*

ISLANDS AND CORAL REEFS

Many islands owe their existence to volcanic eruptions. Others were formed by coral reefs—and some will soon completely disappear.

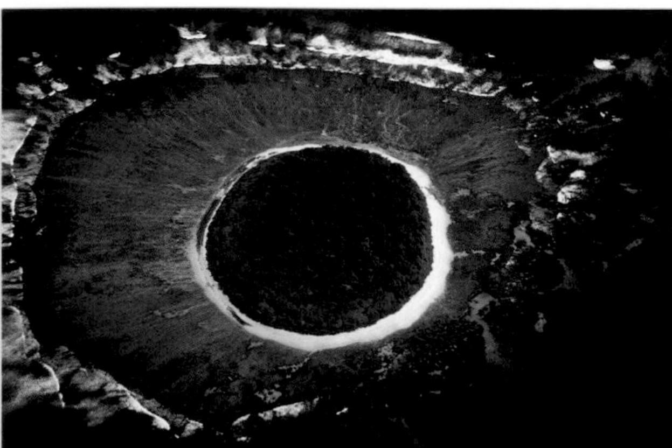

Lifting of the oceanic crust or falling sea levels may cause the lagoon in the center of an atoll to dry out.

The world's largest island is Greenland, with a surface area of over 830,000 miles^2 (2 million km^2); the smallest are nothing more than specks in the ocean. Islands are often associated with a continent. In those cases, the islands are actually elevated areas on the continental shelf (p. 46), which only appear disconnected from the main landmass because of the surrounding sea, such as Newfoundland and Great Britain.

Volcanic islands, such as those rising along the mid-oceanic ridges, are the result of subduction (p. 35). Their formation can also occur over hot spots (p. 35). Iceland and the Azores archipelago, which rise several thousand feet (meters) above the sea floor, are islands of the Mid-Atlantic Ridge.

Atolls are found only between 30° of northern latitude and 30° of southern latitude. This is because they are formed by colonies of corals, which live almost exclusively in warm water. South Pacific atolls such as Bikini have achieved notoriety due to U.S., British, and French nuclear weapons testing between 1946 and 1996.

Underwater Forests

Tropical coral reefs are primarily built by stony corals. Coral animals, or polyps, extract calcium ions and carbon dioxide from the seawater and use it to create a hard exoskeleton made of calcium carbonate. As dead skeletal material is overgrown by living tissue, gigantic reefs gradually form. The Great Barrier Reef off the northeastern coast of Australia extends over 1,250 miles (2,000 km).

The coral polyps live in symbiosis with zooxanthellae, or coralline algae. These organisms settle within the skin of polyps. Through photosynthesis, the algae transform carbon dioxide and water into oxygen and sugar. This helps nourish the coral polyps, which offer the algae protection and nutrients in return.

The Antarctic krill is a type of zooplankton: Tiny animals that drift freely in the water.

The intake of carbon dioxide by the algae also promotes the production of calcium carbonate by the corals. Some stony corals can be found outside the tropics, even at depths of over 19,672 ft (6,000 m). These corals have no zooxanthellae; instead, they extract nutrients directly from the water. Without symbiotic helpers, however, they build significantly smaller reefs.

Submerged Land

The warming of the oceans due to climate change (p. 54) threatens tropical coral reefs. The zooxanthellae are highly sensitive: A temperature rise of only 2 to 4°F (1 to 2°C) causes them to emit toxic substances, and the coral polyps eject partners which are vital to their own survival. Intact reefs serve as wave breaks, among other functions. Without them, low tropical islands will experience more frequent flooding in the future. The rise in sea levels resulting from the melting of polar ice will even cause some islands to disappear. Many island inhabitants are already feeling the effects of repeated floods. The soil and the few sources of fresh water on the island become contaminated with salt.

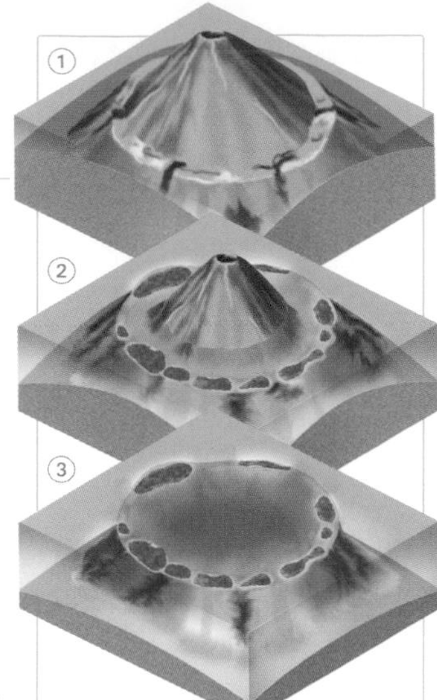

Atoll Formation

In the late 19th century, Charles Darwin developed a theory that would eventually prove accurate: Where an atoll exists today, a volcanic island once stood with coral colonies developing around it (1). Over the course of time, the island was worn away through erosion, or it sank into the sea when the seafloor subsided or sea levels rose. Meanwhile, the light-dependent corals built higher structures (2). As the island gradually disappeared into the sea, the corals continued to grow, and in many cases, the individual reefs fused together to form a ring surrounding a lagoon (3).

above: *Atoll formation in three stages.*

Coral reefs, which are the world's largest biological structures, are even visible underneath the ocean from space.

➲ **see also: Photosynthesis,** *Biology Chapter, p. 66*

HUMANS AND THE SEA

Nearly 100 million tons of fish are taken from the sea each year. These catch levels will soon decline significantly, however, since two-thirds of all fish stocks are currently overexploited.

The bluefin tuna, one of the world's most important types of food fish, is facing ecological collapse. Off the coast of Canada and in the North Sea, the once-plentiful cod populations have nearly disappeared. The same fate threatens the cod of the Baltic Sea. The leading causes for the dramatic declines in fish stocks are excessive catch quotas and illegal fishing operations.

Tanker wreck off the coast of Great Britain's Shetland Islands, 1993

A particular threat is posed by deep-sea trawling. Since the fish of the depths do not reproduce in great numbers due to their difficult living conditions, many species may soon face extinction. Furthermore, the gigantic dragnets of fishing vessels destroy nearly all animal life in their paths as they scrape across the seafloor.

Mariculture

In the meantime, the products that nature can no longer supply are available through marine farming, or mariculture, which has developed into a thriving industry. Today, nearly every salmon offered for sale comes from a fish farm; only two out of every hundred were caught in the wild. Various kinds of shellfish and seaweed are also raised artificially.

However, mariculture may also prove to be a dead end because of its intensive use of fishmeal. Since the fishmeal is derived from conventional fishing operations, ocean fish populations are unable to recover. Strict protective measures such as the introduction of prohibited fishing seasons and minimum mesh sizes for nets—allowing younger fish to pass through—may have a positive effect.

Polluted Seas

Cities often pump untreated wastewater into the sea. Phosphate pollution is especially toxic for many marine organisms. Defunct nuclear submarines rust beneath the Arctic waves. When tankers sink, thousands of tons of oil are spilled into the sea. Double-hulled ships could help prevent such catastrophes, but a number of shipping companies continue to shrug off the risk.

"Blue Energy"

Even a polluted sea, nearly depleted of fish, offers potential energy that can be used to generate electricity. In tidal power plants, the movement of water masses near the shore is used to drive turbines. However, since a tidal amplitude of at least 26 ft (8 m) is required, not every river mouth or coastal zone can be suitable.

The technology of wave power plants is still in its infancy. In these facilities, ocean waves are used to compress and release air, setting a turbine in motion. In the Arctic Sea, offshore power plants are being developed to exploit the sinking of the Gulf Stream system's cold water masses for energy production.

The greatest tidal amplitude in Europe is found in Saint-Malo Bay, Brittany. The tidal power plant La Rance is located here.

21ST CENTURY

IF CATCH QUOTAS ARE NOT REDUCED, *many fish stocks will be fully depleted by 2050.*

DRAGNET FISHING *kills hundreds of thousands of sea birds each year.*

SINGLE-HULLED TANKERS *will be banned from use after 2015.*

PARTICULARLY *advocating action is the Food and Agriculture Organization of the United Nations (FAO).*

THE NORMANS *crossed the Atlantic in the ninth/10th century and discovered Greenland.*

ISAAC NEWTON *recognized the principle of the tides in 1687.*

THE FIRST NORTH ATLANTIC SEAFLOOR MAP *was published in 1854 by Matthew Fontaine Maury of the U.S.*

First-generation pressurized diving suit

The Sea—Discovery and Research

IN 1872, A NEW ERA BEGAN in oceanographic research: The British steamship HMS Challenger undertook a five-year mission to explore the world's oceans. The Mid-Atlantic Ridge was discovered during this expedition. In 1960, the manned diving boat Trieste reached depths of up to 35,790 ft (10,916 m) in the Pacific Ocean's Marianas Trench. The U.S. began building research stations off the California coast in 1964. In the late 1970s, the "black smokers" or deep-sea hot springs (p. 31) were discovered. In 2006, Daniel P. Jackson of the U.S. reached a depth of 1,997 ft (609 m) in a pressurized diving suit.

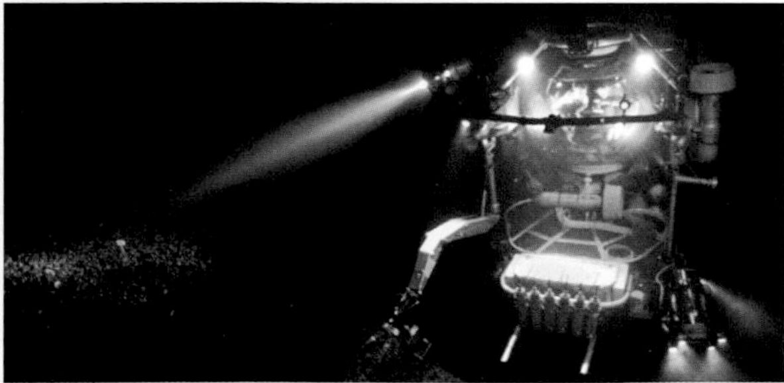

A modern deep-sea exploration vessel with grappling arm in action

Soldiers in protective suits clean a beach contaminated by an oil spill off the Spanish coast in 2002.

The worldwide ban on commercial whaling took effect in 1986, yet continues to be evaded.

➲ see also: **Alternative Energy Sources,** *Physics and Technology Chapter, p. 135*

KEY FACTS

THE EARTH'S ATMOSPHERE *consists of a mixture of gases—primarily nitrogen and oxygen.*

LIFE ON EARTH *is protected by the atmosphere from overheating as well as from dangerous radiation from space.*

AIR POLLUTION *from industry and vehicles influences Earth's climate. The first effects of pollution can already be felt today.*

Earth's atmosphere | Air pollution | Climate system | Climate phenomenon | Climate change

THE ATMOSPHERE—EARTH'S GASEOUS SHIELD

The atmosphere serves as a natural protective shield for our planet. Interactions among the sun, the Earth, and the Earth's atmosphere create an environment in which life can exist. However, since the industrial revolution, human beings have had an increasing negative impact on the atmosphere.

Atmospheric research is one of the leading scientific challenges of our time.

THE FUNCTION OF EARTH'S ATMOSPHERE

All of the Earth's weather phenomena take place in the gaseous layer surrounding our planet; many geological and nearly all biological processes also depend on this mixture of gases.

Only above a certain level of mass does a planet produce enough gravitational force to hold a layer of gases around its surface, and so form an atmosphere. The temperature of the planet also plays a role. As temperature rises, the gas pressure increases and a greater gravitational force is needed to prevent gases from escaping into space.

In our solar system, several planets and moons have atmospheres. However, their composition is different due to varying sizes and surface temperatures of the bodies.

Some 3.5 billion years ago, cyanobacteria initiated the development of our modern atmosphere (p. 31).

Air Providing Life

The gaseous mixture that makes up Earth's atmosphere is composed of 78 percent nitrogen and 21 percent oxygen. The remaining 1 percent includes noble gases, hydrocarbons, and nitrogen compounds. This characteristic mixture, which we call air, is a significant component of the biosphere, or the space in which life exists (p. 52). The oxygen in our atmosphere is vital for the life-sustaining metabolic processes of nearly every living thing on Earth.

Protection and Warmth

Since the Earth's diameter is 7,900 miles (12,756 km) at the Equator, the atmosphere, with a thickness of only about 620 miles (1,000 km), is nothing more than a thin outer layer. Yet it functions as an effective protective shield. Like a filter, it removes most of the sun's harmful ultraviolet rays, while allowing shorter-wavelength radiation—visible light—to pass through.

Thanks to its ability to reflect radiation, the Earth's cloud cover acts as a cooling system for the planet.

One-third of the sun's light is reflected directly back into space from the tops of clouds. This helps prevent the planet from overheating. The remaining two-thirds reaches the Earth's surface, where it is converted into longer-wavelength heat radiation. Only part of this heat is released back into space. The rest is absorbed and reflected by greenhouse gases, such as water vapor and carbon dioxide, thus warming the atmosphere and surface temperature.

Thanks to this natural "greenhouse effect," the Earth's average surface temperature is just over 57°F (14°C). Without it, the average temperature would fall to some 0°F (–18°C), and today's diversity of life would not be possible.

Anatomy of the Atmosphere

LAYERS: The atmosphere is not a single, uniform blanket of gases. Instead, it is divided into layers which vary in chemical composition and temperature. The first 50 miles (80 km) are sometimes called the homosphere, because its gaseous components mix homogeneously. In the area above it, the heterosphere, the gases are separated due to the gradual decline in gravitational force.

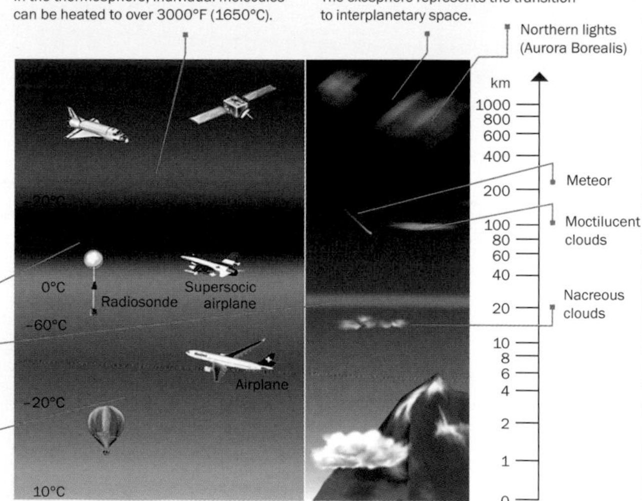

In the thermosphere, individual molecules can be heated to over 3000°F (1650°C).
The exosphere represents the transition to interplanetary space.
Northern lights (Aurora Borealis)
km
1000
800
600
400
200
100
80
60
40
20
10
8
6
4
2
1
0
Meteor
Moctilucent clouds
Nacreous clouds
0°C
Radiosonde
Supersocic airplane
-60°C
Airplane
-20°C
10°C
Most meteors burn up in the mesosphere.
The ozone layer, which absorbs ultraviolet radiation, is found in the stratosphere.
The troposphere contains over 90% of the atmosphere's air and nearly all of its water vapor. The most significant weather phenomena take place here.

see also: Atmospheres of Other Planets, *Universe Chapter, pp. 18–21*

AIR POLLUTION FROM HUMAN ACTIVITY

There is no longer any doubt that air pollution can influence global climate. In many industrialized nations, strict environmental regulations have been put into effect.

By absorbing ultraviolet rays from the sun, the atmospheric gas ozone plays a key role in protecting the Earth. Ozone is produced when the sun's radiation splits oxygen molecules in the stratosphere.

The Ozone Hole

In the late 1970s, scientists observed a thinning of the ozone layer over the Earth's polar regions. Through research, they identified the main cause: Chemicals called chlorofluorocarbons (CFCs), which had been produced industrially since 1930 and were used as propellants and refrigerants. When CFCs escape into the air, they rise into the stratosphere where they are split by solar radiation. This produces active chemical compounds, or radicals, which react with the ozone molecules. A high concentration of radicals can lead to the formation of an ozone hole, which would allow the sun's harmful ultraviolet radiation to reach the Earth's surface unhindered. Since 1995, the use of CFCs has been limited or banned worldwide. According to calculations by the World Meteorological Organization, the ozone holes over the polar regions—where especially high levels of CFCs have accumulated during the long, frigid polar nights—may actually repair themselves by 2075.

In 2006, the ozone hole over the Antarctic reached a record size of 6.5 million miles^3 (27.5 million km^3).

Acid Rain

The burning of fossil fuels such as coal, oil, and natural gas (p. 42) produces large amounts of sulfur dioxide and nitrogen oxides. When these pollutants enter the atmosphere, they react with oxygen and water to produce acids.

The acids, primarily sulfuric and nitric acids, then return to Earth in the form of "acid rain." The soil becomes acidified, harming plant life. Acid rain is cited as a cause of the death of forests in some parts of the world. The acids also dissolve heavy metals and aluminum from the ground, carrying them into nearby bodies of water. Significant declines in aquatic species have been blamed on high concentrations of aluminum.

Acid rain also has destructive effects in urban environments. Since the acids attack sandstone and limestone, concrete structures such as buildings and statues weather much more quickly. Since the 1980s, many industrial countries have begun using filtration systems and catalytic converters to reduce harmful emissions.

The Greenhouse Effect

Burning fossil fuels also produces the greenhouse gases carbon dioxide and methane. The release of these gases increases the Earth's natural greenhouse effect, thus warming the atmosphere. During the past 100 years, the average temperature of the Earth's surface has increased by 1.3 °F (0.7 °C). Worldwide, the shrinking of glaciers has been observed while sea levels have risen 6–7 inches (15–18 cm). These and other phenomena provide evidence that human activity has caused an increase in the atmosphere's greenhouse effect. In 1997, the Kyoto Protocol (p. 55) was negotiated to reduce the production of greenhouse gases. Nevertheless, worldwide emission levels continue to rise.

The destructive effects of acid rain are seen on this statue.

INSIDER KNOWLEDGE

THE GREAT SMOG: *On the evening of December 5, 1952, London experienced one of the worst smog events in the history of industrialized nations. Low-lying fog combined with urban pollution formed a poisonous combination. Thousands of people died from respiratory ailments.*

ICY EVIDENCE: *Core samples taken from polar ice accurately document changes that have occurred in atmospheric greenhouse gas levels since the industrial revolution.*

THE INDUSTRIAL REVOLUTION *began in England in the second half of the 18th century.*

SVANTE ARRHENIUS *recognized the climatic importance of carbon dioxide in 1895.*

CHARLES D. KEELING *explained the greenhouse effect in 1958 and initiated research into the phenomenon.*

A gas company in the 1880s

Industrialization—The Beginning of the End?

HUMAN BEINGS have scarcely taken environmental considerations into account over the course of their developmental history. With the industrial revolution, the use of coal energy—a key contributor to environmental pollution—rose enormously. Environmental damage has also been caused by waste from the chemical industry and increasing vehicle traffic.

THE DEADLY EFFECTS of industrialization on nature and the climate began to be recognized in the mid-20th century. However, world demand for energy will continue to rise sharply since many countries are still in the early stages of their industrial development.

Pollution from automobiles blankets many of the world's cities in smog.

THE CLIMATE SYSTEM

Different climates prevail in various parts of the Earth, from the dry heat of the desert to the chill of polar regions. Taken together, average global climate figures can be calculated.

Climate is defined as the full range of weather conditions experienced in a particular place, including daily and seasonal changes, over several decades or longer. Thus, climate differs from weather, which refers to short-term conditions during a period ranging from a few hours to a couple weeks—or at most, a particular season.

According to the size of the area under consideration, climate can be divided into microclimate, which occurs within an area only a few yards or meters; mesoclimate, which extends over several hundred miles or kilometers; and macroclimate, which refers to the climate of entire continents or even the Earth as a whole.

Due to their dryness, deserts are usually barren of vegetation. Most are found in subtropical zones.

Tropical rain forests near the Equator can receive up to 394 inches (1,000 cm) of rainfall each year.

Climate Observations

Climate arises from the interaction of the Earth's five "spheres": the atmosphere, biosphere (living things), pedosphere (soil), lithosphere (rocks and minerals), and the hydrosphere or cryosphere (water or ice). Taken together, these form the geosphere. A multitude of climatic factors influence each of the spheres, ultimately producing an overall climate in the geosphere.

To describe weather and climate in the atmosphere, scientists collect data about the various climatic elements; e.g., temperature, air pressure, humidity, wind speed, and direction. Using data collected over a long period of time, average values are calculated. When scientists compare these with current data, they can make predictions about long-term climate patterns; for instance, the temperature of the oceans shows a rising trend.

The Earth's Climate Zones

The Earth is divided into a number of different climate zones. One commonly used system is based on average temperatures in particular regions. Thus, the world can be divided into polar, temperate, subtropical, and tropical zones.

The tropics form the "warm belt" near the Earth's Equator. They are bounded by the Tropic of Cancer in the north and the Tropic of Capricorn in the south. Moist grasslands and rain forests are typical tropical landscapes. There are no clearly-defined seasons in this zone, and the average yearly temperature is approximately 77°F (25°C).

The subtropical regions lie between the tropics and the temperate zone, from latitude 23.5° to about 40.0° north and south. The subtropics include dry savannas and deserts, among other habitats. Their yearly average temperatures lie between 54–77°F (12–25°C). They are characterized by hot, tropical summers and winters with moderate temperatures.

If ice in the polar regions melts, it usually happens during the few warm weeks of the polar summer.

The temperate zones are found between the polar circles and latitude 40.0° north and south. Here, clearly defined seasons and changing lengths of day and night are observed. Typical vegetation includes evergreen, mixed, and deciduous forests. The annual average temperature is between 41 and 59°F (5 and 15°C).

The icy and snowy environments of the polar zones lie within the Arctic Circle in the north and Antarctic Circle in the south. With average temperatures of minus 13–34°F (minus 25–1°C), depending on the season, they are very hostile to life.

Factors Affecting Climate

WHAT DETERMINES CLIMATE? Diverse conditions and processes work together to determine the climate of a particular area. Here, a distinction is made between primary and secondary climatic factors. Primary climatic factors include latitude, the elevation and contour of the Earth, and the amount of solar radiation received in the zone. From these, secondary climatic factors arise, such as ocean currents, wind systems, and other natural cycles.

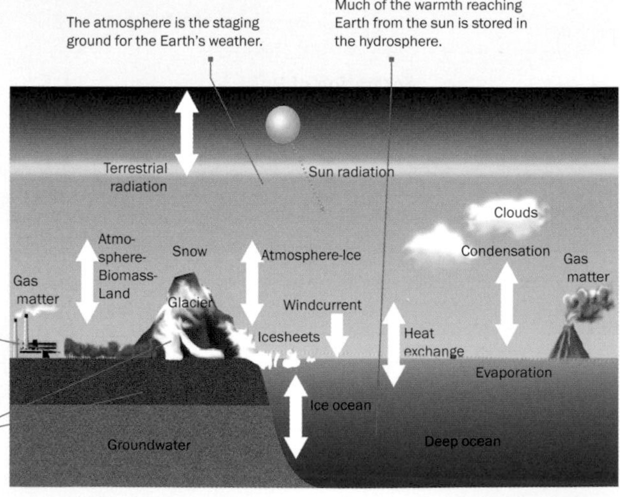

In the biosphere, a distinction is made between natural and anthropogenic—or human-caused—influences on climate.

The lithosphere and cryosphere serve as a "climate archive."

NATURAL CLIMATE PHENOMENA

Climate has gone through natural cycles throughout the Earth's history. This is shown by climate data from past millennia, obtained using core samples from polar ice and mineral deposits.

Driven by the sun's energy, the winds and ocean currents constantly mix the Earth's troposphere and hydrosphere (p. 52), affecting our planet's climate.

The Trade Winds

The "passat" or trade winds are tropical winds that blow in a regular pattern throughout the year. The ongoing circulation is caused by interactions between areas of differing air pressure. The low-altitude trade winds blowing from the subtropics toward the Equator are shifted sideways by the Earth's rotation. Based on the wind direction, a distinction is made between the northeast trade winds in the Northern Hemisphere and the southeast trade winds in the Southern Hemisphere (p. 47). At the Equator, trade winds become warmer and rise through the atmosphere. They then return to the subtropics at a higher altitude. Since they transport great amounts of moisture taken up from the oceans, these winds have a significant influence on global climate.

The Northern Hemisphere is relatively untouched by the effects of El Niño.

H = High Pressure Area

Northeast Trade Wind

Intertropical Convergence Zone

Southeast Trade Wind

The trade winds' circulation systems are known as Hadley cells.

El Niño and La Niña

The southeast trade winds drive the circulation of water in the South Pacific. Cool surface water near the coast of South America is driven westward, warming up along the way. As the current approaches Southeast Asia, it pushes against the cooler water there, which sinks into the depths of the Pacific. This cool water flows across the seafloor toward South America, where it rises to begin the cycle again.

This cold current from the deep Pacific produces an extended high pressure zone and a dry climate in western South America. The water is rich in nutrients, creating highly productive fishing off the shores of countries such as Peru. In Southeast Asia, by contrast, the warm waters produce sustained low pressure zones. As a result, Australia and Indonesia are regularly battered by heavy monsoon rains.

Every three to eight years, an unusual warming pattern is observed off the South American coast. One presumed reason is a weakening of the trade winds, interrupting the water circulation pattern in the Pacific. The results include heavy rains and hurricanes. Without the nutrient-rich cold current, fish stocks drastically decline. In Southeast Asia, severe droughts bring failed harvests and forest fires. Since this often appears around Christmas time, Peruvian fishers named it "El Niño" or "Christ child." When rising pressure differences between South America and Southeast Asia allow the trade winds to gather their strength, the circulation pattern resumes and the original conditions return. This is known as "La Niña" or "little sister." Scientists still do not fully understand either phenomenon.

During El Niño years, many marine animals, including seals and sea birds, struggle to survive.

Formation of Rain

Warmth from the sun causes water to evaporate, and the water vapor rises within the troposphere. As it moves higher, it begins to condense on microscopic particles in the air such as salt, sulfates, dust, or pollen, forming tiny droplets. A collection of droplets produces a cloud. The condensation process releases heat, causing the droplets to rise even higher. Above a certain altitude, they freeze, forming ice crystals. These clump together until they form clusters heavy enough to fall to the ground. If the temperature stays above 32°F (0°C), the ice crystals melt and fall as rain.

left: *Rain replenishes water reserves on land.*

CLIMATE MODELS: *Historical climate patterns can be simulated by computers using climate models.*

TIROS: *On April 1, 1960, the first weather satellite, TIROS I, was launched into orbit around the Earth.*

Over the past 550 million years, the Earth's average temperature has remained at a constant of about 72°F (22°C), with the exception of four cold phases. The current average is about 59°F (15°C).

Today, Pleistocene, Tertiary, Cretaceous, Jurassic, Triassic, Permian, Carboniferous, Devonian, Silurian, Ordovician, Cambrian, Precambrian

72°F (22°C) 63°F (17°C) 54°F (12°C)

Average Global Temperature

The Earth's Climatic History

NATURAL EVENTS such as the formation of the atmosphere, the creation of new land masses, tectonic plate movements, large volcanic eruptions, and meteorite strikes have influenced the Earth's climate over the course of planetary history. Most changes in climate took place very gradually, but their causes left traces that can still be detected today. Plant and animal fossils, as well as the chemical composition of minerals and ice deposits, provide scientists with useful information about the climatic conditions of past eras. Because ice preserves air particularly well, analyses of polar ice are currently among the most accurate and significant sources of climate data from the past.

INSIDER KNOWLEDGE

DENDROCHRONOLOGY: *Trees form thicker growth rings during favorable growing seasons and thinner rings under unfavorable conditions. Thus, growth rings not only give information about the tree's age, but also about climatic conditions in the past.*

THE EARTH

CLIMATE CHANGE

Are floods, storms, and record high temperatures the first signs of climate change, and are humans responsible? Scientists are attempting to answer these questions.

Natural factors exist which can explain the current warming trend in the Earth's climate. However, what is most unusual is the speed at which the change is occurring.

Scientists disagree about whether global warming will increase the frequency of hurricanes.

The reason may be a new influence on global climate: human activity.

Cold Phase, Warm Phase

The alternation between ice ages and warm phases on Earth is part of a natural cycle. On average, a cold or warm phase lasts 100,000 years. Within this period, smaller climate changes occur after about 20,000 to 40,000 years.

In 1920, Serbian astronomer and mathematician Milutin Milankovitch first realized that astronomical forces have a cyclical influence on the intensity of solar radiation reaching the Earth. With its tilted axis, the Earth moves like a top as it traces an elliptical path around the sun. At intervals of 20,000, 40,000, and 100,000 years, this motion alters the distance between the Earth and the sun, as well as the angle at which sunlight hits the Earth—possibly serving as a trigger for climate change. These "Milankovitch cycles" are confirmed by data from sediments on the ocean floor as well as core samples obtained by drilling into polar ice. Whether they are the only reason for cyclical climate change has not been proved.

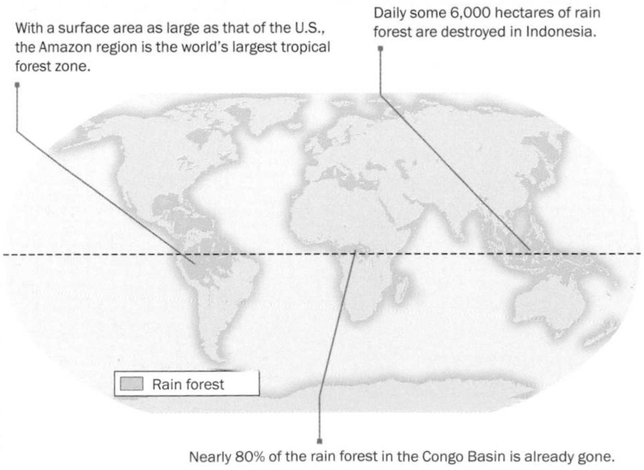

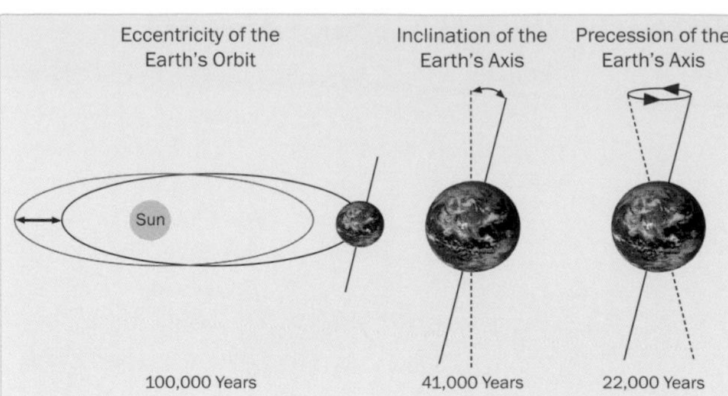
Eccentricity of the Earth's Orbit
Inclination of the Earth's Axis
Precession of the Earth's Axis
Sun
100,000 Years
41,000 Years
22,000 Years

Alterations in the Earth's tilt and its path around the sun change the distance between the two bodies and the angle at which sunlight reaches our planet.

The Earth is currently in the warm phase within an ice age. Therefore it must be assumed that humans are not the sole cause of global warming. A small minority of scientists even assert that human activity has absolutely no influence on the warming process.

Natural Catastrophes

Volcanic eruptions (p. 39) can also affect global climate. A large eruption releases huge amounts of ash and sulfur dioxide into the air. The ash particles spread out into the atmosphere, while the sulfur dioxide reacts with moisture in the air to form sulfuric acid. Under certain wind conditions—as seen near the Equator—the sulfuric acid can make its way to the stratosphere and remain there for years. As "aerosols," or floating particles, both the ash and sulfuric acid reflect some of the sun's rays back into space. The result is an overall cooling of the Earth. In 1991, the eruption of Pinatubo in the Philippines lowered average temperatures on Earth by 32.9°F (0.5°C) for two years.

A similar effect can be caused by an asteroid striking Earth. The impact raises huge clouds of dust, which also act as aerosols in the atmosphere. About 65 million years ago, a huge asteroid or comet struck the Earth off the coast of Mexico, causing climatic cooling which led to mass extinction (p. 33). Of course, eruptions of "supervolcanoes" and asteroids are extremely rare, and they are not involved in the current warming trend.

INSIDER KNOWLEDGE

ICE CORE SAMPLES: *At a depth of 12,200 ft (3,720 m), Antarctic ice is approximately 900,000 years old.*

TEMPERATURE SWING: *On August 29, 1936, temperatures in Spearfish, South Dakota rose from −4°F (−20°C) to 45°F (7°C) in two minutes.*

CATEGORY 5: *During the 2005 hurricane season, three storms reached the highest strength category, with winds over 155 mph (250 kph).*

Green Lungs

TROPICAL RAIN FORESTS serve as important storehouses for water and carbon compounds. No other ecosystem on land stores as much carbon. Clearing and burning of the forest, however, releases large amounts of greenhouse gases. Near the Equator, rain forests help regulate heat and humidity levels within the tropical zones, thus affecting global climate.

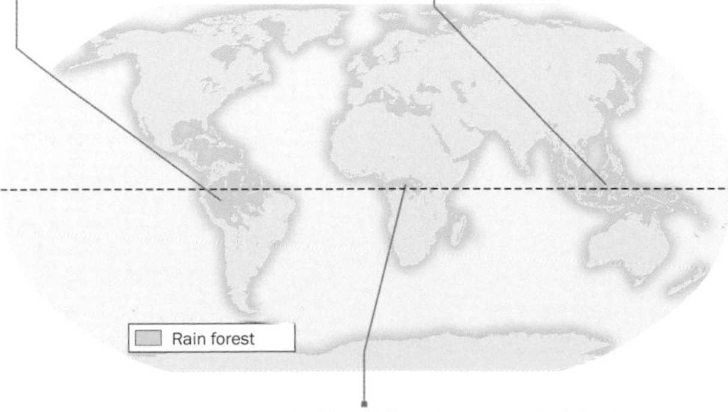
With a surface area as large as that of the U.S., the Amazon region is the world's largest tropical forest zone.
Daily some 6,000 hectares of rain forest are destroyed in Indonesia.
Rain forest
Nearly 80% of the rain forest in the Congo Basin is already gone.

A comparison: Views of Switzerland's Palü glacier in 1891 and in 2003 (right)

Duc to global warming, glaciers are continuing to shrink, which contributes to the rising sea level.

see also: **Climate Changes,** *Politics, Law, and Economy, p. 208*

HUMAN INFLUENCE ON CLIMATE

The Earth's climatic system is slow to change. The climate trends that are occurring today were partially triggered by events that happened decades ago.

Gold mining operations endanger the Amazon ecosystem.

Wood from tropical forests is exported to industrialized countries.

Natural processes lead to constant changes in the Earth's climate. However, since the industrial revolution (p. 51) a new factor has been added: human activity.

Do Humans Affect Climate?

Long-term climate developments can be simulated using computerized models. Based on trends from the past, it appears that historical climate data for recent centuries only makes sense if human activity is included as a factor. In the past 150 years, humans have released increasing amounts of greenhouse gases and other pollutants into the atmosphere. Since the climate reacts slowly, it is unclear whether these emissions are already having an effect today. Scientists also disagree about whether human influence outweighs the natural factors affecting climate.

However, it is clearly foreseeable that human demand for food, housing, and energy will continue to rise, which will thus increase the burden on the environment. The Earth's population is expected to reach some 8 billion by 2025. Depending on the degree of human impact as calculated by experts, the protection of the Earth's climate will demand far-reaching political, economic, and social changes.

Industrial Nations—Leaders or Perpetrators?

Industrial nations consume nearly 75 to 80 percent of the fossil fuels burned each year. Thus, they are responsible for the majority of greenhouse gas emissions. The injured parties are less-developed countries, which lack resources to counter the effects of global warming, such as droughts, floods, and heavy storms.

In light of this situation, the industrialized countries have the responsibility to reduce their greenhouse gas emissions. The Kyoto Protocol of 1997 represented a first step toward the implementation of international climate protection measures. Strategies to address the problem may include the use of renewable energy sources and changes in public policy with regard to vehicles.

Five Minutes to Midnight

However, even if current emissions of greenhouse gases and other pollutants could be stopped completely, it would take decades for the levels of carbon dioxide and other gases to return to those before the industrial revolution. Nevertheless, reducing emissions is the only way to prevent a possible climatics catastrophe. Yet the outlook is poor as the U.S., the largest emitter of carbon dioxide, has rejected the Kyoto Protocol. Meanwhile, the industrial expansion of China and India will lead to further rises in emissions.

GREEN LIGHT FOR INCREASES: *Australia, Iceland, and Norway were granted permission to raise emissions above their 1990 levels.*

HOLD YOUR POSITION: *Russia, Ukraine, and New Zealand can maintain their 1990 emission levels.*

In the future, the industrializing nations will intensify the problem of climate change.

The Kyoto Protocol

A BEGINNING: The UN Kyoto Protocol aims to reduce emissions of six greenhouse gases by 5.2% compared with their 1990 levels. It is viewed by many as a milestone in climate protection; however, critics call it a "drop in the bucket" as long as industrial heavyweights such as China and the U.S. fail to take action. Some scientists also question the effectiveness of confining the discussion almost exclusively to carbon dioxide.

International conference on climate change in Kyoto, Japan, in 1997

Stormy Forecast

Statistically, clusters of storms such as those observed in recent years occur regularly and are among the Earth's natural climatic cycles. However, climate researchers predict that such clusters and other extreme weather phenomena may become more common in the future, in part, because of the increased warming of the oceans.

above: *A storm strikes the Florida coast*

In Sumatra, 3.5 million hectares of rain forest are destroyed each year through burning and clear-cutting.

INSIDER KNOWLEDGE

WARMING: *: Since 1955, the oceans have warmed by an average of 33 °F (0.5 °C).*

ICE AGE: *For the past 11,625 years, the Earth has been experiencing a warm phase within a global ice age. The next cold phase is expected in 15,000 years at the earliest.*

THE EARTH

➲ see also: **Renewable Energy,** *Physics and Technology Chapter, p. 135*

Monographic Boxes

Analytic Boxes

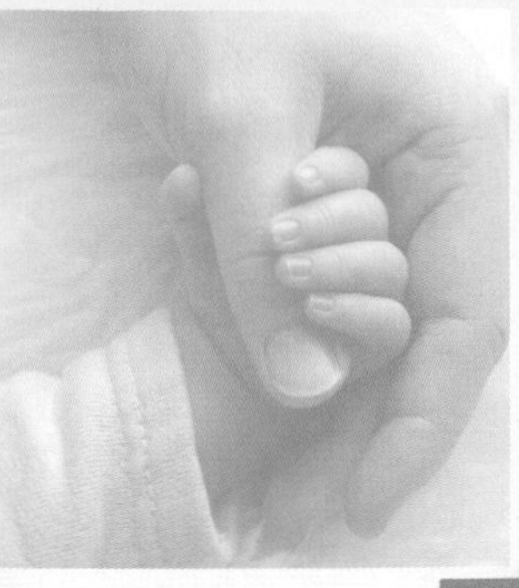

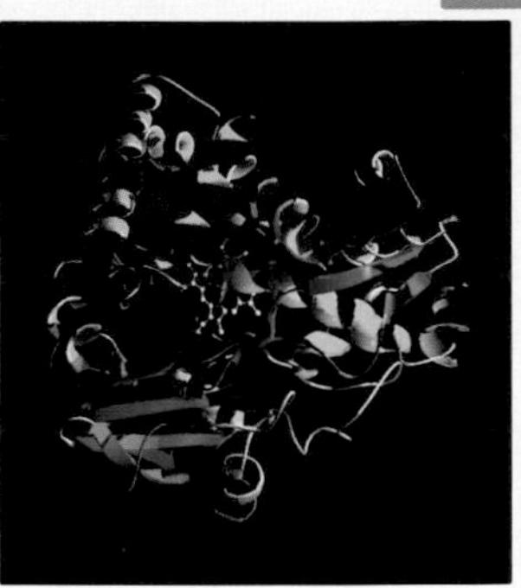

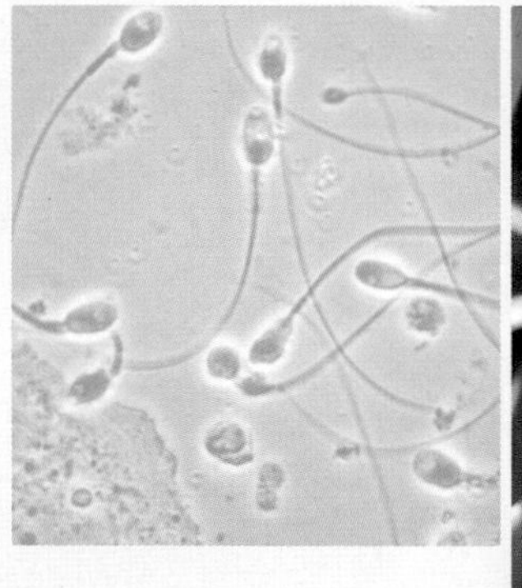

BIOLOGY

Humankind has always been anxious to decipher the phenomenal secrets of nature. Biology has the potential to unravel yet more of these secrets. Investigation has explored how life emerged with such astounding variety; how its smallest component, the cell, functions; how animals, plants, and people behave and adapt themselves to their environment. An understanding of the foundations of biology has also enabled humankind to recreate certain natural processes and to alter them for their own purposes. In the 21st century, our accumulated knowledge in this field is being used extensively in the food industry, agriculture, and the manufacture of medicines.

KEY FACTS

THE ORIGIN *of life on Earth has still not been fully clarified.*

THE PRIMORDIAL SOUP THEORY *suggests life arose from chemical reactions in non-living substances.*

EUKARYOTIC CELLS *developed from symbiotic relationships among prokaryotes.*

THE FIRST MULTICELLULAR ORGANISMS *were probably first present in the Pre-Cambrian era.*

The appearance of life on Earth | The first living things

THE ORIGIN OF LIFE

How life came into existence on Earth may possibly never be proved with complete certainty. Many religious explanations (p. 218) and scientific theories have been presented to try to explain this mystery. It seems likely that simple organic molecules arose and combined, eventually producing cell-like organisms. From these, prokaryotic and later eukaryotic cells developed. These cells were the starting point for the evolution of multicellular organisms such as today's plants, animals, and human beings.

The first single-celled organisms probably appeared some 3.5–4 billion years ago.

BIOLOGY

THE APPEARANCE OF LIFE ON EARTH

The journey from molecules to organized living creatures can only be described by theories, as concrete evidence is still lacking. The primordial soup theory is one such theory.

Scientists working in many disciplines attempted to solve the mystery of the appearance of life on Earth. They have presented many theories. Since Louis Pasteur first observed bacterial cells dividing under a microscope, biology has recognized the basic precept that life arises only from pre-existing life. The initial appearance of life on Earth would appear to present an exception to this rule.

At that time, physical and chemical conditions were very different from today. It seems the first organic molecules were produced through the addition of energy to non-living material about 3.4–4 billion years ago, from which life first developed. The "primordial soup theory" described the mechanisms and individual steps in this process by its re-creation in laboratory experiments in 1953.

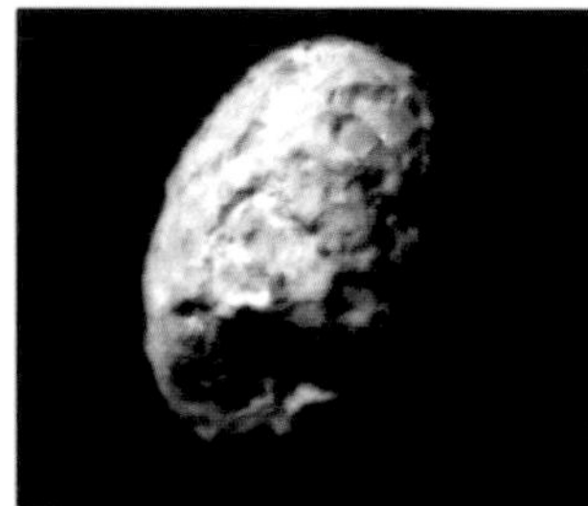

According to the panspermia theory, life on Earth may have arrived on comets.

The Primordial Soup Theory

This hypothesis posits that simple organic molecules were formed out of chemical reactions among inorganic molecules in the primordial sea. Primordial soup refers to early Earth's water containing many dissolved substances. The molecules were exposed to high levels of energy from ultraviolet radiation—since there was no protective ozone layer at the time—and lightning discharges. With this energy input, they were able to combine and form organic building blocks including sugar, fatty acids, and amino acids—the precursors of proteins. These formed the basis for the first protobionts—antecedents of true cells. The protobionts took on closed, bubble-like shapes (resembling single-celled organisms) in which metabolism could take place.

There are many other theories, including that life arose around hydrothermal volcanic vents ("black smokers") spewing particle-rich water from the deep ocean floor.

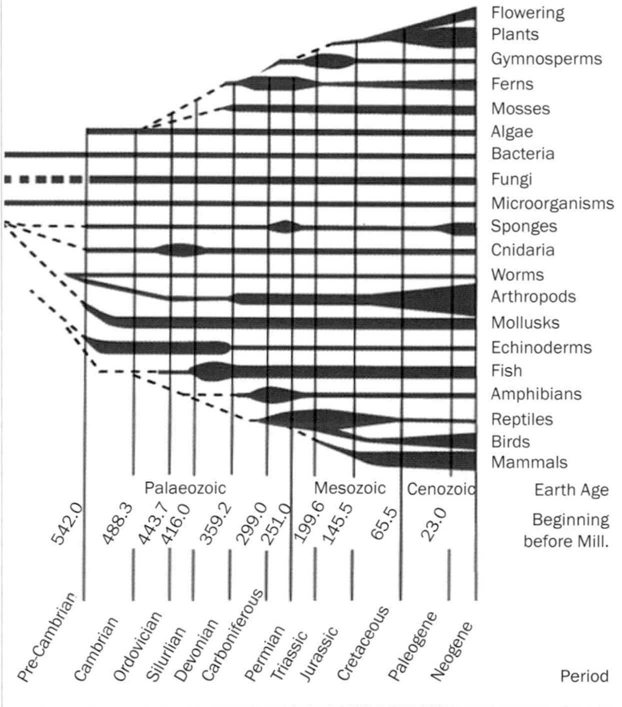

Using layered mineral deposits and their fossils, scientists reconstruct the history of Earth and divide it into time periods.

Lightning may have supplied some of the energy needed to produce life from inorganic molecules.

see also: Origin of the Earth, Primordial Experiment, Black Smokers, *Earth Chapter, pp. 27, 30, 31*

THE FIRST LIVING THINGS

Living things have developed over time from simple structures to increasingly complex forms, such as multicellular and higher organisms.

After the development of the first cell-like structures, protobionts, the path was clear for the evolution of the first true cells: prokaryotes.

Prokaryotes—The First Cells

The first prokaryotes were very similar to contemporary bacteria and cyanobacteria, or blue-green algae. While they lacked a true nucleus, they had a membrane which separated them from the environment, creating an internal space in which metabolic processes could take place.

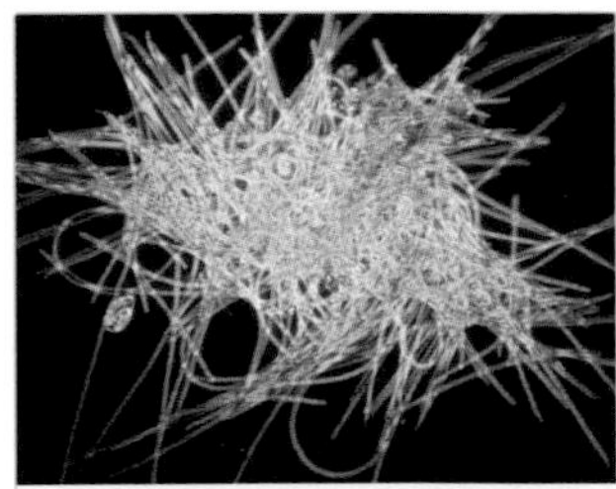

Cyanobacteria were the first to do oxygen-producing photosynthesis.

Some early prokaryotes began to use sunlight to fulfill their energy needs. They carried out an anaerobic form of photosynthesis, oxidizing hydrogen sulfide and giving off sulfur as a waste product. This type of energy production is still used today by purple bacteria.

Stromatolites are calcium carbonate deposits made by marine cyanobacteria.

A major step forward was the development of oxygen-producing photosynthesis (p. 66). Using the sun's energy, carbon dioxide, and the plentiful water supply surrounding them, cyanobacteria began to assemble their own nutrients.

Oxygen—which was poisonous to living things of the time—was released as a waste product from this process. The only other surviving organisms were those that could retreat into oxygen-free habitats (such as sulfurous hot springs), or are able via cellular respiration to use oxygen to produce energy through the oxidation of food. The oldest known prokaryote fossils are stromatolites that are about 3.4 billion years old. Stromatolites are calcium carbonate deposits which form from colonies of cyanobacteria.

Imprint of jellyfish-like organism from the late Pre-Cambrian from Australia's Ediacara region

The First Eukaryotes

The first eukaryotes probably developed about 2 billion years ago from symbiotic relationships among prokaryotic cells. Equipped with a true cell nucleus, they formed a foundation for the development of higher organisms. In addition to single-celled organisms, all multicellular things—plants, animals, and humans—are eukaryotes.

The Endosymbiont Theory

THE ENDOSYMBIONT THEORY attempts to explain the origin of eukaryotic cells. It proposes that they emerged through the fusion of various prokaryotic cells. Larger cells took in smaller ones and closed around them without digesting them. The cells then lived in a community or symbiosis, with both likely profiting from the arrangement. Gradually, the symbiotic partners lost their ability to survive independently and became a single organism: a eukaryotic cell. Within the new cell, the smaller prokaryotes took on the functions of what later became the cell organelles (cell-part with specialized functions). One supporting piece of evidence for this theory is that some cell organelles have their own unique DNA, are surrounded by double-layered cell membranes, and reproduce through division in a way similiar to bacteria.

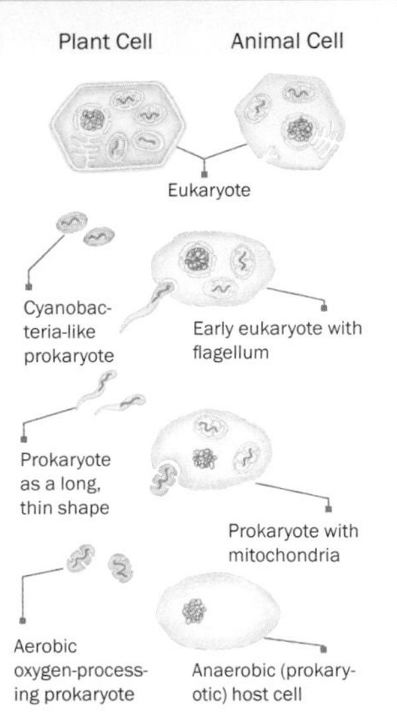

Eukaryots emerged through their incorporation of smaller prokaryots.

Multicellular Organisms

Multicellular life may have arisen from colonies of single-celled organisms, in which daughter cells did not separate from others after cell division. Multicellular life may also have emerged from single-celled organisms with multiple nuclei.

Foraminifera are single-celled shelled organisms that have existed since the Cambrian period.

The first multicellular organisms probably appeared around 700 million years ago in the Pre-Cambrian period. However, there is little fossil record documenting their existence, likely because they did not have any hard physical components such as shells. However, the imprints of soft-bodied organisms that can be found are mostly in the Ediacaran fauna of Australia. In the early Cambrian period, many new species developed within the relatively short time of 50 million years. About 400 million years ago, the first plants came ashore, making way for the colonization of dry land by other organisms.

INSIDER KNOWLEDGE

BACTERIA *have existed for billions of years nearly unchanged and have spread to countless habitats.*

LIVING FOSSILS *are species that have barely changed over millions of years. There are few examples of these among higher, more complex organisms.*

For centuries, humans have used the oldest living things—bacteria—to make cheese.

BIOLOGY

➔ see also: Cyanobacteria, *Earth Chapter*, p. 30

KEY FACTS

THE INVENTION *of the light microscope (early 1600s) allowed researchers to examine living cells.*

A CELL *is the basic unit of life.*

HEREDITY *is the transfer of genetic information from parents to their offspring.*

BREEDING *and genetic manipulation permit humans to intervene in the reproductive processes of many living things.*

Cell structure and division | Heredity

GROWTH AND REPRODUCTION

All organisms go through phases of growth and reproduction during their lives. The basic mechanisms for these processes are nearly always the same; they involve the division of cells, the basic units of life. This division ensures that their genetic information is passed on to daughter cells in the form of chromosomes. Chromosomes are formed from deoxyribonucleic acid (DNA) and various proteins. They contain information about an organism's appearance, character, behavior, and numerous other traits that will affect their lives.

➲ *Every cell contains a complete set of genetic information, which is passed on during reproduction.*

CELL STRUCTURE AND DIVISION

All living things are made of cells, which are generally organized into specialized tissues. Plant cells use sunlight to create their own food.

Biologists view the cell as the basic unit of life, because it is the simplest form of living matter. Some organisms, such as bacteria, euglena, and paramecia, are made up of only one cell, and are thus referred to as single-celled organisms. Others, including humans, are multicellular, or composed of many cells.

Parts of a Cell

Cells are surrounded by a cell membrane and, in plants, a wall. Embedded in a jelly-like substance called cytoplasm, individual structures or organelles perform cell functions. A basic distinction is made between organisms that have cells with a true nucleus (eukaryotes) and those without a nucleus (prokaryotes). The nucleus, enclosed by a nuclear membrane, contains the organism's genetic material in the form of chromosomes. The mitochondria are another type of organelle that powers the cell by producing energy for metabolic processes. The ribosomes use amino acids from food to produce the proteins necessary for all essential processes. Lysosomes and peroxisomes digest foreign and toxic substances that might harm the cell. The Golgi apparatus consists of stacked structures, or dictyosomes, which sort and store substances such as proteins and lipids.

The single-celled organism paramecium is covered with cilia, which allow the cell to move.

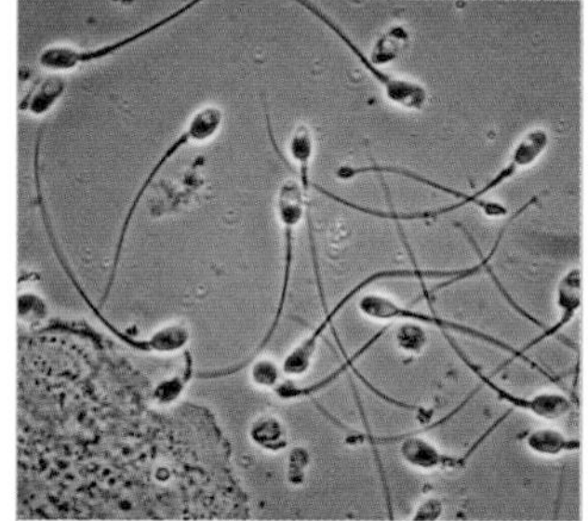

The sperm penetrates the egg cell (left) during fertilization.

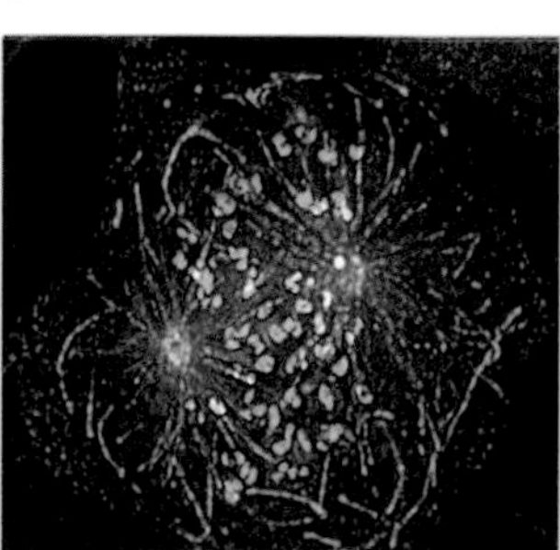

Cell division: The spindle apparatus helps chromosomes divide.

Growth and Division

The growth and reproduction of organisms takes place through cell division. It starts with mitosis, the splitting of the nucleus. This separates the previously doubled strands of the chromosomes, so that each new nucleus contains a complete set of genetic information. The cytoplasm pinches inward, dividing the cell into two identical, smaller daughter cells. The organelles—which have also previously doubled in number—are divided between the daughter cells. The new cells grow to normal size and double the genetic material in their nuclei to prepare for the next mitosis.

Differences Between Plant and Animal Cells

PLANT AND ANIMAL CELLS: *Some organelles are found only in plants (xx), others exclusively in animals (xy).*

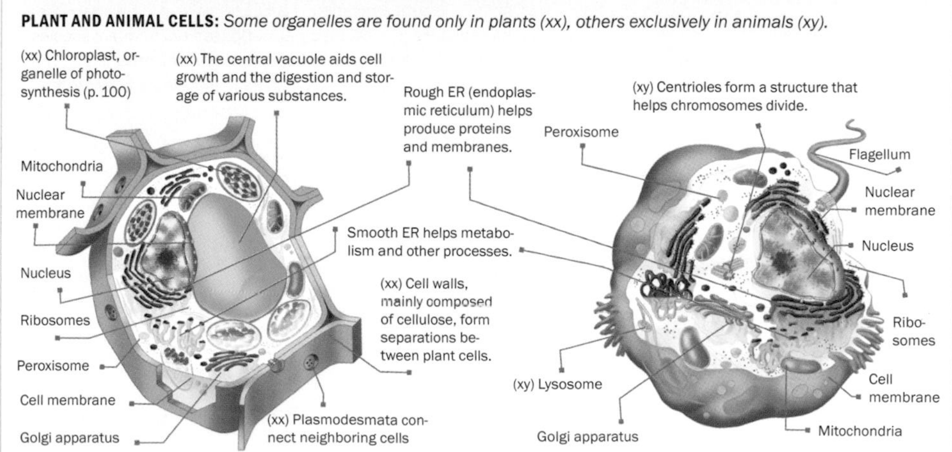

INSIDER KNOWLEDGE

BACTERIA ARE PROKARYOTES: *their genetic data lies free in cytoplasm.*

THE PROCESS OF CELL DIVISION *lasts from 30 minutes to 2 hours.*

HEREDITY

Parents pass on genetic information to their offspring. This material is combined from both parents in sexual reproduction.

Pioneers of Genetics

Charles Darwin, the originator of evolutionary theory, was the first to recognize that all living things developed from older forms of life. They underwent a continuous process of adaptation to their environments through changes in their genes. The science of modern genetics began in 1860, when Austrian abbot Gregor Mendel propagated different plant species and identified the rules of inheritance. Geneticists James Watson from the U.S. and Francis Crick from Britain solved the puzzle of DNA structure in 1953.

above: *Charles Darwin revolutionized the natural sciences—and polarized society.*

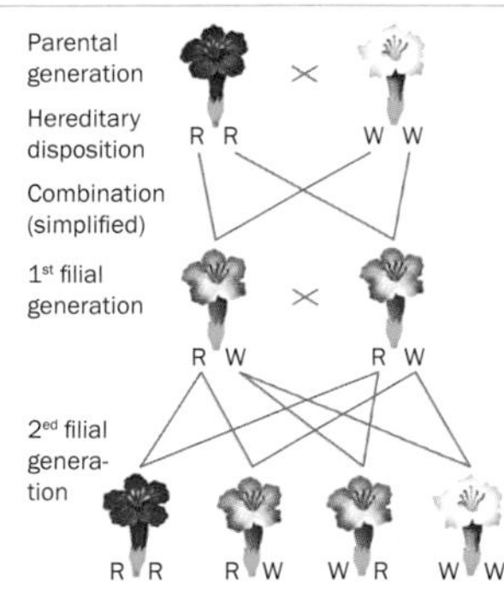

Intermediate inheritance: A red-flowered plant is crossed with a white-flowered plant. The offspring's flowers are pink. When two pink-flowered plants are crossed, the next generation has plants with red, pink, and white flowers.

Most living things produce progeny during the course of their lives. These offspring exhibit traits inherited from their parents as well as their own individual characteristics. Scientific understanding of the mechanisms of inheritance developed only in the 20th century. The groundbreaking discoveries of modern genetics are also used for practical applications, such as the breeding of animals and plants.

How Does Heredity Work?

In sexual reproduction, germ cells, or gametes, fuse together. In both animals and humans, these are the egg cells and sperm cells. Unlike other cells, gametes contain only single sets of genetic material. After joining together, the new cell contains the usual double set of genetic information.

Genetic information is transferred in the form of long strands of deoxyribonucleic acid (DNA) containing individual genes. DNA and proteins make up the chromosomes, whose coiled internal structure was not identified until the 1950s. DNA molecules take the form of a double spiral or helix, with two long, tightly wound strands connected to each other through hydrogen bonds. These molecules contain an organism's complete set of genetic instructions.

Which Gene Will Be Expressed?

Genes are individual segments of DNA within chromosomes. They affect all traits including appearance and character. Reproduction entails a copy of a gene from the father and a gene from the mother joining together to transfer this genetic information to the offspring. The progeny now has two versions of each gene, one from each parent. These may be the same—both may contain the instructions for blue eye color—or different; for instance, one may have instructions for brown eyes and the other for blue. Usually, one gene prevails over the other and is thus called the dominant gene. The suppressed or recessive trait is not lost, however; it can appear in later generations if it is not suppressed again.

Some traits may also be inherited in an intermediate form. For example, crossing a plant with red flowers and one with white flowers can produce a pink-flowered plant.

DNA is a very long molecule with a double helix shape.

Cloning copies an individual organism's complete genetic data. Dolly the sheep, the first healthy cloned animal, was born in 1996 and died aged six and a half years.

GENETIC TECHNOLOGY *refers to processes that allow targeted manipulation of genetic information.*

SELECTIVE BREEDING CAN *both encourage and suppress particular traits in animals and plants.*

PEDIGREE PETS *are often the products of breeding for desired abilities or appearance.*

Humans breed animals for specific traits such as body shape, fur, and eye color.

Genetic Manipulation and Breeding

FOR CENTURIES, people have bred microorganisms for the production of wine, beer, and cheese. Genetic technology takes this process a step further by manipulating specific genes for practical applications in research, medicine, and agriculture.The manipulation of genes resulted in hundreds of new products at the beginning of the 21st century. Genes from different species are often combined by inserting a gene from one organism into another. The tools used by scientists in this process include DNA-splitting enzymes and host organisms, such as the bacterium Escherichia coli.

CONTEMPORARY GENETIC TECHNOLOGIES engineer minuscule organisms that produce antibiotics and antibodies for a great range of medical purposes. Bacteria can be genetically altered to enable them to break down environmental pollutants, and improve the resistance of varieties of agricultural plants.

Genetically modified corn plants can better resist diseases and pests.

BIOLOGY

KEY FACTS

GREEN ALGAE *are the ancestors of modern plants.*

THE OXYGEN *that humans need to survive is primarily produced by plants.*

NUTRIENTS AND WATER *are transported within the plant through specialized vascular tissues.*

PISTILS AND STAMENS *are the key reproductive organs of a flowering plant.*

Evolution | Anatomy | Plants without seeds | Plants with seeds | Photosynthesis | Nutrients

THE WORLD OF PLANTS

Plants are the only living things that create their own sustenance. They use the unique process of photosynthesis to capture and use the sun's light as an energy source. In turn, these autotrophic, or self-feeding, phenomena form the nutritional foundation for animals and humans, who cannot manufacture their own food. Although plants can be highly diverse in appearance, most share characteristic structures such as leaves and roots. Over the course of evolution, they have continually adapted themselves to prevailing environmental conditions.

Plant life left the oceans for land more than 450 million years ago.

THE EVOLUTION OF PLANTS

The ancestors of today's land plants lived in the oceans and seas. They had to develop features to meet challenges such as dehydration in order to adapt for survival on dry land.

Horsetails have simple water conducting systems.

Mosses remain dependent on moisture for reproduction.

The common buttercup belongs to the flowering plants group.

Fossil findings make it possible to distinguish four significant developmental periods in plant evolution. Each of these periods resulted in a new diversification of plant life.

Protection Against Dehydration

Around 460 million years ago, the first land plants evolved from aquatic green algae in the initial period of plant development. During a transitional phase, some species are thought to have adapted to life in bodies of water that would periodically dry up. As a result, modern mosses can survive on land by a waxy layer that protects them from dehydrating.

Appearance of Vascular Systems

During the next developmental stage, the first plants equipped with internal tubes to transport water, including ferns, horsetails, and clubmosses (p. 64), emerged on coasts and other moist environments. Unlike mosses, these first vascular plants already consisted of true roots and supportive stems with water-conducting tissues. They managed to obtain adequate moisture outside an aquatic environment and transport nutrients to each section of the plant.

The First Seeds

The first seed-producing plants (p. 65) appeared during the third developmental period. These differ from spore-producing vascular plants in that the embryo—together with a supply of nutrients—is encased in a shell: the seed. From these plants developed various kinds of plants without protective seed covering, or gymnosperms, such as today's evergreens. Lacking encasement, like within a fruit, their seeds fall freely to the ground to germinate. Seed-producing plants enjoyed significant advantages in the conquest of new environments. They no longer depended on moist environments for reproduction and their embryos were more protected from adverse environmental conditions.

Development of Fruit

Fruit-forming flowering plants called angiosperms, or plants with covered seeds, appeared during the fourth stage of development about 130 million years ago. In contrast to gymnosperms, angiosperm seeds are sealed inside chambers, or ovaries. These develop into fruits with attractive qualities like flavor or color, which promote their distribution. Animals transport the fruit—and the seeds inside—to other locations. This is one reason for the enormous success of angiosperms.

Coal Forests of the Carboniferous Era

APPROXIMATELY 360 MILLION years ago, ferns, giant horsetails, and clubmosses formed extensive, swampy forests. The plant matter that fell to the ground did not decay in the marshy environment, but instead formed thick layers of peat. Over the course of the Earth's history, these swamps were covered by oceans, and marine sediments were deposited on top of the peat layers. High temperatures and pressure gradually transformed the peat into coal.

Giant horsetails no longer exist today.
Ancient giant tree ferns could grow up to 32 ft (10 m) tall; today, they grow only in the tropics.
Lepidendron trees, which could reach a height of almost 100 ft (30 m), are now extinct.

see also: Coal, *Earth Chapter, p. 42* | *Physics and Technology Chapter, p. 132*

THE ANATOMY OF PLANTS

Nearly all vascular plants have the same basic anatomy: stems, leaves to absorb light and carbon dioxide, and roots to absorb water and minerals.

The basic components of a seed plant are the roots, leaves, stems, or shoots, and—at certain times of the year—flowers and fruit.

Roots—Contact With the Soil

The roots of a plant play several important roles. They provide stability by anchoring the plant firmly in the ground. The branches of fine root hairs absorb water and dissolved minerals from the soil. Some plants, such as carrots, have especially thickened roots that are used to store large amounts of nutrients. The plant later draws upon these reserves to produce flowers and fruit.

The Stem—The Support System

In addition to acting as support for the plant's leaves, flowers, and fruit, the sturdy stem transports water upward into the leaves from which it carries nutrients to the rest of the plant. This occurs through narrow tubes in the plant's tissue system called vascular bundles. Shoots generally grow toward light and can become woody, as in the case of bushes and trees.

Leaves—Setting of Photosynthesis

The green leaves of a plant produce nutrients through the process of photosynthesis (p. 66). This occurs in chloroplasts, which are contained within the leaf cells. The sugar produced by photosynthesis is distributed through the vascular bundles to the rest of the plant, where it nourishes individual cells. Water is distributed in the same manner. The vascular bundles can often be clearly seen as the veins on the underside of a leaf. The leaves draw carbon dioxide from the air through slit-shaped openings called stomata, which are predominantly found on their underside. These stomata usually open in the daytime to release excess water and the oxygen produced during photosynthesis. The carbon dioxide is stored in the plant's cells until it is required.

The cuticle, or upper surface of leaves, is often layered with a waxy coating, as is the lower surface sometimes, to protect the plant from dehydration and the sun's harsh rays.

left: *The veins of a leaf comprise the circulatory system for water and nutrients.*
right: *Fruit provides protection for the seeds.*

Flowers and Fruit

Biologically speaking, flowers are modified stems whose growth has been limited. Their anatomy is highly variable, depending on the plant family. Flowers basically comprise several specialized forms of leaves. The sepals—which are usually green and resemble ordinary leaves—protect the inner parts of the flower before it opens. Often strikingly colorful petals serve to attract insects in search of nectar and other animals for pollination. Lying within the ring of petals, the plant's reproductive organs, the male stamens and the female pistil, are divided into the style, ovary, and stigma. The style connects the stigma and ovary, which contains the ovules that develop into seeds. Each male stamen consists of a filament and an anther that holds pollen. After pollination, the ovule ripens into a seed and the ovary develops into a fruit. The fruit surrounds the seeds to protect and disperse them. The appearance of the fruit is adapted to the plant's particular distribution mechanism (p. 64).

The flower, with its pistils and stamens, houses the plant's reproductive organs.

Classification of Plants

Biology organizes living things into groups on the basis of specific shared characteristics. These groups are then arranged within a hierarchical system. The plants can be grouped into the categories of land plants and algae. Modern plants (other than algae) that are found in water are former land plants which re-adapted to aquatic life over the course of evolution.

Land plants can be further divided into mosses and vascular plants. The vascular plants include spore producers such as ferns, club-mosses and horsetails, as well as the seed-producing gymnosperms and angiosperms.

above: *Carl von Linnaeus was the first person to organize a system for naming plants and animals.*

Anatomy of a Plant

MOST SEEDED PLANTS share the basic anatomical design shown in the illustration. The flower is the plant's reproductive organ; the leaves are where photosynthesis occurs to provide nourishment; and the stem is the plant's support system. The roots supply the rest of the plant with water and often serve as a storage area for nutrients.

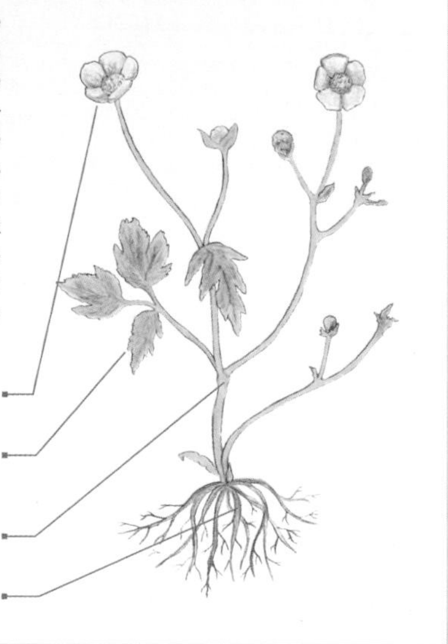
The flower is the plant's reproductive system.
The leaves carry out photosynthesis to provide the plant with nourishment.
The stem transports many substances.
The roots draw water and nutrients from the soil.

SEEDLESS PLANTS: ALGAE, MOSSES, AND VASCULAR SPORE-PRODUCERS

Plants that do not produce true seeds use spores to reproduce. Spores typically develop within specialized structures and are spread primarily by the wind.

Plants without seeds reproduce by means of spores. Spores are organisms in their earliest stages of development, which are composed of a single cell or a cluster of cells. The plants with spores include algae, mosses, ferns, and horsetails.

Algae—The Ancestors

All modern plants are descended from green algae, which are classified with the lower plants. Algae are green monocellular or multicellular organisms equipped with cell organelles such as chloroplasts, containing the pigment chlorophyll.

Botanical researchers continue to study which modern plants are most closely related to green algae. In general, algae live in water and carry out photosynthesis (p. 66), the process that powers all plant growth. While their forms and structures are highly diverse, most have a stringy or leaf-like appearance. In coastal zones, they provide nutrition for fish and other creatures, sometimes forming entire forests on the seafloor. However, excessive algae growth caused by the use of too much fertilizer disrupts the ecological balance of a body of water.

The green color of brown algae is simply masked by brown colored pigments.

Mosses—Little Plants

Mosses are a highly diverse group of plants dependent on water-rich environments. They are small and lack true leaves, stems, and roots. Hence they take in moisture from their surfaces, where a waxy coating prevents dehydration.

Only a small number of species are equipped with the simple cells required to transport liquids. They also require moisture for reproduction, since the male reproductive cells swim to the female cells through a film of water. Only a light coating of moisture from either rain or dew is usually sufficient.

Mosses also grow in dry areas as they survive a long time in a dehydrated state. Without a support structure for vertical growth, most grow no more than a few inches (centimeters) high, although they can spread out horizontally over vast areas.

Long-Leaved Ferns

Ferns are an especially species-rich group of plants, characterized by very long leaves called fronds that usually have indented or feathered edges. In their early growth stages, fronds are curled up in the shape of fiddleheads—resembling the upper end of a violin—that gradually unfurl. Ferns have a branching system of vessels in their stems and fronds for transporting water and nutrients. Their spore packets, called sori, can be seen on the underside of the leaves and catapult the spores up to several yards (meters) away so as to be dispersed by the wind.

Ferns are primarily found living within shady and moist habitats in the tropics, but also grow in temperate-zone forests. Although many are small, large ones such as giant tree ferns can grow up to 98 ft (30 m) in height.

Giant tree ferns grow to impressive heights in the rain forests.

Horsetails

Horsetails have a hollow, vertical stem which is divided into segments, where small spindly leaves form. Some stems have a cone-like structure at their tips containing their reproductive spores, while their rhizome root system reaches deep underground. These spore-producers attained heights of up to 100 ft (30 m) millions of years ago, but currently can grow to about 26 ft (8 m), primarily in moist environments. Horsetails are often used as medicinal plants, such as to staunch bleeding or as a diuretic to stimulate bodily excretion.

Mosses produce spore-containing capsules at the top of thin vertical stalks.

Distribution Mechanisms of Spore-Producing and Seed Plants

Spore-producers such as ferns have spore packets that dry out and burst open, flinging their spores into the air. They rely on wind and water to disperse them. However, many seed plants have developed mechanisms for distributing their fruits and seeds. Some animal species are attracted to specific plants for their nectar as well as for the shape, color, and fragrance of their flowers. Animals often consume a plant's fruits, digest them, and then deposit the seeds in excrement far from the original plant. Other seeds and fruit have burrs and hooks that stick to passing mammals, traveling great lengths before falling to the ground and germinating.

above: *Fern leaves with spores*

BIOLOGY

➲ **see also: Overfertilization,** *Chemistry Chapter, p. 100*

SEED-PRODUCING PLANTS

The embryo, or young plant, of seeded plants is packaged with a supply of nutrients inside its coat. This protects it from dehydration and other environmental hazards.

Pollination occurring by a bee

The apple contains its own seeds.

Seed plants are a highly diverse and widely distributed group of more than 300,000 species. They use seeds rather than spores for reproduction. This group covers two main divisions: Gymnosperms, or plants with seeds lacking a protective cover, such as conifers and cycads, and the much larger group of plants with covered seeds, called angiosperms. In the former group, the seeds fall to the ground and germinate, while the seeds of the latter group are protected within a seed chamber, or ovary, which develops into a fruit.

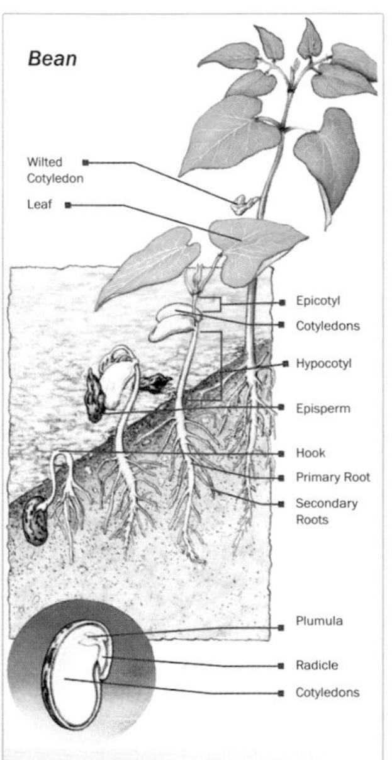

After germination, a bean plant forms a sprout with two leaves.

INSIDER KNOWLEDGE

30 PLANT SPECIES *account for 95% of the world's food supply. Of these, wheat, corn, and rice alone make up 56%.*

FLOWERS *adapt to specific pollinators; red blossoms are often pollinated by birds, as the color is easy for them to see.*

Pollination by Wind or Animals

Gymnosperm flowers are either completely male or completely female. Several bundled blossoms are actually cones, with each tree generally having both male and female cones. The open cones of the conifers release the male pollen, which the wind carries to female cones on the same tree or neighboring trees. The seeds develop after pollination. When they are ripe, they push open the scales of the cone and are distributed by the wind.

The pollination systems of angiosperms are more diverse and can be highly specialized. A single flower contains both female and male reproductive organs. Each species has built-in mechanisms to prevent self-pollination.

With most angiosperm species, insects and other animals transport pollen from male organs to female reproductive cells and are then rewarded for their effort with nectar. Pollination is less a matter of chance for angiosperms than for gymnosperms, which depend on their seeds being dispersed exclusively by the wind. Many species of flowering plants have adapted to a particular animal group, such as birds, bats, and insects. These adaptations may affect the shape, fragrance, and color of the flowers. Some species of orchids—the bee orchid, for instance—even imitate the form and odor of a female insect in order to to lure males to pollinate the flowers.

From Seed to Plant

After fertilization, a seed generally falls to the ground, absorbs water, and forms a sprout through a process called germination. The angiosperms comprise two groups: The monocotyledons, which have a single of seed leaf (cotyledon) during germination and have parallel leaf veins, and the dicotyledons, which have a pair of seed leaves and have a net-like vein structure. The monocots include orchids, lilies, and grasses, as well as important agricultural plants such as corn, rice, and wheat. The dicots are trees such as oaks, as well as smaller plants such as cabbages, cacti, and roses.

21ST CENTURY

PRODUCTIVITY *of agricultural plants is constantly increased by selective breeding and genetic manipulation.*

WORLDWIDE *some 677 million tons of corn are produced per year, around 41% in the U.S. alone.*

GLOBAL DIVERSITY *of plant species is declining due to monoculture and the use of herbicides.*

CONIFER SPECIES *form the largest group of the gymnosperms.*

THE SEEDS OF CONIFERS *ripen within the cones for four months to three years, depending on the plant species.*

THE WORLD'S OLDEST ORGANISM *is the Californian Great Basin bristlecone pine aged 4,778 years.*

Evergreen tree cones—collections of blossoms—release their seeds at the optimal time.

Conifers

CONIFERS OFTEN FORM extensive forests in cold climates and hilly regions. Most are evergreen: That is, they do not lose their leaves in winter. The typical needle-shaped structure of their leaves reduces surface area in order to protect them from dehydration. Furthermore a thick waxy coating also covers the leaves. The conifers include the world's largest plants, such as California's giant sequoias, which can reach a height of 363 ft (110 m) and a trunk circumference of 86 ft (26 m).

Most of the evergreen forests in central Europe and North America were planted.

LIGHT AND AIR

Plants transform and use the energy they obtain from sunlight. This ability means that they create the nutritional foundation for most other living things on Earth.

Plants use the energy from sunlight to produce sugar with water molecules and carbon dioxide.

In contrast to animals, which feed on other organisms, plants are able to produce their own nutrients. Nearly all plants can perform photosynthesis, the process in which energy from sunlight is transformed into chemical energy and stored.

Photosynthesis

The greenery on Earth absorb about 200 billion tons of carbon dioxide from the atmosphere yearly, to produce sugar and many other organic substances, while giving off oxygen as a waste product from this process. Photosynthesis uses visible light with wavelengths of 400–700 nanometers. The process has two stages: Reactions which are light dependent and reactions that are independent of light.

Where Photosynthesis Occurs

Photosynthesis takes place within chloroplasts, which are found primarily in the green leaves of a plant. Hundreds of these lens-shaped sub-cellular organelles are within a single plant cell. Many flat disk-like structures, containing the green pigment chlorophyll, are stacked on top of each other within each chloroplast. Chlorophyll is a molecule that can absorb sunlight and capture its energy to produce other molecules, such as adenosine triphosphate (ATP) and nicotinamide adenine dinucleotide (NADPH), which function as energy carriers. Leaves usually grow toward the sun in order to capture sufficient light for photosynthesis, a response known as phototropism.

The carbon dioxide needed for photosynthesis is taken up through the "stomata," which are microscopic pore-like openings in the leaves. The water necessary for the process is transported upward from the roots. The excess water evaporates and the oxygen produced from the chemical reaction is given off through the stomata. Largely due to this, the climate in open green spaces and especially in forests is particularly enjoyable. The feeling of fresh air is a result of the increased oxygen content and evaporation of water from leaves. Forests and parks thus play an essential role as the "green lungs" of cities and heavily populated areas.

21ST CENTURY

CLIMATE CHANGE: *The causes of global warming include increasing high levels of carbon dioxide emissions which cannot be completely absorbed and processed by the existing plants.*

CLEAR-CUTTING *forests has an enormous effect on animals, plants, and even the Earth's climate. Forests play an essential role in oxygen production and the reduction of atmospheric carbon dioxide.*

The Transfer Molecules ATP and NADPH

The highly complex process of photosynthesis was not fully explained until the 1960s. It was deciphered by Melvin Calvin, who was awarded the Nobel Prize for Chemistry in 1961. In the first stage of photosynthesis—the light-dependent reaction—energy from sunlight is captured within the chloroplasts where it is used to split water molecules and to create the carrier molecules ATP and NADPH. These then construct sugar molecules out of carbon dioxide during the light-independent reaction. The resulting sugar is generally stored in the form of a starch. Sugar molecules are transported to the individual cells when new energy is required by the various sections of the plant.

Cross Section of a Leaf

A MICROSCOPIC CROSS SECTION shows all the essential components of a leaf.

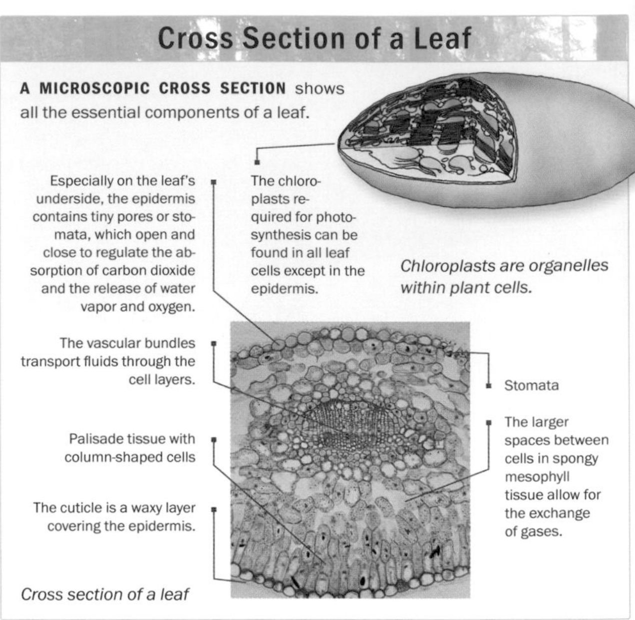

Especially on the leaf's underside, the epidermis contains tiny pores or stomata, which open and close to regulate the absorption of carbon dioxide and the release of water vapor and oxygen.
The chloroplasts required for photosynthesis can be found in all leaf cells except in the epidermis.
The vascular bundles transport fluids through the cell layers.
Palisade tissue with column-shaped cells
The cuticle is a waxy layer covering the epidermis.
Stomata
The larger spaces between cells in spongy mesophyll tissue allow for the exchange of gases.

Chloroplasts are organelles within plant cells.

Cross section of a leaf

INSIDER KNOWLEDGE

PLANT PRODUCTIVITY *increases when the key factors in photosynthesis—such as light intensity and temperature—are optimized, such as is seen in greenhouses.*

PLANTS ARE OFTEN *referred to as the primary producers. This is because nearly all other living things depend on the plants' ability to manufacture nutrients through the process of photosynthesis.*

➲ see also: **Climate Warming,** *Earth Chapter, pp. 54–55* | **CO_2 Fixing,** *Physics and Technology Chapter, p. 132*

WATER, NUTRIENTS, AND TEMPERATURE

Climatic conditions as well as the availability of water and nutrients affect the appearances of plants. They use specific strategies and structures to adapt to their environment.

All plants need air, light, nutrients, and water in order to live, grow, and reproduce. However, the concentrations of nutrients required can be highly variable, depending on the plant species.

Nutrient Absorption

The roots take up water and dissolved minerals in the form of ions. Some of the essential nutrients needed for growth and metabolism include nitrogen, phosphorus, calcium, magnesium, and iron. Potassium is also required to open and close the microscopic pore-like leaf openings called stomata.

To increase their supply of essential minerals, plants often have symbiotic relationships with bacteria or fungi in the soil. These surround the roots and increase their effective surface area. In exchange, the plant provides bacteria and fungi with the products of photosynthesis such as sugar. Nitrogen-fixing bacteria also help plants to obtain molecular nitrogen.

Vascular xylem and phloem vessels transport sugar, water, and minerals within the plant.

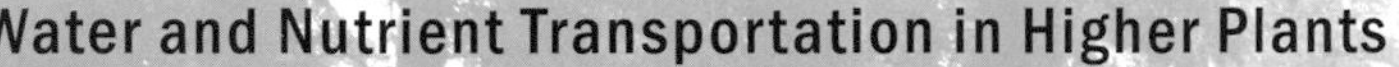

Water and Nutrient Transportation in Higher Plants

IN HIGHER PLANTS, water, dissolved nutrients, and the products of photosynthesis are transported by specialized tissues called vascular bundles. These run through the entire stem as well as the leaves and roots. The tissue called xylem conducts water and minerals upward into the leaves. The fluid is pulled up from the roots as a result of capillary action and the evaporation of water through the stomata openings on the leaves. The products of photosynthesis are transported through tissue called phloem from the leaves to the rest of the plant.

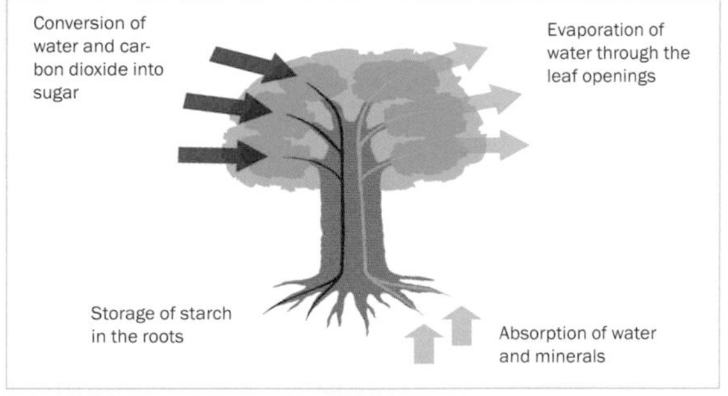

Adaptation to Temperature and Moisture Conditions

Since plants cannot always find optimal levels of the resources needed for growth in every location, they have adapted to a range of environmental conditions. They have developed diverse appearances and different strategies for absorbing and shedding water so as to survive in extreme temperatures.

Plants adapted to hot, dry environments can survive even in exceptionally dry conditions. They have developed many strategies to reduce evaporation. Some, such as mosses (p. 64) and flowering desert plants, retreat into a dried-up, dormant state. Succulents including cacti store large amounts of water in their shoots and leaves, releasing it only sparingly in times of drought. Others produce smaller leaves or reduce the number of their leaves to minimize evaporation. Their roots usually reach deep into the soil or spread quite extensively below the surface to absorb as much water as possible.

Plants in moist environments raise their rate of transpiration—the evaporation of water from their leaves—by producing broad, thin leaves with only a minimal waxy coating or none at all. In variable climates that include periods of frost, most plants lose their leaves in winter. They can also produce a natural anti-freeze substance that prevents ice crystals from forming within their cells. Plants that live in water can absorb it along with dissolved mineral ions over their entire surfaces. Their roots are either degenerated or just anchor the plant.

Many plants have adapted to conditions with little sunlight by developing large leaves with high concentrations of chlorophyll. These allow the plants to carry out photosynthesis efficiently, regardless of the environment.

Desert plants absorb and store large amounts of water during brief rainy periods.

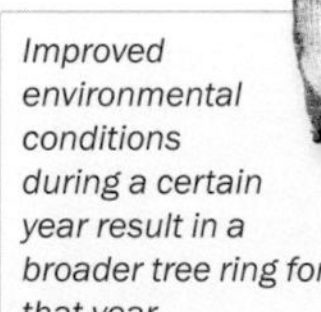

Improved environmental conditions during a certain year result in a broader tree ring for that year.

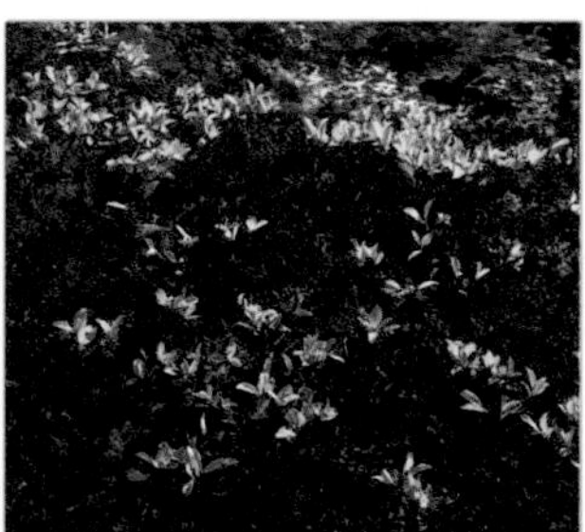

Plants survive severe winter frost by reducing water content in their tissues, among other strategies.

Mangrove trees have adapted to life in tidal zones. Their special roots anchor the plants and take in oxygen.

BIOLOGY

KEY FACTS

SOME 1.5 MILLION *animal species are documented today.*

AQUATIC *creatures account for the majority of all animal species.*

THE ANIMAL KINGDOM *is divided into about 30 groups, or "phyla."*

ARTHROPODS *are the animal kingdom's most prosperous phylum.*

VERTEBRATES *make up fewer than 5% of all known animal species.*

Evolution and the origin of species | Invertebrates | Fish | Amphibians | Reptiles | Birds

DIVERSITY OF THE ANIMAL WORLD

Animals—thus also human beings—trace their origins back to the oceans of the Cambrian period more than half a billion years ago when the first multicellular organisms feeding exclusively on other living things appeared. This explosive development opened up new resources and opportunities and led to the current diversity of animal species. Animals now inhabit nearly every environment on Earth, although most continue to live in water. Only a few vertebrates, along with insects and arachnids have permanently conquered the land.

➲ *Animals are organisms that feed on other living things.*

BIOLOGY

EVOLUTION AND THE ORIGIN OF SPECIES

Evolutionary trees help to illustrate evolution and species origin. Yet they are quite hard to construct, since basic animal structures all developed at about the same time.

Evolutionary tree of the Animal Kingdom

An animal is a multicellular organism that cannot produce its own food molecules through photosynthesis (p. 66) as plants do, but instead feeds on other living things (plants or animals). Other typical characteristics include sexual reproduction, a nervous system, and muscle tissue.

The basic physical structures of modern animals were evident 500 million years ago. Physical, embryonic, and genetic traits are considered in the creation of their evolutionary tree. The resulting groups reflect four milestones in evolutionary history.

The first crucial step was the appearance of "true" body tissue, which sponges—with their porous, sack-like bodies—did not then possess. Developing muscles and connective tissue was a prerequisite for specialized functions such as movement and breathing.

The second milestone was the development of bilateral symmetry and an identifiable head, in contrast to the radial symmetry of organisms, such as jellyfish, who lack a distinguished head and tail. It is this quality that enabled early animals to move purposefully in certain directions.

The third stage was the development of a fluid-filled cavity between the internal organs and the body wall, which is found in all "higher animals" except flatworms. This allowed the internal organs to move irrespective of the motion of the body as a whole.

During the fourth step, the higher animals (echinoderms, vertebrates) developed differentiated mouth structures. This development contrasts these more complex animals from lesser animals with only simple openings known as blastopores (mollusks, arthropods).

The Transition From Water to Land

The ancestor of all "tetrapods" or four-limbed animals (amphibians, reptiles, birds, and mammals) was probably a lobe-finned fish that was similar to coelacanths living today off the Comoro Island's coast. Its muscular pectoral and pelvic fins, supported by a bony skeleton, enabled it to crawl to shore. Yet, without developed lungs and the ability to keep its skin moist, it had to return frequently to the water. Moving onto land was probably a survival strategy. This would have resulted from the necessity of abandoning one shrinking body of water for another, clearly needing to evolve to travel greater distances.

above: *Coelacanth*

INVERTEBRATES

Most animals are invertebrates with a fantastic variety of physical structures, including mollusks (clams, snails), insects (bees, beetles), and many aquatic animals (jellyfish, sponges). They all lack backbones.

Invertebrates make up the largest number of animal species. Individual representatives of the group often display extreme diversity of form.

Sponges are fixed in place.
above: *A giant king crab*

Ancient Sponges

Existing 500 million years ago, sponges are the oldest group of all multicellular animals. Most sponges today continue to live in the ocean, their original environment. Unlike other multicellular animals, sponges do not develop true tissues or organs. Their bodies, supported by a network of calcium carbonate fibers, have a system of channels and pores that end in an internal cavity. They pump large amounts of water through this cavity every day, filtering out drifting food particles and releasing the water through a central top opening.

Worms

Worms use their elongated, limbless bodies to move by creeping. Annelids, such as the common earthworm, have bodies divided into similar segments. Meanwhile nematodes, such as tapeworms, have no segmentation or dissimilar parts. One evolutionary innovation for worms was the appearance of a definable head and tail end, allowing them to move in a particular direction and conquer different environments. Some worm species live in water, such as lugworms. Other useful species burrow in soil, such as earthworms; and a number of parasitic worms afflict people and other animals. Some are dangerous, such as the dog tapeworm which can spread to humans, and the African parasite that causes bilharzia (a condition affecting 300 million worldwide).

Earthworms live in the soil.
above: *Roman snail with shell*

Shelled Animals

Snails, shellfish, and squid belong to the invertebrate phylum of mollusks. They are composed of a head, a foot, and a visceral sac, which contains their internal organs. Many mollusks, like clams or snails, have calcium-based shells that protect their soft bodies. There are exceptions such as slugs and squid, which can have internal calcium structures instead. Octopuses are the most intelligent of the invertebrates; they can even be trained to unscrew the lid of a jar to reach food inside.

Creepy-Crawlies: Arthropods

The phylum of the arthropods includes insects, crabs, and spiders. This successful group composes 80 percent of all known animal species. They feature a segmented body with, at most, one pair of attachments—such as legs, mandibles, or antennae—per segment. They also have exoskeletons hardened by chitin that is continuously replaced through shedding as they grow. They also have a heart, an open circulatory system, and a nervous system that resembles a ladder.

Bird spider

Cnidarians

The phylum Cnidaria contains sea anemones, jellyfish, and corals. Some take the form of polyps, attaching themselves in place with a disk on their "foot," while others, such as jellyfish, move freely. Most live in the ocean. Their delicate tentacles are equipped with stinging cells, which they use for self-defense and capturing food. When the tentacles touch prey, stinging capsules break open and may release paralyzing poisons. The box jellyfish is one of the world's deadliest creatures.

above: *Crown jellyfish emit a colored glow.*

Metamorphosis of Insects

INSECTS DEVELOP from eggs, usually deposited on plants, from which larvae or young insects emerge. The larvae eat, grow, and repeatedly discard their skin. The larvae of some species, such as the grasshopper, resemble the adult insect. However, other species undergo dramatic metamorphosis as they mature. Butterfly and dragonfly larvae radically change form to become pupae, emerging later as fully formed adults.

A larva or caterpillar emerges from an egg and usually sheds its skin several times as it grows.

After the larva or caterpillar has transformed into an adult butterfly, it frees itself from the pupa.

The caterpillar attaches itself to an object and begins to wrap itself in fine threads.

BIOLOGY

FISH

As the oldest group of vertebrates, fish represent the greatest variance, with over 30,000 species; 10 percent live in fresh water.

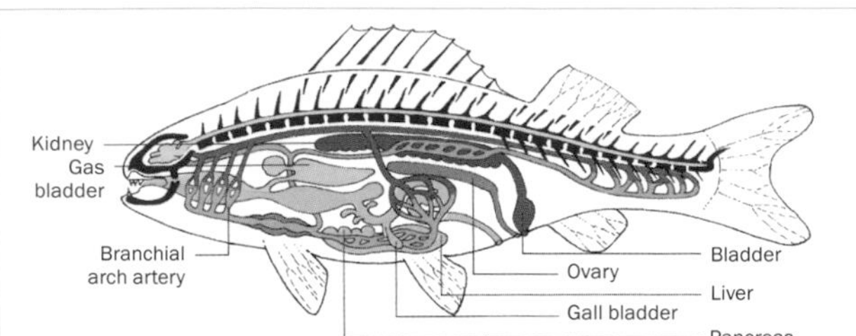

System structures: Yellow—Nervous, Green—Digestive, Light-blue—Pulmonary, Violet—Excretory, Orange—Reproductive, Pink—Muscular

Fish—cold-blooded animals (p. 71) that breathe through gills—are found in all aquatic habitats. Bony fish comprise the overwhelming majority, compared to fish with cartilaginous skeletons. The former inhabit environments ranging from the ocean depths (down to 25,000 ft or 7,620 m) to rivers, lakes—even pools. Some migrate between fresh and salt water. Their skeletons are strengthened with calcium phosphate, in contast to the flexible cartilage of fish such as sharks and rays, which are almost all ocean dwellers.

Fish in tropical seas are often brightly colored. The salmon is a typical migratory fish.

Anatomy of a Fish

The body of a fish is built around its backbone, to which ribs and free "fish bones" are attached in support. The shape is adapted to its particular habits. Some bottom-dwelling species, like the flounder, are flat. Swift hunters such as the pike have torpedo-shaped bodies. The fins assist in steering and forward motion. The paired pectoral and pelvic fins help it to maneuver, while the dorsal, anal, and caudal (tail) fins help stabilize it. The unique swimming motion results from the forward push of the tail fins and simultaneous flexing of the body.

GREAT WHITE SHARKS *can reach 10–23 ft (3–7 m) in length and more than 3,300 lb (1,500 kg) in weight.*

RAYS *have huge pectoral wing-like fins which have merged with their heads.*

WHALE SHARKS *are the world's largest fish; they filter-feed on plankton and other tiny creatures.*

Coloration helps rays blend into their surroundings; some are armed with a poisonous stinger.

Sharks

SHARKS HAVE EXISTED in nearly unchanged form for the past 300 million years as superb swimmers in the open ocean. Possessed of an acute sense of smell, they sense tiny amounts of blood and any other substances given off by their prey within a large radius. Some sharks lay single eggs with large yolks, while others give birth to live young. A specialized pelvic fin is used for internal insemination. Their highly developed teeth, which evolved from hardened scales, are not anchored in the jaw. Sharks may either swallow their prey whole or rip out chunks of flesh with their powerful jaws.

Sharks have dominated the world's oceans for millions of years.

INSIDER KNOWLEDGE

SEAHORSES *are fish, in spite of their unusual outward appearance.*

CLEANER FISH *cleanse parasites and dead skin off other fish.*

MALE *three-spined sticklebacks take on the duties of caring for their young.*

Fish regulate their buoyancy with an air-filled swim bladder. The lateral line on their bodies is a row of organs that sense water currents and detect the proximity of objects, the seafloor, and other creatures.

Fish have thin skin embedded with protective, overlapping scales. The scales are usually made up of bony material.

Nutrition and Reproduction

Fish eat plants, plankton, or other fish. The placement of their mouths is often an indicator of their specific feeding habits.

Most fish reproduce outside the body. The female fish deposits her eggs and the male releases his sperm into the water at approximately the same time. The number of eggs released is dependent upon the species of fish.

Only a few, including the guppy and some shark species, give birth to fully formed young. Eggs are fertilized inside a female by a male with an organ called a gonopodium. After gestation, babies can usually swim alone within 24 hours.

Fish Migration and Fish Ladders

Some fish migrate between fresh and salt water to other habitats. Salmon migrate from the sea to rivers for the purpose of laying eggs, while European eels leave fresh water to breed in the sea. Both species' larvae later return to complete a cycle of this journey. Obstacles such as dams block these migrations. Today, fish ladders function similarly to canal locks to help fish circumvent these obstacles.

above: *Fish ladder in a river*

21ST CENTURY

FISHING *with drift nets can be highly productive since some species (herring and sardines) form schools of up to several million fish.*

THE YEARLY CATCH *of global fishing operations is some 140 million tons.*

WORLDWIDE OVERFISHING *causes huge declines in fish populations.*

AMPHIBIANS

Amphibians are the descendants of the first vertebrates to venture onto shore. They still lead a double life, spending their larval phase in the water and the rest of their life on land.

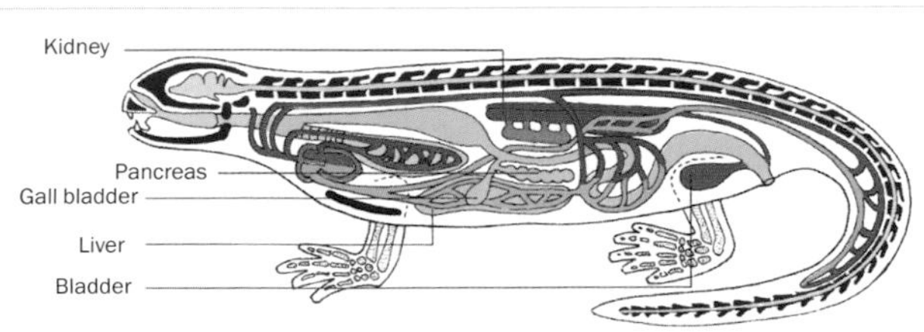
Kidney
Pancreas
Gall bladder
Liver
Bladder

System structures: Yellow—Nervous, Green—Digestive, Light blue—Pulmonary, Violet—Excretory, Orange—Reproductive, Pink—Muscular

The amphibian group includes tailed animals such as salamanders and newts, as well as tailless species such as frogs and toads.

Caudata and Anura

Caudata, including salamanders and newts, comprise some 400 species living in the Northern Hemisphere and the American tropics. They have an elongated body, two sets of similar legs, and a long tail. Large eyes are also a typical trait. The roughly 4,000 species in the group Anura—the frogs and toads—live everywhere except for the polar regions. Their long and powerful hind legs are used for hopping and jumping.

The poison-arrow frog's bright colors signal: "Warning, I'm poisonous!"

Tree frogs have sticky toe pads that make them excellent climbers.

Between Water and Land

As descendants of bony fish that crawled onto land with strengthened fins, amphibians show traits of both water and land vertebrates. The most striking is their metamorphosis from a gilled swimmer such as a tadpole or larva to an air-breathing adult frog or salamander.

Amphibians are cold-blooded; since they cannot regulate their own body temperature, they assume the surrounding one. Many species spend the winter in holes in the ground or piles of leaves.

Their delicate skin—which must not dry out—has a breathing function that supplements the lungs. It is also equipped with glands that secrete toxic or ill-tasting fluids to deter predators.

Why Frogs Croak

Frogs have a well-developed sense of hearing—as well as a strong voice. Males have developed mating calls to lure females. Salamanders, on the other hand, are more likely to attract partners with odorous substances or bright coloration. Amphibian mating rituals can be highly complex.

The male releases sperm to fertilize eggs laid as a cluster in the water (pond frogs), or a packet of sperm is taken up by the female for internal fertilization (crested newts). Egg clusters can be very large (over 10,000 eggs) or small; in some cases, only a single egg is laid. Some amphibians even bear live young. Only a few species breed outside the water, depositing their eggs in rotting leaves or tree cavities.

Lurking Dangers

Many amphibian species, such as frogs, move among aquatic and terrestrial habitats during the year or over the course of their lives. This may involve journeys of several miles (kilometers) or more. Barriers such as roads can be deadly. Another reason for the decline in the world's number of amphibians is the widespread use of weedkillers and insecticides, which eliminate their food sources or are absorbed through their thin skins.

Secretions from the fire salamander's skin glands protect it from predators.

INSIDER KNOWLEDGE

GIANTS AND DWARVES: *Japanese giant salamanders range up to 5 ft (1.5 m) in length, while some tropical frog species are less than half an inch (2.5 cm) long.*

INDIGENOUS *people use the poison-arrow frog's toxic secretions to make their weapons more effective.*

FROG SUNBURN: *Ultraviolet radiation can damage amphibian skin.*

Tree frogs use the sticky pads on their toes to become superlative climbers.

The Amphibian Life Cycle

BOTH TAILED AND TAILLESS amphibians mate in the spring. This is followed by egg-laying, usually in a pond. After emerging from the fertilized eggs, larvae—tadpoles, in the case of frogs—can metamorphose into adults in a few weeks. Frogs and toads undergo an especially dramatic change. They develop legs and lungs as they gradually lose their tails and externally visible gills. Tadpoles are primarily vegetarians; salamander larvae feed on insects.

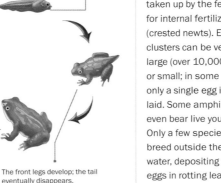

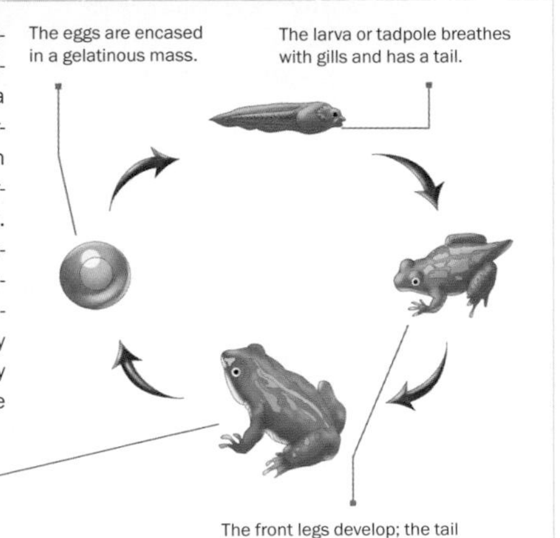
The eggs are encased in a gelatinous mass.
The larva or tadpole breathes with gills and has a tail.
The front legs develop; the tail eventually disappears.
The adult frog has legs and breathes air.

REPTILES

This group includes snakes, lizards, turtles, crocodiles, and the extinct dinosaurs. Reptiles were able to conquer the land on a permanent basis due to several key adaptations.

Reptiles make up an extremely ancient group of animals, from which all mammals and birds developed. During the Permian era, which occurred 300 million years ago, three evolutionary lines diverged: One became turtles and tortoises; another became dinosaurs, lizards, snakes, crocodiles, and birds; and the third, eventually, became mammals.

Numerous adaptations not yet developed by amphibians helped reptiles succeed on land. Scales on their skin protect it from drying out; their lungs are strong and efficient; and their eggs are encased in sturdy shells to prevent damage or dehydration. Reptiles cannot regulate their own body temperature through their metabolism burning calories. Thus, they seek shade during hot weather and spend extended periods sunbathing—despite the risks involved. Yet, needing less food than mammals of the same size, they can adequately survive in nutrient-poor regions such as deserts.

Lizards

Today, lizards are the largest and most diverse species group, even though they are mostly very small in size. They typically bury or cover their eggs, and reduce body activity during cold weather with hibernation. They include many interesting species; some are legless and resemble snakes, while others are visually striking, such as collared lizards which flare their impressive collars when they sense danger. Chameleons are able to change color and have protruding eyes that enjoy a viewing range of almost 360°. Geckos have specialized feet with a very high surface area, allowing them to adhere to smooth walls and even ceilings.

Giant tortoises can live for as long as 180 years.

Crocodiles can be found in both fresh and salt water.

Turtles and Tortoises

Turtles and tortoises have barely changed biologically in the past 150 million years due to the protection provided by their characteristic back and belly shells. These bony structures are covered with skin and bone plates. Most land tortoises and freshwater turtles can draw their head and legs completely within their shells, but sea turtles cannot.

All turtles and tortoises are omnivorous and lay their eggs on land. Sadly, most species are threatened with extinction, as humans continue to encroach upon them and destroy their habitats.

Crocodiles and Alligators

Crocodiles and alligators are the largest living reptiles. Confined to the warm regions of the world, they spend most of their lives in the water, where they breathe through vertically oriented nostrils and wait for prey to approach. At lightning speed, they lunge toward the shore and pull their victims underwater. The prey softens after a few days in the water, then the crocodile spins its own body while tearing chunks of flesh from its prey, as the crocodile cannot chew.

HUNGER ARTISTS: *Boa constrictors can survive a year or longer without food.*

THE WORLD'S 3,000 SNAKE SPECIES *include 300 venomous varieties, 50 of which are potentially fatal to humans.*

MEDICAL APPLICATIONS: *Snake venom is used for treatment of diseases and in medical research for new active agents.*

Boa constrictors coil around and suffocate their prey.

Snakes

THE SNAKE is one of the most emblematic creatures in human mythology, and is perceived to represent both wisdom and evil. Indian mythology considers snakes to be the "bringers of life," while the Bible tells the story of a snake as the first deceiver. Snakes are widespread worldwide, and so is the fear of them.

SNAKES' MOST OBVIOUS TRAIT is their lack of limbs, so they move with a slithering motion. Since they hunt other animals, they have developed a keen sense of smell and the ability to sense vibrations and temperature variations. Venomous snakes use a pair of hollow fangs to inject a paralyzing or deadly nerve venom from specialized salivary glands. Constrictors can unhinge their jaws to swallow large prey. Snakes shed their skins by detaching the outermost layer, as they grow continuously.

The fer-de-lance is the most poisonous snake of South and Central America.

INSIDER KNOWLEDGE

THE LARGEST *reptiles living today are the saltwater crocodiles at up to 30 ft (9 m); on land, the Komodo dragon at 10 ft and 110 lb (3 m and 50 kg).*

THE HEAVYWEIGHT *reptile record holder is the giant tortoise, weighing up to 880 lbs (400 kg).*

RECORD LONGEVITY: *The Galapagos giant tortoise can live 180 years.*

Scales of a snake

The male sand lizard will fight viciously over females.

BIRDS

The conquest of the air sets the birds apart from most other vertebrates. As they are remarkably adapted for this purpose, they display impressive achievements in flight.

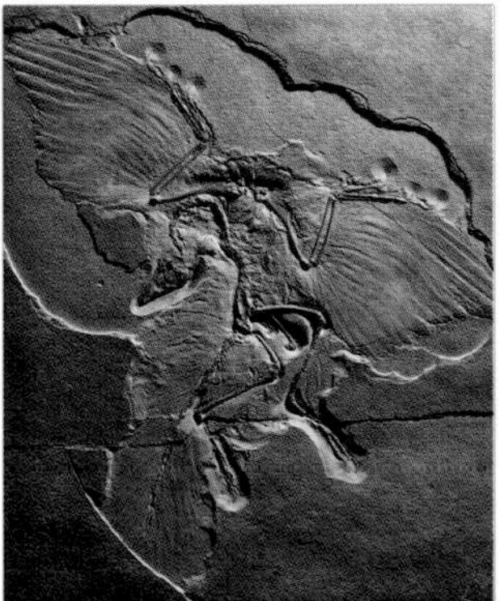

The early bird archaeopteryx displays both bird and reptile traits.

Birds first emerged as flying reptiles, as shown by the spectacular discovery of the 150-million-year-old fossil archaeopteryx. This avian ancestor has evident reptilian traits, such as claws on its wingtips and a long tail. However, the feathered characteristic of birds—seen only in this group of vertebrates—are also already present.

Characteristic Traits

In addition to being able to fly, excellent vision is another notable trait, most highly developed in birds of prey that spot small animals from a great height. Beaks display a variety of forms depending on eating habits: Sharp-edged for raptors, heavily reinforced for woodpeckers, and tube-shaped for hummingbirds. Feathers are also adapted to their unique lifestyle. Birds living in cold climates are protected by thick layers of feathers and insulating down. The colorful plumage on male birds attracts females, while dull colors offer camouflage.

Birds are warm-blooded (p. 74) and have efficient hearts, lungs, and circulation. This allows some species to remain active and search for food in cold climates as well as during the winter. Faced with dwindling food supplies after the summer, many birds migrate to warmer latitudes. Some species will travel up to 6,200 miles (10,000 km) to reach their wintering grounds.

About 8,000 known species of birds exist today. Some, such as the African ostrich and the New Zealand kiwi, have lost the ability to fly. Perching birds, the group known as passeriformes, which includes species such as sparrows, swallows, and finches, make up 60 percent of all avian species.

Bird Migration

The phenomenon of bird migration, movement between summer and winter habitats, or nondirectional flights of young bird groups is observed in nearly all regions. They are guided by geographical orientation, their ability to sense the Earth's magnetic field, imitation, and genetic influences. Most migrations—particularly those in the Americas—occur along a north-to-south axis. Central Europe has two main migration routes: Western storks fly over Gibraltar and the Mediterranean Sea to West Africa; eastern storks cross the Bosporus, the Jordan Valley, the Sinai Peninsula, and the Nile Valley on their way to East Africa. The protection of threatened species requires conservation efforts across several countries, which is a difficult venture to coordinate.

above: *Brent geese in Finland on their way to Siberia*

Mating and Reproduction

Most birds maintain and defend territory to mate and nest. They sing (songbirds) to attract partners or use visual signals such as attractive plumage. Pair bonds in birds vary greatly in duration. Some are limited to the incubation period of the eggs, as with ducks, or are lifelong, as with raptors, owls, nuthatches, and penguins. Some species build elaborate nests, but only a few use the same one for several years. Others—such as Antarctic penguins, which incubate their eggs standing up—do not build nests. All birds lay eggs, but the number varies from one to 20. The eggs are generally white.

INSIDER KNOWLEDGE

THE LARGEST BIRDS *capable of flight are pelicans, swans, and condors.*

FLYING UNDERWATER: *Penguins' flight muscles have adapted for swimming.*

AERIAL ARTISTS: *Hummingbirds flap their wings 80 times per second.*

WHITE STORKS *travel 6,200 miles (10,000 km) twice a year.*

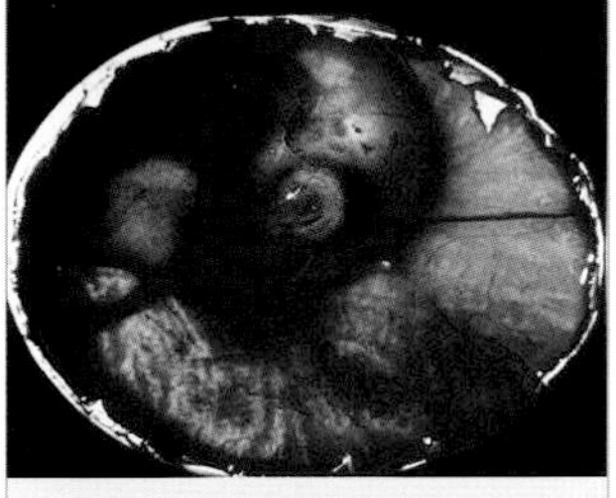

A domestic chicken hatches from an egg after 21 days.

The parent birds take turns sitting on the eggs to ensure a constant temperature for 11 days to 20 weeks. After the chicks hatch, the parents feed them until they learn to fly. Parasitic breeders, such as the cuckoo, lay their eggs in other birds' nests, then abandon them to be raised by unwitting foster parents.

Hummingbirds have long tongues to sip nectar.

How Do Birds Fly?

FOR CENTURIES, humans have been fascinated with the idea of imitating the flight of birds and insects, but have not been able to duplicate their efficiency. Birds use their powerful chest muscles to propel themselves forward by flapping their feathered wings, which are shaped to provide aerodynamic lift. They weigh very little, at most 33 lbs (15 kg), and have extremely light, hollow bones to better facilitate flight.

The honeycomb-like structure of birds' bones reduces their weight.

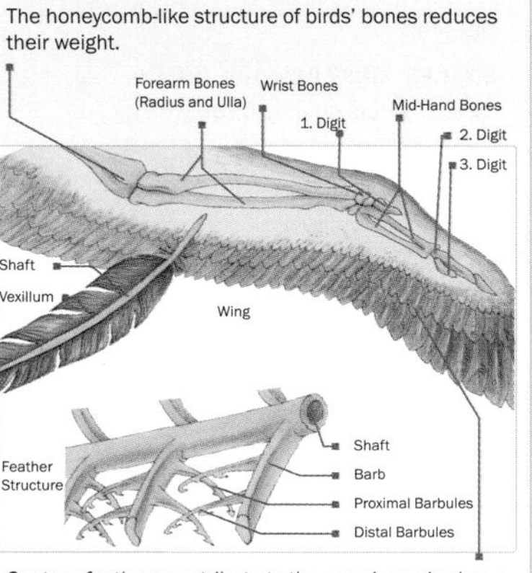

Contour feathers contribute to the aerodynamic shape of a bird's wing.

BIOLOGY

KEY FACTS

MOST MAMMALS *gestate and give birth to live young. The monotremes are the exception, they alone among the mammals lay eggs.*

MAMMALS *have come to inhabit all environments; air (i.e., bats, flying squirrels), fresh and salt water (i.e., otters, whales, seals), and land (i.e., ungulates and carnivores).*

EATING HABITS OF MAMMALS— *herbivores, insectivores, carnivores, and omnivores—are diverse.*

MAMMALS

This diverse group, to which humans belong, is classified as mammals both because the young are fed by their mother's milk and because its members have hair, fur, or skin that covers the body to some degree. There are two subgroups, "prototheria," or original mammals, which includes the egg-laying platypus, and "theria," with mammals such as rodents, primates, ungulates, carnivores, and sea mammals. There are around 5,500 species of mammals existing across the entire world, including even blue whales and elephant seals thriving on their seasonal visits to Antarctica.

Mammals got their name because they feed their young with milk from the female mammary glands.

DIFFERENCES AND SIMILARITIES

At first glance, mammals often show few external similarities. They can be large or small; furry or bare; and bipedal or quadrupedal. However, they share a wide range of biological features that have allowed them to evolve into an extremely successful vertebrate group.

Mammals are distinguished from all other animals chiefly by two features. They maintain a constant body temperature, usually between 96° and 102°F (35° and 39°C) and they develop their young within the womb before they are born. These characteristics have made it possible for mammals to be more independent of changes in their environment than other animals. Their biological structure is geared to protect their young for long periods of time and shield them from harsh environmental challenges. This enables mammals to survive even in extreme habitats, such as polar bears in the Arctic and armadillos in the desert. Their constant body temperature is ensured by the insulating effect of their fur, hair, or skin; the formation of glands in their skin covering; and their efficient food intake and utilization.

Mammals use milk glands to feed their young. Polar bears can survive at the North Pole as a result of their constant body temperature.

Classifications of Mammals

There are some 5,500 different species of mammals arranged within various groups:

Monotremata (platypus, spiny anteater) Characteristics: It lays eggs and has short legs, small eyes.

Marsupialia (marsupials) Characteristics: The developing baby grows in a pouch.

Perissodactyla (odd-toed ungulate) Characteristics: Its weight lies on its middle toe.

Carnivora (carnivores) Characteristics: Flesh-tearing dentition lets it separate meat from bones.

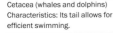

Cetacea (whales and dolphins) Characteristics: Its tail allows for efficient swimming.

Primates (lemures, monkeys, apes, humans) Characteristics: It has a large brain, forward-facing eyes.

Development of the Young

Mammals feed their young in the womb through the placenta, an organ which is connected with the fetus through the umbilical cord. Essential nutrients and oxygen are provided to the offspring through the umbilical cord.

The feeding of young mammals with milk produced by their mother's mammary glands after they are born is a fundamental innovation in the animal world. This enables babies to grow quickly and increases their chances of survival. Additionally a strong mother-child bond is formed that encourages intensive care of the young. This is also reflected in the strongly marked social structures with typical hierarchical or territorial behavior (pp. 82–83).

Generally, altricial mammals can be distinguished from precocial mammals. The former, such as carnivores and primates, are unable to leave their home shortly after birth, while the latter, such as ungulates and whales, follow their mothers almost immediately after birth.

Further Similarities

All mammals' hearts have separated ventricles, which pump blood efficiently to all the regions of the body. They have a superior sense of hearing (their hearing structure includes the malleus, stapes, and incus), a complex brain, and jaw joints that allow different teeth formations. Their original five limbs have been partly modified or reduced over the course of time as with whales, dolphins, and other sea mammals (p. 79). Skin, claws, hoofs, or horns give mammals a protective mechanism against injuries and dehydration.

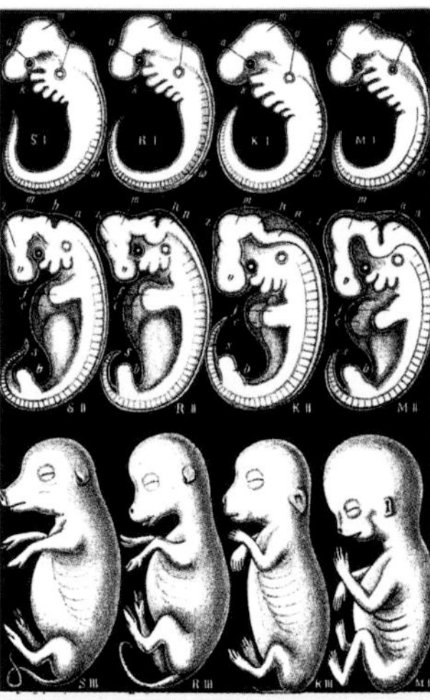

Even though adult animals can appear to be very different from each other, their embryos develop through similar stages in the womb.

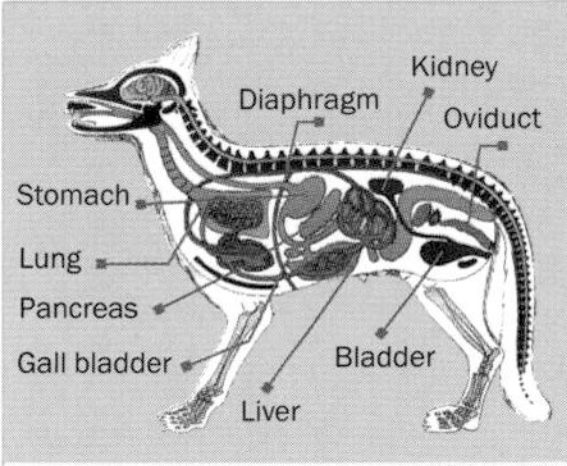

System structures: Yellow—Nervous, Green—Digestive, Blue—Pulmonary, Violet—Excretory, Orange—Reproductive, Pink—Muscular

BIOLOGY

KANGAROOS, KOALAS, AND PLATYPUSES

These early mammals have unique characteristics that are not seen in other mammals. Monotremes lay eggs through the cloaca, whereas marsupials give birth to their young, which then climb into their mother's pouch to mature and to suckle milk.

The monotremes and the marsupials rank among the original mammals, which are primarily found on the Australian continent.

Monotremes

Monotremes are the most original and possibly also the most unusual of all the mammals. They lay eggs through the cloaca, a cavity into which the intestinal and urinary canals open. Depending on the species the female mammal lays one or two soft-shelled eggs about two to four weeks after mating, which then are incubated for up to 10 days before the young hatch. Afterward the babies nourish themselves with the mother's milk, like all other mammals.

The koalas, or koala bears, eat only leaves from the eucalyptus tree. This dependency threatens their survival today due to the shrinking eucalyptus forests in Australia.

The platypus has a duck-like bill protruding from a broad, flat jaw that is strengthened by keratin plates (the material that produces horns). Its flat, beaver-like tail and pronounced webbed paddle-like paws in front allow it to hunt small creatures in the water and sift the catch. It lives in complex self-dug burrows set in the riverbanks of Australia.

On the other hand, echidnas, also known as spiny anteaters, are purely land animals. They have strong digging claws, which help them to dig up ant and other insect nests before they use their long, sticky tongue and tubular snout to eat the insects. In case of danger, they raise their spikes. All representatives of the monotremes are loners and are nocturnal or mainly active in the dawn hours; they live only in eastern Australia, Papua New Guinea, and Tasmania.

Kangaroos are great jumpers in the grasslands of Australia by using their extremely strong hind legs for propulsion and their thick tails for balance.

Marsupials

Marsupials are a group comprising 270 types of mammals with varied habitats and behavior patterns. They live on the Australian continent, in Papua New Guinea, North America, and South America. The marsupials may have developed differently due to their diverse environments after the continents of Australia and South America broke away from Pangaea, but they display the same biological structure nonetheless. The Eutheria mammals, or the placental mammals, developed in much the same way on the northern continents, with the result that the animals in both groups are astonishingly similar in body shape and behavior patterns. Examples include marsupial moles and moles, quolls, and weasels.

Marsupials are so varied that it can make describing common features difficult. However, the predominant shared characteristic is a pouch in which the mothers carry their newly born young so that they can suckle and mature. Young marsupials have a laborious birth, since the tiny baby has to climb independently from the birth channel to the pouch, using only its senses of smell and touch. Once there, it fastens its mouth onto one of the mother's mammary glands and remains until it is ready to leave the pouch.

The platypus lives near rivers and hunts fish. Its breeding burrow is up to 98 ft (30 m) long. Every time the platypus leaves the burrow, it fills in the doors with mud to keep intruders out.

In the case of the red kangaroo, this suckling stage can last up to 235 days. As many as 12 young animals are born during each birth. The number of young varies in accordance with the degree and duration of protection they receive in the pouch. The greater the level of protection, the greater the number of babies that can survive. Because of this, a high birth frequency compensates for a short or less protected duration in the pouch.

Young mammals drink from teats in their mother's pouch, with two teats giving nourishment to two infants at the same time. But a few marsupials, such as the opossum, do not have a pouch.

INSIDER KNOWLEDGE

SPINY ANTEATERS *can live up to 49 years.*

PLATYPUS MALES *have a functional poisonous spur on their hind foot.*

PETAUROIDES *can glide up to 328 ft (100 m) as a result of their winged skin surface.*

RED KANGAROOS *can jump up to 10 ft (3 m) high and 30 ft (9 m) distance.*

➔ **see also: Pangaea,** *Earth Chapter, pp. 32–33*

RODENTS AND LAGOMORPHS

Despite their external similarities, rodents and lagomorphs have evolved independently of each other. However, they can be distinguished easily because of the incisors on their upper jaw.

Rodents and lagomorphs inhabit the entire planet with the exception of Antarctica.

Rodents

Within the category of mammals, rodents are the most various with 1,700 species. The common characteristic of all rodents is their dentition, with a pair of chisel-like incisors located at the front of their upper and lower jaws. These teeth continue to grow throughout their life. The chisel shape is formed through constant wear and tear, since only the front portion of the tooth is protected by a hard layer of enamel. Rodents do not have canine and premolar teeth, which results in a gap between their incisors and molars.

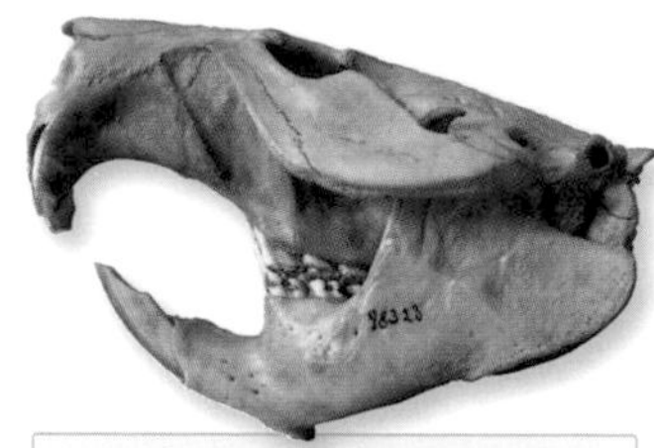

Gnawing teeth, a pair of enlarged incisors on the upper and lower jaws, are a characteristic of the dentition of this group.

Rodents feed primarily on leaves, seeds, fruits, roots, and tubers, but a few also feed even on insects or other invertebrates. Their dentition is supported by extraordinarily strong chewing musculature, which is why all rodents appear chubby-faced. For the most part rodents live socially in groups, e.g., marmots and house mice. Active at all times, day or night, they can be found in all habitats ranging from water to high mountain tops, except not in the air.

Female Ochotonidae (pikas) give birth to an average of 12 young twice or three times a year.

Inhabiting predominately wet environments, muskrats feed on plants that grow in or along water. They are very good swimmers.

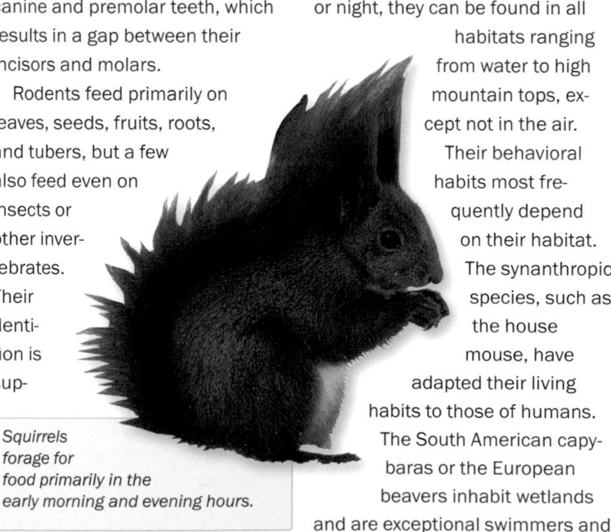

Squirrels forage for food primarily in the early morning and evening hours.

Their behavioral habits most frequently depend on their habitat. The synanthropic species, such as the house mouse, have adapted their living habits to those of humans. The South American capybaras or the European beavers inhabit wetlands and are exceptional swimmers and divers. The African spring hare is an outstanding jumper due to its kangaroo-like hind legs. Squirrels are great climbers because of their long tail that helps them to maintain balance.

Lagomorphs

The lagomorphs include both long-eared animals, such as hares and rabbits, and small-eared animals that are similar to guinea pigs like the North American pikas. Previously, hares and rabbits were considered to be rodents. However, the difference between the two groups is immediately discernible by a glance at the rabbit's dentition.

Like all lagomorphs, rabbits have two pairs of small teeth, or "peg" teeth, that rest behind the large incisors on the upper jaw. Because of this type of dentition, lagomorphs have become well adapted for a gnawing diet.

They typically also have cleft upper lips and skin folds (harelips) as well as rhythmic twitching when they open and shut their nostrils. They have a well-developed sense of touch and hearing, aided by the long sensory hairs around their nose and the lop ears of hares and rabbits. Their hind legs, totally covered by hair, are usually very long. Hares can run fast and powerfully at up to 50 mph (80 km/h), which facilitates their life in open habitats of fields, grasslands, plateaus, and semi-deserts and is particularly important whenever they try to escape a predator.

Lagomorphs are pure herbivores, and metabolize their cellulose-rich diet with the help of intestinal bacteria. To optimally metabolize this diet, lagomorphs excrete soft feces pellets that they ingest a second time. They use burrows or nests to rear their young. Due to their short lifespan, lagomorphs annually have several litters, each with about nine offspring each year. This high birth frequency accommodates the fragility of the young, which are often devoured by predatory animals and birds. The fur of wild hares and similar animals is almost always colored reddish or gray-brown to provide the maximum camouflage.

Nocturnal Activity

Most rabbits and hares are active during the night and dawn. They display marked social behavior within their family communities, such as the mating ritual of endangered hares which, unfortunately, is rarely observed today. They often feed in the late evening hours or during the night to maximize protection against predators. If supplies are meager, hares can cover considerable distances in search of food. They frequently make food provisions for the cold winter months.

above: *Hares hide during the day in hedges and tall grass.*

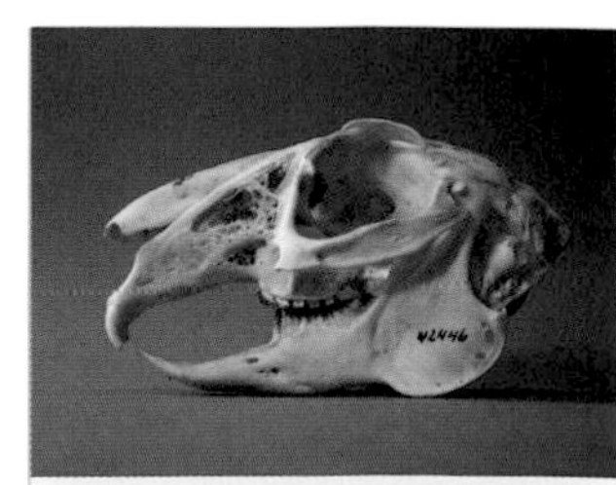

Lagomorphs possess a second pair of incisors. These are developed like pegs and hidden behind the front pair on the upper jaw.

BIOLOGY

UNGULATES

All ungulates are hoofed mammals that feed on plants and are distinguished by their phalanges, or toes, that are encased within a hard covering.

Springboks can jump up to 11.5 ft (3.5 m) vertically from a standing position.

Ungulates are among the largest, most impressive, and most commonly found land mammals. They are all herbivores (with the exception of omnivorous pigs and the insect eating anteater) and have phalanges covered by hooves. The ungulate group includes many domesticated animals, such as horses, cattle, sheep, goats, and pigs, but also elephants, rhinos, and giraffes as well as an ungulate that has returned to the sea, the sea cow (p. 78). Originally they lived on all the continents of the Earth, with the exception of Australia.

Horses are categorized as hot bloods (e.g., Arabians), warm bloods, and cold bloods. This classification is in reference to their temperament, not their body temperature.

Metabolism

All ungulates share the same particularity that, although they are vegetarians, they cannot digest the nutrition from plants on their own, as they lack the enzyme which ensures the decomposition of cellulose. Their digestive system is aided by symbiotic bacteria, yeasts, and protozoa. Many hoofed animal species are ruminants, such as deer and cattle. They can metabolize the cellulose better by repeatedly chewing their pre-digested cud.

Characteristic Features

Most hoofed animals have long limbs, which enable them to flee from predators in their original habitat within grasslands and savannas. In a few groups, the males and sometimes the females have developed additional physical attributes such as horns (for example, cattle), antlers (for example, deer), or even tusks (for example, pigs). Rather than using these features violently, hoofed animals often utilize them to intimidate and assess the strength of opponents.

The hoofed animals can be classified within two groups: The even-toed ungulates and the odd-toed ungulates. The first sub-group includes deer, giraffes, and hippos, while the second sub-group consists of horses, rhinos, and tapirs.

Both even-toed ungulates and odd-toed ungulates display a reduction in the number of their phalanges, to varying extents. For instance, horses in the current day possess only one toe, or hoof, on each leg.

INSIDER KNOWLEDGE

HIGH-PERFORMANCE *cows can produce 8 gal (30 l) of milk daily.*

A HORSE *can run up to 37 mph (60 km/h) and cover 25–30 miles (40–50 km) in one day.*

UNGULATES *are the tallest and heaviest land mammals; Giraffes are 13 ft (4 m) high and elephants weigh up to 8 tons.*

BREEDING PIGS *are highly fertile mammals with 14 young per litter.*

Stone Age paintings from Lascaux, in southern France, depict hunting scenes with wild hoofed animals such as prehistoric horses and European wild bison.

DOMESTICATION *means the taming and breeding of animals by humans.*

FOR MORE THAN 11,000 YEARS, *hoofed animals have been bred for the utilization of their products (meat, milk, and wool) and their services as draft animals.*

"YOU NAME *the horse used by a people, and I shall name their practices and institutions." —G. Cuvier*

Dairy cow at pasture

Domesticated Ungulates

THE HOOFED ANIMALS TAMED by humans and selected through breeding over the centuries (domestication) play an important role today. The close bond between humans and animals was formed as early as the last Ice Age, when people started to settle, cultivate crops, and use implements. Hoofed animals were hunted from approximately 15,000 years ago and were later (from 9000 B.C. in the Mediterranean area) bred as transport and draft animals as well as for products such as milk, wool, and meat. The biological prerequisite for domestication is that newborn hoofed animals adapt themselves to humans through recognizing them as a fellow species and not fearing them.

The oldest instances of the use of implements by man were closely connected with his use of hoofed animals.

THE UTILIZATION of wool from sheep and goats offered people protection against harsh weather conditions. Although using cows for milking was a later development, animals in farming retained their importance right up to this century. There are around 450 cattle species in total, and more than 200 species of horses.

LINEAGE: Domestic cattle were descended from the European wild ox, or bison; the pig was descended from the wild boar; and the horse from the Przewalski horse (also known as the Asian/Mongolian wild horse).

Wool production by sheep became a selection factor in today's breeds only in later years.

BIOLOGY

ELEPHANTS AND SEA COWS

Elephants and manatees are closely related to each other. The elephant is the largest mammal living on land, while sea cows have adapted themselves to living only in water.

Elephants and manatees belong to the ungulate group (p. 77), although elephant hooves have been reduced to vestigial remnants and the hooves of manatees have receded completely.

Elephants

Elephants are also known as proboscideans and pachyderms. These terms refer to their characteristic nose and their thick skin, respectively. Anatomically, an elephant's trunk is really an elongated nose, although the nostrils lie high up on the skull and not at the end of the trunk. The extremely strong muscles in its trunk allow the elephant to use it as a fifth limb. The legendary thick skin of the elephant is actually very sensitive and extraordinarily thin in some places, including the stomach and behind the ears. The skin requires continuous care and cooling, which is why elephants enjoy bathing in water and mud. Since they do not possess any perspiratory glands, they release their superfluous heat only via their large ears. These animals have highly sensitive pillar-legs and possess vestigial hooves that have a tissue padding, which means they can tramp around without making as much noise as might be expected.

Their heavy tusks, which are transformed upper incisors, can grow to up to 11.5 ft (3.5 m) long. Elephants use their tusks to intimidate enemies and defend themselves, but also to dig watering holes and tear bark off trees. The legendary memory of the elephant has been partly confirmed in scientific experiments: Places once seen remain etched in their memory throughout an entire lifetime. Even elephants 70 years old can find their way back to the watering holes of their youth.

Three species exist today: the African elephant, the forest elephant, and the Asian elephant. They live in grasslands, savannas, mountainous areas, and forests.

Sea cows, found in the Indo-Pacific, spend most of their time drifting in shallow, warm water.

Poachers hunt and kill elephants to remove and sell their valuable ivory tusks.

Sea Cows

Sea cows, consisting of manatees and dugongs, are closely related to elephants. However, they display few similarities to elephants except for the short tusks of the dugong. They have totally adapted to life in the water. Instead of forelegs they have developed flippers, their hind legs have receded, and the base of their body tapers to a rounded tail like a paddle. The cylindrical body of a mature sea cow is around 13 ft (4 m) long and weighs up to 1,320 lb (600 kg). These mammals swim slowly or drift in the water, but can also dive for up to 20 minutes.

They are sometimes known as sea cows because of their herbivorous diet. They graze exclusively on aquatic plants and algae. Sea cows live either a solitary life or in small groups. Since they are mammals, the mothers suckle the young, but underwater. A sea cow is born after a gestation period of 12–14 months. Manatees can be found in the shallow waters of the coastal areas and bays of tropical seas, and at the mouths of rivers.

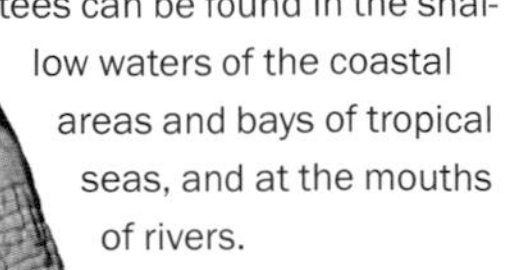

Ancestor Mammoths

This prehistoric proboscidean lived up to 8,000 years ago in the grasslands of North America, Europe, Asia, and Africa. Different mammoth species (e.g., the woolly mammoth) adapted to the coldness of the ice ages through their dense body hair. Even today, the frozen, well-preserved remains of mammoths are retrieved in the Siberian permafrost, and are later exhibited in museums. Their DNA could provide clues about the evolution of the Proboscidea order. Cave paintings from about 11,000 B.C. depict scenes in which mammoths are hunted, but it is still unclear as to whether over hunting or climatic changes toward the end of the ice ages caused their extinction.

above: *Nearly the entire carcass of the mammoth was used by early people after it was killed.*

21ST CENTURY

INTERNATIONAL PROTECTION of the species ensured the survival of the elephant under the Endangered Species Act.

SOME ENCLOSED SANCTUARIES led to local overpopulation and damage to vegetation.

PROTECTION AGAINST POACHING is ensured by sawing off tusks among other measures.

BIOLOGY

WHALES, DOLPHINS, AND OTHER SEA MAMMALS

Cetacea—marine mammals such as whales, dolphins, and porpoises—include the planet's largest living forms. They have exceptional sensory abilities and impressive aquatic skills.

The eyes of seals need to be able to function both on land and underwater.

The history of cetaceans dates back to a time shortly after the dinosaurs, when a group of four-legged mammals first began living in semi-aquatic environments. Over many millions of years, they evolved to become more streamlined and better adapted to long periods under water. This group of marine mammals, the cetaceans, are now perfectly suited to aquatic life. Although they adapted thoroughly over evolutionary time, the recent changes brought about by the impact of human activity threatens them with extinction today.

All belong either to the species-rich group of the toothed whale or that of the toothless whale, also known as baleen whales. These toothless whales, such as blue whales and humpback whales, have whalebone or baleen instead of teeth. These comb-like keratinous plates allow them to filter plankton or krill from the water and to grind smaller fish. Toothed whales prey on fish or squid; among these are dolphins, pot whales, killer whales, and narwhals.

Like some seals, the streamlined bodies of cetaceans have layers of blubber instead of hair to maintain body temperature and forelimbs that have evolved into flippers. Their hind limbs have receded completely. The tail or "fluke" is their principal propellant, as they use their pectoral fins or "flippers" only for steering. Some species of cetaceans can dive for over 90 minutes before surfacing. To allow them to dive down to great depths, they store air within a muscle pigment in their muscle tissue rather than their lungs. The development of baby whales progresses quickly as they must be able to follow the herd. A blue whale calf, which suckles underwater for about seven months, grows 110 lbs (50 kg) heavier and 1.8 inches (4.5 cm) longer daily.

Dolphins

Dolphins have a 40 percent larger brain than humans as well as a fourth brain ventricle that allows them to remain mobile 24 hours a day just like whales. They relax only when half of their brain is switched off for seconds at a time. The other half takes over the duties of watching for danger and controlling their swimming and breathing.

The most important sensory perception of all cetaceans is hearing, as visual conditions underwater are generally poor. Sonar is also used for communication. Sounds produced vary greatly, ranging in frequency from 5 to 280,000 Hz. The use of artifical sonar by man can interfere with echolocation and cetacean communication, and has been linked to mass strandings.

The great killer whale (orca) can dive for 15 minutes and attains speeds of up to 35 mph (55 km/h).

Seals

Seals, sea lions, fur seals and walruses are all pinnipeds, and are divided into three main groups. Eared seals have strong front flippers and use their hind flippers as a rudder. This group includes fur seals, who have been hunted relentlessly by humans for centuries for their dense coats, and sea lions. Earless seals—or true seals—include the leopard seal and are more adapted to water than land. Like cetaceans, they use their front flippers for steering. Walruses, with their imposing tusks, make up the third group alone. Pinnipeds breed and give birth on land or ice. Diets vary between sustenance on mollusks (walruses), fish (seals), or penguins (sea leopards). They may be less adapted to long sojourns in the water than the cetaceans, but they can swim nearly as fast, at around 28 mph (35 km/h).

INSIDER KNOWLEDGE

THE LARGEST ANIMAL *on Earth is the blue whale, measuring up to 109 ft (33 m) and weighing 165 tons.*

WHALES CAN DIVE *up to 8,250 ft (2,500 m) in 30 minutes.*

THE SPRAY *from the whale's blowhole is condensed air.*

POT WHALES *exchange 90% of their inhaled air in their breathing process.*

THE MAXIMUM SPEED *recorded in dolphins is 35 mph (55 km/h).*

WHILE HUNTING, *dolphins can dive down 990 ft (300 m) deep and remain submerged for up to 15 minutes.*

DOLPHINS *are companionable animals and live together in groups.*

Dolphin therapy is often used to successfully treat handicapped children.

The Dolphin—One Intelligent Mammal

THE CLOSE RELATIONSHIP between humans and dolphins was made famous in the series of TV programs and films about Flipper the dolphin. For centuries the Imraguen people of Mauritania and an Indian tribe in Brazil have been fishing with the help of wild dolphins. The dolphins guide the fish inside the hand-cast nets and are rewarded with the escaped or discarded fish.

THESE HIGHLY INTELLIGENT, SENSITIVE MAMMALS are increasingly used for therapeutic purposes to treat disabled people or children with behavioral problems. However, it is difficult to scientifically establish a dolphin's positive influences on the human body or mind.

THE INTELLIGENCE of dolphins is exhibited in aquatic shows, which attract hordes of visitors. However, dolphins thrive only in open water. Therefore, shows involving captive dolphins generate controversy.

Dolphin mother with young in its natural habitat.

BIOLOGY

PREDATORS: DOGS, CATS, AND BEARS

Predators are the hunters among the mammals. Found thoughout the world, they have developed highly diverse lifestyles and strategies for capturing prey.

Animals that kill and eat other animals are predators. They include the carnivorous mammals (such as cats and seals), omnivores (for example, bears), birds of prey and many insects. Often the prey are herbivores, but sometimes predators are hunted in turn. The top predator of an ecosystem is the animal at the top of the food chain, with no known predators.

Hunting and Tearing—Characteristic Traits

Predators share only a few common biological traits due to their diverse lifestyles, the most significant being dagger-like canine teeth and pairs of shearing carnassial cheek teeth. These help predators seize and tear into their prey.

Carnassial teeth, which can shear flesh, are typical of predators.

Running speed and efficiency can be increased by placing only a part of the foot on the ground. Martens utilize half of their foot, while others, such as cats, have evolved to run only on their toes.

Mobilization can also be accomplished by using the entire foot, such as with bears. An outstanding sense of smell leads predators to their prey. Cats, however, rely on their excellent vision, functional even in semi-darkness.

Social organization is closely related to hunting and feeding. Some predators, such as wolves and lions, live and hunt in packs. Others, such as martens, leopards, and brown bears, have become accustomed to hunting on their own. Martens with their slender bodies and flexible backbones penetrate other animals' burrows to trap and kill their prey.

Black bears observe a hibernation period in the winter, but wake up occasionally to eat.

INSIDER KNOWLEDGE

THE FASTEST MAMMAL *is the cheetah, reaching speeds of up to 75 mph (120 km/h).*

THE SMALLEST LAND PREDATOR *is the European pygmy weasel, 4 in (10 cm) long and 1.5 oz (45 g).*

THE LARGEST LAND PREDATOR *is the Kodiak bear, or grizzly bear, at 10 ft (3 m) tall and 1,980 lb (900 kg).*

20/20 VISION: *Cats see 7 times better than humans, even in darkness.*

YOUNG LIONS *first hunt with their mother at 3 months of age; they hunt successfully on their own when they are 2 years old.*

PREY *is usually dispatched with a powerful bite to the throat or back of the neck.*

THE HUNT *is often a group activity; individual animals then eat according to rank.*

The lioness tears up her prey using her razor-sharp carnassial teeth.

The Hunt

HUNTING BEHAVIOR is innate and refined through learning. Depending on the species and habitat of the predator, a wide range of hunting strategies can be used. Wolves and jackals are coursing predators, which tire their prey by chasing it in packs. Wolves communicate through body movements, positioning of the ears, and vocalization. The pack surrounds its exhausted prey and several wolves attack it simultaneously. Group hierarchy determines which animal has the privilege of eating first.

CATS, like the lion, are primarily stealth hunters. They sneak up on their prey on the soft pads of their paws and pounce on it, using their claws to bring down the victim. A well-placed bite to the throat or back of the neck usually results in an immediate death. All domesticated cats would use this strategy if they were to hunt mice.

Young cheetahs must practice before they can hunt successfully.

Predators as Pets

Wild predators were the ancestors of today's domestic cats and dogs. Dogs are the descendants of wolves which were domesticated some 10,000 years ago by Stone Age hunters (p. 77). They were first used primarily for hunting and later also for guarding herd animals. The fireside-loving cat probably descended from the African wild cat or Indian desert cat in the Mediterranean region. There it most likely frequented human settlements as a scavenger and in effect domesticated itself.

above: *Dogs and cats are humans' favorite pets.*

Friend or Foe?

Humans often compete with predators for the same prey and have always hunted them, especially wild cats and bears, for their pelts. Bears, wolves, lions, and tigers were feared and admired in prehistoric times, as is evident from the subject matter of prehistoric cave and rock art.

The recent reemergence of wolves, bears, and lynx in central Europe reawakened age-old dread. However, many species are now in sharp decline as people continue to create agricultural land from their natural habitats. Predation is one way to control wild herds of herbivorous animals, such as deer, and keep them from exceeding the limits induced by food supply.

PRIMATES: MONKEYS AND APES

Most primates (more than 500 species) have a strikingly enlarged cerebrum in the brain. This gives them the capacity to learn and to display complex social behavior.

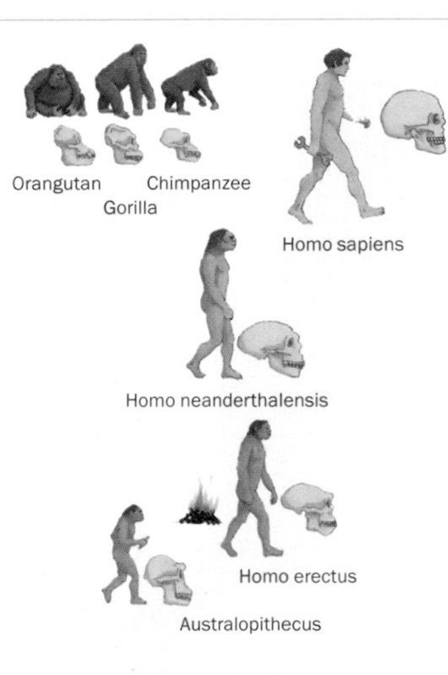

Primates evolved from tree-dwelling climbers to become upright users of tools.

Primates live in the tropical and subtropical forests of Asia, Central and South America, and in the savannas of Africa. This results from their modes of locomotion and mostly herbivorous food gathering. As outstanding climbers, monkeys and apes first lived in trees but some species have adapted to life on the ground. They have a life expectancy of up to 40 years. Primate mothers and other family members take intensive care of their young, giving them plenty of time to learn from their elders. Modern research divides primates into the groups "strepsirrhini," which have wet noses, and "haplorrhini," which have dry noses, but both share some characteristics. Strepsirrhini tend to be nocturnal, a habit associated with their smaller body size and keener sense of smell. Haplorrhini are mostly diurnal, or active in the daytime—with some exceptions such as with tarsiers. Strepsirrhini, earlier called prosimians, include lemurs—such as the mouse lemur and the ring-tailed lemur—lorises, and galagos (bush-babies). Lemurs live only on the Comoro Islands and Madagascar and occupy nearly all available habitats there. The galagos in Africa, and loris in South Asia, both resemble sloths due to their appearance and slow, careful movements. They have powerful hands that give them a secure grip on tree branches.

The haplorrhini, previously known as true monkeys, live in the tropical and subtropical zones of the Americas (capuchin monkeys and marmosets), in Africa (meerkats, gibbons, and great apes), and in South Asia (tarsiers). A further differentiation of primates can be made in relation to their global distribution: New World monkeys are found in the Americas, whereas Old World monkeys inhabit parts of Africa and Asia.

Communication and Social Life

Nearly all primates enjoy highly developed social and familial lives. They live in a family group or in a harem, comprising one male and up to nine females. They communicate through sounds, pheromones (excreted chemicals that can give messages like warning of danger or desire for sex), gestures, and facial expressions involving the eyes and lips. Prominent researchers, such as Jane Goodall, have studied the behavior of chimpanzees, investigating, for example, their ability to solve problems such as undoing a buckle to open a box and retrieve fruit, and their ability to communicate with humans using symbols and sign language.

Genealogy of Primates

Fossil remains indicate that the earliest primates, living approximately 60 million years ago, were tree-dwelling insectivores. The ancestors of most of today's species existed as early as 20 million years ago.

In the 19th century, with the emergence of evolutionary theory by Charles Darwin, Alfred Wallace and others, human beings were said to be related to other primates, which led to significant controversy. After 150 years of research and, more recently, studies of DNA, the kinship between humans and great apes such as chimpanzees, gorillas, and orangutans has been clearly demonstrated. Today, the theory of evolution forms the foundation of biological inquiry.

Tarsiers grow to only 3.5–6 inches (9–15 cm) long—not including tail.

Characteristics of Primates

Primates are distinct from other animals because of their relatively large brains, which enhance their capacity for learning, using tools, and engaging in complex social behavior. They use their large, forward-facing eyes to see in sharp detail and in three dimensions, and they clearly perceive contrast and color. Their supple hands and feet—with flexible thumbs and toes, sensitive fingertips, and nails instead of claws—are admirably suited for feeling, gripping, and holding, while varying sets of teeth allow them to feed on plants and meat.

above: *Primates swing from rope to rope using their flexible thumbs.*

Cerebral Cortex

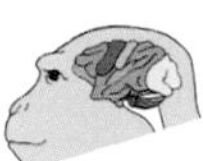

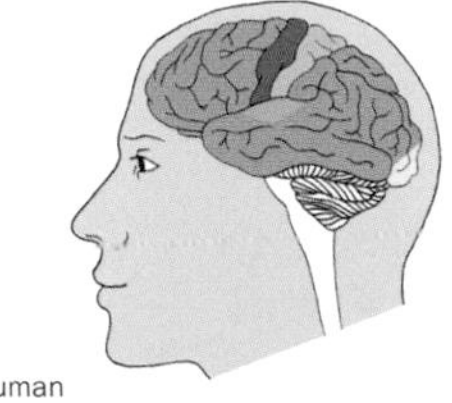

Brain development: The enlargement and increased folding of the cerebrum and cerebral cortex provided greater thinking power.

Adult male gorillas (silverbacks) are true heavyweights at up to 600 lb (270 kg).

KEY FACTS

LEADING PIONEERS *in the field of animal behavior: Nikolaas Tinbergen, Konrad Lorenz, Karl von Frisch, and Ivan Pavlov.*

MOST BEHAVIOR *is partially innate and partially learned.*

COURTSHIP, MATING, *and care of the young propagate the species.*

ANIMAL GROUPS *generally favor the strongest members in hierarchy and feeding priority.*

Courtship, mating, and care of the young | Social behavior and communication

BEHAVIOR: ACTIONS AND REACTIONS

How do animals behave, and what governs that behavior? Specific patterns regulate and simplify processes for individuals of the same, or different, species. These include reproduction, care of the young, communication, interaction, nourishment and defense. Among others, patterns set body postures, movements, and vocalization. Animals normally tend to react to particular stimuli with the same patterned response. A hedgehog confronted by a fox, for example, rolls itself into a ball. In the study of behavior, a basic distinction is made between innate and learned abilities.

➔ *Classical research in behavior studied the question of whether behavior is innate or learned.*

COURTSHIP, MATING, AND CARE OF THE YOUNG

All higher divisions of animals display distinctive behavior patterns (courtship, mating, and rearing of young) in selecting the best partner to produce healthy offspring.

Courtship and mating rituals maintain sexual reproduction, the procreation strategy used by all higher animal groups. Parents feed their young, protect them, and transmit skills. For many species, behavior patterns also form the foundation for complex social structures, such as family groups, which may remain strong for life.

Searching for a Partner

Each animal species has developed unique strategies to help it search for a mate. The goal of courtship is to attract a potential partner. Many species follow a highly specific courtship pattern. The male's display serves three purposes: It helps the female recognize him as the same species, assess his desirability as a mate, and accept or reject him. Since the labor-intensive job of raising the young usually falls to the female, she selects a high-quality partner whose offspring will justify her investment.

Courtship may involve visual stimuli, such as combs on roosters, antlers on deer, and bright colors of dragonflies and birds. Auditory cues, such as bird song, may also be used. Other courtship devices include specific odor-producing substances, or pheromones, which are used, for example, by many insects.

Mating

The act of mating ensures the successful transfer of sperm to egg. Fertilization may be either outside the body (external) or internal. In both cases, sperm produced by the male fertilizes the female's egg cells. These mature into embryos inside the mother's body, in the case of mammals, or in eggs laid by the mother, as with fish, amphibians, reptiles, and birds. Young animals are often relatively helpless and depend on care provided by their parents.

Care for the Young

Nearly all invertebrates, amphibians, and reptiles limit care of their young to the selection or creation of a suitable place to deposit the eggs. This may be a hole or nest that provides protection from predators and harsh environmental conditions. Laying a large number of eggs ensures that at least some offspring survive. However, for mammals, care of the young is substantially more demanding and can continue for several years or more.

Two Barbary macaques mating

The peacock shows off his feathers to attract peahens.

LION TAMARIN *siblings also help raise the young.*

MEERKATS *live in pairs with their offspring within a larger group.*

ELEPHANTS *form close-knit bands of families.*

Emperor penguins have only one chick per year, which is nurtured by both parents together.

Family Life

FAMILY BANDS that live together for many years or even for life are observed primarily among the mammals. Youngsters often remain with their parents even after weaning, since protection by the family group is advantageous for the still-dependent offspring.

EXTENDED NURTURING of the young allows them to actively learn survival skills. Human infants, for instance, learn to walk and talk with parental help and have formative experiences with them. Young elephants also remain with their mothers and close relatives for several years, learning effective strategies for finding and choosing food. Emperor penguin parents take turns caring for their chicks while they are very young.

A cohesive family unit offers protection and security.

SOCIAL BEHAVIOR AND COMMUNICATION

Behavior patterns regulate group interaction and establish ranking order, feeding priority, territorial boundaries, intra-group cooperation, and other aspects of community life.

Female red deer live in herds that sometimes include younger males.

A low-ranked wolf rolls over and presents its throat. This is a sign of submission to avoid a potentially hazardous conflict.

Specific behavior patterns regulate relationships between individuals of the same species to simplify social interaction. For example, a recognized system of ranking order and feeding priority makes it unnecessary to fight over every meal, which would waste valuable time and energy.

INSIDER KNOWLEDGE

HIGH NOTES: *Many animal acoustic signals cannot be heard by humans.*

SCENT MARKS: *Dogs leave messages with their urine—such as "I am female"—to inform other dogs.*

ANTS *communicate by producing odors, or pheromones.*

CHOREOGRAPHY: *Many bird species perform complex courtship dances.*

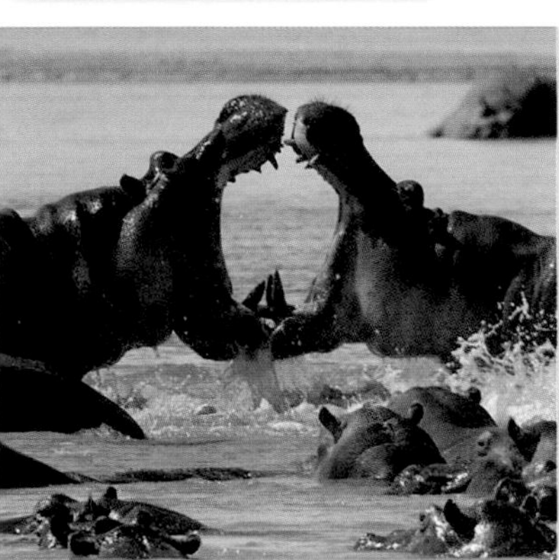

Fights between hippos can be life-threatening.

Eating Hierarchies

Individual animals signal their rank through body language and vocalization, which are recognized by other group members. Higher-ranking animals display behavior such as baring their teeth and hissing (lions) or aggressive pecking (chickens). Lower-ranking animals make submissive gestures, for instance lowering their head and averting their gaze. Conflict is necessary only when significant changes to the hierarchy occur, and even then it transpires in symbolic battles that are usually fought without bloodshed.

Many group behavior patterns appear to favor the highest-ranking animal at the expense of others. The alpha male may receive the largest and most nutritious share of the prey. Furthermore, he is generally the only male that reproduces with several females, ensuring that the optimum genes are passed to the next generation.

Other behavior patterns clearly burden the individual but benefit the group. For example, a marmot attracts a predator's attention when it whistles to warn the group of danger. Cooperative behavior is also seen in group hunting by wolves (p. 80), when all members benefit from the combined effort.

Learning Within the Group

Social behavior is only partially inherited, since it is strongly influenced by observing parents and other adults. This is demonstrated in studies of animals raised in isolation, which exhibit behavior disturbances, as well as twins reared separately, who share the same genes but behave differently.

Communication

Effective communication in a group is a prerequisite for a functioning social life. Information is transferred using visual, acoustic, chemical, and even electrical signals. Social insects such as ants and bees have complex communication systems. Bees report the distance to and direction of an attractive food source, such as a fruit tree or a blooming meadow. Returning worker bees dance in flight to give the directions to their hive mates. The speed of their movements indicates the distance, while deviation from the vertical shows the direction. Bees use odors to signal information about the type of food to be found.

Innate and Learned Behavior

Heated debate continues to inform the issue of the relative importance of innate and learned behavior. Most behavior patterns are now assumed to display both genetic and acquired components. Human infants display innate behavior, such as smiling and making a grasping reflex when their hands are touched. However, these patterns are usually refined through learning. Woodpecker finches, for instance, have an innate tendency to pick up small sticks, but they must learn to use them as tools.

The many different types of learning include practice, imitation, and insight, as well as learning through success and reward.

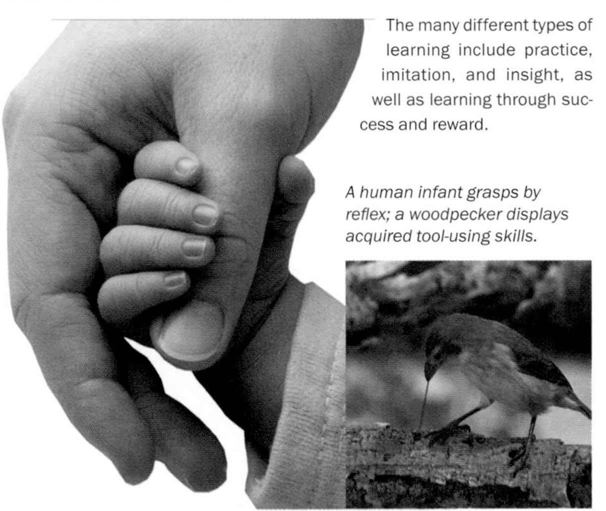

A human infant grasps by reflex; a woodpecker displays acquired tool-using skills.

BIOLOGY

➔ see also: Learning and Behavior in a Group, *Psychology Chapter, pp. 273, 275*

KEY FACTS

*"**MANKIND** stood up first and got smart later,"—Stephen Jay Gould, evolutionary biologist*

***HUMAN BEINGS** today inhabit nearly all environments on Earth.*

***KEY FUNCTIONS** are carried out by the circulatory, respiratory, digestive, immune, and nervous systems.*

***WIDESPREAD HEALTH DISORDERS** include heart disease, diabetes, and obesity.*

HUMAN BEINGS

Although human beings share many biological traits with other organisms—especially mammals—their unique characteristics make them one of the most successful species on Earth. In a way that no other creature has done before, humans shape their own lives through modifying their environment and the living things in it. They are distinguished from other animals by their upright gait, their enormous capacity for learning, and their development of languages, writing systems, and a variety of cultures.

Human beings are remarkable for their cultural achievements.

HUMAN EVOLUTION

The roots of humanity lie in Africa. Humans spread out from that continent to settle other regions of the world, evolving both biologically and culturally.

The modern human or *Homo sapiens*—"wise man"—forms a very young branch of the vertebrates in the broader category of the primates (p. 81), based on shared physical and genetic traits. Fossil finds indicate that the roots of modern humans lie in Africa. They spread out from this continent about 100,000 years ago to settle other regions, in the process pushing out older hominids such as Europe's Neandertals. Chimpanzees are now the closest relatives to humans on the basis of common ancestry. In fact chimps share more genetic traits with humans than with other great apes like orangutans.

Becoming Human

Humans developed characteristics that clearly differentiate them from other species. The early hominid Australopithecus began walking upright about three million years ago. This apparently occurred because of global climate change in the ice ages, which led to the thinning out of forests and the spread of savannas with isolated stands of trees. Tree-dwelling great apes were at a disadvantage compared to a species able to walk upright, since the latter could search for food on the ground, view open territory and use tools.

Early tools included scrapers made from stone.

Early hominids (such as *Homo habilis*) made and used simple stone tools some two million years ago, at a time when their larger brain gave them an advantage over other primate species.

Homo habilis both hunted animals for food and gathered fruit and roots. The larger *Homo erectus* developed some 1.5 to 2 million years ago, and was the first species of early human to move out of Africa into northern climates. One reason might have been that an increased proportion of meat in their diet led to the need for larger hunting grounds. The use of fire may also have played a role in this migration.

The robustly built European Neandertals and the taller, lankier modern humans—*Homo sapiens*—developed from these early hominid species. Modern humans emerged between 200,000 and 150,000 years ago in Africa. Around 100,000 years ago they—like Homo erectus—crossed the Arabian Peninsula and spread into Europe, Asia, Australia, and the Americas where they coexisted with other early humans for several millennia.

In Laetoli, Tanzania, preserved footprints of Australopithecus afarensis show that this early hominid already walked upright.

Cultural Development

Cultural development is a human characteristic that is allied to biological evolution. The continual enlargement and increased folding of the human brain (p. 89), coupled with a longer dependent childhood that allowed more time for learning, enabled early humans to develop language and culture. The four most important psychological developments were abstract thinking, plan-making, innovation, and symbolization.

H. ergaster
H. rudolfensis
H. erectus
H. habilis
H. heidelbergensis
Paranthropus
H. neanderthalensis
Australopithecus
H. sapiens
4.0 3.5 3.0 2.5 2.0 1.5 1.0 0.5 0.1 0.03 Million Years

The evolutionary history of modern humans includes diverse species which often lived at the same time.
above, from left to right: *Australopithecus, Homo erectus, Homo neanderthalensis, and Homo sapiens.*

CHARACTERISTIC HUMAN TRAITS

Distinctive traits distinguish modern humans, Homo sapiens, from all other living things. These include both physical characteristics as well as the intellectual and cultural achievements developed through human evolution.

In contrast to other animals, humans walk stiffly upright on two legs. This posture is supported by a skeleton that has adapted over the course of human evolution. The pelvis is broad and tipped forward while the backbone forms a double-S shape to absorb vertical forces, unlike the arching structure of four-legged animals. The big toe has lost the gripping function used by the great apes; it now lies parallel to the foot rather than spreading out to the side. The bones in the sole of the foot form an arch that cushions it while walking, while the hands have evolved spectacularly since they are no longer needed for movement. Opposable thumbs and a rotating forearm have ensured that the human hand is an ideal instrument for exploration and manipulation.

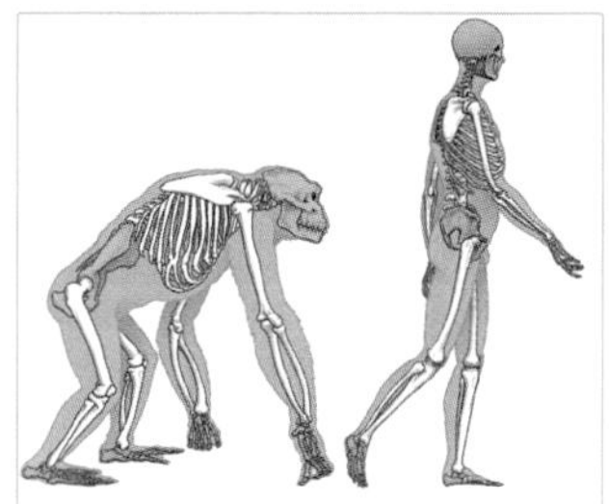

Unlike chimpanzees, humans can walk upright and use their hands freely.

The skull gradually expanded in all directions, with a continually enlarged brain being accommodated behind a high forehead. At the same time, the distinct snout observable in the great apes receded, the brow ridges over the eyes disappeared, and the nose and chin evolved to become more prominent. Human body hair also drastically receded to only a few specific areas.

Human teeth, smaller than those of the great apes, suit an omnivorous (both plants and meat) diet filled with great variety. The unique physical structures that make spoken language possible are constructed mainly from cartilage and soft tissue. The key requirements for speech include a movable tongue, an arched palate, and an appropriately positioned larynx.

Intellectual and Cultural Development

Many of the physical traits just described have a direct connection to the intellectual development of humans. For instance, the period of childhood lasts longer for humans than it does for chimpanzees since human infants must be born at an earlier stage of development so that their large skulls can fit through the mother's pelvis during the act of labor. For much the same reason, significant brain development for humans—further stimulated by the environment—takes place after birth.

Sexuality is a significant component of human behavior.

Increased performance resulted from the larger human brain with its enhanced folds, which made the use of space in the cranium more efficient, consequently leading to higher intelligence and an aptitude for language. The lifelong ability to learn and a capacity to display complex social behavior were crucial preconditions for the emergence of culture. The intellectual and cultural evolution of early humans has been traced through the discovery of "cultural" fossils such as tools.

INSIDER KNOWLEDGE

HUMANS *remain fertile about as long as chimpanzees do, but live longer on average.*

CULTURE *is the transmission of information through behavior, especially teaching and learning.*

THE AVERAGE HUMAN BRAIN *is around 75% water and weighs approximately 3 lb (1.4 kg).*

Human sexual behavior is influenced not only by instinct but also by deliberate choice. Language and conscious intentions such as expressions of tenderness play a significant role in the process. Human sexuality can also affect social structures within cultures, such as lifelong partnerships.

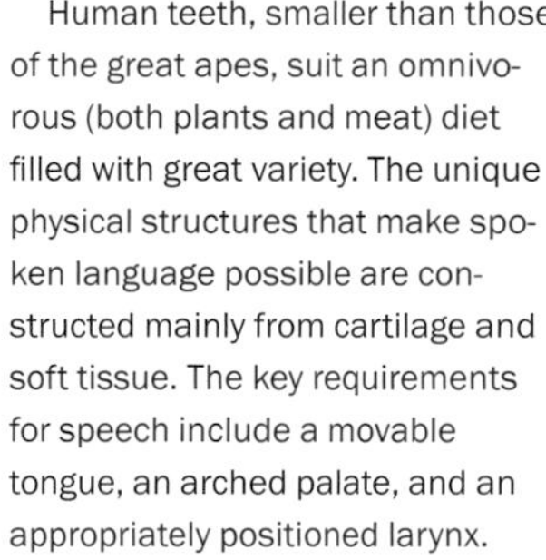

LANGUAGE *is the most important form of human communication.*

WRITING *allows humans to reliably pass on knowledge, observations, and traditions over many generations.*

PREREQUISITES *for spoken language include a larynx and vocal cords.*

Writing, reading, and mathematics form a major part of human culture and education.

Language and Writing

SPOKEN LANGUAGE translates thought into sound. It is the basis of all human social relationships and cultural evolution, although exactly when and why it evolved remains unclear. It possibly preceded a creative explosion some 40,000 years ago, when artistic cave paintings, jewelry, and musical instruments were first observed.

WRITTEN COMMUNICATION began supplementing spoken language about 5000 B.C. The oldest discovered sample of a writing system, from Mesopotamia, is dated from about 4000 B.C. Writing is defined as the communication of messages using a recognized system of symbols. Several high cultures independently developed forms of writing.

Language makes it possible for people to exchange opinions.

MUSCULOSKELETAL SYSTEM—BONES, JOINTS, MUSCLES

Humans have a bony skeleton with movable joints that supports an upright posture. Muscles attached to the skeleton make it possible to control precise movements.

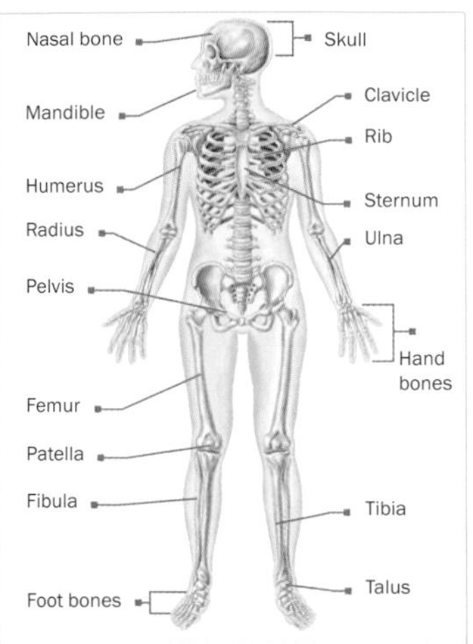

The skeleton supports the body, protects internal organs and provides sites for muscle attachment.

Pectoralis major muscle
Sternocleidomastoid muscle
Biceps
Deltoid muscle
Back Muscles
Abdominals
Triceps
Hand muscles
Gluteus maximus muscle
Quadriceps femoris muscle
Gastrocnemius muscle
Tibialis anterior muscle
Hamstrings

The term musculature refers to the entire set of human muscles, which are attached to the bones.

The human skeleton comprises about 208 individual bones and fulfills three main functions: support, protection, and movement. It supports the body and protects the inner organs—for instance, the skull encases the brain and the rib cage protects the heart and lungs. Muscles are attached to individual bones to make movement possible. The bone and cartilage of the skeleton are connected at the joints by strands of connective tissue. The main body axis, or axial skeleton, consists of the skull and vertebral column. Attached to this is the appendicular skeleton—bones of the arm and leg as well as the shoulder and pelvic (hip) girdles. The vertebral column can absorb a great deal of sudden and heavy force because of its double S curve.

Vertebral Column

In humans, the vertebral column, also called the backbone, consists of 34 vertebrae, which have spinal discs separating each of them. These are made of cartilage and have a jelly-like center. They work as excellent shock absorbers when the spinal column is stressed by running, jumping and similar activities. The spinal cord—central axis of the nervous system—runs through a canal within the vertebral column. It carries information between the brain and the body. An injury to the spinal cord, for instance from a broken vertebra or a ruptured disc, can have very serious consequences, such as permanent paralysis.

The muscles are placed under enormous stress during athletic activity.

INSIDER KNOWLEDGE

INSUFFICIENT EXERCISE *can lead to back pain and damage to the vertebral column.*

MUSCLE CRAMPS *are usually caused by a lack of minerals, especially potassium, calcium, and magnesium.*

MUSCLE ACHES *after exercise are caused by inflammation in the muscular tissue.*

OSTEOPOROSIS *results from the excessive breakdown of bone material.*

The Joints

The joints are the movable connections between components of the skeleton and are specialized for the specific movements they make. Ball-and-socket joints can be moved in all directions. They are found, for instance, at the shoulder and hip, allowing the arms and legs to swivel, swing, and twist. Hinge joints, such as the elbow, can only be moved along a single axis. Pivot joints make twisting movements, such as those made by the forearm.

The Muscles

Every healthy body has more than 600 muscles that can be consciously controlled. Muscles contract and relax to drive the movement of internal and external body parts. Contraction is a conscious process. It is often accompanied by the passive stretching of an opposing muscle (the flexor and extensor). Skeletal muscles are anchored to bones by tendons that move the bones. Regular physical training leads to a thickening of the muscle fibers and higher performance levels, but does not increase the number of muscle cells.

Anatomy of a Bone

THE BONES OF HUMANS AND OTHER MAMMALS are primarily made of calcium phosphate. They are wrapped in a thin layer of connective tissue called the periosteum, and have a compact outer layer and a spongy inner scaffolding. Bone marrow, laced with blood vessels, is located between the cavity of tubular bones and the spaces of the spongy layer. Red and white blood cells and platelets are formed in the marrow. Long bones (such as those in the thigh, shin, and arms) differ from flat bones (such as the skull and ribs), but all constantly break down and reconstruct themselves. Usually, they can repair themselves quite easily after a fracture has occurred.

A protective layer called the periosteum covers bones. It contains blood vessels and nerves and is highly sensitive to pain.

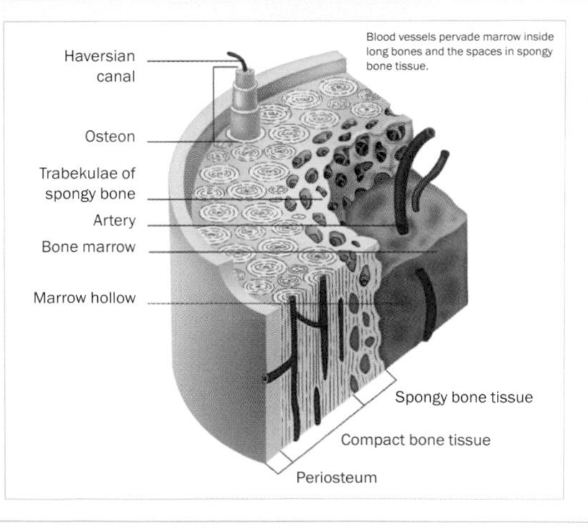

HEART, CIRCULATION, AND RESPIRATION

Respiratory organs—the lungs—take in oxygen, which is transported within the cardiovascular system to all parts of the body.

The heart is the central organ of the human body. It ensures that an adequate supply of nutrients and oxygen reaches the other organs and tissues. Consisting almost exclusively of muscle, an adult's heart weighs about 9 oz (300 g) and is around the size of a clenched fist. The two halves, separated by a wall, are subdivided into two valved chambers: the smaller upper atrium and the larger lower ventricle. Chambers of the heart are stimulated by the sinus nodes, the heart's own nervous system, to contract (systolic) and relax (diastolic) in a steady rhythm. Contractions pump the blood into blood vessels that carry it throughout the body.

The human circulatory system includes the systemic and pulmonary circuits.

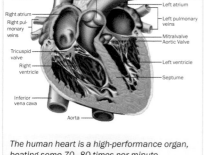

The human heart is a high-performance organ, beating some 70–80 times per minute.

Blood Circulation

Humans have a closed circulatory system: the blood is enclosed within the blood vessels. The left side of the heart pumps oxygen-rich blood through the systemic circulatory system, distributing it through the aorta. As they circulate through the tissues, the red blood cells release oxygen and take in carbon dioxide. Deoxygenated red blood cells flow through the veins back to the heart, where the right chambers pump the stale blood back to the lungs for oxygen. The pulmonary circulation system oxygenates the blood and sends it back to the left chamber.

Blood and Vessels

Blood vessels such as arteries and veins are made up of layers of muscle. They are coated with a thin connective tissue called epithelium. Muscles of the blood vessels promote and regulate the flow of blood through the body. The smallest vessels are capillaries, with no muscles, that exchange oxygen and carbon dioxide through their thin walls. Blood is composed of plasma (water, proteins, and chemical ions) and blood cells. Red blood cells exchange oxygen and carbon dioxide; white blood cells are the body's immune defenses; and platelets ensure that blood clots. Humans have an average of 9.5–10.5 pints (4.5–5 l) of constantly renewing blood in their bodies.

Respiration

Human beings need oxygen to release the energy from food they ingest and provide power for all body functions. They take in oxygen from the air by breathing through their nose and/or mouth. The air then enters the trachea, or windpipe, which splits into two bronchi that lead to the lungs. Like the branches of a tree, the bronchi split further into bronchioles, which bring oxygenated air to miniscule air sacs called alveoli. The alveoli pass oxygen through their lining and into the thin membranes of capillaries.

HIGH BLOOD PRESSURE *caused by stress, hormonal fluctuations, smoking, or excessive alcohol consumption can lead to heart attack.*

HEART ATTACK *risk factors include high blood pressure, nicotine use, excessive weight, an unhealthy diet, insufficient exercise, age, and heredity.*

THE SCIENTIFIC NAME *is a myocardial infarction.*

Smoking increases the risk of a heart attack.

Heart Attack—Causes, Frequency, Treatment

CARDIOVASCULAR SYSTEM DISEASES, significantly heart attack and stroke, are common causes of death in industrialized regions. Blocking blood supply to the heart for more than 20 minutes during a heart attack destroys some heart muscle. Obstructing arteries or capillaries in the brain during a stroke kills nervous tissue. Both conditions are associated with the narrowing or blockage of blood vessels by clots of blood cells and protein fibers.

THE CAUSES of heart disease include a diet with a high level of unhealthy fats, excessive alcohol intake, smoking, and insufficient exercise. Public education about these risk factors aims to complement emergency care and treatment.

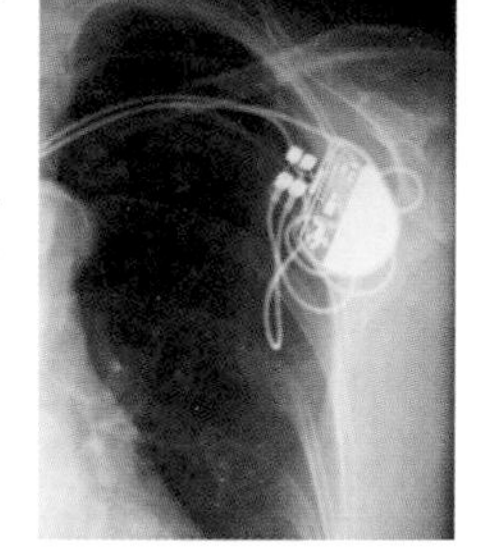

Pacemakers provide electrical impulses to the heart, ensuring that it beats in a regular rhythm.

Lung Diseases

The lungs supply the body with oxygen from the air. However, harmful organisms and pollutants such as dust and smoke can also enter the lungs with each breath. Bacteria, viruses, and fungi can infect lung tissue and cause disease. Bronchitis only affects the bronchi; pneumonia affects one or both lungs. Symptoms of lung disease include a swelling of the bronchi, heavy mucus production, and intense coughing. With lung cancer, abnormal cells appear in the tissue and lead to the growth of a malignant tumor. Smoking is a significant cause of lung cancer, in addition to hereditary reasons.

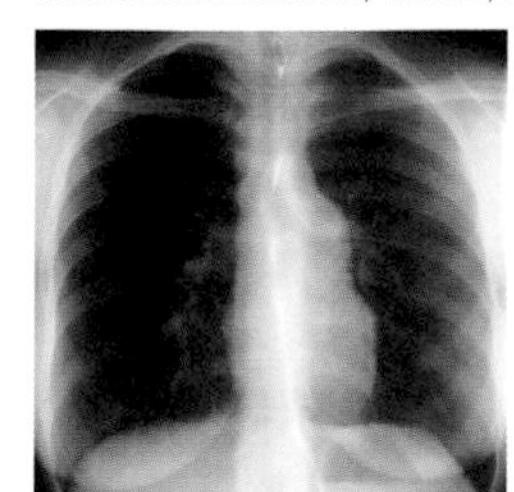
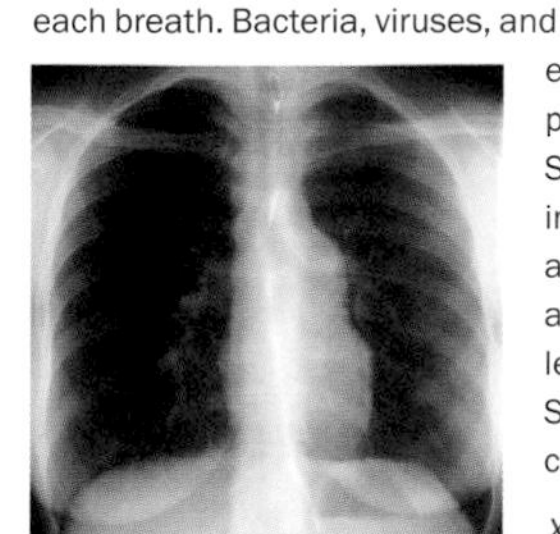

X-ray of the lungs

The red blood cells are responsible for transporting oxygen and carbon dioxide within the body.

SENSORY ORGANS

The sensory organs are the "antennas" humans use to pick up information from the environment. This input is converted into electrical impulses and carried by the nerves to the brain.

Humans perceive the world through the six senses: sight, smell, hearing, touch, taste, and balance. Since the sense of balance is a recent addition, many references continue to be made to the five senses. However, the popular use of the term "sixth sense" is in reference to other forms of awareness such as telepathy, or electrical and magnetic perception in humans and animals. Senses are developed to varying degrees of sensitivity in humans and other living creatures. Information from the senses is communicated and understood with special sensory cells or receptors.

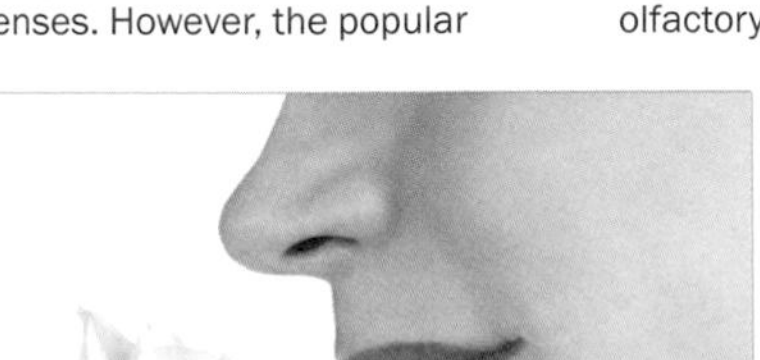
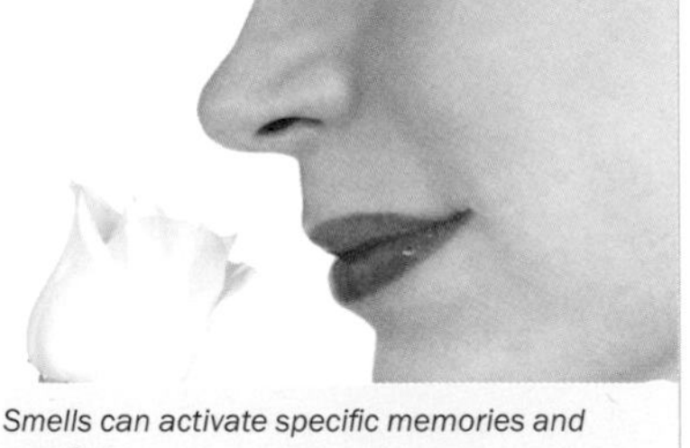

Smells can activate specific memories and emotions.

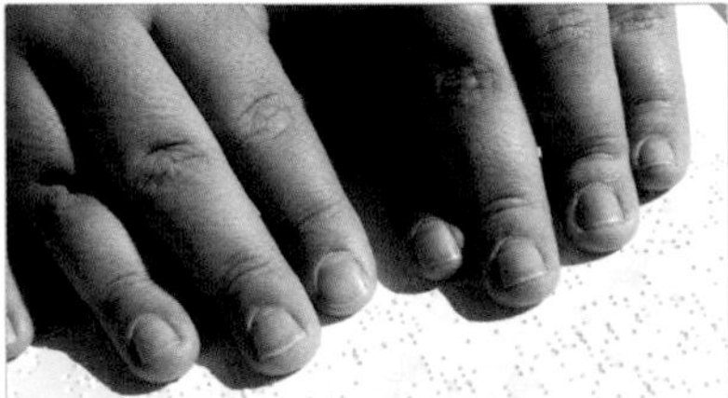

Blind people use their sense of touch to read. With the fingertips, it is possible to scan the raised writing system called Braille.

Olfaction Scents

The process of smelling, or olfaction, takes place in the upper nasal chamber. The olfactory nerve cells located there have branches that protrude into a layer of mucus. Odor molecules breathed in with the air dissolve in this mucus and bind to specific receptor molecules on the olfactory cells. This stimulates the cells to produce electrical signals, which travel over the olfactory nerve to the brain's olfactory center. Humans can distinguish about 10,000 smells.

Taste

Taste is affected by the sense of smell, which provides finer distinctions of flavor, as well as by the visual impression made by food. However, basic characteristics of taste—sweet, sour, bitter, salty, fatty, and savory—are perceived with taste receptor cells. These are organized into taste buds, which are concentrated mainly on the upper surface of the tongue. Receptor cells, stimulated by food, send impulses to the brain to determine the flavor.

Hearing

In humans and other mammals, the ability to detect sound is performed by the ear. Human hearing covers around 30,000–20,000 hertz. Sound waves passing through the ear canal reach the eardrum, a membrane which divides the middle ear. The sound waves cause the eardrum to vibrate, and the tiny ear bones resting on it—the hammer, anvil, and stirrup—strengthen the vibration and convert it into movements. The movements cause pressure waves to pass to the cochlea, or the fluid-filled inner ear. As the fluid moves, it stimulates the cochlea's tiny hairs. These microscopic hair cells produce electrical impulses which are carried over the auditory nerve to the brain's auditory center. Excessive noise and ageing can result in the loss of hair cells in the inner ear, and lead to impaired hearing.

Balance

The sense of balance is regulated by a fluid-filled vestibular system in the inner ear. This system has sensors in the hair roots that register the body's motion and position in space. Since the hair cells are surrounded by a thick fluid, head movements cause different patterns of liquid pressure. The hair cells transmit electrical impulses to the brain to evaluate the position of the head.

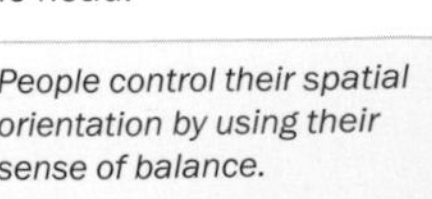

People control their spatial orientation by using their sense of balance.

Vision

VISION DELIVERS SOME 80% of total human impressions and information. The human eyeball, measuring 1 inch (25 mm) across, distinguishes the three primary colors red, green, and blue and perceives black-white contrasts. Sight begins when rays of light from an object enter the eye. Through refraction, an upside-down, smaller image of the object is projected onto the light-sensitive cells of the inner lining of the eye, called the retina.

Incoming light is refracted at the cornea, the curved front of the eye.

Rod- and cone-shaped receptors in the retina detect light and produce nerve impulses. The 7 million cone cells are sensitive to color; the 120 million rod cells are sensitive to black-and-white contrast.

The lens focuses the light.

Light rays pass through the fluid-filled eyeball.

The optical nerve carries impulses from the retina to the brain to process the information.

The Skin as Sensory Organ

TOUCH is governed by the body's largest organ, the skin. Stimuli from contact, pressure and vibration activate receptors in its three layers: the epidermis, dermis, and hypodermis. The hypodermis, the deepest layer, is missing in body parts with very thin skin, such as the eyelids. Touch is sensed by receptors at the follicles of hairs. "Basket cells" directly under the skin react to pressure differences, and receptors in the hypodermis sense vibration.

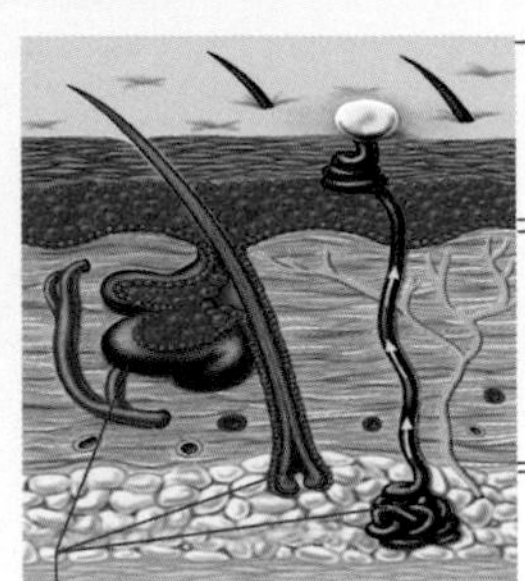
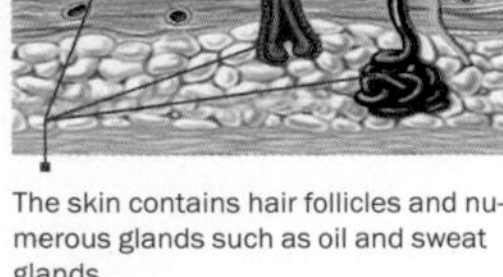

The epidermis is made of several layers of thickened, dead cells.

Composed of connective tissue fibers, the dermis contains blood vessels and nerve receptors.

The hypodermis contains small cushions of fat and sensory cells that react to pressure.

The skin contains hair follicles and numerous glands such as oil and sweat glands.

see also: Optics, *Physics and Technology Chapter, p. 109*

BIOLOGY

BRAIN AND NERVOUS SYSTEM

The human brain and nervous system are the body's control center. The brain contains many billions of neurons and nerve cells.

Understanding the human brain is a long-standing challenge for neurobiologists. The brain is a high-performance organ which registers and processes all the sensory impressions arriving through the nervous system. It is made up of soft brain tissue, consisting of neurons and glial cells. The bony skull, protective membranes, and cranial fluid all shield the brain from potentially harmful influences.

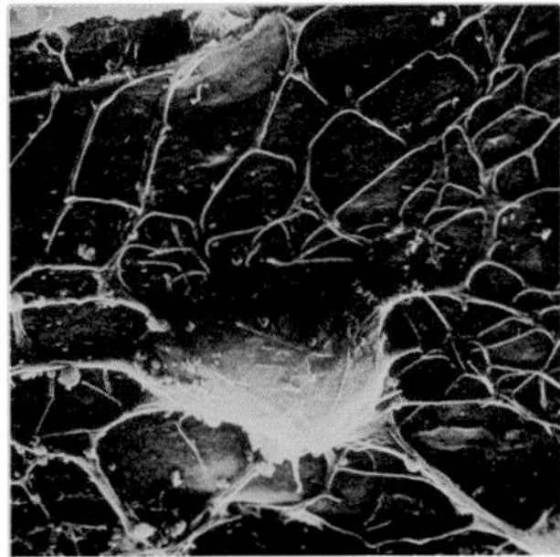

A neuron is made up of a cell body, the soma, as well as dendrites and axons.

Structure of the Brain

The brain has two symmetrical hemispheres that are connected by a bundle of nerve fibers. The left hemisphere, which includes the language center, is mainly responsible for analytical thinking. The more intuitive, image-based processes are carried out in the right hemisphere. The brain's outer layer, or cerebral cortex, is about the thickness of an adult's little finger and contains the highest concentration of neurons. The cortex's numerous convolutions increase the surface area, which raises the brain's performance.

The brain is divided into several parts. The cerebrum is the center of consciousness, perception, thoughts, emotions, and action. It is organized into lobes and includes numerous functional areas.

The inter-brain or diencephalon is the interface between the sensory organs and the cerebrum. It also filters out unnecessary information, protecting the brain from overload. It regulates the body's temperature, fluid levels, and circadian (day and night) rhythm. A portion of the interbrain produces hormones (p. 91), which are released into the bloodstream to regulate other important body functions.

The brain's internal switching station is the midbrain or mesencephalon, which lies under the diencephalon. It transfers information to other areas of the brain.

The cerebellum, located at the back of the head, coordinates body movements. With the balance organ in the ear, it helps maintain the body's equilibrium. Connected to the cerebellum is the medulla oblongata, the center for essential reflexes such as swallowing and vomiting. It is also involved in regulating heartbeat, breathing, and the circulatory system (p. 87).

Neurons—the Building Blocks

The brain and nervous system are built from nerve cells that transmit signals from one part of the body to another. They comprise a cell body, or soma, and several connections called dendrites. Dendrites pick up signals and carry them toward the cell body, while wire-like fibers called axons carry data in the form of electrical impulses toward the brain or specific regions of the body. Special glial cells called Schwann cells surround axons like a layer of insulation. The places where nerve cells meet are called synapses. Electrical impulses are transferred over these gaps with the help of messenger substances, or neurotransmitters.

Multiple Sclerosis

Multiple sclerosis (MS) is an inflammation of the central nervous system. Neurons in the brain and spinal cord are attacked by the body's own immune cells. Damage to the nerve cells produces symptoms such as fatigue, loss of coordination, muscle weakness, and vision disturbances. The symptoms may vary or gradually worsen over time periods that may differ in length. Contemporary therapies can treat only the symptoms, not the cause of the disease.

above: *Multiple sclerosis can lead to impaired mobility.*

21ST CENTURY

MODERN BRAIN RESEARCH *has sparked a large debate regarding the existence of human free will.*

PROCEDURES FOR RESEARCH *into the activity of the brain include magnetic resonance imaging (MRI) and computed tomography (CT).*

INSIDER KNOWLEDGE

GENDER DIFFERENCE: *An adult female brain weighs 2.6 lb (1.2 kg), compared with 2.8 lb (1.3 kg) for an adult male brain, yet they have a higher number of convolutions.*

THE BRAIN *makes up only 2% of total body weight, but requires 20% of the body's blood volume.*

A NEURON *in the spinal cord can reach 3.3 ft (1 m) in length.*

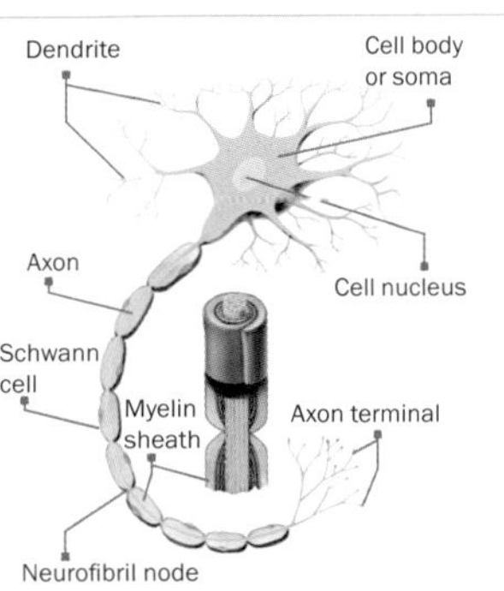

The axons of a nerve cell are surrounded by a myelin sheath, consisting of a fat-containing substance supplied by Schwann cells.

Functional Areas of the Brain

THE CEREBRAL CORTEX comprises deeply folded cortical tissue that is often referred to as "gray matter." It is organized into functional divisions. The motor association cortex controls the skeletal muscles. The sensory cortex receives data from the sensory organs, registering perceptions such as taste, touch, vision and hearing. Association areas compare and coordinate the elements of information, as the full performance of a function requires the participation of all relevant fields.

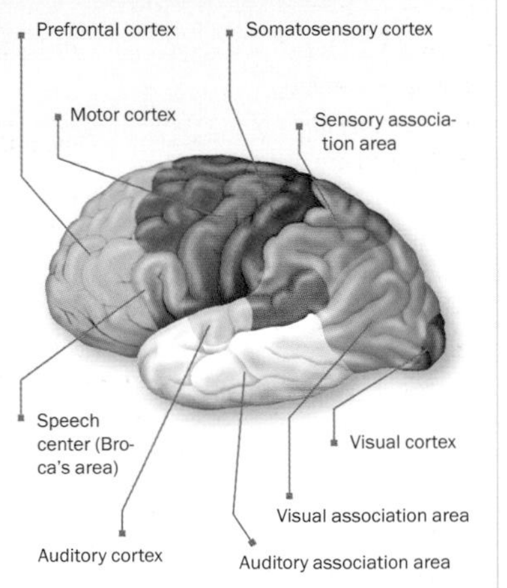

see also: Neuron Net, *Physics and Technology Chapter, p. 141* | Does Free Will Exist?, *Psychology Chapter, p. 272*

BIOLOGY

METABOLISM

Humans, unlike plants, do not produce their own nutrition (p. 66). Instead, they must obtain food and drink to convert into energy in order to maintain their bodies.

Metabolism refers to the intake, movement, and chemical transformation of nutrients within an organism as well as the disposal of its subsequent waste products. Food is primarily required as a source of energy not only to maintain processes such as moving, thinking, and breathing, but also for the growth and renewal of cells and tissues.

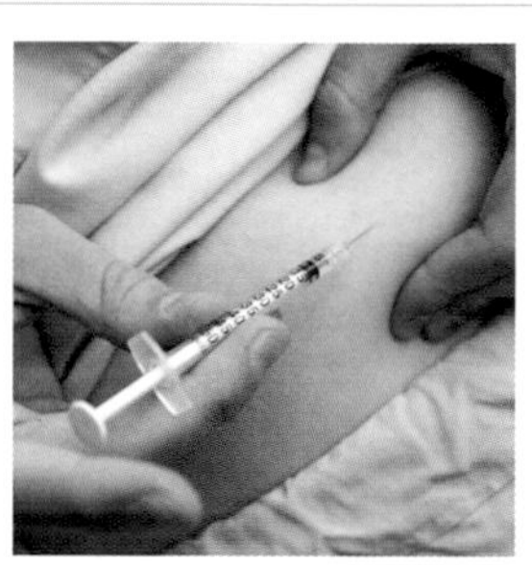

Diabetes

Diabetes is one of the most common diseases, and is known as one of the fastest growing problems affecting industrialized nations today. It weakens the body's ability to productively use sugar. In diabetes mellitus, which affects more than 180 million people worldwide, the breakdown and metabolism of sugar in the blood—normally carried out by insulin produced in the pancreas—does not function properly. Diabetes can be present from birth or may result from an unhealthful diet or metabolic problems connected with ageing. Many diabetics must inject themselves regularly with artificially produced insulin.

above: *Insulin injection*

INSIDER KNOWLEDGE

EATING HABITS: *Proteins and fats should account for 15% and 35%, respectively, of the daily energy ration. Diets in industrialized regions may exceed that target, while developing regions may not meet it.*

What Happens to Our Food?

A piece of food undertakes a journey that starts at the mouth and continues to the esophagus, stomach, and small and large intestines; ending at the rectum and anus. Throughout this process, individual organs of the digestive system fulfill specific functions. Other glands and organs, such as the salivary glands, pancreas, gall bladder, and liver, also contribute to digestion.

Path Through Mouth, Stomach, and Small Intestine

The teeth mechanically break up food inside the mouth, mixing it with saliva from the salivary glands. The flow of saliva may actually begin even earlier as a reflex from the smell of food. Enzymes in the saliva break up starches and animal-produced carbohydrates (glycogen) into smaller sugar molecules.

Swallowing motions push the food mixture through the esophagus into the stomach, where it is combined with digestive juices such as hydrochloric acid. The stomach churns the cell structure of the food. Proteins are split into smaller molecules by enzymes. Two to six hours after a meal, the stomach empties its contents into the small intestine—16.5 ft (5 m) long—where the main digestive processes occur. Bile from the gall bladder dissolves the fats and enzymes from the pancreas digest the fats, proteins, and carbohydrates.

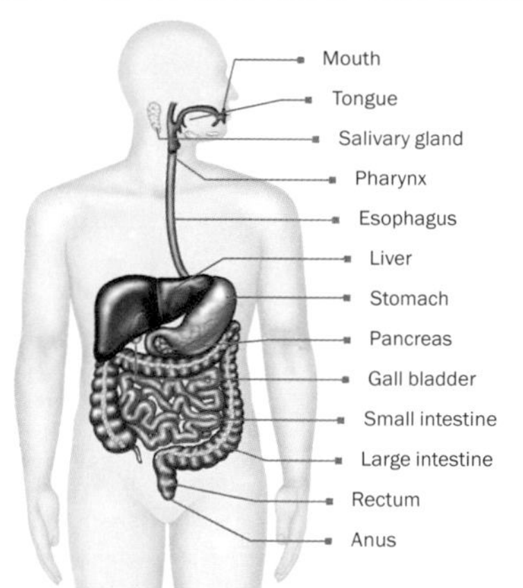

Food passes through many stages of digestion on its way through the mouth, esophagus, stomach, and intestines.

The end products of digestion are sugar derived from starchy and sugary foods such as bread and cakes; peptides and amino acids from proteins in meat, eggs and fish; and fatty acids from fat-containing foods such as butter and oils.

The dissolved food components are then absorbed into the body through the walls of the small intestine. Sugar, amino acids, and short fatty acid molecules pass through the villi, a multitude of tiny finger-like protrusions, which increase its surface area to about 240 yd^2 (200 m^2) and allow greater efficiency by absorbing more nutrients. Through the villi, nutrients are passed to blood vessels for transport to the body's cells.

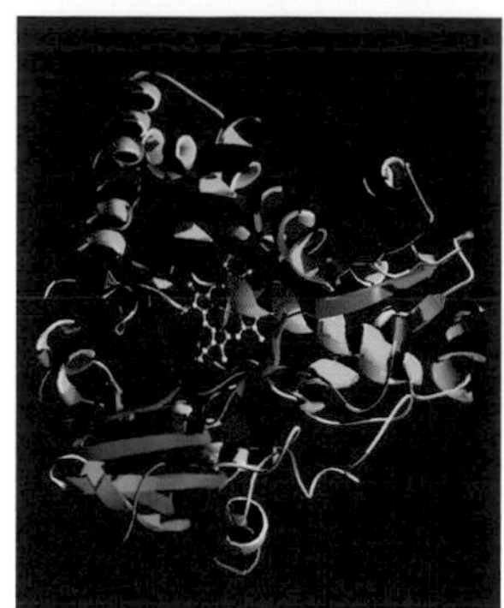

Enzymes play a central role in metabolism.

Enzymes

Enzymes are proteins and are designated as biological catalysts since they speed up chemical reactions within the body. To accomplish this, they reduce the activation energy that must be applied to set a metabolic process in motion. Enzymes are involved in most of the body's biochemical reactions. In digestion, they are responsible for splitting up and dissolving large food molecules such as fats, proteins, and carbohydrates into smaller units that the body can absorb and use.

Large Intestine and Excretion

Substances that cannot be digested, such as fiber, continue to the large intestine, which measures 2.5 inches (7 cm) in width. The large intestine absorbs water from undigested food while the remaining waste substances are excreted via the rectum and the anus. The large intestine is home to beneficial bacteria like E. coli. These organisms feed on the material passing through the intestines and secrete vitamins that the human body cannot produce by itself.

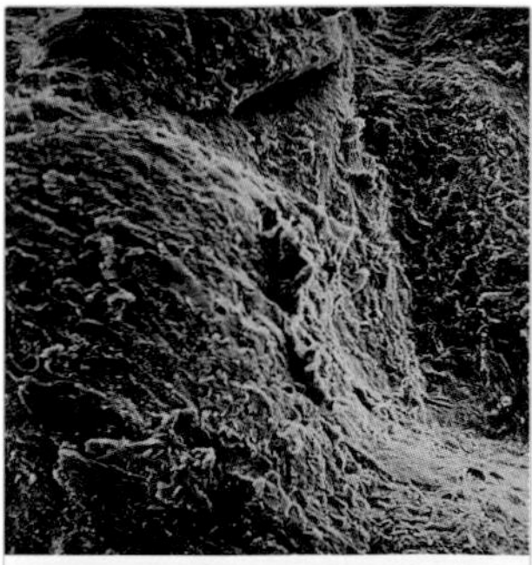

The mucus-coated stomach lining produces the hydrochloric acid needed for digestion. The mucus protects the stomach walls from the acid's corrosive effects.

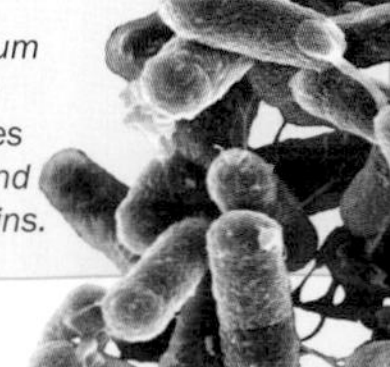

The bacterium Escherichia coli produces vitamin K and other vitamins.

REPRODUCTIVE ORGANS AND HORMONES

Human reproduction is governed by a complex hormonal system and accompanied by typical patterns of behavior. During the process, specific male and female characteristics help stimulate sexual arousal.

The sex drive ensures the reproduction of the species. It can be stimulated by specific male or female sexual characteristics, such as a man's broad shoulders (p. 82) or a woman's breasts.

Male Reproductive Organs

The male reproductive organs include the penis, testicles (or testes), and scrotum, as well as the ducts that transport sperm, carriers of genetic material. Canals within the testes produce more than 250 million sperm cells daily. In humans, and most other mammals, the testes are located in the scrotum, on the outside of the body. Normal body temperature, 98.6°F (37°C), is too high for successful sperm production, but the slightly lower temperature within the scrotum is ideal. The sperm ripen in a long tube called the epididymis until an ejaculation occurs. They then pass through the vas deferens and the urethra within the erect penis to exit the body. The sperm cells are deposited inside the vagina during sexual intercourse.

> **INSIDER KNOWLEDGE**
>
> **FERTILITY** *in industrialized regions is declining sharply due to personal life choices and pollution.*
>
> **THE BIRTH RATE** *in industrialized countries is about 2.1 children per woman.*
>
> **BIRTH CONTROL PILLS** *led to a great reduction in births in many regions.*

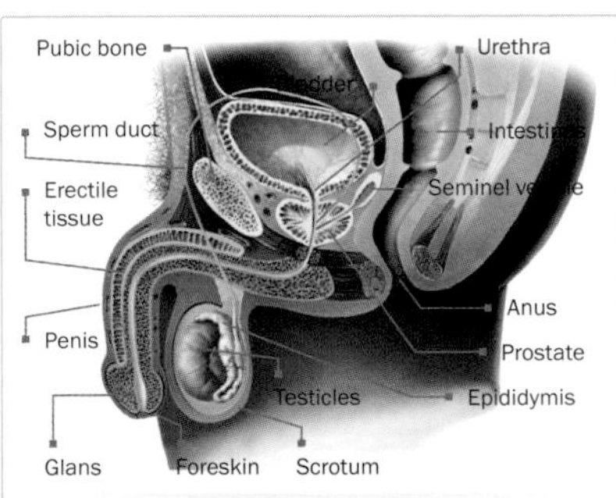

When aroused, blood fills spaces in the erectile tissue, causing the penis to enlarge and harden.

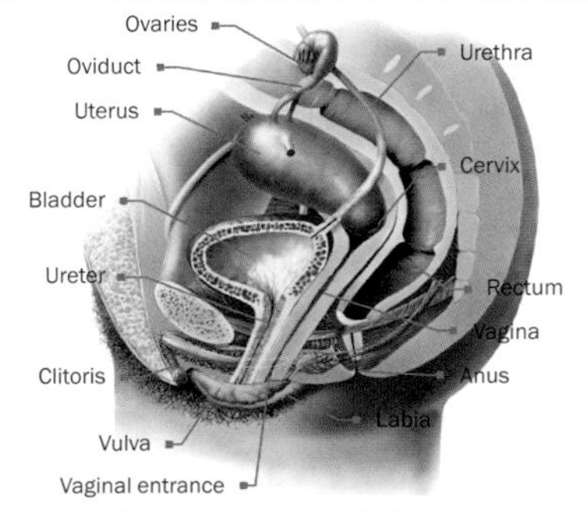

The vagina leads to the cervix, which is the entrance to the womb where a baby develops.

Female Reproductive Organs

The female reproductive organs include a pair of ovaries and Fallopian tubes, the uterus, vagina, clitoris, and two layers of skin protecting the vagina called labia. Before birth, about 400,000 eggs develop in the ovaries. As humans reach puberty, these eggs will periodically mature. The egg is surrounded with several layers of follicle cells that provide it with nourishment as it ripens. Multiple follicles develop during the female monthly cycle, but generally only one grows to full size and is released from the ovary into the Fallopian tube in a process called ovulation.

While the egg cell makes its way toward the uterus, the remaining follicle forms the corpus luteum, which secretes the hormones estrogen and progesterone. These prepare the walls of the uterus for implantation of a fertilized egg. If the egg cell remains unfertilized in its path to the uterus, the corpus luteum and the thickened uterine lining break down, leaving the body during menstruation. If sperm enters the Fallopian tube and fertilizes the egg, a pregnancy results.

Hormones can have a direct affect on targeted cells or organs, and can also stimulate other organs to produce hormones.

Hormones

Hormones produced and secreted by glands are involved in almost all processes in the body. Blood distributes these messenger substances to their sites of action, where they bind to receptors on the surfaces of cells and cause biochemical reactions. Hormone-producing organs include the pineal gland, the pancreas, and thyroid, as well as the adrenal cortex and the cells of the ovaries and testes. Hormones influence metabolism, growth, reproduction, and behavior, among others. Differing amounts of sex hormones such as testosterone and estrogen are present in both females and males. These influence the development and functioning of primary and secondary sexual traits.

Female Hormones and Menstrual Cycle

THE HORMONES estrogen and progesterone thicken the lining of the uterus during the menstrual cycle. The lining exits the body through monthly bleeding (menstruation) from the vagina if fertilization has not taken place. Menstruation occurs from the first to the fifth days of the cycle. The follicular phase follows from the fifth to the 14th day, when the pituitary gland releases follicle-stimulating hormone (FSH) to ripen the follicle around an egg. The follicle produces estrogen to increase luteinizing hormone (LH), triggering ovulation—the egg's release—around the 14th day. The body temperature rises, and the egg travels toward the uterus. The luteal phase, from the 14th to the 28th day, is when the follicle left by the egg becomes the corpus luteum. It releases progesterone and prepares the uterine lining for a fertilized egg, or is otherwise shed.

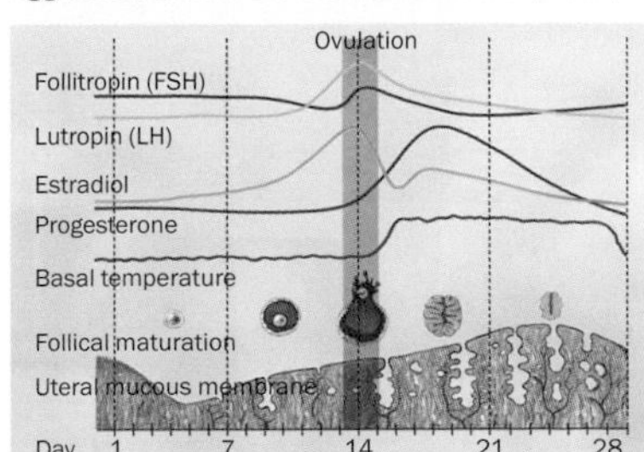

The menstrual cycle lasts approximately 28 days.

BIOLOGY

THE IMMUNE SYSTEM

The human body is constantly confronted with harmful bacteria and viruses from the environment. However, its complex immune system goes into action when it recognizes them.

The immune system recognizes defective cells and substances foreign to the body and combats them with a range of specific and non-specific defensive strategies. Non-specific strategies are innate, or passive, and form the first line of defense against infectious microorganisms. For instance, the skin and the mucous membranes coating the digestive, respiratory, and genital tracts prevent most bacteria, viruses, and parasites from entering the body.

Invading microbes find it difficult to get through the skin's dead surface cells and the oils produced by sebaceous glands. Mucus, tears, and saliva wash away many potentially harmful organisms. The secretions of most of the body's mucous membranes also contain enzymes or antibacterial proteins.

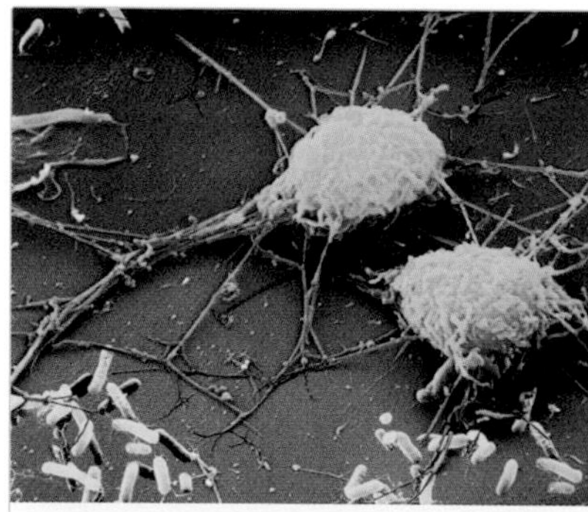
The immune system in action: a macrophage eliminates an invader—a bacterium.

The body's more specific defense mechanisms form what is called the acquired or active immune system. The system triggers an immune response by recognizing specific markers or antigens on the surface of invading foreign cells and forming antibodies to provide a targeted reaction. Organisms that succeed in penetrating the body are attacked and consumed by white blood cells such as macrophages. The inflammation produced in response to invading microbes increases the production and release of macrophages.

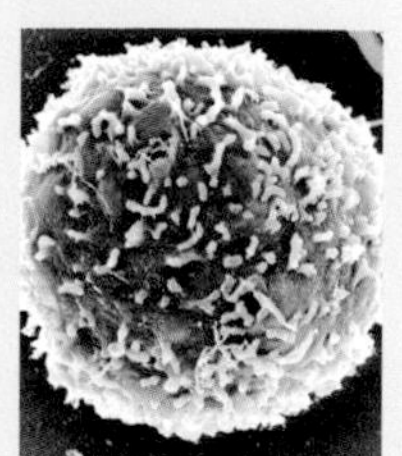

THE WORLD HEALTH ORGANIZATION (WHO) *estimates that some 3.1 million people died of AIDS in 2005.*

EACH YEAR HIV *infects 4.1 million more people.*

60% OF ALL HIV-POSITIVE *people living worldwide live in sub-Saharan Africa.*

HIV is a virus that attacks the white blood cells responsible for immune defenses.

AIDS

AIDS (ACQUIRED IMMUNE DEFICIENCY SYNDROME) is an incurable disease emerging in the 1980s that attacks and weakens the immune system. It is caused by the human immune deficiency virus (HIV), which targets the immune system's defensive cells, copies itself inside them, and in this way destroys them. The immune system weakens until—usually years later—symptoms of the disease manifest themselves. The formation of tumors and the frequency of infections increase drastically.

THE VIRUS is passed on in body fluids like blood, sperm, vaginal secretions, and mother's milk. Since there is still no effective cure—treatments only delay the onset of symptoms—methods that prevent infection, such as protected sex, remain the best defenses against contracting the disease.

right: *Virus that causes AIDS*
left: *Woman suffering from AIDS*

Primary Infection

When an infectious organism enters a body for the first time, this is known as a primary infection. First, the pathogen is picked up by an immune cell and broken into pieces. These pieces are then displayed on the immune cell's surface, stimulating the production of specific defensive cells. Some of these try to consume the invaders through phagocytosis or to kill them by secreting superoxides. The immune system first recognizes an invading pathogen due to chemicals produced or protein markers (antigens) on their surfaces. Other immune cells begin to produce antibodies, which cling to the invaders. After a primary infection, antibodies and memory cells remain, enabling the immune system to react more quickly and efficiently to any new infection by the same organism.

Allergies and Autoimmune Disorders

An immune system can turn against itself when it malfunctions. Self-recognition mechanisms may stop functioning properly, and so-called autoimmune disorders, such as diabetes, can result. Allergies are oversensitive reactions by the immune system to foreign substances in the environment, such as pollen, household dust, animal hair, or specific foods. Specialized defensive cells secrete increased amounts of histamines, which cause symptoms like sneezing—or in extreme cases, anaphylactic shock and failure of the cardiovascular system.

above: *Hay fever is an allergic reaction to plant pollen.*

Protective Vaccination

People protect themselves against infectious diseases through vaccination. In active immunization, a tiny dose of the disease's infecting agent is introduced into the body as weakened or dead cells. In response, the body produces antibodies to combat the pathogen, e.g., the influenza vaccine. In passive immunization, a serum is administered that contains specific antibodies against a particular organism.

INSIDER KNOWLEDGE

EVERY CELL *has distinguishing chemical or protein tags that mark it as known or unfamiliar.*

ORGAN TRANSPLANTS: *The cells of a donated organ are recognized as an infectious organism, so the immune response must be suppressed.*

BIOLOGY

HUMAN TISSUES AND CELL REGENERATION

The human body has specialized cells that organize themselves into tissues and organs. The cells are continually replaced, although this process slows down with age.

All components of the human body can be defined as various types of tissues. Tissues are groups of cells with a unified structure and function, held together by fibers or an outer layer of cells. The body's more than 50,000 million cells are divided into about 200 different types. Body organs are composed of four basic types of cells and tissues: epithelial, connective, nervous, and muscular.

Connective and supportive tissues (clockwise): adipose, blood, cartilage, dense connective tissue, loose connective tissue, osseous.

Epithelial Tissue

Epithelial tissue obstructs infectious organisms, protects against injury, and prevents loss of body fluids. Cells of this tissue type are organized into layers and lie close together. They cover the body's surfaces and its organs, as well as lining its cavities. Epithelial cells lining the lungs and intestines form a single layer. Inside the nose, they are present in multiple layers, in combination with nasal hairs. The epithelial tissues of the skin can regenerate rapidly.

Connective Tissue

The main functions of connective tissue are to support and bind other tissues. Connective tissue can be liquid (blood), jelly-like (tendons), and rigid (cartilage and bone). Typically, the cells of these tissues lie relatively far apart and are embedded in another material, or matrix. The areolar or loose connective tissues are the most common human connective tissues. These connect the skin and organs as well as hold them in place. Various types of fibers make them highly flexible and tear-resistant.

Dense connective tissue is found in ligaments as well as tendons, which attach muscles to bones. Cartilage and bone constitute special connective tissues that support the body. Bone tissue (p. 86) is hardened by deposits of minerals such as calcium phosphate, yet does not become brittle.

Nervous Tissue

Nervous tissue in the spine, brain, and nerves transmits tiny electrical impulses throughout the body. It comprises nerve cells and their surrounding neuroglial cells (p. 89).

Muscle Tissue

The elongated cells of muscle tissue (p. 86) can contract in response to a nerve impulse to cause movement. This tissue—there are about 650 muscles in the body—is the most common human tissue by volume. The muscles can be divided into three types: skeletal, smooth, and cardiac muscle (pp. 86–88). Skeletal muscles are attached to bones by tendons and permit the body to move. Smooth muscles are found in the walls of the digestive tract, internal organs, and blood vessels. While they contract more slowly than skeletal muscles, contraction persists for a longer period of time.

Cell Regeneration and Ageing

All cells divide regularly (p. 60) and are replaced. This process slows down as the body ages, leading to changes in the appearance and performance of tissues and organs. Affected elements include sensory organs, hormone levels, elasticity of connective tissue, reaction time, and memory. Medical conditions such as Werner syndrome, in which young people prematurely take on elderly characteristics, support the hypothesis that ageing is genetic.

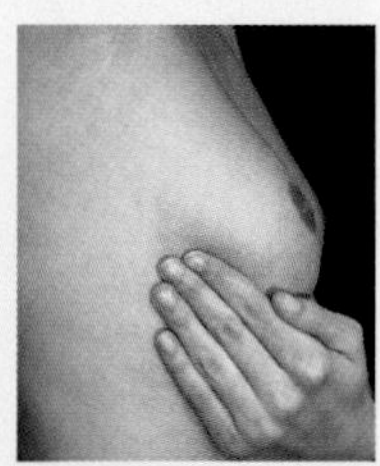

58 MILLION PEOPLE *worldwide died of cancer in 2005—70% of these in developing countries.*

WOMEN MOST COMMONLY *develop breast cancer, while men develop prostate or lung cancer.*

CANCER PATIENTS *are considered "cured" if the disease does not recur for five years.*

Early cancer detection techniques, such as breast examination, look for changes in the tissue.

Cancer

CANCER is defined as a malignant tumor in which cells divide irregularly and destroy healthy tissue. Cancer cells are disconnected from the normal mechanisms controlling cell division and growth. The cause of this process may be a genetic defect or external influences such as a virus, asbestos dust, or ultraviolet radiation. The abnormal cells multiply within a tissue or organ and prevent it from functioning properly. They may then travel to other parts of the body, forming metastases or secondary tumors.

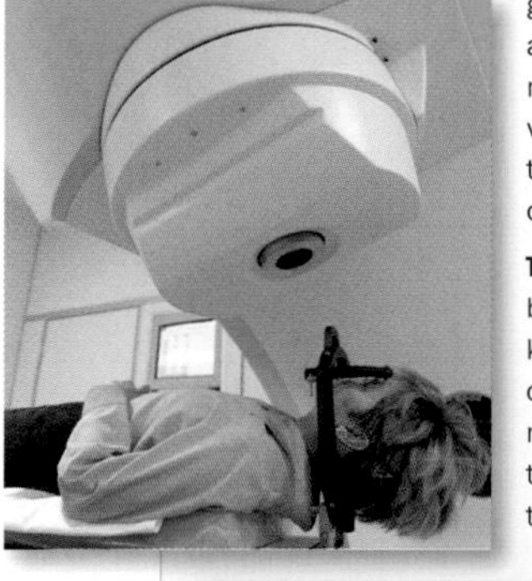

THE EARLIER A CANCEROUS GROWTH is detected, the better the chance of a cure. Cancer therapy aims to kill abnormally growing cells. Depending on the type of cancer, it may be treated with a mixture of treatments including surgery, radiation therapy, medications that interfere with cell reproduction (chemotherapy), and radioimmunotherapy.

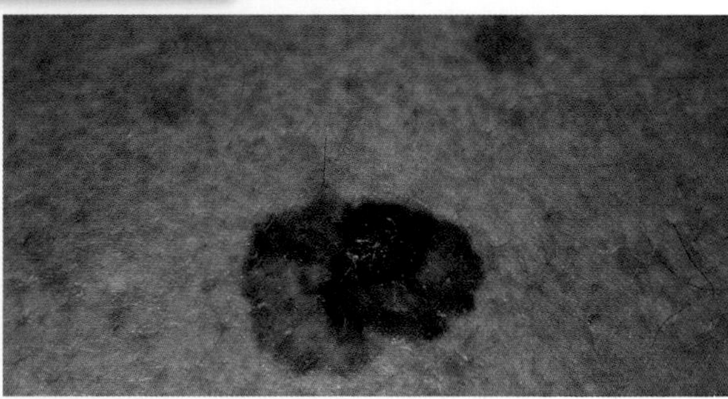

Skin cancer is often triggered by excessive sun exposure without adequate protection. **above:** *Radioimmunotherapy is a cancer treatment that targets marked tumor cells with high doses of radioactivity.*

Monographic Boxes

Analytic Boxes

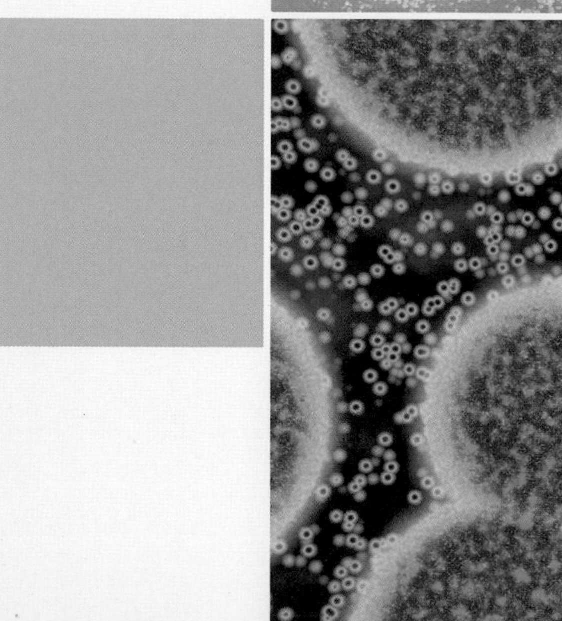

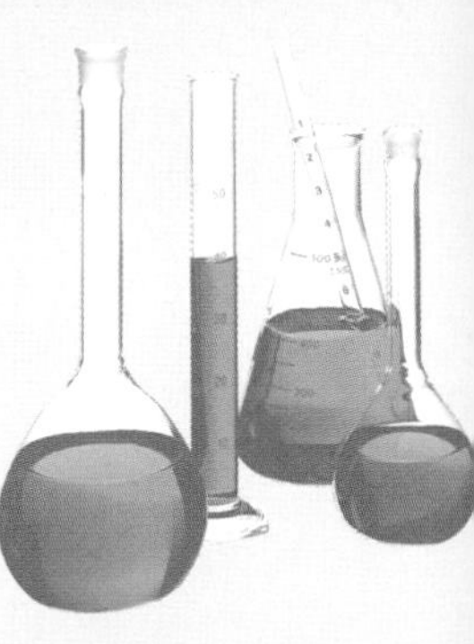

CHEMISTRY

While the concept of chemistry might make most people think of Bunsen burners, explosions, and liquids in test tubes, the scope of what it examines is far grander. Chemistry is concerned with materials, the abundant varieties of matter: their creation, characteristics, and transformations. Matter is what makes up our Earth, our environment, and humankind itself. In the span of decades chemists have come to understand how matter is organized, and they have thus been able to artificially create more chemical materials and products: manure, medicines, plastics, semiconductors, and many other materials without which modern everyday life could not be imagined. At present chemists are developing the materials of tomorrow: more efficient and "more intelligent" than today's.

KEY FACTS

A MIXTURE *can be separated into its basic substances by physical means.*

AN ELEMENT IS A SUBSTANCE *that consists of just one kind of atom.*

THE PERIODIC TABLE *is a system for organizing the chemical elements within a chart of rows and columns.*

MOLECULES *consist of two or more atoms whose particles are chemically bound.*

From matter into elements | Atoms—building blocks of matter | The order of elements | The power of chemical bonds

MATTER—THE WORLD OF SUBSTANCES

Early humans had no explanation for the existence of a vast array of substances and their transformations. Thus they could only attribute chemical phenomena to the acts of the gods. The ancient Greek philosophers believed that all matter consisted of four elements: fire, water, air, and earth. It was not until modern times that chemical researchers succeeded in identifying the building blocks of matter. Through this they were able to give order to the various materials in the world and explain chemical changes between substances.

Matter (Latin: "materia," or "material") exists everywhere except in an absolute vacuum (Latin: "vacuus," or "empty").

CHEMISTRY

FROM MATTER INTO ELEMENTS

Compounds, mixtures, and elements differ by the ways they are separated into component parts. An element consists of atoms and cannot be broken down by physical or chemical means.

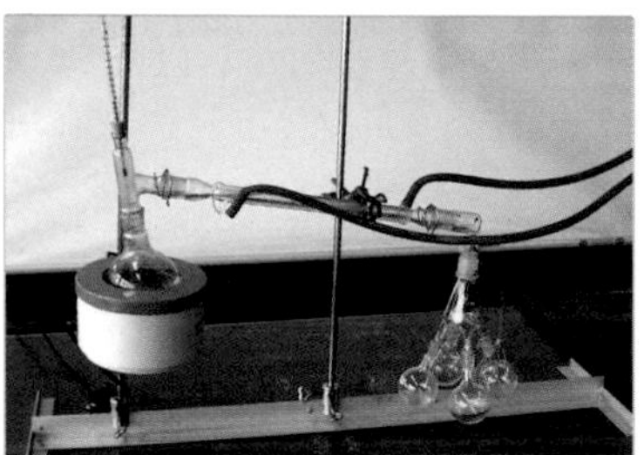

During the distillation process, a mixture is heated. The resulting vapor is condensed into its component parts.

As Anton Chekhov said during the 19th century, "For the chemist there is nothing impure on this Earth." There may have been a deeper meaning in this Russian author's words but from the scientist's standpoint, Chekhov was mistaken. For the chemist there is a big difference between mixtures and compounds.

Separating Mixtures

Wine is an example of a mixture. If wine is heated, it starts to boil at around 172°F (78°C). After a certain length of time, the boiling point will step up to 212°F (100°C). If a pure alcohol such as ethanol is heated, the temperature remains constant at 172°F (78°C). Ethanol is a pure compound, while wine contains a number of substances, mostly ethanol and water. If the fumes that form as wine is heated are directed through a tube and into another container, the fumes condense into a liquid state. The resulting fluid drips into the other container and the ethanol is thereby separated from the wine. This separation occurs because of the different boiling points of both water and ethanol.

In addition to this distillation process, there are other ways to separate the component parts of mixtures. With filtration, it is possible to use the different sizes of particles and with liquid chromatography, the different solubility of substances.

Diamonds and graphite both come from the same element: carbon.

Brass is a mixture of both copper and zinc; bronze consists of copper and tin.

The best reply to the question of how mixtures and compounds differ is that mixtures can be separated by physical means, but compounds cannot.

Kinds of Mixtures

Mixtures such as wine often have an outwardly uniform appearance. Another example is seawater, which consists of salt dissolved in water. Alloys such as brass or bronze are mixtures of metals with special material characteristics. Bronze is copper with up to one-third part tin, and brass is copper with zinc added. In emulsions such as oil-and-vinegar salad dressings, on the other hand, one can clearly see drops of one type of liquid within a second type of liquid.

Compounds and Elements

Although compounds—in contrast to mixtures—cannot be separated into their component parts by mechanical means, most of them can be broken down further by other means. Water, for example, will separate into oxygen and hydrogen when an electric current is applied. Oxygen and hydrogen, just like iron, gold, or sulfur, cannot be further divided by chemical means. All of these substances are elements.

Carbon provides an example of how elements can take different appearances. There are two very common formations of carbon: One modification of carbon can be found on the neck of a wealthy woman (diamond); another helps children in their first attempts at writing (graphite).

The mixture of oil- and water-based liquids creates an emulsion.

Extraction of salt is achieved by crystallizing sodium chloride in seawater.

INSIDER KNOWLEDGE

OVER 30 MILLION *different substances are currently catalogued in the "Chemical Abstracts" database.*

ALMOST 12 MILLION *of these are commercially viable chemicals.*

EVERY YEAR, *400,000 new substances are described in the technical publications worldwide.*

ATOMS—BUILDING BLOCKS OF MATTER

The first step to modern chemistry was the recognition that atoms existed. Today, it is now known that every element consists of a specific kind of atom.

The British physicist Ernest Rutherford examines the structure of the atom.

At the start of the 19th century, John Dalton, a science teacher in Manchester, promoted the theory that all matter is composed of indivisible atoms. The atoms of any element are identical in their mass and chemical make-up.

In the years that followed, atoms were assumed by scientists to be round elastic objects that were uniformly filled with matter. But later in that century, this view was definitively refuted when physicist J. J. Thomson showed that negatively charged particles, electrons, can be separated from their atoms. Furthermore, Henri Becquerel was actually able to observe natural radioactivity. Through these discoveries, physicists began to understand that the atom could be split.

Mainly Empty Space

At the start of the 20th century, Ernest Rutherford bombarded a thin sheet of gold leaf with alpha particles emitted from a radioactive element. Almost all of the particles penetrated the gold leaf with no deflection; but a few were deflected and some even bounced back. "It was unbelievable, almost as if you were to fire a 38 cm artillery shell at a piece of tissue paper and have it come back and hit you," wrote Rutherford later. He concluded that the atoms in the gold leaf consisted mostly of empty space, but at the same time there was a mass in the center of these atoms that could deflect the incoming particles. This led Rutherford to the idea that atoms are constructed of a positively charged core and a negatively charged shell. This idea was further developed by Niels Bohr and other researchers. According to them, the shell of an atom consists of electrons that circle about a nucleus, which is made up of protons and neutrons. Electrons move in fixed orbits, much like the planets.

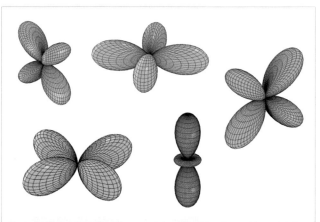

Electrons do not rotate in orbits around the atom. According to this model, they exist in orbitals (blue areas) of probability.

Wave Mechanics and Orbitals

Bohr's model for the atom was not, however, able to explain either the existence of atoms with multiple electrons or how atoms are bound together. Another problem for physicists ranging from Bohr to Schrodinger to De Broglie was that it seemed that for half the time they would be applying the classical laws of physics, and the other half they would be applying the laws of quantum physics.

Today, the wave mechanical view of the atom holds that the position and momentum of an electron cannot be simultaneously determined exactly. From this perspective, there are no more electron orbits. Instead the movement of electrons is described and determined by a mathematical function—the wave function. The wave function value yields the probability of an electron being present within a given small volume. The region in which an electron may be found around an atom has a characteristic shape; this region is called an "orbital."

Bohr and His Atom Model

THE BOHR ATOM MODEL is based on a bold hypothesis. From the perspective of classical physics, the electrons that orbit around the nucleus of the atom would release their energy in the form of radiation. If this was true, the electrons would eventually crash into the nucleus of the atom. The physicist Niels Bohr advanced the proposition that this is exactly what electrons do not do. Starting from this assumption, he developed his own archetype of the atom. Using this model, Bohr could explain the wavelength of the light radiated by hydrogen atoms that were in an excited state.

Electrons move around the nucleus of an atom in an orbit that is identified by an integer "n" called the orbit's primary quantum number.

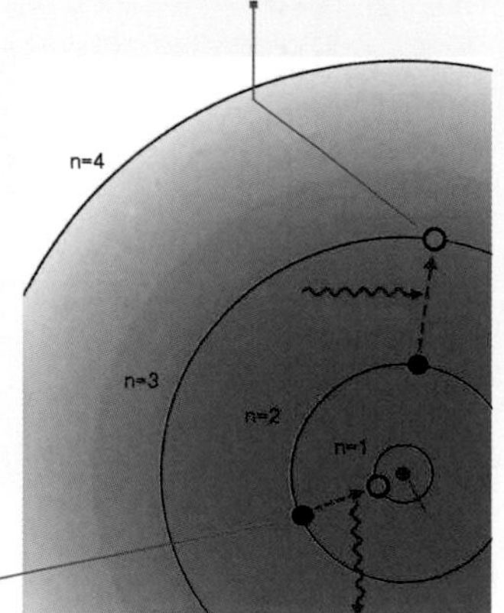

When an electron jumps from an orbit with a larger radius to an orbit with a smaller radius, a photon is radiated. If the electron moves to an orbit with a larger radius, it means the electron "swallowed up" or absorbed a photon.

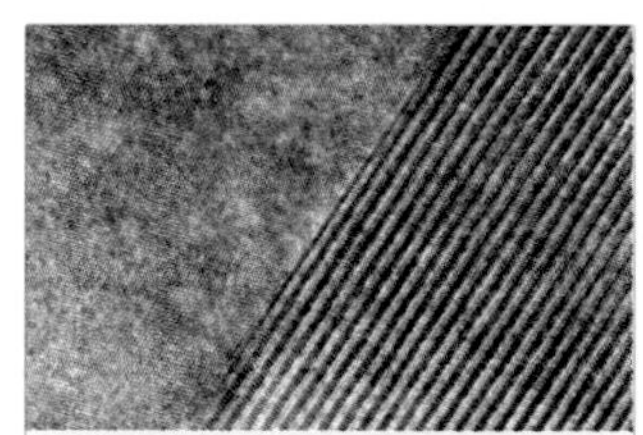

With the use of an electron microscope one can see that the silicon atom has a rough granular structure.

21ST CENTURY

TODAY ONE CAN OBSERVE *directly what was once just a logical concept. New instrumentation and the vast improvement in microscopic resolution permit the actual observation of individual atoms.*

THROUGH THE USE *of a scanning electron microscope (SEM) scientists can even observe electron clouds inside an atom.*

THE ORDER OF ELEMENTS

It hangs on the walls of every chemistry classroom in the world: the periodic table. It currently contains 111 elements, which are arranged according to their properties.

People thought about the possibility of elements being arranged in some kind of order even before Rutherford and Bohr developed their models for the structure of atoms. In 1829, the German chemist Johann Döbereiner observed several groups of three elements each that possessed similar chemical properties. He called these groups triads. One of the triads was composed of the colored gases chlorine, bromine, and iodine. The metals lithium, sodium, and potassium, which are highly reactive with other elements, formed another triad. What caught Döbereiner's attention was that the atomic mass of an element in the middle of the triad is approximately the same as the average of the mass of both of the other elements.

Recognition by the Czars

The mid-19th century witnessed the discovery of numerous new elements—an important step in being able to classify them into a systematic order. In 1869, the Russian Dimitri Mendeleyev and the German Lothar Meyer independently developed the periodic table. Mendeleyev claimed that "the atomic weight determines the character of an element." Accordingly, he classified the elements in ascending order of atomic weights and placed related elements under each other in vertical columns. In the table that he had generated, Mendeleyev left the spaces under aluminum and silicon empty to accommodate elements that had yet to be discovered. The discovery of gallium and germanium about 100 years later, which contained the properties predicted by Mendeleyev, contributed immensely to the acceptance of the periodic table in the scientific world.

Dimitri Mendeleyev devised a systematic relationship between the atomic weight and the chemical properties of atoms.

The Periodic Table Today

The periodic table displays the elements with their chemical symbols and arranges them in rows according to their atomic number, which is also displayed. This is the number of positive elementary particles (protons) in the nucleus of the atom. As atoms are electrically neutral, the atomic number is also equal to the number of electrons in an atom, which are found in the orbitals or "shells" surrounding the nucleus. Hydrogen atoms (element symbol: H) have the simplest structure since the nucleus contains only one proton. As the atomic number increases, so does the mass or weight of the atoms. The uranium atom contains 92 protons and is the largest atom found in nature.

The number of electrons in the outermost atomic shell largely determines the chemical properties of elements. Elements with similar properties are arranged in groups vertically. For example, all elements of the eighth main group ("noble gases") have eight electrons in the outer shell, with the exception of helium, and do not react with other elements. The table's horizontal rows are "periods" (1 to 7) and the vertical columns are "groups" (1 to 18).

21ST CENTURY

NEW ELEMENTS *can be produced by scientists through the nuclear fusion of atoms; however, they possess a short half-life.*

WITH RESPECT TO FUTURE *elements that can be produced by the fusion of atomic nuclei, based on predictions, atoms with atomic numbers of about 114 and neutron numbers of 185 could prove to be relatively stable.*

Periodic Table of Elements

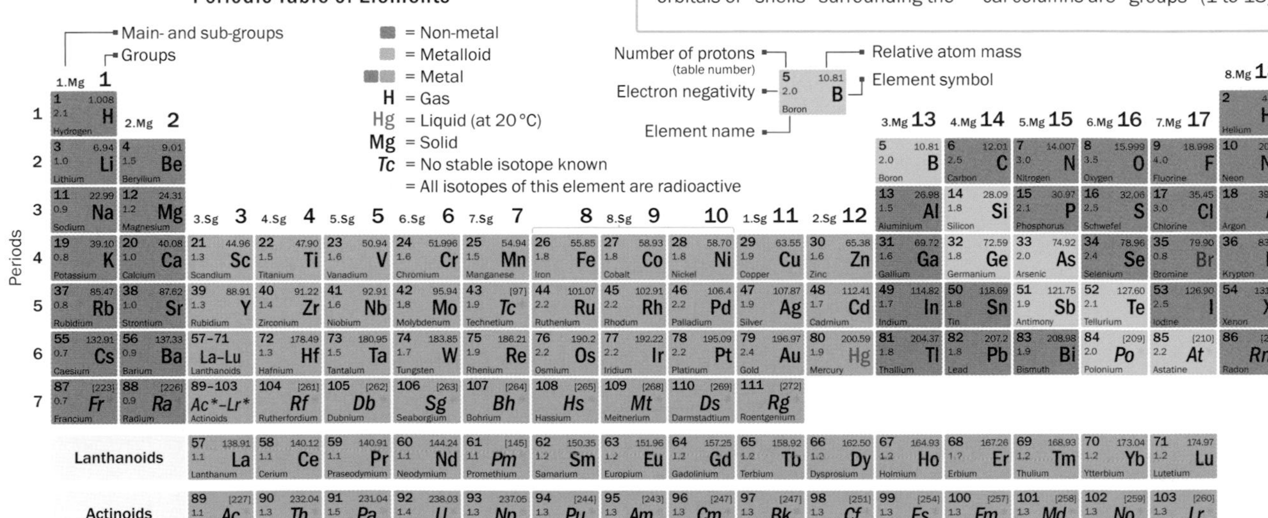

Main- and sub-groups
Groups
= Non-metal
= Metalloid
= Metal
H = Gas
Hg = Liquid (at 20 °C)
Mg = Solid
Tc = No stable isotope known
= All isotopes of this element are radioactive

Number of protons (table number) – Relative atom mass – Electron negativity – Element symbol – Element name (example: 5, 10.81, 2.0, B, Boron)

Periods	1.Mg 1	2.Mg 2	3.Sg 3	4.Sg 4	5.Sg 5	6.Sg 6	7.Sg 7	8	8.Sg 9	10	1.Sg 11	2.Sg 12	3.Mg 13	4.Mg 14	5.Mg 15	6.Mg 16	7.Mg 17	8.Mg 18
1	1 1.008 2.1 H Hydrogen																	2 4.00 He Helium
2	3 6.94 1.0 Li Lithium	4 9.01 1.5 Be Beryllium											5 10.81 2.0 B Boron	6 12.01 2.5 C Carbon	7 14.007 3.0 N Nitrogen	8 15.999 3.5 O Oxygen	9 18.998 4.0 F Fluorine	10 20.18 Ne Neon
3	11 22.99 0.9 Na Sodium	12 24.31 1.2 Mg Magnesium											13 26.98 1.5 Al Aluminium	14 28.09 1.8 Si Silicon	15 30.97 2.1 P Phosphorus	16 32.06 2.5 S Schwefel	17 35.45 3.0 Cl Chlorine	18 39.95 Ar Argon
4	19 39.10 0.8 K Potassium	20 40.08 1.0 Ca Calcium	21 44.96 1.3 Sc Scandium	22 47.90 1.5 Ti Titanium	23 50.94 1.6 V Vanadium	24 51.996 1.6 Cr Chromium	25 54.94 1.5 Mn Manganese	26 55.85 1.8 Fe Iron	27 58.93 1.8 Co Cobalt	28 58.70 1.8 Ni Nickel	29 63.55 1.9 Cu Copper	30 65.38 1.6 Zn Zinc	31 69.72 1.6 Ga Gallium	32 72.59 1.8 Ge Germanium	33 74.92 2.0 As Arsenic	34 78.96 2.4 Se Selenium	35 79.90 2.8 Br Bromine	36 83.80 Kr Krypton
5	37 85.47 0.8 Rb Rubidium	38 87.62 1.0 Sr Strontium	39 88.91 1.3 Y Rubidium	40 91.22 1.4 Zr Zirconium	41 92.91 1.6 Nb Niobium	42 95.94 1.8 Mo Molybdenum	43 [97] 1.9 *Tc* Technetium	44 101.07 2.2 Ru Ruthenium	45 102.91 2.2 Rh Rhodium	46 106.4 2.2 Pd Palladium	47 107.87 1.9 Ag Silver	48 112.41 1.7 Cd Cadmium	49 114.82 1.7 In Indium	50 118.69 1.8 Sn Tin	51 121.75 1.9 Sb Antimony	52 127.60 2.1 Te Tellurium	53 126.90 2.5 I Iodine	54 131.30 Xe Xenon
6	55 132.91 0.7 Cs Caesium	56 137.33 0.9 Ba Barium	57–71 La-Lu Lanthanoids	72 178.49 1.3 Hf Hafnium	73 180.95 1.5 Ta Tantalum	74 183.85 1.7 W Tungsten	75 186.21 1.9 Re Rhenium	76 190.2 2.2 Os Osmium	77 192.22 2.2 Ir Iridium	78 195.09 2.2 Pt Platinum	79 196.97 2.4 Au Gold	80 200.59 1.9 Hg Mercury	81 204.37 1.8 Tl Thallium	82 207.2 1.8 Pb Lead	83 208.98 1.9 Bi Bismuth	84 [209] 2.0 *Po* Polonium	85 [210] 2.2 *At* Astatine	86 [222] *Rn* Radon
7	87 [223] 0.7 *Fr* Francium	88 [226] 0.9 *Ra* Radium	89–103 *Ac*-Lr** Actinoids	104 [261] *Rf* Rutherfordium	105 [262] *Db* Dubnium	106 [263] *Sg* Seaborgium	107 [264] *Bh* Bohrium	108 [265] *Hs* Hassium	109 [268] *Mt* Meitnerium	110 [269] *Ds* Darmstadtium	111 [272] *Rg* Roentgenium							

Lanthanoids	57 138.91 1.1 La Lanthanum	58 140.12 1.1 Ce Cerium	59 140.91 1.1 Pr Praseodymium	60 144.24 1.1 Nd Neodymium	61 [145] 1.1 *Pm* Promethium	62 150.35 1.2 Sm Samarium	63 151.96 1.2 Eu Europium	64 157.25 1.2 Gd Gadolinium	65 158.92 1.2 Tb Terbium	66 162.50 1.2 Dy Dysprosium	67 164.93 1.2 Ho Holmium	68 167.26 1.2 Er Erbium	69 168.93 1.2 Tm Thulium	70 173.04 1.2 Yb Ytterbium	71 174.97 1.2 Lu Lutetium
Actinoids	89 [227] 1.1 *Ac* Actinium	90 232.04 1.3 *Th* Thorium	91 231.04 1.5 *Pa* Protactinium	92 238.03 1.4 *U* Uranium	93 237.05 1.3 *Np* Neptunium	94 [244] 1.3 *Pu* Plutonium	95 [243] 1.3 *Am* Americium	96 [247] 1.3 *Cm* Curium	97 [247] 1.3 *Bk* Berkelium	98 [251] 1.3 *Cf* Californium	99 [254] 1.3 *Es* Einsteinium	100 [257] 1.3 *Fm* Fermium	101 [258] 1.3 *Md* Mendelevium	102 [259] 1.3 *No* Nobelium	103 [260] 1.3 *Lr* Lawrencium

The periodic table of elements represents all elements in order of their atomic number. The elements in this chart are arranged horizontally in periods, and vertically in groups according to their chemical properties. Within the main groups, further differentiation is made based on the element's metallic properties (e.g., electrical conductivity). As compared to the main groups, the elements belonging to the subgroups do not vary greatly from one another.

THE POWER OF CHEMICAL BONDS

When atoms come in contact with each other, their electron shells interact and a chemical bond is formed. These bonds are classified as covalent, ionic, or metallic.

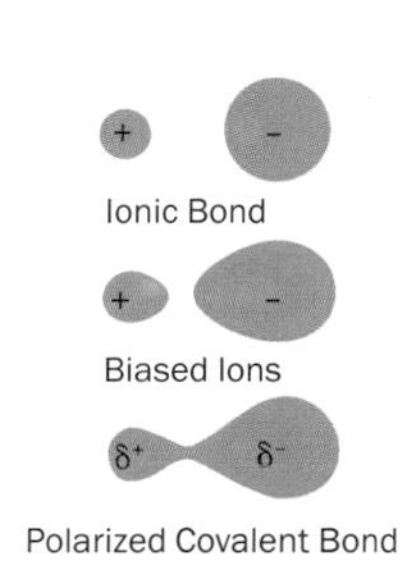

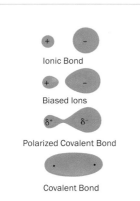

The distribution of bonding (valence) electrons is different for covalent and ionic bonds.

Under certain conditions, atoms create bonds with one another. For example, when two hydrogen atoms are far apart, they do not exert any force on each other. The moment they come into contact, this changes. According to the laws of electrostatics, the negatively charged electron shell of one atom attracts the positive nucleus of the other atom. The electron shells "coalesce" into each other and a zone of negative charge exists around both nuclei.

Attraction and Repulsion

There are, of course, limits to this process. When the nuclei come closer to each other, the force of repulsion between them increases. Hence, the atoms remain at a distance from one another with the forces of attraction and repulsion serving to maintain the distance—both atoms form a molecule.

In the case of a covalent bond between different atoms, such as hydrogen chloride, the bonding electrons are more strongly attracted to the chlorine atom than the hydrogen atom. These simple bonded molecules that come together in chemical bonds are called monomers. When there are two monomers, the compound is called a dimer; with three monomers, a trimer. The distribution of electrical charge in a hydrogen chloride molecule is unequal. Molecules like hydrogen chloride have two poles and the bonding is, therefore, characterized as polar covalent.

Stable Structure of Ions

In an extreme case, an atom can completely acquire the electrons of the other atom. Ions are thereby generated: A positively charged cation and a negatively charged anion. The force of attraction between them is very high because of their opposite charges and they build an ionic structure. Ionic structures are very stable and ionic compounds—common table salt is an example—usually have higher melting points than non-ionic compounds. Like ionic compounds, metals have a definite structure. The electrons in a metal are not bound to a particular atom. Instead they form a sea of negative charge that binds the positive nuclei together.

Molecules that are formed from covalent bonds usually comprise a few atoms—as long as they do not contain carbon atoms: Sulfur dioxide (SO_2), ammonia (NH_3), ozone (O_3), and water (H_2O) are prominent examples.

Carbon atoms not only react with atoms of other elements, they also form bonds with themselves. Most common is the covalent single bond between two carbon atoms, but carbons can also link to form linear and branched chains or rings. Certain complicated molecules are known to contain millions of these carbon atom bonds. These are very important in the production of many man-made products such as pharmaceuticals and plastics.

Ionic bond: Salt has a crystal structure composed of positive sodium atoms and negative chloride atoms.

Electronegativity

Electronegativity (EN) is a measure of how much an atom in a molecule attracts electrons in a chemical bond. Its value can vary depending on the bonding electron. In spite of this, it is useful for determining whether the bonding electrons are completely transferred to an atom. When the EN-difference of the atoms is greater than 1.8, an ionic bond is formed. When the EN-difference is very small, the bond is nonpolar covalent. The most electronegative element is fluorine with an EN value of 4.0.

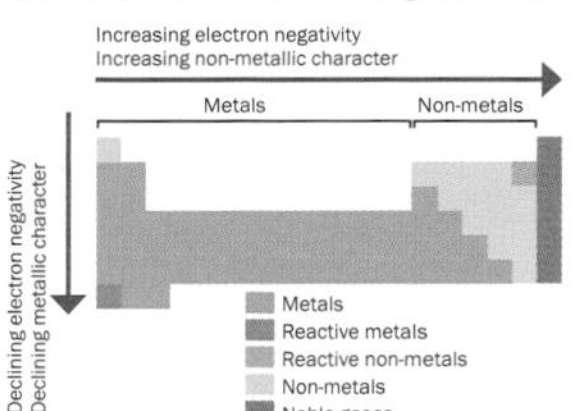

The EN decreases from top to bottom and increases from left to right (exception: noble gases).

Covalent bond: Oxygen and hydrogen share the electron bond in a water molecule.

INSIDER KNOWLEDGE

HAFNIUM CARBIDE *melts at a temperature of 7520°F (4160°C) the highest melting point known for a compound.*

COMMON SALT *(NaCl) has a melting point of 1473.8°F (801°C); the melting point of water is 32°F (0°C).*

THE HIGHEST MELTING POINT *for metals is 6191.6°F (3422°C) and is the melting point of the element tungsten.*

Metallic bond: The atoms are closely packed together.

KEY FACTS

ARTIFICIAL FERTILIZERS *and pesticides can increase crop yield many times over.*

THE ADVANTAGE OF PLASTICS *is that they are indestructible and moldable.*

THE OPTICAL AND ELECTRICAL *characteristics of semiconductors can be altered and controlled.*

ACTIVE INGREDIENTS *in medicines are mostly generated chemically.*

Chemistry and nutrition | Plastics everywhere | Semiconductors for computers and modern life | Medicines and cosmetics

SUBSTANCES OF EVERY DAY—CHEMISTRY DETERMINES OUR LIFE

Almost everyone benefits daily from the products of chemical and pharmaceutical industries. We are indebted to them for many things including a wide range of food items, effective treatment and prevention of diseases, affordable housing and furnishings, clothing, transportation, and modern information technology.

➲ *Discoveries by chemists have changed our world.*

CHEMISTRY AND NUTRITION

Without artificial fertilizers and pesticides there would not be enough food grown on Earth to satisfy our needs, even with equal distribution of agricultural output. Manufactured preservatives help prevent the wasting of food.

Today, a farmer harvests five times as much corn or maize on one acre of land as a farmer did in 1850—the year when the triumph of artificial fertilizers began. The German chemist Justus von Liebig discovered that plants extracted nutrients from the soil, which were then not available to sustain the growth of plants in the next harvest. These nutrients, especially nitrogen, phosphorus, and potassium, had to be returned to the soil in order to maintain the agricultural output. Fertilizers make this possible.

At the present time chemically generated fertilizers are designed for each crop variety based on the plants' specific nutritional requirements. Fertilizers today include calcium, magnesium, sulfur, and sometimes trace elements that play a role in plant nutrition.

Today large areas are fertilized very efficiently by using airplanes to spray the crops.

Pest Control

However, fertilizers alone are not responsible for the increased productivity in agriculture. Chemical compounds began to be used in the second half of the 19th century to fight organisms harmful to crops. For example, farmers used the "Bordeaux mixture" (burnt lime in a copper sulfate solution) against fungal diseases that threatened their yield.

In the 1940s, it was found that chlorinated hydrocarbons and organic phosphorus compounds could effectively destroy insects. Meanwhile, agriculturalists used herbicides to suppress even grasses and weeds that take away light, water, and nutrients from crops.

New pesticides are constantly being developed to make them more effective. One reason this is necessary is that fungi and insects start to resist or become insensitive to the old agents. A farmer 50 years ago might use 11 lbs (5 kg) of pesticides on one acre of crops. Using modern agents, a farmer can get the same amount of pest control with less than 3.5 oz (100 g).

Preservatives

One of the reasons famine was common in earlier times is that food would spoil. Preservatives repel insects and prevent the growth of fungi. In order to preserve food for a longer time, preservatives such as sorbic acid, nitrites, vitamin C, and vitamin E are added, which prevents the multiplication of pathogens. The possible negative effects of food preservatives are being debated today.

Fresh fruits and vegetables are rich in vitamins, but they perish quickly.

The use of preservatives gives many food goods a long shelf life.

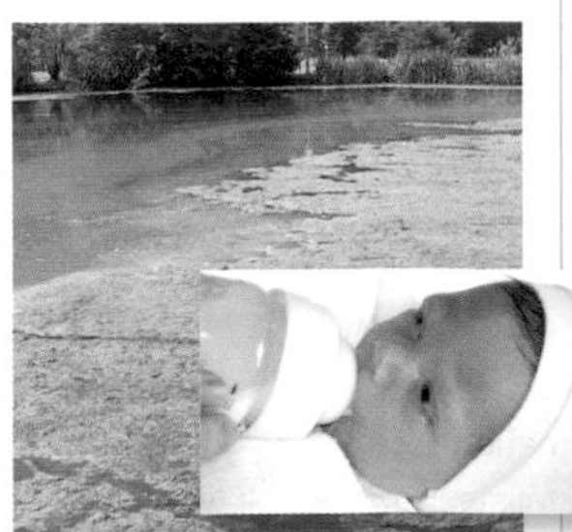

Nitrate

Nitrate is an indispensable component of fertilizers. However, with rain, excess nitrate seeps easily into the groundwater. According to the World Health Organization, drinking water should contain no more than 50 ppm (parts per million) of nitrate. Babies have died because their meals were prepared with well-water that had a high concentration of nitrate. A further problem is that nitrate, which flushes into lakes and rivers, disturbs the biological equilibrium. Algae begin to grow excessively while other water organisms die off.

above: *Strong growth of algae in overfertilized waters; clean drinking water is important for the health of babies.*

INSIDER KNOWLEDGE

"FUNCTIONAL FOOD" *refers to fresh or processed food with health benefits in addition to the nutritional content.*

EXAMPLES *are yogurts containing cultures of live organisms, and bread with omega-3 fatty acids added.*

EXPERTS *estimate that the world market for functional food is around 80 billion dollars (62 billion euros).*

PLASTICS EVERYWHERE

Upholstered furniture, lacquers and paint, DVDs, casings of household appliances, and airbags for cars are some of the things made from plastics. This list could be continued endlessly because plastics are cheap and easy to process.

When plastic melts, it becomes a pliable substance that is pourable.

Plastics have often been regarded as a symbol of waste and contamination of the Earth for environmentalists. However, while this opinion is fairly widespread, there are some voices of praise, such as the French philosopher Roland Barthes who said, "Plastics are the first magical materials that are ready for everyday use." The economic importance of this material is in fact huge. One of the negative qualities attributed to plastics is that they are generally nonbiodegradable. Because of this, the use of recycled plastic products is an imperative part of protecting the environment.

Composition

Plastics consist of macromolecules, which are built up from thousands of small groups of atoms bound together to become one large molecule. For this reason, plastics are called polymers, from the Greek terms *poly* ("multiple") and *meros* ("parts"). Thermoplastics soften and are moldable when they are warmed up. Polyethylene is a thermoplastic and is also the most produced plastic in the world. Other thermoplastics include polyamides and polycarbonates. Thermosetting plastics do not soften when heated, but instead they change color or generally decompose. The most important examples of such plastics are synthetic resins, which are used for lacquers. Elastomers are polymers that can be deformed at room temperature through exposure to extreme pressure or tension, but then are able to return to their original shape. Typical examples of elastomers are foam materials and polyesters.

Shown here in production is polyurethane-leather, which is both wind- and waterproof, but allows sweat to evaporate.

Light and Moldable

Plastics have replaced traditional materials such as wood or metal in many areas because of their beneficial features. Their primary advantages are their lightness and resistance to damage from weather and chemicals. Plastics can also absorb sound as well as insulate electricity and heat.

Yet another advantage has contributed significantly to the ubiquity of plastics. They can be made into any shape cheaply, primarily through injection molding. With this method, the granules of a thermoplastic substance are melted and injected under pressure into the hollow area of what is called a tool or a mold. The mold determines the form and surface of the finished product.

Recycling

Since plastics are frequently used for mainly short-lived products, the result is an increasing disposal problem. Furthermore, the advantage of their chemical stability later becomes a disadvantage as plastics decompose very slowly in trash dumps and clutter roadways. For this reason, the recycling of plastics is particularly important.

What Makes a Plastic Thermoplastic?

MOST PLASTICS that are encountered on a daily basis melt when heated. The reason is that their threadlike molecular chains are not connected to each other by other chemical compounds, as is the case with rubber, for instance. The molecules in thermoplastics are held together only through weak molecular forces, which means that they slide past each other at high temperatures.

The individual molecular chains slide past each other when they are heated if they are not linked with other compounds. As a result the plastic melts.

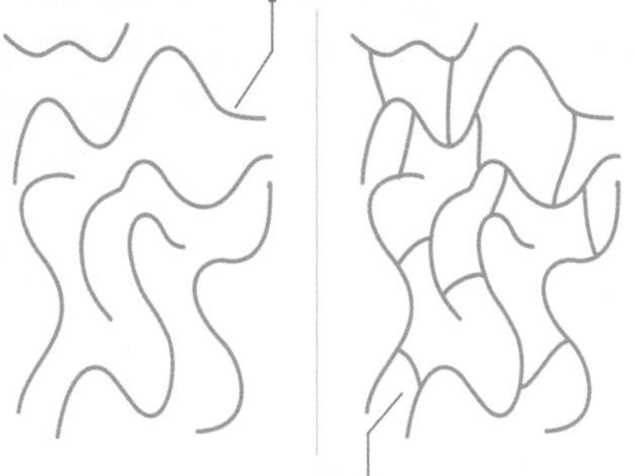

In the case of thermosetting plastics, the molecular chains are cross-linked and break arbitrarily during heating. As a result the plastic decomposes.

Polycarbonate

CDs, CD-ROMs, and DVDs are used today in numbers so large it is difficult to imagine. The 40 billion discs produced just in 2005 would have created a tower about 30,000 miles (48,000 km) high if the discs were stacked on top of one another. Each disc is mainly made up of a polycarbonate.

Thermoplastics made of polycarbonates are widely used because they are transparent, inherently stable, mechanically firm, and resistant to light. Among the many things made out of them are stadium and winter garden roofing, protective glasses and sunglasses, headlights, and covers for signal and control lights.

above: *CDs made of polycarbonate are coated with aluminum varnish.*

During recycling, plastics are collected, sorted, chopped, melted, and then remolded.

21ST CENTURY

ORGANIC LIGHT-EMITTING DIODES *(OLED's) use advanced organic polymers to display bright colors on very thin screens.*

FLEXIBLE, ELECTRONIC *screens made of plastic compounds may replace traditional ink and paper.*

TECHNIQUES *that use plastics to produce raw materials with a high degree of purity will become economically worthwhile.*

CHEMISTRY

SEMICONDUCTORS FOR COMPUTERS AND MODERN LIFE

In the 19th century, it was discovered that the conductivity of certain materials was dependent on temperature. Materials with semiconductor properties are the basis of modern information.

Computers, mobile phones, digital cameras, space travel, medical technologies such as computed tomography, and artificial pacemakers would be unthinkable today without parts made from semiconductors. At 68°F (20°C) these materials conduct electricity better than insulators, but not as well as metals. The conductivity of semiconductors is strongly dependent on temperature; it generally increases with rising heat.

Silicon wafers (in foreground) are semiconductors for electronic components and are used to manufacture microchips.

Upon hearing the word "semiconductor," one commonly thinks of silicon. In fact, it is the most technologically important material, but more than 600 inorganic semiconductors are also known. Some of the most important are the III-V semiconductors—like gallium arsenide. It consists of elements in the third and fifth group of the periodic table.

This small object is a microprocessor, which is the heart of every computer.

Way to the Perfect Crystal

Semiconductors are mostly used in the form of close-to-perfect crystals. They are produced through piece-by-piece melting of a manufactured bar of semiconductor material. By slow cooling, the atoms get arranged in a uniform atomic structure and the semiconductor is crystallized. A variant of this "zone-by-zone" melting is used to clean silicon. In order to produce a very thin layer of crystal, the gaseous semiconductor compounds are condensed on a cold carrier surface. Today, the methods used to structure the crystal's atomic positions have become increasingly important.

The cleansing and transformation of silicon to single crystals is very energy intensive.

Desired Donor Atoms

A semiconductor is a solid whose conductivity can be controlled over a wide range. Semiconductors are technologically important because their conductivity can change by adding impurities. To do this, donor atoms are introduced into the semiconductor's crystalline structure. This "doping" is achieved by firing an ion beam onto the semiconductor. The higher the energy with which the ions collide against the surface of the semiconductor, the deeper they penetrate into it.

Chip Production and Application

To manufacture integrated circuits and microchips, semiconductors must not only be doped, but also provided with tiny structures. The semiconductor layers are covered with photoresist. Then, the model for the structures, the so-called mask, is transferred to the semiconductor through exposure to UV radiation or electron beams. A chemical bath separates selected portions of the coating. At the place where the varnish dissolves, acids can be used to etch away the semiconductor layer. These procedures take place in air-conditioned and clean rooms. The concentration of dust in the air is kept as low as possible. If a dust particle settles in the diminutive circuit of a microchip, then it will not work properly.

Semiconductors not only play an important role in microtechnology and information technology, but also are used to convert light energy and electrical energy into each other. Solar cells convert light into electricity, while light-emitting diodes convert electricity into light. Many common pocket calculators use solar cells for energy, and many electronic instruments use light-emitting diodes for their numerical displays.

INSIDER KNOWLEDGE

***MICROCHIPS** are produced in rooms with a maximum of one dust particle in 8 gal (30 l) of air. By way of comparison, 8 gal (30 l) of city air contains 15 million particles.*

***PERSONNEL** wear special clothes in the clean rooms; otherwise, more than 50,000 small particles could be discharged per second.*

How a Semiconductor Works

THE ELECTRONIC BAND STRUCTURE of solids explains the properties of semiconductors. Just as electrons in free atoms have energy levels, electrons in solids form energy bands. Band gaps are present between the bands of different energy. In a semiconductor, the highest energy level occupied with electrons is called the valence band and the lowest unoccupied energy level is called the conduction band.

Electrons cannot overcome the band gap in insulators. If they do, they will immediately be captured again by the huge attraction of the atomic nuclei. This is why electric current cannot flow.

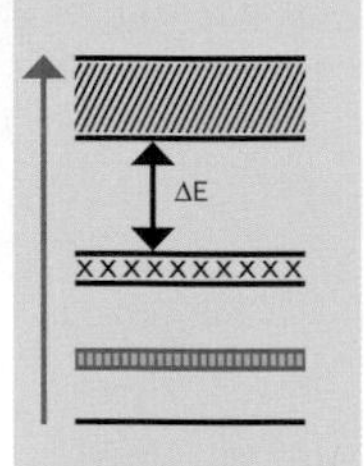

Semiconductors have a smaller band gap than insulators. The electrons can be brought to the conduction band from the valence band at room temperatures.

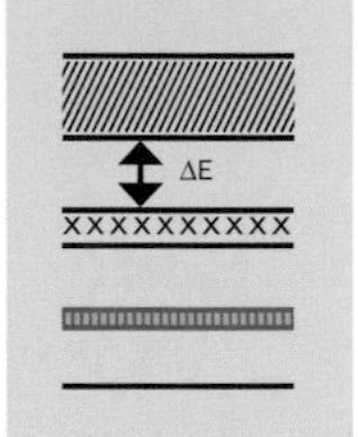

Electrons build an additional narrow band in a doped semiconductor. They can easily reach the conduction band and contribute to conductivity.

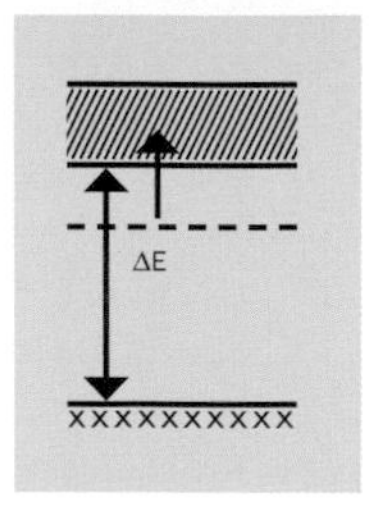

➔ see also: **Solar Cells and Electronic Components,** *Physics and Technology Chapter, pp. 134, 140*

MEDICINES AND COSMETICS

Innovative medications play a decisive role in the prevention and treatment of many diseases. More than 80 percent of the active ingredients in medicines are generated chemically.

Medicines do not guarantee eternal health, but we still owe them a lot. Polio has been eradicated in most parts of the world because of the discovery of vaccines. Those infected with HIV can delay the onset of AIDS significantly by using various drugs. Medicines can heal gastrointestinal ulcers within a week, rendering surgical treatments obsolete. Statins are a class of pharmaceutical agents that lower the cholesterol levels of people who have cardiovascular disease or are at risk of getting it. The list can go on. For example, pharmaceutical companies have suggested that it is entirely conceivable that cancers will be treatable, even in the advanced stage, via medicines or other therapies.

The ingredient salicylic acid in aspirin has been industrially produced for over 100 years.

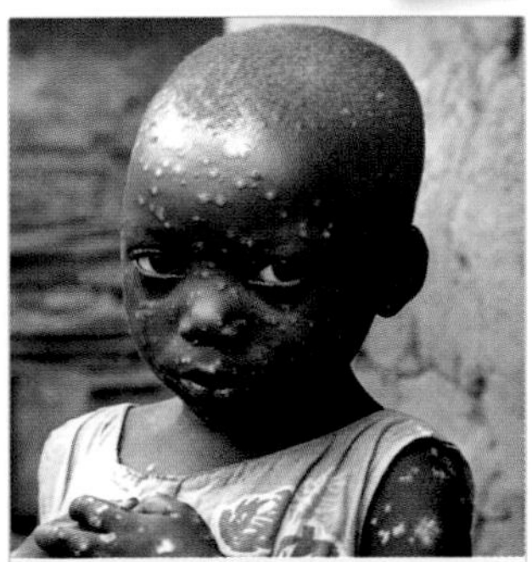

Even though vaccines have been developed, people in poorer areas still die from smallpox.

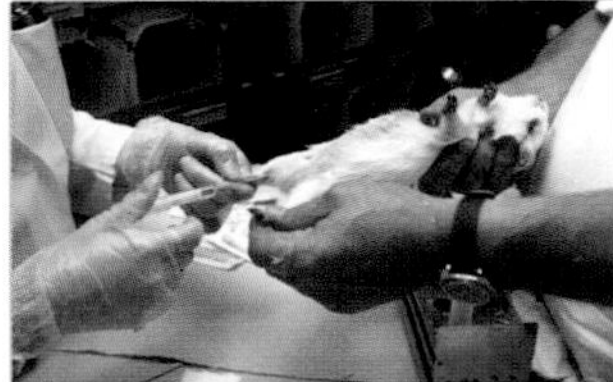

Medical tests are frequently carried out on small animals.

Search for Active Ingredients

The active ingredient is the most important component of every medicine. One example is a plant extract, which is of natural origin or generated genetically. However, many active ingredients are produced by chemical means, and it is believed this will continue to be the case in the future.

Diseases are caused mostly by invading viruses or by the wrong interaction of body molecules. For this reason, researchers, during the development of a new medicine, first try to find a target. This would be, for example, a body or viral molecule that is associated with the disease. As the agent is directed directly against this target, researchers then collect clues as to what molecules can be bound to it. There are usually a lot of possibilities for this. Researchers test hundreds of thousands of different molecules with the help of automation, or they look at the bio-molecules that come into contact with the target molecule. They then try to duplicate its form and function. Finally, they can simulate the accumulation of molecules in the target with the help of computers. If scientists have found the appropriate molecules, they investigate other matters: Are these molecules soluble in fat to the necessary degree? Do possible agents bind only to the target and not to similar biomolecules? If this is the case, the substance will likely cause undesired side effects.

Extensive Tests

Up-and-coming candidates for an active ingredient are first tested on cell cultures and animals. In these tests, the pharmaceutical researchers analyze how the agents change in the organisms as well as how they and the products of their decomposition are distributed. They also ascertain how toxic the substance is and if it damages the organism's genetic make-up.

Around three-quarters of all the agents get rejected during these trials. Clinical trials on human beings begin with the remaining agents, during which first the safety of the medicine and later its effectiveness is established.

INSIDER KNOWLEDGE

THE DEVELOPMENT *of a new medicine takes 12 years on average and costs around 800 million U.S. dollars (593 million euros).*

FOR EVERY 5,000 *active ingredients found, only one medicine reaches the market.*

MEDICINES *with around 25 new active ingredients are yearly certified worldwide.*

21ST CENTURY

MORE EFFECTIVE *medicines to control the level of blood sugar in diabetics will soon be available that do not require injection. There will also be medicines to cure multiple sclerosis.*

PREVENTIVE MEDICINE *will also have an increased focus. Vaccines against cervical cancer and shingles, for example, will also probably be developed soon.*

PRESERVATIVE AGENTS *and cosmetics are made up of a base and an active substance.*

COSMETICS *promise beauty; however, in reality their effect is at best temporary, and the dangers should not be ignored.*

Shampoo lather is caused by washing detergents. Soap molecules reduce the surface tension of water, which enables water bubbles to form and persist.

For Skin and Hair

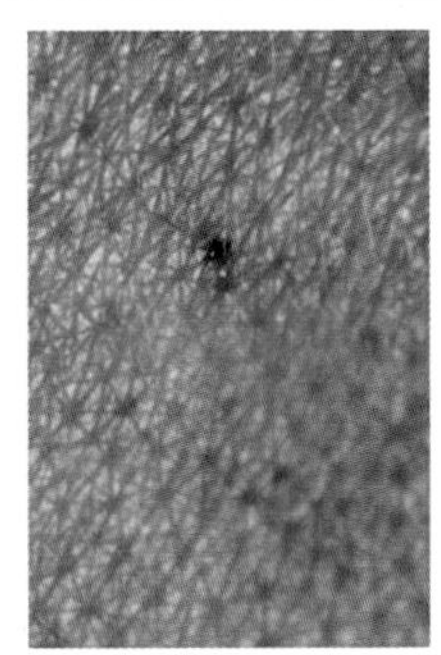

AS WITH MEDICINES there are active ingredients in cosmetics, for example, light protection materials and vitamins. The most important part of a cosmetic is the base, not the active ingredients. For shampoos and shower gels the base consists of water, conditioners, and surfactants, whose molecules reduce the surface tension of the water. For creams and lotions the base consists of water, oils, waxes, and emulsifiers. Oil-in-water creams consist of small droplets of oil dispersed in water that are easier to use and more comfortable than water-in-oil creams.

THE EFFECT OF CREAMS influences the condition and function of the outer protective layer of skin, the stratum corneum. Regardless of advertising, the effect is minimal. Cosmetics are subject to legal restrictions and should not contain any materials that can be taken into the body through the skin and reach the bloodstream.

above: *The skin has an acidic epidermis, which can be supported with preservative agents.*
left: *Scents in perfumes are synthetically produced for the most part.*

CHEMISTRY

KEY FACTS

SUBSTANCES OF THE FUTURE *include superalloys, high-performance ceramics, one-atom-thick nanotubes, and substances with shape memory.*

IN NANOTECHNOLOGY, *materials are modified molecule-by-molecule and are even developed directly from individual atoms.*

ACCORDING TO RESEARCHERS, *nanomaterials are becoming used in a wide variety of applications.*

The performance increases | The miniatures are coming

MATERIALS OF TOMORROW

Compared with the substances of today, materials of the future will be lighter, more stable, more heatproof, and more "intelligent." Science and industry especially are promising a lot from nanomaterials, a world that is visible only with the most up-to-date microscopes as it consists of structures the size of a millionth of a millimeter. Nanomaterials are reckoned to be the bearer of hope for many branches of industry, such as electronics, energy technology, medicine, and mechanical engineering.

The prefix "nano" originates from the Greek word "nanos," meaning "midget."

CHEMISTRY

THE PERFORMANCE INCREASES

Materials like steel and ceramics are still very much a hot topic today. Their properties are constantly being improved by chemists, while being fit to the most demanding requirements.

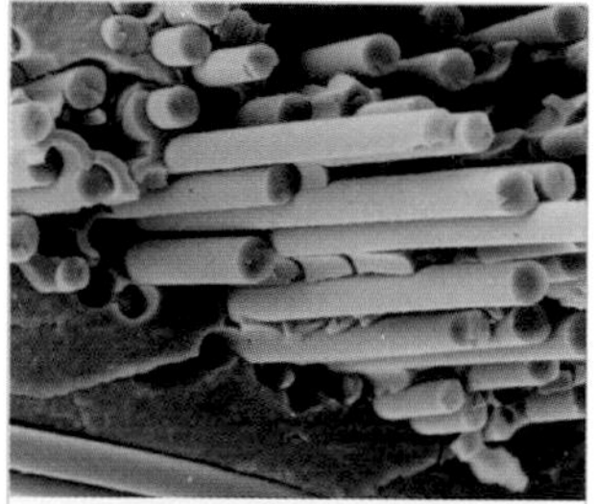

Fiber-reinforced ceramics are characterized by their stability in extreme temperatures.

Not all steel is created equal. Steel consists mostly of iron, but different steels use different alloying elements. For example, researchers have recently developed steel with a 15 percent manganese content and enriched with a 3 percent aluminum and silicon content, which does not rupture even at tensions of 1,100 megapascals. This is equivalent to the weight of ten bull elephants on an area the size of a postage stamp. In contrast, conventional steel for automobile bodies can resist only 700 megapascals.

Another new type of steel can be stretched lengthwise by around 90 percent without rupturing. This means the behavior of automobiles in a crash can be significantly improved upon. Furthermore, the use of this steel will reduce the weight of an auto body by around 20 percent. The production of super steel is very difficult; therefore it will still take a number of years before automobiles will be made with it.

Saving Energy With Ceramic

Materials that profit private companies and consumers do not necessarily benefit the environment. Energy conservationists and environmental protectionists, however, will also be satisfied if the ability of metal alloys and ceramics to withstand heat and stress can be increased further. This would result in more efficient power stations being put into operation. This means gaining more power from fossil fuels and at the same time releasing less carbon dioxide into the atmosphere. Thanks to new superalloys and ceramics, steam power stations already operate at over 1112°F (600°C) and gas turbines at over 2192°F (1200°C). Research is being carried out intensively to increase the performance of power stations even more.

The rotor sheets of a gas turbine are equipped with a protective layer of ceramic.

Present-day high-performance ceramics have almost nothing in common with the earthenware of earlier times. They can be made break-proof by reinforcing ceramic with carbon fibers. Strengthened in this way, ceramics have amazing properties. Fitted at the nose of a space shuttle, they protect it from the enormous heat that is produced during re-entry into the atmosphere of Earth. Ceramics are also used for wear-proof rotor disks for brakes due to its ability to resist corrosion and abrasion.

BESIDES THEIR VISIBLE SHAPE, *memory-metals and memory-plastics have a permanently memorized build.*

SHAPE MEMORY MATERIALS *are used in keyhole surgery (laparoscopic surgery), which is a modern operating technique that uses very small incisions.*

A stent is a tiny wire net that expands inside a diseased artery to allow blood to flow.

Substances With Memory

SELF-REPAIRING FENDERS: There's been an accident and the fender got dented. Wouldn't it be great if the dent just disappeared? This can be a reality with shape memory materials. Such substances "remember" their original shape and the memory is activated by heating. The dent could just be heated away.

MATERIALS WITH SHAPE MEMORY: Alongside plastics with shape memory there are also memory-metals. With the help of a special nickel-titanium alloy, the research satellite ENVISAT-1 could open its "eyes" after it reached its orbit in 2002. Such metals are also used in medicine. Supporting wire nettings called stents are placed in coronary arteries that are constricted by disease. They expand with the warmth of the blood, allowing blood flow to occur. Researchers are experimenting with such materials, like with prototypes for a self-folding valvular transplant to enable flow in an artery.

right: *Earth observation satellite ENVISAT-1*

THE MINIATURES ARE COMING

Products made with nanomaterials are already being produced. It is expected that they will be used more and more in our day-to-day life in the years to come.

A nanometer (0.000000001 m) is to a meter what the diameter of a hazelnut is to the diameter of Earth. Those who produce, analyze, or use controlled structures in an order of magnitude of less than 100 nanometers work in the world of nanotechnology. In this world, the classic principles of physics and chemistry are not necessarily followed. It is this that makes the world of nanotechnology exciting for scientists and businesspeople. Research is primarily focused on nanostructured surfaces, nanoparticles, and mixing nanoparticles with materials such as plastics.

Self-cleaning Lotus effect: Honey does not stick to a spoon coated with nanoparticles.

The Path to Nanoparticles

There are two basically different strategies for the production of nanoparticles. The first is to reduce structures and objects to a desired size. The semiconductor industry currently follows this method when it miniaturizes microchips. Alternatively, objects can be built up through thc controlled manipulation of individual atoms or molecules. A tool used for doing this is the scanning tunneling microscope. Scientists using the scanning tip can move the atoms to-and-fro, much like billiard balls on a tablc. They can also merge them into larger entities. However, this procedure is too time consuming and expensive for industrial mass production. Hence, many researchers are looking for ways to get the atomic and molecular components to organize themselves independently in the final structure.

From Sun Protection to Computers

Nanotechnology has already penetrated a number of areas within daily life through the controlled addition of nanoparticles to many substances. Because of nanotechnology, sunscreens protect against UV radiation much better now than ever before while windshields reflcct sunlight and heat more effectively. Wafer-thin coatings make automobile paint and plastic glasses scratch-free and mirrors that do not mist up. Through the "Lotus effect," nanostructured substances do not allow dirt to gather; this principle has led to the creation of self-cleaning bathtubs and roofing tiles.

Researchers have already achieved results with nanomaterials that will soon be manufactured in other areas. In medicine, there is hope that the surfaces of nanoparticles can be coated with biological matter in such a way that the nanoparticles can lock themselves onto cancerous cells. Nanocontainers can then be loaded with substances that kill the cancer cells. Alternatively, the formation of blood vessels that supply cancerous tumors can be suppressed.

For the computer industry, nanomaterials open the door for even smaller circuits. Transistors and simple logical circuits have been manufactured recently with carbon nanotubes. Carbon nanotubes consist of one-atom-thick graphite sheets that are rolled up into a single seamless cylinder. Transistors made from nanotubes can possibly replace transistors made from silicon, whose miniaturization has reached its physical limits. The use of nanoparticles is in development in many different areas, such as the future production of improved adhesives, higher performance batteries, unforgeable documents, fuel cells, and energy converters.

A model of a carbon nanotube: Using carbon nanotubes, complex circuits can be made that have a very small surface area.

Properties of Nanomaterials

The properties of materials often change in an astonishing way when the size of objects is reduced by nanotechnology. For example, a gold coin is usually thought to be beautiful and precious. It also has very low chemical reactivity. A gold particle of few nanometers, on the other hand, takes on the color of red wine and can accelerate chemical reactions as a catalyst. The reason lies in the changed relationship between volume and surface area. Nanostructures have a larger structure in relation to their volumes compared with objects of the "large world." The larger the surface area, the greater is the possibility of chemical and physical exchange with the environment.

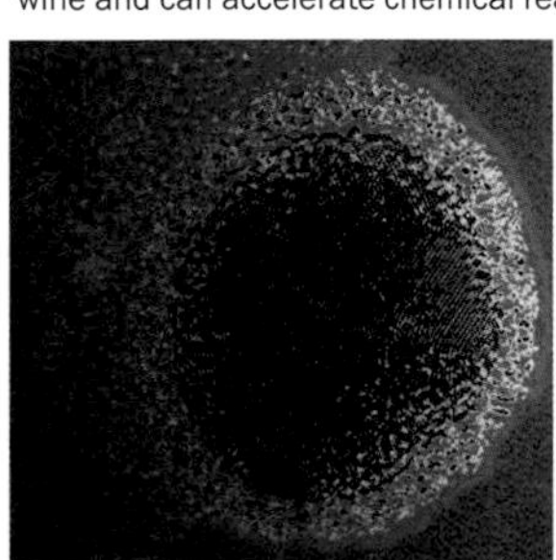

Nanoparticles from crystallized gold are not golden in color, but rather their color depends on their size.

The tip of a scanning tunneling microscope navigating over atoms. A nanostructure can be modified in a very controlled manner.

INSIDER KNOWLEDGE

NANOTECHNOLOGY *is believed to be an extremely promising technology of the future.*

IN 2004, *there was around 1.6 million dollars (1.2 million euros) supporting the industry in the U.S.*

THE EUROPEAN UNION *is investing even more.*

THE WORLD MARKET *for nanoparticles for metallics was estimated to be 900 million dollars in 2005.*

CHEMISTRY

Monographic Boxes

Analytic Boxes

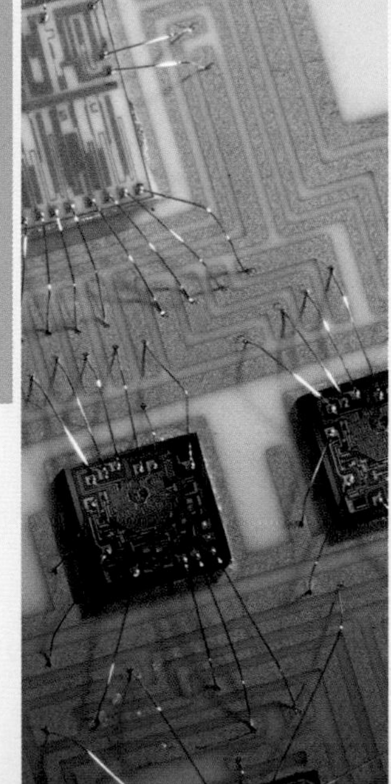

PHYSICS AND TECHNOLOGY

Physics is the science that explores the fundamental cause-and-effect relationship in natural phenomena using mathematics and logics. Its theoretical models are continuously checked against the results of experiments. Research subjects range from electricity and thermodynamics to the theory of relativity. The findings of physics are used in all areas of engineering. This includes the means of propulsion in vehicles, the structure of buildings, the creation of energy, production processes, and electrotechnology such as computers and media like television and mobile phones. Much of the modern world technologies owe their existence to the understanding of the principles of physics.

KEY FACTS

ANCIENT PHILOSOPHERS *developed theories about the material world.*

THE REGULARITY *of physical processes allows predictions to be made about them.*

ALL TECHNICAL APPLICATIONS, *from pulleys to nuclear fission, take advantage of physical laws.*

THE FORMULATION *of a theory of everything is an unattained goal of physicists.*

Mechanics | Optics | Electricity and magnetism | Atoms and radioactivity | Thermodynamics | Theory of relativity

BASICS OF PHYSICS

Scientific research within the field of physics has led to key innovations that are indispensable foundations of modern technologies. New areas of research, along with the classical research areas, have emerged through interdisciplinary approaches, for example, physical chemistry and biophysics. However, the development of a theory of everything that will unify all the known physical theories is, to this day, an unattained and grandiose dream of physicists.

Physics deals with the observation and description of phenomena of an inanimate nature.

MECHANICS

Many mechanical phenomena were applied long before they were investigated scientifically. Intensive research is carried out today in many new areas, e.g., condensed matter physics.

Mechanics studies the movement of objects and the forces acting on them. Among the factors that are considered are: speed and acceleration; weight and force; and momentum and energy. Mechanics also studies periodic motion such as the orbiting of planets, the motion of a pendulum, and the behavior of waves in matter. Devices that use the basic concepts of mechanics include levers, springs, gyroscopes, gears, pulleys, and pendulums.

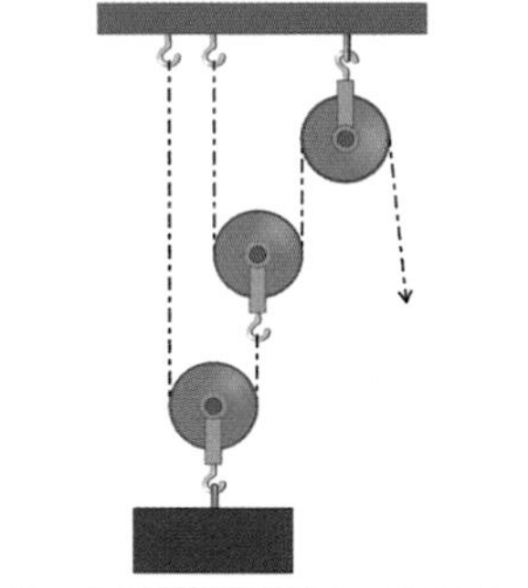

A pulley reduces the force required to lift a body by increasing the distance the force acts through. The work done remains the same.

Newtonian Mechanics

The foundation of mechanics was developed by Sir Isaac Newton (1643–1727). He discovered the basic relationship between force, acceleration, and mass. Newton described speed (v) as a distance (x) that is covered in a certain time (t): ($v = \Delta x/\Delta t$). The acceleration (a) describes how quickly speed itself changes: ($a = \Delta v/\Delta t$). In order to accelerate a resting object to a certain speed in a certain length of time, a force (F) must be applied to the object. The amount of acceleration will depend on the mass of the object. The heavier the object, the greater the force that needs to be applied in order to give it a certain acceleration. The resistance with which an object opposes its acceleration is called inertia.

Complex Systems

More complex than the rectilinear motion of objects are circular motion and other kinds of periodic motion. Calculations are even more complex if ideal conditions are not assumed and friction (for example, aerodynamic resistance) is considered. The rotational motion of three-dimensional objects, such as a gyroscope, is also very complex.

Mechanical Energy

Energy occupies a central significance (p. 130) in many areas of science and technology. In mechanics, energy is the ability to do a certain amount of work (W). If a body possesses energy it is capable of performing work by transferring its energy to another body.

If a liter of water with a mass of 1 kilogram is lifted 1 meter high in one second, one joule of energy is transferred to the water while one watt of power is generated. This one joule of energy is created in the form of potential energy. This potential energy can, for example, be converted into kinetic energy by pouring the water through a water wheel and then to electrical energy with a generator.

The Foucault pendulum always swings in the same direction. What moves is the Earth beneath it.

In a vacuum, without air resistance, the feather falls as fast as the lead ball. The force of gravity is directly proportional to the mass.

Conservation of Linear Momentum

THE CONSERVATION of momentum can be seen with a series of pendulums, one next to the other. Momentum is defined as the product of mass and velocity. If a single ball is raised, it swings down and transfers its momentum to the adjacent ball, which in turn passes the momentum onto the next ball. The end ball swings off in the same direction with the same velocity as the first one. That the mass of the balls is the same is shown by the fact that raising two balls simultaneously causes two balls to swing out on the other side. An ideal system, without air resistance or friction, would swing forever.

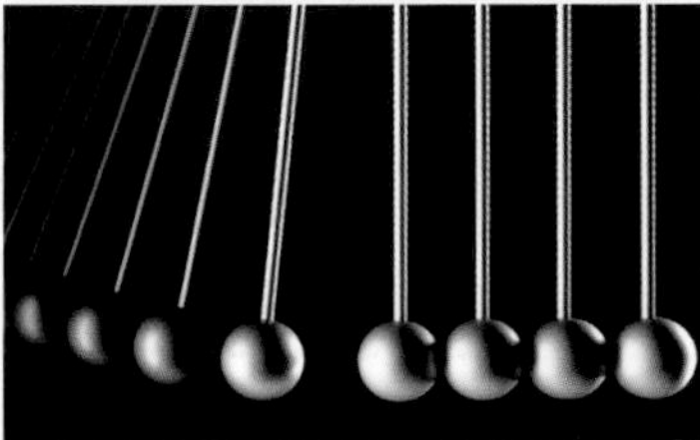

This series of pendulums is a popular desk toy that can be used to demonstrate laws of physics.

OPTICS

Optics means more than making better lenses and encompasses, among other things, research on photons, laser beams, and holography.

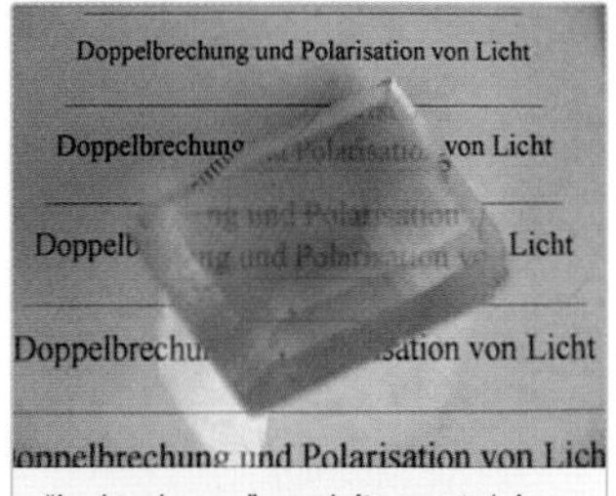

"Iceland spar," a calcite crystal, is double refracting. It splits unpolarized light into two polarized beams, causing two images.

The properties of light have a tremendous impact on our daily life as, for example, when a sheet of glass partly allows incidental light to pass and partly reflects it. The passage of light from one medium into another medium is called refraction. When a light beam strikes the interface between the media at an angle, it changes direction. Because of refraction, a prism will cause white light to be split into the different colors that it comprises. This explains just how water droplets in the atmosphere, refracted by the sunlight, result in the multi-colored occurrence of rainbows.

Magnification and Inversion

A convex lens (magnifying glass) causes parallel light rays to come together at the focal point. The distance from the focal point to the lens is called the focal distance. This effect can be used to create a magnified image of a small object or a small inverted image of a large object. Convex lenses have two convex surfaces. Lenses with concave surfaces cause light rays to diverge and create images smaller than the object. Cameras, telescopes, and microscopes use multiple lenses to create the desired images. Cameras make objects appear smaller and microscopes and telescopes make objects appear larger.

Both photos, which the eyes see, are added together in the brain to form a three-dimensional image.

Wave Particle Duality of Light

Geometric optics considers light to be made up of single rays that travel in a straight line until refracted by entering a new medium. In wave optics, the wavelengths of the different colors of light and the wave properties of light are taken into consideration. Light is considered to be an electromagnetic wave consisting of electric and magnetic fields vibrating in space. The difference between light, microwaves, and radio waves is the length of the wavelength.

Light is emitted by electrons in an atom when the electron jumps from a higher energy level to a lower one. One photon (light particle) is emitted for each electronic transition. Photons are also emitted when an electron decelerates rapidly. X-rays are created when electrons bombard a target in an X-ray tube. Does light consist of waves or particles? Neither model can explain all of the phenomena that can and have been observed. The parallel existence of the two theories is referred to as wave particle duality of light.

Lenses like this loupe either collect or disperse light. This property is used in microscopes, binoculars, and eyeglasses.

Polarized Light, Lasers, and Holograms

Light has other properties besides its wavelength. The electric and magnetic fields vibrate in a plane perpendicular to the direction of propagation. In polarized light the magnetic and electric fields are vibrating in one direction. A polarizing screen is made up of long molecules that are intended to only allow light of a certain polarity to pass through it. Polarizers are used in LCD-screens (pp. 138, 147). Laser rays are mostly polarized light with very high intensity. Other known high-tech applications of optical research are holograms. In holograms, the interference between light waves is used to generate three-dimensional images.

Why Is the Sky Blue?

Sunlight reaching the Earth's surface goes through air molecules and water droplets in the atmosphere causing the light to scatter in all directions. The amount of scattering, just like the reflection of light, depends on the wavelength of light. For example, violet light is scattered 16 times more than red light. The shorter wavelengths are scattered more strongly in all directions, so that more light of this portion of the spectrum is seen by the eye. The sky appears blue, and not violet, because the eye is more sensitive to blue.

above: *The sky only appears blue to humankind due to the biases of our perception of light.*

INSIDER KNOWLEDGE

THE LIGHT SPECTRUM *is greater than human beings can perceive.*

BEES *see ultraviolet light, but cannot see red. They can also detect the direction of polarization of light.*

RED LIGHT *is more visible in a fog than other colors due to its weak dispersion.*

➲ **see also: The Eye,** *Biology Chapter, p. 88*

ELECTRICITY AND MAGNETISM

Electrical and magnetic forces are so closely intertwined that electromagnetism is often referred to as if it were a single process. Both originate within atomic operations.

Electrical current flows when charged particles such as electrons move. Normally, matter is electrically neutral because the charges are balanced and there is no net electrical field acting on the electrons or protons. In static electricity, friction causes positive and negative charges to be separated, as when glass is rubbed by silk, resulting in the electrons transferring from the silk to the glass. A measure of the concentration of positive or negative charges is called the voltage, or electrical potential.

Induction and Electric Fields

Batteries utilize the different electronegativity (readiness to release electrons) of metals (p. 131) to produce a difference in electrical potential. The photoelectric effect converts light into an electric current. Photodiodes use light and semiconductor materials (p. 140) to generate electric currents. In electromagnetic induction, moving a wire in a magnetic field or changing the strength of the magnetic field causes charges to separate and an electrical potential to be created.

The magnetic fields of the sun cause ionized gas to erupt on its surface. The arcs follow the shape of the magnetic fields.

When a wire is connected to a battery, the terminals apply an electric field to the inside of the wire, which attracts the electrons. The greater the speed of the charges and the greater the number of charges, the greater the current. Furthermore, an electrical current flowing through a wire induces a magnetic field in the vicinity of the wire. This can clearly be seen by placing small magnets around a current-carrying wire.

Magnetism

The movement of electrical charge and electrical current generates circular magnetic fields around the direction of the current flow. The moving charges are ions (p. 111). It is believed that the Earth's magnetic field and the sun's magnetic field are caused by the motion of ions in their cores.

Magnetic fields are also generated by permanent magnets, which are made from iron and a few other metals. Atoms in matter are like tiny magnets because of the charges on the electrons and protons. Ordinarily, the atomic magnetic fields cancel themselves out. But in the case of permanent magnets, the spins of the electrons are aligned in such a way that a net magnetic field is produced.

A permanent magnet has a north pole and a south pole. At the north pole, the magnetic field leaves the magnet while at the south pole the magnetic field enters the magnet. Like poles repel each other while unlike poles attract each other.

Magnetic fields exert a force on moving electrical charges called the Lorentz force. The force is perpendicular to the direction of the magnetic field and the direction of motion of the charge. Generators and electric motors, among other devices, are based on the reciprocal effects of the Lorentz force (p. 130).

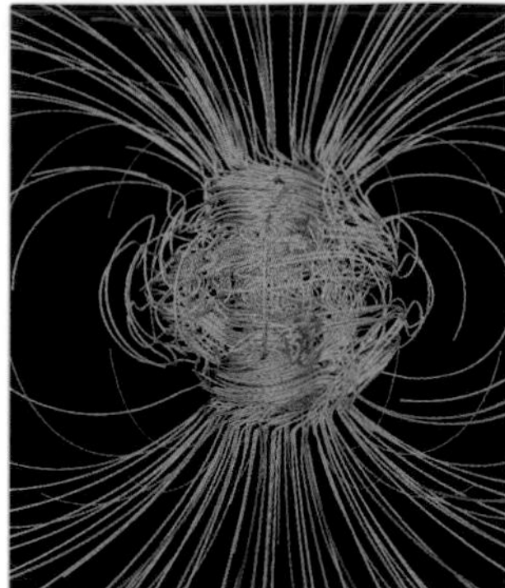

Earth's magnetism may be caused by currents in the core. The magnetic fields change directions every 250,000 years.

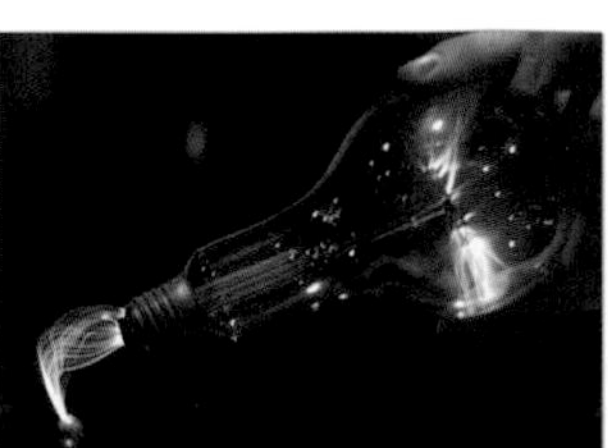

If the voltage is high enough, the current overcomes the air resistance and creates an electrical arc.

Like charges repel each other. The strands of hair on this woman's head have the same static charge on them.

The Law of Resistance

THE RELATIONSHIP between electrical current, voltage, and resistance can be understood with the analogy of a barrel filled with water that has an adjustable nozzle or valve. If the nozzle is closed, it means there is an infinitely high resistance to the water because the water does not flow. An electrical circuit with an infinitely high resistance would be one with a switch that is open, causing a break in the circuit. The current in such a circuit is zero. If the nozzle of the water barrel is opened a little, a small stream of water will come from the barrel. This corresponds to a switch in a circuit that is closed, but the circuit has a high resistance and causes a low flow of current. If the nozzle is opened wide, a lot of water flows. This corresponds to a circuit with a small resistance and hence a large flow of current. With these ideas, we can define the resistance of a circuit as the voltage divided by the current ($R = V/I$). Georg Ohm discovered the experimental fact that the resistance of a circuit does not change when you change the voltage. This gives us Ohm's law: $V = IR$.

The analogy of a barrel to explain voltage, resistance, and current.

see also: **Semiconductor**, *Chemistry Chapter, p. 102* | **The Sun**, *Universe Chapter, p. 14* | **Composition of Earth**, *Earth Chapter, p. 26*

ATOMS

The discovery of quantum mechanics in the 20th century changed the way people look at the world. The search for all the forms of matter in the universe is still being pursued.

The physicist and chemist Marie Curie discovered the radioactive elements polonium and radium.

Isotopes

The number of protons in the nucleus determines its chemical properties and what element it is. Variants of the same element with different number of neutrons are called isotopes.

The sum of neutrons and protons in an isotope is written next to the element's name or symbol. There is only one stable isotope of gold (Au-197). Carbon, on the other hand, has two stable isotopes (C-12 and C-13) and one unstable isotope (C-14). C-14 decays by emitting an electron. There are a number of other isotopes of carbon (C-10, C-11, etc.) and gold that are not found in nature but can be generated artificially in the laboratory.

Different physical models have been developed to describe the structure of atoms. According to the shell model, an atom consists of a positively charged nucleus with electrons rotating around the nucleus in circular orbits. The nucleus is made up of positively charged protons and neutral neutrons bound together by nuclear forces. The number of electrons equals the number of protons, and the electrons move in orbits that are determined by the principles of quantum mechanics. Cations are positively charged and anions are negatively charged. They are atoms with missing electrons or with extra electrons.

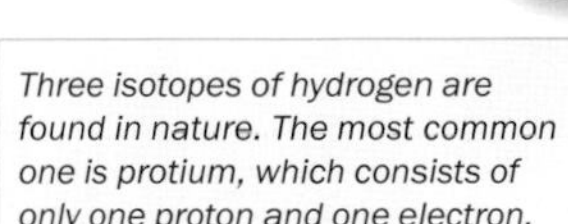

Three isotopes of hydrogen are found in nature. The most common one is protium, which consists of only one proton and one electron.

Nuclear Fission

As the number of protons and neutrons increases in the nucleus, the nucleus becomes unstable. Atoms with large nuclei—for example, plutonium or uranium—split when bombarded by neutrons under specific conditions (p. 133). This process, called nuclear fission, is a source of energy and new isotopes.

Radioactivity and Radiation

Radioactive radiation that consists of particles and energy is produced by nuclear fission. Alpha radiation consists of two protons and two neutrons bound together. It can have a very harmful effect on human health even though it can be shielded with a sheet of paper.

Beta radiation is the emission of electrons and positrons with high speed. Gamma radiation has the highest frequency and is the most energetic form of electromagnetic radiation. To shield against gamma rays, very thick concrete or lead walls are needed.

Harmful amounts of x-rays are released during nuclear fission. Other fission products are radioactive isotopes. Some of these isotopes disintegrate and release radioactive radiation centuries after the initial nuclear fission process.

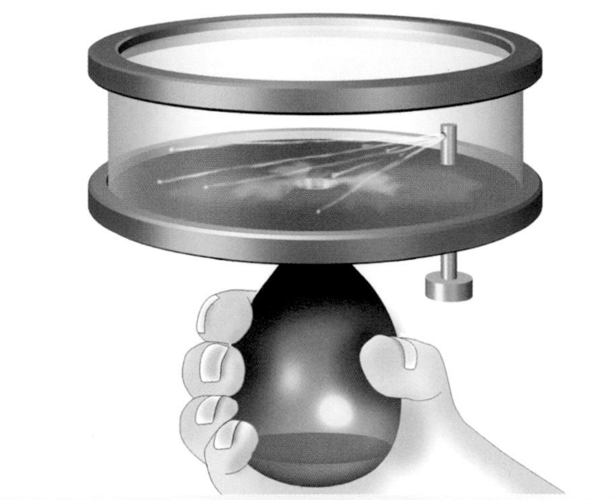

Water vapor in a cloud chamber is condensed by a single ion, leaving behind a visible radioactive trail of its path.

Carbon Dating

Every living organism takes in carbon from food and air. The ratio of the amount of radioactive isotope C-14 to the amount of stable isotope C-12 in living organisms is the same as the ratio in the atmosphere. The C-14 in a dead organism decays with a half-life of 5,730 years, but the amount of C-12 remains constant. The time of death of an organism can be calculated from the ratio of C-12 to C-14 in the organism's remains. Variations in the C-14 content of the atmosphere make this dating method inaccurate for certain time periods.

above: *The Shroud of Turin, believed by many to be the burial shroud of Christ, was created in 1300 A.D. according to the process of carbon dating.*

The isotopes of uranium-235 and plutonium-239 are utilized as fissionable material for atomic power plants and for the manufacturing of nuclear weapons.

INSIDER KNOWLEDGE

THE PROPORTION OF HYDROGEN *isotopes in the polar ice caps gives information about climatic changes.*

EVERY ELEMENT *emits a certain discrete spectrum of light when bombarded by x-rays or electrons. This method is used to determine the chemical composition of materials.*

ATOMIC MODELS *are constantly being developed and expanded upon.*

➲ see also: Atoms, *Chemistry Chapter, p. 97*

THERMODYNAMICS

Thermodynamics is often referred to as "the study of heat energy." However, it also studies all other forms of energy as well as matter.

A locomotive engine does not create energy. It transforms one type of energy into another.

The laws of thermodynamics describe the relationships between temperature, heat, and the internal energy of an object. The melting of solids and the evaporation of liquids are examples of internal energy changing. A closed system is one that does not exchange matter or energy with its surroundings. A closed system can be an insulated test tube, a machine, or the entire universe.

The First Law

A basic assumption of thermodynamics is that there are different kinds of energy: kinetic energy, potential energy, chemical energy, internal energy, the energy of light, and so forth. These different forms of energy transform into each other, but the total amount of energy in a closed system is constant. The first law of thermodynamics is that energy can neither be created nor destroyed.

The Second Law

The second law of thermodynamics places restrictions on the first. Entropy is a measure of disorder in the universe. For example, burning a teaspoon of gunpowder releases combustion gases and generates heat. Thus, the particles become distributed in space and have a greater variety of speeds. Likewise, heat flows from hot objects to cold objects. This means entropy has increased because there is less order or less knowledge about the universe. The combustion process can be reversed, but this requires an input of energy. However, the necessary steps for this would generate more entropy. The second law of thermodynamics is that there is a tendency in the universe for entropy to increase.

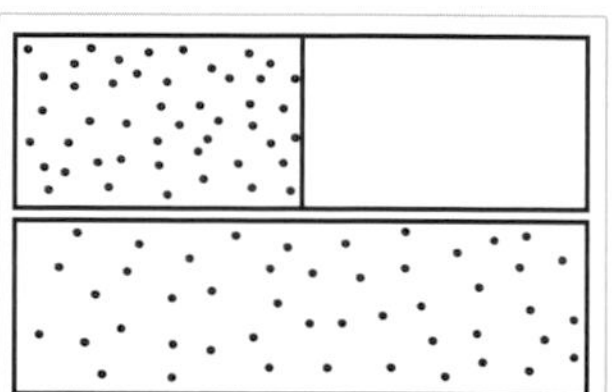

When more space is made available to a gas, it expands to fill the entire space. Its entropy increases because the gas goes from more order to less order.

The Third Law

While it is possible to attain temperatures up to more than a million degrees, the lowest temperature that can be reached is −459.67°F (−273.15°C), or zero on the Kelvin scale. As this is the coldest possible temperature, it is called absolute zero. Theoretically, at this point, matter is devoid of any form of energy because the particles are not moving. The third law of thermodynamics states that it is impossible to reach the temperature of absolute zero. Experimentally, laboratories have reached within 800 trillionths of a degree above absolute zero; however, this point has never been actually attained. The lower the temperature, the harder it is to go any lower.

Significance of Thermodynamics in Science and Technology

Science and technology frequently refer to the knowledge and findings of thermodynamics. In chemistry, for example, it is important to know whether reactions use or absorb energy. In engineering, the efficiency of motors and other kinds of thermal engines is directly related to the second law of thermodynamics.

Heat Death

Since the universe is a closed system, heat death may occur at some point. This would occur when the temperature of the universe became uniform. At this moment, there could be no living entities since the chemical and physical processes that create life would cease. Heat death is the state of maximum entropy and is predicted by thermodynamics. When all the energy transformations have taken place and all particles move with the same kinetic energy, there can be no energy flow.

above: *Even the desert is far from a total energy consumption.*

A PERPETUAL MOTION MACHINE *operates without any external source of energy because it perpetuates its own motion.*

IT IS IMPOSSIBLE *to construct a perpetual motion machine according to the rules of thermodynamics.*

Perpetual motion with a magnet and an iron ball, according to a design by John Wilkins, Bishop of Chester, ca 1670.

Perpetual Motion Machines

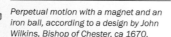

SCIENTISTS HAVE designed perpetual motion machines for centuries. One example: A waterfall propels a waterwheel. A pump is connected to the waterwheel and pumps the water back up. Simultaneously, the waterwheel operates a mill and supplies its own water.

WHY CAN'T such a contraption work? The friction of the motion of the waterwheel results in the loss of the waterfall's energy. Trying to use the waterfall to operate a pump so that the water would never run out would bring about a greater loss of energy through friction. In the case of other possible machines, devices, and engines, energy is lost either because of friction or because heat must be emitted to the surrounding area.

A perpetual motion machine with balls, a wheel, and an Archimedean screw by Ulrich von Cranach in 1664.

INSIDER KNOWLEDGE

PROBABILITY THEORY *and statistical mechanics are important tools used in thermodynamics to understand the behavior of a system.*

TWO SYSTEMS *are in a state of thermal equilibrium when they have the same temperature.*

➲ see also: Probability Theory, *Mathematics Chapter, p. 160*

THEORY OF RELATIVITY

Albert Einstein's theories changed physics and human perception of the world. Experiments cannot verify all the implications of his theories because of the scope of the predicted effects.

In 1905, Albert Einstein published four major papers and became a famous physicist. Among them were works explaining the special theory of relativity and the photoelectric effect. Einstein published the general theory of relativity in 1915. In 1921, he received the Nobel Prize in Physics.

Relativity of Space and Time

A problem facing physicists was whether Newton's theorems (p. 108) were applicable at the atomic level. Einstein clarified this with his work on the photoelectric effect. His approach was not only physically abstract, but also drew inspiration from philosophy and graphic comparisons.

Einstein's Approach

Newton considered space and time to be independent variables that could be used to calculate speed. Einstein considered the speed of light to be the greatest possible speed, as well as a natural constant in computing the true variables of both space and time.

Light requires approximately eight minutes to travel from the sun to Earth. This means the speed of light is about 186,000 miles/sec (300,000 km/sec). Hence, a viewer on Earth does not see the current brightness of the sun, but instead sees how bright the sun was eight minutes ago. Einstein used the implications of this to derive transformation equations between frames of reference.

In his theory of general relativity, Einstein described gravitation as a curve in space-time. Objects with considerable mass, like a star, bend space and cause light to deflect. The theory regarding the existence of black holes was later developed on this basis. A black hole has so much mass that its gravitational field prevents any light from escaping.

Applications and Scope

Einstein revolutionized the concept of gravitation and proved that the supposed ether, the medium through which electromagnetic radiation propagated, did not exist. He was also a founder of quantum mechanics. Nevertheless, Einstein was not an infallible genius. He spent years trying to develop a universal theory of matter, but did not succeed. Einstein's work on the photoelectric effect, the theory of relativity, and general relativity is the basis of modern physics as well as the technological advances that have characterized the 20th century.

E=mc²

An implication of the theory of relativity and the photoelectric effect is the relationship between matter and energy. The famous equation is $E = mc^2$. This means that matter can be converted into energy and vice versa. The source of the sun's energy is the decrease in the mass of helium when it is formed from neutrons and protons. The energy of nuclear fission is similar. The equation became associated with the development of the atom bomb and nuclear fission technology, a field Einstein actually did not work in directly.

above: *Albert Einstein writing an equation for the density of the Milky Way on a blackboard.*

TIME *is dependent on the frame of reference.*

EINSTEIN'S THEORY *was confirmed using two clocks; one travelled at high speed on a plane while the other remained stationary on Earth.*

MINKOWSKI *developed a four-dimensional coordinate system based on Einstein's theories. It has three space axes and one time axis.*

Time goes by slower in a space shuttle.

The Twin Paradox

A PAIR OF TWINS are separated from each other. One of them remains on Earth, while the other travels through space on a spaceship at a speed close to the speed of light. She returns with the spaceship after a period of two years. According to calculations using the equations of the theory of relativity, when she meets her sister she will find that her sister is older by 40 years.

THE FASTER the speed of the spaceship, the slower is the progress of time. Matter with mass cannot move at the speed of light, but in this hypothesis the calculations can be made by assuming a speed near the speed of light. The sister who remains on Earth will age in the usual way. The traveling sister will age more slowly because time passes more slowly in a moving frame of reference.

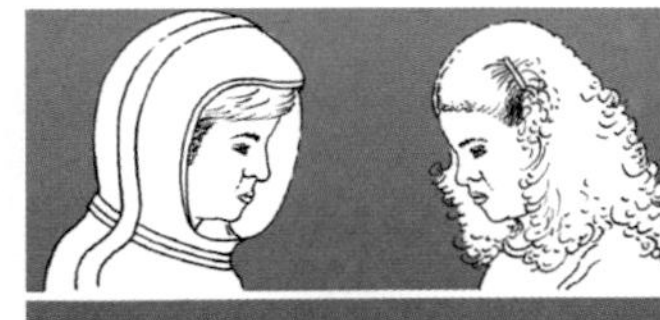

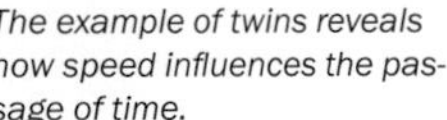

The example of twins reveals how speed influences the passage of time.

Black holes, like every large mass, distort space and time.

➲ **see also: Black Holes,** *Universe Chapter, p. 13*

KEY FACTS

MOBILITY *contributes to and results from a globalized world.*

THE TRANSPORTING *of both people and goods continues to increase.*

EVERY VEHICLE *contributes to an all-round infrastructure through its specific characteristics.*

INNOVATIONS *in automotive engineering are based on advances made in other technical areas, like materials production.*

Automobiles | Two-wheelers | Rails | Ship transportation | Wind and waves | Airplanes | Helicopters | Rockets

AUTOMOTIVE ENGINEERING

In the beginning of the 19th century, success was achieved in beating the cruising speed of horse power and wind energy. The first public steam engine traveled seven times faster than a horse-drawn carriage. This was the start of a revolution in speed that still continues today. New challenges are the improvement of vehicle safety, usage of alternative means of energy in automobile engineering, as well as the integration of information and communication technology.

Means of travel are being increasingly controlled electrically instead of mechanically.

AUTOMOBILES—MOTOR AND BODY

The automobile combines power of transport, mobility, and individuality. There is still no other vehicle that has had a comparable influence on personal and social life.

The heart of a car is the motor, whose task is to convert thermal and either electric or chemical energy into kinetic energy. Gasoline or diesel engines are used most frequently in automobiles and commercial vehicles.

INSIDER KNOWLEDGE

LOREMO LS IS *the first car to get 157 miles/gal (1.5 l/100 km) and sells for about $15,000 (11,000 euros).*

THE SECRET *is minimized wind resistance and reduction of weight.*

CW=0.2 *is its air resistance.*

200 LB (450 KG) *is its overall weight.*

ITS ENGINE IS *a 2-cylinder-turbo-diesel*

100 MPH (160 KM/H) *is its maximum speed.*

THE LOREMO LS *goes into production in 2009 with Loremo AG.*

However, a change is bound to happen in light of rising oil prices. The automobile industry is striving to replace traditional combustion engines with efficient alternatives, like "biodiesel," electric drives, or hybrid drives, which use more sources of energy.

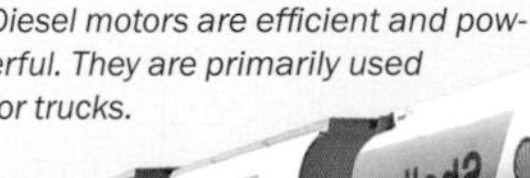

Diesel motors are efficient and powerful. They are primarily used for trucks.

Transmission and Chassis

The transmission lies between the motor and the wheels. It comprises the clutch, manual or automatic transmission, drive shaft and differential. The rotating movement generated by the motor is relayed, distributed, and regulated through this system. The torque produced by the engine is applied to the wheels through the transmission, transaxle, or differential, which accomodate for the different speeds achieved by the inside and outside wheels during a turn. The tires, wheel suspension, suspension, brakes, and steering transmit the engine's energy to the road and affect the handling. All of these components are housed by the chassis and frame, also known as the unibody.

Body

The visual effects of an automobile are determined in large part by its body work. The structure of the body also decides the weight and aerodynamic characteristics, as well as the safety of its passengers.

High-performance engines are deployed primarily in commercial vehicles, like this sports car.

Currently, unitized bodies are common; however, the latest developments favor a skeletal structure composed of hollow sections designed for strength, rigidity, and lightness. The advantage of this structure is the possibility of using lighter materials. Along with steel, frequently aluminum, magnesium, and synthetic materials are used for the chassis.

Automotive Electronics

All the components of an automobile to which tension applies, such as the ignition system, automotive battery, and starter, are called automotive electronics. They are used in modern safety standards and optional comfort features while replacing mechanical controls and security systems.

The Gasoline-Powered Engine

IN GASOLINE-POWERED ENGINES, fuel is finely sprayed and then mixed with air in the carburetor or, in the case of petrol motors, within injection pumps. This mixture is led to the cylinder and compressed through the movements of a piston. A spark plug ignites the mixture as the explosion drives the piston outward. In the four-stroke motors common today, injection of the fuel and discharge of exhaust gases happen by separate strokes of the piston. Petrol motors allow a quicker number of cycles than diesel motors, but have lower efficiency and higher wastage.

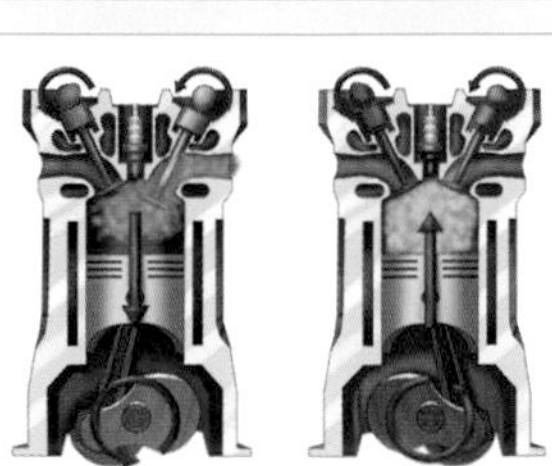

Starting position, intake stroke, and compression stroke

Ignition of fuel, power stroke, and exhaust stroke

The cycle of a four-stroke engine consists of four movements of a piston in a cylinder.

AUTOMOBILES—SAFETY AND ENVIRONMENTAL PROTECTION

Modern automobiles offer not just comfort, speed, and design, they are also able to fulfill the increasing requirements of environmental compatibility and road safety.

Despite the rising density of traffic, in the last couple years there have been fewer accidents resulting in serious injuries or death. One reason for this is the effort made to increase the safety systems of automobiles through innumerable improvements.

The increasing density of vehicle traffic has made it necessary to ensure the protection of both drivers and the environment.

Passive Safety Systems

Passive safety systems are employed to minimize the consequences of accidents for drivers, passengers, and pedestrians. The most well-known components are safety belts, headrests, airbags, and the "crunch zone," which deforms itself softly in the case of impact and hence absorbs the energy. Even predetermined braking points in the steering wheel and pedals, as well as innovative materials like laminated glass for the windshield and carbon fibers in the body structure, reduce the risk of injuries during accidents.

Catalysts reduce the toxicity of harmful fumes from an internal combustion engine.

Active Safety Systems

In order to avoid accidents as much as possible, active security systems are used, which include braking and steering aids as well as warning systems. The greatest progress has been in the area of electronic safety systems. Passive and active security systems as well as electronic vehicle tracking systems are being combined with each other increasingly to improve passenger security further.

Help in Navigation

The driver is relieved of many important tasks, or at least they are made considerably easier, through assisting systems. For example, the electronic vehicle tracking system helps to drive in reverse: If a minimum distance with an obstacle is crossed, a warning signal goes off. It can even warn of tailgating, other vehicles in blind spots, and deviation from the boundaries of a lane. Cruise control helps to maintain a selected speed. If a slower vehicle changes lanes in front of the car, it automatically brakes and later accelerates again if the lane is free.

Environmental Protection

Exhaust emissions are jointly responsible for climate change and increased health risks for humans and animals. Legal regulations enforce environmental protections upon the automobile industry to reduce atmospheric pollution, to conserve nonrenewable resources, and to reduce noise pollution. Through efficient fuel consumption, usage of regenerative fuels like biodiesel as well as the development of alternative systems of driving like hybrids and electromotors can limit the damages to the environment that arise from increasing mobility.

Electronic Stability Control

ESC (ELECTRONIC STABILITY CONTROL) is an active safety system. Different sensors constantly register if a wheel threatens to lock up or spin. A microcomputer evaluates data and in cases of emergency seizes control or activates the braking assistants. If there is a risk of skidding, the wheels are braked independently of each other until stable traction is established again. ESC locks the wheels during braking and carries out full braking automatically if there is an emergency.

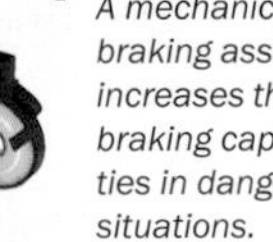

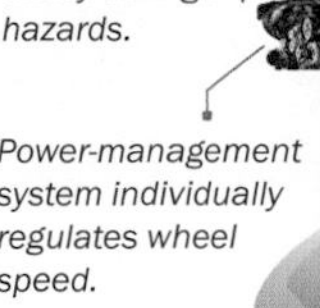

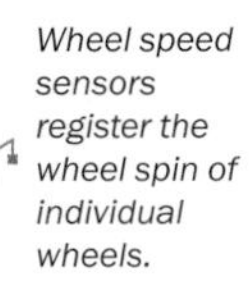

The anti-skid regulation triggers the brakes on individual wheels briefly during slip hazards.

A steering angle sensor controls the automatic guidance.

A mechanical braking assistant increases the braking capabilities in dangerous situations.

Power-management system individually regulates wheel speed.

Wheel speed sensors register the wheel spin of individual wheels.

A yawing sensor registers skids and lateral slips.

Navigation Systems

Navigation systems provide better orientation. The location of an automobile is determined through radio communications with 24 GPS (Global Positioning System) satellites in space. A computer calculates the best route to a specified location and displays this as a digital map on a small screen. Most of the navigation systems "react" to the latest traffic radio information; they warn about traffic jams and redirect the drivers.

above: *On-board computer is equipped with GPS and shows the best route.*

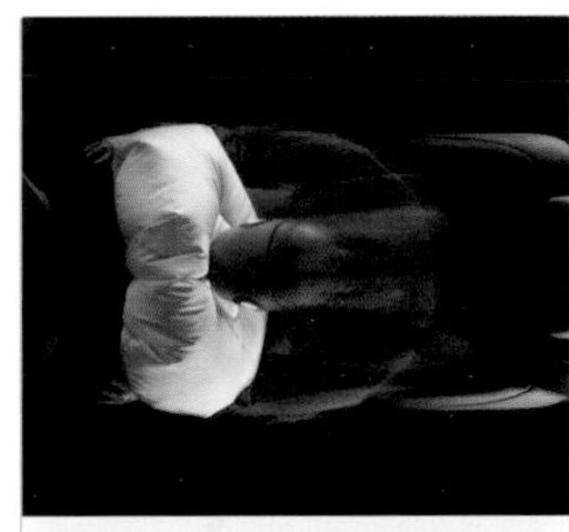

The efficiency of passive safety systems like belts and airbags is checked during crash-tests.

21ST CENTURY

THE EUROPEAN PARLIAMENT *aims to cut CO_2 emissions in new cars to 153 grams per mile (95 grams per kilometer) by 2020.*

VEGETABLE OIL *is a CO_2-neutral fuel: When growing, plants absorb as much CO_2 as they emit when burned.*

WITH NATURAL GAS, *about 25% less CO_2 rises per half mile (about 1 km) than with gasoline or diesel.*

A HYBRID, *in which an electric motor backs a combustion motor, reduces CO_2 emissions 10–50%.*

PHYSICS AND TECHNOLOGY

TWO-WHEELERS WITH AND WITHOUT ENGINES

Between pure muscle power and the horsepower of a motorcycle almost anything is possible. Two-wheelers are simultaneously a means of transport in daily life, sports equipment, and toys.

High-capacity street motorcycles can achieve a speed of up to 186 mph (300 km/h). They are significantly lighter, have lower air resistance and less power loss due to friction than automobiles. For these reasons, two-wheel vehicles naturally have a higher efficiency than four-wheel vehicles.

Centrifugal Force

Bicycle and motorcycle riders enjoy the experience of speed and vehicle control. However, behind the apparently direct steerage exists complex matters of physics. Already at speeds as low as 6 mph (10 km/h), centripetal and gyroscopic forces start to influence the steering of all two-wheelers.

A centripetal force acts on every body that changes the direction it is moving in. The inertia of mass means a force perpendicular to the direction of motion must act on a moving body to cause it to change direction. The magnitude of the centripetal force depends on the mass and speed of the moving body and how much the direction changes. Centripetal forces can be dangerous for a two-wheeler that is moving fast since it changes the balance of forces. On a right turn, the rider experiences a centrifugal force to the left.

High-tech mountain bikes have a strong but light body, adjustable fork and body suspensions, and hydraulic disc brakes.

Therefore, motorcycle riders lean inwards in curves in order to balance the acting forces.

Horsepower

The big difference between motorcycles and bicycles is the method of propulsion. The bicycle rider steps on the pedal causing the front sprocket wheel to rotate. A chain transfers the circular motion to the rear sprocket wheel and to the rear axle. The rear wheel moves faster than the pedaled one as a direct result of the gear ratio.

In the case of motorcycles, the circular motion is usually powered by a two-stroke or a four-stroke combustion engine (p. 114). The power is transmitted to the rear wheel through a chain or wheel drive to an axle and gears, as with an automobile. Before the circular motion reaches the rear wheel, the torque of the motor is raised or lowered by either a transmission or gear box.

INSIDER KNOWLEDGE

CARBON FRAMES *in bicycles are lighter, firmer and more flexible than steel frames.*

GEARLESS HUB DYNAMOS *for generating electricity have an efficiency of 70%. They are low-maintenance and are reliable even in snow.*

HYDRAULIC RIM BRAKES *work efficiently, can be controlled easily, are long lasting, and maintenance-free.*

Innovations in Two-Wheelers

High-tech vehicles have long since been developed from what was originally a simple means of transport. Innovations in bicycles and motorcycles are not just stylish, they also improve security and comfort for the rider. New materials, such as plastics strengthened with carbon fibers, make the frames lighter. Disk and drum brakes have been made more safe. Saddle, fork, and body suspensions have been available for bicycles for the past few years. Apart from easing stress on the body, suspensions improve contact between tires and the road. These technologies have been used for some time in motorcycles. Computers on motorcycles have increased the safety of the rider.

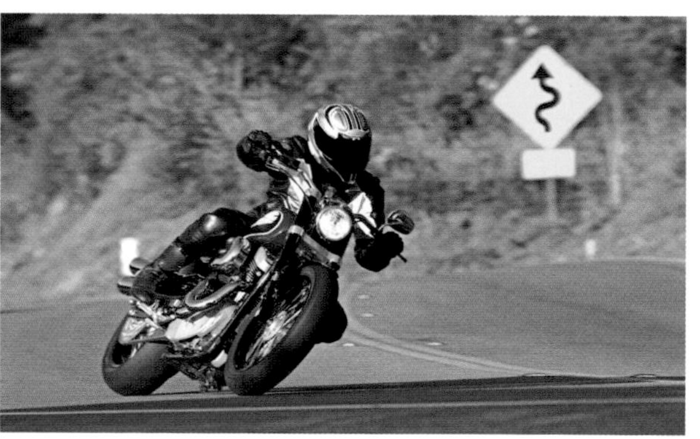

Gyroscopic Effect

From the point of view of physics, a wheel is like a toy top. If a toy top spins fast enough, its rotation stabilizes because of the conservation of angular momentum. The axis of rotation is vertical. Small disturbances to the top's motion made, for example, by nudging it with a finger are resisted, and the top continues to rotate. In a spinning wheel, the rotational axis is horizontal and parallel to the road. When the top slows due to friction, it begins to wobble or "precess" about its vertical axis. The gyroscopic effect contributes to stabilizing a two-wheeler, but plays a far lesser role than the centripetal forces in helping to drive a two-wheeler.

above: *Motorcyclist leans into the curve.*

Gearbox

THE NUMBER OF REVOLUTIONS per minute of a motor is changed in the gearbox. If a small gear on the input shaft seizes a larger gear on the output shaft, the rotational speed is diminished (low gear). If the large gear seizes a smaller one, the rotational speed is increased (high gear). The rotational motion is then transmitted to the wheels from the gear box.

THE CLUTCH transfers the rotational motion of the motor to the gear box. This is done by two disks that are held together by the forces of friction. On releasing the clutch, the disks are separated from each other and power is not transmitted to the gear box. The gears can be shifted during this time.

The clutch allows the gears to be changed.

The clutch on a motorcycle operates according to the same principles as the clutch on a car.

Different-size gears translate the motion of the motor into fast or slow rotations.

RAILS

There are almost a million miles (1.5 million km) of railway track worldwide for surface and underground railroads. Trams are used for passenger traffic and for transporting goods.

Vehicles that ride on railways are more economical than road vehicles because friction is lower and the vehicles can carry a greater payload. However, they are always bound to a system of railways.

There are various methods for constructing railways and tracks. The foundation of track construction is beds made of crushed stone or concrete with dampers for sections where the trains will operate at high speed. Beams of wood or pre-stressed concrete are placed at regular distances in the track bed, while steel rails are fastened to them.

The famous trolley cars in San Francisco are powered by underground pull cables.

Train cars are held to the rails by flanges on the wheels. Additionally, the left and right wheels together form a kind of double "frustum," which increases the stability of the wheel-track connection. The extensive unification of track width or gauge has simplified international train service. Where different standards exist, as is the case near the border between Poland and Belarus, passengers have to change trains and goods have to be reloaded or the cars are transferred in entirety to a different chassis.

Propulsion

Trains are powered by locomotives, which generally do not take any passengers or payload. Locomotives can be powered with steam engines, electric power, or diesel motors. There are also diesel locomotives with diesel-electrical or diesel-hydraulic drives. Electric locomotives use only an electrical power system and are supplied with the needed energy via a bus bar or overhead contact line.

Current Supply

Electrical wagons can be supplied with alternating current or direct current. Direct current is primarily used in underground railways and trams. Most of the large railways use alternating current even though heavy transformers are required. In the transformer stations of railways, current is often converted from current in an industrial network to alternating current with a smaller frequency. Three-phase alternating current drives are not common because it makes speed regulation inaccurate and complex.

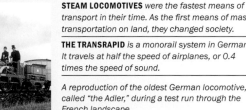

STEAM LOCOMOTIVES *were the fastest means of transport in their time. As the first means of mass transportation on land, they changed society.*

THE TRANSRAPID *is a monorail system in Germany. It travels at half the speed of airplanes, or 0.4 times the speed of sound.*

A reproduction of the oldest German locomotive, called "the Adler," during a test run through the French landscape

From Steam Trains to Transrapid

IN 1825, "Locomotion No 1" in Northern England was the first steam locomotive to operate regularly. It reached a speed of 16 mph (25 km/h). The efficiency increases with the temperature of the working fluid, so using superheated steam enables the engine to work harder. There have been other innovations as well. Speed records of over 124 mph (200 km/h) were set in the 1830s and 1840s.

ALMOST ALL steam locomotives in Europe and the U.S. were replaced with electric and diesel locomotives for reasons of economy. They reached speeds of 174 mph (280 km/h) in special sections of tracks.

THE TRANSRAPID uses magnetic levitation and is a significant innovation. It does not travel with wheels on a track, but moves friction free on a magnetic field (p. 110). This produces a speed of 311 mph (500 km/h).

The Transrapid hovers above the rails because of a magnetic suspension system. Alternating electromagnetic fields provide the power.

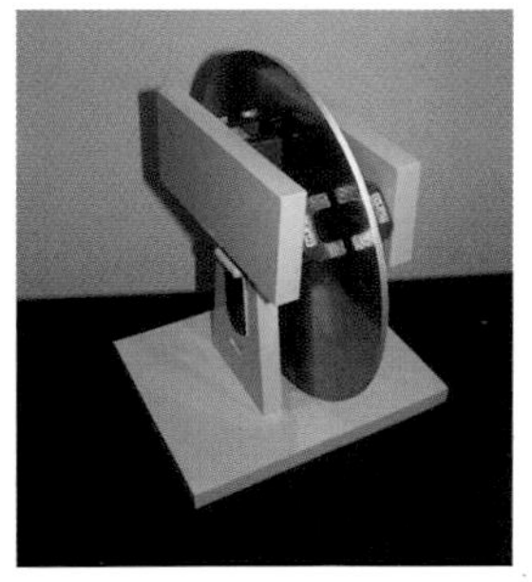

Electromagnetic Brakes

Electromagnetic brakes are based on the principle that magnetic fields are induced by moving electrons and vice versa. A leading metal disk (rotor) rotates within a magnetic field. This causes the electrons in the metal disk to move in circular paths called eddy currents. The eddy currents produce a second magnetic field that opposes the motion of the rotating disk, causing it to slow down. Electromagnetic brakes cannot bring objects to a complete halt since the braking force becomes smaller as the speed is reduced.

above: *Experiment relating to electromagnetic brakes*

INSIDER KNOWLEDGE

THE TRANS-SIBERIAN RAILWAY *is the longest railway stretch in the world at 5,771 miles (9,288 km).*

THE HIGHEST RAILWAY *runs from Tibet to China and reaches a height of 16,640 ft (5,072 m).*

THERE IS AN UNDERGROUND RAILWAY *in Jordan that is 820 ft (250 m) below sea level.*

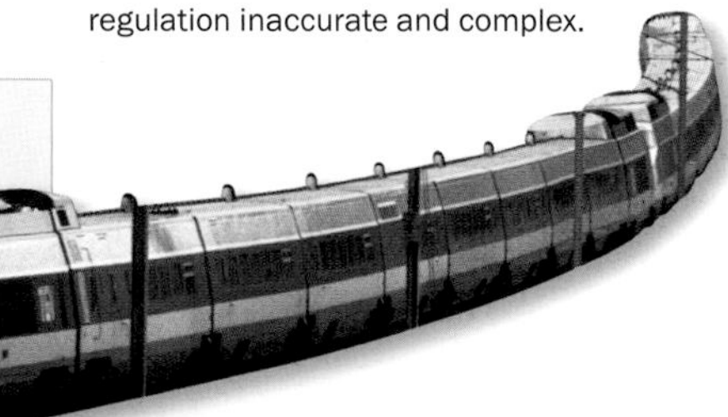

The TGV—Train à Grande Vitesse—has two engines with electromotors, reaching speeds of 357 mph or (575 km/h).

PHYSICS AND TECHNOLOGY

SHIP TRANSPORTATION

The transportation of goods by ships at sea is increasing. Therefore, constant technical innovations are needed to improve security as well as profitability.

Maximum demand: The slim hull of a cruise liner guarantees speed, mobility, low draft, and high capacity.

Globalization is responsible for the increase in the traffic of goods between the continents. Cargo shipping has been registering steady growth rates for years because the sea route is still the most economical means of transporting large quantities of goods and heavy individual items. Historical and archaeological evidence shows that cargo shipping was widespread in the first millennium B.C.

Ship Construction

Shipyards in Europe, North America, and Asia are responding to the demand of shipping companies for fast, safe cargo and passenger ships. However, the main problem of shipbuilding is the same as it was 2,000 years ago. The shape of the hull below the waterline determines the speed and stability of the ship. Container ships are cargo ships that carry all of their goods in truck-size containers. They are wide and relatively flat, which means they are very large and stable, but also slow. They are equipped with 12- or 14-cylinder diesel motors that provide a power of over 100,000 hp each. With a peak cargo of more than 8,000 containers, they can achieve average speeds of around 25 knots (29 mph or 46.3 km/h). Their load carries the bulk of dry goods or manufactured goods. Bulk carriers are used to transport unpackaged bulk cargo such as coal and wheat. Tankers are used to transport bulk liquids like petroleum and chlorine.

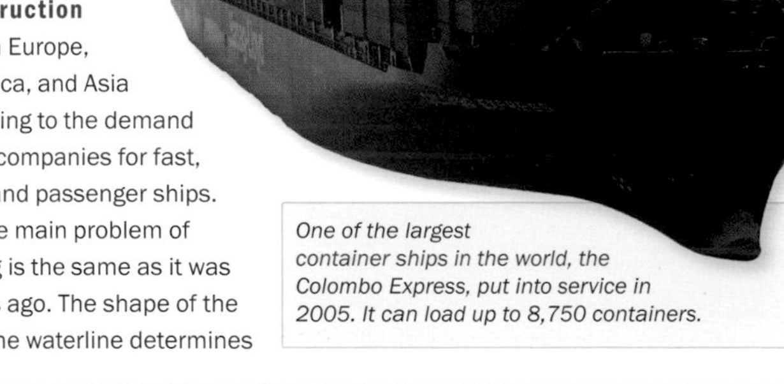

One of the largest container ships in the world, the Colombo Express, put into service in 2005. It can load up to 8,750 containers.

Totally different principles are used for the construction of speedboats where the aim is the maximization of speed, rather than of load capacity. The hull is shaped to traverse the waters quickly with a minimum amount of water displacement. Speedboats, in fact, lift themselves out of the water during high speeds. Motorboats come in a variety of sizes and have engines that are inboard, outboard, or a hybrid of the two.

Engines

The core of every motor ship is the engine. In addition to diesel motors, there are gas turbines and electrical motors. The power of the engine is directly transferred from the motor to the propellers through the ship's drive shaft.

Hovercrafts float on a downward stream of air produced by fans and can travel over land as well as water.

An exception is found in military ships, such as aircraft carriers and nuclear submarines, which use gas turbines. Gas turbines provide jet propulsion and are used because the ships need to travel long distances without refueling.

Submarines and Archimedes' Principle

In order to surface, a submarine must pump air into its tanks and squeeze out the water.

DIVING IS BASED ON a simple law of physics concerning objects put in water. The philosopher Archimedes discovered over 2,000 years ago that the upward force a liquid or a gas exerts on an object is equal to the weight of the volume of fluid displaced by the object. The upward force is called the buoyant force and Archimedes' principle is sometimes called the law of upward thrust.

IF A 20,000-TON HEAVY submarine floats in water, then the weight of the displaced water is 20,000 tons (top illustration). When the submarine plunges under the water, then the weight of the submarine is increased. This is done by replacing the air in a submarine's tanks with water. (bottom illustration).

Displaced water F_{FL} = 20,000 tons

Full tank

F_{FL} = 35,000 tons

21ST CENTURY

REMOTE-CONTROLLED *kites are being tested for use on container ships. These can increase speed and reduce fuel costs by 10-35%.*

DRIVE GENERATORS USING *power from water current are ecological and significant in inland navigation.*

WIND AND WAVES

Ships, boats, or recreational boats that use wind energy, currents, and muscular strength to move need to take optimal advantage of the laws of physics as a prerequisite.

Sailboats lost their importance in international trade at the beginning of the industrial revolution. Steamships replaced them because they were less dependent on the weather, could embark on a voyage quickly, and required less manpower. Sailing remains a very popular form of recreation.

Surfer Rebecca Woods during a competition in Sydney: Two fins at the stern stabilize the motion and the rest is body control.

Physics of Sailing

Sailboats move from power supplied by wind energy. When the wind reaches the sail from the back, a net force on the sail results from the difference in the pressure caused by the wind. If the wind reaches the sail from the sides, the wind is split into two currents by the shape of the sail. The same aerodynamic principle that gives airplanes lift (p. 120) drives sailboats. The air flowing over the windward side moves faster than the air flowing over the leeward side. This results in more pressure on the leeward side. Through this difference in pressure, a force is created that moves the sailboat. The drift is determined by the angle the sail makes relative to the direction of the wind. If the angle of attack is wrong, then the sail begins to flutter and the wind power stops. Sailboats can move in a direction opposite to the wind by a process called tacking. In tacking, the boat sails 45° to the wind for a time and then changes direction. The sailboat nears its target through regular wind maneuvers and by always sailing close to the wind.

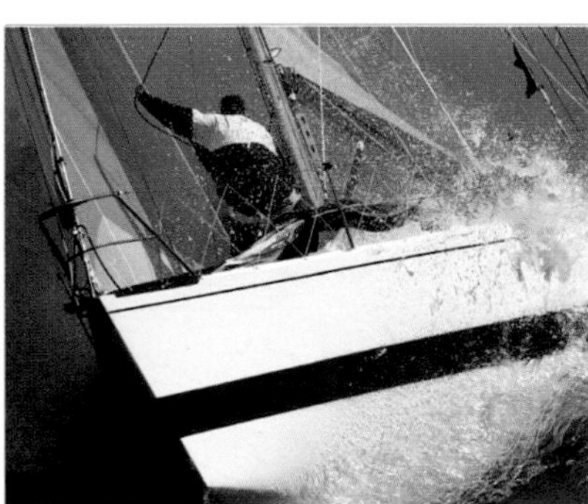

The differences in aerodynamics and forces place each boat within a particular class.

Heeling and Stability

Airflow hitting the sail sideways causes the ship to tilt along its longitudinal axis. This phenomenon called heeling is made worse by sea disturbances, unbalanced loads, and centrifugal forces during tacking. It can lead to capsizing.

The stability of a ship refers to its ability to resist heeling. There is a difference between stability of weight and stability of form. Sailing ships whose bottom makes up to 30–50 percent of the overall weight have stability of weight. With an increase in the angle of tilting, the keel generates a torque that opposes this motion and tends to keep the ship upright. Smaller sailboats primarily rely on stability of form. They do not have a keel, but a centerboard and a wide type of hull. With the wide hull they roll back easily to the upright position. The crew in a small boat can contribute to its stability by moving over to one side of the boat. This procedure is known as hiking. Multiheel ships like catamarans or trimarans naturally have a high stability of form.

Wave and Muscular Power

Other nonmotorized water sports are surfing, wind surfing, and kite surfing, as well as paddling canoes and rowboats. The wind delivers the required power through the sails during wind surfing and through the kites during kite surfing. The surfer determines the direction of movement through their body weight and muscular power. This is also true for conventional surfing or wave riding. The surfers control the speed and direction of their boards so that they constantly remain on the slope of the wave, neither overtaking the wave nor navigating through it.

HYDRODYNAMICS *(Greek: "hydro" or "hydr" for "water," "liquid") concerns itself with currents and the behavior of bodies in water.*

THREE TYPES OF HULLS: *wide displacement hull, narrow semidisplacement hull, and planing hull.*

SHIPS *with a planing hull have the fastest speeds.*

A trimaran with extremely lean hulls can almost completely lift itself from the water.

Hydrodynamics

THE SHAPE of the hull of a boat limits its speed because it produces bow and wake waves during motion. A ship cannot move faster than the bow and wake waves. The maximum speed a boat can achieve is called the speed of the hull. Longer ships achieve higher speeds of hull because they generate longer waves, which disperse rapidly.

THE SPEED of the hull can be exceeded only through planing. Planing occurs when a boat skims over the surface of water as a result of lift forces produced hydrodynamically. Special hulls are developed to enable a boat to do this. They are long and flat hulls with a wide stern. They lift themselves from the water at high speeds because of the dynamics of the heel and the bow waves.

Freight and passenger ships have mostly flat hulls. This enables them to carry large loads, but makes them slow.

HOW PLANES FLY

It was as late as 1903 when the dream of flying became a reality with the first airplane of the Wright brothers. With inland flights, intercontinental flights, and the transport of goods, the amount of flying increased rapidly.

Triangular military aircraft called "flying wings" are tailless and have no separate fuselage.

Airplanes are heavier than air. Therefore, a lifting force greater than the weight of the plane must be provided.

Liftoff

Airflow is produced during the motion of an airplane on the runway, which is split by the curved wings of an airplane. The upper airflow travels a different path than the lower airflow because of the shape of the upper side of the wing. The velocity of airflow is greater on the upper side of the wing than on the lower side. This causes the pressure underneath the wing to be greater than the pressure above the wing because of Bernoulli's principle, which states that an increase in velocity occurs with a decrease in pressure. This produces a net upward force that is called the lift. The force of air resistance opposing the motion of the plane is called the drag.

The angle that the wing presents to the oncoming air (called the angle of attack) helps the airplane achieve lift off from the ground. Increasing the angle of attack increases the slice of air the wing is hitting, hence increasing both the lift and the drag. Accelerating the speed of the airplane or increasing the speed of the airflow with propellers will increase the lift more than the drag. The magnitude of the lift depends on the angle of attack and speed.

A plane can rotate around its three axes with the help of ailerons, rudders, and elevators.

Piloting

Once in the air, the plane is guided with the help of a rudder, elevators, and ailerons. The pilot controls these devices through the control stick, control wheel or side stick, and pedals for the rudder. The pilot's directions can either be transmitted mechanically through control rods and bowden cables or with an electrical fly-by-wire system.

Ailerons regulate the movement around the longitudinal axis of the airplane. This movement is called the rolling of the airplane. They are present on the exterior of the wings and can be moved upward or downward independently of each other. This causes the lift of the wings to change. The plane rolls toward the direction of the wing with the smaller lift.

The rudder controls the movement of the flight around the vertical axis. This movement is called the yaw of the airplane. It is fastened perpendicularly to the tail of the plane, as on a boat. It is used during the approach while landing and balances out the undesired yaw, which is a side effect of the ailerons. The control pedals for the rudder also steer the wheels of the plane on the ground.

Elevators are part of the tail of the airplane and rotate the airplane around its lateral axis, that is, elevators control the pitch of the plane. The angle of attack of the wings is regulated with the elevators. In certain planes, additional small rudders are used to help stabilize the smoothness of its flight.

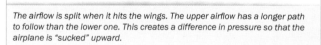

The airflow is split when it hits the wings. The upper airflow has a longer path to follow than the lower one. This creates a difference in pressure so that the airplane is "sucked" upward.

Pilots steer with the control sticks, control wheels, and pedals and must operate numerous controls.

21ST CENTURY

ACCORDING *to estimates, air transport will triple by the year 2015.*

SUPERSONIC *vertical take-off planes are being planned as air taxis for business flights in America.*

FLYING WINGS *may revolutionize aviation technology with fuel savings of around 25–35%, higher payloads, and longer ranges in comparison to airplanes with tails.*

➲ see also: **Flight of Birds,** *Biology Chapter, p. 73*

PROPULSION AND SPEED

Light gliders carry themselves aloft with rising air. In order to propel heavy and faster airplanes, jet engines are required. Supersonic flight is still used only in the military.

Gliders, paragliders, and hang gliders can fly for long stretches without using an on-board source of power. In order to gain height, gliders use rising columns of warm air knows as thermals. These can occur as slope winds at the windward side of a mountain and as lee waves in the downwind side of a mountain. Gliders require an external power source that can give them some height to start with. Commonly used for starting are winches with stationary motors and powered airplanes. Some gliders have their own engines. In order to have an optimal relationship between the loss of height and the distance covered, gliders should be light so they can ascend quickly in thermal columns. However, they should not be too light since greater weight means faster speeds. This is good when little time is spent in thermals. Gliders should be able to make tight turns so they can circle around in a thermal. Another consideration is how easy it is to transport the glider if it lands outside of an airfield (out landing). Some gliders have water tanks in their wings to provide extra weight and adjust the glider's center of mass. The water must be jettisoned before landing to avoid stress on the frame.

Gliders are lightweight and do not carry more than two pilots. They are used for recreation and for aerial photography.

Military Aircraft

Military aircraft are used for transport, reconnaissance, and to carry out air warfare operations. Combat aircrafts are equipped with air-to-surface or air-to-air missiles. They can be deployed as bombers or as interceptor aircraft. There are naval aircraft carriers that bring military aircraft to all parts of the world.

Sonic and Supersonic Speed

Unlike civilian air transportation, military aircraft often travel at supersonic speeds, which are speeds faster than the speed of sound in air.

It is specified in units called Mach numbers. The Mach number is the speed of the aircraft divided by the speed of sound in the air the aircraft is moving in. Mach 1 is the speed of sound and is about 745 mph (1,200 km/h) in normal air. Military jets achieve speeds of around Mach 2 and a few models reach Mach 3. In order to reach supersonic speeds, afterburners or special high-performance jet engines are used.

Camouflage

Military flights are planned with considerations of optical, acoustic, and radar camouflage. The surface of stealth aircraft is broken up into triangles that deflect radar signals instead of reflecting them back to the sender. This is accomplished with stealth technology. Theoretically, there are a number of ways to detect stealth aircraft, but none have been proven to work. There is the possibility, for example, of locating camouflaged flights through a network of radar stations. Further camouflaging is accomplished by using radar-absorbent materials (iron ball paints), which convert electromagnetic energy into heat.

Afterburners give additional thrust to supersonic jets.

Supersonic Flights

When an object moves in a medium, it produces a front of compressed matter. If a plane moves faster than the speed of sound in air, the sound waves cannot move past the front the plane has created. The pressure builds up in this region, creating a shock wave. Spherical shock waves get formed at the tip and rear of the plane and propagate outward. As a result, an overlay of shock waves is formed along the flight path of a supersonic plane. These waves are not sound waves, but when they reach a human ear they are perceived as a single or double bang.

above: *A low-pressure zone is formed at the middle of a plane in flight, causing the condensation of water.*

Turbofans

TURBOFANS are a kind of turbojet and function according to the recoil principle. Air flowing into it is compressed in several stages and heated up to nearly 1112°F (600°C). It is mixed with fuel in a combustion chamber and ignited. During the burn, the flow rate of the gases increases and the gases go through a turbine. This generates the energy for the compressors in the airplane, among other things. The gases are emitted through a nozzle, and the force of expulsion pushes the airplane.

Air is mixed with fuel in the combustion chamber and ignited. It expands due to the heat and accelerates out.

The turbine extracts energy for the compressors.

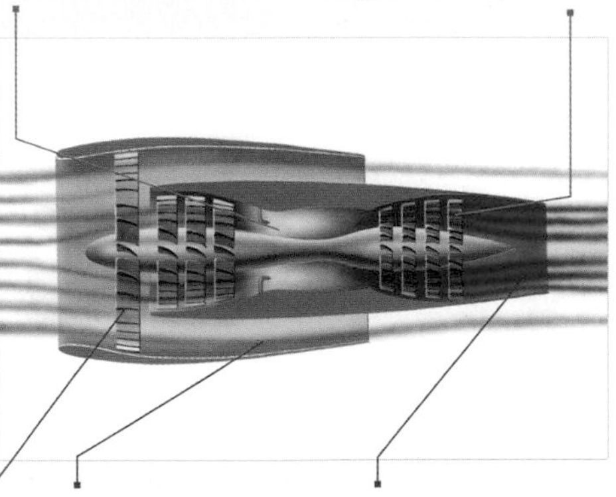

Incoming air is compressed in the compressor.

Bypass of the air stream makes the engine quiet and efficient.

The exhaust gases are discharged to the rear, and this force drives the airplane.

INSIDER KNOWLEDGE

SHARK SCALES *served as models for planes designed for fuel efficiency. By copying its surface structure, fuel savings of up to 5% were achieved.*

SPACESHIPONE *gets aloft with the help of an airplane and can achieve a height of 62 miles (100 km) with rocket propulsion. It is the first manned privately funded spacecraft in the world. It has a unique "feathering" reentry system.*

HELICOPTERS

Helicopters enjoy a unique position as they can start flying perpendicularly, hover over a single spot, fly slowly, and fly backward. For this reason, they have many flexible uses.

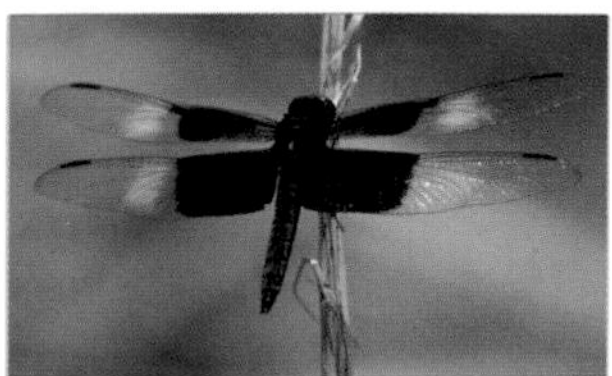

The dragonfly flies like a helicopter. With its independently mobile wings, it can stop in flight, hover, and fly backward.

Since helicopters do not have wings bolted to the aircraft, aerodynamics is not an important element of design. Instead, construction optimizes load volumes, fixed weight, and stability of the helicopter.

All major helicopters are propelled by turbines that power the shaft on which the rotor blades are fixed. Between the turbine and gears there is a centrifugal clutch with a freewheel that prevents the transfer of spinning impulses from the rotor to the turbine. The gear reduces the spinning velocity before transferring the impulse to the main rotor. Almost all helicopters have a tail rotor, which prevents the fuselage from rotating in a direction opposite to that of the main rotor. Helicopters with two main rotors, working in opposite directions, balance the rotational forces and eliminate the need for a tail rotor.

Lift and Steering

Helicopters get their aerodynamic lift the same way fixed-wing aircraft do. Instead of fixed wings, there are rotor blades. The angle of attack of the blades determines the amount of lift. Air flowing over the blade has a higher speed than air flowing under the blade, thereby creating a difference in pressure. By the use of the helicopter's controls, the vertical lift is transformed into a horizontal propulsion. Helicopters change direction on their three axes through rolling, yawing, and pitching. The controls of helicopters are a collective pitch control lever, a cyclic pitch control lever, and pedals for the tail rotor. In order to regulate ascent and descent, the angle of attack of all the rotor blades is changed with the collective pitch control lever. The steeper the angle of attack of the rotor blades, the greater the amount of the air that is blown down from the rotor blades and the greater the amount of lift. The collective control lever is a control usually found at the left side of the pilot.

For pitch (tilting forward and back) or roll (tilting sideways) the angle of attack of the main rotor blades is altered during the rotation at different points in the cycle. If the cyclic pitch control lever is pressed forward, the angle of attack of the rear rotor blade is increased. Pitching forward causes the helicopter to move in the forward direction. To control roll, the right or the left rotor blade is given the steeper angle of attack at the proper point of the rotation.

The pedals that control the tail rotor are called anti-torque pedals and correspond to the rudder pedals on a fixed-wing aircraft. The angle of attack of the tail rotor blades controls the movement of the helicopter along its normal axis (yaw). In the case of helicopters with two main rotors and no tail rotor, yaw control is possible through a cyclical blade adjustment of both the rotors.

Swashplates

THE SWASHPLATES are the central elements of steering-control in helicopters. They are the devices that translate the pilot's steering commands on the controls into movement of the main rotor blades. There are actually two swashplates, and they are located in the rotor shaft under the rotor head. The swashplates are connected to the cyclic and collective control levers. The upper swashplate rotates with the rotor. The lower swashplate is tilted toward the left, right, forward, or backward for cyclical blade control. The swashplates are shifted upward or downward along the rotor axis for collective blade control.

The angle of attack of the rotor blades is steered by the swashplates and the control and driving rods.

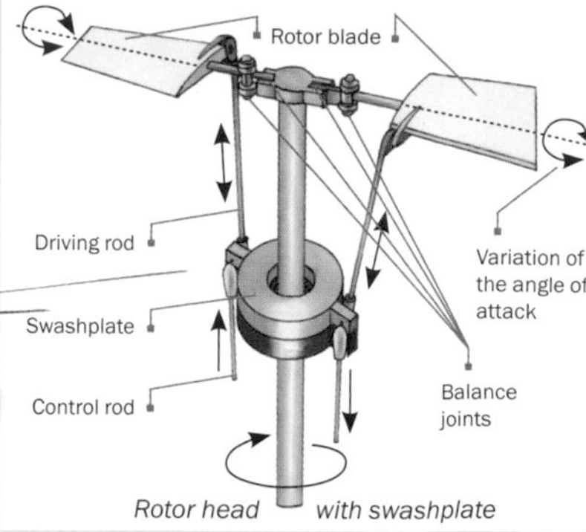

left: *The tail rotor blades keep the helicopter from spinning around.*
right: *The rotor blades are constantly adjusted as they are rotating.*

Combat Helicopters

Combat helicopters, like the Boeing AH-64D Apache, are mobile and efficient weapon systems designed for armed forces. The Apache was developed for the U.S. Army and employed in many military capacities since 1984. With its fire control radar attached to the main rotor, it can identify targets and transmit data to other units. The AH-64D Apache is equipped with an automatic 30mm cannon for combat and has a number of guided and unguided Hydra 70 rocket launchers.

above: *The Apache helicopter*

Schiebel's Camcopter: This is a drone that provides air reconnaissance for the rescue of missing persons or geological research.

Because of their ability to land and start anywhere, helicopters are suited for rescue operations.

INSIDER KNOWLEDGE

THE HIGHEST POSSIBLE *speed a helicopter can reach is approximately 250 mph (402 km/h) because of stability problems with the airflow around the rotor blades.*

IN CASE OF ENGINE FAILURE, *experienced pilots can use the rotation of the rotor blades to slow the descent to the ground.*

ROCKETS AND SPACE TRAVEL

The propulsion of rockets is based on the recoil principle, just like jet airplanes. However, in order to leave the Earth's atmosphere rockets require a much stronger thrust.

Isaac Newton was the first to recognize the symmetry when two bodies exert a force on one another. A body can be accelerated only if another body is accelerated in the opposite direction with a force of the same magnitude.

Rocket propulsion is based on this principle of action and reaction, known as Newton's third law. A mass is discharged from a rocket with a high speed because of a thrust. If the thrust is stronger than the force of gravity, the rocket lifts off.

There are various ways of generating the thrust. Chemical propulsion is currently common, using solid or fluid fuel. The appropriate fuel is ignited in a combustion chamber, and then combustion gases are discharged under high pressure through a nozzle. In the case of a fluid propellant, liquid oxygen and liquid hydrogen are mixed in the combustion chamber. In the case of a solid propellant, fuel and oxidizers are directly combined in the combustion chamber.

After ignition, the contents of the combustion chamber burn continuously. Solid propellants are mostly used in rockets that are attached as boosters for the main rockets when there is a massive payload. Liquid propellants are used for the main rockets, as they can produce pressures of up to 300 bars (300 atmospheres).

The largest part of the rocket consists of its fuel tanks. The payload is at the tip, and the combustion chamber at the bottom.

Starting the Rocket

Rockets carry satellites, astronauts, and components for geosynchronous space stations. In order to overcome the gravitational pull of Earth, they must achieve speeds of up to approximately 18,000 mph (28,800 km/h), which is more than 20 times the speed of sound. The lower portion of a rocket consists of the main engine and boosters. There is a second smaller engine over this huge engine. Cargo is tucked away at the tip of the rocket. The boosters fall off five minutes after the start. They fall into the sea and are salvaged for reuse. At an elevation of around 68 miles (110 km), the main engine is also separated from the rocket. The main engine disintegrates to a significant extent in Earth's atmosphere. The satellite is brought to its final orbit by a small rocket. When the capsule opens, the satellite is released in space.

Space Shuttle

The space shuttle launches like a rocket and lands like an airplane. It consists of the orbiter vehicle, main engine, and solid-fuel boosters. The space shuttle can accommodate eight people and up to 29 tons of payload. Space shuttles are used for research missions in space, for control of space stations, as well as for setting up and repairing of satellites.

THE ISS *is the largest international civil project ever undertaken.*

PARTNERS: *10 European nations, the U.S., Canada, Japan, and Russia.*

MODULES *from different countries are assembled in space. The last will be connected in 2010.*

The International Space Station (ISS) is used for research.

ISS—International Space Station

THE CONSTRUCTION of the ISS began in October 1998. The ISS consists of different modules, such as areas for living and areas for working. Forty installation flights with the space shuttle and unmanned launch vehicles will be needed in order to couple all modules by 2010. Important components of the ISS are systems for position control, life support, electricity supply, and security. After completion, the ISS will measure just over 108m (356 feet) long and over 70m (238 ft) wide. The solar panels have a span of 240 ft (73 m).

IT WILL BE THE LARGEST research laboratory in space. Eight solar cell panels 117 ft (35.6 m) long supply 100 kW of electrical power at 120 volts. The ISS has been occupied since 2000.

Weightlessness in the ISS means many experiments can be carried out; however, it requires a lot of support materials for the scientists.

Guided Missiles

Cruise missiles are unmanned rockets that can transport up to 992 lbs (450 kg) of explosives. They can be fired from submarines, ships, planes, and land. Inertial guidance systems, map-based systems, the Global Position System (GPS), and radar systems mean that cruise missiles can be targeted with great accuracy. With a flight attitude of only 49 ft (15 m) to 328 ft (100 m) above the ground, they are almost invisible to radar. The fastest cruise missile is the BrahMos, manufactured by companies in India and Russia, and travels at 2.8 times the speed of sound.

Guided missiles can be equipped with many different payloads, from simple explosives to nuclear weapons.

21ST CENTURY

ION THRUSTERS *accelerate ionized gas with an electrical field and use the recoil for propulsion. Before the gas leaves the rocket, it must be neutralized.*

SOLAR SAILS *made from Mylar use the radiation pressure of the sun for propulsion in space.*

➔ see also: Humankind Conquers the Solar System, *Universe Chapter, p. 23*

KEY FACTS

CONCRETE AND STEEL *will continue as the most important construction materials in the 21st century.*

ROADS *are highly stressed structures.*

ECOLOGICAL BUILDING *combines traditional construction materials and modern housing technology.*

THE TECHNOLOGY *of construction considers the building, building site, and construction materials.*

Structural and civil engineering | Mechanical and serial construction | Skyscrapers | Ecologically freindly houses

CONSTRUCTION TECHNOLOGY

People have always had to protect themselves from the elements in order to survive. In the beginning, men and women occupied caves and tents. An increasingly sedentary way of life led to the building of houses from materials found in nature and, later on, from manufactured materials like bricks. Centuries ago, huge structures were erected without detailed calculations being carried out. Today, new construction materials and technological advancements, like the software for calculating static equilibrium, facilitate the construction of highly customized buildings.

Technical development, urban development, and space constraints affect architecture.

STRUCTURAL ENGINEERING

Single family houses, apartment buildings, office towers, and concert halls are all built in the form of structures that correspond to their different functions and requirements.

Structural engineering is the planning and construction of structures located on Earth's surface. High-rise buildings such as office towers and apartment buildings fulfill a multitude of functions that determine how they will be constructed. The process of planning these buildings includes fundamental decisions about construction materials and design.

above: *In buildings like the Burj Dubai, a steel framework is used.* **below:** *The plans include calculations of static forces.*

Foundation

Structural engineering begins with the building site and ground. The building site and ground must support the weight of the building as well as its "traffic load." Foundations absorb the forces that are exerted against a building and distribute them so that they can be transferred to the ground without deforming the subsurface.

A wooden frame is the supporting element of this house.

Construction Phases

First, the skeletal framework of the structure is erected on the foundation. The shell of the building consists of the supporting components and basic walls without their inner adornments. The shell of the building (pp. 126–127) can be constructed in a number of ways. Either the walls or the supporting framework are designed to absorb the load and stress of the structure. The walls also perform a protective function against external elements and sound. After the completion of the outer shell of the building, including the roof in certain cases, internal construction begins, which includes the positioning of nonsupporting partition walls and the laying of electrical cables.

Uses and Requirements

Depending on how the building will be used, various safety devices are installed in high-rise buildings.

The Centre Georges Pompidou in Paris has the framework on the outside to create more interior space.

Requirements relating to the stability of the structure and protection against sound, heat, humidity, and fire are affected by factors such as the number of people living within it. In order to fulfill these various requirements, a variety of construction materials with different physical properties are available.

Static Forces

FORCES ACTING in different directions exert pressure on a building. The forces are the building's own weight, the traffic load, the force from wind, the weight of snow, and the lateral forces arising from tremors in the Earth. The loads and stresses are directed to the ground via the structural components and the foundation. It is necessary that the materials used are not deformed by these loads and stresses.

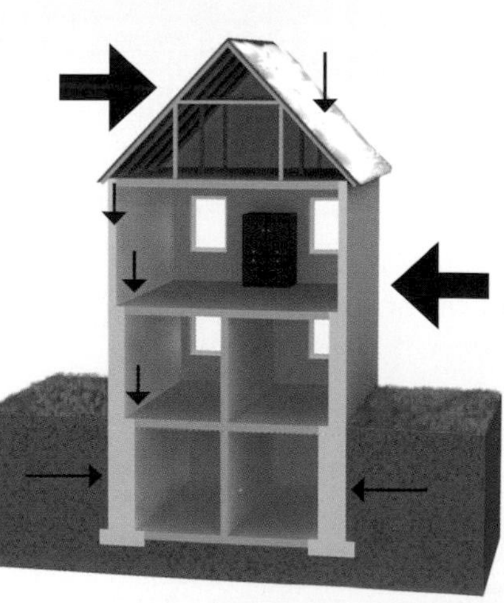

CIVIL ENGINEERING

Civil engineering includes the construction of roads, tunnels, canals, dams, and bridges. A deciding factor in design is the stability of the geological subsoil.

Roads are constructed so they can withstand the load of heavy traffic for decades. A roadway is subjected to compressing and shearing forces, as well as forces exerted by the turbulence of passing traffic. Along curves, in high-speed sections, and in sections subjected to sudden jolts from breaking vehicles, roadways are subjected to additional forces. Besides the stress of passing traffic, forces of nature, such as extreme temperature variations, trigger damage to roadways.

Extreme forces are experienced by roadways, especially at junctions with traffic signals.

Structure of Roads

Roads are made of a superstructure and a substructure, which are designed with a view toward local climatic conditions. The superstructure consists of a surface course or top cover to protect the road construction and a lower base course to distribute the load. If required, a protection against frost is also used.

Tunneling shields are used in making tunnels in order to cut through the rock mass.

The substructure includes an 8 to 32-inch (20 to 80-cm) underlying layer and an embankment that can consist of compacted soil. The substructure can be up to 2 m (6.6 ft) in depth below the roadway depending on circumstances.

Slope of the Road

All roads have a transverse slope, which allows surface water to drain off. When there is a curve in the road, more slope is built in to counteract the centrifugal force of the vehicles. The longitudinal slope of roads is determined by the structure of the terrain. However, the design must change this slope to accommodate the driving speed of vehicles. The faster the traffic on the road, the flatter the road must be.

Tunnels

Tunnels create shorter routes. A geological analysis is the prerequisite for the safe construction of tunnels. Tunnel construction begins with the loosening of the rock mass with hammers, drills, or dynamite. Then, the loosened rocks and stones are removed with the help of tunnel-boring machines. Modern tunnel construction uses concrete, steel arches, and other construction materials to prevent the collapse of any cleared cavity spaces. In addition, ventilation, flow of water, and fire precautions must also be taken into account.

INSIDER KNOWLEDGE

THE USE OF TAR *in the construction of roads has been prohibited since the 1970s, as it releases pollutants in the groundwater.*

ASPHALT, *sometimes confused with tar, is actually composed of bitumen and rock.*

The dam's walls are wider at the base to withstand the pressure exerted by the water.

Dams and Retaining Walls

Reservoir dams and retaining walls are structures that block the flow of rivers and moving earth. Dams found in nature are aggradations of gravel, soil, or boulder rocks. Most artificially made dams are embankment dams and are made of compacted earth. Embankment dams use their weight to hold back the force of the water, as in dams made of concrete. Embankment dams can be made with either earth fill or rock fill.

ARCHED BRIDGES *direct the pressure to the piers.*

SUSPENSION BRIDGES *direct part of the pressure sideways via the suspension cables.*

RHYTHMIC OSCILLATIONS *can cause the collapse of bridges.*

The Roman aqueduct Pont du Gard was built on three layers of arches. The upper layer spans 300 yds (275 m).

Construction of Bridges

BRIDGES SPAN rivers, valleys, and crossroads. Arched bridges can be erected with steel as the supporting material. For massive bridges, pressure-resistant material like concrete can be used. Due to the arch, individual structural components are subjected to tremendous pressure. Arched bridges made of steel arches can have a span of 1,640 ft (500 m).

TO SPAN more than 2,620 ft (800 m), suspension bridges are constructed. These bridges have two high pylons. Two horizontal steel supporting cables are attached to the pylons and a concrete roadway is attached with vertical cables, called hangers. The entire load and stress is transferred to the supporting cable via the hangers and directed to the pylons as a vertical force. Suspension bridges are susceptible to damage from vibrations, which are triggered by the wind.

left: *The Golden Gate Bridge spans 1 mile (1.6 km) across the San Francisco Bay. Distances like this can be achieved only through suspension bridges.*

PHYSICS AND TECHNOLOGY

RESIDENTIAL CONSTRUCTION

Today, traditional designs are usually used for residential houses. These allow for individual tastes and optimal environmental properties. However, the size of the residences is restricted.

Construction materials have various requirements. They should be resistant to bending, moldable, lightweight, resistant to erosion, heat insulating, sound absorbing, cost-effective, and ecologically friendly. Usually, the desired effects are achieved only through a combination of materials.

Straw provides good insulation and protection against rain. However, a straw roof needs a slope of 45%, so the rainwater can drain off.

Wood, clay, and bricks are natural construction elements that possess good insulating properties. They are durable throughout the year because of their ability to absorb and release moisture. These traditional construction materials are used to build block houses, timber-framed houses, and brick houses. They are mostly used for the construction of residential housing, especially single-family dwellings. They are also used for the restoration of monuments and to preserve the look and atmosphere of a location or landscape.

Brick walls today are very seldom erected manually.

Wood

Wood is a versatile construction material that is used for the mass production of log cabins and for timber-framed houses. Modern log cabins are very thick, so they rarely need additional insulating material. However, they are rarely built these days because of the large amount of wood needed. Timber-framed houses are more economical and practical. They consist of a supporting framework made out of horizontal and diagonal beams. The interspaces can be filled up with a composition made from clay and sand, bricks, or plaster. Timber framed construction is used for the renovation of historical buildings. It is coming into vogue because it is ecologically friendly.

Wooden columns can be sheathed with siding, while the spaces between the internal and outer walls can be filled with insulation. Such lightweight structures are very easy to build.

Bricks and Concrete Blocks

Natural stones and bricks have a long record in the history of construction. Bricks have been used for more than 5,000 years. They consist of baked or burnt clay. Normal porous bricks are baked at 1470–1650°F (800–900°C). The massive clinker bricks are baked at 2000°F (1100°C). Bricks are also made from concrete in various compositions. These have insulating and structural properties similar to those of the porous bricks. Both types are durable and have compressive strength. In addition to this, they are nonflammable, are capable of storing heat because of their porous nature, and provide good sound protection.

Clinker bricks can bear more of a load and provide better protection against fire; however, they offer inadequate heat insulation. Since they can be manufactured in various colors, they are primarily used for facades.

Natural Stones

With properties similar to those of clinker bricks, natural stones are frequently used for facades and internal spaces. Since the carving, chipping, and accurate sawing of stone is very time-consuming, stone houses have been replaced by brick houses. Dry-stone walls, on the other hand, have also become popular.

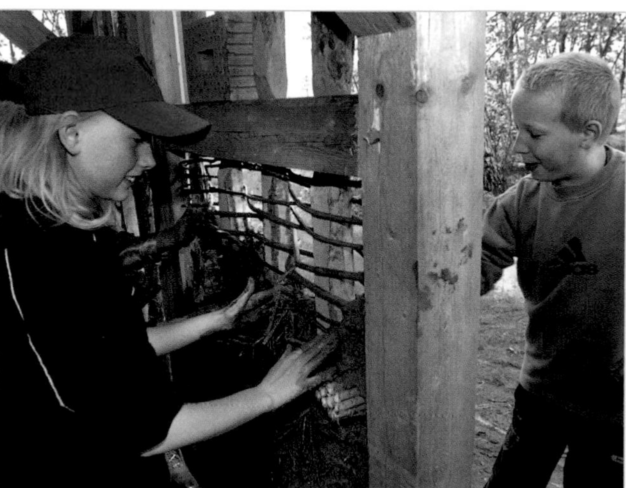

Clay as a construction material is good for air conditioning. Hence, timber framed buildings that use clay are regaining popularity.

Modern Wooden Structures

It is not only the promoters of traditional construction techniques that advocate the use of wood. Today, the construction of the support of almost every slanting roof is made of wood, even when the rest of the building is composed of reinforced concrete. Laminated beams provide higher stability because they weigh less. Wood is often used for ecologically friendly houses (p. 129). Multistoried buildings with a modern look can be constructed entirely out of wood.

above: *Six-storied wooden house in Steinhausen, Switzerland*

PREFABRICATED CONSTRUCTION

Modern architecture is defined by new construction elements such as steel, reinforced concrete, and glass. Experimentation with new materials with different properties is an ongoing process.

Concrete and steel will continue as the most important construction materials of the 21st century. Concrete is produced from cement, water, and gravel or sand in various granulations. Its properties can be changed by adding other materials, for example, aluminum powder.

There are many different kinds of concrete. There is heavy, normal, and light concrete based on its density. Other properties are its compressive strength, tensile strength, and elasticity. Normal concrete is good at insulating sounds, but not so good at protecting against vibrations and heat. However, special insulating concrete has been developed.

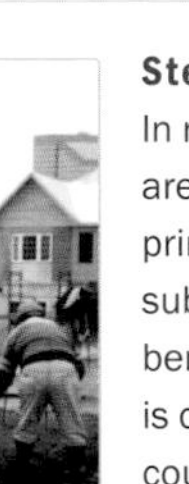

Concrete is poured over the steel surface for an extra floor.

Concrete's importance in engineering comes from its especially high compressive strength. However, since concrete has poor tensile strength, it is frequently reinforced with steel.

Steel and Prestressed Concrete

In reinforced concrete, steel bars are embedded into the concrete, primarily for use in areas that are subjected to bending pressure or a bending force. Reinforced concrete is called ferroconcrete in some countries, and the reinforcing steel is called rebar. This usually has a diameter of 0.2–0.5 inch (4–12 mm). Putting a corrugated surface on the steel bars improves the bonding between steel and concrete.

Reinforced concrete combines the high compressive strength of normal concrete with the high tensile strength of steel. Simultaneously, concrete serves to protect the steel from corrosion because it is waterproof in the right concentration and composition. In prestressed concrete, steel under tension is set in concrete. This significantly increases the material's strength compared with normal reinforced concrete.

Construction With Prefabricated Components

Prefabricated concrete or reinforced concrete elements are used for the construction of residential and commercial complexes, industrial units, and soundproof walls. They are also used for road dividers, canals and conduit systems, and bridges. When prefabricated components are used, the installation of individual components is coordinated with the construction of the entire structure at the building site. While building a side, the wall and roof components are put together along with the window and door openings. Even wood is used for construction with prefabricated components.

On the whole, the use of prefabricated materials is cost-effective because it reduces labor costs and construction time. The manufacturing of construction components improves quality; however, a disadvantage of this type of construction is that it reduces variance in the final product.

Any shape can be created with concrete, a property used by the architect Antonio Gaudi to good effect.

A factory made with steel and prefabricated concrete walls

INSULATED GLASS *is used for large window fronts, a modern structural feature.*

GLASS FACADES *do not supply any support to the structure. They cover the supporting framework like an outer shell.*

MODERN GLASSES *are stable and resistant to extreme pressure, for example, people can walk on glass roofs.*

Many office towers have an inner framework that supports the facade made out of glass.

Glass Structures

UNTIL A FEW YEARS AGO, windows were the points of entry for heat and sunlight in houses. Today, insulating glass enables the use of glass on a large scale, without it leading to a waste of energy. Procedures have been developed in the past decade that improve the thermal insulation properties of glass. Hence, the use of glass in construction now offers a broad spectrum of possibilities: Glass is used in ceilings, facades, staircases, and balconies.

FRONTAL FACADES that are made out of glass do not provide any support; instead they are erected in buildings within a structural framework made out of steel for the purpose of providing an attractive front to the structure and to insulate the building. In the case of glass domes, the sheets are inserted directly in the supporting steel structure.

The glass dome of the Reichstag building in Berlin

21ST CENTURY

TRANSLUCENT CONCRETE *is in production. The inclusion of transparent materials allows new architectural uses.*

SELF-COMPACTING CONCRETE *is more fluid than conventional concrete, and is capable of reinforcing itself without the use of vibrators.*

PREFABRICATED STRUCTURAL *components enable factory floors and halls to be completed in a few days.*

SKYSCRAPERS

Skyscrapers combine height's popularity with economics. Height comes with its own set of dangers; thus safety is an ongoing and important concern.

The building of the investment company Lloyds of London.

Skyscrapers are constructed on a steel frame with economics in mind. The geometry of the building is designed so that a maximum amount of usable floor space is available at the minimum possible supporting cost. In the case of extremely high buildings, resisting the horizontal load from wind is a special challenge. As the height of the building increases, the force of the wind increases exponentially, not linearly. It must be precisely determined for the proper design of the structure.

Steel Frame Construction

Skyscrapers are predominantly built on a skeletal structure made of steel.

Like with a timber-framed building (p. 126), a supporting framework is constructed with vertical columns and horizontal girder beams. As far as possible, the vertical columns direct all load vertically to the ground. The steel frame as a rule consists of vertical, horizontal, and cross-sectional steel girders to which precast reinforced concrete units and external wall panels are added.

Reinforcing Systems

Vertical supports come in several types: steel frames, concrete cores, tube within tube design, and mega-structures. For the steel frames, vertical columns with immovable wall units are placed in the central portion of the building. In the case of tube supports, the building envelope is created as a tubular cross-section. These are considered to be the safest supporting frameworks for skyscrapers.

The 1,053-ft (321-m) hotel Burj al-Arab in Dubai has visible supports.

Safety of Skyscrapers

Skyscrapers also need to withstand extraordinary loads, like those arising from natural catastrophes, fire, and attacks from terrorists. Fire control regulations require that the basic support construction be able to withstand the heat of a fire for quite a while.

In regions prone to earthquakes, skyscrapers need to be able to compensate for unpredictable vibrations. They are constructed on an elastic foundation that vibrates along with the earth without breaking. A newly developed system detects oscillations and uses hydraulic cylinders, controlled by a computer, to adjust the actual position of the building.

There are additional safety measures as well. Elevators and emergency exits are put in place as well as operated in fire-resistant reinforced shells. The control panels of the elevators are placed behind thick steel walls to protect them from malfunctioning. There are also air spaces between the floors to prevent the spread of fire.

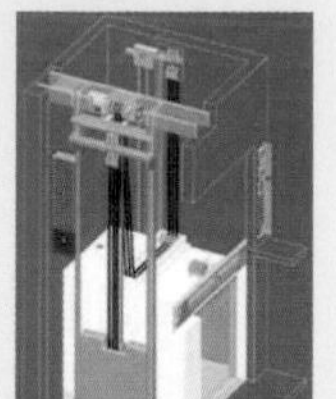

IN 1853, THE ENGINEER *Elisha Graves Otis introduced the first safety elevator with a brake system in the Crystal Palace in New York.*

THE FASTEST ELEVATOR *is the Taipei 101 at a speed of 38 mph (61.2 km/h) and a height of 1,667 ft (508 m).*

ALL SKYSCRAPERS *have a system consisting of multiple coordinated elevators.*

Elevators are suspended from multiple suspension cables and are secured with a brake system.

Elevators

WITHOUT ELEVATORS it is impossible to imagine buildings higher than a few stories. Modern elevators in high-rise buildings use geared traction machines operated with an electric motor to lift the cabins. They operate with the help of friction via a traction sheave.

DUE TO A COMBINATION of safety systems and units, elevators are the safest means of mass transportation. Up to ten cables are used to support a cabin. For a short span of time, safe operation is possible with only one of these cables. Furthermore, there is also a mechanical brake system, which is automatically activated if the speed limit is exceeded and if there is a power failure.

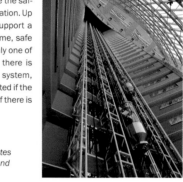

High buildings like the Emirates Tower in Dubai require fast and safe elevators.

The world's highest buildings: Taipei 101, Petronas Towers, Empire State Building, Jin Mao Building, Chrysler Building, Eiffel Tower

➔ see also: Chrysler Building, *Architecture Chapter, p. 331*

ECOLOGICALLY FRIENDLY HOUSES

Alarming reports about global warming, which is caused by CO_2 emissions, and increasing oil and gas prices have led to energy-saving concerns in the field of house construction.

Conventional houses have a yearly heating requirement ranging from 25,360–95,100 Btu/ft² (80–300 kWh/m²). Houses that require less than 25,360 Btu/ft² (80 kWh/ m²) are referred to as low-energy houses. "Three-liter houses" use less than three liters of fuel per square meter and generally have a heating requirement of less than 12,680 Btu/ft² (40 kWh/m²). Passive-energy houses have a yearly heating requirement of less than 4,750 Btu/ft² (15 kWh/m²).

Plus-Energy Houses

Plus-energy houses use photovoltaic equipment and produce more energy than they use. The surplus energy can be given to a public power supply system.

Plus-energy houses and other eco-friendly homes attribute their good energy balance to excellent insulation and housing technology as well as architecture that favors the use of alternative energy sources (pp. 134–135).

Insulation and Construction Materials

Most eco-friendly homes are built from wood because it has especially good insulating properties.

The surface covering insulates the eco-home; large windows allow the sun's rays to enter.

It is also environmentally friendly because it is a renewable raw material. For the roof and outer walls, insulating elements like cellulose made from scrap paper or hemp can be included.

Triple-glazed insulating windows allow sunlight to enter, but at the same time, prevent heat from being released. This effect can be supported with an architectonic design of the living spaces. An example of good design is giving the living room large glass windows facing toward the south. In the case of passive-energy houses, this kind of solar heating suffices to generate a comfortable room temperature. The bedrooms, with small windows, face to the north. Most eco-homes use solar energy and photovoltaic equipment on the roof. In this case, the direction of the roof's surface is toward the south.

Housing Technology

In addition to solar technology, ventilation systems with heat recovery, heating systems that use geothermal energy, rainwater harvesting units, and solar water heating are important components of eco-homes. Wastewater recovery systems use heat from wastewater to heat up fresh water.

Ecological Building

Ecological building does not restrict itself to the energy balance of houses. The entire "life cycle" of a building must be considered. Ecological building begins with procurement of basic construction materials and the manufacture of components used in building. It takes into consideration both the use and reuse of building materials.

The recycling and restoration of construction materials after the demolition of a house is also a goal. Ecological building attempts to find the best possible way of saving energy and using renewable raw materials.

Heat Pumps

HEAT PUMPS can make use of water, earth, air, and sun as sources of energy. In a closed system, a refrigerant absorbs the heat from the environment in an evaporator. A temperature difference of about 16°F (9°C) can cause the liquid refrigerant to vaporize. The pressure of the gaseous refrigerant is increased by a compressor. In this process, the temperature increases more. Finally, pressure reduction occurs when the vapor goes through the expansion valve. The heat is released to the surroundings in the condenser. The freezing agent is liquefied once again and can reabsorb heat.

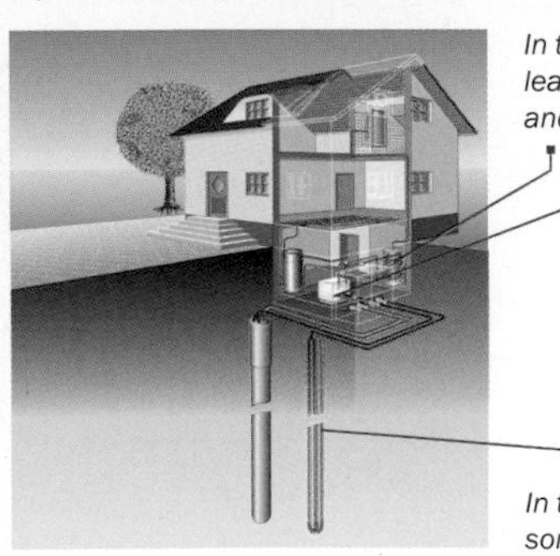

In the condenser, the refrigerant releases heat to water to make heat and hot water.

A compressor increases the energy of the refrigerant, which is stored in the tank. About 75% of energy comes from the environment and 25% from the compressor's power supply.

In the evaporator, the refrigerant absorbs heat from the ground surface.

21ST CENTURY

A FLOATING ZERO EMISSION HOME *was introduced in November 2005.*

THREE RENEWABLE ENERGY *sources: Solar energy with photovoltaic cells, heat pumps, and pellet fuel ensure a continued energy supply.*

MICROFILTRATION *purifies dirty water so that it can be drained into the water system.*

The ventilation system heats fresh air to the required level.

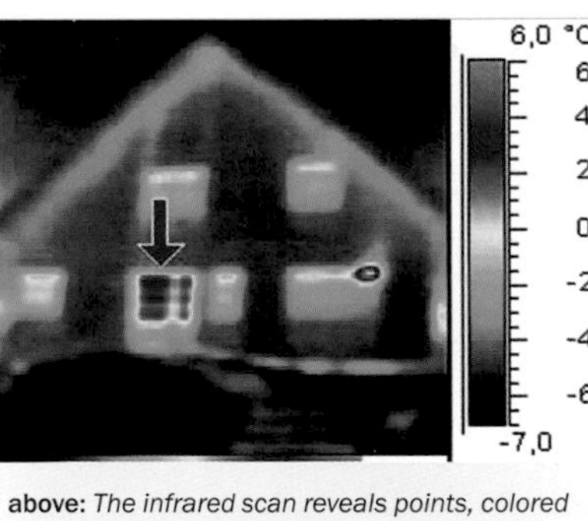

above: *The infrared scan reveals points, colored in red, where heat is lost.*
below: *"Living on water"—This zero emission home acts as a house-boat.*

PHYSICS AND TECHNOLOGY

KEY FACTS

ENERGY IS *the basis of existence of the industrialized nations.*

FROM THE PERSPECTIVE OF PHYSICS, *the use of energy is a complex process of manifold changes.*

TECHNICAL SYSTEMS *put these changes into effect.*

THE CHARACTER *of the energy carriers and of the aims for its use make the implementation of various techniques a necessity.*

Energy production | Energy transport and storage | Fossil fuels | Nuclear technology | Alternative energy sources

ENERGY TECHNOLOGY

Since the discovery of fire, technologies for the production and use of energy have become increasingly more complex and efficient. Early sources of energy included wood and water power, followed by coal and electricity during the industrial revolution. In the 1950s, nuclear power was added to the mix. Today, dwindling reserves of fossil fuels are providing the impetus for new technological developments that promote the use of renewable energy sources. Energy is consumed primarily for heating, transportation, electrical production, and the operation of machinery.

The energy supply is one of the leading issues facing the future.

ENERGY PRODUCTION

Energy is not actually "produced," but merely transformed. One example of this is the transformation of kinetic energy into electricity, according to the principle of induction.

Energy can be present in various forms. For example, it can be stored chemically in gasoline and then made available for use through the process of combustion. A pendulum already set in motion has kinetic energy, while a tensed spring has potential energy. Electricity is considered one of the most refined forms of energy, since it can be transported efficiently and is used for a wide variety of applications.

Energy Production and Use

From the perspective of physics, all technological devices that produce or use energy can be viewed as energy transformers. Energy production refers to when energy from a natural resource (such as coal) is converted into a form that can be easily used by the general public (such as electricity).

The resulting energy can then be employed for a particular application, such as to start up and run a computer. Technological devices that are commonly used to produce energy include generators, thermocouples (for the production of electricity), and furnaces (for the production of heat). Devices that use energy include electric motors, lights, and ovens.

Energy Efficiency

According to the first law of thermodynamics (p. 112), the amount of energy in a closed system remains constant in spite of transformations. If a system (such as a laboratory flask, a machine, or the Earth's atmosphere) does not release any energy to the outside, its total energy cannot decrease; that is, it cannot be used up or lost.

When any amount of gasoline is used, the energy contained is not destroyed, but rather transformed into movement and heat. Similarly, energy cannot be produced from nothing, but can be only converted into a form that is useful to people (such as electricity).

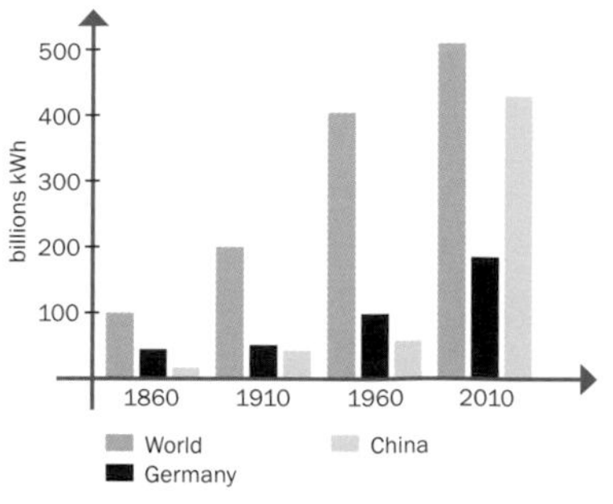

During the past 40 years, world energy consumption has more than doubled. Experts predict that it will increase even more rapidly in the future.

Types of Energy Transformation

GENERATORS—PRINCIPLE OF INDUCTION: When a wire is held against the positive side of a magnet, the positive and negative charges inside the wire move away from each other as it becomes polarized. If the magnet is now turned and held with its negative side toward the wire, the positive and negative charges within the wire switch sides: electricity is starting to flow! The effect is heightened when the wire is wrapped around a spool and the magnet is anchored within the spool and rapidly rotated—this is how generators work.

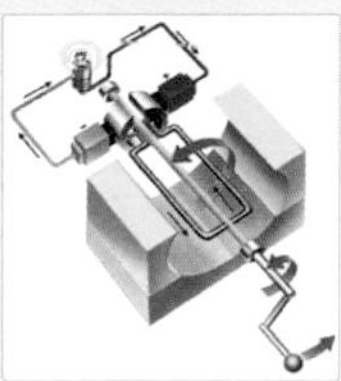

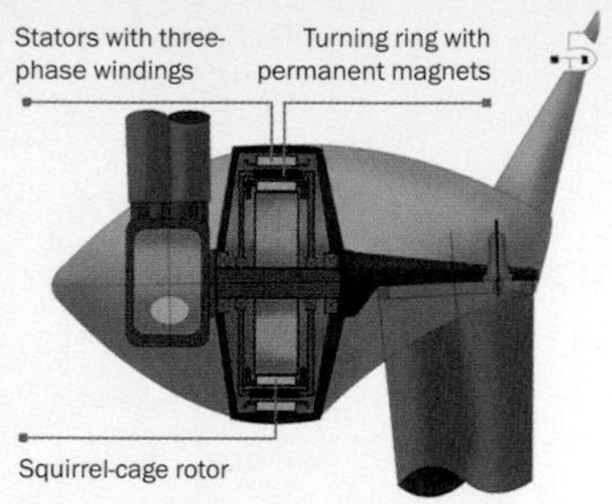

WIND GENERATORS: The rotor of a windmill is turned by the wind. The rotor is connected to an axle, which also turns, and on the end is a magnet within the magnetic field of a spool of wire: an electrical generator. A transformer converts electricity to a desired voltage.

ELECTRIC MOTOR: A motor operates like a generator, only in the opposite sense. An alternating current is applied to a spool of wire, producing an electrical field with magnetic properties. Inside the spool is a magnet or a second magnetized spool. Because the alternating current constantly changes its polarity, the inner magnet or spool is forced to change direction repeatedly and thus turns. This motion is then transferred to gears where it is used to run a device, such as an electric vehicle.

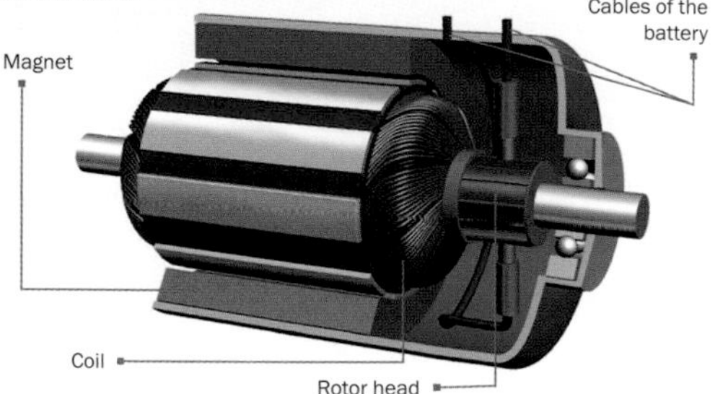

ENERGY TRANSPORT AND STORAGE

A highly mobile communications-based society demands universally available energy. In order to fulfill this demand, a wide variety of technical devices are used.

Energy is not always available where it is needed, and thus it must be transported. An example of this can be seen in a power plant that produces large amounts of electricity intended to serve many households. Electricity can be moved relatively easily over power lines. The transportation of some other kinds of energy, however, is not so simple. Sunlight, for instance, cannot be directly captured and transported. To solve this problem, engineers must convert the energy into a form that is easier to transport. For instance, sunlight is used to split water into hydrogen and oxygen. The hydrogen created by this process is transported in pressurized containers, perhaps to a city. There, the hydrogen can be used to run fuel cells installed in a vehicle. By way of these transformations, solar energy can be used to operate a car.

Toothed gears can transport kinetic energy, as shown by this enormous generator component for a future wind power facility.

Transporting Energy

To transport electricity, copper cables in the form of high-tension wires are used. When electricity flows through a conductor (in this case a wire), the resistance of the conductor leads to a loss in energy. The wire itself "uses" electricity by converting some of the electrical energy to heat. Therefore, in order to minimize these losses, energy is transformed into a different state. Low-voltage electricity is converted to a higher voltage and lower current, so that power can be efficiently transported to the desired destination (p. 110).

Energy Loss During Transformation

Regardless of the form in which energy is transported, the second law of thermodynamics states that energy transformations (almost) always involve a loss of some of the energy (p. 112). For instance, kinetic energy can be transported using gears, belts, or chains. However, at the same time a portion of the kinetic energy is converted through friction into unwanted heat energy. Radiation energy is lost through dissipation; a pendulum is slowed by air resistance, giving off heat.

Energy Storage

Aside from making it easier for transport, storing energy can also be useful for other reasons, such as saving energy for use whenever and wherever it is needed. Electricity can be stored galvanically in batteries or dry cells, or as a charge within a capacitor. Transformation into and back from other forms of energy offers a multitude of additional possibilities. For example, if energy is used to lift water with a pump, the result is stored potential energy in the form of increased water pressure.

INSIDER KNOWLEDGE

ENERGY STORED IN 100 G OF OIL...

REPRESENTS *1 kilowatt-hour or 3600 kilojoules*

EQUIVALENT *to energy found in 1,200 granola bars*

EQUALS *the solar power of 1 hour on a square meter of ground in summer*

IS ENOUGH *to produce 200 hours of light with an energy-saving bulb*

IS USED *up in 3 minutes by a continuous-flow water heater*

CAN BE *produced by a person in 100 hours on a home exercise machine*

IS 1/20 OF THE DAILY *electricity usage in a U.S. household, not counting heating*

Superconductors

Superconductors are substances with no electrical resistance. Thus, they conduct electricity without losing energy. However, technical applications of this principle are hindered by the fact that superconducting properties only occur at temperatures far below zero. In addition, the production of superconducting alloys (like niobium-titanium) is very expensive. Superconductors are used to build highly sensitive measurement devices and friction-free housings for generators and flywheels, as well as in communications technology.

above: *A mixed oxide of yttrium, barium, and copper, which becomes a superconductor at −297°F (−183°C).*

CAPACITY: With an operating potential of 15 volts, a dry cell with a capacity of 4,000 mA/h can power a 60-watt device for one hour.

BATTERY TECHNOLOGY is constantly improving the capability to store more energy in the same space, making longer running portable devices possible.

AA-size batteries store a limited amount of energy.

Dry Cells and Batteries

COMMON FORMS of energy storage include batteries and dry cells. In these devices, electrical energy is stored in a chemical form. Previously, relatively low-performance nickel-cadmium batteries were widely used. These batteries are now being outlawed in many countries because of their environmentally harmful components.

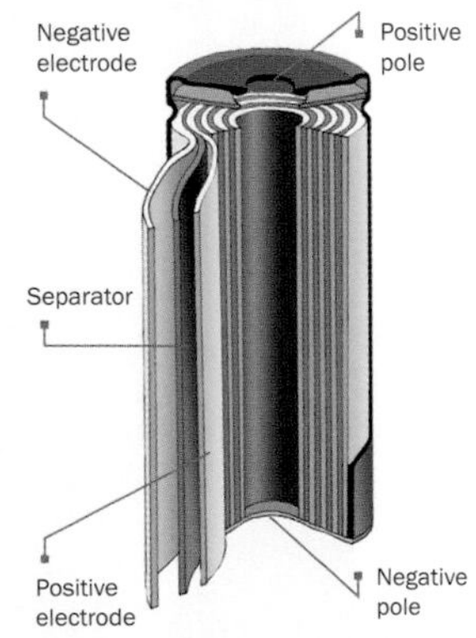

RECHARGEABLE BATTERIES are becoming increasingly popular instead. Lithium-ion batteries, commonly used to power laptops and cell phones, offer especially good performance. The next generation of these devices—lithium polymer batteries—are currently among the most powerful mobile energy storage units. All rechargeable batteries must be charged using devices specially designed for them. If not, they may become overloaded and catch fire or even explode.

PHYSICS AND TECHNOLOGY

COAL, OIL, AND NATURAL GAS

As energy sources, fossil fuels form the backbone of the industrialized world. However, the technical efforts required to satisfy the demand for these resources are constantly increasing.

Even in ancient times, oil from the Earth was used as fuel. The intensive use of fossil fuels as an energy source began during the industrial revolution. Today coal, natural gas, and especially oil form the foundation of all industrial economies. These substances are used for many different applications including fueling vehicles, generating heat and producing electricity.

How Much CO_2 Does a Tree Store?

An average tree produces about 88 lb (40 kg) of leaves and branches each year using CO_2, water, and nutrients from the soil. During this process, it stores about 44 lb (20 kg) of CO_2 and releases oxygen as a by-product. One acre (0.4 hectares) of sustainable forest can sequester as many as 4 tons of CO_2 annually. To store the CO_2 output of a country such as Germany, which produces around 800 million tons per year, it would need approximately 200 million acres (80 million hectares) of forest. However, many factors, such as the species of the trees, affect the total CO_2 that a forest can store.

above: *Smoke from the RWE company's Neurath power plant*

Production and Use

Oil has by far the greatest importance as a fuel, heat source, and raw material for the chemical industry. Before oil can be used or transformed into usable energy, however, it must be refined. In a refinery, sulfur is removed from crude oil. The resulting oil is then separated through distillation between its lighter and heavier components: gasoline, diesel, heating oil, and tar. To improve engine performance and reduce wear, various substances are added to gasoline.

Coal, on the other hand, often needs only a mechanical cleaning before it can be used. With so-called "cracking" techniques, it is also possible to produce liquid fuel from coal, for instance to power vehicles. However, this process is technically complex and currently uneconomical.

Natural gas contains 85–98 percent methane, along with other hydrocarbons, carbon dioxide, and sometimes helium. For easier transport and for use as a fuel, it is compressed and partly liquefied. The heat produced during this compression process can be used for many purposes, including to heat homes or run swimming pools.

Huge power shovels used in brown coal mining can remove up to 240,000 tons of coal and rock each day.

Energy Production

The chemically stored energy in gasoline and other fuels is released and used in various ways. Combustion engines, for instance, convert this energy into movement (p. 114). Similarly, electricity production in many power plants begins with the combustion of fuel. The energy stored within the fuel is released and converted into heat, which turns water into steam. The high pressure generated from this process is used to turn a turbine. The turbine's rotation then drives a generator, which produces electricity through the principle of induction (p. 130). Thus, the energy from coal, oil, or natural gas must undergo numerous transformations before it can be used in the form of electricity. During electricity production, excess heat is also given off. This heat can be transferred to other locations, for example to heat buildings. This process of power-heat coupling or cogeneration makes better use of the same amount of fuel. These power plants are therefore highly efficient and reduce the total consumption of fossil fuels. This is as important as filtering the emissions, as the combustion releases CO_2 into the atmosphere, causing the greenhouse effect.

PRODUCTION of fossil fuels worldwide: some four million tons of oil and 95.3 billion ft^3 (2.7 billion m^3) of natural gas per year.

1 BARREL (BBL) = ca 42 gal (159 l) = 300 lbs (136 kg) of oil.

THE MIRACLE OF RISING *oil production with decreasing reserves cannot continue for long.*

Oil platform in the Magellan Strait, Chile

Oil and Natural Gas Production

TENS OF THOUSANDS OF PRODUCTION FACILITIES worldwide tap the Earth's reserves of oil and natural gas on land and at sea. Producing countries estimate their combined reserves at approximately 1.2 billion barrels of oil (160 billion tons). Based on this figure, the supply should last for another 40 to 50 years.

USING PIPES equipped with diamond-tipped drill heads, oil fields lying deep under the surface of the Earth or the sea can be exploited. At first, the deposit's natural pressure is often enough to bring up the oil. Later, pumps or injections of water or natural gas may be needed, followed by complicated special procedures as the reserve is depleted. Even with the latest technology, an oil field cannot be fully exploited; some 20–40% of the oil remains in the ground. Pipelines or tanker ships transport the oil and natural gas to refineries where they are processed further so as to make the product useable.

In refineries, oil and natural gas are purified and separated into their component substances.

21ST CENTURY

"PEAK OIL" *is the point at which oil production reaches its highest possible level and then begins to decline. Experts expect Peak Oil to be reached between 2007 and 2020. From that point on, oil prices will rise sharply.*

OIL IS THE PRICE LEADER *among energy resources: When oil prices rise, the prices for natural gas and coal also increase.*

AN ENERGY CRISIS LOOMS: *Rising prices and energy shortages cause difficulties for business and agriculture; standards of living will reactively decline.*

see also: **Fossil Resources**, *Earth Chapter, p. 42*

NUCLEAR FISSION AND FUSION

In its early days, nuclear technology raised hopes of unlimited energy. Soon, however, its potential dangers were recognized. It nevertheless remains a component of the energy supply.

Nuclear technology is based on the fact that the splitting (fission) of atomic nuclei releases large amounts of energy (p. 111). To initiate this process, fissionable material, such as uranium or plutonium, is bombarded with neutrons. When a neutron hits an atomic nucleus at just the right speed, it causes the nucleus to break apart. The breakup produces smaller atoms, additional free neutrons and energy. The released neutrons can then split other nuclei, thus unleashing a chain reaction.

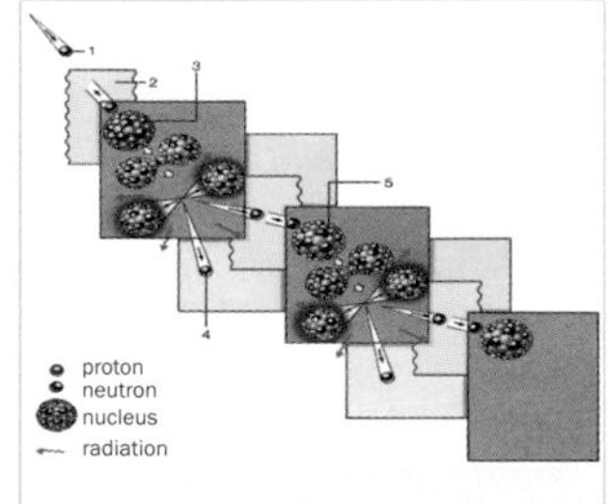

Diagram of a chain reaction in nuclear fission

The concrete sarcophagus around Reactor Block 4 of the Soviet nuclear power plant in Chernobyl, which exploded in 1986. The accident exposed millions of people to radiation, and thousands died.

Technical Operation

In the core of a nuclear reactor, a process of controlled atomic fission takes place. The fissionable material takes the form of fuel rods connected together in bundles. In order to slow the neutrons to the appropriate speed, moderators, such as water or graphite, are used. Control rods slow down or stop the chain reaction when needed. The energy arising from nuclear fission is collected in the form of heat by a coolant substance. Kinetic energy derived from this heat is then used to drive turbines and generators.

Types of Reactors

Reactor types can be differentiated based on the materials used for rods, coolant, and moderators, as well as the organization of the fission process. Boiling water reactors have only one cooling cycle: the same water that cools the reactor also drives the turbines in the form of steam. Pressurized water reactors, on the other hand, have separate primary and secondary circulation systems. In "fast breeder" reactors, liquid sodium metal is used as a coolant. During the fission process, this type of reactor "breeds" additional fissionable material, thus obtaining significantly more energy from a given amount of uranium. Pebble-bed reactors, which use helium as a coolant, have spherical units of fissionable material instead of rods.

Risks of Nuclear Technology

The different types of reactors present various kinds of hazards. With boiling water reactors, a defect in the turbine housing can allow radioactively contaminated water from the primary circulation system to escape into the environment. In pebble-bed reactors, the helium is heated to more than 1832°F (1000°C). If it comes into contact with water, it can abruptly vaporize and cause an explosion. Even when reactors are functioning properly, the radioactive waste they generate poses dangers for thousands of years.

Future of Nuclear Power

In spite of all the risks, the use of nuclear energy will probably continue. Research is being conducted into more effective safety mechanisms and more efficient utilization of fissionable material.

Nuclear Fusion

In a nuclear fusion process, such as that which occurs within the sun, small atomic nuclei (e.g., deuterium and tritium) are fused together. This can only happen when material is in a plasma state at an extremely hot temperature, since the nuclei repel each other at lower temperatures. This process could theoretically be used on Earth to release enormous amounts of energy. However, scientists have not yet been able to find a controlled fusion process, which produces more energy than is consumed to create the plasma. It is estimated that another 50 years is needed until this technology has matured sufficiently to be used for electricity production.

above: *Experimental plasma facility for nuclear fusion in Germany*

A Pressurized Water Reactor

THE FIRST REACTOR of this type was placed in operation in the late 1950s. Today, some 250 power plants and 600 ships (including submarines) are equipped with pressurized water reactors. This makes these reactors the most common type worldwide. Their average electricity production ranges from one to two gigawatts. The newly developed European Pressurized Reactor, EPR, which is scheduled to be placed in operation in 2010, is a pressurized water reactor.

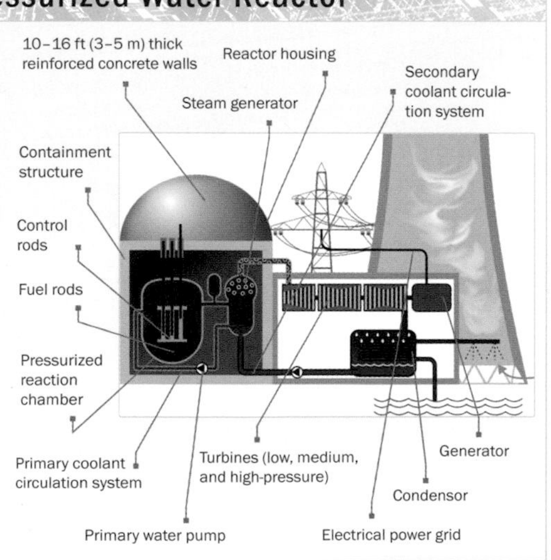

INSIDER KNOWLEDGE

THE HALF-LIFE *of a material is the time it takes for half of its radioactivity to be released. The half-life of cesium-137 is 30 years, while uranium-238 is over four billion years.*

MEASUREMENT *of radioactive decay is done with a Geiger counter. The measurement unit is the becquerel: 1 Bq = decay of 1 nucleus per sec.*

GRAY (GY) *is the measurement for the emitted energy of radioactive decay. One Gray is one Joule per kg.*

➲ **see also: Atoms,** *Chemistry Chapter, p. 97*

SOLAR TECHNOLOGY

The sun's radiation can be transformed into useful energy—without the release of harmful emissions. Developing solar technologies is now the subject of intense research.

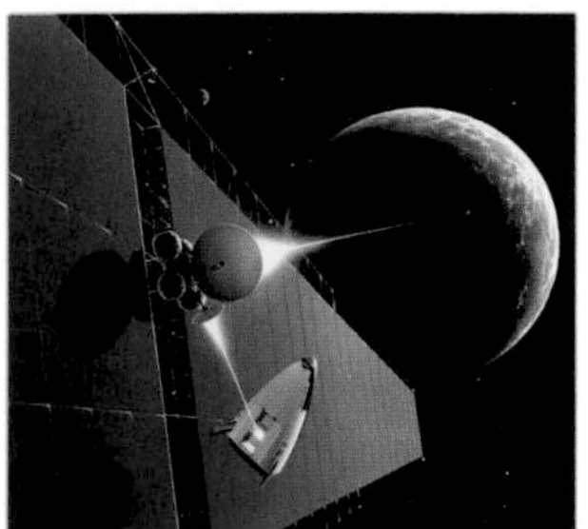

Solar arrays supply the International Space Station with energy.

10.7 ft² (1 m²) of solar cells can produce approximately 1 kilowatt in an hour in bright sunlight—or in 20 hours under cloudy skies. 64–75 ft² (6–7 m²) of cells are needed to fully supply a one-person household.

Solar Energy—Heavenly Possibilities?

The sun can be compared to a gigantic nuclear reactor. In it, atomic nuclei are constantly fusing together, releasing huge amounts of energy, which reach the Earth as powerful solar radiation. The aim of solar technology is to make this energy useful to people. If it were possible to make use of the sun's entire energy output, around 2,500 times more energy would be available than is used around the world today.

The Pros and Cons of Solar Technology

The term "solar technology" includes various types of systems. Photovoltaic devices, for example, use the LED (light-emitting diode) principle in the opposite direction. Light is converted into electricity using silicon-based semiconductors. Commonly used solar cells are capable of converting 8–16 percent of the light they capture into electricity. Solar thermal devices, on the other hand, use the sun's energy to heat water, which is then stored in "solar batteries" (insulated water tanks). Other technologies using solar power include solar chimneys, solar-chemical, and photochemical installations. The great advantages of solar technologies can be seen in their low-cost and emission-free operation. There are also significant disadvantages, however. The lifespan of solar cells is only about 20 to 30 years. Furthermore, their production is extremely costly and is often dependent on government subsidies.

Research and Development

In the future, mirrors and magnifying lenses will be used to increase the efficiency of solar cells by supplying them with more light ("concentrator cells"). In addition, multiple layers of semiconductors are expected to allow solar cells to exploit a wider spectrum of light. Using an extremely thin coating of silicon for the cells may also significantly reduce production costs.

Devices That Use Solar Technology

Solar devices can be classified according to their power levels. For example, they may use some tens of watts (such as parking meter machines), a few kilowatts (residential home systems), or up to several megawatts (large "solar parks" or arrays of solar panels). In the higher power classes, the production and use of energy are often independent processes, with the sun-derived electricity being transported over large distances (e.g., from solar parks to faraway households). In smaller systems, the energy is often produced for a specific purpose and used directly.

above: A solar-powered radio

The Solar Electricity Cycle

SOLAR CYCLES IN A SINGLE FAMILY HOME: The system shown here feeds the solar power it produces into the public electricity grid. Appliances and electrical devices in the home draw their electricity, as usual, from the electric utility. This principle makes sense when the solar power produced has a greater value than the cost of power from the local utility.

IN SELF-SUFFICIENT "island systems," solar power is stored in batteries, which are used to power devices.

A photovoltaic system: solar modules convert sunlight into electricity.

Solar thermal system: a pump supplies cold water to the solar collector.

The direct current travels over wires to an inverter system and is converted into alternating current.

Water is heated by the action of sunlight.

If the solar energy is insufficient, a conventional furnace is used to supplement the solar collector.

The solar power produced is fed into the public electricity grid.

Electricity to run devices in the home is taken from the public utility.

The warmed water is available as hot water (e.g., for bathing) and can also be used for heating the home.

Hot water is stored in a "solar battery."

OTHER ALTERNATIVE ENERGY SOURCES

In recent decades, emphasis has been placed on the development and use of renewable energy sources. Are they useful alternatives to conventional energy supplies?

Seaflow Turbines

Since 2002, a pilot program of seaflow turbines has been in operation off the British coast. Ocean currents from the tides cause huge rotor blades, 33 ft (10 m) long, to turn. This energy is then transferred to a generator. Due to the high density of water, a current of some 8 ft (2.5 m) per second is enough to produce 350 kilowatts of relatively constant electrical power, independent of the weather. The company responsible for the project envisions installations with a capacity of one megawatt each, consisting of twin-rotor towers. These facilities would be capable of supplying 40% of Great Britain's electricity needs.

above: *Seaflow turbines*

Using water at 302°F (150°C) from a depth of 1.8 miles (3 km), 5,000 houses are supplied with electricity.

Energy is found in various forms in nature whether it is heat from deep within the earth or kinetic energy in ocean waves, rivers, and wind. A wide range of technical processes can be used to make this energy useful to people, through the production of electricity, heat, or fuel. Some of these processes have already proven cost-effective and are being used to deliver reliable energy supplies, while others are still in the testing phase or exist only on paper. Motives for the use of renewable energy sources include the need to reduce emissions of carbon dioxide (CO_2) and the desire for independence from fossil fuels.

Wind and Water Power

Wind energy facilities and most hydropower plants convert kinetic energy into electricity using generators (p. 130). Examples of this include windmills and low-pressure hydropower plants installed in rivers. High-pressure power plants located within dams first transform the potential energy of the reservoir water into kinetic energy. Innovative new tidal power stations use the movement of seawater to produce an air current which drives a propeller. Still in the experimental stage, osmotic devices use various combinations of fresh and salt water to create pressure. And wave generators use the up-and-down motion of waves to produce electricity through the principle of induction (p. 130).

Biomasses

The term "biomass" covers a range of renewable fuel sources. "Biodiesel" can replace petroleum-based fuels, while wood pellets can be used instead of oil in home furnaces. Large power plants are able to produce both electricity and heat. Sources include wood, plant oils, gases from fermentation or dumps, biologically produced alcohol, and fermented animal products, among others. One of the most versatile raw materials, biomass can easily be stored and derives most of its energy from renewable resources.

In spite of its high-voltage discharge packed into a few milliseconds, a lightning bolt has less energy than a liter of heating oil.

INSIDER KNOWLEDGE

THE PROPORTION *of energy from renewable sources in the EU is 15%; the goal is 20% by 2020.*

WORLDWIDE, *the proportion is approximately 8%.*

LEADING NATIONS *in wind power are Germany, Spain, and the U.S.*

NORWAY *covers 99% of its energy needs using hydropower.*

Geothermal Energy

Geothermal technology makes use of the high temperatures found in deep layers of the Earth. Hot water is brought up from a drilled borehole and then utilized directly for heating or transferred to a heat pump to produce electricity. Through a second borehole, an equal amount of cold water is returned to the ground. A variation is the "hot dry rock" method, which is used in places with high temperatures and without natural water supplies. Water is pumped into the ground and then returned to the surface in heated form. Geothermal power is viewed as one of the strongest potentially renewable energy sources, although its implementation is still in its beginning phases.

Alternative Energy Production Technologies

WIND GENERATORS, high-pressure hydropower stations, and solar parks are mature technologies which are already being used in many places. To date, seaflow turbines have only been operated in prototype form. Although solar cells have become relatively widespread, the proportion of electricity generated by solar technology lies well below that of wind or water power.

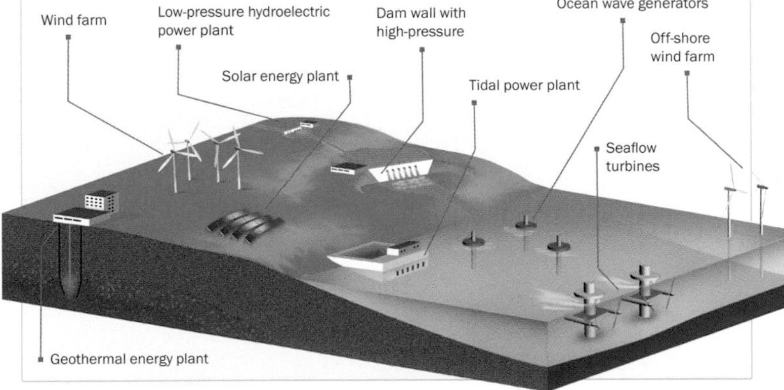

PHYSICS AND TECHNOLOGY

KEY FACTS

ELECTRONIC COMPONENTS, *silicon chips, and digital signal processing are basic components of the information age.*

AN INTERNET CULTURE *has been established that affects everyday life.*

COPYRIGHT AND DATA PROTECTION *are the most significant problems of new 21st century technology.*

AROUND 1.5 BILLION *users are connected to the internet today.*

Distribution | Components | Input and output | Storage | Electronics | Circuits | Internet

COMPUTER TECHNOLOGY

The first digital computer was developed in the 1940s. Today, they are a fixed component of our everyday life. Computers have become indispensable wherever information is collected, processed, and transferred. We even talk about an "information age" because of the central role computers play in private and public life. Research and development aim at making computers more compact, increasing the number of tasks they perform, making computer technology more universal, and improving both the speed and reliability of computers.

Computers consist of programmable circuits and process digital data through complex calculations.

THE UBIQUITOUS COMPUTER

Initially only large enterprises could afford computers. Today there are PCs in children's rooms that outperform all the large mainframes of the 1960s.

In 1977 Ken Olsen, president of the Digital Equipment Corporation, is reported to have said, "There is no reason for any individual to have a computer in his home." Times have changed.

The First Computer

The German engineer Konrad Zuse built the first working programmable computer in 1941: the Z3 (Z1 and Z2 were prototypes). The computer weighed around one ton and used relays as switches and for calculations in aircraft design. Independently, in 1943, the ENIAC, Electronic Numerical Integrator and Computer, was built in the U.S. The name "computer" comes from this device. It did not have any relays, but used electron tubes as switches and was, hence, the first electronically programmable computer. The military computed the flight paths of projectiles with the ENIAC. Several large computers were developed, which were operated by governments, universities, and large companies.

Konrad Zuse with a version of his Z1. The original was made in 1938 and was the first programmable computer in the world.

Even third grade students are learning their way around computers.

In Use Everywhere

How far computer technology has penetrated daily life was shown by the "Millennium problem." At midnight on New Year's Eve, no plane was in the air. Experts feared that there could be accidents if the built-in computer microchips wrongly interpreted the time change from "99" to "00."

Many devices used today, from toasters to pacemakers, are controlled by microchips.

Into the Future

The computer industry is the most dynamic and important part of the world's economy. New computers with higher performance ratings and with more functions are being continually introduced onto the market. Along with the development of high performance supercomputers, the use of decentralized computational power is gaining significance. NASA, for example, provides data packets for downloading (p. 142) to private users so they can use their unused computer time to make the extensive calculations demanded by NASA. This is "grid computing." A problem requiring time to solve on one computer is divided into small parts, distributed to thousands of computers in the grid for computation, and the returned calculations are assembled into an answer.

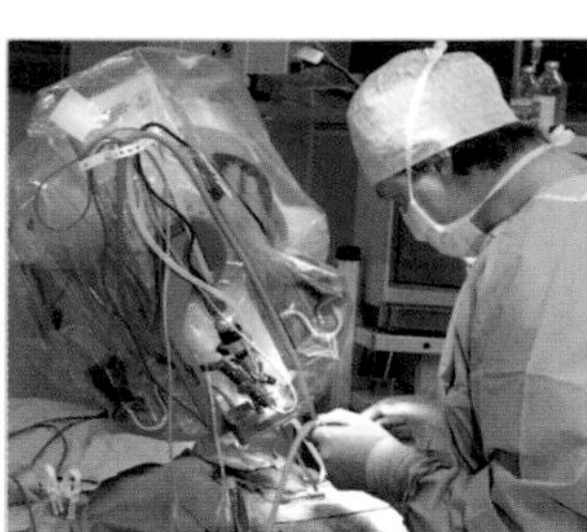

Computer-controlled robots are used increasingly in the operating room. The surgeon, however, remains in ultimate control.

"High-End" Computers

"High-end" means possessing the most modern and efficient technologies. In the field of computer technology, there are different high-end systems. Supercomputers are distinguished by an extremely high computational power, like the Blue Gene/L of IBM with 280 teraflops (a billion calculations per second). Highly miniaturized computers and individual microchips that achieve extremely high computational power or combine entire computer systems into a single component are also high-end.

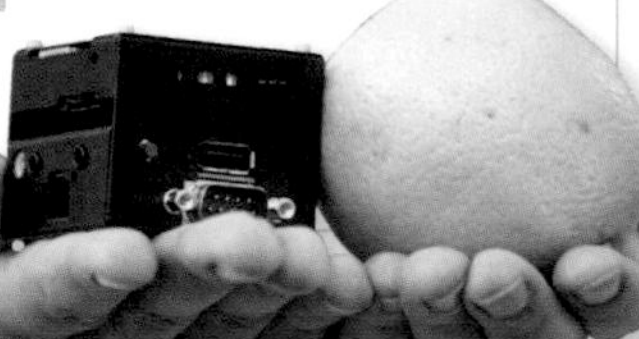

above: *The supercomputer BlueGene/L of IBM in the Livermore National Laboratory in California* **right:** *The Teacube computer made in Japan and an orange used for scale*

COMPONENTS OF A COMPUTER

The spectrum of computer types is broad, but its basic components are few in number. The selection of components in a computer determines the efficiency of the system.

Computers made their way into businesses and homes in the early 1980s. The architecture of various computing systems was different back then, but they have many similarities with the computers of today. Personal computers are used primarily for office applications as well as for personal use as typewriters and recreation. Large computers are used by big companies and government agencies as high-performance central computers that can be accessed simultaneously by many users. Even these use the same components as personal computers.

Elementary Components

A central element of computers is a printed circuit board called the motherboard, through which almost all of the computer's components communicate with each other. The BIOS (Basic Input Output System) is present in a small chip in the motherboard and is a small program that provides access to the hardware components of the computer. Even the processor, the central computing unit of the computer, is attached to the motherboard, which is cooled by a fan.

High-end graphic cards with a high-performance 3D-microchip provide even real-time games with realistic images.

The processor carries out most of the computing operations, hence is the most important determinant of the character and efficiency of the entire system. Data that has to be made available to the processor quickly is loaded in the main memory. If the main memory is small, programs that need to process large volumes of data quickly (i.e., video programs or games) will run slowly.

Data is exchanged between the components through a bus, a connecting device consisting of multiple conductors. The transfer rate within the system is significantly dependent on the amount of information that the bus can transfer in a unit of time.

In order to connect a computer to a local area network (LAN) or the Internet, modems and network cards are attached to the bus (p. 142).

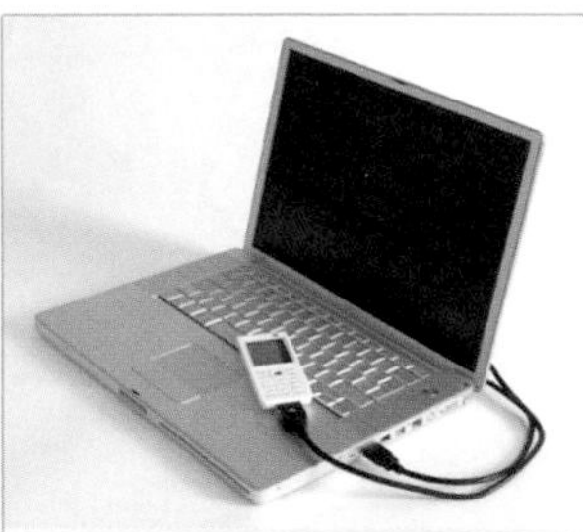

With universal serial bus (USB) connections, many different devices can be connected to the computer and supplied with power.

INSIDER KNOWLEDGE

THE PERFORMANCE *of processors has been doubling itself every 18 to 24 months.*

1971: *Intel 4004, 0.1 MHz*

1985: *Intel 80386, 12–30 MHz*

1993: *Cyrix 486–33, 100 MHz*

1999: *Advanced Micro Devices K7 Athlon, 500–1200 MHz*

2007: *Intel Pentium 4 Prescott, 3800 MHz*

Miniaturized Systems for Mobile Computers

To be transportable, laptop computers have to be as small and light as possible. The small dimensions are achieved by using compact components, which are often more costly than normal components.

A further requirement for mobility is an efficient battery. In order to achieve as much operating time as possible without recharging, laptops are equipped with special "mobile" processors that perform during low current consumption. PC cards allow expansion cards to be more easily attached. Even more miniaturized than laptops are handheld computers, personal digital computers (PDAs), and mobile telephones.

Components of a Computer

APPLE INC. PLAYED a decisive role in the history of the development of the computer. The use of a graphical input device, such as a graphical tablet for the user to draw on, was first introduced by Apple Inc. in the 1980s and only later by other companies. Apple computers were considered superior to other personal computers in the field of graphical processing for a long time. At present, they continue to be at the forefront of software and hardware design. The recently released iMac desktop computers are housed entirely within a flat panel display screen, with the keyboard and mouse as the only visible, external attachments. Apple Inc. uses stable Unix-based operating systems that rarely experience system crashes, and tend to be very highly regarded by users.

There are different connections for the monitor, keyboard, mouse, loudspeaker, network cable, external drives, USB-memory, and much more.

INPUT AND OUTPUT DEVICES

Input and output devices enable people to communicate with the computer's processor. These devices are critical in determining how effectively a user can work with the computer.

Computers were still huge machines in the 1960s. Levers and buttons were used to input numbers and mathematical operations while the outputs were followed by observing sets of control lights. It was years before a "monitor" was borrowed from air traffic control stations to represent outputs more clearly. Teleprinters probably served as models for the introduction of the keyboard.

The continued development of input and output devices was directed toward making the computers more ergonomic, i.e., more adapted to human movement and thinking patterns. Less fatigue, precise control, and simple operations were optimized in this way because huge amounts of data had to be entered as quickly and as simply as possible.

Diodes constantly generate light in liquid crystal displays (LCDs). The amount of light passing through a "sandwich" of polarizing filters and liquid crystals is determined by applying an electric field.

Input Devices

The most important input device is the keyboard, which enables an operator to type in characters and give the computer many instructions. The characters are arranged somewhat differently in every country. Touch pads and trackballs have been developed as alternatives for the mouse, another important input device. They are used for laptop computers and tamper-proof computer terminals in libraries or museums. Public computers like those provided at railway stations and movie theaters to buy tickets use touch screens instead of a keyboard. The touch screens give very clear and explicit instructions on how to operate the computer. Game pads have been developed as input devices, especially for certain gaming consoles. Optical information is recorded through scanners, and acoustic information through microphones. Microphones are also used for the operation of phonetically controlled computers.

Output Devices

The most important output device is the monitor. It presents the user with graphical displays of results. Editing text and pictures, for example, would be impossible without the monitor. The bulky cathode ray tubes are increasingly being replaced with flat screens. Other output devices are loudspeakers, which have been part of standard equipment since the 1990s, and the printer. The Internet can be considered as an output device that contains many possible connections.

Simulators: Complex Input and Output Devices

Normally, the user sits near the computer and interacts with only the screen, mouse, and keyboard, using only some of their senses. Actions take place symbolically, such as the movement of icons on the screen, for example, for the perception of the user. The limitations of a monitor are broken through in simulators. In simulators, computers generate virtual events in a pseudo-environment, as for instance in flight simulators for pilot training. The operating instruments and display devices, which are available to a pilot in a real cockpit, serve as input and output devices. Simulators are technically complex but are effective learning tools because of their accurate simulation of reality. Simulators are also widely used in the entertainment industry.

The Mouse

In the case of a mechanical mouse, a ball is moved through the motion of the casing by the user. Two perpendicular axes, to which perforated discs are fastened, rotate with the ball. The light of a diode shines through the holes of the discs onto a light sensor. If an axis is rotated, the ray of light that falls on the sensor is interrupted again and again. The sensor sends the state "light" or "no light" as a digital signal to the computer. From the number of light signals received from the two axes, the mouse's pointer on the screen is moved.

above: *Mechanics of a computer mouse*

Virtual Worlds

VIRTUAL REALITY makes it possible for a person to interact realistically with a computer-generated environment. Motion sensors translate physical movements, such as grasping or head turning, into the virtual world. Sensory feedback is provided through the visual display and often audio. This allows immersion in the experience and creates the illusion of reality in fantasy environments and artificial simulations of real-life.

Headphones produce 3D sound effects.
The movements of the user are translated as visual feedback.
Visors have monitors instead of lenses.
Force feedback: Motors are placed in joysticks, for example, in order to simulate the sense of touch.
Inductive mats on the floor use the position of the foot as input.

STORAGE MEDIA

The security of data is important in this modern age of communication. There are a variety of different physical phenomena and properties of matter that are used for this purpose.

High technological standards are set for data storage. Increasingly, larger quantities of data must be securely stored over a long period of time. The medium of storage has to be as compact and transportable as possible, allow for quick access, and be connectable for many systems—all this at an attractive price.

Standard Mobile Storage Media

Floppy disks and Zip disks (flexible disks) have been replaced to a large extent by compact discs with read-only memory (CD-ROMs). Since 1996, Digital Versatile Discs (DVDs) have been available and are more efficient. High-Definition DVDs (HD DVD) and Blu-ray Discs (BD) were developed as competition and offer up to 50 GB memory storage. Multi-sided devices with a faster access time are hard disk drives with a USB connection (p. 137). Hard disk drives can be connected to almost all computer systems without any special reading devices. USB memory sticks use flash memory (memory that can be electrically erased and reprogrammed) and have capacities of many gigabytes and a USB connection. They are small and simple to handle.

What Is a Megabyte?

The smallest memory unit is a bit and can have two values (0 and 1) that can be represented by two charges (positive and negative). In order to represent all the characters of a PC-keyboard, 256 characters need to be encoded. For this purpose 8 bits are called a byte since (2^8 = 256 or 0 to 255). A megabyte is 1 million bytes. However, since computer memory comes in powers of two, 1 megabyte = 2^{20} = 1,048,576 bytes in the units used for computers. Around 2,000 pages of pure text, 7 seconds of uncompressed music, or a quarter-second of high quality video can be saved in one megabyte.

A 1 GB memory chip can store the equivalent of two million pages of text.

Storage Media With Special Tasks

In the primary storage or main memory of the motherboard, data is only temporarily saved for quicker processing. Even graphic and video cards have their own main memory. BIOS, by contrast, is a kind of permanent memory in which the manufacturer stores important system data. This data cannot normally be modified by the users. Memory that allows only the reading but not the saving of data is called read-only memory (ROM). On the other hand, hard disks and USB memory sticks use random-access memory (RAM) that can save data.

CD-ROMS and DVDs are the most common medium of storage.

Development of New Storage Technologies

More efficient materials and novel ideas for data storage are being actively researched. A Japanese research group hangs its hopes on an optical storage medium in which plastic balls of 500 nanometer diameters are provided with a fluorescent colorant. A section of the ball is modified during saving in such a way that the colorant lights up during reading—every ball is a bit. Using this method will produce memory size several times higher than a DVD's. In the search for storage media that can withstand nuclear attacks, data has been translated into DNA molecules and implanted into bacteria as if it was genetic information. The data can be read unmodified even after hundreds of generations of the bacteria. It remains to be seen if this ambitious research ever results in a marketable product.

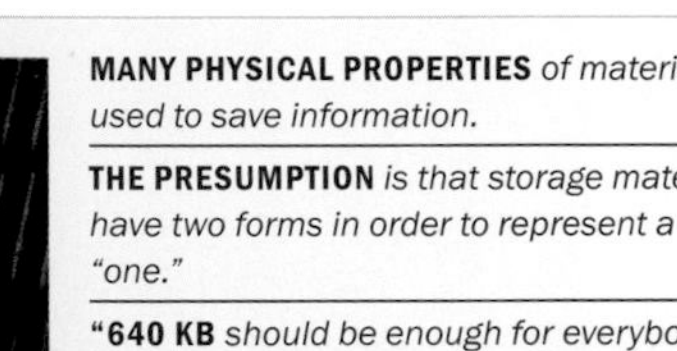

MANY PHYSICAL PROPERTIES *of materials can be used to save information.*

THE PRESUMPTION *is that storage material must have two forms in order to represent a "zero" or "one."*

"640 KB *should be enough for everybody."*
—Bill Gates, founder of Microsoft, 1981

Scanning tunneling microscope (STM) photo of a hard disk with grooves for magnetic data storage

Physics of Data Storage

A HARD DISK can be compared to a huge field of aligned bar magnets placed next to one another. The polarization of the smallest magnetic units (north or south) represents the digital status "zero" or "one." The smallest storage units of a USB memory stick are tiny transistors (electronic switches, p. 184) that either conduct or block currents. Information is stored in the surface of a CD-ROM as indentations called lands and pits and scanned by a laser beam. A one-bit land has a width of around 300 nanometers (three ten-thousandths of a millimeter) and can contain one bit of information. In the case of magneto-optical disks, a laser is used to modify the magnetic state of the data medium, which is a ferromagnetic material sealed beneath a plastic coat.

USB memory stick

INSIDER KNOWLEDGE

MAXIMUM CAPACITY *of different storage media:*

3.5 INCH DISC: *1.4 MB*

ZIP DISK: *100 to 750 MB*

CD-ROM: *650 to 900 MB*

FLASH MEMORY CARD (COMPACT DISC): *4 MB to 16 GB*

DVD: *4.7 to 17 GB*

BLU-RAY DISC (BOTH LAYERS): *up to 50 GB*

USB STICK (UNIVERSAL SERIAL BUS STICK): *16 MB to over 100 GB*

ELECTRONIC COMPONENTS

Electronic components are the basic elements inside computers and in the technology of communications. Highly complex circuits are combinations of many electronic elements.

The electronic components used in a computer have different operating voltages. In the operation of a light-emitting diode, for example, less current is required as higher currents can damage the device. If such a diode is directly connected to the main power source, it will melt down immediately. In order to reduce the current flow, the resistance of the circuit containing the diode must be increased (Ohm's law, p. 110). To do this a component can be inserted into the circuit that is named after its function—a resistor. A high resistance, as long as the voltage does not change, will lower the voltage so that the diode operates properly. The combination of current, voltage, and resistance is the basis of all electronic circuits. In the manufacture of computers, for example, a large number of components are assembled. Each component itself is made up of many smaller components and many printed circuit boards.

From the Enormous to the Tiny

There are different kinds of electronic components designed for different kinds of operations. In the field of power electronics, components with high voltage and current ratings are used. On the other hand, components in signal and communication electronics operate at voltages well under 100 volts and currents under one ampere. Corresponding to the different areas of application, components have different forms and dimensions. A switch used in an electric power system can weigh several pounds (kilograms), while the sensitive and precise switches of signal technology are frequently assembled with tweezers.

The ongoing miniaturization in computer technology has brought about new types of components. Older components have contacts in the form of small legs, which are stuck to the circuit board through holes, soldered to the other side, and connected by wires. A new class of components is used in computer and communication technology called surface mounted devices (SMDs). SMD components, which were developed in order to fit more components into a circuit, are soldered directly to the surface of a printed circuit board. Printed circuit boards are used to mechanically support and electrically connect components.

Production Technology

The mass production of electronic devices mostly takes place in fully automated assembly lines. In the development, control, and repair of components, technicians work with fine tools, soldering stations, magnifying glasses, and measuring and testing devices.

Electronic components are very sensitive to static charges and are called electronic sensitive devices (ESD). Technicians will often stand on a grounding mat and wear shoes with metal strips. ESD-safe foam and ESD-safe bags are required for shipping such components.

The arrangement and linking of the components of a computer circuit board determine its function.

Electronic Components of a Processor

Knowledge of the function of individual components is very important for an understanding of electronic circuits. Diodes exist as light-emitting diodes (LEDs) and in other forms. Diodes allow current to enter in one direction but not the other. They transform alternating current, for example, into direct current. Diodes are also used for voltage protection and power regulation and are made from semiconductors. Inductors consist of a wire wrapped around a post to form a coil. They can modify the flow of alternating voltage and increase or decrease voltages, as in a transformer. Transistors can be used as amplifiers or to store information. Resistors do not just limit current, but can also be used to change voltages. Condensers can store a charge in order to balance out voltage fluctuations. If after switching off the monitor, the display flickers for a few more seconds, the condenser is responsible.

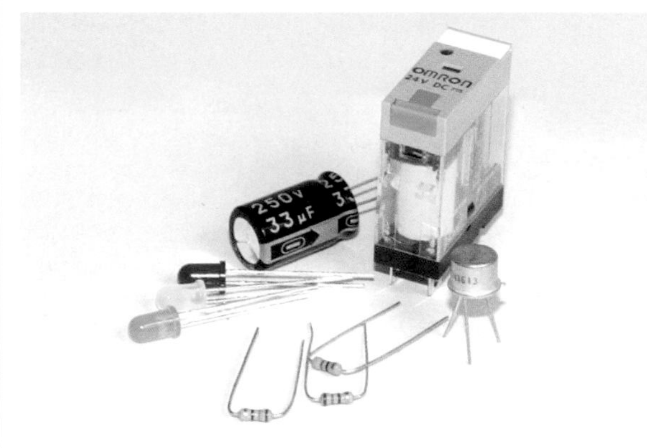

Transistor as a Circuit

TRANSISTORS are mostly made up of silicon or germanium (p. 102) and replaced triode vacuum tubes. If a transistor is connected to a light-emitting diode in an electric circuit, then initially it will not let current flow and is comparable to a closed circuit. If a voltage is applied at the base of the transistor, the transistor becomes conductive. Now it corresponds to an open circuit, current flows, and the diode emits light. A transistor can represent a digital value ("zero" or "one") through its conductive and non-conductive states. This means it corresponds to the smallest logical unit (p. 139). This is why there are more than a hundred million transistors in a computer processor.

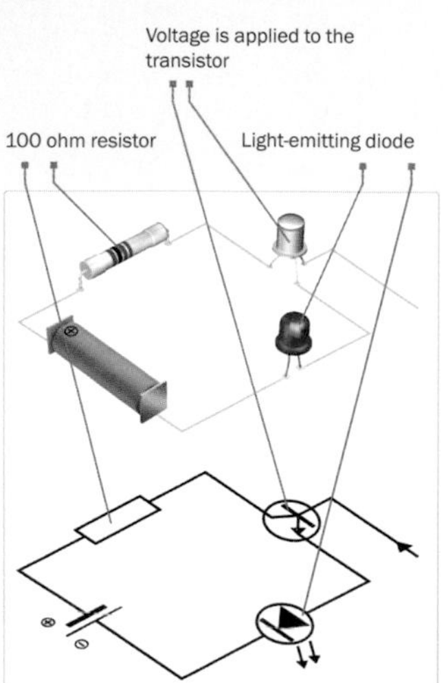

A battery supplies the operating voltage.

➲ see also: **Silicion Wafer,** *Chemistry Chapter, p. 102*

CIRCUITS

Electronic circuits have replaced mechanisms made from metal in many areas. Innovative circuits simulate the way the brain processes information.

At first sight, a circuit board looks like a colorful chaos of electronic components. There are, however, regularities that all circuits follow. The operating voltage comes from a voltage source that can be a power supply or battery. There are inboxes and outboxes for data in signal and computer technology. The function of a circuit is determined by the type and size of the components used.

The precision of a circuit depends on the tolerances (acceptable deviations) of the ratings of the components. If during operations it is possible to modify the function of the circuit (for example, potentiometers with a variable resistance or any element with a changeable value) or to interrupt the individual conducting paths (for example, with buttons or keys), the changes are integrated into the circuit without a change in function. The knobs of some potentiometers protrude out of an opening on the cabinet. An example is the volume and tone controls on a hi-fi audio system. In addition, there are options for setting different parameters on circuits that are accessible only to a technician. The receiving unit on a cellular phone is an example. For troubleshooting circuits, measurements can be made at points whose correct voltages are recorded in tables.

Contacts on the lower surface of an IC base.

INTEGRATED CIRCUITS *(ICs) are components that contain a multitude of smaller circuits.*

AND, OR, NAND, NOR, AND XOR *are logic gates and perform logical operations in a computer.*

PROCESSORS *are especially efficient ICs that have an extremely large number of circuits in them.*

Numerous microcircuits are connected to each other in a computer chip.

Circuits

A CANDY VENDING MACHINE dispenses a packet of bubble gum only if the buyer has inserted a coin AND pressed the button after selecting his or her choice. These actions are performed by an integrated circuit (IC). The machine gives 5 volts to each of two pins of an AND logical gate of the integrated circuit. Since both of the pins are getting a high input, the conditions 1 AND 2 are both high; and the output of the gate, a third pin, produces 5 volts. This signal is used to disburse the bubble gum from the drawer. If payment can be made with a dollar bill, an OR logical gate can query if the amount was paid EITHER as coins OR as a bill. In an OR gate a high output occurs if one pin or the other pin or both pins have a high input.

XOR GATES are OR gates that allow the fulfillment of exactly one condition. NAND gates exclude the AND case, and NOR gates exclude the OR case. Through the coupling of different logical gates, an IC can carry out increasingly complex queries.

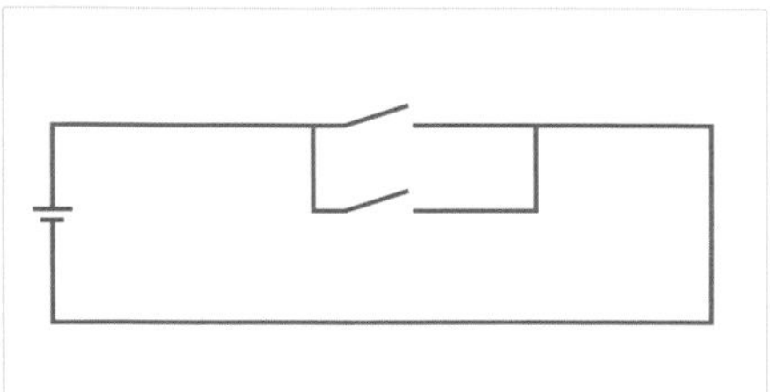

Circuit with an OR gate

Signal Transmission

The generation, processing, transfer, and storage of information and signal electronics have become very important in the information age. An important requirement of the technology of signal transmission is that the information be fully and correctly transmitted.

Many factors can disturb a transmission, for example, the resistance of long cables and electrical fields produced by other devices. For this reason, controls and redundancies are part of planning an information transmission system. Redundancies are additional, not required, standbys and duplicates. A few systems repeat a received message so that the sender knows that the transmission has taken place without errors. Such a transmission, however, gets delayed and unnecessary data is sent.

Modern technology appends control information to the data packets that enable the receiver to make sure that the message was received without errors by a built-in analysis. An example of this is the Transmission Control Protocol (TCP/IP) used on the Internet, which is part of a suite of conventions and standards used to transmit data. TCP/IP is used for email, file transport protocol, and the World Wide Web.

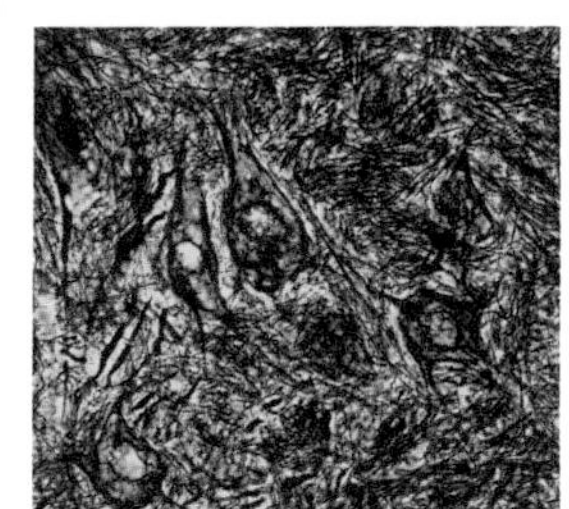

Neural Network

The human brain is more efficient in many ways than any of the computers available today. Scientists expect to gain some useful knowledge from research on the brain. Artificial neural networks (ANN) process information in a way that is similar to the way the brain processes information. Traditional computer systems process tasks serially, one computation after the other. Parallel processing means computations occur at the exact same time. Simultaneous processing is the goal in the development of ANN. ANNs do not work logically, but rather on the basis of trial and error. They also use probabilities and approximations. ANNs are used in economics and meteorology for simulation and prognosis.

above: *Microscopic picture of nerve cells*

In data communications, "handshaking" means the transfer of data starts only after the receiver has signaled readiness. This helps to secure a good transfer of data. For example, a printer gives the computer the message "online" before data is sent. With the message "Paper tray empty" the transfer is interrupted so that no data is lost.

21ST CENTURY

THE ASCENDANCY OF ROBOTS *is the subject of many movies. Their dominance, however, will probably remain science fiction in the 21st century.*

THE DEVELOPMENT *of neural networks and artificial intelligence is still in the beginning stages.*

THE CREATION *of artificial intelligence that is multifunctional and adaptive is far away.*

➲ see also: Nerve Cells, *Biology Chapter*, p. 89

THE INTERNET—STRUCTURE

"Internet" is an abbreviation of "Interconnected Network," standing for a global network of interconnected computer networks. Its main uses are communication and information storage.

In 1958, the U.S. wanted to develop a technology that would allow many users to simultaneously access the computing power of mainframes. Computers of four universities were connected to a network in 1969 and the Advanced Research Projects Agency Network (ARPANET) was set in operation. Additional computers were connected to the network in the 1970s, and the protocol that defined the way messages were sent was improved. New services, such as email and the transporting of files, were developed. The emergence of special data networks, to run in parallel to the telephone network, allowed quicker transfer of data. In 1972, a new technology was developed under the term "Ethernet." Ethernet is a diverse family of technologies that enabled the setting up of local area networks (LANs). A LAN is a computer network covering a small geographic area like a home, office, or group of buildings.

The Internet—A Decentralized Computer Network

The Internet transfers data in packets; that is, the information to be transmitted is divided into small units. These individual packets can be sent from the sender to the receiver in many different ways. Unlike the circuit-switching technology of telephones, there is no single cable between a client and the host system. Rather, there is a complex system of computers and nodes through which the data finds its way. Nodes are computers programmed as a router. So that a router knows where to forward the incoming data, every data packet contains the target address as the first bit of information. Through this principle of intelligent nodes, the Internet works without a central steering point. Even if a part of the network fails, the Internet can continue to function because information can be transferred ("routed") in other ways.

INSIDER KNOWLEDGE

NUMBER *of hosts on the Internet:*
1969: *4*
1981: *213*
1989: *80,000*
1991: *375,000*
1998: *over 30 million*
2003: *172 million*
2008: *over 500 million*

Structure and Devices

A host-computer provides a service (e.g., a Web page), and a user accesses it from a distant place. The information is forwarded through a multitude of networks before it reaches its target. A gateway is a node that serves an entrance to another network so that different networks are connected. For example, a company's computer network can be connected to the Internet. The connection between the Internet and individual users is frequently made available by an Internet provider for a fee. The data from the Internet is transferred to the provider who makes the final connection with the end users. The connection between a PC and the telephone network is made by a modem, an amalgam of the words "modulation" and "demodulation." The modem converts the digital data of the computer into acoustic signals (analog modem) for the telephone network or in other digital data formats (ISDN). Every computer in the Internet is identified with a unique Internet Protocol (IP) address made up of four bytes of data, so that each component can range from 0 to 255. For example, one of the computers that offer the contents of Wikipedia has the address 60.230.200.100. In order to make it easy for non-experts to use the Internet, a name is assigned to the address. The Domain Name System (DNS) translates the name of the computer (e.g., www.wikipedia.net) into the IP address. This way, the router can find the correct host without having to know the IP address.

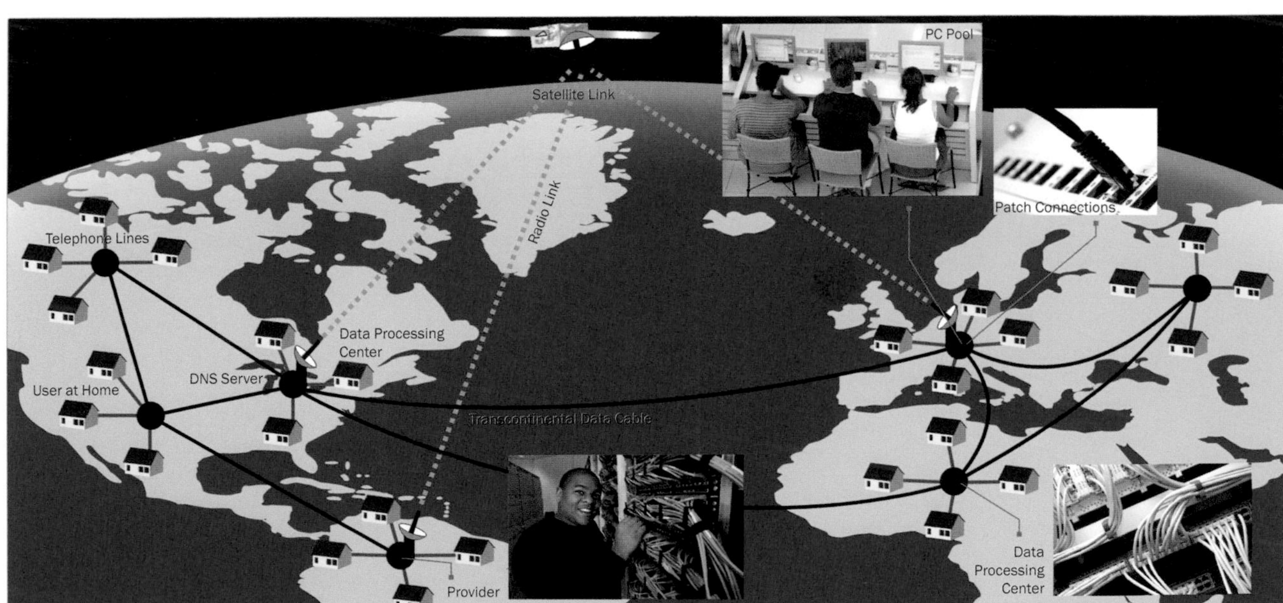

Internet service providers have servers and routers, and the data packets are transmitted through cable and satellite connections. The connection between the local computer and the main host is usually through the telephone network. The individual computers are connected to it with modems and routers.

THE INTERNET—SERVICES

The Internet is much more than a network of cables and computers. Numerous protocols and services are available to a user who wants to chat, search for information, or send an email.

The first service of the ARPANET (p. 142) was to organize the data exchange between the connected computers. ARPANET implemented the Transmission Control Protocol (TCP) that determines uniform data formats as well as enables radio and satellite transmission of data. Computers can be operated remotely through telnet (teletype network) developed in 1971. The File Transfer Protocol (FTP) enables files to be transferred between computers and is widely used today. The email service also originated in 1971. The small program was developed by Ray Tomilson in order to send electronic messages to users on different computers. He did not suspect how quickly his invention would spread.

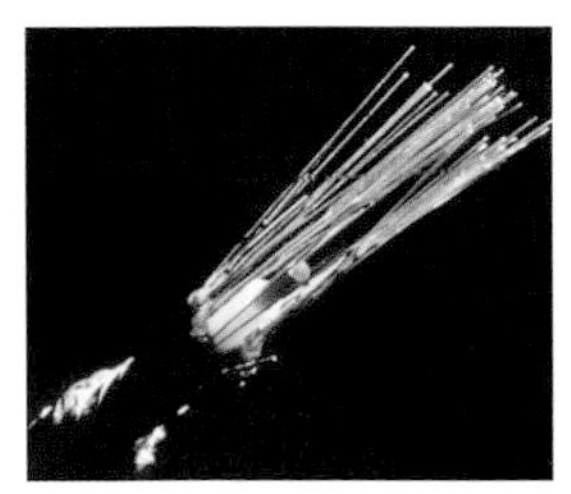

Internet Backbones

Internet backbones are a large collection of connections between individual networks. They consist of optical fiber cables that connect the Internet exchange points of computer centers in different countries to each other and carry data at very high rates. In the beginning, Internet backbones were maintained by national organizations. Today they are mostly in the hands of private providers. An important Internet backbone is the EuroRing with capacities of up to 10 gigabytes per second. The most important exchange point in Europe is the Amsterdam Internet Exchange (AMS-IX) and it is the largest in the world.

above: *Fiber optic cable*

Bulletin board systems (BBS) began in 1979 on the Internet in order to send messages along with uploading and downloading software. From sorting of the contributions published on BBSs, the USENET emerged with tens of thousands of newsgroups. The Internet Relay Chat (IRC) was introduced towards the end of the 1980s in order to exchange text messages in real time. The character of the Internet changed fundamentally in 1991 with the release of the World Wide Web. The Web gave the nonscientific public access to the Internet. With the abolition of the ban on advertisement, the Internet became a mass medium. Communication between individuals, sales, and entertainment became the most popular applications. Streaming processes have enabled the real-time transfer of radio and video data since 1995. In streaming, the transmissions are divided into small units and transferred. In order to avoid interruptions in replay, a buffer temporarily saves the data and bridges moments of lower transfer rates. The rapid transfer of films and sounds increases the attractiveness of the Internet for the advertising and entertainment industry. In 2008, it was estimated there were over 1 trillion Web pages accessible to the public.

Current Developments

Electronic payment procedures allow the Internet to be used as a market place. Along with making material goods and services available for purchase, Internet sites are increasingly making products available to an online user for a fee and securing their credit card or personal bank information with secret encoding.

Increasingly, private and business contacts are made over the Internet so that now hardly any company can get by without an Internet presence. Because of the increasing number of participants, the Internet Protocol version 6 (IPv6) has been developed to replace the current IP (IPv4). This protocol will expand the number of IP addresses from around 4 billion (2^{32}) to 340 sextillion (2^{128}).

There are different ways of connecting a computer to the Internet: With modem and cable, with a wireless local area network (WLAN), and with Bluetooth.

THE WWW *was developed at the research institute CERN in Geneva, Switzerland, and spread worldwide within a few years.*

THE FORMATTING LANGUAGE HTML *creates Internet pages through the specification of colors, fonts, and hyperlinks.*

ADDITIONAL SERVICES *of the Internet are email and file transfer under the FTP protocol.*

Screenshot of YouTube

WWW—World Wide Web

THE WORLD WIDE WEB is a service offered by the Internet. Important elements in Web pages are images, text, and hyperlinks to other servers, as well as the possibility of accessing other services such as email or newsgroups. Web pages are built using HyperText Markup Language (HTML), which combines text with extra information to create Web pages. The successor to HTML is Extensible HTML (XHTML), which is expandable and corresponds to the Extensible Markup Language (XML) structuring language. New programming languages enable the representation of multimedia and interaction with the user. The Adobe Flash animation software enables clips of moving graphics to be included on the Web pages.

A screenshot of an email account: Along with personal emails, unsolicited emails sent to large numbers of people (spam) also circulate.

PHYSICS AND TECHNOLOGY

KEY FACTS

DIGITALIZATION *is the coding of information into binary numbers (0 and 1) to replace analog systems.*

NEW MEDIA *forms allow even private individuals to publish their creative output.*

INFORMATION AND ENTERTAINMENT *continue to go hand in hand with new media formats.*

MINIATURIZED DEVICES *are universally used.*

Landline telephony | Cell phones and multi-purpose devices | Radio | Television | Photo and video | Audio devices

COMMUNICATION AND ENTERTAINMENT TECHNOLOGY

Digital technology has replaced analog technology in telephony as well as in radio, television, photography, movies, and music. There is an increasing trend towards eliminating the boundaries between various media. Multifunctional devices can be used to make a call, send a text message, take photos, record short movies, play music, and make an entry in a calendar.

The word "digital" comes from the Latin word for finger, "digitus."

LANDLINE TELEPHONY

Since the 1990s, digital technology has enabled new services to be added to landline telephones. Many providers are now offering a telephone connection, Internet access, and cable TV.

During the course of the 20th century, the telephone has evolved from a privilege to a means of communication used by everyone. The end of the 20th century witnessed the switch from analog to digital technology and a new era in telephony.

Today, instead of analog wire wrap connections, digital control boxes are used at distribution points, which are similar to Internet routers.

Digital Landline Telephones

Terminals and distribution centers need to be equipped for a digital telephone network. The data is now transferred in packets just as on the Internet (p. 142). However, unlike the Internet, telephone networks are centrally administered and customers are billed.

The spectrum of services was significantly extended with digital technology. Caller identification, call forwarding, voice mail, call waiting, and teleconferencing were introduced. Other services, like telefax, were significantly simplified. The telephone network facilitates services such as the remote control of household devices. Thus, the homeowner can control an alarm system at a distance with the help of surveillance cameras.

This and similar technologies of home automation are sometimes referred to as "Smart Home" or "Intelligent House" technologies.

Merging of Networks

The upgrading of cellular networks has led to further developments in landline telephony, for example, the use of a Short Message Service (SMS) on landline phones and voice mail. Also, wireless network adapters for landline instruments and various other services have been introduced.

The use of telephone connections as Internet access points created demands to increase data transfer capacities. Since the capacity of copper cables is limited to a certain extent, landline telephone service providers are currently placing fiber optic cables directly into individual households.

On the other hand, the Internet is giving serious competition to telephony with Voice Over Internet Protocol. This technology means that with the help of an adapter the Internet can be used for long-distance conversations.

Companies belonging to various other industries are also providing telephone services, e.g., cable TV. Technology has made it possible to provide telephone and Internet services via TV cables or high voltage current networks.

Also, broadband telephone and data connections can be established via radio and satellite technology, totally independent of a fixed network.

The first overseas telephone cables were laid down in the middle of the 20th century, compete to this day with satellite connections.

The technology of Voice Over Internet Protocol transfers speech and video images on the Internet.

Digital Computation of Tones

AN IMPORTANT CRITERION for designing telecommunication instruments is the ability to replicate language and tones. Technically, it is possible to operate voice/telephone networks with a very high quality. However, to limit the amount of data that has to be transmitted, the frequency range is reduced to that of human speech, which is between 300 and 3400 Hertz.

FOR DIGITAL TELEPHONES, the sound waves are analyzed and translated into a digital signal, in sequences of 0s and 1s. These are then transferred as electrical impulses or as "light" and "no light" states in fiber-optic cables.

Conversion of sound waves in digital data

CELL PHONES AND MULTI-PURPOSE DEVICES

No other communication device has found such a large market in such a short time as the cell phone. Not just a telephone, mobile phones now perform many other functions.

Cell phones have rapidly penetrated our daily lives. Remote and thinly populated regions have especially benefited from the possibilities of wireless communication. Low prices make the cell phone an excellent alternative to a landline.

Transmission and Distribution Technology

Like the digital telephone network, the cellular phone network is computer based, centrally controlled, and delivers information in packets (p. 142). Transmission towers erected close to one another are needed for the operation of a cell telephone network.

Headsets with earphones and microphones keep the hands free when on a call.

Not all service providers possess their own individual transmission technology. Instead, they rent or lease the infrastructure of another company. There are also various arrangements between cellular companies that allow their customers to use the service networks in different geographical areas. This arrangement is called "roaming."

Besides transmission towers and distribution centers, gateways are installed to establish connections between landline networks and the Internet. This enables calls to be made from a mobile phone to a landline phone and other services, like text messaging or email.

Cell phones cannnot operate in a subway because metallic structures act like a Faraday cage to block signals. However, antenna and radio receivers can be installed in the tunnels to provide mobile phone service to subway riders.

"Electrosmog"

Electrosmog refers to the danger to the environment from the electromagnetic radiation that is emitted from mobile phones and broadcasting towers, TV and radio transmitters, and high-voltage power lines. Critics are fearful of adverse effect on the health of humans, for example, headaches, lack of concentration, and even more serious illnesses. The issue is controversial, but there is no definitive scientific proof of adverse effects.

above: *Satellite dish and transmitting tower for mobile phones*

ALONG WITH *the development of the mobile phone, new services have been established that were not provided by any other device.*

THE SALE OF RINGTONES *is a lucrative business.*

BACK TO BASICS: *In Japan, mobile phones that are only used for the purpose of making calls are popular.*

Most young people today do not leave the house without their mobile phone.

Services

SMS (Short Message Service, or text messaging) has been available since 1991. Technically, an SMS consists of an address (header) and a message (body) that is different from email. Compared to a telephonic conversation, the quantity of data is small. There can only be 1,120 bits in an SMS because of the signaling protocol. Messaging services and a tsunami early-warning system are some of the other technical innovations that have been developed. An SMS can also be used for the remote control of distant devices. In 2004, 500 billion SMSes were sent worldwide, up from 17 billion in 2000.

MMS (Multimedia Messaging Service) allows multimedia objects, such as photos, video clips, and tickets of admission, to be included in the message. Other services are SMS chats, which link messages from the same conversation together. Wireless Application Protocol (WAP) enables access to the Internet from a cell phone.

Swiss Federal Railways (SBB) has a ticket purchase system for cell phones. After a credit card payment is confirmed, an MMS image with a code serves as a ticket.

Cellular Networks

The growth of cellular telephony began in the 1980s, especially in Europe. Currently, a major portion of mobile communication takes place in the GSM (Global System for Mobile Communications) network. The GSM service is used by over 2 billion people in 212 countries. GSM networks operate mainly in four different frequency ranges. The U.S. and Canada use the 850 MHz and 1900 MHz bands while Europe uses 900 MHz and 1800 MHz.

At the beginning, cell phones could only use one of the bands at a time. Dual-band cell phones permit the use of two different bands, and tri-band cell phones facilitate telecommunications in Europe as well as in the U.S.

Advanced transfer protocols for the GSM network have been developed to increase the transmission capacity. The Universal Mobile Telecommunications System (UMTS) is a third-generation (3G) mobile phone technology. Service providers anticipate an intensive use of multimedia and Internet applications because of the greater rate of data transfer. Likewise, laptops can be used to establish cellular connection to the Internet via cell phone or UMTS cards. Currently, further development of UMTS technology promises to produce a fourth-generation network.

Many people possess one or two older cell phones in addition to the one in use.

A personal digital assistant (PDA) can make calls, receive and send emails, access databases, change a schedule, and more.

RADIO

In the 1920s, radio became the first real-time medium of mass communication. The switch to digital technology brings major changes in transmission and reception technology.

Radio-transmission towers are put on mountains to increase the range.

Radio technology transmits sound over long distances through the air. The sound waves are converted into electromagnetic waves and then reconverted back to sound waves (p. 109). Musical sound is a mechanical wave with frequencies between 40 Hz and 14 kHz. Electromagnetic waves, or radio waves, travel in a vacuum. The radio waves used by AM radio stations have frequencies ranging from 520 to 1610 kHz, and those used by FM radio stations have frequencies ranging from 87.9 to 107.9 MHz.

Analog and Digital Modulation

Radio waves consist of a carrier wave (e.g., an even sine wave with the frequency of 100 MHz in the UKW range) that is modulated to reproduce music and speech. The process of frequency modulation (FM) changes the frequency of the carrier wave, that is, the number of oscillations per second. The process of amplitude modulation (AM) changes the amplitude or the strength of the radio wave. The receiver extracts the fluctuations in the carrier wave and processes them to produce modulated sound. FM radio produces a higher quality of reception. AM radio is technically easier to implement; however, it is more susceptible to atmospheric disturbances such as thunderstorms. Digital radio broadcasters use various technologies like Digital Radio Mondiale (DRM) and Digital Audio Broadcasting (DAB). These protocols describe the formats of the digital data packets, which transport the sound data within the digital radio network.

A multiband radio with a built-in generator

Digital radio broadcasts are transmitted via satellites with frequencies of 2.5 GHz in North America and 1.4 GHz elsewhere.

INSIDER KNOWLEDGE

RADIO WAVES *are part of the electromagnetic spectrum.*

THE RADIO TRANSMISSION TOWER *in Warsaw was the tallest at 2,119 ft (646 m) until it fell in 1991.*

WEATHER *influences the range of radio broadcasts.*

Currently, a large portion of radio broadcasts still use analog technologies. The EU, however, plans to completely switch over to digital transmission and reception by the year 2012.

Reception Technology

Antennas receive the radio waves, which are eventually converted into electrical oscillations by an oscillatory circuit that includes inductors and condensers. A particular radio station is selected by setting the oscillatory circuit to a specific resonance frequency. The length of the antennas depends on the wavelength of the radio wave that one wishes to receive. AM radio waves have longer wavelengths than FM radio waves and can be up to 1,893 ft (577 m). Radio transmission can be performed by a cable network. In this case, the data is not transmitted in the form of electromagnetic waves; instead, it is transmitted in the form of high-frequency electrical oscillations. In addition to AM and FM radio, there are satellite radio programs that use either antennas or satellite dishes for reception, depending on the frequency range of the broadcast. Digital receivers or set-top boxes can be used for analog signals as well as digital broadcasts.

A Four Seasons miniradio in a plastic bubble with suction pads.

Extras of the Digital Era

Digital radio technology offers many extras besides improved reception. For example, it is possible to display additional information about the broadcast on the receiver. Internet radios use an audio-streaming technology (p. 142) to achieve a real-time transmission of audio data, which is an entirely different technology. Audio streaming can be directed to one user or broadcast to all users.

Radio

Radio and wireless telegraphy are information systems that propagate through space. In the early part of the 20th century they were an important component in coordinating complex operations across the globe and accurately determining the position of ships. Today, communication via radio is an inseparable component of air, shipping, and rail traffic. There is ongoing research into ways of improving wireless information systems, for example, by developing a flight control system that uses microwaves.

above: *Ship personnel use a radio for on-board communications with a port.*

Transmission of Radio Waves

IMPORTANT FOR BROADCASTING TECHNOLOGY AND TRANSMISSION PROPERTIES is the length of the radio waves used. Most regional radio broadcasters use the very-high-frequency range (VHF: 30 MHz to 300 MHz). VHF waves provide good sound quality; however, their range is limited. Short waves (SW: 3 MHz to 30 MHz) have longer wavelengths and are therefore used by national broadcasters. The sound quality is, however, lower than with VHF waves. Medium-frequency waves (MF: 500 kHz to 1500 kHz) have a sound quality that depends on the time of the day. They have broader range, especially at night, because they can be reflected from the ionosphere. Likewise, low-frequency waves (LF: 150 kHz to 300 kHz) cover long distances. They are used by European radio stations, but not by radio stations in the U.S.

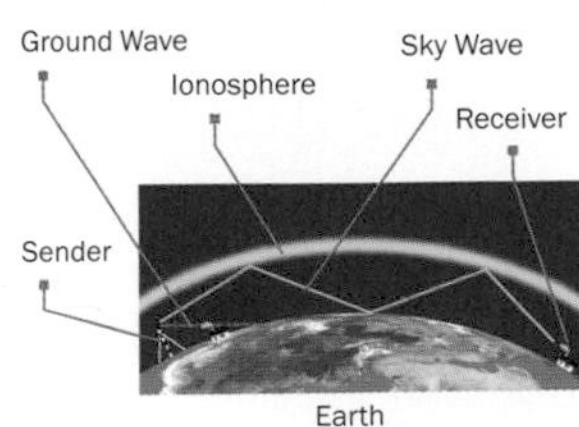

Very-high-frequency waves are transmitted from high transmission towers directly to the receivers, whereas short waves are reflected by the ionosphere.

TELEVISION

Technology increasingly governs the quality and success of a television broadcast. The switch to digital technology has led to comprehensive changes behind the scenes as well.

Live action sports: Huge LCD screens facilitate the public showing of television programs.

The first prototype of a television was developed in 1928, but commercial distribution began in the 1950s. Transmission via satellites has been operational since the 1960s. The switch to digital technology has brought about many profound changes.

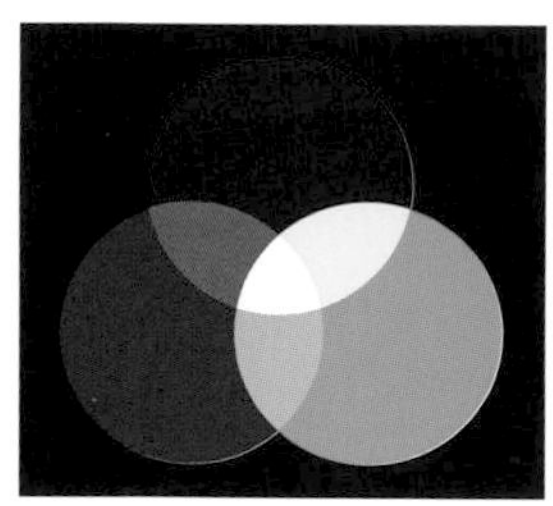

Additive Color Mixing

Daylight contains all the colors of the spectrum (p. 109). A colored substance reflects the part of the spectrum corresponding to the observed color with the rest of the spectrum being absorbed. Since dyes reduce the luminosity, subtractive color mixing is sometimes used. In the case of additive color mixing, colored light is mixed. The more colors, the greater the luminosity. The mixing of red and green light results in yellow; and the mixing of red, green, and blue results in white light. Televisions and monitors are developed according to these principles.

above: *Additive color mixing*

Technology in TV Broadcasts

Film videos need to be recorded and edited with great technical expertise before they can be transmitted to the public. Efficient computer networks and digital devices are a fundamental part of the majority of modern broadcasts.

Teleprompters are used so that the news reporters can look into the camera without reading from notes. These devices are mounted on the cameras and superimpose the news items in text form. Anchors wear radio headphones, which gives them additional information when and if required.

The image together with the accompanying sound is stored in magnetic tape cassettes or directly on a hard disk. The playing devices automatically communicate with the computer used for editing. In order to edit the recordings, the studios use special computers with extremely large memories and hard disks with capacities measured in "terabytes."

The final edited versions of the broadcasts are transmitted by tall antennas. For analog broadcasts, formats like PAL, SECAM, and NTSC are used. For digital broadcasts, there are a variety of different transmission technologies and formats that are available.

Digital Extras

Digital transmission technology allows for an entirely new range of possibilities. "Movie on demand" allows the user to order films from television service providers at any time. This means programs need not be broadcast to the entire region. Interactive broadcasts, where the user can intervene and take an active part in the events of the screen using the telephone network, are possible. This is done, for example, with televised computer games or audience polls. Because of digital technology, television sets are no longer needed to receive and view broadcasts. Computers can be used to watch television when they are equipped with video cards. Likewise, newer mobile phones can receive television broadcasts.

TELEVISION PRODUCTION *today uses many different technologies, not just cameras, microphones, and lighting.*

THE TECHNOLOGY USED *has a great influence on the quality of the television transmission.*

A LARGE PART *of the technology that is used in studios remains unknown to the viewer.*

Studio camera on a trolley

Digital Technology

IN TELEVISION STUDIOS, a Betacam type of camera is frequently used. They are always mounted on trolleys so that they can create a clear picture—trolleys are mounts with wheels that move on the floor or hang on ropes/wires over the stage. For quick and mobile input, Mini-DV cameras are also employed, which deliver a slightly lower picture quality. Both types of cameras contain professional video microchips that support programs used for editing.

THE TRANSMISSION of television is similar to the transmission of digital radio (p. 146). It takes the form of high-frequency signals sent via cables, antennas, satellites, or streaming on the Internet (p. 142). The formats for digital transmission differ internationally and include Digital Video Broadcasting (DVB) in Europe and Advanced Television Systems Committee (ATSC) in the U.S.

Control console in a mixing room of a television studio

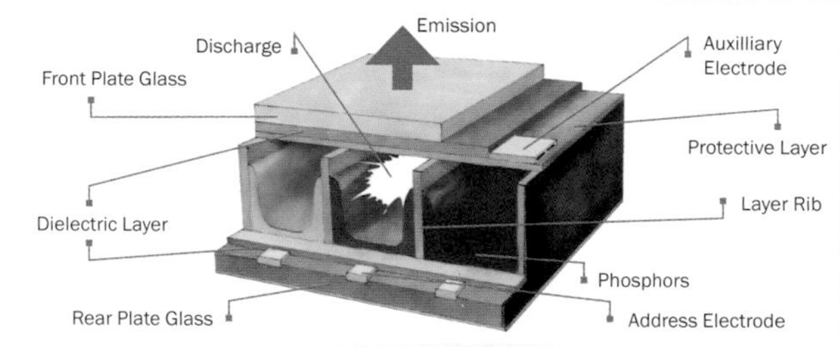

In plasma screens, every pixel is composed of three subpixels with red, green, or blue phosphors. Neon and xenon gases are ionized by electrodes and become a plasma that produces ultraviolet (UV) light. When the UV light strikes the phosphors, the different colors are produced.

Screens must be tested for their functionality and safety before being introduced into the market.

PHYSICS AND TECHNOLOGY

PHOTO AND VIDEO

Photography and video film are taking advantage of the digital revolution. Recording and playing devices are becoming smaller, making them more mobile and less expensive.

In 2000, for the first time ever, more video films were sold on DVDs than on video cassettes. At the present time, only DVDs are being produced.

Digital Video Technology

Analog video formats like VHS have been replaced by digital formats like MiniDV, Digital8 video tapes, and DVD and Blu-ray discs. The size of a modern MiniDV camera is the same as a pocket-sized camera. Analog cameras used to be heavy and unwieldy. Besides being able to record large amounts of data, digital video technology improves postproduction processing and optimizes picture quality.

Additional functions include producing color effects and being able to edit the recording in a personal computer. Recording times of more than five hours are possible because of energy saving techniques and efficient batteries. Photographic zoom lenses are capable of increasing the size of the original image 2 to 15 times. In a digital television camera, the size of an original image can be increased 700 times. The new and bigger images are created with a minimal loss of data. A video camera often includes a stereo microphone.

Many private individuals use small digital video cameras and make their own films with video editing programs.

High-definition video cameras allow consumers to record events with exceptional picture quality.

Digital Photography

An important benefit of digital technology is that a picture or an image can be viewed immediately after the shutter has been clicked. The image can also be deleted from the camera's memory immediately.

Digital cameras with two lenses give good picture quality even when light conditions are extremely poor.

There are different ways of identifying the quality of a digital camera, such as by the number of pixels captured in an image. This figure, called the resolution, has risen from a few hundred thousand to 50 million in high-quality cameras.

A high resolution is very often the criterion for making a purchase. However, it is not that relevant for viewing images on a monitor or for making prints in the standard sizes. To a great degree, the quality of images and pictures is determined by the optical properties and the sizes of the lenses. Shutter speeds and aperture settings have been supplemented with digital effects, for example, digital zoom, color balance, and contrast control.

The variety of storage media that can be used is very wide. Manufacturers try to promote their standards into the market. The most promising formats are those that can also be used in cellular phones. Cameras have USB connections to computers to transfer photos so that special picture card reading devices are rarely used.

Digital Photography

DIGITAL PHOTOGRAPHY requires several conversion processes to save images or pictures as digital data. The incident light is focused by microlenses and directed to light-sensitive semiconductor detectors. These are charge-coupled devices (CCD) and can convert colors and the intensity of light into electrical signals. The parts for each pixel are scanned for red, green, and blue light. Depending on the picture format used, the colors can be stored with different degrees of detail. For example, each pixel for 8-bit color graphics is represented by one byte. Other formats are "highcolor" (15/16 bits) and "truecolor" (24/32 bits). Finally, picture contrast is optimized as the data is compressed for storage.

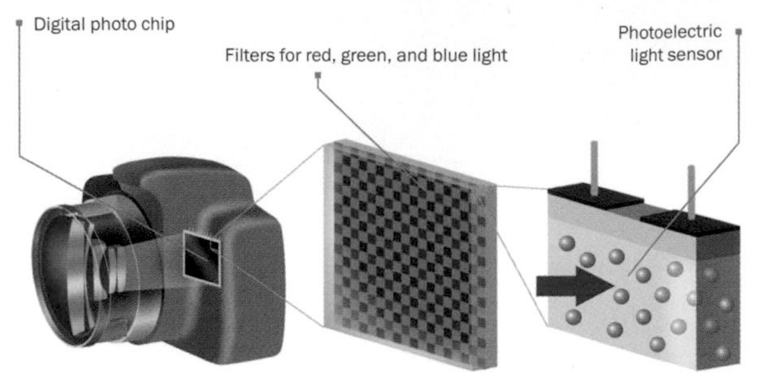

Surveillance cameras are a common sight in daily life.

Road to a Universal Medium?

By and large, there has been an amalgamation of various devices. Video cameras can now take still pictures, and digital cameras can record short video clips with sound.

INSIDER KNOWLEDGE

OPTICS *are more important in digital cameras than a high resolution.*

VIDEO CAMERAS *support editing programs that assign a number to every image or picture.*

THE PREDOMINANT METHOD *for capturing color today is to use a color filter mosaic in front of a CCD to selectively record the red, blue, and green information in the picture.*

Added to this, there are other kinds of devices that perform image and video recording, such as cell phones and personal digital assistants (PDAs). Dedicated devices continue to be superior to the multifunctional devices. It remains to be seen whether there will be a complete amalgamation of devices, or whether a reverse trend leading toward high quality devices with one single perfected function will develop.

➲ see also: USB Connections, *Physics and Technology Chapter, p. 137*

AUDIO DEVICES

From miniature radio to surround sound in cinemas, high-quality audio technology is available today at attractive prices. Digital audio players (e.g., iPods) make music available everywhere.

In 1979, the invention of the Walkman opened up the possibility of music that is available anywhere and anytime. It was the beginning of an era of mobile entertainment electronics and an expression of a new attitude towards life. Today, this role has been taken over by digital audio players that use the MP3 format. Concepts like "duration of play in minutes" have been replaced by their digital equivalents.

Headphones with active noise suppression generate a sound wave that cancels out the sound reaching the ears by destructive interference.

Audio Technology

Audio technology has become mobile and has penetrated into the realms of day-to-day existence. Miniature radios are given out as "freebies," and MP3 players are integrated into cell phones as extras. Portable CD players displaced the Walkman from its position in everyday life. Modern CD players are capable of playing alternative computer formats like WAV and MPEG.

Miniaturization has resulted in the loss of sound quality. In a reverse trend, extensive stereophonic systems are being developed that produce the impression that the listener is at a live event. A Dolby Surround soundtrack is produced with four channels of sound that are reduced to two channels of digital information. Dolby Pro Logic adds hardware and "firmware" to Dolby Surround to improve the quality of sound reproduction for cinemas and home-theater systems. Dolby Digital 5.1 has five loudspeakers with one low-frequency speaker called a subwoofer. There are other systems that use eight or more speakers in order to simulate sounds as effectively as possible.

Virtual Dolby Digital, on the other hand, is an attempt to achieve similar sound effects in a room with only two loudspeakers. Special software computes the sounds and tones in some computer games so that the players feel like they are in the actual place and situation, such as in the midst of football game.

Data Extraction

There are a number of ways music and video clips can be exchanged free of charge on the Internet. This unofficial exchange is referred to by some as piracy, and in the 1990s it led to revenue losses for the music industry. Music can now be downloaded legally for a fee from official Internet sites. The copying or downloading of selected tracks only is called "grabbing". The process of extracting files from one type of media and copying them to another, usually encoded into a new playback format, is called ripping. Most discs sold include copy protection files to prevent ripping and redistribution.

Recording Technology for Sound and Music

All that is needed to record and reproduce speech is to connect a microphone to a computer with a sound card and an audio player.

Loudspeakers

THE MUSICAL EXPERIENCE is not just dependent on the storage medium and computer equipment. Loudspeakers play a decisive role. "Multiway boxes" divide the music into different frequency ranges. The diaphragm of a small loudspeaker has a higher resonant frequency and is better at reproducing higher tones. Larger diaphragms are better at replicating the lower frequencies. The tuning and coordination of the equipment and loudspeaker, the design of the cabinets and the material used to make them, as well as the placement of the loudspeakers in the room, are important for good sound quality.

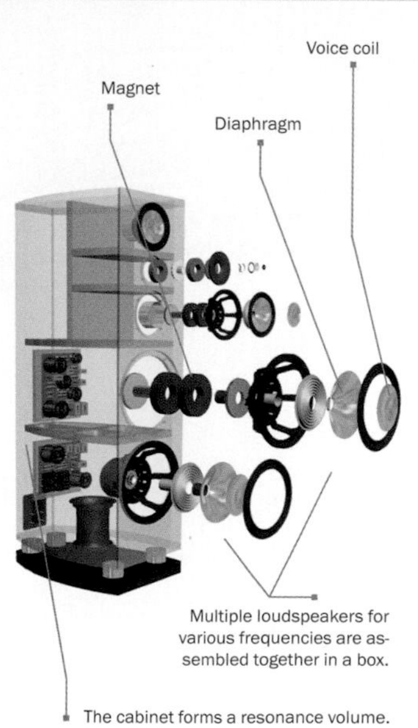

Cross-section of a high performance loudspeaker

MP3 Encoding

Various psychoacoustic phenomena are used for MP3 encoding. For example, our hearing does not perceive soft sounds immediately after having been subjected to loud noises. Another example of noise masking is how we block out background sounds. Likewise, our ability to hear at the borders of the audible range of frequencies is limited. In order to save storage memory, certain components of sounds are not included in the compression of the data with MP3. In combination with mathematical compression, MP3 encoding can reduce music files to a considerable degree without any distinguishable loss of sound.

above: *The MP3 player can hold up to 10,000 CD quality songs.*

Similar results can also be achieved with a USB memory stick with a device for dictation and sound recording. Better sound quality can be achieved with minidisc devices used in combination with external microphones. Sounds can be edited after recording with programs such as Adobe Audition and GarageBand.

In-ear headphones today can use hi-fi components that will provide a very high quality of sound and tone.

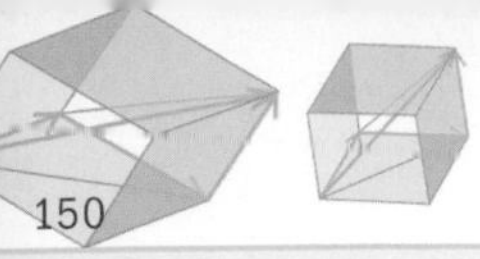

Monographic Boxes

Analytic Boxes

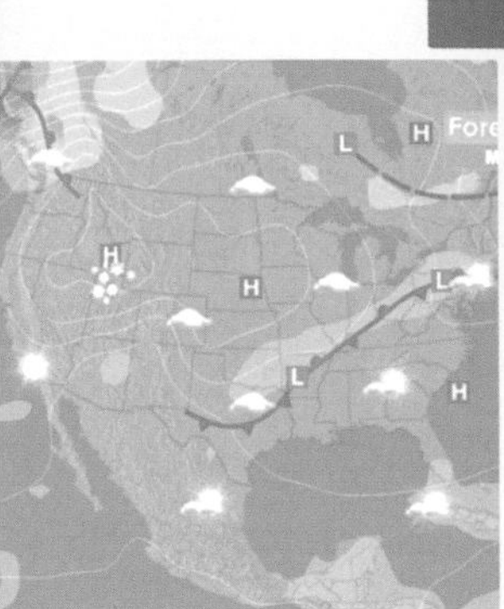

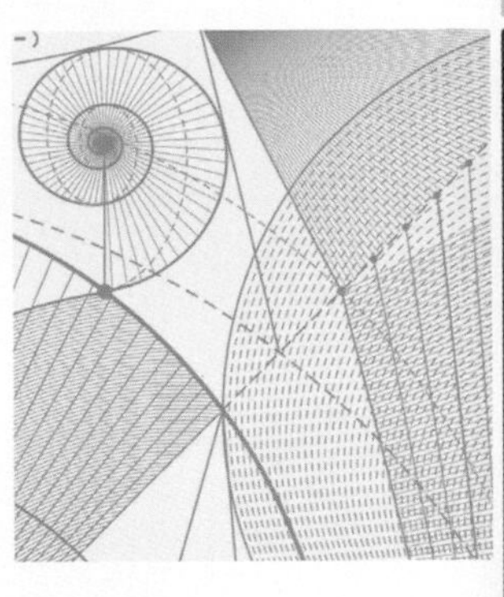

MATHEMATICS

Mathematics, as an academic discipline, is primarily one of the "humanities." In contrast to the natural sciences, that examine concrete objects and processes, mathematics is concerned with the abstract objects and structures created by humankind. Its validity, however, extends over many academic fields and so the tools of mathematics serve almost all other sciences. The boundaries between pure and applied mathematics are blurred. What today is considered as "art for art's sake" can help to develop new technologies tomorrow. Mathematics augments our perception of beauty and elegance and helps to formulate thoughts clearly through a decisive language.

KEY FACTS

ARISING FROM PRACTICAL APPLICATIONS *the first generally accepted principles of mathematics were formulated at around 3000 B.C.*

THE FIRST SCIENTIFIC USE *of abstract mathematical concepts took place at around 500 B.C.*

TODAY, MATHEMATICS IS *studied as an abstract science and is used to solve practical problems facing humankind.*

The first mathematicians | The subject of mathematics

THE SUBJECT OF MATHEMATICS

Mathematics was established as a science in Greece in ancient times by Pythagoras of Samos. Pythagoras and his teacher Thales of Miletus are civilization's first philosophers. Mathematics was considered then to be a branch of philosophy, but is now considered an independent field closely aligned with logic. The content and concepts of mathematics are based on objective reality. However, mathematics is abstracted from any concrete entities and is based on axioms, definitions, and logical deductions. Thus, mathematics can be used to solve concrete problems.

The study of mathematics began long before the term "mathematics" was used.

THE FIRST MATHEMATICIANS

People in ancient China, India, and the Americas were occupied with mathematical problems long before mathematics even became a science.

The first use of what we now call mathematics goes back 5,000 years. The motivation for using mathematics comes from daily life. At first, mathematics enabled people to simplify a number of practical tasks.

Abstract Power of Numbers

Humankind was not given numbers in the cradle. They were needed, however, to determine the size of a herd of animals with little effort. What we now consider commonplace was the result of a long and winding process of development and discovery. A general description of quantity must use the same numerals for the same quantity of objects. The number three is not assigned to just three plates but also to three spoons, three oranges, and so forth. The concept of the number three is thus the result of abstract reasoning. Even today there are cultures that use mathematically unsophisticated number systems, for example, three boats may be called something different than three coconuts. Larger quantities are simply called "many."

The angle of a pyramid's faces are calculated exactly so that they come together at the top.

Application of Numbers

The beginning of mathematics is found in the first advanced civilizations. Where art, architecture, writing, justice, and philosophy began to develop, the systematic study of computations and geometry were also initiated. Business and commercial trade not only brought goods to other people, but also transferred knowledge about common experiences and new insights. The Arabic numerals, for example, actually originated from India. They reached Europe through the work of Arabic mathematicians.

The first insights into geometry were related to practical needs. The yearly inundation of the Nile River delta in Egypt, for example, gave farmers fertile soil but also kept blurring and confusing the borders of their fields. This meant the fields had to be measured and calculated every year, obviously requiring advanced methods. Calculations and geometric tools were also required in architecture. For instance, during the planning of monumental structures, architects had to not only take the operating physical forces into consideration, but also the religious guidelines concerning orientation.

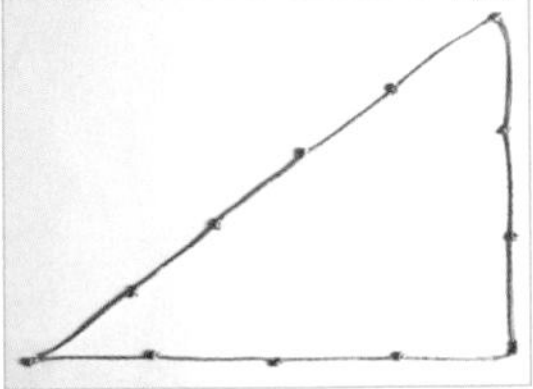

The 12-Knot Cord

Babylonian and Egyptian temple architects and surveyors used closed loops of rope with knots in them that could be put into the shape of a triangle. The distance between the knots was the same and constituted a unit of length. If a triangle had sides that were three, four, and five knots long, then it was a right triangle. It was Pythagoras who came up with this general rule of right-angled triangles. Pythagoras' theorem is one of the founding moments of mathematics, and is demonstrative of the ingenuity the Greeks brought to the field.

above: *The 12-knot cord is based on the Pythagorean theorem:* $3^2 + 4^2 = 5^2$.

Number Systems

NUMBERS are an elementary concept of mathematics. Numbers, especially their structure, have changed over a period of thousands of years. Numeral representation followed an ordinal system until the Middle Ages. There was one line or notch on a stick for the number one while larger numbers had many notches. So that the numbers did not become too long, the lines were bundled. One wrote "V" instead of "IIIII" and two times "V" was noted as "X."

POSITIONAL NOTATION based on addition began in Europe during the 10th century with the introduction of the number zero. All natural numbers can be represented by using only ten digits.

European	0	1	2	3	4	5	6	7	8	9
Greek		α	β	γ	δ	ϵ	ς	ζ	η	θ
Chinese	〇	一	二	三	四	五	六	七	八	九
Urdu Naqsh	ز	ز	ژ	س	ش	ص	ض	ط	ظ	ع
Devanagari (Hindi)	०	१	२	३	४	५	६	७	८	९
Roman	0	I	II	III	IV	V	VI	VII	VII	IX

X–ten
C–hundred

L–fifty
D–five hundred

The decimal system with 10 digits from zero to nine is used throughout the world. The way the digits are represented, however, differs.

Roman numerals are not suitable for arithmetic

Thales of Miletus brought geometrical proficiencies to Greece from his travels in Egypt.

THE SUBJECT OF MATHEMATICS

Mathematics is frequently seen as being connected with numbers and geometric figures. However, it is essentially a logical science that concerns itself with structure, space, quantity, and change. Mathematicians try to learn the relationships between these concepts.

Mathematics is a science that works on theories it itself creates. A theory is a system of statements about objects. In mathematics, the characteristics of objects are not as important as the relationships between them. These relationships generate a structure, which is why mathematics is known as a structural science. A theorem is derived from basic statements or axioms that are taken to be self-evidently true, but cannot be proven without making further assumptions.

For coordinating logistics of goods going in and out of a warehouse or depot, the quantity, mass, and volume need to be accurately calculated.

Mathematics gains practical importance from the power of its theorems. As long as a question can be described mathematically, it can be answered mathematically. Mathematics allows for abstraction and disengagement from concrete objects. It then provides for a retranslation back into the world.

For example, through observation one can find out how many times on average it is possible to roll a certain number on the dice with every sixth throw. With the help of mathematics, however, one can calculate the chances of rolling a "six" without even having to throw the dice. Furthermore, these mathematical methods can be applied to many other situations involving probabilities.

INSIDER KNOWLEDGE

NUMERICAL SYSTEMS *develop and study algorithms, which are fixed sequences or sets of instructions that lead to the solution of a problem. Algorithms can then be represented by formulas and ultimately processed automatically.*

Fields of Application

Mathematics today encompasses a variety of different branches of study involving various concepts. These branches are not sharply isolated from each other. This means that problems can be solved in a number of different ways, which makes solutions more easily attainable.

Mathematicians differentiate between pure and applied mathematics. This distinction, however, has more to do with the goals of the mathematician than the branch of mathematics that is being studied.

The major branches of mathematics are number theory, topology (which is an extension of geometry), numerical analysis, and discrete mathematics (which deals with finite countable structures), along with disciplines often taught in schools, such as algebra and geometry.

Numerical analysis and discrete mathematics were essentially developed in the 20th century with practical applications in mind. Real events, like the flow of goods or traffic, are modeled with the help of mathematics. Relationships between critical quantities such as size, cost, or time are described exactly and ultimately optimized.

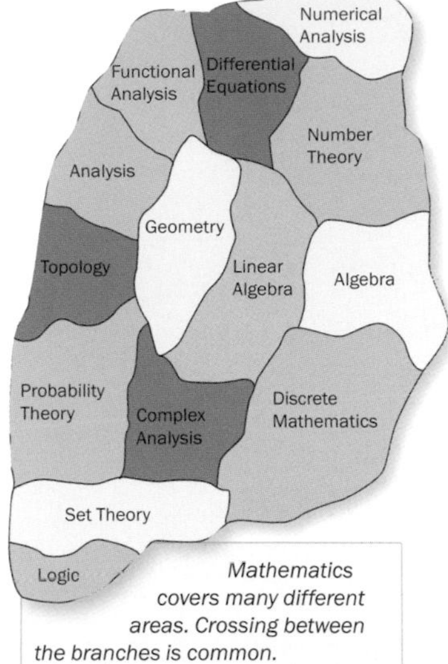

Mathematics covers many different areas. Crossing between the branches is common.

Public transportation should be efficient, that is, less waiting time with fewer vehicles. Even problems such as this can be solved using mathematics.

Axioms

AXIOMS *are fundamental statements or assumptions that are taken to be self-evident.*

AN AXIOMATIC SYSTEM *defines a consistent set of axioms and principles while using logic to derive new principles.*

MATHEMATICAL THEOREMS *are derived from axioms as in classical geometry.*

"Every straight line contains at least two different points." —Euclid

AXIOMS FORM the basis of a logical system by defining its basic terms and characteristics. Several basic statements can form an axiomatic system as long as they can be formulated consistently. From these axioms, other propositions can be derived.

FOR EXAMPLE, the natural numbers are defined through two axioms. The first is that zero is a natural number. The second is that every number "n" has the successor "n + 1." It is clear that there are infinitely many natural numbers because it is possible to add "one" to every number. Another example is the axioms of Euclidean geometry (pp. 156–158). The axioms of geometry introduce concepts like points or lines and the basic relationships between the defined objects. All the theorems of Euclidean geometry can be derived from axioms with the help of logic.

The building of a tunnel: The shortest distance between points is a straight line.

The distance of heavenly bodies cannot be directly measured but can be ascertained with the help of mathematics.

MATHEMATICS

KEY FACTS

GEOMETRY AND ARITHMETIC *were the first branches of mathematics.*

CLASSICAL GEOMETRY *deals with points, straight lines, surfaces, and three-dimensional objects.*

NUMBERS AND ARITHMETIC OPERATIONS *are the central themes of arithmetic (number theory).*

THE RANGE OF NUMBERS *was gradually expanded by arithmetic operations.*

Geometry | Arithmetic

CLASSICAL MATHEMATICS

Geometric forms, numbers, and calculations are the classical themes of mathematics. The most famous communicator of classical geometry was the Greek mathematician Euclid of Alexandria. In his most popular work, "Elements," he deals with geometric figures on a plane and in three-dimensional space. Another classical branch of mathematics is arithmetic (number theory), which is the science of numbers and includes among other things basic arithmetic operations and the divisibility of numbers.

The roots of mathematics are present in operations with numbers and geometrical objects.

GEOMETRY

Classical geometry is based on the axiomatic system written down by Euclid. Geometry describes the relationship between geometric structures.

Measurement is the comparison of an object with a known and an easy-to-reproduce standard: an angle, a length, or a surface. This was the original extent of geometry. Euclidean geometry uses clear definitions of points, lines, and straight lines. It can be developed to an extent without the use of numbers as we see them.

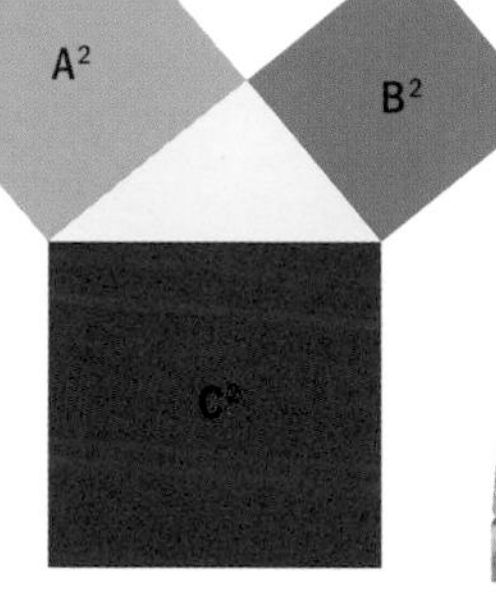

Protractors and Rulers

Classical basic operations are, for example, bisecting a line or an angle without having to know its size. Every operation can be reduced to elementary steps: Drawing a straight line between two given points, drawing a circle around a given point and through a second given point, and duplicating a given length. All these operations can be carried out with protractors and rulers even if they do not have scales.

The platonic solid is formed from equivalent polygons. All the sides, edges, and angles of the platonic solid are the same.

$$(a+b)^2 = 4\tfrac{1}{2} \cdot a \cdot b + c^2$$
$$a^2 + 2ab + b^2 = 2ab + c^2$$
$$a^2 + b^2 = c^2$$

The area of a hypotenuse square (c^2) is equal to the sum of the areas with two legs (a^2 and b^2).

The Pythagorean theorem is fundamental in geometry.

Geometry With Numbers

Geometrical constructions also form the basis of arithmetic operations. For example, the joining of two lengths corresponds to addition. A rectangle corresponds to the multiplication of lengths. Therefore, numbers can be used for both sides of the rectangle and their product is the surface area of the rectangle.

A special case is the question of the length of the diagonal in a square. This can be calculated by using the Pythagorean theorem: $c^2 = a^2 + b^2$ where c is the length of the diagonal. If "*1*" is substituted for the sides of the square (a and b), the equation becomes $c^2 = 1^2 + 1^2 = 2$.

This leads to yet another question: Which number multiplied with itself results in the number two? What is the square root of two? This leads to the creation of a new class of numbers in arithmetic.

Construction of a Right Angle

IN ORDER TO CONSTRUCT a right angle to a given straight line at a given point, M, a circle is first drawn around the point. The intersections of the circle with the straight line, A and B, are obtained. A circle with a greater radius is now drawn around A and B each, with the same radius for both. The intersections of the two circles, S1 and S2, are joined. The line joining S1 and S2 intersects the given line at a right angle at the given point.

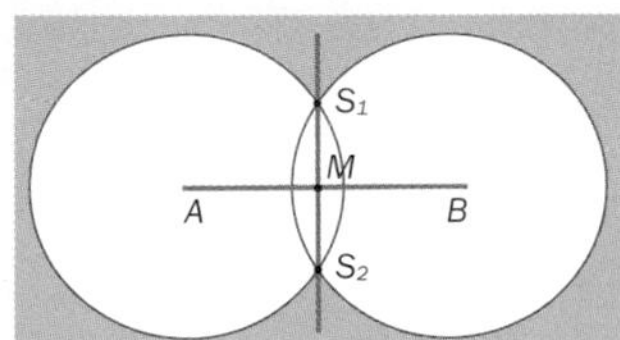

Construction of a right angle with circles and lines

IF THE LINE AB IS GIVEN, then one follows the same procedure to get the perpendicular bisector of line AB. A circle, S1, is drawn around the point A, and a second one of the same radius, S2, is drawn around B. The center point (M) is obtained by connecting S1 and S2.

From Angles to Time

A circle can actually be divided into any number of parts, and an angle can have any value. The definition of 360° for a circle by the Babylonians has the advantage that after repeated divisions, whole numbers still remain, which means that angles have integral values. The reason for this is that the number 60 has the most divisors (*2; 3; 4; ...*) of any number between 1 and 100. If 60° is divided twice, 15° is obtained, which becomes a bridge for the measurement of time: 15° *(=360° : 24)*. Thus, the rotation of Earth corresponds to an hour. An hour has 60 minutes, and 60 times 60 seconds.

above: *Angles of the sun's rays are used to measure time.*

The square root of two is called an irrational number, which means that it cannot be represented as the ratio of two whole numbers.

A compass is a tool for drawing geometrical figures.

ARITHMETIC

Arithmetic, or number theory, strictly defined, encompasses calculation with numbers. Moreover, it examines and develops the principles of different types of numbers.

Arithmetic primarily deals with calculations. The basic rules of calculations come from an intuitive and natural handling of objects. For example, it is immaterial whether a person first adds two sheep to three and then adds four or if he first added three sheep to four and then added two. The general formulation is called the associative law: $(a+b)+c=a+(b+c)$.
The associative law applies to all numbers in the number system, not just the natural numbers.

The abacus was developed around 1100 B.C. and was used to make arithmetical calculations.

Why Are New Numbers Needed?

The arithmetic operations of division and subtraction cannot generally be executed with the natural numbers (*1; 2; 3; ...*). The distribution of eight coins to three people is not physically possible, just as when ten coins are to be distributed to only eight people. These problems can, however, be solved mathematically by creating new kinds of numbers. A third of a dollar does not exist nor does a negative human being, but the introduction of fractional and negative numbers makes calculations possible. Concerning the two problems, eight divided by three results in $^8/_3$ and eight minus ten is a negative two.

Each initially unsolvable task thus brings an extension number with it.

Number Ranges

Addition and multiplication can be carried out unconditionally with the set of natural numbers $\mathbb{N}$. The set of integers $\mathbb{Z}$ is obtained through the introduction of negative whole numbers ($-1; -2; -3; ...$). Subtraction can then be carried out unconditionally.

The number range is expanded with a set of fractional numbers $\mathbb{Q}_+$ in order to carry out divisions. $\mathbb{N}$, $\mathbb{Z}$, and $\mathbb{Q}_+$ together form the set of rational numbers $\mathbb{Q}$, which enables all the basic arithmetic operations to be carried out with the exception of dividing by zero. Every rational number can be expressed as a fraction a/b, where a and b are whole number integers.

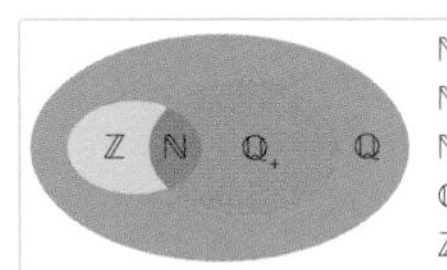

$\mathbb{N} \subset \mathbb{Z}$
$\mathbb{N} \subset \mathbb{Q}_+$
$\mathbb{N} = \mathbb{Z} \cap \mathbb{Q}_+$
$\mathbb{Q}_+ \subset \mathbb{Q}$
$\mathbb{Z} \subset \mathbb{Q}$

The set of rational numbers $\mathbb{Q}$ includes fractions as well as both negative and positive integers.

An expansion of the rational numbers to irrational numbers is required to express nonterminating nonrecurring decimal fractions. For example, the relationship between the circumference and diameter of a circle (π) can be understood. Likewise, the calculation of square roots becomes possible without restrictions if irrational numbers are introduced. If the rational numbers are expanded with irrational numbers, such as π or the square root of two, the set of real numbers $\mathbb{R}$ is obtained.

Another set of numbers can be constructed that do not seem to have any relation to the real world. They are called imaginary numbers and are defined in the following way: "i" is the solution of the equation $i^2 = -1$. In other words, "*i*" is the root of minus one. The term "imaginary" points to the fact that the numbers are purely thought-up. Nevertheless, they have very real applications. Calculations in physics and engineering become easier with the help of complex numbers, which encompasses the areas of real and imaginary numbers.

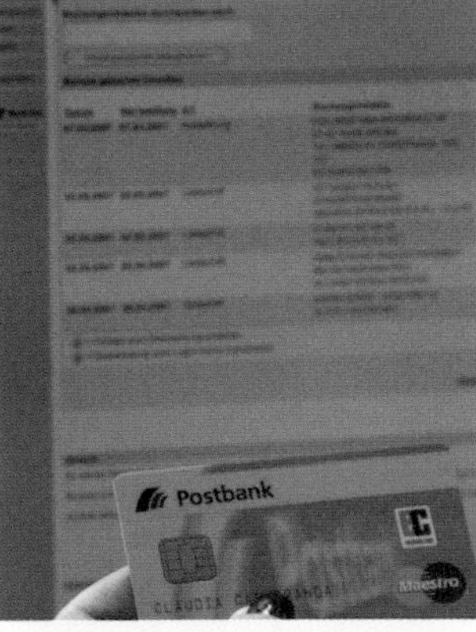

Online banking uses number theory

INSIDER KNOWLEDGE

THE CODING OF DATA *is becoming very important and is considered to be a practical application of number theory. Solutions of complicated problems in number theory serve as the key for accessing data, for example, in online banking.*

Music is closely linked to mathematics: By locating the frets of a guitar in certain numerical ratios, the notes of a musical scale are produced.

COMPUTING LAWS *contain partially mathematical statements that are provable.*

RULES *such as "multiplication and division before addition and subtraction" are based on definitions.*

MATHEMATICAL *formats can be identified and transformed.*

Basic arithmetic principles are fixed components in every school curriculum.

Computing Laws

COMMUTATIVITY: The addends are exchangeable in addition, and the factors are exchangeable in multiplication.

COMMUTATIVE LAW

$a+b=b+a$

$a \cdot b=b \cdot a$

ASSOCIATIVITY: It is immaterial whether the sum or product is calculated first. However, calculation should begin with whatever lies inside the brackets.

ASSOCIATIVE LAW

$a+(b+c)=(a+b)+c=a+b+c$

$a \cdot (b \cdot c)=(a \cdot b) \cdot c=a \cdot b \cdot c$

DISTRIBUTIVITY: When addition and multiplication are combined, every addend in a bracket must be multiplied by the factor before or after the bracket. If there are common factors, the multiplication can take place after the total sum is calculated. The binomial theorem is based on this principle.

DISTRIBUTIVE LAW & BINOMIAL FORM

$a \cdot (a+b)=a \cdot b+a \cdot c$

$a^2+2ab+b^2=(a+b)^2=(a+b) \cdot (a+b)$

Any number can be substituted for the letters.

KEY FACTS

ANALYTIC GEOMETRY *combines geometry and algebra.*

GEOMETRIC FIGURES *do not need to be drawn since they can be represented by equations relating variables of a coordinate system.*

SYMBOLS *with arrows are used to represent vectors.*

VECTOR CALCULATIONS *play an important role in both physics and technology.*

Coordinate geometry | Vector geometry

ANALYTIC GEOMETRY

All problems in geometry are solved graphically. Through the interplay of algebra and geometry, the same problems can be solved using calculations with variables. Mathematical objects with length and direction are called vectors, and can be represented by arrows placed on a coordinate system. These abstract structures are also used to describe physical quantities. Vectors are also denoted by letters set in boldface type or with tiny arrows on top.

Structural relationships between objects can be described universally with a coordinate system and vectors.

MATHEMATICS

COORDINATE GEOMETRY

In coordinate geometry a set of axes is selected, and every point is allotted a fixed place in the coordinate system. Sets of points can be represented graphically or with equations.

A person arriving in a new city would need to orient himself through a fixed reference point. This can be a frequently visited building, for example. If he wanted to visit somewhere else, it would be necessary to know the distance between the destination and the reference point as well as the direction. This is the way points are described in a coordinate system.

In daily life, huge buildings frequently serve as reference points for orientation.

Coordinate lines are used on most maps to give exact locations, such as this one of New York City.

In an orthogonal coordinate system, two perpendicular axes are selected. The origin of the coordinate system is where the axes intersect *(0, 0)*. The coordinates *(2, 3)* refer to a point two units to the right of the origin and three units above the origin. Each point is specified by a pair of numbers.

Representation of a Point Set

In order to describe a set of points—e.g., a straight line—instructions are needed since a straight line consists of an infinite number of points. There is an easy way to do this.

The equation $y = 2x + 3$ describes a straight line. If the algebraic solutions of the coordinate points are understood, then it is possible to map out the points. If the number one is substituted for x, then y would be five; if the number two is substituted for x, then y is seven. These are the coordinate points P_1 *(1, 5)* and P_2 *(2, 7)*, which are both on the same straight line. Coordinates of each point (x, y) on a straight line satisfy the equation.

Geometry and Algebra

A certain amount of cooperation occurs between geometry and algebra because geometric problems can be described and solved algebraically, that is, with the help of algebra. On the other hand, one can find the solutions of an equation or a set of equations by using graphical methods.

Graphs are frequently used in cases when an exact solution is impossible or too difficult to obtain. Both geometry and algebra answer the question of how many points, if any, are common to two or more sets of points, and how many solutions are present.

Apart from its significance within mathematics, coordinate geometry can also be an important tool for other sciences. In physics, for instance, it is possible to graphically depict the trajectory of an object by choosing time as the independent variable.

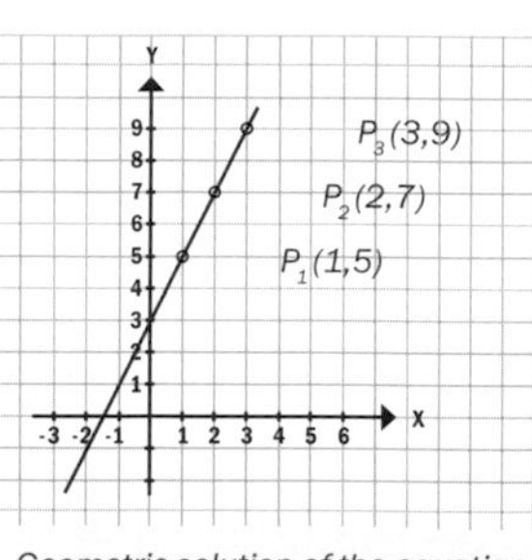

Geometric solution of the equation $y = 2x + 3$ in a coordinate system.

INSIDER KNOWLEDGE

A POINT SET *connotes a fixed assemblage of points in a space.*

A FUNCTION *assigns exactly one element (y-value) in the output set to each element (x-value) of the input set.*

A GRAPH *shows all the pairs (x, y) assigned by a function. The graph is a straight line if the function is linear.*

Cartesian Coordinate System

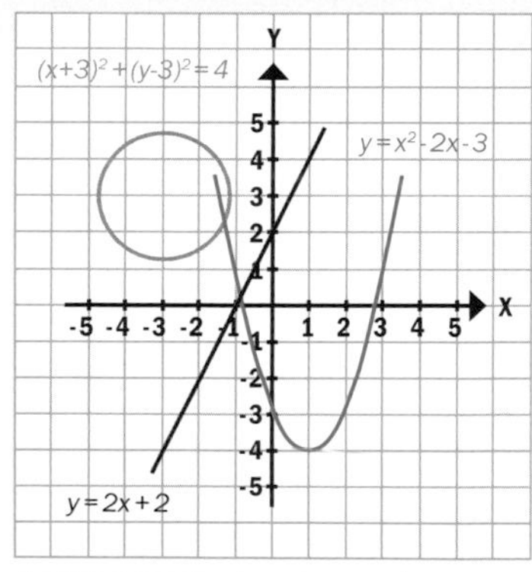

A set in a coordinate system can be represented by a graph or by an equation.

THE LOCATIONS of points in the sets (shown as a straight line, a circle, and a parabola) are described by an equation. From the structure of the equation alone, it is possible to determine the point set.

THE GRAPHS show that the straight line and the parabola have a common point: *(−1, 0)*. It is possible to easily see that there is another such point not shown on the graph: *(5, 12)*. The surest way of locating intersection points is to solve the equations algebraically.

VECTOR GEOMETRY

Movements in planes and space can be described with vectors. Vectors are represented in a coordinate system by their components in *x, y,* and sometimes *z* directions.

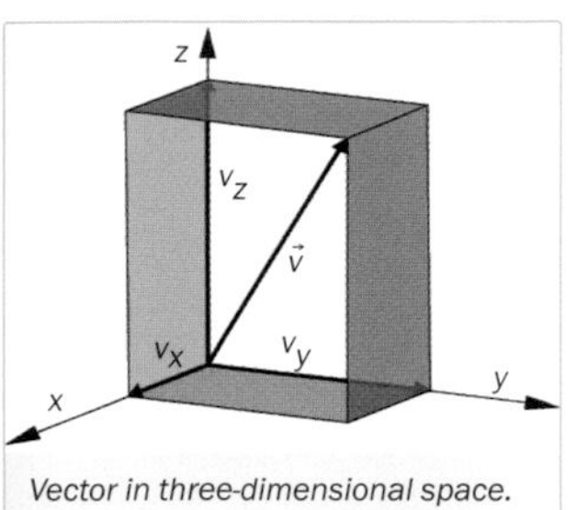

Vector in three-dimensional space. Every point P (x,y,z) is defined by the vector: $\vec{p}=\begin{pmatrix}x\\y\\z\end{pmatrix}$ whose coordinates are x, y, and z.

Vectors are frequently drawn as arrows. Every arrow represents the movement of a point in space. A vector quantity has both a direction and a magnitude. The length and direction of an arrow mirror the vector's magnitude and direction, respectively.

In geometry, all arrows with the same direction and the same length represent the same vector. A vector can be placed anywhere on a coordinate system. Vectors can also be defined by pairs of numbers or triplets of numbers, it being understood that the beginning of the arrow is at the origin.

A vector space is an algebraic structure, which consists of a set of vectors together with various specific operations. Analytical geometry is one of the many possible applications of vector calculations. Since the structural content is independent of real quantities, vector calculations are used in physics and engineering.

Elements of a vector space and their sum

Points and Point Sets

A vector can be used to describe many different quantities. The position vector defines the location of a point relative to the origin of a coordinate system. The velocity vector defines the direction and speed of an object.

In order to describe a point set, one must start with a single point and then give instructions in order to reach the other points. The single point is specified by a position vector. Normally, a set of points contains an infinite number of points while a defining equation contains a variable with an infinite number of values.

The linear equation, for example, defining the set of points on a straight line is: $\vec{x}=\vec{a}+r\vec{b}$ To reach point $\vec{x}$ of the straight line, begin at point a then travel in the direction specified by $\vec{b}$ a distance equal to r times the length of $\vec{b}$.

A plane can similiarly be represented by: $\vec{x}=\vec{a}+r\vec{b}+s\vec{c}$. An office building can serve as an illustration of this equation. Each floor of the office is specified by the position vector $\vec{a}$ and can be reached by the stairs or the elevator. If a person walks a certain number of steps *(r)* along the corridor (first directional vector $\vec{b}$) and then walks a certain number of steps *(s)* along a hallway (second directional vector $\vec{c}$), the destination on the new floor would therefore be reached.

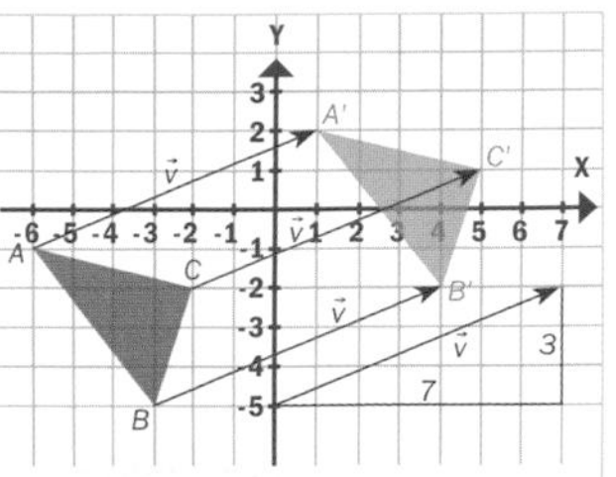

The movement of all points of triangle ABC is represented by the vector $\vec{v}=\binom{7}{3}$.

Geometry Without Drawings

Through calculations, similar simple descriptions of geometrical objects are possible without having to make actual diagrams. Common points of different sets of points can also be found this way while distance calculations can be carried out with little effort. In this way, complex problems in which vectors play a role are solved through pure calculation. This occurs frequently, for example, in physics and computer graphics.

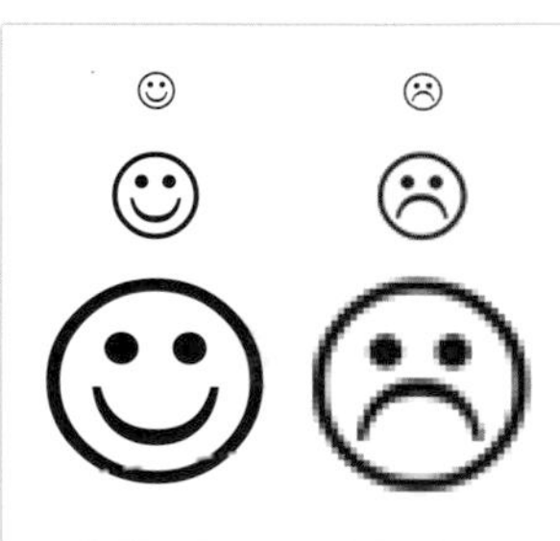

Vector graphic images (left) can be enlarged with continous picture resolution, while raster images compiled of a bitmap (right) will become pixelated.

21ST CENTURY

VECTOR GRAPHICS *uses points, lines, and curves, which are described mathematically and precisely with vectors, to represent images in computer graphics. Compared with graphics consisting of pixels, it is possible to maximize or minimize images from vector graphics without any loss of quality. Computer animations use vector graphics which is why there are full-length animated films with realistic representations of humans, etc.*

IN PHYSICS, *the use of vectors to describe quantities with both direction and magnitude is very common.*

FORCE AND ACCELERATION *of a single object always point in the same direction.*

MASS OR ENERGY *do not have directions and are called scalar quantities.*

The direction of the wind is from the side, but the boat moves forward.

Vectors in Physics

FORCES ACTING ON A BODY are added vectorially. If two locomotive engines are pulling a goods train, the contributions are added since the direction of the forces is the same. Forces can also cancel out. If a tractor traveling near the track is pulling the train, then only the components of the force in the same direction as the tracks cause the train to move. Components that are perpendicular do not contribute to the train's motion.

A NEWS SATELLITE orbits the Earth at a regular speed. Its motion is continuously accelerated because the direction of the motion is constantly changing. In the absence of another force, a moving object will travel in a straight line due to inertia. The force of gravity changes the direction of the satellite. The velocity of the satellite has a component tangent to the orbit and a component directed towards the Earth.

Since lateral forces do not contribute to the movement of the boat, the horse must pull extremely hard.

KEY FACTS

AN INFINITESIMAL *is greater than zero, less than any positive number expressable as a decimal.*

DIFFERENTIAL CALCULUS *concerns changes in the function and shape of its graph.*

INTEGRAL CALCULUS *concerns the cumulative value of a function.*

IN AN APPLICATION *a relationship is described as a mathematical function.*

Differential calculus | Integral calculus

INFINITESIMAL CALCULUS

Infinitesimal calculus means calculating with infinitely small numbers; however, it also includes calculations with infinitely large numbers. More accurately, infinitesimal calculus studies how certain mathematical relationships change when a variable approaches a certain limit. Infinitesimal calculus is part of analysis, which is essentially the study of functions. The behavior of a mathematical function is described in differential calculus and integral calculus by looking at functions in infinitesimal sections.

Differential calculus is to a certain extent the inverse of integral calculus.

DIFFERENTIAL CALCULUS

Differential calculus describes the behavior of a function in infinitely small parts. Its two most famous founding fathers were Sir Isaac Newton and Gottfried Wilhelm Leibniz.

During a hike up a mountain, a person finds themselves high above sea level. However, what is most interesting is how steep the mountain is at various points. The mathematical term for steepness is slope. Differential calculus is concerned with the slope of graphs of functions.

Slope, Secant, Difference Quotient

The term slope is commonly used to describe the steepness of a straight line. A graph with a curved line has a constantly changing slope.

The secant cuts the graph of a function in two points: x_1 and x_2. The slope can be ascertained from the sides of the triangle.

Constructed for calculating slopes, a secant is a straight line that cuts the graph of a function *f(x)* at two points, x_1 and x_2. The average slope of this section of the graph can be calculated from the following ratio, which is called the difference quotient: $\frac{f(x_2)-f(x_1)}{x_2-x_1}$

Using secants, the slope of a curve can therefore only be approximately determined for a certain section of the curve.

Boundary Value, Tangent, Derivative

In order to measure the slope of a curve at a particular section as precisely as possible, the distance between the points should be as small as possible. The distance should actually be reduced to zero. However, since the distance required for the calculation of the slope is in the denominator, it cannot be zero. Zero is understood to be the desired boundary value that remains unattained.

Another way of expressing this is that the secant should cut the curve so that it produces an infinitely small section, i.e., an infinitesimal section. Such a straight line is referred to as a tangent (Latin: *tangere* = to touch) and, graphically speaking, it perches on the "back" of the graph of a function. A tiny triangle can be constructed on the tangent line in order to measure the steepness by measuring the "rise" and the "run." The slope of the tangent line is called the "limit" (Latin: border) of the slope of the secant and is expressed mathematically as $\lim_{\Delta x \to 0} \frac{\Delta y}{\Delta x} = \frac{dy}{dx} = f'(x)$.

This exactly corresponds to the slope of the curve at this position. It is called the derivative of the graph at point *x*. The slope of a nonlinear function at a certain position is called its derivative and is written *f'(x)* or *df/dx*.

Upon release, the hammer moves in a straight line across the field. This flight path corresponds to the tangent of the circular orbit at the point of release. The tangent can be determined using vector-based calculus.

Leibniz's notational system for infinitesimal calculus, including the difference quotient, was accepted.

Applications

Differential calculus finds an application in the mathematical formulations of real processes. The derivative is used to specify the rate of a process at different points. Marginal costs, for example, can be described in this way in business economics. Through the help of differential calculus, a company can determine its marginal costs by taking the derivative of its total costs as a function of quantity produced. This means companies can determine how far costs can be reduced—through infinitely small steps—without endangering profit.

INSIDER KNOWLEDGE

LEIBNIZ AND NEWTON *developed infinitesimal calculus independently of one another at the end of the 17th century, but somewhat under the influence of Newton, the scientific Royal Society of London accused Leibniz of stealing the idea. However, from what we know today, this was not the case.*

Newton's Approach to Infinitesimal Calculus

While Leibniz searched for mathematical solutions to mathematic problems geometrically, Newton approached the matter from a completely different perspective. The problem that interested him was determining the instantaneous speed of an accelerated body. He supposed the curved graph of a body's position to be the result of a constant acceleration. He also considered a point to be an infinitely small line. The time interval in which the speed of the body is observed is so short that the change in position disappears. Thus, the slope or the derivative of the position graph is the instantaneous speed of the body.

Sir Isaac Newton

INTEGRAL CALCULUS

During integration, a function *F* is sought for a given function *f* such that the derivative of *F* is the given function *f*. *F* is the integral of *f*.

In integral calculus, the area under the graph is calculated by adding an infinitely large number of infinitely small areas.

Many Narrow Strips

During ancient times, Archimedes developed a method of integration that was later generalized by Leibniz and Newton in modern times. The area under a curve cannot be calculated with a simple geometric formula if the graph is curvilinear. To do the calculation, one can first assume that the curve does not go below the x-axis. Since it is easy to compute the area of a rectangular surface, the area under the curve is divided into many rectangles with the same width. The width of each rectangle is equal to the distance between two neighboring x-values, i.e., Δx. The area of each rectangle is calculated as its width multiplied by its height, which is the value of the function at at an appropriate value of x. The following equations are valid for the individual strips: $A_1 = f(x_1) \cdot \Delta x$, $A_2 = f(x_2) \cdot \Delta x$.

The total area is obtained by adding the individual strips and factoring out Δx: $A = \Delta x \cdot (f(x_1) + f(x_2) + \ldots)$

The sum becomes more precise as Δx gets smaller. As Δx approaches zero, the sum becomes the integral of the function *f(x)*.

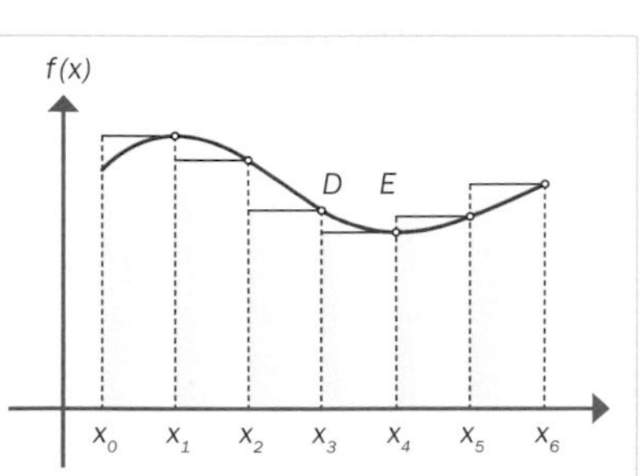

The approximate calculation of an area under a curve through summation of rectangles.

Primitive and Definite Integral

Leibnitz and Newton developed the idea that the derivative of the integral of a function *F* leads back to the original function *f*:

$F'(x) = dF(x)/dx = f(x)$.

The function *F* is the primitive or indefinite integral of the function *f*. In this way, the two branches of infinitesimal calculus are connected. The fundamental principles of differential and integral calculus establish this connection and simultaneously provide a method of calculating integrals that is valid as long as *F* is a differentiable function.

$\int_a^b f(x)dx = F(b) - F(a)$.

Above is the limit of the summation of an infinite number of areas: $f(x) \cdot dx$. The symbol of integration is a long drawn-out "S" from the Latin word *summa*. The entire expression is called the definite integral of *f* from *a* to *b*. On the right, there are the following instructions: Find a function *F*, for which $F'(x) = f(x)$. Then find the difference between the values of the function at *a* and *b*.

As an example, consider the function $f(x) = x^2$. In order to integrate this function from 0 to 1, one requires the primitive or indefinite integral *F* whose derivative is *f*.

Solids of revolution emerge if a plane figure is rotated about an axis. The volume is calculated with integral calculus.

This is $F(x) = \frac{1}{3}x^3$. This formula is provable by taking its derivative with the difference quotient.

The value of the definite integral is:

$\int_0^1 x^2dx = F(1) - F(0) = \frac{1}{3}1^3 - \frac{1}{3}0^3 = \frac{1}{3}$

Applications

Integral calculus is used in many areas of physics. For example, the mechanical work done on an object by a force acting over a distance is equal to the product of force and distance when the force is a constant: $W = F \cdot s$. When the force varies over the distance, calculus is used with formula: $W = \int_{s1}^{s2} F(s)\,ds$.

METHOD OF EXHAUSTION *is a process for calculating areas by inscribing large numbers of polygons.*

ARCHIMEDES *used this approach for calculating area and volume.*

HE CALCULATED *the area of the region between a parabola and an intersecting line by inscribing polygons in that region.*

Archimedes lived in the third century B.C.

"Integral Calculus" in Ancient Times

THE AREA UNDER A PARABOLA can be approximated using the integration method of Archimedes. The width of the inscribed rectangles can be factored out (see main text). In this way only the sum of the squares of numbers remains in the formula for the area. Archimedes arrived at the value $\frac{1}{3}$ for the area under the parabola from 0 to 1 (see example in main text).

AREAS UNDER CURVED LINES: Areas under curved lines could not be calculated exactly. In a very special case, Hippocrates determined the area of a crescent formed by a semicircle and a quarter-circle with a trick in the fifth century B.C. He showed that the area of the crescent was exactly equal to that of the right triangle that subtended the quarter circle, hence $\frac{1}{2}a \cdot b$.

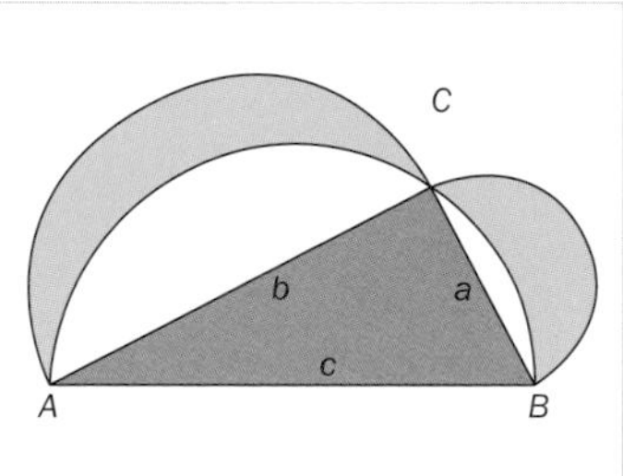

The blue surfaces together are exactly as large as the orange triangular surface.

KEY FACTS

STATISTICS *describes the connections between large sets of data.*

STOCHASTIC PROCESS *is a sequence of changes in which chance plays a role.*

PROBABILITY *expresses the relationship between certain specified events and all possible events.*

PROBABILITY THEORY *is the mathematic study of random phenomena along with the likelihood of their occurrence.*

Mathematical statistics | Probability theory

WHEN NUMBERS LIE

Of course, numbers themselves cannot lie. If numbers result in misunderstandings or even harm, the fault lies with the presenter or interpreter of the statistics. Properly used, probability theory and statistics help to describe events with numbers. Predictions can be made regarding the probability that certain events will occur while forecasts can be made with a certain degree of confidence. There are applications for mathematical statistics in almost all the natural sciences as well as in the scientific study of social relationships and human society.

➔ *Stochastic analysis is used to model processes in nature and society.*

MATHEMATICS

MATHEMATICAL STATISTICS

After the close of polls during an election, pollsters make projections that forecast the final vote quite precisely. Statistics delivers the necessary tools for making these predictions.

Age	0	1	...	20	...	70	...
Frequency	22	16	...	43	...	47	...

Children 0 to 13	Adolescents 14 to 17	Adults 18 to 59	Seniors 60+
327	156	1,546	1,021

Initially a rough list showing the raw data is created, and then a tabular division into groups is made.

Descriptive statistics is concerned with the representation of collected data. It often deals with very large quantities of information about individual events, which are summarized according to certain variables. This is in order to represent the data clearly, often through a graphic display.

Generation and Capturing of Data

After the data is collected, a rough list is created. In doing so, the characteristics of units in a population are identified—for example, the ages of people in a city. In the case of a very large population, one can use a representative sample. Each characteristic listed, such as an individual's age in years, can obviously repeatedly occur. Hence, the next step is the creation of a frequency table.

Frequency in this case means the absolute frequency, i.e., the actually counted number of times a characteristic occurs. The relative frequency is occasionally interesting and meaningful. For example, if there are 3,050 inhabitants in a village and 47 of them are 70 years old, the relative frequency of 70 year-olds in the city is $f = \frac{47}{3050} = 0.01541$. This corresponds to 1.541 percent.

Frequency tables, however, are not generally used to present the data. Instead it is usually presented in a graphic.

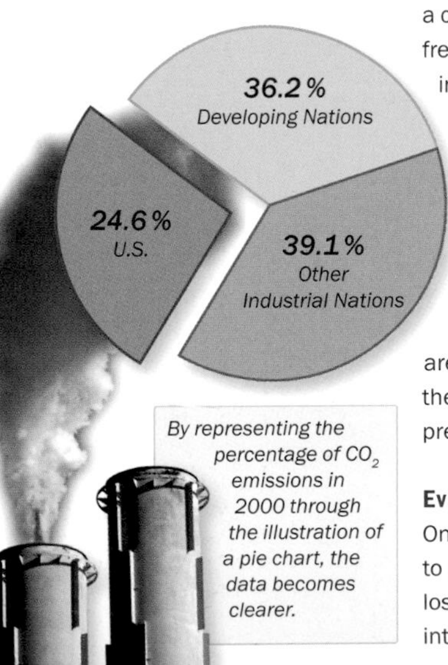

By representing the percentage of CO_2 emissions in 2000 through the illustration of a pie chart, the data becomes clearer.

Evaluation of Data

One of the goals of statistics is to summarize data with a minimal loss of information. If one is only interested in the number of inhabitants of the village in a certain age group, then feature summaries are used. An important parameter of statistics is the mean value, which is the average of the collected data. Frequently, individual data values vary greatly from the mean value. These observed differences are a measure of statistical spread. In another measure of spread, the deviations of the individual values from the mean value are squared, added and divided through by the number of measured values. The square root of the result gives the standard deviation. This value is important for many reasons. For instance, the manufacturer of a battery for cellular telephones cannot promise the customers that the battery will last exactly 70 hours. However, by using standard deviations after sufficient testing of the battery, the producer can say with a high degree of confidence that the lifetime of the battery is 70 hours, give or take five hours.

Lying With Numbers

The way in which data is presented always requires an interpretation and understanding of the information as well as its social relevance. In a graphical presentation, a scale for the data must be decided upon. This means a totally neutral and value-free presentation of the data is almost impossible. Depending on the selection of the scale for plotting the data on an axis, a socially important parameter, like unemployment or the gross domestic product, can look like it follows a flat curve or a steep curve. A wrong impression can also be created by truncating part of the graph.

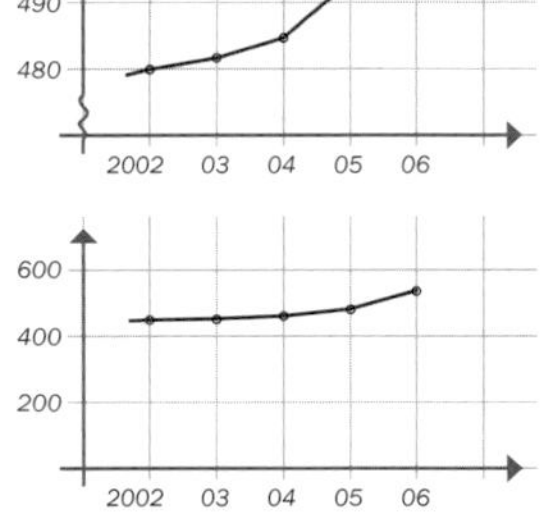

Number of armed robberies in the last five years: According to the presentation and scaling, the increase can appear to be very sharp while it is actually only 2%.

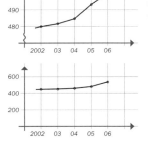

The percent of people in individual continents in the total population of the world at different points of time can be represented with side-by-side bar diagrams.

PROBABILITY THEORY

Probability theory is the mathematical study of processes with random output. It is used to plan complex processes and estimate costs.

Probability theory is one of a few disciplines in mathematics that was oriented toward practical applications right from the start. It actually developed from questions about chance in gambling.

Generally speaking, probability theory is used for decision-making if the consequences of future events have to be estimated.

The cost of accident insurance, for example, should not be too high, but must be enough to cover the expenses of the insurer. The risk to the insurer is the mathematical probability of an accident occurring. If the insurer knows that the probability of an accident happening in one year is five percent, then the yearly premium paid by the insured will be at least five percent of the average cost of an accident.

The chances of winning in a game of dice can be calculated with the help of probability theory.

INSIDER KNOWLEDGE

INTUITIVE ESTIMATIONS *of the probability of an event occurring are frequently wrong. What is the probability that some pair of students in a class of 23 students will have the same birthdays? Most people estimate the answer to be around 5%. The actual probability is around 50%. In their casual estimations, people consider only the chance that one particular birthday will be duplicated.*

Calculation of Probability

In probability theory, an event is a collection of specific possible occurrences called outcomes. In order to assess the probability of an event occurring, the basic calculation is to divide the number of outcomes in that event by the number of all possible outcomes. The event "an even number will appear with the toss of a die" has a probability of 50 percent (0.5), as there are three favored outcomes (numbers two, four, or six) and six possible outcomes. In this calculation, it is assumed that all the possible outcomes are equally probable.

Calculations become complex if the outcomes are part of subevents. In these cases, it has to be determined if the subevents are dependent on each other or not. In drawing cards successively from a single deck, the probability of drawing a particular card keeps increasing as the size of the deck diminishes, becoming zero once the card is actually drawn. However, with throwing a die multiple times, the throws are independent of each other, so the probabilities remain the same. The probability of several independent events occurring is found by multiplying the probabilities. The probability of throwing a six twice is $\frac{1}{6} \cdot \frac{1}{6} = \frac{1}{36}$, which is around 2.8 percent.

No infallible system of winning roulette has ever been discovered.

Limits of Probability Theory

The use of probability theory in science, especially in economic or social questions, is highly refined and well developed. This is because this branch of mathematics is particularly useful for making responsible decisions.

Some probabilities cannot, however, be calculated accurately. The probability that two people will sit down next to each other in a waiting room might be calculated to be 0.5, as long as there are two seats available. However, there are additional influencing factors. For example, where the two people sit will depend on whether or not they know each other.

Probability Distributions

The device developed in the 19th century by Sir Galton is a model for events occurring multiple times consecutively. Balls are dropped onto the obstacles at the top. Each ball falls either to the left or to the right. Since there are eight rows of obstacles, there are $2^8 = 256$ ways for a ball to fall,but most of the balls fall into one of the more centrally located compartments. The probabilities can be calculated from the coefficients in the generalized binomial theorem.

above: *The Galton board demonstrates the probability distribution in the case of independent events having a probability of 50%.*

Probabilities in Modern Physics

For atoms and particles smaller than atoms, the deterministic rules of classical physics do not apply. An electron moving around the nucleus of an atom is considered to be both a wave and a particle in the theory of quantum mechanics. The motion and location of the electron is determined by its quantum mechanical wave function. The wave function of an electron only describes the probability of finding an electron at any particular point in space. The wave functions of all subatomic particles are used to calculate the probabilities of various nuclear and atomic events.

Graphical representation of the wave function of an electron in a hydrogen atom. The probability of finding an electron at a particular location diminishes with increasing distance from the nucleus.

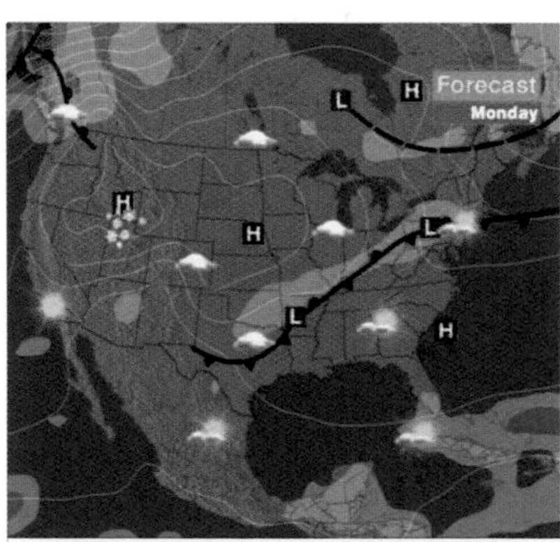

Stochastic methods are used to make weather forecasts by calculating, for example, the probability of rain.

MATHEMATICS

see also: Orbit Model, *Chemistry Chapter, p. 97*

KEY FACTS

MATHEMATICAL PROOFS *describe the steps that connect the proposition being proved to a set of axioms and/or already proven propositions.*

EXPEDIENCY *selects the method used to prove a proposition, but intuition often plays a role.*

COMPUTERS *can process formalized steps (algorithms). However, they are not generally used as a means for proof.*

The domino principle | Modern mathematics

OLD AND NEW MATHEMATICS

A logical proof based on pure thought is the foundation of mathematics. At the same time, proven statements are generally accepted truths. For this reason, there has always been a conflict in mathematics over whether it is an end in itself or a tool for science. In the beginning of the 20th century, there were strong movements to reduce mathematical objects to their fundamental characteristics, in other words, to achieve the highest possible level of abstraction. Simultaneously, life has made more and more demands on mathematics.

Understanding and creativity remain the most important tools of mathematics.

THE DOMINO PRINCIPLE

A mathematician is not satisfied when a statement applies to hundreds, thousands, or millions of cases. A mathematical statement should be valid for all conceivable cases.

The idea of mathematical induction is that after the first domino falls all the others follow it.

Why should one try to prove statements for infinitely many mathematical objects? According to astrophysicists, there are only around 10^{78} elementary particles in the universe. So why try to prove statements for a greater number than this? The question goes to the very nature of mathematics because it is a science that does not limit itself to finite entities.

In reality, for practical purposes, scientists and applied mathematicians are content to make approximations and obtain results that are limited. On the other hand, human beings have a drive to know everything, which leads to a desire to learn and understand pure mathematics. Whether the knowledge gained from these efforts has a practical use can only usually be decided later on. The alternative paths to knowledge are intuition or knowledge gained from scientific experiments.

How should spheres be arranged to minimize the volume occupied? What is well known by experienced fruit vendors has not yet been rigorously proven mathematically.

Proofs in Mathematics

A proof is a logical derivation from known, proven, or assumed statements. Based on these statements, it is possible to advance step-by-step until the proven statement is formulated. But how can a statement for infinitely many mathematical objects be proven in a finite length of time?

Statements about all natural numbers can be proven because of the inductive character of natural numbers. Every natural number n has the successor $n + 1$. Because of this, a proof can be constructed based on the principle of falling dominoes: All the dominoes fall if two conditions are satisfied. First, one domino must fall, and, second, every falling domino must hit the next one. Applying this to natural numbers: If a statement is valid for the first number, i.e. 1 (the "base case") and it is possible to prove that whenever it is valid for a number n it is also valid for $n+1$ (the "inductive step"), then the statement is valid for all natural numbers.

In describing an infinitely large number of mathematical objects, a particular characteristic is specified. Thales' theorem, for example, states that a triangle is always a right triangle if its base is a diameter of a circle and its vertex a point on the circle. Such a statement is true for an infinite number of circles, not just one particular circle with a defined diameter.

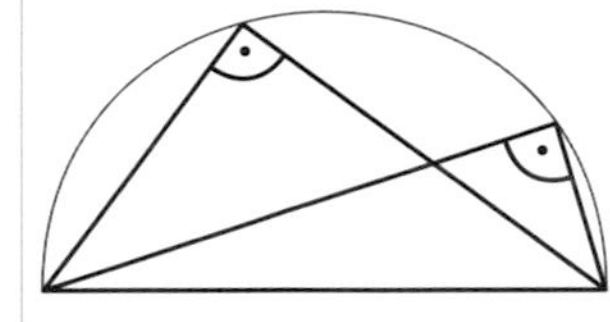

Thales' theorem was proven 2,500 years ago.

Proof by Contradiction

Another way of proving statements is to change the logical structure. Instead of proving the statement true, one proves that the opposite statement is false. An example is Euclid's theorem, which states that there are infinitely many prime numbers. First one hypothesizes the existence of a "greatest" prime number, then contradicts this by finding another that is even larger.

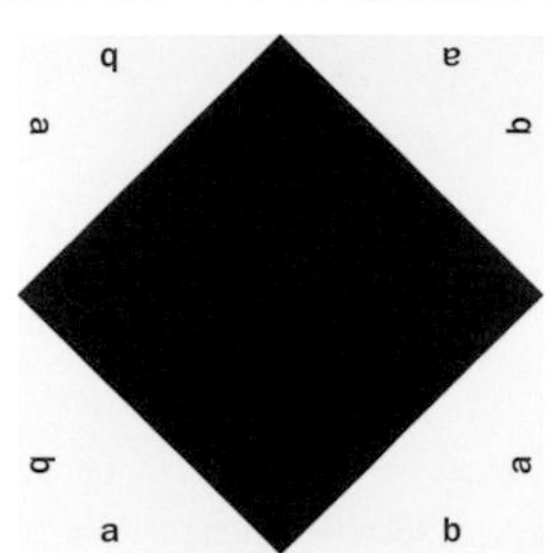

Direct Proof

A direct proof of Pythagoras's theorem comes from breaking down a large square into four congruent triangles and a smaller square. The large square has sides of length $a + b$ and an area of $(a + b)^2 = a^2 + 2ab + b^2$.

This region is made up of a square with an area c^2 and four congruent triangles with the sides a, b, and c. The area of each triangle is: $\frac{1}{2}ab$.

Thus, the total area is: $c^2 + 2ab$.

By comparing the two expressions we see that $c^2 = a^2 + b^2$.

INSIDER KNOWLEDGE

DIRECT PROOFS *are logical deductions made from already proven statements or axioms.*

INDIRECT PROOFS *confirm the statement by demonstrating that the negation of the statement is false.*

INDUCTIVE PROOFS *derive a statement about a general case from individual cases.*

MODERN MATHEMATICS

No one in this century can possibly grasp the whole of mathematics. Mathematics is increasingly a cooperative effort requiring the employment of new methods.

At the start of the 20th century, Kurt Gödel showed that the compatibility of consistency and completeness in mathematics is not unlimited.

Mathematics provides us with models for describing natural phenomena. If there is ever such a thing as a "world formula," i.e., a model for all the fundamental interactions in nature, it will not consist of a single equation, but will be a complex mathematical structure. This structure will conform with experimental findings and will be logically consistent.

The World as a Village

The Internet is a model for the increasing amount of social and economic interactions that take place. It is not just data that is exchanged in this virtual world. In the 21st century more people are traveling and more goods are being transported around the world than ever before. It is the task of mathematics among other things to describe these global interactions so that they can be carried out as efficiently as possible. Even the strategic decisions of large enterprises provide a range of tasks for applied mathematics. The implementation of business plans and the management of projects with the aid of computers require evaluating many individual factors.

$(x^2 + y^2 + z^2 - 1)^3 = x^2 z^3 + y^2 z^3$

$x^2 yz + x^2 z^2 = y^3 + y^3 z$

$(x^2 + y^3)^2 = (x + y^2) z^3$

These pictures of breathtaking beauty were generated by computers and represent the solutions of equations. This is mathematics.

"Pure" Mathematics

The question of whether new knowledge will bring economic gains has to come after the new developments. At the start of the 20th century, the mathematician David Hilbert formulated the proposition that there should be a complete and consistent axiomatic system—an "inner-mathematical world formula"—from which additional mathematical and scientific knowledge could be derived.

Just a few years later, Kurt Gödel proved the impossibility of such a system. According to Gödel's incompleteness theorem, when sufficiently complex relationships between two objects are set up, a system is formed that is either incomplete or contradictory. This means that mathematics must concern itself with the limits of knowledge: There are statements that are not provable.

Furthermore, there are structural relationships and bridges between disciplines, such as those between geometry and algebra. Every bridge between individual disciplines of mathematics brings about an enormous source of new knowledge since the content of each discipline can be used to generate content in the other discipline.

Mathematics will answer a few questions in the 21st century, keep a few open, and possibly even raise new questions. Whatever the case, mathematics will remain, for people who study it professionally or only during their leisure time, a source of inspiration and a tool for sharpening their understanding of the real world.

THE STRICTLY FORMAL LANGUAGE *of computer programming has influenced mathematics.*

COMPUTERS *cannot yet develop highly sophisticated mathematical proofs, but they can perform lengthy calculations and routine tasks.*

Operating instructions in computers are given by zeros and ones.

Mathematics With Computers

FOR COMPUTER-AIDED PROOFS, the problem is first deconstructed into individual steps by mathematicians. Computers are then used to process these steps. The actual creative work is still done by humans, and only the handling of individual steps is done by the (computer) machine. The proof that a computer can operate without making errors does not exist since there can be errors in programming. For some mathematicians, the use of computers for proofs is not satisfactory because of this possibility.

THE FOUR-COLOR THEOREM is possibly the most famous problem of mathematics to be solved with the help of a computer. The question of whether more than four colors are needed to color all the regions on any map was raised by Francis Guthrie in the middle of the 19th century. This was finally proved in 1977 by Wolfgang Haken and Kenneth Appel, after many hours of computer calculations.

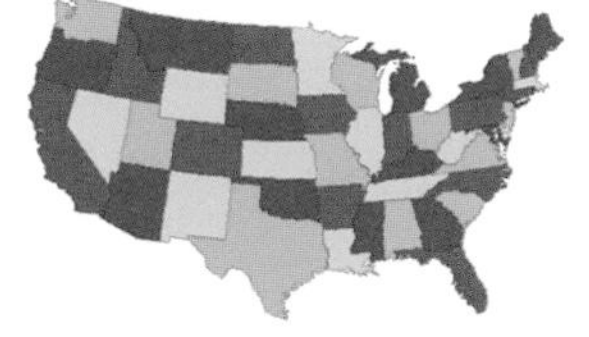

Four different colors are enough to differentiate regions of a map from one another.

INSIDER KNOWLEDGE

THERE IS NO *Nobel Prize for Mathematics since Alfred Nobel considered mathematics to be just an "auxiliary science."*

THE FIELDS MEDAL *is considered the highest award for mathematicians and is awarded once every four years.*

THE PRIZE MONEY *currently is 15,000 Canadian dollars.*

21ST CENTURY

IN THE FUTURE, *mathematics will be indispensable for modeling, simulation, and the optimization of various other processes and methods used in science and technology.*

ONE IN THREE OF ALL *mathematicians work in engineering and other technical fields and play an important part in the development of science and new technologies.*

Monographic Boxes

Analytic Boxes

POLITICS, LAW, AND ECONOMY

As the Greek philosopher Aristole was able to identify, a person is inherently "a political being." Every individual is always a part of a larger social unit, a family, a community, and a country. The task of politics and its institutions is to set up binding rules for a national community, to make these decisions universally valid, and to execute them. Herein lies the challenge for both national and international law. The more the economies and media of different countries grow together, the more important become the joint decisions on national boundaries and the awareness of global partnerships. The study of economics analyzes the production, distribution, and consumption of goods and services.

KEY FACTS

THE FIRST STATE STRUCTURES *were developed in Egypt and China.*

AN EARLY FORM OF DEMOCRACY *developed in the ancient Greek states.*

FEUDAL COMMUNITIES: *Rule in the Middle Ages was based on interdependency and inheritance.*

THE MODERN TERRITORIAL STATE *developed in the absolutism of the 17th century.*

Groupings and kingdoms | Feudal and territorial states | Modern age through revolution | Democracy—nature and history

SOCIETIES, FORMS OF STATE, AND GOVERNMENT

From family groupings to the bureaucratic centralized state of the modern age, the social systems of humankind developed from simple communities to increasingly complex structures. The great revolutions of the 18th century broke with the privileges of the aristocratic upper class and introduced a process of comprehensive democratization in state and society.

At the beginning of the 21st century, large areas of the world professed themselves to be democracies.

FROM FAMILY GROUPINGS TO THE FIRST KINGDOMS

The family made up the first form of organization in human communal life. These grew into clans and tribes and from these communities of restricted size, the first state-like structures of history developed within the first empires.

The foundation of the earliest social systems was the family. A shared identity grew from common ancestry. Family members helped each other with tasks such as providing food and defense. In Stone Age cultures, the family members of many generations joined together in villages to form larger communities. At the same time, family relationships regulated social cooperation. The particular rank that an individual had within the kinship structure determined their role in the community.

Persia was one of the first empires. Darius the Great (522–486 B.C.) was one of its rulers.

Larger tribal communities often developed from small family groupings having a mutual bond through a common language, lineage, or shared myth of origin. They made no claims to a defined territory and hardly possessed any organizational structures beyond personally regulated ones.

In the kingdoms of the ancient Orient, such as Egypt, attempts were made for the first time to centrally control and streamline agriculture.

Early Kingdoms

A form of centralized state power began to develop around 3000 B.C. in the advanced cultures of Egypt, Mesopotamia, China, and India.

With the founding of these first kingdoms the binding principles of kinship were replaced with organization in support of a religion; thus these states emerged with a god-like ruler placed at the head. He ensured his power by building up an administration loyal to him. Officials levied taxes, planned building projects, and set regulations or prepared for wars.

The building up of this complex administration was made possible primarily through the development of writing. This advancement allowed information to be recorded and passed on. Enforceable laws could be documented and contracts would be bound.

The early empires, however, had too few officials to administer the whole of the conquered territories. The Romans were the first who were able to substantially organize their domain. They sent magistrates directly to the provinces to rule. Regardless of their maneuvers, the colossal Roman Empire around the Mediterranean broke apart due to its size and cultural diversity. The Roman Empire disintegrated around 500 A.D. in the great migrations of people. In time, states in the Middle Ages assumed the Roman legacy.

The Divine Ruler

Within the ancient monarchies, it was common that kings, along with their political importance, were also accorded great religious significance. They were regarded as the personification of a god, or his son, or at least appointed by a god. Thus, in their position of power, they were more or less conceived as sacrosanct. The Egyptian pharaohs such as those in the Early Dynastic and Old Kingdom (up to ca 2400 B.C.) were considered to be divine. According to Egyptian thought, the office of king was an institution that the gods had created for humankind. Each individual holder of the office was a direct descendent of the god Horus. This deified position allotted the population only a passive and subservient role.

above: *Pharaoh Tutankhamun's gold mask (18th Dynasty)*

FROM FEUDAL STATE TO TERRITORIAL STATE

In the Middle Ages, rule was exercised by the holding and allocation of land. The modern territorial state, centrally led by kings or princes, developed in the 17th century.

The Christian society of medieval Europe was hierarchically divided into classes. The clergy and the aristocracy, headed by the king, composed the upper classes. Beneath them came the majority of the population: merchants, craftsmen, peasants, and serfs. Society was for the most part fixed in its structure. Each person stayed within the class into which he or she was born and was integrated into the respective social community.

The structure of society was determined by the relationship between the feudal lord and his vassal.

Rule in the Middle Ages

The sovereignty of the kings in the Middle Ages did not rest on a central administration within a defined territory, but rather on a network of relationships of personal loyalty. In an agrarian society, the amount of power a king possessed was determined by how much land he was able to grant to his fiefs. He turned land over to his noble minions or chief tenants, who were vassals of the crown, for their personal use. In return they were required to loyally serve and follow him in times of war.

The vassals of the crown, for their part, loaned the lands to subvassals, or vavasours. This complex structure of sovereignty, known as the feudal state, thus developed within itself a number of superiors and subordinates. In addition to the royal fiefs, the vassals of the crown as a rule also owned their own land. For this reason, the king was always dependent on their good will and was anxious to gain new lands.

Paths to the Modern State

The rigid, medieval social order began to break apart in the 15th century. The increasing impact of finance and trade weakened the aristocracy while it strengthened the middle class. In the 17th century, the modern territorial state with its defined borders and centralized powers replaced the feudal structure. France's development is characteristic of this. With the help of a standing army and a bureaucracy loyal to him, King Louis XIV was able to win over the aristocracy and concentrate power in his court, thus establishing a monopoly that granted him the sole right to wield authority.

The king had a vast amount of power—he led the affairs of state, and was lawgiver and supreme judge. He expanded the infrastructure, introduced state economic policies, and integrated the Church into the state system. The process of nationalization did not lead to centralized nation-states everywhere. The princes in the German Empire remained independent and established numerous regional points of power. It was not until the 19th century that a central state was forcibly established.

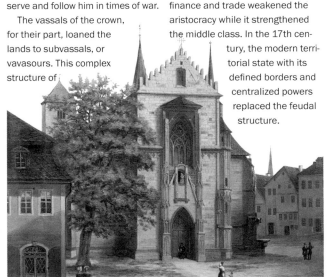

There was a great rivalry in the Middle Ages between secular and ecclesiastical authority. The emperor and the pope quarreled over who held supreme power.

INSIDER KNOWLEDGE

A STRICT DRESS CODE *clearly separated the classes from one another during the Middle Ages.*

TOWN-DWELLING CRAFTSMEN *were organized in guilds.*

CITY AIR IS LIBERATING: *Serfs who had lived in a town for a year without being called back by their lords were granted freedom in the Middle Ages.*

THOMAS HOBBES, *born 1588 in Westport, died 1679 in Hardwick Hall.*

WAR OF ALL AGAINST ALL: *His theory of state is founded on a pessimistic view of humanity.*

ABSOLUTE STATE AUTHORITY: *The state must guarantee peace and security to the individual.*

Hobbes was the first to theorize that the state derives its power from the individual.

The "Leviathan" by Thomas Hobbes

THE ENGLISH PHILOSOPHER Thomas Hobbes is considered the first political theorist of modern times and the "father of absolutism." He did not consider political authority to be God-given or natural. Instead, it could only be justified through its benefit to the individual. He considered the state as a contract between the ruler and the ruled, both seeking to secure the common interests of the citizens. Hobbes, who lived through the brutal civil war in England, saw the task of the state as primarily existing to provide for peace and security. Against this backdrop, he developed a theory of the all-powerful state in 1651 in his work "Leviathan."

HOBBES assumed a negative image of man. He posited that humankind is by nature driven by ruthless self-preservation and is constantly striving to extend their individual power. This course leads to conflict and so, in order to avoid the "war of all against all," people relinquish part of their authority to a sovereign, who is responsible to no one. This monarch alone sets the rules, which all his people must obey to resolve conflicts.

Title plate of Hobbes' "Leviathan": The state is the super ordinate, all-powerful authority that unites all people in it.

THE BIRTH OF THE MODERN AGE THROUGH REVOLUTION

The revolutions of 1776–1789 launched the breakthrough of democracy in Europe during the 19th century. The working class emerged out of industrialization.

Fall of a symbol: The "storming of the Bastille" on July 14th, 1789, marked the beginning of revolution in France.

In the 17th century, the middle class gained social influence through education and money. It became the motor of the European Enlightenment in the 18th century, which in part questioned traditional political authority. In countless publications, the privileges of the aristocracy were attacked, a political voice demanded, and inalienable rights (p. 176) formulated that were the state's responsibility to protect. These ideas formed the intellectual breeding-ground for the revolutions that radically altered the forms of society in Europe and America in the following decades.

The "Sans-culottes" were a radical republican group in the French Revolution.

Revolutions in the U.S. and France

The American Revolution began with the Declaration of Independence in 1776. In it, the British colonies officially disassociated themselves from the motherland in the name of freedom and equality. The governors of the British king were removed from office, and, in 1789, the Constitution of the United States of America was ratified, providing for a presidential republic (p. 179), a separation of powers, and basic rights (p. 176). It also prescribed a binding commitment to law and justice. It remains in force today, making it almost the oldest democratic constitution in the world. Taking a revolutionary step in 1789, the representatives of the Third Estate middle class in France declared a National Assembly and passed a series of groundbreaking decisions. Among others, they abolished the aristocracy while proclaiming human and civil rights (p. 176). The constitution of 1791 founded a constitutional monarchy that was a model for other European states.

Victory of the Middle Class

For a short time the excesses of the French Revolution dragged the civil ideals of liberty through the mud, but in the meantime the traditional noble elite's dominating position had irrevocably run out. Almost everywhere in Europe in the 19th century, civil movements forced the authorities to accept constitutions and to more or less limit royal influence on political decisions. In this way, the middle class, to a great extent, ensured itself of having a voice in the political process. It became a decisive factor in a society that had been radically changed through technological progress.

Social Upheavals

The industrialization of economic production brought forth a new class of laborers who initially were without rights. Labor unions and socialist parties (p. 184) soon demanded equal rights as well as a political voice. They were also instrumental in forming the foundations that made the establishment of modern democracies (p. 169) in Europe possible at the beginning of the 20th century.

The establishment of a communist dictatorship in 1917 in Russia (p. 172) allowed nationalist and fascist forces to gain strength. As a response, many democracies, especially in Europe, turned into totalitarian regimes (p. 170). Communism came out of the World Wars more powerful, while in western Europe new democracies were founded. After the collapse of the Soviet Union, a great portion of the newly autonomous regions pledged themselves to the ideals of a liberal democracy (pp. 176–177).

A result of democratic revolutions: politicians must now be convincing.

"TERROR, WITHOUT WHICH VIRTUE IS IMPOTENT." Robespierre deliberately erected a reign of terror in 1793 and 1794 in France.

"RULE OF REASON": Robespierre was inspired by the teachings of the philosopher of the Enlightenment, Rousseau.

Maximilien de Robespierre (1758–1794) was known as the "the Incorruptible."

Virtue and Terror

SOCIAL REVOLUTIONS in the name of the people are always in danger of turning into murderous tyranny through the messianic missions and extremes of individual revolutionaries. Maximilien de Robespierre, who was an integral part of the radicalization of the French Revolution after 1791, is the exemplary embodiment of this historical experience. The talented speaker and fanatical supporter of the Republic held a position in France of almost unlimited power after 1793.

HIS GOAL WAS to put into practice the teachings of Jean-Jacques Rousseau, according to which a true democratic society must recognize a "general will" ("volonté generale") over the will of the individual. Robespierre believed he knew this "general will," thus, he attempted by force and deterrence to establish a "rule of virtue." He sent thousands of supposed opponents of the "Revolution" to the guillotine before he himself was executed in 1794.

Robespierre considered King Louis XVI a "criminal of humanity." He was executed by the French people on January 21, 1793.

➲ see also: Enlightenment and Rousseau, *Philosophy Chapter, pp. 258–259*

DEMOCRACY—NATURE AND HISTORY

The Greek city-states of antiquity founded the democratic system of government. Modern democracies with representative bodies and universal suffrage were first established during the 20th century.

The first communities in which the people themselves determined their own political rule was in ancient Greece. In the small, manageable city-states of the fifth and fourth centuries, the citizens regularly met together in the marketplace to discuss and decide on all public affairs and to sit in judgment. They also gave this form of government their name: democracy, the "rule of the people."

In ancient Athens, the people's assembly met in the Acropolis ("high city"). Today, it is the most famous landmark of the Greek capital.

In the beginning of the parliamentary system, the ruler (here Elizabeth I of England) was no longer able to make solitary decisions, but rather was made dependent on having the consent of Parliament.

The Principle of the Sovereignty of the People

Various forms of democracy (p. 178) developed in the course of history, and in modern complex societies a direct democracy is hardly possible. Despite that, the Greek legacy, the principle of sovereignty of the people, remains the decisive criterion for every democratic system of state. All political power must derive from the will of the people, which as a rule is determined indirectly through members of the representative bodies of the people. This is primarily achieved through the majority election (p. 177) of members to representative bodies by the people. Further important features of a democratic system today are the control of the exercise of state power, the guarantee of fundamental and minority rights, and the right to equal political participation for all citizens (p. 176). The last criterion in particular was not implemented in many states until the 20th century.

Origin of Parliamentary Systems

The start of modern democracy reaches back to the 13th century when the nobility in England forced the king to accept the instituting of a Parliament. This later was divided into the aristocratic upper house and a lower house where elected commoners met.

The Parliament slowly evolved from a council to an independent arbitrator. In 1688, the king was generally deprived of power, and the Parliament became the actual sovereign of politics with the right to legislate laws. Over time, the upper house increasingly lost significance and the elected lower house assumed more and more authority. English parliamentarianism became the model for the revolutions in America and France (p. 168). Yet the majority of the population still remained excluded from the political process.

Suffrage for All

The right to vote in most of the other constitutional monarchies of the 19th century, which for the most part had weak parliaments, remained bound, as it had been for varying lengths of time, to property and class. Universal suffrage was introduced first in France in 1852, then in the German Empire in 1871, and finally in England in 1918—although in part only for the male population. The introduction of universal female suffrage took even longer. Whereas women in France had to wait until 1944 before they were allowed to have a say in the composition of the parliament, women in Liechtenstein were denied the right to vote until 1984.

INSIDER KNOWLEDGE

THE DEMOCRACY OF THE IROQUOIS *(a union of North American natives) was influential in the shaping of the Constitution of the U.S.*

POLAND *ratified Europe's first democratic constitution on May 3, 1791.*

ARISTOTLE, *the Greek philosopher, belittled democracy as the "vacillating rule of the many."*

Democracy in the age of media: In the presidential election of 2000, the candidates George W. Bush and Al Gore courted the voters through television.

Athenian Democracy

THERE WAS NO PARLIAMENT and no parties in the Athenian democracy of the fifth century. All free citizens of Athens—not including women and slaves—exercised direct legislative, governmental, and judicial power, as well as control in the assemblies. Public offices were allocated only for a limited time either by vote or by drawing lots.

The Assembly: center of power in which all decisions were made according to the majority; voting took place by raising hands.

Areopagus
Homicide court

Government
Committee of 50 councilmen

9 Archons

10 Strategists (1 per Phyle)

Council of 500 (50 per Phyle)

6,000 Judges (600 per Phyle)

Through an election

Through a lot

Open Town Meeting
All Athenians over 20 years old

Council of 500: Set the agenda for the assemblies. Each of the ten Phyle (tribe or clan) chose 50 representatives by lottery.

Prytanies (delegations from the ten tribes): prepared the assemblies.

Constitution of Cleisthenes 507 B.C.

KEY FACTS

A DICTATORSHIP *is the concentration of power in the hands of a few.*

TOTALITARIAN DICTATORSHIPS *attempt to politicize even people's private lives.*

LENIN'S CADRE PARTY *had a decisive influence on the communist world.*

NATIONAL SOCIALISM *combined fascist state organization with murderous racial hatred.*

Dictatorship | Theocracy | Leninism | Stalinism | Maoism | Military dictatorship | Fascism | National Socialism

DICTATORIAL FORMS OF GOVERNMENT

A dictatorship is the rule of an individual or small group. Throughout history, numerous and varied forms of dictatorial power has been exercised. Since antiquity, power-mad tyrants, oppressive do-gooders, and nationalist military cliques have existed. A characteristic of the 20th century was the attempt of many dictatorships not only to secure their own authority, but to do it in the name of some large-scale social utopia that sought to fundamentally revolutionize society as a whole. Millions of people fell victim to these ambitions.

The term dictator comes from the Latin dictare, to "order" or "dictate."

DICTATORSHIP—NATURE AND VARIANTS

Forms of government are termed dictatorships when all power is in the hands of an individual Some dictatorships violate the personal liberties of citizens more than others.

Dictatorship and democracy are forms of government that fundamentally exclude each other. While the democratic exercise of power is tied to the will of the people and subject to a systematic control (p. 176), complete power in a dictatorship is concentrated in one person or group. Many democratic states, however, allow for the possibility of a temporary assumption of power that is sometimes similar to a dictatorial form of government. This form of governing is typically implemented to overcome states of emergency. In Germany, for example, basic democratic rights (p. 176) can be limited in a crisis. In France, the declaration of a state of emergency can suspend all basic rights for a period of 12 days while in Great Britain, the War Measures Act grants additional authorities to the government during war. The implimentation of these laws is a very serious matter.

Charismatic Rule

Totalitarian dictators often attempt to establish a quasi-religious relationship between themselves and the people. They achieve what is often referred to as a "cult of personality." The ruler is presented as a demi-god at enormous mass demonstrations or in persuasive films to awaken a yearning for salvation in the people. This is intended to breed a mass of devout followers, who faithfully and devotedly obey the will of the dictator. In his speeches, Adolf Hitler often spoke of the destiny that sent him to the German people as their "savior."

above: *Enthusiastic followers of Hitler in Berlin in 1935*

Dionysus I ruled from 406–367 B.C. over the Sicilian city-state of Syracuse; he is considered one of the cruelest tyrants of antiquity.

Characteristics of a Dictatorship

Despite their varied historical manifestations, all dictatorships display typical commonalities. To speak of a dictator in the actual sense, a permanent and unlimited claim to power must be made. A suspension of the division of powers (p. 176) is also central. The courts and the parliament—if there is one—are filled with loyal followers. Basic democratic rights and participation in the political process are curtailed or abolished (pp. 176, 181) and all opposition is more or less violently suppressed. Many dictators, particularly in the 20th century, came to power through democratic processes. They legitimized their rule through staged elections, giving it a pseudo-democratic appearance.

Totalitarian Dictatorships

Political forms of government that seek to establish a new, comprehensive system of values in society, as well as to extend their authority to the personal spheres of the general public, are termed "totalitarian" dictatorships. Massive propaganda is also characteristic, aiming to intellectually manipulate the populace from childhood in order to integrate them all into the state or state-affiliated organizations. Arbitrary terror against "enemies of the state" is meant to break free will and to turn the population into a submissive, maneuverable mass. The communist (p. 172) and fascist (p. 174) dictatorships of the 20th century can be regarded as typical.

General Alfred Stroessner, who was of German descent, dictatorially ruled over Paraguay with the help of the military from 1954 to 1989.

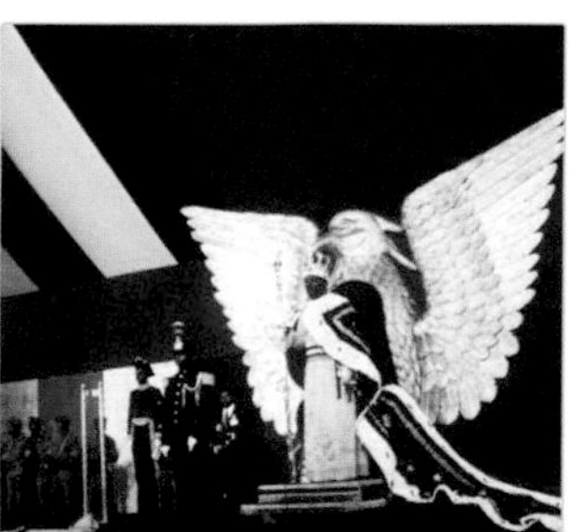

Jean-Bedel Bokassa set up a dictatorship in 1966 in the Central African Republic. In 1977 he had himself crowned emperor.

MODERN DICTATORSHIP—THEOCRACY, NATIONALIST REGIME

Modern dictatorships most often try to substantiate and ensure their authority through an exaggerated display of national patriotism. Religious regimes, like that in Iran, cite the will of God in their governmental decisions.

Modern dictatorships as a rule rely on an ideology to justify autocratic rule to the populace. Here, the most important point of reference is the nation, with the exception of the communist systems that were initially internationally oriented (p. 172). Common culture, religion, origin, or tradition is propagandistically inflated so as to differentiate the nation from others. This primarily serves to increase the individual's identification with the government.

Many of the military dictatorships (p. 174) of Latin America, as well as most of the clan-led governments of Africa like the Hutu, had and continue to have such nationalistic traits. However, many communist dictatorships deliberately employ such nationalistic elements. This was how the Soviet dictator Stalin (p. 172) sought to build up communism in his own country, Russia.

From 1974 on, the Romanian dictator Nicolae Ceauçescu referenced to himself as the "leader of all Romanians" and included himself in the ranks of the great national heroes. At present, the last remaining Stalinist (p. 172) system, in North Korea, increasingly appeals to nationalistic sentiments.

Frequently extreme nationalism leads to the persecution of ethnic or religious minorities and also serves as a basis for aggressive foreign policy.

Ayatollah Khomeini, still revered today, was the spiritual leader of the Islamic revolution in Iran in 1979 and until 1989 its Supreme Leader.

In the Name of God: Dual Government in Iran

A special form of ideological dictatorship is theocracy, which presents a divine law as its justification. At its head is a "divine" or "divinely chosen" ruler or priesthood. State and religious systems become one. Early state systems like those of Egypt, China, and India (p. 166) were often theocracies. In the Western cultural area, this only exists today in the Catholic nation Vatican City.

Since the "Islamic Revolution" of 1979, the most powerful theocracy in existence is Iran. Although the "Islamic Republic" has a democratically elected parliament and head of state, its power is greatly reduced. A 12-man "Council of Guardians" must approve all laws and regulations by checking their compatibility with the principles of Islam. A religious leader, the Supreme Leader, is chosen by the Assembly of Experts and holds the highest authority. He is supreme commander of the armed forces, appoints the supreme judiciary, and he alone controls the direction of state policies. In issues of dispute, it is always the clergy that makes the final decision.

Nicolae Ceauçescu ruled Romania from 1974 to 1989 with the help of the "Securitate," the all-powerful secret police.

North Korea's Stalinist ruler, Kim Jong-il, completely isolated his country from the world.

NATIONALIST REGIMES *aim for one ethnic or religious "purity" of their state population.*

HISTORICAL VICTIMS OF DISPLACEMENT: *Jews and Muslims were driven from Spain with the Reconquista, Native Americans onto reservations.*

20TH CENTURY VICTIMS OF GENOCIDE: *Jews in Europe-Russia; Armenians in Turkey; Kurds in Iraq*

Murdered Tutsi members after the massacre by the Hutu ruling powers in Rwanda in 1994.

"Ethnic Cleansing"

NATIONALIST REGIMES put their own ethnic group above all others and strive for an ethnically or religiously homogenous population within their borders. If necessary, this is achieved through force. Especially during the 20th century, there were regular systematic expulsions or genocides of undesirable groups in the population, providing more advantageous housing or living conditions for the dominant ethnic group. A historical example is the mass murder of Armenians in Turkey during 1915. At the beginning of the 21st century, this was causing continuing mass expulsions in the West Sudanese region of Darfur.

IN EUROPE in 1991, the divided multi-ethnic nation of Yugoslavia ignited years-long wars between the former member republics over the individual national boundaries. These were accompanied by brutal crimes against minorities perpetrated by all sides. The Serbian president Slobodan Milošević is regarded as one of those mainly responsible for the escalation. In 1999, he was brought under charges before a UN court.

Around 1.5 million Christian Armenians died in 1915 and 1916 during deportation by the Young Turks.

POLITICS, LAW, AND ECONOMY

LENINISM AND STALINISM

Lenin established a regime in Russia in the name of socialism (p. 184). His concept of a "dictatorship of the proletariat" greatly influenced later communist states. Stalin, his successor, built the party dictatorship into a murderous autocracy.

Lenin founded the Union of Socialist Soviet Republics, the USSR, in 1922.

In the 19th century, the German philosopher Karl Marx regarded the transition from capitalism to a dictatorship of the proletariat as a necessary historical process in which the power of the state would be automatically transferred to the proletariat (p. 184). On the other hand, at the turn of the 20th century, the Russian socialist Vladimir Lenin developed the doctrine that only a "new kind of party" would be able to lead the propertyless working class, the proletariat, to victory in the class struggle. Thus a core of politically trained professional revolutionaries must bring about the dictatorship of the proletariat with force, and educate the general population to become socialists. Because Russia was underdeveloped, the capitalist stage, referred to as "historically necessary" by Marx, would be skipped and the revolution brought about as soon as possible. The Revolution of 1918 against the czarist empire was the beginning of the worldwide communist revolution.

Dictatorship of the Cadre Party

When Lenin's followers, the Bolsheviks, came to power in Russia through a coup in 1918, they began to systematically impose their authority on the state and society. The freely elected parliament was disbanded, non-socialist press and parties were banned while the influence of the church was restricted. The courts were required to administer socialist jurisprudence, which judged the behavior of an individual only according to his function in the socialist society and did not recognize universal human rights (p. 176). Opponents of this new doctrine were branded as "enemies of the revolution" and persecuted by the state secret police. An enormous administrative apparatus was created in commerce and industry to centrally plan and control all the production in the state. After 1923, when opposition to the state economy mounted, particularly among the farmers, Lenin allowed them to sell their crops on the open market instead of giving them to the state. The power of the party over the country was, as yet, not unlimited.

The Stalin cult was also strong in the satellite states of the Soviet Union, with assemblies such as the one seen here in 1948 in former Czechoslovakia.

Glorification of Stalin: Art was used as state propaganda.

Stalin's Terror Regime

After 1928, under Lenin's successor, Josef Stalin, the country once and for all developed into a totalitarian dictatorship (p. 170). Farming was ruthlessly and forcibly collectivized—that is, made part of a state collective—while extreme industrialization was pushed forward. Actual and presumed political opponents were eliminated when the party, army, and administration regularly "purged." By 1938, Stalin had murdered almost all of the old party and state elite while replacing them with loyal functionaries, who put an unprecedented personality cult into motion. The Leninist dictatorship of the Communist Party changed into the dictatorship of one man that cost millions of lives. Today, regimes that mask the absolute power of one person or small group with socialist ideology are termed "Stalinists."

Comintern

On Lenin's initiative, all communist parties joined together in 1919 in the "Communist International" (Comintern) to achieve the worldwide "dictatorship of the proletariat." The member parties were required to be subordinate to the leadership. National parties increasingly lost their independence due to the great influence the Soviet party had from the very beginning. Under Stalin, "Comintern" became purely a foreign policy instrument of power for the Soviet dictator. He also arbitrarily dissolved the organization in 1943.

above: *Second Congress of the Communist International, 1920, Petrograd; Lenin at center*

The GDR regime under Soviet leadership was also Stalinist until its overthrow in 1989.

INSIDER KNOWLEDGE

STALIN *actually wanted to become a priest, but because of his revolutionary intrigues he was expelled from the seminary.*

LENIN, *in his treatise "Testament," warned about Stalin's thirst for power.*

ONLY WITH GERMANY'S HELP *was Lenin able to return to Russia from exile in Switzerland in 1917.*

➲ see also: **Socialism**, *Philosophy Chapter, p. 180*

MAOISM—COMMUNISM OF THE PEASANTS

Mao Zedong created his own variation of Marxism-Leninism on China. Despite a restructured economy, today the state and party leadership still draw inspiration from Mao.

Under the leadership of Mao Zedong, a communist regime was put into force in China. The establishment of a People's Republic in 1949 expanded Lenin's doctrine and adapted it to the specific conditions of China. Mao's interpretation of how the communist revolution should take power fundamentally differed from pure Marxist-Leninist doctrine. He believed that agrarian developing countries like China rather than the highly industrialized West or even the Soviet Union must be the vanguard of a worldwide communist revolution. He also saw the peasants in the countryside, instead of the urban proletariat, as the bearers of the revolution. A guerrilla war against the landowners would carry the revolution in China to the cities, and there ignite a people's war that would launch a socialist revolution.

A portrait of Mao decorates the entrance to the Forbidden City on Tiananmen Square in Beijing.

The Permanent Revolution

In practice, Mao Zedong differed little from Soviet ideology. Without compromise, he also imposed the autocratic authority of the Communist Party and, much like Stalin, had himself venerated as a great nationalist hero of the people. First and foremost, he pushed ahead with the collectivization of agriculture.

However, simultaneously, in order to catch up with industrial progress in the West, he forced heavy industrialization in the country from 1958 to 1960 with his "Great Leap Forward." It was characterized by a massive steel campaign and the foundation of communes that was meant to take advantage of China's large population. Millions lost their lives in the process.

According to Maoist philosophy, the unity of the masses, the party and the whole country is essential, therefore the attitudes of the people should be scrutinized. Special camps were set up for socialist "reeducation" of the people. The Cultural Revolution that Mao launched in 1966, which only officially ended with his death in 1976, was aimed at "purging" the Chinese society of "internal enemies" and removing "bourgeois-decadent" thought. Fanatic party cadres destroyed the Chinese cultural wealth; the educated elite were publicly humiliated.

Mao sought to force industrial progress in China with major technological projects.

Mao is revered to this day as the "Great Chairman."

Mao's Legacy

The Maoist model influenced many communist movements, especially in neighboring developing countries like Vietnam, North Korea, and Laos. In Albania in 1961, Maoism was even proclaimed official state doctrine.

After the fall of the Soviet bloc 1989 and 1991, Maoism changed. The state and party leadership in China has been progressively opening up the country's economy to the West ever since Mao's death in 1976, while professing a "socialist market economy." Furthermore, communes were disbanded and more individual rights granted.

Up until today, Mao's ideas are still adhered to officially. One idea is truly alive and well: the monopoly of the Communist Party, with power that tolerates few political opponents.

KHMER ROUGE *was a guerrilla troop that emerged from the Communist Party of Cambodia.*

POL POT AND THE KHMER ROUGE *radicalized the Maoist theory of peasant communism.*

CITY DWELLERS *were deported to the countryside and particularly intellectuals were killed.*

Pol Pot installed one of the most absurd terror regimes of the 20th century.

"Stone Age Communism" of the Khmer Rouge

IN CAMBODIA, the Khmer Rouge under the leadership of Pol Pot established a particularly murderous deviant of Maoism from 1976 to 1979. They subjected the country to a process of social reshaping that was aimed at creating a communist peasant state. The total population of the cities—children, elderly, and even the sick—were resettled in the countryside, where they were forced to serve as slave laborers for the farmers.

WHEN THE AGRICULTURAL PRODUCTION did not increase as expected, Pol Pot had whole sections of the population systematically murdered. Intellectuals—wearing glasses was enough to qualify—were especially targeted and murdered by the thousands as "useless eaters." About 2 million Cambodians fell victim to the terror. In 1979, Vietnamese troops drove Pol Pot from power. In 1998 he committed suicide.

A total of close to 2 million Cambodians fell victim to the terror.

FASCISM AND MILITARY DICTATORSHIPS

Fascist ideology with a supreme leader was characteristic of the early 20th century, particularly in Europe. This thought also prevailed in some authoritarian military dictatorships.

The pretense to power of fascist regimes is reflected in art and architecture (grounds of the 1942 World Exposition in Rome as planned by Mussolini).

After WWI, a nationalist movement gained ground in Italy around the former socialist Benito Mussolini. They called themselves "Fascists" after the ancient Roman symbol of power, a bundle of birch rods (Latin: "fasces"). In 1924, Mussolini took advantage of a state crisis to lever out the democratic institutions and set up a completely new kind of leader dictatorship. It soon became the model for the right wing nationalist movements to subsequently gain political influence worldwide. By 1945, fascist systems of government had replaced parliamentary democracies in Spain, Germany, and Portugal.

Fascism as Anti-Ideology

The goals of the fascists were so different in various countries that one can hardly speak of a single, united doctrine of fascism. Ideologically, they primarily held in common an opposition toward the political currents of the modern age. Their orientation was markedly anti-communist, anti-capitalist, anti-democratic, and anti-liberal. Violence as a political means was glorified and the nation was aggrandized through propaganda. Fascist movements were structured like military organizations, and a cult was built around a central leader. The people were understood as a will-less, arbitrarily malleable "mass" that must unconditionally obey the will of the leader. The aspirations of the fascists to invade all areas of society and to impose an absolute unity of leader and people were almost achieved in National Socialist Germany (p. 175).

Italian "Duce" Benito Mussolini was a model for the fascists.

21ST CENTURY

RIGHT WING EXTREMISTS *and "neo-fascist" parties have grown in popularity in the last couple of years in France and Italy.*

LEFT WING PARTIES *today still like to place their political opponents under suspicion of being fascists.*

IN BOLIVIA AND VENEZUELA *authoritarian tendencies are recognizable in the current left wing, populist presidents.*

Authoritarian Military Governments

The clichés of fascist ideology, such as anti-communism, military ideals in the education of the youth, and an excess of national pride, were later adopted in part by authoritarian military dictatorships. Especially in the socially unstable countries of South America and Africa, groups of officers in many places pushed their way to power after 1960—usually with the claim of seeking to stabilize the land and reform its structures. In Chile (1973–1990), Argentina (1976–1983), and Greece (1967–1974), for example, brutal dictatorships were first established, democratic rights were subsequently suspended, and eventually thousands of people from the leading opposition camp were arrested or murdered.

Later, as so often is the case in other military dictatorships—e.g., in Brazil (1963–1988) or today in Pakistan—spurious democratic elements have been allowed to be integrated into the dictatorship, as long as its own hold on power was not jeopardized. This included limited free elections and a less restricted freedom of speech. A slow process of democratization began in most of these countries; however, the military remains an important factor in the struggle for power, usually linked to but at times somewhat independent from that of the dictator, especially in the case of developing countries.

General Augusto Pionochet came to power in 1973 in Chile through a military coup.

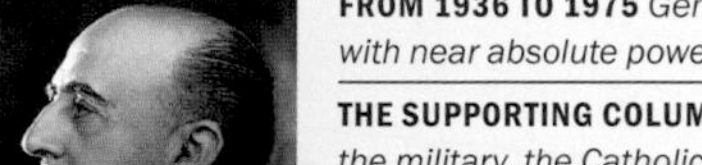

Francisco Franco

FROM 1936 TO 1975 *General Francisco Franco ruled with near absolute power in Spain.*

THE SUPPORTING COLUMN *of his rule was, along with the military, the Catholic Church.*

AFTER 1945, *Spain developed into an authoritarian system.*

The Franco Regime

IN 1936, FRANCISCO FRANCO established a partly fascist, partly authoritarian dictatorship in Spain that was finally ended through free elections in 1977. The nationalist Franco overthrew the republican government with the help of the military, proclaimed himself "leader of all Spaniards," and brutally suppressed all opposition. Franco's position of absolute authority rested on the loyalty of the fascist Falange state party, the military, and, surprisingly, the Catholic Church. He granted it numerous privileges and declared Catholicism to be the only religious denomination of the Spanish nation.

FRANCO REMAINED NEUTRAL during WWII. In 1947, he officially restored the monarchy, but retained all power for himself. Under international pressure, the economy was liberalized in 1959, censorship loosened, and a restricted amount of system-friendly civil rights were granted to citizens. After Franco's death in 1975, Spain peacefully transformed into a parliamentary monarchy under his successor King Juan Carlos.

Francisco Franco surveys a parade after his victory over the Republicans.

NATIONAL SOCIALISM—VIOLENCE AND RACIAL FANATICISM

Adolf Hitler installed a regime contemptuous of humankind in 1933 in Germany that was only brought down after a bitter war. The totalitarian "Fuehrer" (German: "captain") state was marked by a confusing juxtaposition of competing power structures.

A variation of fascism, National Socialism came to power in Germany in 1933 with Adolf Hitler as its central figure. The extreme racism, however, also gave it an ideology completely of its own.

Hitler was a talented demagogue who cast a spell over the masses.

A New European Order

Hitler sought a complete reorganization of Europe along the principles of his racial theory, which decreed that the racially "valuable" people, the Aryans, should rule over the "inferior" races as the master race. With this goal, he began a war in 1939, which cost millions of people their lives, especially in Eastern Europe. It was not until the complete defeat of Germany by a coalition of the leading international powers—England, France, the U.S., and the USSR—that the National Socialist system of power was destroyed. The ideology has since been internationally outlawed.

The Dual State

While in exile in 1940/1941, the German political scientist Ernst Fränkel analyzed the principles of power of National Socialism in a study. According to him, the German terror regime could be broken down into two structurally different systems of government, both conditional to one another. The normative state, in which fixed laws were in force and maintained the appearance of normalcy, and the prerogative state, in which these laws were broken and arbitrarily pre-empted according to political discretion.

above: *Ernst Fränkel*

Political and Social Nazification

Within a very short time, Adolf Hitler had transformed the German democracy into a totalitarian Fuehrer dictatorship (p. 170) and had imposed the National Socialists' claim to the universal validity of their ideological precepts on all levels of politics and society. Basic rights were rescinded, the media were made compliant, and all political parties except the official state party, Hitler's NSDAP (Nazi Party), were banned. The military was made to swear a personal oath of loyalty directly to Hitler himself. Those active in industry were compulsively organized in party-controlled mass associations. Even spare time was organized by the regime while a special value was placed on the education of youth. From 1940, children between the ages of 10 and 18 were forced to join the party's youth organizations.

Instrument of Terror: The SS

At the head of the National Socialist state there was no hierarchically organized ruling bloc. Rather there was a chaotic co-existence of rival state and party organizations. Their only point of reference remained Hitler. The whole system of suppression was at first composed of a thick tangle of state and party organs. Heinrich Himmler, however, gradually built up the "SS" (Schutzschaffel) from a small elite unit to the regime's main instrument of power. He tied the SS and the police tightly together and finally controlled the whole system of terror of the National Socialist state. The SS was in charge of the concentration and extermination camps within German-controlled territories, in which "undesirable" persons were systematically tortured and/or murdered. The Allied military court in 1946 declared the SS to be a criminal organization.

Exemplifying nationalism, the Germans citizens of Berlin adorned Koenigstrasse with Nazi banners in August of 1936.

THE NATIONAL SOCIALISTS *considered the Jews to be the "corrupters of humankind."*

SINCE 1933 *the Jews had been systematically forced out of society. In the "Night of Broken Glass" (Nov. 9–10, 1938), Jewish houses, stores, and synagogues were destroyed.*

ABOUT 6 MILLION JEWS *fell victim to systematic mass murder.*

Anti-Semitic propaganda in Germany

The Genocide of the Jews

THE MAJOR ENEMY from the National Socialists' point of view was "International Jewry," which was seen as ruling over all international movements and destroying the national "purity" of the people. Directly after assuming power in Germany, the National Socialists began to systematically force all citizens with Jewish backgrounds out of every area of life by judicial, economic, and criminal means.

WITH THE BEGINNING OF WWII IN 1939, Jews were first deported to ghettos and work camps. Mass executions after the invasion of the Soviet Union in 1941 heralded bureaucratically organized genocide. Jews from all over Europe were transported to planned killing centers and murdered there. In the largest Nazi "death factory," Auschwitz-Birkenau, at least one million people died, primarily from poison gas.

Extermination camp Auschwitz-Birkenau

KEY FACTS

IN REPRESENTATIVE DEMOCRACIES *the citizens decide who governs them.*

CITIZEN INVOLVEMENT *is crucially decisive in the quality of democracy.*

DEMOCRATIC RULE *serves the protection of human rights.*

DEMOCRATIC STATES *intervene in a more or less regulatory manner in the free marketplace.*

Basic rights, separation of powers | Civil society | Basic forms of democracy | U.S. and British system | Participation

PRINCIPLES OF DEMOCRACY

The democratic systems of government that are in practice within the world today are very diverse. All functioning democracies are based on the fundamental principles of human rights, separation of governing powers, and the right of every citizen to vote during political elections. The various political decision-makers are elected for a specific period of time, and the state institutions are constrained by legislation and justice systems. This type of system allows for social interests to develop freely.

"Democracy is the worst form of government except all those other forms..." —Winston Churchill

BASIC RIGHTS AND SEPARATION OF POWERS

The guarantee of basic rights combined with an institutionalized control of state power are essential structural elements to prevent a misuse of power in a democracy.

UN: Universal Declaration of Human Rights

"All human beings are born free and equal in dignity and rights." Thus begins the universal "Declaration of Human Rights" that the UN General Assembly adopted on December 10, 1948. The member states almost unanimously committed themselves to the protection of civil and political rights (e.g., the right to freedom of speech) as well as the social rights of each individual (e.g., the right to work). Although not legally binding, the declaration increased the political and moral pressure on nations and contributed to human rights standards' becoming the uniformly applied standard for the legitimacy of state actions today.

above: *The UN Human Rights Council, founded in 2006, aims to protect civil rights worldwide.*

Democracy stems from the idea of self-determination of the government by the citizens. Although citizens can influence politics, this does not mean no rule is exercised over them. All citizens are bound by laws, and offenses are prosecuted by the state. There are two main principles that prevent the misuse of state power in a democracy. One is a separation of powers into different, individual bearers of power; the other is the existence of legally protected basic rights of freedom and protection for each individual that in their essence cannot be revoked.

Individual Rights

Each person is entitled to individual rights of protection—a concept that dates from the age of Enlightenment (p. 258). The abstract human rights to freedom and equality to all citizens are, as a rule, expressly guaranteed by modern democratic constitutions. Such fundamental rights are enforced through legal action in politically neutral courts.

Every democracy is based on fundamental rights. First and foremost, the basic rights represent the citizen's right of defense against the state, but also normally guarantee the right to participate in the state's political life. In a functioning democracy, all decisions of the state are bound to the constitution. Ultimately, a legitimate democratic system of governance protects an individual's rights to freedom.

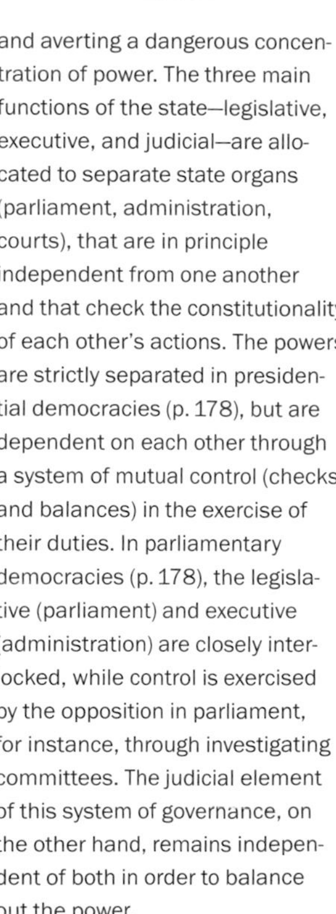

Baron de Montesquieu originated the system of separation of powers in 1748 in his work "The Spirit of Laws."

Balance of Powers

The overlapping principle of separation of powers in democratic constitutions is directed at guaranteeing these civil freedoms in the polity and averting a dangerous concentration of power. The three main functions of the state—legislative, executive, and judicial—are allocated to separate state organs (parliament, administration, courts), that are in principle independent from one another and that check the constitutionality of each other's actions. The powers are strictly separated in presidential democracies (p. 178), but are dependent on each other through a system of mutual control (checks and balances) in the exercise of their duties. In parliamentary democracies (p. 178), the legislative (parliament) and executive (administration) are closely interlocked, while control is exercised by the opposition in parliament, for instance, through investigating committees. The judicial element of this system of governance, on the other hand, remains independent of both in order to balance out the power.

The declaration of human rights by the French National Assembly marked the way to a democratic constitutional state.

see also: **Enlightenment**, *Philosophy Chapter, p. 258*

CIVIL SOCIETY AND THE WELFARE STATE

A stable democracy requires the active participation of its citizens. State organs protect the democratic order and also guarantee, to varying degrees, economic welfare to its citizens.

State employment agencies and private job centers find work for job seekers.

As important as the effective control of the government's decision-making processes is, the quality of a nation's democratic culture depends primarily on an active citizenry. Citizens not only cast their votes in elections as they arise, but also actively support their interests in day-to-day life, by joining political parties, clubs or citizens groups, and committees (p. 181). In this way, concerns and problems of the citizens become public, influencing and structuring the political decision-making process in democratic institutions. This requires a public arena that is open to various civic groups to have equal opportunity to articulate their interests. Such a civic society is promoted in a federally organized system, such as that of the U.S., in which the decision-making authorities are decentralized as much as possible. This means that a good deal of power and authority lies with the communities or, as in the case in the U.S., with the individual states, and less with the central government.

Socio-Political Balancing Mechanisms

Socio-political balancing mechanisms and economic freedom can hardly be separated from political freedom. At the same time, a free economy (p. 199) can perfectly well endanger democracies. It creates social and economic imbalances, placing the legitimacy of democratic order in question.

For that reason, democratic states all intervene to a certain extent in a regulatory manner, referred to as the principle of the free marketplace. Businessmen, for example, are required to adhere to specific labor, health, and environmental standards. A comprehensive system of security like unemployment, retirement, and health insurance is meant to protect the people from undue social risks. In emergencies, state social welfare guarantees a minimum economic standard.

The extent of a state's social services ultimately depends on the political orientation of the government. For instance, the social democratic (p. 184) orientated Scandinavian countries aim to provide comprehensive care for their citizens, whereas the state-guaranteed social security in traditionally liberal states (p. 183) like the U.S. is more weakly developed. There citizens carry the responsibility of protecting themselves against the varying levels of risk they might encounter by taking out specific insurance policies.

An outwardly fortified democracy; soldiers swear loyalty to the state (Germany pictured).

Communal self-government is stressed in federal states.

Sovereign Functions of the State

The democratic state has two core functions: to ensure the functional ability of state organs like the courts and police, and to protect the liberal constitution. Above all, protection against anti-democratic forces within the society is difficult to manage in a democracy. To what extent the state can partially intervene in an open opinion-making process and the basic rights it can suspend are debatable.

SECRET SERVICES *are meant to protect the constitutional order in democracies.*

BASIC RIGHTS *of an individual can be suspended.*

AN EFFECTIVE CONTROL *of the secret police is difficult even in a democracy.*

Emblem of the Federal Bureau of Investigation (FBI), the federal police of the U.S.

High Anxiety

SPECIAL STATE AUTHORITIES are empowered to collect covert information that is important to the security of the state and to pass it on to political decision-makers. The investigations are directed primarily towards attempts against the democratic order, in the course of which basic civil rights like the privacy of telephone or postal communication are suspended.

IN DEMOCRACIES, secret organizations are usually subject to the control of parliament in order to avoid arbitrary misuse of their power, though their effectiveness is often disputed because control of secret service activities does not take place publicly. Following September 11, 2001—as well as a number of other terrorist attacks—the authority of the security agencies in many states, especially in the U.S., has been greatly expanded.

Ready for a major "eavesdropping attack" on the citizenry: a microtransmitter, a bug, and a telephone circuit board

BASIC FORMS OF DEMOCRATIC GOVERNANCE

Modern democracies can be divided into presidential and parliamentary systems of government. In the former, the people elect the head of state; in the latter, parliament does.

In parliamentary democracies such as Germany, the head of government must justify his policies to parliament.

In representative democracies, the people do not vote directly on political issues as they did, for example, in ancient Athens (p. 169). Rather, the people elect representatives to state bodies provided for in the constitution, where they make political decisions for them. As a rule, the representatives are responsible only to their own consciences, but must stand for re-election by the people at regular intervals. Two basic forms have developed in the various representative democracies that differ from each other primarily in the form of the relationships between parliament, administration, and head of state.

Parliamentary Democracies

In parliamentary systems of government like those in England, Germany, and Italy, the head of state is elected by parliament, which can also force his resignation. The government is therefore dependent on the confidence of parliament, which is usually accompanied by close cooperation with the parliamentary majority. If the government loses the majority in parliament, the head of state often has the right to force new parliamentary elections. The head of government is either a president, who is elected, or—as in England and the Netherlands—a monarch, who chiefly fulfills representative and ceremonial functions.

Presidential Democracies

In presidential systems of government like in the U.S., parliament, or the legislature, and the government are clearly separate from each other. A state executive is elected directly by the people and functions as both head of state and government. He is independent of the legislature and cannot be voted out of office by it. In turn, he cannot dissolve the legislative branch.

In many countries there is a mixed form of presidential and parliamentary democratic elements. In France and Finland, for instance, a directly elected president and a prime minister are dependent on the confidence of parliament and share the powers of government.

Direct Democracies

In all representative democracies there are limited forms of direct citizen participation (p. 177). Especially in federally structured states, citizens at the regional level can introduce a bill to parliament with sufficient signatures in support of a specific matter. The government and parliament can also poll the public about important subjects and topics through referendums, though such decisions are not always binding for the government.

RULERS *are also freely elected in democracies that have not fully developed.*

IMPORTANT AREAS OF SOCIETY *in a democratic culture like the press or interest groups are merely underdeveloped.*

Corruption and inscrutable decision-making structures are characteristic of many nominally democratic states in Africa. Kenya's president, Mwai Kibaki, dissolved his cabinet in 2005.

Authoritarian Democracies

IN THE 1990S, particularly in Africa, Asia, as well as former communist states of Europe (e.g., Russia), many technically democratic systems of government with authoritarian tendencies were formed. Though they guarantee free elections and have democratic institutions, the protection against state intervention in citizens' civil rights and control of governmental power are generally insufficient.

FREQUENTLY, free democratic structures are missing outside of parliament out of which a living civil society can develop. Freedom of the press can be restricted, as a rule. As most of those states were former dictatorships, this condition may represent just a short transitional stage on the way to developing democracy.

In defective democracies, demonstrators against governmental policies are not always protected against repressive measures by the state.

Heads of state in parliamentary democracies, like the reigning British queen, have very little political power.

INSIDER KNOWLEDGE

IN TIMES OF PRONOUNCED POLITICAL DISAFFECTION, *the call for a more direct democracy becomes louder.*

THE FREE PARLIAMENTARIAN *must often in practice give in to party discipline.*

ENGLISH MONARCHS *have not used their right to dissolve Parliament for centuries.*

Directly elected presidents of state, such as Nicolas Sarkozy in France, have enough authority to make independent decisions.

THE SYSTEM OF GOVERNMENT IN THE U.S.

Characteristic of the U.S. governmental system is a resistance against too great an accumulation of power by an individual group or person. Despite the politically strong position of the President, rule is divided. For instance, only Congress may formally introduce legislation.

The U.S. is a federal state comprised of 50 individual states. The Constitution of 1787 provides for a republic with strict separation of powers and is still in force today (p. 176). The executive power lies with the President, the legislative with Congress, composed of the Senate and the House of Representatives, and the highest judicial power with the Supreme Court (p. 196). The individual states can make decisions in many areas independent of the federal government. Their political structure is overall the same as that of the federal state, except that a directly elected governor is at the head of the government.

The constitution of 1787 begins with the words "We the people."

The President

The President is the focal point of power in the U.S. at the federal level. He is elected along with his Vice President for a term of four years. He is elligible for reelection, but can only serve two presidential terms. The President represents the country abroad, shapes foreign policy, and alone has the right to conclude international treaties. As warranted by the Constitution, he is also commander in chief of the armed forces. He is in charge of the White House staff, which advises him in all political fields and prepares recommendations. The President can be removed from office only through impeachment by Congress, which must determine his violations of the Constitution. But the extent of presidential powers only appears immeasurable. The President's influence is dependent on his assertiveness with the other branches of government.

The U.S. President may only address Congress once a year in his "State of the Union."

Institutionalized Control of Power

An important limitation to the President's power lies in the structure of the executive branch, which he formally heads. The political responsibility for an individual area of policy is spread over many different offices, whose authority often overlaps and who often in part pursue opposing political goals. It is then a challenge for the President to coordinate all these strands and achieve his will.

Congress authorizes and funds the executive. The legislative branch alone, composed of the Senate and the House of Representatives, passes bills and can declare war. Treaties become effective only upon ratification by the legislature. The executive office may not formally present a bill to Congress, but must rather enlist individual representatives to take the initiative and introduce the bill. The President has the power to veto a bill, but Congress can override with a supermajority. Investigative committees are used to oversee the legality of government actions. The free media also plays a part by helping to hinder abuses of power within the government.

Presidential Election

The President is elected in a multistaged process. After an election campaign within the party, the candidate is nominated by their party's national convention. The people actually only elect the Electoral College. Each state sends to the college only as many electors as it has representatives in Congress. Electors in most states are informally bound to vote for their party's candidate. However, few ever stray from their promised commitments. As all of a state's electoral votes fall to the majority elected candidate, it is possible that a candidate receives a majority of the electoral votes and becomes President without winning the majority of the nationwide popular vote (Election 2000).

above: *Citizen casting vote*

Checks and Balance

IN ACCORDANCE WITH THE CONSTITUTION OF THE U.S., the authority of the three governmental branches is balanced in a system of mutual control. This is done in order to prevent any majority to rule the country without having to answer to anyone. The legislative branch is divided so as to balance the interests of the individual states. The Senate is composed of two senators from each state, serving six-year terms. The senators then face reelection, which is determined by the voting citizens of the state. In the House of Representatives, on the other hand, the 435 seats are allocated according to the size of each state's population, with the Members serving two-year terms.

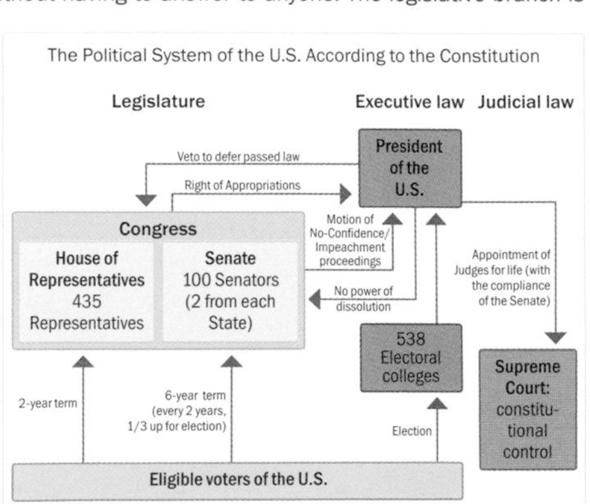

The Capitol is the seat of Congress.

POLITICS, LAW, AND ECONOMY

GOD SAVE THE QUEEN—THE BRITISH SYSTEM OF GOVERNMENT

Great Britain is considered to be the motherland of parliamentarianism. Although officially a monarchy, actual power lies with the government head, who is accountable to Parliament.

Westminster Palace is the seat of both chambers of Parliament.

The United Kingdom with its member countries, England, Wales, Scotland, and Northern Ireland, is a parliamentary monarchy. It is based on an unwritten constitution, i.e., it has not been formulated into a single document. The political institutions—the monarchy, the government, and the parliament—along with their relationships to one another have developed out of enacted laws and common law (p. 191) over the course of centuries. Thus, all power is ultimately derived from the legislative authority called Parliament. Until recently, the UK was centrally governed and administrated from its capital of London. The individual countries, with the exception of England, have their own parliaments (an Assembly in Wales) with the authority to make independent decisions regarding their specific areas.

Constitutional System Overview

IN CONTRAST TO THE STRICT SEPARATION of powers in the U.S. political system, Great Britain's executive and legislative branches are closely entwined. British parliamentarianism has even been described as a temporary "elective dictatorship" because, with the help of the parliamentary majority, the government has almost unlimited powers of achieving its will in decision-making. The democratic control consists foremost in the competition between the government and the opposition party. In terms of a separation of powers, the independence of the judiciary is to be strengthened in the future. Instead of the "Law Lords," a supreme court of law is to be made separate from the upper house.

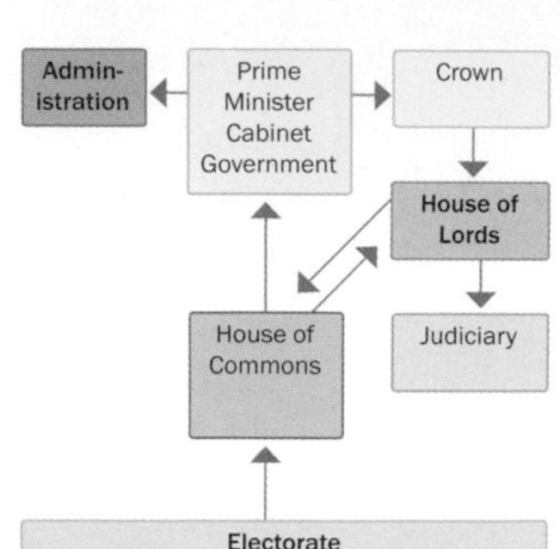

The "House of Commons" is the only institution that is directly democratically legitimized.

Monarchy and Parliament

The monarch is the head of state of the kingdom and theoretically has combined executive, legislative, and judicial powers. In practice, however, these powers are separated as in every democracy (p. 176). For centuries, according to common law, the monarchy has had only a limited political role. Today, it embodies the historical continuity of the nation and assumes ceremonial functions. The head of state usually gives the annual "Queen's Message," which is formulated by the government.

Legislative power lies exclusively with a bicameral parliament consisting of the House of Lords (upper house) and the House of Commons (lower house). The House of Lords formerly was only the hereditary nobility. Today, ecclesiastical dignitaries hold seats there along with commoners who have been raised to peerage because of their services to the state. The earlier functions of the House of Lords as a supreme court of justice as well as its participation in legislation have since been greatly reduced. Yet, it can recommend laws and block them for one year. Actual legislative authority lies with the democratically elected House of Commons. It controls the government and can force its dissolution.

Power of the Prime Minister

The center of power of the government is presided over by the prime minister, who, along with his Cabinet, exercises the executive power. The politician obtaining the majority in the House of Commons is named prime minister by the monarch. He appoints the members of his Cabinet—usually from outside the House of Commons—coordinates their work, and determines the guidelines of the government's policies. He can designate the exact date of the next elections within a five-year time period.

The Commonwealth

A community of states, the "Commonwealth of Nations," emerged out of the former British colonial empire, devoting itself to cultural exchange. Today it includes a total of 53 sovereign states in all corners of the world. These states either recognize the British queen as a nominal head of state or she is represented by a governor-general. Among them include India, Australia, South Africa, and New Zealand. Every two years there is a summit conference that serves to resolve mutual problems of the Commonwealth.

above: *The Queen visits Commonwealth member state Australia.*

The prime minister speaks before the House of Commons.
right: *Members of the upper house*

PLURALISM AND PARTICIPATION

Besides casting their vote in elections, people can take part in the democratic decision-making process by being active in political parties or interest groups.

Not only state organs like parliament and government are part of the political reality of a liberal democracy. Rather, it is also of prime importance that institutions exist through which citizens can exert influence on political decisions, such as political parties, associations, and the media.

Parties present candidates to the people for election to public offices.

Tasks of the Parties

The political parties are the most important mediators between the state and society. Citizens who have similar opinions about the organization of the polity join together in them. The parties bundle ideas into a political platform, make it public, and cultivate political leaders. In Europe, for the most part, they are tightly organized; in Germany they even have constitutional status and are partially financed by public funds. In the U.S., on the other hand, they are less of an organization with a unified philosophy, but rather more like a loosely knit association of individual groups. Their main purpose is to nominate candidates for public offices. Members of Congress are free to make decisions independent of party affiliation. Because candidates are chosen by state party organizations, the party leadership in Congress has less influence over how Senators vote in Congress than is the case in the UK, where the national party controls who can run for office. In the UK, party leaders in the House of Commons can impose a "whip," while a backbench rebellion would be seen as undermining the authority of its leadership.

Pressure of Individual Interests

Every citizen in a democracy has the right to join clubs and associations to articulate personal interests. Besides professional associations, there are politically active groups in various fields: in the field of economics, business associations and trade unions; in social welfare, charities; and in sociopolitical fields, environmental groups. As a general rule, all of these political groups attempt to make their goals public so as to bring pressure on political decision-makers. The organization of these groups varies internationally. For example, in Germany there are many central umbrella organizations, while labor unions and business associations in the U.S. are pluralistic and self–organizing. The more socially significant an organization is, the more directly contact is sought with the deciding bodies. Lobbyists, or representatives of interest groups, worldwide attempt to influence politicians when decisions touch their issues of interest.

Many workers are organized in labor unions that represent their interests.

COMMUNICATION: *The Internet enables new forms of political participation.*

VISION: *Some dream of a civil society linked together through the Internet.*

WHETHER THE INTERNET *actually leads to more democracy is debatable.*

Politicians like Tony Blair can communicate directly with the people over the Internet.

The Electronic Democracy

THE INTERNET has not only revolutionized economic life, but also offers the chance to have a more direct democratic voice in politics. Especially for the young, the Internet has become an important medium to gain the information and orientation vital for making key political decisions. Opinions can be exchanged interactively in discussion forums or campaigns organized by the various parties or by impartial organizations.

NEW POSSIBILITIES have also opened up for politicians. Their own digital monologues ("blogs") increase the transparency of decisions and allow a direct dialog with the people. The fact that Hillary Clinton first announced her candidacy for President online on January 20, 2007, shows the status of the Internet in politics. A virtual public marketplace has been created that has some dreaming of a worldwide civil society linked together through the Internet. It is clear that the administrative process can be made organizationally more transparent and closer to the people through use of the Internet.

The Internet is the marketplace for political opinions.

Election Systems

There are basically two procedures for transforming votes into a political composition of parties in Parliament. In Great Britain and the U.S., among others, a first-past-the-post electoral system is used and all positions being contested are given to the few parties with the most number of votes irrespective of the exact ratios. The votes for other parties are no longer of consequence. This is to ensure a stable parliamentary plurality for one party. In most European states, however, the mandate in the constituency is divided among the parties according to the number of votes they received (proportional representation), so that the will of the people is reflected as exactly as possible in Parliament.

above: *U.S. final 2004 presidential electoral chart according to state*

KEY FACTS

CONSERVATIVES *want to maintain traditional values.*

LIBERALS *stress the responsibility and self-determination of the individual.*

SOCIALISTS *want to build a society exhibiting solidarity upon the principle of equality.*

GREENS *stress environmental protection and seek to establish a greater level of democracy.*

Conservatism | Liberalism | Socialism | Alternative politics

POLITICAL IDEOLOGIES

In their actions, politicians follow their basic convictions, such as how society should be constituted or, above all, how it would function ideally. Today, the classic political conceptual structures of conservatism, liberalism, and socialism still form the foundations of the major parties as well as the guidelines for concrete political actions and decisions. There are, of course, many subfactions of these core ideological groups. Also, in the last decades, alternative political concepts—the Green parties for example—have gained importance.

Ideologies motivate people's political behavior.

CONSERVATISM—THE POWER OF TRADITION

Security and continuity remain the central principles of conservative ideology. At the same time, the conceptual positions have shifted greatly since the 19th century.

The conservative Austrian statesman von Metternich wanted to reorganize the power structures of Europe in the 19th century.

Basically to have a fundamentally conservative attitude means to want to protect and maintain the existing social order. To a conservative, the state, society, and culture are historically evolved structures held together by the customs as well as practices of the people. Innovations are desired only when they are proved to be mandatory for the stability of the political framework.

An election poster of German conservatives in 1957 warns of "socialist experiments."

State Power and Individualism

Conservatism first developed at the end of the 18th century as an independent political position in a defensive reaction to the ideas of the French Revolution. Political theorists like the English philosopher Edmund Burke defended the old social order based on privilege and ecclesiastical authority. The aristocracy and landowners supported the conservative parties of the 19th century in continental Europe. The state was assigned a central role in securing social structures and was to take over welfare services if necessary. The course of development was completely different in England and the U.S., where the conservatives were early to support the personal responsibility of the individual. Traditionally, the English "Tories" and the American "Republicans" assume an anti-socialist assistance position.

Conservatism Today

Classic conservatism lost its aristocratic base after World War II. Conservative parties everywhere now back democracy and the free economy. Meanwhile, a Christian orientation grew, particularly in Italy and Germany. Beyond national peculiarities, the modern conservative is characterized by advocating a strong state from within and outside as well as a distinctly anti-socialist sentiment. The old conservative attitudes that are seen today are primarily in a close relationship with religion and, if existing, with the monarchy.

Politically conservative and economically liberal: Ronald Reagan and Margaret Thatcher.

COMMUNITARIANISM *places a sense of community in the center position.*

THE COMMON GOOD *stands above the interests of the individual.*

A CIVIL SOCIETY *should be strengthened, the demands of the state lowered.*

Communitarians want solidarity between communities instead of a faceless state apparatus.

Communitarianism

COMMUNITARIANISM is the term given to a political theory movement that emerged in the 1980s whose most important advocates are considered to be the U.S. intellectuals Michael Walzer and Amitai Etzioni. They criticize the exaggerated individualism in modern society.

THE COMMUNITARIANS, in contrast to the liberals, consider a person as a social being whose community is primarily shaped by culture and tradition. Individual self-fulfillment along with egotistical pursuit of profit destroy group solidarity and with it the foundation of a free, democratic society. According to their demands, politics must orient itself more toward the common good and increase local communities' power to shape them in order to develop the responsibility of the individual for the community. Politicians such as the British Prime Minister Tony Blair have referred to communitarian ideas.

Values such as tolerance and solidarity should be learned as early as possible.

LIBERALISM—INDIVIDUAL FREEDOM AND SELF-FULFILLMENT

The most important principle of liberalism is to protect the freedom of the individual from intrusions by the state. The primary liberal demands are fulfilled today in modern democracies.

Liberalism focuses on the free development of the individual and takes a negative standpoint on external coercion. In its view, the state primarily has the task of enabling each person to determine his or her own life. The core liberal concerns are maintaining individual civil rights and establishing constitutional restrictions of political power.

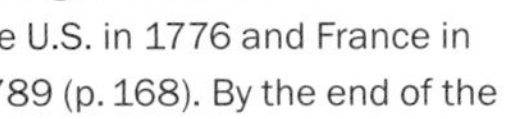

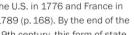

John Stuart Mill demanded in the 19th century that the individual should be sovereign over himself.

The Constitutional State

Based on the ideas of the Enlightenment, political thought was socially sustained in the 18th and 19th centuries primarily by the rising middle class (p. 168). To oppose the absolutist pretension to power, they promoted the state protection of the people's right to privacy in all areas and their political participation. The power of the state had to be restricted through a constitution in which the basic rights (p. 176) and the possibility of citizen participation were bindingly specified and enforceable.

Freedom and national unity were demands of the German liberals in the 19th century.

Liberal constitutional states emerged out of the revolutions in the U.S. in 1776 and France in 1789 (p. 168). By the end of the 19th century, this form of state also prevailed in all of Europe.

Separation of powers (p. 176) and the rule of law became the principles of the modern systems of government.

Capitalism and Social Liberalism

Classic economic liberalism is based on the teachings of the 18th century Scottish philosopher Adam Smith. According to him, the egotistical pursuit of gain, as well as that of necessity, also promotes the common good. Free competition alone creates wealth and economic progress. The state's only economically-related task is to protect private property.

As a matter of fact, the liberalized economy of the 19th century did create immense wealth, but it also concealed a social time-bomb. The owners of industrial means of production made huge profits at the expense of their workers. In reaction to the achievements of the labor movements that formed against it, strong liberal social currents developed in the 20th century that advocated state intervention in the economy. Aside from the consideration of civil rights, the term "liberal" in the U.S. stands above all for the state control of economic forces and social betterment.

Victoried to Death?

After the Second World War, the rule of law and a more or less bridled economy became the chief concerns of almost all democratic parties. Organized liberalism increasingly lost its influence. Today, only in Canada and Australia are there still major liberal parties. At present, modern liberalism faces the question of how values of freedom and the control of power can be secured in a globalized economy (p. 204) with the various states of the world sharing ever-increasing levels of political, cultural, and economic interaction with one another.

Liberalization of the economy was a significant catalyst of industrialization in the 19th century.

JOHN LOCKE, *born 1632 near Bristol, Great Britain, died 1704 in Oates.*

THE STATE IS LEGITIMIZED *through protecting the freedom and property of its citizens.*

THE CITIZEN *has a right to resist the power of the state when necessary.*

John Locke is regarded as the progenitor of liberalism and greatly influenced the Constitution of the U.S.

John Locke, the Liberal Guide

THE POLITICAL TREATISE "Two Treatises of Government" by John Locke, published anonymously in 1689, is considered the key work of liberalism because it theoretically ties together his political and economic demands. Locke considers humankind as free by nature and hence able to decide the fate of the fruits of their labors. People join together of their own accord in a community and make elections according to the principle of majority rule government that is divided into executive and legislative powers.

IT IS THE TASK of the government, according to Locke, to safeguard individual property. If the state is not capable of that, then the individual has a right to revolt. Locke does not regard property primarily as an instrument to increase profit, but above all as a guarantee of the people's political independence and reason for their engagement in the civic world.

The protection of personal property (here an English mansion) remains to this day the main liberal creed.

see also: Enlightenment, *Philosophy Chapter*, p. 258

SOCIALISM—EQUALITY FOR ALL

Socialists strive for a social order based on communal solidarity in which all layers of society have an equal share in the commonwealth.

Social democrats everywhere in the world organized themselves in the "Socialist International" (here in Rome in 1997).

In general, endeavors and teachings that criticize liberal economic social systems are termed socialist (p. 179). They are directed at creating a more humane society based on the principles of equality and solidarity. In contrast to liberalism, they stress the social responsibility of the individual. The economic system of private capitalism encourages the enrichment of few. It acts as a proponent of social inequality, and thus should be placed more or less under state control so that the resources are generated justly and divided for the common good of all.

Reformism vs. Revolution

During the period of industrialization in the 19th century, socialism became a movement against the impoverishment and political exclusion of the working class. Everywhere in Europe, workers joined together in labor unions to fight for their rights. Socialist parties gained great popularity with the masses and were elected to parliaments. It was only in the U.S. that the socialist idea never gained a foothold.

With political successes, the two main currents within the labor movement, the reformists and the revolutionaries, suddenly saw their differences grow violent. While the one sought a gradual transformation to better social conditions, the other urged for a quick, and if necessary, violent revolution in order to see results.

Social Democrats vs. Communists

At the beginning of the 20th century, the labor movement split once and for all between Social Democrats and Communists. In 1918, the Communists pushed their way to power in Russia (p. 172) and established a regime in the name of socialism. They ruled dictatorially under Lenin, and later Stalin, and placed the economy under state control. Totalitarian socialism spread out into many countries (p. 173) after the Second World War. In the dispute with the "real-existing socialism," democratic socialism stressed that no society can be considered humane without individual civil rights and democracy in all social areas.

After 1945, most social democratic parties in Europe basically accepted the market economy and attempted to equalize income and divide property only within certain areas. The establishment of a distinct social welfare state (p. 177) was primarily the work of the Social Democrats. The present crisis of the social welfare state in Western democracies is causing many European Social Democrats to gain notice. "New Labour" in Great Britain managed a transition to a pronounced market economy since coming to power in 1997. In contrast, the old socialist ideas seem to be experiencing a rebirth in the countries of Latin America.

INSIDER KNOWLEDGE

COMMUNIST *parties in Western democracies distanced themselves from Soviet dictatorship.*

THE GERMAN SOCIAL DEMOCRATIC PARTY *was banned from 1878 to 1890 and became the largest party on the continent during that time.*

International solidarity, as propagated in this woodcut, was the main principle of the labor movement.

Ferdinand Lassalle (1824–1865) is considered the founding father of German social democracy.

KARL MARX, *born 1818 in Trier, Germany, died 1883 in London.*

A PROLETARIAN REVOLUTION *was in his opinion an historical necessity.*

COMMUNAL PROPERTY *leads to a communist society free of domination.*

Karl Marx was the father of communist theory.

Karl Marx and Communism

THE GERMAN PHILOSOPHER Karl Marx founded "scientific socialism." Together with Friedrich Engels, he wrote in 1848 the "Communist Manifesto," a historico-philosophical theory that formed the ideological foundation of communism in the 20th century. They ascribed to the proletariat the historical task of liberating humankind from oppression and bringing about a domination-free society.

MARX SAW WORLD HISTORY as a series of class struggles between the rulers and the ruled. He asserted that the free development of each individual will be possible following the historically inevitable victory of the proletariat over the bourgeoisie. The means of production must be taken over by the community, so that each individual can live free of all coercion. All forms of domination become obsolete in a communist society.

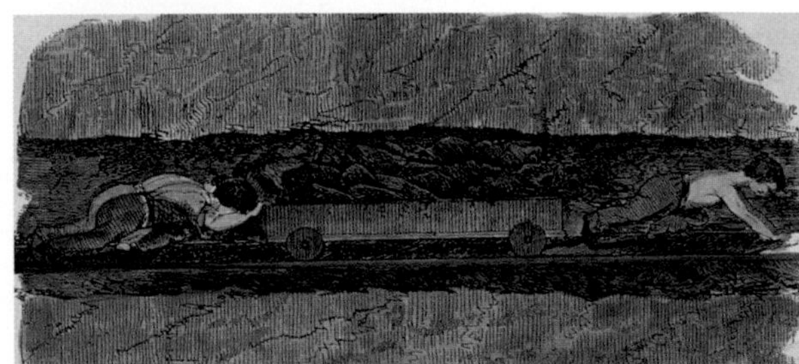

The vision of a society free of exploitation and coercion was full of promise to the maltreated laborer of the 19th century.

see also: Historical Materialism, *Philosophy Chapter*, p. 261

THE GREENS—ALTERNATIVE POLITICS

When the Greens emerged from different social protest movements in the 1980s, they brought a new political current that has established itself most notably in European parliaments.

The Green policies support the development of alternative sources of energy, e.g., wind power stations.

Anti-authoritarian movements of the 1960s led to an increase in social protest movements in Western democracies. From outside the established political party structures, they demanded social changes in specific areas. Since the 1980s, Green parties have developed worldwide out of a broad variety of individual factions like the environmental, peace, civil rights and feminist movements and have since become an integral part of the political party landscape, particularly in Europe. In Europe there are at present 12 Green parties represented in national parliaments. In Sweden, France, and Germany, among others, they have already held governmental positions of responsibility. In countries with pronounced two-party systems like Great Britain and the U.S., the Greens' influence on a national level remains limited, despite strong regional success.

Ecology and Emancipation

The major focus of their platform and the trademark of all Green parties is their consistent engagement for comprehensive environmental protection and especially new environmentally-friendly forms of energy sources. Often they assume positions in other matters that do not fit into the classic left-right spectrum and that are weakly or not convincingly represented by the established parties; the central value standards used here are social responsibility of the individual, the right to self-fulfillment, and suspicion toward those in authority. Typical demands include worldwide peace policies, less imposition of bureaucratic will, improved protection for minorities, more active support of women, and, above all, a political voice for all citizens.

Peace activists repeatedly drew attention to their cause through spectacular actions.

Distinctly Combative

This call for more participation in all political processes and the legacy of the protest culture are also reflected in the relatively democratic basis and decentralized organizational structure of most Green parties. The party leadership is more bound to the members' votes than in most other parties. Rules like gender quotas and a ban on accumulating offices are also meant to make Green values secure within the party and to avoid an exalted caste of functionaries. Powerful party heads, as a rule, better their chances against the other parties, but represent to some, a betrayal of party ideals.

STUDENTS DEMANDED *more participation and democracy in Western societies.*

THEIR ARGUMENT: *Rigid social norms suppress the free development of the individual.*

ROCK MUSIC AND CLOTHING *were as much a means of protest as were demonstrations and disruptive actions.*

"Make love, not war": For some of the youth, the open treatment of sexuality was also a protest.

The Anti-Authoritarian Movement of 1968

IN THE 1960S, a student protest movement started in the U.S. and was taken up in the entire Western world. It was first ignited by the U.S.'s military engagement in Vietnam, but soon expanded to a fundamental opposition against political conditions. While the American students took up the cause of African-American civil rights, those in Europe primarily demanded social democratization under socialist conditions.

POLITICAL PROTESTS were accompanied by the complete rejection of "authoritarian power structures." With inappropriate clothing and music, many youths sought to make clear their utter rejection of the traditional system. The pacifist "hippie" movement rebelled against the pressure to achieve, as well as against middle class values, with their glorification of free sex and drugs.

The works of the philosophers Herbert Marcuse and Max Horkheimer formed the ideological armor of the rebellious students.

The Limits of Growth

This sensational study by the "Club of Rome," an international think-tank, initiated an ecological rethinking in 1972 inside Western societies. If the industrial over-exploitation of nature continued unabated, according to the thesis, the natural resources of raw materials, energy, and soil would near depletion in 100 years at the latest. The result would be famine and the loss of prosperity. Environmental protection and a sparing of resources have since found their way into everyday politics.

above: *Green parties have planted the protection of the environment into the general consciousness.*

21ST CENTURY

ALL THOSE *in political power recognize in principle the necessity of energy sources that would spare the environment.*

WHETHER A MARKET ECONOMY *or a planned economy holds a better solution to protecting the environment is still debated in many Green parties.*

THE KENYAN *Green politician Wangari Maathai was awarded the Nobel Peace Prize in 2004.*

➲ see also: Renewable Energy, *Physics and Technology Chapter, p. 135* | Frankfurter School, *Philosophy Chapter, p. 265*

KEY FACTS

IN THE UN, *nations attempt to find joint solutions to world problems.*

THE EU *is a close confederation of nations with some degree of supranational collaboration.*

NATO *is a military alliance of governments with commonly shared political values.*

NONGOVERNMENTAL ORGANIZATIONS *are international players in the global civil society.*

United Nations | European Union | NATO | Amnesty International | Greenpeace | ATTAC

INTERNATIONAL ORGANIZATIONS

In principle, it is the function of international organizations to find international solutions for the political, economic, military, or social tasks the members agree to handle. The UN, NATO, and the EU are free associations of nation-states established under international law with their own organs and areas of responsibility. International organizations like Greenpeace and Amnesty International, on the other hand, are independent of national governments and are committed worldwide to a clearly defined cause.

The more the world becomes economically cross-linked, the more important international politics become.

UN—THE UNITED NATIONS

Almost all of the world's nations have joined the UN to ensure peace. The UN has only as much power as the member states allow.

The United Nations (UN) was founded in 1945 after the Second World War by 51 nations and has its seat in New York. In 2003, there were 191 members of the UN, almost all of the world's nations. With their membership, the states commit themselves to maintain world peace, to resolve disputes peacefully, and to respect human rights, among other things. The extent to which the UN can honor its goals depends on the members' willingness to cooperate. The UN is not a "world state" with its own instruments of power, but rather a free association of—in principle—sovereign states.

THE NOBEL PEACE PRIZE *was awarded to the UN for its work toward a better world in 2001.*

THE MANY UN PEACE MISSIONS *successfully contributed to establishing peace in conflicts.*

THE BUILDING *of new state and social systems is increasingly becoming the primary objective of multiple UN missions.*

In the former war zone of Kosovo, UN-ordered soldiers are ensuring the safe return of refugees.

UN Peace Missions

TO MAINTAIN WORLD PEACE, the Security Council of the UN can decide upon military action. The member states must make troops available for this, because the UN maintains no troops of its own. The troops can be deployed directly against an aggressor. The Security Council then grants individual states permission to restore peace with force, for example, in the Iraq-Kuwait conflict of 1990.

THE MAJORITY OF THE MEASURES are peacekeeping missions following a conflict. In these cases, multinational troop contingents—also called "blue helmets" because of their UN emblems—position themselves as neutral buffers between the belligerents and manage the ceasefire. Peacekeepers are at present stationed in the Congo, and on the Israeli and Lebanese and the Indian-Pakistani borders, among other places. In the current UN peacekeeping missions in Afghanistan and Kosovo, the boundaries between keeping the peace and forcing the peace are increasingly becoming blurred. UN troops are allowed to take military measures against troublemakers and experts support the buildup of civilian infrastructures.

UN soldiers safeguarding the Israeli-Jordanian border.

The General Assembly examines and approves the UN budget.

General Assembly and Security Council

In the complex structure of the world organization, the General Assembly is formally the supreme body. All member states are equally represented in this "unelected world parliament." The General Assembly can, among other things, pass non-binding resolutions and elect a general secretary to outwardly represent the UN. Associated with it are special organizations like the children's fund, UNICEF.

The actual center of power of the UN is the Security Council. It determines if world peace is in jeopardy and, if necessary, sets courses of action that can range from economic boycotts to military engagements. It has five permanent members (the U.S., Russia, Great Britain, France, and China) and ten members elected for two years. The five permanent members must pass all resolutions unanimously.

Further key bodies of the UN are the International Court of Justice (p. 195), as well as the Economic and Social Council, which coordinates the economic and social activities of the UN along with working together with many special organizations like the World Bank.

Discussions of Reform

Since the Cold War, there have been discussions of how fundamental reforms to the UN could address the new problems and challenges of the 21st century more effectively. The subjects include an expansion of the Security Council, more authority for the General Secretary, the formation of a world environmental organization, and an autonomous UN military.

THE EUROPEAN UNION

Following the Second World War, the European states interwove politically and economically more and more with each other. Today, the EU is a close union of autonomous states that makes cross-border decisions in many areas.

After 1945, the European states step by step began to unify the continent both politically and economically. The goal was to make wars impossible in the future in Europe. The first step was taken in 1951 when six countries, including West Germany and France, created a common market for coal and steel. In 1957, the European Economic Community (EEC) was formed and, through various treaties, steadily dismantled customs barriers and other obstacles to trade for other industrial sectors.

Breakthrough to a Political Union

A milestone on the way to a united Europe was the 1992 treaty on EU (Maastricht Treaty). With it, the EEC free-trade zone was further developed into the close political and economic union of today. The resolution to introduce a common currency was groundbreaking. In 2002, the euro replaced the local currencies in 11 EU countries. The political union was also pushed ahead and a common foreign security policy and cooperation in the areas of the judiciary and internal affairs were decided upon.

Besides that, the EU handles questions that directly affect the lives of the people in the member states. Job creation is supported and an alignment of the living conditions in the different states is a goal. Also, everyone belonging to a member state is an EU citizen with special rights. All EU citizens have an unlimited right of residence in all EU countries and voting rights at the municipal level in the country in which they live.

The European Commission is the guardian of the European community. Its president represents the EU to the rest of the world.

Character and Institutions

The EU has developed into a confederation of states, each retaining its own individual character. It is neither a federation with an independent central power like the U.S. (p. 179) nor an international organization, in which sovereign governments work together like the UN (p. 186).

The member states remain in principle autonomous, but join together at the European level to gain international clout and to democratically clarify issues of common interests. In many areas, the member states have voluntarily conferred—partially or totally—legislative authority to the EU institutions they created.

The highest EU authority is the European Council, consisting primarily of the heads of state and government of the member states. It sets fundamental political goals and appoints the head of the 25-person "European Commission" with the approval of the "European Parliament," which is reelected every five years.

Among other things, the Commission monitors the implementation and proposal of EU laws. Only the "Council of the European Union" or sometimes "Council of Ministers," and the European Parliament, can pass laws. The "European Court of Justice" acts as a judicial organization that ensures the observance of these passed laws.

The euro is the official currency in 18 European countries, 13 of which belong to the EU.

THE WORLD'S LARGEST DOMESTIC MARKET *currently, the EU includes 27 states and close to 490 million inhabitants.*

STATES WANTING MEMBERSHIP *must meet political and economic requirements.*

THE EU *also sees itself as a community of shared democratic values.*

In 2004, Poland joined the EU.

EU Expansion

THE UNITED EUROPEAN MOVEMENT has been a great success so far. Only West Germany, France, Belgium, Italy, Luxembourg, and the Netherlands took part in the first steps toward unification in the 1950s and 1960s. But one after the other, almost all West European states joined: Denmark, Ireland, and Great Britain in 1973, Greece in 1981, Spain and Portugal in 1986, and in 1995, Austria, Finland, and Sweden.

THE COLLAPSE OF communism in 1989–1991 presented the EU with the chance to unify the whole continent ideologically as well. Political and economic criteria were set up for those former Eastern bloc states seeking membership: A stable democracy, a constitutional system, as well as a functioning market economy and competitive ability within the EU. In 2004, ten new countries joined the EU all at once: Estonia, Latvia, Lithuania, Poland, Czech Republic, Slovakia, Hungary, Slovenia, Malta, and Cyprus. In 2007, Romania and Bulgaria were added. Negotiations with further aspirants are in preparation. The possible admittance of Turkey is the most fiercely disputed for many different reasons.

The European family of nations gained additions in 2004 and 2007.

NATO—DEFENSE ALLIANCE AND CRISIS MANAGER

Until 1990 NATO was a defense alliance of Western nations against the communist Eastern bloc. Today its focus lies in the prevention of conflicts and military reaction to crises.

In 1949, the U.S., Canada, and many European nations came together to form NATO (North Atlantic Treaty Organization), an alliance for military and political defense. Later, West Germany, Greece, Turkey, and Spain also joined. Its prime goal until 1990 was to deter communist expansion attempts, namely those of the Soviet Union and its satellite states.

In its Articles of Treaty, which have remained unchanged to the present, NATO members states a pledge to come to each other's aid in case of attack (collective defense action). In doing so, each state can independently take the measures it deems necessary. There is no automatic military obligation of mutual assistance. With membership, the states commit themselves to political, economic, and cultural cooperation along with the military.

The goal of the alliance is also the defense of certain values. From the outset, the member states were required to accept the constitutional state and private property as principles of liberal democracies.

THE NATO STATES *stood face-to-face with the highly armed states of the communist "Warsaw Pact" until 1991.*

THE PRINCIPLE *of military deterrence was meant to secure the peace in Europe.*

PROXY WARS *in developing nations replaced a confrontation between the superpowers.*

The signing of the NATO treaty in 1949; in the center, President Harry Truman

The Cold War

NATO WAS FORMED in 1949 as a defense alliance against the communist states in the East, which joined together in the Warsaw Pact in 1955. The alliance was meant to counter the perceived threat of the military presence of the Soviet Union with a strong armed forces capability in Western Europe. The fundamental concept of the Cold War was to make clear to the opponents that an attack would have deadly consequences even for them. The result was an arms race of weapons of mass destruction, which put both sides theoretically in a position to wipe out all of humankind several times over.

DESPITE DISARMAMENT negotiations, armament surges occurred again and again during this period, leading to mass paranoia. The arms race ended with the collapse of the Soviet empire in 1991. However, NATO continues to possess many nuclear weapons.

Apocalypse as deterrent: a nuclear test in Nevada

Institutions and Functions

NATO is divided according to its aims into a military and a political organization. The supreme body, made up of political representatives from the member states, is the NATO Council with its headquarters in Brussels. It has the authority to make essential political policy decisions. Coordinative to it is the planning commission on issues of defense and nuclear policy composed of the defense ministers of the member states. Assisting the Council are numerous technical committees that handle special matters. NATO has its own bureaucracy headed by a general secretary who is responsible for the conducting of daily affairs. The highest military body is the Military Committee, on which the alliance partners' top generals sit. It advises the NATO Council and executes its directives. NATO armed forces consist of national units that in an emergency are placed under NATO command according to a prescribed procedure.

The NATO star, the symbol of the alliance, stands in front of the headquarters in Brussels.

Alliance With a Future?

NATO lost the original purpose of its founding with the collapse of Communism in 1989–1991. Today, NATO sees its most important tasks, alongside mutual defense, to be worldwide deployment for peace and defense against terrorism, for instance, on behalf of the UN (p. 186). A rapid reaction corps is being built up that can be quickly and flexibly dispatched to the crisis regions of the world.

In addition, the former Eastern bloc states are being introduced into NATO through new accords and new structures and cooperation is being intensified. Bulgaria, Estonia, Latvia, Lithuania, Romania, Slovakia, and Slovenia have since officially joined. Even Russia has been loosely tied to the NATO structure. But it has been observing the expansion of the military zone of influence of its former opponent toward its own borders with suspicion and mistrust.

NATO currently has 26 members. France and Iceland are still not members.

NONGOVERNMENTAL ORGANIZATIONS

Organizations like Greenpeace are active worldwide in the name of particular social concerns without an official mandate. They have increasingly gained in importance on the world stage over the past decades.

Internationally active interest groups with large memberships are today usually termed nongovernmental organizations (NGO). They are privately organized, non-profit orientated, have a working structure capable of acting, and are financed by donations or membership fees. Each organization pursues aims within a specified area. Preferred areas of focus are general humanitarian, social, and ecological concerns. They attempt to sensitize the public to their concerns and to influence the decision-makers in politics and business through the collections of signatures, petitions, or even demonstrations.

Members of "Doctors Without Borders" provide help in war zones or disaster areas with medicine and technical medical equipment.

Human Rights and Environment

NGOs in humanitarian fields are not a phenomenon of the 20th century, however. One of the most well-known, the International Red Cross and Red Crescent Movement, with organizations almost everywhere in the world, was founded in the 19th century. Their mission is to alleviate the suffering of the victims of armed conflicts and natural catastrophes and support national civil defense and the medical corps of armed forces. Such classic humanitarian tasks are also performed by medical organizations like "Doctors Without Borders."

Many NGOs dedicate themselves specifically to the protection of human rights, e.g., the safeguarding of children (Terres Des Hommes). The best-known and most influential human rights organization with more than 1.7 million members worldwide is "Amnesty International." On the basis of the UN's Universal Declaration of Human Rights (p. 176), it has been investigating violations of human rights and publicly denouncing them in regularly published reports since 1961. Professionally organized and internationally carried out campaigns, such as the recent "Stop Violence Against Women," are meant to heighten the awareness of human rights.

21ST CENTURY

MANY NGOS *have been founded in Africa in recent years primarily established with funds from Western development aid.*

DYNAMIC GROWTH: *There were officially 7,306 NGOs worldwide at the end of 2004. In 1964, there were only 1,470.*

PUBLIC SOCIAL PRIVATE PARTNERSHIP: *Private enterprises are increasingly participating in the financing of social projects.*

How to make one's concerns known by effective use of the media is demonstrated time and time again by Greenpeace—the largest international environmental organization. It has successfully taken action to stop nuclear tests and the commercial killing of whales. Since its founding in 1971, it has grown from being a small citizens action group of American environmentalists to a globally acting network with hierarchically organizational structures and its own research divisions.

Influence and Democracy

NGOs have become an important part of international democracy. Because of their increasingly professional organizational forms, governments and supranational organizations are recognizing many NGOs as advisers. Among others, the Economic and Social Council of the UN works closely with NGOs. NGOs also participate as a rule in international conferences within the framework of the UN. While many NGOs profess to speak for all humankind, their internal structures are often not entirely democratic. Moreover, most NGOs originated in rich industrial nations and in part represent their interests.

Greenpeace has become known worldwide for its spectacular actions for the environment.

BY ITS OWN ACCOUNT, ATTAC has over 90,000 members worldwide.

ITS NETWORK is still relatively loosely structured and ideologically heterogeneous.

ATTAC wants to increase its cooperation with organizations with similar aims.

Closing demonstration of the fourth World Social Forum of anti-globalists in Mumbai, India.

ATTAC—Against Economic Globalization

IN 1998, an association was founded in France that advocated democratic controls of the global financial markets. This ATTAC association—the French acronym for the "Association for the Taxation of Financial Transactions to Aid Citizens"—is today an active network worldwide that criticizes the "neo-liberal" excesses of capitalism. With the slogan "The world is not for sale," it is calling for global political, social, and environmental changes directed at a balancing out of disparities between rich and poor nations.

ALTHOUGH TENDING to be grounded at the left of the political spectrum, the association sees itself as being open to all political persuasions that pursue similar goals. Not having a centralized leadership, the national divisions for the most part freely decide topics and the organizational form of specific actions. Only violence is fundamentally rejected.

Example of globalization: The American fast food chain has set up restaurants all over the world.

KEY FACTS

JUSTICE *is the guiding moral principle around which all legal orders are oriented.*

EARLY LEGAL ORDERS *were based on rules of religion.*

IN DEMOCRACIES, *parliaments or assemblies create the laws.*

PEOPLE DEBATE *whether man-made laws are, or should be, based on more fundamental laws of nature.*

Rights and justice | Rights and law | Natural and positive law | Roman law | Religious foundation | Internatinal law

JUSTICE AND ORDER—BASIS OF LAW

The search for basic principles of justice and equality in human society is the fundamental purpose of all legal systems. While these principles are expressed in the form of laws, an individual's natural, inalienable rights exist independent of them. Earlier codes of laws were legitimized through ethical and religious authorities, such as the code of Hammurabi in Babylonia, the Laws of Manu in India, and the Mosaic code in Palestine. Later systems of law were based upon more secular theories.

Laws are rules of conduct and proceedings that are established in order to promote an ideal situation in society.

RIGHTS AND JUSTICE—THE SEARCH FOR THE IDEAL

In principle, laws seek to bring about the ideal of equality through a system of legal directives. These directives set forth the rights and duties of an individual in relation to society.

The search for justice forms the central goal of all legal and societal orders. Justice stands as one of the highest ethical norms on which a society can be oriented. This ideal is the standard against which all legal systems must be measured. Demands for more justice and equality are the underlying reason for most historical revolutions and uprisings. Using these norms, legal systems should ensure that justice permeates the form of permanent laws and regulations. In cases of doubt, these laws should be able to be legally challenged. However, this remains an elusive ideal because laws must also take into account individual liberties and natural rights.

JOHN RAWLS *(1921–2002) was a professor of political theory at Harvard.*

RAWLS *is recognized as the one responsible for the contemporary revival in liberal political theory.*

JUSTICE *is, according to Rawls, not distributive, but procedural.*

John Rawls wrote "Political Liberalism" and "The Law of Peoples."

John Rawls's "A Theory of Justice"

"A THEORY OF JUSTICE," written by the U.S. philosopher John Rawls, aroused much attention when it was published in 1971. Understanding justice as fairness, he believed it could be distinguished by principles of political and legal equality, individual freedom, and an equal opportunity in society. Much like the 17th-century thinkers Thomas Hobbes (p. 167) and John Locke, Rawls based his theory on the idea of a social contract. Unlike the earlier thinkers, however, who believed that such a contract was part of the natural and historical condition of human societies, Rawls viewed the contract as a hypothetical device for thinking about the basic principles of a just social order.

ALSO LIKE HOBBES, Rawls begins with the idea of the "rational ego" of people. An individual does not know what position or status they will have in society. This means that people should only enact laws that give everyone equal access to positions and are benficial to all. Laws that favor specific groups could end up putting them at a disadvantage. Rawls accepts that social and economic inequalities will develop, but this is not problematic as long as these are combined with opportunities that are open to everyone and benefit all.

Fairness in practice: A soccer player helps an opposing player to his feet.

Distributive and Commutative Justice

The definition and utilization of justice has been pondered by political thinkers since antiquity. According to Aristotle, the law should follow a principle of "to each his own." It is through this that justice is defined as each person receiving their due—equals are treated equally. Aristotle thus made a distinction between "distributive justice," relating to the sharing of wealth and power, and "commutative justice," relating to the equal treatment of people. Both of these interpretations of justice are ideals in most modern legal systems. Within them, distributive justice means that people should be treated according to their own individual abilities with respect to the allocation of social advantages and honors. Ensuring this is, above all, the duty of the state. Commutative justice is established among members of a society. Achievements and the compensations one receives for them remain in a balanced relationship, which means that comparable jobs have equal rewards.

Aristotle was the first important theoretician of justice.

Justitia holds a scale in her hand as the symbol of justice. The sword represents the punishment one would face for breaking the law.

RIGHTS AND LAW: THE FLEXIBLE APPLICATION OF THE LAW

Laws must encompass the principle of justice. They set forth a code of behavior and, in general, must be formulated to minimize controversy.

The understanding of law is no less complex than that of justice. The law itself does not exist; there are only concrete laws. Together they provide a legal order that governs the life of a community. Laws work as a set of directives and are oriented around the moral principle of justice. Rights and laws form a "what ought to be" guide, which describes what society would look like if everyone respected all rights and laws and also managed to live in accordance with them.

The Ten Commandments from the Old Testament is one of the oldest known set of legal norms.

In contrast to customs, habits, and common practices that also regulate the life of a community, compliance with laws can be demanded by the state as protector of the community's order. When a law is broken, the state can threaten and impose penalties or sanctions. This aspect of the law is the responsibility of the courts.

The Laws

Laws are enacted according to a specific procedure. In democracies, for example, legislative power lies with parliaments or other representative assemblies, which must follow the constitution of the country.

Laws provide for as well as govern the rights and duties of all members of a society in relation to the collective as well as between individuals. Laws, such as the German "Basic Civil Law" (p. 176), set forth societal principles that are general and abstract in design. There is, therefore, a certain flexibility in determining whether a specific act or situation is covered by a law or not. Broad legal language allows judges to be flexible when applying laws; however, this flexibility as a rule must not lead to arbitrary litigation or legal uncertainty.

In a state based on constitutional law, all rules and regulations should be published in a form that is accessible to all citizens, in order for them to know the laws and regulations of their own country.

The Constitutional State

All laws in a democracy should either maintain, encourage, or establish a legal order and serve the principles of justice and equality. This is what one refers to as a constitutional state.

The moral principle of justice can be broken down into three aspects of the law: equality, social justice, and legal certainty.

Equality means equality before the law: People should be treated on equal terms by the legal system in spite of differences between them such as religion, skin color, or wealth. However, in order to be fair to each individual, laws today may be interpreted flexibly in specific cases.

Social justice means that certain inalienable rights are guaranteed. Legal certainty is the idea that laws must be formulated as precisely and clearly as possible and also, in order to give citizens direction and security, not continually changed.

IMMANUEL KANT, born 1724 in Königsberg and died there 1804.

ONE SHOULD follow their duties based on reason.

INDIVIDUAL PERFECTION and societal bliss were for Kant the duty and goal of ethics.

Kant was one of the most important theorists of the Enlightenment and renovated ethics and law.

Kant's Idea of the "Categorical Imperative"

IMMANUEL KANT BELIEVED STRONGLY in the necessity of morality not simply because it was prescribed by religious authorities, but rather because he could use his powers of logical reasoning to demonstrate its necessity. One key concept of his moral stance was the "categorical imperative." The most succinct definition of this that Kant gave us was: "Act only according to that maxim whereby you can at the same time will that it should become a universal law."

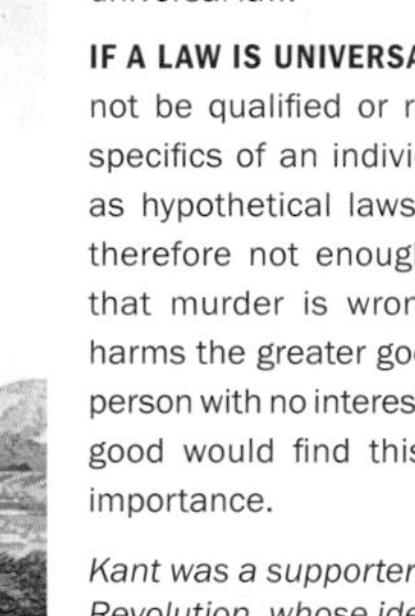

IF A LAW IS UNIVERSAL then it cannot be qualified or refuted by the specifics of an individual situation as hypothetical laws can be. It is therefore not enough to stipulate that murder is wrong because it harms the greater good, because a person with no interest in the greater good would find this law of little importance.

Kant was a supporter of the French Revolution, whose ideals—Liberty, Equality, Fraternity—were inspired by the Enlightenment.

Equality of all citizens before the law was a requirement, even in antiquity. This was also the basic principle of the legal statutes of the Athenian Solon (center) from 594 B.C.

➲ see also: Immanuel Kant, *Philosophy Chapter, p. 258*

NATURAL LAW OR POSITIVE LAW?

Many scholars believe that legal orders can be derived from natural laws, which apply to all people and are inherent, as opposed to man-made or "positive laws."

The greatest debate in the history of law deals with the relationship between natural law and positive law. Natural laws are described as the rights of all people "derived from nature" and form the basis for all man-made laws. Natural law is seen as having priority over human laws (positive laws).

Natural Law

Even in ancient times people assumed that humans were beings with reason, language, and free will who had certain basic rights.

Even today, the legal decisions of the biblical King Solomon are seen as symbolizing wise and just judgments.

CONVERGENCE THEORY: *Every legal declaration is in principle provisional, meaning it can be corrected when new facts become known.*

A NEW SOCIETAL CONSENSUS *on legal questions is the product of rational discussions that explore all possible opinions on the issue.*

The legal system must continually adapt in order to remain consistent with an ever-changing society.

The "Convergence Theory" of Law

AN IMPORTANT CONTRIBUTION to the further development of jurisprudence comes from the modern convergence theory, which addresses the special nature of human beings.

THE HUMAN BEING is understood as both existing and changeable, which means each person has a distinctive and unalterable identity (their existence), but at the same time, there exists as a collection of relationships with people and things. However, relationships are never static, but rather undergo a process of constant change. This dynamic must be taken into consideration by the law. Therefore jurists should not consider crimes and perpetrators in isolation, but must take into account the circumstances of the crime, including the motives, the situation, the emotional condition of the perpetrators at the time of the act, etc., and place them all in perspective.

Judge from high court in Germany: A judge should flexibly interpret the law.

These have at times been perceived as inalienable, meaning one could neither give them up, nor could such rights be disputed by others. During the Christian Middle Ages, the natural rights of antiquity were included in the Christian view of creation: that since all of humanity were creatures of God, were created in his likeness, and were given free will, they thus possessed certain rights that must be respected by the political and legal order. From the Enlightenment on, reliance has once again been placed more heavily on a person as a rational being while natural law is now interpreted as basic human rights.

A problematic aspect of natural law is that it uses nature, as diverse as it is, as the basis for ordering human society as it should be. It can, therefore, be used to legitimize very different legal principles. As a result, both the idea of the legal equality of all individuals and the idea that power belongs to the strongest can be supported by the theories of natural law.

Positive Law

Man-made laws, i.e., positive laws, are continually compared to the widespread, unwritten ideas of natural law. Since the Enlightenment, great value has been placed on precise, written positive laws because they use humanity's power of reason to demarcate abstract natural law. In the 19th century, this focus on rationality led to a doctrine that strictly separated the process of making a law from its content (legal positivism). Laws were considered valid under this doctrine regardless of their content. They obtained authority by being formally and correctly enacted. This position was discredited when 20th century dictators, using formal and legitimate legislative procedures, enacted laws considered criminal and unjust.

Nominalism

The dispute over universals in philosophy during the late Middle Ages concerned the relationship between general principles and reality, which had a definite influence on theories of rights. Realists believed that ideas were real, whereas nominalists believed that ideas were mere abstractions that would be understood through comparison and combination with things that actually existed. Looking at the judiciary, this doctrine holds that concrete cases should be the only reality of the law and that general legal ideas may only be formed and introduced.

above: *Legal scholarship is important, thus it fills entire bookshelves.*

During the Enlightenment, the idea of human rights, which included equality for all, grew out of religiously based natural law.

➲ **see also: Dispute of Universals,** *Philosophy Chapter, p. 252*

ROMAN LAW AND ITS LEGACY

Roman law is reflected in both content and form of all Western legal systems. Any differences arose from the various existing regional legal customs.

The Roman models of state organization and legal systems are, even today, stamped on the Western cultural tradition. Many legal principles that are still recognized today were laid down by this system. In doubtful cases, one must decide in favor of the accused (*in dubio pro reo*); contracts must be honored (*pacta sunt servanda*); and both parties must be heard in a court of law (*audiatur et altera pars*).

Roman law (here the decision announcement of King Dolmitian) is not based on the Greek model. It was the standard source of law in Europe until the 19th century.

Roman Law

The Roman legal system was based first of all on unwritten, customary law that arose from long periods of practice. The first written, fixed law was the Twelve Tables from approximately 451 B.C. It included almost all areas of law that are still differentiated today: public and private law, religious law, criminal law, and administrative law.

Roman jurists regularly expanded and commented upon the laws while adapting them to the ever-changing empire with its many different provinces and legal traditions. Well-known legal scholars, such as Labeo, commented less on the system in general than on specific legal disputes.

In this way, Roman law acquired a practical, case-specific orientation that was able to survive the downfall of the Roman Empire. Subsequent rulers took large parts of this law and carried it throughout Europe and northern Africa.

Regional Differences

Roman law had an influence on the laws in the Early and Late Middle Ages. Although Roman law was legitimized through Christianity, a distinction soon grew between secular and ecclesiastic law. The sovereign of a country was also seen as the highest authority in respect to all worldly matters.

The subdivision of the German nation by the Roman Empire, and later the Holy Roman Empire, propagated the development of strong regional differences. Thus, different legal systems evolved that were specifically suited for the needs of individual states and created the basis of today's legal systems in Germany.

In the Middle Ages, the secular rulers were also the highest judge. England's Richard II is here holding court over opposition leaders.

This tendency toward regional differentiation is particulary evident in Anglo-Norman law. The common law that was developed in the 13th century in England was based less on written law than on precedent, giving much more room for interpretation in judicial decisions regarding specific cases.

The Enlightenment and Civil Rights

Beginning in the Enlightenment, the principles of Roman law underwent an important expansion. The rights that were formerly believed to be applicable only to certain groups (e.g., free citizens in old Rome or certain classes in the Middle Ages) now applied to all people. These rights were independent of one's religion, heritage, or position, but were instead based only on one's "humanness."

The emphasis on equality was associated with the propagation of individual rights. In comparison with those of the state, these were formulated as basic rights, which included the right to property, physical safety, and freedom of religion. This led to the demand that the state apply the concept of basic rights in its laws dealing with the lives of individuals. The British "Habeas Corpus Act" of 1679 was a relative milestone for this, because a commitment was made that no one could be imprisoned without legal reason or investigation.

Codex Justinianus

Many Roman emperors systematized the ever growing body of law and commentaries in order to standardize the legal system. An important guide for Western jurisprudence was the legal codex of the Byzantine Emperor Justinian I, which was published in 534 A.D. This body of civil law, also known as Codex Justinianus, included over 4,600 laws and statutory provisions in a collection of 12 books. The Codex firmly established the basis of the Western legal system—specifically continental Europe's private, penal, and administrative laws. For example, it instituted how many witnesses must be present at the drawing up of a will, the rights of married women, and the level of taxes.

above: *Justinian I ruled from Constantinople over the entire former eastern part of the Roman Empire—Byzantium.*

The "Habeas Corpus Act" of 1679 opened many prisons in Great Britain and freed many innocent people.

A RELIGIOUS FOUNDATION FOR LAW

Until the late Middle Ages, laws were primarily based on religion. Traces of religious norms and values can still be found today in many legal systems.

The earliest legal systems were based on religious principles; a deity, like God, was the source as well as reason for justice and law. Legal systems were seen as holy manifestations emanating from rulers, priests, or prophets. If need be, these persons were empowered to interpret God's law.

Religious Law

Religious law rests on two principles: First, people need a legal order in order to live together. This order is not found within oneself, but relies on heavenly guidance. Second, God's laws provide basic rules for society and are seen as unalterable and absolute, because God himself enacted them. Details can then be regulated by human laws. Laws given by God generally do not differentiate between worldly and spiritual realms, but describe an all-encompassing way of living. A separate ecclesiastical law was formulated in the Early Middle Ages.

Rights and Faith

One of the earliest known legal systems is the Babylonian Code of Hammurabi from approximately 1700 B.C. Schamasch, the God of Justice, is said to have given the Code to the King. The biblical God presented his laws written on stone tablets to the people of Israel through Moses when he was on Mount Sinai. The core of these laws is the Ten Commandments. They set forth duties to God and humans as well as basic prohibitions against immoral behavior. They are seen in legal history as a short version of religiously based natural rights.

In Europe during the Middle Ages, an individual looked to religion to reach judgments. In order to prove guilt or innocence, the accused was tried by oath, or by compurgation. These "trials" were seen as court competitions and whoever won was innocent. Only when law was freed from its religious underpinnings did rational forms of proof such as confessions move to the forefront in determining the outcome of a case.

Religion and Law Today

For almost all people, religious law has become a part of the customary law within current legal systems. The religious principle of the "Sanctity of Life" can be found in many legal codes, including prohibitions against murder or protection against libel. Legal privileges granted to the institutions of marriage and family, but not to other alternative living arrangements, are also grounded in religious belief.

Today, the law ordained in the Qur'an, the Sharia, still plays a large role in most Islamic nations, but has actually mixed with elements of modern legal rights. In addition to the Qur'an, the Sunna is a source of law derived from the modeled life of the Prophet Muhammad. He created a social and legal order in Medina.

The tablet with the Code of Hammurabi, a legal code compiled by the Babylonian King Hammurabi (1728–1686 B.C.)

ALL MAJOR RELIGIONS *recognize legal systems for the regulation of earthly affairs and try to influence these systems.*

THE CHRISTIAN "TWO KINGDOMS DOCTRINE" *describes Christians as citizens of two worlds, the earthly state with its state and legal system, and the God-given holy order.*

Through the Great Flood, God destroyed the disobedient and sinful humankind.

Guilt or Weakness?

IN THE OLD TESTAMENT, it is repeatedly explained how people disobey holy orders and laws. God sends forth—usually after a warning—a penalty, an example of which is the Great Flood. Offenses were attributed to individuals who were called to account for them.

CHRISTIANITY, in contrast, attempted to explain the cause of the offense: After the expulsion from the Garden of Eden, people fell into the deficient condition of original sin, whereby individuals are subject to the weaknesses of their human nature. This condition led inexorably to conflict and violence between men and for this reason humankind needed, on earth, a God-given, legal, and political order that would control humanity's natural weaknesses and promote social stability. In Christian societies the theory grew out of this view that legal and political measures should lead to the good of the whole and to the establishment of a righteous peace.

Adam and Eve are expelled from paradise by the Archangel Gabriel.

The Islamic Sharia assigns physical penalties, such as whipping, for forbidden activities.

see also: The 10 Commandments, The Sharia, *Religion Chapter, pp. 232, 241*

INTERNATIONAL LAW

International law regulates the relations between sovereign nations. International organizations such as the UN have throughout the 20th century tried to establish general, binding, and acceptable legal standards.

The ex-president of Serbia and Yugoslavia, Slobodan Milošević, had to answer to the UN's Court of International Justice in The Hague for serious war crimes.

Legal codes have governed relations between people and states throughout history. Fundamental to modern international law, which dates back to these times, is the understanding that individual states are also subject to laws. This means that all states, especially their rulers, have equal rights and may make independent decisions regarding internal and external affairs.

Freedom to Sign Treaties

All states, therefore, may enter into treaties and accords with other states for their mutual advantage. These may address policies such as border issues or economic trade. In principle, there is no generally accepted, overarching, mediating body such as the court system of a national legal systems which can resolve disputes over rights or treaty interpretation. States are, therefore, instructed after signing, that the treaty will be accepted and honored by all treaty partners. The *pacta sunt servanda* (Latin: "pacts are to be respected") holds that even nations should be bound by the fundamental legal principle that promises should be kept.

International Conflict Resolution

Lacking a mediating authority, it is important that the principles of international law be consistent with national legal systems. Therefore, attempts were made to make natural law, and later human rights (pp. 190–191) "international." After the bloody World Wars of the 20th century, it was believed necessary to establish international institutions (such as the League of Nations in 1918 and the UN in 1945) that tried to solve problems and conflicts between nations authoritatively. The charter of the UN (p. 182) can be viewed as the constitution of international governments as well as international organizations.

In 1988, an international court was established to try and judge war criminals among other criminals meriting a trial of this magnitude. Although not yet accepted by all countries, the UN is nonetheless the organization to which nations in crisis turn to stop the violation of international legal standards.

Law Through Consensus

Because sovereign states are treaty parties in international law, they can institute new laws through treaties, when all the parties are in agreement. These sovereign states can create a solution for a particular problem, which then leads to a valid law. Through membership in international organizations, like the UN or the EU, treaties between nations are often coupled with the legal requirements of these organizations. For example, two treaty partners within the EU may only compensate their employees as much as all other employers in other EU countries.

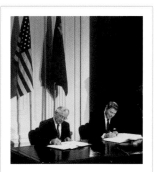

above: *The two national leaders Gorbachev and Reagan sign an arms agreement in 1988.*

21ST CENTURY

THE CALL *for a worldwide legal order creates a fear that regional traditions will be lost.*

IT IS DEBATABLE *whether international law can successfully enforce human rights and if the use of necessary force should be authorized.*

THE IDEA *of national sovereignty loses some of its meaning in the age of globalization.*

HUMAN RIGHTS VIOLATIONS *are difficult to charge and punish through international organizations.*

INTERNATIONAL INSTITUTIONS AND ORGANIZATIONS: *The European Congress of Human Rights, Amnesty International, Office of the High Commissioner for Human Rights, Human Rights Watch, etc.*

A UN agreement demands the protection of refugees, but not every country adheres to this policy.

The Violation of Human Rights

BASIC HUMAN RIGHTS, such as the right to live, are universally recognized, which means they apply to all people, in all nations, independent of the nations' legal traditions. Almost all member states of the UN have agreed to the 1948 Human Rights Convention (p. 172). Nonetheless, fulfilling the ideals of this convention proves increasingly difficult and highly problematic in many countries.

THE MOST COMMON HUMAN RIGHTS VIOLATIONS next to government-sanctioned murders and torture, is the oppression of ethnic or religious minorities. The opportunities of the UN are therefore limited, because many nations do not, in principle, accept any limitations on national sovereignty. A group of nations can, for example, attempt to impose a trade embargo in order to isolate the country. Internal political interests or long-lasting debates often frustrate and slow attempts to sanction nations that violate human rights.

The newly installed 2006 UN Human Rights Commission deliberates on, and judges compliance with, the protection of human rights all around the world.

KEY FACTS

A PROPER COURT OF LAW *includes professional and lay people, state attorney (prosecutor), and lawyers (defense attorney).*

A VERDICT MAY BE APPEALED *to the next highest court in the hope that the decision of the lower court will be reversed.*

SENTENCING *occurs only after a conviction following a legitimate trial. It must take into account both the perpetrator and the crime.*

The court | Public and civil rights

THE APPLICATION OF THE LAW

A trial in civil or criminal courts follows strict procedures and involves the work of several different groups. The prosecutor or state attorney represents the state before the court, while the defense lawyer represents the accused. A judge then makes a decision, often with help from experts. If the court finds the accused guilty, the judgment will help decide a punishment, which depends upon the severity of the crime and must, by law, consider the circumstances of the accused and the crime.

Courts establish the criminal offense and then judge it in order to determine the extent of the punishment.

THE COURT: JUDGE, ATTORNEYS, AND LAY PEOPLE

In the court system, judges are required to be impartial and independent. The prosecutor represents the state and the defense attorney represents the accused.

The court is an example of jurisprudence in practice. It determines whether a criminal act has occurred according to the law, rules on the charges, and sentences the perpetrator. During a trial, different parties work together to reach a verdict including the judge, the state attorney, and defense lawyers.

Judges and Their Decisions

In all constitutional states, every official court is overseen by at least one legally educated judge. The judge decides on the issues before the court. In criminal processes, the judge either sentences or absolves the accused; in civil cases, the judge rules on the issue disputed by the parties. The judge must be impartial and independent, and is, in general, a government employee. In reaching a verdict, a judge must act in accordance with valid laws, human rights, and their own conscience. In the U.S., juries composed of lay people are most often used in criminal cases. The judge leads the trial and determines the legal aspects of the case; the jury decides and agrees on a verdict.

Justices of the Peace played a large role in early Anglo-Saxon justice.

Lawyers and Lay People

The state attorney prosecutes the accused and offers suggestions regarding the degree of punishment as well as its enforcement. In preparing for trial, they may carry out an investigation. Most leave this function to the police, and the state attorney then decides whether to proceed with charges.

Like the state attorney, lawyers are also legally trained jurists. Whether chosen by the accused or appointed by the court, they defend their client at trial.

THE HIGHEST COURTS *review the constitutionality of laws and announces ultimate decisions in specific cases.*

THE COURT SYSTEM *is hierarchical. Every judgment can be appealed to the next higher court.*

Some are critical because the highest constitutional courts hand down increasingly political decisions.

Highest Courts

IN NATIONAL LEGAL SYSTEMS, the highest court takes a prominent position. Examples include the U.S. Supreme Court and the German Federal Constitutional Court. They decide, for example, issues of competence between the different state entities or review whether laws or government measures violate norms set by the constitution. In principle, every citizen whose basic rights have been infringed upon by government action has the right to lodge complaints before the highest court.

THE DECISION of the highest courts cannot be contested, and as a rule, are binding for all lower courts. The constitutional courts often emphasize that their decisions are legal, not political. Their decisions can nonetheless be politically very explosive.

The U.S. Supreme Court is seated in Washington, D.C.

The Power of the Judge

Judges have a relatively high degree of freedom in making their decisions, particularly in Anglo-American systems. This results in a better disposition of each individual case. The judgment should be consistent with principles of rationality and fairness (i.e., the natural sense of justice), and also be appropriate, meaning the sense as well as the purpose of the existing law should be respected. If a decision violates these principles, the verdict or ruling will generally be overturned or reversed by the next higher court.

above: *A judge must consider many factors in his decision-making.*

The judgments of the Nazi "People's Court" were a perversion of state legal procedures.

PUBLIC AND CIVIL RIGHTS

Civil proceedings decide disputes of civil law, which governs the majority of legal relationships. Like criminal proceedings, these follow specific court procedures.

In the U.S., some disputes may be shown on television and are accompanied by great publicity.

Criminal law regulates relationships between the state and individuals. Meanwhile, civil law manages the interactions of individuals as well as between persons and things. Modern states that follow the rule of law thus allow citizens to enter legal relationships without the involvement of the state, but provide a government forum for the resolution of disputes. This area of law is primarily concerned with contracts that range from purchase and lease contracts to transfers of property rights. To have a valid legal transaction, like a contract, it is mandatory that the contracting parties (there must be at least two) be legally competent, which in general occurs at the age of 18.

A state attorney represents the state before the court and explores the issues from the opposite side to the defense attorney.

INSIDER KNOWLEDGE

BEFORE THE OPENING *of the main proceedings, the defendant is referred to only as the "accused" by the court.*

THE DEFENSE ATTORNEY *may reveal information given by the defendant only if their client specifically allows it due to attorney-client privilege.*

IN CRIMINAL PROCEEDINGS, *the victims of the crime greatly impact the verdict with their testimonies.*

The Course of Criminal Proceedings

Disputes between citizens are handled by civil courts. Criminal offenses are, by contrast, handled by the criminal process in which the state appears as a party. Most often these cases involve crimes against life including murder and sexual assault, or crimes against property, such as theft or fraud.

A criminal trial follows many steps. Based on an arrest by the police or independent inquiry by the state's attorney, an investigation process is begun to determine the facts of the case and identify the perpetrator. The state attorney's office lodges a formal charge if a crime has occurred. Before a trial, a hearing allows the court to review the concrete basis for any presented accusations.

If the accusations are confirmed, the normally public proceedings can begin. During the main phase, the defendant must first confirm his identity and then the prosecutor reads the charges. The proceedings then move to the "evidence phase" where, by listening to witnesses who are questioned by the state attorney as well as by the defense lawyers, an understanding of the act is reached. Witnesses are informed of their obligation to tell the truth, and must swear an oath before the court.

Once all of the evidence has been presented, the judge closes the evidence phase of the trial. In the next stage, the state attorney and the defense attorney must each give a closing statement arguing for the guilt or innocence of the accused as well as for a specific sentence. The defendant has the final word. Finally, the court recesses to deliberate. Upon reentering the courtroom, the judge announces the verdict, the sentence, and the right of the accused to an appeal. In some cases the state attorney's office or the defendant may ask for an appeal within one week of the verdict. If this request does not succeed, the judgment becomes legally binding and will be enforced.

Only in extraordinary cases may the court keep the interested public out of the proceedings.

IN TRIALS INVOLVING JUVENILES, *evaluators or experts (p. 195) are often brought to proceedings.*

JUVENILE PENAL CODES *set forth more lenient penalties than those imposed on adults.*

THOSE FOUND GUILTY *must take full responsibility for their actions.*

For small transgressions, juveniles are often ordered to work community service hours.

Accountability

IN MOST NATIONS full legal responsibility begins at the age of 18. Minors are deemed partially responsible after age 14. With young adults (between 18 and 20), the decision on whether to charge and sentence as an adult or as a juvenile is at the discretion of the court. In most cases, the nature of the crime is the determining factor. Juvenile penal laws offer milder sentences than those for adults; thus, the longest sentence (e.g., for murder) is ten years. The development and education of juveniles, alongside their punishment, is a primary concern in their sentencing.

CRIMES COMMITTED BY PERPETRATORS UNDER THE AGE 14 are becoming more common, so many localities are discussing the possibility of lowering the age of partial responsibility to 12. In the U.S., the crime itself, the view of the state attorney, and the state policy are all large determinants in underage proceedings.

Increasingly younger criminals are being brought to the court for drug abuse and trafficking, theft, as well as violence.

KEY FACTS

GDP, *or Gross Domestic Product, is generally accepted as one of the best measures of a country's economic strength.*

FREE MARKET ECONOMIES *are economies that receive little or no interference from the government.*

IN COMMAND ECONOMIES, *the government makes all economic decisions predominantly through a large planning agency.*

Types of economic systems | Modern macroeconomics and the role of the state

NATIONAL ECONOMIES

Economic activity is the source of wealth for any country. Therefore, government control and regulation of the economy has a decisive effect not only on prosperity and growth, but also on political and social well-being. Economic systems in which the government primarily exerts control over economic production and activity are referred to as command economies. On the other hand, economic systems that allow competition to determine prices are referred to as free market economies. A mixed economy has characteristics from both command and free market systems.

Economics is the study of how people allocate resources for different uses.

TYPES OF ECONOMIC SYSTEMS

The organization of national economies has varied over time as a result of social, political, and technological changes. Free-market democracies now dominate the global economy.

The free market economy and the command economy are on opposite ends of the scale of economic organization. In the real world, all national economies are mixed economies—lying somewhere in between the two polar extremes of free-market and command systems—and share important attributes of both.

KEYNES'S MAGNUM OPUS, *the "General Theory of Employment, Interest, and Money," came out in 1936.*

WITH A STRONG INTEREST IN THE ARTS, *Keynes was an active member of the Bloomsbury group in London.*

IN 1942, *Keynes was made Baron of Tilton in the County of Sussex and sat in the House of Lords.*

John Maynard Keynes, through his service and writings, was a defining force in 20th century economics.

John Maynard Keynes

THE GREAT DEPRESSION led John Maynard Keynes to analyze the workings of national economies in order to explain how recessions occur and turn into depressions. Keynes was aware that economies appear to go through business cycles that keep repeating themselves. A full business cycle is a period of strong economic activity following a period of economic weakness. His analysis of a business cycle laid the foundation of modern macroeconomics.

AS AN INTERVENTIONIST, KEYNES ARGUED that the government should enact fiscal and monetary policies to counter the negative aspects of the business cycle. Thus, when businesses are not building new factories and producing more goods because of concerns over profit, the government should reduce taxes, borrow large amounts of money, and commission large projects in order to help stimulate the floundering economy.

Keynes represented the UK during the foundation of the Bretton Woods institutions.

Free Market Economy

In a free market economy, economic activity takes place with little or no interference from the government. The term *laissez faire* (French: "let it be") was coined to describe the attitude of government toward businessmen, workers, and consumers in a pure free market economy. For economists, a "market" is any physical or virtual place where buyers and sellers of goods and services can meet and transact business. Private ownership and largely unrestricted individual freedom are other key characteristics of a free market economy. While no pure market system exists today, the U.S. economy demonstrates one of the most profound free market tendencies.

Command Economy

In a command economy the government makes all decisions regarding the production and allocation of goods and services, usually through a large and bureaucratic planning agency. A key characteristic is the government ownership of all buildings and equipment that are used to produce goods and services. The government also determines the role that individuals have within the production process. There is little to no private ownership and individual freedom is restricted.

Western metropolises have come to symbolize the capitalist system.

Command economies existing today include Cuba and North Korea.

Mixed Economy

Mixed economies that combine aspects of a pure market economy and a command economy are most prevalent today. Both privately owned and state-owned enterprises exist. Citizens living with a mixed economy have a number of freedoms: They can own land, travel, buy and sell goods and services, hire and fire people, organize businesses, and join trade unions. The government takes an active role in the economy through providing tax-funded, subsidized, and state-owned services such as transportation. People retain autonomy over a large part of their finances, but must contribute to welfare, social security, and other social services. The government also passes laws and regulations to protect its citizens through product safety laws, minimum wage legislation, and intellectual property laws.

MODERN MACROECONOMICS AND THE ROLE OF THE STATE

The 20th century saw global competition between two very different economic spheres. The question at the heart of the struggle was what role the government should play in the economy.

Eastern Economics

Led by the USSR, a centrally-planned command economy was established in the Eastern bloc, which was associated with very little individual freedom and heavy government intervention in economic decisions. At the head of the Soviet economy was the State Planning Committee, or *Gospan*, which outlined multiple economic "five-year plans" to boost production. These five-year plans called for rapid industrialization and unrealistic production targets. This system of Gospan was reorganized in 1985 by Mikhail Gorbachev with his *perestroika* ("restructuring"). While certain, more capitalistic enterprises, such as the private planning of factories, were enacted, economic opportunity was still limited for the individual. By 1990, the Soviet government lost its centralized control over the economy and as there were no adequate free-market mechanisms installed to replace it, it fell. This was one factor that led to the eventual breakup of the Soviet Union in 1991.

Through state-directed five-year plans, the Soviet Union improved infrastructure at the cost of an increasingly inefficient use of natural resources.

Germany's Social Market Economy

AFTER THE DEFEAT of the totalitarian Nazi ideology and the destruction of much of Germany's economic infrastructure in World War II, the West German Federal Republic needed a new economic system that would be compatible with a democratic constitution. German economist Alfred Müller-Armack defined the principles of the social market economy in 1947. It was put into practice by the acting chancellor of West Germany, Ludwig Erhard, which led to the "German economic miracle" of the 1960s. The aim of this social market economic system is to combine the principle of free markets with that of social equity. As a result, the state actively promotes competitive free markets and an economically active middle class; but, it encourages market oriented income distribution while avoiding sharp differences in income and wealth. This is meant to ensure strong social and welfare services for all its citizens. The government aims to stabilize the national economy, and avoid inflation and unemployment. Economic measures are designed to conform to market principles.

Ludwig Erhard enacted West Germany's Deutsche Mark in 1948.

Western Economics

In response to economic shocks and under the influence of Keynes, the free-market-mixed economies of the West were developed. Institutions were created that allowed these economies to avoid the devastating consequences of mass unemployment and inflation. The Depression era saw the launch of the "New Deal" in the U.S. under President Franklin D. Roosevelt. Influenced strongly by the work of Keynes, this policy would shape the American economy for decades to come. In post-WWII Europe, the German economic miracle that owed much to the development of the social market economy came to influence other European countries, which implemented their own variations. By the 1970s, Keynes's remedies against the negative effects of the business cycle were becoming less effective. A number of economists argued for a greater role of the market and less government intervention in Western mixed economies. They became particularly influential in the U.S. and Great Britain. President Ronald Reagan's "Reagonomics" and Prime Minister Margaret Thatcher's "Thatcherism" during the 1980s were strongly influenced by the ideas of the economists Friederich A. Hayek and Milton F. Friedman. These gifted economists both became winners of the Nobel Prize for Economics. They argued that the free market was a prerequisite for the freedom of the individual. They also asserted that the type of government intervention recommended by Keynes, which aimed to tame market forces, was largely futile or even counterproductive to long-term economic success. In the 21st century, the economic systems of the U.S. and Great Britain remain close to the free-market end of the scale. Meanwhile, the economies of Germany, France, and Scandinavia are examples of systems that lie in the middle of the scale.

Shortages are a problem of centrally planned economies, as shown by the long line in this store in East Berlin, 1962.

The relative stability of the post-WWII world supported a huge expansion in goods, manufacturing, and consumption.

INSIDER KNOWLEDGE

MODERN ECONOMICS *began with the publication of Adam Smith's book "The Weath of Nations," published in 1776.*

INTRA-COMPANY TRADE *(the movement of goods within multinational corporations) accounts for almost half of global imports and exports.*

KEY FACTS

MACROECONOMIC PERFORMANCE RESULTS *are an important decision-making tool for people and organizations in industry.*

CENTRAL BANKS *are responsible for ensuring that the business cycle within a country is kept stabilized.*

THE TOOLS USED *by central banks include fiscal and monetary policies that are either expansionary or contractionary.*

Measuring performance | GDP | Growth and stability | Governments and central banks

MANAGING THE ECONOMY

Governments, businesses, and private individuals want to know how the economy is performing so they can make decisions about policy, investment, and consumption. GDP, growth of inflation, unemployment, and interest rates are four key measures widely used to gauge economic performance. Economists, governments, and businesses monitor these indicators closely and try to interpret future performance from the current trends in order to make decisions about the allocation of resources to meet current and future needs.

The Federal Reserve System is the name of the central bank in the U.S.

MEASURING MACROECONOMIC PERFORMANCE

If we think of an economy as a car in motion, its dashboard needs to have devices that tell us how fast we are going, what the engine temperature is, and how much gas is in the tank.

Macroeconomic performance is determined primarily through four key measures: Gross Domestic Product (GDP), growth of inflation, unemployment, and interest rates.

GDP

GDP is the market value of all final goods and services produced within the geographic boundaries of a country during a certain period of time, usually a year or a quarter. GDP can be seen as a basic measure of the material wealth created by an economy. The greater the GDP, the more goods and services are produced within the economy to meet the needs of its citizens.

Inflation

Another indicator of economic performance is the rate of inflation. Economists define inflation as a general increase in the price levels of an economy in relation to a standard level of purchasing power. In order to measure inflation, economists and statisticians put together baskets of goods and services and follow the price of these baskets over time. Inflation erodes the purchasing power of money. Thus, people who are holding money will be able to buy fewer goods and services at the end of a period of inflation than at the beginning.

Unemployment

The rate of unemployment is the percentage of the civilian work force that is actively seeking employment, but not currently employed and not engaged in the production of goods and services. Unemployment causes financial hardships and social disruption to the people directly affected by it. For the economy as a whole, a rising rate of unemployment suggests that firms are producing fewer goods and services to meet demand in the economy. The result is both rising financial distress which can over time lead to increased poverty levels and rising government payments to the unemployed, which can hurt public finances. A high and persistent rate of unemployment tends to be associated with economic and social instability.

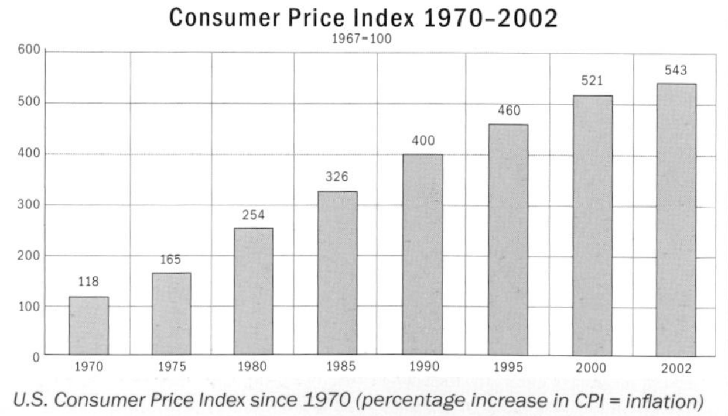

U.S. Consumer Price Index since 1970 (percentage increase in CPI = inflation)

Due to the size and stability of the economy of the U.S. in the 20th century, the dollar has long served as a global reserve currency.

Role of the Government

As the government's role in the economy has increased, government finances have assumed a greater importance in the health of an economy. The government's budget deficit or surplus and the level of government borrowing have an impact on the economy to the extent that they affect inflation expectations and interest rates or incentives to work and save if interest rates have to increase.

The Interest Rate

A key signal that affects saving, investment, and economic growth is the interest rate. This is the "price of money." Households receive interest on the money they save, and businesses borrow money to invest in land, machinery, and equipment, with which to expand production, sales, and profits. Interest is the compensation lenders receive to defer consumption now in favor of consumption later. The higher the interest rate the more attractive it is to save money and the less attractive it is to borrow money short-term. Finally, the difference in the value of goods and services exported from a country, and goods and services imported into a country either adds to or subtracts from domestic economic growth. A surplus in the balance of trade (goods) and the current account (goods and services) is a net stimulus to the economy and increases a country's foreign savings. A deficit on the trade and current account reduces domestic growth and increases foreign borrowings.

INSIDER KNOWLEDGE

ALAN GREENSPAN, *chairman of the Board of Governors of the U.S. Federal Reserve system (1987 to 2006), was considered one of the most successful monetary policy makers of his time, but faces criticism in light of the 2008 economic crisis.*

COMPONENTS OF GDP—DASHBOARD OF THE ECONOMY

To calculate GDP, government economists and statisticians survey, measure, and apply sophisticated estimation techniques for decision-makers.

Circular Flow Model

Economists have developed the circular flow model to represent the macroeconomy. It illustrates how economic activity has both flows of goods and services, and flows of money between the participants in the economy of a country.

At the basic level, a circular flow model of a national economy can be drawn consisting of households and firms. Households purchase and consume goods and services. They also provide the firms with the means by which to produce goods and services. Economists call these the factors of production. The factors of production are labor, land/buildings, capital, and entrepreneurship. Labor receives wages, land receives rent, capital receives interest payments and entrepreneurship receives profits made by business. In "markets for goods and services," firms and households exchange goods and services for money. Markets also exist for the exchange of factors of production by household against money paid by firms. Of course, not every household provides all types of factors of production. Some may provide labor, while others rent land.

In labor, effort becomes wages, which are converted to goods.

Role of GDP

GDP, one of the key indicators of the macroeconomy, is measured as the money that flows from households to firms in exchange for goods and services during the period of one year via the markets for goods and services. In addition, it includes the goods firms have produced but have yet to sell; this is called inventory. The flows in a circular flow diagram are continuous, as the economy never stops. Firms need to earn profit and people need to sell factors of production in order to buy goods and services.

Application

Economists have made the circular flow diagram a more realistic model by adding the government, foreign economies, and financial markets. Households still buy goods and services and consume them. Firms combine resources (such as labor and raw materials) to produce goods and services. They also make investments in land and equipment, which they use for producing goods and services, which they intend to sell. The government includes central and local government institutions and agencies. Its main functions are to regulate the economy through passing laws, to collect taxes, and to provide common services, such as social security. When taxes do not provide sufficient funds for these tasks, a government can borrow money in the financial markets. Foreign economies include households, businesses, and government agencies outside the borders of the national economy. Together these four sectors purchase the entire production of the economy.

Circular Flow Model

THE FOUR SECTORS OF THE ECONOMY (i.e., households, firms, government, and foreign economies) interact on three markets. In the product and services market goods and services are purchased with money. The seller is primarily the business sector; the buyers are all four sectors. In the resource market, the business sector buys, mainly from households, the labor, land, equipment, and the entrepreneurship it needs in order to accomplish the production of goods and services. In the financial markets, savings earn interest and money is borrowed by paying interest. Savings are mainly placed by households and money is borrowed by businesses to make investments in the land and equipment necessary to produce goods and services. The price for savings and investments are interest rates. A higher interest rate makes saving more attractive, a lower interest rate makes investing more attractive. With lower interest rates firms pay less for the money they borrow and therefore the potential profit from the investment they make with that money will be higher.

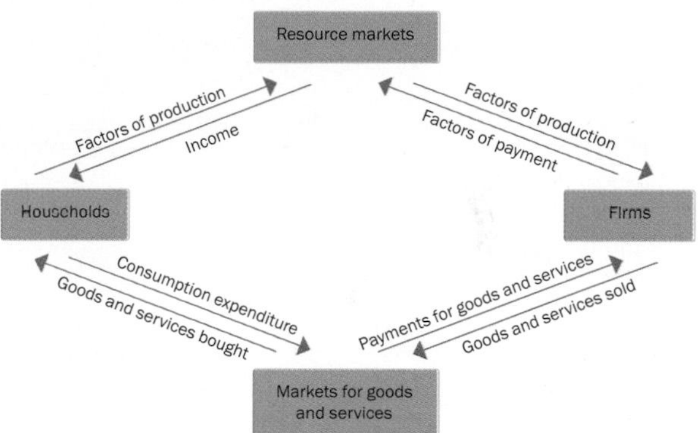

With the circular flow diagram economists show us that the macroeconomy is a dynamic system that keeps on turning, with money flowing one way, being exchanged for goods, services, and factors of production, which flow in the opposite direction, going around, never stopping.

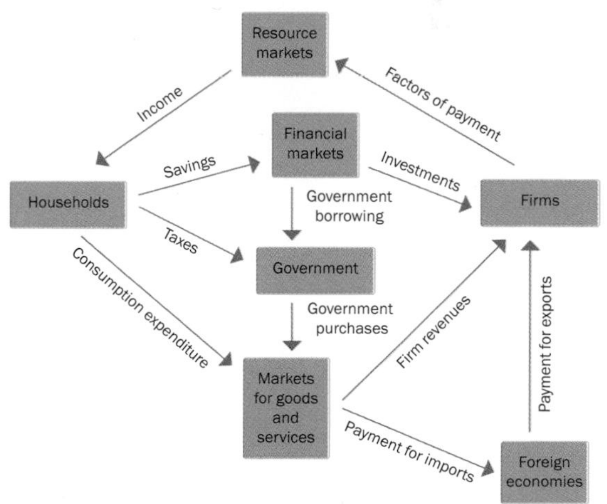

The diagram above shows the more realistic circular flow diagram with government and the financial markets. It shows the money flows that take place within the system of a macroeconomy and does not show the flows of goods services and factors of production that flow in the opposite direction.

AIMING FOR GROWTH AND STABILITY

Governments adopt policies to increase employment, control inflation, and ensure the sustainable growth of the economy in the context of changing economic circumstances. Fiscal or monetary policies assist in this goal.

Over the longer-term, economies are subject to periods of growth (expansion) and decline (contraction) in line with the business cycle. As the business cycle unfolds, unemployment, inflation, and real economic growth follow predictable patterns. The challenge for macroeconomic policy is to reduce the severity of the swings in the business cycles, in order to maintain sustainable (non-inflationary) growth and employment over time.

The Business Cycle

The business cycle exhibits distinct stages. During a contraction in the business cycle, real GDP growth will slow or decline to its lowest point at the "trough." It will subsequently recover on a period of expansion to its highest point at the "peak" of the business cycle. A straight line connecting the midpoints of expansion and contraction represents the long-term trend.

The excesses of the business cycle can level to painful, sometimes devastating episodes of unemployment and inflation. The Great Depression in the U.S. and hyperinflation in Germany were major economic shocks that caused massive disruption.

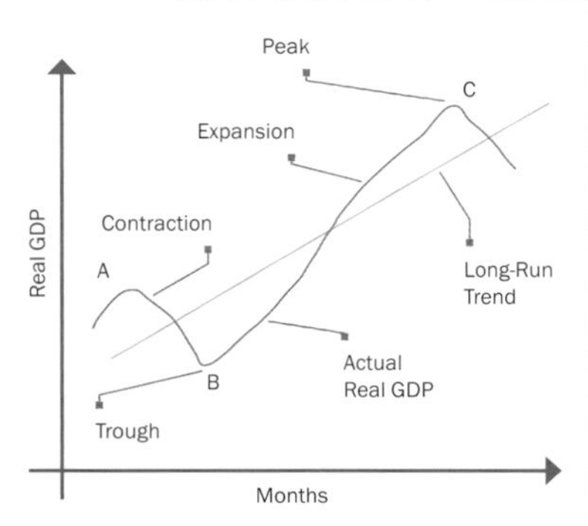

A graph of a typical business cycle clearly shows the contraction, recovery, and bubble.

Ever since, government policy has sought to better manage business cycles in order to "smooth out" peaks and troughs.

Fiscal and Monetary Policy

Fiscal policy refers to how a government raises revenues (taxes and borrowing) to fund spending (for defense, services, projects, etc.). Monetary policy refers to how the government, treasury, and central bank influence the amount of money in circulation and the level of interest rates in the economy.

Monetary and fiscal policies are expansionary or contractionary as necessary to offset the respective stages of the business cycle. For example, if the business cycle is expanding too quickly, contractionary policies such as increasing the interest rate will help stabilize the economy as people are less likely to use credit cards due to a higher cost of borrowing.

In this way, governments use monetary and fiscal policy measures to intervene in business cycles to avoid recession, to maximize growth and employment while avoiding overheating of the economy.

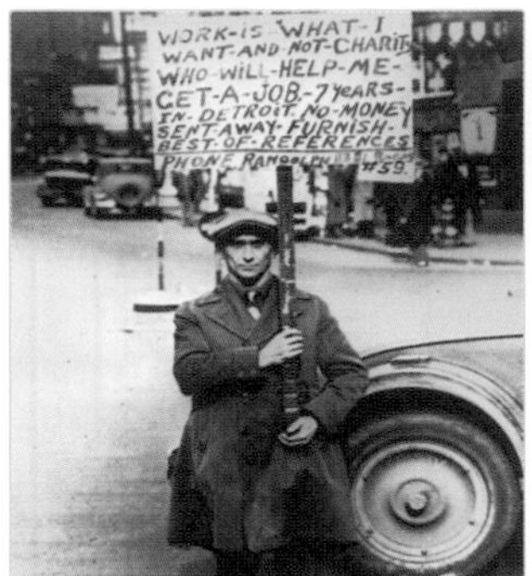

The Great Depression in the 1930s demonstrated the need for government intervention in the economy.

Globalization

Greater global economic interdependence has increased the impact of one nation's economic policies on other nations and on the world economy. International forums such as the G8 and G10 industrial and multilateral institutions such as the International Monetary Fund and the World Bank have taken on increasing importance as a means of changing views and to some extent coordinating policies internationally.

Balance of Trade

THE BALANCE OF TRADE measures the difference between exports and imports of goods. The current account measures the difference between exports and imports of good and services. A current account surplus means more are exported to other countries than are imported from them. A net deficit means more goods and services are imported from other countries than exported to them. A current account surplus is not necessarily "good" or a deficit "bad." A surplus suggests producers in the export sector are performing better than their foreign competitors, but implies that domestic consumers in the aggregate are consuming less and lending abroad. A current account deficit suggests that domestic consumers as a whole are consuming more and borrowing abroad, while domestic producers may be underperforming in competition with foreign producers.

Containers full of goods await shipping at this container yard in Shenzhen, China. By maintaining a trade surplus, China has accumulated the largest foreign currency reserves in the world.

GOVERNMENTS AND CENTRAL BANKS

By managing the money supply and the level of interest rates in an economy, a central bank seeks to control inflation and promote sustainable economic growth.

Twelve privately managed Federal Reserve Banks act as agents for the U.S. Treasury.

The central bank, independent from the government, utilizes various policies to stabilize fluctuations in a country's economy.

Banks Today

Government leaders in democratic countries are elected for periods ranging from four to six years. Economic performance during these tenures often determines whether they will be reelected. Leaders accordingly may be tempted to intervene in the economy to promote expansion in order to get reelected. Politically motivated expansion may be detrimental to sustainable economic growth.

In the latter part of the 20th century, many democratic countries have moved toward dynamic macroeconomic systems, which give the central banks greater responsibility for monetary policy and a great degree of independence from government intervention. Central banks are expected to focus on long-term economic performance regardless of the political cycle. They are expected to be guardians of the value of money with the primary responsibility of avoiding inflation. The tension between the treasury or the ministry of finance of the government, on the one hand, and the central bank on the other is designed to ensure that monetary and fiscal policy measures both address and control the risks of unemployment and inflation.

Expansion or Contraction?

Expansionary policies aim to avoid or overcome the effects of a recession. Expansionary fiscal policies consist of increasing government expenditures or reducing taxes. Increasing government expenditures, through a highway construction program, for example, directly boost demand for goods and services within an economy. Reducing taxes indirectly raises demand by putting money in people's pockets that they can spend on goods and services. The advantage of cutting taxes is that individuals, not the government, decide what they want to spend the money on. A potential drawback is that people who are uncertain about their prospects may be cautious with their extra money, saving rather than spending it. Expansionary monetary policies increase the amount of money in circulation. As the money supply increases, interest rates—the price of money—decline. Lower interest rates encourage borrowing and investment, thereby boosting economic activity.

Contractionary policies aim to avoid or overcome an overheating of the economy as a result of overly rapid expansion. Contractionary fiscal policies consist of increasing taxes or reducing government expenditure. This has the effect, respectively, of reducing the amount of money people have to spend on goods and services, and reducing government spending on goods and services from the businesses. Contractionary monetary policies reduce the amount of money in circulation, and raise interest rates, which in turn discourages borrowing and investment.

Before the 1970s, all major currencies were backed by government reserves of gold. Many nations continue to hold reserves.

DENMARK, SWEDEN, AND THE UK *maintain their own national currencies.*

CYPRUS, MALTA, AND SLOVAKIA *are slated to adopt the euro by 2009.*

THE NETHERLANDS AND FINLAND *do not mint the one- and two-cent coins, thus transactions are rounded to the nearest five cents.*

The euro is managed by the European Central Bank based in Frankfurt, Germany.

Joining the Euro-zone

A RECENT REAL-LIFE EXAMPLE of the macroeconomy "dashboard" in use is the introduction of the euro for countries of the European Union (p. 187). In deciding to adopt a common currency, policy-makers recognized the potential difficulties of countries diverging too much in their economic policies on performance. In the "Maastricht treaty" on monetary union, named after a city in the Netherlands, close to the borders of Belgium and Germany, EU countries defined and agreed on approximate targets for specific economic indicators, or "convergence criteria." An EU member wanting to join the monetary union with the euro as its currency, would have to conform to the convergence criteria on a strict timetable. This was necessary to ensure that public finances and debt levels would be consistent with low inflation with stable currency values of the core countries, especially Germany.

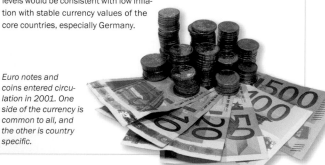

Euro notes and coins entered circulation in 2001. One side of the currency is common to all, and the other is country specific.

KEY FACTS

GLOBALIZATION *is one of the more influential forces in the 21st centruy.*

THE LIFTING OF TRADE BARRIERS *between countries remains to be contentious issue worldwide.*

DEVELOPING NATIONS *face unique problems as a result of globalization.*

THE WTO *is the only global organization that coordinates international trade policies among governments.*

Global economy | International trade and organizations for trade | Future Trends | Environmental impacts | Global aid

GLOBALIZATION

Rapid technological developments have contributed to the expansion of world trade. Production processes can be spread across multiple international locations, with each developing its own specialty and the end product assembled in a location close to where it is sold. Enormous advances in transport logistics have contributed to the growth of international trade. The development of information and communication technologies, notably the Internet, has been a further major driving force for growth in international trade.

Globalization is the concept of a diffusion of common cultural experiences and ideas.

FROM NATIONAL ECONOMIES TO THE GLOBAL ECONOMY

Over the last 50 years, international trade has been an important driving force for global economic growth. The total volume of world merchandise trade was over 21 trillion dollars in 2005.

Nothing has changed the face of the global economy more than the expansion of international trade. Its impact has been decisive on large and small economies alike. Most global trade is among industrialized countries, but developing countries are gaining an increasing share of world trade, which was about 30 percent in 2005.

With the expansion of global trade, the rapid growth has occurred of large multinational companies producing, selling, and assembling in an array of locations worldwide, often managing globally recognized brands everywhere. Hand in hand with the growth of exports of goods and services has come an expansion in foreign direct investment (plant and equipment), as multinational industrial groups establish factories and offices to take advantage of opportunities to produce more cheaply and to open up new markets. Multinationals such as IBM, Nestlé, Toyota, and Unilever manage global production and sales networks that provide high-quality products to customers worldwide. But international trade is not reserved for large multinational corporations. The Internet is a channel that has allowed both small and multinational businesses to have access to global markets.

Shanker Annaswamy is the managing director of IBM, the world's largest computer-service provider, in India.

INSIDER KNOWLEDGE

IKEA, *originating in Sweden, is the world's largest furniture retailer with stores in about 30 countries in the worldwide.*

NEARLY 90% *of the world's PCs ran on a Microsoft operating system in 1993.*

Services too are increasingly produced and sold across borders. These include financial services such as international insurance from Lloyds of London, or international business services such as call centers in Bangalore, India, that serve clients in the U.S.

Current Trends in Globalization

At the beginning of the 21st century, most business leaders, economists, and politicians are convinced that further trade liberalization offers enormous scope for boosting global growth and prosperity, or estimate a boost of the U.S. dollar: 500 billion per annum is achievable. The economic argument is that economics that adapt position themselves to compete will create new and better jobs that the ones that are lost. They argue that low-wage, labor intensive production processes should move to developing countries while skill- and capital-intensive processes thrive in industrialized countries. In Great Britain the output of the labor-intensive textile industry fell from 9.4 percent to 3.6 percent of the total output of the British economy between 1970 and 2003. In the same period the business services sector grew considerably, was able to compete internationally and gained an important share of exports.

However, globalization is not without its problems. Many countries seek to protect local industries from increased competition and oversight authorities such as the World Trade Organization (WTO).

The availability of inexpensive labor in countries like China has caused many Western firms to move all manufacturing overseas.

As countries like India continue to experience rapid growth, global brands like Citibank are quick to take advantage of the expanding market.

EXPANDING INTERNATIONAL TRADE

Since 1945, international trade has contributed significantly to worldwide economic growth. This has benefited both rich nations and emerging economies such as India, Brazil, and China, but remains a divisive issue for many.

Inevitably, one country's exports are another country's imports, but whereas expanding export markets are seen as beneficial to economic growth, increasing openness to imports is often seen, by both governments and ordinary people as threatening. Many countries view increased imports replace goods and services produced in the home country with those produced abroad, thereby threatening employment in import-competing industries in the home country.

Difficulties of Global Expansion

Proponents of free trade argue that not only industrialized and middle-income developing countries will benefit, but low-income developing countries will as well. However, international trade raises concerns in many countries. Some worry that lifting of trade barriers will favor only the rich and some rapidly growing developing countries, such as China, India, and Brazil, while leaving the poor countries worse off. At the same time, in industrialized countries, there is a concern that international competition would threaten economic activities that sometimes are deeply connected to a country's culture and are unable or unwilling to adjust costs, quality, and/or marketing to re-position their products. France, for example, has a rich tradition of viniculture and wine production that is threatened by competition from the U.S., Australia, South Africa, and Chile.

This Hyundai shipyard in South Korea is filled with cars ready for export to the global market.

Nongovernmental organizations are concerned that the least developed countries that have low productivity and weak institutions will not be able to meet the competition from the rich and powerful industrialized nations. Many African countries' agricultural sectors are currently competing with heavily subsidized agricultural products from the EU. They stand to benefit very little until EU agricultural subsidies are phased out.

Protectionism

Governments have therefore taken measures to protect domestic industries from foreign competition. These measures include putting tariffs on imports, subsidizing domestic firms with tax-payers' money, and encouraging exports with tax-relief for the exporting company. Huge agricultural subsidies in the EU and the U.S. are examples of the protection of the agricultural sector. Monetary policy can also be used to encourage exports by keeping the value of the domestic currency low against that of the foreign competitor. At the beginning of the 21st century, China's enormous trade surplus is, to a significant level, keeping the value of the Chinese currency artificially low against other major currencies. Governments also devise non-tariff barriers to trade, such as imposing arbitrary technical standards or requiring burdensome import licenses. Japan has developed a reputation for being inventive in this regard.

Some have argued that profits by large corporations rarely benefit the developming countries in which they are made.

INSIDER KNOWLEDGE

CHINA, *the fourth largest economy, is one of the fastest growing as well, with a yearly growth of 10% in the past four years. This has been fuelled in a large part by its exports.*

INDIA'S *barriers to international trade and investment make it a relatively closed protectionist economy.*

Thyssen Krupp, one of the biggest steelworks in Germany, exports to the worldwide market.

Comparative Advantage

THE BRITISH ECONOMIST David Ricardo (1772–1823) showed with his principle of comparative advantage that each country should specialize in the production of goods and services that it is best at producing and sell those goods and services to other nations that do the same.

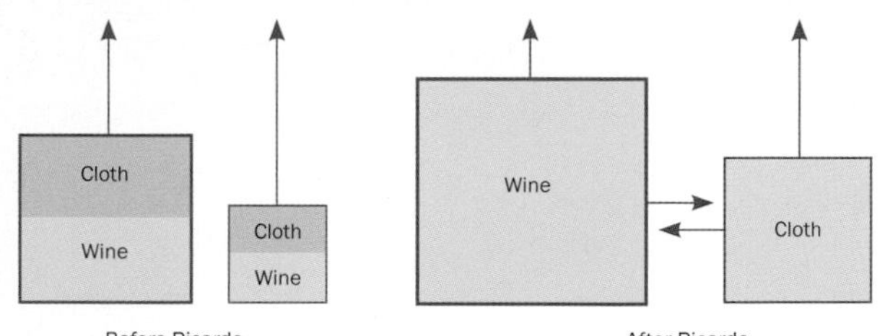

TWO FICTIONAL COUNTRIES produce only two goods: cloth and wine. Country A is more efficient than country B at producing both cloth and wine, and so has an absolute advantage in both. Before Ricardo, economists would have said, Country A has nothing to gain from trade with country B. Ricardo argued that if each country specialized in producing the good in which it had comparable advantage—i.e., the good they could produce more efficiently—total output of both cloth and wine would rise and both countries would benefit through trade.

POLITICS, LAW, AND ECONOMY

INTERNATIONAL ORGANIZATIONS FOR TRADE

With the growth of trade and globalization, it has become essential for governments to negotiate and form unified and accepted trade practices. The WTO is the major coordinating body.

Given the number of countries participating in international trade, it would be inefficient for individual countries to negotiate trade arrangements with each other.

Trading blocks have naturally emerged to set out rules of trade among members with goals to facilitate trade among members, typically reducing or abolishing trade barriers. The North American Free Trade Area (NAFTA) comprising the U.S., Canada, and Mexico emerged as a result of this and the EU is another example. To facilitate trade among the entire global community, it has been necessary to create organizations to oversee trade processes in the global community.

Pascal Lamy, Director-General of the World Trade Organization, attends a panel session on the frozen WTO trade talks in Davos.

21ST CENTURY

AS OF 2007, *the WTO has 153 members, with the most recent being Tonga who joined in 2007, and Cape Verde and the Ukraine who joined in 2008. Russia is still notably absent as a member and its accession is still currently in negotiation.*

Development of Global Trade Oversight

The General Agreement on Tariffs and Trade (GATT) was formed in 1947 at the Bretton Woods Conference that followed World War II. The GATT framework served to reduce barriers to international trade.

Then in 1986, the largest international governmental trade negotiation round ever, involving 123 countries began. Based in the city of Punta del Este in Uruguay, the Uruguay Round took seven years to negotiate. Outcomes included significant import tariff cuts by developed countries, more market orientation in agricultural trade, agreed food safety standards, gradual liberalization of textile trade, protection of intellectual property, restrictions on the use of subsidies, and provisions against the practice of "dumping" (i.e., competing unfairly by selling surplus goods at prices far below their cost). The most important aspect of these negotiations resulted in the establishment of the WTO.

The World Trade Organization

The WTO, with headquarters in Geneva, was formed to assist producers, importers, and exporters in conducting their global business. It is currently the only organization in the world with this role.

Main aims, among others, include setting and enforcing international trade rules, providing forums for trade liberalization, and resolving trade disputes. Negotiations between nations are formalized through "WTO agreements" which are signed by most of the trading nations and ratified within the country's own parliaments.

There are currently 153 members, including the largest four traders (the U.S., the EU, Canada, and Japan) and its membership continues to increase.

Agriculture Subsidies

THE COMMON AGRICULTURAL POLICY (CAP) of the EU is one example of agricultural protectionism. More than 60 percent of the central budget of the EU goes toward the CAP. The CAP raises farmers' income in three ways: keeping agricultural prices at a high level, buying produce when prices fall below a certain level, and imposing import tariffs on foreign produce. This can have damaging effects on developing countries that are unable to profitably export their agricultural goods to richer countries who thus benefit from a comparative advantage. It also hurts consumers in the EU who not only pay directly for the subsidies with taxes, but also pay a higher price for produce.

Agriculture is one of the most protected, and thus least efficient, areas of trade.

Recent WTO Rounds

In November 2001, at a WTO conference in Doha, Qatar, the Doha Development Round was launched. The key goal was to open agricultural markets in the industrialized nations to agricultural produce from developing countries, by reducing the very high agricultural subsidies and import tariffs and other trade barriers. These are prevalent in the EU and the U.S. In return, developing countries should reduce import tariffs on industrial goods. In 2006 the Doha Development Round failed, with different parties blaming each other for causing its failure. A notable occurrence during the negotiations was the formation of a coalition of fast-growing developing countries led by Brazil and India, showing their muscle and newly found self-confidence in the negotiations with the industrialized countries. Attempts to revive the Doha Development Round in 2007 and 2008 have failed.

above: *A recent meeting of WTO participants in Geneva, Switzerland.*

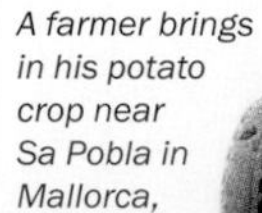

A farmer brings in his potato crop near Sa Pobla in Mallorca, Spain.

CURRENT AND FUTURE TRENDS

As globalization affects many aspects of society, decisions made by global organizations such as the World Trade Organization, the World Bank, and the Group of Eight come under intense scrutiny.

As proliferation of global corporations increases, meetings of organizations such as the WTO and the Group of Eight consistently attract large protest rallies. Decisions made by organizations such as these have an enormous impact worldwide and attract criticism from opponents of globalization.

The Anti-Globalization Movement

Anti-globalization is a term that encapsulates different causes including environmentalism, anti-capitalism, and opposition to multi-nationals. Most of the existing opposition to globalization stems mainly from concerns of exploitation of the world's poor, workers, and the environment. In particular, it is argued that in the current context, it is easier for large multinationals and rich industrial nations to act with less accountability for their actions. Opponents also express concern over the homogenization of cultures worldwide, particularly due to the profileration of large mutinational organizations such as McDonald's. Environmentalists and Third World activists are worried that globalization will reduce the ability of governments and democratic institutions to manage domestic economic development.

Activists are not the only ones expressing concern. Labor unions fear loss of jobs to cheaper locations. They fear WTO agreements have nothing to offer the poor and will give little attention to their concerns in favor of the purely economic interests of the powerful Western industrialized countries.

To these activists, the WTO represents all that is threatening in the move toward globalization. WTO agreement meetings have accordingly been accompanied by violent protests from these groups. Some of these non-governmental organizations have tried to influence government negotiators to take their concerns into consideration, rather than completely rejecting efforts to build an open global trading system. Activists also target meetings of the International Monetary Fund, the Group of Eight, and the World Forum.

Future Directions

In the 21st century, it is expected that greater direct debate and engagement between governments and NGOs such as Greenpeace and Oxfam will take place regarding globalization.

The G8 meeting in Rostock, Germany in 2007 generated several decisions that impacted a number of areas relevant to globalization today, which included new initiatives regarding climate change and increased assistance to Africa. Resolutions included a 60-billion-dollar pledge to fight AIDS, malaria, and tuberculosis in Africa and to aim to reduce global emissions of greenhouse gases by 2050 between all eight nations by 50 percent or limit the rise of global temperatures. Critics are, however, still skeptical. Before the summit, Oxfam claimed that the G8 were already on track to missing their previous 2010 aid target by 30 billion dollars. Also, regarding climate change, the U.S. would only agree to reduce emissions in line with China and India, so as to not reduce the competitiveness of American industry.

The work of the WTO remains controversial, and security at its meetings is often very tight.

South Korean farmers shout slogans during a protest against the World Trade Organization near the convention center in Hong Kong, China, in 2005.

21ST CENTURY

THE INTERNET *has allowed anti-globalization campaigners to acquire large numbers for protest rallies.*

IN 2006 *the "Live 8" concerts, which took place in Europe, Japan, Canada, and South Africa, accumulated 30 million signatures for a campaign regarding G8 policies.*

FOUNDED IN 1971, *the WEF meets every year in Davos, Switzerland.*

WHIL E VERY INFLUENTAL, *the forum has been critisized for representing the wealth and not the population of the world.*

THE EVENT *is often a target of anti-globalization protesters from around the world.*

World leaders such as British prime minister Tony Blair are regular speakers at Davos.

World Economic Forum

THE WORLD ECONOMIC FORUM (WEF) is a private foundation created by an economics professor from Switzerland, Klaus Schwab. Its aim is to engage business leaders and leading political figures around the world in shaping global, regional, and industry agendas. The WEF organizes an annual meeting that usually takes place in Davos, Switzerland. Here, business leaders and politicians from around the world can discuss and reflect on developments in the economy and global political issues. Top business leaders and politicians around the globe value the unique networking opportunities the WEF provides. Not surprisingly, the WEF has become the focus of criticism and protests of environmentalists and third world activists. To counter the media attention on the annual meeting of the World Economic Forum, these groupings have begun organizing a meeting of their own, the so-called World Social Forum, which takes place simultaneously, usually in a developing country location.

Bill Gates, Chairman of Microsoft, addresses a plenary session on Web 2.0 during the World Economic Forum (WEF) in Davos.

GLOBALIZATION AND ENVIRONMENTAL IMPACTS

Globalization continues to be an issue of contention among environmentalists. The largest economies in the world also tend to be the biggest polluters. In particular, climate change and greenhouse emissions are discussed extensively by both governments and non-government organizations.

One concern with globalization is the impact of rapidly rising international trade on the environment. The concern ranges from the depletion of valuable rain forests and other ecological systems, to the explosion of carbon emissions from increased use of vehicles, planes, fossil-powered energy plants, and others. In particular, energy intensive economic activity is an increasingly important factor to be priced into cost benefit calculations due to the increased scrutiny of the environmental impact of global trade expansion on climate change.

Global Warming

As the first decade of the 21st century draws to its end, scientists agree that humanity is contributing significantly to climate change. A report produced for the British Government by the economist Sir Nicholas Stern in 2006 indicates that political and economic decision-

Rock star Bono and German Chancellor Merkel represent two different groups who share an interest in the developing world.

makers are beginning to take this problem seriously.

This is for good reason as the Earth's average surface temperature, which has been increasing by about 1.2° to 1.4°F since 1900, is expected to increase another 2° to 11°F above 1990 levels by the end of this century. This amount of change can have drastic effects for developing nations. The Akosombo Reservoir in Ghana, which contributes to Ghana's economy, is now only half full due to droughts and less rainfall attributed to global warming. Ghana has been forced into rationing and finding new energy sources. Since the reservoir, at one time, supplied 95 percent of the country's energy needs and also allowed the country to export energy, these changes have negatively impacted the economy.

International Efforts Toward Climate Change

There have been several initiatives to address climate change but the most important to date is the Kyoto Protocol. Proposed in December 1997, the Kyoto Protocol to the UN Framework Convention on Climate Change (UNFCCC) is an interna-

At the G8 summit in June 2007 in Germany, world leaders discussed climate change.

tional treaty, which came into effect in February 2005. The aim is to reduce the emission of six greenhouse gases in 38 developed countries by a commitment period of 2008–2012. Negotiated in Kyoto, Japan, it is currently the largest global effort to reduce greenhouse emissions to date.

Carbon Emission Trading

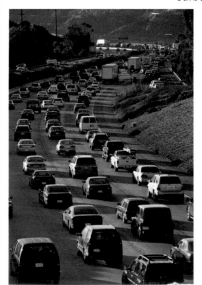

It is becoming clear that the negative consequences of climate change will be very unevenly distributed throughout the world, with poorer developing countries being hit much harder than most rich industrialized nations. Climate change will be one of the biggest challenges, requiring a long-term global effort to start immediately. An interesting economic aspect associated with climate change is the use of economic mechanisms as part of the strategy to address it. An example is carbon emission rights trading. For example, governments assign limits on carbon emissions to companies, and then allow a global market for trading carbon emission rights to develop. In this way, companies that take measures to reduce carbon emissions can financially benefit by selling the carbon emission rights to other companies who exceed their limits. In this way the power of the market can be harnessed to provide incentives for corporations to act to reduce the negative impact they have on the environment. The creation of an international fund to help developing countries with adjustments to climate change and the development of environmentally friendly technologies are further economic measures that will become an important new aspect of the world economy in the 21st century.

The increased usage of automobiles continues to contribute to the emissions of greenhouse gases.

Traffic in Asia's congested cities (here in Jakarta) is a leading contributor to pollution that deteriorates the Earth's atmosphere.

However, the effectiveness of this treaty remains questionable. There have been indications that many countries under the agreement will fail to meet their targets. Secondly, not only is the leading emitter of green house gases, the U.S., not a party to the treaty, but China, which emits the second highest proportion of greenhouse gases, is not required to restrict its emissions. Among other things, economic considerations continue to be a hindrance in progress toward climate change.

➲ see also: **Humans Effect on the Climate,** *Earth Chapter p. 55*

DEVELOPING NATIONS AND GLOBAL AID

More than one fifth of the world lives in extreme poverty, on less than $1 per day. However, industrialized countries find it in theri interest to assist poor countries with social and economic development.

Poverty often goes hand in hand with political instability; countries with extreme social and economic problems can be fertile recruitment grounds for internationally active groups that are ready to use violence to achieve their goals. From drugs via illegal immigration to political and religious extremism, rich industrialized nations can themselves be impacted by the socio-economic problems of developing countries. Helping countries to develop their economies can also bring significant economic benefits to rich industrialized countries through international trade.

The sale of these 99 euro hotdogs in Sweden went to support the UN Development Program.

Between 1990 and 2002 the proportion of the world population living in extreme poverty was reduced by 8 percentage points from 28 percent to 21 percent. The general picture, however, is one of very uneven distribution of this improvement. In the Sub-Saharan regions of Africa droughts and the effects of HIV/AIDS have contributed to another 150 million people falling below the poverty line during the same period.

Forms of Development Aid

Development aid can take many forms. Most often it consists of financial and technical assistance. It can be provided bilaterally from one country to another or multilaterally through international organizations. A number of intergovernmental organizations play a major role in international aid. The United Nations, the World Bank, the International Monetary Fund, and the Paris based Organization for Economic Cooperation and Development (OECD) are just some of the organizations that keep track of developments, promote, and perform scientific research, and provide financial and technical assistance to developing countries.

In the 1990s, movements of concerned citizens dedicated to doing something about poverty and the extremes of the uneven distribution of wealth rose to prominence in the rich countries and took on an ever more active role. These civil society movements gave rise to organizations outside the control of governments, which engaged in financial and technical aid. These nongovernmental organizations (NGO's) (p. 189) have been instrumental and increasingly successful in moving the ethically motivated economic issues of developing countries to a higher place on the agenda of Western governments.

The Future of Aid

A number of global initiatives to improve economic and social conditions in poor countries were launched. Of these, the United Nations' Millennium Development Goals (MDG) initiative is the most comprehensive and ambitious. It aims to eradicate extreme poverty and hunger by 2015, achieve universal primary education, promote gender equality and empower women, reduce child mortality, improve maternal health, combat HIV/AIDS, malaria and other diseases, and ensure environmental sustainability.

A group of women in Madagascar gather with their children outside a health clinic provided by an international NGO.

Cambodian babies, affected by HIV/AIDS, lay in their cribs and are cared for by a local nongovernmental organization.

MOHAMMED YUNUS *received the Nobel Peace Prize in 2006.*

IN 2005, *Grameen Bank had about 5 billion U.S. dollars of small loans on its books.*

BUSINESS LOANS TO THE POOR *have since spread to the U.S. and UK.*

Mohammed Yunus lectures frequently on poverty reduction and microfinance.

Microcredit

THE BANGLADESHI ECONOMICS PROFESSOR and banker Mohammed Yunus implemented an innovative method of reducing poverty on a large scale. He observed that poor Bangladeshi farmers and their families, who needed small loans to buy crops and raw materials, were charged excessive rates of interest by local lenders. Because the loans were very small and they could not offer assets to secure loans, conventional banks were not interested in lending to them, so farmers were at the mercy of local loan sharks and avoided borrowing money, if at all possible.

MAKING his first loan of 27 U.S. dollars in 1974, Yunis went on to start his own bank, Grameen Bank, lending small amounts of money to farmers and would be entrepreneurs at reasonable rates of interest. Through these loans, a large proportion of which were made to women, microcredit helped many households to escape poverty.

One of the most successful microcredit ventures is a loan to start a cell phone rental business. Women are very often the recipients.

KEY FACTS

PRODUCERS AND CONSUMERS *are the buyers and sellers in the economy.*

A SUPPLY AND DEMAND CURVE, *assists decision makers in determining the socially optimal price for a good or service.*

MONOPOLIES, OLIGOPOLIES, CARTELS, AND ASYMMETRIC INFORMATION *can disrupt the efficient allocation of resources in a free market economy.*

Harnessing the power of markets | Market failures

ECONOMICS AND BUSINESS

Economists have contributed valuable knowledge about how markets work and what can make them fail. In the 21st century businesses are focusing on knowing their markets and adapting to them to achieve greater profits. Economists and governments are focusing on getting an accurate picture of the economy, and adopting policies to ensure stable growth and avoid market failure. Tools such as the supply and demand curve, which determines optimal prices and and production, assists in this task.

The word economy is derived from the Greek word "oikonomos," which means alteration.

HARNESSING THE POWER OF MARKETS

At the core of capitalist societies are markets. Here businesses strive to maximize their profits by offering products and services which consumers desire and are able to afford.

In any economy, producers and consumers are sellers and buyers of goods and services. The market is where buying and selling takes place. When these transactions take place in a free market economy, the two groups negotiate according to the law of supply and demand, to achieve the socially optimal price and quantity. Originally dependent on a physical location for buying and selling, in the 21st century transactions are increasingly resolved through communication on the Internet.

The Internet has broadened the market with an explosion of suppliers, and the ability to reach many more customers.

Competition of Businesses

Businesses need to understand their markets to be profitable and create value for their shareholders. Economists and policy-makers need to understand the problems that can cause markets to malfunction or "fail" to maintain a safe and healthy society. There are various policy options available to balance the force of the market with the ideas of social welfare, so that the benefits of competitive price and production signals can be harnessed for the benefits of the economy and society as a whole.

In a situation where numerous firms produce identical products and face many customers, firms will compete and produce the socially optimal output at the minimum possible cost. Economists call this situation perfect competition. The fact that a socially optimal outcome is reached while individual firms and consumers are each rigorously pursuing their own self-interest was a stunning early result of the study of economics. The most famous Scottish economist of the 18th century, Adam Smith, called it "the invisible hand of the market."

Markets Today

At the beginning of the 21st century, the market mechanism is considered a good way to organize much of the world's economic activity. Global currency and commodity markets appeared in unexpected places, for example in the command economy of communist China and public services sector in European mixed economies.

In the 21st century markets will continue to play a central role in the global economy. The success of auction sites such as eBay on the Internet shows how modern technology has allowed the age-old concept of the market to be extended into many homes. The Internet has lowered the cost of connecting with a greater number of customers by eliminating the need for a physical store location.

In most places, power generation is an example of a monopoly, as the cost of entering the market is so high, it cannot sustain competitors.

Especially when products are similar, brand identity is an important factor in capturing market share.

Supply and Demand

THE PRINCIPLE of supply and demand is used to describe the quantity and price of a good, based on the relationship of sellers to buyers. Each group is represented by a curve. The point at which the two curves meet is called the equilibrium and indicated the socially optimal price and production quantity for any given good. The slope of each curve indicates the degree of elasticity of either supply or demand, and is useful to determine how the quantity of a good might increase or decrease with a change in price.

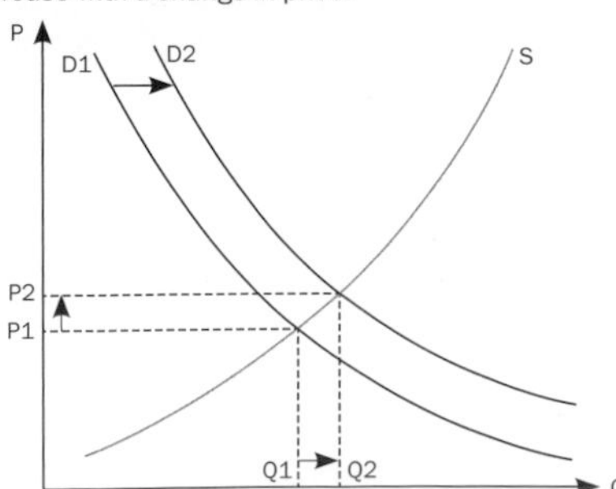

This graph shows a simplified supply and demand curve, graphed as price against quantity of the good produced.

MARKET FAILURES

While free markets function naturally to achieve an efficient allocation of resources, monopolies, cartels, and asymmetric information can serve to be a barrier.

In Western societies, free monopolistic competition exists in which many firms with slightly different products compete with each other. Production costs are slightly higher than in perfect competition, but potential buyers benefit from product differentiation. In industrialized countries where this form of competition is widespread, consumers have choices among many different brands of family cars, etc.

Buyers and sellers barter, and the prevailing price is the market price.

Monopolies and Oligopolies

Not all markets consist of a large number of suppliers facing a large number of consumers. When a single supplier provides for many consumers the supplier has a monopoly. An example is when only one electric-generating company supplies all the households in a particular area. It has no competitors and, if unchecked, will tend to restrain output to drive up prices, thereby producing less than the social optimum output. Accordingly, when monopolies exist, governments intervene to check their monopolistic tendencies and promote output and price levels that ensure long-term supplies at fair prices to consumers.

With so many brands of car available, consumers are forced to differentiate on many factors.

In an oligopoly, a relatively small number of firms dominate a market and face a large number of consumers. The soft drinks and beer industries are sometimes oligopolies. Oligopolies will often fiercely compete with each other; Coca Cola and Pepsi are an example of this. On the other hand, oligopolistic firms may conspire to set prices and quantities in order to maximizes their profits at the expense of consumers. Companies that band together to limit competition in order to gain a monopoly typically form a cartel.

Cartels

The formation of a cartel is an attempt to transform an oligopoly into monopoly. In most countries cartels are illegal. Governments carefully evaluate market data to determine whether firms are conspiring to form cartels and impose sanctions when they find that is the case.

Cartels are by nature unstable. Cartel members who do not adhere to production restraints can increase their profits at the expense of other cartel members by simply producing more. With multiple firms seeking to maximize returns, oligopolistic behavior presents complex choices best understood through the aid of applied mathematics and game theory.

Other Failures

In addition to monopolies and cartels, markets fail in other ways. For example, if property rights are unclear or absent, individual behavior can lead to negative externalities (cost imposed on third parties). The ecologist Garrett Hardin popularized this conflict between individual interests and the common good in a 1968 essay entitled "The Tragedy of the Commons."

Asymmetric information is another instance of market failure. If a buyer or seller has private information that gives one party an advantage over the other that party stands to make excess profits. If the other parties know the unfair advantage, the market may collapse. The used car market is a classic case: The used car salesman knows more about the quality of the used car than the buyer. There is no accepted base of information on which a fair price can be negotiated. Possible solutions include requiring the seller to offer a warranty or the buyer getting an expert opinion.

When buying a used car, the consumer is at a disadvantage, as the seller may not reveal all information about the history of the car.

Avoiding "The Tragedy of the Commons"

IN A FARMING VILLAGE most land is privately held, except for one large field of common land where everybody may graze their cattle. On the private land, the owner has incentive to limit cattle grazing. If he puts too many cows out to graze he may increase his short-term profit, but depletes the field and lowers profits in the long term. The owner has incentive to carefully balance the number of cows and the availability of grass. On the common field, however, nobody is charged for grazing, everyone has incentive to put cows there, and the common field soon becomes overgrazed and useless. In this case, individuals pursuing their self-interest are not persuaded to think of the social outcome by the "invisible hand of the market." The property rights make all the difference. Economists advance two solutions: Turn the common field into private property or issue grazing permits. Property rights and licensing will be critical features in dealing with problems of the environment in the 21st century.

21ST CENTURY

IN APRIL 2000, MICROSOFT *was judged in a U.S. court of law as an "abusive monopoly" and was ordered to split into separate units. This has since been partially overruled on appeal by Microsoft.*

ANGOLA, ECUADOR, AND SUDAN *announced their desire to join the OPEC oil cartel. Sudan and Ecuador are still waiting.*

KEY FACTS

PLANNING *is an important stage in starting a business as it assists in assessing potential issues before they arise.*

PRICING STRATEGIES *assist enterprises in optimizing profit and market share.*

PERFORMANCE MEASUREMENT TOOLS *are important for both managers and investors in the ongoing operations of an enterprise.*

Strategy and planning | Pricing and revenue | Legal structure and raising capital | Measuring performance

OPENING AND RUNNING A BUSINESS

It takes more than a great idea to run a successful enterprise. Opening and running a business requires extensive analysis not only at the planning phase, but also on an ongoing basis throughout the entire lifespan of a business venture. The entrepreneur must look at internal and external factors to make informed decisions. This is especially important today, when external factors such as the Internet play an important role.

Modern economic theory stresses the importance of the entrepreneur in economic growth.

STRATEGIC PLANNING

When entrepreneurs want to start a business they will have to check its feasibility and draw up a plan before they can put their idea into action.

A great business idea can be the worst enemy of an entrepreneur. When it seems evident that a new product or service will meet certain market requests and that it only needs to be produced to sell, failure is likely to sit on the doorstep: While opening a business may be spontaneous, running it successfully will need strategic planning rather than tactical day-to-day decisions.

Strategic Planning Tools

A qualified analysis of the prospective products, their markets, and the means to produce and sell them and of all budgets is the indispensable start of all plans. There are a number of tools that help founders of a new company to ascertain the viability of their potential business venture, to determine a strategic direction and to identify potential weaknesses.

The SWOT analysis is a rather basic but very helpful method to identify options and threads of most situations, products or decisions in business life. It consists of a list of internal strengths (S) and weaknesses (W), and external opportunities (O) and threads (T). Differentiated in this manner complex problems with their interdependencies and ambiguities become clearer and easier to access. Strategies are long-term plans that must be evaluated regularly. A business plan which describes in detail the company, its products, markets and its projected growth is a good base on which an ongoing controlling system can be built.

Checklist for Start-Ups

Product/Service: What is the benefit to the user? Which comparable products are existing or may be introduced by competitors? What makes the new project better than existing products? What would be the suggested retail price?

Target group: What are their needs and expectations? Which price will they pay?

Competitors: Which companies offer comparable products and what is their standing in the market?

Distribution channel: Through which channels can the target group be reached? Who are the players in the concerned channels and what are their expectations?

Product life: How long will the product stay in the market? (worst, middle, best case scenario)

Production: Make or buy? Who can supply what in sufficient quality? What are the quantities needed in which time?

Own organization: What staff, which facilities are needed in house and freelance?

Budgeting: What are projected costs and income?

Finance: How much money is needed, where does it come from?

The entrepreneur must undertake an extensive analytical planning process to ensure that a project is viable before going ahead.

INTERNET E-COMMERCE *was enabled through the introduction of the first graphical browser software in 1993, which made the Internet more accessible to customers.*

AMAZON.COM, INC., *a "virtual bookstore," started in a garage in Seattle, Washington, in 1995. In 2006, net profits totaled $10.7 billion.*

E-commerce is an important strategic consideration for many businesses.

E-Commerce as Strategic Segment

A CONSIDERATION during the planning phase for new enterprises is the utilization of the Internet. The Internet has provided many businesses an effective and efficient method of reaching millions of customers worldwide without the need of setting up physical stores. "E-commerce" through the Internet revolutionized the business world and allowed even small businesses to challenge the large corporations. It is not, however, without its disadvantages. With many online companies competing for business, the profit margins are low or non-existent.

AMAZON.COM, INC. is an example of how small business have used the Internet to challenge the traditional large retailers. Jeffrey Bezos, founder and CEO, saw the potential in using the Internet as an alternative channel to access customers. In a little over 10 years, the company has developed from a small business in the founder's garage, to being listed on the NASDAQ 100 stock exchange.

Jeffrey Bezos, founder and CEO of Amazon.com, Inc., was Time Magazine's1999 Person of the Year.

PRICING AND REVENUE

One of the main goals in any organization is profitability. This is achieved by maximizing revenues while keeping costs low.

Profit is the income of an enterprise, which is calculated simply as revenues after costs are deducted. Revenues are the inflow through an enterprise's activities during a given period of time and costs are the amounts paid by a company to other parties during the same period of time. To maximize profit, revenue must be kept at the highest level possible while keeping costs optimally low. There are many ways through which a business can achieve these goals.

Revenue and Pricing Strategies

Revenue is generated primarily through selling products and services. Therefore, revenue is maximized primarily by the pricing decisions of management. Decisions concerning price are affected by a variety of factors, which include consumer demand, competition, and cost. First, the manager must determine how much a customer is willing to pay for a product or service. If the price is too low, the customer is not charged as much as they may have been willing to pay, hence revenue is not optimized. On the other hand, if the price is too high, there may be no incentive for the customer to buy, which may result in revenue lost to the company. In addition to this, competitor prices must be considered during the decision making process, particularly if the competition offers an alternative to the enterprise's product or service. If a competitor charges a lower price, all businesses which sell a similar product are eager to charge the same price or lower to ensure that consumers will not purchase the competitor's products. Finally, as cost is a factor in the calculation of profit, the price must be sufficient to ensure that profits are made.

Decision-making may seem like gambling at times, but should always reflect objectives.

Cost Optimization

Costs are classified as either fixed or variable. Variable costs are costs that change in line with certain activities within a business. Fixed costs stay the same regardless of the level of activity within a business. Using an ice cream shop as an example, the more hours an employee with an hourly wage works to sell ice-cream, the higher the variable cost to the business. On the other hand, the rent on the premises will not change in proportion to any activity undertaken.

Costs must be kept optimally low to ensure that profitability to the business is maximized but at the same time, cost-cutting must not compromise the goals of the company: if a company aims to make quality products, costs must not be set so low that quality is endangered. In general, a cost reduction program focuses on eliminating three types of activities: over-resourced, poorly managed and non-value-adding. Over-resourced costs occur where one task is currently performed using too many resources. For example, in an ice cream store, a manager can identify that one could perform a task currently performed by two employees simultaneously. Poorly managed activities can increase costs unnecessarily but can be identified and rectified through exception reporting. The ice cream store manager who has hired several new employees may note that wastage through errors has increased due to the highly technical nature of the espresso machine. Once this has been identified, the manager solves the issue by assembling a quick use guide that employees can refer to while working. Lastly, non-value adding activities add costs to a product or service that a customer would be unwilling to pay extra for. Therefore the elimination of these costs will not impact optimal quality. For example, in a street where the lowest priced ice cream attracts customers, premium vanilla ice cream will most likely become waste. A technique utilized in industry to assist in identifying these activities is "value engineering" which, among other things, involves analyzing steps in a production process and defining which steps do not add value. These steps in the process are subsequently eliminated while costs that are essential to reach the organization's goals are kept which optimizes the level of spending that an organization undertakes.

Most hourly wages are defined as a variable cost as they are closely related to the product or service sold: The more beers are served the longer the waitress works.

Pricing Strategies in the Luxury Goods Market

The luxury goods market pursues a strategy of differentiation. Through high quality products and exclusivity, this market targets the high-end consumer who is willing to pay extra to own a product. Being able to price significantly over cost requires careful marketing and branding, a high level of service and in most cases, careful control over distribution channels. The LVMH Group is an example of a conglomerate that owns luxury brands that many are familiar with, including brands such as Dom Perignon, Christian Dior, and TAG Heuer.

On average, the LVMH Group charge approximately 180% over the cost of production. This is a large markup when compared, for example, to the Kmart group, employing a cost leadership strategy, which charges about 25% over their cost. The ability to charge large mark-ups is predominantly due to the exclusivity of the brands and the high level of service that is provided to customers. Also, this is evidenced by the fact that such brands are unlikely to be found in discount outlets, showing a tight control over distribution channels. Prices are also kept high to ensure that customers who pay the extra to own a product will be differentiated from other consumers as the majority of the population is priced out of the market.

However, when there is a major downturn in the economy, the sales of luxury goods are always expected to reduce.

LEGAL STRUCTURE AND RAISING CAPITAL

Determining the legal structure is an important decision to make during the process of setting up a business. For small businesses, the most common ways are the sole proprietorship and the partnership.

One of the first strategic tasks of an entrepreneur is determining the legal structure of a business. The legal form must fit internal and external relations—i.e., partners or shareholders inside and customers or banks outside—and it has an effect on tax rates. The legal structure can be changed as the business is growing or changing, but this may have complex and costly implications on several functions such as book keeping, contracts, and investor relations

Forming a partnership allows individuals to combine their skills toward benefiting one organization.

Sole Proprietorship

First, an entrepreneur will have to choose the legal structure that is most suitable for the type of enterprise they have. The two major company structures that a small enterprise will tend to utilize are sole proprietorship and partnership. A sole proprietorship is the simplest structure. It only requires one person to start up and operate, and is generally exempt from onerous legal requirements applying to an incorporated entity. The business's profits are actually taxed as the entrepreneur's own income. One of the advantages of this lies in the deductibility of costs outside the concerned business: if a business is profitable, but the entrepreneur suffers a loss in another venture he is engaged in, this loss can be offset so the individual is taxed at a lower rate. However, the major drawback of this type of legal entity is that the individual is liable for anything that may happen to the business. For example, if the enterprise is sued, the owner has to bear all costs and pay any compensation out of his or her own pocket.

INSIDER KNOWLEDGE

THE SARBANES OXLEY ACT *of 2002 was brought in due to the large corporate failures of companies such as Enron and Worldcom. This created more accountability for corporate executives for their actions which included longer jail terms and larger fines for contraventions.*

Partnership

The second most common form for small businesses is the partnership, in which two or more people have ownership of the entity. In this case, one of the few necessities is a contract be drawn up between the partners which rules rights and duties of each party and will thus help in possible (legal) disputes in the future.

This form is commonly used where the talent and experiences of two people are required to ensure that an enterprise is run appropriately, and dual ownership is a better way of ensuring that the partners are remunerated appropriately. A major disadvantage is that the partnership is automatically terminated when one of the partner dies, leaves the partnership or a new partner joins which can be a time consuming and costly. A partnership is a simple and good form for two or more entrepreneurs whose expertise in certain fields add to each other and are equally relevant to the success of the business. Limited partnerships are the same but have limited liability, comparable to a company.

Sole proprietorships often borrow money through personal loans in order to open their own businesses.

Finding Capital

There are several means through which an enterprise is able to raise funds, each with its own advantages and disadvantages, and the budding entrepreneur must choose which is the optimal way.

In both forms—sole proprietorship and partnership—it is likely that the individuals will have to borrow money. The higher risk a company is, the more expensive debt will be, as the bank will charge more interest for loans made. When an organization is high risk, it is less likely to use debt to fund the company, as banks will either charge too much interest to compensate them for the additional risk or not fund the enterprise at all. In this case, it is more likely that a higher risk enterprise will use "equity" i.e., investor funds. In a sole proprietorship, this is not possible if the owner does not want to relinquish ownership of the organization. In the partnership form, investors can also be brought in as "silent partners."

Legal Entity: Corporation

As a small business expands, it may find that the current entity structures of sole proprietorship or partnership may no longer be a suitable structure to meet its needs. This is often the case when small businesses need a new means of raising capital due to rapid expansion. In this case, the "corporation," or the limited liability company, may be an appropriate option.

In a corporation, shares of the company are sold to selected investors or publicly sold on a stock exchange. The shareholders are the owners of the company, but they are generally not liable for any complaints made against the company: the risk to owners generally only extends to the amount they paid for each of their shares.

Another advantage of a corporation is that the company can easily stay in operation past the death or departure of the management as the company has a legal identity separate from managers or owners. Yet corporations are expensive to set up and maintain, mainly due to onerous legal requirements.

above: *The New York Stock Exchange in Wall Street has seen and fueled the rapid growth and sudden crashes of many corporations.*

left: *Manhattan is home to most of the largest incorporated entities in the world.*

MEASURING PERFORMANCE

Measuring performance allows both managers and investors to ascertain the success of an organization against their goals.

There are various tools that allow investors, owners, and managers to ascertain the success of an enterprise both the long and the short term. Typically, this aim is achieved through the analysis of financial measures. Financial measures arise from financial information, i.e., profits, assets, liabilites, etc. However, non-financial measures can also assist the entrepreneurs and investors in comparing their achieved successes to the core goals of an enterprise.

Measuring performance allows investors to make informed decisions regarding the profitability of their investment in a business.

Financial Measures

Financial measures are an important indicator to a business owner or manager to, first and foremost, ascertain the profitability of an enterprise. Numbers arising from the balance sheet (see right for an example), income statement, and cash flow are the primary sources of information within financial measures, and can help the manager or investor, among other things, ascertain profitability.

Financial ratios can also be used to assist in the analysis of an enterprise's performance. However, financial indicators do not give a full picture, as they do not predict the future success of an enterprise. In particular, financial results tend to be more inwardly focused. In this regard, non-financial indicators assist in this task.

Non-Financial Measures

Non-financial indicators allow the manager to analyze the degree to which an enterprise reaches its goals that are not primarily economic. For example, a high level of employee turnover may be a sign of employee dissatisfaction. As employees are one of the key components toward the success of an enterprise, it is important to monitor fluctuation and react to it in order to ensure the future success of an organization.

Additionally, there may be goals that are non-financial, but still play an important role in the company's business philosophy and therefore must be controlled, as, for example, to be environmentally conscious.

21ST CENTURY

TRIPLE BOTTOM LINE REPORTING *is a new concept in economics that is utilized by many large corporations as a response to the public's concern of corporate ethics. This involves the reporting of social and environmental results, as well as economic.*

Balanced Scorecard

The balanced scorecard approach assists in aligning performance measures with an organization's strategy. This method emphasizes the importance of utilizing non-financial measures in an analysis of an enterprise. The approach uses four quadrants which analyze the company in the perspective of financial measures, customer relationships, internal (operational competence), and learning (innovation). This forces the manager to consider all measures, both financial and non-financial, to reach their goals as each quadrant is as important as the other.

The Balance Sheet

On December 31:	2007 ($)	
Assets		
Current assets:		
Cash and cash equivalents	18,000	
Short-term financing receivables	25,000	
Inventories	7,000	
Total current assets	50,000	D
Non-current assets:		
Property, plant, and equipment	57,000	
Less: Accumulated depreciation	(22,000)	
Long-term financing receivables	20,000	
Total non-current assets	55,000	
Total assets	105,000	A
Liabilities		
Current liabilities:		
Accounts payable	22,000	
Total current liabilities	22,000	E
Non-current liabilities		
Long-term debt	42,000	
Total non-current liabilities	42,000	
Total liabilities	64,000	B
Equity		
Stockholder's equity:		
Common stock	31,000	
Retained earnings	10,000	
Total stockholder's equity	41,000	C
Total liabilities and stockholder's equity	105,000	

One of the main financial tools used by investors is a financial statement that consists of a balance sheet, income statement, and cash flow. A financial statement only provides the investor with a snapshot of the company's performance, but the numbers can also be utilized for further analysis.

ANALYSIS USING BALANCE SHEET FIGURES:

A) ASSETS: items which a company utilizes in order to generate wealth. Current assets display the items used within a year. Assets assist in determining the short term viability of a company as well as its prospect for growth.

B) LIABILITIES: items that a company owes in order to obtain assets. Current liabilities are to be paid within one year. The total of liabilities should not exceed that of assets, as this would imply that a company may not be able to generate wealth in the future.

C) STOCKHOLDER'S EQUITY: Assets less liabilities. Indicates the amount that cumulatively belongs to the companys owners, i.e., shareholders. Equity is used by companies as an alternative to borrowing cash in order to acquire assets. Equity is a lower risk form of financing than having debt.

RATIO ANALYSIS:

Ratio analysis is another common tool that is used to measure performance. This method utilizes the base numbers to create meaningful ratios that can help to further analyze a business. Ratios can be compared with other ratios, perhaps from previous years or within different industries.

$$\text{Debt to equity ratio (\%)} = \frac{\text{Total liabilities (B)}}{\text{Stockholders equity (C)}}$$

The debt to equity ratio indicates the proportion of debt funding opposed to equity. A higher ratio shows that operations are primarily financed with debt which may mean an aggressive growth strategy is pursued. However, the additional expenses generated by interest will have to be offset by additional revenue.

$$\text{Current ratio} = \frac{\text{Current assets (D)}}{\text{Current liabilities (E)}}$$

The current ratio shows the business's ability to pay back its debts within one year. A higher ratio implies better solvency in the short-term, a lower one may mean they have issues with solvency.

Monographic Boxes

Analytic Boxes

RELIGION

The belief in some higher entity that exercises power over the course of the world and the people on it is common in all cultures. There are of course many differences. The religions of East Asia, for example, have developed as simple calls to ethical action such as Buddhism or as codes of conduct derived from grandiose pantheons such as Hinduism and Taoism, while the religions of the Middle East believe in a single God and establish rules in order to maintain a relationship with their own God, such as in Judaism, Christianity, and Islam. It does not matter, however, whether it concerns a mountain, a wise teacher, a personal God, or an entire Lord of Hosts—religious attempts to communicate with the holy are always marked by their rituals and rites.

KEY FACTS

RELIGION IS *a transcendence from this world into a "different" higher reality.*

RELIGIOUS SENTIMENT *often presents itself somewhere between reverence and a feeling of security.*

RELIGIOUS ACTIVITIES *bring an individual closer to higher powers and show respect.*

THE EXPERIENCE *of a community is linked with the practice of religion.*

What is religion? | Religions of Africa | Religions of Oceania and Australia | Religions of Central, South, and North America

FOUNDATIONS OF RELIGION AND TRADITIONAL RELIGIONS

Religion is the result of an attempt by people to contact a higher reality. The religious experience provides comprehensive explanations and interpretative models of the world. Traditional religions are based on an intense ceremonial exchange of the living with their ancestors as well as the surrounding spiritual world.

Traditional religions do not differentiate between this world and the spiritual realm.

WHAT IS RELIGION?

Through cults, sacrifices, ceremonies, and prayer, people attempt to establish contact with a higher power. They do this for protection, but also due to a certain degree of fear.

Stories of Creation

Nearly all religions believe that the world and humanity itself was created by some type of higher entity. In monotheistic (one god) religions, god is unanimously considered to be the creator, adviser, and preserver of the world. Within polytheistic (multiple gods) religions, there is often one particular god responsible for creation. The extent to which creation stories can be interpreted literally or symbolically is a matter of dispute among religious followers. They do, however, reject that life originated as a mere "chance" within the frame of natural history.

above: *Biblical creation*

The basic fundamental experience of all religions is the "transcendence" from the visible world to a spiritual one. This concept of a higher world is often perceived on a personal basis and relates to a god or gods. It permeates existence—world and people—while providing individuals with a sense of purpose.

Religious Sentiment and Cults

Religious sentiment is conflicting: A divine being creates and controls the world, therefore an individual gains a sense of comfort and completeness through worship. However, they are also "frightened" by this omnipotent and perhaps omniscient higher being. Sacrifice, prayers, and cultic festivities serve to bring people closer together with this perceived divine power—making it more accessible for protection and guidance. In many religions, god or a higher power is also considered the guiding principle for ethical conduct. Hence, holy commandments and prohibitions direct an individual on Earth.

Community of Believers

An important aspect of all religions is communal religious practice. Of course there are private types of religious worship, but no entirely private religion. Usually worship ceremonies entail songs, prayers, dances, and rituals—all of which ensure solidarity among believers in a community as well as an individual's sense of belonging.

The "higher power" is represented in many religions by a god; Shiva is one of the foremost gods in Hinduism.

THE CONCEPT OF MORTALITY *has been a part of religious belief since its very inception.*

MANY RELIGIONS BELIEVE *in judgment of the dead so as to differentiate between the blessed and the cursed.*

LIFE AFTER DEATH *is determined in many religions by a person's actions during life.*

The burial and commemoration of the dead belong to some of the oldest religious practices.

Immortal Life? Death and Afterlife

RELIGION AND DEATH: A central question in religion is whether a person, or rather their soul, continues to exist after death.

LIFE AFTER DEATH: There are varying perceptions regarding "life after death." Most commonly, post-death existence is influenced by the actions of an individual during life and whether they meet the requirements dictated by their religion. This concept is supplemented by the cycle of rebirth seen in Hinduism and Buddhism, as well as the "holy judgment" present in religions such as Christianity and Islam.

Christianity and Islam consider paradise as the abode of the blessed.

The wheel of life is an important symbol for Buddhism.

The cross and fish were the symbols of early Christians.

A crescent moon: An Islamic symbol since the Ottomans.

INDIGENOUS RELIGIONS IN AFRICA

Contact with ancestors, initiation rites, myths, and magical healing practices that are present within community life play an important role in African religions.

Through Voodoo religious ceremonies, the living make contact with their gods and ancestors. Such ceremonies originated in Benin and Togo in the Caribbean.

The indigenous religions of Africa are mostly based on the communal belief in the forces of nature and ancestors of a tribe. Traditional religious knowledge, e.g., origin myths and healing practices, has been passed on orally. As a result, summarizing this vast variety of religions and cultic practices is difficult. Today, 50 percent of Africans are Christians and 40 percent are Muslims—many are practitioners of syncretic (mixed) variants of these world religions and traditional religions.

Ancestor Cult and Myths

Within surviving traditional tribes, individuals consider themselves especially affiliated with their ethnic group or tribe, and feel closely linked to their ancestors. Ancestors or, as the case may be, spirits of the dead, are present among the living and play an active role in their fate; hence rituals are performed in their honor. Gods, on the other hand, are rather distant beings exhibiting both good and evil characteristics who arbitrarily inflict blessings and punishments upon humanity. Hence in many communities, ancestors are considered to be mediators between gods and people. Tribal myths and stories primarily deal with the origin of the world, animals, and people.

INSIDER KNOWLEDGE

TRADITIONAL HEALERS *consider disease and death as "disturbances" from the world of god and spirits.*

THE YORUBA *in Nigeria believe that their ancestors return to their village on a specific day each year and advise the living.*

VARIOUS INITIATION RITES *include circumcision. The Dogon tribe in Mali believes that male children come into the world with a dual "man-woman" identity, thus circumcision gives them the appropriate sex.*

Rites and Initiations

Rituals play a central role as they establish a balance between humanity, gods, ancestors, and nature while granting an individual protection and the ability to overcome problems of daily life. The integration of an individual into the community starts during adolescence through preset admission rites (initiations) that are often accompanied by tests. Initiation rites symbolize the "death" of the earlier person and subsequent "rebirth" to a higher stage with new rights and duties. As a rule, initiations and religious ceremonies are subject to strict taboos and regulations. Any violation has dire consequences for the perpetrator as it disturbs the balance of the forces and enrages the higher powers. Even burial rites play an important role, as the dead now transcend into the role of ancestors and take on a new role within the community.

In principle, a fetish can be any object that has been given magical powers by a priest.

Magic and Healing Knowledge

Magical practices lie at the center of various rites and ceremonies. Traditionally, there exists both "black" and "white" magic. Thus there are both evil spells and spells used to heal ailments or protect oneself against dark forces. Furthermore, it is common that magic be used in matters of the heart or to predict the future. In certain localities, "witches" and "sorcerers" are persecuted and expelled when they are linked with specific cases of bad luck.

CIRCULAR DANCING INTO A TRANCE *in certain religions serves to contact the "other world" and higher entities.*

VARIOUS RITUAL DANCES *are an integral part of festivities, harvests, or hunts.*

DANCING ALSO *plays a role in funeral ceremonies, particularly in death and ancestor cults.*

The symbolism of a dance is often portrayed through masks.

Ritual Dance

SELDOM ARE DANCES not present in an African religious ceremony. They are distinctive with a specific sequence of steps and robust rhythms. The dancers concentrate on the "consonance" of bodily and spiritual experience. They often dance right up to the point of exhaustion, then collapse and fall into a trance. According to voodoo beliefs, the bodies of these dancers are "possessed" by gods and spirits.

RITUAL DANCES are usually intended to summon the power of a particular entity such as the sun or of an animal during a hunt. Through the dance, the energy from that which is sought is symbolically represented by the dancer.

above: *Ritual dance of the Matakam in Cameroon*
right: *Mask dance of the Dogon tribe in Mali*

RELIGION

RELIGIONS OF OCEANIA AND AUSTRALIA

The religions of Oceania and Australia are based on beliefs that draw strong links between their followers and the world of ancestors and spirits. This "other world" is always present in daily life.

Ayers Rock, also known as "Uluru," is considered to be holy by the Aborigines. The site is believed to possess great spiritual powers.

The religions of the Australasian indigenous people, such as the islanders of Oceania, the Maori in New Zealand, and the Australian Aborigines, are extremely diverse. Only a few basic similarities can be detected in their world perceptions.

The Religions of Oceania

The concept of religion used by Western culture does not represent the beliefs of Polynesians, who do not differentiate between spiritual and observable worlds. Ancestors, spirits, and gods are believed to be present in daily life. They are thought to inhabit the world alongside the living, connected by magical bonds to the people, animals, and plants.

This reciprocative diffusion of "both worlds" has strong effects on the public life of Polynesians, which is mostly composed of strong hierarchical layers. Almost all activities like handicraft, art, hunting, fishing, festivities, and battles are subjected to strict regulation and purification ceremonies. For example, some places should be visited only at specific times or by certain people.

The tradition of oral instruction is common to all Oceanic religions. Their narratives and tales usually pertain to creation myths, which describe and narrate stories related to the origin of their island and the people therein. The reverence of gods and spirits also varies from region to region and is related to individual communities. The ancient ancestors of these tribes are often considered to be in close proximity to the (creator) gods. On certain islands, god-kings are revered as direct descendants of gods. It is found quite frequently that extraordinary natural locations such as mountains and, above all, volcanoes are considered the home of the gods.

Mana—Ancient Concept of Religion?

The quest for a possible "ancient concept" of religion leads us to the Oceanic "mana." Mana is a very comprehensive concept originally meaning "great power." It refers to a spiritual and universal energy that pervades both the invisible and visible realm, while facilitating contact between the two. At the same time every object, every living being and every person is said to have a personal mana that characterizes the individual persona, equipping a few with extraordinary powers to achieve great accomplishments.

above: *Fetishes are objects that have been provided with mana.*

INSIDER KNOWLEDGE

NARRATIVES *about the Dreamtime are constantly being edited and modified in "dream trails."*

ANCIENT ANCESTORS AND TOTEM SPIRITS *are revered by individual clans in forms of both animals and people.*

Dreamtime of the Aborigines

According to the traditional beliefs of indigenous Australians, human lives are closely linked with the "Dreamtime", an earlier time during which the world, plants, animals, and later humans were created.

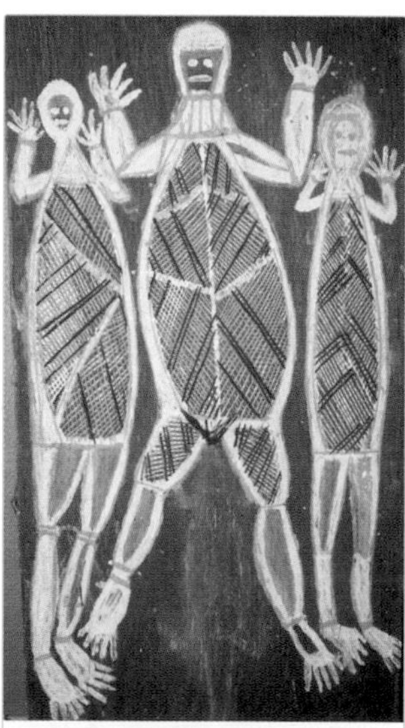

Spirits or entities of the Dreamtime are portrayed in animalistic and humanistic forms.

The ever present spirits, ancestors and mythological beings are contacted through meditation and communal ceremonies. Dreamtime has lasting effects on the present as the spiritual entities that entered the world during "dreaming" left behind forces in special locations, which continue to influence life today. During dreamtime, spiritual beings ("sky heroes") established human culture, communal laws, and harmonious co-existence with nature. As these are considered valid to date, myths are also still important as they are considered to embody community knowledge and are passed on through the oral narrative tradition.

Cargo Cults

The cargo cults in Melanesia originated from the 19th century as a result of the natives coming into contact with Western explorers and their goods, which arrived by sea to the island. The Melanesians believed these goods were gifts from their ancestors. The cults prepared themselves for further gifts and the arrival of an apocalyptic "redeemer." As more packages landed in the island, not reaching their intended destination, especially in WWII, the doomsday vision increased, igniting an outbreak of social unrest.

above: *The arrival of James Cook at New Hebrides in 1774*

Australian Aborigines during a religious ceremony for the Emu Totem sometime before 1928.

RELIGION

NATIVE AMERICAN RELIGIONS

Today, the indigenous people of South America have preserved pieces of their religious faiths; those of North America are once again retracing their original shamanistic religions.

While only remains are found from the religions of the advanced ancient cultures of Central and South America, elements of the North American indigenous people, including both the Native Americans and the Inuit of northern Canada and Greenland, have been maintained.

The chieftain of a tribe had religious responsibilities alongside legal and political functions.

Legacy of Advanced Cultures

When the Spaniards conquered Central and South America in the 16th century, they systematically destroyed the native religions in the region: the Aztec, Incas, and Maya. Within their martial city-states with state-controlled agronomy, myths regarding the gods and creation, astrological calculations based on constellations, their own independently created calendar, and cultic ceremonies that included human sacrifice all played an important cultural role. Christianity, which was later actively propagated amid the native population, intermingled with the traditional cults and mystical ceremonies originating from the ancient religious culture to create a unique religion referred to as "Mayan Catholicism," which is still practiced to date.

Religions of North America

The indigenous people of North America are often referred to as Native Americans. Originally, they were primarily hunters and gatherers. They placed great importance on their relationship with the animals they hunted and the spirit guardians of each species. Hunting ceremonies gave thanks and nurtured these relationships. The sedentary, agrarian communities conducted religious ceremonies during occasions such as maturity rites, harvests, or periods of drought. Priests often led these ceremonies, while shamans and healers also held sacred functions.

All the tribes shared the common belief in supernatural, often impersonal powers associated with the surrounding environment. However, there were also personal guardian spirits that were represented by the forces of objects and living beings. Some tribes also revered a higher spiritual being, named "Wakan Tanka" by the Sioux and "Manito" by the Algonquian.

One special phenomenon was the reverence of the dead, be it a plant or an animal. The dead were revered with special emotional connection. The name of a particular tribe was often attributed to its totem animal, which drew lines of demarcation between various groups. There were also "medicinal alliances" named after animals such as the Eagle, Bear, Buffalo, or Otter alliances. These groups often shared their medical or sacred knowledge.

Totem poles erected near residential dwellings or tents depict the heraldic animal of a family.

Many indigenous North Americans converted to Christianity in light of the European conquest of the continent and the accompanying Christianizing mission. Hence, this saw an abrupt discontinuation of traditions. The revived Indian religions of this era are innovations emerging from traditional and Christian elements.

Stepped pyramid temples that were dedicated to the gods are common of the pre-Columbian (before Columbus) religions of Central America.

SHAMANS *are equipped with extraordinary powers and are mediators between various worlds.*

THE KNOWLEDGE OF HEALING: *A few Shamans specialize in specific ailments such as fractures, arrow or gunshot wounds, and births.*

MANY NATIVE AMERICAN CHIEFS *were also popular as healers, such as the Apache chief Geronimo.*

Healer from the Apsaroke tribe

Healers and Shamans

SHAMANS EXISTED in nearly all hunting-gathering cultures. They could be either male or female. They undertook functions as priests, healers, preserver of tribal cultural knowledge, and interpreters of dreams. Primarily, their responsibilities centered around their ability to establish contact with the "other world" of spirits, ancestors, and totem animals. For this purpose, they would enter a trance-like state through meditation, dance, drumming, or even, at times, psychedelic drugs.

THE "JOB" OF SHAMAN cannot be learnt, but rather it is believed that the spirits select the shaman to whom they wish to communicate. The shaman usually begins his initiation with a life threatening crisis or illness. After this, he is "reborn" as a new person.

A magic healer during a cultural ritual performed on the land of the pre-Columbian Inca ruins of Rumicucho.

RELIGION

KEY FACTS

BELIEFS: *Unity of man and worldly souls (man-nature unity), the transmigration, pantheon of gods, and temple worship.*

SIGNIFICANT SCRIPTURES: *Text canons of the Vedas and the Bhagavad-Gita.*

HINDU SOCIETY *is significantly characterized by the traditional caste system, which dictates rigid social stratification.*

HINDUISM—A WORLD RELIGION BETWEEN UNITY AND DIVERSITY

Originating nearly 3,000 years ago, Hinduism is the world's third largest religion with approximately 900 million followers spanning from East to West. At the same time, Hinduism acts as a collective term to refer to the adherents of various religious rituals and beliefs who are without a common god, founder, church, or scriptures.

The Persians named the inhabitants of the banks of the Indus River "Hindus."

HINDUISM'S TEACHINGS OF WISDOM

Despite the great diversity of Hinduism, there are a few similar beliefs that are held by all Hindu practitioners. These fundamental beliefs include reincarnation, liberation from the state of samsara through moksha, and the laws of karma and dharma. The Hindu way of life is shaped around such concepts.

The Hindu's view of the world is fundamentally based on the concept of *samsara*, the cycle of rebirth. According to samsara, every person has a divine inner truth or soul—the *atman*. This is similar to the infinite cosmic spirit that encompasses everything in the world—the *Brahman*. The atman is believed to be subjugated by the illusory power of *maya* (Sanskrit: "illusion-magic"), which causes a person to identify with all that is worldly and perishable. Trapped by this imagined reality, the atman wanders through various existences, unable to escape samsara. Only when the atman recognizes its true nature through intuitive realization, namely by unifying with the immortal Brahman, it attains *moksha*—salvation. This marks the atman's exit from the cycle of rebirth and the law of karma. Yoga, asceticism, meditation, and worshipping the gods are paths to moksha.

TRACES OF HINDUISM *are found as far back as the second millennium B.C.*

THE ARYANS *brought the Vedic religion to India with their migration to the region.*

IN BRAHMANISM, *priests function as intermediaries between the gods and people.*

Agni, the Vedic god of fire, was an important facet of Brahmanism. Giving sacrificial offerings to him dominated various rituals.

The Origin of Hinduism

THE ROOTS OF HINDUISM can be traced to the Indus Valley, or Harappan, civilization. This highly advanced and urban culture existed in current-day Pakistan from the third to the second millennium B.C. While very little is known about the Harappan religion, surviving inscriptions on seals reflect the worship of a female deity and a horned predecessor to Shiva. Trees and animals also held religious significance.

BRAHMANISM, an early form of Hinduism, dates back to the Vedic religion of the Aryans, nomads from Central Asia who migrated to India in ca 2000 B.C. Their culture was defined by a multitude of rituals, the utilization of Sanskrit, the Vedas, and the worship of Brahman and gods like Indra, Agni, and Vayu.

Shiva is thought to have originated from the Vedic god Rudra. Both Rudra and Shiva control the opposite forces of destruction and preservation.

Karma and Dharma

Hindus believe in the cosmic law of karma, the "fruits of action." The effects of moral actions are carried over after death to the next existence, influencing the subsequent birth either positively or negatively. There is a believed consequence for every selfish action of the atman, who is tied to the cycle of birth, death, and rebirth. Staunch Hindus try to adhere to the law of dharma. Holding *dharma* (Sanskrit: "proper conduct") as the universal truth, Hindus strive to preserve it through daily ceremonies. Today dharma stands as an ethical guide for Hindus, providing an individual with a code of conduct. While *sanatana* dharma holds virtues such as non-violence and purity as the public law for every Hindu, *svadharma* is a more personal version of the concept of dharma.

The Kathakali dance is a combination of dance, theatrics, mimicry, music, and ritual that narrates stories from the great Indian epics.

Cows are seen as a gift of the god Brahman and are therefore considered holy by the Hindus. This can possibly be traced back to the Aryans, whose nomadic lifestyle was closely linked to cattle breeding.

LITERATURE AND THE GODS

A characteristic of Hinduism is the existence of a large pantheon of gods that have evolved over the centuries to include Vedic gods, various local deities, and popular gods.

Religious Texts

Hinduism's holy scriptures were composed in the holy language of Sanskrit. They are composed of two types of texts: sruti and smriti. The *sruti* (Sanskrit: "heard") texts were created through the transmission of eternal truth and knowledge by the gods to a transcriber. Texts written in this manner, known collectively as the Vedas (Sanskrit: "knowledge"), contain instructions for sacrificial rituals, mantras, and hymns. The *smriti* (Sanskrit: "remembered") texts have been passed down through generations. These include epics such as "Mahabharata" and "Ramayana," legal texts, and other mythological tales.

above: *For centuries, the Vedas were passed down through the generations by oral recitation.* **right:** *The "Bhagavad-Gita" is a popular chapter of the "Mahabharata." It tells of Krishna's instructions to Arjuna, the warrior.*

The disruptive fury of goddess Kali is not directed toward mortals; instead it is aimed at demons. She is seen by Hindus as a protective mother figure over humankind.

There are six schools of philosophy in Hinduism: Yoga, Samkhya, Nyaya, Vaisheshika, Purva Mimamsa, and Vedanta. There are various notions regarding the gods of Hinduism. A few Hindus believe that the gods are manifestations of the worldly soul, Brahman. Some Hindus believe that Vishnu is the origin of all that exists and the source of human consciousness. Others believe in Shiva or Krishna as the incarnations of Vishnu. There is, however, one common belief among all these variations. The popular gods have been ingrained within the local traditions and subsequently have a large following. Three of these gods—Vishnu the benevolent preserver, Shiva the force of destruction, and Brahman the creator—form a trinity, the Trimurti.

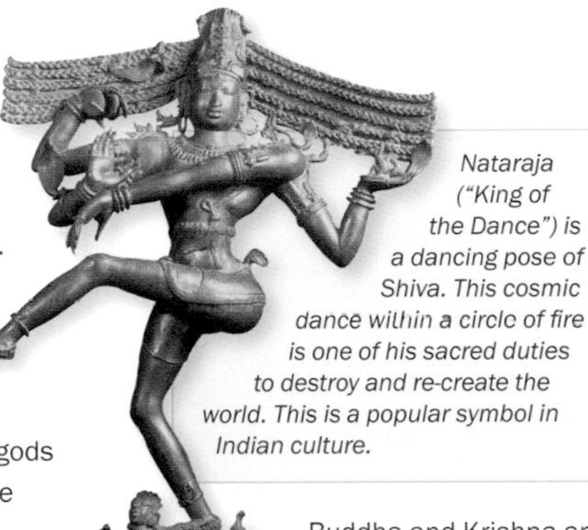

Nataraja ("King of the Dance") is a dancing pose of Shiva. This cosmic dance within a circle of fire is one of his sacred duties to destroy and re-create the world. This is a popular symbol in Indian culture.

While Brahma does not have a wide following today, Shiva is worshipped in various manifestations including Nataraja (King of the Dance) and as an ascetic seated on a tiger and his body smeared with ash. As most Indian gods are assigned animals as their symbolic modes of transport, Shiva is pictured with a trident on the bull Nandi. Vishnu is the mild preserver of the world and reveals himself to people in various forms, both human and animalistic. The Vaishnavas, the followers of Vishnu, believe that Buddha and Krishna are incarnations of Vishnu and that he will emerge again in yet another form. The image of the calm Vishnu reclining on his *naga* (snake) is very common. He is often pictured with a conch, discus, lotus, and mace. His mount is Garuda, a mythical beast—half human and half eagle.

Pictured here within their marriage procession, the myths of Rama and Sita are often entwined within the epic of Ramayana. Also featured are the monkey king Hanuman, Rama's brother Lakshmana, and the demon Ravana.

The Female Deities

Shaktism holds great significance in Bengal, Assam, and Kashmir. This tradition attributes all existence to a female power of creation, Shakti. The worship of Shakti is personalized by Indian idol worship; goddesses like Lakshmi, Durga, and Kali are worshipped as aspects of Shaktism. Within modern Hinduism, Kali has the largest number of followers. She is mostly depicted as an eight-armed destroyer with a chain around her neck made up of the skulls of demons. Kali and Parvati, a more gentle embodiment of Shakti, are often pictured with the male god Shiva. Another goddess, Saraswati, was actually one of the earlier Vedic goddesses but was integrated into the Hindu pantheon of gods. In the Vedic Ages, she was worshipped as the river goddess while today she is considered the goddess of learning, and is often seen playing an instrument with two of her four hands.

Ganesha

The elephant-god is probably one of the most popular gods of India. According to one popular version of the myth, Ganesha's elephant head is attributed to a fit of rage suffered by his father Shiva. When Shiva left his wife Parvati in pursuit of ascetic pleasures, she created Ganesha through her own divine powers. This angered Shiva who subsequently beheaded Ganesha, throwing Parvati into a state of utter despair. As Shiva realized the rashness of his behavior, he replaced Ganesha's head with that of the first living creature that passed his way: an elephant. Ganesha, the god of luck, is believed to help one overcome life's troubles. His mount Vahan, the rat, is a symbol for the strength that is possessed by even the smallest living being.

above: *Ganesha is often depicted seated on his mount, the rat, along with a bowl of sweets and a lotus. He is worshipped across India, but enjoys predominant significance in Mumbai (Bombay).*

HINDU SOCIETY

The life of a Hindu is shaped by many rites of passage, social and religious norms, and religious festivities. Among them are sacrificial rituals to the deities and fulfilling familial duties.

The life of a traditional Hindu is divided into four phases, or *asramas*. The first asrama is the phase of a student during which the Hindu receives religious education from a guru. This is followed by the stage of beginning a family and the third phase of retreat and seclusion. The final, and completely voluntary, phase is the complete renunciation of the secular world as one lives as a wandering, homeless ascetic.

Rites of passage are associated with each of the asramas. The very first is the *upanayana*, which initiates the start of the first stage of studentship and a second birth; born into society after the first birth of being born in nature. Marriage is another important rite of passage that is often arranged by the parents. Aside from caste affiliation and horoscopes, additional factors including color of skin, education, and age are considered in arranging marriage. Male offspring hold significant value to the male figurehead of every Hindu family. Only a son can perform the rituals following the death of his father, which ensure that the deceased, according to some, will not be reincarnated.

There are fewer rites of passage within the lives of Hindu women. Their major life event is marriage, after which the bride moves into the home of her spouse's family. She is then subordinate to her mother-in-law and assumes responsibility for housekeeping. Holding considerably less power than men, Hindu women live a life that is centered on the household and the birthing of children.

Diwali, the festival of lights, is celebrated across India with fireworks and brightly lit streets.

It is considered especially significant to give an offering of puja at the holy Ganges River.

Kumbh Mela is one of the largest Hindu festivals held at different locales once every 12 years. In 2001, about 70 million believers took part in celebrations.

The Way of the Yogi

YOGA IS A PHILOSOPHY and religious practice that concerns itself with integrating the inner soul of the Atman with the divine soul of the Brahman. Through yoga, a yogi gains physical and mental self-control that results in a higher state of consciousness. Practitioners believe the human body contains channels, or *nadis*, through which subtle energy flows. The nadis intersect at points called *chakras*, centers of energy found along the spinal column. Meaning "the wheel of life" in Sanskrit, chakras are believed to control the body's systems and organs.

The lotus position is one of the most important postures in yoga.

There are six chakras, or centers of energy, present in the body. They are all controlled by an additional chakra, the Sahasrara or crown chakra of consciousness that binds an individual to the spiritual world.

The Muladhara or base chakra is the seat of human creative potential.

The Caste System

Hindu society is structured according to the social and religious hierarchy of the caste system. Originally four large castes or "varnas" existed forming the hierarchy of India: The "sudra" (laborers), "vaishya" (merchants), "kshatriya" (warriors), and at the top the revered "brahmin" (priests). Today, numerous subcastes or "jatis" are based on occupations. Although the caste system was abolished in 1949, it continues to define Indian society even now.

above: *Casteless people, or "untouchables," form the very bottom of the hierarchy.*

Religious Practices

The prayer ritual of puja stands at the center of Hindu religious practice and is performed both within the home as well as temples. Food offerings of *ghee* (clarified butter), rice, and flowers are often placed before visual depictions of the gods. Holy Sanskrit verses are recited during puja while holy food is distributed among the participants. Pilgrimage is another cornerstone of Hindu life. Holy sites and cities in India such as Varanasi, Puri, and Haridwar are popular with pilgrims due to the activities of gods and mythological heroes. Pilgrimages are often associated with visits to religious festivals such as the Kumbh Mela, Holi, or Dussehra.

21ST CENTURY

THE DALIT MOVEMENT: *Casteless Indians are referred to as Dalits or "untouchables." Today they still compose the lowest level of Hindu society and are often seen working in lowly occupations including latrine cleaning and leather-working. The Bahujan Samaj Party, among others, fights for the rights of dalits and is one of the largest parties in the populous state of Uttar Pradesh since the elections of 2002.*

RELIGIOUS SCHOOLS, DIVISIONS, AND COUNTER-MOVEMENTS

Apart from traditional religious denominations, numerous schools of neo-Hinduism exist today. In contrast, Sikhism and Jainism have risen to an important position in Hinduism.

Two very important branches of Hinduism are Vaishnavism and Shaivism. The central point of their religion is the veneration of either Vishnu or Shiva. Followers of Vaishnavism worship Vishnu as well as his various incarnations (p. 223), primarily Rama or Krishna. Within Vaishnavism, there are numerous sects, such as Gaudiya Vaishnavism and Swaminarayanism.

Likewise, the followers of Shiva reflect various divisions and schools. The Pasupata sect worships Shiva in the form of Pasupati, lord of animals. They are ascetic Shaivas who follow animal vows, ritualistically smear themselves with ash, and live in isolation. Another extremist Shaivite sect is the Kapalikas, or "bearers of the skull-bowl." Worshipping Shiva in the form of Lord Bhairava, the Kapalikas imitate him by living on cremation grounds and use skulls as bowls.

A form of worship that has come to infiltrate many Hindu sects is *bhakti* (Sanskrit: "path of devotion"). While its distinctive details are dependent upon the beliefs of the sect, bhakti in general refers to selfless sacrifice for a deity. Furthermore, the heart rather than the spirit acts as an intermediary between an individual and god. It is this direct connection that has led to bhakti being followed by a large number of Hindus.

Vaishnavas, followers of Vishnu, wear white marks on their forehead frequently in the shape of a U, T, or Y.

Neo-Hinduism

Since the 1950s, neo-Hinduism has evolved from within the multiple movements of Hinduism that have been initiated by contemporary gurus. Some of these newly emerging sects have spread to the West, for example, the Hare Krishna movement or the neo-Sannyasins, the followers of the guru Osho. Other famous gurus are Vivekananda, Yogananda, and Aurobindo. The teachings of these Gurus are often associated with a certain practice of yoga.

Jainism

Developing at the same time as Buddhism (p. 226), came Jainism, whose founder Mahavira is known by his followers as Jina, "the victorious one." Along with Buddha, Mahavira was an opponent of the caste system and believed that the path of salvation was open for every human being. He was the last of the 24 Jain Tirthankars or "ford-makers." Mahavira strove to show people the path toward salvation. Like Hinduism, Jainism also believes that the Atman, or soul, is trapped within the cycle of rebirth. Liberation is dependent on the strict adherence to ethical laws, the most important of which is Ahimsa, the vow of non-violence against living beings. The Jains wear a mouth guard to avoid inadvertently swallowing insects, while others sweep the ground before their feet to prevent anything from being trampled. The Jain community is divided between lay followers and ordained monks or nuns.

The worship of Hanuman, the monkey god, is closely connected with the mythical hero Rama. Hanuman has experienced a large following ever since.

SIKHISM *was founded in the 16th century in Punjab by Guru Nanak.*

SIKH MEANS "DISCIPLE": *Male Sikhs often bear the surname Singh or "lion" while female Sikhs are called Kaur or "princess."*

An orthodox Khalsa-Sikh can be identified from the five Ks: Kesh (uncut hair), Kanga (comb), Kachera (knee-length garment), Kara (circular metal bracelet), and Kirpan (ceremonial dagger).

Sikhism: Bridging Islam and Hinduism

SIKHISM HAS around 23 million followers, a majority of whom live in the Indian state of Punjab. Its basis of faith borrows aspects from Islam as well as Hinduism, but it does not identify itself with any of these religions. Sikhs believe in only one god that is present within every individual. Sikhs search for this proximity through meditation and inwardly repeating the name of god. They believe that one can be liberated from the cycle of rebirth only through deep devotion to god during their life.

SIKHISM REJECTS many aspects of Hinduism including the caste system, worshipping visual depictions of deities, and gender inequality. The sect's teachings and ideals are contained in their holy book, "Guru Granth Sahib." Because they consider all life as having holy origin, vegetarianism is prevalent among Sikh practitioners.

The Golden Temple in Punjab is the main shrine for the Sikhs.

A Jain follower with a mouth guard during a visit to a temple.

KEY FACTS

BUDDHISM ORIGINATED *in India. From here its holy teachings spread as far as East Asia.*

CORE PHILOSOPHICAL TEACHINGS *are the Four Noble Truths and the Eightfold Path.*

THE BUDDHIST COMMUNITY *is called sangha. It consists of lay followers, monks, and nuns.*

THERE ARE *over 300 million practicing Buddhists worldwide today.*

The life of Buddha—facts and myths | Lectures of the cycle of existence

BUDDHISM—THE MIDDLE PATH TO NIRVANA

The Buddhist religion does not have a deity. It encourages the self-awareness of its followers and also the critical scrutinizing of the Buddhist teachings of salvation. The central teachings of the Buddha are the Four Noble Truths as well as overcoming earthly suffering through following the Eightfold Path.

➔ *The philosophy of Buddhism is based on the teachings of Buddha Siddhartha Gautama.*

THE LIFE OF BUDDHA—FACTS AND MYTHS

Buddha, meaning the "Enlightened One," is one of the four titles for Siddhartha Gautama. While his teachings are the basis of Buddhism, his life is surrounded by numerous tales.

One myth of Buddha's birth has him coming out of Queen Maya's right hip during a journey.
right: *Indian Buddha from Gandara*

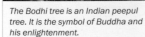

The Bodhi tree is an Indian peepul tree. It is the symbol of Buddha and his enlightenment.

According to Buddhist mythology, the young Siddhartha lived an isolated life within a grand palace. One day he was curious about the outside world and decided to leave his palace, undertaking four excursions. In doing so, Siddhartha saw an elderly man, a diseased man and a corpse for the first time in his life and was shattered by these experiences. During his fourth excursion, he came across a begging monk. Siddhartha was so struck by the monk's calmness and serenity that he decided to abandon worldly life and concern himself only with the questions of existence.

Asceticism and Enlightenment

For six years, Siddhartha strictly practiced asceticism; however, he did not gain any insight into the true nature of things. He did, however, understand that there had to be an intermediate path between a life of asceticism and a life of luxury. He decided to meditate under a Bodhi tree as long as he could until he could find the solution to human suffering. After battling his inner demons and primal cravings, Siddhartha became internally free and achieved enlightenment.

Wheel of Life

After attaining enlightenment, Buddha found himself amidst a rapidly increasing number of lay followers, monks, and nuns. In light of this, he began to make sermons about his path to salvation and launched his "Wheel of Life." Buddha dedicated his entire life to traveling and preaching about the middle path to salvation. He later succumbed to food poisoning at the age of 80. According to the Buddhist belief, with his death he reached Nirvana.

LIFETIME: *around fifth or fourth century B.C.*

LINEAGE: *from the Shakya line*

LEGENDS: *There are various legends on the life of Buddha, many about his birth and youth.*

The Mahabodhi temple (completed in the 14th century) was constructed in front of the Bodhi tree, where Buddha reached enlightenment.

The Historical Buddha

THE EXACT LIFETIME OF THE HISTORICAL BUDDHA cannot be accurately dated. According to island chronicles from Sri Lanka, Siddhartha Gautama lived from 560 B.C. until 480 B.C. This statistic, however, is doubted today. Instead, his lifetime is roughly estimated to be around fifth and fourth century B.C.

VERY LITTLE FROM THE LIFE OF BUDDHA can be historically proved. It is certain that Buddha descended from the aristocratic Shakya tribe, which lived in the Republic of Kapilavastu on the border between India and Nepal. Additionally it is believed that Siddhartha Gautama was married and had a son before taking up the ascetic movement at the age of 29.

The travels of Buddha

LECTURES OF THE CYCLE OF EXISTENCE

The cycle of samsara and the teachings on suffering are fundamentals of Buddhism. The main Buddhist teachings seek primarily to provide a method of liberation from all suffering.

Samsara means "continuous movement" and is often translated as a cycle or reincarnation. Much like in Hinduism, Buddhism holds the concept that there is a cycle of birth and consequent decay that is shaped by suffering.

According to the teachings of Buddha, the cycle of rebirth is perpetuated by 12 factors that build upon one another. The first is nescience or ignorance regarding the Four Noble Truths and the sorrow of all beings. From these samsaras, spiritual and physical intended actions come into being. In this complex process called "Chain of Causation," Buddhism explains the thirst for continuous existence by describing the interaction between name and form, the arising of sensation, feeling, disposition, and consciousness. Ignorance (avijja) as the starting point, gives rise to attachment or clinging to pleasant states or aversion to unpleasant states, leading to wrongful actions and further suffering. In this way, ignorance leads to desire for existence and thus, birth inevitably leads to old age, sickness and death. Buddhism proposes the Eightfold Noble Path as a way to the cessation of suffering and a liberation from this endless cycle of rebirths. Within ignorant creatures, the experience of these feelings results in a thirst for further sensations.

Laughing Chinese Buddha

Thirst and ignorance lead to the embracing of another birth from which a similarly sorrowful life follows along the path of its predecessor, including old age and death.

Samsara is not the same as transmigration of the soul. Buddhism rejects the conception of an eternal, constant soul for living beings. According to Buddhism a person is made up of five factors of existence, the skandhas: body (*rupa*), feelings (*vedana*), perceptions (*samjna*), mental formations (*samskara*), and consciousness (*vijnana*). The identification of a person with their feelings and thoughts or the presumption of being a unique person in possession of an individual eternal soul was dismissed by Buddha as self-conceit.

Indian emperor Ashoka made the Buddhist teachings accessible to his subjects through stone edicts.

21ST CENTURY

"BUDDHISM LITE" *is a popular way of life in the U.S. and Europe. The aim is to adapt Buddhism to Western lifestyles while keeping mainly to the basic principles of wellness and relaxation.*

The Four Noble Truths

The Four Noble Truths form the basis of the Buddhist teachings. The first truth, *dukkha*, is that suffering exists. Buddha stressed that everything in life was linked with sorrow: birth, sickness, old age, death, anger, rage, and pain. Likewise, separation from something one likes and union with something one does not like are also sorrowful. According to the second truth, *samudaya*, the source of human suffering is *tanha*, or craving, which, along with ignorance and hate, forms the root of all evil. Buddha teaches in the third truth, *nirodha*, that suffering can end and must be accepted as something not absolute. The fourth truth, *magga*, details the end of suffering, which is the Eightfold Path.

The Eightfold Path

The Eightfold Path in Buddhism leads to the end of sorrow. It is divided into three catagories: wisdom, ethical control, and mental discipline. By following the path, a person achieves liberation from desire and selfishness, both of which are the route to samsara and continuous rebirth into a world of suffering.

The Indian flag shows the Wheel of Life. It is today a symbol for movement and unity of Indians.

Bowing before a Buddhist statue is an exercise of humility.

RELIGION

The Buddhist World View

MANY BUDDHISTS envisage five or sometimes six realms of the world. The three bottom levels are the hell realm, the realm of hunger and the realm of animality, then follows the realm of humanity and the realm of heaven, where the asuras live. Asuras are demons, who are ruled by their jealousy of the gods. The pretas, hungry ghosts, have enormous bellies and tiny mouths so that they can never satisfy their hunger.

Withdrawal from samsara is possible only through rebirth as a human being. The Devas, gods, cannot understand the necessity of Buddhist salvation due to their happy existence.

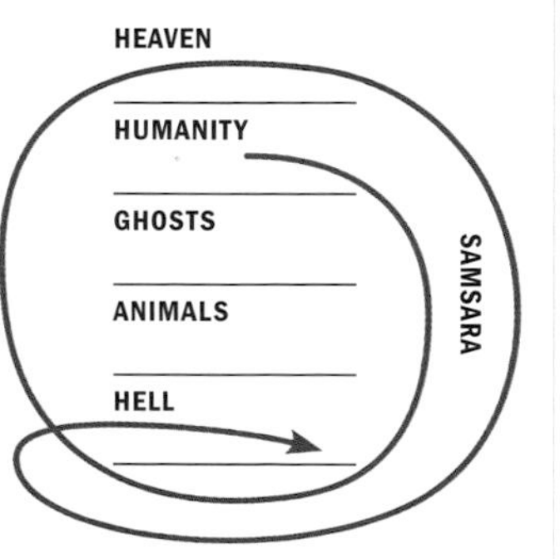

Animals cannot attain enlightenment because of their instincts. Buddha has, however, also addressed them in his lectures.

The realm into which a person is born depends on their karma. The ultimate goal being to ascend the realms.

KEY FACTS

THE TEACHINGS AND RELIGIONS *of China and Japan are a hallmark of their cultural perceptions of empire.*

MOST TEACHINGS *draw influence from other religions, like Buddhism.*

SHINTO AND CONFUCIANISM *were used to glorify the East Asian emperor and state cults.*

ALL TEACHINGS DEVELOPED INTO *folk religions that were thus made accessible to normal believers.*

Shinto—Japan's way of the gods | Confucianism and Taoism

THE RELIGIONS OF CHINA AND JAPAN

The religions of Japan and China are responsible for the perpetuated appreciation of ancestoral and familial ties, traditions, and state institutions within both countries. Shinto and Confucianism in particular developed honorable codes of behavior that included a valued observance of tradition as well as service to the community. The religions of East Asia were flexible in terms of acceptance and change, and could therefore accommodate the religious and cultic needs of all layers of society.

The religions of Japan and China are closely linked with the cultural and historical development of these countries.

SHINTO—JAPAN'S WAY OF THE GODS

The followers of Shinto revere forces of nature and "kami" (gods), who are called upon during ceremonies. Although no longer a state religion, it is historically linked to the Japanese emperor-cult.

Emperor Akihito during a ritualistic rice harvest, which is a part of the ceremonial duties of the "tenno."

Shinto means "the way of the gods" and is the indigenous animistic religion that has shaped, and continues to shape, Japanese culture. Comprising numerous cults and various forms, Shinto is practiced by more than 80 percent of Japanese people today. With the passage of time, there has been a multifaceted intermingling of Shinto concepts with Confucianism and Buddhism.

The Kami

Shintoism has a multitude of gods (*kami*) as each extraordinary event arouses religious veneration, such as natural phenomena which are ascribed to animistic spirits. Hence, kami are not personal beings, but instead are forces of nature, extraordinary places like mountains or springs, as well as the souls of the dead. Even significant personalities are considered divine. The kami life force can also "transcend" to people and make them capable of performing special feats.

The followers of Shinto should live in harmony with kami, offer prayers in their honor, and show thanks by visiting shrines. The predominant cultural activities include purification rites, reverence of nature, and religious festivities that are often accompanied by games and competitions.

Mythology and the Emperor-Cult

Shinto mythological tales on the origin of the Japanese state, detail its creation through the union of married gods Izanagi and Izanami with the imperial dynasty. Due to this divine lineage, the Japanese emperor (*tenno*) was soon considered a god.

Amalgamation of Shinto and Confucianism (p. 229) influenced the rigid code of the samurai, whose greatest honor was to fight and die in the service of the emperor. In the 19th century, this took on a nationalistic and imperialistic connotation. After the capitulation of Japan in 1945, the emperor officially ended his claim to "divinity." To this day, the tenno continues to participate in important public Shinto ceremonies.

During marriages, the bridal couple is blessed and spiritually cleansed by a priest.

The holy rocks at Futamigaura are yearly bound together with ropes. This is to symbolize the connection between the two gods who gave rise to Japan.

AMATERASU *was originally a tutelary deity and was represented on battle armor.*

EACH YEAR *approximately 6 million pilgrims visit the Grand Shrine at Ise.*

THE MAIN SHRINES *are the inner shrine (Naiku) and the outer shrine (Geku).*

The former flag of Japan depicted the symbol of the sun-goddess Amaterasu.

Amaterasu and the Grand Shrine at Ise

SUN-GODDESS AMATERASU is the most revered goddess in Japanese mythology. The Grand Shine at Ise stands as proof of the degree to which she is esteemed, comprising over 65 complex structures. This is the main shrine of the Shinto and a "symbol of the state and unity of the Japanese people." The holy symbols of Shinto and the insignia of Amaterasu—a sword, mirror, and jade stone—have been preserved in the innermost shrine.

ACCORDING TO MYTHOLOGY, Amaterasu's grandson Ninigi no Mikoto descended to Earth, thus initiating the tenno lineage. His grandson was the first emperor Jimmu, who is thought to have started the emperor cult.

The structures in the Grand Shrine at Ise are demolished and rebuilt every 25 years, thus ensuring that every generation can be involved.

CONFUCIANISM AND TAOISM

While Confucianism was originally a set of ethical teachings, Taoism began as a religious community that concerned itself with the search for elementary forces of the universe.

The most important religious traditions in China are Buddhism, which originated in India, and Taoism. Beginning as an ethical philosophy, Confucianism gained religious elements only at a later stage. Both indigenous Chinese religions include references to ancient Chinese concepts such as "yin and yang" as well as the cult of ancestor worship.

Children continue to learn about the Confucius rules of life today.

Confucianism—Ethics of "Humanity"

Confucianism developed as a secular ideology regarding an ethical-political view of the world. It continues to define the moral views and code of conduct for the Chinese people. Teachings can be traced back to the civil servant and scholar Confucius. While he does not make any statements about the nature and function of gods, he does, however, strongly advocate the observance of traditional rites, reverence of ancestors, and preservation of family ties. All of this brings stability to the lives of every member in the community. Thus "humanity" is the central concept—interaction with fellow human beings. The ideal person, who is held as "superior" (*Junzi*), is proficient in almost every art form by virtue of their "life-long learning" and puts their insights into practice in daily life. They use their knowledge and abilities to serve the community.

The symbol for yin and yang, demonstrating the reciprocity and harmony of energies.

Taoism professes the belief in five mythical mountains that are considered the home of the gods.

Mencius, the second great thinker of Confucianism, updated teachings in the fourth century B.C. to emphasize the concept of *yi*, which means "justice appropriateness and sense of duty." It assumes that an individual by nature is good; however, one's character needs constant education and refinement. This is provided by adhering to certain necessary principles, like ancestor reverence and loyalty to the ruler or the state.

From 200 B.C., Confucianism became state ideology and for a period of about 2,000 years it was used as part of the training of civil servants until the Chinese Revolution beginning in 1911/1912. Simultaneously, Confucianism acquired religious qualities.

Taoism—Principle of Harmony With the World

Compared with Confucianism, Taoism has several clear traits that qualify it more as a religion. Lao Tzu (ca fourth century B.C.) is considered to be the founder of Taoism with his authoring of "Tao Te Ching." Since the second century A.D., an affiliated church, a monastery, and a complex set of divine doctrines have developed. Most of the gods named within these doctrines are references to historical figures who held particular significance. Like Confucius, Lao Tzu was lauded as a savior of the world.

"Tao" literally translates as "way," however; it refers to the principle of the world and the ultimate basis of all beings, from which the cosmos originated. Each person has an individual tao, which should not be disturbed by conscious immoral acts; instead it should develop freely. Taoists are involved with various practices such as meditation, rituals, and alchemy to achieve harmony with tao.

Lao Tzu, founder of Taoism, retreated to the mountains after imparting his teachings.

INSIDER KNOWLEDGE

IN MODERN CHINA, *people are once again reflecting upon the teachings of Confucius; this is after a long period of him having being declared a "reactionist" by Mao.*

THE TAOIST CHURCH *was long controlled by the "celestial teachers," also referred to as "Taoist priests."*

CONFUCIUS *lived from 551–479 B.C. In 1906 he was equated with the highest deities.*

AN EMPIRICAL EDICT *decreed in 267 A.D. that a "great sacrifice" take place four times a year in honor of Confucius.*

DESPITE REFORMS *and "neo-Confucianism" since the 18th century, state Confucianism has displayed signs of religious consolidation.*

Statue of Confucius in Qufu

The Deification of Confucius

STATE CULT: As Confucianism became the state ideology of China, the people raised his status to that of a holy man and ultimately to a god. This was promoted by the state as in this manner the societal ideal of Confucianism was incorporated and implemented among the masses. In 194 B.C., the emperor gave sacrificial offerings in the house and temple of Confucius in Qufu for the first time.

STAGES OF AGGRANDIZEMENT: Since the first century A.D., sacrifices were offered in honor of Confucius and his 72 pupils in all Chinese schools. In 555, the emperor decreed the construction of temples in honor of Confucius in every district capital. In 739, Confucius was declared "king"; in 1008, the "quintessential wise one"; and in 1086, "emperor." He was named "most holy scholar" in 1657 and finally deified in 1906.

The 2,557th birthday of Confucius was celebrated with great pomp in Qufu in 2006.

➲ see also: Taoism, *Philosophy Chapter, p. 250*

KEY FACTS

JUDAISM *is the oldest monotheistic religion in the world.*

A COMMON JEWISH FAITH *first emerged with the Babylonian exile.*

THE TORAH *is the primary holy book of Judaism, making up the first five chapters of both the Hebrew Bible and Christianity's Old Testament.*

DEVOTION TO GOD *and a lineage reaching back to Abraham unite Jews all over the world.*

Origin and beginning | From destruction of the temple until today | Learning and teaching | Piety and festivities

JUDAISM—LIFE ACCORDING TO GOD'S COMMANDMENTS

Judaism is a lively and diverse monotheistic world religion that shares characteristics with both Christianity and Islam. Its creative contribution to cultural history is immense. Jewish holy scripture, the Torah, is fundamental for the organization of Jewish life across the whole world. Various Jewish communities can today be found in all parts of the world.

The Jewish religion is closely linked with the history of the Israelites.

RELIGION

THE ORIGIN AND BEGINNING OF "GOD'S CHOSEN PEOPLE"

The Jewish religion actually developed after the time described in the Bible. Within the Bible, mythical and historical events were interpreted in terms of the Jewish beliefs.

According to ancient tradition, Judaism emerged between the Euphrates and Tigris rivers. The nation of Israel in the Bible originates with Abraham of Ur, who worshipped a unique God that permeates everything. Six generations later, descendants of Abraham lived in Egypt as slaves. Moses rose up as a leader among them, taking his people across the Red Sea and back toward the "promised land." During the Exodus, Moses received the Ten Commandments, a set of laws central to the Jewish religion.

Settled in the promised land, the 12 tribes of Israelites finally unite as a single nation under Saul, who ruled from 884 to 882 B.C. After him, David, then Solomon served as powerful leaders, building the temple of Jerusalem, considered the most important altar of the God Jehovah and the spiritual center of the Jewish religion. After the death of Solomon, the Israelite nation split in two. Israel, the northern kingdom, was captured by the Assyrians while the southern kingdom was taken over by the Babylonian king Nebuchadrezzar in 597 B.C. Ten years later, he destroyed the temple of Jerusalem and deported large portions of the upper and middle classes to Mesopotamia. This period of time, called the Exile, unified Jews in their belief in Jehovah and their return to the promised land.

God's covenant with Israel made them his chosen people. The promise was conveyed by the agreement with Noah after the flood, the promise of children to Abraham, and the transmission of the Torah to Moses.

The Promised Land

After the Persians (538 B.C.) captured Babylon, many Jews returned to Israel and reconstructed the temple in Jerusalem. The country was the tributary province of the Persian kingdom and remained so even after the victory of Alexander the Great over the Persians in 333 B.C. With this, the Hellenistic culture reached Judaism. When the Seleucid king Antiochus IV banned the temple culture in 168 B.C., a Jewish resistance movement arose.

Four years later, they, under the leadership of the Maccabees, drove out the occupying forces and newly consecrated the temple. The Romans, called to settle a dispute between two Maccabee brothers, captured Jerusalem in 63 B.C. Later, Herod was made Judah's vassal king, during whose rule Jesus of Nazareth (p. 234) was born.

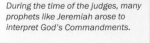

Holy Scriptures

The Jewish Bible or "Tanakh" is the product of more than 1,000 years of history. During the rabbinic period (ca 70 A.D.–sixth century), the tripartite canon (traditionally counted as 24 books) was created. These holy Hebrew scriptures are considered inspired and consistent, and include the five books of Moses (Torah), prophetic writings, (Nevi'im) and hagiographies or writings, (Ketuvim), which include the Psalms. The organization of the books into chapters can be traced back to the Middle Ages; the numbering of the verses to the 16th century.

above: *Jewish scripts often contain magnificent artistic images.*

During the time of the judges, many prophets like Jeremiah arose to interpret God's Commandments.

The arch of Titus in Rome was constructed to commemorate the capture of Jerusalem. It shows, among other things, the plundering of the temple.

see also: **Hellenism**, *Visual Arts Chapter, p. 289*

FROM THE DESTRUCTION OF THE TEMPLE UNTIL TODAY

The destruction of the temple in Jerusalem in 70 A.D. is considered the start of the Jewish diaspora. Jews lived as a minority in non-Jewish societies until the foundation of Israel in 1948.

The diversity of modern Judaism can be traced to the different interpretations of the Torah. Orthodox Jews (left) adhere strictly to the commandments; meanwhile in liberal Judaism there are even female rabbis (right).

From the second century, many Jews arrived in Spain, France, and the later Holy Roman Empire as refugees or slaves. At the same time, a circle of scribes gathered in the Palestinian city of Jabneh and performed legal functions on behalf of the Jews, thanks to the tolerance of the occupying Romans. They are known as the first rabbis (p. 232).

In 132 A.D., a Jewish revolt broke out against the Roman Empire under the leadership of Simon Bar Kokhba, which saw a Jewish defeat after three years of warfare. With this, the Jews were removed from Jerusalem and its surrounding regions in the diaspora, the "spreading out." Thus, the rabbi circles located in Palestine and Babylon started to exert even greater influence. As the Roman emperor's support for Christianity increased, so did the amount of pressure exerted on the Jewish minority. Jews enjoyed legal security under Muslim rule, but were subject to many restrictions.

Middle Ages to the Early Modern Period

Judaism achieved a cultural period of bloom in the Middle Ages, primarily on the Iberian Peninsula and the German cities. However, it also experienced persecutions and expulsions. High points of terror came with the Crusades, which were increasingly accompanied by pogroms—organized persecution—of the Jews as well as their expulsion from England (1290) and Spain (1492). Around 12,000 Jews lived in Germany at the start of the Early Modern period. The first Jews settled in North America in 1646.

Enlightenment to the Foundation of Israel

Different branches of Judaism began developing from the 19th century onward in Western Europe and the U.S. as a reaction to the Enlightenment. While Orthodox Jews chose a more isolationist position, others sought assimilation. More than ever before, Jews strove to gain equal rights within societies in which they were a minority. This was first achieved in France following the French Revolution. The Nazi ascension to power in Germany in 1933, resulted in unprecedented anti-Semitic actions. With the Wannsee conference on January 20, 1942, the systematic mass murder of Jews living in the German-controlled regions was decided. On May 14, 1948, David Ben Gurion proclaimed the state of Israel, which was successfully established.

THERE WERE *pogroms against the Jews during the Crusades.*

THE NATIONAL SOCIALISTS (NAZIS) *murdered over six million Jews.*

TODAY, ANTI-SEMITISM *is growing in the Arab world.*

The "Judensau" was ridiculing propaganda against the Jewish religion in the Middle Ages.

Anti-Semitism

JEWS HAVE BEEN suppressed and persecuted since antiquity due to their religion and lifestyle. Anti-Semitic conceptions increasingly shaped the politics of the Christian kingdoms since the fourth century. They never experienced full civic equality, even under Islamic rule. During the Crusades, numerous Jews were either forcibly baptized or murdered throughout Europe. Slanderous allegations of well poisoning or murdering children continued up to the modern age.

RACIAL IDEOLOGY AND MASS MURDER: Since the 19th century, anti-Semitic demagogues claimed that the adherents of Judaism were a threat to public interest. The instrumentalization and spread of this illusion by the Nazi Reich in WWII resulted in the murder of around six million people.

THE ARABIC WORLD has seen a growth of anti-Semitism in the recent decades. Combining the claims of traditional religious superiority with aggression against the state of Israel, this sentiment greatly increases the defensive attitude against the Western world.

above: *The Jewish badge served as a discriminatory identification during the Nazi Third Reich.*
left: *The Dreyfus Affair is an example of modern anti-Semitism.*

Zionism

Due to widespread anti-Semitism, Jewish scholars since the late 19th century have hoped for the modernization of the Jewish people through the establishment of Israel as a nation. Theodor Herzl (pictured) is considered as the founder of the Zionist movement with his work "The Jewish State" (1896). The seventh World Zionist Organization in Basel voted for the establishment of Palestine as the homeland for Jews throughout the world. In May 1948, the Israeli Declaration of Independence was publicly read in Tel Aviv.

The ascent to power by the National Socialists in Germany overshadowed the 18th Zionist Congress in Prague in 1933.

21ST CENTURY

SINCE ANTIQUITY, *Jews have been living in Palestine.*

THE ANCIENT CITY OF JERUSALEM *is the holy city for three world religions. In 1980, it was made the lawful national territory of Israel.*

OVER 5 MILLION JEWS *live in Israel. It is the only country in the world in which Jews hold the majority.*

RELIGION

LEARNING AND TEACHING

The foundation of the Jewish faith is the Torah. Within these scriptures are the Commandments, expanded by the rabbinical tradition of scriptural interpretation. They are the sources of the Halakha—the Jewish code of religious laws.

The central beliefs of Judaism are staunch monotheism, or the belief in one universal God, and the central prominence of the Torah, the five books of Moses, as direct revelation from God. Over many centuries, Jewish rabbis, or religious teachers, have studied and commented on the Torah. Their writings contribute to the Halakha, a code of laws, cultural instructions, and norms that provide the basis from which the Jews structure and live their lives. The intellectual task of coming to understand the Torah and God's laws is a living challenge for Jews and their leaders. Because of this, there is no final or definite interpretation of the Halakha but rather it is continuously modified and developed. Different interpretations of the Halakha have resulted in various movements within modern Judaism. While the Halakha is considered absolutely binding within Orthodox Judaism, conservative Jews have a more flexible interpretation. Reform Jews more or less accept the understanding of the Halakham, but believe that they no longer have binding power over their lives.

This page of the Talmud concerns Genesis.

Scholarly Tradition

Jewish scholars believe that Jewish teachings have been passed down through the generations virtually unmodified since Judaism's very inception in Sinai. Today, rabbis maintain this chain of continuity of the scholarly tradition. The Palestinians (Tannaites), until the beginning of the third century, followed by the rabbi schools of Palestine and Babylon (Amorians), involved themselves in collecting, bequeathing, sorting, and writing their understandings and interpretations of the Torah and the basis of the Halakha to be stored within libraries. Thus, the collections at Mishnah and Tosefta, the Midrashim, and the Jerusalem and Babylonian Talmud emerged. In the Early Middle Ages, the Babylonian Talmud was the highest authority of the Jewish justice system.

The Rabbi

The rabbi was primarily a scholar of the Torah who was revered by virtue of his charisma and competence. The authority granted to rabbis by the Jewish community was restricted to questions pertaining to the interpretation and application of the Torah to everyday life, but held no religious functions. From the High Middle Ages, rabbis acted in the service of the Jewish community and were expected to deal competently with all questions regarding religious laws. By the modern ages they received a position of increasing importance as the religious and moral authority representative of the Jewish community, especially when faced with non-Jewish authorities. In modern Judaism, duties of the rabbi came to include pastoral duties such as leading worship services. Since the 19th century, the majority of traditional Talmudic schools have become academic rabbinical seminaries. As a result of the progressive Jewish reform movement going on since the 20th century, even women have been ordained as rabbis.

Rabbis are apprenticed scholars of the Torah. Today their responsibilities include ceremonial tasks and acting as pastor to the community.

THE TORAH *is enshrined in the eastern wall of the synagogue.*

THE CANTOR, OR CHANTER, *leads Jews in prayer, sung in the Hebrew language.*

PRAYER TIMES *are in the morning, afternoon, and evening.*

The Torah is preserved in the synagogue in a special Torah shrine (Aron-Ha-Kodesh).

The Synagogues

SYNAGOGUES symbolize the preservation of the collective Jewish way of life and often house social, cultural, and administrative facilities. While significant for many ways to the Jewish community, the synagogue is most importantly the center of various religious services and community meetings.

THE TORAH SCROLLS, which are read out during services of the synagogue, are held within the ark. The prayer leader stands upon a raised platform and begins recitations of consecutive sections of the Torah. During the main religious services on the Sabbath and holidays, chapters from the books of the prophets are also read. Local liturgical customs, prayers, and hymns continue to play an important role in the synagogues. Traditional Judaism insists upon women being seated in a separate gallery.

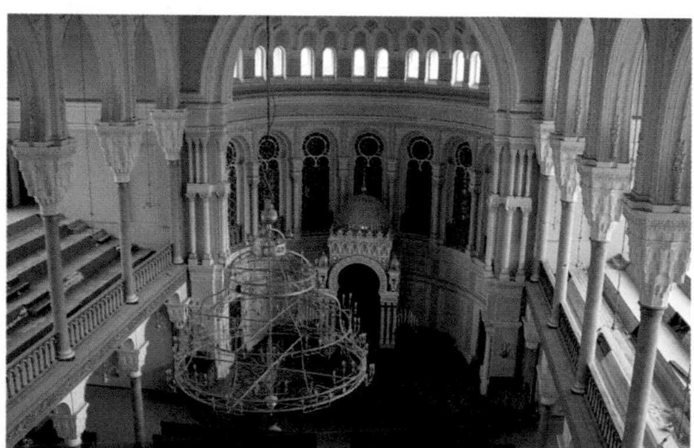

Synagogues (e.g., this one in Russia) always face eastward. The ark, which encases the Torah, is on the eastern wall.

21ST CENTURY

THE HEBREW BIBLE *is the fundamental text of the Jewish religion and culture.*

THE COMMANDMENTS OF THE TORAH *are considered by the Jews as a gift of God and as the holy path.*

ABOUT 13 MILLION PEOPLE *in the world believe in the Jewish faith.*

ALL JEWISH COMMUNITIES *are autonomous and not subordinate to any central authority.*

PIETY AND FESTIVITIES

Jewish piety is determined by the Commandments of the Torah and by centuries of "midrash," or scholarly interpretation of the Torah and its meaning. They seek to live a life in accordance with the will of God and provide structure and significance for day-to-day life and celebration days.

The Torah brings salvation and orientation in all aspects of Jewish life. Fundamental aspects of the Torah Commandments include circumcision, observation of the Sabbath, purity provisions, and dietary laws. The purity of people reflects upon the sanctity of God. Impurities include types of skin diseases, bodily excretions, blood, and, above all, contact with the dead. People can retain purity by immersion within a ritual bath (mikvah) while impure objects also can be made fit for use through a method of purification.

During the Sabbath, the table is laid out with Sabbath breads, salt, and a carafe of wine.

Laws of Everyday Life

Dietary laws include avoiding certain types of meat, such as pork, as well as prohibiting the common storage and consumption of meat and dairy products together. All foods that are permissible to eat by the Commandments of the Torah are referred to as "kosher."

Every week Jews observe the Sabbath, the seventh day of the week, as a day off from work. Celebrated in the home or synogogue, it is permissible to break the Commandment of the Sabbath only when danger is perceived to life and body. In addition, personal piety involves prayers, fasts, and good works.

Worship Services and Festivities

The public ceremonies of Judaism are celebrated in the synagogue. According to Orthodox Judaism, ten adult Jewish males must be present during sermon. As common prayer and reading of the Torah are the focal points of service, within a one year (three years within Reform communities) the entire text is recited. Today, the Hebrew Torah is commonly recited within a sermon held in the local language. Main prayers of the Jewish service are the *shema* ("Hear Israel") and the *amidah* ("18 blessings"). In Orthodox Judaism, a *tefillin* (prayer belt and jacket), a *tallit* (prayer cloak or shawl), and a *kipa* (cap) are worn during prayer.

The annual Jewish festivals and customs were mostly linked with luminary movements and the vegetative cycle. They were first established as celebrations of the actions of God such as the Exodus from Egypt.

Community rituals celebrate each stage of life: The circumcision of male infants on their eighth day; the religious ceremony ("Bar Mitzvah") associated with males in their 13th year coming of age (in Reform Judaism females hold a similar celebration, the Bat Mitzvah); both the proposal and act of marriage, and then finally death. Important annual festivals are Rosh Hashanah (New Year), Hanukkah, and Yom Kippur (Day of Atonement).

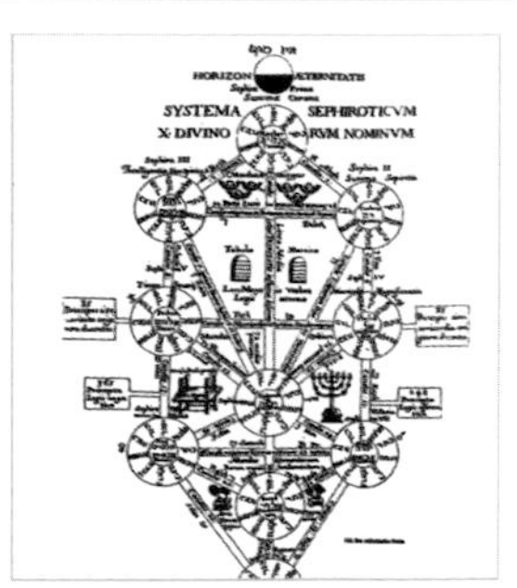

Kabbalah and Hasidism

The term Kabbalah ("to receive") refers to an esoteric movement of Judaism that emerged in the 13th century. Kabbalah followers believe that there is an invisible event behind every visible one. Practitioners believe that the human being is a work in progress, which can reach its full potential through pious works. The East European Hasidic philosophy is a popular Jewish movement that emerged in the 18th century. Linked to the Kabbalah tradition, the Hasidic believers seek an internalization of piety. Based on the view that God is responsible for all of creation, they consider all actions during the course of life granted by the will of God.

above: *The tree of life represents the ten Sefirot—the ten manifestations of God. It is an illustration of the levels of understanding God.*

Annual Festivities

THE JEWISH RELIGIOUS CALENDAR sets holidays within specific months according to lunisolar cycles. It is based on calculations rather than observation. Due to the fact that 12 months in a lunar year run short by 11 days in comparison to a solar year, an intercalary month is inserted to make adjustments to the shortage of days in the lunar calendar.

Holidays (blue) that were mandated by the Torah include Passover, which celebrates the exodus from Egypt, and Sukkot, the Feast of Tabernacles.

Introduced by rabbis, a few commemoration days (red) were mandated including Hanukkah and Purim, which commemorates the rescue of the Persian Jews by Esther.

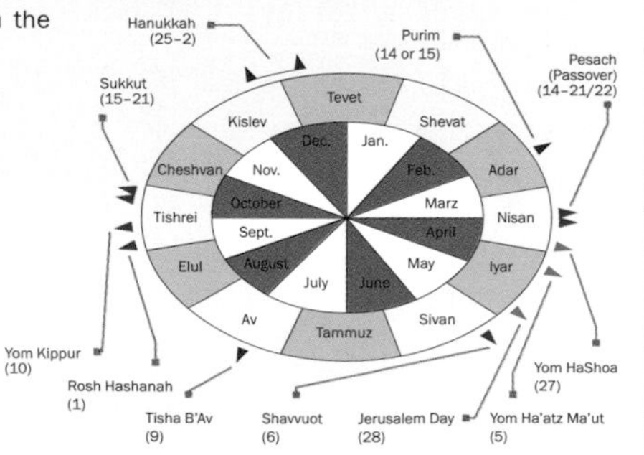

Civil and religious holidays (green) include Yom HaShoah, in memory of those murdered in the Holocaust, and Yom Yerushalayim or "Jerusalem Day," which celebrates the Israeli victory of the Six Day War in 1967.

The holiday of Hanukkah celebrates the miraculous replenishment of the lanterns of the temple in 164 B.C. Each day one candle is lit within a "menorah."

RELIGION

KEY FACTS

THE INSPIRATION FOR CHRISTIANITY *is Jesus of Nazareth, whose birth marks the start of the Western era.*

CENTRAL BELIEFS *are the teachings of Jesus, deemed the son of God, and interpretations of his death and resurrection.*

THE CHURCH *as it is known today was first constituted in the fourth century.*

A VIBRANT FORM OF CHRISTIANITY *is found today in South America.*

CHRISTIANITY—FROM JEWISH SECT TO A WORLD RELIGION

Christianity is one of the most significant monotheistic religions in the world. Its beliefs are closely linked to Judaism, from which it originated. The central focus of the Christian faith is based upon the belief of salvation made possible through the crucifixion and Resurrection of Jesus of Nazareth, the son of God.

"Christ" corresponds to the Jewish sovereign title of "Messiah" or in Hebrew, "the Anointed One."

JESUS OF NAZARETH

Jesus of Nazareth is the central figure of the Holy Bible and Christianity. The basis of the Christian faith is considered to be the profession of Jesus Christ as the path to salvation.

Located in the New Testament of the Bible, the Gospels, of which the Gospel of Mark is the oldest, describe the ministry of Jesus of Nazareth. Christian beliefs were promoted after Jesus' death by retelling his parables and lessons within the emerging Christian communities. Initially retold orally, Jesus' ministry was later collected and organized within a literary format. The beliefs of early Christian authors are reflected in the stories of Jesus' birth and life as a young man.

JESUS IS THE *Greek form of the Aramaic name Joshua.*

THE LIFE AND ACTIONS *of Jesus are rooted within the Jewish tradition.*

THE GOSPELS DESCRIBE *the life and teachings of Jesus, which act as the constituents of faith.*

Early versions of the Bible record an ox and donkey at the Nativity scene.

The Life of Jesus

BIRTH AND BAPTISM: Jesus was born during the rule of the Roman emperor Augustus (27 B.C.–14 A.D.) in the Galilean province of Nazareth. His entrance into the public sphere occurred during the rule of the Galilean prince Herod Antipas (ca 20 B.C.–39 A.D.). Jesus was baptized in the River Jordan by the Jewish preacher John the Baptist. For many years Jesus traveled through Galilee spreading his teachings as a charismatic itinerant preacher.

SPHERE OF INFLUENCE AND DEATH: As reported in the Gospels, Jesus healed the sick and preached in synagogues during his ministry. He called upon the people of Israel to convert and follow him. There was a steady rise in the number of his followers, many of whom existed on the fringes of society. Eventually Jesus was arrested, prosecuted, and executed by the Roman provincial government in Jerusalem on charges of blasphemy and political agitation around 30 A.D.

In the Gospel of Mark, the story of Jesus begins with his baptism by John the Baptist.

Message of Jesus

The main message of Jesus was the renewal of Judaism in accordance with the kingdom of God. As the preachings of Jesus were often portrayed through allegories of rural life, stories of him healing the sick and helping the fringe groups of ancient Jewish society conveyed the Christian message to his mainly agrarian audience. The Sermon on the Mount (found in the Gospels of Luke and Matthew) compiled these teachings. Their primary theme was love, both for God and for one another. This message responds to intensely restrictive commandments in the Jewish Torah, which placed limits on behavior and promised exacting punishment for wrongdoing. Jesus instead encouraged inclusive love and charity as a guide to behavior and social organization.

Identity of Jesus

Jesus considered himself a messenger of God while others declared him specifically as the "Messiah." By addressing God as "Father," Jesus relayed a remarkably close relationship. Arriving in Jerusalem, the religious and political center of Judaism, this provocative claim was bound to trigger conflict between Jesus and the temple aristocracy, working under the law of the Romans. Arrested on charges of blasphemy, Jesus was executed. The descriptions of his death in the Gospels emphasize the fulfillment of prophecies of a Messiah, sent by God to redeem humankind, found in the Old Testament.

Farmers and fishermen from Galilee were the first followers of Jesus. Traces from the era of the New Testament can still be found today by the Sea of Gennesaret.

The miracles of Jesus, such as the feeding of 5,000 people, are told in the Gospels.

THE EMERGENCE OF CHRISTIANITY

The early Christians formed a local community that was attractive to many people. From its start as a small Jewish sect, Christianity soon exploded into an expansive religious movement.

Crucifixion was a cruel method of execution that was practiced in ancient times. To Christians, the death of Jesus on the cross represents his willing self-sacrifice in payment for the sins of all humankind.

The early Christians believed that Jesus was the Messiah and had been resurrected following his crucifixion. Furthermore, they were highly apocalyptical, expecting the end of the world was near. They initially met privately in Jerusalem, but soon numerous other communities emerged. Eventually the members of these Christian communities interacted with one another; praying together, meeting at mealtimes and providing each other with support. Within early Christian society, all men were equal while women were also allowed to take on important communal positions.

First Conflicts

Soon the followers of Christ were accused of heresy and threatened by the majority of population who held other religious beliefs. Many fled to Samaria and a few to Antioch, where they were first referred to as "Christians." In Antioch, they were joined by followers of the Hellenistic-Roman cults. Christian communities often exempted their members, whether converted Jews or Gentiles (non-Jews), from strict Jewish laws including circumcision, cleanliness requirements, and food restrictions. Christian leaders believed in baptism as the symbolic ritual of cleanliness and, after that, purity of the spirit and actions as the way to follow in the path of Jesus.

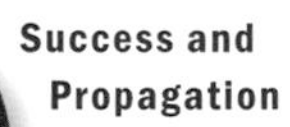

The apostles Peter and Paul emerged as the primary preachers within early Christianity. With his letters, Paul provided the basis of Christian theology for new communities.

During the period of Christian persecution by the Roman Empire, the Christians buried their dead underground in catacombs that were often painted with Christian motifs.

Success and Propagation

The transmission of the new religion saw increased influence over the following decades. Overall, the remarkable lifestyle of the Christians aroused interest to join. Entire households, including both families and their slaves, made the decision to convert. Christianity spread rapidly from the Middle East, attracting both the educated and wealthy as well as the poor and enslaved.

The main reason for the success of Christianity was the promise of salvation and resurrection. Furthermore, the solidarity of early Christian communities was attractive as wealthy Christians made donations to the poor, the elderly, and the sick. The community saw to the burial of its members, transmigratory Christians were housed, and healers worked without payment. Once it was recognized that the end of the world would not occur as soon as had been expected, gradually more importance was attached to the Christian lifestyle. As the communities came to adapt to the norms and values of their environment, hierarchies emerged, the social structures that would later become the foundation of the organized Church.

Regular communion services were characteristic of the collective lifestyle of early Christians.

Christian Persecution

Affirming the Christian faith did harbor risk for followers. In 64 A.D., the Roman Emperor Nero decreed the imprisonment and execution of Christians on charges of alleged arson. Many in the Roman Empire refused to concede in the face of public sacrifice. Their resistance and persecution saw the eventual acceptance of Christianity during the second and third centuries A.D.

From Messiah to Christ

In the Hebrew version of the Bible, the Messiah (Hebrew: "the anointed one") came to represent one who was chosen by God as the rightful ruler of the Israelites descending from the line of King David. The Christian concept of the Messiah as the apocalyptic bringer of salvation was expressed in the prophetic books of the Bible. As early Christians reflected on the meaning of the crucifixion and Resurrection of Jesus, they came to identify him as the Messiah and Christ (Greek: "the anointed one"). This identification of Jesus as the Christ is the central point of the Christian faith.

The Resurrection of Jesus is the central event of Christianity, represented here in the "Isenheim Altar" by Matthias Grünewald.

RELIGION

THE ANCIENT CHURCH AND THE MIDDLE AGES

Christianity spread with the support of kings and emperors. It subsequently developed into various streams of beliefs, which soon became an important factor of power in Europe.

The persecution of the Christians ended in the fourth century under Emperor Constantine I. His successor Theodosius I declared Christianity the state religion of the Roman Empire. From this time on, the development of the Christian Church was closely tied to political power. Rome was considered the Holy See, or seat of power, and the home of the Church's leader, the pope. Leadership under the pope is held by bishops. Church councils, or meetings of bishops, dictated Christian theology by agreeing on creeds—expressions of belief. The Roman Empire split in 395, leading to separate Roman and Byzantine churches.

During the Crusades, the concept of a pilgrimage was associated with the idea of a "just war" against pagans.

Spread of Christianity

Autonomous churches also arose in the Middle East and North Africa. The spread of Christianity in various countries and the foundation of monasteries is primarily attributed to traveling monks. The baptism of the French king Clovis I in Rheims (489) marks Christianity's propagation across Europe. In North Africa and the Iberian Peninsula, the influence of Christianity was thwarted in the seventh and eighth centuries by the Islamic expansion.

Middle Ages—Pope and King

The Church during the Middle Ages was closely linked to temporal rule. Numerous European rulers of the Middle Ages secured alliances with the Church through the pope and bishops. Thus, military undertakings, such as the Crusades, served spiritual as well as worldly interests. European Crusaders sought to conquer the Holy Land, especially the city of Jerusalem, and bring it under Christian rule. These efforts failed. With time, increasing power struggles arose between the pope and the secular rulers—culminating with the Investiture Conflict of 1122. The papacy itself experienced a crisis in the Great Western Schism (1378–1417) when two men claimed authority, Clement VII from Avignon, France, and Urban VI from Rome.

Reformation

Various movements arose in the monasteries for a spiritual reform of the Church. Mendicant orders emerged, which advocated the renouncing of all possessions as a break from the secular. Medieval theology also originated within the monasteries, such as scholasticism, which combines Christian teachings with classical philosophy.

Inquisition and Mission

In the 12th century, Church leaders sought to punish heretics with the Inquisition. By the 15th century, the Inquisition was an enormous force in Europe as the Church announced it was rooting out "witches." The Inquisition in Spain reached its most gruesome peak after the Christian monarchs reclaimed Spain from the Muslims in 1492 (Reconquista). Also at this time, America was discovered, which was followed by the conversion of the indigenous population to Christianity. The colonizing actions also at times involved seizing territory, suppressing native cultures, and enslavement.

SINCE THE 11TH CENTURY, *a pope has chosen his own papal name.*

THE TITLE OF THE POPE *is "holy father," his self-designated name is "servant of God's servants."*

THE POPE *is selected by the cardinals.*

"You are Peter, and upon this rock I will build my Church." —Matthew 16:18

Papacy

THE POPE IS THE SUPREME HEAD of the Roman Catholic Church. The tradition of the bishop of Rome as a successor of the Apostle Peter has its origins in the second century A.D. From the fourth century, the Roman bishops claimed increasing power and control over the entire Church. In the fifth century, Pope Leo I was the first to claim superiority as an heir of Peter. During the barbarian invasions, the political authority of the papacy strengthened. Since the early Middle Ages, the pope's position gained considerable political influence and power. The aggrandizement of the political claim to power by the popes during the Renaissance era was one of the main points of criticism of the Reformation (p. 237). The first Vatican Council (1869–1870) declared papal infallibility while emphasizing his role in office as shepherd and teacher of all Christians.

above: *In the 21st century, the papacy tries to unite Christian tradition and modern life.*
left: *In the Middle Ages, the emperors were crowned by the pope.*

Layout of the Bible

The Christian Bible contains both an Old and New Testament. The Old Testament corresponds to the collections of Jewish holy scriptures. Christians read in the Old Testament prophecies and predictions that foretell of the coming of Jesus Christ, as expressed in the New Testament. The canon of the 27 New Testament scriptures evolved from the third century. It consists of the Gospels, stories of the apostles, letters (primarily by Paul) and the revelation of John. In 1546, the canon of the Catholic Church— the official list of contents of the Holy Bible—was decreed at the Council of Trent.

above: *Gutenberg Bible, printed ca 1455*

➲ see also: **Scholasticism**, *Philosophy Chapter, p. 252*

FROM THE REFORMATION TO THE CURRENT DAY

Martin Luther initiated the greatest change in the history of the Western Church with his shocking assault on traditional Christianity, the starting point for present-day Protestant religions.

The Reformation movement was triggered by Martin Luther, who protested against Church officials who wielded political and financial power through their claims to be intermediaries between people and God and who sold dispensations, or promises of spiritual salvation. His beliefs became the foundation for the Protestant forms of Christianity. The Reformation soon led to a split of the Church between Catholicism and Protestantism. Subsequently, multiple non Catholic autonomous communities were founded: From 1525, Lutheran state churches emerged; Ulrich Zwingli had already initiated a reformed Church program for Zurich in 1523; in 1535 the Church of England was established; John Calvin led a Protestant Church in Geneva in 1541. In reaction to the Reformation, the Council of Trent was called in order to determine significant aspects of the Catholic faith. The Peace of Augsburg, a religious treaty (1555), stated that within Germany, the territorial ruler was to decide the belief of his subjects. However, tensions between the denominations continued to increase substantially until culminating with political consequences that resulted in the Thirty Years' War (1618–1648).

In 1517, Martin Luther sparked the Reformation in Wittenberg with his 95 theses against the sale of indulgences by the papacy.

Enlightenment and Revival

The epoch of the Enlightenment in Europe from the 17th century saw Christianity being challenged. Religious beliefs began being based on human reason rather on blind faith. After the French Revolution, a radical secularization process began across Europe. Thus the church and the state continued to drift apart from each other.

In the 18th century, Christian revival movements emerged, especially in English-speaking regions, founded on earlier communal ideals with an emphasis on personal piety. Already in 1609, the first Baptist congregation was organized in Amsterdam. In 1629, John Wesley founded the Methodist Church along with his brothers. The influence of the Baptist preacher William Miller led to the emergence of the Adventists. In 1830, Joseph Smith founded the Church of Latter-day Saints (Mormons). The Pentecostal movement began at the start of the 20th century and especially emphasized the influence of the Holy Spirit in its various manifestations.

At the first Vatican Council in 1869 the pope's infallibility was dogmatized, further distinguishing the Catholic and Protestant Churches.

The Church in the 20th Century

During the 20th century, many Protestant denominations developed and grew in membership. The Catholic Church continued to define itself in response to Protestantism and secular humanism. The Second Vatican Council opened the church to a broader membership. Latin was replaced by modern languages in worship services, and the Church's dedication to all humanity was declared.

Simultaneously, fundamentalist and evangelical religious movements emerged throughout the developed and the developing worlds. Highly emotive communal experiences, such as the trancelike practice of "speaking in tongues," often characterized these new religious expressions.

Differences Between Denominations

According to the Catholic understanding of faith, the teachings of the Church are based on the Bible and Christian tradition. The word of God is explained through Church doctrines. The Reformers stressed their belief that the Bible alone was sufficient for the promulgation of faith, thus contesting the Church's traditional domination over religious interpretation. While the Church assumed that a person "pays dues" in the process of receiving God's salvation, Luther contended that God's grace was passive; thus faith alone was sufficient. The hierarchically structured Church was considered to be the sole mediator between God and humanity; however, Luther emphasized a "priesthood of all believers." Luther accepted only the first three of the Church's seven sacraments (baptism, Eucharist, penance, confirmation, matrimony, priesthood, and unction). Zwingli, on the other hand, considered baptism and the Eucharist to be mere symbols of faith.

"Erasmus Among the Reformers" (1520) by Lucas Cranach: Johannes Forster, George Spalatin, Martin Luther, Johannes Bugenhagen, Erasmus of Rotterdam, Justus Jonas, Caspar Cruciger, and Philipp Melanchthon

21ST CENTURY

ALMOST ALL *spheres of the Western culture are heavily influenced by biblical and Church traditions.*

DIALOGUE WITH *Judaism and Islam is one of the tasks of the Christian Church in modern times.*

IN THE 21ST CENTURY, *Christianity is increasingly disassociating itself from its Europe-centered character.*

Baptism of the natives after the Spanish conquest of Mexico: Up to the 20th century, mission and colonialism often went hand in hand.

The great multitude of cultures and traditions is a hallmark of Christian life. An especially animated form of Christianity is practiced in South America.

➔ **see also: The Reformers and Music,** *Music Chapter, p. 364*

KEY FACTS

ACCORDING TO ISLAM, MUHAMMAD *is the last prophet sent by God to Earth.*

THE DIVINE REVELATION *exists in the text of the Qur'an, God's final message to humankind.*

SEVENTH CENTURY A.D. *witnessed a split between Shiites and Sunnis.*

THE FIVE PILLARS OF ISLAM *are the religious duties performed by every practicing Muslim.*

ISLAM—SUBMISSION TO ALLAH

Islam is the one of the major world religions. Since its start on the Arabian Peninsula in the seventh century A.D., it has been propagated all across the world. Currently Muslims make up the second largest religious community in the world, the largest being Christians. Most Muslims reside in Asia and North Africa; however, their presence has also been established in America and Europe through migration and conversion in the 20th century. There is a broad span of beliefs and practices among Muslims today, but all consider Muhammad their prophet.

Islam means "submission to God."

PROPHET MUHAMMAD AND THE BEGINNING OF ISLAM

In pre-Islamic Arabia, tribes worshipped their own tutelary deities. Muhammad voiced his belief in one God. For this, he faced anger, suspicion, and violence.

Muhammad, a merchant trader, received his calling in 610 when archangel Gabriel named him the messenger of God, entrusting him with the duty of bringing God's word to others, while invoking them to submit to the universal God (Allah). From that night onward, Muhammad opened himself to receive the words of God, impressed upon him by Gabriel. The messages he received form the holy scripture of Islam, called the Qur'an, from the Arabic for "to read" or "to recite." The first to follow the religious path laid out by Muhammad were members of his family and close associates. The prophet, however, experienced great resistance, including threats to his life from his own tribe, the Quraish rulers of Mecca. They felt threatened by Muhammad's attempt to establish a community that surpassed all tribal boundaries and encouraged a common belief. Muhammad accepted an invitation from tribal leaders in the city of Medina to come and teach his religious vision there. He and his followers secretly left Mecca and went to Medina. Their migration, called the Hegira, is considered the starting-point of the Islamic religion.

PROPHET MUHAMMAD, THE FOUNDER OF ISLAM, lived around 570–632.

TO DATE HE IS CONSIDERED the ideal person, serving as a model for every aspect of life.

AYESHA, Muhammad's youngest wife, was one of the principle heirs to his spiritual legacy.

The first mosque of the world emerged from Prophet Muhammad's residence in Medina.

The Life of Muhammad

PRIOR TO HIS calling, the first 40 years of Muhammad's life are not well-known. Muhammad was born around 570 in Mecca. Orphaned at an early age, he grew up under the guardianship of his uncle Abu Talib.

PRIVATE LIFE: Muhammad was a businessman and worked in the service of a rich widow, Khadija, whom he later married in 595. He was a loyal and loving husband, and a successful and honest trader. Even before his calling, he lived a conspicuously religious life, which included frequent retreats into the desert for the purpose of prayer. Only after Khadija's death (619) did Muhammad marry several wives.

POLITICAL AND RELIGIOUS LEADER: Muhammad led military campaigns against hostile tribes, who aimed to extinguish his life and his message. In 632, he died in Medina without having decreed anyone as a successor. This later brought conflict that resulted in a split in Islam.

Tale of Muhammad ascending to heaven after his "night journey" from Mecca to Jerusalem.

The Umma in Medina

With emigration to Medina, Muhammad became the religious and political head of the Muslim community or *Umma*. The provisions of Medina's communal code sought to promote a harmonious coexistence between the Muslims and local Jewish tribes. However, after the hegira (migration), disputes led to the Jewish tribes leaving Medina.

This period also saw battles between Muslims and the Quraish leaders. The war ended in 630 with the conversion of the entire Quraish tribe to Islam and the non-violent entry of the Prophet into Mecca. Other tribes from the Arabian Peninsula joined the new Umma, creating a powerful confederation of tribes in the name of Islam.

Sunnah and Hadith

Muslims wish to follow in the Sunnah, or way of life, of Prophet Muhammad. For that, they look not only to the Qur'an but also to the Hadith, a collection of stories and sayings reported to be first-hand accounts of the deeds and words of the prophet. These writings were originally transmitted orally, then collected and put into writing a century or two after Muhammad's death. There is some controversy over their reliability. The Hadith collections now considered the most authentic date from the ninth and tenth centuries (or, in Muslim terminology, from the second and third century A.H., or anno hejiri, years after the hegira).

above: *Hadith illustration*

PROPAGATION AND SPREAD OF ISLAM

Within the 120 years following the death of the prophet, Islam had spread to the east and west. At the same time, conflicts over leadership caused a major split in the religion.

Following the death of Muhammad, the search was on for a suitable successor who could take over his political and military functions as leader of the Muslim Umma.

The Four Rightly Guided Caliphs

The first four successors to Muhammad are considered the "rightly guided caliphs," because during their leadership the religion experienced harmony even as it spread to many new cities and regions through trade and conversion as well as military might. The first caliph, Abu Bakr (632–634), was the father of Muhammad's youngest wife. Then came Umar (634–644) and Uthman (644–656). The fourth caliph, Ali bin Abi Taleb (656–661), was the husband of Muhammad's daughter, Fatima.

Harun ar-Rashid's fame is attributed to his fairy tale "1001 Arabian Nights."

This era is characterized by the explosive expansion of Islam. By the time of Ali's death, the Muslims had dominated the entire region of the Sassanid Empire (Iraq and part of Iran). They had also infiltrated north toward Central Asia and west across the former Byzantine regions of Syria and Palestine as far as North Africa. Within the conquered regions, the Muslim leaders did not demand the immediate conversion of the local inhabitants. Instead recognition of Islamic rule was initially stressed. Non-Muslims were granted protection and freedom of religion upon the payment of a civil tax.

Great Islamic Empires

Upon the death of Ali, Muawiyya, the Umayyad caliphate (661–750) that ruled over Damascus, began to select appointees for the Syrian governorship. The legitimacy of this action by the first Muslim dynasty's founder was debated from the very beginning. The Islamic expansion, however, continued uninterrupted. The Muslim armies conquered the Byzantine areas of North Africa and Spain, marching as far as southern France. They even went as far as the Indian subcontinent and threatened to capture the capital of the Byzantine Empire, Constantinople.

In 750, the Umayyad caliphate was overthrown by the Abbasid dynasty. The rule of Abbasid Harun ar-Rashid began a prosperous period for the caliphate and its capital in Baghdad. The end of the Islamic Empire began in the following century with the counter-caliphates in Spain (Cordoba) and Egypt. The Abbasid caliphs lost their political power to non-Arabic Muslim dynasties in the 11th century. The role of the caliph was reduced to legitimizing the selection of a political leader, taking the title of sultan from the mid-11th century. In the 13th century, the Mamluks in Cairo displaced those in Baghdad. Beginning in the late 14th century, Muslim leaders in Turkey and the Middle East pressed on toward the Christian city of Constantinople. Mehmet II, an Ottoman king, conquered the Byzantine capital in 1453 and the city's name was changed to Istanbul. At its peak, the Ottoman Empire comprised European, North African, and Asiatic regions. However the caliphate, which had become weak by the turn of the 20th century, was dissolved by Atatürk in 1925.

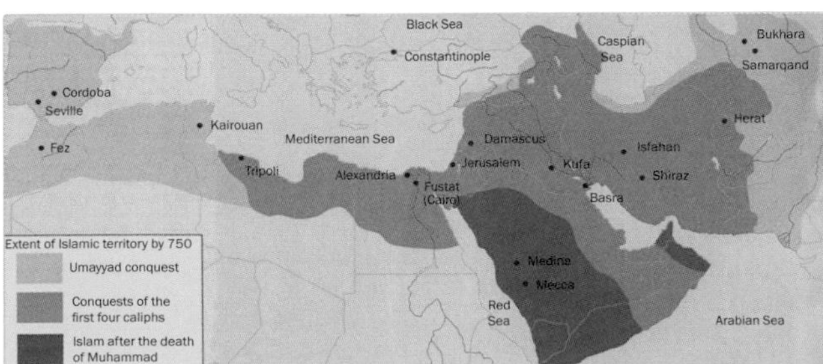

The propagation of Islam during rule of the rightly guided caliphs.

THE TERM SHIITES *is derived from Shiat u-Ali: The followers of Ali.*

THE LARGEST SHIITE GROUP *is the Twelver Shi'a who recognize twelve Imams.*

THEIR FOUNDING *is considered by some to have been in 680.*

The sepulchers of Imams, like the Golden Mosque in Baghdad, are important sanctuaries.

The Shi'a

THE SPLIT: The Shiites split from the Sunni majority soon after the death of Muhammad. The split was induced by their refusal to accept the legitimacy of the rule of the first three caliphs. They considered Ali's and Fatima's (the Prohet's daughter) descendants as Muhammad's only legitimate successors and leaders (Imams) of the Umma. According to the Shiites, the legitimate Imams (male descendants of Ali and Fatima) were infallible, possessed supernatural qualities, and died as martyrs for their communities.

BELIEFS: From the point of view of the Twelver Shi'a, the largest Shiite sect, the Umma has been without legitimate leadership ever since the disappearance of the 12th Imam in the ninth century. Before he returns, the void is filled by religious scholars. A strict Shiite hierarchical clergy has thus evolved.

The Shiites commemorate the martyrdom of Hussein on Ashura.

INSIDER KNOWLEDGE

IN EGYPT *during the 11th century, the Sunni population was ruled by the Fatimid Shiite caliphs.*

DURING THE SAME *period, the Shiite Buyids protected the Shiite caliphate in Baghdad.*

IN THE 13TH CENTURY, *Egypt was ruled by the Mamluks, former military slaves.*

IN SPAIN, *Judaism under Islamic rule flourished—a fact that is little known.*

LIFE IN ISLAM—THE FIVE PILLARS

The religious duties of Muslims, referred to as the five pillars of Islam, have been adopted from the Qur'an. These are mandatory for every practicing adult Muslim.

Conversion

The first pillar is the confession of faith, or Shahadah. This declaration converts a person to Islam, i.e., makes him a Muslim, provided it is done in true faith: "There is no god but God and Muhammad is the messenger of God."

Prayers

The second pillar of Islam is performance of ritual prayers, or *salat*. They are performed five times a day at times determined by the place of the sun in the sky. Ablutions, or ritualistic washing, precede every prayer. The devotee performs each of the prayers in the direction of the the Kaaba in Mecca. The Friday afternoon congregational prayer includes a sermon and is led by an *imam* (religious scholar) in the mosques, and if possible Muslims are expected to attend.

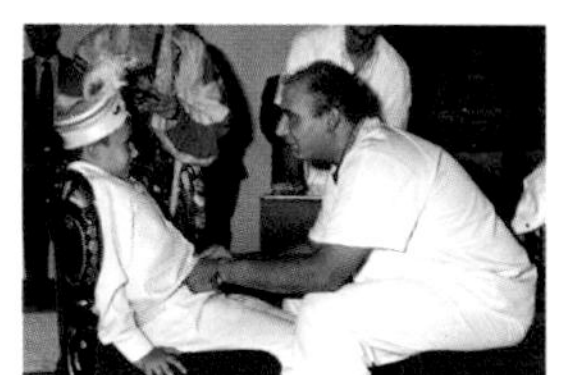

Holidays and Festivities

The Qur'an does not mention any feasts, but the sunnah or practice of the prophet specifies two religious festivals: The small feast at the end of Ramadan and the Eid ul-Adha, marking the end of Hajj on the tenth day of the month of pilgrimage. Shiites celebrate the Day of Ashura, which commemorates the murder of the prophet's grandson, Hussein. In some countries, even the birthday of the prophet is celebrated, though normally Islam disallows celebration of the birthdays of holy men.

above: *Circumcision of the foreskin is a pre-Islamic ritual that is not mentioned in the Qur'an.*

The flag of Saudi Arabia displays the Shahadah: There is no god but God (Allah) and Muhammad is the messenger of God.

Duty of Charity

The third pillar of Islam is charity given to the needy for self-purification (*zakat*) in the belief that such deeds please God. For many modern Muslims, zakat has come to mean a promise to give a share of their wealth annually to worthy causes or needy individuals.

Fasting

Fasting (*sawm*) during the Ramadan is the fourth pillar. Ramadan is the ninth month of the Muslim calendar, determined by the moon's phases. From daybreak to sunset for a period of 29 or 30 days the healthy are expected to not eat, drink, smoke, or have sexual contact. Fasting aims at cultivating self-control, compassion, and awareness of God. Its purpose is not hardship. If ill health prevents an individual from fasting on a regular basis, then compensation is required in the form of charity, especially feeding the poor, if financially possible.

Seven rotations around the Kaaba in Mecca are an important facet of the Great Pilgrimage.

The Hajj

The fifth pillar requires every Muslim (within reason) to make the pilgrimage to Mecca, or Hajj (occurring during the 12th lunar month), at least once in a lifetime. Pilgrims to Mecca perform ceremonies reliving events in the life of the Prophet Muhammad, including circumambulations of the Kaaba, a massive black stone building representing the heart of the faithful, cleansed of pagan gods by Muhammad and said to have been built by Abraham (or, in some traditions, by Adam).

21ST CENTURY

THE HAJJ *today is booked as a package tour with an inclusive tour guide.*

NEARLY 3 MILLION *followers from 160 countries made the pilgrimage to Mecca in 2008.*

PRAYER REMINDERS *on a cell phone often replace a muezzin.*

THE MOSQUE is a house of worship where Muslims perform their five daily ritual prayers.

MEN AND WOMEN pray separately in the mosque.

FRIDAY PRAYERS are the only ones featuring a sermon, which often refers to current events. Demonstrations linked to the Friday prayer are common.

From the minaret, a "muezzin" invites the followers of the Islamic faith to pray five times a day.

The Mosque

PLACE OF WORSHIP AND CONGREGATION: In Muslim countries, there are prayer rooms in every public building and in every residential area. The Great mosque or even the Friday mosque which can hold large numbers of worshippers are used for daily prayers as well as the more widely attended Friday and festival prayers. The larger mosques generally have religious schools, in which instruction in Quranic Arabic and other religious matters is given.

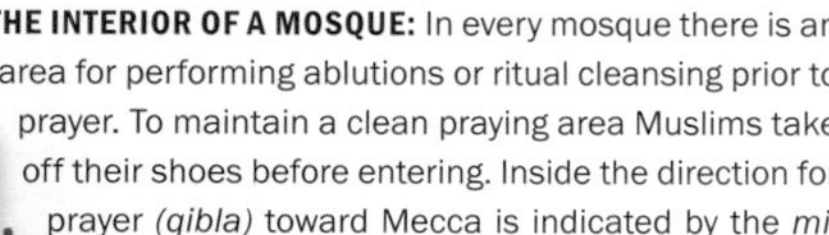

THE INTERIOR OF A MOSQUE: In every mosque there is an area for performing ablutions or ritual cleansing prior to prayer. To maintain a clean praying area Muslims take off their shoes before entering. Inside the direction for prayer *(qibla)* toward Mecca is indicated by the *mihrab*, a niche in the wall. Once a week, the Friday afternoon prayers are led by an imam.

right: *The mihrab, which is often richly decorated, symbolizes the presence of the prophet during prayer.*
left: *During Friday's sermon (*khutbah*), the Imam stands on a sermon pulpit, the* minbar.

ISLAM TODAY

The start of the 21st century is witness to the fact that Islam is, geographically, the most wide-ranging religion. Today 69% of Muslims live in Asia, 27% in Africa and about 3% in Europe.

The Organization of the Islamic Conference (OIC) estimates that there is currently a total of 56 countries where Islam is either the religion practiced by the majority or is the official state religion. Among them are Turkey, Indonesia, Sudan, Kazakhstan, Saudi Arabia, Iran, Iraq, and Lebanon. Overall, the respective cultural inheritance existing before Islam exerts a profound influence on the religious lives of Muslims. Local traditions merge with the imported Arabic-Islamic culture. This is clearly seen through attire and architecture, as well as rites associated with marriage, funerals, and circumcision. For example, female circumcision is practiced in East Africa while in Egypt the deceased are interred within burial chambers, or sepulchers.

Today, the Sunni Al-Azhar Mosque in Cairo exerts the greatest influence worldwide.

Also, on the personal level, there exists a broad spectrum of religiousness that has evolved over the years: From piety that is laden with superstition to rational and mystical Islam.

Religious Authorities

Sunni Islam does not recognize a hierarchical clergy and does not have a religious head since the dissolution of the caliphate. However, there are religious institutions and training centers whose scholars (*sheikhs*) are renowned across the world. In addition to this, in all Muslim countries there is a state-appointed, supreme religious scholar (*mufti*) whose legal opinion (*fatwa*) may be formally considered. Growing Islamic movements as well as various apolitical believers do not recognize these state-controlled authorities anymore; instead they believe in independent preachers. Alongside popular sheikhs with classic training, there are also preachers who advocate a new style and reach out to their audience through media such as cassette recordings, TV, and Internet.

Renewed Inclination to Islam

Interest regarding religious issues and the need to have religious orientation in daily life has sharply increased within Muslim societies, even though this is set against a backdrop of terrorism taking place in the name of Islam. A conservative trend is thus noticeable, which emphasizes the importance of external characteristics such as attire, head-dress and observance of religious duties. Additionally, a considerably large number of fatwa inquiries are also received by the religious scholars on a daily basis. The followers living within the ever growing Muslim communities in Europe and America are faced with the problem that the clergy hail from Muslim countries. They are therefore not well versed in the reality of life pertaining to Muslims living in Western societies. The challenge for the 21st century is to develop European Islamic institutions, which can relevantly infuse ideals of Islam into the Western culture.

It has become a trend in the 21st century that more Western-educated Muslim women are freely opting to wear a headscarf (the hijab).

Islamism

Islamism is a reaction to colonialism, and intruding foreign policy of some Western powers. It reduces Islam to a superficial political movement to regain political power against the West. They sometimes combat even their own governments. While some radical Islamists resort to violence in order to disrupt a particular government, many pursue their goals by working within the system, especially through social work and education. Such groups often succeed in effective charitable work. Governments may see them as dangerous, as they highlight any failing efforts, and some have been barred from political participation or persecuted.

Various followers of Islam demonstrating against Western culture's influence on Muslim societies.

SHARIA is the path or way of life, the Islamic law for daily behavior, derived from the Qur'an, the life and example of the prophet Muhammad, the wisdom of Muslim teachings, and rational thought.

IT REGULATES many spheres of Islamic life.

Legal opinions (fatwa) regarding the sharia can be issued by every religious scholar. However, usually the government appoints a supreme mufti for these interpretations.

The Sharia

THE ISLAMIC SHARIA, or law, refers to the totality of commandments and prohibitions contained within the Qur'an and the Sunna. The sources, however, have been detailed in only a few places so that they can actually be applied as the word of law. In the early stages of Islam, legal scholars sought to "find laws." This resulted in the founding of four highly differentiated Sunni Islam law schools that exist to date. The sharia does not actually exist as a universal set of laws, but is rather dependent upon interpretation. This explains why, for example, family law that is based on the sharia varies so greatly between the various Muslim countries.

ISLAMIC CRIMINAL LAW may astound those unfamiliar with it due to its often unequal treatment of the sexes and harsh punishments for certain crimes, such as the stoning to death of married men and women who commit adultery. However, these laws are variably enforced in only a few Muslim countries, and normally only in dictatorships.

A prenuptial agreement is an integral part of the Islamic marriage ceremony.

KEY FACTS

NEW RELIGIONS *often mix the core teachings of traditional religions with other elements.*

CULTS *often require from their members a radical break with their environment and a strictly religious "new beginning."*

CHARACTERISTICS *of the age and modern trends are often incorporated into the teachings of new religions, even more so in cults.*

Manifestations of new religions | Cults—between longing for salvation and modern trends

NEW RELIGIONS AND CULTS

In response to an increasingly ambiguous globalized world, individuals are turning to religion in their search for explanatory models and help in managing their lives. Almost all new religious movements have split from large traditional religions while making appealing offers to believers that seem more relevant, and perhaps even more "modern," for their lives. Religious organizations that pursue commercial interests and use questionable tactics such as manipulative practices are negatively referred to as cults.

New religions and cults mostly combine the faith of different religions.

BETWEEN ACCEPTANCE AND INDEPENDENCE—MANIFESTATIONS OF NEW RELIGIONS

New religions are mostly formed through a combination of topics, teachings, and organizational forms of different preexisting religions.

Religion is gradually becoming more and more a private matter. Within Christianity in particular, the church has lost authority over individual lives. Times of crisis automatically lead to the search for "new" ways, which is found in a mixture of traditional religious elements and newer ones from other religions, spiritual trends, psychology, or philosophy.

NEW AFRICAN-AMERICAN RELIGIONS *emerged during enslavement, especially in Latin America.*

DIFFERENT RELIGIONS: *Voodoo, Xango, Candomblé, Macumba, Umbanda, Maria Lionza, Rastafari*

The sea goddess Yemonja in Candomblé, worshipped here, has traits similar to those of the Christian Virgin Mary.

New African-American Religions

THE KIDNAPPING AND ENSLAVEMENT of native Africans on the American continent and the Caribbean islands since the 16th century was also associated with a ban on their traditional religions in accordance with an intensive Christianizing mission. As a result, religions emerged in various locations which blended traditional African beliefs with Christianity.

PARTICULARLY DYNAMIC is the Voodoo religion, practiced in Caribbean, as well as the Umbanda and Candomblé of Brazil and neighboring countries. The mystic-spiritual religion of Umbanda combines African influences with Catholic, Indian, and esoteric ones, and even has a large following among non-Africans. In contrast, Candomblé in Brazil is almost exclusively practiced by African descendants.

Sacrifice, natural rites, and magical practices characterize the Brazilian Umbanda.

New Forms of Old Religions

New religious movements often form out of arising conflict with already existing religions. Most of them criticize the rigid organizational forms of traditional religions and their questionable arrangements with powers of the state. They also at times attempt to revive certain aspects of traditional teachings and return to core beliefs. They often show a remarkable flair for modern and innovative types of teachings and communion.

In Christianity, variant groups have emerged such as Jehovah's Witnesses, Mormons, or the Pentecostal Churches. In Islam, the Ahmadi movement surrounds a "new" prophet while the Bahá'í faith seeks to bind all large religions and their teachings into one tolerant universal religion. The Bhagwan or the Hare Krishna movement is an adaptation of Hinduism. Numerous new religions sprang up, especially in Japan, primarily as an answer to defeat in the Second World War.

Back to the Roots

Many new religious communities have emerged in regions where heavy missionary activity occurred as a return to native cults. This has widely taken place in Latin America, but also in Oceania (pp. 220, 221). In North America, Native American religions have seen a revival along with Germanic and Celtic religions in the U.S. and Europe. Other new religions owe their encounters with the different religions and cultural circles since the 19th century primarily to modern "esotericism." This term refers to using esoteric knowledge which promotes personal spirituality. While it is not a unified religious system, the doctrine, originating in Asia, offers teachings and practices as an alternative to Christianity.

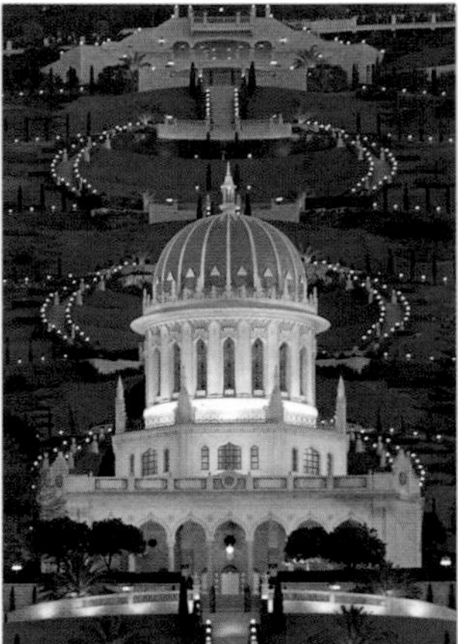

The Bahá'í faith, which emerged in the middle of the 19th century in Persia, is centered in Haifa, Israel.

The Pentecostal Church is widespread primarily among African Americans. Its charismatic preachers call for strict Christian moral conduct.

CULTS—BETWEEN LONGING FOR SALVATION AND MODERN TRENDS

In contrast to newer religious movements, the term "cult" generally takes on negative connotations. A radical break from society, strict discipline, and financial sacrifice are often required from its members.

The term "cult" has generally come to be known as a negative connotation of "sect," from the Latin word "*secta*" or "teaching, school, party," which derives from "*secare*," meaning "to separate, split." A cult is known as an unorthodox group whose faith and actions challenge societal norms and taboos, thus bringing about conflict with the majority of society.

Contents and Features

Working within so-called communal experiences, cults take current trends and modern thoughts, such as those on need, and meditative practices to a much higher degree than new religions. Many of them were referred to as "youth religions" in the 20th century since they primarily addressed younger generations and banded with those who had little to do with conventional religions and lifestyles.

The Unification Church founded in 1954 by Korean Sun Myung Moon organized a spectacular mass-wedding of its followers.

Many cults exert complete control over their members, often with controversial psychological practices and obedience exercises. Additionally, many of them seal themselves off from the outside world thus making it extremely difficult to exit the cult. Their protest against society manifests itself in special clothing, hairstyles, signs, and symbols. It is common for members to blindly follow a cult leader or master, often referred to as a "guru."

In the View of the Public

Negative headlines detail cults who demand of their members a complete break from their existing lives and social contacts, limitless—at times even sexual—devotion, and participation in dubious financial practices. Equally as dangerous are the different occults and satanic cults that are "destructively" aligned and the doomsday cults, which anticipate or have attempted to bring about the "end of the world" with attacks (such as Aum Shinrikyo in 1995) or mass suicides (such as the Order of the Solar Temple from 1994–1997).

Asahara Shoko is the leader of the Japanese cult Aum Shinrikyo, which carried out a gas attack on a subway in Tokyo in 1995.

Many countries and traditional churches attempt to protect youths through "cult representatives" and information centers to, at the very least, guard the impressionable through knowledge and, in some small way, subject cults to a certain amount of control.

OSHO'S FOLLOWERS *are estimated to be around 1 million "sannyasis" ("renouncers") worldwide.*

RAJNEESH CHANDRA MOHAN *called himself Bhagwan in 1971, and then Osho in 1989.*

AFTER RAJNEESH'S DEATH *it became apparent that his closest workers were involved in illegal financial transactions and criminal machinations.*

Bhagwan or Osho Shri Rajneesh (1931–1990)

The Bhagwan Movement

WITH THEIR SAFFRON GARB AND NECKLACES the Bhagwan-Youth generated great public interest in the 1980s. In 1970, Rajneesh Chandra Mohan founded the Neo-Sannyasin movement. Its community, "Rajneeshpuram," was located in Antelope, Oregon (1981–1985). Since Osho's death, a 21-member committee has led the community.

BHAGWAN'S LIFE-AFFIRMING TEACHINGS combined Eastern psychology, the sexual openness of tantric Buddhism, and the mysticism of Taoism and Sufism. According to him, the spiritual and profane worlds form a unit while every individual can become a "holy being" through certain meditation techniques.

BHAGWAN FULFILLED all the clichés of a hypocritical cultic guru when he traveled past his ecstatic followers waving at them from his oppulent Rolls-Royce.

Bhagwan followers dancing

Scientology Church

In 1954, L. Ron Hubbard founded the Church of Scientology with a doctrine based on combined religious, philosophical, and psychological elements. The primary aim of a believer is to achieve higher efficiency and sovereignty through "spiritual health." Certain, very expensive courses are available, which help an individual to become an "operating thetan." With this state, a person is able to rule their universe of material, energy, space, and time. Hubbard considered this a universal method for solving all of humanity's problems. The Church of Scientology stepped into public consciousness primarily through its persistent and media-savvy pitch for recognition as a religious community as well as through its missions and numerous business enterprises.

Scientology recruits with publications and personality tests.

21ST CENTURY

THE ACCEPTANCE *of some cults in the context of religious freedom represents a big challenge for many societies.*

IT IS AN OPEN QUESTION *as to how far world religions can absorb the need for religious change without losing their identities.*

➲ see also: Taoism, *Religion Chapter, p. 229* | *Philosophy Chapter, p. 250*

Monographic Boxes

Analytic Boxes

PHILOSOPHY

Philosophy is a daunting business. Unlike any other field of study, philosophy seeks to find a greater understanding of, or even the definitive and elusive "answer" to, everything. The gaze of the philosopher ranges over concepts as diverse as language, science, history, morality, gods, minds, beauty, time, love, and death. A physicist can measure the speed of a rocket, a chemist can mix acids together, a biologist can dissect a body, but to further complicate the job of the philosopher, the luxury of being able to prove their hypotheses outside of abstract theorizing is rarely possible if not impossible. And yet over the span of a few millennia the perspectives, methods, and findings of philosophy have provided us with some of the most exquisite, powerful, and convincing examples of human thought.

KEY FACTS

WESTERN PHILOSOPHY *originated in the city-states of Greece, particularly in Athens.*

THE PHILOSOPHERS OF ANTIQUITY *replaced beliefs and superstitions with observation and reason.*

COMPLEX ARGUMENTS AND METHODS *developed among different philosophical schools.*

LOGIC, *the "art of reason", became the basis of thinking.*

Pre-Socratics (sixth century B.C.) | Socrates and Plato | Aristotle | From the cynics to neo-Platonism (fifth century B.C.)

PHILOSOPHY: THE BEGINNING

The first philosophers of antiquity wanted to explain the world without any reference to divine influence. Essentially, what forms the basis of existence? Later, they also began to critically examine social values and organizational forms. They asked themselves under which conditions can humankind best develop and be happy? In a quest for the answers, various disciplines of philosophy developed. This movement away from superstition toward seeking reasons and explanations have formed the basis of philosophy up to the present day.

Western philosophy began with a quest to understand the true nature of reality.

PHILOSOPHY

PRE-SOCRATICS

The foundation for Western thought was established when the first philosophers countered ancient mythology with a natural philosophical explanation of the world.

Philosophy (Greek: "love of knowledge") was founded in the Greek city-states at the turn of the sixth century B.C. The forerunners of Socrates (p. 247) were referred to as the pre-Socratic philosophers.

Pythagoras studied both mathematical and philosophical problems.

Mathematics and Philosophy—Matter and Thought

The pre-Socratics sought new approaches to explain the world, without mythology or god. Out of this came two prominent mathematicians: Thales of Milet and Pythagoras of Samos. Having made radical breakthroughs in mathematics, they began drawing parallels with the nature of the world.

Other philosophers pondered original matter, or the first principle (*arché*) behind the existence of the world. Parmenides differentiated between a world of experience inaccessible to reason and a world of thought that comprises the truth of existence. In contrast Heraclitus saw the world to be an ever changing reality. Empedocles held that four basic elements were propelled by the opposing forces of love and hate.

Subsequent philosophers, like the atomists Leucippus and Democritus, sought to merge these contradictory propositions.

Practical Philosophy?

The Sophists, such as Protagoras, Gorgias, and Cratylus, avoided these debates. They were hired to teach rhetorical skills to students pursuing legal and political careers. Accordingly, the Sophists oriented their thoughts and actions toward everyday life from an individual perspective, not a generalized one. Social conventions were to be observed purely out of personal interest. The Sophists doubted man was capable of recognizing a final truth. They considered all values and philosophical interpretations to be relative.

Parmenides considered the everyday experience of motion to be an illusion. Instead, he believed the real world to be a static entity.

Arché

Early philosophers searched for the original principle or substance (Greek: *arché)* from which all development began. The pre-Socratic philosophers had very concrete concepts of arché. Thales thought it was water; Empedocles believed it was the four elements (fire, earth, air, and water). Others considered it to be an abstract principle. Anaximander postulated it to be the infinite *(apeiron)*, while Anaxagoras envisaged a world-encompassing mind *(nous)*. Atomic theory, which is based on the concept of discrete indivisible units, mediated between what is abstract and what is concrete.

According to Thales, water is the "primary substance."

HERACLITUS OF EPHESUS, *born about 550 B.C., died in 480 B.C. in Asia Minor*

PANTA RHEI *(Greek: "everything is in flux"): Heraclitus saw the whole world as subject to constant change as characterized by internal contradictions.*

THE HERACLITEAN NOTION *of endless change was the earliest predecessor of the 19th century concept of dialectical materialism (pp. 260–261).*

Heraclitus (painting from 1628)

Heraclitus and Dialectics

DIALECTICS (Greek: "to make statements and counter statements") describes the art of rational debate.

HERACLITUS was one of the first dialectic philosophers. He perceived the world as being shaped by opposites. Only constant disagreement and resistance make change possible. Contradictions can be temporarily harmonized or blended together to form new contradictions that will be confronted by contradictions. Thus, everything is caught in permanent flux. According to Heraclitus, we cannot step into the same river twice because although the banks and bed may remain as they were, every second new water is flowing into it, changing its very nature. And as we are also ever changing, we will also be different. Reality is like a river; it changes with every motion in space and time and, consequently, is never the same.

According to Heraclitus, "War is the father and the king of all."

see also: **Pythagorian Theorem and Thales' Theorem,** *Mathematics Chapter, pp. 152, 162*

SOCRATES AND PLATO

Classic Greek philosophy began with Socrates and Plato in the fifth century B.C. in Athens. Both thinkers primarily studied humankind and its life.

Nothing in writing has survived from Socrates, the first classic philosopher. But Plato, his most important disciple, recorded a number of his didactic positions. Unlike the natural philosophers before him, Socrates did not study nature, but rather human life and its conditions. He argued with the Sophists that, as a "lover of wisdom" (*philosophia*), a person cannot possess the truth (*sophia*) but can only strive toward it. That is why the basis of Plato's critical reasoning was the sentence: "All I know is that I know nothing."

Reaching the Good Through Questions

Socrates believed that the ultimate goal of all human action was "good" and "justice." A person does good when he knows what good is. Thus, knowledge must be increased. But, instead of being given to one directly, one must seek it within oneself. For that reason, Socrates would never lecture his listeners; instead, he questioned them.

above: *Socrates (470–399 B.C.) founded classic philosophy.*
right: *Plato (427–347 B.C.) founded the famous philosophical school, the Academy (Academeia), in an olive grove near Athens.*

In his numerous dialogues, Plato depicts Socrates as a partner in a dialogue who does not patronize his opponent, but rather assists him in recognizing the inconsistencies in his own opinions. This "art of the midwife" (the Socratic method) is meant to help ideas gain acceptance in a discussion. Later Plato also practiced this method in his own school. In 399 B.C., Socrates' critical intellect brought him in conflict with the authorities in Athens. He was accused of impiety and corrupting the youth. Refusing the opportunity to escape, he accepted the death sentence and, having spent the night in his cell with his friends discussing the nature of the afterlife and the immortality of the human soul (the scene is related in Plato's "Phaedo"), he drank a cupful of poisonous hemlock.

According to Plato, our search for a significant other is really a quest for immortality.

Love and eroticism are discussed in Plato's work "Symposium" during a drinking party.

Plato—Socrates' Most Important Student

In Plato's philosophy, ideas form a realm of truth to which humanity has no direct access. As in his allegory of the cave, reality envelops people with imperfect reflections of ideas. In spite of this, we are able to access these higher truths because our souls were given the knowledge of these true ideas before birth. Through reason we can retrieve this forgotten innate knowledge from our unconscious. In this sense, cognition is memory.

Platonic Love

Plato examines the nature of love in his dialogue "Symposium" (Greek: "banquet"). He presents the idea that love is a search for immortality: Our instinct to breed is a mark of this. But Plato further affirms that to give spiritual birth to ideas is far better than to give bodily birth to children. In this sense, one can best attain immortality through the ideas that are the fruit of philosophic relationships.

Consequently, physical love, although also important, is only the prelude to the actual and more worthwhile love of beauty. This love then detaches itself from the person being loved, and becomes a love of the idea of beauty in general. This ideal lies at the base of Platonic love as the quintessence of non-physical love.

Ontology and Phenomenology

Ontology and phenomenology are two different disciplines that have shaped philosophical argument over the centuries.

Ontology (Greek: "knowledge of being") is the study of the nature of all existence. It assumes that we have only a partial knowledge of our environment and of that which is observable. Behind the concrete manifestation, however, lies a deeper truth that can be revealed to us through philosophy.

Phenomenology, the study of the forms of appearance, is concerned primarily with concretely observable things. It analyzes the possibilities of human cognition and seeks deeper truths.

above: *Philosophers seek the deeper truth behind the "mask" of reality.*

The Allegory of the Cave

ACCORDING TO PLATO, people cannot recognize the essence of things using their common sense because they see only incomplete reflections of things that are projected into the darkness of their cognition. As if in a cave, they lie captive, chained by their ignorance and superstitions. In order to free themselves, they must throw off the chains and make their way out into the sunlight. Of course, they will at first be blinded by the sunlight, but as their eyes become accustomed, they will soon realize where reality actually lies and then start to understand its essence.

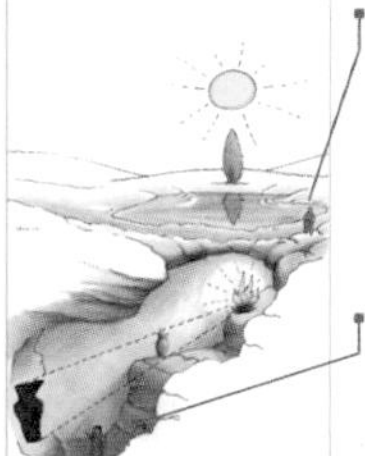

A person must free himself of ignorance and leave the cave to reach the light of knowledge.

A person in his cave does not perceive reality, but only its projected shadow, this renders common sense considerably less effective.

PHILOSOPHY

ARISTOTLE

Next to Plato, his student Aristotle is regarded as one of the most influential philosophers of antiquity. He sought the ideal conditions for an individual's self-fulfillment.

Aristotle was the most important student at Plato's school of philosophy in Athens (p. 247). He studied ethics and politics as well as logic, aesthetics, and the philosophy of science and epistemology. But Aristotle considered the most important philosophical discipline to be metaphysics (Greek: "that which exists behind nature"). Prior to subdivision into individual sciences, metaphysics examined the basic principles, causes, and structures of existence in general.

Political Animal

Aristotle viewed man as a "political animal," a social creature capable of finding happiness only in a community. In general, everyone has the ability to find self-fulfillment, unless hindered by their environment. In Aristotle's works such as the "Nicomachean Ethics" and "Politics," he sought the ideal communal living and structural conditions for this self-fulfillment as well as the goals humanity should pursue.

How Does One Become Rational?

A person chooses his actions well when his reasoning is trained. Unlike animals, Aristotle said, every person has a rational mind. A person learns the correct use of his mind through logic (Greek: "art of reason"), which Aristotle called analytics. Aristotle assumed that all thought occurs in concepts. These concepts are connected into sentences, and conclusions are drawn from the sentences.

Aristotle organized the knowledge of his time and established a system of thought. Among his many methods of proceeding are the notions of induction (reasoning from the particular to the general) and deduction (from the general to the particular). His accomplishments in this field remained valid well beyond the Middle Ages, and were very influential with regard to the formation of the great monotheistic religions (pp. 251–252).

above: *Aristotle (384–322 B.C.) founded his own school of philosophy in Athens, the Lyceum.*

below: *Slave labor provided the material basis for the intellectual blossoming in Greece.*

Know the World

Unlike Plato, Aristotle proceeded on the assumption that, in principle, a person perceives the world itself and not just a dubious reflection of it. He has a basic belief in our senses' ability to relay accurate information. According to Aristotle, potential things at first consist of an unformed material (bricks). Then a specific form evolves that is not inherent to the material, but rather denotes its essence as a particular thing (house). The specific form corresponds to the "idea" that occurs in Plato's "world of forms" (p. 247), but it has become concrete and is implied in the things.

It was mostly Muslim scholars who preserved Aristotle's works for posterity. They were readapted by the scholastics (p. 252) in the Christian West (medieval illustration of Aristotle's "The Ethics").

ATHENS *experienced its political and cultural golden age in the fifth and fourth centuries B.C.*

THE ATHENIAN DEMOCRACY *formed the ideal basis for the blossoming of classic philosophy.*

THE PHILOSOPHY SCHOOLS *of Athens such as Plato's Academy, Aristotle's Lyceum, and the Stoa were famous throughout the world.*

Athens around the mid-fourth century B.C.

Polis and Philosophy

THE STRONGHOLD OF PHILOSOPHY in antiquity was the city-state Athens with its democratic constitution. Here many of the citizens developed a lively interest in discussions about politics, ethics, and morals. However, only the male taxpayers were allowed to participate in public discourse. Women, the poor, and the enslaved were excluded.

IN HIS WORK "THE REPUBLIC," Plato designed his ideal state, which was also based on a strict separation of social classes. The philosophers should rule as guardians of virtue; the warriors should protect the state; and the craftsmen as well as the farmers should sustain everyone. Birth or origin would not decide the membership of the classes, but rather abilities and education. Always controversial, in recent times his ideas have been linked with those of totalitarianism.

MAJOR CONCEPTS like "freedom," "community," and "democracy" had different meanings than they do today. The ancient societies and their economies were often based on slavery. Thus, freedom was not something that inherently belonged to humanity. It was much more a social status that one could gain or lose, for instance, as a debtor or prisoner of war. Even in the Athenian democracy, the community of equals applied only to the wealthy.

The philosopher Plato points above to the realm of the ideals. His student Aristotle holds his hand horizontally, pointing at what we can learn from the real world (fresco by Raphael, 1508–1511).

21ST CENTURY

ARISTOTLE'S *models of ethics and politics are still being adopted today. For example, his demand for a balanced and just community influenced Martha Nussbaum, an American philosopher born in 1947. With regard to humankind's potential for development, Nussbaum analyzed the concepts of growth and poverty within the context of society as a whole entity.*

see also: **Democracy**, *Politics, Law, and Economy Chapter, p. 169*

FROM CYNICS AND EPICUREANS TO NEO-PLATONISM

Various philosophical schools emerged from classic Greek philosophy. They influenced Roman philosophers, whose thinking in turn affected Christianity.

Even after its political decline, Athens remained an intellectual center. Not only were the teachings of Plato and Aristotle carried further, but new philosophy schools developed. These schools, along with individual philosophers, primarily pursued the question of the possibility of a happy life.

The philosophy of Epicurus has often been mistaken as a license for debauchery and sensual pleasures.

A Happy Dog

Diogenes of Sinope sought happiness in independence (*autarky*) from all conventions and necessities. He often offended decorum and, therefore, was called *kyon* ("dog") by his fellow Athenians. His teachings were thus referred to as Cynicism. Diogenes once demonstrated his "doggishness" to an Athenian who asked him whether man was a two-legged, upright-walking creature without feathers. Instead of answering, Diogenes plucked a chicken and threw it at the feet of the Athenian.

Diogenes' disciples, the Cynics, were ascetic wanderers who lived from alms. They wanted to distance themselves from a society that they considered had taken many wrong turns, and sought to dispose of its values in order to achieve happiness in harmony with nature and themselves.

The Stoics met with their students in the Stoa Poikile, a colonnade on the marketplace of Athens.

The Misunderstood Epicurus

Epicurus founded a new school in Athens in 306 B.C. His goal was to provide the individual with an optimum of happiness during his lifetime. Contrary to later misinterpretations of his teachings, he was not concerned with the pure gratification of desires. Instead, reason should control lust and provide man with peace of mind (*ataraxy*). Reason should also take away the individual's fear of gods, priests, and death. Moderate satisfaction of one's cravings and prudent avoidance of apathy would make a happy and conflict-free life possible for anyone.

Reason vs. Passion

To counter the teachings of Epicurus, Zeno of Citium founded Stoicism around 300 B.C. He taught in the Stoa Poikile ("painted porch"), which gave its name to his philosophy. Stoics considered reason as the means to happiness and they considered passion absolutely contrary to reason. Therefore their greatest goal was to be free of all passion.

Much like the Cynics, they thought man should free himself from striving for worldly goods. Unlike the two aforementioned schools, however, the Stoics produced not only an orally transmitted dogma but also a system of thought that was refined over time and made comprehensive by including reflections on physics, metaphysics, and logic.

Roman Offshoots

Roman philosophers did not produce any new teachings, but carried on the Greek tradition, which they adapted to the circumstances of Roman society. In the first century B.C., Cicero and Lucretius served primarily as mediators, while in the first century A.D., Seneca mixed the approaches of the Epicureans, Cynics, and Stoics, and aspired to a peaceful and tranquil life in harmony with nature. Marcus Aurelius, the "emperor philosopher," combined political science and religion with a stoic ethic in the second century. In the third century, Plotinus founded neo-Platonism, which had a great influence on the Church doctrines of Augustine (p. 251), among others.

According to Epicurus (341–271 B.C.), a life of harmony and joy leads to happiness.

INSIDER KNOWLEDGE

CHRISTIANITY *was, in its early years, heavily under the influence of classic philosophy. But later the Christians turned against individual philosophizing. One of the most famous victims was Hypatia, who held the chair for Platonic philosophy in Alexandria, Egypt. She was murdered in 415 by a fanatic Christian mob. The last school of philosophy in Athens was closed by the religiously devout Emperor Justinian I in the sixth century.*

Diogenes is said to have lived completely unpretentiously in a barrel. When Alexander the Great offered to fulfill a wish for him, Diogenes asked him to move out of the sun.

Lecturers at the Berlin Humboldt University protesting against budget cuts in the colleges; they did not want to have to make do with a barrel as Diogenes once did.

➲ see also: Early Christianity, Religion Chapter, p. 236

KEY FACTS

NEW RELIGIONS *emerged in Asia with distinctive philosophical systems as their focus.*

DURING THE MIDDLE AGES, *philosophy was used in the service of theology in Europe, the Middle East, the Christian Western world, and in areas where Islam held influence.*

IT TOOK *many centuries for faith and knowledge to be separated from one another in philosophical thought once again.*

Asian wisdom | The servant of theology | In God's name—scholasticism | Renunciation of faith

KNOWLEDGE AND FAITH

How closely philosophy and religion—or knowledge and faith, as the case may be—really are connected is illustrated by Asian teachings related to wisdom. They emerged around the same time as the philosophy of classical antiquity, but soon these teachings took on religious connotations. During the transition from antiquity to the Middle Ages, Christian as well as Jewish and Muslim scholars started to debate the relationship between philosophy and theology. It would take several centuries before a gradual separation of faith and reason began to occur in the Christian West.

Approaches to harmonizing faith and reasoning developed in Asia that were radically different from those in the West.

ASIAN WISDOM

The three doctrines of wisdom from Buddhism, Taoism, and Confucianism quickly acquired a religious-cultural orientation, without, however, losing their relation to philosophy and ethics.

The three greatest Asian worldviews arrived at different solutions to basic human problems. They ranged from a radical break with the world to an acceptance of one's own nature through subordination to strict standards and norms.

Buddhism

Around 500 B.C., Indian Siddhartha Gautama, or the Buddha ("the awakened one"), proclaimed that he had found the way out of the eternal cycle of birth, death, and re-birth. Based on his teachings, Buddhism developed a comprehensive set of ethics that would lead the follower to enlightenment.

All acts, good or bad, bring about retaliation—primarily longing, hate, and ignorance—that leads to new suffering. Release from this can be brought about only through the complete killing of all passions. Accomplishing this leads to nirvana ("extinction") during which a person exits the cycle of rebirth. The path to nirvana includes the acquisition of knowledge, kindness, and an unquestioning nature, so that one learns to understand and accept the world.

The teachings of Confucius, which include respect for elders, are still observed in modern China (photo, 2002).

Taoism included old teachings on nature like the two all-encompassing basic forces yin and yang.

Taoism

The Chinese teaching of Taoism also skeptically pitted human knowledge and will against each other. Taoism, called *daojiga*, emerged in the fourth century B.C.

Tao (Chinese: "path") is the indefinable basis of all existence. It penetrates everything, unifies all contradictions, and generates yin and yang—the first pair of complementary contrasts. Yin and yang are not meant to be adversaries; rather they need and work with each other. They are light and darkness, heaven and Earth, man and woman, and so on. In Taoism, even a person is considered to be part of nature. Yet it is one's very capability for reflection and self-determination that can lead to misdirection. Rather than acting against them, it is better for a person to understand their nature and tao. Societal values are considered to be artificial. If one ascribes too much importance to them and strives strongly toward them, then one disturbs the tao and becomes unhappy. With this, Taoism abandoned Confucian doctrinal rules.

Confucianism

In a time of political and social unrest around 500 B.C., the Chinese philosopher Confucius developed a doctrine that combined philosophical, socio-ethical, and political aspects.

If Buddhism and Taoism are searching for a way to leave the world, Confucianism deals primarily with the position of the individual within society. Society is held together through virtues such as allegiance, respect for elders and ancestors, as well as observance and adherence to customs and rituals. The Chinese imperial state acknowledged the advantage of these teachings and made Confucianism compulsory for all goverment officials. From the second century B.C., Confucius himself was worshipped as a god within the official state religion. In later times, the rigid hierarchy maintained by Confucianism was heavily criticized. Some even saw in it the reason for China's social and economic backwardness at the beginning of the 20th century.

Philosopher Lao-tzu is considered the founder of Taoism. He is said to have lived in the sixth century B.C., although the first works attributed to him appeared 200 years later.

The Chinese philosopher Confucius is still religiously worshipped by some.

see also: **Buddhism, Taoism, and Confucianism,** *Religion Chapter, pp. 226–227, 229*

THE SERVANT OF THEOLOGY

Christian, Muslim, and Jewish scholars put philosophy, formerly the "queen of sciences," in the service of theology. In this way, they used it to bolster the foundation of faith.

For many centuries, the Christian churches controlled intellectual life in Europe. Under these conditions, to philosophize meant reconciling philosophical traditions with faith, or in essence, providing proof for the truthfulness of Christianity's teachings.

St. Augustine

From the beginning there was a conflict with non-Christians and dissenters against official Church doctrines. Around 400, in the time of the downfall of the Roman Empire and invasion by Germanic peoples, Bishop Augustine found justification for the war against nonbelievers and their ideas. Inspired by neo-Platonism (p. 249), Augustine developed a world plan based on divine laws of history in "De civitate Dei" ("The City of God"). The chosen and enlightened Christians would take on the nonbelievers until good triumphed with divine intervention. Until then, Augustine surmised, it is legitimate for Christian rulers to wage the *bellum Iustum* ("just war") against nonbelievers. With his doctrine that only faith leads to knowledge, Augustine's writing became the touchstone for thought in the Middle Ages.

left: *Figurine of a lady as a symbol of the Church (sculpture, 13th century).* **right:** *Medieval philosophy was subordinate to Christian teachings (carving, 16th century).*

Consolation of Philosophy

About 100 years later, while in jail awaiting execution at the beginning of the sixth century, the Roman philosopher and statesman Boethius authored his main work "De consolatione philosophiae" (The Consolation of Philosophy).

In it, Lady Philosophy visits an inmate inside a dungeon and explains to him why he is unhappy. External things like riches and power cannot make a person really happy, as one will always strive for more riches and power. Happiness, acquired through philosophical knowledge, can come only through self-sufficiency and confidence in the goodness of God and his destiny. In this way Boethius, an important translator and commentator on the works of Aristotle, tried to connect faith with knowledge, or, as the case may be, Aristotelian ideas with Christian ones.

Ontological Proof of God's Existence

Archbishop Anselm of Canterbury also wanted to comprehend and justify faith with reason. With his work "Proslogion," written around 1080, he tried to prove the unquestionable existence of God.

In doing so, Anselm defined God as something beyond which nothing greater could be conceived (the greatest thing). His second assumption was that something that exists in reality must be greater than that which occurs only in the mind. Anselm's greatest thing thus had to be surpassed in reality because if it occurred only in the mind, it would not be the greatest thing anymore. Hence the greatest thing, or God, must exist in reality.

Anselm's ontological (p. 247) proof of God was later criticized by scholars such as Thomas Aquinas, who believed it was illogical to attempt to go from ideas to reality, or from a definition of God to God's existence in reality.

One of the most important Church scholars, Augustine (354–430) shaped medieval philosophy.

INSIDER KNOWLEDGE

THE CULTURE OF PHILOSOPHIZING *declined somewhat with the end of classical antiquity.*

PHILOSOPHICAL WORKS *were casually studied in monasteries depending on which texts were available in the library.*

SOURCES OF ANTIQUITY *were barely accessible. For example, Aristotle's "Organon" was the only one of his works known until the 12th century.*

AVERROES, *born 1126 in Cordova, Spain, died in 1198 in Marrakech, Morocco.*

AVERROES *considered rationality to be independent of theology. He was attacked and persecuted by Islamic clergymen for this.*

AVERROISM, *a philosophical movement in the Christian Western world, was based on the analysis of Aristotle and the teachings of Averroes.*

Averroes (fresco, ca 1365)

Averroes and the Arabian Exile

SCHOLARS IN THE ISLAMIC-JEWISH WORLD al-Kindi (died ca 870), al-Farabi (died 950), Avicenna (Ibn Sina; died 1037), and Moses Maimonides (died 1204), among others, contributed to the revival of Aristotle's works. They preserved and further developed the teachings of philosophers from antiquity. One of the most significant Muslim philosophers was Averroes (Ibn Rushd), who was long considered to be the best commentator on Aristotle. "Averroism" later developed through his own analysis of Aristotle's works.

IN SPITE OF IDEOLOGICAL and geopolitical contrasts—for example, at the time of the Crusades—the transfer of texts and commentaries was successful due to the fact that the philosophy of the Islamic world dealt with the same basic problem as that of the Christian world: the mediation between faith and knowledge. During the Middle Ages, exiled ancient philosophy found a home in the Islamic world. Even Jewish scholars profited here from the tolerant atmosphere, compared to that of the Christian Western world.

Arabian book illustration (ca 1204)

IN GOD'S NAME—SCHOLASTICISM

Throughout the Middle Ages the connection between Christian faith and knowledge was strengthened and formalized. This was primarily achieved by the so-called scholastic method.

The term "scholasticism" (Latin: *scholastica*, meaning "that which belongs to the school") refers to the philosophy and theology developed in Christian schools that strongly influenced thinking during the Middle Ages in the Christian Western world.

Aim and Method of Scholasticism

The scholastics tried to connect Christian teachings from the Bible and early patristic writers with philosophical traditions, using dialectical reasoning. A question (*quaestio*), based on a given book or author, would be developed, in which terms were clearly and distinctly demarcated (*distinctio*) so that a logically driven debate could ensue (*disputatio*).

The goal of these debates was to find agreement in both sides of the argument instead of contradictions, and to match the accepted teachings of spiritual authorities (*auctoritates*) like St. Augustine. This process guaranteed a stability of the knowledge system but hindered any real innovations.

Thomas Aquinas

Scholasticism developed primarily through the rediscovery of Aristotle's writings. Through these writings, neo-Platonic conceptions of faith and knowledge were deemed questionable and in need of reform. Aristotelian philosophy was given new momentum by Albertus Magnus (ca 1200–1280) and his pupil Thomas Aquinas. Thomas Aquinas was opposed to the radical reading of Aristotle's teachings called Averroism (p. 251). Aquinas was afraid that the radicals' one-sided emphasis on rationality could lead to a separation of philosophy and theology. According to contemporary opinion, Thomas Aquinas overcame this contradiction between faith and knowledge. In his book "Summa Theologica" he synthesized the neo-Platonic and Aristotelian approaches in defense of the foundations of the Christian faith.

Via Antiqua and Via Moderna

However, Aquinas's work could not end one of the great debates of the Middle Ages: the problem of universals. Rather it developed into the conflict between the old "realistic" path (*via antiqua*), supported by Aquinas, and the "nominalistic" approach (*via moderna*) to which William of Ockham subscribed. This marked the beginning of the separation of faith and knowledge, or of the secular and heavenly orders.

THOMAS AQUINAS, *born 1224/1225 near Aquino, died 1274 in Fossanova, Italy.*

VIA ANTIQUA: *"the old way," taken up by the realists (concepts exist in reality).*

VIA MODERNA: *"the new way" of the nominalists (concepts exist in the mind).*

Thomas Aquinas (sculpture, 16th century)

Aquinas and the Problem of Universals

THE UNIVERSALS or general concepts (Latin: *universalis*, "general") were a matter of dispute with regard to their actual existence. The nominalists saw only names (Latin: "nomina") in universals, which were not real but abstracts of reality. The realists, on the other hand, claimed that the general concepts represented true reality while actual reality was only an imperfect image. In this they oriented themselves with Plato's allegory of the cave (p. 247). Several other intermediate positions were unable to win over any majority.

THOMAS AQUINAS proposed a solution from the standpoint of the realists. He differentiated Universals in three ways. First, there are concepts, which are similar to Plato's ideas and are created by God before the real thing ("ante rem"). Second, there are concepts which, in the sense of Aristotle, are present in the individual things ("in re"). These things by themselves communicate to us how they are to be thought. Finally there are concepts which were formed after the creation of things ("post rem"). Therein lies the biggest source of human error.

"This is not a pipe," this painting by René Magritte (1928–1929) says; rather it is only a picture of a pipe. In the same way the nominalists opined that the term "pipe" represents only the abstract conception of a pipe.

Analogy of Faith

Thomas Aquinas wanted to describe the relationship between God and His creations through "analogia entis" (Latin: "analogy of being"). He posited that all existence explains itself through an incomplete similarity with God. In this way the earthly hierarchy copies the heavenly one. However, there is no clear separation between the two spheres. One example is the pope, who as the representative of God on Earth is still a part of the heavenly order, as a ruler by God's grace. Subsequently the similarity and therefore the closeness to God can grow like the steps that make up a ladder.

above: *A Jacob's ladder leads monks on the path to Christ.*

Thomas Aquinas is enthroned between philosophy, astronomy, theology, and grammar while the defeated Averroes lies at his feet.

RENUNCIATION OF FAITH

Gradually, doubts began to grow regarding the acceptance of philosophical justifications of faith. Humanism began to focus on humankind and its social arrangements.

From the High Middle Ages, the Church began to lose more and more of its monopoly over the interpretation of all spheres of human life and sciences.

Faith Without Knowledge

William of Ockham (ca 1285–1349) was one of the first thinkers of the Middle Ages to separate theology and philosophy. He assumed that God created the world out of free will. Therefore coincidences and arbitrary things related to creation defy logic. God's will is not fathomable because it cannot be understood through human rationality, but rather only through faith and theology. Philosophy was to consider only concrete phenomena.

John Duns Scotus (ca 1266–1308) arrived at a similar separation. According to him, philosophy can act independently; however, unlike theology, errors can occur. Furthermore, philosophy can concern itself only with being and not with God, which often leads to skepticism as it does not stand in the certainty of faith. Theology, on the other hand, instructs people to be immersed in the love of God and is therefore helpful in life.

Nicholas of Cusa (1401–1464) deepened the gap between rational and theological knowledge. In a type of "negative theology," he claimed that one could not formulate any positive statements about God due to God's incomprehensibility to human reason. All one can do is to acknowledge this impossibility. In this way Cusa exempted philosophizing from theological activities.

Allegory of disintegration of the inherited political order in the Peasant's War: The mice attack the cats.

In later times, there were numerous similar attempts by scholars to differentiate between the secular and the theological. None were more successful than Martin Luther and his "doctrine of two kingdoms," which decisively broke with the "analogy of being" (p. 252), separating the corporeal from the spiritual.

Humanism and the Renaissance

After philosophy was absolved of the task of legitimizing faith, it could concern itself with humans as individuals and their characteristics. The scholarly circle of humanists (from Latin *humanus*, "humanly") excelled in this regard. They first formed in northern Italy in the 14th century and in the course of the Renaissance spread throughout the whole of Europe.

Humanists started to read the ancient texts of Roman authors with the goal of revitalizing the ideals of life and scholarship of antiquity. Their questions were pragmatic in nature and aimed to elicit answers for how one could live a good life or engage in useful thinking.

Along with these spiritual historical processes, several discoveries and inventions broadened human horizons: Columbus arrived in America, Copernicus proved that it was the sun and not Earth that was at the center of the universe and the printing press enabled quicker dissemination of opinions.

In this way, the medieval view of the world and humanity was gradually overcome. Even the clerical-feudal order was questioned, for example in the Peasant's War in Germany or through the rise of the working class. This paved the way for a more sober perception of reality, which prompted many new ways of thinking such as a new type of political philosophy.

Erasmus of Rotterdam (ca 1469–1536) was one of the most significant Humanists. His critique of the Church preceded the Reformation.

INSIDER KNOWLEDGE

A NEW WAY OF THINKING *began at the end of the Middle Ages in which rationality had its own kingdom.*

UTOPIAN WORLD PATTERNS *and "sober" political philosophies have had a big influence on the development of politics to the present day.*

THE HUMANIST IDEALS *of education started to determine the methods of teaching in both schools and developing universities.*

NICCOLÒ MACHIAVELLI (1469–1527) worked for the Florentine government. When he was suspected of betrayal, he was tortured, but later he achieved amnesty.

THOMAS HOBBES (1588–1679) was critical of the Church in his "Leviathan," and had to be temporarily exiled in France.

Niccolò Machiavelli (painting, 16th century)

Sober Policies

"IL PRINCIPE" ("The Prince") appeared in 1513 as the main work of Niccolò Machiavelli. In it, ethics and politics are analytically separated for the first time. Politics, it says, serves the development and receipt of power. Virtue has nothing to do with morals and at best serves to deceive illiterates. Tactical maneuverings to preserve the ruler's position of power are alone important.

THOMAS HOBBES CHARACTERIZED a state of nature shaped by the lack of morals with the words "Homo homini lupus est" ("Man is a wolf to man") wherein a "war of all against all" rages on. In order to achieve freedom, humans must transfer all their rights to an absolute sovereign, who controls the adherence of freedom: the Leviathan. The only right that cannot be taken from humans is the right of survival. The Leviathan must defend this right. If he fails to do so, he may be overthrown.

Title page of Thomas Hobbes's "Leviathan" (copper engraving, 1651)

➔ see also: Martin Luther and Reformation, *Religion Chapter, p. 237* | Renaissance, *Visual Arts Chapter, pp. 294–297*

KEY FACTS

THE MODERN CONCEPT OF *"subject" is established; philosophy and psychology are thus enhanced.*

REASON AND REALITY *become the central subject matters of philosophy.*

MORALITY, *due in part to scientific revolutions, is severed from religion, and is radically scrutinized.*

NEW POLITICAL IDEALS—*Freedom, Equality, Fraternity—are formulated and cause unrest in Europe.*

Withdrawing from tradition | Spinoza and Leibniz | Sensualism and empiricism | French materialism

THE BEGINNING OF THE MODERN ERA

The Reformation of the Church in the previous century along with unprecedented scientific progress allowed 17th-century philosophical criticism to distance itself from religious dogma, abandon the medieval conception of the world, and give birth to the ensuing age of Enlightenment. The philosophers of this era examined a world ruled by reason and re-centered around man. They began to doubt old traditions and authority, thus completely rebuilding the foundation of scientific argument. Their criticism of socio-political conditions would eventually lead to the French Revolution.

Modern philosophies began with a renunciation of classical and medieval tradition.

PHILOSOPHY

WITHDRAWING FROM TRADITION

Up to 1637 and the publication of Descartes' "Discours de la méthode," philosophical texts always drew upon works of earlier authors. Descartes broke with this tradition.

The French philosopher Descartes lived in a time of radical crisis: Religion was split among denominations, the medieval order was broken, and humanistic beliefs regarding the intelligence of humankind were questioned in light of the atrocities of the Thirty Years' War.

As a young man, Descartes witnessed this war and was struck by a vision: He should find the way to universal human knowledge. But he resolved to look for it no further than in himself and in the world, thus breaking with tradition and religious dogma.

RENÉ DESCARTES *was born in 1596 in La Haye and died in 1650 in Stockholm.*

METHODICAL DOUBT AND RATIONALITY *(Latin: "ratio") formed the central point of Descartes' thinking. He was a precursor of the Enlightenment.*

CARTESIANISM: *The teachings of Descartes (Cartesius in Latin) found many supporters, but also inspired critics with new theories.*

René Descartes (painting, ca 1640)

Descartes and the Foundation of the Subject

DESCARTES DOUBTED that one could trust sensory perception or human thinking as both were prone to deception. He likened these deceptions to a demon that persuaded people that wrong information was true.

ONLY ONE CERTAINTY remains: He who thinks, exists. Since one can neither trust perception nor traditional thinking, the conscious subject, the thinking "I," is all one can be sure of. "Cogito, ergo sum" ("I think, therefore I am") is Descartes's most famous utterance and is the basis on which his principle of knowledge rests.

THE MODERN CONCEPT OF THE SUBJECT is founded on the philosophy of Descartes. Earlier the term "subject" (Latin: "underlying basis of all") was considered as a carrier of characteristics realized during the learning process. With Cartesianism one begins to differentiate between the perception of subject and object. Descartes developed the subject of "I," which identified and evaluated the outer and inner worlds. It can also become its own object and thus develop self-consciousness.

"The Thinker" by Auguste Rodin

Through Doubt to Truth

Descartes assumed that all knowledge had to be doubted. Any idea that could be doubted had to be rejected in order to find a foundation for genuine knowledge. This "methodical doubt," rejecting perception as unreliable and admitting only deduction as a method, led him to one basic principle: Thought exists. And since thought cannot be separated from the thinking subject, I also exist. Only the sentence "I think, therefore I am" is in itself conclusive and hence serves the foundation of the subject.

All further derivatives of Descartes rested on this universal doubt. He developed dualism (from Latin: *duo*, "two"), which divided the world according to two substances. The *res cogitans*, or "the thinking thing" (inner world), covers the entire range of thinking and perception while the *res extensa* or "extended matter" (external world), covers the entire spatial expanse and all the objects within it. These two entities are entirely self-sufficient, with the only connection between them being the intervention of God. Descartes' rationalism later inspired the philosophies of Spinoza and Leibniz (p. 255) and was thoroughly opposed by the Empiricists (p. 256).

Not a question new to the time of virtual reality: Descartes had centuries earlier asked how it is possible to differentiate sensations between truth and illusion.

Mass executions, rape, and plundering were an everyday part of the Thirty Years' War. Between 1618 and 1648, the armies of German and foreign rulers devastated large parts of central Europe.

SPINOZA AND LEIBNIZ

Although they were rationalists, Spinoza and Leibniz contrasted Descartes's dualism, developing monism as well as monadology. Both attached great importance to the Christian creator-God.

Spinoza and Leibniz combined craftsman-like skill with scientific knowledge and complex philosophical thought. Descartes's teaching was thus developed further in critical and creative ways.

Everything Is One and God Is Everything

Baruch de Spinoza had already criticized the Jewish faith as a young man. As a result, the Amsterdam Jewish community, to which he belonged, expelled him. Even the Christian Church was unhappy with the thinker, and in 1674 banned his "Tractatus theologico-politicus."

Spinoza established pantheism, a doctrine that God is found in everything. With this, he assumed that the creator could not have been created, as that would require something more powerful than the creator. Hence, the creator must have been the cause of his own creation—he is *natura naturans* (nature doing what nature does). Since creation always happens in space, it requires a place. God created the world in the image of himself, *natura naturata* (nature already created), and thus God is always present in everything. According to this idea, a person wishing to become one with God should first become one with nature. In principle, this is possible since both the spatial world and nature are expressions of the creator. By acknowledging the unity of all existing things and their necessity, it is possible for one to become closer to God.

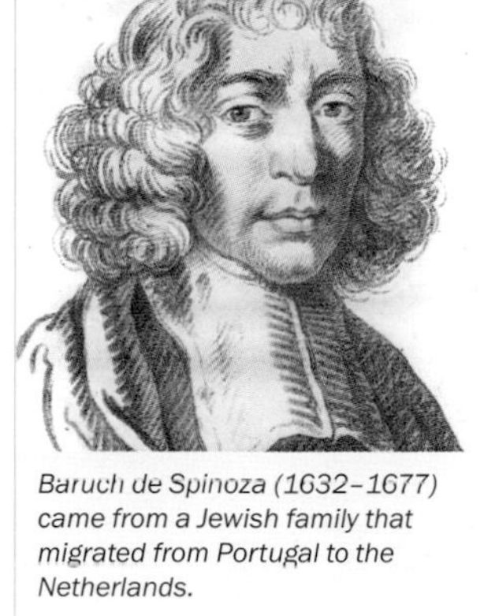

Baruch de Spinoza (1632–1677) came from a Jewish family that migrated from Portugal to the Netherlands.

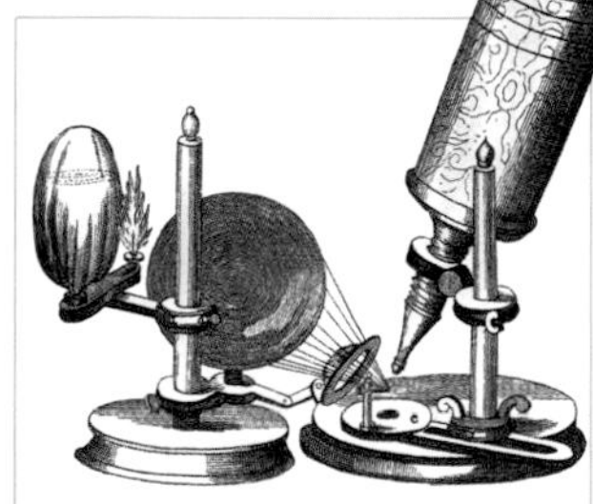

Spinoza earned his livelihood by cutting optical lenses for microscopes.

Spinoza at first agreed with Descartes's dualism in the sense of differentiating the thinking world from the spatial world; however, he believed the creator's same ultimate substance permeated both of these spheres. To differentiate himself from Descartes, he founded the philosophical idea of monism (Greek: *monos* or "alone").

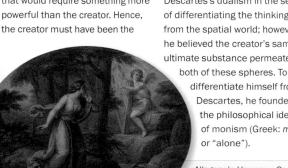

Allegory in Harmony: God can be traced in all manifestations of nature.

Monadology

Gottfried Wilhelm Leibniz was a wide-ranging thinker who designed financial programs and submarines, and invented the binary system, which is used by today's computers. Alongside Newton, he also independently developed calculus. In 1714, he published his treatise "Monadology," which proposes that physical reality is composed of monads. A monad (Greek: *monas*, "unity" or "single") is the smallest possible unit of being that is both indivisible and self-enclosed. It is the metaphysical equivalent of what an atom is for physics. Leibniz explained that God too is a monad and the harmony of all monads is proof of his existence. These monads make up all possibilities for the universe, but only some are realized. There is an infinite number of possible universes, and only one of them can be actual. Thus, the existing world was pre-decided by God, although he did not create all that was possible.

How then did "evil" come to exist in God's creation? In his "Theodicy" (justice of God), Leibniz wrote that the existing world is the best of all possible ones. This theory became both influential and infamous, and would later become the subject of Voltaire's satire "Candide." According to Leibniz, because the world is God's creation it must be perfect. Thus the imperfections of the world are actually due to humankind—specifically to their finiteness and their God-given freedom to choose between good and evil.

The German philosopher, mathematician, and historian Gottfried Wilhelm Leibniz (1646–1716) was an important universal scholar.

Monism and Dualism

In monism, form and growth are attributed to only one basic principle. One example, *nous* (spirit), was identified by the pre-Socratic philosopher Anaxagoras. Dualism is effectively based on two fundamental principles, similar to Descartes in his distinction between spiritual (*res cogitans*) and spatial (*res extensa*) substances. Since both these substances are basically different and not connected, problems exist. How is it possible to negotiate between the two and still be able to orientate oneself in the world? Descartes assumed negotiation took place in the pineal glands, where he believed the "heart of the soul" was located.

Descartes' diagram of the negotiation of a sensory perception from the toe by nerves to the pineal gland.

INSIDER KNOWLEDGE

MISUNDERSTOOD *as atheism, Spinoza's ideas triggered the "pantheism controversy."*

NAPOLEON BONAPARTE *used a battle plan of Leibniz's for his war in Egypt.*

AFTER 1968, *Spinoza was rediscovered as a political thinker.*

LEIBNIZ'S BINARY SYSTEM *provided the basis for digitization.*

PHILOSOPHY

➲ see also: Leibniz and Differential Calculus, *Mathematics Chapter, p. 158*

SENSUALISM AND EMPIRICISM

The British philosophers of the 18th century opposed rationalism, developing the concept that human thoughts are not a result of inherent ideas, but are based on sensory impressions.

Empiricism (Greek: *empeiros* or "experience") concludes that only experiences lead to knowledge. Sensualism (Latin: *sensualis* or "sensual") further restricts this and places emphasis only on the meaning of sensory experiences: *Nihil est in intellectu, quod non prius in sensu fuerit.* (Nothing exists in understanding that has not been previously experienced by the senses). This clearly states the main essence of their epistemology (or "theory of knowledge").

Human Intellect: Tabula Rasa

John Locke, the founder of empiricism, perceived the human mind as a *tabula rasa*, or "clean slate." The senses gradually fill the mind with input from worldly experiences. Hence ideas and images of the surrounding world are formed, enabling the person to find his or her way through the environment while interacting with it creatively.

The human intellect does not merely receive information from the external world, but also from within. The body responds to pain, happiness, hunger, thirst, etc., thus this sensory data can also form simple ideas. Ultimately, the function of the intellect lies in combining simple ideas with complicated ones, which can then be applied to reality. But it is also because of this that ideas and reality are detached from one another, thus making fantasies and dreams possible.

The British philosopher John Locke (1632–1704) also distinguished himself as a political thinker. His theories hallmark the concept of a liberal constitutional state.

The Scotsman David Hume (1711–1776) perceived the experience of the senses as the basis for all knowledge. Even morals and ethics are determined by emotions.

In 1690, Locke wrote his most famous work, "An Essay Concerning Human Understanding," to contest Descartes's notion that ideas are an inherent trait of humanity and that they can extrapolate the reality of situations without being influenced by the external world. According to Locke, a person can know of or perceive reality only in an incomplete form by virtue of the input from sensory impressions. Contrary to Descartes, Locke does not doubt the existence of reality, as it is that which evokes sensation.

To Be Is to Be Perceived

Like Locke, the Irish Bishop George Berkeley also concluded that all knowledge originates from sensory experience. However, he radicalized Locke's empiricism with the formula *esse est percipi* ("to be is to be perceived"). Accordingly, all that is not concretely perceivable would merely be a figment of the imagination because it would not officially exist. In this sense, Berkeley rejected abstract ideas that were senseless, such as the color "red" or the shape "triangle."

In "A Treatise Concerning the Principles of Human Knowledge" from 1710, Berkeley further qualified his theory through a discussion about a substance that cannot be perceived, but instead perceives: The infinite and ever-present spirit of God. Since God perceives everything, he guarantees all existence even when it is not concretely perceivable. This explains seemingly concrete ideas that have not been experienced in reality, such as angels. Last but not least, he discusses which perceptions are induced by God and which by reality.

The "Is-Ought" Theory

David Hume, a main proponent of empiricism, differentiated between direct perceptions and derived associations. Thus, cause-effect sequences, which are characteristic of many laws of nature, were constructed on the basis of similar experiences. Out of pure habit, though not always through direct experience, one can link specific causes ("the sun is shining") to specific effects ("it will be hot"). Hume thus questioned the principles of scientific knowledge that prevailed to this date.

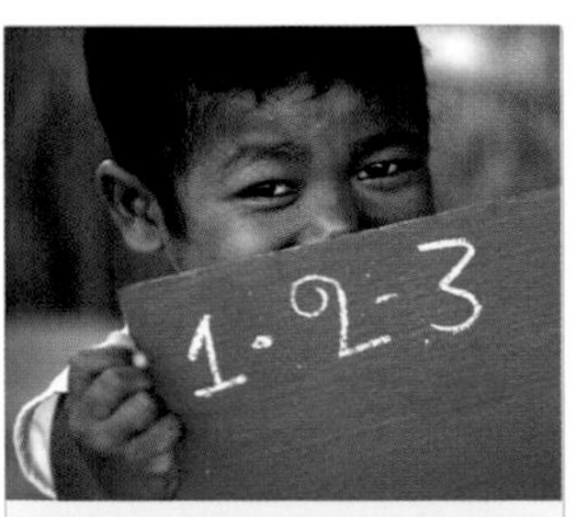

Tabula rasa: The human intellect is like a clean slate that is filled with worldly experiences through the gradual influence of the senses.

In 1748, Hume criticized the concept of the "self" or "I" with his work "An Enquiry Concerning Human Understanding." Since we cannot perceive ourselves as whole and static, subjectivity is an illusory idea. Hume's understanding of morals is also radical. He states one cannot derive prescriptive statements from descriptive ones. We cannot infer what ought to be from what is: "No ought from an is."

The Fable of the Bees

It was during the beginning of the 18th century that Bernard Mandeville, a Dutch doctor based in London, described the principles of pre-capitalist economic conditions and their social structure. According to Mandeville, this structure was based on the exploitation of the poor and the interplay of individual egoistic interests, among various other factors. War, luxury, and other vices promoted prosperity and development far more than virtue and morality. The philosopher George Berkeley—other idealists and men loyal to the Church—criticized the fable as an attack on religion and the middle class.

above: *A beehive acts as a metaphor for human society.*

see also: **John Locke's Political Influence**, *Politics, Law, and Economy Chapter, p. 257*

FRENCH MATERIALISM

In the mid-18th century, French philosophers pursued the ideal of comprehensive Enlightenment, thereby preparing the theoretical base of the French Revolution in 1789.

French materialism (Latin: *materia* or "material") detached itself from traditional philosophical ideas and problems. The Materialists focused on how life was lived concretely and sought to understand nature better in order to further human happiness in the political realm.

The "Encyclopédie"

Between 1750 and 1772, Jean Baptiste le Rond d'Alembert and Denis Diderot released the 28 volume "Encyclopédie," which contained over 75,000 entries. Numerous scholars including philosophers Voltaire and Rousseau (p. 259) were involved with this piece of work. They were referred to as the "Encyclopedists."

The "Encyclopédie" is considered to be the epochal work of French materialism. Its purpose was to provide an overview on the state of all sciences, from art to trade. It laid the philosophical foundation of systematics, which was based on empiricist concepts. The consolidation of all knowledge was intended to eliminate superstition and unfounded beliefs, thus establishing a rational future.

ENCYCLOPÉDIE,
OU
DICTIONNAIRE RAISONNÉ
DES SCIENCES,
DES ARTS ET DES MÉTIERS,
PAR UNE SOCIETÉ DE GENS DE LETTRES.
Mis en ordre & publié par M. DIDEROT, de l'Académie Royale des Sciences & des Belles-Lettres de Prusse; & quant à la PARTIE MATHÉMATIQUE, par M. D'ALEMBERT, de l'Académie Royale des Sciences de Paris, de celle de Prusse, & de la Société Royale de Londres.
Tantùm series juncturaque pollet, Tantùm de medio sumptis accedit honoris! HORAT.
TOME PREMIER.
A PARIS,
Chez BRIASSON, rue Saint Jacques, à la Science. DAVID l'aîné, rue Saint Jacques, à la Plume d'or. LE BRETON, Imprimeur ordinaire du Roy, rue de la Harpe. DURAND, rue Saint Jacques, à Saint Landry, & au Griffon.
M. DCC. LI.
AVEC APPROBATION ET PRIVILEGE DU ROY.

The "Encyclopédie," or "Dictionnaire Raisonné des Sciences, des Arts et des Métiers," was written by the French Encyclopedists (title page of the first volume, 1751).

Denis Diderot (1713–1767) was one of the main proponents of the French Enlightenment.

The term "sadism" has been derived from the French philosopher Marquis de Sade (1740–1814) and the sexual fantasies that he described in his works. Spending many years in prison, de Sade eventually died in a mental asylum.

The Encyclopedists saw knowledge as an instrument of power that could free them from political bondage. People must free themselves from propagated ideas and false notions in order to step into the realms of liberty, fraternity, and equality.

On many occasions, the "Encyclopédie" was subjected to censorship because it was suspected of promoting atheism and immorality. However, this did not stop the widespread success of the work, as censorship was rarely implemented.

The French Materialists also attempted to propagate their ideas and gain a larger following through other mediums, such as newspaper articles, public letters, philosophical discourses, novels, and poems. They allied themselves with other proponents of Enlightenment, even Europe's absolutist monarchs such as the Prussian King Frederick II, the Great (p. 256) or the Russian Czarina Catherine II, the Great.

Reason and Passion

With his novels and philosophical texts, the infamous Marquis de Sade went so far as to declare all morals as irrational, with desire the only guiding factor of action. He stated that this was natural and thereby also rational. His wild life and his radical views continuously brought de Sade into conflict with the law. Having freed their attention from contemplating the position of God in life, de Sade and other French Materialists began turning toward rationality instead. Their ideas inspired and fueled the French Revolution of 1789, which ended the absolute rule of the monarchy and abolished the traditional privileges of the nobility and the clergy.

The storming of the Bastille on July 14, 1789, was the trigger that sparked off the Revolution. One of the few imprisoned inmates was Marquis de Sade, who composed his first works in a luxuriously decorated cell.

With Napoleon Bonaparte's accession to power in 1799, materialism lost its political influence. Today, however, its ideals are at the root of all Western democracies and are the basis for the Universal Declaration of Human Rights.

Mechanical Materialism

ONE OF THE ENCYLOPEDISTS, Paul-Henri Thiry, Baron d' Holbach, conceptualized the world as a causal linking of matter (bodies) and movement. When specific bodies affect other bodies in a specific way (cause), the desired effect is thus necessarily obtained. The causes that result in reciprocative effects are determined by the respective matter.

MAN–MACHINE: In his work "L' Homme Machine" in 1747, Julien Offray de La Mettrie concludes that an individual should follow his desire. As the consequences of action are predetermined, one must not be concerned with morals.

Cause and effect are intertwined with each other like a clock. This interrelationship cannot be changed.

21ST CENTURY

ATHEISM: *A world without God is conceivable and likely.*

SECULARIZATION: *In Western industrial societies, the Enlightenment relaxed the bond of religion. Rationality and knowledge are considered to be the foundation of human activity.*

THE VALIDITY OF MORALS *cannot be proved. Moral conceptions have no validity in their own right.*

➔ see also: French Revolution, *Politics, Law, and Economy Chapter,* p. 168

KEY FACTS

ENLIGHTENMENT: *Rationality was to lead humankind out of ignorance.*

IDEALISM: *Hegel saw the driving forces of every cultural and historical development in ideas.*

MARXISM: *Karl Marx developed a political philosophy that had lasting influence on the 20th century.*

NIHILISM: *Nietzsche declared God to be dead. The "superman" was to overcome traditional ideals.*

Enlightenment (mid-18th century) | Romanticism | Idealism | Materialism | Existential philosophy (mid-20th century)

PHILOSOPHICAL SYSTEMS AND SYSTEM-DETRACTORS

Until the 20th century, philosophers like Kant, Hegel, and Marx founded large systematic edifices of teachings. Several individual authors objected to the closed nature of these systems with their comprehensive claim to universal validity. They focused their interests on the concrete human individual—his life and his emotional world.

At the end of the 18th century, philosophy was diversified by various approaches and systems.

PHILOSOPHY

PHILOSOPHY OF THE ENLIGHTENMENT

"Dare to know" was one of the guiding principles of the Enlightenment, which primarily went against superstitions and intolerance. Instead, it claimed, people should be driven by rationality.

The Enlightenment found a home in Prussia during the second half of the 18th century, when King Frederick II brought French Enlightenment philosophers like Voltaire to his court and even wrote works himself. A multitude of German Enlightenment philosophers flourished there due to the atmosphere of relatively high tolerance, relaxed censorship, and considerable freedom of opinion.

IMMANUEL KANT *(1724–1804) was professor of logic and metaphysics in Königsberg from 1770.*

HIS "CRITIQUES" *gave philosophy a new basis.*

KANT'S CATEGORICAL IMPERATIVE *requires that the acts of the individual be put to scrutiny in universally valid ways.*

Immanuel Kant (painting from 1791)

Kant's Critiques

KANT INFLUENCED others less by original ideas than by the systematic use of his own philosophy. In his three analyses ("Critiques") he structured and summarized a multitude of ideas that were circulated in the 18th century.

Critik
der
reinen Vernunft
von
Immanuel Kant
Professor in Königsberg.

Riga,
verlegts Johann Friedrich Hartknoch
1781.

THE "CRITIQUE OF PURE REASON" is an attempt to define the nature of objective knowledge. In it, Kant bridges the gap between rationalism and empiricism, by claiming that although knowledge starts with experience it is also formed by reason. Experiences are not direct but rather are shaped through space, time and categories such as causality, which are inherent to reason but make experience possible. In the "Critique of Practical Reason" Kant elaborates a strict moral philosophy while the "Critique of Judgment" deals with his aesthetic theory.

The title page from the first German edition of Kant's "Critique of Practical Reason"

Berlin Enlightenment

One German Enlightenment philosopher with wide appeal was Gotthold Ephraim Lessing. In essays, articles, and plays, he vividly represented the Enlightenment ideals of tolerance, humanity, and public participation in politics. He criticized the privileges of the aristocracy and the orthodoxy of the Church. His "Parable of the Three Rings," from his 1779 play "Nathan the Wise," refers to the common origins of Judaism, Christianity, and Islam.

Closely associated with Lessing, Moses Mendelssohn brought a Jewish perspective to the Enlightenment with his works on religious and aesthetical questions. He set about making rationality the guiding principle of action—such as the emancipation of Jews, who at that time still did not have "normal" citizen status. Only on the level of education and culture, like in salons, did Jews have the chance to maintain intellectual contact with the Christian middle class.

Alongside Lessing and Mendelssohn, the publisher and author Friedrich Nicolai was one of the most influential propagandists of the German Enlightenment. According to him, philosophy should be used for society to help better shape humanity.

Allegory of the Enlightenment: The light of rationality drives out ignorance and superstitions.

Kant's Systematic Clarification

Far from Berlin, in the east Prussian city of Königsberg, lived the most important representative of German Enlightenment: Immanuel Kant. He defined the Enlightenment as a method through which individuals could escape their self-inflicted immaturity, by subjecting rationality to precise analysis, thus scrutinizing the objectivity of experiences claimed by Empiricists (p. 256).

Lessing and other representatives of the Enlightenment tried to mediate between religions while espousing religious tolerance.

see also: The Enlightenment, *Literature Chapter, p. 344* | **Categorical Imperative,** *Politics, Law, and Economy Chapter, p. 191*

ROMANTIC PHILOSOPHY

A specific Romantic philosophy was especially common and accepted in Germany. In other European countries, however, it was considered to be too emotional and irrational.

At end of the 18th century, Friedrich Schelling, the poet Friedrich Hölderlin, and Georg Wilhelm Friedrich Hegel (p. 260) founded Romantic philosophy. Together these three men formulated a "systematic program of German idealism." Following Kant, all ideas, such as freedom, morality, divinity, or beauty, were to be unified into one comprehensive system. Unlike Kant, however, the group took a strong stance against the Enlightenment's emphasis on rationality and its neglect of feelings and needs.

Friedrich Schleiermacher sought to find a connection between theology and philosophy.

Fichte's I-World

The "system-program" was under the influence of Johann Gottlieb Fichte. He saw the individual "I" as the creative spirit and self-confident subject at the center of discussion, underscoring the uses of practical philosophy. According to Fichte, there is no objective reality or universal worldview. Instead, each individual shapes his or her own world. Certain principles do exist, which Kant also tried to comprehend, but only through constructive handling of these principles is it possible for people to form their own perceptions—their own "I-world"—not through theoretical contemplation.

Athenaeum.

Eine Zeitschrift

von

August Wilhelm Schlegel

und

Friedrich Schlegel.

Ersten Bandes Erstes Stück.

Berlin, 1798.

Athenaeum

For approximately three years, Friedrich Schlegel and his brother, under the assistance of Schleiermacher and others, edited the magazine "Athenaeum." This was the literary journal of early Romanticism. The content, short and spirited thoughts corresponding to the basic assumptions of the authors, suggests that thinking aims for the absolute, and thus can never be satisfied. However, through a kind of common philosophizing, a person could come close to it. Therefore, people should do away with rational systems and embrace the truth of natural thought.

above: *Title page of "Athenaeum"*

Schelling and Schlegel

Schelling, in his considerations, also proceeded from the "I." He found that it was in a terrible situation because it was far removed from the past when it had existed in harmony with nature. Philosophy now had the task of analyzing the dichotomy between "I" and the world, between nature and spirit, and in the process help to bridge the split.

Schelling felt that art was an important midpoint toward achieving this end. He believed it provided a practical example of what could be acheived by philosophy.

Friedrich Schlegel developed ideas similar to Hegel's and Schelling's, but took them even further. He sought a universal poetry, between religion and philosophy, that would replace the two, and through which humanity would view all other fields of knowledge.

The art of the German Romanticists reflects the ideas of this time: turning toward the "I" and studying its relationship with nature.

Return of Religion

This close connection between philosophy and religion as a remedy for a too rational human world was also characteristic of Friedrich Schleiermacher. Through his concepts of "absolute knowledge" and "absolute identity," he succeeded in connecting theology with the ideas of the Enlightenment. Both terms represent God, as it is only through contemplating his infiniteness that one can become aware of one's own finiteness.

JEAN-JACQUES ROUSSEAU *(1712–1778), due to his criticisms of the Enlightenment, is considered one of the earliest proponents of Romanticism.*

HIS "SOCIAL CONTRACT" *influenced modern conceptions of democracy.*

IN CONTRAST WITH THE FRENCH MATERIALISTS, *he rejected the claims of culture and civilization (p. 257) while praising the simple joys of nature.*

Jean-Jacques Rousseau (painting, 1766)

Rousseau and Nature

A PERSON IS GOOD BY NATURE. In the primitive state, people lived in harmony with nature and were happy. However, by the 18th century, historical "progress" had given birth to private property, agriculture, and the feudal system. This meant that people's conditions worsened as they were gradually alienated from their natural roots. It is therefore imperative that the ideals of the natural situation, such as freedom and equality, be integrated into modern society.

IN "THE SOCIAL CONTRACT" Rousseau developed his idea of the "social citizen." Social order and political power should be bound by rules that the citizens themselves have laid out. This guarantees a higher level of individual freedom for everybody.

Rousseau idealized the "noble savage," who was uninfluenced by civilization, and still lived in the original state of unfiltered connection with nature.

PHILOSOPHY

➜ **see also: Romanticism,** *Visual Arts Chapter, p. 304* | *Literature Chapter p. 347*

IDEALISM—HEGEL'S END OF PHILOSOPHY

Hegel created a system in which he wanted to explain all of the developments regarding the human conscience and their manifestations in art, history, religion, etc.

Hegel was considered a "world-spirit at the writing table." From 1818 until his death in 1831, he was a philosophy professor in Berlin.

Idealism was based on ideas such as "the absolute" or "the all" that exist independently of experience. Subsequently with Romantic philosophy (p. 259), Hegel gave German idealism a comprehensive system of thought.

Phenomenology

Schelling had already understood dialectics (p. 246) as a process of thesis, anti-thesis (negation), and synthesis (negation of negation), in which developments were completed. However, it was Hegel who first made dialectics an all-encompassing and generally valid approach toward explanatory processes of consciousness.

In his "Phenomenology of Spirit" in 1807 (p. 247), Hegel examined the nature and development of the mind through a series of ever new dialectic processes. In these, the thinking subject always overreaches itself. The different consciousness levels of the mind can be viewed in their many forms, from primitive appearances (phenomena) through the manifestations of the mind, as in art, religion, or history. Hegel believed the final unity of these evolving dialectical processes to be "absolute ideas."

The Master and Slave Dialectic

Hegel used his dialectic method to analyze historic development and the balance of power. In the open struggle between people for mutual recognition, the winners become the masters while the losers become slaves. If the slaves conform to their role, the masters can force work upon them. However, the masters also become dependent on their slaves, who then have the possibility of reversing the balance of power if they become aware of their might and position. They can thus overcome their masters and affirm themselves as equals.

The dialectic here shows itself in a sequence of thesis (desire for recognition), negation (death or slavery), and negation of negation (overcoming the masters and the acknowledgment of equality).

Napoleon was primarily a bearer of hope for Hegel. He overcame the terror and anarchy that followed the French Revolution and reorganized Europe according to his conception of the "absolute spirit on a horse."

INSIDER KNOWLEDGE

SELDOM DID *philosophers of the 19th century fail to make reference to Hegel—either positively or negatively. In this way, Hegel did not end philosophy as he had intended, but rather he inspired it.*

The Spirit of History

According to Hegel, the absolute spirit is behind all developments in history, all of which work toward its ultimate realization, as the highest of all ideas. Hegel wrote the "Science of Logic" between 1812 and 1816 in order to trace this spirit. Hegel's view of history is a progressist one, since everything leads toward the realization of the absolute spirit and only makes sense in that light. In this sense, his is a total system that explains and rationalizes every occurrence.

On Aesthetics

In his "Lectures on Aesthetics" given between 1820 and 1829, Hegel dealt with the manifestations of ideas in art. Here too, he saw the history of art as a series of dialectical processes. In the beginning, he claimed, there was the symbolic form, in which the idea sought its true expression in art without finding it. This was followed by the classic form in which the idea found its harmonious external manifestation. In the end is the Romantic form, in which ideas transcend individual representation and become infinite spirituality.

According to this idea, the art expressed in philosophy should disappear at this point, so that the unified idea could be conceptually understood, and even generalized. With his work, Hegel believed that he had accomplished everything, and that there remained nothing left to be achieved. In this way, he considered his work to be the "end of philosophy."

Left and Right Hegelians

For an idealistic philosophy like Hegel's, the simple reality is not important, but rather the idea itself. Hegel's followers were divided on issues like his statement, "That which is rational, is real; and that which is real, is rational." According to the interpretation of the Right Hegelians, this sentence meant that the existing Prussian state was rational, despite its autocratic ruling system. On the contrary, the Left Hegelians argued that since the state was irrational, it was also not real. One of their most significant followers was Ludwig Feuerbach. He saw history not necessarily as the effect of an absolute spirit in the sense of Hegel, but rather as a result of the emotional needs of a person for food, shelter, and love. He also considered religion to be a human projection. The young Marx (p. 261) also identified himself with the Left Hegelians before elaborating his own theories.

above: *Ludwig Feuerbach: "You are what you eat."*

➔ **see also: French Revolution,** *Politics, Law, and Economy Chapter, p. 168*

MATERIALISM—MARX'S NEVER ENDING HISTORY

Changes wrought by the industrial revolution provoked new developments in political philosophy. Karl Marx showed the working class the way out of the past and present to the future.

Unlike idealism, with its emphasis on abstract ideas, materialism turned towards concrete material things as the reason for all thinking and human development. Karl Marx and Frederick Engels adapted idealist dialectics by "setting it back on its feet," implying that Hegel had set it on its head, or upside down.

Marx and Engels published the "Communist Manifesto" in 1848 and founded dialectic materialism (monument in East Berlin).

Capitalism and Communism

Marx primarily occupied himself with economic theory. His aim was communism (from the word "common") in which a classless society existed where everyone could develop their capabilities and live according to their requirements. Marx saw the chance for self-realization of people through work. According to him, contemporary capitalist society had developed as a direct result of the previous stages of primitive communism, ancient slave-holding society, and feudalism. In capitalism, the freedom of the workers existed only in selling their manpower. Hence, for the common good of everyone, the means of production, such as machines or raw materials, had to be expropriated and nationalized. By doing this, capitalism would be overthrown and the path would be established for the worldwide conversion to a communist society.

Vladimir Ilyich Ulyanov, alias Lenin, created the Soviet Union, founded on communist principles.

Freedom and Necessity

In his dialectic historical analysis, Marx termed the history of humankind as a series of class struggles. Finally, the middle classes had fought the system of feudal nobility and had expanded an already partially existing system of capitalism.

However, Marx believed this trendsetting action operated only up to the beginning of the 19th century. After that, the middle class curbed any further social development of the working class. Hence, a revolution was necessary to encourage the already prescribed path of social development. Freedom, in the Marxist sense, exists in the knowledge of this necessity. It is not consciousness (the ideal) that determines existence (the material or living circumstances), rather existence determines consciousness. If people see this and recognize the laws of social development, then they can be free to act consciously.

Lenin and Trotsky

Lenin took up and adapted Marx's approaches. For him, there were only two possibilities: Either a person was for or against the revolution—with all its consequences. Furthermore, one party should collectively represent all of the working class. His aim was not a civil democracy, but rather a Soviet republic. During the civil and political strife following the Russian Revolution of 1917, Lenin converted his concept into a "dictatorship of the proletariat" as a preliminary form of the ideal communist state.

As Marx and Engels had not specified any future political form of communism, there was plenty of room for interpretation. Leon Trotsky, a comrade of Lenin, insisted that communism should be constantly changing as a permanent revolution. He strongly believed the Marxist idea that man was ever adaptable. Many 20th-century philosophers were strongly influenced by Marx.

"Das Kapital"

THE STARTING POINT OF MARX'S MAIN WORK "Das Kapital" explains that earlier goods were exchanged for one another. As division of labor and trading conditions became more complex, goods were exchanged through a third commodity, in which the value of all the goods could be expressed through money. Money lost its purely intermediary function in capitalism: It serves the increase of profits as capital. It is used again and again to gain more profits. However, an increase in value does not arise through higher sales—as purchase price in the market. According to the "added value formula," value is added when the manpower used in the production of a commodity is not fully compensated. Capital is always concerned with the exploitation of labor.

The means of production such as factories, coal mines, and raw materials are privately owned in capitalism.

"Advance constant capital": machines, raw materials, etc.

"Added value": Result of unpaid overtime work or exploitation

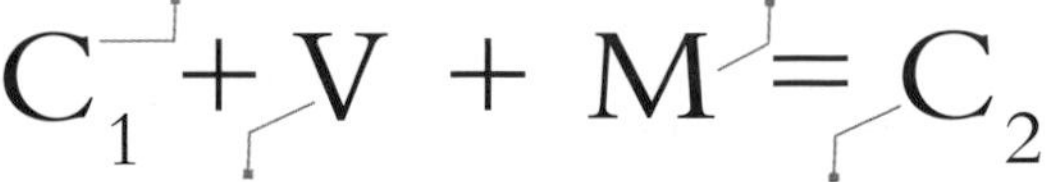

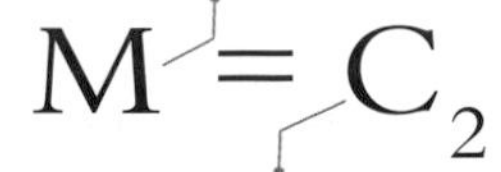

$$C_1 + V + M = C_2$$

"Variable capital": workers' wages

"Enhanced capital": profit

Dialectical and Historical Materialism

The basic teaching of dialectic materialism was to draw lively conceptions from the abstract (idea, law) to the concrete (examination in practice). Historical materialism researched history according to its development principles. The basic question was: How is the all-determining economy (the foundation) becoming transformed in society and how does society see itself, for example, through the eyes of religion?

above: *The Russian revolutionaries sought to put Marxism into practice.*

see also: Leninism, Communism, *Politics, Law, and Economy Chapter, pp. 172–173*

PHILOSOPHIES OF LIFE

A few philosophers strove toward finding a "more vivid" access to reality. They challenged traditional morality and intensely disputed the pretenses of scientific knowledge.

Contrary to previous thinkers, who created rigid systems with an emphasis on a few constant ideas or concepts, the philosophy of life aimed at a more holistic approach. Dynamic and creative life forces should be the determining factors of reality in its entirety.

Philosophize With a Hammer

Influenced by the ideas of Arthur Schopenhauer (p. 263), the German thinker Friedrich Nietzsche set about a radical criticism of traditional philosophy. He did not elaborate a clear system; indeed he was opposed to all "systems" as he believed they masked old superstitions under scientific jargon. His writings contain polemic perspectives regarding morality and history. They are intended to liberate "life" as an intuitive and rich force. One of Nietzsche's beliefs was that Judaism and Christianity were expressions of "slave-morality" because they glorified the weak and denounced the strong, thus keeping humanity back from expressing its life force totally.

Because Nietzsche's work consists mainly of often cryptic aphorisms, it has been subject to various interpretations. In the 20th century, his work was immensely influential among artists and thinkers, although it also gained notoriety for being claimed by extreme groups on both ends of the political spectrum.

Ironically, Nietzsche stated: "When thou goest to woman, take thy whip"; seen here with Lou Andreas-Salomé (left, seated) and Paul Rée (center); he later on fell out with them.

The Birth of Tragedy

In the "The Birth of Tragedy" (1872), Nietzsche explains how the ancient Greeks gradually distanced themselves from life. Their world was originally a harmonious balance of the "Dionysian and the Apollonian," concepts named respectively after the gods of wine and poetry. Desires and passions were either lived out directly or were experienced vicariously through art.

At Socrates' time (p. 247), doubt and reason triumphed over the life forces. Thought replaced action, marking the beginning of human decadence. Highly critical of classic philosophy, Nietzsche turned toward the long forgotten pre-Socratics (p. 246).

Henri Bergson's (1859–1941) intuitive epistemology questioned the sciences.

FRIEDRICH NIETZSCHE, *born in 1844 in Röcken near Lützen, Germany, died in 1900 in Weimar.*

AGAINST PHILOSOPHICAL SYSTEMS, *Nietzsche developed a new expression for a philosophy freed from tradition.*

NIETZSCHE STATED, *"God is dead", denying all existing dogmas and moral concepts.*

Later in his life, Nietzsche became mentally ill ("Nietzsche on his sickbed," 1899).

Nietzsche and the Superman

"HUMAN, ALL TOO HUMAN" was the problem, as Nietzsche saw it, and to overcome it was his avowed objective. He considered his contemporaries too outdated, too moralistic, and too conventional.

IN "THUS SPAKE ZARATHUSTRA," a philosophical novel symbolizing humanity's development, the hero realizes that life is a battle and the will for power is the basic underlying force behind all human action. Thus, moralistic arguments are neither true nor false; instead they are mere tactics in pursuit of a strategy that facilitates subjugation or submission. Man must free himself from these shackles in order to transcend his petty existence.

IF HE DOES THIS, he can become a "superman," and the force of life unhindered flows freely.

THE ETERNAL RETURN, the idea that everything one does will be eternally repeated, is a sort of test of the affirmation of life.

The superman's aim should be liberated laughter over a senseless world: "Laughing have I consecrated; ye higher men, learn, I pray you—to laugh!"

The Love of Fate

In his second "Untimely Meditations" (1874), Nietzsche criticized the science of history, which generated a plethora of facts with no practical significance to life. Instead of studying life, one should simply live it. His philosophy aimed at achieving the highest goal of *amor fati* (Latin: "love of fate"). This basic acceptance and love of life should be accompanied by liberated laughter, with which one can overcome all that is tragic, petty, and moralistic.

Bergson's concept of élan vital spread through the material world like a creeper growing in a jungle.

Life and Experience

Henri Bergson was an important French philosopher of life. Bergson calls humanity's natural creative impulse *élan vital*, or vital impetus, and likens it to the force behind Darwin's evolutionary theory.This stimulus for free creative development constantly challenges the inertia of material. He believed more in the force of creative intuition than in intellect.

PHILOSOPHIES OF EXISTENCE

The philosophers of existence studied the human as an individual, and how one perceives the world, while at the same time dismissing the established philosophies taught in universities.

Material or ideal facts are not the subjects of interest for the philosophers of existence. Instead they deal with the possibilities and conditions of individual action.

The World as Will

In his main work "The World as Will and Representation" (1818–1844), Arthur Schopenhauer points out that the individual cannot detach conscious thinking from the general thought of the world. There is a will that permeates the entire world.

Everyone can experience this: On one hand, we want to do something with our bodies; on the other hand the environment, society, and other bodies also have their own demands and wants. For as much as the will strives for perfection in various ways, it cannot attain it. It is forever unfulfilled and thus one is condemned to suffering. At best, one can abandon one's desires and demands, surrendering the will to live. Schopenhauer's ideas were much influenced by Buddhism (p. 250).

Arthur Schopenhauer (1788–1860) opposed Hegel's systematic approach (p. 260).

The Danish theologian Søren Kierkegaard (1813–1855) is considered the father of existentialism.

To Exist in Religion

Søren Kierkegaard, like Schopenhauer, oriented philosophy to the concrete individual. He believed that there were three stages of existence: First a developmental phase, in which the individual's behavior is purely aesthetic. Thus he experiences luck and misfortune as an observer, without active participation. Then, regardless of whether he so chooses, he enters the second "ethical" phase. In this, one has the freedom to personally choose: For example, the choice between short-term gratification and long-term satisfaction. However, as man refers himself to other human beings, the fear of loneliness, of living and dying alone, emerges. The individual can overcome this fear only in the third "religious" phase. All one can do is to hope that God exists, and die with this uncertainty. Herein lies the irrational element of faith.

Existentialism was a part of the protest culture of the youth during the 1950s in Paris.

The myth of Sisyphus, who has to undergo constant struggle, illustrated the substance of human existence for Camus.

Condemned to Be Free

Initially, the philosophies of Schopenhauer and Kierkegaard did not find any academic acceptance; their reach did, however, broaden in the 20th century. It was in the 1920s that Karl Jaspers and Martin Heidegger gave a new start to the philosophy of existence. Jean-Paul Sartre revised Heidegger's thoughts. In "Being and Nothingness" (1943), he advanced the idea that we live with a part of nothingness that allows us freedom of choice. The choice is the limit of our freedom: Every free act contains a negative aspect, as every choice one makes eliminates all other possible choices. Thus man is "condemned to be free." This daunting responsibility one has over one's free will led Sartre to postulate that people use "bad faith" to escape their moral obligations. Sartre also had a pessimistic vision of human interaction. When we are with others, we objectify them and they objectify us. Thus: "Hell is other people."

The Myth of Sisyphus

Albert Camus was a friend of Sartre's, until they had differences regarding political involvement. Camus's "The Myth of Sisyphus" (1944) is typical of his beliefs: The gods condemned Sisyphus to a life of pushing a rock up a hill, and it kept rolling down. Sisyphus's hardships represent the absurdity of the human condition. Personal goals can only be fulfilled conditionally. However, people keep making plans, which fail and prove the senselessness of existence. The question is whether one should tolerate this absurdity or choose suicide as an escape.

Because both Camus and Sartre were successful writers of fiction, their books and plays gained them a wide following throughout the 1950s.

Jean-Paul Sartre (1905–1980) and his life-long friend, the author and feminist Simone de Beauvoir (1908–1986).

INSIDER KNOWLEDGE

SCHOPENHAUER, *like Hegel, taught at Berlin University. Whereas Hegel had an audience of 300, Schopenhauer had merely three.*

THE CURE *recorded the pop song "Killing an Arab" in 1978, inspired by Camus's "The Stranger."*

SARTRE *rejected the Nobel Prize for Literature, as he did not want to become a Western institution.*

see also: Existentialism, *Literature Chapter, p. 357*

PHILOSOPHY

KEY FACTS

LOGIC *contributed significantly to the technical progress that dominated the 20th century.*

STRUCTURALISM *seeks structures in all areas of thought.*

THE ESTABLISHMENT *of subjective and socially critical theories after 1945 laid the groundwork for the 1968 movement.*

POSTSTRUCTURALISM *reflects the development of ideas and systems.*

Logic and structuralism | Frankfurt School and the linguistic turn | Discourse analysis | Poststructuralism

PHILOSOPHY AT THE TURNING POINT

Since the second half of the 20th century, philosophy has been characterized less by a dominant trend than by various cooperating and competing approaches. The analysis of language and communication in logic and structuralism seemed to be the ideal way to understand the modern world. Along with newer philosophical methods, such as discourse analysis and deconstruction, they have introduced a fruitful phase of theory construction. This includes gender research as well as media theory and the new political philosophies relating to globalization.

At the turn of the 21st century, the diversity of philosophical approaches corresponds to the increasingly complex world.

LOGIC AND STRUCTURALISM

While linguistic analytic philosophy in English-speaking countries was based on logic, French structuralism postulated an unconscious handling of language.

Logic as a science of reasoning is closely related to sciences such as mathematics. It deals with translating arguments into structures that lead to true or false statemants.

Logic and Sciences

Aristotle (p. 248) laid down the foundations of classical logic in his "Organon." Charles Sanders Peirce and Gottlob Frege modernized it in the late 19th century by independently developing predicate logic. This further formalized and advanced philosophy, and allowed statements to be analyzed in different ways. This was essential for analytical philosophy, the underlying idea being that if one can correctly translate arguments into logic, one will avoid making errors in reasoning. Bertrand Russell was a father of analytical philosophy and one of the most significant logicians of the 20th century. He made an attempt to ground mathematics in logic.

Later, the principle of bivalent logic (true and false) came under fundamental criticism. Thus, "possible" was introduced as a third category. Consequently, diverse multi-valued or polyvalent logic resulted from this three-valued logic. This was also utilized for the development of computer programs.

Structuralists Michel Foucault, Jacques Lacan, Claude Lévi-Strauss, and Roland Barthes (left to right) as the "savage minds." In his work "The Savage Mind," Lévi-Strauss examined the worldviews in "primitive" cultures.

Language and Signs

Ferdinand de Saussure, the linguist who is regarded as the founder of structuralism, believed that language follows an underlying structure. This observation was transferred to systems of relationships by the ethnologist Claude Lévi-Strauss. These systems follow fixed structures that unconsciously regulate social relations. Semiotics (from the Greek *"semeion"*: sign) further expanded Saussure's approach. Roland Barthes, Umberto Eco, and others analyzed signs, their meanings, and their influence on thoughts.

Psyche and Politics

The psychoanalyst Jacques Lacan applied structuralism to the unconscious, claiming the latter was "structured like a language." He differentiated three orders in the formation of the ego: the imaginary, the symbolic, and the real.

Julia Kristeva associated political and psychoanalytic perspectives with language. Only through expression in language can thoughts become free. She emphasized the ambiguities of language rather than its aptitude for specfic, denotative meaning. This led her into poststructuralism, joining, among others, Michel Foucault (p. 266).

In the "Mythologies," French philosopher Roland Barthes describes how everyday objects can be loaded with extra meaning; the Citroën DS became the goddess "déesse."

Linguistic Signs

FERDINAND DE SAUSSURE examined linguistic signs, which he understood as a link between the word and the designated object. He differentiated between the spoken and written word, the "signifier" and the abstract meaning, the "signified." The latter, in turn, referred to the "referent," the extra-linguistic reality. The linking of signifier and signified is chance. The signified "tree" has, for example, a number of signifiers like "Baum" or "arbre." The connection within a language is only fixed when all other signifiers mean something else. Thus, the signified "tree" can only be assigned the series of sounds "tree." Although de Saussure's theory is considerably more simple than what was to follow, his point of view that a language can be understood only within a system prepared the way for the development of structuralism theory.

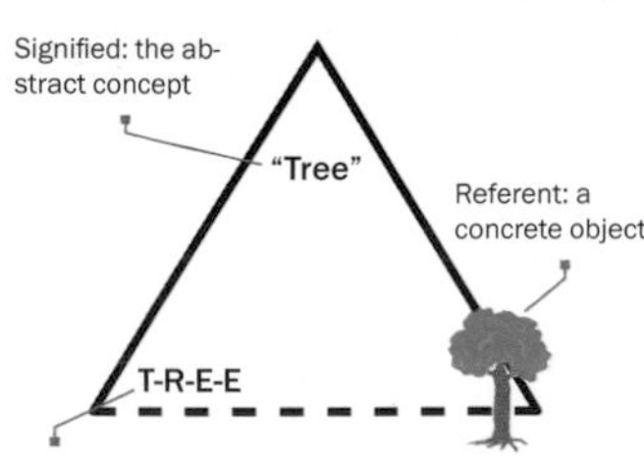

above: *Language is based on the learning of sounds*
left: *Relationship of the signs according to Saussure*

see also: Developmental Psychology, *Psychology Chapter, p. 276*

THE FRANKFURT SCHOOL AND THE LINGUISTIC TURN

In the second half of the 20th century, philosophy acquired new perspectives in reference to languages and society that were to have a strong influence on people's lives.

The sociologist and philosopher Max Horkheimer developed the Frankfurt Institute for Social Research in the 1930s into a center of political philosophy.

The Personal Becomes Political

Horkheimer founded the Frankfurt School and its "critical theory" together with Theodor W. Adorno, Erich Fromm, and Herbert Marcuse. Influenced by Marxist social theory, they concentrated at first on capitalism and related phenomena, such as the tendency to view everything and everyone as a commodity. Later they dedicated themselves primarily to the analysis of fascism. For Horkheimer, this was a crisis form of capitalism: "Whoever does not want to talk of capitalism should be silent about fascism."

A psychoanalytical perspective was added to the Marxist view of the world (p. 261). It placed the oppression of man's collective unconscious in relation to political oppression. In particular, Herbert Marcuse saw the way to true political freedom through the freeing of the collective unconscious. He thus became one of the philosophical mentors of the 1968 student movement in Germany. Through the movement, the Frankfurt School had a decisive role in the liberalization of society.

Jürgen Habermas, held to be one of the most important students of the Frankfurt School, put forth his "Theory of Communicative Action" in 1981. In this, he claimed that rationality was located in the structures of communicative linguistics and not within the thinking subject. He described an ideal speech situation in which all participants would be equal and could thus produce rational discourse and actions.

Jürgen Habermas (born 1929) propagated a domination-free communication and the tying of state power to the processes of public opinion shaping.

Linguistic Turn

With his interest in communication, Habermas pursued the "Linguistic Turn," which relates to the philosophy of language. After this turn, language was no longer regarded as just a neutral mediator of information but rather as a discourse, as communicative space. Only in this space are statements and cognition possible, and truths determined. Every development of human knowledge and thinking follows linguistic structures.

In the anglophone world dominated by analytic philosophy, a change in the other direction took place. Richard Rorty moved toward a so-called post-analytic philosophy. For him, there were no universally valid truths. Instead, he championed the freedom of the individual's ability to (re)create oneself.

The Personal Becomes Political: The 1968 generation consciously turned against the domination and moral concepts of the middle class.

Justice and Solidarity

In 1971, in the field of political and moral philosophy, John Rawls advanced "A Theory of Justice," which rested on the equality of the members of society. He stressed a liberty of the individual that would not be restricted by an abstract principle of "justice" but would instead be based on the solidarity of humankind, so that the position of the rich will benefit the poor.

INSIDER KNOWLEDGE

ADORNO *also composed modern classical music. He detested pop music, which he considered a product of the culture industry.*

DURING THE NAZI ERA, *the Frankfurt Institute for Social Research relocated to New York.*

RICHARD RORTY *was one of the most controversial philosophers of recent times, not least because of his position on American foreign policy.*

THEODOR W. ADORNO *was born in 1903 in Frankfurt am Main, Germany, died 1969 in Visp, Switzerland.*

IN THE HOLOCAUST, *Adorno saw an epoch-making cultural break that required a radical reorientation of philosophy.*

THE STUDENT MOVEMENT *of the 1970s and 1980s was greatly influenced by Adorno.*

Theodor W. Adorno, 1968

Dialectic of the Enlightenment

IN A WORK co-authored with Max Horkheimer from 1944 to 1947, Adorno opined that the Enlightenment had reached its end. Reason had demystified the world and helped to master nature, in the course of which reason itself was glorified and exploited as a legend. The individual subject had lost his significance and had to be subordinated to the rationalization of all spheres of life, as well as the domination of the economy and technology. The masses were ready to submit to totalitarian ideologies like fascism.

THE ARTS also had nothing left to counter rationalism. Comprehensive economization had replaced them with a manipulative culture industry. This was meant to distract the masses from reality.

Adorno considered the amusements of the masses to be a sell-out of culture that was meant to lead to a targeted dulling of their minds.

➔ see also: **1968 Movement,** *Politics, Law, and Economy Chapter, p. 185*

DISCOURSE ANALYSIS AND THE HISTORY OF SCIENCE

One of the most successful innovations in the humanities and cultural sciences was Foucault's discourse analysis. This has had a great influence on the history of modern systems of thought.

"Discipline and Punish," Foucault's work about the development of a disciplinary society, moves from the public torturing and execution of the assassin Damien in 1757 to the foundations of the modern penal system.

Since the 1940s, an attempt was being made in France to find a new way to examine the sciences. While cognitive theories were primarily concentrating on human subjects, epistemology analyzed the basic structures and thought patterns of scientific theory construction. Here the focus was on the *episteme* (Greek: "knowledge" or "science"): the underlying historical conditions that make scientific theories possible. Proponents of epistemology included Gaston Bachelard, Georges Canguilhem, and the Marxist Louis Althusser, who had a direct influence on Michel Foucault.

The Order of Things

In his works "Madness and Civilization," "The Order of Things," and "Discipline and Punish," Michel Foucault describes how systems of knowledge change under certain historical conditions. In 1966 with "The Order of Things," he focused on the role of the episteme in the formation of scientific discourse and the influence of the latter on society. He advanced the idea that the episteme, the historical conditions that produce a "truth," shift from one period to another.

A special chair was created for Michel Foucault (1926–1984) in Paris, "Professor of the History of Systems of Thought"

Foucault challenged traditional intellectual history with his discourse analysis. He showed how many generally accepted concepts in various spheres of life were in fact the result of historical conditions. For example, in "Madness and Civilization," he shows how the political, social, and scientific framework of the 19th century formed the concept of insanity as a treatable disease, whereas in the previous century, it was almost considered a crime.

The development of movable type-printing up to modern media and information technology changed the worldview and perception of humankind. This resulted in new questions and perspectives developing in philosophy.

Truth and Power

In the 1970s, Foucault's work took a new direction. Whereas he previously examined what made certain knowledge come to be regarded as true, now he became interested in the effect of knowledge in connection to power. For example, in the first volume of "The History of Sexuality," he describes how psychoanalysis borrowed from the confession techniques of the Catholic Church and similarly invested itself with power.

Power is not only exercised from above. Even those subjected to power have a share in it. People are interconnected in complex webs: The boss exploits the worker and the worker lets himself be exploited.

Foucault asked why we let ourselves be subjugated with such relish.

Body and Submission

In "The History of Sexuality," Foucault asks why people are so enthusiastically submissive. He claims that, since antiquity, discourse has built up around the body that concerns, among other things, sexuality, nutrition, and hygiene. They all work towards self-discipline of the body. This control that the subjects impose on themselves creates the space for all other forms of submission.

Science and Progress

Others have also examined the historical development of science. In "A History of Scientific Thought: Elements of a History of Science," Michel Serres shows how close the humanities and natural science are despite claims of the 19th century. Isabelle Stengers and Bruno Latour, among others, doubt the influence of exacting methods and historical circumstances on the formation of systems of knowledge. Thus, at present, the belief in lineal progress and provable truths is being critically examined.

Media Theory

IN "THE GUTENBERG GALAXY" (1962), Marshall McLuhan analyzed how various forms of media, through changing how we perceive the world, affect society, politics, etc. Thus he traced most modern values to print technology, and argued that with electronic interdependence the world would become a "global village." He later also famously claimed that "the medium is the message," meaning that the form of a given media affects us more than its content.

IN "DRIVING THE SPIRIT OUT OF THE HUMANITIES" (1980), Friedrich Kittler described technological media as a historical precondition of the humanities. Without them, Lacan's differentiation of the three orders of perception, the real, the imaginary, and the symbolic, would not have been possible.

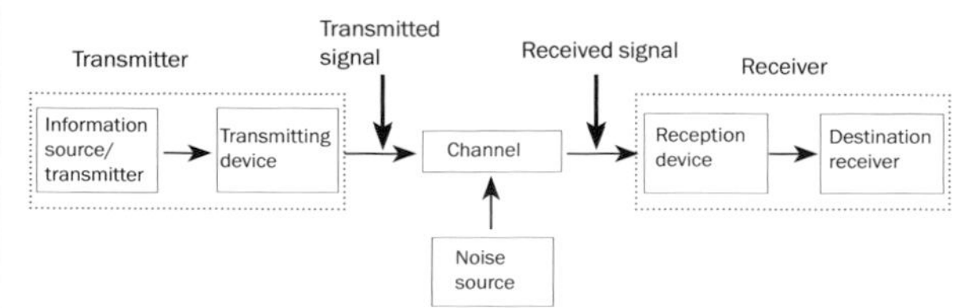

Model of the process of media transmission: The noise in the "channel" can lead to distortion of the transmitted information.

DIFFÉRANCE PHILOSOPHY AND POSTSTRUCTURALISM

Many philosophers doubt that structuralism is also capable of describing dynamic processes and the ambiguous facts of a situation.

From the 1970s onward, many philosophers critically analyzed thinking that assumed fixed structures and systems.

Différance and Différence

In "Writing and Difference" (1967), Jacques Derrida criticized the central position of spoken language in structuralism. With the term *différance* he referred to the importance of writing. This artificial word has the same sound as the known word *différence* (French: "difference"); the distinction is recognizable only in writing. Writing is therefore not only a medium, but also something independent. The différance is a reference to something inexplicable and disquieting in the relationship between writing and language. Derrida did not want to develop a new system but to "deconstruct" all the statement systems and their claims to truth. This demonstrates that every system undertakes irrational repressions and exclusions that do not correspond to the actual multiplicity of possible meanings.

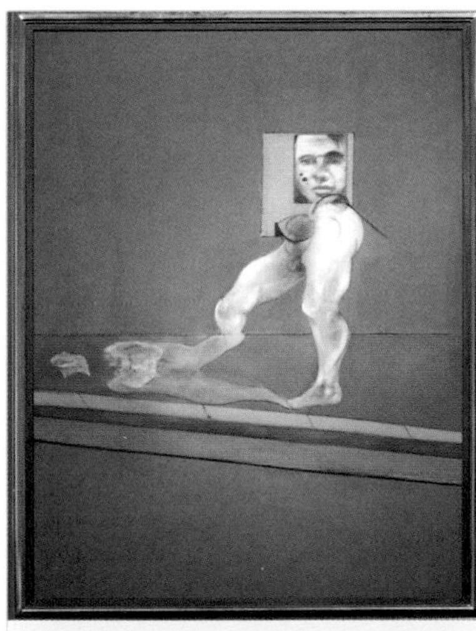

Francis Bacon, "Study from Human Body and Portrait", 1988. In "The Logic of Sensation" Gilles Deleuze describes Francis Bacon as a painter of différance who, with his deformed bodies, created a new school of painting between the abstract and the figurative.

The philosopher Jacques Derrida (1930–2004) placed writing at the center of his ideas and founded deconstruction.

In deconstructive architecture, traditional building forms dissolve.

Global Deconstruction

The relative simplicity of Derrida's fundamental approach earned him great notoriety. His method was adopted not only in the humanities, but also in architecture and literature. The concept of the différance was also significant for French-speaking feminism, represented by authors like Luce Irigaray, Hélène Cixous, and Julia Kristeva. They described the position of women as that of différance. In and of itself, there is no female identity; rather this gender difference has been created as a result of male systems that should be deconstructed.

War Without Battle Lines

In 1972, Gilles Deleuze published the books "Anti-Oedipus" together with the psychoanalyst and philosopher Félix Guattari. This fundamental criticism of structuralism in linguistics, psychoanalysis, and ethnology was considered a major statement of so-called "poststructuralism."

Deleuze was interested in decentralized systems of thought that were capable of describing the complex shape of the world. To that end, together with Guattari, he developed a series of terms like rhizome, schizoanalysis, line, micropolitics, war machine, nomadology, etc.

In contrast to Derrida, whose interests lay with philosophy's internal issues, Deleuze sought to grasp the world, not as it is, but rather as it will be. For him, the process of becoming was the important thing. Deleuze had clear political directives. He still wanted to abolish capitalism in the 1990s and re-define socialism. Philosophy was meant to be a kind of guerrilla, who wages a "war without battle lines." The philosopher Michel Foucault said that perhaps one day the 20th century would be called "Deleuzian."

21ST CENTURY

PRESENT DAY PHILOSOPHIES *are complex and differentiated not least of all because the world appears complicated. Designs of an individual art of living are related to approaches that criticize globalization and its effects on the environment, humankind, and culture. Without socio-cultural improvements, humankind will not be able to fully develop itself.*

State of Emergency

In "Empire" and "Multitude—War and Democracy in the Age of the Empire" (2000–2004), Tonio Negri and Michael Hardt developed a theory of globalization and resistance to globalization based on the work of Deleuze and Foucault. The Slovenian psychoanalyst and philosopher Slavoj Zizek deemed "Empire" to become as influential in the 21st century as Marx's "Communist Manifesto" had been in the 19th and 20th centuries. It describes the supposed normality of the present as a historical state of emergency, and predicts that after the collapse of the socialist states, an alternative system will emerge. The basis for this is the unbearable position of scores of workers and the unemployed. Their existence has been permanently reduced to a subsistance level of bare survival.

above: *Job hunters wait before a job market in Moscow*

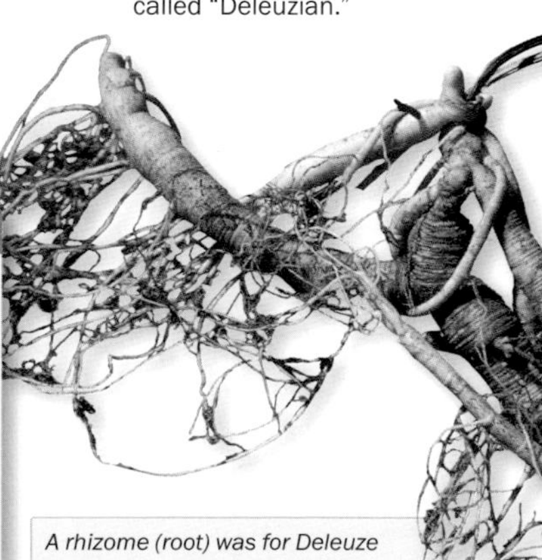

A rhizome (root) was for Deleuze the model of a non-hierarchical, variable, and diverse order.

Monographic Boxes

Analytic Boxes

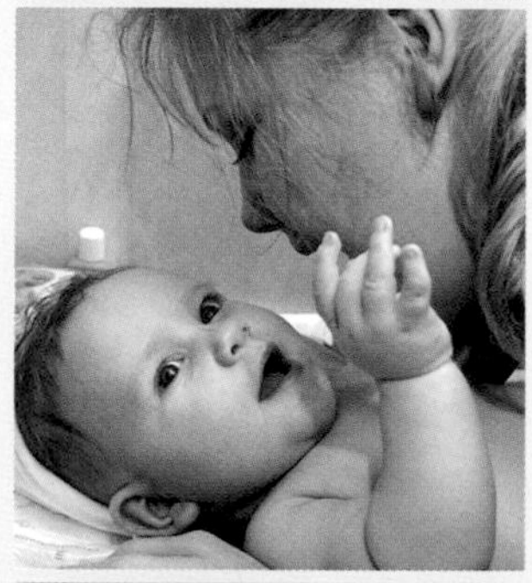

PSYCHOLOGY

Psychology is concerned with how people behave, what they think and feel. It is not simply limited to what one can externally observe, but rather it relates a lot to the internal processes of human thought and feeling: Why we forget pieces of information and retain some others our whole lives; how do prejudices arise; why do we find certain people attractive; why do we feel content in certain situations while anxiety attacks us in others? Much of this knowledge finds very concrete uses in our everyday life, and in the most disparate of areas: from the upbringing of children, to an individual's job prospects and advertising, to name but a few.

KEY FACTS

THE WORD "PSYCHE" *is the Greek word for "soul."*

PSYCHOLOGY *developed into a modern science during the 19th century.*

THE AMERICAN PSYCHOLOGICAL ASSOCIATION *is the world's largest organization of psychologists with about 148,000 members and it based in Washington, D.C.*

FIVE BASIC MODELS *of humanity coexist in the field of psychology.*

The beginnings of psychology | Models of humanity

THE EMERGENCE OF PSYCHOLOGY AS A SCIENCE

The origins of the study of psychology reach far into the past. As a branch of modern science, however, it has existed only since the 19th century. Through the course of its development, psychology has split into various segments with diverse theories arising to explain human development and behavior.

Psychology, as a modern scientific discipline, is only about a century old.

THE BEGINNINGS OF PSYCHOLOGY

Early in history, scholars—primarily philosophers—began to analyze the mind. Psychology did not become an independent science, however, until researchers began to carry out experiments.

It is evident that people have contemplated psychological questions since ancient times. Plato, for example, believed that the body and the soul were two separate systems. On the other hand, Aristotle proposed that body and soul belong together, forming one unified entity. Until the Enlightenment, psychological questions remained the subject of abstract philosophical speculation. At that time, however, interest grew in researching human personalities and other aspects of life. People tried, for example, to "read" the character traits of individuals from their physical peculiarities, such as facial profiles. People also began to focus on the development of children, which can be seen as the earliest beginnings of developmental psychology (p. 276). Much attention was paid to the subject of human behavior in groups and communities. This then led to the development of social psychology, which today is largely associated with the discipline of sociology (p. 275). Also during this period, psychological disturbances began increasingly to be viewed as ordinary disease processes and subjects for scientific study.

Experimental Breakthroughs

Psychology's path to becoming a modern science reached a milestone with the use of scientific methods such as laboratory experimentation. Instead of relying on subjective reports of individuals' thoughts, feelings, and experiences, or simple observations of their behavior, 19th century researchers carried out experiments in an attempt to obtain universally valid data. As a result, psychology gradually became a branch of the natural sciences. The birth of modern psychology was in 1879 when German researcher Wilhelm M. Wundt founded the world's first laboratory for the "investigation of psychological phenomena" at the University of Leipzig. Psychology soon became an established science.

Ernst H. Weber was among the first researchers to carry out experiments to study human cognition.

Wilhelm M. Wundt founded the world's first laboratory for psychological research in Leipzig in 1879.

IN 1887 G. Stanley Hall founded the "American Journal of Psychology."

LEADING WORKS BY STANLEY HALL: "Adolescence" and "Aspects of Child Life and Education."

HALL PARTICIPATED IN THE FOUNDING of four American scientific journals on psychology.

Cover page of the first edition of the "American Journal of Psychology."

G. Stanley Hall—Pioneer of Psychology

DURING THE LATE 19TH CENTURY, psychology developed into a recognized science and psychology laboratories were established in numerous countries. In the United States, G. Stanley Hall is viewed as a pioneer in the field. In 1881, he became the first professor of psychology and pedagogics at Johns Hopkins University in Baltimore. Here he created the country's first experimental psychology lab. He founded the American Psychological Association in 1892, which today remains the world's largest organization of psychologists, as well as the country's first scientific publication in the field, the "American Journal of Psychology." Within his own research, he studied multiple topics but focused largely on child and adolescent development.

HALL STUDIED for some time with Wilhelm M. Wundt in Leipzig, carrying out joint research. He was also interested in the then-modern theories of psychoanalysis (pp. 282–285) and invited renowned thinkers such as Sigmund Freud and Carl G. Jung to speak at a conference at Clark University in Massachusetts.

Gathering of psychologists at Clark University, 1909. Front: S. Freud, G. S. Hall, C. G. Jung. Rear: A. A. Brill, E. Jones, S. Feren.

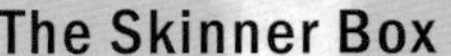

MODELS OF HUMANITY

Psychologists study human behavior from a variety of perspectives. Over the course of time, five fundamental points of view have emerged about the nature of humanity.

In psychology, different explanations may be offered for the same problem or phenomenon. Why is this so? Over the history of the field, different methods have been used to study human experience and behavior. Some researchers have focused exclusively on observable behavior while others have included studies of the subject's thought processes in their considerations. Some psychologists have tried to produce explanations by observing people within their environments. Others have focused on breaking down psychological processes into their smallest elements as far as individual nerve signals. Behind each of these methods lies a different "model of humanity" that describes how and why people act as they do, what role is played by mental and biological processes, and why individuals are different from each other. In all, there are five main schools of thought.

A Pure Bundle of Nerves

Biological psychology assumes that all human thoughts and actions can be explained by natural, organic processes. According to this model, learning, for example, is simply a change within the brain's networks of neurons. When considering a complex psychological phenomenon, adherents of this model do not view it as a whole, but as a multitude of individual biological events within a person.

External Stimuli vs. Thoughts

The school of behaviorism concerns itself exclusively with what can be physically observed. In this view, external stimuli are chiefly responsible for human behavior. Mainly, people learn to do things for which they are rewarded.

The opposite of behaviorism is cognitivism. Followers of the cognitive school place central importance on human thought processes, contending that people actively process data and transform it into new information. Therefore, humans are not only passive receivers of stimuli, but agents who can actively plan and make decisions based on their past experiences (p. 272). People can successfully apply what they have learned in the past, to completely new problematic situations.

Driven by the Subconscious

Adherents of psychoanalysis base their ideas on the work of Sigmund Freud (p. 282). For them, human beings are creatures of conflict and are filled with subconscious desires, which they cannot fulfill because of societal restrictions. According to this theory, human behavior reflects the constant struggle between an individual's personal needs and the demands placed on them by society. Many human actions arise from the desire to reduce this innate tension. The humanistic model sees people predominantly as active beings engaged in the endless pursuit of self-actualization. This view also takes individuals' personal life histories into account.

These different viewpoints are often in competition with each other. However, it is also possible to apply more than one model to a particular case. For example, a psychologist may explain the origin of a child's fears using humanism, while interpreting the same child's attempts to learn to walk according to behaviorism. All of these schools are influential in the field of psychology today.

According to the cognitivist point of view, information processing within the brain occurs between the stimulus and the response. Stored experiences influence human behavior.

The Skinner Box

BEHAVIORIST B. F. SKINNER became famous for his experiments with rats in the "Skinner box" (although Skinner used the term "operant conditioning chamber"). The box contained a lever that was connected to a light source. A rat placed in the box will naturally sniff and touch the lever. If it touches the device at the same time as the light goes on, food is dispensed into the box. This raises the likelihood that the animal will touch the lever more often. Gradually, the rat learns that it must press the lever in order to get food—without any interference from the researcher. These experiments show that specific behaviors can be learned through a reward process (see Learning, p. 273).

When the animal presses the lever at the same time as the light goes on, the food dispenser opens and a food pellet drops out.

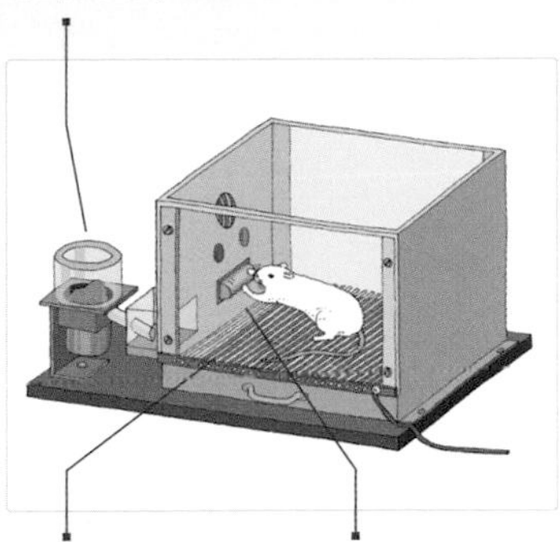

The box is sometimes equipped with an electrified wire grid. Pressing the lever shuts off the flow of electricity. In this case, the reward is not food, but the cessation of the electric shock.

Over a certain period of time, if the rat is consistently rewarded with a food pellet it learns to press the lever when the light goes on.

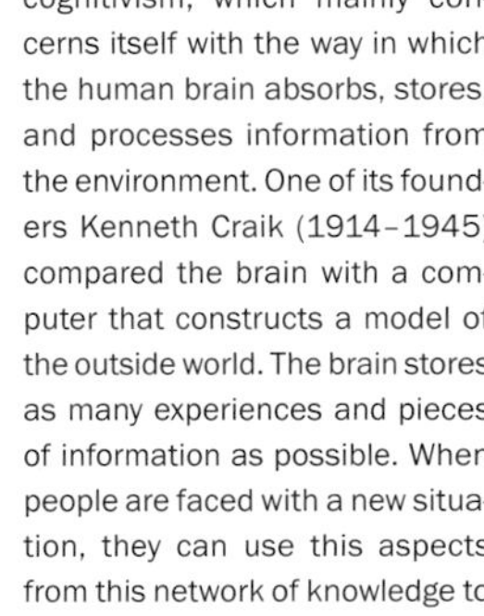

Kenneth Craik's Brain-Computer Model

Another school of psychology is cognitivism, which mainly concerns itself with the way in which the human brain absorbs, stores, and processes information from the environment. One of its founders Kenneth Craik (1914–1945) compared the brain with a computer that constructs a model of the outside world. The brain stores as many experiences and pieces of information as possible. When people are faced with a new situation, they can use this aspects from this network of knowledge to work through various possibilities for action in their minds. Thus, past experiences help them to react appropriately in the present.

above: *Craik's metaphor for the brain—a computer's hard drive.*

21ST CENTURY

IN ITS PURE FORM, *the behaviorist model is an extremist position that is no longer held among modern psychologists.*

TODAY'S BEHAVIORISTS *do not reject thought processes as the subject of study and experimentation.*

HUMANIST THEORIES *concentrate on human potential: A person's ability to strive toward self-actualization and to make the most of his or her individual possibilities.*

KEY FACTS

PSYCHOLOGY *describes, explains, and predicts human behavior.*

NEWBORN BABIES *already have unique personalities and differing temperaments.*

MEMORY *stores information within meaningful patterns that makes it easier to remember.*

PLAYING WITH CHILDREN *is beneficial for both their cognitive and social development.*

FOUNDATIONS OF PSYCHOLOGY

Psychology studies how people think and feel, what motivates them and how they behave. It is interested in discovering processes shared by people as a whole, for instance the development of particular skills during childhood, as well as the factors that distinguish individuals from each other and give them distinct personalities. An additional field of study is human interaction: How people communicate, what kinds of groups they form, and the causes of aggressive behavior.

Psychological processes cannot be directly observed. For this reason, precise descriptions are important.

REASONING, THINKING, AND DECISION-MAKING

Solving problems and making judgments are closely related processes of human thinking. Central to both of them is the collection and processing of information.

Thinking is a constantly active process. People are always taking in information and facing the need to solve problems, plan, and make decisions. To carry out these tasks quickly and reliably, people use cognitive strategies to rapidly process the incoming stream of information to ensure that important facts are easily retrievable when needed.

Making Decisions

New information is organized into specific categories and placed within the context of related existing knowledge. This system provides the information with meaning. For example, a person who is allergic to citrus fruits may place a lemon into the mental category "Warning—Allergy," even if he or she has never eaten one. Organizing information into categories allows people to apply information from prior experiences to entirely new situations and hence make quick decisions based on relatively few details. Each individual has a unique method of categorization that reflects his or her experiences, expectations and predispositions.

At times, a person's categorization system may even influence the absorption of new information. People, for example, often pay exclusive attention to information that supports their own opinions (confirmation bias).

Language and Thinking

A close connection exists between human thought and language. The influence between the two is double-sided. One example of this is "thinking out loud." People who talk through the steps of their reasoning can often solve problems more effectively. Repressing this "inner monologue," on the other hand, has a negative effect on problem solving, even when the solution does not directly require the use of language. Language, in turn, is preconditioned on human thought.

HUMAN FREE WILL *is once again a subject of controversy.*

FREE WILL *means, above all, that people can freely and consciously make decisions.*

"FREE WIL": *Probably an illusion to avoid despair." —Janosch*

Politicians such as Tony Blair base their lives on a belief in their strong force of will.

Does Free Will Exist?

ALREADY DURING THE ENLIGHTENMENT, free will was understood to be limited by external factors. Some modern experts believe that human behavior is orchestrated by unconscious activity in the brain while free will is an illusion. As evidence, they point to the Libet experiment. During this study, participants were asked to lift one of their hands at an arbitrary moment decided by them. Readings reflected observable activity in the brain even before the subject consciously carried out the act of raising their hand.

OTHER SCIENTISTS STRESS that the decision-making process includes a series of steps occurring on various levels. The conscious decision should be understood as the final stage of a complex process—a limitation on free will, but not a contradiction.

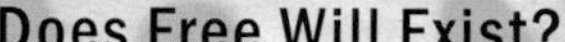

right: *Is an individual a type of robot, controlled exclusively by unconscious brain activity?*

Artifical Intelligence

Computers that can simulate complex human thought processes are called Artificial Intelligence (AI). They are capable of gathering information—for example, in the form of language or symbols—storing it, and assigning meaning to it, so that it is accessible when needed and can be used appropriately. Ideally, an AI should be able to construct a system of categories similar to those used by humans, and thus apply existing information suitably to new situations. An expert system is an AI that has stored knowledge about a highly specialized area. Through a special questioning process, it can assist human experts in making decisions.

above: *The main characters in the film "AI: Artificial Intelligence" are humanoid robots.*

LEARNING AND MEMORY

Learning refers not only to storing information and gaining new skills, but also accumulating experiences. In this process, memory plays a central role.

Learning takes place through a number of different mechanisms.

Learning Through Conditioning

One basic learning mechanism is the principle of classical conditioning. During this process, a connection is made between two triggers or stimuli. Biologist Ivan Pavlov demonstrated this mechanism in the 19th century through his experiments with a dog. Before feeding the dog, he would consistently ring a bell. The dog gradually learned that hearing the sound of the bell meant food. Eventually, the dog reacted to the sound alone with the natural reflex of saliva production. Conditioned responses such as this one can later disappear if the two stimuli are separated from each other.

Learning Through Rewards

A more active form of learning is called instrumental conditioning (or operant conditioning), based on the work of B.F. Skinner. In this process, a person recognizes a connection between his or her behavior and its consequences. If people are rewarded for a certain behavior, they will tend to repeat it. If there is no reward, they will display the behavior less often. As a rule, the faster the reward follows the behavior, the stronger the learning effect.

An especially effective result is seen when a behavior is rewarded at irregular intervals. For example, if a person does not know when they will win at a game of chance, they tend to pursue the behavior (e. g., gambling) more frequently.

Learning by imitation: People learn most social rules through copying others' behavior.

Learning Through Insight and Imitation

One important aspect of human learning is insight, or the ability to recognize connections. Humans can solve an unfamiliar problem by thinking it through, rather than randomly trying out various possibilities (trial and error). They can consider various solutions and evaluate each one's chances for success. Once identified, the solution can be applied to similar situations in the future.

To learn complex social rules and behaviors, people (especially children) seek role models who they can observe and imitate. In addition to known individuals, role models may be from sports, books or movies.

A case in which rewards at irregular intervals can present a significant potential for addiction: A woman gambling in Las Vegas.

Memory: A Three-Level System

Memory gathers, stores, and recalls information on three different levels. The first level is sensory memory, which temporarily stores input from the senses. Short-term memory, the second level, captures information and prepares it for storage in long-term memory. Long-term memory, which represents people's knowledge about themselves and the world, stores information for an unlimited time. It contains personal experiences, emotions, skills, and rules. Information storage takes place when networks are formed, connecting elements of knowledge to each other.

21ST CENTURY

MODERN MNEMONIC TECHNIQUES *such as mind mapping help to store information in long-term memory.*

BIOFEEDBACK *is a new form of conditioning that allows a person with technical support to learn to perceive unconscious biological processes, such as changes in blood pressure, and consciously direct them.*

The Act of Remembering and Forgetting

Remembering can be described as a process of finding and retrieving information. This is easiest when the circumstances of storage and remembering are similar. Therefore, if a student was already nervous while studying for an exam, they may actually be able to recall the stored knowledge more effectively during the test.

For knowledge to remain in memory, it is necessary to repeat it often. This rehearsal serves to solidify the mental path to the appropriate information. Thus, forgetting does not always mean that the knowledge itself has been completely lost, but rather that the actual path to it has faded.

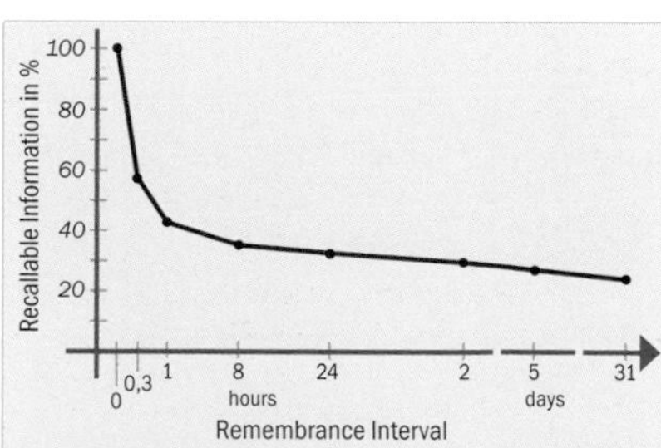

The Forgetting Curve: People exposed to new information forget a great deal of it during the first hour. What remains after eight hours usually stays in memory.

Why Punishments Do Not Help

For a long time physical punishment was viewed as a useful child-rearing tool. However, it is now recognized that it generally does not lead to the desired behavioral outcome. This occurs, among other reasons, mainly because the punishment focuses attention on the negative behavior rather than the desired alternative. Parents who spank a child for an inappropriate action are not providing an example of the correct behavior; thus, the child cannot learn it. Physical punishment also evokes strong negative feelings in a child that he or she connects to the person applying the punishment, not between the negative feelings and a particular behavior.

above: *Wilhelm Busch's character "Professor Lämpel" insisted on draconian physical punishment.*

MOTIVATION AND EMOTION

What sets human behavior in motion and keeps it going? The concept of motivation explains why people strive to achieve particular goals. People are motivated by multiple factors, above all emotion.

Human behavior is influenced—as well as motivated—by a variety of factors. While some "motivations" are biological and directly promote survival, others are learned. Thus, motives may be either conscious or unconscious.

The Origin of Motivation

Biological motivations, such as hunger, are also called "drives." Within an organism, a form of tension arises to satisfy a drive, like hunger, that is reduced by a corresponding behavior, such as eating. The motivation for action is associated with this reduction in tension. However, people eat not only to satisfy their hunger, but also for social and emotional reasons. Stress may induce a person to overeat while an external stimulus may also serve as a motivator, such as if a cake looks especially delicious. These motivators can induce people to eat even if they are not hungry. A similar phenomenon occurs when participants in a competition see the prizes in advance. The tangible sight of a potential reward motivates them to improve their performance.

External incentives also act as a motivator for a certain type of behavior or action.

Motivation for Achievement

People strive for success, which motivates them to continuously strive for greater achievements. However, the strength of this motivation or "need to achieve" can vary greatly from person to person. Among other things, it depends on the value an individual places on his or her own performance. People lacking self-confidence tend to give up on a task much sooner than people with a strong belief in their own abilities.

People's levels of motivation are also connected to their beliefs concerning the causes of events. Do things tend to happen because of one's own individual skills, or because of external factors such as random chance? These beliefs have an important connection to a person's self-esteem as well as their motivation to work toward their personal goals and believe in future success. People who blame a failed effort on their own poor performance will give up more readily than those who believe that bad luck was involved.

Emotions are most effectively communicated through facial expressions. It is in this way that all humans speak the same language.

The Origin of Emotion

Because emotions such as anger, fear, and affection can both trigger and maintain behavior, they are motivators of human actions. Emotions arise on various levels. First, the emotion is instigated by something such as a situation, or perhaps simpler such as a thought or memory. The next step is a subjective evaluation of the emotional trigger. It is here that the individual's personality plays an important role. Their value system and level of self-confidence determine, for example, whether they feel angry and insulted in response to a provocation or dismiss it as unimportant. Purely physical reactions, such as a pounding heart and rapid breathing, can also contribute to strengthening emotions.

Locus of Control

Life Event		Internal	External
	Positive	"I passed the test because I studied hard"	"I passed the test because I got lucky"
	Negative	"I failed the test because I'm not smart enough"	"I failed the test because teacher doesn't like me"

Some people tend to ascribe the results of activities, such as a test, to their own skills (internal locus of control) while others point to outside factors (external locus of control).

Emotions are an innate characteristic of being human and, therefore, can be found in every person in the world. Correspondingly, there are also universal facial expressions that express basic emotions and can be identified by all people, regardless of language or nationality. Eight fundamental emotions grouped into opposing pairs have been identified by researchers: joy and sadness; anger and fear; surprise and anticipation; acceptance and disgust. All other emotions can be seen as variations or combinations of these basic fundamental types.

Maslow's Hierarchy of Needs

DURING THE 1950S, American psychologist Abraham Maslow in his paper "A Theory of Human Motivation" presented the thesis that people are motivated by two different systems of needs. A deficiency need, such as hunger, drives a person to restore their internal balance. A growth need, on the other hand, spurs people to make use of their potential and work toward goals, thus reaching a higher stage. Maslow then concluded that all people have a hierarchy of needs, which he presented in the form of a pyramid diagram. In this model, the more primitive, mainly biological, needs comprise the base, or the bottom. Lower-level needs command attention until they are satisfied; only then can one work toward fulfilling higher-level needs.

Maslow viewed self-actualization as the highest level of his hierarchy.

Self-Actualization
Pursue Inner Talent
Creativity • Fulfilment

Self-Esteem
Achievement • Mastery
Recognition • Respect

Belonging-Love
Friends • Family • Spouse • Lover

Safety
Security • Stability • Freedom from Fear

Physiological
Food • Water • Shelter • Warmth

Someone who is physically satisfied, feels safe, and has a functional network of relationships can then work on building self-esteem and achieving recognition at work and the social environment.

THE POWER OF THE SITUATION

Human behavior depends above all on where an individuals find themselves in (social) situations. Group membership, role expectations and the presence of authorities influence people's reactions and opinions about others.

Humans are social beings. In daily life, they constantly find themselves in situations of interaction with other people, both friends and strangers. Psychologists who study human behavior and perceptions in social situations study, among other things, group dynamics, role expectations, prejudices, and the power of authority.

Groups and Role Expectations

Groups are often created around a common goal through which members identify with the group and one another. Generally, individual members take on diverse roles or functions within the group that are according to the group's expectations. Groups also tend to have specific norms, such as rules that are expected of an individual member. People often behave in conformity with their group, especially in cases where the group has a strong sense of unity, other group members are perceived as more competent, and also if the group faces a difficult or ambiguous task.

Observations have shown that people tend to fold when faced with social pressure from their group. When fellow members agree about a solution to a problem, an individual will often agree, regardless of whether they would have made a different decision in isolation. This behavior reflects two fundamental human needs: The need to belong and the need to test one's own perceptions, thus reducing uncertainty.

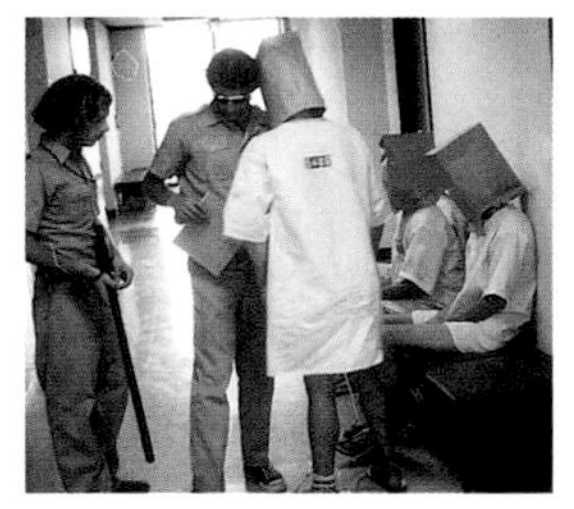

The Stanford Prison Experiment

In 1971, Stanford University psychologist Philip Zimbardo recruited volunteers with the following advertisement: "Male college students needed for psychological study of prison life. $15 per day for 1-2 weeks (...)." The aim of the experiment was to examine the effects of social roles on behavior. After participants were divided into "prisoners" and "guards," they were housed in a prison-like university building. Although the experiment was supposed to last two weeks, it was stopped after six days due to alarming behavior on both sides. The "guards" used harassment techniques that bordered on sadism. This experiment illustrated the power dynamics of social situations.

above: *Very quickly, participants lost their sense of the boundary between role-playing and reality.*

Group norms often affect what people wear. Even without an explicit dress code, group members tend to dress similarly.

The Bystander Effect

Numerous studies have shown that a person's sense of individual responsibility tends to decrease as the size of the group increases. This helps explain cases in which many people witness a crime in progress but do not come to the aid of the victim. However, this effect also seems to depend on the nature of the emergency situation. It is usually enough for one person to take the initiative; others will then offer their help.

Judging Others

People often judge others at first sight using stereotypes based on the characteristics of clothing, appearance or behavior. Even before getting to know anything about a person, an observer may mentally assign him or her to a particular category. This categorization process serves to quickly give the observer a rough idea of what might be expected from the new person. However, these kinds of prejudices are highly stable. If the person shows unexpected behavior, it may be ascribed to other causes: for instance, if John is convinced that Anna is especially intelligent, he may blame her poor exam performance on unfair testing methods, rather than adjusting his original view.

IN THE MILGRAM EXPERIMENT, *obedience to authority was more pronounced as the distance from the victim increased.*

SOME 2,000 PEOPLE *of varying ages, professions and levels of education participated in these experiments.*

The "punishment" of inmates in the Buchenwald concentration camp reflected extreme brutality.

Authorities and Obedience

MORE THAN ANYTHING ELSE, the events of Nazi Germany raised the question of how people can be induced to offer unconditional obedience.

THE MILGRAM EXPERIMENT showed that ordinary people are willing to give a potentially deadly electric shock to another person, if they are instructed to do so by an authority figure (the researcher).

CERTAIN CONDITIONS have been identified that make people more likely to blindly obey authority. Especially in ambiguous situations, it is hard for a person to know when to withdraw compliance, particularly when the first steps were easy. If the authority figure is seen as the legitimate representative of society and trust is placed in him or her, then people will follow more readily because the responsibility lies within the authority figure.

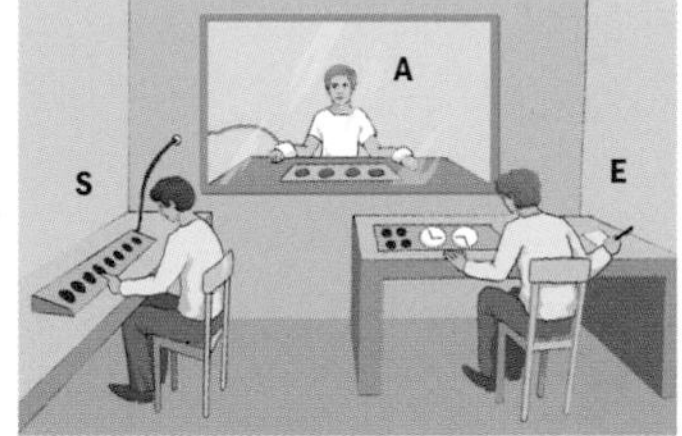

The setup of the Milgram experiment: the researcher (E) is in the same room as the test subject (S). When the "student" (A) in the next room gives the wrong answer to a question, (S) punishes him with an electric shock. It should be noted that A is an actor, and the shocks are fake.

INSIDER KNOWLEDGE

AUTHORITARIAN SYSTEMS *arise when people transfer their rights of action to a leader or organization.*

ANONYMITY *tends to favor more aggressive behavior; e.g., the probability that a group will turn into a "lynch mob" increases with the size of the gathering.*

AGGRESSION *between different groups is easiest to resolve if they have to work together toward a common goal.*

PSYCHOLOGY

DEVELOPMENTAL PSYCHOLOGY

Each phase of life, such as childhood, brings new challenges. People develop basic skills such as abstract thinking and the use of language.

Stage	Age	Abilities
Sensorimotor	0–2	*Simple cognitive and motor-skills*
Preoperational	2–4	*Language learning, discovery of self-concept along with individual experiences*
Preoperational-Intuitive	5–7	*First judgments and conclusions about experiences, not verbalized*
Concrete Operational	7–11	*First logical operations though only about concrete things*
Formal Operational	12–15+	*Logical and abstract thinking, drawing of conclusions, hypothetical positioning interpreting*

In Jean Piaget's model of cognitive development, each stage is associated with the mastery of specific thinking skills.

During early childhood, a range of factors can affect development. Malnutrition in an infant's first months of life, for example, can have a long-term impact on their mental abilities since the brain grows rapidly during this time. It is also important for the child to take advantage of these critical phases. During these periods, children show optimal readiness to gain a particular new skill. If the ability is not acquired at this time, the child will have difficulty catching up later.

Cognitive Development

As they grow, children develop their capacity to think abstractly, solve problems and create a mental picture of the world. Jean Piaget's research shed significant light on these processes. Above all, Piaget was interested in how children's thought processes and their understanding of the outside world change during the various stages of development.

All children go through four stages of mental development. The order of these stages is always the same, although the pace of development may be different. During the sensorimotor period (0–2 yrs), infants learn that objects continue to exist even if they cannot be perceived at the moment (object permanence). Thus, the child can be said to have an inner representation of the object. The next step is the preoperational phase (2–7 yrs), in which children learn that objects retain their identities even if they change externally, e.g., children now know that a cat cannot turn into a dog. At this time they can also imagine a situation from another person's perspective. During the concrete operational stage (7–11 yrs), children begin to rely more heavily on concepts than on their own perceptions. They realize, for example, that a particular volume of liquid does not change just because it has been poured into a different container (conservation of volume). During the final period, the formal operational phase (11+ yrs), the adolescent gains the ability to solve abstract problems and pose hypothetical questions.

Social Development and Gender Role Acquisition

Social development begins with an emotional bond between mother and child. This forms a foundation for later social relationships. Parental attention is vital for a harmonious parent-child relationship. It helps the establishment of a stable bond that lays the groundwork for increased cooperation in later childhood. Children begin to learn gender-related behavior patterns at a very early age. On one hand, this takes place through rewards for behavior seen as gender appropriate and on the other hand through imitation. Same-sex parents also serve as role models.

ON AVERAGE, *girls enter puberty two years earlier than boys.*

IN RECENT DECADES, *adolescents have been reaching sexual maturity and initiating sexual activity at earlier ages in the industrialized nations.*

HOMOSEXUAL EXPERIENCES *in adolescence are not uncommon, even among heterosexuals.*

During the process of identity formation, it is often that a political opinion will take shape.

Puberty

DURING ADOLESCENCE, young people break away from their parents, become independent, and begin making their own plans for the future. This process has no fixed beginning or end point. It depends, among other factors, on the tasks young people must complete to reach adulthood in their particular culture.

AMONG THE MOST significant challenges for adolescents are moving out of the parents' home, developing their own social and sexual identities, and planning for their future path in life. Each of these challenges helps the young person construct his or her own identity.

AFTER MOVING OUT of the parental home, young adults focus on other social contacts and take on new social roles. The development of an independent social identity takes place, above all, within their peer group. As a young person's orientation shifts toward the peer group, relationships within the parental home also change, which can lead to disagreements. However, arguments between parents and adolescents usually focus on superficial aspects of youth culture, rather than representing true intergenerational conflicts.

above: *The first sexual experience usually, but not always, occurs within a romantic relationship.*

The Competent Baby

At birth, infants already possess a wide range of abilities. Although they initially have blurred eyesight (in fact they are legally blind) all the other senses are well-developed from the start. They prefer pleasant sensations, such as sweet tastes, and try to avoid unpleasant stimuli like loud noises and harsh lights. From birth, humans are social beings. Even newborns prefer human voices to other sounds and are more interested in faces than other views. At only a week old, a baby can identify its mother's voice and distinguish her from other people. Infants are born with the ability to communicate. Thus, they are immediately ready to begin interacting with their environment and learning from their experiences.

above: *A newborn interacts with its mother by responding to her voice.*

Starting at around age 7, children begin to realize that the volume of a liquid does not change when it is poured from one container into another.

PERSONALITY: WHAT IS IT?

Individuals differ from others on the basis of their unique patterns of personality characteristics and skills, as well as their self-concepts.

People react differently to situations mainly because they have different personalities. A personality is what makes a human being an individual. It includes unique psychological traits—that is, an individual's self-concept, characteristics and skills—which remain stable over an extended period of time.

Characteristics as Markers of Personality

Early theories regarding personality proposed categories of traits into which people could be classified. One well-known model distinguishes two main pairs of opposites: introversion/extroversion and stability/neuroticism. According to this, an individual's personality can be described by their position along these two dimensions. Another model uses five key qualities (the "big five"), which are exhibited to varying extents by different people: neuroticism (emotional stability or instability), extroversion, openness to experience, agreeableness, and conscientiousness. In turn, each of these basic dimensions is connected to a set of behavioral traits. Thus, for example, people with a high level of extroversion will more likely be talkative, open, adventurous, and sociable. People with a lower level of extroversion tend to be calm, careful, reserved, and withdrawn.

If the ideal self and the real self do not agree, this can lead to internal conflicts and emotional disturbances.

Categorizations of this kind can indeed describe a range of personalities. However, since they do not take the social situation or the individual's self-concept into account, they fail to explain many kinds of reactions and cannot accurately predict behavior. They merely act as possible metaphors to help understand the complexity of human personality.

Unstable
moody
afraid
rigid
sober
pessimistic
reserved
unfriendly
calm
Introvert
passive
meticulous
thoughtful
amicable
controlled
reliable
balanced
pensive
Stable
sensitive
anxious
aggressive
excitable
changeable
impulsive
optimistic
energetic
Extrovert
genial
sociable
talkative
open-minded
laid-back
vivacious
carefree
leading

British psychologist Hans Eysenck defined individual personalities using a matrix of opposing traits: introverted/extroverted and stable/neurotic.

Social Situations and Self-Conception

A person's behavior can be very different depending on the situation. For instance, a father may be helpful, affectionate and attentive with his children, but selfish and aggressive in another context. In fact, individual traits are highly dependent on the situation in which they are expressed. It appears that specific situations activate different patterns of experience, which then influence behavior. On the other hand, people also actively shape their environment, altering it so that its effects on them will be more positive.

Another factor that influences personality and behavior is self-conception, or the perception of oneself. A person's self-conception is formed from innate qualities, such as temperament, combined with social experiences. However, self-conception does not necessarily reflect reality. In order to maintain their inner picture of an ideal self, people tend to distort information so as to support their self-conception. Negative experiences may be completely disregarded or re-interpreted to make them more positive. In general, people with more accurate self-concepts tend to be happier and more satisfied with life.

21ST CENTURY

ATTRACTIVENESS: *The more similar people are in appearance, attitudes, and values, the more attractive and agreeable they will perceive each other.*

ESCAPE INTO EMAIL: *People who tend toward emotional instability prefer to express differences of opinion by email, while extroverts generally seek face-to-face conversations. Emails help reduce uncertainty and increase the writer's control over the situation.*

Extroverts enjoy being in the center of things and surround themselves with other people while introverts tend to be withdrawn. Most people lie somewhere between the two extremes.

Testing Intelligence

INTELLIGENCE IS UNDERSTOOD to be a relatively stable personal characteristic, thus is a part of personality. But what is intelligence and how can it be measured? Intelligence refers to the capacity to absorb knowledge, comprehend language and ideas. Furthermore, it also refers to nonverbal skills such as logical reasoning and visualizing objects in space. Because it consists of such a great variety of abilities, it is often believed that a person's precise intelligence is indeterminable. However, it can be estimated by tests that assess each of these abilities. A person's intelligence quotient (IQ) can thus be calculated in comparison with his or her norm group; that is, people of the same age and level of education. Since intelligence does not depend on verbal skills, language independent intelligence tests have been developed, which present tasks in pictorial form.

The block test: An example from HAWIE, the Hamburg-Wechsler Intelligence Test for Adults

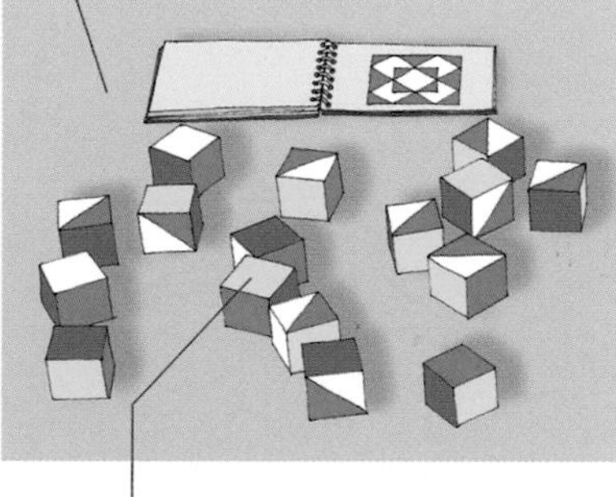

In the mosaic problem, subjects are asked to assemble blocks into a given pattern as quickly as possible. This tests their perceptual organization skills.

PSYCHOLOGY

KEY FACTS

EDUCATIONAL PSYCHOLOGY *focuses on a child's upbringing within the family, as well as education and training in school and at work.*

FORENSIC PSYCHOLOGY *evaluates the reliability of witnesses and defendants in court.*

THE DIAGNOSIS AND TREATMENT *of mental illnesses is carried out by clinical psychologists. Various forms of therapy may be used.*

Bringing up a child | Everyday life: work | Mental illnesses and their diagnosis | Types of treatment

APPLICATIONS OF PSYCHOLOGY

Psychology plays a role in many aspects of everyday life—starting from birth. Psychologists are interested in determining what kinds of child-rearing practices are optimal for a young person's development; how school lessons can be structured so that students will learn effectively and enthusiastically; what conditions help employees feel comfortable in the workplace; and how unemployed people can successfully come to terms with their situation. The best-known area of psychology is the care and treatment of the mentally ill.

Psychologists concern themselves not only with individuals, but also with organizational structures, such as companies.

PSYCHOLOGY

FAMILY AND SCHOOL: BRINGING UP A CHILD

A child's upbringing takes place both within the family and at school. An important aspect of this process is the reaction of parents and teachers to specific behaviors.

A child's upbringing begins as soon as he or she is born. While later forms of education often depend on language, the parents' reactions to a baby's smiles, sounds, and eye contact play an important role in infancy (p. 276). At a very early age, babies learn that specific behaviors such as smiling or crying result in certain consequences. These experiences help the child to understand connections, giving him or her a feeling of security and control. However, if parents are unable to recognize and respond to a child's needs, he or she will not be able to develop a reliable control system. In that case, the baby observes no connection, or only a weak one, between its own behavior and the parents' reactions.

Parenting Styles

An essential task for parents is passing on values, role expectations, and rules of social behavior. In this process, they may use various parenting styles, which can be distinguished based on their levels of support and control. In an authoritarian parenting style, parents exercise a high level of control over their children, but provide little support in the form of recognition, respect, and trust.

Communication with parents is of key importance for a child's healthy development.

Group work has been accepted as a successful model for classroom learning. Students work together to find solutions.

Children reared in an authoritarian style are often aggressive and tend to have lower levels of self-confidence. This is because they have limited opportunities for independent action, so they enjoy fewer experiences of success. Parents who take a "hands off" approach and provide little control or support to their children, on the other hand, are said to employ a permissive parenting style.

Especially positive effects on a child's development are seen when the parents offer support while at the same time providing opportunities for the child to face everyday age-appropriate challenges. This involves both positive feedback for appropriate behavior as well as negative feedback for any undesirable actions.

School: Learning and Upbringing

Schools are responsible, above all, for imparting knowledge. However, they also play a role in the child's general upbringing. Students must learn to integrate themselves into the classroom community and follow group rules. One important insight of psychology that is now being generally applied is the fact that students are more motivated and learn more effectively when they are actively involved in the lesson and have the chance to figure out answers for themselves. One special challenge for today's teachers is adapting their approaches to students' specific needs and their increasingly diverse backgrounds. Providing individual attention to each child is also especially important during the learning phase.

E-Learning

INTERACTIVE MEDIA are gaining importance as learning aids utilized both inside and outside of school. One advantage of using them is that students can individually determine the pace of their progress. In addition to simple programs for learning the alphabet, for example, more complex "tutorial" programs allow students to independently gain knowledge about a certain subject at various learning levels. When the user successfully answers a question, the program provides positive feedback before moving on.

INTERACTIVE MEDIA GAME

Tasks are appropriate for the target learners and relevant to their environment.

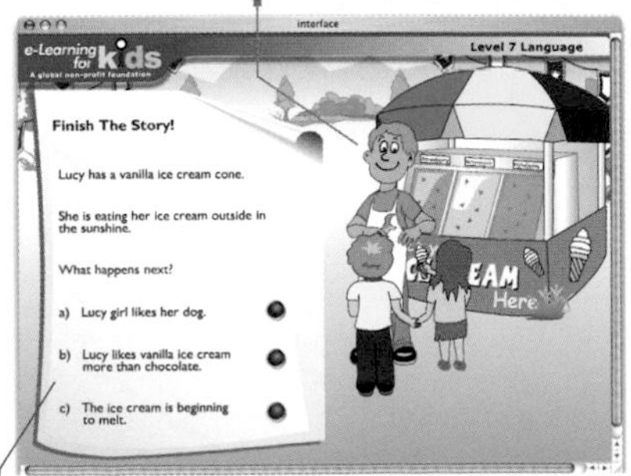

Answers are offered in multiple choice format.

When the user chooses the right answer, immediate positive feedback is given.

EVERYDAY LIFE: WORK

Psychologists have interested themselves with the mechanisms of the working world. Through their work, people not only earn a living, but also strive toward personal goals.

The well-being of its employees is just as vital to a company's success as an appropriate business structure and division of labor. Stress and harassment in the workplace, on the other hand, are counterproductive.

Employees who participate in decision-making processes are more motivated and feel more responsible for the company's success.

Satisfaction on the Job

Contented workers perform more effectively, tend to be more actively engaged in the workplace, and have fewer absences. Numerous factors contribute to job satisfaction. One important aspect is the feeling that pay is appropriate to performance. While underpayment nearly always leads to decreased motivation, pay raises by themselves do not automatically produce job satisfaction. Workers' levels of motivation tend to rise when their achievements are recognized, when they take on increased responsibility, and when they see future prospects for themselves, such as the potential for advancement.

Taylorism

In the late 19th century, F. W. Taylor developed a system to increase workers' productivity at a given rate of pay. The work process was divided up into many small steps while each worker was given a single, monotonous activity. Planning and organization remained exclusively in the hands of management. Money was used as a motivator in the form of bonus payments for higher performance. As a result, workers' sense of identification with their job decreased, along with their motivation to work for the good of the company. Higher workloads also negatively affected employees' health. For these reasons, Taylorism was later corrected in favor of a more "humanized" workplace.

above: *Charlie Chaplin as a factory worker in "Modern Times"*

An Effective Leadership Style

Also central to business success is whether the manager is able to motivate employees to work toward specific goals. Research has shown that what makes a good boss is not their personality, but his or her ability to react appropriately to a range of situations. Most importantly, treating employees fairly strengthens their commitment to the company as well as their confidence in the manager's authority.

Stress and Harassment

One of the greatest problems in the workplace is stress. In extreme cases, it can even lead to physical and mental disorders. However, what people perceive as stressful depends on their individual assessment of a situation as well as their personal resources for managing stress. These include, for example, support from a spouse or partner. One of the most significant sources of workplace stress is the fear of losing one's job.

Both under- and overloading at work can lead to stress. In other words, stress tends to arise from an imbalance. This can be seen, for example, when the time available is disproportionate to the volume of work, or assigned tasks are poorly matched to a worker's skills. To reduce this burden, both institutional measures (such as altering job requirements) and individual initiatives (skills training or relaxation therapy) can help.

Harassment in the workplace harms not only the targeted person, but the organization as well, since it can lead to absences, decreased motivation and productivity, and even the loss of the employee. Harassment consists of hostile attacks from colleagues or superiors over an extended period of time. Workplace bullies may openly and directly insult their victim or use subtler methods, such as isolation or spreading rumors. Often, harassment only stops when the company takes measures to combat it.

ADVERTISING *is designed to attract attention, so that the product stays in customers' minds.*

"KEY STIMULI" *are triggers that create positive associations with the product.*

ADVERTISING DOES INFLUENCE *consumers, but the actual decision to buy remains theirs alone.*

Small children do not yet recognize the methods used by advertisers to influence them.

How Does Advertising Influence Consumers?

ADVERTISING IS AIMED, first of all, at making potential buyers aware of a product. Then, consumers should remember the product as long and as positively as possible, so that it is foremost in their minds when the time comes to make a purchase. To achieve this, advertising messages are repeated often. In addition, advertising uses the insight that people tend to remember something more effectively when it is connected to an emotion (p. 274). Advertisers thus seek to link the product to good feelings, through the use of humor, sexy images, beautiful scenes, evocative music, etc.

ANOTHER TECHNIQUE is to have celebrities, who function as role models for the target consumer group, present the product.

To ensure that a product is prominent in people's minds, advertising must draw attention to itself.

INSIDER KNOWLEDGE

PRINCIPLES OF *advertising are based on theories of learning (p. 273).*

PRE-EMPLOYMENT TESTS *are designed, and often administered, by psychologists.*

IN ASSESSMENT CENTERS, *everyday job situations are simulated. Managers aiming for leadership positions are tested in this manner.*

PSYCHOLOGY

MENTAL ILLNESSES AND THEIR DIAGNOSIS

People with mental illnesses display disordered forms of thought and behavior. These symptoms can be acute enough to make patients a danger to themselves or others.

Mental illnesses can be caused by a combination of various factors such as: Physical (genetic) disposition to illness, triggers such as trauma or stress, and the social environment. In many cases, patients are aware that they are ill; in others, their perception is too distorted to assess the severity of their condition.

Schizophrenia is often accompanied by paranoia, as the film "A Beautiful Mind" memorably depicts.

Depression

An common disorder is depression. Its effects may be so acute that a sufferer is unable to pursue everyday activities and has a negative view of the future. It can sometimes lead to suicide as depressed individuals feel extremely sad while lacking self-confidence and motivation. Fortunately, depression can be treated relatively successfully.

ANXIETY DISORDERS *occur approximately twice as often in women as in men.*

MORE THAN 14% OF ALL PEOPLE *develop a phobia over the course of their lives.*

THE MOST COMMON *phobias include the fear of heights or of specific animals.*

Fear of heights, or acrophobia, is among the most prevalent anxiety disorders; one famous acrophobic was Johann Wolfgang von Goethe.

Anxiety Disorders

MANY PEOPLE SUFFER from fears in varying intensities. These are considered disorders, or phobias, only when they reach the point of irrationality. Specific phobias are directed at a particular object, animal, or situation (e.g., the fear of heights or spiders). Social phobias involve particular situations of human interaction, such as the fear of public speaking or approaching a stranger. It is symptomatic for phobics to attempt to avoid the feared object or situation at any cost.

A SPECIAL TYPE of anxiety disorder is a panic disorder. In this syndrome, the sufferer has sudden attacks of high-intensity fear. For no obvious reason, the affected person experiences a racing heartbeat, shortness of breath, or sensation of dizziness.

A TRAUMATIC SITUATION such as an accident, rape, or war can lead to post-traumatic stress disorder. Symptoms of this condition include nightmares, intense fears, and constant reliving of the traumatic event in the patient's mind. Obsessive-compulsive disorder also falls within the category of anxiety disorders. Compulsively repeating an activity can help reduce fear and anxiety.

Bodily symptoms
Cognition
Thoughts ("distress")
Fear
Bodily changes

The "vicious circle of fear": Fear creates physical symptoms, which are interpreted by the affected person as signs of potential danger. This, in turn, leads to increased fear. The sufferer falls into a spiral which is difficult to escape.

A special type of depression is bipolar disorder, in which depressive moods alternate with a phase of manic euphoria.

Eating Disorders

The number of patients diagnosed with eating disorders has been rising in recent years. These afflictions can be divided between anorexia, in which the affected person subjects himself or herself to extreme starvation, and bulimia. Bulimics often engage in eating binges and then try to rid themselves of the excess food afterward by vomiting or using laxatives. A number of factors have been identified that predispose a person to eating disorders. The more of these that are present, the greater the risk of developing the condition. Factors include genetic inheritance, the example set by the parents' eating habits, and social pressures to be thinner.

Schizophrenia

In schizophrenia, earlier called dementia praecox, sufferers lose the ability to function effectively in the everyday world. For many, the content of their thoughts is disrupted. They may suffer from delusions—ideas or beliefs that do not correspond to facts or reality, although they may be passionately convinced that they are true. Paranoid delusions are the most common type. Schizophrenia is usually treated with a combination of psychotherapy and medication.

Of Sound Mind?

When a defendant appears before the court, psychologists are often asked to certify whether he or she is "compos mentis," or of sound mind. If the person is pronounced incapable of understanding the consequences of his or her actions—mostly in connection with a serious mental illness—the next step is usually involuntary commitment to a psychiatric institution. However, mentally ill criminals tend to profit from therapy only when they are willing to work with the therapist toward common goals. Therapy undertaken against the patient's will has little chance of success.

above: *Psychiatric facility*

Personality Disorders

Each person has a set of traits that make up his or her personality. While healthy people can react flexibly to different situations and tasks while adapting themselves to the changing conditions of everyday life, people with personality disorders cannot. They often have great difficulty interacting with other people. People with a narcissistic personality disorder, for example, want to be admired. Those with a paranoid personality disorder are mistrustful.

Anorexics often have distorted bodily perceptions. In spite of their emaciated physique, they believe they are of normal weight or even fat.

TYPES OF TREATMENT

The leading types of treatments used today are psychodynamic therapy, behavioral therapy, cognitive therapy, and some humanistic therapies.

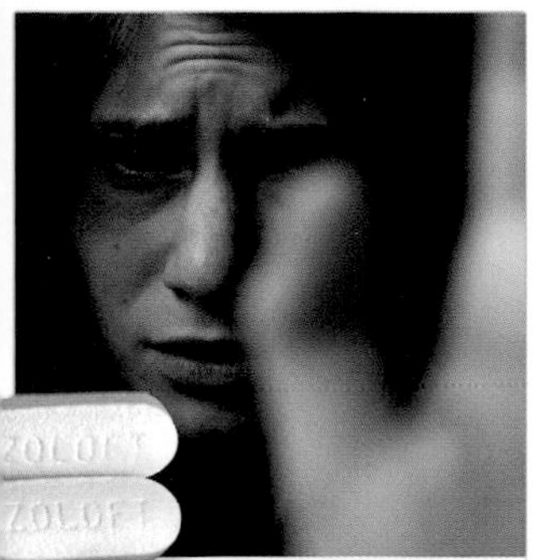

Depression can often be successfully treated with a combination of cognitive therapy and medication.

Psychological treatment methods are called psychotherapies. Their goal is to help the patient change his or her inappropriate thoughts, interpretations, and behavior. The methods used are highly diverse.

Psychodynamic Therapy

Psychodynamic theory begins with the assumption that adults' mental disturbances (neuroses) are caused by unresolved conflicts and traumas from childhood. Therapy consists of conversations aimed at helping the patient recognize the relationship between the hidden, unresolved conflict and his or her current difficulties.

Behavioral Therapy

Behavioral therapy places its focus on abnormal behavior. Here, behavior is understood to include everything that can be influenced by the learning process (p. 273); thus, it also extends to thoughts and feelings. Principles of learning are systematically applied to increase the occurrence of desired behaviors and reduce the frequency of problematic ones. Social skills training is also a form of behavioral therapy. This group-based treatment is aimed at people with social anxiety. Participants gain the opportunity to practice situations they fear within a group, such as asking a stranger for assistance. Role playing and other exercises are used for this purpose.

Cognitive Therapy

Abnormal behavior can arise from faulty thought patterns or mistaken ideas that may not be fully clear to the affected person. For example, a man may wrongly believe that events occurring in his environment are specifically directed at him, or he may overestimate their importance. In cognitive behavioral therapy, these mistaken thoughts are revealed, and the patient learns to evaluate their experiences more appropriately.

Humanistic Therapy

The best-known humanistic form of treatment is the "person-focused talk" therapy developed by Carl R. Rogers, which is centered on the relationship between therapist and patient. The therapist's main objective is to make the patient feel safe and protected. Within this environment, patients can make their own discoveries and decisions. During this process, the therapist should simply support, not direct, the patient. By providing a patient with unrestricted affirmation, the therapist helps him or her develop a stronger self-concept.

In family therapy, the family is viewed as an interactive system.

INSIDER KNOWLEDGE

DISORDER-SPECIFIC THERAPIES *are focused on the needs of patients with a specific condition.*

WHEN SEVERAL MENTAL *disturbances are present at the same time, a combination of various therapy modules may be most effective.*

THERAPY SHOULD ALSO HELP *the patient recognize signs that the disorder is recurring and take steps to prevent it.*

Couples and Family Therapy

Relationships and families can be viewed as systems with their own dynamics. When problems arise between partners or family members, therapists take a closer look at the patterns of communication occurring within this dynamic. Communication is also seen as including interpersonal behavior, or nonverbal communication. During therapy, participants work on effective forms of communication.

Effectiveness of Therapies

All forms of therapy have the same ultimate goal: To reduce the patient's suffering and improve quality of life. The patient is supported in efforts to develop more effective strategies to handle stress and the demands of daily life. According to the type of psychological disturbance, various forms of treatment have differing levels of effectiveness. In some cases, it is helpful to combine more than one type of therapy.

Confronting Fears

IN ONE BEHAVIORAL THERAPY TECHNIQUE for the treatment of phobias, patients are encouraged to confront the object or situation they fear. If the fear is highly intense, there is a risk that the patient may be overwhelmed by it. In that case, a gradual desensitization process may be used. A hierarchy of frightening situations is worked out, ranging from situations that cause the patient little anxiety to those which arouse the greatest fear. The patient is challenged to imagine each situation, starting with the easiest one, as realistically as possible. Relaxation techniques are also employed.

THE THERAPY: In the presence of the therapist, the feared situation is introduced. It is continued until the patient's tension subsides and she becomes gradually calmer.

SUCCESSFUL LEARNING: The negative consequences feared by the patient do not occur and she gains a new, more positive outlook.

PSYCHOLOGY

KEY FACTS

HUMAN BEINGS *are characterized by conflict in their lives and are constantly forced to balance internal and external demands.*

THE HUMAN PSYCHE *is made up of unconscious, preconscious, and conscious levels. The dynamics between them are intricate.*

PSYCHOANALYTICAL THEORY *is continuously being developed further to improve the methods it employs.*

The origins of psychoanalysis | Mind and personality | Motives of actions | Psychoanalysis as therapy

PSYCHOANALYSIS

Psychoanalytic theory starts with the assumption that the human psyche has three levels, which are constantly interacting and even in conflict with each other. One of its key ideas is that not all regions and contents of the psyche can be accessed by the conscious mind. Instead a person remains unconscious of them, yet they exert a strong influence on his or her thoughts and behavior. Unresolved conflicts, which can result in mental disturbances, are revealed and then processed during psychoanalytic therapy.

Psychoanalysis tries to shed light on the content of the unconscious.

THE ORIGINS OF PSYCHOANALYSIS

In the late 19th century, Sigmund Freud developed a theory about the human psyche that included unconscious processes. The content of the unconscious, he postulated, has a significant influence on an individual.

Sigmund Freud (1865–1939) developed psychoanalysis as both a theory about the human mind and a technique for treating mental disturbances.

Born in Moravia in 1856, Freud grew up in Vienna where he studied medicine. He was soon recognized in the city as a leading neurologist. To continue his education, Freud studied with Professor Charcot in Paris. There he learned the technique of hypnosis, which was being used as a new treatment for hysteria. Returning to Vienna, Freud opened his own medical practice and began working on the development of psychoanalytic techniques. He first used the term "psychoanalysis" in 1896. Parallel to his research into the unconscious mind, he founded the "Psychological Wednesday Society" in 1902, which consisted of himself and four other Viennese physicians. In 1911, the International Psychoanalytic Association arose from this organization. Already at an early stage, various branches broke off from Freud's view of psychoanalysis—for example, C. G. Jung and Alfred Adler founded their own psychoanalytic schools. After the Nazi occupation of Austria, Freud and his family immigrated to London. It was from there that psychoanalysis spread out into the world.

Psychoanalysis compares human consciousness to an iceberg, most of which is hidden underwater.

Topological Model

According to Freud, the human mind consists of three levels: the conscious, the preconscious, and the unconscious. In the psychoanalytic view, most of the psyche remains hidden, just as an iceberg floating in water. Only a small part of the content that determines human perception and behavior is available to the conscious mind—only the tip of the iceberg. Although the majority lies "underwater," it exercises an enormous influence on a person. It contains hidden fears, repressed conflicts, and traumatic experiences, as well as innate drives and instincts. This content is organized in layers according to the various phases of development. The lowest level—the unconscious—is unavailable to the person and includes instincts, genetic traits, and the milestones of psychosexual development. Although there is no direct access, they can be uncovered by using certain psychoanalytic techniques such as hypnosis and dream interpretation (p. 285). The middle level—the preconscious—is partly accessible, as one can concentrate in order to bring its contents into the conscious mind. The preconscious contains fears, personality traits, and repressed conflicts.

An exhibition on psychoanalysis in Vienna, marking the 150th anniversary of Freud's birth.

The Case of Anna O.

Anna O. is often viewed as an important starting point for psychoanalysis. Josef Breuer, a physician and friend of Freud, succeeded in curing Anna O. (the alias of Bertha Pappenheim) of various symptoms, including partial paralysis, visual disturbances, and a tendency to fall into trances. In addition to medication with morphine, the treatment consisted of a "talking cure." Breuer hypnotized his patient and let her speak freely—what Freud later called "free association." With this therapy, her physical symptoms, which Breuer believed were psychological in origin, disappeared. Later investigations showed, however, that Anna O. was probably not entirely healed by the "talking cure."

STRUCTURE OF THE MIND AND DEVELOPMENT OF THE PERSONALITY

According to Freud, the human personality consists of three components: id, ego, and superego. Maturity is viewed as a series of stages associated with specific developmental tasks.

The "structural model" stands at the center of Freud's theory of personality. In it, three forces are distinguished within the human psyche: the "id," the "ego," and the "superego." These forces are constantly interacting and can conflict.

Id, Ego, and Superego

The id is where impulses from drives or instincts—needs, feelings, and desires—are located. This part of the human psyche operates without any regard for morality, logic, or order. The goal of the id is the direct satisfaction of its impulses. The ego, on the other hand, represents conscious thought and action. Constrained by reality, it governs interactions with the environment, conscious thought, and acts of will. The ego serves as a mediator between the other two forces—the id and the superego—and decides which drive impulses will be put into action. The superego can also be seen as the conscience. It encompasses a person's values, boundaries, and morals while serving as an internal power that controls, warns, and even punishes an individual.

Freud explained the interaction of these three forces through an analogy: The ego can be represented as a rider on horseback, with the id as the horse, and the superego as the riding instructor. With this model, Freud formulated a view of mentally healthy behavior: actions in which the ego succeeds in harmonizing impulses from the id and standards of the superego.

Developmental Theory

Freud believed that people are capable of having sexual experiences starting from birth, whereby sexuality is understood in a generalized way as the pursuit of pleasure. According to Freud's theory of psychosexual development, personality, sexuality, and the body mature together during a series of four developmental phases. In the "oral" phase, an infant's main pleasure is suckling at the mother's breast. During this time, a baby develops a sense of basic trust. Between the first and third year of life, a child's focus of pleasure shifts to the anal zone: He or she begins to exert conscious control over the evacuation process. During this "anal phase," the child learns social rules of behavior and how to handle conflict. This is followed by the "phallic phase," in which the child develops a gender identity and discovers the opposite sex, at first through play. During this phase, a phenomenon occurs that Freud called the Oedipus complex. A boy unconsciously desires his mother and views his father as a rival, fearing that he may take revenge with castration. Feeling guilty and fearing punishment, the boy increasingly represses his attraction to his mother and identifies with his father. He adopts the father's value system and moves away from the mother. Before puberty, a child also goes through a "latency period," in which interest in bodily sources of pleasure tends to be dormant and repressed. The endpoint of psychosexual development is the "genital phase." If a person cannot move past one of these phases, this "fixation" has an effect on personality. For example, people with an "oral" personality have a weakness for sources of oral gratification such as eating, drinking, and smoking. They seek security by clinging to others or avoiding new experiences. A fixation at the anal phase can be expressed as greediness or an excessive love of order, as well as compulsive behavior.

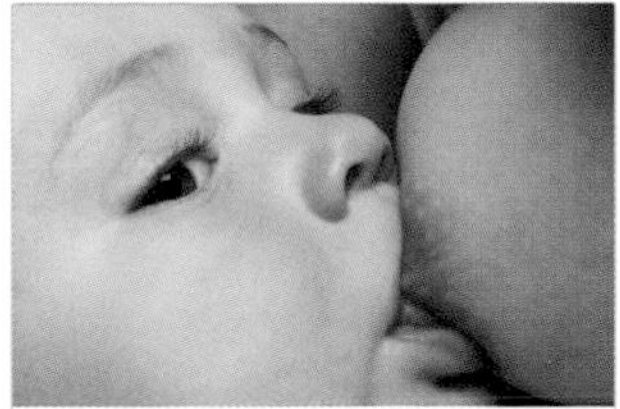

An infant's erogenous zone is the mouth, which is why Freud called infancy the oral phase.

Scrooge McDuck, according to Freud's theory, is a classic example of an anal personality: greedy, miserly, obsessed with order, and hungry for wealth and power.

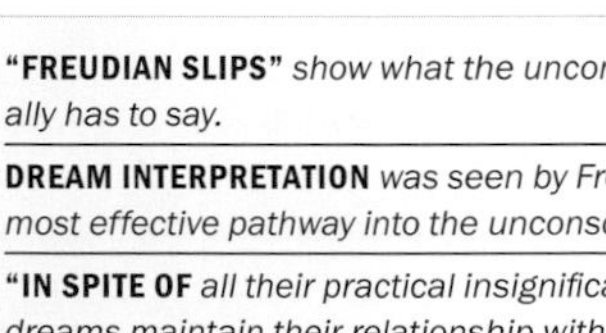

"FREUDIAN SLIPS" *show what the unconscious really has to say.*

DREAM INTERPRETATION *was seen by Freud as the most effective pathway into the unconscious.*

"IN SPITE OF *all their practical insignificance, dreams maintain their relationship with the great interests of life."*

Freud used hypnosis to uncover memories of repressed childhood experiences.

Access to the Unconscious

FREUD DEVELOPED SEVERAL methods to reveal the contents of the unconscious. Through hypnosis, early childhood experiences that have been buried within the unconscious can be uncovered. The subject remembers and relates them during hypnosis sessions. Thus, unconscious conflicts can be revealed and resolved.

SLIPS OF THE TONGUE are no accident, according to Freud. Instead, they are a message from the unconscious. If someone mishears, arrives late, gets lost, oversleeps, or forgets or loses something, conclusions can be drawn about repressed desires, feelings of guilt, aggressive impulses, and so forth. During free association, subjects are asked to say everything that comes to mind, even if it appears to be nonsense. Every thought is promptly followed by another, thus showing which ideas are connected or associated.

DREAMS ARE the disguised fulfillment of hidden desires arising from the id, according to Freud. In the dreaming state, the ego is weakened, but is still capable of disguising the nature of an actual wish. With the help of interpretation, the dream's true or latent content can be revealed.

Dreams can often take bizarre forms—in this way, the ego attempts to disguise their true content.

MOTIVES OF ACTIONS

The motives of human activity are rooted in the id and are therefore unconscious. In order to prevent the id's impulses from entering into consciousness, people develop various techniques: defense mechanisms.

Freud assumed that people are directed, above all, by drives. A drive is a basic need that continually arises. People can postpone fulfilling a drive, but not indefinitely, since its intensity continues to increase. The most important drive is the libido (sex drive), which is oriented according to the various developmental stages: oral, anal, phallic, and genital (p. 283). Freud viewed the human psyche as a "process," which is maintained by energy from the libido. Only when objects or ideas are associated with the libido do they become meaningful to the person. For example, the first target of interest for a baby's libido is the mother's breast—thus, it becomes a meaningful object within the infant's perception.

Defense Mechanisms

People attempt to prevent the many impulses originating in the id from coming into consciousness, either because they seem unacceptable—they do not meet the superego's standards—or they are not compatible with reality. For this purpose, defense mechanisms are brought into play. These defensive systems find ways to redirect the id's impulses, enabling a person to avoid inner conflict. However, if defense mechanisms are used too regularly and too often, neuroses can thus arise (p. 285).

The most common defense mechanism is *repression*: A person suppresses unwanted impulses so that they do not come into awareness. However, they can still emerge as Freudian slips or in dreams (p. 283). *Regression* often arises in reaction to a frustrating experience: The person behaves in a manner associated with an earlier developmental stage. Instead of consciously addressing the problem, he or she reverts to "immature" substitute behavior.

Conscious awareness forms only a small part of the human psyche. Defense mechanisms prevent unconscious and preconscious material from entering a person's consciousness.

A person engaging in *rationalization* will attempt to justify behavior through logical reasons—which are, however, not their true motives. In projection, people deceive themselves by attributing their own unconscious desires, guilt, or fears to objects or other people. Alternatively, imitating another person's way of thinking and behaving can help protect against feelings of inferiority. When someone imitates not merely a particular trait, but another person's entire personality, this is known as *identification*.

In *compensation*, a person attempts to balance a weakness in one area by over-satisfying needs in another. For example, a man with feelings of inferiority because of his small stature may try to overcome this through outstanding achievement in another field. The mechanism of *displacement* can be seen when impulses are directed toward a different object. For instance, after a dispute with his boss in the office, a man may vent his anger on his family at home.

All of these defense mechanisms serve to bury unpleasant events within the unconscious; thus, allowing the person to avoid facing and resolving the associated conflicts out of fear of the consequences. However, the conflicts are not completely eliminated by these actions; they remain active and continue to have a variety of influences on an individual's behavior.

The defense mechanism of sublimation allows sexuality to be expressed in a socially acceptable form, such as dancing.

TRANSGENERATIONAL INHERITANCE: *Symptoms of trauma are passed on through the generations.*

CHILDREN OF OFFENDERS *suffer from their parents' actions; their symptoms are associated with feelings of shame and guilt.*

THE STRONGER THE TRAUMA *experienced by parents, the greater the children's mental anguish.*

The traumatization of Holocaust survivors continues to cast its shadow over the third generation.

A Lasting Legacy

EXTREME TRAUMAS, such as those experienced by Holocaust survivors, can continue to affect the second and third generations. Symptoms of the trauma are unconsciously passed on to children and grandchildren, especially when the experiences are hushed up or considered taboo. In that case, young people are keenly aware of gestures, references, breaks in conversation, etc., without understanding their meaning. They seek to support their parents by offering their own pain to remedy their elders' suffering.

AN INDIVIDUAL'S LIFE STORY is thus strongly tied to his or her parents' past, which is often passed on to the third generation as well. In therapy, patients must therefore not only reconstruct their own life histories, but those of their parents and/or grandparents, so that they can learn to distinguish between their own and others' experiences.

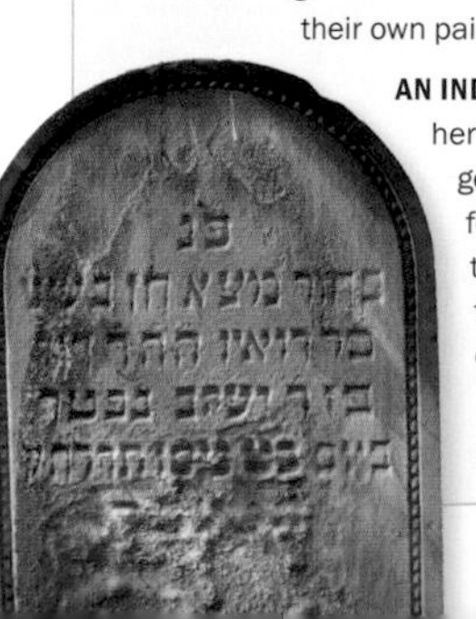

Victims of war, torture, and violent crime suffer from extreme traumatization.

PSYCHOANALYSIS AS THERAPY

According to psychoanalytic theory, incompletely processed conflicts are the cause of mental disturbances. The aim of therapy is to reveal and resolve them.

The psychoanalytic view of mental illness holds that the use of defense mechanisms (p. 284) generally reflects a disordered process. However, a person is considered to have an established neurosis only when a certain line is crossed and the disordered behavior affects his or her professional and social activity. A neurosis can be seen as an acquired disorder, the result of incomplete repression by the ego of impulses from the id. To prevent the repressed impulses from entering conscious awareness, the psyche produces neurotic symptoms. One example of this is compulsive washing: Repressed feelings of guilt seek a path into consciousness by evoking a constant sensation of having dirty hands. To combat this feeling, the person washes his or her hands again and again.

Unresolved conflicts within the psychosexual development process (p. 283) can also lead to psychological disturbances, mostly in the form of regression—that is, falling back to the affected phase of development. These repressed or unresolved childhood experiences can express themselves in so-called psychoneuroses; these include all forms of hysteria, phobias, compulsions, and character neuroses.

The Psychoanalytic Method

Psychoanalysis's aim is to help the patient gain deeper insight into the context of his or her suffering. The analyst seeks to help free the patient from unexamined or unconscious barriers of self-defense mechanisms and resistance. This allows for a restructuring of the personality elements responsible for the provoking and maintaining of a disorder.

During a therapy session, the patient is asked to express everything that comes into his or her mind in an unrestrained manner. In this "free association" technique, the patient thus takes on the active speaking role, while the analyst merely asks clarifying questions, offers interpretations and seeks to create an atmosphere in which the patient can speak freely.

The analyst remains in the background, representing a kind of "blank wall" upon which the patient can project significant people from his or her life history (such as family members). This so-called transference process is a key element in every analysis. Thus, special attention is paid to the relationship between analyst and patient. Psychoanalysis aims to bring past conflicts that were experienced as traumatic into consciousness, so that they can be resolved in a manner appropriate to the now-adult patient. During this process, a great deal of resistance must be overcome, which takes up a large portion of the psychoanalytic process. Classical psychoanalysis continues for a period of three to five years. Today, however, shorter psychoanalytic therapies are increasingly being used.

Freud's couch in London: Classical psychoanalysis demands that there is to be no direct eye contact. Thus, the patient lies on a couch while the analyst sits behind him, so as to encourage free association.

Psychoanalysis According to C. G. Jung

After working with Freud for some time, C. G. Jung developed his own theory, which he called "analytical psychology" or the "psychology of complexes." Jung divided the unconscious into two forms: personal and collective. Here, the personal unconscious roughly corresponds to Freud's idea of the unconscious, which contains the individual's forgotten or repressed thoughts and feelings. The collective unconscious, on the other hand, is shared by all of humanity. Its content is independent of a person's culture, ethnicity, or life history. Many basic human themes can be found, for example, in legends and fairy tales. These so-called archetypes are similar across diverse cultures and time periods. Some examples of these archetypes include characters such as heroes and monsters.

above: *C. G. Jung (1875–1961)*

21ST CENTURY

MEDIUM-LENGTH *or short-term therapies are mostly preferred by today's psychoanalysts.*

NEUROSCIENTISTS *are also investigating the effectiveness of psychoanalytic treatment.*

THE COUCH IS OUT. *Today, patient and analyst engage in dialogue.*

FREUD IN EVERYDAY LANGUAGE: *the Oedipus complex, unconscious, repression, Freudian slips, etc.*

Self Psychology

In the 1960s, U.S. neurologist Heinz Kohut founded a school of thought called "self psychology." This view considers people within the context of their entire individual development in relation to others, rather than as isolated individuals. The development of the self is highly dependent on significant persons in childhood, who must communicate to the child a sense of his or her own value so that a strong self can emerge. People with weak selves often protectively deceive themselves, pretending that they are better or more capable than they really are. If they are unable to maintain this self-image, they may fall into a depression. In therapy, the focus lies on the development of the self and the individual's network of relationships. This is reflected in the complex bond between analyst and patient.

above: Receiving recognition and protection from important people in a child's life are important for the development of a strong self.

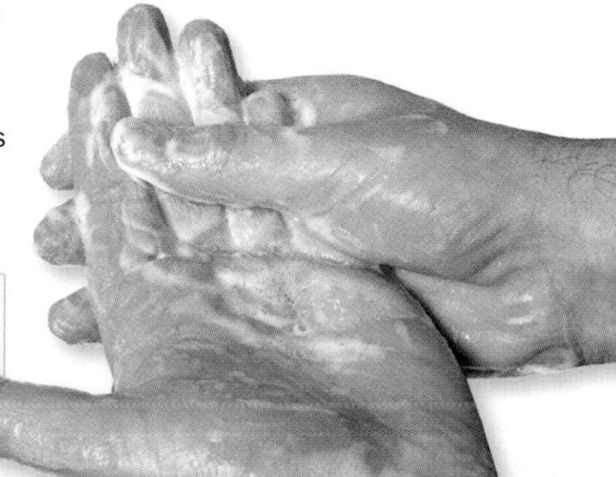

Repressed feelings of guilt can be the cause of compulsive washing.

Monographic Boxes

Analytic Boxes

VISUAL ARTS

Art is always a mirror of the times in which it emerged. Therefore, the pictorial works of earlier eras enable an informative insight into the contemporary world of the artist: They show us how the people lived, what was important to them, and how they saw their world. In comparison to the obvious representations of the world in historic pictures, the modern art of the 20th century can often seem very opaque and inaccessible. It does not necessarily follow any fixed rules any more: Abstract figures or distortions of everyday objects are often used to confound our viewing habits and conventions of "beautiful art." They show us the world in such a fashion as to reinvigorate our perception of it and thus inspire our imagination and thinking.

KEY FACTS

MAKE-UP PALETTES *from around 3000 B.C. are the oldest evidence of Egyptian relief art.*

HIEROGLYPHS *appeared for the first time about 3000 B.C.*

MUCH GREEK SCULPTURE *is known today only through Roman copies.*

NOT ONLY WAS ROMAN ART *inspired by traditional Italian subject matter, but also by the archetypes of Hellenistic Greece.*

Egypt (3000 B.C.–395 A.D.) | Greece (1100–100 B.C.) | Rome (200 B.C.–565 A.D.)

ART IN ANTIQUITY

The cradle of art lies in ancient Egypt. Over the millennia on the fertile banks of the Nile, an independent style of art was developed that was conceived to last for eternity. It became an influence, from the seventh century B.C., on the art of Greece and later that of the Roman Empire. Greek art began developing from the late Cretan and Mycenaean styles on the Greek mainland at the end of the 11th century B.C. Artistic works of Greece, especially during Hellenistic times, eventually became a paradigm for Roman art.

➔ *The art of antiquity invented an image of man caught between rigidity and animation, perfection, and reality.*

EGYPTIAN ART

Rigidity, symmetry, and great attention to detail are the unmistakable characteristics of Egyptian art. Once established, these rules remained in force for 3,000 years.

Ancient Egypt was relatively isolated by the surrounding desert. With the establishment of a centralized kingdom around 2900 B.C., a completely individual style developed in relief, sculpture, and painting. In accordance with the Egyptian belief in an afterlife, their art was concentrated in burial complexes and shrines. The graves of deified pharaohs, their families, and high officials included wall-paintings and contained a variety of burial objects that were meant to guarantee a suitable afterlife.

Art According to a Template

Painting in particular provides an exact portrayal of everyday life in Egypt. The pictures were not only meant to capture earthly life, but also to depict the Egyptian gods and the awaiting afterlife.

The figure forms in paintings and reliefs followed strict rules. Among these were prescribed proportions, the division of the picture area into strips (registers), and a fixed reference line as a base. The characteristic lack of a foreshortened perspective, shading, and only a hint of background, conformed to the rule of a clear and complete rendering of the images that recalled the lives of the deceased.

The depiction of the human figure switched continually from profile (face, arms, and legs) to a frontal view (eyes and torso). In addition, the illustrated figure size was relative to an individual's importance, and male figures were given a darker skin tone than females.

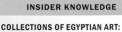

Stone relief of Pharaoh Narmer as the unifier of Egypt (ca 3000 B.C.)

INSIDER KNOWLEDGE

COLLECTIONS OF EGYPTIAN ART:
Egyptian Museum, Cairo

The British Museum, London

Brooklyn Museum and The Metropolitan Museum of Art, New York

Musée du Louvre, Paris

Ägyptisches Museum, Berlin

Ny Carlsberg Glyptotek, Copenhagen

STATUES *were meant, just like mummies, to receive the soul of the person after death.*

"HE WHO KEEPS ALIVE" *(s-ankh) was the term for sculptors in ancient Egypt.*

A LESS RIGID, MORE INDIVIDUAL STYLE *("Amarna style") appeared during the Amarna period under Pharaoh Akhenaton (1364–1348 B.C.).*

The bust of Queen Nefertiti, wife of Pharaoh Akhenaton (ca 1355 B.C.)

Portraiture

THE EGYPTIANS preserved their dead as mummies for a life after death. The embalmed body, wrapped in cloth strips, was considered the sanctuary of the soul. Portraits served the same purpose and were produced in various designs as burial objects.

THE SCULPTOR translated a person's essential characteristics into stone. The likenesses, however, showed no physical similarity to the person. Attributes such as clothing indicated the social standing of the person portrayed. Larger statues were carved out of a block with the subject either sitting or standing. These statues, as was the case with all Egyptian art, were subject to strict rules; such as always looking ahead.

Double statue of Pharaoh Menkaure and his wife, Queen Khamerernebti II (ca 2520 B.C.)

Gold relief from tomb of Pharaoh Tutankhamen (14th century B.C.)

Fresco from the tomb of Nefertari, wife of Ramses II (1300 B.C.)

GREEK AND ROMAN ART

The central theme of Greek art was the human figure in mythology and everyday life. During the Roman Empire, art was essentially used for political propaganda.

Protogeometric and geometric art were the first styles of Greek art from 1050 to 700 B.C. During this period, vases were decorated with precisely measured ornamentation and later with meandering lines as well as static representations of human and animal figures.

Kore from Chios, found on the Acropolis in Athens (sixth century B.C.)

Kouros and Kore

In the archaic period from the mid-seventh century B.C., there arose two types of monumental sculpture: *kouros* and *kore*. The kouros was a nude male representing either a youthful god or a warrior. It imitates both the symmetry and forward-facing, striding stance of Egyptian sculpture. The female counterpart was the kore, a standing young female figure wrapped in a robe. Often used as votive offerings, both are often pictured with the "archaic smile," which is emblematic of the majority of Egyptian sculpture.

Portrayal of Reality

The black-figure technique in vase painting developed on the Greek mainland in the sixth century B.C. This was followed by the red-figure technique developed in the first half of the fifth century B.C. In the classic period both achieved a narrative, realistic style.

What had been only hinted at in the animation of kouroi gained its full form in the classic sculpture of the fifth and fourth centuries. In the transitional phase from archaic to classic, in the first half of the fifth century B.C., the artists developed the austere style, with a special interplay of body movements (*contrapposto*) as well as foreshortened perspective. Representatives of the Rich style also attempted to capture the "expression of the soul."

Vase with red figures representing Dionysus, god of wine (volute-handled crater, fifth century B.C.)

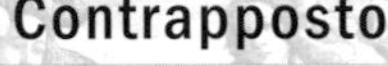

Contrapposto

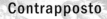

THE INVENTION of the contrapposto is ascribed to the sculptor Polykleitos. His statues embody the image of man in classic Greece and symbolize democracy. With a supporting leg and the free leg, as well as the combination of movement and countermovement (ponderation), it represents both balance and harmony.

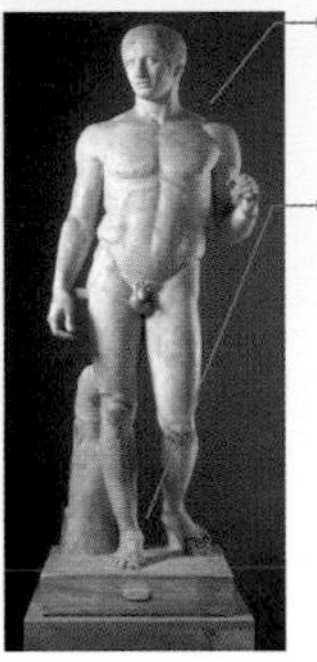
The tilt of the hips causes the left shoulder to be higher than the right.
The right foot is firm on the ground; the left is placed to the rear.

Doryphoros (Greek: "spear-bearer"), Roman copy in marble (before 79 A.D.) after the original in bronze by Polykleitos (ca 440 B.C.)

Spread of Hellenism

Greek art spread during the empire of Alexander the Great. Limbs and the arrangement of folds of material became increasingly more dynamic during the Hellenistic period between Alexander's death in 323 B.C. and the first century B.C. Static forms became dramatically animated works.

Roman Art of a World Empire

Coinciding with the decline of the Hellenistic states in the second century B.C., an individual art form began to take shape in Rome, which radiated out into the steadily expanding empire. The Romans imitated earlier Italian and Hellenistic models in their sculpture and ornamentation. However, they developed their own individual imagery in portraits and relief. Busts that faithfully reproduced the subject were popular due to traditional ancestor-worship during the Republican period until 27 B.C. In the subsequent Augustan age, ending in 14 A.D., a more uniform style that stressed the sublime began in portraiture. Statues of rulers, reliefs on tombs, triumphal arches, and columns told of military and historical events.

The statue of Augustus shows the first Roman emperor in a contrapposto position (ca 19 B.C.).

Roman wall paintings in the Villa of the Mysteries in Pompeii show women being inducted into the secret Dionysus cult (100 B.C.).

The relief on Trajan's column in Rome memorializes the war victories of Emperor Trajan (113 A.D.).

➔ **see also: Greek Polis,** *Politics, Law, and Economy Chapter, p. 169*

KEY FACTS

CHINESE ART AND CULTURE *spread to Korea and Japan from the fourth to sixth centuries A.D. in the wake of Buddhism.*

BECAUSE ISLAM FORBIDS *the depiction of figures, artists concentrated on producing artistic calligraphy as well as intricate geometric patterns and rich floral ornamentation.*

EUROPE *profited from the lively cultural exchange with East Asia and the Islamic world.*

East Asian Art (fifth century B.C. until today) | Islamic Art (seventh century A.D. until today)

ASIAN AND ISLAMIC ART

The Chinese culture is one of the oldest in the world. Its traditional art forms and techniques, which especially influenced Japan and Korea, continue to be cultivated to this day. Europeans became intrigued, especially in the 18th and 19th centuries, by East Asian art, which they regarded as exotic. Islamic art creatively combined different cultural influences from the Mediterranean and the Middle East. The Islamic prohibition against depicting figures led to the development of rich ornamentation and beautiful calligraphy.

➔ *East Asia and the Islamic world closely combined religious and secular, aristocratic art.*

EAST ASIAN ART

China influenced the East Asian cultural sphere both politically and artistically for centuries. Korea and Japan later developed forms and techniques of their own.

As one of the first high cultures in the world, Chinese art first manifested itself within the colorful ceramics of the Yangshao culture, which existed from 5000 to 3000 B.C. Their rhythmic lines foreshadowed the later characteristic traits that would develop in later Chinese art.

THE MAUSOLEUM OF QIN SHI HUANG DI *was built in the third century B.C.; in 1987 it was declared a World Heritage site.*

A FARMER *discovered the first figurines in 1974 while digging a well.*

OVER 7,000 LIFE-SIZE TERRA-COTTA WARRIORS, *including horses and war chariots, guarded the underground burial palace of the first Chinese emperor.*

Crossbow man (third century B.C.)

Army of Tomb Guards

CHINA'S FIRST EMPEROR Qin Shi Huang Di (died in 210 B.C.) united China into one empire. He built the Great Wall, and built in honor of himself a grandiose tomb. It measured 226,042 ft^2 (21,000 m^2) and took 38 years to complete. Inside was stationed an army of infantry and a cavalry of horses and chariots. The figures were produced in giant ceramic workshops in which each head was individually formed and the soldiers were given "real" weapons.

The clay soldiers in the monumental tomb of the first Chinese emperor.

Handicraft and Artistic Work

Starting in the 15th century B.C., the Chinese made tools, weapons, and images from bronze. In the 11th century B.C., they invented the process of making porcelain. Mural paintings from the third century B.C. reflect contemporary daily life in China. Paintings on silk from this time period have been found captivating, as has lacquer work. Lacquer, a technique of preservation with resin, was used especially by the Japanese to decorate commodes, folding screens, and boxes.

Art and Buddhism

Buddhism inspired an aura of lightness and eternity in East Asian art. Initially, religious art was limited to symbolism, as artistic creation was thought of as a type of meditation. It was not until as late as the first century A.D., about 600 years after the death of Buddha, that the Chinese first depicted him in stone and bronze.

Bronze Buddha statue from Korea, seventh or eighth century A.D.

White-and-blue Chinese vase with a dragon motif, 18th century

Artistic Developments

From the Ming dynasty to the 17th century, porcelain boomed. Especially popular was a Persian technique reaching China in the 14th century—white porcelain painted with cobalt blue glaze. From the 10th century, artists preferred painting landscapes and animals. Others set high standards in carving jade, weaving silk, printing books, and coloring wood cuts. Japanese calligraphy was refined as it was connected with Zen Buddhism.

"Pair of lovers" (colored woodcut by Utamaro Kitagawa, 1788)

➔ **see also: Chinese Architecture,** *Architecture Chapter, p. 321*

ISLAMIC ART

Along with the spread of Islam in the seventh and eighth centuries, Islamic art reached Spain and North Africa from Syria and southeastern Europe and northern India via Iran and Iraq.

One characteristic trait of Islamic art is the absence of figures, particularly within the religious sphere. Since the seventh century, artists mainly concentrated on the creation of rich ornamentation and complex calligraphy.

Classical Heritage

Islamic artists during the Umayyad dynasty in the seventh and eighth centuries drew their style from the late classical Byzantine legacy. They developed various complex forms of braided and intertwined ornamentation.

Due to the Islamic belief in the Qur'an as a divine revelation, it was important to follow the prohibition on representing living things. Therefore, artists strove to present the text of the Qur'an in the most beautiful

Ivory canister from Spain with human figures (10th century)

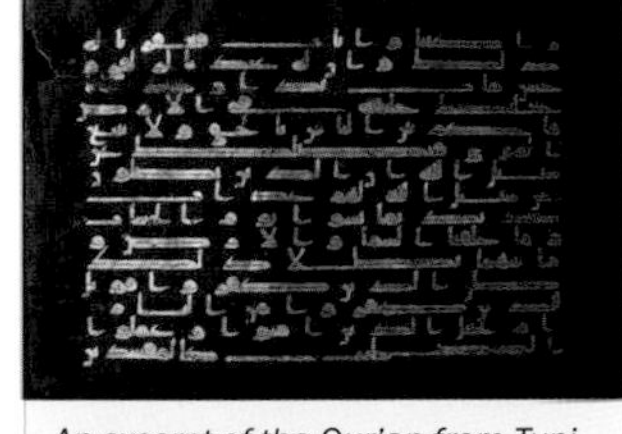

An excerpt of the Qur'an from Tunisia in the kufic style of calligraphy.

calligraphy decorated with braided motifs and other abstract forms.

Within the mosques, complexly intertwined geometric designs (*arabesques*) decorated the pulpits carved from wood (*mimbars*) as well as rugs, textiles, ceramics, and bronze vessels.

Artistic Styles of the Islamic Dynasties

The different styles of Islamic art are primarily named after the contemporary dynasty that was ruling when it was popular. For instance, the Turkish Tulunids, as viceroys of the Abbasid caliphs of Baghdad, brought their art to Syria and Egypt in the ninth century. An important development in the Iraqi Samarra for the production of ceramics was luster glaze, which gave objects a metallic sheen. Since the 10th century, carvings of ivory that represented human figures were created under the Fatimids of Cairo.

The Anatolian Seljuks, who ruled an expansive empire in the 11th and 12th centuries, produced brilliantly decorated manuscripts. In the 13th century, the oldest existing knotted rugs were hand-woven in Konya, the Seljuk capital. In the 12th and 13th centuries, the painting of miniatures flourished—especially in the region of present-day Iraq. Literary works, be they scientific or historical, were given elaborate illustrations. East Asian motifs like lotus blossoms, fabled animals, and bands of clouds entered the treasury of Islamic art forms, especially that of Persia, with the Mongols.

Glass blowing blossomed under the Mamluk, who ruled Egypt and Syria until the 16th century. At the same time, the Moorish style established itself on the Iberian Peninsula with the Alhambra palace existing as an outstanding example. Hand-knotted "hunt rugs" reflect the brilliant carpet weaving styles of the Persian Safavids during the 16th and 17th centuries.

Islamic, Persian, and Hindu styles combined to produce a naturalistic style on the Indian subcontinent under the Mughal emperors. At the same time, the *saz* style, which employed looser, less geometric patterns, emerged in the Ottoman Empire.

Persian illustration from "Khamseh" by Nizami (16th century)

Wood carving with floral motives from Jerusalem (eighth century)

INSIDER KNOWLEDGE

A ROCOCO MOTIF *known as "chinoiserie" exemplifies the popularity of the exotic in the West. Japanese art influenced Impressionism. The artistic inheritance of the Fatimids influenced Norman art in southern Italy in the 11th and 12th centuries. The Moorish style of the Iberian Peninsula affected the architectural style in Latin America.*

Tiles as Building Decoration

Since the ninths century, ceramic tiles were used to decorate exterior and interior walls. They were produced by different processes for different purposes. Glazed tiles comprising one color were used for mosaics. There were also large tiles painted in varying hues with glazed paint, e.g., the "cuerda seca" (Spanish: "dry cord") method used in the Spanish city of Granada. Under-glazed painting was widespread in the Ottoman Empire.

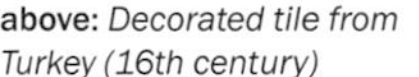

above: *Decorated tile from Turkey (16th century)*

right: *Dome of the Lutfallah mosque in Isfahan, Iran, built 1602–1619*

➲ see also: Islam, *Religion Chapter, pp. 238–241* | Islamic Architecture, *Architecture Chapter, p. 320*

KEY FACTS

IN BYZANTIUM, *the eastern ancient Roman Empire, the tradition of classical art endured for a long time.*

ROMANESQUE *was the first artistic style to spread all over Europe.*

SYMBOLS AND ALLEGORY *were more important than life-like depictions.*

GOTHIC *was expressive, elegant, and experimental.*

THE ARTISTS *of the Middle Ages mostly remained anonymous.*

Byzantine art (fourth/eighth–15th century) | Romanesque (11th–13th century) | Gothic (12th–16th century)

ART OF THE MIDDLE AGES

The art of the Middle Ages united several traditions. Classical culture survived in Byzantium and spread not only to western and eastern Europe, but also to Islamic countries. Aside from the classical heritage, another important element was Christianity. Throughout the Middle Ages, art was almost exclusively religious. With Romanesque and Gothic, the Middle Ages developed new, very independent styles, which eventually led from Late Gothic to the Renaissance. The Middle Ages were, therefore, not a time of cultural decay but rather a time of transformation.

➲ *Medieval art had primarily religious content in paintings, manuscript illustrations, and architectural decorations.*

BYZANTINE ART AND ROMANESQUE STYLE

More than anywhere else, the classical tradition lived on in the Byzantine Empire. While artistic styles were confined mainly to particular regions, Romanesque was the first pan-European style.

Between the fourth and eighth centuries, the Byzantine Empire developed an independent style of its own. Sacred paintings of saints, called icons, were created according to a particular set of rules. Magnificent wall mosaics, which depict saints next to rulers, serve as impressive evidence of Byzantine art. These mosaics were not meant to accurately portray individual persons. They expressed the illustriousness and sublimity of the personages depicted and made them look as if they were in heaven.

Byzantium achieved an enduring influence on religious art in the countries of eastern Europe, where Orthodox Christianity prevails. Here the icon painters still follow the old rules.

THE RABULA GOSPELS *from sixth century Syria contain the oldest surviving biblical illustrations.*

THE EXPRESSION "MINIATURE" *for book illustrations comes from the red pigment minium that was used for drawing with pens.*

ILLUSTRATION CENTERS *in the 14th–15th centuries were France, Burgundy, and the Netherlands.*

In the initial "R," St. George is pictured fighting the dragon (book illumination, 12th century).

Illuminated Manuscripts

CODICES, parchment, or paper pages bound together as books, replaced scrolls in the course of the fourth century. The Church used the new medium to preserve and promulgate religious works. Scriptoriums, or writing rooms where manuscripts were copied by hand, were set up in monasteries. These manuscripts were decorated with ornamental or figure miniatures within or on the border of the text or on separate pages. Gold leaf was often used with these decorations. Book covers were decorated with precious stones, gold, or ivory.

FOR THE FINE ARTS, manuscript illumination was of the greatest importance. Artistic achievements could be disseminated quickly through easily transportable books.

The picture for the month of May from the book of hours, "Très Riches Heures du Duc de Berry," was created by the Brothers Limburg in 1416.

Monastic Schools

Religious works of art were also created in other parts of Europe. Monasteries were the centers of artistic creation. In scriptoriums, illuminators decorated expensive manuscripts with pictures based on antique models. These artists, however, had no interest in creating individual artworks or a sense of space. The covers of the manuscript books were often decorated with ivory or gold.

This ivory carving from the 10th century demonstrates Byzantine influence in the Holy Roman Empire.

Romanesque

With the start of the Romanesque style around 1000 A.D., sculptors ceased carving free-standing statues. They were now connected to buildings, especially church portals and interiors. They conveyed the basics of Christianity to churchgoers, most of whom could not read or understand the Latin Mass.

This relief from the 11th century shows the churchgoer what pain could await one in hell.

This mosaic from the sixth century depicts the Byzantine Empress Theodora with a saintly halo.

➲ **see also: Romanesque,** *Architecture Chapter, p. 322* | **Medieval Literature,** *Literature Chapter, pp. 338–340*

THE GOTHIC

Artists working in the Gothic style strove for a close imitation of nature, molding, and expressiveness. They gradually rose out of anonymity and became known by name.

Benefactors wanted to record their pious deeds in portraits (Naumburg Cathedral, 13th century).

Around the middle of the 12th century, new forms of sculpture that were part of the architecture emerged in France, marking the artistic transition from the archaic Romanesque to the light and fine-limbed style of Gothic.

The Wilton Diptych, an altar painting from about 1395, is reminiscent of Byzantine icons with its gold-colored background.

Previously only rulers and the Church commissioned art, but now they were joined by town elites who had become rich through commerce, trade, or money lending. Portraits of donors and tomb sculptures expressed persistent self-awareness. Mendicant orders promulgated the veneration of Mary. The figure of Mary became a central theme of art along with the Last Judgment and the incarnation of Christ. By the 14th century free-standing sculptures increasingly appeared.

From Frescos to Panel Paintings

Beginning in the 12th century, stylistic elements of Byzantine art and its classical tradition began to reach middle and southern Europe as a direct result of the Crusades. Byzantine mosaics had already exerted great influence, especially in Venice and Sicily.

Byzantine models inspired Italian panel and fresco paintings. At the beginning of the 14th century, artists like Duccio di Buoninsegna and Giotto di Bondone were influenced by the "Maniera greca-byzantina" (Greek-Byzantine manner), which manifested itself primarily in the portrayal of faces and clothes. They tried to create greater naturalness and individuality. In particular, Giotto strove to give his pictures depth by including landscapes instead of the customary gold backgrounds. He is considered one of the forerunners of the Renaissance (p. 294). From the mid-14th century, wood panel paintings in contrast to wall paintings were predominantly used for altar pieces and devotional pictures.

Since there was little room in Gothic churches for wall paintings except on pillars and vaults, monumental stained-glass windows developed. Exceptions included Giotto's fresco cycles in Assisi and Florence and the wall paintings of Pietro Lorenzetti (1320–1348) in the Palazzo Pubblico in Siena. Their new delineation of space and lively scenes showed the way forward in the second half of the 14th century.

The Court Style

Starting around 1400, the delicate, elegant "Court Style" of Gothic developed north of the Alps in Bohemia, France, and Flemish Burgundy. Typical of this style is a Madonna with an S-curved figure and voluminous clothes.

In addition to the typical religious works, more secular books were now being illuminated. Book illustration was no longer confined to monasteries but was also done in workshops in cities. For example, in 1416 the Brothers Limburg illustrated a devotional book for the Duke of Berry. The miniatures that decorate the "Très Riches Heures du Duc de Berry" unite a love of story telling, delight in depicting the beauty of nature, and satisfaction in noting precise details.

A Madonna bears herself in the typical S-curve (about 1400).

In the Late Gothic period in Germany, artists such as Tilman Riemenschneider, and Veit Stoss created highly expressive wood carvings.

Giotto's fresco, "The Lamentation Over Christ" (ca 1303–1305)

INSIDER KNOWLEDGE

THE TERM "MIDDLE AGES" *was coined in the 15th or 16th century. At that time, the epoch between antiquity and Renaissance was considered a time of cultural decay.*

DUE TO ICONIC VENERATION, *disturbances erupted in Byzantium during the eighth and ninth centuries.*

"GOTICO" *("foreign," "barbaric") was originally a word of disgrace.*

The Flemish painters Robert Campin and Jan van Eyck (p. 297) were already anticipating the styles that would emerge with the Renaissance through their naturalistic styles of painting (p. 294).

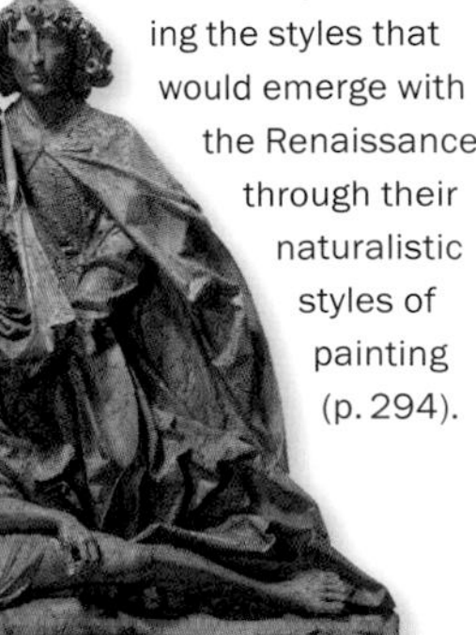

Tilman Riemenschneider conveys deep sorrow and empathy with his wood carving "Lamentation Over Christ" from 1515.

➔ see also: Gothic, *Architecture Chapter, p. 323*

KEY FACTS

THE RENAISSANCE *brought the rebirth of classic ideals.*

THE CENTRAL PERSPECTIVE *went hand in hand with a whole new perception about humanity and its place within the world.*

ART *would no longer be seen as a mere handicraft.*

THE ARTISTS *of the Renaissance were interested in applying wide ranging and refined techniques.*

RENAISSANCE AND MANNERISM

The era of the Renaissance marks the transition to modern times. The artists liberated themselves from the visual conventions that dominated the Middle Ages and turned toward depicting observable reality through linear perspective. Alongside biblical and mythological themes, portrait and landscape painting gained importance. Natural science studies as well as the orientation on the classical art of antiquity led to a new manner of artistic representation that characterized Western art for centuries.

The term "Renaissance" characterizes the rebirth of the arts from the spirit of classical antiquity.

EARLY RENAISSANCE

Endeavoring to reproduce the world as exactly as possible, the artists undertook intensive studies of nature and educated themselves about the classical art of antiquity. Characteristic of the Early Renaissance was a style stressing lines with clearly outlined contours.

Exploratory expeditions, expanding trade relations, and scientific discoveries in the 15th century meant a person no longer saw himself as a cog in the divine structure of things, but rather attained a sense of awareness as a self-directed individual.

The new positioning of humanity at the center of creation also resulted in artists shifting their focus to the world about them. They no longer relied on accepted theories and instead began to reproduce the reality about them as precisely as possible. With a scientific spirit of research, they began to uncover the laws that govern nature. The insights gained through observation and deliberation served from then on as "building plans" for their art.

"Bacchus and Ariadne" (painting by Titian, 1522)

Central Perspective

One of these laws is central perspective (p. 297). The mathematical construct developed by Leon Battista Alberti made possible the achievement of the illusion of depth in a two-dimensional image.

Masaccio was one of the first to employ this method in the fresco "The Holy Trinity" (1427). The illusion was further developed in the works of Piero della Francesca and Andrea Mantegna through the sculptural modeling of figures and a moving play of light and shadows.

Sandro Botticelli's "Birth of Venus" from 1482–1486, has the love goddess in the pose of classic sculptures, the counterpoise.

Classic Paradigms

Toward the end of the century artists were so well versed in painting perspective space that compositions which still appeared contrived in the beginning became more polished. Botticelli's "Birth of Venus" is a typical example of the flowing lines that exemplified the elegant style of draftsmanship of the closing years of the 15th century.

Venus is represented with her weight balanced on one foot in the so-called counterpoise (p. 289). This form of movement was known from the art of antiquity, which was to become the great paradigm for the Renaissance artists. They saw the Humanist ideal realized in the life-like form of classic Greek and Roman sculptures.

Michelangelo's (p. 296) famous "David" is also depicted in the counterpoise. The monumental sculpture derives its compelling power of expression not least from its successful blending of the ancient ideal of beauty and its naturalistic likeness to the human form.

This artistic packaging of ideal and reality within their artistic representations characterizes the art of the High Renaissance (p. 295), whose center was Rome.

A New Artists' Image

The artists liberated themselves in the Renaissance from the role of anonymous craftsmen and developed a new self-image and a sense of mission. In his self-portrait Albrecht Dürer (p. 297) portrays himself with obvious similarity to Christ to make visual the deep relationship between divine power of creation and the artist with creative abilities bestowed upon him by God. The idea developed in the Renaissance of the artist as a personality endowed with exceptional abilities persisted until the modern era.

above: *Albrecht Dürer's self-portrait in 1500: The Renaissance put artists on a divine pedestal.*

see also: Humanism and Renaissance, *Philosophy Chapter, p. 253* | **Renaissance,** *Architecture Chapter, pp. 324, 325*

HIGH RENAISSANCE

The art of the High Renaissance was thoroughly influenced by harmony and proportion. Brilliantly painted worlds were created on the basis of balanced patterns of composition.

The perfect reproduction of space, forms, light, and movement allowed the artists at the beginning of the 16th century not only to artistically imitate reality but, on the basis of artistic laws, also to create realistic appearing images of worlds that sprang from their own imagination.

Michelangelo portrayed "The Creation of Adam" in compelling vividness (p. 296). His imagined scenario of the bestowal of "the divine spark" not only translates the biblical text in an expressive way, but also envisages the Neoplatonic concept that a reflection of divine beauty is to be found in the beauty of the human body. Among the outstanding artistic personalities of the era were Leonardo da Vinci, Michelangelo, Raphael, and Titian. While Raphael and Michelangelo helped work on the remodeling of the Vatican compound under the commission of Pope Julius II and so represent Roman art, the name Titian is closely associated with Venice, which also developed a flourishing art scene in the first half of the 16th century.

Veronese combines biblical stories with idealized architecture, which is reminiscent of his hometown Venice: "The Marriage at Cana" (painting, 1562–1563).

Venetian Painting

In contrast to the classic-oriented Roman art created by papal commission, Venetian painting was characterized by an opulent splendor of colors, sensuality, and a certain worldly subject matter.

Paolo Veronese staged the "Wedding at Cana" as a boisterous celebration in sumptuous Venetian architecture. Alongside such worldly interpretations of biblical stories, mythological scenes enjoyed great popularity. Arcadian idylls, bacchanals, and feasts of the gods were laid out in glowing colors and—as seen in Titian's painting "Bacchus and Ariadne"—with a pronounced sense for dynamic motion, illustrative description full of fantasy, and an interest in human expression.

21ST CENTURY

RENAISSANCE ART *embodies an individualistic ideal for people that still seems fitting today: striving through self-reflective criticism toward beauty and self-realization.*

Landscapes and Portraits

Venice with its lagoons and islands demonstrated a special feeling for atmospheric lighting, which may have encouraged their change of direction towards landscape painting. Landscapes, which had to this point functioned only as a backdrop, now advanced to become a medium for creating mood and atmosphere and thus an essential part of the painting. Giorgione's painting "The Tempest" (ca 1505), is the first independent landscape painting in art history.

Portrait painting also experienced a reassessment. Painters such as Giovanni Bellini and Titian became concerned not only with capturing the likeness, but also the character of the models.

LEONARDO DA VINCI, *born 1452 in Vinci, Italy, died 1519 in Clos Lucé in France.*

LEONARDO WAS NOT ONLY A PAINTER, *but also an architect, engineer, and a natural architect.*

WITH HIS WIDE INTERESTS, *Leonardo embodied the artistic and humanistic ideals of the Renaissance.*

Leonardo da Vinci (painting, 19th century)

Leonardo da Vinci

HE WAS THE EMBODIMENT OF THE RENAISSANCE MAN. After his training in Florence, he was employed by the court in Milan, and until his death was in the service of the French king.

LEONARDO WAS NOT ONLY AN OUTSTANDING PAINTER and draftsman, but also a brilliant inventor. His universal talent and inexhaustible thirst for new knowledge earned him great admiration. He was ahead of his time with many of his ideas, for example, designing a flying machine. He was not always in line with the Church authorities and out of fear of being accused a heretic, he recorded parts of his scientific findings in a secret code.

THE "MONA LISA" is one of the most famous paintings in all of art history. The hard-to-define facial expression and the "object of the soul," as Leonardo called it, have fascinated viewers for hundreds of years. Even if it is not known what was going through the young lady's mind, one thing has been verified: the model was Lisa Gherardini del Giocondo. She is seated in front of a broad landscape; the figure and background are bathed in a warm light. Leonardo used light and color perspective, for which he is commonly attributed; however, it had already been used in early Netherlandish painting.

The smile of Leonardo's "Mona Lisa" is mysterious (1503–1506).

"THE LAST SUPPER" portrays Christ speaking of the impending betrayal. The composition reflects the drama through the wildly gesticulating disciples while Jesus sits as a calming influence in the center. The mural demonstrates da Vinci's subtle use of color, delicate line-work, and balanced structure. The soft tonal transitions ("sfumato") as well act to imbue this painting with a luster.

"The Last Supper" (painting by Leonardo da Vinci, 1495–1497)

see also: Neo-Platonism, *Philosophy Chapter, p. 249*

RENAISSANCE AND MANNERISM

The art of mannerism is characterized by an extremely turbulent and unnatural method of depiction. The pointed emphasis on artificiality, the deliberate "maniera" (Italian: "style") of the form, gave the art movement its name.

INSIDER KNOWLEDGE

CREATIVE FANTASY, *the artist's individual style of interpretation and rendering, gained its own independence against the trends in the Renaissance.*

Although Rome and Venice wallowed in painted splendor, the second half of the 16th century proved to be a time of crisis and war. The Copernican revolution shook the view of the world conveyed by the Church, and the belief in a well-ordered world harmony increasingly waned. The classic patterns of composition no longer seemed suitable for portraying a world that had been turned upside down. The perspective space continuum was abandoned in favor of making visual space more dynamic.

Surmounting of the Renaissance Ideals

In Parmigianino's painting "Madonna of the Long Neck," the abrupt juxtaposition of fore and background is unsettling, while Tintoretto created visual ravines through using extreme diagonals in his artistic works.

With the destruction of illusionistic space, the mannerists opened up a new dimension in art. The deliberately unnatural and exaggerated style of rendering, which did not pay heed to human anatomy and displayed bodies in sinuous and twisting coils (*figura serpentinata*), was to appeal to the viewer's emotions and open a reality behind visual appearance that is only accessible to the inner eye.

El Greco's ecstatic interpretations of biblical stories are like images flickering up in a dream. While working for the Spanish court, he abandoned all visual realism, showing signs of modern art. His figures seem to be driven by inner demons, a sensation emphasized by strong contrasts of gloomy darkness and ghostly, lurid brightness. The mannerists' goal had explicitly been to not create a deceptively real picture space where the viewer imagined he could enter at any time. The supernatural, mystical atmosphere, a suggestive style in painting where the real and unreal, spirit world and perceptible world are no longer distinguishable, had been alien to painters of the Renaissance. In the Baroque (p. 298), from about 1600, the intellectual worlds created by the mannerists reached their zenith.

Contradicting Nature

Slender limbs, stretched to the extreme, bodies spread out, twisting and turning, contradicting all traditional laws of proportion, form the characteristics of mannerism. Parmigianino also gave his Madonna unusually long limbs. Particularly striking is the delicately bowed swan neck that earned the picture the title "Madonna of the Long Neck." The painter intensified the idealized features of Raphael's organic figure moving into a stylish elegance, which contemporaries admired for its grace.

Parmigianino manipulated the proportions of his figures, like with "Madonna of the Long Neck" from 1534.

MICHELANGELO BUONARROTI, *born 1475 in Caprese / Tuscany, died 1564 in Rome.*

MICHELANGELO'S ART *forms a single corpus of work in the field of painting, sculpture, and architecture.*

THE CREATIVE HUMAN FIGURE *with all its beauty, power and suffering is at the center of his art.*

Michelangelo (copper engraving, 16th century)

Michelangelo Buonarroti

THE CREATION OF ADAM is fresco painted on the ceiling in the Sistine Chapel, Michelangelo's most major and famous work. In fresco painting, paint is applied directly to wet plaster ("fresco," Italian: "fresh"). Rapid, self-assured work is required as it dries quickly. Making corrections by painting over is barely possible. It was only with reluctance that the multi-talented artist took on the commission as he considered himself a sculptor. A sculptural three-dimensional quality is intrinsic to his powerfully painted nudes. In a virtuoso manner, the artist composed the Creation as a convergence of the dynamic and the static; it is only the divine spirit that breathes life into Adam.

right: *The statue of "David" from 1501–1504 is over 16.4 ft (5 m) tall.*

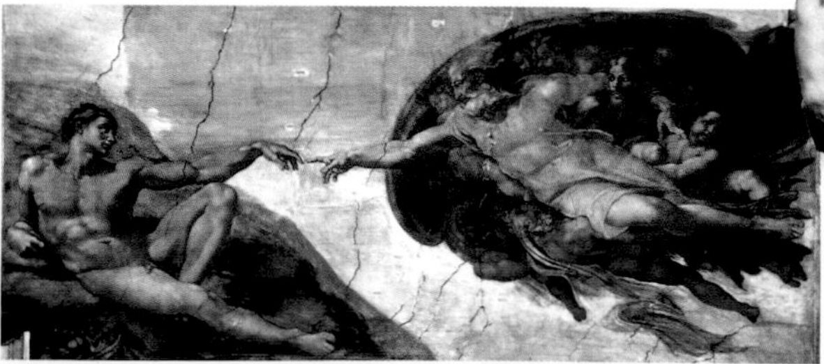

Michelangelo's world-famous fresco "The Creation of Adam" records the instant during which God gave life to humanity.

El Greco's paintings like "The Resurrection" (1584–1594) are emblematic of modern art today.

➲ see also: Copernicus Worldview, *Earth Chapter, p. 27*

One-Point Perspective—Rendering of Illusionistic Spatial Depth

IN ONE-POINT PERSPECTIVE the lines of geometric forms or spaces (3) converge at one vanishing point. The resulting grid makes a spatial representation possible conforming to the natural optical law that things appear smaller the greater the distance (2).

THE GOTHIC (p. 293) "importance-through-size" perspective was surmounted by the introduction of one-point perspective. One-point perspective accommodated the artistic need for precision in rendering and, because of its mathematical calculability, complied with the non-material claim of the Renaissance man to approach the world through intellectual achievement.

ANOTHER POSSIBILITY OF CREATING DEPTH is provided by aerial perspective. This style, where objects in the background lose intensity of color and contour (1), was named by Leonardo da Vinci.

The entire image format of Raphael's "Marriage of the Virgin" from 1504 sets the building in the very center of the painting.

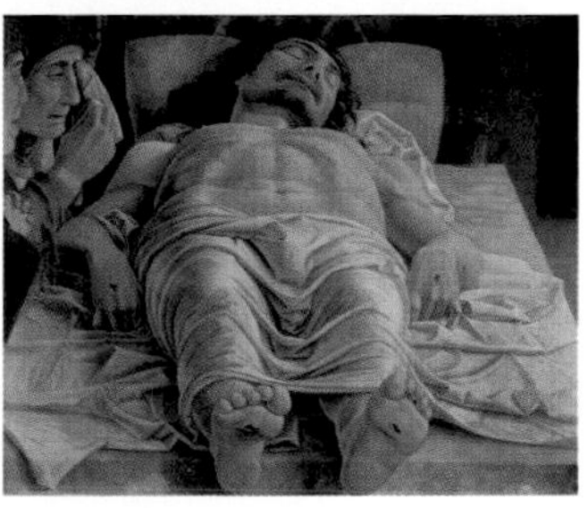

Virtuosic contact with perspective: "Lamentation Over the Dead Christ" (painting by Andrea Mantegna, ca 1490)

IN MANTEGNA'S "LAMENTATION OVER THE DEAD CHRIST," the body is shown dramatically foreshortened. The artist thereby provides proof not only of his virtuosity as a craftsman but also plays with the suggestive power of this unusual angle of view. The viewer has the feeling he is standing at the feet of the deceased and is part of the group of mourners recognizable in the upper left corner of the picture.

NORTHERN EUROPE

An awakening interest in visual reality also began to emerge at the beginning of the 15th century north of the Alps.

In contrast to Italian art, early Dutch painting was not based on the study of antiquity or research in natural science but rather on the exact observation of common objects and a knowledge of their material composition.

Dutch Painting

Painters like Rogier van der Weyden and Jan van Eyck were brilliant masters in capturing the composition of diverse surfaces. Thanks to oil painting having spread early in the north, the artists achieved a textural brilliance that made material appear to the viewer real enough to touch. In contrast to the fresco and tempera painting used in Italy, which became dull when dry, supple oil paint allowed the building up of a painting by means of translucent layers of color (glazes), imbuing faces, and clothing with a unique vitality and brilliance.

The works of Hieronymus Bosch and Pieter Bruegel the Elder also reveal a pronounced love for detail. They held up an admonishing mirror to their contemporaries with their drastic depictions of virtuous and depraved behavior. Their morally-based scenes smoothed the way for the picture style that came to full bloom in the following century during the Dutch Baroque (pp. 300–301).

In Bosch's "Hell" from around 1504, music instruments are used as tools for torture.

Everyday Scenes

The Dutch fondness for everyday scenes and meticulously precise details is evident in van Eyck's "Portrait of Giovanni Arnolfini and His Wife." Despite the microscopic rendering of the bridal couple and their witnesses in the mirror, the composition preserves an atmospheric unity. This is achieved through the naturalistic light that plays equally about the scene.

above: *Van Eyck's "Portrait of Giovanni Arnolfini and His Wife" from 1434 is full of symbols, such as the dog representing loyalty.*

German Renaissance

The intellectual and aesthetic ideals of the Italian Renaissance also arrived in the German language area in the early 16th century. Famous works of the Early Renaissance had been distributed as copper etchings and numerous artists took educational tours to Italy. Albrecht Dürer (p. 294) gained a lasting impression of the Italian view as his balanced, symmetrically composed self-portrait illustrates. As a painter, but above all as a superb wood and copperplate engraver, he introduced ideals of the classic form to northern European art.

Nevertheless, under the influence of the Reformation, northern art remained less opulent than in the Catholic South. Among their most significant representatives, besides Dürer, were Lucas Cranach and Hans Holbein.

➲ see also: The Reformation, *Religion Chapter, p. 237*

KEY FACTS

FROM ROME, *the center of Catholicism, the Baroque style spread across Europe.*

THE CHURCH AND THE ROYAL HOUSES *used Baroque art to shape their public images.*

STILL LIFES, *landscapes, and everyday scenes became independent genres in painting.*

COMMONERS *also appeared as collectors and commissioners of art.*

Baroque in Italy | Baroque art in the European courts | Baroque in Holland | Baroque genres

BAROQUE

The term Baroque is used in art history to cover a wide variety of styles in a single epoch. Beginning in the 17th century, separate genres of the Baroque style developed according to the national and confessional affiliations of the individual countries in a Europe wracked by religious wars between the Protestants and the Catholics. In the Catholic countries, there was a tendency toward ecstatic monumentalism. While absolutist France preferred classic elegance, Protestant Holland saw the development of a middle-class realism.

In Baroque art, naturalism and idealism merge into a world of opulent images.

COMMISSIONED BY THE CHURCH—BAROQUE IN ITALY

The art of the Italian Baroque was closely tied to the Counter-Reformation. Magnificent works of art were meant to imbue the Catholic faith with a new persuasive power.

Ceiling painting in the Jesuit Sant'Ignazio Church, Rome (fresco by Andrea Pozzo, 1688)

In its effort to make Catholic teachings vivid and attractive, the Church began in the 17th century to rely on the seductive and suggestive effects of art. As a result, Rome became a major artistic center.

Dramatizing the Faith

Since the High Renaissance (p. 295), artists had been creating vivid worlds outside of their own experience, such as the mythological Elysian Fields. In the Baroque, biblical traditions and stories were now dramatized with breathtaking, dynamic realism full of pathos and surprising effects.

On the ceiling fresco of the Jesuit Sant'Ignazio Church in Rome, Andrea Pozzo incorporated the architectural elements of the building into his painting. With the opening of heaven, reality and vision merged. Art and architecture had become a Baroque synthesis of the arts.

The development of art in Rome was closely tied to Gianlorenzo Bernini, who was celebrated during his lifetime as the 17th century's Michelangelo (p. 296). Also universally gifted like the great Renaissance artist, Bernini played a decisive role as the architect for the renovation of Saint Peter's Basilica. As a sculptor, he created statues distinguished by their dramatic expression, narrative intensity, and sensuousness.

A great innovator in the art of painting, Caravaggio was known for his use of dramatic lighting. He had a lasting influence on artists of later generations, including Artemisia Gentileschi, one of the few female painters known today from that time period.

above: *"Susanna and the Elders" (painting by Artemisia Gentileschi, 1610)*
left: *"Apollo and Daphne" (sculpture by Gianlorenzo Bernini, 1622)*

Baroque in Bavaria: "The Assumption of the Virgin" (stucco sculpture by Egid Quirin Asam, 1717–1725)

MICHELANGELO MERISI DA CARAVAGGIO, *born 1571 in Milan, died 1610 in Port'Ercole, Italy.*

IN OPPOSITION TO THE STYLIZATION *of mannerism, Caravaggio consciously employed a powerful and life-like realism.*

THE "CARAVAGGISTS" *imitated Caravaggio's style, above all the contrasts between light and shadow.*

"Sick Bacchus" (self-portrait as Bacchus, detail, ca 1593)

Caravaggio

HIS UNSTABLE LIFESTYLE made Caravaggio the "l'enfant terrible" of the Italian art scene. Known to have been involved in various brawls, he was in trouble with the law more than once.

CARAVAGGIO'S "CHIAROSCURO" (Italian: "light-dark") painting, with its dramatic contrasts between light and dark, also led art onto new paths outside of Italy. As if lit up by a spotlight, the figures emerge out of dark backgrounds. Caravaggio often employed ordinary people as models, whom he put on canvas without any idealization. His secular portrayals of biblical stories earned him high admiration, but also accusations of profanation.

"Judith Beheading Holofernes" (painting by Caravaggio, ca 1598)

see also: **Baroque Architecture,** *Architecture Chapter, p. 326* | **The Counter-Reformation,** *Religion Chapter, p. 237*

BAROQUE ART IN THE EUROPEAN COURTS

In addition to the Church, the ruling houses of Europe emerged as significant commissioners of art. They used the fine arts as a means of glorifying their power.

"Et in Arcadia Ego" (painting by Nicolas Poussin, ca 1638–1639)

"The Newborn" (painting by Georges de La Tour, ca 1640s)

Parallel to the sweeping imagery of the Italian Baroque, Baroque classicism developed a clear, calm manner of representation that was modeled after classic antiquity (p. 289) and the High Renaissance (pp. 294–297). The paintings of Caravaggio also found many imitators. The candlelight paintings of the French "Caravaggist" Georges de La Tour are full of reverence and tranquility.

Sublime Beauty

Baroque classicism found its purest form in 17th-century France. The most important representatives were Nicolas Poussin and Claude Lorrain, although they worked mainly in Italy. While Lorrain painted ideal landscapes flooded with light, Poussin developed the genre of "heroic landscapes" with atmospheric moods and mythological scenes.

Poussin's drawing style and balanced compositions corresponded to the ideals of the French Academy of Arts. Founded at the time of King Louis XIV and dependent on the patronage of the court, it was the state's most important authority on art. Not only a school, the academy also regulated commissions and monitored adherence to a classically influenced style.

"Rape of the Daughters of Leucippus" (Peter Paul Rubens, ca 1618)

Baroque Opulence

Flemish painter Peter Paul Rubens was a complete anti-classicist. He defined his work with exaggerated, dynamic, full-bodied figures and compositions made with colors reminiscent of Venetian painting (p. 295) from the 16th century. Rubens staged mythological and biblical scenes as a feast for the senses. As a highly sought-after artist, he had a flourishing workshop in Antwerp, received commissions from the courts of Europe, and worked in Rome.

Court Portraits

The most talented of Rubens's students was Anthony van Dyck, who established his own elegant style as a portraitist at the English royal court in the early 17th century. At the same time, Diego Velázquez served the Spanish crown. In Catholic Spain, stronghold of the Counter-Reformation, the repertoire of paintings was mainly limited to religious themes and court portraits. But gradually, similar to Dutch works of the same period, the paintings called *bodegónes* (Spanish: "still life") also began to reflect depictions of contemporary everyday life.

Courtly Elegance—the New Royal Image

Nobles were usually presented in an idealized form, equipped with the attributes of their power. Anthony van Dyck developed a new archetype with his portrait of the English king Charles I. The king posed as an elegant gentleman enjoying his favorite pastime—hunting. The gaze directed slightly downward from above, the casual pose and the carefully crafted understatement illustrate the sovereignty of the king more powerfully than the traditional portrayals could ever have.

above: *"King Charles I" (ca 1635)*

VISUAL ARTS

INSIDER KNOWLEDGE

RUBENS *had a successful career as a diplomat for the Spanish crown.*

CARAVAGGIO *was in prison several times on suspicion of murder.*

NEARLY 70,000 PICTURES *were produced annually in Holland during its "Golden Age."*

A Masterwork Poses Riddles

VELÁZQUEZ'S "LAS MENINAS" (Spanish: "The Maids of Honor") from 1656 stands out above all for its multi-layered image structure, along with its artistic virtuosity. Velázquez arranged the scene as if it were on a stage. To the left it is possible to see the painter at work. But what is he actually painting there? Through the clever overlapping of layers of reality, his picture tells a story that we can reconstruct upon closer examination. The work inspired the painter Pablo Picasso to create a series of paintings in the 20th century.

Velázquez portrays himself standing behind his easel painting the royal couple.

The royal couple is recognizable in the mirror behind the painter. They stand somewhere outside of the visible picture frame, close to where the viewer is situated, probably posing at that moment for the painter.

The little infanta Margarita and her meninas (Spanish: "maids") are shown indirectly as observers sitting at the portrait. Her look is directed at the royal couple outside the picture.

THE DUTCH GOLDEN AGE—BAROQUE IN HOLLAND

Dutch Baroque was the art of the emerging middle class. Religious themes were pushed aside by the mundane as a flourishing art market began producing new genres of pictures.

"The Banquet of the Officers of the St. George Civic Guard" (painting by Frans Hals, 1616)

In 1648, the Northern Netherlands gained its independence from Spain and rose to become one of the leading economic powers of Europe. Thus began in Holland the "Dutch Golden Age," an era in which the artistic repertoire and the art market were fundamentally changed.

Mirror of Their Own World

In contrast to Southern Netherlands, which remained primarily Catholic and under Spanish domination, the portrayal of biblical scenes played only a subordinate role in the Protestant North. The typical Dutch interest in secular subject matter, already characteristic of early Dutch painting (p. 297), and the Calvinist ban on images led to a closer focus on reality. The rise of religious images within the Catholic Church had been challenged by John Calvin, who felt that it detracted from the religious sermon. As a result, Dutch painters chose subjects for depiction that were never before considered worthy of painting, such as the landscape of one's native land, scenes from domestic life, and arrangements of common, everyday objects.

As a rule, Dutch painters no longer produced for ascertained clients, but rather for an anonymous market. To meet the growing demand for particularly popular genres, the painter often specialized in a single type of picture and presented himself exclusively as master of a certain subject—be it paintings of flowers, vast seascapes, or still life.

Not only the subject, but also the size of paintings changed. Art collecting was no longer the privilege of the ruling class. Having achieved wealth, the middle class also liked to decorate their living rooms with fine antiques and paintings. Small format "showpieces" fit the needs of this new circle of clients.

"Belshazzar's Feast" (painting by Rembrandt, ca 1630)

Pots from Rembrandt's Amsterdam studio

Commemorative Group Portraits

The monumental large-scale format, on the other hand, remained for public, representational purposes, e.g., pictures of the civil guard units. These group portraits had a special place in Dutch portrait painting. Here, it was not about the individual, but rather a community of comrades. Despite that, much emphasis was naturally placed on each member being easily recognizable since each had to pay to be immortalized in the picture.

In his painting "The Banquet of the Officers of the St. George Civic Guard" from 1616, Frans Hals skillfully connected the individual portraits with each other through a tightly interlaced composition. The separate figures were formally brought together through their glances as well as the posing of their heads and hands, which established the impression of a closed company. A few of the militiamen are turned toward the viewer, welcoming them into their ranks with friendly glances.

"Archduke Leopold Wilhelm in his Art Collection in Brussels" (painting by David Teniers the Younger, 1653)

REMBRANDT HARMENSZOON VAN RIJN, *born 1606 in Leiden, died 1669 in Amsterdam.*

HIS ABILITY *to empathize gave patterns of depiction a new dimension that included the psyche.*

"THE NIGHT WATCH" *defied convention by presenting people acting out their official roles as civic militia in a non-stately and informal style.*

Rembrandt (self-portrait, etching, 1630)

Rembrandt

THE MOST FAMOUS AND MOST ATYPICAL painter of Dutch Baroque is Rembrandt. He also ran a successful workshop that produced paintings still puzzled over today by experts. Which paintings were created by him and which by his students is still in question. He never specialized in one particular genre so that along with landscapes, self-portraits, and individual and group portraits, he also painted mythological and biblical themes. In paintings executed with a powerful brush stroke, he skillfully combined the light and shadow painting of Caravaggio (p. 298) with the dynamism of Rubens. Rembrandt's psychological interest in his figures was an innovation. Rather than biblical stories, the world of humanity was foremost.

"The Night Watch" of 1642 shows an Amsterdam civil guard unit preparing to march. It resembles other paintings that were highly regarded in this period.

BAROQUE GENRES—ART AS MORAL INSTRUCTION

Still life, landscape, genre painting, and interiors became the most popular types of pictures. They combined a realistic depiction of everyday life with symbolic content.

Among the subjects that developed into separate picture styles during the period of the Dutch Baroque were the portrayals of rural and middle class day-to-day life—genre painting.

Genre and Interior

With a love for detail, painters like Jan Steen and Gerrit Dou in the 17th century depicted tavern brawls, lusty family celebrations, titillating seduction scenes, and working housewives. On one hand, the pictures were a mirror of contemporary everyday life while on the other, they graphically presented the viewer with the right and wrong ways of life as moral lessons. Jan Steen's anecdotal description of quarrelling peasants in a tavern unmistakably shows where addiction to alcohol and gambling will most likely lead.

The moral message the timelessly calm *interieur* paintings (French: interior) of Jan Vermeer is less obvious. The painter repeatedly refers to allegorical figures and symbols that were immediately understood by the educated public. Although Vermeer's "Girl With a Pearl Earring" is completely free of moral undertones, it demonstrates his intuition for the effect of the colors and textures of objects.

The "Girl With a Pearl Earring" (painting by Jan Vermeer, called Vermeer van Delft, ca 1665)

INSIDER KNOWLEDGE

ART EDUCATION *at the academies was, until modern art, based on Poussin's classical style.*

THE LIVES *of Bernini, Caravaggio, Rembrandt, and Vermeer have provided material for novels and films.*

NO ARTIST *before Pablo Picasso painted as many self-portraits as Rembrandt.*

Still Life and Vanitas Symbols

In the hierarchy of genres—at the top of which stood historical painting—still life was the lowest ranked, preceded by portraiture and landscape painting. It was, however, very popular with collectors. The artistically draped objects in the still life were not meant to be just pleasing to the eye, but to serve as reminders of the transience of earthly splendors. Objects such as hour-glasses, low-burning candles, wilting leaves, or skulls as *vanitas* (Latin: vanity) symbols, further served to make visual the insignificance of all worldly beauty.

Landscape Painting

The native landscape paintings of artists like Jacob van Ruisdael or Jan van Goyen, who sometimes based their work on sketches made in the countryside, often had a double meaning in content. Comparable to the vanitas symbols in still life, dead trees and ruins point out the transience of life. For today's viewer, pictures of the mighty heavens full of atmosphere and clouds over flat landscapes seem much more natural and true-to-life than the idealized "heroic landscapes" of the Baroque classicists. However to their contemporaries, they were also allegorical. In the face of nature's might, humankind is small and vain.

Still Life—Trompe L'Oeil

Shimmering glass, polished silver, choice food, fine linen, exotic fruits, and similarly precious objects were rendered in Dutch still life with the finest painting techniques that made the textures of the objects deceivingly life-like. To intensify the realism further, individual items like a knife, the rim of a plate or a lemon peel would occasionally jut out beyond the edge of the table that defined the borders of the painting so that it seemed that they reached out into real space. This effect is called "trompe l'oeil" (French: "deceive the eye"). Trompe l'oeil, a style of painting that took the illusion of a painted reality to the extreme, rose to become one of the most popular specialty forms of still life at the end of the 17th century.

above: *"Still-Life With Oysters" (painting by Pieter Claesz, 1638)*

below: *"The Old Mill" (painting by Jacob van Ruisdael, ca 1670)*

A look at the everyday life of the simple folk in Holland of the 17th century: "Quarrelling Peasants in a Tavern" (painting by Jan Steen, ca 1668/1672)

KEY FACTS

AS THE AGE OF TRANSITION, *the 18th century set the stage for the coming modern age.*

ROCOCO, *the art of aristocratic society, was delicate, pleasing, and erotic.*

IN NEOCLASSICISM, *art was seized by reason; it had to be clear, logical, and moral.*

WITH INCREASING *independence, artists interpreted traditional subjects.*

Rococo (1715–1780) | Neoclassicism (1750–1830)

THE 18TH CENTURY

Rococo and neoclassicism developed in the 18th century against the backdrop of the beginning of the industrial revolution and the Enlightenment, which placed rational and self-determined man at the center of creation. The two artistic movements could hardly have been more different in their styles. The decorative, fanciful, and cheerful Rococo that lasted far into the 18th century came face to face on the eve of the French Revolution with the formal severity and static image content of neoclassicism.

➔ *Rococo and neoclassicism secularized traditional picture subjects. For the first time, art styles were also contemporary.*

ROCOCO

At the beginning of the 18th century, the emotionally charged style of the Baroque gave way to the light and delicate Rococo. The new style loved the decorative, elegant, and intimate.

The transition from Baroque to Rococo was smooth since Rococo was considered part of late Baroque. In contrast to Baroque, Rococo did not seek to overwhelm and convince, but rather to adorn and please.

Sweet Life of the Aristocracy

With a preference for rich textures, the Rococo painters depicted the elegant world of the aristocracy, who in turn, as art collectors, celebrated themselves through these works. Besides oil paints, the artists used watercolors and pastels, which were popular due to their transparency.

With sleek strokes and iridescent colors, François Boucher and Jean Honoré Fragonard created scenes with an erotic touch or, like Antoine Watteau in his "The Pilgrimage to Cythera," used mythological themes to portray contemporary society.

"The Pilgrimage to Cythera": Several couples are enjoying flirtation and seduction on the island of the Greek goddess of love, Aphrodite (painting by Antoine Watteau, ca 1717)

"The Kitchen Maid" (painting by Jean-Baptiste S. Chardin, ca 1738)

"Robert Andrews and His Wife" (painting by Gainsborough, ca 1749)

New Sentimentality

The Frenchman Jean-Baptiste-Siméon Chardin's world of images was not quite so fashionable. In quiet still lifes and simple pictures, similar to Dutch genre painting, he mainly focused on the modest lifestyles of the lower classes, depicted in muted tones.

In England, Thomas Gainsborough created sensitively crafted portraits of people and landscapes, while Joshua Reynolds remained true to classical ideals with his portraits. The satirist William Hogarth made his mark as a critical chronicler of society but also worked on realistic portraiture.

"Reclining Girl" (painting by François Boucher, 1752)

WILLIAM HOGARTH, *born 1697 in London, died there in 1764*

MODERN CARICATURES *were inspired by Hogarth through his satirical and socially critical pictures.*

A COPYRIGHT LAW *in England, called the Engraver's Act, was first advocated by Hogarth to protect the copyright of his graphically reproduced works.*

"Self-portrait With His Pug" (painting, 1745)

The Inventor of the Caricature

HOGARTH DESCRIBED the decadence and double standards of the upper classes in his series of narrative pictures. But he also took an equally critical look at the living conditions of the poorer population. The print "Gin Lane," which denounced excessive alcohol consumption, was part of a successful campaign that Hogarth carried out together with the writer Henry Fielding against the abuse of gin.

A TRAINED copperplate engraver, Hogarth reproduced his own paintings as etchings so that his "moral pictures" had a large circulation.

"Gin Lane" (copperplate print and etching by William Hogarth, 1751)

NEOCLASSICISM

Clear lines, smooth application of color, and static compositions characterize neoclassicism, which was inspired by classic antiquity. From France it spread throughout Europe and America.

Neoclassicism developed in the mid-18th century as a style that held clarity and conformity to natural laws as its highest principles. Entirely committed to the spirit of rationality and the rigors of science, the artwork was meant to appeal to reason rather than emotion.

In Imitation of Classic Antiquity

As it had 100 years earlier, the art of classic antiquity (p. 289) once again served as model to an emerging art movement. Quiet grandeur, sublime simplicity, and realism recognized in the works of antiquity, and missing in Rococo, were now considered decadent. And yet, neoclassicism was far more than just an alternative aesthetic direction to the predominant style. Greek and Roman antiquity embodied the democratic and republican ideals being intensely discussed on the eve of the French Revolution.

"Pauline Borghese" (sculpture by Antonio Canova, 1804–1808)

The Painted Manifesto

A key work of neoclassicism is the "Oath of the Horatii" of 1784 by Jacques-Louis David. Not only did the clearly constructed picture technically conform to the new taste, but the content is based on a theme from antiquity. This instantly made the painter famous. David used the story of the Horatii triplets, who swore to defend the freedom of Rome with their lives, to illustrate a conviction.

"Bather of Valpinçon" (by Jean Auguste Dominique Ingres, 1808)

The painting was immediately understood in pre-Revolutionary France as a political manifesto—a symbol of a new social order in which free citizens make political decisions and assume responsibility.

The Elegant Line

Far removed from any political objectives, but just as clearly inspired by classic antiquity, are the works of the Italian sculptor Antonio Canova. His tranquil sculptures of Princess Pauline Borghese clearly distinguish themselves from the swirling figures of Baroque and Rococo. The princess, a sister of Napoleon Bonaparte, caused a scandal by modeling in the nude.

Jean Auguste Dominique Ingres also followed a firm set of rules. The harmonious outline of a figure was, to him, the decisive element in creating perfect beauty out of the perfect line. Even though Ingres's approach is similar to that of a draftsman, his pictures impress viewers through his fine, lustrous painting style.

Art Academies

Scientific methodology did not exclude art. Training at the art academies replaced apprenticeships in artisan workshops. It consisted mainly of copying old masters as well as drawing from plaster and nude models. The formulaic curriculum and artistic traditionalism met with increasing criticism. Women were banned from studying at art academies until the 20th century.

above: *"Drawing from Life at the Royal Academy" (1811)*

INSIDER KNOWLEDGE

KNICK-KNACKS: *The discovery of porcelain promoted the mass production of decorative sculptures.*

JACQUES-LOUIS DAVID *just barely escaped execution by the guillotine during the revolution.*

THE LOUVRE, *the former French royal residence, became the first public museum after the revolution.*

VISUAL ARTS

The Constructed Picture

DESPITE ITS FORCEFUL GESTURES, the scene appears strangely stiff. This is because the painting is composed using a grid of verticals, horizontals, and diagonals that restricts the action of the figures. The use of the triangular form is conspicuous. This triangle directly blocks the dynamic movement of the diagonals with a countermovement that brings it to a static rest. This pattern can be found repeatedly in the picture.

The paralleled diagonal positioning of the legs results in a spatially-confined scissor pattern.

"Oath of the Horatii" (painting by Jacques-Louis David, 1784)

Form analogy: The fanning of the swords reflects the staggered arrangement of hands raised to take the oath.

A shield-like triangle compositionally holds the men together.

As a counterpoint to the triangle, a pyramidal form encloses the women.

see also: French Revolution, *Politics, Law, and Economy Chapter*, p. 168

KEY FACTS

PHOTOGRAPHY *and other technical innovations led to the development of a new repertoire of imagery.*

PARIS *became the trend-setting art metropolis of the world.*

WITH THE BIRTH OF THE AVANT-GARDE, *artists opposed the traditional art promoted by the numerous art academies.*

LIKE-MINDED ARTISTS *formed circles and schools.*

Romanticism (1790–1830) | Realism (1840–1880) | Impressionism (1860–1880) | Post-Impressionism (1880–1910)

THE 19TH CENTURY

Technical progress and extensive realignment of society during the 19th century made lasting changes not only to people's view of the world, but also to the arts and the role of the artist. Liberated from all patrician and clerical ties, artists were free to follow their individual convictions and artistic ideals. Their creations reflected this, and divergent style movements emerged with increasing rapidity, replacing or running parallel to each other. Thus art became a commodity on the open market.

An unprecedented diversity of styles dominated the arts at the end of the 19th century, marking the start of modern art.

VISUAL ARTS

ROMANTICISM

Romanticism introduced subjectivity, intuition, and emotion into the arts. Set free from the traditional repertoire of imagery, artists realized their own ideas.

"The Wanderer above a Sea of Fog" (painting by C. D. Friedrich, 1818)

In the late 18th century, Romantic artists started to radically challenge classicism's (p. 303) faith in reason. Emphasizing the importance of emotion, painters did not just depict what they saw in front of them, but also what they saw in themselves. This redefinition of art as a "voice from inside" forms the foundation of the modern understanding of art and shapes the image of the brilliantly creative artist who takes inspiration from within.

Atmospheric Landscapes

Romantic artists preferred landscape paintings because they expressed moods especially well. These were often communicated to the viewer through figures portrayed from the back. In "The Wanderer Above the Sea of Fog" by the German painter Caspar David Friedrich, the viewer feels the effects of the vastness and grandeur of a mountain panorama.

Friedrich's landscapes often convey world-weariness, longing and solitude. In reaction to the war against Napoleon, they occasionally took on a patriotic tone. With the advent of the tranquil Biedermeier period in the mid-1800s, Romanticism finally died away in Germany.

"Liberty Leading the People" (painting by E. Delacroix, 1830)

In a Rapture of Colors

The Englishmen John Constable and Joseph Mallord William Turner also used landscapes to express emotional states. Their works, however, were not based on spiritual inwardness, but rather on the precise study of nature and a fresh, sometimes bold artistic rendering that hinted at the later movement of Impressionism (p. 306). The Frenchmen Eugène Delacroix and Théodore Géricault composed monumental, historical paintings with great daring, echoing the pathos of Baroque. The lively brushstrokes along with the increased luminosity caused by the method of contrasting complementary colors impart a rousing dynamic to the famous painting "Liberty Leading the People" by Delacroix.

FRANCISCO DE GOYA Y LUCIENTES, *born 1746 in Fuendetodos, died 1828 in Bordeaux.*

IN FORM AND CONTENT, *the wide variety of his work broke with the conventions of his time and cannot be assigned to any particular style.*

GOYA'S VISIONARY MOTIFS *and expressive painting gave modern art significant inspiration.*

Francisco Goya (self-portrait, 1815)

Goya

BASED ON ROCOCO, Goya developed a lively language of imagery with his colors and originality that cannot be classified as belonging to any certain style, even though it is similar to Romanticism.

AS PAINTER TO THE SPANISH COURT, he created realistic but not always flattering portraits of the rulers. He also produced pictures with socially critical content. Particularly in his prints, he drew a dark vision of human error and political evils.

"THE THIRD OF MAY 1808: THE EXECUTION OF THE DEFENDERS OF MADRID" shows the brutality of the Napoleonic occupation troops in Spain and the powerlessness of the victims. The dramatic use of light and color impart a gripping intensity to the picture. The painting has become a general condemnation of all military force.

above: *"The Third of May 1808" (painting, 1814)*
right: *"The Sleep of Reason Brings Forth Monsters" (1797–1798)*

see also: French Revolution, *Politics, Law, and Economy Chapter*, p. 168

REALISM

The painters of realism broke away from all biblical, mythological, and literary models. True to nature, unembellished, and committed, they reflected upon everyday reality.

The revolutions of 1848 in European countries and advancing industrialization worldwide led to great upheavals in society.

Gustave Courbet's "Burial at Ornans" from 1849 depicted for the first time common people and their daily lives on a monumental scale.

However, official art remained dominated by classic ideals or romantic reverie, both of which had nothing to do with the realities of life.

Some artists reacted to this disparity around the middle of the 19th century by pointedly turning to the world of everyday reality, which they sought to depict as honestly as possible. Although attempts to portray reality have occurred throughout art history since the Renaissance (p. 294), realism now voiced ethical and political appeals instead of just portraying a scene.

Real Life

Parallel to new trends in the natural sciences and humanities, the realists focused on fact and perception, thus rejecting art that was based only on imaginary worlds. However, they never sought to simply imitate reality since that would have been easier with photography, which had just recently been invented.

Instead, painters like Gustave Courbet, Adolf von Menzel, Jean-François Millet, and Honoré Daumier wanted to illustrate social conditions within their art. In particular, artists chose motifs taken from industrial and rural worlds of life and labor.

Previously, these subjects had been handled at most in small, anecdotal genre paintings. Courbet broke with this tradition and provided art history with its first public scandal with the painting "Burial at Ornans." It portrayed an ordinary burial and the rural mourners on a monumental scale, challenging the accepted norms of the art establishment at that time.

The Work of the Painter

"THE IRON ROLLING MILL" by Adolf von Menzel is a key artistic work of German realism. In order to achieve honest, realistic depictions in his compositions, Menzel spent several weeks in the most modern steel mill of his time. While he was there, he produced over 100 sketches and studies in both pencil and chalk, some even in color, of the men and the machinery. A visual memory, these sheets served as the basis for the later execution of the painting within his studio. This meticulous preparation enabled Menzel not only to render an exact representation of the industrial process, but also to capture physical likenesses of the individual workers.

"The Iron Rolling Mill" (painting by Adolf von Menzel, 1872–1875)

Partial study for the painting: With a dense atmosphere and attention to detail, he portrays the hard labor, heat, and noise of a modern industrial plant.

Everyday Beauty

Millet also portrayed common life, though far less provocatively and militantly than his socially committed contemporary Courbet. Without glossing over reality, he depicted the toils of daily peasant life in "The Gleaners." At the same time, however, he imbued the scene with a kind of solemnity through clear styling, measured rhythm, and subdued light.

Millet was a member of a group of artists led by Camille Corot, which became known as the Barbizon School. Its members were the first in the mid-19th century to produce their paintings *en plein air* (French: "in the open air") and not in the studio. Later, en plein air painting became of vital importance for the artists of the Impressionist movement and its frequent depictions of nature.

New Technology—New Perception

The invention of the locomotive not only changed people's mobility, but also their perception of the world. Speed blurs firm contours. J. M. W. Turner, who was intensely interested in optical laws like the relationship between light and color, made use of this phenomenon in his painting of the Great Western Railway. Turner's shimmering, almost abstract style of painting broke away from the concrete portrayals of his earlier paintings and conveyed sensory impressions.

above: *"Rain, Steam, and Speed—The Great Western Railway" (painting by Turner, 1844)*

"The Gleaners" (painting by Jean-François Millet, 1857)

21ST CENTURY

REALISM *experiences continuous revivals to this day. As a countermovement to expressive and abstract tendencies, new forms of realism appeared in the 20th century: New Objectivity or Neue Sachlichkeit, Nouveau Réalisme, Photo realism, and Pop Art. Socialist realism glorified a political ideology.*

VISUAL ARTS

THE BEGINNING OF MODERN ART—IMPRESSIONISM

The Impressionists led art down new paths. With brilliant colors and loose brush strokes they created landscapes flooded with light and portrayed life in the modern large city.

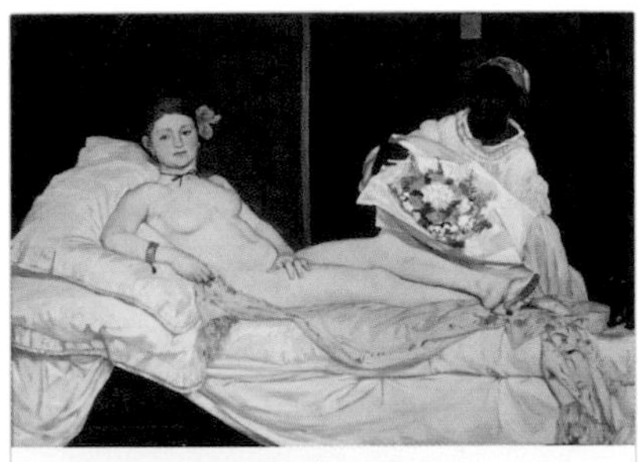
"Olympia" (painting by Édouard Manet, 1863)

Although Impressionists are included among the realists (p. 305), their pictures contained no political overtones. In the second half of the 19th century, painters like Claude Monet, Pierre-Auguste Renoir, Edgar Degas, Alfred Sisley, Camille Pissarro, and Berthe Morisot turned to more cheerful subjects in their paintings, capturing the bustle of the Parisian boulevards, pleasure gardens, and day excursions out to the countryside.

The light dances: A festive mood in the Parisian open-air café "Le Moulin de la Galette" (painting by Pierre-Auguste Renoir, 1876)

Breaking with all artistic conventions, their new way of painting was not understood at first by the public or art critics. These pictures, portrayed with loosely dabbed color and random snapshot-like details of reality, were regarded at best as sketchy "impressions," but not as finished works of art.

Reality of the Moment

However, the superficial style of painting was intentional. The Impressionists wanted not only to paint what they saw, but also how they saw it. Instead of staying in the studio, they consistently painted in nature, (*en plein air* painting), to capture as purely as possible the visual impression, play of light, and atmosphere. Renoir even painted the large-format view of "Moulin de la Galette" entirely at the open-air café shown in the painting.

"The Burghers of Calais" (bronze replica of the sculpture by Pierre-Auguste Renoir, 1884–1886)

The capturing of direct sensory impressions demanded that the artists work rapidly. The colors were only roughly mixed beforehand and then, with quick, short brushstrokes, applied to the canvas. Lacking details and contours, an Impressionist painting viewed up close appears to be a carpet of colors in turmoil. Viewed from a distance, however, a clear picture materializes. With their brushstrokes, the Impressionists made visible the painting process itself as painting.

Manet and Rodin

Although Édouard Manet was not part of the inner circle of Impressionists, he shared the anti-academic ideals of his colleagues. Often his work provoked a scandal, particularly his paintings of naked women outside of a mythological context. Even though his "Olympia" was inspired by a painting by Titian (p. 295), Manet's picture showed a real woman, a well-known prostitute in all likelihood, who openly and self-confidently displayed her nakedness.

Equally revolutionary was the effect Auguste Rodin had on sculpture when he freed his figures from typical statue poses and, in the true sense of the expression, took them off their pedestals. His "The Burghers of Calais" is realistically animated and conceived without any heroic glorification.

A play of light and air: "The Gare Saint-Lazare in Paris" (painting by Claude Monet, 1877)

To the Point—Pointillism

GEORGES SEURAT further developed the Impressionistic way of painting in the mid-1880s, dissolving not only forms, but also colors. Seurat divided the color of an object, the so-called local color, into many little points, or dots, solely consisting of the primary colors. The mixing of shades of colors no longer took place on the palette but in the eye of the observer where the points were blended in the retina to the desired hue.

above: *Seurat's sketch explains his pointillist method of painting. The finished painting also consisted of many individual points.*

"The Circus" (painting by Georges Seurat, 1891)

see also: **How Eyes Function**, *Biology Chapter*, p. 88

POST-IMPRESSIONISM

Post-Impressionism marked the beginning of classic modern art, when artists freed themselves of exact replication and stressed the inherent laws of art.

After 1880, a long tradition came to an end and a new era began with post-Impressionism. Ground breaking post-Impressionists like Paul Cézanne, Vincent van Gogh, Paul Gauguin, James Ensor, and Edvard Munch broke with natural reproduction and color as well as with the rules of perspective used since the Renaissance.

In doing so they turned away from the illusory rendering of reality employed by the Impressionists. Instead effect and expression was to be communicated through the means of painting itself, i.e., through the choice of colors and forms. Not the "what" but rather the "how" of a painting was made the main focus.

"The Kiss" by Gustav Klimt from 1908 is one of the best known works of art nouveau.

From Impression to Expression

While Cézanne analytically reduced the world to its component parts, Van Gogh, Ensor, and Munch worked spontaneously, guided by their emotions. With bold brushstrokes, distorted forms, and "unnatural" colors, they created oppressive scenarios of various emotional states.

In comparison, the world of Gauguin's paintings appeared to be a harmonious paradise. Warm, bright colors, designs with flowing lines, and rounded, distinct forms impart both a balance and unity to the pictures. But Gauguin's paintings, above all the South Sea pictures, often contained symbolic allusions. His works thus showed a closeness to the Symbolists, who were popular around 1900 and to which Munch also belonged.

Symbolism—Pictures of the Soul

In the search for a "deeper truth" beyond the visual world, the symbolists explored the depths of the human soul in their pictures. Sigmund Freud later termed this "the unconscious."

Eros, fear, and death are the dominating themes of the stylistically heterogeneous and often dream-like worlds in the pictures of Odilon Redon, Arnold Böcklin, and Franz von Stuck. Their dark moods mirrored the general feeling of insecurity at the *fin de siècle* (French: "turn of the century").

Gustav Klimt's "The Kiss," on the other hand, clearly carried traces of art nouveau, whose decorative ornamentation was found not only in the fine arts, but above all in the applied arts such as interior design, tableware, jewelry, and typography.

Foreign Worlds

As early as the mid-19th century, artists were fascinated by foreign cultures, above all the Orient. The artists of early modernist art also developed an attraction to the exotic. The artists in the time of imperialism were primarily interested in the "primitive" cultures of Africa or the South Seas. Gauguin sought purity, naturalness and innocence in Tahiti, which he felt was lacking in the art and lives of world-weary Europeans. The clear forms of Japanese woodcuts also inspired numerous artists.

above: *"Motherhood" (II) (painting by Paul Gauguin, 1899)*

INSIDER KNOWLEDGE

NO ARTIST *was reproduced more often in the 20th century than Vincent van Gogh.*

GAUGUIN *settled in Tahiti and became one of the first dropouts in art history.*

THE SEVERELY DISABLED *Toulouse-Lautrec lived on the margins of society in a world of pimps and prostitutes despite his aristocratic origins.*

VINCENT VAN GOGH, *born 1853 in Zundert, died 1890 in Auvers-sur-Oise.*

HIS POWERFUL STYLE *of painting was not meant to reproduce visual impressions but rather was an expression of his state of mind.*

AFTER A QUARREL *with Paul Gauguin, with whom he occasionally worked, the psychologically unstable artist cut off a part of his ear.*

"Self-portrait with bandaged ear" (1889)

Vincent van Gogh

BEGINNING AS A REALIST, van Gogh created dark-toned pictures of farmers and workers in his Dutch homeland. Only after he moved to Provence did his paintings brighten. Inspired by the works of the Impressionists, he developed a language of imagery using vivid colors. His work was later an important stimulus for Expressionist artists (p. 309).

AFTER A BOUT OF MENTAL ILLNESS, about which nothing to this day is known, van Gogh increasingly intensified his use of color and brushwork. The canvas virtually pulsates and vibrates in "Starry Night." Swirling spirals make the sky appear to be an energy-laden force field. The suggestive effect of the picture is the result of color choice and the way paint was applied to the canvas, which are the primary tools of painting itself.

"Starry Night" (painting, 1889)

With easily distinguishable forms and strong colors, Henri Toulouse-Lautrec revolutionized poster art. His works were already a coveted collector's item during his time (poster for the choral singer Aristide Bruant, 1892).

VISUAL ARTS

➲ see also: Sigmund Freud, *Psychology Chapter, p. 282* | Art Nouveau, *Architecture Chapter, p. 331*

KEY FACTS

MODERN ART *is above all interested in imperceptible reality.*

THE ARTIST *is considered autonomous; there are no more limits of themes, styles, and categories.*

THE VIEWER *is stimulated to make interpretations of what they see.*

IN THE ART MARKET *millions are exchanged worldwide, while the search for every new talented artist continues.*

THE 20TH CENTURY

The artists of the 20th century broke with all the previously arranged artistic traditions of the preceding artistic generations. To understand the modern world in its entire complexity, artists set aside all earlier artistic conventions and turned to the abstract. Subjective expression and creative innovation superseded the mastery of the craft. By using "non-artistic" materials, the traditional repertoire of painting and sculpture expanded to include even more new categories. The question "What is art?" now received a radically different answer.

The foundation of modern art was laid in the first half of the 20th century.

ROADS TO THE ABSTRACT—CUBISM, FUTURISM, AND FAUVISM

Experiments with form and color led in the early 20th century to ever more abstract discoveries in art. Visible reality was analytically dissected or translated into highly emotional paintings.

The post-Impressionists (p. 307) broke with the rules of traditional painting. They were followed by a generation of artists who created new styles of art, new manners of painting, and new ways of seeing.

Cubism

Pablo Picasso (p. 310) and Georges Braque created in 1907 an entirely new style: cubism. Inspired by Paul Cézanne, they divided the world into individual facets. Whereas Cézanne clung to the one dimensional point of view, Cubists, on the contrary, showed their subjects from different viewpoints and fused them into one fused form.

Thus they destroyed the pictorial space based on a central perspective that had prevailed in Western art since the Renaissance. In its place rose a free artistic construction that was not based on appearance but on knowledge of the character of things. In this way, the Cubists combined several viewpoints into a single perception, which in reality the viewer could only see individually by walking around an object.

Futurism

For the Italian Futurists the dimension of time as well as speed and movement in space played central roles.

In their paintings, Umberto Boccioni and Gino Severini piled different perspectives and phases of movement on each other. Boccioni applied this principle of simultaneousness also to sculpture. His walking figure seems completely absorbed with movement—up to the polished surface.

Fauvism

In his painting "The Dance," Henri Matisse treated the theme "movement" more poetically than Futurism, with its inclination towards technical apperance, would have. Matisse, founder and chief representative of the French group of artists known as "Fauves" ("wild animals"), created bold picturesque worlds of clear, rhythmic forms in dark, unmixed colors.

"Still Life With Violin" (painting by Georges Braque, 1911)

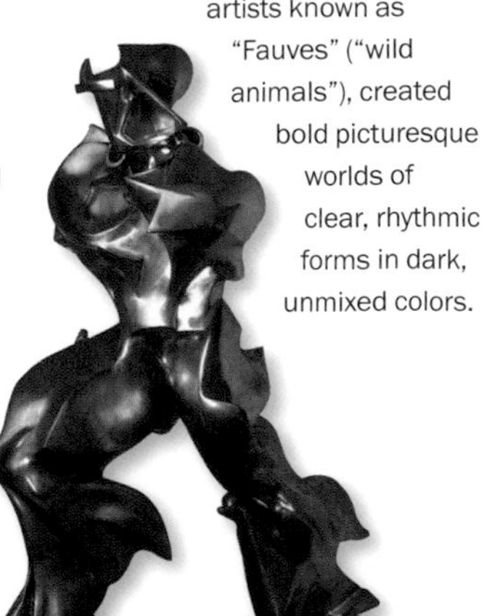

"Unique Forms of Continuity in Space" (bronze sculpture by Umberto Boccioni, 1913)

PAUL CÉZANNE, *born 1839 in Aix-en-Provence in France and died there in 1906.*

ILLUSORY DEPTH *replaced flat forms in Cezanne's paintings.*

THE OBJECTS THEMSELVES *did not interest him, but rather their geometric structure.*

HE IS KNOWN *as the "Father of the Modern."*

"Self-portrait with Bowler Hat" (sketch, 1885)

Paul Cézanne

CÉZANNE'S PAINTINGS are marked by strong structures, calm lines, and finely blended, subdued colors.

ART SHOULD NOT COPY NATURE, but rather form a "harmonious parallel to nature;" i.e., an independent world, subject to its own laws, like nature has its laws. In order to approach this inner structure, Cézanne proceeded in an analytical way: He reduced the visible reality to basic two- or three-dimensional geometric forms. From these building blocks, he created a composition that was loosely connected to visible reality. However, in its construction it followed exclusively requirements posed by the painting itself.

CÉZANNE STROVE to create a perfectly constructed picture. He desired to convey to the viewer through his paintings an "idea" (but not a copy) of nature. Through these efforts, Cézanne formed the whole basis of what is modern, abstract art.

"Mont Sainte-Victoire" (painting by Cézanne 1902/1906)

EXPRESSIONISM

The Expressionists conveyed subjective experiences and personal feelings through strong colors and exaggerated forms. They wanted to communicate emotionally with the viewer.

Simultaneously with the French Fauves, the artist community "die Brücke" formed in Germany and a while later "der Blaue Reiter."

"Die Brücke" and "Der Blaue Reiter"

The group of artists known as "die Brücke," meaning "the bridge" used sharp, woodcut-like contours, intense colors, and simplified forms. The young painters around Ernst Ludwig Kirchner wanted to free themselves from the norms of what they saw as a cocooned society by using "primitive" forms of painting. "Uncorrupted and direct" read their manifesto; they wanted to express an "ecstatic enjoyment of life."

They found this initially outdoors and later in Berlin with its millions of inhabitants. Kirchner conveyed the dynamic, metropolitan city in his "Street Scene" through a nervous, angular style of painting. By distorting the perspective, it seems as if the ground is disappearing from beneath the people's feet.

The group known as "der Blaue Reiter," meaning "the blue rider," also saw art as a means of making "the invisible visible." Wassily Kandinsky, Paul Klee, Franz Marc, and Alexei Jawlensky certainly followed a more poetic and sensitive path than the impetuous Brücke painters. They put the "spiritual," that is, the subtle feelings which a painting, like a piece of music, may arouse, in the foreground, making the works characterized by subjectivity and the self.

To come closer to this "inner sound," the painters freed themselves more and more from depicting concrete objects. In 1910, Kandinsky painted the first picture In the history of art completely abstracted from objective reality. This picture evoked an emotional response from the viewer solely through its colors and forms. The same effect was produced by the artist's "Composition VII" (p. 310).

Dadaism

Dadaists such as Hugo Ball, Max Ernst, Jean Arp, Kurt Schwitters, John Heartfield, Marcel Duchamp, and Hannah Höch criticized expressionism for circling around emotions and being an unrealistic "margarine of the soul."

After the horrors of World War I, they wanted to create provoking and jarring art. Their common criticism of society and art unified the Dadaists instead of a common style of painitng. As a loosely consolidated group, they agitated throughout the world with centers in Zurich, Berlin, Cologne, and Paris. Their anti-art, consisting of collages, montages, and collections of everyday items, contradicted all hitherto held concepts of beauty in art. Dadaism and its critique of traditional art were taken up after 1945 by Nouveau Réalisme, Pop Art (p. 312), and Conceptual Art (p. 313).

"Degenerate" Art

Well into the 1920s, expressionism was one of the dominant art forms in Germany. However, after 1933, National Socialism caused its sudden death. Its leading representatives, such as Max Beckmann, Oskar Kokoschka, Marc Chagall, the painters of "die Brücke" and "der Blaue Reiter," as well as all Jewish artists, were branded as "un-German" and "degenerate." The Nazis removed their works from museums and destroyed or sold them overseas. Artists who were forbidden to work and threatened with persecution were forced to flee into exile. Those threatened to a lesser degree retreated from life as artists into an "inner emigration."

above: *"The Night" (painting by Max Beckmann, 1918/1919)*

"Berlin Street Scene" (painting by Ernst Ludwig Kirchner, 1913)

Collage, Assemblage, and Ready-Made

EVERYDAY ITEMS BECOME WORKS OF ART: In 1912, Braque and Picasso glued newspaper clippings on their paintings and thereby invented the art form known as "collage" (French: "to glue"). Photo montages were developed in the 1920s; these pictures consisted entirely of fragments of photos. The Dadaist Kurt Schwitters combined abstract painting with everyday objects in his so-called Merz pictures. In his "ready-mades," Marcel Duchamp spurned all artistic treatment of profane objects as, for example, a urinal, and simply declared them works of art. The formation of a work of art from everyday, three-dimensional objects was called "assemblage" (French: "fitting together"). It experienced its greatest popularity in the Nouveau Réalisme (p. 312) of the 1960s.

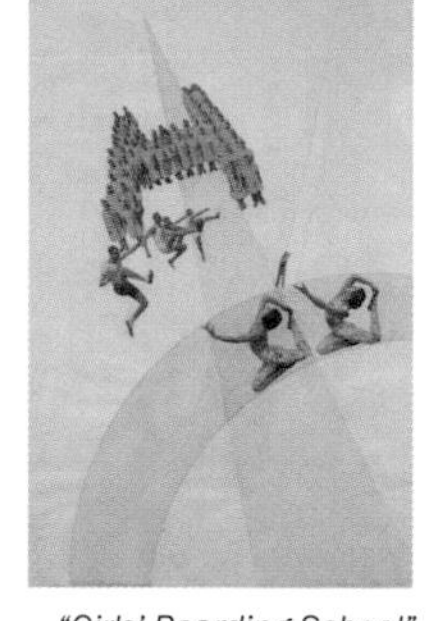

"Girls' Boarding School" (collage by László Moholy-Nagy, 1925)

From banal article to art object: "Fountain" (ready-made by Marcel Duchamp, 1917)

The "Unpicture" is one of Kurt Schwitters's Merz pictures (assemblage, 1919).

INSIDER KNOWLEDGE

WITH THE BEGINNING OF THE MODERN ERA, *women could more easily gain footholds in the world of art hitherto dominated by men. Artists like Frida Kahlo, Hannah Höch, Georgia O'Keeffe, or Meret Oppenheim count today among the great names of early 19th-century art. The "re-discovery" of many forgotten women artists continues to this day.*

see also: National Socialism, *Politics, Law, and Economy Chapter, p. 175*

VISUAL ARTS

ABSTRACT AVANT-GARDE—CONSTRUCTIVISM

Constructivism is a school within abstract art which uses only clear, geometric forms. Constructivist tendencies are recognizable in some works of art today.

Inspired by cubism (p. 308), the content of paintings became even more abstract in the first decades of the 20th century. Russian artists took a leading role in this new development.

"Black Square" (painting by Kasimir Malevich, ca 1921)

below: *"Corner Counterrelief" (sculpture by Wladimir Tatlin, 1915–1925)*

Russian Avant-Garde

Already Wassily Kandinsky (p. 309) had freed himself from depicting recognizable subjects. Nevertheless, his pictures included movement and forms that permit interpretation. In contrast, Kasimir Malevich's "Black Square" shows nothing but a black square on a white background surface.

Malevich combined philosophical reflections about time and place with this radically simple form, which he repeated in many variations. Simple, basic geometric forms perfectly expressed pure sensation for him. He called his style of painting "Suprematism" (Latin: *supra* or "above"), because he considered it superior to the styles that still allowed concrete associations.

Such an intellectual concept of art was increasingly questioned in Russia after the October Revolution of 1917.

Artists such as Wladimir Tatlin or Aleksander Rodschenko considered themselves more like art engineers who wanted to participate productively in the building of the new socialist society. They worked in different disciplines of art, were inspired by industrial techniques and material, and made the construction process the central theme of their art.

Tatlin's "Counterreliefs," which were assembled from different materials, as well as the mobile "Light-Space Modulators" of the Hungarian Lászió Moholy-Nagy, gave a new definition of the concept of sculpture. However, in 1934, the Soviet dictator Stalin prohibited all avant-garde art in the Soviet Union, thus demanding "Socialist realism" (p. 311).

By positioning his canvas so that a corner points upward, Piet Mondrian adds objective character to his picture ("Tableau No. IV," 1924–1925).

De Stijl

Much like Malevich, Theo van Doesburg and Piet Mondrian, both from the Netherlands, reduced their pictorial language to plain lines and clear colors. In 1917, they founded the Dutch group of artists, "De Stijl." They used the expression "concrete art" to make clear that their strictly geometric forms were not the result of an abstraction process but used for their own sakes as independent conveyers of expression. In fact, when a person studies one of Mondrian's paintings, an inner rhythm and dynamic is identifiable in the ruler-straight lines and smooth fields of color. The viewer is aware of this animation without having to actually name or even describe it definitively.

Walter Gropius incorporated the creative principles of the De Stijl artists and elements of Russian Constructivism into the Bauhaus. In 1919, he established this movement of art combining both art and industrial shapes in Dessau, Germany.

The shapes and colors in Kandinsky's "Composition VII" from 1913 should produce an emotional "inner sound."

PABLO PICASSO, *born 1881 in Málaga, Spain, died 1973 in Mougins, France*

ONE OF THE MOST CREATIVE *and innovative artists of the 20th century, Picasso worked as a painter, drawer, graphic printer, and sculptor, as well as creating ceramic pieces.*

PICASSO IS CONSIDERED *the cofounder of cubism (p. 308) and discovered collage (p. 309).*

Picasso at work on a bowl (1948)

Pablo Picasso

NO NAME IS so intimately connected with modern art as Pablo Picasso. He began figure painting during his Blue and Rose Periods. In 1917, Picasso entered an artistic new world with his "Les Demoiselle d'Avignon." The fragmented depiction of the nudes shocked its viewers since it was not the way people were used to seeing figures. This picture is considered today the key work of modern art, which prepared the way for the abstract. After a cubist phase in the beginning of the 1920s, Picasso returned to a classically inspired realism and also briefly joined the Surrealists.

"Les Demoiselles d' Avignon" (painting by Pablo Picasso, 1906)

"GUERNICA"—A PICTURE OF HORROR: With this painting of 1937, the pacifist Picasso expressed his revulsion over the destruction of the Spanish town of Guernica during the Spanish Civil War. Elements of his later style are evident: The painting looks drawn, and the scene is divided into many flat surfaces. Picasso continued to paint until a very old age. The composition is a clear condemnation of fascism and war in general.

"Guernica," 1937

➔ **see also: Bauhaus,** *Architecture Chapter, p. 331*

SURREALISM AND REALISTIC TRENDS

With their works, the Surrealists searched the hidden corners of the soul. Others sought anew to depict objects realistically and to focus on daily life.

Different artists searched for new conceptions of reality. They returned, in part, to earlier styles of art or utilized new scientific fields such as psychology.

Surrealism

Like the Dadaists (p. 309), the Surrealists displayed the grotesque, the illogical, and the absurd. However, they did this not to question the bourgeois concept of art but to reach greater depths of conscious-

"Women and Bird in the Moonlight" (painting by Joan Miró, 1949)

ness. Artists such as Salvador Dalí, Max Ernst, or Giorgio de Chirico found inspiration in Romanticism and symbolism (pp. 304, 307). However, the decisive impulses

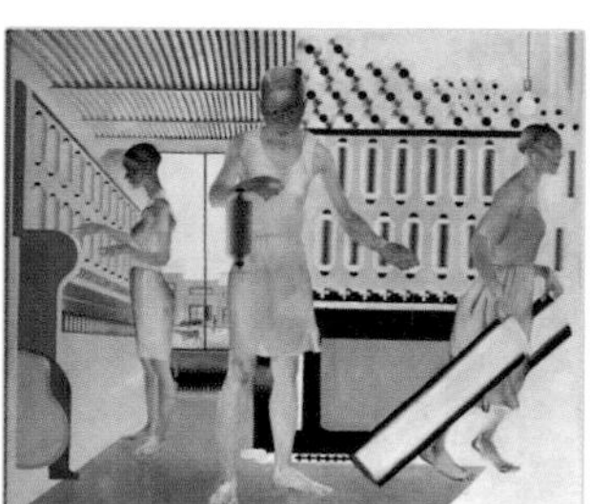

Socialist realism glorified the world of work, for example, in the "Textile Workers" (painting by Alexander Deineka, 1927).

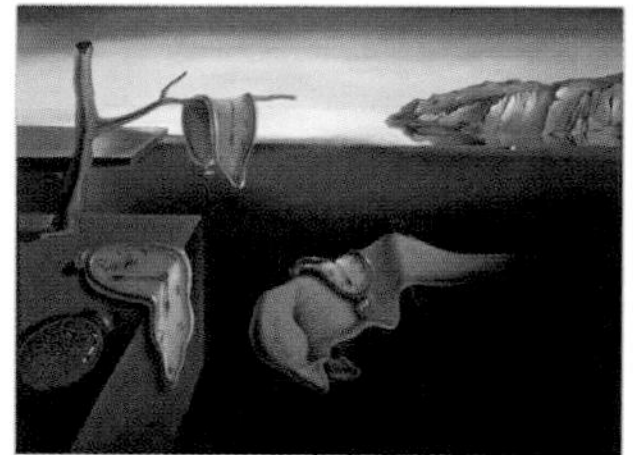

"The Persistence of Memory" (painting by Salvador Dalí, 1931)

came from Sigmund Freud's psychological interpretation of dreams.

Dalí's visions, full of inexplicable portents and allusions, look like dream visions dragged into the light of day. Less depressing but equally perplexing is the picture world of the Belgian René Magritte. He renders everyday objects surreal to make the viewer see the difference between the reality of life and the reality of paintings. The abstract figures of Joan Miró, on the other hand, are both joyful and playful. His fine, swinging lines and dancing patches of color give wings to fantasy.

A similar lightness is found in the mobile sculptures of Alexander Calder. They react to the slightest breath of air and alter their forms as chance will have it. Chance and a spontaneous shape, uncontrolled by the mind, played a decisive role for the Surrealists. In this way, they hoped to come especially close to the powers of the unconscious.

New Objectivity and American Realism

After World War I, many artists countered ecstatic expressionism (p. 309) and spiritualized abstraction with the depiction of tangible objects. Thus, some painters, male and female, turned to "New Objectivity" and to contemporary, everyday life. With critical eyes, Otto Dix and George Grosz, for example, captured the glittering big city life of Berlin with its entertainments, but also its social misery.

At the same time, some artists in the U.S. also focused their attention on reality and treated it truthfully as well as critically. While Grant Wood depicted country people in stylized portraits, Edward Hopper described the loneliness of modern city people in quiet pictures.

Socialist Realism

The painters of "Socialist realism," which was the prescribed style in the USSR until 1989, also turned toward everyday life, but in a clearly idealized form for its use as propaganda. While modern art forms had existed in Russia in the 1920s, they were relinquished in the 1930s in favor of a traditional style of painting that modeled its style and execution on the pre-modern art of the 19th century. socialist realism became the unifying form of art in all communist countries. A similar approach to the creation of art was also enforced for a time in the People's Republic of China.

"Crinkly with Red Disk" (mobile by Alexander Calder, 1973)

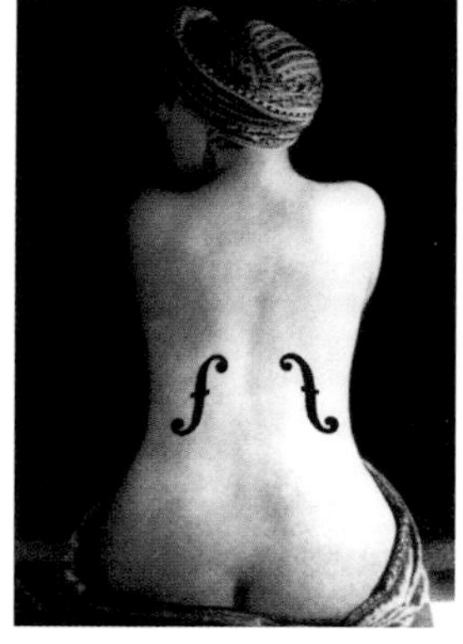

Photography Becomes Art

Since its beginning in the 19th century, photography has competed with painting. Early photographers attempted to give their photos a "painted" effect. However, in the beginning of the 20th century, photographers developed an artistic style of their own in documentary shots, detail studies, and portraits. In the art of Bauhaus, New Objectivity, and Surrealism, photography established itself as an independent artistic medium. It has occupied an undisputed place in the history of art ever since.

above: *"The Violin" (print after photography by Man Ray, 1925)*

"Nighthawks" (painting by Edward Hopper, 1942)

VISUAL ARTS

see also: **Sigmund Freud,** *Psychology Chapter, p. 282* | **Music in the USSR,** *Music Chapter, p. 382*

FROM ABSTRACT EXPRESSIONISM TO POP ART

After World War II, abstract art completely dominated the art world. However, in the 1960s, new artistic markets as well as Pop Art widened the concept of art.

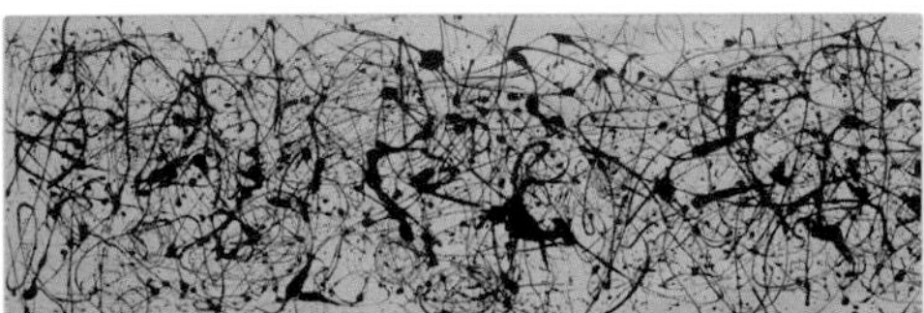

"Painting Number 7A" from 1948, one of Jackson Pollock's "action paintings."

The Cold War divided the world into two ideological camps, which affected the art of the post-war world. In contrast to the realistic art of the Eastern bloc, artists in the West produced free, associative paintings in continuation of the style of the Expressionists and Surrealists.

The New Role of the Viewer

The new style of art was called abstract expressionism in the U.S., which now assumed a leadership role in the world of art. This style ranged from the compositions of Willem de Kooning, which were still oriented to actual objects and painted in sensuous, deep hues, to Jackson Pollock's filigreed web of lines.

In both their styles, neither artist follows the classical rules of composition or wanted to convey a definite, concrete message. They challenge the viewer to give his own meaning to the picture, to impose his own thoughts and feelings. This "meaningful viewing" assigned the observer an entirely new role, but also led people to feel that modern art is "difficult to understand."

Robert Rauschenberg's "combine paintings," like "Canyon" (1959), mixed collage with painting.

Pollock went a step further with his "action paintings." Rather than applying paint in the traditional way, he flung, sprayed, or dripped colors on the canvas that lay on the floor. His "dribbling" (as Pollock called it) left tracks of paint that were, of course, extremely abstract. However, they also made it possible to retrace the creation process. They formed in their own way a slice of reality.

Return to Reality

Robert Rauschenberg also looked for a means of connecting with reality. Like the Dadaists (p. 309), he integrated everyday objects into his work. His pictures ("combine paintings") are paintings that loosely incorporated various three-dimensional objects. His spontaneous, but demonstrative, use of everyday materials and things made Rauschenberg a forerunner of Pop Art, which introduced an entirely new realism in the 1960s.

POP ART REVOLUTIONIZED ART. *It raised articles of consumption and trivial picture motives to the rank of works of art.*

ARTISTS MADE MULTIPLE COPIES *of their work or made screen prints to combat the idea that only one of a kind possessed value.*

THE MOST GLITTERING STAR *of Pop Art, Andy Warhol, artfully stylized himself.*

"Marilyn Monroe" (print by Andy Warhol)

Everything Is Pretty—Pop Art

POP ART was the planned counter design to abstract art. Art was to depict actual objects again. The creators of Pop Art used a pictorial language familiar to all from the consumer and entertainment industries.

BANAL MOTIFS FROM daily life were picked by Andy Warhol, Tom Wesselman, David Hamilton, Roy Lichtenstein, and Claes Oldenburg from pictures, objects, or installations. Enlarging, repeating, or outlining them made them appear alien and strange. Lichtenstein used the technique of enlargement to make us aware of the special aesthetic of comics. Art and trivia penetrated each other, and the line between high and pop culture became blurred.

With total accuracy, Roy Lichtenstein transferred comics onto large-scale canvases ("Whaam!," 1963).

Action Art, Happenings, Performances

Like the Dadaists before them, the "Nouveaux Réalistes" around Yves Klein, the "Fluxus" movement, as well as individual artists such as Joseph Beuys and Allan Kaprow orchestrated a revolution against the traditional concepts of art with the "happenings" in the 1960s. Several artists would perform a provocative action critical of art or society, which sometimes incorporated the observers. This was replaced in the 1970s by the "performance" during which an artist performed dramatic experimentally staged scenes.

above: *The projects of "wrap" artists Christo and Jeanne-Claude are in the tradition of action art such as the wrapping of the German Parliamentary Building in 1995.*

Willem de Kooning painted with dynamic brush strokes and radiant colors ("Woman II," 1952).

VISUAL ARTS

see also: **Music after 1945,** *Music Chapter p. 383*

CONTEMPORARY ART

In the past decades, a large variety of art styles and techniques have developed. Contemporary artists know no limits, whether in style, material, or themes.

The development of an understanding of what constitutes art through Pop Art, neo-Dadaist action art, and an intensive analysis of purely aesthetic phenomena led to today's abundant diversity of art forms and styles.

"Who's Afraid of Red, Yellow, and Blue IV" (painting by Barnett Newman, 1969-1970)

More Than Colorful Surfaces?

At the end of the 1950s, some artists developed a style called post-painterly abstraction as a counter movement to abstract expressionism (p. 312). One trend was known as "color field painting," which was influenced by classical "Constructionism" and De Stijl (p. 310). Represented by Barnett Newman and Ad Reinhardt, these artists focused on the expressive power of pure color. Newman's monumental paintings let the viewers immerse themselves in an unending field of color.

On the other hand, the practitioners of the style called "hard edge painting" created sharply divided fields of color to which they assigned no higher meaning. To them, a colored surface was simply that. To emphasize this, Frank Stella shaped his canvases to conform to the shape of his paintings, giving the colored surfaces an objective presence.

Three video projectors and six monitors show singer Rinde Eckert: "Anthro/Socio. Rinde Spinning" (installation by Bruce Nauman, 1992–1993).

Minimal Concepts

Practiced especially in the field of sculpture, "minimal art" also freed itself from the idea that a piece of art must have a hidden meaning. Donald Judd assembled simple geometric elements so that the viewer would perceive the empty spaces between them—the nothingness—as part of the picture.

From here it was only a small step to "conceptual art," which eschews even the execution of a work and emphasizes instead its "idea." The viewer is supposed to give it mental form by viewing sketches, notes, etc.

In her photographs, Cindy Sherman puts herself in the scene, for example, in 1989 as Martha Washington.

New Media and Old Paintings

The art of painting lost its predominance in the 1970s with the triumphant entry of conceptual and "performance art," and also photographic and video art, whose pioneer was the Fluxus artist (p. 312) Nam June Paik.

The most important artistic medium today is "installation art," the assembling of different objects in a given space. These may consist of everyday items, including natural materials (as with Joseph Beuys or in *arte povera*), colored lights, or video sequences (as with Bruce Nauman). The practitioners of this non-painting art form want to create a space for experiences that stimulate new ways of observing, feeling, and thinking.

However, painting has not completely disappeared. It achieved a high point again with photo-realism. Artists such as Gerhard Richter or Francis Bacon would not or could not let go despite all anti-painting trends. Richter makes his photographic models appear outlandish by blurring effects, thereby calling into question the idea that artificial pictures can really mirror reality. Photographer Cindy Sherman also questions whether pictures and clichés can reflect reality. She pointedly questions female imagery in traditional male-dominated art through dramatizing the role of women in her self portraits.

21ST CENTURY

IN THE POSTMODERN ERA, *it is no longer possible to definitively assign a work to just one particular style. Today's artists borrow from the rich heritage of art and mixed media categories, styles, and techniques as their creativity desires. Which art prevails is decided by the worldwide art market.*

"Betty" (painting by Gerhard Richter, 1988)

Even the nothingness in between the shelves is an integral part of this work by Donald Judd from 1990.

below: *The only purpose here is putting colored spaces in order: Frank Stella, "Ctesiphon III," 1968.*

VISUAL ARTS

Monographic Boxes

Analytic Boxes

ARCHITECTURE

Humans were designing structures to live in since before *Homo sapiens* walked upon the Earth, using materials in the natural environment to construct the first simple shelters against the elements. As more complex societies emerged, new materials and building techniques were discovered and perfected, allowing new forms and structures to come about. Roman arches, Gothic arches, concrete, and all manner of other developments have had a great impact on the way we construct the world that we see around us. These material factors, together with the politics, philosophies, and artistic styles of different cultures and eras, have created a world of variation in the monuments which humanity has left, marking time and space on the face of an increasingly human-centered planet Earth.

KEY FACTS

PALEOLITHIC *buildings consisted of stuctures made of natural materials, built by Homo erectus around 500,000 years ago.*

HUNTER-GATHERERS *erected large stone temples during the Neolithic period around 9000 B.C.*

EARLY CIVILIZATIONS, *which first appeared around 3500 B.C., farmed the land intensively and constructed irrigation systems, palaces, roads, and sewers.*

Settling down | Architecture of the early civilizations | Early civilizations: 3500–500 B.C.

THE BEGINNING

Knowledge of ancient cultures is largely made possible through the study of their architectural remains. The menhirs and henges of prehistory stand testament to the ability of groups of people, living thousands of years ago, to achieve impressive feats of engineering while using much simpler tools than are available today. The development of farming and city-based cultures increased the scale of architectural projects to the level where enormous structures, such as the pyramids of Egypt, could be built.

The first buildings were constructed before modern humans even existed.

SETTLING DOWN

Climatic changes around 10,000 B.C. changed the global environment so that in certain areas of the world humans started to farm and live in dense settlements.

The earliest dwellings used by humans tended to be temporary and movable, reflecting the nomadic lifestye of the hunter-gatherers who used them. Easily transportable materials, such as animal hide, bone, wood, clay, and mud were the main building materials during this time, and little remains of these structures. At present, the oldest shelters discovered appear to gave been built by *Homo erectus* 500,000 years ago at a site near Chichibu, Japan, where post-holes were found dug into a layer of volcanic ash. More recent remains, dating from 400,000 years ago, have been found at the site of Terra Amata, France, where lines of stones supported shelters made of sticks.

Excavations at Terra Amata near Nice, France, have turned up the remains of Paleolithic shelters.

Hunter-Gatherer Architecture

Until recently, it was believed that only settled, agricultural populations had the capability to erect major monuments. Recent discoveries at the site of Göbekli Tepe in Turkey have changed this view.

The monolithic temples at Göbekli Tepe, dating from ca 9000 B.C., could only have been constructed by hunter-gatherers, since at that time, agriculture had not developed anywhere in the world. The structure consists of monolithic T-shaped pillars of limestone, carved with animal designs, up to 23 ft (7m) tall and 50 tons in weight. This site is the first in the world to show hunter-gatherers to have been capable of constructing large, complex permanent strctures. Whether part of a religious ceremony or a scientific project, the question of their motivation remains unanswered.

Göbekli Tepe, ca 9000 B.C., is the oldest sanctum known.

Çatalhöyük

During the Neolithic period (8000–3000 B.C.), the change in climate alowed for the development and spread of farming, which created settled societies that began to invest their energies in building more permanent homes from wood, wattle and daub, brick, and stone. Çatalhöyük is one of the earliest and most extensive known Neolithic sites, and the settlement that existed there around 7000 B.C. had a population of about 8,000 people. There were no streets in the settlement, rather rooftops served as paths and inhabitants accessed their mud-brick houses via holes in the roof. It appears that the settlement also lacked public buildings. Vivid murals have been found on interior and exterior walls.

Stonehenge, England: a megalithic structure built around 3000 B.C.

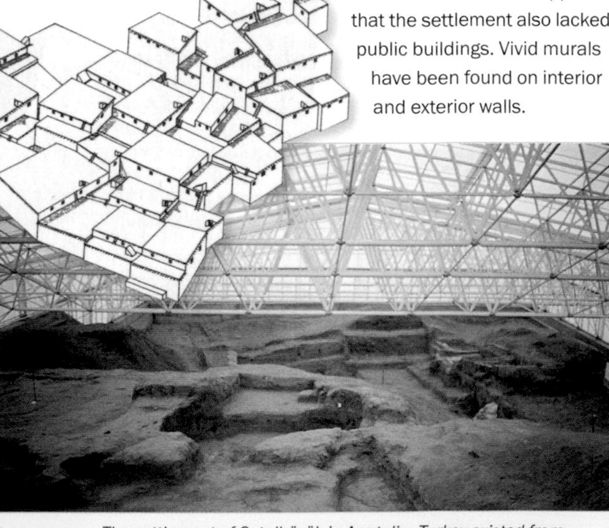

The settlement of Catalhöyük in Anatolia, Turkey existed from around 8000 B.C. to around 6500 B.C. At its peak, it is thought that up to 10,000 people lived in the village.

ARCHITECTURE OF THE EARLY CIVILIZATIONS

Early settlements had water management systems by the sixth millennium B.C., and by the third millennium B.C. roads, multi-level buildings, and sewage systems were constructed.

The Great Pyramid at Giza (built 2570 B.C.) was the tallest building in the world until 1300 A.D.

The earliest civilizations arose in a number of locations around the world, including the Americas and China. However, those which arose in the Middle East, around the Mediterranean, and in northern India are among the oldest and the best researched to date.

The Concentration of Power

The first civilizations generally arose with the development of irrigated farming. The concentrated, settled communities which developed under these conditions had a societal organization that allowed for the simplification of the task of building and maintaining irrigation systems and other large building projects.

Ancient Egypt

Because ancient Egyptian cities were made of mud-brick and constructed on the Nile floodplain most of their remains have been lost. That which has been recovered shows various styles of temples, constructed with stone columns and lintels or carved into rock faces, and the pyramids.

Pyramids, the imposing tombs of the Pharaohs, developed from the more modest mastaba—rectangular aboveground structures built over underground burial chambers. The building of sequencial mastabas that decrease in size led to the creation of the first step pyramid around 2700 B.C. In 2600 B.C., the first smooth-sided pyramids were built, the largest of which is the Great Pyramid of Giza.

The Indus Valley

The Indus Valley civilization, the remains of which were first discovered in the 1800s, existed from 3300 to 1700 B.C. and shows an incredible level of architectural accomplishment for the time. Streets were laid out on a regular gridiron pattern, and the rectangular buildings were all provided with a sewage system, laid out so as to keep waste water and clean water separate. The people of the Indus Valley civilizations were also among the first in the world to use the arch.

Greece and Crete

Crete was home to the earliest known European civilization—the Minoans. The Minoans built elaborate palaces and settlements with paved roads by 2000 B.C. The palace of Knossos, built around 1500 B.C., consisted of over 1,000 rooms on multiple floors, was supplied with water through an aqueduct, and had sanitary and sewage systems.

A distinctive feature of Minoan architecture is the shape of the columns, which were narrow at the base and increased in diameter with height. This was because the cypress tree trunks that were first used as columns were stuck in the ground upside down in order to prevent resprouting. This aesthetic was maintained even when the Minoans began to use stone columns. The Mycenaeans, contemporaries of the Minoans, lived on the Greek mainland. Their building style was characterized by the creation of massive limestone structures and fortified settlements.

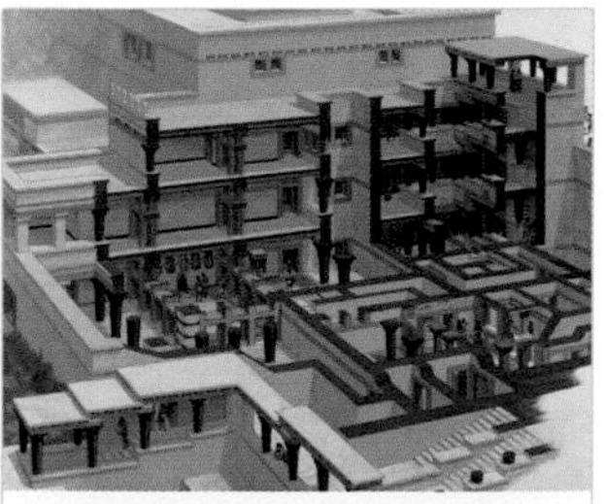

The Palace of Knossos, Crete (built between 1700 and 1400 B.C.)

A reconstruction of the Ishtar Gate of Babylon, built around 575 B.C.

21ST CENTURY

ÇATALHÖYÜK, GÖBEKLI TEPE, *and other ancient sites continue to be excavated with ever improving techniques in order to discover how our ancestors lived.*

TODAY'S SYSTEM *of dividing clocks and, therefore time, by multiples of 12 is inherited from Sumeria.*

RECENT EXCAVATIONS *in Peru show that the Caral Supe civilization was building pyramids at the same as the ancient Egyptians.*

MESOPOTAMIA *refers to the region between the Tigris and Euphrates rivers in present day Iraq.*

THE TOWER OF BABEL *of the Bible is thought to be based on the ziggurats built by the Babylonians.*

Mesopotamia

THE ARCHITECTURAL HISTORY of Mesopotamia began in 4000 B.C. with the Sumerians. Although the area later came under the rule of the Assyrians and Babylonians, the various Mesopotamian civilizations demonstated a high level of continuity in their architecture.

THE MOST DISTINCTIVE of all buildings developed in the region were the ziggurats: vast stepped pyramids made mainly of sun-dried brick, with fired brick exteriors that fended off the elements. These structures were not used as tombs, as in the case of Egypt, but rather as temples, which were accessible to priests only. Houses in the cities were composed of mud-brick, but because mud-brick is vulnerable to erosion, buildings often required renovation. New structures were built on the debris of the old, meaning that the ground level of the settlements slowly rose, resulting in cities raised upon artificial hills.

The walled city of Babylon, built on the banks of the Euphrates, was the capital of the Babylonian empire.

KEY FACTS

THE ANCIENT GREEKS *made use of post and beam architecture for the construction of stone temples.*

ROMAN *architecture was based on the use of arches and vaults which were constructed with stone, brick, and concrete.*

ENTASIS *is a technique that counters the illusion of structural narrowing that arises with depth perception by giving straight lines and surfaces a slightly convex shape.*

Ancient Greek and Hellenistic architecture ca 800 B.C.–146 B.C. | Imperial Roman architecture ca 300 B.C.–300 A.D.

CLASSICAL ARCHITECTURE

Ancient Greek architecture functioned primarily as public and religious buildings such as temples and theaters. Roman architecture continued Greek traditions, but incorporated important innovations such as the arch and the use of concrete. Later architectural styles, such as those of the Byzantine, Frankish, and Renaissance states, were developed on the foundations set by classical architecture. Modern architecture has continued to use the styles and inventions of antiquity as a reference point.

The classical period began with the Greeks around 700 B.C. and ended with the Romans around 600 A.D.

ARCHITECTURE

ANCIENT GREEK AND HELLENISTIC ARCHITECTURE

The temples and theaters of ancient Greece have become the architectural archetypes for the Western world.

Around 800 B.C., in the wake of the Minoan and Mycenaean civilizations, a Greek national identity, with common myths, cults, and festivals emerged.

Ancient Greece

The great buildings of the ancient Greeks were temples and theaters. Temples were post and beam constructions consisting of closed rectangular structures with low roofs raised on columns. Theaters consisted of stepped rows of seating built into circular depressions. Greek architecture inherited many elements from other places and times. The Doric column first appeared in mainland Greece, and combined the Mycenaean capital, with a vertically tapered column shaft in the style of the Egyptians, with whom the Greeks had contact from the seventh century B.C. In time, the Doric column was replaced by the Ionic column, which originated in Asia Minor. The Corinthian column, which first appeared at the temple of Apollo Epicurius at Bassae, is based on the Ionic, but has an elaborate floral capital. Later, this style was popular with the Romans.

Hellenistic Style

After Athens lost the Peloponnesian war to Sparta, Greece fell into economic and political chaos. It was only with Alexander the Great and the creation of a Hellenistic empire that the Greeks once again became wealthy. The new empire allowed the further spread of Greek styles, and their new wealth allowed for the expansion of imposing architecture into the private realm. Grand staircases became a popular motif, the previously modest houses of the Greeks became palatial in scale and colonnaded streets were decorated with statues of wealthy citizens. These later developments have been seen as decadent by some, embodying the excess of empire and the abandonment of the spare simplicity of earlier Greek architecture, which has come to be thought of as the Western world's architectural precursor.

Simple but effective: the theater of Epidaurus, built ca 350 B.C.

"ACROPOLIS" *means "upper city" in Greek.*

THE PARTHENON, *dedicated to Athena, is one of a number of temples built on the Acropolis of Athens and restored under the rule of Pericles.*

MUCH OF THE DAMAGE *to the Parthenon occurred in 1687 when the Turkish ammunition store there was hit by a Venetian projectile.*

Three-dimensional statues serve as columns at the Erechtheion temple on the Acropolis.

The Acropolis and Parthenon

THE PARTHENON, situated on the Acropolis of Athens, built between 447 and 436 B.C., replaced an earlier temple destroyed by the Persians. Greek temples originally consisted of a brick cella (inner chamber) surrounded by timber columns and protected from the elements by a gable roof. With time, they came to be built of more durable limestone. Quite unlike the usual Greek temple with six columns, the Parthenon has eight columns along the front, and is constructed mostly of marble. The lines of the Parthenon are slightly convex. This technique, called entasis, actually makes the lines appear straighter.

The Parthenon, Athens built 447–436 B.C.

The Greek Column Orders

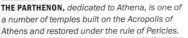

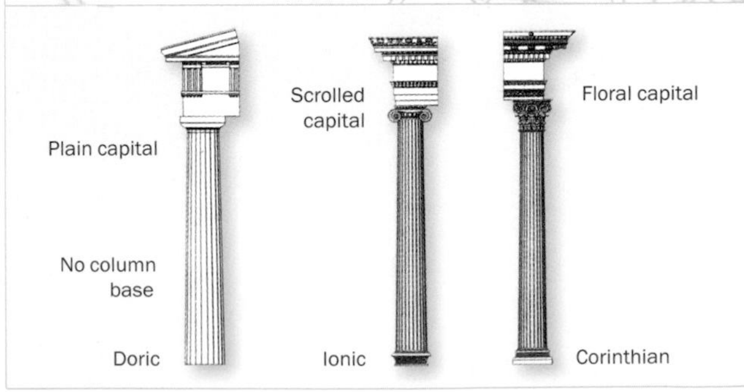

ROMAN ARCHITECTURE

The Romans pioneered the use of large quantities of concrete in architecture, as well as the application of arches, vaults, and domes. They inherited much of their style from the Greeks.

Roman civilization began in northern Italy, which had been dominated by the Etruscans, from whom the Romans inherited arches, vaults, and domes. The Greeks, who had colonies in Italy and whose lands became part of the Roman Empire in 146 B.C., were another important influence on Roman architecture.

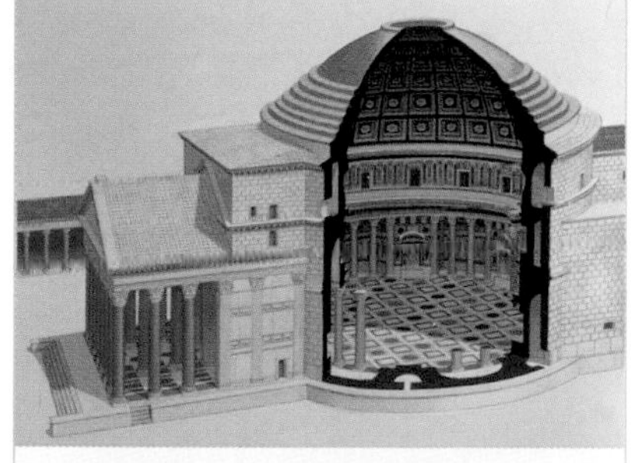

The Pantheon in Rome was built 118–128 A.D. The dome spans 142 ft (43.3 m).

Tradition and Innovation

The classical Greek contribution to Roman architecture was great, but Greek elements were used more for decoration and facades. The structure of Roman buildings depended more on the use of arches and walls of brick and concrete than on the post and beam architecture of the Greeks. Vaulting and domes, enabled the Romans to enclose ever larger spaces without the use of intermediary supports. Roman innovations in the mixing of concrete, which was manufactured using lime, rubble, water, and volcanic ash allowed even greater spans to be covered. The area covered by the dome of the Pantheon in Rome was not surpassed until the Renaissance.

Expressing Power

Roman settlements were planned on a grid pattern around two large roads which formed north-south and east-west axes. The forum, an ancestor of the modern town square, was based on the Greek agora and stood at the intersection of these two roads, surrounded by public buildings such as the basilica (halls of justice and commerce), temples, and triumphal arches. Roman architecture expressed, and was enabled by, Roman power. The government had a monopoly on natural building materials, bricks were produced by state-owned brick-works, and commissions for the construction of civil buildings were carried out by the army. Throughout the empire roads and bridges allowed the rapid movement of goods, information, and troops—all necessary for the vast Roman Empire. The wealth of individual Roman citizens was embodied in the Roman villa with gardens, terraces, and colonnaded halls. In the crowded cities, the Romans used mass construction techniques to create high-rise buildings.

21ST CENTURY

SOME ROMAN AQUEDUCTS *in the Andalusian town of Almuñécar, Spain are still in use today.*

MODERN SPORTS STADIUMS *derive their design from the amphitheaters and stadiums of the Greeks and Romans, such as the Colosseum in Rome.*

The Roman Arch

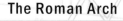

ROMAN arches were semi-circular in shape, and allowed the efficient spanning of great distances by structures such as aqueducts and viaducts.

BUILT by a process known as centering, Roman arches were built around a semi-circular wooden frame, which was removed once the keystone, the top center piece was inserted and the arch was completed.

THE FORCES generated in semi-circular arches tend to cause the sides to bulge outward. For this reason, early arches and vaults were constructed underground. The Romans countered these lateral forces by supporting arches with abutments.

Triumphal Arch, Leptis Magna-Lebda, Tripoli, Libya

Aqueducts

The Romans were not the first to use aqueducts, but the scale on which they did so was unprecedented. Growing populations in various urban centers throughout the empire, particularly Rome, meant that local water sources became inadequate and easily contaminated. The Romans used the arch to great effect in the construction of arcades, which carried clean water to urban centers, spanning whole river valleys in the process. Once in the city, raised aqueducts were used to maintain a useful supply of water and keep water free of contamination.

above: *Pont du Gard, France (built in the first century A.D.)*

Collapse

The growth in power of the Roman Empire was reflected in the increasing grandeur of its architecture. In the third century A.D. an increase in external threats, crises in state finances, and the near collapse of the empire stalled architectural development. The empire was ruled by a rapid succession of emperors whose building projects rarely came to fruition.

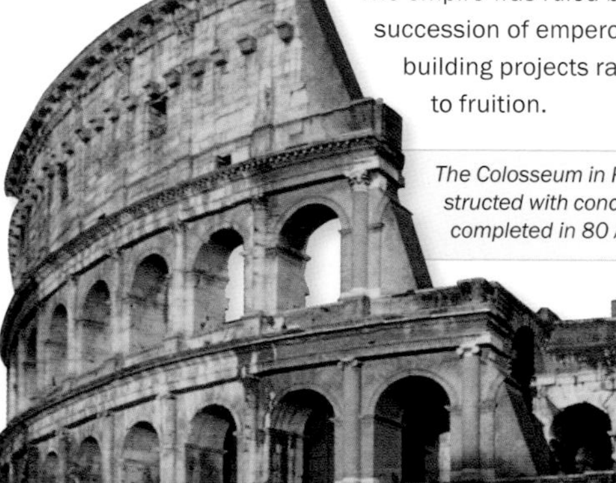

The Colosseum in Rome, constructed with concrete, was completed in 80 A.D.

KEY FACTS

ISLAMIC ARCHITECTURE *has a continuos tradition from the foundation of Islam to modern times.*

THE RICH AND ADVANCED *architecture of the Native American cultures came to a rapid end with the conquest of the Americas.*

SOUTH OF THE SAHARA, *multiple very large complexes of stone buildings were built during the Middle Ages.*

ARCHITECTURE OUTSIDE OF EUROPE

Outside Europe, hundreds of cultures were developing their own ways of building, long before the Greeks and the Romans, from whom most European architecture originally derived, even existed. The Chinese began work on the Great Wall in the fifth century B.C., and the native cultures of the Americas have long established traditions of impressive architecture, which continued to be developed until the time of the European conquest.

Some of the most extensive architectural ruins in Southern Africa are those of medieval Great Zimbabwe.

ISLAMIC ARCHITECTURE

The early Islamic world consisted mainly of nomadic tribes with no use for major architecture. As Islam spread, it adopted various building styles as well as developing its own.

With the initial expansion of Islam, it was often the case that buildings constructed for older religions were converted into mosques, but soon purpose-built mosques were constructed.

Early Islamic Architecture

Muhammad's house in Medina was taken as the model for the mosques. Typically, for houses of the area, it consisted primarily of a covered hall with palm trunk columns supporting a flat roof. Mosques based on this design are referred to as hypostyle. The most important feature of a mosque was the mihrab, a niche in a wall, indicating the direction of Mecca, the direction of prayer. Running parallel or perpendicular to this wall were rows of columns topped by arcades which, again, helped in orientation for prayer. Outside the prayer hall was a courtyard with a fountain used for washing before prayer, as well as a minaret; a tower used to call the faithful to prayer.

The Sultan Ahmet Mosque, Istanbul, by Sedfkar Mehmet Agha: a dome mosque (built 1610–1616)

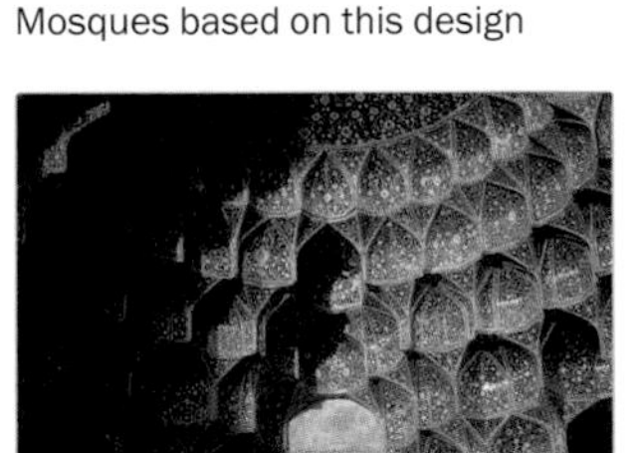

Dome of Sheikh Lotfollah mosque, Isfahan, Iran (built 1602–1619)

below: *The Taj Mahal, India: a mausoleum modeled on a mosque (built 1630–1653)*

Empire

The Islamic empire grew rapidly between 1300 and 1600 and Islamic architecture came to incorporate many of the styles of its conquered territories. In this manner, Byzantine, Roman, Persian, and Egyptian styles became part of the Islamic architectural vocabulary. Islamic Spain, under the Umayyad dynasty, saw a flourishing of Islamic architecture. The Alhambra, built around 1300, was the residence of the last Muslim princes in Spain. It was a vast complex of pools, fountains, and buildings whose contours were blurred by stalactite vaults and other decorative detail. Later Islamic empires introduced their own architectural styles. The Ottomans made Constantinople their capital and the Hagia Sophia, constructed by the Byzantines, was converted into a mosque. It became the inspiration for a new style; that of the central-dome mosques. The Iwan is the third major style of mosque, inherited from the Persians. An iwan is a pointed vault with one end left open, an example of which is the main entrance to the Taj Mahal.

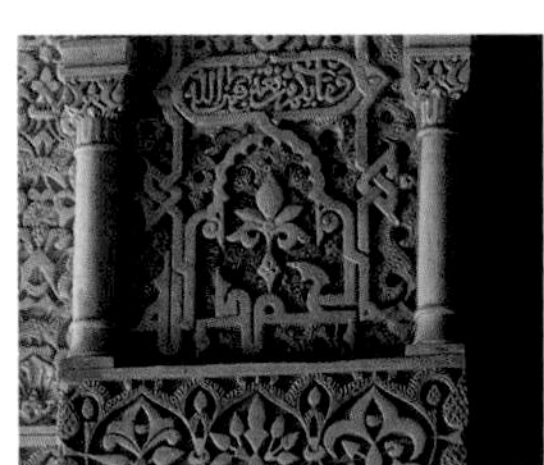

Arabesque

The Islamic ban on the depiction of human and animal forms forced Islamic art to develop in a very different direction from that of Europe. Arabesque is the term used to describe the elaborate patterns employed in Islamic art. These consisted of repeating geometric and floral forms, as well as calligraphy, which became a highly developed art form as verses from the Qur'an were used for the decoration of buildings.

above: *Arabesque ornamentation in the Alhambra, Spain (built 1338–1390)*

Defense

Islamic architecture was not only religious. Islamic architects also designed defensive works such as massive towers of packed earth and walled and gated cities in order to maintain the borders of Empire.

ARCHITECTURE OF AFRICA, ASIA, AND PRE-COLUMBIAN AMERICA

As a result of local conditions, availability of building materials, religious practice, and cultural diffusion, a range of distinct architectural styles developed across the globe prior to the prevalence of European-derived architecture.

Human societies the world over have developed thier own impressive architectural traditions.

China

Most of the remains from very early Chinese history are mausoleums and graves, which were made of stone. Chinese Imperial Architecture is among the grandest in the world. The roughly 1,500 mile (2,400 km) long Great Wall of China is visible from orbit, and the Mausoleum of Quin Shi Huang, the first emperor of China, is the size of a small city. Traditional Chinese houses are generally constructed of wood, which makes for more earthquake-proof structures. They have a rectangular plan, and a tiled roof supported on a system of cantilevers and beams. Perhaps the best known Chinese building type is the pagoda, a development of the stupa, which was an import from Buddhist India.

Africa

The most extensive ruins south of the Sahara are those of the trading city of Great Zimbabwe, built between 1100 and 1450. The layout of the buildings at this site is based on that of traditional pallisaded or mud-walled African farming compounds, scaled up in size and built with large, thick drystone walls up to 32 ft (10 m) in height.

The Hall of Supreme Harmony in the Forbidden City, Beijing: The building of the Forbidden City began in 1406.

The Old Mosque of Bobo Dioulasso, Burkina Faso, (built in the late 19th century) it is an example of the mud architecture of the Sahel region of Africa.

El Castillo, Chichen Itza, Mexico (built by the Maya ca 1100 A.D.) The pyramid is in many ways like those of Central Mexico, which suggests cultural exchange.

North and Central America

Very few major native constructions remain in North America, apart from the mounds of the Mississippian cultures and the still-used settlements of the Pueblo peoples of the American Southwest. Further south, the situation is different. The civilizations of Central America shared many building types, most notably large I-shaped courts for ritual ball-games and stepped pyramids topped with temples, which were used for religious purposes. New temples were often built over old ones, resulting in huge pyramids such as the Great Pyramid of Cholula, the largest pyramid by volume in the world.

South America

The Inca were the last and most powerful in a long line of native South American civilizations. Incan roads, paved with stone, traveled almost the full length of the Pacific coast of South America, with rope suspension bridges crossing gorges and rivers. Inca buildings were made of large square or polygonal blocks of stone, some several tons in weight, fitted so closely together that a knife blade could not be inserted between them. Many features of Inca architecture, such as mortarless stonework and lightweight thatched roofs, were developed in order to fortify buildings against earthquakes.

Angkor Wat, Cambodia: an example of classical Khmer architecture built in the reign of King Suryavarman II in the early 12th century

Cliff dwelling, Mesa Verde, Colorado (built ca 1200 by the Anasazi)

INSIDER KNOWLEDGE

CORBEL ARCHES *are not as stong as true arches, relying on the principle of the cantilever.*

THE GREAT PYRAMID OF CHOLULA *is the largest pyramid in the world by volume.*

NATIVE AMERICA *never developed the true arch. The Maya used the corbelled arch instead.*

KEY FACTS

BYZANTINE ARCHITECTURE *was the building style of the old East Roman Empire, known as Byzantium.*

ROMANESQUE ARCHITECTURE *developed in western Europe after the collapse of the West Roman Empire. It was the building style of the Holy Roman Empire.*

GOTHIC ARCHITECTURE *has three distinct characteristics: pointed arches, ribbed vaults, and flying buttresses.*

Byzantine architecture 395–1453 | Romanesque architecture 1000–1200 | Gothic architecture 1144–1500

MEDIEVAL ARCHITECTURE

The collapse of the Roman Empire split Europe in half. The East Roman Empire became the Byzantine Empire, which lasted until the invasion of the Ottomans in 1453. The West Roman Empire collapsed entirely, and it took many centuries until a unified Holy Roman Empire arose in the West. The term Romanesque is used to refer to the style of architecture which developed in Western Europe during this period. By the 11th century, a new style developed from Romanesque architecture, that of Gothic, which went on to structurally and aesthetically dominate Europe.

In the medieval period, the Church was dominant in society, and most of the buildings were ecclesiastical.

BYZANTINE AND ROMANESQUE ARCHITECTURE

Byzantine architecture can be seen as a continuation of Roman architecture, while Romanesque architecture only came into being with the founding of the Holy Roman Empire.

Byzantine Architecture

Byzantine architecture, based on Roman forms, still had some influence from the East since the capital, Constantinople, was in what is now Turkey. Imperial mausoleums were the model for martyrs shrines, thermal baths were the model for baptisteries, and the circular Roman temple, exemplified by the Pantheon, became the model for Byzantine buildings such as San Vitale in Ravenna (527–548) and the Hagia Sophia (532–537) in Constantinople. These centrally planned, domed, radially designed buildings continued to be the model for Orthodox churches long after the Byzantine Empire fell to the Ottomans in 1453.

Romanesque Architecture

Romanesque architecture, the first unified architectural style in western Europe after the fall of Rome, was mostly ecclesiastical, reflecting the dominance of the medieval Church. In the West, early churches developed from the Roman basilica, whose layout was changed to suit its new function. The entrance was moved to the west of the building, while the eastern section was set aside for the altar and the apse, where the clergy would stand. In the Romaneque period, a westworks was added, fronting on to the western end, and the main body of the church was divided into the nave in the west, reserved for the public, and the sanctuary in the east, reserved for the clergy. With time, the secular westworks of churches became much grander, incorporating towers and even a gallery for the secular ruler. This trend physically embodied the growing power of the Frankish kings. By the end of the Romanesque period, buildings became lighter as cross barrel or groin vaults standing on pillars replaced the earlier barrel vault, whose massive walls counter the lateral thrust of the vault produced very gloomy interiors.

PILGRIMAGE CHURCHES *such as St. Sernin housed the relics of saints and were laid out to serve the needs of large crowds of pilgrims.*

THE LAYOUT *of St. Sernin was first developed with the construction of St. Foy, Conques which was begun 30 years earlier in 1050.*

View down the nave of St. Sernin, Toulouse

St. Sernin

ST. SERNIN, TOULOUSE, is the largest Romanesque pilgrimage church in existence. The church, which was built between around 1080 and 1120 demonstrates the development of earlier Christian church plans which occurred at this time. It is vaulted rather than flat-roofed, has a number of chapels radiating from the apse, and the two wings of the transept give the church the shape of a crucifix. Another Romanesque innovation was the crossing tower, built where the transept crosses the main axis of the church, which is supported by four enlarged piers.

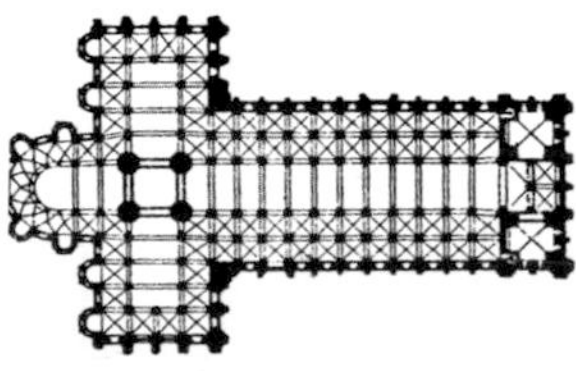

EXTERNALLY, the church displays a typically Romanesque massing of volumes, with small chapels clustered around the the apse and the crossing tower rising above everything. The spire was added in the 15th century.

left: *Plan view of St. Sernin*
above: *St. Sernin*

Hagia Sopia, Constantinople: Originally a Byzantine church, it was converted into a mosque.

San Vitale, Ravenna: a centrally planned Byzantine church

INSIDER KNOWLEDGE

WESTWORKS *are the imposing western entrances which characterize Romaneque churches.*

CROSS BARREL VAULTS *consist of two superimposed barrel vaults.*

"GOTICO" *(Gothic) was first a contemptuous term used in Italy for styles regarded as barbarous.*

GOTHIC

Gothic architecture began with the building of the Abbey of St. Denis, France, in 1144 and the style grew to dominate Europe architecture for the next 400 years.

Gothic architecture, in striking contrast to Romanesque designs, was the result of architects identifying the forces acting on the building structure, and directing them along piers, columns, ribs, and external buttresses.

The Doge's Palace in Venice is indicative of the Italian Gothic.

Reaching for Heaven

The focus of architecture at this time was still ecclesiastical, and the new system grew out of a desire to create impressive cathedrals with very tall walls and vaults, arching up as if to heaven. The pared-down system of piers, buttresses, and arches had the advantage of allowing the spaces in between piers to be filled with windows, flooding churches with a volume of light not possible under the massive Romanesque style of building.

Arches and Vaults

Romanesque architects occasionally emphasized the edges of cross-vaults with decorative ribbing. Gothic architects put these ribs to a new use, and turned them into the main structural elements of the roof, constructing them as roughly semi-circular arches, and then filling in the cells between the ribs with pointed Gothic vaults. This resulted in a much stronger, lighter design. On meeting a column or wall, pointed arches and vaults have the advantage of transferring more force straight down, thereby producing less lateral thrust than a semi-circular arch or vault. Building massive walls in order to absorb lateral thrust went against the Gothic desire to create high, light, airy buildings. Instead, Gothic architects devised a variety of strategies to help absorb thrust. One was to supplement the structural pillars with colonettes, semi-columns that continued up into the ribs and buttressed the thrust from the vault. External buttressing of walls in the form of piers, further supplemented by flying buttresses, which arched over to lower, more distant piers, dealt with the remaining lateral thrust. All of these features kept structural mass out of the interior, and allowed as much light as possible in through the perforated walls.

Castles

The political instabilities of Europe during the Middle Ages meant that the Gothic period saw the construction of many castles and fortifications. These were used both as places of residence for those in power and as military strongholds. Much European military architecture was adopted from what the Crusaders found in Byzantium and the Holy Land, but castles of the Gothic period also incorporated features such as pointed arches, vaults, and Gothic decorations.

Gothic Politics

The spread of Gothic architecture through Europe physically embodied the spread of French political influence. Eagerly adopted in post-Norman England, it met greater resistance in the Germanic east of Europe, which clung to the Romanesque architecture of the old Frankish Empire for some time. Italy also felt the impact of Gothic style, but adopted only certain elements, tending to avoid the use of the external buttressing so common in the rest of Europe and retaining the wider proportions of Romanesqe architecture. The Italian Gothic period is also referred to as the Proto-Renaissance.

King's College Chapel in Cambridge has English-style fan vaults.

The Cathedral of Amiens

THE CATHEDRAL OF AMIENS, *France, begun in 1220, is regarded as one of the best examples of Gothic architecture. The elaborate system of Gothic vaults and arches, piers, flying buttresses, and columns is typical of the style.*

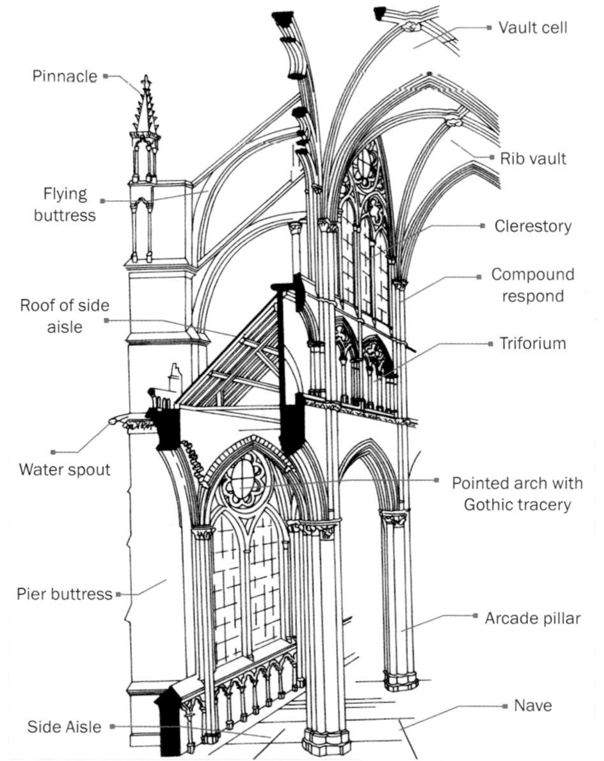

KEY FACTS

RENAISSANCE *refers to the rebirth of the classical arts and sciences.*

MANNERIST *architects used classical elements to create new and unconventional designs.*

BAROQUE *architecture was intended to overwhelm the observer with decoration and effects.*

ROCOCO *architects aimed to create a light-hearted atmosphere by using excessive ornamentation.*

Early and High Renaissance 1420–1530 | Mannerism and Late Renaissance 1530–1600

EARLY MODERN ARCHITECTURE

Beginning in the mid-15th century, the development of Renaissance architecture was triggered by the rediscovery of ancient Greek and Roman architectural forms. With time, the new style spread across Europe, but it was not long before architects started to explore new avenues of design, and in the Baroque period a new, highly decorative style of building came into being, which reached the extremes of decorative excess in the designs of the Rococo period, which was then abandoned for the simpler lines of neoclassical architecture.

Architecture in the early Renaissance had an influence on neoclassicism in the 1700s.

ARCHITECTURE OF THE ITALIAN RENAISSANCE

Renaissance architecture began in 15th-century Italy in Florence, but soon spread to the rest of Italy and beyond, becoming the dominant style in much of Europe.

In 15th-century Italy, the trading class was becoming increasingly secular and humanistic, particularly in the city of Florence, which had become very wealthy through commerce. Powerful families supported the arts, people studied the classics, translated ancient Greek and Latin documents, and excavated ancient ruins.

Early Renaissance

After centuries in obscurity, "De Arcitectura," written around 25 B.C. by the Roman engineer and architect Vitruvius became the focus of much interest. This architectural treatise emphasized symmetry and harmony and analyzed the temples and the orders of Greek architecture, allowing the rediscovery of distinctly Greek and Roman styles. For the first time since antiquity, private homes became a focus in this wealthy society of northern Italy, resulting in the Palazzo, a town house modeled on the fortified homes of the Middle Ages. Palazzi had the appearance of a stronghold. The external walls of the ground floor consisted of rough stonework and small rectangular windows. Upper floors were more open, with lower ceilings.

Santa Maria Novella, Italy: facade completed in 1470 by Leon Battista Alberti.

Mannerism

The mannerism of the Late Renaissance used classical motifs in an expressive, sculptural way by breaking the rules of proportion and order. Michaelangelo's Laurentian Library exemplies the work of this influential Renaissance architect. Here, columns become an element of decoration, sunk into the walls, rising from volutes, and not even extending to the floor.

above: *Vestibule with staircase, Laurentian Library, Florence*

High Renaissance

The High Renaissance saw architects gaining mastery of classical forms. The Donato Bramante's Tempietto San Pietro demonstrates the new understanding of classical architecture, taking a number of elements traditionally used in rectilinear Greek and Roman buildings and translating them into a circular form. Another architect, Andrea Palladio (1508–1580), based his purist style on the Greek Temple, and his writings on the subject went on to lauch English Palladianism in the mid-1600s.

The Tempietto San Pietro, Rome, exemplifies the High Renaissance reinterpretation of classical style.

BRUNELLESCHI *painted the first known image with linear perspective, and is considered to have discovered the concept. Alberti later formalized the geometry.*

THE PANTHEON *inspired Brunelleschi to come up with his design for the dome of Santa Maria.*

THE DOME *of Santa Maria, the largest masonry dome in the world, was in part made possible by the use of a herringbone pattern of brickwork.*

Filippo Brunelleschi

Brunelleschi and the Dome

BRUNELLESCHI pioneered the architectural Renaissance. The dome he designed for the cathedral of Santa Maria del Fiore, Florence, consisted of two nested shells and, unlike Gothic structures, the load-bearing ribs were hidden. This approach not only had structural benefits, but also allowed the inner and outer domes to be designed to suit their respective contexts.

DOMES saw a revival in the Renaissance. The circle was seen as sacred, symbolizing perfect harmony and balance, the ultimate expression of the Vitruvian delight in proportion and symmetry. Studies such as da Vinci's "Vitruvian Man" (derived from specifications in "De Arcitectura") showed how the proportions of the human body, created in God's image, related to the circle.

Santa Maria del Fiore, Florence

see also: The Renaissance and Mannerism, *Visual Arts Chapter pp. 294–297*

THE RENAISSANCE OUTSIDE ITALY

As Renaissance architecture spread through Europe, different countries took to different aspects of the style, with regional variations resulting from history and political circumstances.

Gothic was firmly established in Europe in the early 16th century. It took some time before the Renaissance style could assert itself outside Italy.

France

Renaissance architecture first reached France by way of the Italian architects summoned by French aristocratic families. In 1516, King Francis returned to France from northern Italy with a number of Italian architects, which resulted in Chateau de Chambord. This building was a fusion of French tradition and Italian style, incorporating the traditional layout of a medieval castle, complete with cylindrical towers at the corners, with a clear Renaissance geometry of repeating arches; large, rectangular windows; and a rectangular plan. The roof, consisting of such a confusion of chimneys and towers that it looks like the skyline of a city, is an extreme example of the Gothic tradition of steep roofs richly decorated with structures. This feature appears in almost all French Renaissance castles.

Spain

When Renaissance style first came to Spain, it was assimilated as plateresque, a style of decoration on buildings which otherwise continued to be medieval in their construction. It was El Escorial (1559–1584) which marked the Spanish transition from richly decorated Gothic and plateresque architecture to a sparse, rather severe style of Renaissance classicism. Built outside Madrid, it is a vast complex in which Phillip II and his architects consolidated a fortified palace with a monastery, a royal burial ground and, dominating everything, a church which echoes St. Peter's in Rome.

El Escorial, Madrid by Juan Batista de Toledo and Juan de Herrera (completed in the late 1590s)

The Queen's House in Greenwich was designed by Inigo Jones and built from 1616–1635.

Germany and the Low Countries

For the most part, Renaissance architecture reached the Netherlands and Germany by way of copper engravings and the architectural texts of Vitruvius, Palladio and others. In contrast to Southern Europe, however, Germany, and the Netherlands had no Greek or Roman architecture to refer to and a purer High Renaissance style of classicism did not occur. Instead, many elements were adopted such as large rectangular windows, string courses between floors, and gables crowned with obelisks. Domed buildings, however, were hardly ever constructed.

England

The Renaissance was especially late in coming to England, where Gothic still kept a very firm hold, especially in the case of religious buildings. During the 1530s there was even an official ban on Italian architecture—a consequence of Henry VIII's struggles with the pope. Secular architecture only started to show Renaissance characteristics by the late 16th century, largely thanks to the works of the Italian architect and author Andrea Palladio, whose work was inspired by the simple geometries of the Greek temple. The foremost English architect of the time, Inigo Jones, spent time studying in Italy and was inspired by the works of Palladio. The Queen's House in Greenwich, designed by Jones in what came to be known as the Palladian style, is a cubic white block, consisting of a lower storey of rusticated stone in the Italian tradition, large rectangular windows, Ionic columns and a flat roof. Buildings such as this inspired great enthusiasm for the writings of Palladio, who had a dominating influence on English architecture until the 18th century, by which time other parts of Europe were exploring the architectural successor to the Renaissance; Baroque.

Place des Vosges

While Renaissance squares in Italy were surrounded by public buildings, Henry IV surrounded Place des Vosges with private residences, which were given unified facades. This style spread from France, inspiring architects such as Inigo Jones to build similar squares of terraced houses for the rich in London. The terraced house was to become a very important building style during the Industrial Revolution, when it was used to house the vast numbers of poorly-paid industrial workers in crowded British cities.

above: *Place des Vosges, Paris (built 1605–1612)*

Chateau de Chambord, France, by Domenico da Cortona and Pierre Nepveu (built 1519–1547)

ARCHITECTURE

see also: Baroque Art, *Visual Arts Chapter, pp. 298–301*

BAROQUE ARCHITECTURE

The Baroque architectural style developed from mannerism and aimed to dominate and overwhelm the observer with dynamism, illusionism, and extravagant ornamentation.

The term "Baroque" began as a derogatory term for what were seen as the misshapen and unclassical creations of Italian architects such as Bernini, Borromini, and Guarini. The term is now widely used to refer to the sweeping, richly ornate styles of these architects and others. The Baroque aesthetic went on to become the dominant architectural style of 17th and 18th century continental Europe and was used to as a tool of the Counter-Reformation.

Trevi Fountain by Nicolo Salvi, Rome, built 1732–1762, and Palazzo Poli, facade by his student Luigi Vanvitelli

From Mannerism to Baroque

While the Mannerists of the Renaissance had, to some degree, explored classical themes, the Baroque period saw architects move even further away from the restrained harmonies of classicism, and doing so with the express aim of producing buildings that were designed to impress, dominate, and overwhelm. This trend stemmed partly from the ecclesiastical architecture of the Counter-Reformation, when the Catholic Church sought to reestablish its authority in the wake of the heresies of Protestantism and humanism. Architecturally, this was expressed in the tension between Renaissance centrally planned, circular church layouts and the more traditional rectangular, axial layout of churches which were based on the early Christian basilica. Bernini's design for St. Peter's Square in Rome can be seen as an early Baroque compromise between these two forms, consisting of a grand, perspective-deforming trapezoidal collonade which opens into a circle half-way along its length. Rome's Il Gesù, completed the return to the traditional layout, reasserting the basilical plan over the central plan. Il Gesù became the model for Baroque churches built in the next two centuries.

Piazza at St. Peter's, Rome, by Giovanni Bernini (built 1656–1665)

Ornamentation

While Renaissance architecture is characterized by circles and straight lines, the Baroque was the era of ovals and undulating walls which alternated between concave and convex. Baroque buildings became ever more elaborately ornamented. Interiors were covered in paintings, and windows and doors were capped with complex shapes. Garlands, vases, urns, cartouches, and scrolling were used for decoration. Composite capitals and other variations on the ancient orders were used. Pilasters (columns partly attatched to walls) appeared on façades in great abundance, as did non-structural columns and herm pilasters. In order to appear more monumental, columns and pilasters were paired and often extended over two or more stories, forming what is called the colossal order. In order to maximize drama and grandeur, architects came to incorporate the spaces around buildings themselves in their designs. The manipulation of the surrounding environs was highly controlled. Shrubs and hedges were cut into cubic shapes, flowers were planted in geometric patterns, and the gardens and woodlands surrounding palaces were penetrated by straight rays of avenues. This total control molded the viewer's entire experience of the space.

Il Gesu, Rome by Giacomo Barozzi dadade Vignola 1568 - 1575

Church of St. Ivo della Sapienza, Rome (built 1642–1662)

INSIDER KNOWLEDGE

ANTIGUA GUATEMALA *has the most intact Baroque architecture in the Americas.*

THE BAROQUE STYLE *was particularly propagated by the Jesuits.*

see also: The Reformation, *Religion Chapter, p. 237*

THE LATE BAROQUE AND ROCOCO

During the late Baroque period of the 18th century, many local variations on the style developed, and European architecture became even more elaborate and decorative.

During the late Baroque period, the Baroque style spread far beyond the borders of Italy—not just across Europe, but across the Atlantic to the Americas.

France

Baroque architecture reached France through the work of Louis Le Vau, who designed a number of buildings using Italian architecture as inspiration. His works included Château Vaux-le-Vicompte and together with Jules Hardouin-Mansart, much of the Palace of Versailles. Versailles incorporates a distinctly French Renaissance element; the *cour d'honneur*, an open-fronted couryard for the receival of honored guests. The Palace's Hall of Mirrors exhibits the extremes of Baroque ornamentation.

Pilgrimage Church of Wies, Bavaria, by Dominicus Zimmermann (built 1744–1754)

The Palace of Versailles, France by Louis Le Vau and Jules H. Mansart (built 1661–1698)

The Architecture of Conquest

Baroque architecture developed as Spain and Portugal claimed continents, and Baroque was the first architectural style to be carried to be exported by European expansionism. The Churrigueresque style, characterized by the sumptuous sculptural decoration of walls, arose in Spain. Churrigueresque was influenced by the Spanish Renaissance, Moorish themes, and the indigenous decorative traditions of the recently conquered colonies in Latin America. The colonies themselves had their own architectural styles. Indigenous themes were incorporated into the elaborate decorations on church facades, which served to express European imperial power and impress the native peoples into piety.

The Church of the Convent of La Merced, Guatemala (built 1552)

The German Baroque

Only in the early 18th century, once the area had recovered from the devastation of the Thirty Years' War, did Baroque architecture begin to appear in Germany. It quickly became very elaborate in character, adopting opulent Rococo aesthetics. Bavaria in particular was traveled by many Italian artists, and some German towns adopted Baroque architectural elements and painted trompe l'oeil ornamentation. The ornate style flourished in Bavaria, Franconia, Dresden and Potsdam, but is rare in towns closely aligned with the Reformation.

England

Architecture in 18th century England was relatively restrained, and while much of Europe was building elaborate Baroque structures influenced by Rococo aesthetics, England was more inclined toward a pared-down version of Baroque which tended in the direction of classicism. Sir Christopher Wren's major architectural work, rebuilding of St. Paul's cathedral in London after the Great Fire of 1666, epitomizes the English Baroque. The dome of St. Paul's is a triple-shelled construction; an imposing high-arched dome on the outside, a shallower dome within, invisible and purely structural, and an even shallower dome situated on the inside, designed to suit the internal proportions of the building. The building as a whole is Baroque, but it retains a strong classical feel, and has a Greek-style temple facade.

Rococo

Rococo began in France with the end of the reign of Louis XIV. It was an extremely ornate form of the Baroque style, and replaced the dramatic grandeur and seriousness of the earlier years with a sense of playfulness. Pastel shades and flowing masses of decoration were added to walls and ceilings. Their curvaceous forms were composed of cherubs, leaves, flowers, and birds. The word Rococo derives from the French "Rocaille," referring to the loose water-worn shells and stones that were often featured.

above: *The Zwinger, Dresden, by M. Pöppelmann and B. Permoser (built 1709–1732)*

St. Paul's Catheral, London, by Sir Christpher Wren (built 1675–1710)

INSIDER KNOWLEDGE

ŒIL-DE-BOEUF *is the architectural term used to describe the oval-shaped window that appeared on buildings in the Baroque period.*

HERM PILASTERS *are attached columns which terminate with the upper body of a man.*

TROMPE L'ŒIL *is a technique of painting objects onto surfaces so realistically that it appears that they really are there.*

NEOCLASSICISM AND GEORGIAN STYLE

During the mid-1700s the Enlightenment backlash against politics and the neoclassical reaction against Baroque architecture manifested as many different styles.

The Enlightenment of the 18th century resumed the secular and democratic movement which had begun in the Renaissance. This change was reflected in the world of architecture.

The Capitol, Washington D.C. (built 1792–1827), was built in the "Federal style" of neoclassical architecture, which was used for many American public and government buildings. The original design was still unfinished when it was burnt down by the British in 1814.

Changes in Society

The 18th-century European monarchs and Church found themselves losing the absolute power which they had exercised during the Baroque period. This led architects to abandon the decorative excesses of Rococo and return to ancient Greek and Roman architecture, which had long been associated with secular, democratic ideas. Churches and palaces lost their significance to museums, libraries, theaters, banks, stock exchanges, and universities.

Excavations

Even during the height of the Baroque period, British Palladianism had never really ceased to be practiced, and classical architecture had also survived in France, to a degree. The 1700s saw Greek and Roman architecture become popular all over Europe, and in a far more authentic form than ever before. This was because architects were able to refer to the various archaeological excavations that had started to take place in the first half of the 1700s. The excavations also affected interior design. Prior to the 1700s, classicist designers had merely decorated building interiors with variations on exterior features, such as columns and temple facades. The excavations of Herculaneum (1738) and Pompeii (1748) allowed a more historically accurate style of interior decoration to develop, based on what was found at these sites.

Classicist interior of Syon House in London by Robert Adam (built 1762–1769)

Greek Revival

It had long been difficult for Europeans to see Greek architecture for themselves, as Greece was under Ottoman rule. In the mid-1700s English and French scholars managed to visit the ruins in Greece for themselves, and brought knowledge of what they had seen back to Europe, writing books such as "The Antiquities of Athens." In 1758, James Stuart, one of the authors of this book, went on to build the first Greek-style building in England, a Garden Temple at Hagley Hall.

Architecture in the U.S.

Neoclassical architecture was the civic architecture of the U.S. from very early on in the country's history. Thomas Jefferson himself was the architect of a number of buildings, including the first buildings of the University of Virginia, the Virginia State Capitol, and his own house "Monticello." Architecture of this type went on to become known as the "Federal style" of architecture, and was used to establish most early official buildings, associating the U.S. historically with the power of the Romans.

Revolution Architecture

In his 1755 work "Essai sur l'Architecture," the French abbot Laugier called for a more "honest" architecture to emphasize structure over decoration. Architect Claude-Nicolas Ledoux later wrote that buildings should employ an "architecture parlante" to communicate their function to viewers. French Revolution architecture was characterized by the use of massive geometric forms such as spheres, and a degree of grandeur so extreme that many designs were never attempted.

above: *Etienne-Louis Boullee's unbuilt design for a cenotaph for Isaac Newton. The sphere would have reached about 492 ft (150 m) in height and was to function as a planetarium.*

Théatre d'Anatomie, Paris: a late 1700s design by Jacques Gondoin

INSIDER KNOWLEDGE

KING FRANCIS I *of Naples found some of the art recovered from Pompeii, which had been buried when Mt. Vesuvius erupted, so explicit that he had it locked away. The collection was re-opened in 2000.*

HISTORICISM

European architects of the 1800s took their inspiration from a variety of styles—not just Roman and Greek, but also, Gothic, Romanesque, Renaissance, Chinese, and Indian.

The late 1700s and the 1800s were a time of great change in Europe, and particularly in Britain due to colonialism and the Industrial Revolution. The architecture of this time employed a wide variety of building styles drawn not just from the European past, but also from the traditions of countries which had been incorporated into the new British Empire.

A Hidden Revolution

By propagating the historic styles, Historicist buildings hid what were ultimately buildings enabled by industrial wealth and production techniques beneath facades of the past. During the 1800s in Britain, the growing class of industrialists wanted to imitate the architectural style of their former feudal masters and equate themselves with the kings and lords of the past. Industrial production meant that materials could be easily and cheaply produced, and expensive craftsmen were no longer needed. The factories, water works and power stations that allowed for this new prosperity and affordability, began to be hidden away, disguised as castles, town halls, and churches.

INSIDER KNOWLEDGE

HISTORICIST *themes varied from country to country. The French tended towards neo-Baroque, the English to neo-Gothic, and the Germans to neo-Byzantine and neo-Romanesque.*

Historicism

Historicist architecture, largely constructed in the 1800s, was not so much a single style, but an approach to architecture which looked to the past not just for inspiration, but as a source of styles to be directly imitated.

DURING THE 19TH CENTURY *European cities started to fill up with Egyptian obelisks and other souvenirs which European travellers brought back with them from the East.*

THERE WAS A FASHION *during the 1800s for tombs in the shape of Egyptian pyramids.*

The Woolworth Building, New York by Cass Gilbert: a Historicist skyscraper built 1910–1913

Exoticism and Eclecticism

EUROPEAN COLONIZATION resulted in the importation of foreign styles to Europe between 1750 and 1850. This led to the creation of buildings such as the Pagoda in Kew Gardens, built by William Chambers, who had spent some time in China studying the local architecture. Chambers's experience of China meant that his re-creation of a pagoda was relatively faithful to Chinese aesthetics, but many other architects had little real idea of the styles they were trying to imitate, and their creations were often informed as much by their imaginations as by real research.

SOME ARCHITECTS quite deliberately started to mix various architectural traditions. John Nash's Royal Pavillion in Brighton, England, is an eclectic mixture of Gothic towers, Moghul onion domes, and chinoiserie for internal decoration. Iron was used structurally, and the building exterior was covered with concrete.

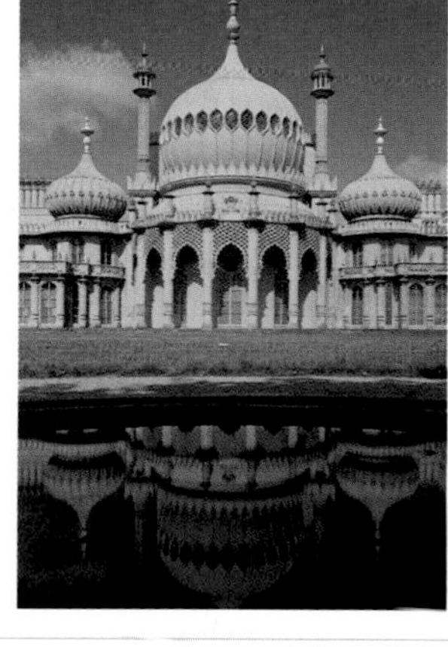

Royal Pavillon, Brighton, England (built in 1818 by John Nash)

Schloss Neuschwanstein

In the 1800s, the architecture of the Middle Ages was often reproduced in a romantic, nostagic form. King Ludwig II of Bavaria, comissioned the building of the dramatic neo-Romanesque castle of Neuschwanstein. It was designed by artist and set designer Christian Jank and inspired by Richard Wagner's operas. The building was the inspiration for Disneyland's Sleeping Beauty Castle in Florida.

above: *Schloss Neuschwanstein, Bavaria (built 1868–1886)*

The Gothic Revival

Historicism first arrived in England in the form of the Gothic Revival, which was a result of the Romantic interest in the middle ages. Once revived, the Gothic style went on to have great religious and national significance. It became the default style for the building of new churches, and when the competition was run for a design for the new British Houses of Parliament, the rules specified that the building had to be Gothic or Elizabethan in style. Typically, for Historicist building, the Houses of Parliament have a style borrowed from another age, but used in a manner quite different from that of the original (ecclesiastical) context. The structural iron columns and bars of the building are hidden from view.

Rewriting History

The wealth of the 1800s resulted in the completion of buildings which had, for various reasons, lain unfinished for centuries. Also, the restoration of various castles and churches became popular. Art historians were beginning to learn about the styles of the past during this time, but restorers were often over-zealous in their work, "correcting" stylistic inconsistencies in old buildings and destroying earlier alterations. It was during this period that the cathedrals of Cologne, Ulm, and Bern were completed. During this time new buildings were erected in imaginative versions of antique styles, such as the fantastical Schloss Neuschwanstein in Bavaria.

The Houses of Parliament, London (built 1836 to 1868)

KEY FACTS

THE INDUSTRIAL REVOLUTION *began in Britain with advances in the transportion technology and production, primarily enabled by the invention of the steam engine.*

INDUSTRIAL PRODUCTION *made new materials available to architects, enabling the creation of new kinds of buildings.*

INTERNATIONAL STYLE *is characterized by the abandonment of historical styles.*

Industrial architecture 1775–1900 | Early modernism 1900–1945 | Modernism and later styles 1945–present

ARCHITECTURE FROM INDUSTRIAL TIMES ONWARD

The industrial revolution not only enabled a new kind of architecture, but also demanded it. The exploding urban populations of new industrial centers, the destruction of the two World Wars, and the new structure of industrial and post-industrial society meant that only an industrial level of building could provide homes to the masses.

Since the industrial revolution new building materials and technologies have changed the face of architecture.

ARCHITECTURE OF THE INDUSTRIAL ERA

The industrial revolution made iron available in quantities which made it viable as a building material. The World Fairs of the Victorian era were a showcase the new possibilities.

The Crystal Palace, London

By 1775, industrial improvements in the techniques of iron production had reached the stage where it was financially possible to construct an entire bridge from cast iron parts over the River Severn in England. During the Historicist period which followed iron was increasingly used in the construction of buildings, but the new structural material was hidden behind facades.

The Crystal Palace

In 1851, iron as a building material burst onto the scene in the form of the Crystal Palace, built to house the Great Exhibition of that year. The designer, Joseph Paxton, was a head gardener, and had designed his first iron-framed glasshouse while working for the Duke of Devonshire. The Crystal Palace was the first building to be made entirely of pre-fabricated and standardized parts and consisted of a 111-ft (34-m) high iron framework filled in with glass panels. The building, which took only 17 weeks to erect, covered an area of 20.7 acres (8.4 hectares), and at the end of the exhibition, it was dismantled and re-erected in Sydenham, London.

Wainwright Building, St. Louis by Louis Sullivan, built in 1891.

Functional Buildings

While record-breaking buildings were being built for World Exhibitions, industrial architecture was also applied in the construction of everyday buildings of the industrial revolution such as railway sheds, bridges, factories, and department stores. These constructions were not considered to be proper architecture at the time. Instead, they were referred to as "functional buildings," and Historicist facades were often used to hide the structures of such buildings as St. Pancras Station in London.

Skyscrapers

In the 1870s in America, taller and taller city buildings were being built. The use of iron frameworks meant that tall buildings no longer required thick walls because the framework absorbed the weight of the structure. As skyscrapers became taller, there was a tendency to simplify their appearance into columns and bands of brick filled in with panes of glass. Tall buildings had been constructed before, most notably the cathedrals of medieval Europe, but what set skyscrapers apart was that they were used daily as living spaces and offices. The development of safe and effective elevator technology in the late 19th century was important for the skyscraper.

21ST CENTURY

WHILE THE EIFFEL TOWER *can still be seen today in Paris, the Crystal Palace was destroyed by fire in 1936, and the Galérie des Machines was dismantled in 1910.*

21ST CENTURY TECHNOLOGY *will continue the revolution in building materials and systems which began in the 1800s.*

SINCE *the late 20th and early 21st centuries, there has been a move away from the dogma of modernism to more eclectic approaches.*

The International Exposition

FOR THE INTERNATIONAL EXPOSITION OF 1889, which took place in Paris, the engineer Gustave Eiffel designed the Eiffel Tower, an iron structure which easily became the tallest building in the world, reaching a record-breaking height of 1,063 ft (324 m). Before 1889, the world's tallest man-made structure was the 558-ft (170-m) Washington Monument. This height was only exceeded in 1930, with the construction of the Chrysler Building. The other record breaker of the Paris Exhibition was the Galérie des Machines, a 383-ft (117-m) wide iron and glass hall, constructed in the form of a three-hinged arch.

Galérie des Machines, Paris built in 1889 by Charles Dutert and Victor Contamin

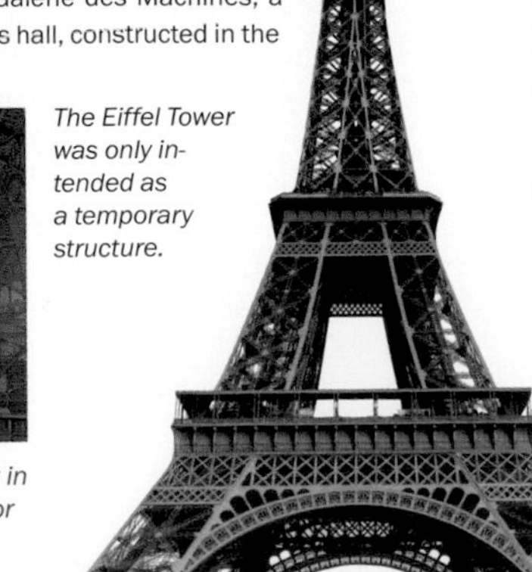

The Eiffel Tower was only intended as a temporary structure.

EARLY MODERN ARCHITECTURE

The 1900s witnessed architects exploring the new possibilities that were opened up by the industrial revolution. They no longer hid their creations behind historicized facades.

In the very late 1800s, designers and architects began to reject the historicism and eclecticism of the Victorian period and turned to other sources for inspiration.

Art Nouveau

Art nouveau drew much of its aesthetic from the natural world, and is characterized by stylized floral and plant-like forms. The architects of this time had decided that form should follow function, that decoration should be derived from structure, and that beauty arises when form and function coincide. Influenced by the Arts and Crafts movement, they sought a constructive human-centered relationship with new technology and believed that industrial production could be taken advantage of in order to bring art and beauty to the masses. There was much stylistic variation within the movement, from the curved, organic structures designed by Hector Guimard and Antoni Gaudí to the rectilinear work of Charles Rennie Mackintosh.

The Arrival of Modernism

In the early 1900s, the tide turned against decorative architecture. German architect Adolf Loos went so far as to declare that "ornament is a crime." In 1907, Peter Behrens was appointed artistic advisor to the German firm AEG, for whom he built the Turbine Factory, a monolithic structure of steel, glass, and reinforced concrete whose design followed the modernist ethos that form should follow functon. Around 1910, a number of designers came to study under him, including Ludwig Mies van der Rohe, Le Corbusier, and Walter Gropius. These three went on to become among the most influential architects of the 20th century.

The Avant-Garde

The avant-garde styles of the interwar years were not as widespread as Bauhaus, but their extreme forms have exerted a strong influence on 20th-century architecture. The Futurism of Fascist Italy and the Constructivism of Soviet Russia had much in common. They sought to create hyper-modern architecture which expressed the possibilities of the new industralized era in an arresting and aggressive mannner. Expressionist architecture, as pioneered by the German group "die Brücke," sought to find an expressive architectural language free of academic influences. The interest of Expressionist architecture comes not from surface decoration, but rather from the unusual forms of a building's structure.

International Style

International style, as practiced by Le Corbusier, Gropius, Mies van der Rohe, and, to an extent, Frank Lloyd Wright and was greatly influenced by Bauhaus. The style was characterized by flat roofed buildings standing on thin metal or concrete pillars, with ribbons of windows stretching horizontally across the entire facade, and the avoidance of decoration.

Art Deco

Art deco defined the architectural styles of skyscrapers in the 1920s and 1930s. The movement began with a number of French designers whose 1925 "Exposition Internationale des Arts Décoratifs et Industriels Modernes" first brought the style to a large audience. Art deco architecture took its inspiration from a great variety of sources, such as art nouveau, Bauhaus, Constructivism, modernism, and Futurism, as well as the architecture of the Aztecs and the ancient Egyptians.

above: *The Chrysler Building, New York City (built in 1929)*

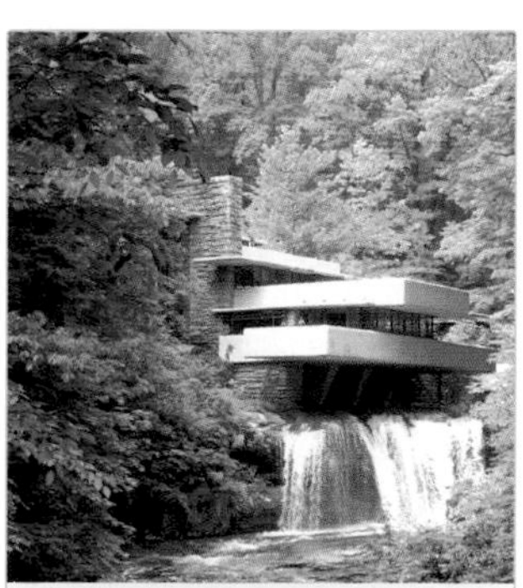

Fallingwater, Pennsylvania by Frank Lloyd Wright (built 1934)

THE NAZI REGIME *disapproved of Bauhaus and modernist architecture in general, although in Italy, modern architecture was very popular among the fascists at the time.*

WALTER GROPIUS'S *first wife was Alma Mahler, widow of the composer Gustav Mahler.*

Walter Gropius, 1920

Walter Gropius and Bauhaus

A STUDENT OF PETER BEHRENS, Walter Gropius founded the Bauhaus School in 1919 with the aim of creating an institution to combine art with advanced technology. The artists Wassily Kandinsky, Paul Klee, and Josef Albers were all teachers at the Bauhaus. Bauhaus architecture used glass, steel, and reinforced concrete to create buildings whose rectilinear apperance was influenced by the Dutch art movement De Stijl, and whose overall philosophy continued with the idea that form should follow function.

THE POLITICAL TENDENCIES of Gropius and others in the Bauhaus made them unpopular in the conservative town of Weimar and in 1924 the Bauhaus moved to Dessau, where Gropius designed the new premises. When the Nazis later took power the Gestapo closed the school and Gropius left Germany, first moving to Britain, and then to America.

The Bauhaus, Dessau by Walter Gropius (built 1925)

Entrance to the Paris Métro by Hector Guimard (built 1900)

➔ **see also: Walter Gropius and Bauhaus,** *Visual Arts Chapter, p. 310*

ARCHITECTURE

LATE MODERN AND POSTMODERN

The post-war period saw many of those architects who had established their reputations as modernists continue in their work, but by the 1960s a backlash had begun.

Modernism became the dominant building style after the war, but soon many came to question the universal use of functionalism and minimalism in modernist design.

The Modernists

After World War II, International Style, the branch of modernism which first came into being in the 1920s, became the dominant style used in the construction of large buildings. The functionalist philosophy articulated by the first modernists of achieving the maximum possible utility with the materials available created a relatively unified minimalist aesthetic, where added decoration was eschewed in favor of buildings whose beauty was intended to arise from their proportions and methods of construction. Modernists, such as Le Corbusier, no longer saw themselves as mere designers of buildings, but as shapers and improvers of society and in the wake of the war, architects were given the opportunity to be just this, as European governments sought to rebuild the shattered urban environment and provide affordable accomodation for all. While Le Corbusier was creating residential tower blocks in Europe, Ludwig Mies van der Rohe had immigrated to the U.S. and was designing the first steel and glass corporate skyscrapers. The Seagram building, New York, a monolithic skyscraper of bronze and glass, was built in between 1954 and 1958 and became the standard for corporate architecture for the next 30 years.

Le Corbusier's Unite d'Habitation, Marseilles (built 1946–1952)

R. R. Donnelly Center, Chicago, by Ricardo Bofill (built 1992)

Sydney Opera House by Jørn Utzon (built between 1957 and 1973)

After Modernism

By 1960, the limited palette of international style resulted in a new movement; the Postmodernists. The Postmodernists rejected the stylistic formulas of modernism for a more varied approach. During the following decades, decorative features and stylistic references returned to the built landscape. During the last decades of the 20th century, this movement away from modernism continued as certain architects also abandoned the idea of functionalism, regarding their buildings as more sculptural and expressive forms than anything else. Another development during the same period was that of High-Tech architecture, which retained a functionalist philosophy. High-Tech architects aim for a Futurist aesthetic, seeking to display the technology of their buildings as clearly as possible. The Centre Pompidou achieves this by putting structural supports, pipework, and escalators on the outside of the building. Yet another response to the standard aesthetic of modernism was critical regionalism which, though commited to the use of modern building techniques, seeks to bring a sense of place back to architecture, designing buildings which make use of local elements, both natural and cultural. The best known example of this approach is the Sydney Opera House, a building whose concrete structure echoes the shape of seashells and the waves which come up the harbor.

Centre Pompidou, Paris, by Richard Rogers and Renzo Piano (built between 1972 and 1976)

Postmodernist Architecture

THE THEORETICAL FOUNDATIONS of postmodernism were laid in 1966 with the publication of "Complexity and Contradiction in Architecture" by Robert Venturi. The Postmodernists, tired of the limited designs offered by the then prevalent international style, started to design buildings which quite deliberately went against internationalism.

BRINGING DECORATION and historical and cultural references back into their buildings, the philosophy of Postmodernist architects was succinctly summarized by Venturi, who stated, in postmodern contradiction to Mies van der Rohe's famous maxim "less is more" that, rather, "less is a bore."

above: *The Portland Building, Portland, Oregon, by Michael Graves (built 1980)*

left: *The Humboldt Library, Berlin, by Charles Moore (built 1988)*

➔ see also: **Postmodernist Art**, *Visual Arts Chapter, p. 313*

THE 20TH CENTURY

The 20th century was a time of great architectural innovation, and the 21st is set to prove yet more spectacular, as new materials and new needs inform the way we build.

The 21st century has already seen its first record-breaking skyscraper, and its successor is already under construction. The 21st century promises a wealth of surprising and exciting developments in the world of architecture.

Information Technology

A major development in architecture in the 1990s was the use of computers in designing buildings. The complex curves of the Guggenheim Museum, Bilbao, were planned out using CATIA software, which was originally developed for designing aircraft. The late 20th and early 21st century deconstructivist style, where buildings are given the spectacular appearance of having been thrown together or of being in the process of collapse, was greatly assisted by computer software, and the 21st century will continue to see the impact of information technology on the evolution of architectural forms.

Frank Gehry's titanium-covered Guggenheim Museum in Bilbao (built in 1997)

Ever Higher

International competition to build the world's tallest building continues. Taipei 101, completed in 2003, is 1,474 ft (448 m) tall, but the not yet completed Burj Dubai, in the United Arab Emirates, will soon exceed this, reaching a final height of around 2,625 ft (800 m). Another building in Dubai, currently in its planning stage, is set to reach over a mile in height—more than three times the height of Taipei 101.

New Shapes

Recent architecture has tended to move ever further from the forms of 20th century modernism. Deconstructivist architecture is one expression of this tendency. Another expression comes in the work of Santiago Calatrava, who combines studies of natural forms with his training as an engineer to produce buildings with organic, insect-like, skeletal forms. In contrast, the skewed rectangular forms of Beijing's CCTV building, designed by the Office of Metropolitan Architecture, appear to defy gravity, forming a giant crystalline loop. The pattern of girders on the outside of the building reflects the distribution of forces within the structure.

Computer model of China Central Television Headquaters, Beijing, by Rem Koolhaas and Ole Scheeren (completed in 2008).

Energy Efficiency

Environmental concerns, economic incentives and the availability of relevant technologies such as solar panels and control systems for vents and windows have recently led many architects to design their buildings with reduced energy consumption. 30 St Mary's Axe, London, also known as "The Gherkin" (completed 2004) was designed by Foster and Partners so that the airflow within the building can be controlled in order to maintain a comfortable temperature without always having to use air conditioning.

New Technologies

The explosion in architectural creativity during and after the industrial revolution resulted from the new abiliy to make iron, glass, and concrete cheaply and in bulk. As these same trends of technological development continue, the 21st century will witness the creation of buildings which take advantage of these new possibilities. The improved strength and resilience of structures built with new materials and technologies, such as ultra-strong glass, carbon fiber, and new plastics means that today's architects are in a constant process of making the impossible possible.

see also: Skyscrapers, *Physics and Technology Chapter, p. 128*

Sustainable Architecture

A growing awareness of environmental issues in the 20th century has led many architects to try to address these concerns in their designs for buildings. The California Academy of Science, scheduled for completion in 2008, exemplifies this. The roof of the building will be planted with 2.5 acres of native plant species, while its perimeter will consist of an array of photovoltaic cells. The windows of the building can all be opened by hand (an unusual feature in large modern buildings) and the building has been laid out to maximize penetration of natural light to working areas.

above: *Computer model of the new California Academy of Science in San Francisco by Renzo Piano*

Part of the Ciutat de les Arts i de les Ciencies, Valencia, Spain, by Santiago Calatrava (built in 1996)

21ST CENTURY

THE MILLAU VIADUCT *The Millau Viaduct, designed by Norman Foster, has piers which are taller than the Eiffel Tower.*

THE LARGEST GREENHOUSE *at the Eden project, in Cornwall, England, is big enough to accommodate the Tower of London. It was designed by Nicholas Grimshaw.*

Monographic Boxes

Analytic Boxes

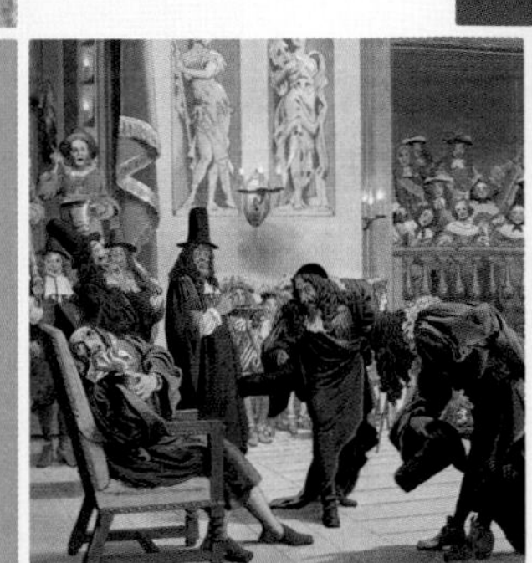

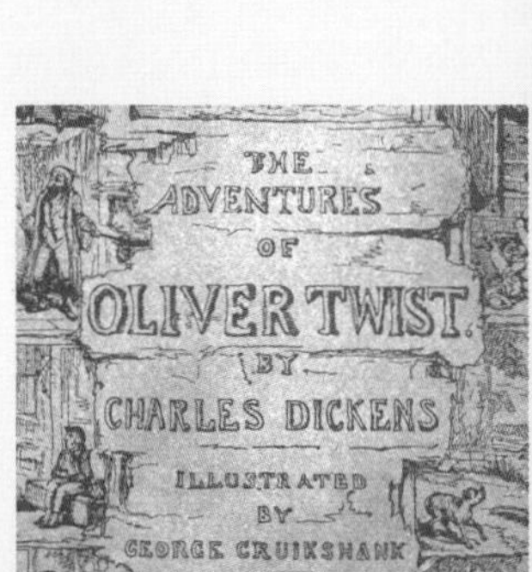

LITERATURE

Literature is seductive. From nothing more than words arranged on a page the mind of the reader can be transported into new worlds, by turns fantastic, ludicrous, stark, haunting, poetic, or gritty. The aims of the author can range from simple entertainment and striking thrills to didactic instruction or mind-bending prose. Literature's cardinal tool, language, allows for such an array of direct meanings and ambiguities that the reading of a work always involves a complex dynamic between what the author intended and what the minds of the various readers interpret. It is this dynamic that ensures that from reader to reader or even from reading to reading a novel or poem can "say" or "mean" entirely different, fresh, and interesting things.

KEY FACTS

HOMER'S EPICS *are considered to be the oldest literary work of antiquity.*

THEATER *played a central role in Greece.*

THE ROMANS *found all important genres present in Greek literature.*

CICERO *made Latin the language of literature.*

THE APEX *of Latin literature was about the time of the birth of Christ.*

From myth to art | Golden times

CLASSICAL ANTIQUITY—ARCHETYPE AND ORIENTATION

The written recording of the Greek mythology made possible the development of a rich literary tradition. The emergence of multiple genres in ancient Greece testifies to the Greeks' intense preoccupation with literature. The Romans inherited this tradition and developed it even further. Today, authors continue to orient themselves on the ancient literature.

➔ *Literature was the basis of ancient culture.*

LITERATURE

FROM MYTH TO ART

In Greece, mythical tales were passed down through the generations, just as in previous cultures. The "Iliad" and the "Odyssey" from 800 B.C. are considered the oldest literary works of the Western world. They initiated a literary movement in which tragedy played a starring role.

The Greek theater was constructed so that one could hear and see everything from all places.

The oldest literary texts of Greek antiquity are epics, which are attributed to the Greek Homer. Although they are known to us as preserved in written form, it is assumed that before they were recorded in script, the stories had a long history of oral recitation and singing. Two major themes are at the center of these epics: the battle over Troy and the travels of the hero Odysseus.

Troy and a Hard Homecoming

Troy was a commercial city located at the entrance of the Black Sea in the region of present-day Turkey. The epic "Iliad" describes the ten-year siege of the city by the Greeks during a war triggered by the abduction of the beautiful Helen, wife of the Greek Menelaus, by Prince Paris of Troy. Cruel battles, primarily between the heroes Achilles and Prince Hector of Troy, permeate the action. As is typical with most Greek literature, the gods watched the action from Mount Olympus and arbitrarily intervened. The epic concludes with the devastating fall of Troy, the end of the war, and the deaths of both Achilles and Hector. As Homer only described the last 51 days of the siege of Troy in the "Iliad," he allows the entire process of the conflict, its causes and consequences, to flow along with the action.

One of the most famous episodes of the "Iliad" is the "Cunning of Odysseus." In it, Odysseus suggests that the Greek soldiers hide inside a wooden horse and be smuggled behind the walls of Troy. The plan was successful and subsequently decided the war. It was perhaps because of this that Odysseus became the hero of the second epic, in which he returns from Troy to his home in Ithaca. While his wife Penelope awaits and is pursued by other men, Odysseus must overcome numerous dangers on his way back. When he finally arrives home, he kills the unsolicited guests.

The Greek Tragedy

Theater had a special significance in Greek literature (p. 337), primarily the great tragedy. The works of the Great Three—Aeschylus, Sophocles, and Euripides—are today considered masterpieces of the genre. Aeschylus is believed to be its founder, while his followers continued to make improvements. The theory of poetics, not only of tragedy, was later developed by Aristotle (p. 337). Almost always, tragedy arises when an individual acts against the gods. The heroes are always extraordinary, making their misery even more frightening.

BORN *possibly 800 B.C. in Smyrna, present-day Izmir in Turkey.*

HOMER *was already considered an exceptional poet in antiquity.*

HIS EPICS *formed the base for the entire Greek concept of humanity and the gods.*

There is no contemporary depiction of Homer. All the portraits, like this one from 200 B.C., are idealized.

Homer

THERE IS SO LITTLE KNOWN about Homer that even his existence is doubted. It is assumed that he was born into an aristocratic family during the eighth century B.C. and lived on the island of Chios.

IT IS ALSO UNCLEAR whether Homer himself authored the "Odyssey" and "Iliad," or if he had his students write parts, or even all, of the "Iliad." Continuously, other works have been attributed to Homer. Whether they are his or not, works attributed to Homer have had a large effect on Greek literature, for which they were considered the archetype. Homer's epics were sources of instruction for children because they were taught to read from his lyrics.

Odysseus sails past the two sirens, Scylla and Charybdis, who attempt to corrupt him with their singing (mosaic from Dougga, mid-third century A.D.).

GOLDEN TIMES

Within Greek literature, the Romans found texts of the highest order. However, the Romans also produced classical authors of world literature.

It is no wonder that the first Roman poet was actually a Greek. Lucius Livius Andronicus was a Greek slave who translated works from his homeland for the Romans. Among these works were a Greek tragedy and a comedy, which were performed on stage in 240 B.C. as well as the "Odyssey" epic. However, the actual founder of Roman literature was Quintus Ennius from Calabria born in 239 B.C. He authored the "Annals" epic on Roman history, thus providing the Romans with their "Iliad." This epic was considered the national epic for two hundred years until between 30 and 19 B.C. when Virgil wrote the "Aeneid," which became the undisputed model for all epic poetry. Both Roman epics, by Ennius and Virgil, details the founding of Rome by the Trojan hero Aeneas after fleeing destroyed Troy.

One of Ovid's tales of metamorphosis was the transformation of Zeus into an ox to seduce the beautiful Europa.

"What Times!"

Virgil wrote poetry during a time of cultural bloom in Rome under the rule of Emperor Augustus. Sometime earlier in the epoch between the republic and the empire, the lawyer and politician Marcus Tullius Cicero made Latin a language comparible to Greek with his speeches, letters, and philosophical writings. His appearances in court or in the Roman senate are legendary while his rhetorical teachings are still discussed today. His texts are full of principles and mottos, the most famous of them being "*O tempora, o mores!*" ("What times! What customs!"). This period of supposed decay was the subject of many satires—poems, which polemically criticized society and politics.

In his masterwork "Germania" (ca 98 A.D.), Tacitus described the decisive enemies of the Romans: the Germanic tribes.

Subjective Sentiment

Even lyrics reached its zenith during the first century B.C. Catullus, born 84 B.C. in Verona, died when he was just 30 years old. He was especially known for the love song Lesbia, which was inspired by the Greek poetess Sappho. Catullus belonged to a literary movement whose members sought to establish a modern, subjective form of poetry that expressed one's feelings, the Neoterics. The diversification of lyrics into different forms like love elegies, odes, and epigrams began with Catullus. Horace, considered the master of odes, achieved huge success during the Middle Ages and within humanism, but not within his own lifetime.

Literature in the Emperor's Court

Under Emperor Augustus, literature became an affair of his court and under his authority. Augustus, during whose rule Christ was born, primarily supported writers who praised his fame and glorified Rome, just like Virgil, who was mentioned before. He sent dissentors into exile, including Ovid in 8 A.D. Ovid penned love poems and the popular "Metamorphoses," a summary of numerous transformation myths. After the golden period under Augustus, the Roman Empire gradually began to disintegrate. During this time, one of the most important historians of antiquity, Tacitus, composed works such as "Histories" and "Germania." He wrote in a style of his own, demonstrating an exquisite skill in written Latin.

The Greek Theater

THE BASIC CONSTRUCTION OF ALL GREEK THEATERS is fairly similar. At the center of the "theatron" (the area where the spectators sat) was a semi-circlular space where the orchestra and the choir would enact the drama. Like today, there were better seats (made of stone) placed in the front and inferior ones (wooden without backrests) placed in the back, sometimes way up high. Scaffolding, the proscenium, was 26.2 ft (8 m) wide and 9.8 ft (3 m) deep, while stairs would lead to the orchestra.

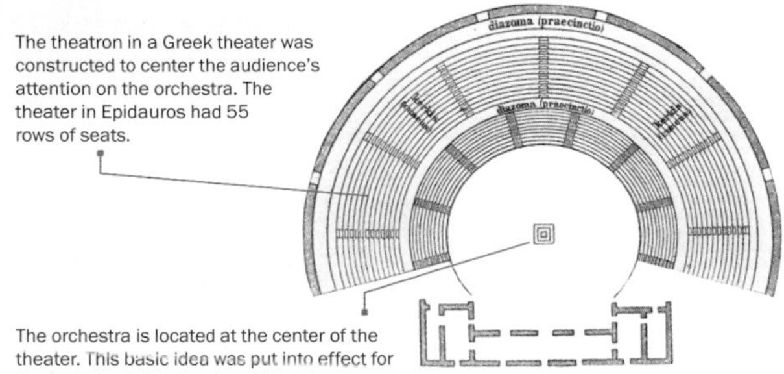

The theatron in a Greek theater was constructed to center the audience's attention on the orchestra. The theater in Epidauros had 55 rows of seats.

The orchestra is located at the center of the theater. This basic idea was put into effect for the first time in the theater of Megalopolis (around 370 B.C.).

The Poetics of Aristotle

The philosopher Aristotle concentrated on poetry, drama, and their genres in his "Poetics." He asserted that all poetry was based on imitation (mimesis), i.e., it had to be in some way realistic and convincing. In order to have an effect, the action must be visible and complete in itself. Furthermore, the reader should be able to identify with the hero. When the character is in an unhappy situation, the reader will be overwhelmed by feelings of compassion and fear, followed by a feeling of relief, which will thus invigorate their emotions (catharsis).

above: *Aristotle (384–322 B.C.)*

INSIDER KNOWLEDGE

THE "ILIAD" *contains 24 books and 16,000 verses while the "Odyssey" has 24 books and 12,000 verses.*

HOMER *wrote his epics in an artistic language that nobody ever spoke.*

VIRGIL *decreed that the "Aeneid" should be destroyed after his death, but this was prevented by Augustus.*

ANCIENT GREEK THEATERS *offered enough space to hold up to 15,000 spectators.*

➔ **see also: Aristotle,** *Philosophy Chapter, p. 248*

KEY FACTS

SONGS PRAISING HEROES *reflect the events of the great migrations.*

THE MOST IMPORTANT GENRES *during the Middle Ages were the courtly novel and lyrical love poetry.*

THE COURT AND THE CHURCH *formed the divergent literary centers of the Middle Ages.*

NON-EUROPEAN LITERATURE *gained prominence with the emergence of great masterpieces.*

Songs in praise of heroes | From adventures to love songs | The court, state, and monastery | East Asia, Persia, and Arabia

THE MIDDLE AGES—BELIEF, LOVE, AND HEROISM

The period between the fifth and the 15th centuries was decisive for the development of national vernaculars. Both inside and outside of Europe, texts of the highest quality were compiled in the prevalent languages of the era. Works such as heroic narratives and aesthetic lyrical poetry arose and dominated literature. Technical advancements saw the development of the printing press.

Versed novels and love songs dominate medieval literature.

SONGS IN PRAISE OF HEROES

Songs about the deeds of great heroes were an important facet of literature during the European Middle Ages. The rendering of such songs was so popular that it soon developed as a new way to earn a living. Poets called skalds and singers entertained the public, especially during festivals.

The migrations of Germanic tribes in the fourth century brought the Roman Empire into a state of crisis. The great empire's fate was sealed when the Germanic tribe leader Odoacer deposed the Western Roman emperor in 476. This marked the beginning of a chaotic and violent new era in Europe. Migrating tribes continued their search for settlement areas and a few of them, such as the Burgundians, even perished in their efforts. The heroic tales of this period were kept alive through verbal transmission and narratives within the respective local vernacular. In order to preserve these songs for posterity, they were eventually recorded in written format in later periods.

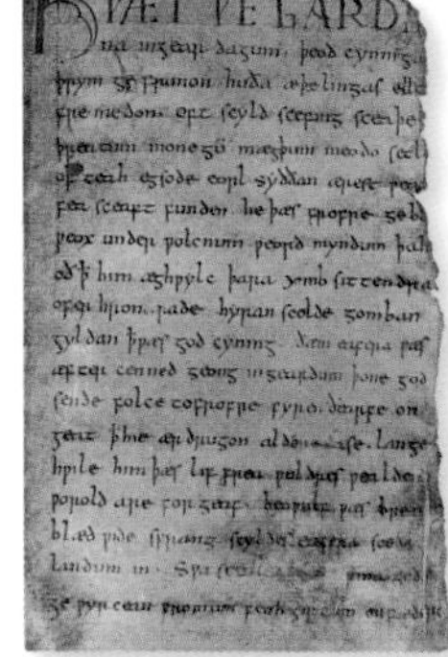

The oldest surviving manuscript of the "Beowulf" epic originated in about 1000.

Scene from the "Prose Edda" in which Thor fights with the Midgard Serpent (painting from 1788)

Battling Monsters and Dragons

The oldest European record of heroic poetry is presumed to be the epic "Beowulf," which details the adventures of an Anglo-Saxon of the same name. It is believed that this epic was compiled in the eighth century by a monk who was inspired by Virgil's "Aeneid" (p. 337). It details two of Beowulf's greatest deeds at the beginning and at the end of his life. First, the young Beowulf saves the Danish King Hrothgar and his mother from the clutches of a man-eating monster named Grendel. Then 50 years later, he fights a dragon, but is killed in the process and is given a hero's burial.

The Eddas and the Skalds

Narratives and songs detailing heroic deeds during the migration period thrived across all of Europe, such as the tales of the knight Roland who, while in the service of Charlemagne, fought against the Saracens. In fact, a few stories spread all the way to Iceland between the eighth and the 12th centuries. Here, they were recorded in Old Icelandic script, along with collections of songs chronicling Nordic gods, within the poem collection of the "Poetic Edda." The Eddas provided a rich souce of inspiration for artists. The stories were spread and passed through generations all across Iceland and Norway. During the Viking era (ninth–11th century), the *skalds* (Scandinavian and Icelandic poets) were encouraged to present their songs in the princely courts. A few of them were in fact stars in their own right, with biographies written about their lives and work. Their heritage was further preserved by Snorri Sturluson's "Prose Edda" (1220–1230): a textbook of skaldic poetry.

The Nibelung Tradition

The stories surrounding the defeat of the Burgundians were the focal point of approximately 1,200 Middle High German Nibelung songs. The 35 manuscripts dating between the 13th and 16th centuries bear witness to the saga's popularity. Siegfried, the dragon-slayer, is caught in an ambush while visiting the court of Worms and is killed by Hagen. His wife Kriemhild learns that his brother Gunther played a role in Siegfried's murder. She takes revenge on him years later with her remarriage to Attila the Hun. She invites the Burgundians to her court to take part in the celebrations, where they subsequently face a gruesome death.

above: *Siegfried bidding farewell to Kriemhild prior to his murder*

Setting up of the tent and departure of knights: A scene from the "Song of Roland," an French epic poem (between 1075 and 1110)

see also: Music of the Middle Ages, *Music Chapter, pp. 362–363*

FROM ADVENTURES TO LOVE SONGS

The royal courts were the centers of medieval literature. It was here that the noble minnesingers, traveling musicians, and professional poets presented their works to the public.

The emergence of a courtly culture within the royal courts changed the face of literature. Epics about the lives and deeds of heroes came to be challenged by courtly epics—verse novels about chivalrous adventures. The poets obviously authored their works while keeping the ideals of their patrons in mind, manipulating the accounts of the heroes. At this time, France became a cradle of literary innovation.

The Courtly Novel

One of the most successful court novels of this period was "Tristan" by Thomas d'Angleterre. The story entails Tristan's journey to Ireland to pick up the Irish princess Isolde and bring her back to marry his uncle, the English King Mark. During the return journey, Tristan and Isolde mistakenly drink a love potion that was originally meant for Mark and Isolde. Bound in eternal love, Tristan and Isolde manage to hide their love affair from the unsuspecting Mark until eventually caught together in an intimate moment. Disclosing themselves, they are forced to break apart and flee. A new literary development observable in "Tristan" was the increasing interest in the thoughts and feelings of the characters. Contrary to the Anglo-Saxon Beowulf, Tristan was not a hero without flaws; instead his temperament changes as he laments, deliberates, and finally decides on his course of action.

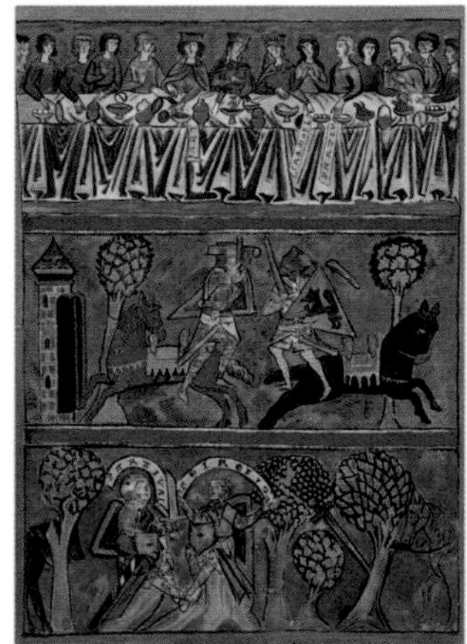

Scenes from the "Parzival" by Wolfram von Eschenbach: Parzival with Arthur; in a duel with Feirefiz; realizing he has a half-brother.

Arthur's World of Chivalry

The movement toward characterization is even more apparent in the epics surrounding the legendary court of King Arthur. These literary works demonstrate the medieval ideals of chivalry, which valued courage in war, service to God, and compassion. The featured hero of the epics would face a series of adventures in order to be deemed acceptable to be a member of the Round Table. Hence, the knights sought honor through their adventures so as to be worthy, as with Percival and his quest for the Holy Grail. In a tale filled with saving damsels in distress, savage battles between knights, and quests to capture relics and objects of special significance, Percival defeats the naivety of his youth and becomes a king.

Chaucer

The most renowned poet to have written in Middle English is Geoffrey Chaucer. He was born some time between 1340 and 1344 and died in 1400 under circumstances that have led to speculation that he was murdered. Alongside his work as a poet and author he held many bureaucratic and even parliamentary positions. Thus, he was intricately bound to society of his time. His most famous work, "The Canterbury Tales," describes a socially mixed group of pilgrims on their way to Canterbury and frames the tales they tell to keep themselves occupied. It is a mixture of cutting satire, bawdy comedy, poetry, and well-observed characters.

Numerous epics dealt with the British King Arthur and his legendary knights of the Round Table (here in a miniature from the 15th century).

MIDDLE HIGH GERMAN MINNESANG *from ca 1150*

IMPORTANT POETS: *Walther von der Vogelweide, Friedrich von Hausen, and Heinrich von Morungen*

"I WILL ALWAYS RUSH TO THE PERSON I LOVE/ *Indeed the destination of my hope is nowhere near,/but I strive everyday for its attainment."*
—Reinmar von Hagenau

Text and notes to a song from the Late Middle Ages by the poet Oswald von Wolkenstein

Minnesingers and Troubadours

WHILE ANCIENT HEROIC EPICS were mostly passed on anonymously, the troubadour poets (known as "trouvères" in France) of chivalric works, as well as the "minnesingers" of the German-speaking region, were anything but humble. The theme of the minnesingers was a special kind of courtly love, or "minne" in Middle High German, whereas the troubadours focused on knightly or chivalric deeds. The two groups had much common, however, as courtly love was an ideal of chivalry in its own right as knights would rescue "damsels in distress" or court their favor as part of their duties. The concept of romantic love did exist, but its poetic description mostly worked within this framework.

WALTHER VON DER VOGELWEIDE revolutionized this genre after it had reached its peak under the court poet Reinmar von Hagenau (ca 1200). Vogelweide propagated reciprocal love ("true love of the heart") in his songs. This concept became the central theme of the minnesang style and remained as such until the end of the 15th century. The French Chrétien de Troyes, who wrote of the Percival legend, and William IX, the Duke of Aquitaine, are also important to the genre.

High Middle German minnesinger Heinrich von Veldeke, illumination in Codex Manesse

THE COURT, STATE, AND MONASTERY

During the Middle Ages, literature made a place within the royal courts, and later transcended to the cities. The monasteries preserved this cultural heritage in their libraries.

Even rulers like Emperor Frederick II emerged as prominent poets or minnesingers.

During the Middle Ages, literature was a matter of the court and was often recorded in the chronicles of rulers as poets. This was the method of many compilations like the Codex Manesse of Heidelberg from the 14th century, which contains songs of the Holy Roman Emperor Henry VI, among others. The Hohenstaufen Frederick II (1194–1250) collected a group of poets, the "Sicilian School," at his court in Palermo. He composed five poems and a book about the tradition of falconry. His sons Enzio and Manfred were also a part of the circle of poets at his court, along with the king of Jerusalem. Most of the other members were lawyers. Their lyrics were propagated across the European continent.

Universities were established in many cities during the late Middle Ages (depicted here: A theological reading at the Sorbonne in Paris).

Cities—New Cultural Centers

Cities began to develop as important centers of power in the 11th century. With this, there was also a growing interest in literature and culture. After the decline of the Hohenstaufens, the central and northern Italian cities of Bologna and Florence emerged as strongholds of literary production. Frederick's son Enzio, who was in Bologna under "knightly detention," brought the students of the University of Bologna (established 1119) the poetic style coined by the Sicilian School. The many Tuscans studying there had, in addition to their legal education, also brought their knowledge of poetic composition from their homeland of Florence. This marked the beginning of the *Dolce Stil Nuovo* (Italian: "Sweet New Style"), which came to influence works of authors such as Dante Alighieri. The cities already had a stimulating literary atmosphere, which was accelerated further by the establishment of various universities all across Europe from the 12th century.

Safeguards of Knowledge

Prior to the establishment of universities, the monasteries were the sole custodians of education and knowledge. The transcription of manuscripts by the monks resulted in the first libraries. Through their efforts, important texts were saved from the threat of extinction—transposition was later simplified by the printing press. In their various works, monks such as Notker of St. Gall (ninth century) or St. Francis of Assisi (13th century) have continuously displayed their talents. The mystical works of Meister Eckhart and Mechthild of Magdeburg are particularly famous (13th century).

Latin—Popular Vernacular

Around 1224, Francis of Assisi wrote the "Canticle of the Sun," a 33-verse piece in praise of the Lord. He composed it in a language, that today is classified as far from Latin, so that this poem is commonly seen as the "foundation of the Italian language." Hence, Italian broke apart from Latin much later than the other popular vernaculars emerging in Europe, which had already developed in the eighth century through biblical translations. Overall, Latin was fostered as the language of the educated and elite.

"St. Francis of Assisi Preaching to the Birds" (fresco by Giotto di Bondone)

The Printing Press

Gutenberg's printing press was constituted of massive wooden beams and a moving spindle. Its inspiration was the wine and paper press of that era.

The ideal composition for the movable type was a mixture of tin, lead, antimony, and bismuth. This type did not harm the paper and could easily be smelted for future reuse.

In order to facilitate an exact print, the paper was affixed to a platform and pushed through the printing plate.

The first printed edition of a book by Gutenberg was presumably a book on Latin grammar by Aelius Donatus.

THE INVENTION OF THE printing press by Johannes Gutenberg of Mainz around 1450 had an enormous impact on the entire culture of knowledge. Texts no longer had to be tediously recorded by hand, but rather could be printed in batches by movable type for quicker and larger distribution. Prior to this moveable type, the printing plate was in common use; however, every new print page required tedious carving of a wooden block, on which the paper would later be placed. With Gutenberg's invention, various single type pieces of characters were made from lead that could be used for printing in various combinations. With the rationale of the printing process, new professions emerged such as printer, type founder, publisher, and bookseller.

EAST ASIA, PERSIA, AND ARABIA

The narratives and poems of the Asian, Persian, and Arabian regions offer insight into an abundance of matters and motives in styles that have been present since their very inception.

The fable of the gazelle, the raven, the tortoise, and the mouse; miniature from the "Kalila Wa Dimna."

While the Roman Empire disintegrated in Europe, another type of world literature emerged in the courts of the Indian kings, a form of Buddhist literature. Dramas and fables were especially popular. The collection of narratives in the form of the "Panchatantra" (the five chapters) has more than 200 versions and has been translated into more than 50 languages. The five chapters have been assigned to five subjects: controversy with friends, winning friends, war and peace, loss, and hasty conduct. All the narratives impart wisdom, often through animal fables, and serve as an educational guide for adolescent princes.

Heike Monogatari

Between 1190 and 1220, a war narrative emerged in Japan entitled "Heike Monogatari." The tale consisting of 12 volumes portrays the samurai clan Taira, which is headed by Kiymori (1118–1181), and their defeat by the Minamoto family clan in 1185. The story has a special place in the tradition of the Japanese Monogatari epics, which were recited by traveling monks. The experiences of the Taira family were recorded along with other stories in 1371.

above: *"Minamoto No Yoshitsune," the ideal knight*

China as an Inspiration

The Tang dynasty (618–907) is considered to be the literary peak of Chinese literature, especially its poetry. The poet Li Bai established a cultic status during his time and continues to be considered as the master of poetic art to date. Simultaneously, a genre of visionary novels also emerged that portrayed the expanse of the Chinese narrative tradition. Their characters step into dream worlds and meet with the spiritual beings. The Chinese literature of the Middle Ages provided an impulse for literary developments in neighboring countries.

The Chinese poetic master, Li Bai (Woodcut)

HAFIZ, *born 1320 in Shiraz and died there 1390.*

ORIGINALLY HE *was known as Shams al-Din Muhammad.*

HAFIZ IS ACTUALLY *the Arabic honorary title for a person who has mastered the Qur'an.*

MOST IMPORTANT PERSIAN POETS: *Jami, Firdausi, Hafiz, Nizami, and Rumi*

Hafiz in a bar (wood engraving from 1880)

Hafiz and Persian Literature

THE PERSIAN POET HAFIZ from Shiraz won everlasting fame with his collection of poems, the "Diwan." Today he is considered to be the greatest Persian poet and has inspired authors like Goethe ("West-östlicher Diwan"). It is believed that he received religious education and then worked as a baker. He later gave up this occupation to become a court poet and Qur'an scholar.

The "Diwan" contains approximately 500 poems. Ultimately, they deal consistently with topics such as friendship, love, nature, and wine. Nevertheless, all the poems with their mystical language are directed toward a connection with God.

Even before Hafiz, literature existed in the Persian region, especially focused on hero sagas and love poetry. The hero chronicles were compiled by Firdausi (940–1020) in the "Book of Kings" (Shah Namah).

One of the most important Persian works is the "Shah Namah" (Book of Kings) by Firdausi, completed in 1014 (manuscript illumination, 1567).

Japan: Poems and Novels

As was the case in Europe and China, poetry established itself within the courts of Japan. One important genre was "renga," a linked verse poem. The "Pillow Book" by Sei Shonagon, a lady of the empress' court, acts as a narrative about the daily life of the court around 1000. The first Japanese novel was also written during this time, also by a woman. In it, Murasaki Shikibu, another lady of the empress' court, details the saga of Prince Genji ("Genji Monogatari").

Arabic Literature

The most important form of literature from the classical Arabic era was lyrical poetry. Poets composed works of praise as well as satire, and were engaged in stiff competition with each other. However, love poems were also common—the *ghazals*. A popular subject was the unlucky love between Layla and Majnun, which is comparable to Romeo and Juliet in Arabic. Undoubtedly, the pinnacle of Arabic lyricism is the rhyming prose of the Qur'an.

Works about heroes also were propagated by the Persians. A prominent example are the "Makamat" (literary assemblies) by al-Hariri of Basra (1054–1122), which describe the adventures of the clever Abu Zaid. Still popular today are the Indian animal fables of "Kalila wa Dimna," which were adapted by eighth century Arabic writers.

21ST CENTURY

ARABIC LITERATURE *continues to draw influence today from the lyrics and recitations of the Qur'an.*

THE SHAH NAMAH *is the Iranian national epic.*

THE JAPANESE SCRIPT SYSTEM *was established during the Middle Ages.*

KEY FACTS

THE RENAISSANCE *sought to refer back to the time of antiquity and its academic pratices.*

SOCIAL AGITATION *in the Early Modern period facilitated a high cultural phase.*

ITALY AND ENGLAND *were the leading cultural nations of the Renaissance.*

ART FLOURISHED *in the Baroque courts; death was a frequent motif in literature.*

Renaissance: rebirth of antiquity (1400–1600) | The Baroque: suffering and delight (1600–1720)

EARLY MODERNITY—REFORM AND OPULENCE

The Early Modern period was a time full of contrasts, which facilitated rich literature. The ascent of the middle class, the power of courts, Reformation, and many wars inspired a plethora of texts in which the contemporary intellectual and social developments were reflected upon by authors. All the genres were equally represented and important.

The Early Modern period was a time of Baroque abundance and political insecurity.

LITERATURE

REBIRTH OF ANTIQUITY

During the Early Modern period, a cultural boom occurred that oriented itself to the spirit of classical antiquity. Literary masterpieces emerged in Italy and England.

With the development of cities in northern Italy, not only were educational establishments like universities formed, but also trading companies. During the 12th and 13th centuries, economic markets expanded in such a way that Italy was doing business with the entire known world. Previously locked to their social station, commoners now had the opportunity to gain wealth and influence. These increasing social dynamics resulted in the general upswing of reform movements, which, evident in Italy as early as the 13th century, became noticeable throughout the rest of Europe in the 14th or 15th century. The stage was set for a high cultural period: the Renaissance.

The "Decamerone" by Boccaccio (above: first page) became the framework for the novella.

Rebirth of Antiquity

During the Middle Ages, there was almost no intellectual debate regarding classical ideas of antiquity, as discourse in Christian Europe was focused on theology. However, no one had actually broken with ancient scholarship, it was just perceived as irrelevant. Only with the advent of modernity was antiquity acknowledged as a closed epoch that had to be revived. Thus, this period was termed in the 19th century the "Renaissance" (from French: "rebirth"). The rising circles of authors and scholars saw themselves as representatives of classical scholarship and its development: the "humanists."

Crowns of Literature

The new movement was accompanied by a return to the languages and texts of antiquity, which were used for the refinement of one's own language and literature. In this way, the traditions of existing genres were preserved while still allowing for the development of new ones. The role model in the Renaissance was Italy. Three Italian poets obtained special glory in the 13th and 14th centuries, and continue to be considered the "three crowns of literature": Dante Alighieri, Francesco Petrarca, and Giovanni Boccaccio. Boccaccio found a new literary genre with his "Decameron" (1350–1353): the novella. England developed into a great cultural nation with the reign of Queen Elizabeth I (1533–1603).

Dante Alighieri's "Divine Comedy" (1307–1321) describes the journey through hell and purgatory to paradise.

WILLIAM SHAKESPEARE, *born probably in 1564 in Stratford-upon-Avon, died there in 1616.*

NO WORKS *that were handwritten by Shakespeare himself have survived.*

CLAIMS that Shakespeare never existed keep finding support.

Shakespeare is today the most performed stage author of the world.

Shakespeare

LITTLE IS KNOWN about the life of the famous poet from the Elizabethan era. It is assumed that he moved to London in 1585 and joined a troupe of actors. He wrote most of his plays for this group, which was under the protection of the English King James since 1603.

HE AND HIS TROUPE opened the Globe Theatre in London in 1599, which achieved spectacular financial revenues. After it burnt down in 1613, Shakespeare returned to his hometown of Stratford-upon-Avon. After his death in 1616, his friends brought a book with his plays to the market. It contained 36 dramas divided into three groups: histories, comedies, and tragedies. His most well known plays are the comedy "A Midsummer Night's Dream" as well as the tragedies "Macbeth" and "Romeo and Juliet."

"Romeo and Juliet" is the most famous love story in the world.

The Globe Theatre in London was built sphere-shaped like most of the theaters of that time. No member of the audience sat at a distance of more than about 65 ft (20 m) from the stage.

see also: **Start of Modernity,** *Philosophy Chapter, p. 254* | **Renaissance,** *Visual Arts Chapter, pp. 294–295*

BAROQUE—SUFFERING AND DELIGHT

While those in the royal courts lived in luxury and kept up the artistic tradition, multiple wars led to misery for the general population—a contrast that was reflected in literature.

The court position at the center of culture did not threaten the increasing power of the cities. On the contrary, an important part of cultural development can be traced back to lively competition between cities and courts. The exact character of this relationship varied greatly among the individual countries. In absolutist France, for example, everything was centered on the court of Versailles, where one of the most remarkable rulers of the 17th century resided: Louis XIV, known as the sun king.

Blooming Courts

Absolutist monarchies reached their peak in Europe with the reign of the sun king. No other king after Louis had comparable power. He maintained a courtly city—the variety, wealth, and splendor of which soon became the model for every European royal court. Louis XIV's sumptuous style served to characterize the entire era of the Baroque (French: "bizarre"). Louis brought eminent artists as well as the playwrights Racine, Corneille, and Molière to his court.

Utopia

"Utopia," meaning "no place" in Greek, is named after one of the literary genres typical of the Early Modern period: the Utopia. It began with Thomas Moore's authoring of "Utopia" in 1516. In it, a sailor by the name of Hythlodaus gives his impressions of the island he is stranded on, which is completely different from his native England. Utopia offered the possibility of an ideal state and criticized the contemporary political and social conditions, which made it one of the most popular literary genres.

above: *View of the moon-shaped island of Utopia, according to its description by Thomas Moore*

Wartime Atrocities

While the courts indulged, Europe was overrun by several wars. The atrocities of the Thirty Years' War were reflected in many contemporary narratives, novels, and poems.

The terrible battles of the Thirty Years' War, such as the Battle of White Mountain in 1620, remind people of the uncertainty of life.

JEAN-BAPTISTE POQUELIN, *alias Molière, born 1622 in Paris and died there in 1673.*

MOLIÈRE *is said to have written 300 comedies, of which only 32 survive.*

TODAY'S MOST WELL KNOWN WORKS: *"The Miser," "The Imaginary Invalid," "Le Misanthrope"*

Molière is considered to be a classic author of French literature. His themes have been transferred to the present through modern productions.

Molière

MOLIÈRE attended a Jesuit school and later became a lawyer. When he decided to become an actor against his father's wishes in 1643, tragedy was the accepted theatric genre while comedy was frowned upon as a pleasure without a standard. It was Molière who made it acceptable.

AFTER HE had traveled for a long time as an actor in a traveling theater, he himself started to write. He eventually gained the patronage of Louis XIV and from then on performed in his royal court. Molière parodied his contemporaries through his comedies and hence was subject to repeated hostilities. "Tartuffe," which deals with religious hypocrisy, triggered a scandal in 1664.

Molière first performed his plays in the royal palace of Louis XIV in 1661.

The general attitude toward life was shaped by the permanent presence of death. "Everything is transitory," begins one of the poems by the German poet Andreas Gryphius.

His contemporary Martin Opitz, who strove to make German poetry equal to the rest of European literature, died in 1632 in Danzig of the plague, or Black Death. The "Simplicius Simplicissimus" (1669) by Grimmelshausen, who was at one time a soldier, was a part of the genre of the Spanish picaresque novel and detailed the war experiences of an imbecile who ends up as a recluse.

Changes in Britain

The great social upheavals that occurred in Great Britain during this period were reflected in its literature. After the Thirty Years' War, a civil war removed and executed the monarch Charles I in favor of a Puritan republic headed by Oliver Cromwell. The failure of this revolution, and restoration of Charles II to the throne, prompted John Milton to write his magnus opus "Paradise Lost," which masterfully depicts Lucifer's revolution against God. It also ushered in a revival of the bawdier delights of the past exhibited in the "restoration comedies" of playwrights such as Oliver Goldsmith and R. B. Sheridan. The 17th century in Britain also brought the amusing satires of Jonathan Swift and Alexander Pope.

INSIDER KNOWLEDGE

3,000 *visitors could find a place in the "Globe," the theater of Shakespeare's acting troupe.*

MANY READERS *thought the island in Thomas Moore's "Utopia" actually existed as they could not understand the Greek title.*

MOLIÈRE *collapsed on stage in 1672 while performing the lead character role in "The Imaginary Invalid."*

LITERATURE

see also: **Baroque,** *Visual Arts Chapter, pp. 298–299* | *Music Chapter, pp. 366–369*

KEY FACTS

THE IDEALS OF THE ENLIGHTENMENT *were tolerance, humanity, rationality, and equality.*

NOVELS AND DRAMAS *should provide culture and education to help condition these ideals.*

THE LITERATURE OF THE ROMANTIC *rebelled against fixed rules and went with genius and feeling.*

IN NORTH AMERICA, *literature of independence developed.*

Enlightenment (18th century) | Theater and novel | Genius cult | Romanticism (1795–1830)

RATIONALITY AND FRENZY—FROM ENLIGHTENMENT TO ROMANTICISM

The 18th century was characterized by the emancipation from traditional authorities and the search for individuality. This also had a clear effect on literature—both on the content and form of the works as well as the theoretical considerations of authors and critics. The formal rules were rejected while constraints were removed and new ground broken.

➜ *The 18th century was a time of overcoming tradition through rationality and geniality.*

LITERATURE

TOLERANCE AND SELF-DETERMINATION

Rationality, humanitarianism, and tolerance were the ideals of the Enlightenment. Literature was discovered as a medium for disseminating knowledge. Thus, a rich literary market emerged.

While the Church was still considered to be the place of refuge in the 17th century, many found its spiritual dominance to be too oppressive by the 18th century. Its claims to authority seemed to oppose the desire for a rationality driven and self-determined life. Additionally, the voices that challenged the claim to absolute power by the rulers started increasing. It was this line of thinking that led to social unrest and even revolution—especially in France during 1789. Immanuel Kant's bold invocation, "Have courage to use your own reason," can be considered as the motto of the Enlightenment. One of the most influential philosophers of the time, Kant was once asked, "What is Enlightenment?" To this, he answered that it is for a human to accept responsibility to fulfill duties in his entrusted office but to have the courage to use reason in public.

Nathan the Wise

Gotthold Ephraim Lessing wrote the drama "Nathan the Wise" in 1779, which depicted the time of the Crusades in Jerusalem in which Christianity, Judaism, and Islam clashed. One scene in particular became very famous in which Sultan Saladin asks Nathan what the true religion is, to which Nathan answers with the parable of the three rings: A father of three sons makes two copies of a ring and then divides them among his sons. Later, the original ring cannot be distinguished just as religions cannot be divided into categories of true and false; rather one should live according to all their learned doctrines.

above: *Lessing's friend, the Jewish Moses Mendelssohn, was perhaps the inspiration for Nathan.*

left: *Frederick the Great appointed many scholars and poets in his court. He is pictured here in a scholarly conversation with Voltaire.*

Tolerance as an Ideal

The Prussian king Frederick the Great is still considered today as the quintessential example of an Enlightened ruler. He was gifted in the fine arts, interested in literature, and maintained correspondence with the famous French philosopher and author Voltaire. Frederick granted his subjects the right to decide for themselves which religion they wanted to practice. The various denominations in the 18th century made tolerance particularly important. This ideal was best demonstrated by a figure from the works of the German poet Gotthold Ephraim Lessing: Nathan the Wise.

Thirst for Knowledge

The Enlightened ideal of tolerance was based on rational negotiation. This made education especially important. Literature, especially the theater, was discovered as the suitable medium to educate people. For the first time books were printed in large quantities as multiple literary magazines emerged and the call for freedom of the press became louder. Interested citizens would gather in the salons to exchange their views and discuss various issues. The natural sciences and their experiments inspired the public. Whoever could, participated in this quest for education. The collected knowledge of this epoch was made available to the wider public through the "Encyclopédie," which was published by Denis Diderot between 1751 and 1780 and contained around 60,000 articles.

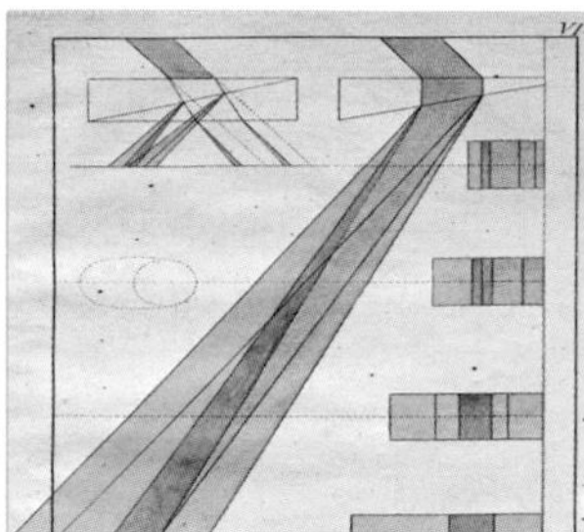

Like many poets of his time, Goethe applied himself to the natural sciences. With his theory of color, he occupied himself with the problems of perception.

The Enlightenment was the high point of discussion: Lessing, Johann Kaspar Lavater, and Moses Mendelssohn in conversation.

➜ see also: **Enlightenment,** *Philosophy Chapter, p. 258*

THEATER AND THE NOVEL

The theater and the novel were supposed to impart the knowledge and rationality of the Enlightenment. How this was to be achieved in public remained disputed.

The most outstanding texts of the Enlightenment were those that were best suited to impart education and culture comprehensively. Besides textbooks for numerous areas of knowledge and various target groups (e.g., women), there were primarily dramas and novels.

The most important form of drama was considered to be the tragedy, which was associated with Aristotle and then with the French dramas of Racine and Corneille.

From Rules and Norms...

In the early Enlightenment, dramatists had to follow an array of rules that were mostly derived from the "Poetics" of Aristotle. First, they had to search for a theme that they wanted to convey to the public. Then they would have to find an action that would illustrate this to the audience. Mostly historical events were used in which emperors, kings, princes, or other high-ranking personalities were involved. Tragedy was considered very effective if the character was initially very rich and powerful, but then succumbed to trouble. This rule of a "high fall" further ensured that no "common" plots of "ill-favored" people came to the stage.

The writer had to further adhere to the three "unities" of action: time, space, and place. For example, there should be a closed plot with a start and end that should not stretch for more than a couple of hours and there should not be constant changes to the stage. In order to learn from the play and experience the effect (catharsis), the viewer had to concentrate entirely on the single theme.

...to Compassion and Emotion

Gotthold Ephraim Lessing heavily contradicted these rules, which had general validity at the start of the 18th century. The decisive element in tragedy was sympathizing with the event on the stage. The viewer had to identify with what he saw so that he could internalize the fate of the tragic hero. Lessing overthrew the "high fall," while turning to psychology and characterizations. These aspects soon became important and tragedies were performed throughout Europe in which common people were at the center. The "bourgeois tragedy" was born.

Gotthold Ephraim Lessing (1729–1781) negated the rules of poetry. He favored the drawing of characterizations in literature.

The genre of comedy primarily served the purposes of amusement and entertainment and so stereotypes were often employed. Lessing lent characters to his players: In his comedy "Minna von Barnhelm," even the minor characters like the chamber maid were individual personalities. The French playwright Beaumarchais handled politically explosive topics in his comedies like "The Marriage of Figaro" (1784).

The young Werther reports on the pains of unfulfilled love in his letters. He commits suicide in the end.

In the era of the Enlightenment, along with courtyard theaters, there were many traveling theater groups that spread the new civilian dramas.

Letters and Adventures

The new high esteem of real characters in drama was brought to authors by a new model: Shakespeare. The young Johann Wolfgang Goethe praised Shakespeare's characters in 1771 for their fidelity to nature. The general view was that Shakespeare had captured the emotions of humanity like none other, without adhering to the superfluous rules of the poetic. The representation of the individual emotions and thoughts now became the main task of literature.

Samuel Richardson devised the tender epistolary novel with "Pamela," which became a trend in Europe. Even Jean-Jacques Rousseau ("The New Heloise") in 1761 and Goethe ("The Sorrows of Young Werther") in 1774 also participated in this trend. The novels of adventure also evoked plenty of excitement during this time. In 1720, a novel was published in England that depicted the experiences of a castaway, Robinson. With it, Daniel Defoe founded the new genre of narration, the "Robinsonade." The reflections of Robinson as he overcomes the hardships faced within his involuntary isolation reflect the rational behavior of an enlightened Englishman when placed in the "savage" context of an uncolonized island.

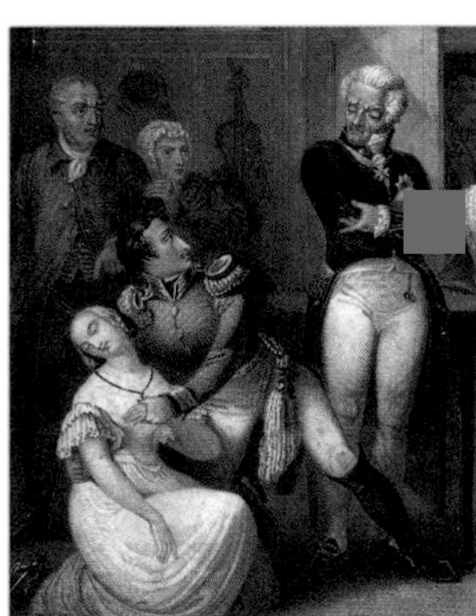

The tragedy "Intrigue and Love" by Friedrich von Schiller provoked zealous riots during its initial performance in 1782.

INSIDER KNOWLEDGE

COMEDIES AND TRAGEDIES *could be distinguished from one another by the ending; either full of marriages or packed with deaths.*

THERE WAS A WAVE OF SUICIDES *after the publication of Goethe's Werther novel.*

DANIEL DEFOE *was already 60 years old when he wrote his first novel, "Robinson Crusoe."*

LITERATURE

BIRTH OF A GENIUS

The thirst for individuality and independence peaked around 1800 with the cult of genius. North America also was on the search for a literary sense of national identity.

The displeasure of the citizens in Europe began to increase with the lack of political influence. The rejection of fixed rules in literature reflected the need for individuality. The young authors of the late 18th century strived for individuality and realism, as communicated by the works of the philosopher Jean-Jacques Rousseau. While this atmosphere of departure led to a revolution in France, it appeared in more moderate forms in other European countries, but could certainly be felt everywhere.

The French word "genie" became the leading term of this time. A person was considered to be a genius if they created something new and original without following any traditional rules. Ideally, a genius was in a permanent natural state in which reasoning took a back seat to the heart and emotion. With the rejection of rationality in art and the commitment to emotions during this time, literary works were considered dangerous. Unrestrained emotions threatened to push the poets into insanity. With the fate of a few—for example, Friedrich Hölderlin—this fear was confirmed.

Melancholy and World-Weariness

Living according to these rules and the literary search for an individual style were closely intertwined. Hence, the authors of the early 18th century could not be allocated to any group as their works were shaped through their individual personalities. Instead, they founded their own schools or styles that adhered to their own writing and lifestyle.

The model for this era was Lord Byron (1788–1824), whose eccentricity was legendary even in his own lifetime. He traveled to the Middle East, fought with the Greeks against the Turks for their independence, and maintained his status as a social outsider. His writings are full of melancholy and world-weariness, but also of self-sacrificing devotion and love. After Byron succumbed to malaria at a young age, the authors in Europe tried to copy his lifestyle and ideas. Such authors were found everywhere, including Germany, Italy, France, and Russia. The new literary term of Romanticism started to prevail for this new style.

An entire generation oriented itself to him: Lord George Byron lived an animated life as a Don Juan, traveler, and poet.

JOHANN WOLFGANG VON GOETHE, *born 1749 in Frankfurt am Main, died 1832 in Weimar.*

IMPORTANT WORKS: *"The Sorrows of Young Werther," "Faust," "Torquato Tasso," "Wilhelm Meister's Apprenticeship and Travels"*

MANY WOMEN *influenced Goethe's works; however, he married only Christiane Vulpius (1806).*

Goethe created works in a great range of literary genres; (portrait, 1828).

Johann Wolfgang von Goethe

THE GRAND DUKE OF SAXONY-WEIMAR appointed the 26-year-old Johann Wolfgang Goethe as administrative officer and advisor of his court in 1775. Nobody could have thought that he would go on to create a body of work in the next 60 years that would have captivated the following generations as it did. He created a furor with his play "Götz von Berlichingen" (1773) and the novel "Werther." With his "Storm and Stress," Goethe became the representative for texts that tried to escape the common existence.

HOWEVER, HIS NEW POSITION in Weimar brought him a disciplined life, which was filled with administrative work, writing, natural scientific studies, conversations, and love affairs. A pivotal experience was his sojourn in Italy from 1786 to 1788 in which he lived a free, unbound life studying the art of antiquity and the Renaissance. From 1794 to 1805, he maintained intensive contact with Friedrich von Schiller, with whom he shaped the style of "Weimar classicism." Somewhat contrary to the roughly hewn nature of his earlier phase of "Sturm and Drang," the classicism that Goethe achieved later on in life strived for equilibrium and a timelessness in its style.

above: *Pages from the manuscript of "Faust"*
left: *A well-known portrait: "Goethe in the Roman Campagna"*

Beginnings of Literature in North America

Considerable literary output came about in North America from the end of the 19th century. It was primarily in the service of building a national identity during the process of cutting the "umbilical cord" from England. Edgar Allan Poe is considered one of the first significant American writers. He is well known today for his poems, such as "The Raven," his thrillers, such as "The Fall of the House of Usher"(1839), and his short stories. Shortly after, Herman Melville published his adventure novel "Moby Dick" (1851). James Fenimore Cooper showed the world in his stories and the special features of North America with his "Leatherstocking" tales from 1821 that became synonymous with adventure.

above: *North America became a nation not just through wars, but also through literature.*

Romanticism was not just limited to literature. Romantic emotionalism was also reflected in art and music.

see also: **Rousseau,** *Philosophy Chapter, p. 259* | **Romanticism,** *Visual Arts Chapter, p. 304* | *Music Chapter, p. 374*

LITERATURE BETWEEN THRILL, SENSATION, AND CONFLICT

Fantasy, empathy, and battles for freedom shaped the literature of Romanticism. Individual geniuses led to the emergence of diverse literature.

Literature that is summarized under the term "Romanticism" is actually a movement in which the most important aspect is variety. There was, namely, one principle that all the Romantic poets felt bound to: The actual subject is at the forefront with its individual characteristics. Three contextual tendencies could be differentiated: show, sensation, and conflict.

Eerie Fantasy

The creation of a monster by the scientist Frankenstein without knowing the consequences of his actions has to be one of the most well known stories of world literature. It was written in 1818 by the daughter of the first English feminist Mary Wollstonecraft, Mary Shelly, who is considered one of the most important Romanticists of England. Shelley oriented herself to the style of Gothic fiction, which was prevalent at that time. It dealt with devils, witches, magicians, and ghosts—fantasy knew no boundaries.

The idea of freedom is at the center of the works by Friedrich von Schiller (1759–1805).

Natural Sensations

Wordsworth's famous opening lines, "I wondered lonely as a cloud/That floats on high o'er vales and hills," perfectly evoke, in an exquisitely constructed rhythm, the calming sensation of nature. The pure elation the poem's narrator feels when these images of nature pass before his "inward eye" allow his heart to "dance with the daffodils." The point where nature ends and feelings begin is made hazy, bringing them into unity. The sensations nature evokes, such as yearning, wonder, and peace, made it an ideal focal point for much of Romantic literature.

Nature was often presented as a force in its own right, or as the visible façade of a supernatural world of complex forces. The protagonist in Samuel Taylor Coleridge's "The Rime of the Ancient Mariner" incurs the volatile wrath of supernatural spirits for the crime of killing an albatross. The spirits haunt and thwart his voyage and he ends up cursed to eternally tread the Earth to retell his tale.

In the Battle for Freedom

Romantic excesses met with much mockery and criticism. German poet Heinrich Heine repeatedly mocked their transfiguration of nature. He saw it as pleasing, but "not a world" on its own.

Friedrich von Schiller came to criticize their neglect of the intellect through a bias towards emotion. He rejected the restrictions that an abundance of subjective feeling put on literary works, since he tried to keep humankind as a whole in view during his writing process. The idea of freedom was already the focal point of his first drama "The Robbers." Subsequently, he dealt with problems that resulted from the yearning for freedom and the responsibility of individual actions. Schiller, like many poets of his time, sympathized with the French Revolution.

Romantic Irony

Irony was always a form of disguised criticism through formulating the opposite of what is supposed to be said. This use of contradicting statements, without having to decide between one or the other, attracted the Romanticists. They made irony part of their stylistic program. Not only could they make statements without meaning them, but they could also distance themselves from their own work and remove any dogmatic truth.

above: *Caricature is a way of expressing criticism humorously, but also clearly. In this illustration from "Gulliver's Travels," Napoleon's physical stature is being mocked absurdly.*

ONE DIFFERENTIATES between folk tales, which were passed on orally, and literary fairy tales.

JACOB AND WILHELM GRIMM collected and edited fairy tales and published them as "Children's and Household Tales" (1812–1815).

ROMANTIC FAIRY TALE AUTHORS: Hans Christian Andersen (1805–1875), Wilhelm Hauff (1802–1827)

Hans Christian Andersen ca 1865

Fairy Tales

FAIRY TALES belong to one of the most beloved genres of the Romanticists since they deal with literature that can be traced back to oral traditions, which were spread through the "naturalist" method of narration. In order to preserve and research them, a few Romanticists like the Grimm brothers collected the proofs of folk poetry. Others wrote stories themselves in the style of folk tales.

THE FAIRY TALES of the Danish Hans Christian Andersen were published in multiple collections and became especially popular. Even though he found inspiration for his stories in traditional sayings and legends, he gave his narrations a fully new form—which became literary fairy tales. One of the most famous tales is that of the little mermaid who falls in love with a human. Wanting to become human herself, so as to be able to live with this man she loves, she undergoes terrible agonies, but ultimately fails and becomes a spirit. Talking objects and animals are typical of Andersen's fairy tales.

The little mermaid asks the witch to help her become a human.

21ST CENTURY

HANS CHRISTIAN ANDERSEN'S *stories like "The Emperor's New Clothes" or "The Ugly Duckling" continue to provide material for adaptations, operas, and films.*

J. R. R. TOLKIEN *transferred the fairy tale into the literary genre of fantasy.*

THE ROMANTIC THRILLER *was the inspiration for the emergence of the horror genre.*

KEY FACTS

REALISM *concerns itself with describing the harshness of reality through elegant literature.*

NATURALISM *tries to illustrate reality as lifelike as possible.*

THE NATURALISTS *criticized the inhumanity of modern living conditions, especially in large cities.*

THE IMPRESSIONISTS *countered realism with an emphasis on a subjective perspective.*

Realism: human fate (1830–1890) | Naturalism: real life (1880–1900)

REALISM AND NATURALISM—PRECURSORS TO MODERNITY

The literature of realism and naturalism disclosed people's living conditions and behavior. Authors aimed to change the literary presentation of reality. The naturalists sought to keep their depictions as lifelike as possible. Although attempting to represent the banality of human life, the realists maintained a beautified stylistic ideal in their writing.

➲ *People and their existence were illustrated through life-like representations.*

LITERATURE

HUMAN FATE AND TRAGEDIES

The aim of realism was to pitilessly and critically represent reality through artistic forms and representations. This pan-European literary movement saw the emergence of the most significant novels and narrations of world literature.

Through his work, Honoré de Balzac sought to provide detailed descriptions of the habits and actions of people in the different levels of society. With an incomprehensible number of novels, the often indebted author strove toward this goal. He had originally planned to capture the characteristics of French society in 137 novels. In 1829, he began "La Comédie Humaine" to show human passions—primarily the greed for money and power present at all levels. Balzac managed to write only 90 novels as he died at age 51; however, his work deeply influenced the spreading realist movement.

Seen by his contemporaries as a corruptor of customs and today as one of the most important realists: Honoré de Balzac (1799–1850).

Charles Dickens's societal novel "Oliver Twist" (1838) describes the life story of an orphaned child.

An International Movement

Stendhal and Gustave Flaubert followed Balzac's footsteps in France. They considered literature to be the medium of observation as well as a chance to dabble in psychological issues.

Prose fiction, which granted plenty of space for narration, developed into the main genre of realism. A conversation about reality took place that sought to sustain truthful representation. Important realist works emerged in North America, northern Europe, and England.

Criticism Through Description

The narrations that criticized difficult life conditions with ambitious literary descriptions were still at the center of interest. Charles Dickens is considered to be the most important English author of socio-critical novels during the early period of industrialization. His "Oliver Twist" in 1838 and "David Copperfield" in 1850 touched his readers and later inspired many modern directors to make film adaptations.

The revolution of 1848 in Germany saw the spread of realism in proponents like Theodor Fontane with his illustrations of life in Prussia in his novels such as "Effi Briest" (1895). In the U.S., "Uncle Tom's Cabin" (1852) by Harriet Beecher Stowe portrayed the abusive life of African-American slaves, which helped promote the Abolitionist movement. Another American author, Henry James, developed a more psychological realism with his works ("Portrait of a Lady," 1881, and "The Turn of the Screw, 1898").

WORKS BY FYODOR DOSTOEVSKY *(1821–1881): "The Gambler" (1866), "The Idiot" (1868), "The Brothers Karamazov" (1880)*

WORKS BY IVAN TURGENEV *(1818–1883): "Fathers and Sons" (1862), "Smoke" (1868)*

WORKS BY LEO TOLSTOY *(1828–1910): "War and Peace" (1868), "Anna Karenina" (1877)*

Count Lev Nikolayevich Tolstoy, portrait 1884

Russian Realism

REALISM IN LITERATURE was a pan-European occurrence; the individual works differ only in their tone dealing with various aspects. The special esteem of the works by Russian realists (such as Dostoevsky, Tolstoy, and Turgenev) rests on the special attention paid to detailing the fates of individual characters. With his final novel, "The Brothers Karamazov," Dostoevsky devised a cosmos full of psychological necessities, emergencies, and existential questions. The four brothers search for a way to master life, but each fails.

At first glance, the novel "The Brothers Karamazov" is a crime drama (scene from the film adaptation by Richard Brooks).

REAL LIFE AND LITERATURE

The naturalists attempted to illustrate as faithfully as possible whatever was observable to them within their literary works. They wanted to disclose and change the dominant states of things in all areas of life.

While the focal point of realists was the illustration of reality through primarily elegant literature, the naturalists wanted to come as close to reality as possible. As far as they were concerned, beauty lay in the strictly dispassionate representation of reality.

Even the Impressionists created landscapes and idylls in a lifelike manner. Camille Pissarro: "Entrance to the Village of Voisins."

The reason for this radicalization of the fundamental idea of realism was the visible deterioration of the living conditions of the lower classes in the 19th century, which were also criticized by the realists. Large cities became the focus of literature due to deplorable housing conditions, factories, diseases, and all-pervasive hunger. The individual was faced with external pressures that made it impossible for them to fulfill their own personal needs and dreams were considered and presented as a small part of a far larger machine.

Science as an Approach

The forerunners of this new movement were primarily French authors. Edmond and Jules de Goncourt brought scientific methods of description and classification to literature, which they recommended to their contemporaries in the preface to their novel "Germinie Lacerteux" in 1864.

Inspired by science, Émile Zola (1840–1902) explained literature in terms of social experiments through various essays. He tried to clarify the terms and conditions of human life through test trials. Most impressive was his 20 volume novel cycle "Les Rougon-Macquart," which was written between 1871 and 1893. In them, he describes the lives of individual members in three families over the course of five generations.

Immorality and Idyll

Guy de Maupassant devoted himself to an unsparing representation of reality. His novels and novellas are characterized by a mode of narration that renounced empathy and psychological analysis.
With his novel "Bel Ami" (1885), he portrays an unscrupulous seducer who utilizes the corrupt society to his own aims without any moral qualms.

Although similarly striving for accurate accounts of reality, the Impressionist movement emerged in opposition to the naturalist radical depictions of horrifying living conditions. The Impressionists devoted themselves to the subjective illustration of simple rural life—the idyll. The Norwegian Knut Hamsun, who won the Nobel Prize for literature in 1920, not only described the downfall of the idyllic because of modernization, but also conceptualized a new rural life as an alternative.

Gerhart Hauptmann's "Die Weber" (1892) documented the rebellion of a Silesian weaver in 1844.

New Ways

The accurate illustration of reality led to the search for new linguistic possibilities. For example, Arno Holz discovered a style of writing in which each action was translated into words. In drama, the lower classes were characterized through milieu dialects, especially those by Gerhart Hauptmann. Henrik Ibsen of Norway founded the modern realistic drama, which had interpersonal communication at its center. With his later plays, such as "The Master Builder" (1892), he used symbolism, which would influence future playwrights.

THE FEMINIST COMMITMENT OF *Virginia Woolf was rediscovered only in the 1960s.*

JANE AUSTEN *wrote psychological realistic novels about society like "Pride and Prejudice."*

THE WORKS OF THE BRONTË SISTERS *were published under masculine pseudonyms.*

The best known of the three Brontë sisters is Emily, who published "Wuthering Heights" in 1848 (from left: Charlotte, Emily, and Anne).

Women's Emancipation and Literature

THERE WERE ALWAYS female writers; however, they were long considered, if known at all, to be an anomaly, as literature was supposed to be the task of men. This changed only with the first wave of international movements from the middle of the 19th century that demanded political and civil rights for women. These first feminists primarily fought for their voting rights and hence were also called "suffragettes." They additionally demanded the right of female education and gainful employment.

IN ORDER TO PROVE what women could do, women's rights activists and later feminists searched for models in the past and were not disappointed: Sophie von La Roche, Jane Austen, the Brontë sisters, and many others, who had actually published their works anonymously. Virginia Woolf (1882–1941), one of the founders of the modern English novel, became the icon of women's literature. With the essay "A Room of One's Own," written in 1928, Woolf presented the female role and struggle to assert oneself in literature to her female audience at Cambridge University.

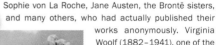

Suffragettes in the battle for women's rights in 1905

INSIDER KNOWLEDGE

BALZAC DESCRIBED ABOUT 250 *food dishes in his works surrounding the mundanity of everyday life.*

DOSTOEVSKY *was placed in a labor camp (1847–1849) because he was associated with a revolutionary secret organization.*

AUTHORS THEODOR FONTANE AND HENRIK IBSEN *were also learned apothecaries.*

KEY FACTS

AT THE TURN OF THE CENTURY, *a language crisis shaped literature.*

WRITERS SOUGHT *to discover new and often wildly experimental forms of narration.*

FUTURISTS AND EXPRESSIONISTS *formulated some of the literary concepts of modernism.*

THROUGH COLONIALISM, *the examination of foreign cultures and literatures was initiated.*

1900–1933: Fin de siècle | New narratives | Expressionism | New objectivity | Colonial and political literature

MODERN PLURALISM—EXPRESSION AND OBJECTIVITY

The technical progress and political upheavals that characterized the start of the 20th century were reflected in literature. The rising literary movements were hardly distinguishable with the influx of individual styles and techniques. These ranged from accurate descriptions of reality to completely senseless rhymes without any real point, or even Enlightenment dramas.

In the first years of the 19th century, great literary plurality emerged that came to shape the modern age.

LITERATURE

TIMES OF CRISIS

At the turn of the century, a general sense of doom and crisis reigned. Language seemed to be no longer a viable medium for the communication of facts and ideas.

Already at the end of the 19th century, a pessimistic view of the world was reflected in literature that dealt with middle class morality and modern progressive thought. The fear of a cultural decline ("decadence") could be perceived all over Europe and North America at the turn of the 20th century. The plurality of forms of literary representation resulted in a loss of orientation, which made the authors doubt whether their writing had anything to do with reality at all. In his "Lord Chandos Letter" from 1902, Hugo von Hofmannsthal describes a man despairing about the limitations of language to describe reality. In the end, the character ultimately loses his ability to speak.

Beauty and Symbolism

As a reaction against this uncertainty, many authors opposed the naturalistic view that one could and must describe the world accurately. Literature was no longer meant to teach, explain, or describe. According to the emerging symbolists, literature was not even in a position to do so. An author could only employ textual images that give an insight into the contexts of the world without having any direct reference to reality. Thus, language no longer serves the purpose of communication, but rather only symbols enable perceivable access to reality.

The literary works of symbolism are characterized by an emphasis on beauty ("aestheticism") and a playful youth style ("art nouveau"). The key figure of this literature was the individual who is free from the middle class and moral conventions. Literary works were profoundly influenced by the new insights provided through psychology and psychoanalysis.

LITERATURE AT THE END OF THE 19TH CENTURY *was influenced by the development of psychoanalysis by Sigmund Freud.*

DECADENCE *describes cultural decline in connection with the impending end of an age.*

POETS OF FIN DE SIÈCLE: *Hugo von Hofmannsthal, Stefan George, Arthur Schnitzler*

Hugo von Hofmannsthal (1874–1929) authored libretti for operas by Richard Strauss.

Fin de Siècle

THE DECADENT MOOD at the turn of the 20th century found literary expression that placed a special emphasis on physically and psychologically extreme situations. Dreams, death, drugs, melancholy, and illness—all that is removed from understanding and deviates from the normal condition—was described and fathomed.

ASIDE FROM PARIS, Vienna developed into a center of this movement. The authors of "Viennese modernism," primarily Hugo von Hofmannsthal, Karl Kraus, and Arthur Schnitzler, discussed the possibilities of the new writing genre during their meetings at coffee houses. One particularly famous author who turned to symbolism of this era was the German Stefan George. He worked closely with Hofmannsthal and rejected any literature that actually pursued a purely rational purpose.

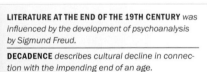

left: *Art nouveau was the art of the fin de siècle ("Portrait of Emilie Flöge," Gustav Klimt).*
right: *Portrait of Stefan George*

The "Youth" magazine gave the decorative movement of art nouveau its name.

The founder of the modern French novel: Marcel Proust

The film "Eyes Wide Shut" is based on the Surrealist novelette by Arthur Schnitzler.

see also: The Beginning of Psychology and Psychoanalysis, *Psychology Chapter, pp. 270, 282* | Art Nouveau, *Visual Arts Chapter, p. 307*

THE NEW NARRATIVE

Multiple paths led out of the language crisis at the turn of the century. Authors searched for new possibilities of narration at the beginning of the 20th century—each one on their own.

Yiddish Literature

Yiddish was the dialect of the Jews living in Eastern Europe—a mixture of Slavic, Hebrew, and German linguistic elements. Although initially writing in Hebrew with little success, Mendele Mocher Sforim eventually became the founder of Yiddish literature. His novel "The Mare" (1873) appealed to Jewish readers to reflect upon their traditions. He compared Judaism to an old horse, within which actually a prince is hidden. Like him, the authors Isaac Leib Peretz and Sholom Aleichem also wrote about Jewish life in Eastern Europe.

above: *Sholom Aleichem (1859–1916) immigrated to the U.S.*

Ernest Hemingway lived for a long time in Cuba (photo, 1946).

In the crisis period at the turn of the century, several movements emerged that sought to create literature although its medium of language had proved to be unreliable. Increasingly, authors ended up diverging drastically from one another. Although many could not be entirely classified as an adherent for any particular movement, they still belonged to literary circles that emerged in cities such as Vienna and Paris.

The Mann brothers, Thomas and Heinrich, were authors. but with quite different styles and aims.

At the turn of the century, Vienna was an important literary center.

The Mann Brothers

With his merciless depiction of the decline of the Buddenbrook family, Thomas Mann justified his worldwide fame in 1901, which reached its peak in 1929 with the award of the Nobel Prize for Literature. His works are characterized by a fine irony and the skillful combination of realistic portrayals, discussions of the narrator, and psychologically complex characterizations. With this, he continually pointed out how rigid the apparently stable life structures can be. His brother Heinrich, on the other hand, identified himself as a political writer. Through his work, he sought to communicate democratic values and influence social changes.

Enigmatic Existences

A totally new literary world was created by the Prague author Franz Kafka. His mysterious and nightmarish descriptions of human existence continue to be interpreted by readers today. Characteristic of Kafka's writing is the sudden intrusion of the unreal into a seemingly normal world, which incites fantastical dimensions. In "The Metamorphosis" (1915), for example, the salesman Gregor Samsa wakes up one morning as a cockroach. With Kafka's "The Trial," the lead character Mr. K is arrested and dragged into a labyrinth of judicial bureaucracy without even once hearing the accusation against him or the reason for his ultimate execution.

Merciless Portrayals

Through the intermingling of dream and reality, Kafka created an atmosphere of hopelessness in his work. Ernest Hemingway achieved the same sentiment through relentless, realistic clarity. His narration is characterized by a sober language, a economical style, and the direct stating of facts without the mediation of a knowing narrator. Thus, Hemingway acquired the reputation of a chronicler, which was enhanced further by his real-life reports on the Spanish Civil War.

The devastated Franz K awaits his prosecution (drawing by Franz Kafka in his novel"The Trial").

In a similarly direct manner, Elias Canetti brought the insane worlds of his characters to his readers. For example, in "Auto-da-Fe" (1931–1932) they must share the experience as Dr. Peter Kiens continues to remove himself farther from reality until he finally sets fire to himself and his books.

INSIDER KNOWLEDGE

HUGO VON HOFMANNSTHAL *founded the Salzburg Festival plays along with Richard Strauss in 1917.*

MARCEL PROUST *worked within a secluded room that was completely lined with cork.*

FRANZ KAFKA *instructed that his works be destroyed after his death.*

Elias Canetti (left) received the Nobel Prize for Literature in 1981.

THE WILD MODERN WORLD

The 20th century began on a stormy note. The Futurists, Expressionists, and followers of other avant-garde movements made people aware of the chaos and speed of modern life.

In 1909, a text with the title "Futuristic Manifesto" by Filippo Tommaso Marinetti appeared in the magazine "Le Figaro." In it, he swore by a new technical era and demanded a radical break with old values and traditions in favor of speed and movement; technology would from then on determine the arts. The manifesto gave rise to Futurism, which found numerous followers all over Europe.

Futurism was significant for the development of other modern literary movements like expressionism.

Filippo Tommaso Marinetti (1876–1944) founded Futurism with his manifesto in 1909.

However, the Futurist movement did not survive long. It was soon avoided by most artists because of its fascist tendencies and its promotion of militarism.

Later in Italy, Futurism became political as it transformed into a support of fascism. Outside of Italy, the movement gained large support in Russia until it was thrust out by the revolution.

Futurist Stylistic Devices

The most important stylistic device of the futurist authors was the montage, in which individual portions of text from different origins are combined with each other. The result was an impression of the simultaneousness of actions and occurrences ("simultaneous technique").

Expressionism was dominated by the examination of life inside the metropolis.

The art form of literature, which by nature must reconcile itself with the fact that words can only be read one after the other and thus actions are perceived only in succession, was now in a position to suggest complexity and simultaneousness.

The Big City Novel

This new simultaneous technique was especially suited to describe the complex processes in a metropolis. A precursor of this innovative form of narration was John Dos Passos, who wrote the first modern "big city" novel with "Manhattan Transfer" in 1925. Further prominent literary examples of this genre are "Ulysses" (1914–1921) by James Joyce and Alfred Döblin's "Berlin Alexanderplatz" (1929).

Expressionism

The successor of Futurism was expressionism (from Latin: *expressio*, "expression"), which primarily identified itself as a protest movement.

Affected by atrocities including the horrifying violence of the First World War, the representatives of expressionism wanted to draw attention to the dangers of modern life. They communicated suffering, death, bad luck, pain, insanity, and other extreme human conditions in a direct manner through poetry, prose, and drama.

Expressionism, which in its dynamics was reminiscent of the energy and rebellion during the German *Sturm und Drang* (p. 346) literary period during the 18th century, leaned on futurism and its montage technique in its form of representation as well as on the then young medium of cinema. Thus, the expressionist episodic dramas had the same effect as film sequences: A highlighted figure is continually brought into new situations, which are influenced and changed by the character's experiences.

Like Futurism, the expressionism that led to the emergence of many poetic circles in the big cities also lost its significance in the 1920s. The international revolutions gave way to a resigned attitude, which sought to counter the chaotic reality of life with content that was sure and factual.

21ST CENTURY

THE EVENTS ORGANIZED *by the Dadaists were precursors of "happenings" art.*

ERNEST HEMINGWAY *is considered one of the most important modern writers from the U.S.*

IN THE GLOBALIZED WORLD, *the literature of foreign countries increasingly gains significance.*

PSYCHOLOGY *is a fixed component of modern literature.*

Dada

The origins of the artistic movement of Dadaism lay in the cabaret, nihilism, and anarchism as well as a departure from exaggerated aestheticism. To be precise, its representatives identified themselves as anti-artists. Radiating from Zurich, where Hugo Ball organized dada evenings in his "Cabaret Voltaire," Dadaism spread across Europe. Its message was that the insanity of modern times must be countered with nonsense. The name itself, "Dada," has no meaning and is actually meant to connote baby language. Texts that transported no messages, but rather mere sounds and noises, as well as collages made of disjointed materials were the most important means of expression in Dadaism.

left: *Collages were a typical stylistic device of Dadaism. (Here, a parodic title page from 1921: "Fox-Trott for the Idiot").*
right: *The universal artist Kurt Schwitters occasionally worked closely with dada artists, but was apolitical.*

➔ see also: **Futurism, Dadaism, Expressionism,** *Visual Arts Chapter, pp. 308–309*

NEW OBJECTIVITY AND FOREIGN WORLDS

After about 1920, literature was defined by the desire to describe objectively familiar and foreign worlds. Worldwide, literature was once again increasingly used for political ends.

Mahatma Gandhi (right) and Rabindranath Tagore (left) in Tagore's residence in Santiniketan, India.

As opposed to the emotionally charged expressionism (p. 352), many writers worldwide strove for objectivity after 1920. The day-to-day life of people was meant to be documented, thus in this context firsthand reporting became a recognized literary genre as authors like Egon Erwin Kisch or Ernest Hemingway became famous through their eyewitness accounts. Even the historical novel, the literary biography, and the radio play gained mass interest. The American author Orson Welles was able to convince his radio audience that Martians had landed on Earth through a skillfully realistic production in 1938.

Distant India

With technical progress, the number of topics that could be dealt with in literature grew. Thus, remote countries were also brought into reach thanks to modern means of transport. Furthermore, the quest for independence by many colonized lands drew the attention of the West. Especially India, for whose independence Mahatma Gandhi fought peacefully since the 1920s, was much discussed—even in literature.

Through the Bengali poet Rabindranath Tagore (1861–1941), the Western world came in contact with foreign culture for the first time. Tagore undertook several journeys to England and to the U.S. while attempting to bring European and Indian cultures closer together through his works. However, he was faced with enthocentrism, rejection, and incomprehension in most parts in Europe.

Tagore, who received the Nobel Prize for Literature in 1913, was received by the Western audience primarily as a wise and exotic brahmin. However, he also contributed to the West's examination of the foreign world and the creation of its own notions of a mysterious, mystical land. The novels of Western authors about colonized territories better appealed to the taste of Western readers than did original, native literature. Rudyard Kipling's narratives and novels, primarily the "Jungle Book," published in 1894, were actually regarded as authentic representations of India. Kipling received the Nobel Prize for Literature in 1907.

In Service of Politics

The start of the 20th century was characterized by political changes for which literature, just as before, was put in the service of creating diverse new movements of departure. With the founding of diverse left-leaning organizations, a worker's literature evolved that benefited from the newly developed literary stylistic devices of the time. Literature was used for the dissemination of political content—as a means of propaganda and appeal for action. Most notably, drama was held in great esteem since it could directly affect the masses, thus developed further during this period. With the "Three Penny Opera" (1928) in Berlin, Bertolt Brecht became the founder of new political theater.

Bertolt Brecht's "epic theater" was supposed to incite reflection.

Kipling's "The Jungle Book" decisively influenced the Western image of India (illustration from 1919: Mowgli kills the tiger, Shere Khan).

LU XUN WAS *born in 1881 in Shaoxing, China, and died in 1936 in Shanghai.*

WITH THE "MAY FOURTH MOVEMENT," *Lu Xun opposed the Confucian state ethics and imperialism.*

LU XUN COMPOSED *narratives, poems, and political essays in the service of the Enlightenment.*

Lu Xun was a professor of Chinese literature in Xiamen and Canton.

Lu Xun—Founder of Chinese Modernism

AT THE CENTER OF THE NARRATIVE "The Diary of a Madman" from 1918 lies the recordings of a madman who believes that his fellow human beings wish to devour him. The author, Lu Xun, was alluding to the "cannibalistic" and frozen traditions of China. He is widely regarded as the founder of modernist Chinese literature.

LU XUN PLEADED for the reformation and renewal of the Chinese state and society. He identified himself with the "May Fourth Movement," which began with a demonstration in 1919 and united all in the collective desire for national unity for the first time in modern Chinese history. Lu Xun's scientific and artistic work decisively supported this process.

Students demonstrated in the Chinese city of Nanjing in the 1920s.

LITERATURE

KEY FACTS

LITERATURE IN FASCISM: *Authors were silenced or received a writing ban and went into exile.*

AFTER 1945 *authors committed themselves to a political and social new beginning.*

LITERATURE, *especially theater, became a political instrument.*

THE GLOBAL BOOK MARKET AND INCREASED COMMERCIALISM *is influencing literature today.*

Literature and fascism (ca 1925-1945) | Postwar literature (1945–1955) | Theater reform | Global book market

DEDUCTION AND DEPARTURE

The terrors of war and the Holocaust completely spurred on literary experiments. Still in shock, authors after 1945 searched for methods in which to express the terror that had been experienced. Literature, especially the theater, was supposed to help in making it impossible for such a catastrophe to be repeated. Later, literature gave expression to the younger generation's quest for self-realization and women's emancipation. In today's era of globalization, literature has become increasingly important as a cultural mouthpiece with worldwide listeners.

➜ *After the Second World War, literature attempted to deal with the horror and to make a fresh start.*

LITERATURE

THE INTERWAR PERIOD

The 1920s saw an economic boom that was followed by the Great Depression in the 1930s. The expansion of fascism and National Socialism in Europe also affected literature.

The American Dream

In "The Great Gatsby" by F. Scott Fitzgerald in 1925, the main character, Jay Gatsby, embodies the essence of the American Dream as a self-made, idealistic man who lives the wealthy life of a bootlegger during the era of Prohibition. As a thorough believer in the American Dream, Gatsby uses his new wealth to win back an old love, Daisy Buchanan. Through the perspective of a narrator named Nick, Fitzgerald examines the "Roaring Twenties," filled with parties and excess of wealth, but also society's failure to meet its potential. The lavish lifestyle of the characters is paired with their carelessness, which later results in the unwarranted murder of Gatsby at the hands of George Wilson. Through the character of Gatsby seeming to realize that his idea and the pursuit of Daisy are more rewarding than actually having her, Fitzgerald portrays the disillusionment of society during this time.

GABRIELE D'ANNUNZIO *was one of the most dazzling figures of Italian Futurist literature, as well as a major proponent of fascism.*

AS AN ITALIAN SOLDIER, *he introduced the black shirt that was to become the fascist uniform.*

HIS WORKS *usually involved individual heroes.*

Several works by D'Annunzio were filmed. For example, he contributed to the film "Cabiria" (1914).

Fascism and Literature

THE RIGOROUS equalization politics pursued in National Socialist Germany sought to quiet all possible opposition. It was during the initial phase of their rule that the Reich Culture Chamber decided who was allowed to write in the Third Reich. Those who were deemed "unsuitable" authors were persecuted and arrested. On May 10, 1933, a public book burning was organized in Berlin at Opernplatz that spread throughout Germany. This demonstration of Nazi power spoke to their merciless determination to persecute all anti-Nazi writers, especially Jewish and Marxist ones.

SEVERAL AUTHORS fled from Germany, like Thomas Mann, who escaped to the U.S. through Switzerland. However, not all were able to cope with a life in exile, such as Ernst Toller and Stefan Zweig, who both committed suicide.

right: *With the Nazi book burnings, even students and professors threw books into the fire.*

The Depression

The prosperity of the 1920s was short-lived as an economic crisis hit the international world. This was primarily characterized by inflation, decreased trade, falling prices, and high unemployment. The Great Depression in the U.S. during the 1930s left nearly two-thirds of the workforce unemployed. These hard times were written about by the American author John Steinbeck. In his masterwork, "The Grapes of Wrath" (1939), Steinbeck centered on a family who, after being evicted from their farm, are traveling to California in search of work.

Fleeing Authors

The expansion of fascism and National Socialism in Europe from about 1920 interrupted the era of literary experiments. In Germany and Italy in particular, authors were mostly left with just three possibilities: falling silent, writing from the underground, or immigrating. In fact, a few authors allowed themselves—at least temporarily—to be used by the regime. Among these was Gottfried Benn; however, he also received a writing ban in 1938. The allegiance of another collaborating author, Ernst Jünger, continues to be debated today.

An Austrian Jew and pacifist, Stefan Zweig lived with his wife in exile in Brazil from 1940.

Mia Farrow as Daisy Buchanan plays the object of Gatsby's affections in a film portrayal of "The Great Gatsby" (1974).

➜ see also: **Decadent Art,** *Visual Arts Chapter, p. 309* | **Music and Fascism,** *Music Chapter, p. 382*

LITERATURE AS A POLITICAL INSTRUMENT

"Never again" was the slogan of the survivors of the Second World War. Never again would inhumanity of that sort be accepted; literature was meant to contribute toward this end.

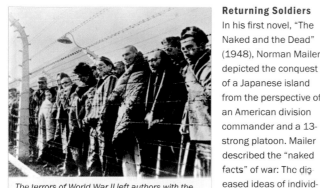

The terrors of World War II left authors with the question of how to deal with the aftermath.

Literature after the Second World War reflected the both to make a fresh start and to deal with the experienced horror. It was felt that it should never again be possible to lead people into a similar catastrophe. Authors sought to use literature to gain perspective as well as to politically educate and encourage self-reflection of the public.

Returning Soldiers

In his first novel, "The Naked and the Dead" (1948), Norman Mailer depicted the conquest of a Japanese island from the perspective of an American division commander and a 13-strong platoon. Mailer described the "naked facts" of war: The diseased ideas of individual soldiers, the senselessness of violence, and the deprivation of American society into which the soldiers had to later be reintegrated. This blunt depiction by the 25-year-old author shocked the American public and made him the focus of discussion.

The outcast sentiment felt by returning soldiers—wrenched from the social structure beyond all moral conceptions—influenced much of postwar literature, such as works like "The Man Outside" (1947) by German author Wolfgang Borchert.

Socialist Demand for Change

Writers began criticizing their contemporary political systems. Since the 1960s, the Russian author Aleksandr Solzhenitsyn exhorted the political leadership of the Soviet Union to reestablish itself upon traditional values and begin anew. Even in his first narrative, "One Day in the Life of Ivan Denisovitsch" (1962), which depicts the living and working conditions in a Stalinist workers' camp, Solzhenitsyn revealed how important a fresh start was for the USSR, which was increasingly abusing individual liberties.

Political Satires of the West

In light of the fall of fascist regimes and the political terrorizing of the USSR, Western authors like the American Ray Bradbury and the British George Orwell wrote satirical novels. In "Fahrenheit 451" (1953), Bradbury's lead character, Guy Montag, is a fireman who burns books, which have been outlawed by the government. In "1984" (1949), Orwell depicts a future totalitarian society that is ruled by "Big Brother." This force is everywhere and maintains control over society through propaganda and even "thought police." Satirizing the implementation of socialism in the USSR, Orwell's "Animal Farm" (1945) depicts the revolt of farm animals against their owners so as to create a society of equality that is free of oppression. Leading the animals are the pigs, who twist their predecessor's original ideal of animal equality into something entirely opposite.

Norman Mailer writes against war even today. He has been awarded the Pulitzer Prize twice.

INSIDER KNOWLEDGE

"ALL ANIMALS *are equal, but some animals are more equal than others." —quote from "Animal Farm"*

SOLZHENITSYN'S *works were first published in the USSR during "perestroika."*

NORMAN MAILER *was once friends with Marilyn Monroe.*

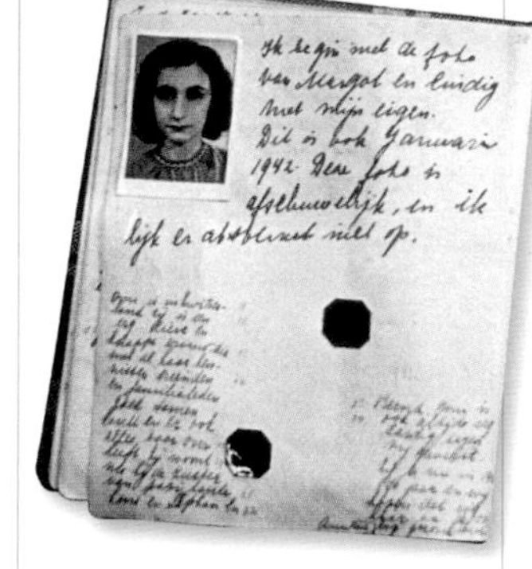

Holocaust Literature

Describing the indescribable is what Holocaust literature had to attempt to do. German authors like Paul Celan attempted to use an abstract language in their work in order not to employ the same language as the culprits and thus make "the terrible" understandable. On the other hand, authors like the Hungarian Imre Kertész or the Spanish Jorge Semprún depict directly and unsparingly the life in the resistance or in the concentration camps. One of the most compelling works is the diary of a young Jewish girl named Anne Frank who, after being forced into hiding with her family, eventually died in a Nazi concentration camp.

above: *Anne Frank died at age 15 (page from her diary).*

right: *Solzhenitsyn's regime-critical works and speeches saw his imprisonment and exile—as well as his award of the Nobel Prize for Literature in 1970.*
above: *The "Socialist realism" co-founded by Maxim Gorky was also transmitted to art, for which this portrait of Gorky is an example.*

see also: **Socialist Realism**, *Visual Arts Chapter, p. 311* | **Music in the Soviet Union**, *Music Chapter, p. 382*

THEATER REFORM

Not illusion but criticism was at the center of theater after 1940. Through its direct contact with the audience, the theater was the ideal medium for communicating new ideas.

Theater was especially well suited for the new beginning following the Second World War. It was the most direct medium through which to reach the public. Aside from existentialist, absurd, and documentary theater, there were numerous stage experiments after 1945 that repeatedly formed the topic of public discussions.

The playwriter Arthur Miller (1915–2005) criticized American society and politics throughout the course of his life.

Burst Dreams

Arthur Miller's drama "The Crucible" belongs to the American scandal dramas of the 1950s, which subtly exposed the political conditions of the McCarthy era. Through bringing the Salem witch trials of the 17th century to the stage, the spectators quickly recognized their parallels to the persecution of communists and other unpopular minority groups by Senator Joseph McCarthy. Even before this, Miller had become famous with the play "Death of a Salesman" (1949), which describes the last day in the life of the salesman Willy Loman. He commits suicide because of his feelings of inadequacy when faced with challenges after he is fired. The "American dream" promoted during this time period was burst like a soap bubble.

Epic Distancing

Not all the authors trusted that the theater audience would automatically understand the plays in the intended manner. Thus, they repeatedly attempted to make it clear to their public that visiting the theater was not merely for the purpose of entertainment, but rather to draw lessons from the play offered onstage. It was therefore important for the viewer to create a distance from the actions on the stage so as to faciliate interpretation of the content.

This idea was developed by Bertolt Brecht with his "epic theater," which used alienation to prevent the identification of the public with the figures of the drama. Through these often shocking tactics, the viewer maintains a critical distance from the action so as to analyze it better. Through interspersed narration and commentary (hence the description "epic"), the viewers are given hints to better understand the play while the conclusion is left open so as to leave them free to draw their own conclusions.

In 1949, Brecht (center) founded the Berlin Ensemble with his wife, actress Helene Weigel (left) (here, during the rehearsals for "Mother Courage and her Children").

Criticism and Responsibility

After Brecht, playwriters like Peter Weiss and Heiner Müller employed the form of epic theater. The Swiss author Friedrich Dürrenmatt likewise used estrangement techniques in his dramas, but often twisted the action on stage into grotesque and contradictory content.

His dramas, along with those by the English Harold Pinter, question the validity of subjective perception. In "The Landlord" of 1962, Pinter depicts how quickly a person can develop authoritarian characteristics if he holds a sense of superiority to others. Overall, the modern drama of the post-war era, similar to the drama of the Enlightenment, committed itself to inciting the theater viewer to critical self-reflection and responsible behavior.

IMPORTANT AUTHORS: *Samuel Beckett (1906–1989), Eugène Ionesco (1909–1994), Arthur Adamov (1908–1970), Jean Tardieu (1903–1995)*

ALFRED JARRY *was the pioneer of absurd theater with his work "King Ubu" (1896).*

Eugène Ionesco sought to prove the senselessness of social conventions. Thus, he brought figures on stage who manifested clichés and would speak at cross-purposes with each other.

Theater of the Absurd

BANAL CONTENTS, GROTESQUE SITUATIONS, senseless talking, and complete incomprehension by the viewer were characteristics of the absurd dramas, which originated in France during the 1950s. The main representatives of this style are the French author of Romanian origin Eugène Ionesco and the Irishman Samuel Beckett. Their aim was to expose the absurdity of human existence that lay within a society devoid of sense.

IN BECKETT'S DRAMA "WAITING FOR GODOT" of 1952, the tramps Estragon and Vladimir wait for Godot without knowing who or what he is, nor why they are doing it in the first place. Their waiting becomes emblematic of the senseless content of life through which its permanent presence in the dialogues absurdly gives the play orientation. However, the dialogues do not lead to any solution and the spectator is left confounded.

In "Waiting for Godot," only four characters appear throughout the play. **above:** *Samuel Beckett received the Nobel Prize for Literature in 1969.*

SELF-REALIZATION AND EMANCIPATION

The authors of the second half of the 20th century continued to search for the essense of human existence. However, the means of self-realization became ever more extreme.

Jack Kerouac penned his novel "On the Road" on a 118-ft (36-m)-long roll of paper—allegedly in a mere three weeks.

Henry Miller once described Jack Kerouac's novel "On the Road" of 1957 as stylistically undisciplined. In fact, this text defies traditional reader expectations. The unbridled colloquial style mirrors the content: The unrestrained vagabond existence of a young American named Dean who withdraws from all social compulsions after being expelled from reformatory school.

Henry Miller

After the 1934 publication of his novel "Tropic of Cancer" in the U.S., Henry Miller was criticized as a pornographer. However, his descriptions of the debauched life of an American without means in Paris are actually more than mere depictions of sexual freedom. The characters in the novel are searching for a new identity that reaches beyond the rigid social structures of the middle class. Miller's novels and narratives had a strong influence on the authors of the beat generation as well as the sexual liberation of the 1960s.

above: *Henry Miller (1891–1980)*

Always in search of the next "kick," Dean is accompanied the next two years by a young author named Sal, who narrates.

With this work, Kerouac created the novel genre of the "beat generation," a group of American writers who gave expression to the attitude towards life of the American postwar youth group. They were concerned with intense experiences and penetrating new levels of consciousness—even with the help of drugs. Beside Kerouac, Allen Ginsberg and William Burroughs were pioneers of this new literary movement, which evolved in New York during the 1940s. This beat movement became the starting point for numerous literary experiments. William Burroughs experimented greatly with the style of his work, as seen in his novel "Naked Lunch" (1959). Written as the memoir of a drug addict, hallucinations and reality are presented as permanently intertwined.

Emancipation and Individuality

Self-realization, individual consciousness, and its extension built the basis of literary works from the 1950s. Yet, the paths taken by the authors were highly individualistic. In the wake of new subjectivity, the rights of the emancipated individuals were to stand in opposition to politicized "normative" society. Field reports, diary writings, as well as views from outsider and marginal groups primarily compose the literature of the 1970s.

One of these marginal groups was women, who increasingly became recognized writers (p. 349). In the wake of the women's movement and resulting feminism, the female role in society became the topic of discussion.

After Modernism

The decisive catchword for art and literature during the second half of the 20th century was the term "postmodernism." It signals the desire for the continued development of modern artistic devices. It also expresses the demand for the playful handling of all possibilities of literary creation and the destruction of traditional stylistic forms.

21ST CENTURY

HAROLD PINTER *repeatedly intervenes in politics and criticizes George W. Bush and Tony Blair's policies in Iraq.*

THE BEAT GENERATION *had a great influence on pop culture—especially in music.*

THE STEREOTYPICAL TREND *of the black-clad existentialist was also carried over to intellectual groups in general.*

PHILOSOPHY: *Existence precedes essence, i.e., the human being gives sense to their existence through freedom of choice.*

AUTHORS: *Albert Camus ("The Stranger," 1942; "The Pest," 1947), Jean-Paul Sartre ("Nausea," 1938; "The Flies," 1943), Simone de Beauvoir ("The Mandarins of Paris," 1954)*

Albert Camus received the Nobel Prize for Literature in 1957; Sarte declined his in 1964.

French Existentialism

FRENCH EXISTENTIALISM was philosophically substantiated by Jean-Paul Sartre. As writer, he wanted to incorporate philosophy into literature, which decisively influenced French modernism. Sartre's conviction that every human being had a right to freedom, which obligated an individual to act responsibly, also presupposed a critical selection of one's own moral values and maxims for action.

OTHER REPRESENTATIVES OF FRENCH EXISTENTIALISM include Sartre's well-known associate Simone de Beauvoir, author of "The Second Sex" (1949) which became the standard for feminism, as well as Albert Camus, who emphasized the absurdity of existence in his essays and novels.

Sartre and Simone de Beauvoir were the focus of media interest.

➲ see also: Existentialism, *Philosophy Chapter, p. 263*

STORIES FROM ALL OVER THE WORLD

At the end of the 20th century, the gaze of the Western book market extended in sudden bursts to the literature of other countries. The authors narrate the stories of their native countries.

The writer as a mediator and representative of his native country gained new significance in the second half of the 20th century in the wake of globalization. Authors provided readers with an insight into the history of their native country.

Latin American Narrators

One of the first to become famous in this manner was the Chilean Pablo Neruda, a key figure of Chilean culture both as a diplomatic representative and an author.

The Russian cult author Vladimir Sorokin settles scores with totalitarian ideas and regimes.

In his verse collection "Canto Generale" of 1950, Neruda portrays the history of the Latin

The poet Pablo Neruda (1904–1973) was politically committed throughout his life (here, during the award of the Nobel Prize).

American continent in more than 300 individual poems. Therein, he manages to swear by ancient myths and traditions (e.g., the Aztec and Inca cultures) while drawing attention to political and social problems. In a thought-provoking style, Neruda appeals to a worldwide readership to take measures against oppression and assist Latin America. For his work, Neruda received the Nobel Prize for Literature in 1971. His participation in assisting victims of Pinochet's dictatorship brought him huge recognition.

Neruda had worthy successors. In 1982, a novel that pinpointed the problems of Chile more accurately than any political speech caused a furore: "The House of Spirits" by Isabel Allende. This family chronicle spans four generations up to the military dictatorship. The author is a niece of the State President Salvador Allende, who died in 1973 during the coup. She gained large recognition and has lived in the U.S. since 1988.

Another great Latin American writer comes from Colombia: Gabriel García Márquez. His novel "One Hundred Years of Solitude" from 1967 leads the reader through both the mystical as well as cold reality of Latin America while following the Buendía family across several generations until their downfall. Márquez received the Nobel Prize for Literature in 1982.

New Freedom in Eastern Europe

In the wake of the break-up of the Eastern bloc from 1985, the nearly unknown literature of Eastern Europe shifted to the center of international attention. Long suppressed authors like Michail Bulgakow ("The Master and Margarita," written in 1929–1939) were now made accessible worldwide. Young writers such as Vladimir Sorokin were finally able to showcase their narrative skill. With his novels, Sorokin repeatedly became the topic of discussion with his attacks against the former Soviet Union.

However, the authors living in exile also reflected the literature of Eastern Europe. One example was the Czech author Milan Kundera who received a publishing ban in his country in 1970 and immigrated to France. His novel "The Unbearable Lightness of Being" from 1985 deals with a pair of lovers living in what is now the Czech Republic.

The Global Book Market: New Countries of World Literature

German literature in Japan, Chinese novels in England—the global book market with its extensive translation industry enables one to gain insight into literary worlds that were nearly inaccessible just 50 years ago. Based on a widely diversified and highly specialized book trade as well as the possibility to order books through the Internet, nearly any book printed anywhere in the world can today be bought anywhere or even downloaded in digitalized form. However, booksellers and publishers are continuing to complain of sinking sales figures.

above: *International book exhibitions are a platform for exchange.*

Isabel Allende's "The House of Spirits" was filmed with an international star-studded cast including Meryl Streep, Jeremy Irons, and Armin Müller-Stahl.

LA INSOPORTABLE LEVEDAD DEL SER

Philip Kaufman filmed the novel by Milan Kundera, "The Unbearable Lightness of Being," in 1982.

LITERATURE OF DEPARTURE

Through globalization of the book market, present day literature can be received anywhere. Authors all over the world are using this to their advantage and raising their voices.

Contemporary literature is characterized by a general atmosphere of departure. More and more authors are discovering the possibility of making their own contributions to an international cultural legacy. They have long ago stopped writing only for their fellow countrymen or native language speakers. Books on such varied themes as life in an Israeli kibbutz or about conflicts in an Anatolian town can make it onto bestseller lists around the world.

Commercialization

The most important bestseller lists and the respective bookshelves in the bookshops are known to every reader. In the book industry, sales figures have become more important than the actual books. The new publications of famous bestselling authors are accompanied by huge advertising campaigns. Traditional reading increasingly takes a backseat. Additionally, the international rights of a successful book are sold and marketed severalfold—through filming, radio play adaptations, or as an audio book.

above: *Every new "Harry Potter" novel is advertised spectacularly.*

Insights

Contemporary authors are aware of their new dual responsibility to both inform and entertain their readers. Thus, the Israeli author Amos Oz—until recently the professor for Hebrew literature in Be'er Sheva—writes not only for his countrymen. He critically examines his country's history, the Holocaust, and Israel's relations with neighboring countries in a way that makes it possible for an outsider, such as a European, to gain perspective of the societal context of Israel.

This is one way Nadine Gordimer wrote herself and South Africa into the international consciousness. With her literary studies of life under apartheid, characterized by confrontations and racial violence, she has relentlessly exposed South Africa's problems.

Already in the 1960s, the Egyptian author Naguib Mahfouz had started to bring attention to the problems in his country and expose them to the outside world. In his novels, he portrays life in Cairo and critically examines fundamentalist movements. His support of Egypt's modernization and of the adaptation of Arabic culture to modernity has brought him into potential contention with Islamic fundamentalist groups.

Amos Oz has become the cultural mediator for Israel.

Nadine Gordimer brought apartheid into the consciousness of the world.

INSIDER KNOWLEDGE

PABLO NERUDA *had to finance his first book himself in 1923.*

ORHAN PAMUK *was the first Muslim author to condemn the fatwa against Salman Rushdie.*

NAGUIB MAHFOUZ *was unable to make a living from writing and was a civil servant for 34 years.*

Authors in Political Disputes

Along with Mahfouz, other authors such as the Indian Salman Rushdie and recently the Turk Orhan Pamuk prove that writers have an important voice in public. There is no other explanation for Rushdie being sentenced to death by a fatwa from the Iranian Ayatollah Khomeini on the grounds that his novel "The Satanic Verses" from 1989 was deemed blasphemous. Pamuk was accused by his country of "revilement of the Turkish identity" because he publicly held Turkey responsible for the deaths of one million Armenians and Kurds. However, his trial was discontinued at the beginning of 2006.

above: *Naguib Mahfouz became internationally famous initially through his "Cairo Trilogy."*
right: *The literary works of the Nobel Prize winner Orhan Pamuk are mostly apolitical.*

Monographic Boxes

Analytic Boxes

MUSIC

Music has engaged people since time immemorial. It followed the first ritual activities, was an essential part of the medieval world, and indispensable for the Renaissance and the Baroque. In the 19th century, concert halls and operas houses served as stages for bourgeois self-expression. Music acted as a refuge for a society developing on the path of industrialization as listeners wondered at the dexterity of the virtuosi. The large caesura of the 20th century, the Second World War, also brought far-reaching changes for music: After many had experienced a world of fascism, war, and exile, they felt as if unbroken contact with the past was no longer possible. After 1945, a pluralism of the styles prevailed, that have carried on into the present in an age of globally heard sounds.

KEY FACTS

AESTHETICS: *The study of music theory was central to the understanding of the comprehensive nature of sacred harmony.*

SOCIAL PICTURE: *The divine, rather than human creativity, was the focus of attention in the Middle Ages. Composers remained anonymous until the 13th century.*

CHANGE OF PERSPECTIVE: *In the Renaissance, interest shifted to consideration of human experiences.*

Medieval music: 5th/6th–14th century | Renaissance music: 15th/16th century

MIDDLE AGES AND RENAISSANCE

Exactly how music was made during the Middle Ages and when the first polyphonic pieces of music emerged remain largely unknown, as many works were simply handed down orally. Singing at Christian religious services marked monastic musical life, while instrumental music was more prominent in secular folk music and dance. Independent musical forms first developed during the Renaissance. Polyphonic compositions for voices reached their high point in the 15th and 16th centuries. The magnificent courts of Italy were the centers of musical life at that time.

➲ *Antiquated ideas shaped music theory during the Middle Ages and the Renaissance.*

SACRED MUSIC IN THE MIDDLE AGES

Christian churches and monasteries were places of knowledge in the Middle Ages. Here, musical texts were copied for later generations; instrumental music was rejected as too secular.

The oldest surviving musical texts date from the 8th and 9th centuries. They describe plainchant (liturgical singing) and are notated using symbols known as neumes. They may have been used as a base for improvisation as well as for singing in unison.

Early Polyphony

The first available source concerning polyphony is the anonymous "Musica enchiriadis" (ca 850). It was written for a single vocal melody; however, others were to improvise while singing at fourth or fifth intervals. This early form of polyphony is known as organum. Polyphony specifically composed with counterpoint (some voices singing different melodies) first appears in the 12th century. The building of huge French cathedrals such as Rheims and Rouen in the early 1200s hastened the emergence of church music for two and three voices. The first names mentioned in connection with polyphony, around the middle of the 13th century, are the master composer Leoninus and the choirmaster Perotinus. Both are thought to have worked in Paris at Notre Dame Cathedral, which, due to its exceptional reputation, became synonymous with music of the period 1163–1250. During this time, the first works for three and four voices with independent melodies arose. This complex music led to the development of a lavish notation system, since improvisation was no longer a realistic possibility.

Singing monks are assembled around a vocal book during the ceremony of Mass.

History of Notation

NEUMES FROM THE 9TH CENTURY were early mnemonic devices written above or next to the text to indicate tonal changes. The five-line stave, thought to be a Spanish invention, has indicated pitch since the 13th century, while written musical notes have indicated length since the 14th century. Modern notation indicating measures appeared around 1600 while practical instructions for musical performance were notated from 1800.

The five-line stave is used in this 16th century antiphonary. Early notation indicating C clef can be seen on the left-hand side.

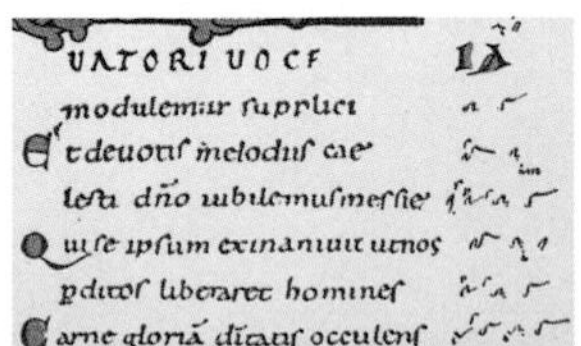

In this 9th century Easter liturgical sequence, neumes are written to the right of the text.

Romantic era composers indicated precise volume, intonation and tempo.

Monastic Musical Life

Music played an important role in daily monastic life, which was divided into eight hours of prayer. The day began with morning prayer at sunrise ("lauds") and ended with compline two hours after sunset. There was more prayer at early dawn ("matins"). This daily cycle adapted to the seasons. There were also as many as two daily Masses. Anyone actively participating in these religious services spent half of each day singing. Initially, it was call and response, performed either by two groups of similar size (antiphonal) or by a soloist and a group (responsorial). Instruments were forbidden in monasteries and churches as they were linked with pagan cults and believed to distract from religious teachings, a prohibition still upheld by the Eastern Orthodox Church. Bellows organs reappeared around the 10th century, although the first water organs date back to the third century. However, the organ was still considered a secular instrument, although composers such as Hildegard von Bingen chose to use instruments as they believed it enhanced the liturgy.

The Benedictine nun and mystic Hildegard von Bingen (1098–1179) is considered the most important composer of the Middle Ages. Her highly individualistic work was unusual for its time.

➲ see also: **Court, State, Monastery,** *Literature Chapter, p. 340*

SECULAR SONGS AND INSTRUMENTAL MUSIC

Music was a highly regarded sideline or subject for theoretical study in the Middle Ages, although professional musicians were still regarded as social outsiders.

The antecedents of the lute, guita and violin arrived in Europe from the Arab world through Spain, but singing remained the most important factor in secular music.

Troubadours and Minnesong

The unattainable lover was a central theme of refined courtly entertainment, which developed around 1070 in southern France. Singers such as William of Aquitaine were known as troubadours (*trouvères* in northern France), which came from the verb "*trobar*" meaning "to compose," as they were regarded as both poets and composers. Noble lyric poets sang solo, mostly in the medieval Romance language now known as Provençal. However, they permitted accompaniment—primarily on the vielle, harp, and lute. The German counterpart lasted from 1150 until the decline of chivalric orders in the 14th century. Medieval stories and Arab love poetry were the models for the *minne* (the Middle High German word for love). The most famous minnesinger was Walther von der Vogelweide.

Bernart de Ventadour, the most famous troubadour of southern France, made his name at the court of Eleanor of Aquitaine.

Song Craft: The Meistersinger

Guilds comprising organized Meistersingers—considered craftsmen—formed in European cities during the 15th and 16th centuries. Songs were based on biblical subjects, but later expanded to include history and other themes sung according to strict rules. Seated on a stool, the singer introduced his new song, which was assessed by a judge behind a black curtain. The most famous singer was Nuremberg-based cobbler Hans Sachs, who composed more than 4,500 master songs. A central function of the master's art was the transmission of knowledge, since many guild members could not read or afford books.

Music in Medieval Educational Curriculum

Music was an important part of every educational program at the Latin schools and universities. All students of medicine and theology had to study music as one of the seven liberal arts. It was considered a science, as the ancient concept of comprehensive harmony was proved by the sound of simple harmonic relationships having a calming effect (an octave will generate, by division of the string, a wavelength in a ratio of 1:2). The special position music held in the educational system shaped the cultural life of large student centers like Paris, where church music and university studies were closely connected. Masters of large cathedrals such as Notre Dame not only directed the choirs, but also instructed students of music theory at the cathedral school.

21ST CENTURY

GREGORIAN PLAINCHANT *is adapted by many contemporary composers.*

HANS SACHS *was immortalized as Beckmesser, a petty music critic, in Richard Wagner's only comic opera "Die Meistersinger."*

CARMINA BURANA *(ca 1300), a collection of sayings, love songs, drinking songs, and dances, was set to music by Carl Orff. It played to sold-out audiences at a Czech sports arena in 2004.*

Music and the Seven Arts

From the Middle Ages through the 18th century, music was considered one of the "seven liberal arts" forming a significant part of every education. The first three were language arts ("trivium") comprising grammar, rhetoric, and dialectic. The remaining four were the mathematical subjects ("quadrivium") of arithmetic (mathematics), geometry, astronomy (astrology), and music. Music held a special position because of its structure, since it was related to both mathematics and also language (especially rhetoric).

above: *Representation of the seven liberal arts*

PERFORMER, JUGGLER, MINSTREL: The many names by which traveling musicians were known reflect their expansion across Europe.

THE PERFORMER'S TASKS were closely interwoven with stories and themes from all strata of medieval society.

The poet Heinrich von Meissen is surrounded by performers with instruments: drum, flute, schal mai, psaltery, and dudelsack.

Traveling Singers and Musicians

THE FIRST MENTION of traveling performers dates to the 8th century. They were considered the primary caretakers of the medieval musical culture, yet most belonged to the lowest social classes. Men and women traveled alone or in groups to earn money with their songs, dances, acrobatics, and performing animals from people in public squares, pubs, bathhouses, and houses of pleasure. Performances consisted primarily of a greeting, a prelude, the main performance, and perhaps an encore.

PERFORMERS HAD CLOSE LOCAL CONNECTIONS as they often played music for processions and weddings. Some even performed as respected accompanists for lyric poets, or by themselves as singers of heroic or epic poetry before an educated public. Despite being regarded as outsiders, many proudly passed on their profession to their children. Their constant and extensive traveling made them central to cultural exchange in medieval Europe.

above: *The crank on a hurdy-gurdy strikes its internal stri to create sound.*
right: *The vielle was a precursor of the violin, with five str and additional vibrating strings.*

see also: Adventures and Love Songs, *Literature Chapter, p. 339*

MUSIC

SACRED MUSIC OF THE RENAISSANCE (1430–1600)

Polyphonic masses and motets in Latin were the dominant forms of Renaissance church music. Yet the role played by music in religious life was controversial during the Reformation and Counter-Reformation and was the subject of much discussion.

Church singers at mass. Religious worship followed an increasingly fixed order called the liturgy.

The 15th and early 16th centuries were considered the age of Franco-Flemish vocal polyphony, as its leading composers came from the Netherlands and present-day northern France.

Franco-Flemish Polyphony

Entire polyphonic masses set to music were the focus of church music. Shorter sacred compositions for several voices were called motets. Compositions blended multiple and individual voices in a rich tapestry of sound, a major development from parallel singing in the Middle Ages (p. 362). Notable composers in the 15th and 16th centuries included Guillaume Dufay from Burgundy, Flemish Josquin Des Prés in Italy, and Adrien Willaert, who set up a school in Venice. Their style had a great influence on all of Europe, especially Italy, where Roland de Lassus became known as Orlando di Lasso, Europe's "prince of musicians."

The Mass

THE MASS, the main form of Christian religious worship, started developing in the ffith century. It celebrates the Eucharist—the ceremony with the bread and wine at the Last Supper—and comprises five fixed elements (Kyrie, Gloria, Creed, Sanctus, and Agnus Dei) and others that vary according to the liturgical calendar. During the 15th and 16th centuries, the permanent parts (the Ordinary) were set to music using increasingly complex polyphony. The musical foundation was either a liturgical chorale or a secular melody known as the "cantus firmus," or fixed song.

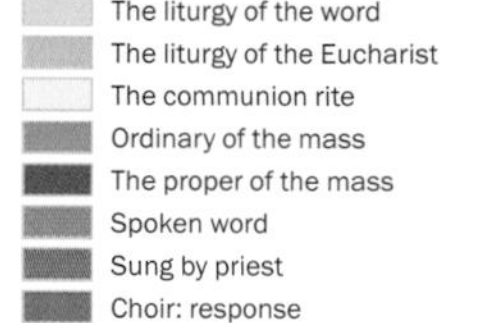

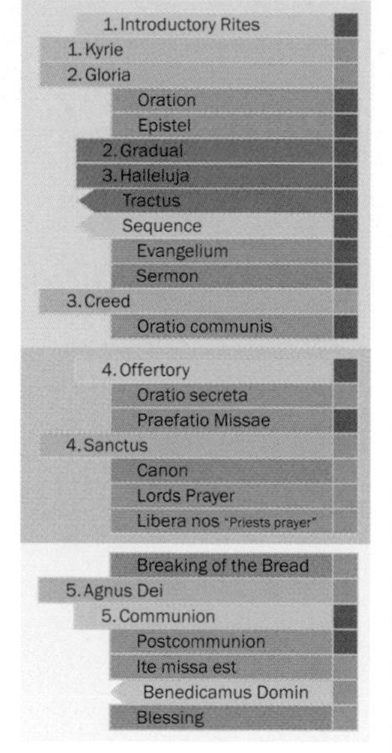

Music of the Reformation

Protestant churches formed in the 16th century after the 1521 Schism with the Roman Catholic Church, but retained the Latin mass. Songs in the vernacular (chorales) were introduced gradually into worship services after religious reformer Martin Luther translated the mass into German. Johann Walter's compilation of songs, the "Wittenberg Gesangbuch" (1524), became the model for many later Protestant choral collections. Luther regarded music as an important component of religious worship, but opinions on this subject varied. Zurich-based Ulrich Zwingli disapproved of music in worship, while John Calvin permitted plainchant in Geneva.

The Council of Trent

The Council of Trent, held between 1545–1563 during the Counter-Reformation, aimed to distinguish Roman Catholic teachings from those of the Reformation. Church music came under discussion, particularly the unintelligibility of text in polyphonic music, the frequent adaptation of secular melodies for church music, and increasing artistic independence. Giovanni Pierluigi da Palestrina is considered to have saved polyphony for religious use with his six-voiced "Missa Papae Marcelli" (1555). The famous composer at Rome's papal court showed the council that his a cappella masses could be intelligible.

In polyphony, individual voices are musically and rhythmically independent. Homophony was the form featuring soloists, with other accompanying voices singing in unison.

Luther and His Music

Martin Luther considered music and religious worship to be fundamentally connected to the concept of divine origin, and to the church ceremonies of praise and proclamation. This philosophy formed the basis for major developments in Protestant church music into the 20th century. Luther played both the lute and flute, and wrote many song texts that were set to music by Johann Walter. He adapted popular secular melodies for some compositions, such as the Christmas carol "From Heaven on High."

above: *Martin Luther (1483–1546)*

The Roman Catholic church commended compositions of Giovanni Pierluigi da Palestrina, shown here in audience with Pope Julius III.

➲ see also: Reformation, *Religion Chapter, p. 237*

SECULAR MUSIC OF THE 16TH CENTURY

Although Franco-Flemish composers influenced all of Europe, each region developed its own style from the 16th century onward.

The Renaissance was noted for the vibrancy of its musical styles and the wealth of activities concerning the arts. Music leadership, however, was taken over by the many courts and churches of Italy. The Flemish composer Willaert was music director of the Cathedral of San Marco in Venice in 1527. He educated Italians Andrea Gabrieli, Giovanni Gabrieli—the most famous Venetian composer of his time—and European musician Heinrich Schütz, creator of great oratorios.

Madrigals

The composed short poem called the madrigal was the most significant form of Italian secular music in the 16th century. The text was based on poetry by the rediscovered medieval poet Petrarch or new poetic works imitating his style. Madrigals were performed at courts, colleges, and salons held by the nobility, which evolved into the Florentine Camerata. Female professional musicians also became prominent in performances at court during this time.

Growing Independence of Instrumental Music

Instrumental music developed into an independent form during the Renaissance. Existing vocal works were performed on instruments initially, although it is not known exactly when certain instruments were first used. Independent musical forms, such as the *ricerare*, developed as a result of increasing improvisation as the phrasings of vocal music were adapted for instruments. This held especially true for the *chanson*, first mentioned as an instrumental form in 1523. Chansons were adaptations of French songs or original compositions written in the style that became overwhelmingly popular in many regions. They were played by ensembles of instruments, especially in England, where music lovers kept entire collections of instruments at home so that guests would not have to bring their own viola or flute.

In Venice, instruments were used for multichoir church music performances while composers adapted their compositions to their particular characteristics and tonal colors. However, the focus on text remained central to music-making well into the Baroque era. The instruments of the time—besides the recorder and viola—included percussion instruments (harpsichord and virginals) and wind instruments (cornet, pommer shawm, and crumhorn). The lute was the preferred instrument for the home, as it was ideal for accompanying solo and consort singing. The organ, which developed its own tradition in the 15th century, was still considered an endless source of rich musical sound one hundred years later.

Spanish Vihuela

In the latter part of the 16th century, Spanish musicians and composers began to favor the *vihuela*, a guitar-like instrument. Virtuoso players created the first truly independent music for an instrument, basing this music on the tonal colors appropriate for the instrument and not merely transposing vocal melodies directly.

Magnificent Venice

The independent city-state of Venice was at the zenith of its power in the 15th century. The nobility displayed ever-greater magnificence in their courts, and music played a key role in church and state formal functions. The position of choir director at the Cathedral of San Marco was one of the most sought-after appointments in all Italy. It attracted composers such as Willaert and the Gabrielis, and the so-called Venetian School specialized in multichoir performances for many high-ranking personalities of the time. The music publisher Ottavio Petrucci, the first to print music using movable type, was based in Venice.

above: *Piazza San Marco in Venice, painting by Canaletto*

THE CONCEPT OF THE RENAISSANCE, *the rebirth of classical thought, also applied to music according to the Florentine Camerata.*

PORTRAYING HUMAN PASSIONS, *desires, and emotions at the center of musical dramas imitates classical thinking.*

One of the oldest preserved operas is Giulio Caccini's "Euridice" (1602), with libretto by Ottavio Rinuccini.

The Florentine Camerata

THE FLORENTINE CAMERATA was a forum for discussion and debate comprising nobles, musicians, intellectuals, and poets at the castle of Count Giovanni Bardi in the 1570s–1580s. The most influential member was the composer and music theorist Vincenzo Galilei, followed by composers Giulio Caccini and Piero Strozzi. Music from Greek antiquity was a favorite topic of discussion. The group was critical of the contemporary use of polyphony and instrumental music, and attempted to imitate the emotional effects of ancient music upon the human spirit. One example was Greek monody, or solo singing with kithara accompaniment.

THE CONCEPT OF THE FLORENTINE CAMERATA extended to Jacopo Corsi's private academy, which started to support performances of so-called pastoral dramas in 1594. These were performed by soloists with simple instrumental accompaniment, and regarded, with the form called intermedia, as the antecedents of opera. Corsi staged the first opera, "La Dafne," at his palace in 1597-1598 with the help of poet Ottavio Rinuccini and Medici court composer Jacopo Peri. Only excerpts of this opera remain.

Peri performed as a singer in intermedia, or interludes performed between the acts of other plays.

The lute was one of the best loved instruments of the time. The theorbo, shown here in a Caravaggio painting, is a bass lute.

MUSIC

KEY FACTS

IMPORTANT INSTRUMENTAL FORMS *of the Baroque: concerto grosso, suite, and trio sonatas.*

OPERA SERIA *(serious opera) reflected the pomp of absolutism.*

THE FUGUE *was seen as the musical depiction of a divine order.*

FUGUE SUBJECTS *were melodic, rhythmic themes that master performers turned upside-down and inside-out.*

Baroque (1600–1750) | Courtly musical culture | Opera | Cantatas and oratorios | Instrumental music

BAROQUE—ABSOLUTIST SPLENDOR

The music of the Baroque era, named after the elaborate architectural style of the period, reflected the splendor of absolute rule. Ambitious court music and the new form of opera were artistic representations of earthly power. The new genre of oratorio was also grandiose, but was based on biblical themes. As George Frederick Handel composed choral and other pieces in London, Johann Sebastian Bach wrote almost 300 sacred and secular cantatas—a new form of church music—in Germany.

Baroque splendor: opera seria—Baroque instrumental music: concerto grosso.

COURTLY MUSICAL CULTURE

European courts developed a magnificent style of court music during the Baroque era. Ballet, opera, and orchestral music were fixed components of an absolutist demonstration of power.

The focus on music in the Italian Renaissance courts like Mantua and Ferrara greatly aided its development. New forms such as opera emerged and orchestras became professional, allowing composers to compose for a specific number of instruments in ensembles. This preoccupation with music continued into the 17th century as a fixture of absolutist court ceremonies including feasts, dances, parades, and hunts—even the church and stage. Demands made by performing musicians grew in proportion to the diversity of their duties. Professional singers and musicians performed increasingly magnificent works as composers discarded the speech rhythms previously used in church music for dance rhythms.

Versailles as Model

Versailles became the stylistic role model for courtly music from the 17th century onward. Under Louis XIV, court music experienced an upswing. The "sun king" loved opulent stage spectacles with music and dance, in which he himself participated as a dancer. Many famous artists understood they had to compose and perform according to Louis's tastes if they wanted to affiliate themselves with his court. In addition to the court composer Jean-Baptiste Lully, the French harpsichordist and composer Elisabeth Jacquet de la Guerre was connected with the Court of Versailles.

The Court of Versailles was the center of music in the 17th century.

INSIDER KNOWLEDGE

MUSIC-MAKING WITH DEADLY CONSEQUENCES: *Lully conducted with a long, heavy, lavishly decorated baton, reflecting the opulence of the Court of Versailles. He used to indicate the initial beat by hitting the baton on the floor, but one time he hit his foot instead. The wound did not heal and inflammation set in. Lully died a few days later of gangrene.*

Jean-Baptiste Lully

JEAN-BAPTISTE LULLY, *born 1632 in Florence, Italy, died 1687 in Paris.*

THE GRACIOUS MAGNIFICENCE *of Lully's music reflected the splendor of the Court of Versailles.*

LULLY CREATED *comedic ballet—a mixture of comedy, ballet, and song.*

Jean-Baptiste Lully

EDUCATED AS A DANCER AND VIOLINIST, LULLY came to France at the age of 15 as a page. He had an unparalleled career at the Court of Versailles. In 1656, he founded the Petits Violons, a well-known elite orchestra. In 1661, he was appointed "Surintendant de la musique instrumental du roi," one of the most influential positions in court music at Versailles. To accommodate the tastes of the dance-obsessed Louis XIV, Lully collaborated with poet and playwright Molière to reform the court ballet.

BEGINNING IN 1673, a new opera was created for Versailles each year. These lavish stage works combined music and dancing with magnificent stage sets, and resulted in spectacular works of art.

Louis XIV as character "The Rising Sun" in "Ballet of the Night," 1654

Courtly music entertained as festival music (above: at the 1760 wedding of Joseph II to Isabella of Parma), dance music for balls, outdoor music for hunting, church music for worship, and stage music for the opera and ballet.

BAROQUE OPERA

The first opera house opened in Venice in 1637, creating momentum for the new genre of sung drama called opera.

The Renaissance courts of northern Italy were especially fond of intermedia: Musical interludes for theatrical works, most of which had little to do with the plot of the play. They developed into independent works of musical theater. The singers portrayed individual characters and the plot was accompanied by music especially composed for it. A new genre was born: opera.

The Masque

The masque evolved as a particularly English form of opera in the early 17th century. It combined dancing, spoken dialogue, and singing. The first English opera was Henry Purcell's "Dido and Aeneas" (1689), composed for a girls' school. Purcell, who was made organist at Westminster Cathedral at the age of 20, wrote five subsequent semi-operas, all closely following the developing masque form.

above: *Henry Purcell*

The First Opera House in Venice

At first, opera remained an exclusively courtly form of entertainment. Claudio Monteverdi composed his opera "Orfeo" to celebrate the wedding of the Duke of Mantua in 1607. Opera enjoyed a wider audience after the first commercial opera house opened in Venice in 1637. Venetian opera was hugely successful, and soon more opera houses were built in Italy. Many different opera styles quickly developed, as groups of opera performers traveled extensively throughout the land.

Opera Seria and Opera Buffa

Two main types of opera evolved: *opera seria* ("serious opera") and *opera buffa* ("comic opera"). The first evolved from the Venetian operatic traditions. In the 18th century it made an impression on the Neopolitan Opera School, which included Alessandro Scarlatti among its students.

Opera seria was usually based on ancient mythological and historical plots. The cast was similar in each work—usually two couples involved in some form of intrigue. Musically, opera seria alternates between recitatives and *arias* (ensembles). Recitatives are spoken musical numbers which advance the plot, while arias are musical excerpts depicting the character's emotions. Opera buffa, the opposite of opera seria, has comic characters appearing in the tradition of the stock caricatures of the Commedia dell'Arte. Most works feature lovers' quarrels and mistakes.

Querelle des Bouffons

Opera expanded throughout Europe in the second half of the 17th century and developed independent traditions outside Italy. Jean-Baptiste Lully developed a new tradition in France in the 1670s. However, in reaction to a 1752 performance of Giovanni Battista Pergolesi's opera "La Serva Padrona," a serious fight erupted between the followers of Italian opera buffa and those of the French tradition, which was called *querelle des bouffons* (war of the comic actors).

Naples (above: Teatro di San Carlo in Naples) became the center of Italian opera in the 18th century. Opera seria at the Neapolitan Opera School defined European opera production for decades.

MONTEVERDI, *born 1567 in Cremona, Italy, died 1643 in Venice.*

HIS "ORFEO" OF 1607 *is considered the first opera in the history of music.*

LATER OPERAS: *"Il ritorno d'Ulisse in patria" (1639-1640), "L'incoronazione di Poppea" (1642)*

HIS STYLE *of composition is marked by "monody."*

Claudio Monteverdi

Claudio Monteverdi

EDUCATED IN CREMONA, Claudio Monteverdi came to Mantua in 1590, where he worked as a musician and court conductor from 1607. The last of the great madrigalists, he contributed to the exploration of the possibilities of the orchestra through the introduction of pizzicato and tremolo in the string sections. He shaped the development of a new, definitive form of opera.

HE COMPOSED LATER OPERAS in Venice after moving to the city in 1613. He held the position of "Maestro di Capella" at the Cathedral of San Marco, where he wrote many sacred and secular songs, and many books of madrigals.

L' ORFEO
FAVOLA IN MVSICA
DA CLAVDIO MONTEVERDI
RAPPRESENTATA IN MANTOVA
AL SERENISSIMO SIGNOR
D. FRANCESCO GONZAGA
M D C IX.

above: *Title page of "Orfeo," Venice, 1609 edition*

Modern production of the opera "L'incoronazione di Poppea" at Berlin premiere in 2006.

CANTATA AND ORATORIO

The oratorio, a type of sacred opera, brought religious themes into the concert hall. Johann Sebastian Bach made the cantata the centerpiece of Protestant Church music.

"Oratorio" was the term used in Rome to denote halls of worship, in which congregations assembled for prayer, religious debate, and song. The term was gained an extended meaning in the 16th century to describe the form of music performed there; singing together gave people a means of pondering questions of faith in a more entertaining manner. Based predominantly on Christian religious themes, the oratorio is a multi-part composition for soloist, choir, and orchestra.

Handel's London Oratorios

The oratorio, although composed for religious worship, expanded beyond the liturgy. It was usually a lavishly performed work, reminiscent of opera because of its rich musicality and artificially contrived storylines, but without scenery. George Frideric Handel described his early oratorio "Esther" (1732) as "a sacred opera." He tried to make a career in London in the 1740s as a composer and producer of opera, but few productions covered their costs. Instead, Handel focused his attention on composing oratorios as highly theatrical biblical operas, sung in English. His "Messiah," which debuted in Dublin in 1742, was one of his most successful works.

George Frideric Handel was influential in Germany and England.

The Cantata

The cantata (from Latin *cantare*, to sing) is closely related to the oratorio. This multi-movement composition for singing and instrumental accompaniment was also fashioned in Italy. The chamber cantata was a social form of entertainment for the aristocracy there: A soloist performed a demanding literary text, accompanied by one or more instruments. The Italian "chamber cantata" (*cantata da camera*) was dedicated to secular themes: love, pleasure, and life. Less common in Italy was the "Cantata da Chiesa" (church cantata), which dealt with sacred texts. However, it found a larger following in Protestant Germany. In Leipzig, Johann Sebastian Bach composed a cantata for every Sunday and holy day of the liturgical year for more than two years (1723–1725).

Bach's Leipzig Cantatas

Bach developed a standard form for the cantata: An orchestral introduction that could be lavishly scored with timpani and trumpets, followed by an introductory chorus, and then a recitative and aria for one or more solo voices. This scheme inspired by opera seria (p. 367) was repeated as desired, depending on the length of the cantata. The cantata then closed with a four-voice chorale. Bach used the cantata form to perfect the principle of his theory of emotional response: he held that music could depict or even provoke such responses. He set edifying religious texts to music in his cantatas, in which he highlighted individual words or phrases through especially musical characters.

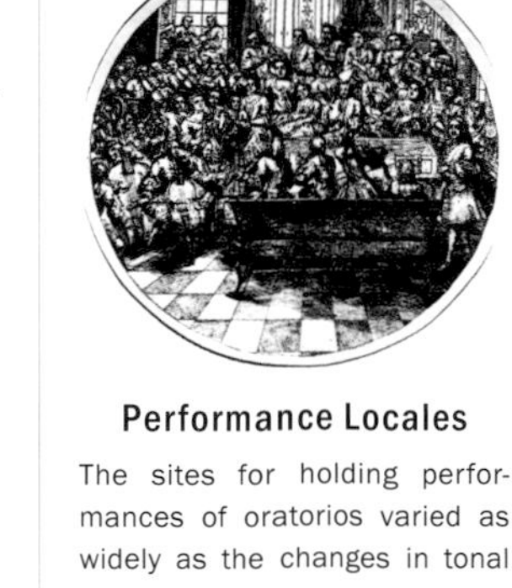

Performance Locales

The sites for holding performances of oratorios varied as widely as the changes in tonal sound for these sacred operas, which were not equivalent to a Mass and did not have stage sets. The appropriate place to perform an oratorio was initially a place of worship such as a church. Performances later took place in noble courts and private dwellings. As these were not large enough, theater stages were used to accommodate the many musicians and choristers involved. The changing locales for performance are illustrative of the characteristics shared with other forms: Its opulent staging and dramaturgy are borrowed from opera, and its subjects from church music.

above: *Handel and an oratorio*

JOHANN SEBASTIAN BACH, *born 1685 in Eisenach, Germany, died 1750 in Leipzig.*

WELL-KNOWN WORKS: *"Saint Matthew Passion," "Christmas Oratorio," "The Well-Tempered Clavier," "The Brandenburg Concertos"*

FOR HIS SECOND WIFE, *singer Anna Magdalena Wilcken, he wrote "The Little Organ Book."*

Johann Sebastian Bach, painting from 1746

Johann Sebastian Bach

BACH CAME FROM a musical family. His parents died when he was young and he was raised and educated by his brother Johann Christoph. After working in Lüneburg, Arnstadt, and Mühlhausen, he was appointed chamber musician at the Weimar court in 1708. He became Kapellmeister at the Anhalt-Cöthen court in 1717. What made his career, however, was when he was named Cantor of St. Thomas Church in Leipzig in 1723. He was responsible for the city's musical life as well as teaching choirboys at St. Thomas School.

MANY OF HIS 20 children were musicians: Johann Christoph Friedrich ("Bückeburg Bach"), Johann Christian ("London Bach"), Wilhelm Friedemann, and Carl Philipp Emanuel.

left: *St. Thomas Church in Leipzig*
right: *Cantata manuscript personally inscribed by Bach*

THE WIDE VARIETY OF BAROQUE INSTRUMENTAL MUSIC

New forms of instrumental music developed in the second half of the 17th century to show the instrumentalists' skills to his best advantage: the concerto grosso, suite, and trio sonata.

The rapid development in the construction of instruments such as the violin and harpsichord had a significant influence on Baroque instrumental music. Italy, with its centers of violin construction in Brescia and Cremona, was especially influential. Larger ensembles of well-trained musicians were established there, and artistic performance techniques developed to facilitate very demanding compositions for stringed instruments. Major composers, including Arcangelo Corelli, Antonio Vivaldi, and Giuseppi Tartini with his "Devil's Trill Sonata," were often virtuoso violinists, who composed pieces to test their craft.

François Couperin was court composer at Versailles from 1700 and royal court harpsichordist from 1717.

Concerto Grosso

The Baroque *concerto grosso* is a composition for a larger instrumental ensemble, in which a group of solo instruments plays in concert with an ensemble (orchestra). The concerto grosso was among the most popular forms of Baroque instrumental music. Corelli's concerti grossi of 1714 were considered standard works. Bach's six Brandenburg Concertos (p. 368) were composed in this form.

Antonio Vivaldi

One of the most influential violin virtuosos and composers of the Baroque era was Antonio Vivaldi, famous not only for composing 60 concerti grossi but also for more than 400 concertos. These were created for public concerts held at the Ospedale della Pietà, a girls' orphanage in Venice where Vivaldi was employed as a music instructor from 1703. These orphanages, established in many Italian cities, gave children and young people a substantial music education. They were the forerunners of modern music conservatories.

Antonio Vivaldi (1678–1741) was known as "il prete rosso" (the red priest) because of the red color of his hair.

Dance Movements in Succession: The Suite

Instrumental music, especially the suite, had a wide following in Germany and France. Various movements follow each other in succession ("suite" comes from the French word meaning "follow"), and their rhythm and character support dances. Two movements always form a pair: The first is a slower (stepping) dance, the second a faster (jumping) dance. A common dance sequence was: *allemande* (slow), *courant* (fast), *sarabande* (slow), *gigue* (fast). Other possible sections were the air, the *minuet*, the *chaconne*, or the *passacaglia*. Among François Couperin's most important works were 27 harpsichord suites, published in four volumes between 1713 and 1730.

Baroque Instruments

The extremely popular lute of the 15th and 16th centuries was widely replaced in the Baroque era by keyboard instruments. While in England and the Netherlands the virginals (rectangular, with keyboard running parallel to the strings) found broad appeal, the spinet (triangular) was especially beloved in Italy and Germany. However, the most important keyboard instrument of the Baroque period was the harpsichord, which was replaced around 1760 by the pianoforte, predecessor to the contemporary piano. The family of string instruments includes, largely unchanged in form since the 16th century, the violin, viola, violoncello, and contrabass.

Antonio Stradivari, 1690

MUSIC

The Fugue

A FUGUE IS a contrapuntal, polyphonic composition comprising many voices that are of equal in importance, each one imitating and adapting the first. Its complex principles of construction made many people in Baroque times consider it an expression of divine world harmony. The pinnacle of Baroque fugue composition is featured in Bach's "The Well-Tempered Clavier" (1722, 1744) as well as his "The Art of the Fugue" (1749-1750). The fugue is usually preceded by a prelude or other free-form movement.

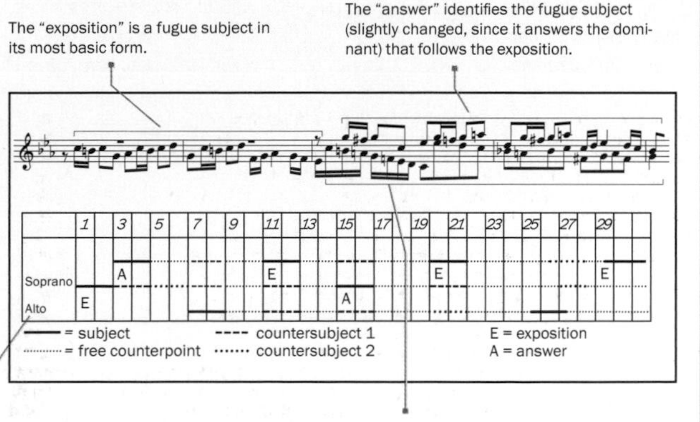

The "exposition" is a fugue subject in its most basic form.

The "answer" identifies the fugue subject (slightly changed, since it answers the dominant) that follows the exposition.

Soprano, alto, and bass signify the individual voices of a three-voice fugue—and indicate that they are also concerned with an instrumental composition.

The countersubject is the opposite of the fugue subject, and composed in free counterpoint or contrapuntal voices.

21ST CENTURY

CREMONA-BASED *Antonio Stradivari made instruments with a distinctive sound, possibly due to the composition of the lacquer—a secret until the 21st century. The roughly 500 remaining Stradivarius violins, known by the names of prior owners, continue to break auction records. The Hammer was sold for 3.5 million dollars (2.8 million euro) in 2006.*

➔ see also: Baroque Art, *Visual Arts Chapter, p. 298*

KEY FACTS

VIENNESE CLASSICAL MUSIC *is connected most closely with Haydn, Mozart, and Beethoven.*

PUBLIC CONCERT LIFE: *Concerts became generally accessible as ticket prices became affordable.*

THE PIANOFORTE *became the main instrument of the period: versatile, virtuoso, and sonorous.*

OPERA *moved away from the rather stiff form of opera seria.*

Classical (1760–1820) | Sonata and string quartet | Concerto and symphony | Orchestral sound | Opera reform

CLASSICAL ERA—CLARITY OF FORM

The music of the Viennese classical era emerged amid the aesthetic and social upheaval that shaped the late 18th century: the Enlightenment, the end of absolutism, and the discovery of emotional responsiveness. New musical forms were greatly demanded in this new cultural climate. Thus, this saw the rise of the string quartet as music for "expert" music lovers as well as the solo concert and symphony for the concert hall, which was open for the first time to all (paying) guests. The most important composers were Mozart and Beethoven.

➲ *Classical music followed the ideals of the Enlightenment.*

MUSIC

NEW IDEAL SOUND: THE STRING QUARTET AND PIANOFORTE

Classical chamber music targeted discriminating experts and music lovers with a great curiosity for all things new.

Social upheavals of the late 18th century were a significant driving force in the new aesthetic consciousness and forms of musical life. Music was now performed not just at royal courts, but also in the homes of the nobility and bourgeoisie. Consequently, a large quantity of suitable music was required, particularly chamber music for small ensembles aimed at a broader musical taste.

Vienna at the time of Mozart and others was one of the most important music centers in Europe ("View of Vienna from the Belvedere," painting by Canaletto).

Music for Connoisseurs

In addition to music for music lovers, an elaborate style also developed that was consciously directed toward connoisseurs. String quartets, in particular those by Mozart and Beethoven, made the greatest demands upon both performers and listeners.

The piano sonata evolved beyond its purpose as an entertaining diversion. The catalyst for this change occurred in 1760 with the improved technical performance of the pianoforte, in contrast to that of the harpsichord. This new instrument, also known as the fortepiano, made possible a differentiation in volume; for example, the playing of loud (forte) and soft (piano). Compositions for the piano became more complex and, because of their tonal and technical details, easier to contemplate. This can be heard in the 32 piano sonatas by Beethoven, who maintained close relationships with the best piano manufacturers of his time, such as Nanette Stein-Streicher, to maximize the tonal possibilities of these newly developed instruments.

WOLFGANG AMADEUS MOZART, *born 1756 in Salzburg, Austria, died 1791 in Vienna*

A PRODIGY *on the piano and violin, Mozart was well-known at an early age throughout Europe.*

WELL-KNOWN OPERAS: *"The Abduction From the Seraglio," "The Marriage of Figaro," "Don Giovanni," "The Magic Flute"*

"Wolfgang Amadeus Mozart," silverpoint drawing by Dorothea (Dora) Stock, 1789

Wolfgang Amadeus Mozart

MOZART AND HIS OLDER SISTER Maria Anna (Nannerl) showed early signs of great musical gifts, which their father, Leopold, a respected music teacher, subsequently developed. Both prodigies became well known throughout Europe as they toured to play at the major courts. Like his father, Mozart served the Prince-Archbishop of Salzburg, but left this position in 1781. He set up business in Vienna, where he achieved great success as a piano virtuoso and freelance composer. He composed numerous piano concertos for his own performances. He was also a successful opera composer, especially in Vienna and Prague.

above: *Mozart appeared at many European courts as a musical prodigy (here with Empress Maria Theresa and her family).*
right: *Program for the premiere of Mozart's "The Magic Flute" in Theater auf der Wieden in Vienna (1791).*

The String Quartet

Joseph Haydn was the primary influence on the development of the string quartet, from its early days as the Baroque trio sonata, in the second half of the 18th century. He established the four-movement form in 1769. Mozart used this model initially, but surpassed it in his later works. Beethoven composed 16 string quartets, which are still part of the standard repertoire for every quartet ensemble. The instruments in a quartet comprise two violins, a viola, and a violoncello.

above: The Juilliard quartet

➲ **see also: Enlightenment,** *Philosophy Chapter, p. 258* | *Literature Chapter, p. 344*

THE CONCERT AND SYMPHONY

Classical music targeted a new public. The nature of the concert in the 18th century required brilliant concertos, colorful programs, and dazzling virtuoso players.

The character of the concert changed fundamentally with the emergence of concert promoters. In Paris, the first important public concert series, Concerts Spirituels, was established around 1725 and shaped concert life in this musical metropolis until the French Revolution. The public concert, also known as the academy, replaced the courtly musical events which had been offered only to an invited group of listeners. The program consisted of assorted works: Symphonies (or individual movements from these), overtures, operatic arias, choral works, and chamber music were selected depending on the availability of musicians and soloists.

New public performance spaces were required. Concert halls were built, and other places of assembly were adapted: guest houses, gardens, and, as above, guild halls.

Mozart's Viennese Academies

Among Mozart's most lucrative appearances were his academies, in which he appeared as the interpreter of his own works. The piano concertos from his time in Vienna were composed for these occasions. They matched the astonishing virtuosity, lightness, and refinement prevalent in Viennese musical tastes of the late 18th century. Mozart adapted his compositions to the productions of the time. While some concertos were composed for a conspicuously small, almost chamber music-like orchestral group, others displayed the complete magnificence of the luxuriously rich orchestral sound.

The Symphony: From Haydn to Beethoven

The development of the symphony between 1759 and 1824, is demonstrated by the number of works. During this time, Haydn composed more than 100 symphonies, while Beethoven composed only nine. This development spanned the Rococo-like lightness of Haydn's first symphonies, to his 6 Paris and 12 London symphonies for the public there, and the profound depth of Beethoven's individual works.

The musical conception of the symphonies assumed correspondingly different forms: Four movements contrasting in speed and tonal color, simple orchestration (especially for the wind instruments), and the largely restricted thematic motif placed Haydn's symphonic style squarely within the classical genre.

Beethoven, however, went beyond these dimensions: Double sections of woodwind and brass instruments strengthened the sound and expanded the possibilities for tonal color. The classical minuet, typically the third movement, developed into a more variable scherzo. The musical structure of the entire work solidified as the individual movements became related to one another. Beethoven applied the idea of the pure instrumental symphonic form to the vocals of his Ninth Symphony by incorporating additional soloists and a choir. Its premiere on May 7, 1824, was a sensational success.

Sonata Form

MOST MULTI-MOVEMENT works of the classical period, like concertos and symphonies, open with a first movement based on the sonata movement form. This became the epitome of Viennese classical music and shaped musical form until the 20th century.

The entire movement is divided into four parts: exposition (introduction of two opposing themes), development (expansion of these themes), recapitulation (almost identical repetition of the exposition), and coda (end).

Exposition :			:	Development	Recapitulation				Coda
First Subject Group (Main Theme)	Transition	Second Subject Group (Secondary Theme)	Codetta	Manipulation of the Themes and Subject Groups	Main Theme	Transition	Secondary Theme	Continuation/Codetta	Secondary Theme
Tonic	Modulation	Tonic Parallel		Modulation	Tonic		Tonic		Tonic

The individual components are thematically and harmoniously related to each other.

LUDWIG VAN BEETHOVEN, *baptized 1770 in Bonn,Germany, died 1827 in Vienna, Austria.*

"FIDELIO" premiered in 1805. Beethoven revised his only opera many times.

THE "HEILIGENSTADT TESTAMENT" of 1802 is a letter to his brother in which Beethoven bemoans his deafness.

Portrait ca 1815 by W. J. Mähler

Ludwig van Beethoven

BEETHOVEN RECEIVED his first musical education in Bonn, his birthplace, as chamber musician at the court there, but went to Vienna in 1792 to study with Haydn, Antonio Salieri, and Johann Albrechtsberger. The great musical city remained central to Beethoven's life: As a composer, he was patronized by the Viennese nobility, and as a pianist he was admired by the Viennese public. His patrons included the Archduke Rudolph, whom he also taught, princes Lichnowsky and Lobkowitz, and counts Waldstein and Kinsky. Beethoven dedicated many works to them.

IN 1795, HE DEVELOPED a noticeable hearing problem, which resulted in total deafness by 1819. Beethoven was forced to stop giving concerts, and he withdrew from public life. He communicated primarily through conversation books as his deafness worsened.

Beethoven's parents, Johann and Maria Magdalena, lived in an apartment in the attic of the Beethoven House in Bonn (left).

21ST CENTURY

"FREUDE, SCHÖNER GÖTTERFUNKEN" *(Beethoven's Ninth Symphony) is based on Friedrich Schiller's "Ode to Joy." It is the anthem of the European Union.*

UNESCO MEMORY *of the World Register appended Beethoven's autograph score of the Ninth Symphony in 2003.*

MUSIC

THE BIRTH OF MODERN ORCHESTRAL SOUND

Small court, great impact. Mannheim was the location for Europe's leading orchestra in the second half of the 18th century. It was here that Johann Stamitz created a new orchestral sound.

The new style of concerts required new spaces. The Gewandhaus ("cloth house") in Leipzig was turned into a concert hall in 1780.

Mannheim and its court of the Palatinate Elector Carl Theodor may have appeared insignificant when compared to Paris, London, and Vienna. Yet in the concluding half of the 18th century, Mannheim became a magnet for musicians yearning for the opportunity to play together on a continual basis. The court orchestra evolved a rich sound and can be considered the first orchestra, in a modern sense.

The Mannheim Court Orchestra

The Elector hired the Bohemian violinist Johann Stamitz to direct his instrumental music. He was joined by Franz Xaver Richter, Ignaz Holzbauer, Christian Cannabich and his son Carl, and other renowned musicians of the time. By 1777, the orchestra comprised about 50 musicians, all of them virtuoso players of their instruments. The significant advantage that Mannheim had over other orchestras did not concern the gifts of individual musicians, since many orchestras were staffed by virtuoso performers. However, since it was common for orchestras to be assembled spontaneously and for musicians to be hired according to availability, a fixed ensemble, such as the Mannheim, gave its musicians the additional benefit of extended periods of practicing and playing together. This exceptional orchestra inspired many new compositions, which showed off its particular abilities: unusual virtuoso tutti passages (for the entire orchestra, not just soloists), experiments with tremendous increases in volume (dynamics), and other bravura passages. A love of instrumental music emanated from Mannheim and thus resonated throughout Europe.

At the Mannheimer Hof (above, the Hoftheater) a unique orchestral tradition resulted from the sponsorship of Carl Theodor.

The violinist Johann Stamitz came to the Mannheim court around 1741. His leadership made the court orchestra renowned in Europe. Carl Stamitz, his son, later worked as a composer in Paris.

From Concertmaster to Conductor

One of the major innovations for the orchestra was the manner in which it was conducted. Baroque orchestras were usually conducted by their harpsichordists, while orchestras in the classical era assigned the duty to their first violinists (known as concertmasters), perhaps because the harpsichord was losing popularity. The violinist used his bow to indicate entrances, dynamics, and tempos. The concertmaster's duty was reassigned in the 19th century to the newly created post of conductor—who was armed with a baton instead of a violin bow.

New Instruments

Wind instruments and their technical innovations were largely responsible for the specific orchestral sound, which characterized music of the late 18th century. The keyed trumpet, which evolved into the contemporary common valve trumpet, was developed in Vienna in 1793 and technologically refined a few years later in Paris. Woodwind instruments such as the clarinet and the flute were also improved—new key mechanics facilitated clearer tones played in a virtuoso manner.

above: *Clarinet and French horn*

The Classical Orchestra's Structure and Seating Chart

THE BAROQUE ORCHESTRA was divided into a continuo group, including cello and harpsichord as well as a group of melody instruments such as violins, flutes, and oboes. The classical orchestra was laid out in a four-part string section: four each of first and second violins, violas, and cellos/double basses. The standard complement featured two oboes, two horns, and two bassoons. Trumpets and timpani created a festive sound. A more extensive wind section with piccolo, contra-bassoon, and trombones, along with a larger percussion section, supplemented the arrangement according to the compositions to be performed.

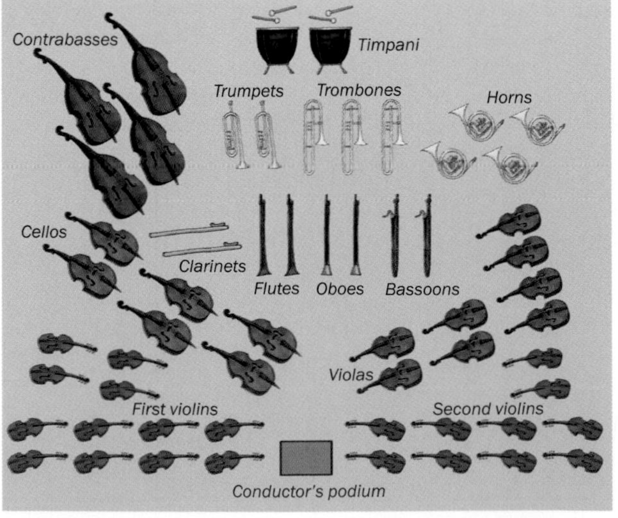

OPERATIC REFORMS: DEPARTURE FROM OPERA SERIA

The era of opera seria came to an end in the second half of the 18th century, when music conjuring emotions of contemporary experiences replaced its pathos.

Christoph Willibald Gluck led operatic reforms in the 18th century.

The basic nature of opera seria was stiff and inflexible: Singing interrupted the story line to try to clarify the characters' emotions. The music took precedence over the text, plot, and acting onstage (*prima la musica, poi le parole*). Its great heroic themes and grandiose set designs served as representations of absolute power.

Gluck's Opera Reform

Opera seria originated in Italy and was widespread in France under the name grand opèra. It underwent a fundamental change at the hands of Christoph Willibald Gluck, who aimed to remake the stiff, artificial opera into a more dynamic, realistic form of music. His innovations ensured that the text (libretto) would be dramatic and comprehensible by the public and that the score should be appropriate to the text and acting motives, and not merely serve as a performance in itself. Gluck replaced the then predominant virtuoso bel canto singing with simple, often song-like lyrics. Another major innovation was the change of the overture from an independent piece of music into an indication of the plot, so that the audience could anticipate the story to come.

Mlle. Maillard sings Armide in Gluck's 1777 opera of the same name.

Orfeo—A Revolution

Gluck's "Orfeo ed Euridice" was the ultimate manifestation of these innovations. The opera premiered in 1762 in Vienna, where Italian opera—represented by court composers Antonio Salieri and Giovanni Paisiello—had predominated. Gluck's close contacts in Paris helped him stage his operas there in the 1770s. His "Orfeo," revised for Paris, "Alceste" and "Armide" greatly influenced French opera composers such as François-Joseph Gossec, A. E. M. Gretry, Luigi Cherubini, and Étienne Nicolas Méhul. Even Richard Wagner (p. 377) referred to Gluck in his musical dramas.

Antonio Salieri was one of the most influential opera composers in Vienna (title vignette of his opera "Falstaff ossia Le tre burle," 1799).

Musical Comedy Reform: Singspiel

Italian opera buffa (p. 367) evolved into singspiel in Germanic regions: a comic prose piece (with German text) sung to simple pieces of music such as ballads, ariettas, and small ensembles. Johann Wolfgang von Goethe produced many texts for singspiel set to music by actress and composer Corona Schröter ("Die Fischerin") and others. In Vienna, Kaiser Joseph II restructured the form of singspiel when he opened the Vienna National Singspiel in 1778. Mozart's "The Abduction From the Seraglio" was very successful there. Singspiel influenced the development of Romantic opera in 19th-century Germany, especially composers such as Carl Maria von Weber and Albert Lortzing. Dramatist John Gay evolved a new type of parody opera, called ballad opera, with the London production of "The Beggar's Opera" in 1728, with score arranged by Johann Pepusch.

It was a precursor of 19th-century comic opera such as those by Gilbert and Sullivan, and was adapted by Bertolt Brecht and Kurt Weill 200 years later as "The Threepenny Opera."

Giovanni Paisiello, court Kapellmeister in St. Petersburg, was one of the most successful composers of his time.

Opera Forms in the 18th Century

OPERA SERIA was the primary form of serious opera between 1720 and 1780.

OPERA BUFFA was the comic counterpart to opera seria.

OPÉRA COMIQUE, a popular form of opera, consisted of spoken dialogue and music. It emerged about 1750 in France as an alternative to courtly tragédie lyrique.

TRAGÉDIE LYRIQUE, the French counterpart to opera seria, is also known as grand opéra.

SINGSPIEL was a popular dramatic work set to music, which gave the performers of both text and score considerable autonomy in their interpretation.

above: *Mozart's "The Marriage of Figaro" (title page of score) belongs to opera buffa.*

21ST CENTURY

THE PRIMA DONNA *was the leading female singer (generally a soprano) in opera seria. Her performance, as well as that by the primo uomo (tenor or castrata), was thought to guarantee the success of a production. The cult followings that formed around 18th-century prima donnas have lost none of their appeal: Singers such as Maria Callas (1923–1977) and Cecilia Bartoli are considered modern prima donnas.*

KEY FACTS

LITERATURE AND MUSIC *became closely connected.*

THE PIANO *was the most important musical instrument of the period.*

SIGNIFICANT MUSICAL FORMS: *song, musical drama, chamber music, and symphonic poems.*

VIRTUOSO *players of the violin and piano ruled the stage.*

OPERATIC FORMS: *grand opèra and musical drama*

Romanticism (1820–1890) | Public and personal music | Virtuosos | Opera | Symphonies | National music

ROMANTICISM—THE VIEW INWARD

Musical Romanticism is a term that covers a number of different aesthetic views and developments: the poeticizing of piano music, the immense interest in song, and a general return to chamber music as well as music-making in the home. During this time period, a star cult developed around the great virtuoso performers. The Romantic operas in Italy, France, and Germany as well as musical drama demanded much larger stages as national musical trends emerged across Europe.

Musical Romanticism was not a unified concept at this time.

SALON MUSIC

The bourgeoisie discovered new locales for music—everything from simple attics and drawing-rooms to the prestigious salon. The performer stood firmly at the center of it all.

The time of the restoration encouraged a general retreat into the private realm—a tendency that also affected musical life. Many pieces of chamber music were created: instrumental music, as wordless art, was particularly suitable for expressing thoughts that could not be stated explicitly due to public opinion and sometimes censorship. Locales for chamber music held an advantage over halls for symphonies requiring many players. The salon was a private space—noble and fashionable, middle-class and simple, or artisan and bohemian.

Robert Schumann composed poetic music and also wrote about music.

Music and Poetry

Literature and music became closely intertwined in the Romantic era. E. T. A. Hoffmann, known today as a poet, was also a conductor and composer. The composer Robert Schumann founded a journal called *"Neue Zeitschrift für Musik,"* at which he worked as an editor and music writer. Romantic piano music can be viewed as the poetizing of music: Mood pieces replaced the sonata. Poetic titles, built-in word and letter puzzles, and even the musical form itself as "songs without words" emphasized its literary content.

The Song

Song format also profited from the close proximity of music to literature: Poems were no longer simple folk songs set to music; rather, their linguistic subtlety was expressed musically. The presence of music helped to interpret the text and, therefore, added a new level of meaning. The song became one of the most beloved forms of music in the Romantic period.

Franz Schubert met like-minded friends at the "Schubertiaden" to make music together.

The Musical Salon

The informal meetings in the salon were of a completely different kind: the Parisian salons, in which Frédéric Chopin caused a sensation as a pianist, were fashionable and elitist. The Berlin salons, like Fanny Hensel's "Sonntagsmusiken," were artistically ambitious; the Viennese "Schubertiaden," on the other hand, were quite lively and spontaneous. The salons were different, but the basic idea of making music with others remained the same.

above: *As Chopin was considered withdrawn in public, each performance was a sensation.*

FANNY HENSEL, *b. Mendelssohn, 1805–1847.*

FELIX MENDELSSOHN BARTHOLDY, *1809–1847.*

BOTH SIBLINGS *were composers, but only Felix was allowed a career in music.*

THEIR TRADEMARK PIECES *were "songs without words" for piano.*

A portrait of Fanny Hensel in 1842, shortly after the completion of her piano cycle "Das Jahr."

Fanny Hensel and Felix Mendelssohn Bartholdy

BOTH SIBLINGS displayed great musical gifts when young and received an excellent musical education with Goethe's friend Carl Friedrich Zelter and others. While Felix consciously prepared himself for a musical career, Fanny's ambitions were quickly cut short. Their father advised his 14-year-old daughter not to make music her profession, but rather to consider it a decorative hobby. Felix enjoyed an internationally successful career as a composer and conductor. Fanny, who married the painter Wilhelm Hensel in 1829, remained in Berlin and organized numerous "Sonntagsmusiken," music salons in her home, where she performed her own compositions as well as those by other composers.

Felix Mendelssohn Bartholdy at the beginning of his international career (1829)

see also: Literature of Romanticism, *Literature Chapter, p. 347*

STAGE STARS AND THEIR PUBLIC

It is impossible to chart the 19th-century public music scene without including a wealth of virtuoso players: Niccolò Paganini, Franz Liszt, Clara Schumann, and many others.

Virtuoso performers of the highest technical caliber and individual programs dominated the 19th-century concert scene. In extensive and often lucrative concert tours, they enchanted the public—occasionally even moving listeners to hysterics—with their playing.

Photograph of Clara Schumann at the piano (ca 1875).

Piano Virtuoso Players

The 19th-century piano virtuoso performers included Mozart's student Johann Nepomuk Hummel, Sigismond Thalberg—a contemporary of Franz Liszt—Clara Wieck, who later married Robert Schumann, and Venezuelan pianist Teresa Carreño, who at one time was married to another European pianist of repute, Eugène d'Albert.

It was often the pianist's personal charisma that charmed the public. The young Clara Wieck enchanted listeners with the sensitivity of her playing, while the combative couple Carreño-d'Albert were often the subject of gossip columns. Robert Schumann once wrote of Franz Liszt that he understood how, with his playing and the atmosphere at his concerts, he could enslave his audience. Frédéric Chopin's manner was also self-assured. He avoided—atypical for a virtuoso—big stages and preferred to play in Parisian salons, where he caused a stir with his mazurkas, polonaises, and études.

Virtuoso Tours

Traveling was unavoidable for virtuoso musicians. Performing concerts in just one place could end a career, since the public constantly wanted to see and hear new artists. Clara Schumann's concert tours illustrate the extent of the touring. As an 11-year-old piano prodigy, she traveled from Leipzig to Dresden, where she performed within the homes of the nobility. In 1832, she made her first trip to Paris, which was followed by numerous concert tours through Germany and the Austrian-Hungarian Empire.

After her marriage to Robert Schumann, Clara continued to be in great demand as a piano virtuoso across Europe: She gave concerts until 1888 in Germany, France, Denmark, Russia, Austria, the Netherlands, Belgium, Hungary, Britain, and Switzerland.

The Virtuoso as Composer

Since most virtuoso performers were also simultaneously composers, it was completely natural for them to compose or even improvise works at their own performances. Because of this, compositions were structured to showcase their exceptional abilities: technical refinements, great jumps in register, speed, and brilliance. Of course, performers also paid particular attention to public tastes: The violinist Louis Spohr for his first performance at Milan's La Scala opera house composed a violin solo that was similar to a singing scene.

Virtuoso Techniques on the Violin

PAGANINI COMPOSED numerous works for solo violin, in which he effortlessly surpassed previous technical boundaries. His preferred performance techniques included frequent large jumps in register using string changes and shifts of position (1). He used many techniques to great effect: double-stops, in which strings are played simultaneously, and extended trills (2). The combination of these technical refinements with speed (3) resulted in brilliance and intense musical expression.

right: *Paganini was the perfect example of many Romantic virtuoso players. The brilliance of his violin technique was astonishing, and his appearance equally forceful. The combination of passion and intensity made him the embodiment of the Romantic artist.*

Choirs in the 19th Century

The political climate in Europe, particularly in the wake of the revolutions of 1848 in multiple countries, prompted the founding of many choirs. While retaining their political and national aspirations, people were yet able to come together in song—in everything from folk songs to the contemporary repertoire of that time. This enormous interest in choral singing created a demand for new oratorios, cantatas, and motets. Mendelssohn Bartholdy, Schumann, and Liszt composed many such works, as did Héctor Berlioz, Charles Gounod, Camille Saint-Saëns, and Augusta Holmès.

above: *Festival concert by the Vienna Männergesangverein*

Franz Liszt enjoyed performing for his devoted public (caricature, 1845).

INSIDER KNOWLEDGE

CONCERTS WERE SPECTACULAR *events where violin strings snapped or entire instruments were broken. It is said that if Paganini's E-string broke during a performance, he would continue playing on the other three strings until he had finished.*

ROMANTIC OPERA IN ITALY

Opera in 19th-century Italy was overshadowed by the bel canto form until Giuseppe Verdi replaced the generation of Rossini, Bellini, and Donizetti. He brought dramatic individual characters to the operatic stage: Othello, Macbeth, and the courtesan Violetta.

The compositions of Gioacchino Rossini reinvigorated the form of opera, especially opera buffa. This form common to 19th-century opera became obsolete with the 1816 premiere of Rossini's "The Barber of Seville" in Rome. The second production of "The Barber of Seville" prompted a triumphant tour to all the major European opera houses, where audiences responded favorably to the opera's new liveliness and tuneful melodies.

Vincenzo Bellini became known primarily for his operas "La Sonnambula" and "Norma."

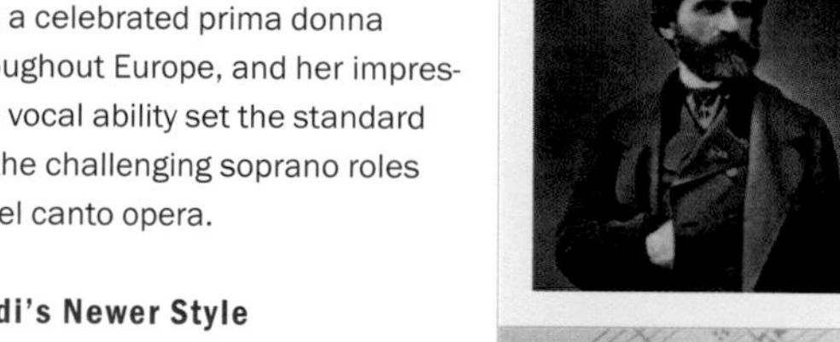

Rossini's opera composing career was short yet brilliant: he wrote 39 operas between 1810 and 1829.

INSIDER KNOWLEDGE

VERDI (VITTORIO EMANUELE RE D'ITALIA) *was daubed on many walls in Italian cities in the 1840s. A popular composer's slave chorus from "Nabucco" was used as a nationalistic anthem by the Italian Risorgimento. However, the graffiti on the walls alluded to Vittorio Emanuele Re D'Italia, the king of Sardinia-Piedmont, who many hoped would unify the country.*

Bel Canto

The melody in bel canto (Italian: "beautiful singing") was the most important aspect of the opera for composers and it dominated the Italian music scene. Vincenzo Bellini wrote more significant parts for coloratura singers, which was rather unusual since singers at that time decided how they interpreted their parts. Rossini, Bellini, Gaetano Donizetti, and other bel canto composers collaborated with the soprano Giuditta Pasta. She was a celebrated prima donna throughout Europe, and her impressive vocal ability set the standard for the challenging soprano roles of bel canto opera.

Verdi's Newer Style

The bel canto generation was separated from Giuseppe Verdi by only a few short years. Verdi wrote his first few operas in the bel canto style, but with his third opera, "Nabucco," he began to develop his own melodramatic approach. He aimed to make stage productions more vivid and dramatic by composing scores more responsive to absorbing plots. The characters in opera began to resonate with the audience as the story line and their fate became easier to understand.

Verismo

Italian opera composers of the next hundred years continued down this path blazed by Verdi, trying to bring real life to the operatic stage by using literary realism as a blueprint. Themes taken from everyday routines and customs were set to music and portrayed in different ways ranging from the realistic to the dramatic. The verismo opera "Cavalleria Rusticana" by Pietro Mascagni ended in a duel with knives, a finale in which the score was given no quarter. It gloried in realistic acoustic elements, discordant confusion, and singing parts that dissipated into spoken parts.

Working with realistic portrayals, Giacomo Puccini's "La Bohème" was clearly identifiable as a depiction of the then bohemian lifestyle in Paris. Lyrics with echoes of bel canto dominated in this opera, as is notable in Puccini's body of operatic works including "Madame Butterfly," "Tosca," and "Turandot."

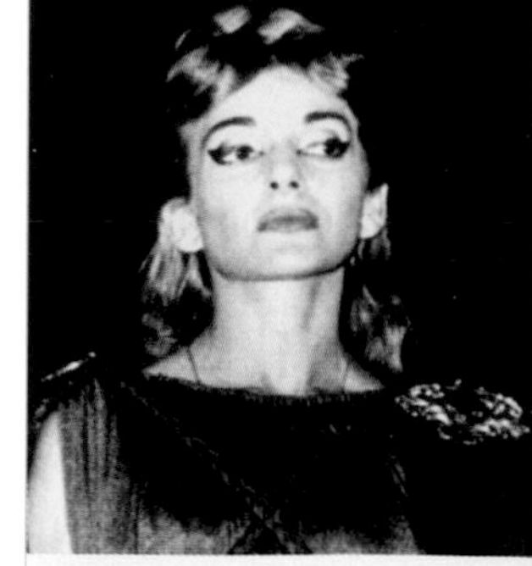

Bellini's Norma was a role for prima donnas such as Maria Callas.

GIUSEPPE VERDI *b. 1813 Busseto, Italy, d. 1901 Milan, Italy.*

VERDI WAS INVOLVED *politically with the Italian unification movement.*

WELL-KNOWN OPERAS: *"Rigoletto," "Il Trovatore," "La Traviata," "Aida," "Don Carlos," "Otello," "Falstaff"*

Photographic portrait, Paris, ca 1870

Giuseppe Verdi

VERDI ROSE TO FAME from a humble background. Despite being rejected by the conservatory, he received private musical instruction through the support of a patron. The success of his third opera "Nabucco" (1842) catapulted him straight to the top of the list of Italian opera composers. His family did not share in his success: His wife and children died in 1839.

AFTER PARTICIPATING IN ITALY'S 1848 revolutionary uprising, Verdi withdrew to his estate Sant'Agata, and the period of his greatest success began.

Today, Verdi's operas constitute some of the most beloved opera programs (above: "La Traviata" at Salzburg Festspiele, 2005).

➔ see also: **Realism**, *Literature Chapter, p. 348*

ROMANTIC OPERA IN GERMANY AND FRANCE

Meyerbeer and Wagner are the complete opposites of composers of great Romantic opera: Meyerbeer represents grand opèra, while Wagner idealizes music drama.

Paris became one of Europe's most important centers for opera in the 1800s. It was here that Italian composers first developed grand opèra: Gaspare Spontini's opera "Die Vestalin" of 1807 was a sensational success, while Rossini brought Italian bel canto (p. 376) to Paris in 1824.

The grand operas of Meyerbeer were hugely successful in Paris.

Meyerbeer and the Grand Opèra

Giacomo Meyerbeer (born Jakob Liebmann Mayer Beer in Berlin) also appears to have been influenced by bel canto. Meyerbeer studied in Venice before arriving in Paris in 1831, where a distinct middle-class consciousness emerged after the July Revolution of 1830. Monumental stage presentations, multiple story lines, scenes with ballet segments, dramatic turns, and varied orchestration were now required of productions. "Robert le Diable," Meyerbeer's first opera in Paris, corresponded perfectly with public tastes and was followed by the successful "Les Huguenots."

Drama Lyrique and Opéra Comique

As an alternative to large scale grand opera, drama lyrique, such as Charles Gounod's "Faust" and Ambroise Thomas's "Mignon," developed in Paris from about 1850. These productions had intimate plots concerned with individuals and featured sentimental melodies.

In the first half of the century, opéra comique (p. 373) was able to hold its ground by featuring spoken dialogue, musical numbers, and cheerful, sentimental characters. However, the influence of drama lyrique changed the older form. From about 1850, it incorporated more serious themes and lyrical or dramatic characters, such as the leading singer in George Bizet's "Carmen."

Romantic Opera in Germany

Romantic opera in Germany became known for its treatment of legends and fairy tales. Nature and its more tempestuous qualities like deep forests and thundering storms inspired many musical imaginations. E. T. A. Hoffmann wrote "Undine" based on the story of a seductive water nymph who falls in love with a mortal and is brought into human disorder. One of the central themes of the German Romantic era was that the resolution of a plot could only be achieved through the phenomenon of devotion, such as love between a human and a water nymph in this opera. Carl Maria von Weber's opera "Der Freischütz" encompassed themes of the power of love and the fear of the supernatural, such as in its Wolf's Gorge scene.

Wagner's Musical Drama

Richard Wagner started composing Romantic opera with his works "The Flying Dutchman" and "Lohengrin." He employed musical memory motifs, which already played a big role in Weber's work. Wagner subsequently developed these into his idea of *leitmotif* "leading motif." His opera aesthetic was based upon the exposition of ancient legends, which he attempted to transfer to opera through the form of music drama.

Forest ranger Max deals with the devil to win a marksmanship contest in Weber's "Der Freischütz."

RICHARD WAGNER *born 1813 in Leipzig, died 1883 in Venice*

MUSIC DRAMA *focused on the composition of a total work of art.*

MAJOR WORKS: *"The Ring Cycle," "Die Meistersinger," "Parsifal," "Tannhäuser"*

Wagner with his wife Cosima, 1872
right: *"Tristan und Isolde" in a 2000 production by the Berlin State Opera (Harry Kupfer)*

Richard Wagner

WAGNER BEGAN HIS career in 1833 as chorus master in Würzburg. In 1839, he was forced to evade his creditors and flee to London with his wife, Minna, after which they lived in impoverished conditions in Paris. Wagner had his first operatic success with "Rienzi" and became court conductor in Dresden. After Dresden's May Uprising in 1849, in which Wagner actively participated, he was pursued by the authorities and fled to Switzerland. Wagner's love affairs (especially with Mathilde Wessendonck) greatly influenced works such as "Tristan und Isolde."

WAGNER'S SUCCESS began in 1864 when Ludwig II of Bavaria brought him to Munich and provided financial support for him to work on his operas. The love affair with his later wife, Cosima von Bülow, began around the same time. The first productions took place in Bayreuth in 1876.

The Festspielhaus in Bayreuth was built according to Wagner's music philosophy.

Notable Premieres Between 1820 and 1890

1821 Weber: "Der Freischütz"
1831 Meyerbeer: "Robert der Teufel"
1837 Lortzing: "Zar und Zimmermann"
1843 Wagner: "The Flying Dutchman"
1849 Meyerbeer: "Der Prophet"
1859 Gounod: "Faust"
1865 Wagner: "Tristan und Isolde"
1875 Bizet: "Carmen"
1882 Wagner: "Parsifal"
1884 Massenet: "Manon"

above: *Many opera houses were constructed in European cities, such as Palais Garnier in Paris, in the latter half of the 1800s.*

ROMANTIC SYMPHONY

Symphonic form was the subject of much disagreement in the 19th century. Conservative advocates of absolute music were outraged at the new direction of the symphonic poem.

Berlioz evoked criticism with his gigantic orchestral apparatus (caricature, 1846).

Beethoven's Ninth Symphony (p. 371) wielded great influence on composers in the 1800s. Some considered it the final development of the classical symphony, while others questioned how any composer—in the sense of musical progress—could write anything symphonic after this monumental work.

Early Romantic Symphony

Early Romantic composers such as Schubert, Mendelssohn Bartholdy, and Schumann were independent composers in that they adopted Haydn's and Mozart's symphonic forms and embellished them with Romantic tonal language. Mendelssohn composed 12-string symphonies, deliberately scoring these for smaller orchestras. He wrote five more symphonies, including the "Scottish" and the "Italian," between 1824 and 1837. Both these compositions were influenced by the musical characteristics he experienced in his travels.

Beethoven's Successor: Brahms

Johannes Brahms was generally regarded as being the symphonic successor to Beethoven, and this put pressure on him to achieve great results with his composition. His First Symphony was 21 years in the making; it finally premiered in Karlsruhe in 1876. Ultimately, it borrowed so heavily from Beethoven that conductor Hans von Bülow nicknamed it "Beethoven's Tenth." Brahms composed three more symphonies in quick succession.

Louise Antoine Julien, founder of the popular promenade concerts in London, achieved wonderous symphony performances.

Program Music and the Symphonic Poem

The close relationship between literature of great passions and themes and music of the Romantic era inspired the development of program music, in which the dramatic symphony was given narrative content through a written program. One example is Hector Berlioz's "Symphonie Fantastique."

21ST CENTURY

TONE POEM COMPOSITIONS *were so popular in the 1800s that only a few symphonies were composed in the next two centuries, such as 15 symphonies by Dmitri Shostakovich and eight by Karl Amadeus Hartmann.*

Franz Liszt developed the genre of symphonic tone poem, more in the tradition of the single-movement overture than the multi-movement symphony. It was the basis for communicating extra-musical content through plays, novels, and poems.

The symphonic poem became successfully independent from the symphonic tradition, which was the subject of a fight between the "New German School" and advocates of absolute music. The idea that symphonic poems could convey non-musical content made them especially attractive to the national music movements (p. 379) of the latter half of the 1800s. Bedřich Smetana composed the great cycle of tone poems "Ma Vlast" from 1872 to 1879, in which he conveyed the need for an expression of national independence.

New German School and Brahms's Followers

One of the bitterest disagreements in music history broke out in the middle of the 1800s between conservatives and progressives. The musicians of the future, including Franz Liszt and Hector Berlioz, were referred to as the "New German School" although there were no German composers in this group. The cornerstone of their aesthetic was considered to be program music (symphonic poetry) and Richard Wagner's music drama. Johannes Brahms was named head of the opposition party; his music was considered to be traditional. Eduard Hanslick, Viennese critic and musical aesthetician, labeled compositions by Brahms as "absolute music."

"Eduard Hanslick instructs Richard Wagner as one composes."

"Symphonie Fantastique"

Berlioz's "Symphonie Fantastique" introduced program music, in which a symphony "told" a story through program notes describing the settings of the music. For its 1830 premiere, the program depicted episodes from the life of an artist. The first movement described the burgeoning love of a young musician (alias Berlioz) for an idealized woman (alias Harriet Smithson, Berlioz's intermittent wife). The second movement showed her at a ball—in the arms of another man, making the jealous musician flee the city for the solitude of nature. The third movement had a distant thunderstorm portending disaster, followed by the fourth, in which the protagonist wished to have his lover murdered and was brought into court. The final movement was a grotesque witches' Sabbath.

above: *Original manuscript page*

Brahms was close to Robert and Clara Schumann. His friendship with Clara lasted until her death in 1896.

MUSIC

NATIONAL MUSIC

The rediscovery of folk songs and dances unlocked new sources of musical inspiration. They were also imbued with a political statement: a desire for national independence.

The political landscape in Europe changed dramatically after the Napoleonic wars. Many regions were more inclined to national independence, such as in the Habsburg hereditary lands of Bohemia and Moravia, as well as in Russia as a result of its democratic reform. These political movements sought national roots as a cultural means for establishing their identity. Music offered several possibilities such as national opera and folk songs.

Ruth Crawford-Seeger collected and published American folk songs. She was an avant-garde composer of the New American Music genre in the 1920s.

National Opera—Prague

Bohemia and Moravia lost their independence to the Habsburg monarchy in 1526. In the course of history, the revival of a pan-Slavic musical culture was regarded in the 19th century as a possible means of asserting national autonomy. Bohemian national music reached its zenith with operas by Bedřich Smetana, including "The Bartered Bride" in 1866 and "Dalibor" in 1868. Smetana composed the opera "Libuse," which dramatized the legendary founding of Prague, for the 1881 opening of the National Opera in Prague. Construction of the opera house, which in contrast to other locales in Prague was supposed to perform Czech repertoire only, was financed by the city's residents. Antonín Dvořák's "Rusalka" premiered here in 1901.

National Opera—Russia

In response to the enormous influence of Italian opera in Russia, an attempt to create an independent tone language was already under way by the 1830s. Mikhail Glinka, with his two operas "A Life for the Czar" (1836) and "Ruslan and Lyudmila" (1842), launched the Russian national school of composition. At first, only subjects from Russian history and mythology were performed on opera stages, and Glinka further reinforced the Slavic element through folk song-like melodies and instrumentation. Alexander Dargomyzhsky, in his operas "Rusalka" (1856) and "The Stone Guest" (1872), put Russian prose to music. He influenced Modest Mussorgsky, who went on to compose song cycles for voice and piano including "The Nursery" and "Songs and Dances of Death."

Folk Song Collections

Musicians in the Romantic era regarded folk song as a primitive form of national expression. Yet collecting folk songs spread across Europe in the later 1800s. Writing down folk music proved challenging, as many were passed down only by oral tradition. So while different variations of a folk song existed, typical folk melodies and rhythms did not necessarily lend themselves as songs in the classical music canon. Thus, collections of idealized folk songs were assembled in the 1800s and were adapted by composers.

Spain: Isaac Albeniz

From his earliest years, Spanish pianist Isaac Albéniz led an unsettled life traveling between the U. S., Spain, and the rest of Europe. He went to South America at the age 12. His piano skills were legendary, despite his blindness. A meeting with composer Felipe Pedrell, who encouraged him to incorporate Spanish folk music into his piano compositions, proved significant. The high point of his work is "Suite Iberia" written in the last years of his life. Other Spanish composers included Enrique Granados and Manuel de Falla.

above: *Isaac Albeniz (1860–1909)*

Antonín Dvořák used Slavonic musical themes as inspiration in his "Slavic Dances."

THE FIVE: *Mili Balakirew, Modest Mussorgski, Nikolai Rimski-Korsakov, César Cui, Alexander Borodin*

MOST MEMBERS *of this group, set up around 1860 as the first Russian conservatory, were specialists in other fields and had little professional musical training.*

Modest Mussorgsky, painting by Ilya Repin

The Five

THE FIVE, also known as the "Mighty Handful," broke through the harmonic impasse of the Western musical tradition to develop a national body of work in Russia during the 1860s. Mily Balakirev headed the group.

MANY WERE CONVINCED that an independent form of music was possible in Russia. They researched Russian folk songs, selecting national and mythological subjects for operas. These included Mussorgsky's "Boris Godunov" and Borodin's "Prince Igor," and symphonic poems such as "In the Steppes of Central Asia" by Borodin and "Sadko" by Rimsky-Korsakov.

Nikolai Rimsky-Korsakov, painting from 1898

right: *Feodor Chaliapin sings the role of Boris Godunov in Mussorgsky's eponymous opera.*

Music around 1900 | Music after 1900

MODERN MUSIC

Musical movements near the turn of the century were aesthetically diverse and somewhat contradictory. Late Romantic music was quite influential until World War I. At the same time, the ideas of Impressionism were also quite popular—especially in France—in the 1890s. In addition, expressionism provided the stimulus for a musical development toward atonality. In post-World War I France, neoclassicism assumed an important role. Arnold Schönberg introduced his 12-tone technique in public in 1923.

Several stylistic trends existed simultaneously around the turn of the century.

KEY FACTS

END OF MAJOR-MINOR TONALITY: *free atonality and 12-tone.*

THE ORCHESTRA *of the late Romantic era: large and diverse.*

GROUPS OF COMPOSERS: *Second Viennese School, Les Six*

FOLK SONG ANTHOLOGIES HAVE *ethnographic claims.*

SCANDAL: *Schönberg's concerts in Vienna, Stravinsky's "The Rite of Spring" in Paris.*

MUSIC AROUND 1900—DEPARTURE AND UPRISING

The decadent, fin-de-siècle consciousness created a cult of beauty and a search for exotic sounds. Impressionism experimented with new tonal colors.

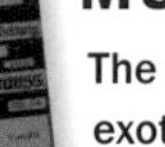

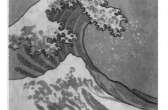

Salome's "Dance of the Seven Veils" shocked audiences. Never before had a soprano danced so seductively in such a scanty costume.

Many composers and musicians associated the turn of the century with the fear or expectation that the late Romantic period would finally come to an end at the same time as the 1800s.

Large Symphonic Works

The 19th century passed down the great legacy of the concept of the symphony. Since the Mannheim School (p. 372), the orchestra had increasingly expanded in size and this led to increased possibilities for more nuanced sounds. This evolution reached its apex and its end point in Europe around 1900: Richard Strauss composed numerous symphonic poems, such as "Thus Spake Zarathustra" in 1896, while the symphonies of Gustav Mahler translated philosophical interpretations of the world into music. Claude Debussy created nature paintings in shimmering colors of sound, free from musical formalism, which were labeled as Impressionist—a reference to the style of painting at the time. In Britain, Edward Elgar and Ralph Vaughan Williams defined their own style of an Impressionist representation of nature.

Sound and the Exotic

The celebrated cult of beauty around the turn of the century also influenced music and was expressed in the search for a more sensual sound. The size of the orchestra, comprising more than 100 musicians, and the many instruments available offered many opportunities to explore new tonal colors. This exploration was combined with unusual exotic content: Strauss effectively linked the exotic sensuality of the music in his one-act opera "Salome" (1905) with the eroticism of Salome and Herod's decadent court. Similarly, Igor Stravinsky used a variety of orchestral sound colors in his early ballets such as "Petrushka" and "The Firebird."

Béla Bartók and Zoltan Kodály traveled in Hungary to research folk music. Much of this material inspired the composers in their own works.

Debussy set the force of the sea to music in "La Mer" by using Impressionist coloring.

Like Bartók, Leoš Janá ček went on several trips to research folk music.

GUSTAV MAHLER, *born 1860 in Kalište, Bohemia, died 1911 in Vienna.*

HE WROTE HIS SYMPHONIES *for the large orchestras of the late Romantic era and often included vocal parts.*

MAHLER INCORPORATED *folk music elements as his symphonic themes.*

As director of the Vienna State Opera, Mahler was one of the leading conductors of his time.

Gustav Mahler

MAHLER STUDIED IN VIENNA, but spent much of his time as a conductor traveling to cities like Olomouc, Kassel, Prague, Leipzig, Budapest, and Hamburg. He was appointed director of the Vienna State Opera in 1897. In 1907, he resigned and went to New York. His heavy workload as director relegated his composition time to his vacations only. His body of work includes orchestral songs and nine symphonies. His tenth symphony remains unfinished.

MAHLER MARRIED the composer Alma Schindler in 1902. She stopped writing music after she married. They had two daughters: Maria, who died at a young age, and Anna, who became a sculptor.

Mahler's Eighth Symphony is also known as the "Symphony of a Thousand" (left: rehearsal for premiere in 1910).

see also: Impressionism, *Visual Arts Chapter, p. 306*

MUSIC AFTER 1900

Until well into the 1920s, avant-garde tendencies gained increasing acceptance in the face of conservative forces—not without protest and even public scandals.

Public concerts, in which composers from the Second Viennese School introduced their works, resulted in frequent scandals. Arnold Schönberg, who in 1907–1908 left traditional harmonies behind to venture into atonality, caused great indignation among conservative members of the public.

From around 1920, jazz influenced European composers such as Ernst Krenek (photo: a scene from "Jonny Strikes Up," 1927).

Scandal in Paris

Sergei Diaghilev, the Ballets Russes impresario in Paris, hired Igor Stravinsky, a young, unknown composer from St. Petersburg who had studied instrumentation with Rimsky-Korsakov. The first ballets which Stravinsky wrote for the ballet company were sensational successes because of their mixture of the exotic and erotic, and a fascinating sensuality of sound. This was followed in 1913 by the scandalous "The Rite of Spring." The basis of Stravinsky's music was its penetrating, unconventional rhythm, combined with a nearly brutal tone language.

Opera After 1900

Richard Wagner (p. 377) was still the most influential of opera composers in the new century. Claude Debussy consciously opposed Wagner's operatic philosophy when he wrote his opera "Pelléas et Mélisande" in 1902—yet without being able to completely separate himself from the older tradition. His opera was a direct response to Wagner's "Tristan und Isolde" but with a less traditional tonal base and harmonic structure. Impressed by the sensual sounds of the late Romantic orchestra, numerous operas built on the themes of the times: the cult of beauty and ugliness in Alexander Zemlinsky's "The Dwarf," or the artist and his place in the world in Franz Schreker's "Der ferne Klang." Pervading much of this debate was the question of the relationship between the sexes.

Nadia Boulanger was one of the most influential music professors of the 20th century.

Historicism, Historical Consciousness, Neoclassicism

In searching for new sound possibilities, many people rediscovered music of the past: research into medieval music became a central theme, not only at newly founded university departments for the study of music, but also in performance. For the first time in centuries, reconstructed music of the Middle Ages (pp. 362–363) and the Renaissance (pp. 364–365) rang out from modern stages. The return of past music took place alongside the development of neoclassicism in France. Composers looked upon 18th century French and Italian music as well as on antiquity.

Twelve-Tone Music

Schönberg developed a new principle of musical arrangement, "Composition with 12 Tones" (dodecaphony), between 1920 and 1923. This is based on the idea that the foundation of a composition is a tone row rather than a melody. Fashioned from the 12 tones of an octave, no note could be repeated until all the others were sounded in this preordained tone row. The basic arrangement of the tone row (1) can be varied according to a number of principles: retrograde (2), where the tones are played in reverse order; inversion (3), in which, beginning with the first tone, all tones and/or intervals, as they relate to the preceding tone, are played inverted. Retrograde inversion (4) combines retrograde (2) and inversion (3).

ARNOLD SCHÖNBERG'S *students included Alban Berg and Anton von Webern.*

COMPOSITIONS *by the Second Viennese School were not received well by the public.*

The Second Viennese School's influence remains noticeable. The systematic composition of serial music (p. 383) invokes aspects of the 12-tone technique developed by Schönberg (left).

The Second Viennese School

ARNOLD Schönberg was a charismatic teacher in Vienna, and socialized with a circle of like-minded people including Alban Berg and Anton von Webern.

THE SCHÖNBERG circle broke with major-minor harmony (tonality) around 1907, and explored atonality. In 1918, Schönberg founded the Society for Private Musical Performances. Its members performed weekly musical works composed from the time of Mahler—including the newest sounds and techniques. In 1923, the Schönberg circle began composing in the 12-tone technique.

right: *Alban Berg (left) and Anton von Webern (right).*

INSIDER KNOWLEDGE

SCHÖNBERG *published special programs for his concerts to explain the system on which he based his music.*

UNIVERSITIES *started to set up departments for the study of music from around 1900.*

Stravinsky (left) arrived in Paris from Russia in 1910 and collaborated with many notable musicians, artists, and dancers of the time, including Pablo Picasso, Vaslav Nijinsky, and Jean Cocteau (right).

KEY FACTS

PERSECUTION, MURDER, AND EXILE *during and after World War II resulted in enormous changes to musical life in Europe and the U.S.*

"NEW MUSIC" *utilized a wide range of styles and concepts.*

ELECTRONIC MUSIC *provided new possibilities for generating sound.*

MODERN MUSICAL THEATER *broke with traditions regarding scene, plot and music.*

New Music (1930s to present) | Music and Fascism | Music after 1945

NEW MUSIC—A VARIETY OF POSSIBILITIES

The musical culture of Europe, North America and elsewhere changed dramatically during World War II. Political ideologies in many regions determined what was to be considered beautiful and of artistic value, as well as who was permitted to compose and perform. After 1945, when the war ended, composers revived and pursued avant-garde ideas from the turn of the century.

New Music utilized new principles for artistic creation, new sounds, and new listening habits.

MUSIC AND FASCISM

The power of music and its great influence was consistently used for political means. Music regularly helped reinforce ideologies and communicated them to the public.

The fascist regimes of the 20th century aimed to manipulate music for their own ends. They followed political doctrine to determine exactly which composers were allowed to continue to write and publish music, what they composed, and which works were performed.

USSR: Shostakovich

Soviet politics under Josef Stalin not only set guidelines for the creation of artistic works, but also punished anyone who dared deviate from them.

Dmitri Shostakovich was allowed to try out relatively inoffensive avant-garde methods of composing, but in 1936 after a performance of his opera "Lady Macbeth of Minsk" he was criticized severely in the government's newspaper *Pravda*. During the rule of Stalin, this clearly meant the composer had fallen out of favor. Shostakovich was aware of the implications, as some of his colleagues were convicted as criminals or deported. He withdrew his recently completed Fourth Symphony and composed his Fifth Symphony to conform to the party line.

The 1938 exhibition "Degenerate Music" in Dusseldorf featured works by persecuted composers as well as music of the avant-garde.

Shostakovich used Jewish themes in some compositions.

INSIDER KNOWLEDGE

MANY OF THE MOST SIGNIFICANT-COMPOSERS *and musicians in post-1930 Hollywood were smong those who fled the Nazi regime for refuge in the U.S. They included Max Steiner, Franz Waxman, Erich Wolfgang Korngold, Dimitri Tiomkin, and Miklós Rózsa.*

Germany 1933–1945

The racial-ideological doctrine of National Socialism in Germany from the early 1930s caused serious upheaval in music. Jewish musicians were forbidden to work; works by Jewish, politically undesirable, or overly avant-garde composers were boycotted; and composers such as Felix Mendelssohn Bartholdy and Gustav Mahler were libeled in music histories written by government hacks. Countless musicians fled the country and went into exile to escape Nazi prosecution.

Composition "After Auschwitz"

After World War II, artistic debate erupted over the topics fascism, exile and war. Many composers wrote pieces based on their wartime experiences including Karl Amadeus Hartmann, who spent 1933–1945 in Nazi Germany's policy of "internal emigration," Arnold Schönberg, who wrote "A Survivor from Warsaw" in 1947, and Benjamin Britten, whose "War Requiem" was premiered in 1962. The composer Lenie Alexander used themes from her double exile in many of her compositions: in 1939 she fled Nazi Germany for Chile, but after 1973 she lived in exile in Paris because of her support for Salvador Allende.

Cellist Pablo Casals boycotted Germany between 1933 and 1945 then went into exile after Francisco Franco seized power in Spain.

Music in Theresienstadt

The concentration camp Theresienstadt, near Prague, was used by Nazi rulers to convince foreign observers that the camps were run according to humanitarian principles. In pursuit of this propaganda, the camp leadership tolerated a certain cultural life: concerts were organized, operas and operettas were performed. Some imprisoned composers wrote works for the limited possibilities in the camps. The notable artists and musicians confined in the camp (Viktor Ullman for one) used the minimal opportunities available to create a fairly refined musical life in Theresienstadt, despite the conditions.

above: *Theresienstadt (1945)*

see also: Fascist Regimes Under Stalin and Hitler, *Politics, Law, and Economy Chapter, pp. 172, 175*

MUSIC AFTER 1945

New Music includes a variety of compositional forms and styles. Common to all is the search for new principles of tone and arrangement.

The years after World War II produced many compositional methods which distanced themselves, at least in part, from the compositional principles of previous centuries. With the advent of electronics, the production of sound was no longer limited to traditional instruments. Instruments employed new, noise-intensive methods of playing such as the prepared piano. New methods of musical notation were created, for example graphical representation, in order to do justice to the expanded repertoire of performance techniques and understand extra-musical elements. The relationship between space and sound was also re-interpreted, which called into question the previously accepted distribution of space between stage and audience.

Serial Music

Arnold Schönberg's 12-Tone Technique (p. 381) was refined in the 1950s by serial music. This concerned itself not only with equal treatment for all 12 tones of an octave, but with the "equality of all elements in a composition" (Karlheinz Stockhausen), including pitch, duration, loudness, and articulation. Many compositions were so complex, however, as to be nearly unplayable. The logical extension was electronic music, from which a corresponding precision was exacted, and aleatoric (chance) music, which relied heavily upon chance for the sequences and repetition of sounds in compositions by Pierre Boulez, Witold Lutosławski, and others.

MUSICAL THEATER *worked with the sounds and technical achievements of New Music.*

FOR LIBRETTI *musical theater often relied on interpreting classical works by von Büchner, Gogol, Shakespeare, and others.*

Romanian-German composer Adriana Holszky composed numerous works that experimented with musical theater form.

Modern Musical Theater

MODERN MUSICAL THEATER was shaped by experiments with total concepts and means of production. These included using no plot or absurd plots (György Ligeti's "Le Grand Macabre") and varying cast sizes. Composers wrote for sharply reduced casts (Mauricio Kagel's "Match" in 1965) and extremely complex casts (Karlheinz Stockhausen's "Licht" in 1978–2005).

COMPOSERS of politically outspoken musical theater included Giacomo Manzoni in "Atomtod" in 1965, Hans Werner Henze "El Cimarrón, 1970," and Luigi Nono in "Al gran sole carico d'amore" in 1975.

"Le Grand Macabre" by György Ligeti at Salzburg Festspielen 1997

New Sound Sources, Intervals, and Modes

After World War II, Pierre Schaeffer developed a principle of composition known as "musique concrete" which, in imitation of the style of "found art" using ordinary objects to create artistic works, utilized the acoustic possibilities of objects found in nature and everyday life.

Czech composer Alois Hába required specially constructed instruments, such as a quarter-tone piano, for his music. He divided the octave not into 12 half-tone steps, but into still smaller intervals called micro intervals. Olivier Messiaen used modes, or six- and ten-step scales, as the basis for his compositions. He also used real birdsong, which he recorded himself, as an element in his compositions.

Minimalism

In the U.S. around 1965, minimalism as a style was initiated and made famous by composers including Steve Reich and Philip Glass. It was influenced by the Fluxus movement in art as well as East Asian philosophy. Characteristics of minimalism include meditative music-making and listening as well as slightly perceptible changes in sound within the composition.

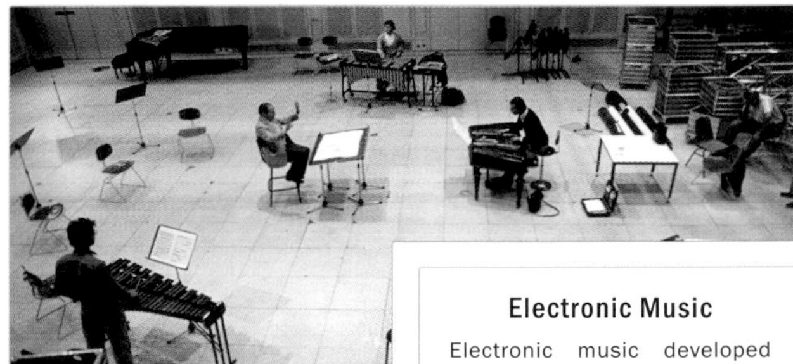

Electronic Music

Electronic music developed around 1950 with the launch of the magnetic cassette recorder, which allowed the pre-production of electronic parts of compositions. Karlheinz Stockhausen headed a studio in Cologne in 1951, Luciano Berio and Bruno Maderna were active in Milan from 1953, and Pierre Boulez started a studio in Paris in 1975. From the early 1960s, composers combined electronic music and its interpreters onstage. The invention of the synthesizer facilitated the performance of live electronic music.

above: *Pierre Boulez conducts a rehearsal in Paris in 1984 at IRCAM (Institut de Recherches et de Coordination Acoustique-Musique).*

John Cage, considered the chief representative of experimental music, explored conventional listening practices, among others.

Finnish composer Kaija Saariaho in conversation with violinist Gidon Kremer in 1996.

➔ see also: **Fluxus**, *Visual Arts Chapter, p. 312*

MUSIC

Monographic Boxes

Analytic Boxes

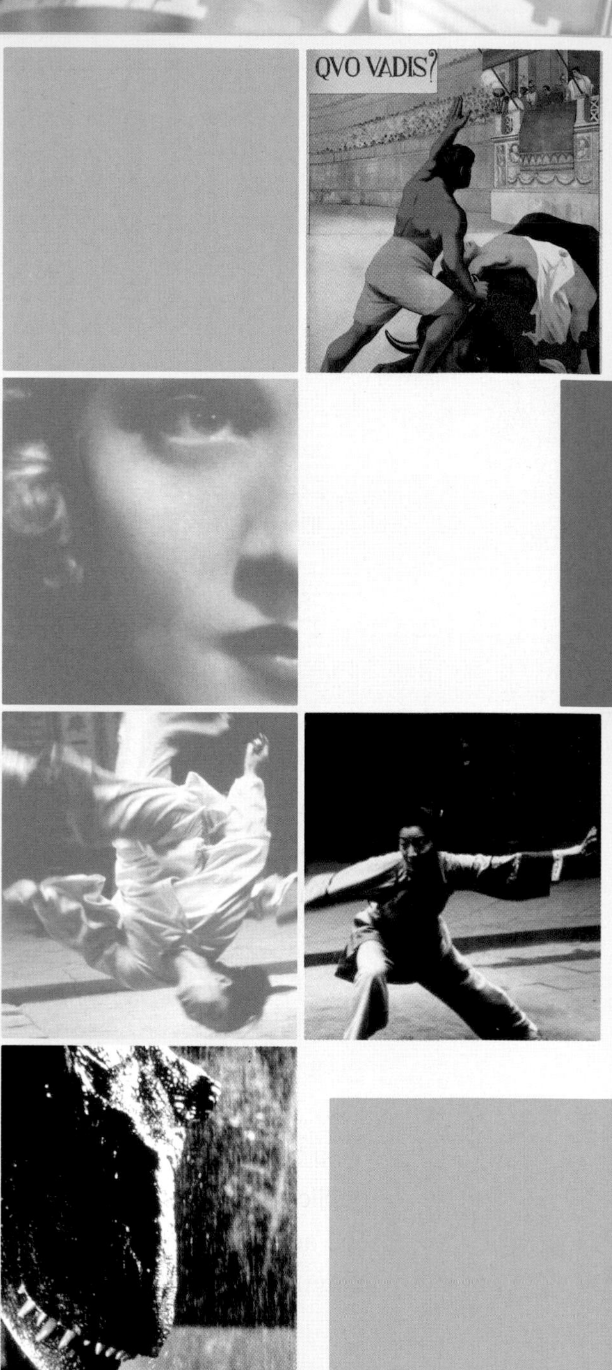

FILM

At the end of the 19th century, the pioneers of motion pictures screened their first short films to the fascination of the world. But at that time no one was able to predict that film would develop as one of the most influential media in the 20th century. Since film started as a scientific feat its development has remained closely linked to technology. Early innovations such as the invention of sound films boosted the potential of the movie theaters as public attractions and lucrative sources of income. The advancements that have been made in the recent past have been even more astounding, leaving some people to wonder if anything can still be called "unfilmable." Cinema has grown dramatically into an industry worth billions upon billions. Yet filmmakers continue to stand as artists in this exciting and young medium.

KEY FACTS

THE LUMIÈRE BROTHERS *exhibited films to the paying public for the first time in 1895.*

"THE JAZZ SINGER," *the first sound film, came to the theaters in 1927.*

AFTER WORLD WAR II, *the U.S. film industry became one of the most influential in the world.*

IN THE 1980S AND 1990S, *expensively produced blockbusters determined films worldwide.*

Invention | Birth of film industry | Silent films | Sound films | Post-War period | Modification | Blockbuster | Outlook

FILM—THE SEVENTH ART

The first moving screen pictures revolutionized cultural life. Through the constant improvement of camera and projection techniques, cinema became the most important medium of the 20th century. It came to shape the world like no other art form had before. The development of cinema was not led by artistic ambitions alone, but rather social, political, and economic interests played large roles. It was in this way that moving pictures blurred the borders between high culture and popular entertainment.

➲ *Cinema is the shortened form of the term "cinematography" (Greek: "recorded movements").*

INVENTION IN TEAMWORK

Cinematography was in the air at the end of the 19th century. A number of inventors simultaneously worked on its technical development by combining and enhancing existing inventions.

Human attempts to create a photo-mechanical image of reality have a long history. The camera obscura developed by the Arab Abu Ali Al-Hasan around 980 and the *laterna magica* invented in the 17th century are considered to be the early forerunners of modern camera and projector technology, respectively.

The Pioneers

The invention of flexible celluloid in the 19th century was very significant for the emergence of cinema. The American George Eastman produced the perforated roll film that he patented in 1889. However, the pictures did not learn to move until the discovery of stroboscopic effects. It is caused by a frame rate of 12 images per second, during which the human eye can no longer recognize individual images, thus creating the impression of movement. This was already employed as an attraction at fairs in devices like "phenakistoscope" or "praxinoscope" used by Charles-Émile Rexnaud.

In the laterna magica, a light source inside the apparatus enabled the projection of images.

Another important innovator of film was Eadweard Muybridge, who documented the bodily movements of humans and animals through his series of photos.

The Lumière Brothers created glowing excitement during the first screenings of their shorts such as "L' Arrivée d'un Train en Gare de La Ciotat" (1895).
left: *In the beginning, the screenings of the Lumières were exclusively for upper class audiences (advertisement, 1896).*

Edison and Other Forerunners

The inventors of the first exhibition machines drew upon these pioneering achievements. Thomas Alva Edison showed the first films in 1893 with his Kinetoscope that was intended for only one viewer. At the time of industrialization when mass consumerism had formed in the cities, this invention could not become widespread. The German Skladanowsky Brothers showed films with their bioscope in the Wintergarten Hall in Berlin, but that proved to be too laborious due to its double 50 mm rolls. The real birth date of cinema is considered to be

Edison invented the Kinetoscope in the 1890s, which worked without projection.

December 28, 1895, when the brothers Louis and Auguste Lumière showed a moving picture with the cinématographe in the Parisian Grand Café to a paying audience. Many technical achievements and various other factors had contributed to making cinema a reality. The cinématographe can be understood as the perfection of many technical developments.

Cinématographe & Co.

THE CINÉMATOGRAPHE of the Lumière brothers had both camera and projector in one, while Edison's Kinetoscope served only the playback function. A filmstrip in the still typical 35-mm format was directed at an object with a jerky movement and exposed. Oskar Messter perfected the film transport in 1896 through his Maltese cross, which decisively reduced the flickering of images. Later on this technology became standard in projectors.

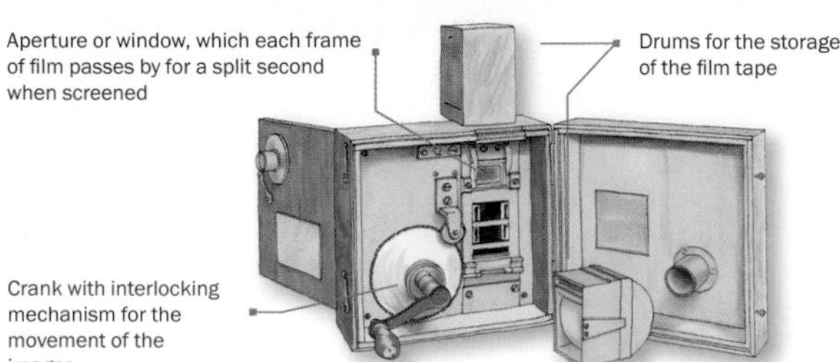

Initially projections were made at the speed of 16 to 40 images per second. It was only later that the standard of 24 prevailed.

➲ **see also: Photography and Video,** *Physics and Technology Chapter, p. 148*

BIRTH OF THE FILM INDUSTRY

After the initial excitement surrounding the optical sensation, cinema began to establish itself as a new artistic medium in which economic interests played a major role.

Technical progress was only one aspect in the development of moving pictures as a popular art form. Exclusive screenings of motion pictures in *varietés* soon yielded a professional film industry. Cinema became an economic factor.

Georges Méliès made use of techniques in "Le Voyage dans la Lune" (1902) that are still in use today.

Art for the Masses

The Lumière Brothers used their cinématographe only to document everyday life. The French theater operator Georges Méliès, on the other hand, understood the potential of the new technology to create illusions. Méliès created the so-called magic films, in which fictive settings arose from the backdrops of studios. His fairytales, horror, and ghost stories were based on sequential shooting. His film "Le Voyage dans la Lune" became a cinema milestone in 1902 as the first long film of around 15 minutes.

THE FIRST AMERICAN MOVIE THEATER *opened in 1902 in Los Angeles.*

FILM DISTRIBUTION *began in 1904, which made it possible to better control screenings and profits.*

The temporary "nickelodeons" were removed from film theaters in 1905; cinema with Wurlitzer organ, 1920.

The Influence of Capital

CINEMA IN COURT: The initial years of American cinema were characterized by many legal disputes that dealt with patents (for film material, etc.) and thereby the control of the film industry. A trust was founded in 1909 with the Motion Picture Patents Company (MPPC) in New York, in which all patents (among them Edison's) were bundled. The MPCC's monopolistic position led to a flurry of lawsuits.

FOUNDING OF HOLLYWOOD: The most effective weapon of the anti-trust movement was innovation. The new form of long films led to an increased number of viewers of independent productions. Many independent film companies started to move to Los Angeles after 1910 as the influence of the MPCC located in New York was felt less here. Furthermore, the climate offered ideal conditions for film making. By 1914, Hollywood became the center of American cinema.

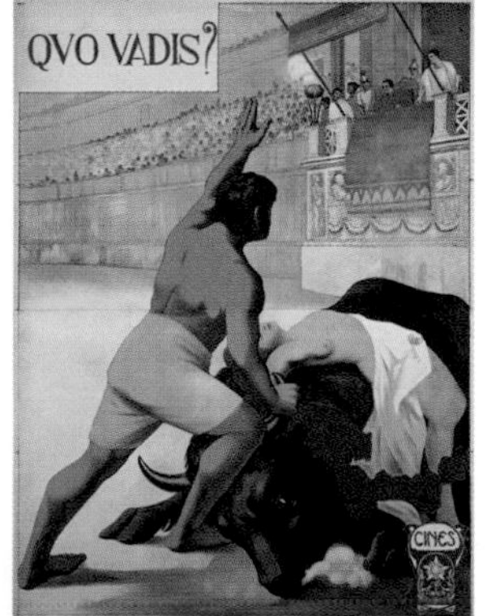

The monumental Italian film "Quo Vadis" of 1912 influenced many later film epics.

Economic factors proved to be crucial in turning films into mass spectacles. The Lumière brothers had made their films according to their own direction, but had sold the patents in 1897 to the showman Charles Pathé. As the founder of the French film industry, he wielded considerable influence in the worldwide film trade until the outbreak of World War I. Pathé's service was to make the Varieté-Attraction that was originally reserved for very few viewers accessible to a broader public. His company, Société Pathé Frères, covered all aspects of shooting. It employed directors, who churned out ten new films weekly in the company-owned studios. Pathé bought cameras and projectors and operated 200 film theaters in Belgium and France.

National Idiosyncrasies

Film industries started to be built in this way in other countries with national peculiarities. Edwin S. Porter filmed the first western, "The Great Train Robbery," in 1903 in the U.S. Porter was the first to make artistic use of editing in his films.

After France, Denmark was the most significant film-producing country in Europe. Modeled on Pathé's example, Ole Olson founded a film production company in Denmark, the Nordisk Films Kompagni. It created a furor in 1906 with Viggo Larsen's adventure film, "Løvejagten."

In Italy, historical topics were preferred, which led to the making of early monumental films, while the comedy genre established itself in France. Films began to boom in Germany only at the end of the first decade of the 20th century. At first, melodramas were made, mostly love stories in which a rogue threatened the happiness of the hero and the heroine. Increasingly, filmmakers started to work together with well-known authors such as Gerhart Hauptmann.

The auteur film, in which the director has full creative control, was born. From 1910 onward, the first film stars arrived on the scene, such as the actresses Asta Nielsen in Europe and Mary Pickford in the U.S. Even they were a sign of the growing power and professionalism of the film industry.

Corkscrew curls as brands: Stars like Mary Pickford (above in "Little Annie Rooney" from 1925; right in "Coquette," from 1929) were marketed through targeted advertisement and press. Screen darlings in stereotypical roles ensured cinema halls were sold out.

German film art: The doppelgänger theme in "The Student of Prague" (1913) was skillfully intensified through lighting effects.

FILM

THE TRIUMPHANT PROCESSION OF SILENT FILM

While the European film industry plunged into crisis, Hollywood experienced a blooming of a variety of genres as new allies were artistically tested.

Double-edged milestone: The epic "The Birth of a Nation" was marred by the racism of the white American middle class.

World War I marked a radical turning point in the film industry. The number of films produced in Europe decreased drastically.

Politics in the Theater

The influence of politics in the film industry grew. In 1917, private film companies in Germany joined together under the name Universium Film AG (UFA). A third of the basic capital of this company came from the state, which wanted to use this new medium to spread its ideology. The influence of politics was more distinct in the 1920s in Italy and Russia, where cinema was used as a propaganda tool of the fascist and communist governments.

In the U.S., the film companies lost their artistic independence in a different way, although it was the very opponent to the film trust (p. 387) that led the business. The huge popularity of the movies led to quick growth of branches that could only be financed through borrowed money and stock markets.

The most important film companies, therefore, came under the control of big companies. As a consequence, films were lacking intellectual quality or revealed racist tendencies. The entire U.S. film industry was more or less under a cloud of self-censorship.

Nevertheless, this period was the boom time of silent films, led by D. W. Griffith and his three-hour Civil War epic, "The Birth of a Nation" (1915).

Multiplicity of Genres

The U.S. did not owe its preeminence in the world of film to the war and the decline of the European film culture alone. Hollywood's industrially organized studios put an emphasis on economic growth and made use of the popularity of long films and stars. A great variety of genres emerged: Comedies starring Charlie Chaplin, adventure films starring Douglas Fairbanks, or melodramas starring Greta Garbo.

The Russian Revolution films worked with new editing techniques, which were perfected by Sergei Eisenstein in "The Battleship Potemkin."

A radically different idea was pursued by the Communist film avant-garde in the Soviet Union. The focus here was not on sentimental, but rather critical viewers. In France, Abel Gance made the eight-hour-long monumental film "Napoleon" (1927–1928), whose innovative visual style was marked by the use of a hand-held camera.

In addition, René Clair and Jean Renoir produced expressive socio-critical films ("poetic realism"), which brilliantly played with the possibilities of silent cinema. The most important aesthetic contribution was made by German Expressionist cinema of the 1920s, in which the subconscious and dreams were given shape. The Spaniard Luis Buñuel along with the painter Salvador Dalí made the first Surrealist film, "An Andalusian Dog" (1929).

Asymmetric walls and somnambulistic design in Robert Wienes' Expressionist masterpiece, "The Cabinet of Dr. Caligari" (1919).

No One Likes Sound Films

"It can be said today with certainty that the continuous usage of dialogue is the wrong way," wrote the German critic Siegfried Kracauer. Like many of his contemporaries, he saw the power of images being threatened by the talkies. Similar skepticism accompanied nearly every technical innovation. During the introduction of television, video recorder, or digital technology, the end of theater was also predicted.

above: *With "Sunset Boulevard"(1950), Billy Wilder memorialized silent movie stars like Gloria Swanson (pictured) and Buster Keaton.*

Paramount has produced more than 2,000 films since 1914.

21ST CENTURY

PARAMOUNT WAS BOUGHT *by Gulf + Western after the end of the studio era and taken over by the media concern Viacom in 1994.*

UNITED ARTISTS WAS FOUNDED *in 1919 by Charlie Chaplin, Mary Pickford, Douglas Fairbanks, and David Wark Griffith.*

METRO-GOLDWYN-MAYER (MGM) *was originally divided into three studios. MGM was sold repeatedly later. A cooperation agreement was made with Sony in 2004.*

➜ **see also: Expressionism,** *Visual Arts Chapter, p. 309* | *Literature Chapter, p. 350*

SOUND FILMS AND THE LARGE STUDIOS

Classical Hollywood cinema reached its heyday during World War II, after both filmmakers and actors had fled Nazi Germany.

The introduction of sound technology in 1927 fundamentally changed the film industry. Entirely new genres arose, like the film musical. Many actors were at the end of their careers, including the comedian Buster Keaton and the silent film diva Gloria Swanson. Until the mid-to-late 1930s, sound films were produced in two or three language versions simultaneously, often with different casts and at a great cost. Synchronization, or dubbing, of films into foreign languages was developed in the late 1930s. With the gradual introduction of color, cinema became more realistic. During that process, all the technical requirements were created that characterize cinema to this day.

INSIDER KNOWLEDGE

THE EIGHT LARGEST STUDIOS *raked in 90% of the film profits in the U.S. at the end of the 1930s.*

RECORD SUM: *In 1946, Hollywood earned 1.7 billion dollars.*

MICHAEL CURTIZ *made 44 films in just the 1930s. Altogether he made over 100 films—"Casablanca" being his most famous work.*

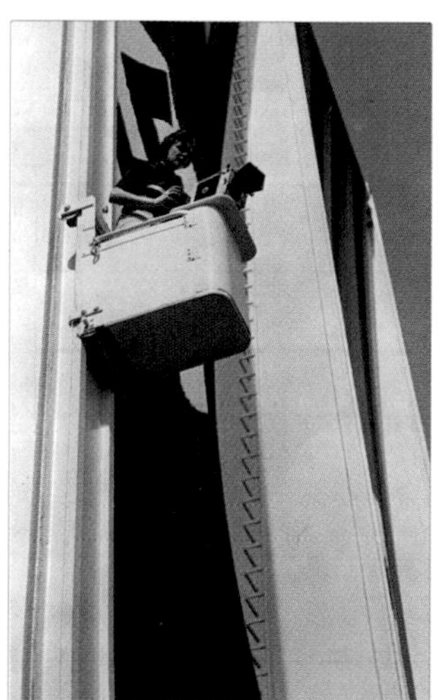

Contract work for Hitler: Leni Riefenstahl staged the Nuremberg political convention in the "Triumph of the Will" (1935).

Films in National Socialism

European cinema entered its second crisis with the Nazis (National Socialists) seizing power in Germany in 1933 and the start of WWII in 1939. Many military films in the late 1920s in Germany showed a tendency toward nationalism. German nationalist publisher Alfred Hugenberg became the owner of the UFA.

Enforced conformity and racial politics ensured that the best film makers emigrated to the U.S., including director Fritz Lang, script writer Billy Wilder, producer Erich Pommer, and actor Peter Lorre. The Nazis exploited the popularity of films to their advantage by making anti-Semitic and propaganda films in which they also appealed to the German audience to make sacrifices for the good of their country. In addition, seemingly apolitical entertainment films were made that suggested an ideal world to the public.

Most successful melodrama of all time: "Gone With the Wind" brought in about 2 billion dollars.

Power of the Studios

Apart from a certain magnitude in France (Jean Renoir, Marcel Carné) and England (Alfred Hitchcock), the U.S. dominated cinema at this time. The period until the end of World War II is considered the peak of Hollywood's power. Five large studios (MGM, Warner, Paramount, 20th Century Fox, RKO) and three smaller (Universal, United Artists, Columbia) controlled the entire market. During the Depression in the 1930s, films were distributed in "Block-Booking" packages. Cinema operators could only borrow a very attractive movie together with cheaper productions. These "B-films" gave the studios a full workload on the one hand and on the other offered a platform for trying out new types of films.

In the profit-oriented film business, the studio bosses had the last word on artistic content. It was the studios that featured their own style. An exception was the singular achievement of Orson Welles's "Citizen Kane" (1941).

"The Jazz Singer" from 1927 was the first sound film in history. Yet it still reflected much of silent film characteristics.

MARY PICKFORD *earned $10,000 per week at the height of her fame.*

ERROL FLYNN *became an overnight star with his role in the adventure film "Captain Blood." He subsequently shaped this genre like no other star.*

Marlene Dietrich made a career in Hollywood after her sensational success as Lola in "The Blue Angel" in 1930 and attained world fame.

Stars

MASS HYSTERIA: Rudolph Valentino did not become a legend through his films, but rather through his death. With around 80,000 people attending his funeral, a mass hysteria was triggered in 1926. As a "latin lover," he belonged to the first generation of stars who became a role model through targeted promotion. For example, Humphrey Bogart was neither particularly good looking nor an extraordinary actor. However, an entire generation of men could identify with his typical lone-wolf characters.

IMAGE PROBLEMS: When Mary Pickford started to act in roles other than the innocent girl toward the end of the 1920s, it signaled the end of her career. Later, the ironic association of an actor with his screen image was simpler. The actor Marlon Brando characterized the sex symbol as an older man in 1996 in "Don Juan de Marco," which he indeed was at one time.

Greta Garbo, the "divine," played aloof characters her entire life. She quit the film business in 1941 when she was just 36 years old.

➲ see also: National Socialism, *Politics, Law, and Economy Chapter, p. 175*

CINEMA IN THE POST-WAR PERIOD

The period following the end of World War II promoted a new cultural variety in film. The invention of television resulted in cinema losing its older viewing audience.

Amidst ruins, Roberto Rossellini dealt with transgression and guilt: "Germany, Year Zero" (1948)

After the end of World War II, cinema gained increasing popularity worldwide. The new political freedom promoted the exchange between various film cultures. The internationalization of film manifested itself in the entries for the great European film festivals during this time (Cannes 1946, Berlin 1951). For example, Japanese director Akira Kurosawa became world famous with his movie "Rashomon" (1950) winning at the Festival in Venice in 1951.

Blooming of Cinema Worldwide

Japanese films opened up to Western influences in the 1920s. They themselves became an inspiration for filmmakers all over the world. Among others, John Sturges directed "The Magnificent Seven" in 1960 based on Kurosawa's sword fighter film "The Seven Samurai" (1954). It was a transfer of Japanese work to American culture.

In Europe, the end of the totalitarian rule in Western Europe revealed an enormous diversity in style. Italian directors like Roberto Rossellini ("Rome—Open City," 1945) or Vittorio de Sica ("The Bicycle Thief," 1948) developed a quasi-documentary, neorealist style. Their blatant realism was a conscious opposition of Italian monumental films and Mussolini's fascist propaganda. In Sweden, Ingmar Bergman used cinema to express the general insecurity that prevailed in the post-war era. French filmmakers like Alain Resnais ("Last Year at Marienbad," 1961) directed innovative and bold films in which the plot was secondary. Apart from a few exceptions, West German films refrained from dealing with the Nazi period. Instead, kitschy, sentimental films were shot in idealized settings, as well as war movies euphemizing the atrocities committed by the armed forces. The East German DEFA (Deutsche Film AG—German Film Stock Holding) seemed far more critical in comparison; for example, Konrad Wolf's films dealt with the Holocaust and Nazism.

Films in the living room—visiting the cinema becomes unnecessary. Family in front of the TV, ca 1960

Rejuvenation Through Television

New genres came into being in Hollywood after the war: Sci-Fi, Film Noir, and the thrillers of Alfred Hitchcock. Individual fears determined the content of these films triggered by the political situation (Cold War, McCarthy era) and technological progress. Cinema audience became more quality-conscious and selective. The rise of television meant that larger segments of the older population turned away from cinema. Thus, the protagonists became younger while the scripts were customized to a youthful target audience.

Film Noir

Film Noir was influenced by the poetic realism of France and the expressionism of Germany (p. 388). Criminal plots and detective stories with graphic representations of crime and violence served as master plots. In the center of these gloomy black-and-white films stood the hero with an unhappy past who is disillusioned and lives in a world without morals. Insecurity and uncertainty are reflected in the male lead character's dealings with the opposite sex. Heroines like Lauren Bacall and Rita Hayworth emerged as attractive emancipated women in tune with the femme fatale image they portrayed.

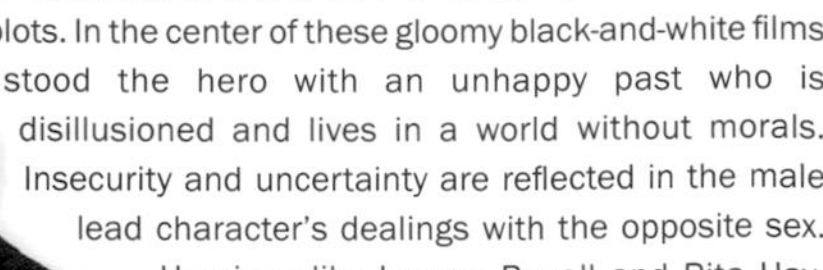

Humphrey Bogart was unsurpassed in his portrayals of the disillusioned hero—one who stands powerless against the big terrible world.

STAR WARS, *the most successful science fiction film to date, grossed $775 million at the box office.*

THE FIRST SCI-FI FILM *in full feature length was the Soviet propaganda piece "Aelita" in 1924. The plot tells about the love between the Queen of Mars and a Soviet researcher.*

Stanley Kubrick worked with NASA experts for three years for the production of "2001—A Space Odyssey."

Science-Fiction

MIRRORING THE PRESENT: As early as the 1920s, Fritz Lang had conceptualized the idea of society as utopia ("Metropolis" in 1926, "Woman in the Moon" in 1929). This genre experienced a boom during the Cold War. The nuclear threat and the anti-communist hunts propagated a feeling of fear in society, which was reflected in films like Franklin J. Schaffner's "Planet of the Apes" (1968) or Don Siegel's "Invasion of the Body Snatchers" (1956). Starting in the 1960s, the theme of rapid technological development gained popularity.

The radio broadcast of H. G. Wells' novel "War of the Worlds" in 1938 triggered widespread panic; it was made into a film by George Pál in 1953.

INSIDER KNOWLEDGE

IN 1952, *there were already 15,000,000 TV viewers in the U.S.*

JOHN CARPENTER'S *"Dark Star" (1974) is a spoof on Stanley Kubrick's "2001."*

THE FILM FESTIVALS IN VENICE *are some of the oldest in the world.*

THE 1960S AND 1970S: RENEWAL THROUGH INDEPENDENCE

The golden age of cinema was over. A new generation of filmmakers, who had grown up with film, emerged on the scene during this period of crisis.

The success of television worldwide led to a decline in cinema culture; Hollywood was struck by a recession. Much later, studios acknowledged the new possibilities of television and opened their archives for the purpose of re-use or began producing films for this new format. Initially they tried to compete with television with short-lived innovations such as the extra large CinemaScope format or 3-D film. However, this was to no avail as the studio system was completely outdated (p. 389). Former screen idols such as John Wayne and Cary Grant lost their popularity as classic genres like the Western became insignificant. Conglomerates gradually took over the entire film industry.

Filmmaker Jean-Luc Godard did things that differed from the norm. ("Breathless" 1959, scene with Jean-Paul Belmondo and Jean Seberg).

The Fresh Spirit of the Time

At a certain point, films underwent a renewal as many Western societies were characterized by generational conflict and a fundamental change in values. France, during the end of the 1950s, was witness to the rise of new group pf filmmakers, who raised their voice against the old authorities. These directors of the *Nouvelle Vague* ("new wave") like Jean-Luc Godard, Louis Malle, Claude Chabrol, and François Truffaut did not adhere to fixed genre types and conventions. They radically changed the portrayals of characters in film. These directors consciously emphasized montage, as opposed to the inconspicuous editing in older films.

The Nouvelle Vague also spread to other countries and influenced similar schools of filmmaking. The style of the "New German Cinema" emerged in Germany. Rainer Werner Fassbinder, Werner Herzog, Alexander Kluge, and Wim Wenders did not stick to the restorative cinema style that dominated the 1950s, but devoted themselves to the most pressing conflicts of the present.

Sexual liberation was part of this new awakening: For example, the Italian director Bernardo Bertolucci significantly deviated from the typical portrayal of male characters in his scandalous film "Last Tango in Paris" (1972). Pop culture also increasingly influenced films. This is especially evident in Italian filmmaker Michelangelo Antonioni's film "Blow Up" (1966), which portrays the attitude of the younger generation toward life in "Swinging London."

THE LATE 1960S: *African-Americans for the first time became lead characters in popular films.*

BETWEEN 1970 AND 1975, *almost 200 "Blaxploitation" films were made—films that were influenced by the African-American civil rights movement.*

JULIA ROBERTS *received the Oscar in 2000 for the environmental drama "Erin Brockovich."*

Pam Grier became an icon of African-American cinema with action films like "Coffy" (1973).

Politics in Films

STAR ROLLS: The films of Hollywood mostly reflect a heterosexual, male point of view. Many productions from the heyday of American cinema were primarily characterized by latent racism. Minorities such as African-Americans or homosexuals were largely cast as criminals, servants, or clowns. The role of women in the 1950s was reduced to that of a sex object (Marilyn Monroe) or an innocent virgin (Doris Day).

POLITICAL FILMS: Film stereotypes began to break apart during the 1970s. Social and political grievances were primarily the subjects of such movies. Films with an underlying political agenda can sometimes be just as popular as pure entertainment fare; a recent example is "Brokeback Mountain" (2005). However, such films are few and represent a minority.

The "Shaft" films with an African-American detective (Richard Roundtree) as a hero were a box-office hit in the 1970s.

Worldwide Awakening

Everywhere there was a renewal of film and cinema. In Latin America, the Brazilian Glauber Rocha provided the impetus for *Cinema Novo* with his cinema as political allegories. In the U.S., a group of young directors, actresses, and actors responded to the creative standstill of the large studios—the first being Dennis Hopper and Peter Fonda with their naïvely pessimistic interpretation of the American dream in "Easy Rider" (1969). George Lucas ("THX 1138," 1970) and Steven Spielberg ("Duel," 1971) made their debut. Martin Scorsese ("Mean Streets," 1973; "Taxi Driver," 1976; "Raging Bull," 1980) and Francis Ford Coppola ("The Conversation," 1974; "The Godfather," 1972; "Apocalypse Now," 1979) directed their best films. The decade of "New Hollywood" was a stroke of luck for cinema and the film industry.

War in the city: Robert De Niro as deputy sheriff of his own morals in "Taxi Driver" (1976).

BLOCKBUSTERS: SEQUELS WITHOUT END

The power of the producers curtailed the freedom of the artists during the 1980s. Movies evolve into opulent spectacles and mirror technological progress.

The end of the era of "New Hollywood" (p. 391) was ushered in by Michael Cimino's epic "Heaven's Gate" (1980). This film with its $50 million budget forced United Artists into financial ruin. Cimino, who had received an Oscar for "The Deer Hunter" in 1978, became a symbol of very demanding directors, who ran high risks with their perfectionism, shooting plans, and inflated budgets. The verdict on "Heaven's Gate" was made even before the film, which was originally five hours long, was released in a compressec form in cinemas. It went down as the biggest flop in film history.

End of Auteur Movies

The downfall of "Heaven's Gate" signaled the end of auteur movies and the zeitgeist of the 1970s. The U.S. and Europe witnessed political change. Thus, the anti-union strategies of Ronald Reagan affected Hollywood as the studios regained control over the film industry. Only in a few exceptional cases did the directors decide on the final cut of their films.

Two other factors contributed to the decline of the aesthetic quality of cinema in the 1980s. First, video technology made its impact felt worldwide, creating a new market for film through wide-scale distribution. Simultaneously, however, the pressure on cinema to become more commercially successful increased. Second, television changed and consequently so did the viewer's expectation. Private cable channels offered a wide variety of entertainment programs, including the music channel MTV with its music videos.

Genre-Mix: "Star Wars" was a combination of adventure, sci-fi, fairy tale, and action. The figures R2-D2 and C-3PO provided the comic relief.

> **INSIDER KNOWLEDGE**
>
> **THE FIRST FILM** *that cost more than $200 million to make was Peter Jackson's "King Kong" in 2005.*
>
> **THE MOST SUCCESSFUL FILM** *of recent times is James Cameron's "Titanic"(1997), making over $1.8 billion at the box office.*

New Stars: Action Heroes

The elaborately staged and highly advertised "blockbuster" became a symbol of the growing commercialization of Hollywood. The financial success of these films was increasingly dependent on their international marketing, which blurred national specifics. Sequels, remakes, and literary screen adaptations promised predictable cinematic success.

The dominant genre of the 1980s was the brutal action film—fast paced and full of special effects. The new stars were Sylvester Stallone ("Rocky," "Rambo") and Arnold Schwarzenegger ("The Terminator"), whose simplistic screen personas were ideal for sequels. A number of directors from "New Hollywood," who had kept them selves abreast of new developments, had successes in crossing into this new age: George Lucas ("Star Wars") and Steven Spielberg ("Jaws," "Indiana Jones").

Hollywood's Influence

European cinema was clearly oriented toward Hollywood. At the beginning of the 1980s, the British production company Goldcrest celebrated worldwide success with "Gandhi" and "The Killing Fields." In Germany, the producer Bernd Eichinger achieved success with international productions like "The Name of the Rose" (1986) and "The House of the Spirits" (1993). Hollywood reacted to this competition by hiring European film artists in their productions. Directors such as Paul Verhoeven ("Robocop," 1987) from the Netherlands, Wolfgang Petersen ("In the Line of Fire," 1993) from Germany, or Peter Weir ("Dead Poets Society," 1989) from Australia, directed their most successful films in the U.S. Chinese cinema and directors (Chen Kaige, Zhang Yimou) drew greater international attention for the first time toward the end of the 1980s.

Home theater: The video cassette created new target audiences. B-movies, mostly horror and trash films, were released on video.

Arnold Schwarzenegger in blockbuster movie "The Terminator" (1984).

True to Life: The Documentary

In the 1920s, the Russian Dziga Vertov ("The Man With a Movie Camera," 1929) propagated the documentary as "cinematic reality" and an independent medium. The development of the light 16-mm camera facilitated the production of "direct cinema" in the U.S. in the 1960s by Frederick Wiseman, D. A. Pennebaker, and the Maysle brothers. Based on Vertov's concept of "film truth," ("kino-pravda"), French filmmakers such as Chris Marker developed "cinéma vérité" in the 1960s, using the camera as an "eye."

Michael Moore popularized documentaries with "Fahrenheit 9/11" (2004) and "Bowling for Columbine" (2002).

OUTLOOK: GLOBALIZATION AND DIGITALIZATION

Today, Hollywood blockbusters are stylish, aggressively marketed media events. Apart from mainstream cinema, a new independent form of cinema has also emerged. Moreover, digitalization has fundamentally changed films of this current day and age.

Today the rivalry between traditional cinema and pay-per-view TV, digital piracy, and illegal DVD copies is more rampant than ever before. In reaction to this increasing economic pressure, highly profitable sequels have been produced since the 1990s: A sequel has been filmed for almost every successful film. Today, many films are shot from the beginning with the intention of releasing them as a series ("Matrix," "Lord of the Rings").

Path to Success

Screen adaptations of successful books ("Harry Potter") and superhero comics ("Batman," "Spiderman"), as well as the recent adaptations of video games ("Tomb Raider," "Resident Evil"), ensure success at the box office. To attract adult audiences, films are presented as cultural events. The marketing for a blockbuster in the meantime takes up tens of millions of dollars in the entire budget.

"Indie" film from Miramax: With a budget of $8 million, Quentin Tarantino's "Pulp Fiction" (1994) grossed over $100 million at the box office.

Simultaneously, gigantic film budgets are becoming more common since "Titanic" crossed the 100-million-dollar mark in 1997.

The early 1990s also witnessed the emergence of new auteur movies in the U.S. The impetus for such new "independent films" came from the film distribution company Miramax, owned by the brothers Bob and Harvey Weinstein. They chose small, innovative, but nevertheless effective productions that made an impact on the public. Thus, Steven Soderbergh's farewell to the 1980s "Sex, Lies, and Videotape" (1989) cost only $1.2 million, but generated $25 million at the box office in the U.S. and won the Golden Palm at the Cannes Film Festival.

Hollywood Shoots in Prague

The biggest influence on film in the last 15 years besides digitalization is the globalization of the film industry. Due to budget contstraints, there has been an increasing turnout of American animation movies in Asia, and Hollywood productions are being made in Eastern Europe. An international marketing machinery has evolved, which works for productions that span across genres and cultures. This, however, also strengthens the national film culture through worldwide distribution via the Internet and DVDs, providing easy access to unknown cinema cultures.

Digitalization

The progress in digital technology has enormously broadened the realm of possibilities in cinema, creating a boom in fantasy films at the end of the 1990s. A countertrend to this sophisticated digital imagery emerged when Lars Von Trier, Thomas Vinterberg, and other Danish filmmakers published their "Dogma" manifesto in 1995. It propagated the exclusive use of hand-held cameras in natural locations without artificial light and sound.

Film projectionists are also facing a new threat: Movies are being pirated during the screening and then distributed digitally.

Hong Kong movie for Hollywood: Ang Lee's "Crouching Tiger, Hidden Dragon" (2000) as homage to the martial arts films of the 1970s

Computer Generated Films

The dinosaurs in "Jurassic Park" are animated computer graphics that were introduced in the post-production stages.

Today, many films that come to the screen contain visual effects, which can only be generated by the computer. The technique of "morphing" allows the digital crossover between two images, making elaborate blending unnecessary. "Compositing" allows mass production of scenes through the compilation of various individual recordings. The first films to be completely generated using the computer with the "rendering" technique were released in theaters during the mid-1990s.

"Toy Story" (1995) contains only animated computer graphics.

Exotic Dream Factories: Bollywood

Over 250 of the 900 films that are produced each year in India (three times more than Hollywood) come from Mumbai. The Indian film industry is popularly called "Bollywood," from a blending of "Hollywood" and "Bombay," the previous name for Mumbai. The typically three-hour melodramas are a mix of dance, action, song, comedy, and religious elements. This form developed in the 1950s and 1960s. Since the 1990s, Bollywood films have gained popularity in the Western world as well.

above: *Shah Rukh Khan*

INDEX

NATIONAL GEOGRAPHIC

The Knowledgebook

Published by the National Geographic Society
John M. Fahey, Jr. President and Chief Executive Officer
Gilbert M. Grosvenor Chairman of the Board
Tim T. Kelly President, Global Media Group
John Q. Griffin President, Publishing
Nina D. Hoffman Executive Vice President; President, Book Publishing Group

Prepared by the Book Division
Kevin Mulroy Senior Vice President and Publisher
Leah Bendavid-Val Director of Photography Publishing and Illustrations
Marianne R. Koszorus Director of Design
Barbara Brownell Grogan Executive Editor
Elizabeth Newhouse Director of Travel Publishing
Carl Mehler Director of Maps

Staff for this book
Judith Klein Project Editor
Jennifer A. Thornton Managing Editor
Gary Colbert Production Director

Manufacturing and Quality Management
Christopher A. Liedel Chief Financial Officer
Phillip L. Schlosser Vice President
John T. Dunn Technical Director
Chris Brown Director
Maryclare Tracy Manager
Nicole Elliott Manager

Library of Congress Cataloging-in-Publication data available upon request.

ISBN: 978-1-4262-0518-7 (Trade), 978-1-4262-0205-6 (Deluxe), 978-1-4262-0265-0 (Regular)

Printed in Singapore

Founded in 1888, the National Geographic Society is one of the largest nonprofit scientific and educational organizations in the world. It reaches more than 285 million people worldwide each month through its official journal, *National Geographic,* and its four other magazines; the National Geographic Channel; television documentaries; radio programs; films; books; videos and DVDs; maps; and interactive media. National Geographic has funded more than 8,000 scientific research projects and supports an education program combating geographic illiteracy.

For more information, please call 1-800-NGS LINE (647-5463) or write to the following address:

National Geographic Society, 1145 17th Street N.W., Washington, D.C. 20036-4688 U.S.A.

Visit us online at www.nationalgeographic.com/books

For information about special discounts for bulk purchases, please contact National Geographic Books Special Sales: ngspecsales@ngs.org
For rights or permissions inquiries, please contact National Geographic Books Subsidiary Rights: ngbookrights@ngs.org

13/PDVG/3

Staff at Peter Delius Verlag

Authors
Corinna Baum (Psychology), Anke Bremer (Islam), Anja Brug (Visual Arts), Matthias Dell (Film), Clive Dennis (Architecture), Dr. Frank Frick (Chemistry), Diana Friedemann (Physics and Technology), Julia Fröhlich (Hinduism, Buddhism), Jana Galinowsky (Moden Life/Media), Uwe Gloy (Earth), Victor Habermann (Mathematics), Markus Hattstein (Cultural History, Law, Traditional Religions, Religions of China and Japan, New Religions, Sects), Dr. habil. Christian Jäger (Philosophy), Dr. Christiane Jakob (Biology), Prof. Ursula Kocher (Literature), Dr. Anna-Carola Krausse (Visual Arts), Christoph Marx (Politics), Martin Mohn (Physics and Technology), Michael Müller (Universe), Alex Radzyner (Economics), Prof. Britta Sweers (Music), Dr. habil. Michael Tilly (Judaism, Christianity), Dr. Melanie Unseld (Music), Dr. Marc Filip Wiechmann (Earth)

Academic consultants
Dr. Lowell Abrams, Associate Professor of Mathematics, The George Washington University; Dr. George Allen, Doctor of Chemistry; Dr. Ghazala Anwar, Professor of Philosophy and Religious Studies, University of Canterbury; Dr. Michael Barzelay, Professor of Public Management, London School of Economics and Political Science; Dr. Christopher L. Cahill, Associate Professor of Chemistry, The George Washington University; Michael Cromartie, Vice President, Ethics and Public Policy Center, Washington DC; Dorothea Diehl, Dipl. Biologist, formerly biologist at the Museum for Natural History, Lübeck; Dr. Maria L. Dittrich, Assistant Clinical Professor, Department of Psychology, The George Washington University; Dr. Robert P. Donaldson, Professor of Biology, Department of Biological Sciences, The George Washington University; Susan Tyler Hitchcock, Doctor in English, University of Virginia; Dr. Keichi Kodaira, President of SOKENDAI/Japan; Dr. Susan Norland, Lecturer for German Literature, The George Washington University; Dr. Saulo Rodrigues, Geologist, Center for Sustainable Development, University of Brasília; Dr. Peter Rollberg, Associate Professor of Slavic and Film Studies, The George Washington University; Dr. André Rosowsky, SACLAY/France; Dr. Suwanna Satha-Anand, Professor at the Department of Philosophy, Chulalongkorn University, Thailand; Dr. Robert W. Tuttle, Professor of Law, The George Washington University

German editorial staff
Juliane von Laffert (Editor in chief), Detlef Berghorn, Tanja Berkemeyer, Sven-Oliver Kiesow, Johanna Knipper, Christoph Marx, Julia Niehaus, Ute Wielandt

Translators
David Andersen, Gary Grassl, Mary Hollerich, Patricia Linderman, Cathy Marich, Orange Tree Language Solutions

English editorial staff
Michele Greer (Editor in chief), Thomas Ashley Bartz, Charles Booth, Celeste Vallarta Ceguerra, Elizabeth Corso, John Eddlemon, Colin Green, Heather Hogue McCullough, Gilles Kennedy, Marc Knox, Generosa Gina Protano, Brad Steiner, Suellen Stover, Marissa van Uden, Elena Ziebarth

Picture management
Susanne Boenig, Claudia Casagranda, Jacek Slaski

Management Berlin
Tanja Berkemeyer, Sabine Kahl

Management Washington, D.C.
Antje Witzel

Graphic Designers
Dirk Brauns (Design Director), Markus Binner, Torsten Falke

Illustrators
Johann Brandstetter, Dirk Brauns, Uwe Gloy, Cybermedia India, Anna Krenz, Michael Römer

Arrangement of the notes
Stefan Schickhaus

Images from: akg-images Berlin/London/Paris; © VG Bild-Kunst, Bonn 2008: Beckmann, Braque, Calder, Chagall, Dalí, Duchamp, Judd, Kandinsky, Koolhaas, de Kooning, Lichtenstein, Magritte, Man Ray, Miro, Moholy-Nagy, Munch, Nauman, Newman, Picasso, Pollock, Rauschenberg, Schwitters. © The Estate of Francis Bacon/VG Bild-Kunst, Bonn 2008. © Salvador Dalí, Fundació Gala-Salvador Dalí/VG Bild-Kunst, Bonn 2008: Dalí. © Succession Marcel Duchamp/VG Bild-Kunst, Bonn 2008: Duchamp. © Art Judd Foundation. Licensed by VAGA, New York/VG Bild-Kunst, Bonn 2008: Judd. © The Willem de Kooning Foundation, New York/VG Bild-Kunst, Bonn 2008: de Kooning. © Man Ray Trust, Paris/VG Bild-Kunst, Bonn 2008: Man Ray. © Succession H. Matisse/VG Bild-Kunst, Bonn 2008: Matisse. © Successió Miró/VG Bild-Kunst, Bonn 2008: Miró. © The Munch Museum/The Munch Ellingsen Group/VG Bild-Kunst, Bonn 2008: Munch. © Succession Picasso/VG Bild-Kunst, Bonn 2008: Picasso. © Pollock-Krasner Foundation/VG Bild-Kunst, Bonn 2008: Pollock. © Robert Rauschenberg/VG Bild-Kunst, Bonn 2008: Rauschenberg; Artifice Images, Astrofoto, big stock photo, Canstockphoto, Claudia Casagranda, dpa Deutsche Presse Agentur, Digitalstock, ESA–European Space Agency, ESO–European Organisation for Astronomical Research in the Southern Hemisphere, fotolia, Interfoto, Istockphoto, Lebrecht Music + Arts, Museum für Naturkunde Berlin, NASA–National Aeronautics and Space, Photographers direct com, Pixelquelle, Seilnacht, Wikipedia commons, ZAK Archive, Delius Producing, University of Washington; Berliner Verkehrsbetrieben (BVG), Stand:10.12.06; Biologiebuch, Linder/Verlag; BMW Motorrad München; Bundesverband WärmePumpe (BWP) e. V.; Canton Elektronik GmbH + Co KG; © Cooling-Station.net; ©Copyright 2007, Linden Research, info@aphaline.com, APHALINE Krim AG; ©MT Aerospace AG; ©Ebay; Firma Cannondale/Modell Perpetrator 1; Fachhochschule Lippe und Höxter, Abt. Physik, Lemgo; Forschungszentrum Jülich; ©Giga-Byte Technology Co., Ltd; Uwe Gloy; Dr. Hebert; Inc.; Medvedev@piclease; ©Kodak; „La Quinzaine Litteraire“; © 2007 David Lindroth Inc.; Pflanzenliebe.de; ©Philipps; Kompetenzzentrum HanseNanoTec, SPM-Gruppe von Prof. Roland Wiesendanger, Universität Hamburg; Georg Mader; National Geographic Society; Georg Oleschinski; pangea.stanford.edu; Pressereferat; (c) R.E Wallace/ U.S. Geological Survey; medienzentrum. klinikum.uni-heidelberg.de; Mercedes-Benz.de; © 2006 MSI Technology GmbH ©Jane Reed/Harvard News Office; Ramgeis; Schiebel Elektronische Geraete GmbH; Dieter Schulte; ©Siemens AG, München/Berlin; Stochastik/edition.cnn.com; ©Peggy Seeger; ©shure-europe-GmbH; ©solarcosa.de; ©Sony; Dirk Trebbels; University of Washington; ©Wikipedia/GNU; Wikipedia/ ©Herrenknecht; ©Werksfoto DG Flugzeugbau, Bruchsal; ©www.ddesignmedia.de,; ©www.otis.com; ©www.marineturbines.com; ©www.globetrotter.de; ceo@sharkbay.wa.gov.au; cs@suesswassertauchen.com; www.Affenberg-Salem.de; www.fzk.de/imvt; www.freigeist.cc; www.e-learning-for-kids.org; www.eberspaecher.com/; www.conti-online.com; (www.schiebel.net); © www.itk-messtechnik.de; www.livingonwater.de; www.mtfoto.dk/malene/Zimbardo/www.prisonexp.org; http://pen.physik.uni-kl.de/medien/MM

Cover Illustrations, Front cover: All photographs from Shutterstock except hydrogen bomb by U.S. Air Force/Defense Nuclear Agency, Berlin Wall by Knud Nielsen/iStockphoto, and shuttle Discovery by NASA. Back cover: All photographs from Shutterstock except dinosaur bird by O. Louis Mazzatenta/NGS Image Collection and meteorites illustration by Davis Meltzer/NGS Image Collection. For detailed credits and picture captions please visit the website www.TheKnowledgePage.com